Marketing for Hospitality and Tourism

Philip Kotler • John T. Bowen • James C. Makens • Seyhmus Baloglu

SEVENTH EDITION

PEARSON

Boston   Columbus   Indianapolis   New York   San Francisco
Amsterdam   Cape Town   Dubai   London   Madrid   Milan   Munich   Paris   Montreal   Toronto
Delhi   Mexico City   São Paulo   Sydney   Hong Kong   Seoul   Singapore   Taipei   Tokyo

Vice President, Editorial Director: Andrew Gilfillan
Executive Editor: Daryl Fox
Editorial Assistant: Lara Dimmick
Program Management Team Lead: Laura Weaver
Program Manager: Susan Watkins
Project Management Team Lead: Bryan Pirrmann
Project Manager: Maria Reyes
Senior Art Director: Diane Six
Cover Designer: Melissa Welch, Studio Montage
Vice President of Sales and Marketing: David Gesell
Senior Product Marketing Manager: Darcy Betts

Field Marketing Manager: Thomas Hayward
Senior Marketing Coordinator: Les Roberts
Digital Studio Project Manager: Leslie Brado
Manufacturing Specialist: Deidra Smith
Vendor Project Manager: Melissa Sacco,
    Lumina Datamatics, Inc.
Full-Service Project Management and Composition:
    Revathi Viswanathan, Lumina Datamatics, Inc.
Printer/Binder: LSC Communications
Cover Printer: LSC Communications
Cover Art: © Jeff Miller/Getty Images

Library of Congress Cataloging-in-Publication Data
Names: Kotler, Philip, author.
Title: Marketing for hospitality and tourism / Philip Kotler, John T. Bowen, James C. Makens,
    Seyhmus Baloglu.
Description: Seventh edition. | Boston : Pearson, 2016. | Includes bibliographical
    references and index.
Identifiers: LCCN 2015050364| ISBN 9780134151922 (alk. paper) | ISBN 0134151925
    (alk. paper)
Subjects: LCSH: Hospitality industry–Marketing. | Tourism–Marketing.
Classification: LCC TX911.3.M3 K68 2016 | DDC 338.4/791–dc23
LC record available at http://lccn.loc.gov/2015050364

2

ISBN 10:   0-13-415192-5
ISBN 13: 978-0-13-415192-2

This book is dedicated to Nancy, my wife and best friend, with love.

P. K.

With love to my wife, Toni, and children, Casey and Kelly.

J. T. B.

*To my wife Kay and to Lynn Ebert whose assistance
was greatly appreciated.*

J. C. M.

To my wife, Zerrin, and our two sons, Derin and Deniz, with love.

S. B.

BRIEF CONTENTS

CONTENTS

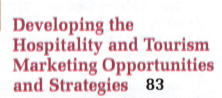

PART IV Managing Hospitality and Tourism Marketing 483

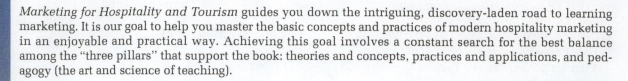

TO THE STUDENT

Welcome to the seventh edition!

Marketing for Hospitality and Tourism guides you down the intriguing, discovery-laden road to learning marketing. It is our goal to help you master the basic concepts and practices of modern hospitality marketing in an enjoyable and practical way. Achieving this goal involves a constant search for the best balance among the "three pillars" that support the book: theories and concepts, practices and applications, and pedagogy (the art and science of teaching).

The hospitality and travel industry are undergoing rapid changes. Some of the applications you learn today you will use immediately, while others you may not use until later in your career. Thus, it is important that you have an understanding of the marketing theories and concepts. This will allow you to analyze future situations and make the proper decisions. Practices and applications are provided to give you examples of how we currently apply the concepts to industry situations. Finally, we have included marketing highlights, opening cases, written cases, color illustrations, and other features to make learning about marketing interesting and enjoyable. Throughout the text, we provide examples to illustrate how companies are using the marketing principles covered in the book.

Marketing is both an art and science. The art adds some ambiguity to marketing, which makes it difficult for some students. We recommend reading each chapter quickly and then going back and reading it more slowly the second time. This will give you a good understanding of the material in the chapter.

This book has been written with you in mind. The development of each edition has involved students who tell us which illustrations to use, which examples they find interesting, and which ones we should replace when we are writing the newest edition. It is our goal to develop a book that is student friendly and clearly explains and illustrates the application of marketing concepts.

We hope you enjoy *Marketing for Hospitality and Tourism* and we wish you success.

Philip Kotler, John Bowen, James Makens, Seyhmus Baloglu

An Indispensable Guide to Successful Marketing in the Hospitality Industry

This book has been written with you in mind—explaining the how and why of everyone's role in marketing. Because customer contact employees are part of our product in hospitality and tourism marketing, marketing is everyone's job. *Marketing for Hospitality and Tourism* gives you an innovative and practical introduction to marketing. Its style and extensive use of examples and illustrations make the book straightforward, easy to read.

Text Organization

PART I: Understanding the Hospitality and Tourism Marketing Process—Introduces you to the concept of hospitality marketing and its importance.

PART II: Developing Hospitality and Tourism Marketing Opportunities and Strategies—Helps you understand the role of consumer behavior and how it affects the marketing environment.

PART III: Developing the Hospitality and Tourism Customer Value-Driven Strategy and Mix—Identifies and explains strategies for promoting products and the various distribution channels.

PART IV: Managing Hospitality and Tourism Marketing—Highlights the latest trends in social media, electronic marketing, destination marketing, and planning for the future through development of a marketing plan.

Chapter 2 Service Characteristics of Hospitality and Tourism Marketing

Marketing was initially developed in connection with selling physical products, such as cars, steel, and equipment. In Chapter 2, we cover the essence of why hospitality and travel products, which are intangible, have marketing concepts that are different from goods-producing firms. The principles found in Chapter 2 become the foundation for the rest of the book.

Chapter Opening Cases

Each chapter opens with a mini case showing you how actual hospitality and travel companies have successfully applied marketing. The cases help you understand and remember the concepts presented in the chapter. For example, Chapter 1 illustrates how Chipotle created socially responsible practices 20 years ago, long before it was a trend. Learn how Chipotle has used social networking and word of mouth to reduce its promotional costs to 1 percent of sales when the industry average is 4 percent.

Introduction: Marketing for Hospitality and Tourism

Chipotle Mexican Grill

Envision this. You're sitting in a restaurant where the people, from the chief executive officer (CEO) on down to the kitchen crew, obsess over using only the finest ingredients. They come to work each morning inspired by all the "fresh produce and meats they have to marinate, rice they have to cook, and fresh herbs they have to chop," says the CEO. The restaurant prefers to use sustainable, naturally raised ingredients sourced from local family farms. It's on a mission not just to serve its customers good food but to change the way its entire industry produces food. This sounds like a gourmet specialty restaurant, right? Wrong. It's Chipotle Mexican Grill. That's right, it's a fast-food restaurant.

In an age when many fast feeders seem to be using ever-cheaper ingredients and centralization of food preparation to cut costs and keep prices low, Chipotle is doing just the opposite. The chain's core sustainable mission is to serve "Food with Integrity." What does that mean? The company explains it the following way:

Chipotle is committed to finding the very best ingredients raised with respect for animals, the environment, and farmers. It means serving the very best sustainably raised food possible with an eye to great taste, great nutrition, and great value. It means that we support and sustain family farmers who respect the land and the animals in their care.

When founder and CEO Steve Ells opened the first Chipotle in Denver in 1993, his primary goal was to make the best gourmet burrito around. However, as the chain grew, Ells found that he didn't like the way the ingredients Chipotle used were raised and processed. So in 2000, Chipotle began developing a

Objectives

After reading this chapter, you should be able to:

1. Understand the relationships between the world's hospitality and travel industry.
2. Define marketing and outline the steps in the marketing process.
3. Explain the relationships between customer value and satisfaction.
4. Understand why the marketing concept calls for a customer orientation.
5. Understand the concept of the lifetime value of a customer and be able to relate it to customer loyalty and retention.

Boxed Marketing Highlights

The boxed segments introduce you to real people and real industry examples, connecting the chapter material to real life.

Marketing HIGHLIGHT 11–1 Segmented Pricing: The Right Product to the Right Customer at the Right Time for the Right Price

In most hospitality, travel and entertainment products capacity is fixed, but demand varies. In these situations, a common price may result in many people not being able to access the product during prime times and empty seats during off-peak periods. In some products such as airline transportation and events, all seats many not be the same. Live performances, including sporting events, theater, and concerts, will charge more for seats with great views and less for seats father away from the event. Some airlines charge more for aisle and window seats. Customers wanting better seats with the capacity to pay for these seats will have the opportunity to purchase the seats they want. Those who want to see the event or want to get to a certain destination but want to spend less can purchase less expensive seats. Susan Greco gives an example of an opera company, which went from a single price for all seats to pricing based on the location of the seat, increasing the price for better seats and lowering the price for seats in the back. Seat prices on the weekends were increased and those during the week were reduced. The variety of prices allowed the customers to choose what they would pay and the opera company increased its overall revenue by 9 percent. Some customers who previously could not afford to attend now had the opportunity to attend by selecting tickets further from the stage on weekday nights.

The opera company had introduced a simple form of revenue management. Airlines, hotels, and restaurants call it revenue management and practice it religiously. Robert Cross, a longtime consultant to the airlines, states there are opportunities for all companies to gain from revenue management. He states, "This will allow you to attract customers by having the right product at the right price for the right customer."

Segmented pricing and yield management aren't really new ideas. For instance, Marriott Corporation used seat-of-the-pants yield-management approaches long before it installed its current sophisticated system. Back when J. W. "Bill" Marriott was a young man working at the family's first hotel, the Twin Bridges in Washington, DC, he sold rooms from a drive-up window. As Bill tells it, the hotel charged a flat rate for a single occupant, with an extra charge for each additional person staying in the room. When room availability got tight on some nights, Bill would lean out the drive-up

Theaters often apply revenue management by charging more for seats with better views and during times when demand is higher. Courtesy of Richard Cummins/Corbis.

Full-Color Visuals

Color format with lively photographs, drawings, and tables will maintain your interest and provide visual aids to learning.

■■■ Important Memory Tools

Chapter Objectives

At the start of each chapter, the list will help you focus and organize your thoughts as you are reading. The learning objectives summarize what you need to know after studying the chapter and doing the exercises.

Key Terms

Key marketing and hospitality terms, highlighted and defined in each chapter, provide you with a convenient source for learning and reviewing the professional vocabulary needed for effective communication on the job. These terms are found in each chapter, and a glossary of all the terms can be found at the end of the book.

Chapter Review

At the end of each chapter, a summary of chapter content in outline form helps you review and retain key information. The format for the chapter review was the suggestion of a student.

■■■ Applying Your Knowledge

Experiential Exercises

These exercises are designed to provide experiences that will illustrate the concepts presented in the chapter and provide experiences that you can draw on in the future.

Internet Exercises

The Internet has become both an important marketing tool and a source of marketing information. The Internet exercises introduce you to information sources on the Internet and show how others are using the Internet.

■■■ Applying Your Critical Thinking Skills

Case Studies

The case studies at the end of the book represent real situations that can be used to analyze actual business situations and come up with solutions to your organization's problem. Sometimes, your instructor will use these cases as the basis of class discussions.

Discussion Questions

These end-of-chapter questions will challenge you to address real-world situations and consider appropriate methods of action.

PREFACE

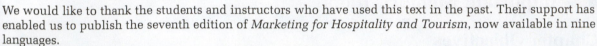

We would like to thank the students and instructors who have used this text in the past. Their support has enabled us to publish the seventh edition of *Marketing for Hospitality and Tourism*, now available in nine languages.

This book is written with the hospitality and travel student in mind. The solicited and unsolicited comments we received from students and instructors have been incorporated into the sixth edition. Students have told us *Marketing for Hospitality and Tourism* is readable and interesting. One student wrote, "I enjoyed reading this book—it didn't seem like I was reading a textbook." In this newest edition we strive to maintain the same tone. For instructors, we made the text flow more smoothly from a teaching perspective.

The authors have extensive experience working with hospitality and travel businesses around the globe. Our understanding of the hospitality and travel business ensures that the end result is a book that clearly explains marketing concepts and shows how they apply to real-life situations.

The book has an international focus, which is especially important in this era of increasing globalization. Business markets have become internationalized—domestic companies are expanding overseas as foreign companies seek to enter U.S. markets—therefore, it is crucial that today's students be exposed to business and cultural examples from other parts of the world. Rather than have one chapter devoted to international marketing, we have incorporated examples throughout the text.

This text has truly evolved as a team project. Without the support of our students and faculty at other universities and colleges, this book would not have developed into the leading book in its category. We thank you for your support and acknowledge below some of the people who have been involved in the development of the book.

■■■ Instructional Support

The support for those using **Marketing for Hospitality and Tourism** includes an Instructor's Manual, a test bank, and PowerPoint slides. The 18 chapters create a comprehensive text. Some instructors may have chosen to use 16 or 17 chapters depending on the scope of their program. The completeness of the text allows this flexibility. There are a number of YouTube and other videos that will engage your students. A Web site for hospitality and tourism marketing professors, htmktgprofessors.com, lists many of these videos. For information on how to access these videos, contact jbowen@uh.edu.

■■■ We Welcome Your Comments, Suggestions, and Questions

We would like to hear your comments on this edition and your suggestions for future editions. Please address comments to John Bowen, Conrad N. Hilton College of Hotel and Restaurant Management, University of Houston, jbowen@uh.edu.

■■■ Acknowledgments

We would like to thank the students and the instructors who have used earlier editions of this book and provided feedback that added value to the users of this edition. Tazeem Gulamhusein, a student at the University of Houston, helped with the research and development of the seventh edition. Thanks go to the following group who provided comments and feedback for this seventh edition: Deepak Chhabra, Arizona State University, Tempe; Dan Creed, Metropolitan State University, St. Paul; Jamal Feerasta, College of Applied Science and Technology, University of Akron; Juline Mills, University of New Haven; David Schoenberg, LaGuardia Community College, CUNY; and Nancy Warren, Highline Community College.

The following people provided reviews of past editions: Jennifer A. Aldrich, Kimberly M. Anderson, James A. Bardi, Jonathan Barsky, David C. Bojanic, Mark Bonn, Jane Boyland, Bonnie Canziani, Harsha E. Chacko, Deepak Chhabra, Dan Creed, Tim H. Dodd, Geralyn Farley, Andy Feinstein, Michael Gallo, Richard M. Howey, Jeffrey Ivory, Dianne Jolovich, Ed Knudson, Robert J. Kwortnik, Ingrid Lin, Ken McCleary, Juline Mills, H. G. Parsa, Edward B. Pomianoski, Hailin Qu, Allen Z. Reich, Howard F. Reichbart, Joan Remington, Emily C. Richardson, Kisang Ryu, John Salazar, Ralph Tellone, Muzzo Uysal, Anna Graf Williams, and Gregory R. Wood.

The following people helped with past editions when they were students to make sure the text was student friendly: Shiang-Lih Chen McCain, Jason Finehout, Michael Gallo, Tazeem Gulamhusein, Walter Huertas, Ming (Michael) Liang, Marvel L. Maunder, Tracee Nowlak, Michelle North, Sarah Robinson, and Carrie Tyler.

We appreciate the support and enthusiasm of the companies that provided advertisements and illustrations for this book. These organizations put forth a great deal of effort in finding and providing the materials we requested; working with them was one of the most rewarding parts of producing this book. We would also like to thank our Pearson Team: Daryl Fox, Susan Watkins, and Lara Dimmick. Finally, we would like to thank our families for their support and encouragement.

■■■ What's New in the Seventh Edition

The 7th edition of *Marketing for Hospitality and Tourism* is a landmark entry in the long successful history of the market leader. With the 7th edition, great care was taken to provide an introductory guide to hospitality and tourism marketing that truly reflects the modern realities of marketing. We've thoroughly revised the seventh edition of *Marketing for Hospitality and Tourism* to reflect the major trends and forces impacting marketing in this digital age of customer value, engagement, and relationships.

- More than any other developments, sweeping new online, social media, mobile, and the internationalization of tourism are affecting how marketers, brands, and customers engage each other. User generated content on social media can make or break a restaurant, while at the same time providing a useful source of customer information. The seventh edition features new and revised discussions and examples of the explosive impact of exciting new digital marketing technologies shaping marketing strategy and practice-from online, mobile, and social media engagement technologies discussed through the text including chapters 1, 4, 5, 6, 11, 12, 13, 16 and 17. With chapter 16 having been completely rewritten and now includes social media and mobile marketing in the title to highlight the importance of these concepts.

- One point of differentiation of the text is it has an international focus. The seventh edition provides new discussions and examples of the growth in global marketing. As the world becomes a smaller, more competitive place, marketers face new global marketing challenges and opportunities, especially in fast-growing emerging markets such as China, India, the Middle East, Eastern Europe and Southeast Asia. In the first chapter we discuss the growing internationalization of the tourism business. To help your students understand the importance of the global aspect of tourism we include international examples and illustrations throughout the text. Chapter 9 now includes expanded coverage of branding practices in hospitality on global level and gives examples of generational and lifestyle brands. In Chapter 17 new sections on branding tourist destinations and tourism competitiveness have been added to help students understand how to compete in a global market. The cases include multinational companies and businesses outside of North America. This international approach makes the text relevant to students outside of North American, while showing North American students they can find a truly rewarding career in the area of international business.

- The distribution channels for hotels are ever changing. Meta-search engines such as TripAdvisor are now selling hotel rooms. Priceline and other online travel agencies (OTAs) are highly profitable, giving Priceline a market capitalization that is three times larger than Marriott. OTAs have developed their own loyalty program to compete with brand loyalty programs. The changing role of distribution systems in the hospitality industry is discussed in Chapters 1 and 12.

- Other emerging trends changing hospitality and tourism marketing include the sharing economy, crowdsourcing, live-like-a-local, sustainable marketing and corporate social responsibility. These concepts are introduced in Chapter 1. Chapter 17 includes a discussion of managing the tourist experience through the cocreation of the visitor experience and providing live-like-a local experiences. Chapters 3, 4, 7 and 17 discuss sustainable marketing and social responsibility.

- This edition also recognizes the role of non-profit organizations in Tourism and Hospitality. This is demonstrated in Chapter opening vignettes for Chapter 4 and 14 and a Marketing Highlight in chapter 14.

- The seventh edition provides revised and expanded coverage of developments in the fast-changing area of integrated marketing communications. It tells how marketers are blending traditional media with new digital and social media tools- everything from Internet and mobile marketing to social media- to create more targeted, personal, and engaging customer relationships. Marketers are no longer simply creating integrated promotion programs; they are practicing content marketing in paid, owned, earned, and shared media. No other hospitality and tourism marketing text provides more current or encompassing coverage of these exciting developments.

- The seventh edition continues to improve on its innovative learning design that has made it the market leader. The text's active and integrative presentation includes learning enhancements such as annotated chapter-opening stories, a chapter-opening objective outline, and marketing highlights that provide industry examples of the marketing concepts discussed in the chapter. Figures and Tables illustrate concepts presented in the text, while definitions of key terms are found in the margins as well as a comprehensive glossary at the end of the text, providing students with a knowledge of vocabulary used in the industry. Each chapter ends with a summary outline, discussion questions, experiential exercises and Internet exercises. The book also contains a collection of case studies covering all the chapters in the text. This innovative learning design facilitates student understanding and eases learning.

Philip Kotler
John Bowen
James Makens
Seyhmus Baloglu

Philip Kotler is S. C. Johnson & Son Distinguished Professor of International Marketing at the Kellogg School of Management, Northwestern University. He received his master's degree at the University of Chicago and his PhD at MIT, both in economics. Dr. Kotler is the author of *Marketing Management* (Pearson), now in its fifteenth edition and the most widely used marketing textbook in graduate schools of business worldwide. He has authored dozens of other successful books and has written more than 100 articles in leading journals. He is the only three-time winner of the coveted Alpha Kappa Psi award for the best annual article in the *Journal of Marketing*.

Professor Kotler was named the first recipient of four major awards: the Distinguished Marketing Educator of the Year Award and the William L. Wilkie "Marketing for a Better World" Award, both given by the American Marketing Association; the Philip Kotler Award for Excellence in Health Care Marketing presented by the Academy for Health Care Services Marketing; and the Sheth Foundation Medal for Exceptional Contribution to Marketing Scholarship and Practice. His numerous other major honors include the Sales and Marketing Executives International Marketing Educator of the Year Award; the European Association of Marketing Consultants and Trainers Marketing Excellence Award; the Charles Coolidge Parlin Marketing Research Award; and the Paul D. Converse Award, given by the American Marketing Association to honor "outstanding contributions to science in marketing." A recent Forbes survey ranks Professor Kotler in the top 10 of the world's most influential business thinkers. And in a recent *Financial Times* poll of 1,000 senior executives across the world, Professor Kotler was ranked as the fourth "most influential business writer/guru" of the twenty-first century.

Dr. Kotler has served as chairman of the College on Marketing of the Institute of Management Sciences, a director of the American Marketing Association, and a trustee of the Marketing Science Institute. He has consulted with many major U.S. and international companies in the areas of marketing strategy and planning, marketing organization, and international marketing. He has traveled and lectured extensively throughout Europe, Asia, and South America, advising companies and governments about global marketing practices and opportunities.

John T. Bowen is professor and former dean of the Conrad N. Hilton College of Hotel and Restaurant Management at the University of Houston and the Barron Hilton Distinguished Chair. Professor Bowen has presented marketing courses and seminars in Asia, Australia, Central America, Europe, and South America. Dr. Bowen is a consultant to both large and small hospitality corporations. Before becoming an academic, Professor Bowen held positions in restaurant management at both the unit and corporate level. Professor Bowen is on the editorial boards of the *Cornell Hotel and Restaurant Administration Quarterly*, *Journal of Services Marketing*, *International Journal of Contemporary Hospitality Marketing*, and *Worldwide Hospitality and Tourism Themes*. He is coauthor of *Restaurant Marketing for Owners and Managers*. Professor Bowen has received numerous awards for his teaching and research, including the UNLV Foundation Teaching Award, the Sam and Mary Boyd Distinguished Professor Award for Teaching, Founder's Award for Lifetime Support of Hospitality Graduate Education, and the Board of Regents Outstanding Faculty Member. The Graduate Education & Graduate Student Research Conference presented him with the Founder's Award, to recognize his contribution to graduate education. The Hotel and Lodging Association of Greater Houston recognized him with their lifetime achievement award. He has been a three-time recipient of the annual award from the International Council on Hotel, Restaurant and Institutional Education (CHRIE) for superior published research in the hospitality industry, and he received the John Wiley Award for Lifetime Research Achievement from CHRIE. Professor Bowen was recently cited as one of the five most influential hospitality management faculty in an article published in the *Journal of Hospitality and Tourism Education*. The Mayor of Houston proclaimed November 21, 2014, as John Bowen Day, in recognition of Dr. Bowen's contribution to the hospitality industry and hospitality education.

Dr. Bowen's formal education includes a BS in hotel administration from Cornell University, an MBA and MS from Corpus Christi State University, and a PhD in marketing from Texas A&M University.

James C. Makens is actively involved with the travel industry. He has conducted executive training for the Sheraton Corporation, Regent International Hotels, Taiwan Hotel Association, and Travelodge of Australia. He has also conducted marketing seminars for tourism ministries or travel associations in Australia, New Zealand, Canada, Indonesia, Singapore, Malaysia, and many nations of Latin America. Dr. Makens serves as a consultant and has written marketing plans for travel industry companies and tourism promotion boards. Other books he has authored or coauthored include *The Travel Industry* and the *Hotel Sales and Marketing Planbook*. His professional articles have appeared in the *Cornell Hotel and Restaurant Administration Quarterly*, *Journal of Travel Research*, *Journal of Marketing*, *Journal of Marketing Research*, and *Journal of Applied Psychology*. Dr. Makens earned an MS, an MBA, and a PhD from Michigan State University. He holds a BS from Colorado State University. He served as associate dean in the School of Travel Industry Management of the University of Hawaii. He was also an associate dean of INCAE, an affiliate of the Harvard Business School in Central America. Dr. Makens recently retired from the faculty at the Babcock Graduate School of Management at Wake Forest University.

Seyhmus Baloglu is professor and Harrah Distinguished Chair at the William F. Harrah College of Hotel Administration, University of Nevada Las Vegas (UNLV). He earned a BS in hotel administration from Cukurova University, an MBA from Hawaii Pacific University, and a PhD in hospitality marketing from Virginia Tech. Professor Baloglu has presented marketing courses and seminars in Asia, Australia, Europe, and the Caribbean. Before joining academia, he held management positions and had diverse background in the industry, including restaurants, hotels, resort clubs, and travel agencies. Professor Baloglu has published extensively in leading journals, including *Journal of Business Research*, *Cornell Hospitality Quarterly*, *Journal of Hospitality & Tourism Research*, *International Journal of Hospitality Management*, *Annals of Tourism Research*, *Journal of Travel Research*, *Tourism Management*, *Journal of Travel & Tourism Marketing*, and *Tourism Analysis*. He received grants, contracts, and consulting projects from tourism destinations, gaming resorts, hotels, airports, nightclubs, and supply-chain organizations. He has been named as one of the significant contributors to the hospitality and tourism literature. His work has been cited extensively across multiple disciplines and fields. His research credentials have earned him both an international reputation and placement on the editorial boards of numerous leading journals. He has presented his work at many national and international conferences, seminars, and symposia and served as keynote speaker and panel participant for numerous international conferences. Other books he has coauthored are *Managing and Marketing Tourist Destinations: Strategies to Gain a Competitive Edge* and *Handbook of Scales in Tourism and Hospitality Research*. Professor Baloglu is the recipient of numerous and prestigious teaching, research, and service awards. He has been named as the recipient of UNLV Alumni Association's Outstanding Faculty Member of the Year and the John Wiley & Sons Lifetime Research Achievement Award from the International Council on Hotel, Restaurant and Institutional Education (ICHRIE). His other major honors include annual research awards from ICHRIE, the Sam and Mary Boyd Distinguished Professor Awards, the Ace Denken Research Award, and the Claudine Williams Distinguished Chair.

Understanding the Hospitality and Tourism Marketing Process

1

Introduction: Marketing for Hospitality and Tourism

Chipotle Mexican Grill

Envision this. You're sitting in a restaurant where the people, from the chief executive officer (CEO) on down to the kitchen crew, obsess over using only the finest ingredients. They come to work each morning inspired by all the "fresh produce and meats they have to marinate, rice they have to cook, and fresh herbs they have to chop," says the CEO. The restaurant prefers to use sustainable, naturally raised ingredients sourced from local family farms. It's on a mission not just to serve its customers good food but to change the way its entire industry produces food. This sounds like a gourmet specialty restaurant, right? Wrong. It's Chipotle Mexican Grill. That's right, it's a fast-food restaurant.

In an age when many fast feeders seem to be using ever-cheaper ingredients and centralization of food preparation to cut costs and keep prices low, Chipotle is doing just the opposite. The chain's core sustainable mission is to serve "Food with Integrity." What does that mean? The company explains it the following way:

Chipotle is committed to finding the very best ingredients raised with respect for animals, the environment, and farmers. It means serving the very best sustainably raised food possible with an eye to great taste, great nutrition, and great value. It means that we support and sustain family farmers who respect the land and the animals in their care.

When founder and CEO Steve Ells opened the first Chipotle in Denver in 1993, his primary goal was to make the best gourmet burrito around. However, as the chain grew, Ells found that he didn't like the way the ingredients Chipotle used were raised and processed. So in 2000, Chipotle began developing a supply chain with the goal of producing and using naturally raised, organic, hormone-free, and nongenetically modified ingredients. Pursuing this healthy-food mission was no easy task. As the fast-food industry increasingly moved toward low-cost, efficient food processing, factory farms were booming, whereas independent farms producing naturally rose and organic foods were in decline.

To obtain the ingredients it needed, Chipotle had to develop many new sources. To help that cause, the company founded the Chipotle Cultivate Foundation, which supports family farming and encourages sustainable farming methods. Such efforts have paid off. For example, when Chipotle first started serving naturally raised pork in 2000, there were only 60 to 70 farms producing meat for the Niman Ranch pork cooperative, an important Chipotle supplier. Now, there are over 700. And as an added bonus, the more the supply chain of sustainable farmers grows, the more the cost comes down.

Today, 100 percent of Chipotle's pork and beef comes from producers that meet or exceed its "naturally raised" standards (the animals are raised in a humane way, fed a vegetarian diet, are never given hormones, and are allowed to display their natural tendencies). Chipotle's goal is to meet that same 100 percent mark for its chicken, dairy, and even its produce. It then plans to tighten its standards even more.

Sourcing such natural and organic ingredients not only serves Chipotle's sustainability mission, it results in one of the most nutritious, best-tasting fast-food burritos on the market—something the company can brag about to customers. Although some fast-food companies intentionally obscure the sometimes less-than-appetizing truths about their ingredients, Chipotle doesn't play that game. Instead, it commits fast-food heresy: Proudly telling customers what's really inside its burritos.

Chipotle chose the "Food with Integrity" slogan because it sends the right message in an appetizing way. "Saying that we don't buy dairy from cows that are given the hormone rBGH is not an appetizing message," says Ells. So the company is building its marketing campaign around the more positive message that food production should be healthier and more ethical. Chipotle communicates this positioning via an integrated mix of traditional and digital promotion venues, ranging from its Farm Team invitation-only loyalty program—by which customers earn rewards based not on frequent buying but on knowledge about food and how it is produced—to its Pasture Pandemonium smartphone app, where players try to get their pig across a pasture without getting trapped in pens or pricked by antibiotic needles.

While Chipotle doesn't spend much on traditional media advertising, the company uses both traditional and nontraditional promotional methods to broadcast its message. Chipotle made a big splash a few years ago during the broadcast for the Grammy Awards with its first-ever national television ad, "Back to the Start"—a two-and-a-half-minute stopmotion animation film showing the negative effects of industrialized farming. The ad received critical acclaim and racked up millions of views online.

As a follow-up, Chipotle released "The Scarecrow," another animated video indicting the industrial food industry. Accompanied by Fiona Apple's cover of "Pure Imagination," the star character leaves his job at a factory farm and opens his own little shop selling freshly prepared food under the banner "Cultivate a better world." The online ad directed people to the campaign's centerpiece—an arcadestyle game app. So far, the video has racked up more than 12 million views on YouTube and more than 9 million people have downloaded the app. Today, Chipotle has moved well beyond ads. The coconscious burrito maker is now producing sitcoms with a message. For example, it partnered with Hulu for the original comedy series, *Farmed and Dangerous*, attacking the sins of big agriculture and promoting the company's commitment to Food with Integrity.

Chipotle is proving that a company can be both socially responsible and produce a profit. And the chain is growing fast, opening a new restaurant about every two days. In the past five years, Chipotle's stock price has quintupled, suggesting that the company's investors are as pleased as its fast-growing corps of customers.

Founder and CEO Ells wants Chipotle to grow and make money. But ultimately, on a larger stage, he wants to change the way fast food is produced and sold—not just by Chipotle but also by the entire industry. "We think the more people understand where their food comes from and the impact that has on independent family farmers [and] animal welfare, the more they're going to ask for better ingredients," says Ells. Whether customers stop by Chipotle's restaurants to support the cause, gobble down the tasty food, or both, it all suits Ells just fine. Chipotle's sustainability mission isn't an add-on, created just to position the company as "socially responsible." Doing good "is the company's ethos and ingrained in everything we do," says Chipotle's director of communications.

A growing focus of companies is social responsibility. Chipotle was ahead of its time, when it started focusing on socially responsible polices almost 20 years ago. Today smart managers are realizing the importance of sustainability, taking care of their employees, treating members of their supply chain fairly, and giving back to the communities they serve. It is an exciting time to be involved in hospitality marketing.[1]

■■■ Your Passport to Success

As a manager in a global economy, marketing will greatly assist your personal career and the success of the enterprise you manage. In today's hospitality/travel industry, the customer is global and is king or queen. This title is bestowed not because of hereditary rights but because customers have the ability to enhance or damage your career through the purchase choices they make and the positive or negative comments they make to others.

The travel industry is the world's largest industry and the most international in nature. International travel has receipts of over $1.33 trillion and over 1.25 billion travelers.[2] China's 1.4 billion people take over 3.3 billion domestic trips each year, spending U.S. $375 billion. The rapid growth of domestic tourism in China, combined with over 135 million inbound tourists, has led to a rapid growth of hotels, resorts, airport facilities, and other facilities to support tourism.[3] China is not alone in its promotion of tourism; other national, regional, and local agencies across the globe are also aggressively promoting their destination.

Each region has unique features that will be perceived as benefits to specific markets. The title "The World's Best Airport" belongs to Singapore. The world's best hotel, according to TripAdvisor, is Gili Lankanfushi in the Maldives. There are 17 countries that are home to the top 25 hotels in the world. The best international airline is Qatar Airlines. The best restaurant in the world is El Celler de Can Roca in Spain.[4]

The world's travel industry is alive, exciting, and competitive. Hospitality companies and destination marketing organizations (DMOs) hire thousands of college graduates each year. As the competitive environment becomes more complex and marketing management changes at an ever-increasing rate, there is a great demand for people who have the knowledge, skills, and attitude to compete in today's environment.

Welcome to marketing! Your passport to success!

Today marketing isn't simply a business function: it's a philosophy, a way of thinking, and a way of structuring your business and your mind. Marketing is much more than a new ad campaign. The task of marketing is never to fool the customer or endanger the company's image. Marketing's task is to provide real value to targeted customers, motivate purchase, and fulfill consumer needs.

Marketing, more than any other business function, deals with customers. Creating customer value and satisfaction is at the heart of hospitality and travel industry marketing. Many factors contribute to making a business successful. However, today's successful companies at all levels have one thing in common: They are strongly customer focused and heavily committed to marketing. Accor has become one of the world's largest hotel chains by delivering L'esprit Accor, the ability to anticipate and meet the needs of its guests, with genuine attention to detail.[5] Smashburger says "Smashed fresh, Served delicious" to let

Gili Lankanfushi in the Maldives was chosen by the users of TripAdvisor as the best hotel in the world. Courtesy of Smileimage9/Shutterstock.

customers and prospective customers know that it uses fresh ingredients that are carefully crafted to produce a great burger.[6] These and other successful hospitality companies know that if they take care of their customers, market share and profits will follow.

As a manager, you will be motivating your employees to create superior value for your customers. You will want to make sure that you deliver customer satisfaction at a profit. This is the simplest definition of marketing. This book will start you on a journey that will cause your customers to embrace you and make marketing your management philosophy.

■■■ Customer Orientation

Purpose of a business. To create and maintain satisfied, profitable customers.

The **purpose of a business** is to create and maintain satisfied, profitable customers.[7] Customers are attracted and retained when their needs are met. Not only do they return to the same cruise line, hotel, rental car firm, and restaurant, but they will also post pictures with favorable comments on social media.

"What about profits?" Some hospitality managers act as if today's profits are primary and customer satisfaction is secondary. This attitude eventually sinks a firm as it finds fewer repeat customers and faces increasingly negative word of mouth. Successful managers understand that profits are best seen as the result of running a business well rather than as its sole purpose. When a business satisfies its customers, the customers will pay a fair price for the product. A fair price includes a profit for the firm.

Managers who forever try to maximize short-run profits are short-selling both the customer and the company. Consider the following episode:

A customer arrived at a restaurant before closing time and was greeted with "What do you want?" Somewhat surprised, the customer replied that he would like to get a bite to eat. A surly voice informed the customer that the restaurant was closed. At this point, the customer pointed to a sign on the door stating that the restaurant was open until 9 P.M. "Yeah, but by the time I clean up and put the food away, it'll be nine, so we're closed." The customer left and went to another restaurant a block away and never returned to the first restaurant.

Let's speculate for a moment. Why was the customer treated in such a shabby manner? Perhaps,

- the employee wanted to leave early to go to a party.
- the employee was suffering from a headache.
- the employee had personal or family problems.

Cruise ships have traditionally been competition for resorts. Disney uses its brand recognition to create a market for its cruises. Disney also combines a vacation at Walt Disney World with a cruise from Florida to the Caribbean. Courtesy of Dmitrijs Mihejevs/Fotolia.

What really happened in the restaurant episode is that this employee once served a customer immediately before closing time, resulting in the employee working until 10:30 P.M. Instead of the corporate office thanking her for serving the customer and staying late, it reprimanded her for putting in extra time. The corporate office wanted to keep down overtime expenses. The employee's response was to close the business by 9 P.M. whatever the cost. Now the corporate office is happy—they just don't realize they are losing customers and future business. Much of the behavior of employees toward their customers is the result of management philosophy. The alternative management approach is to put the customer first and reward employees for serving the customer well.

It is wise to assess the customer's long-term value and take appropriate actions to ensure a customer's long-term support. Two studies document this. The Forum Company found that the cost of retaining a loyal customer is just 20 percent of the cost of attracting a new one.[8] Another study found that an increase of five percentage points in customer retention rates yielded a profit increase of 25 to 125 percent.[9] Accordingly, a hotel that can increase its repeat customers from 35 to 40 percent should gain at least an additional 25 percent in profits.[10] The former president of Scandinavian Airlines summed up the importance of a satisfied customer as follows:

> Look at our balance sheet. On the asset side, you can still see so-and-so many aircraft worth so-and-so many billions. But it's wrong; we are fooling ourselves. What we should put on the asset side is the last year SAS carried so-and-so many happy passengers. Because that's the only asset we've got—people who are happy with our service and willing to come back and pay for it once again.[11]

Without customers, assets have little value. Without customers, a new multi-million-dollar restaurant will close, and without customers, a $300 million hotel will go into receivership, with the receivers selling the hotel at a fraction of its book value.

■■■ What Is Hospitality and Tourism Marketing?

In the hotel industry, marketing and sales are often thought to be the same, and no wonder: The sales department is one of the most visible in the hotel. Sales managers provide prospective clients with tours and entertain them in the hotel's food and beverage outlets. Thus the sales function is highly visible, whereas most of the non-promotional areas of the marketing function take place behind closed doors. In the restaurant industry, many people confuse marketing with advertising and sales promotion. It is not uncommon to hear restaurant managers say that they "do not believe in marketing" when they actually mean that they are disappointed with the impact of their advertising. In reality, selling and advertising are only two marketing functions and often not the most important. Advertising and sales are components of the promotional element of the **marketing mix**. Other marketing mix elements include product, price, and distribution. Marketing also includes research, information systems, and planning.

Marketing mix. Elements include product, price, promotion, and distribution. Sometimes distribution is called place and the marketing situation facing a company.

The four-P framework calls on marketing professionals to decide on the product and its characteristics, set the price, decide how to distribute their product, and choose methods for promoting their product. For example, McDonald's has a fast-food product. It uses quality ingredients and developed products that it can sell at prices people expect to pay for fast food. Most people will not spend more than 15 minutes to travel to a McDonald's restaurant. As part of its distribution plan, McDonald's must have restaurants that are conveniently located to its target market. Finally, McDonald's appeals to different market segments and has many units throughout a city. This allows McDonald's to make effective use of mass media, such as television. The marketing mix must be just that—a mix of ingredients to create an effective product/service package for the target market.

If marketers do a good job of identifying consumer needs, developing a good product, and pricing, distributing, and promoting it effectively, the result will be attractive products and satisfied customers. Marriott developed Moxy Hotels; Darden designed the Olive Garden Italian Restaurant. They designed differentiated products, offering new consumer benefits. Marketing means "hitting the mark." Peter Drucker, a leading management thinker, put it this way: "The aim of marketing is to make selling superfluous. The aim is to know and understand customers so well that the product or service fits them and sells itself."[12]

This does not mean that selling and promotion are unimportant, but rather that they are part of a larger marketing mix, a set of marketing tools that work together to produce satisfied customers. The only way selling and promoting will be effective is if we first define our target market, understand their wants, and then prepare an easily accessible and available value package.

■■■ Marketing in the Hospitality Industry

Importance of Marketing

Hospitality industry. Made up of those businesses that offer one or more of the following: accommodation, prepared food and beverage service, and/or entertainment.

As we have seen, the **hospitality industry** is one of the world's major industries. In the United States, it is the second-largest employer. In more than half of the 50 states, it is the largest industry. In this book, we focus on the hospitality and travel industries.

Marketing has assumed an increasingly important role in the restaurant sector of the hospitality industry. Marketing today in many ways is the same as it was 20 years ago. We must understand our customers and develop a service delivery system to deliver a product they want at a price they will view as being fair. And do all this while still making a profit. In other ways marketing is ever changing and is changing very rapidly. Social media has given the customer a powerful voice; dashboards track comments customers are making about our product on social media; millennials are replacing baby boomers as the most important travel segment, and their wants are very different than the boomers.

The hotel industry is undergoing a consolidation, with companies such as Accor, Hilton, and Starwood buying hotel chains and operating different brands under one organization. The marketing expertise of these large firms has created a competitive marketing environment. While the director of marketing is a full-time marketer, everyone else must be a part-time marketer. All managers must understand marketing. By applying the principles of marketing to your job search, you will be able to enhance your career opportunities and hopefully end up in a job that you will love.

Tourism Marketing

The two main industries that comprise the activities we call tourism are the hospitality and travel industries. Thus, throughout this book we refer to the hospitality and travel industries. Successful hospitality marketing is highly dependent on the entire travel industry. Meeting planners choose destinations based on the cost of getting to the destination, the value of the hotels, the quality of restaurants, and evening activities for their attendees.

Visitors to international destinations, such as these tourists on the Brazilian side of Iguacu Falls, often purchase packages that include airfare, ground transportation, and hotel accommodations. Courtesy of Fabio Lotti/Fotolia.

The success of cruise lines is really the result of coordinated marketing by many travel industry members. For example, the Port of Boston wanted to attract more cruise line business. Massport (the port authority) aggressively marketed Boston to cruise lines. Having convinced them to come, they then promoted Boston to key travel agents. This was critical because travel agents account for 95 percent of all cruise line business. The result was that Boston doubled the number of port calls by cruise lines and added $17.3 million to the local economy through this combined marketing effort.

That's only the beginning of travel industry marketing cooperation to promote cruise lines. Airlines, auto rental firms, and passenger railways cooperatively develop packages with cruise lines. This requires coordination in pricing, promotion, and delivery of those packages. Like Massport, government or quasi-government agencies play an important role through legislation aimed at enhancing the industry and through promotion of regions, states, and nations.[13]

Few industries are as interdependent as travel–hospitality. This interdependence will increase in complexity. The travel industry will require marketing professionals who understand the big picture and can respond to changing consumer needs through creative strategies based on solid marketing knowledge.

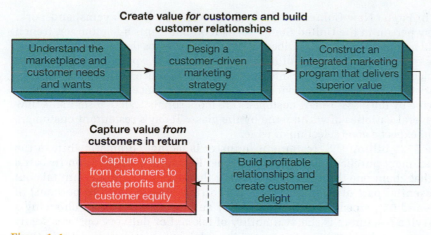

Create value *for* customers and build customer relationships

| Understand the marketplace and customer needs and wants | → | Design a customer-driven marketing strategy | → | Construct an integrated marketing program that delivers superior value |

Capture value *from* customers in return

| Capture value from customers to create profits and customer equity | ← | Build profitable relationships and create customer delight |

Figure 1–1
A simple model of the marketing process.

Although we normally think of marketing as being carried out by sellers, buyers also carry out marketing. Today's digital technologies, from online sites and smartphone apps to the explosion of social media, have empowered consumers and made marketing a truly two-way affair. Thus, in addition to customer relationship management, today's marketers must also deal effectively with customer-managed relationships. Marketers are asking not only "How can we influence our customers?" but also "How can our customers influence us?" and even "How can our customers influence each other?"

Definition of Marketing

Marketing. The art and science of finding, retaining, and growing profitable customers.

Marketing must be understood in the sense of satisfying customer needs. If the marketer understands customer needs; develops products that provide superior customer value; and prices, distributes, and promotes them effectively, these products will sell easily. Here is our definition of **marketing**: Marketing is the process by which companies create value for customers and build strong customer relationships in order to capture value from the customers in return.

The Marketing Process

Figure 1–1 presents a simple five-step model of the marketing process. In the first four steps, companies work to understand consumers, create customer value, and build strong customer relationships. In the final step, companies reap the rewards of creating superior customer value. By creating value for customers, they in turn capture value from customers in the form of sales, profits, and long-term customer equity.

■■□ Understanding the Marketplace and Customer Needs

As a first step, marketers need to understand customer needs and wants and the marketplace within which they operate. We now examine five core customer and marketplace concepts: (1) needs, wants, and demands; (2) marketing offerings (tangible products, services, and experiences); (3) value and satisfaction; (4) exchanges and relationships; and (5) markets.

Customer Needs, Wants, and Demands

Needs

Human need. A state of felt deprivation in a person.

The most basic concept underlying marketing is that of **human needs**. A human need is a state of felt deprivation. Included are the basic physical needs for food, clothing, warmth, and safety, as well as social needs for belonging, affection, fun, and relaxation. There are esteem needs for prestige, recognition, and fame, and individual needs for knowledge and self-expression. These needs were not invented by marketers, but they are part of the human makeup.

Wants

Human want. The form that a human need takes when shaped by culture and individual personality.

Human wants are the form human needs take as they are shaped by culture and individual personality. Wants are how people communicate their needs. A hungry person in Papua New Guinea needs food but wants taro, rice, yams, and pork. A hungry person in the United States needs food but wants a hamburger, french fries, and a Coke. Wants are described in terms of objectives that will satisfy needs. As a society evolves, the wants of its members expand. As people are exposed to more objectives that arouse their interest and desire, producers try to provide more want-satisfying products and services. Restaurants were once able to serve generic white wine by the glass. Today, customers are more sophisticated; restaurants now serve several varieties of white wine by the glass. Today's restaurant customers want and expect a good selection of wine.

The $725 billion U.S. restaurant industry is facing a dramatic shift in the way customers purchase meals. The National Restaurant Association research shows that about one-third of consumers say that purchasing restaurant takeout is an essential part of their lifestyle. In addition, nearly half (46 percent) of adults—and 61 percent of millennials—say an important factor in choosing a table service restaurant is the availability of takeout or delivery options. Many customers want the restaurant to prepare the meal, but they want to eat it in their own home.[14]

Many sellers often confuse wants with needs. A manufacturer of drill bits may think that customers need a drill bit, but what the customer really needs is a hole. These sellers suffer from "marketing myopia."[15] They are so taken with their products that they focus only on existing wants and lose sight of underlying customer needs. They forget that a physical product is only a tool to solve a consumer problem. These sellers get into trouble if a new product comes along that serves the need better or cheaper. The customer will then have the same need but want the new product.

Demands

Demands. Human wants that are backed by buying power.

People have almost unlimited wants, but limited resources. They choose products that produce the most satisfaction for their money. When backed by buying power, wants become **demands**.

Outstanding marketing organizations go to great lengths to learn about and understand their customer's needs, wants, and demands. They conduct customer research. Smart companies also have employees at all levels—including top management—stay close to customers. For example, at Southwest Airlines, all senior executives handle bags, check in passengers, and serve as flight attendants once a quarter. All Disney World managers spend one week per year on the front line—taking tickets, selling popcorn, or loading and unloading rides. Understanding customer needs, wants, and demands in detail provides important input for designing marketing strategies. The city of Santa Fe, New Mexico, has a beautiful and historic opera house, but only a small percentage of the population participated in operas. As Catherine Zacher, former president of Santa Fe Economic Development, Inc., said, "Most Americans don't enjoy being yelled at in Italian." However, they did want other forms of entertainment. When the opera house was made available for a variety of musical concerts, the demand created for this contemporary entertainment sold all available seats.[16]

Market Offerings: Tangible Products, Services, and Experiences

Consumer needs and wants are fulfilled through a market offering: a product that is some combination of tangible, services, information, or experiential product components. We often associate the word *product* with a tangible product or one that has physical properties (e.g., the hotel room or the steak we receive in a restaurant). In the hospitality industry, the intangible products, including customer service and experiences, are more important than the tangible products. Managers of resorts realize that their guests will be leaving with memories of their stay. They try to create experiences that will generate pleasant memories. At a Ritz-Carlton resort

The Gamboa Rainforest Resort offers an experience of a lifetime, allowing guests to explore Panama's rainforest and then relax at a resort enjoying a meal while watching ships traverse the Panama Canal. Courtesy of Bern Hotels & Resorts.

every evening at sunset managers set up chairs on the beach, hire a cellist to play relaxing music, and serve champagne to guests. They realize this event not only creates value for the guest, but it is also an experience that will create a lasting memory of their stay. Marriott provides dolphin safaris at its Newport Beach property and a water rafting trip at its Utah property. Marriott uses the resources of the destination to create guest experiences that the guest remembers for a lifetime.

A market offering includes much more than just physical goods or services. Consumers decide which events to experience, which tourist destinations to visit, which hotels to stay in, and which restaurants to patronize. To the consumer these are all products.

Customer Value and Satisfaction

Customer value is the difference between the benefits that the customer gains from owning and/or using a product and the costs of obtaining the product. Costs can be both monetary and nonmonetary. One of the biggest nonmonetary costs for hospitality customers is time. New electronic forms of registration through smartphones will make the hotel registration redundant. One of the challenges for hotel managers will be to replace the welcoming reception guests received from front desk clerks with another form of welcoming, perhaps through a lobby ambassador. Domino's Pizza saves the customer time and provides convenience by delivering pizza. Limited-service hotels provide value to the overnight traveler by offering a free continental breakfast. One of the biggest challenges for management is to increase the value of its product for its target market. To do this, managers must know their customers and understand what creates value for them. This is an ongoing process, as customers and competition change over time.

Customer value. The difference between the benefits that the customer gains from owning and/or using a product and the costs of obtaining the product.

Customer expectations are based on past buying experiences, the opinions of friends, and market information. If we meet customer expectations, they are satisfied. Marketers must be careful to set the right level of expectations. If they set expectations too low, they may satisfy those who buy but fail to attract new customers. If they raise expectations too high, buyers will be disappointed.

Customer expectations. Expectations based on past buying experiences, the opinions of friends, and market information.

In the hospitality industry it is easy to set high expectations because guests will not be able to judge the product until after they have consumed it. For example, an owner can advertise that his or her restaurant serves the best seafood in the city. If this is not true, many customers will leave dissatisfied; the experience did not meet their expectations. However, if one sets expectations too low, there will be no customer demand. We would not want to advertise that we are an average seafood restaurant. We must understand how we create value for our market and communicate that to our customers and potential customers. For example, we might specialize in fresh locally caught seafood. Customer satisfaction depends on a product's perceived performance in delivering value relative to a buyer's expectations. Smart companies aim to delight customers by promising only what they can deliver and then delivering more than they promise.

Managers must realize the importance of creating highly satisfied customers, rather than just satisfied customers. On a 7-point scale, with 1 very satisfied and 7 very dissatisfied, most managers are happy to receive a 2. However, from Figure 1–2,

Figure 1–2
Scores of 1, 2, and 3 are all on the satisfaction side of the scale; that is, they are all better than a score of 4 (neither satisfied nor dissatisfied), which is the midpoint of the scale. You can see that satisfying the guest is not enough. Only when guests leave very satisfied are they likely to come back. Your goal is to have all guests leave very satisfied.

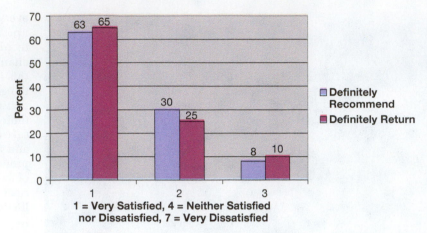

1 = Very Satisfied, 4 = Neither Satisfied nor Dissatisfied, 7 = Very Dissatisfied

Even though 3 is still a "positive" score on the above 7-point scale, few customers giving that rating will return.

which shows the results of a guest survey at a Boston hotel, you can see the huge gap between a guest who rates a hotel a 1 and one who rates it a 2.[17] Think of the last time you went to a restaurant and were just satisfied. Would you go back? Probably not. But when you walk out of a restaurant and say, "Wow, that was great!" you will probably return and tell others about your discovery.

Exchanges and Relationships

Exchange. The act of obtaining a desired object from someone by offering something in return.
Transaction. Consists of a trade of values between two parties; marketing's unit of measurement.

Marketing occurs when people decide to satisfy needs and wants through exchange. **Exchange** is the act of obtaining a desired object from someone by offering something in return. Marketing consists of actions taken to build and maintain desirable exchange relationships with target markets. Beyond simply attracting new customers and creating **transactions**, the goal is to retain customers and grow their business with the company. Marketers want to build strong relationships by consistently delivering superior customer value.

Markets

Market. A set of actual and potential buyers of a product.

The concept of transactions leads to the concept of a market. A **market** is a set of actual and potential buyers of a product. These buyers share a particular need or want that can be satisfied through exchange relationships.

Marketing means managing markets to bring about profitable customer relationships. However, creating these relationships takes work. Sellers must search for buyers, identify their needs, design good market offerings, set prices for them, promote them, and deliver them. Activities such as product development, research, communication, distribution, pricing, and service are core marketing activities.

◼◼ Designing Customer Value-Driven Marketing Strategy

Marketing management. The art and science of choosing target markets and building profitable relationships with them.
Marketing manager. A person who is involved in marketing analysis, planning, implementation, and control activities.

Once it fully understands consumers and the marketplace, marketing management can design a customer-driven marketing strategy. We define **marketing management** as the art and science of choosing target markets and building profitable relationships with them. The **marketing manager**'s aim is to find, attract, keep, and grow target customers by creating, delivering, and communicating superior customer value. To design a winning marketing strategy, the marketing manager must answer two important questions: What customers will we serve (what's our target market) and how can we serve these customers best (what's our value proposition)?

Selecting Customers to Serve

The company must first decide who it will serve. It does this by dividing the market into segments of customers (market segmentation) and selecting which segments it will go after (target marketing). Some people think of marketing management as finding as many customers as possible and increasing demand. But marketing managers know that they cannot serve all customers in every way. By trying to serve all customers, they may not serve any customer well. Instead, the company wants to select only customers that it can serve well and profitably. For example, Ritz-Carlton Hotels profitably target affluent travelers; McDonald's restaurants profitably target families.

Choosing a Value Proposition

Value proposition. The full positioning of a brand—the full mix of benefits upon which it is positioned.

The company must also decide how it will serve targeted customers—how it will differentiate and position itself in the marketplace. A company's **value proposition** is the set of benefits or values it promises to deliver to consumers to satisfy their needs.

Such value propositions differentiate one brand from another. They answer the customer's question, "Why should I buy your brand rather than a competitor's?" Companies must design strong value propositions that give them the greatest advantage in their target markets.

Marketing
HIGHLIGHT 1.1   Jet Blue Delights Its Customers

There's an old adage in the airline industry: "You're not flying planes, you're flying people." These days, however, it seems that many big airlines overlook the people factor. Instead, they focus on moving their human cargo as efficiently as possible while charging as much as the traffic will bear. The American Customer Satisfaction Index rates the airline industry near the bottom among 47 industries in customer satisfaction, barely ahead of perennial cellar-dwellers subscription TV and Internet service providers.

Not so at JetBlue Airways. From the very beginning, young JetBlue has built a reputation for creating first-rate, customer-satisfying experiences. Its slogan—YOU ABOVE ALL—tells the JetBlue faithfuls that they are at the very heart of the company's strategy and culture. JetBlue is on a heartfelt mission to bring humanity back to air travel.

At JetBlue, customer care starts with basic amenities that exceed customer expectations, especially for a low-cost carrier. JetBlue's well-padded, leather-covered coach seats allow three inches more legroom than the average airline seat. Although the airline doesn't serve meals, it offers the best selection of free beverages and snacks to be found at 30,000 feet (including unexpected treats such as Terra Blues chips, Linden's chocolate chip cookies, and Dunkin' Donuts coffee). Every JetBlue seat has its own LCD entertainment system, complete with free 36-channel DirectTV

and 100+ channels of SiriusXM Radio. JetBlue rounds out the amenities with a recently launched industry firstFly-Fi, an in-flight high-speed Internet service with free basic browsing on all equipped planes.

JetBlue continuously innovates to find new ways to delight customers. Its "Even More Space" seats give customers the option of going from "roomy to roomier," allow early boarding, and give early access to overhead bins. Its "Even More Speed" service provides VIP passage through airport security screening. And JetBlue's Mint service puts a new spin on first-class air travel, offering front-of-the-plane, lie-flat "sweet seats," some of them in enclosed suites with their own doors. According to JetBlue, Mint services deliver "unexpected, individualized 'me-mints' that revive and engage, keeping you in mint condition during your travels."

Such tangibles help keep JetBlue travelers satisfied. But JetBlue CEO David Barger knows that the tangibles are only a small part of what really makes JetBlue special. "The hard product—airplanes, leather seats, satellite TVs—as long as you have a checkbook, can be replicated," says Barger. "It's the JetBlue *culture* that can't be replicated. The *human* side of the equation is the most important part of what we're doing." It's that JetBlue culture—the near-obsessive focus on the customer flying experience—that creates not just satisfied JetBlue customers, but *delighted* ones.[18]

Marketing Management Orientations

Marketing management wants to design strategies that will build profitable relationships with target consumers. But what philosophy should guide these marketing strategies? What weight should be given to the interests of customers, the organization, and society? Often, these interests conflict with each other. There are five alternative concepts under which organizations design and carry out their marketing strategies: production, product, selling, marketing, and marketing 3.0.

The Production Concept

The production concept is one of the oldest philosophies guiding sellers. The **production concept** holds that consumers will favor products that are available and highly affordable, and therefore management should focus on production and distribution efficiency. The problem with the production concept is that management may become so focused on production systems that they forget the customer.

A visitor was staying at a hotel in the Swiss Alps with a beautiful view of Lake Geneva. The dining room had an outdoor balcony to experience the beauty of the surroundings. Enjoying breakfast on the balcony was a perfect way to start a summer day. To the guest, the balcony was a great benefit; to the hotel, it was a nuisance. The balcony was at the edge of the dining room and thus the farthest spot from the kitchen. There were no service stations near the balcony, so all supplies had to come from the dining room. There was only one entrance to the balcony, making access difficult. Simply put, serving customers on the balcony was not efficient.

The hotel discouraged customers from eating on the balcony by not setting up the tables. If one asked to eat on the balcony, he or she received a pained expression from the service person. One then had to wait 15 minutes for the table to be set. Once the food was served, the service person disappeared, never to be seen again. This was the hotel's way of reminding the guest that no one should eat on the balcony. Yet the hotel should have viewed the balcony as providing a competitive advantage. The production concept promotes efficiency, but often at the expense of being effective.

Production concept. Holds that customers will favor products that are available and highly affordable, and therefore management should focus on production and distribution efficiency.

The Product Concept

The **product concept**, like the production concept, has an inward focus. The product concept holds that consumers will favor products that offer the most in quality, performance, and innovative features. Under this concept, marketing strategy focuses on making continuous product improvements.

Product quality and improvement are important parts of most marketing strategies. However, focusing only on the company's products can lead to marketing myopia. Consumers are trying to satisfy needs and might turn to entirely different products to better satisfy those needs, such as bed and breakfast (B&Bs) instead of hotels or fast-food outlets in student centers instead of cafeterias.

Victoria Station was a restaurant chain that specialized in excellent prime rib. It was very successful and expanded quickly into a 50-restaurant chain. Management focused on how to make its product better and at a lower cost. It came up with the right number of days to age its beef. The rib roasts were slow cooked to maintain the juices and avoid shrinkage. It had an excellent product and became a popular restaurant brand. Unfortunately, customer wants changed; red meat became less popular. Victoria Station did not keep up with these changes in the wants of its guests. It still produced great prime rib, but many of its customers no longer wanted prime rib. Victoria Station had a product orientation when it should have had a marketing orientation. Its customer counts declined, and it ended up filing for bankruptcy.

Product concept. The idea that consumers will favor products that offer the most quality, performance, and features, and therefore the organization should devote its energy to making continuous product improvements.

The Selling Concept

The **selling concept** holds that consumers will not buy enough of the organization's products unless the organization undertakes a large selling and promotion effort. The aim of a selling focus is to get every possible sale, not to worry about satisfaction after the sale or the revenue contribution of the sale.

Selling concept. The idea that consumers will not buy enough of an organization's products unless the organization undertakes a large selling and promotion effort.

The selling concept does not establish a long-term relationship with the customer because the focus is on getting rid of what one has rather than creating a product to meet the needs of the market. Restaurants often advertise when sales start to drop, without first analyzing why sales are dropping. They do not try to change their product to fit the changing market. They sell harder, pushing their products on the customer through increased advertising and couponing. Eventually, they go out of business because their product no longer satisfies the needs of the marketplace.

The Marketing Concept

Marketing concept. The marketing management philosophy that holds that achieving organizational goals depends on determining the needs and wants of target markets and delivering desired satisfactions more effectively and efficiently than competitors.

The **marketing concept** is a more recent business philosophy and one that has been adopted in the hospitality industry. The marketing concept holds that achieving organizational goals depends on determining the needs and wants of target markets and delivering the desired satisfaction more effectively and efficiently than competitors.

The marketing concept starts with a well-defined market, focuses on customer needs, and integrates all the marketing activities that affect customers. It meets the organizational goals by creating long-term customer relationships based on customer value and satisfaction. As Herb Kelleher, former CEO of Southwest Airlines, stated, "We don't have a Marketing department: we have a Customer department" (Figure 1–3).

The Societal Marketing Concept

Societal marketing concept. The idea that an organization should determine the needs, wants, and interests of target markets and deliver the desired satisfactions more effectively and efficiently than competitors in a way that maintains or improves the consumer's and society's well-being.

The **societal marketing concept** questions whether the pure marketing concept overlooks possible conflicts between consumer *short-run wants* and consumer *long-run welfare*. Is a firm that satisfies the immediate needs and wants of target markets always doing what's best for its consumers in the long run? The societal marketing concept holds that marketing strategy should deliver value to customers in a way that maintains or improves both the *consumer's* and *society's* well-being. It calls for *sustainable marketing*, socially and environmentally responsible marketing that meets the present needs of consumers and businesses while also preserving or enhancing the ability of future generations to meet their needs.

Two of the sustainability efforts of restaurants include reduction of food waste and locally sourced food, eliminating the carbon fuels used to transport foods. The Sustainable Restaurant Association (SRA) has helped create campaigns that reduce food waste and encourage locally sourced food products. The results of their research found most customers do not ask to take uneaten food home because that 34 percent of the respondents never thought about taking uneaten food home, 25 percent felt embarrassed to ask to take food home, and 24 percent thought restaurants were not allowed to let uneaten food leave the restaurant. Eighteen percent said they would not eat the food at home or thought it was not hygienic. The SRA has been working with restaurants to reduce food waste. Wahaca, a London-based restaurant group, encouraged customers to take home uneaten food through its "Too Good to Waste" campaign. They noticed a 20 percent reduction in plate waste over a six-month period. Pret a Manger, through its "Made Today Gone Today" program, gives over 500,000 meals a year of unsold food to charities.[19]

Even more broadly, many leading business and marketing thinkers are now preaching the concept of *shared value*, which recognizes that societal needs,

Figure 1–3
The selling and marketing concepts contrasted.

Starting Point	Focus	Means	Ends
Factory	Existing products	Selling and promoting	Profits through sales volume

The selling concept

Market	Customer needs	Integrated marketing	Profits through customer satisfaction

The marketing concept

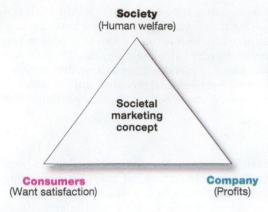

Society
(Human welfare)

Societal marketing concept

Consumers
(Want satisfaction)

Company
(Profits)

Figure 1–4
Three considerations underlying the societal marketing concept.
Source: Kotler, Philip; Armstrong, Gary, Principles of Marketing, 16th Ed., ©2016, pp. 12, 24, 50. Reprinted and Electronically reproduced by permission of Pearson Education, Inc., New York, NY.

not just economic needs, define markets.[20] The concept of shared value focuses on creating economic value in a way that also creates value for society. A growing number of companies known for their hardnosed approaches to business are rethinking the interactions between society and corporate performance. They are concerned not just with short-term economic gains but also with the well-being of their customers, the depletion of natural resources vital to their businesses, the viability of key suppliers, and the economic well-being of the communities in which they produce and sell.

One prominent marketer calls this Marketing 3.0. "Marketing 3.0 organizations are values-driven," he says. "I'm not talking about being value-driven. I'm talking about 'values' plural, where values amount to caring about the state of the world." As Figure 1–4 shows, companies should balance three considerations in setting their marketing strategies: consumer wants, company profits, *and* society's interests.

Preparing an Integrated Marketing Plan

The company's marketing strategy outlines which customers the company will serve and how it will create value for these customers. Next, the marketer develops an integrated marketing program that will actually deliver the intended value to target customers. The marketing program builds customer relationships by transforming the marketing strategy into action. It consists of the firm's marketing mix, the set of marketing tools the firm uses to implement its marketing strategy.

The major marketing mix tools are classified into four broad groups, called the four Ps of marketing: product, price, place, and promotion. To deliver on its value proposition, the firm must first create a need-satisfying market offering (product). It must decide how much it will charge for the offer (price) and how it will make the offer available to target consumers (place). Finally, it must communicate with target customers about the offer and persuade them of its merits (promotion). The firm must blend all of these marketing mix tools into a comprehensive, integrated marketing program that communicates and delivers the intended value to chosen customers. We explore marketing programs and the marketing mix in much more detail in later chapters.

Building Customer Relationships

The first three steps in the marketing process—understanding the marketplace and customer needs, designing a customer value-driven marketing strategy, and constructing a marketing program—all lead up to the fourth and most important step: building and managing profitable customer relationships. We first discuss the basics of customer relationship management. Then, we examine how companies go about engaging customers on a deeper level in this age of digital and social marketing.

Customer relationship management (CRM). It involves managing detailed information about individual customers and carefully managing customer "touch points" in order to maximize customer loyalty.

Customer Relationship Management

Customer relationship management (CRM) is perhaps the most important concept of modern marketing. In the broadest sense, CRM is the overall process of building and maintaining profitable customer relationships by delivering superior customer value and satisfaction. It deals with all aspects of acquiring, engaging, and growing customers.

Relationship Building Blocks: Customer Value and Satisfaction

The key to building lasting customer relationships is to create superior customer value and satisfaction. Satisfied customers are more likely to be loyal customers and give the company a larger share of their business.

Customer-perceived value. The customer's evaluation of the difference between all the benefits and all the costs of a market offering relative to those of competing offers.

CUSTOMER VALUE.   Attracting and retaining customers can be a difficult task. Customers often face a bewildering array of products and services from which to choose. A customer buys from the firm that offers the highest **customer-perceived value**—the customer's evaluation of the difference between all the benefits and all the costs of a market offering relative to those of competing offers. Importantly, customers often do not judge values and costs "accurately" or "objectively." They act on perceived value.

To some consumers, value might mean sensible products at affordable prices. To other consumers, however, value might mean paying more to get more. For example, limited-service restaurants serving food selections usually found in more expensive table-serve restaurants have become popular with customers who are willing to stand in line and place their order at a counter. They then have their food delivered to them at the table rather than having a server come to the table to take their order. They save 10 to 20 percent on an equivalent meal at a full-service restaurant and often will tip less than they would at a full-service restaurant, creating a perceived value for some customers. Other restaurant customers like to relax with their guests, enjoy conversation, and do not want to stand in line to place an order. To these customers the perceived value of a full-service restaurant is higher than a limited-service restaurant, and they are willing to pay the extra costs of a full-service restaurant.

Customer satisfaction. The extent to which a product's perceived performance matches a buyer's expectations.

CUSTOMER SATISFACTION.   **Customer satisfaction** depends on the product's perceived performance relative to a buyer's expectations. If the product's performance fails short of expectations, the customer is dissatisfied. If performance matches expectations, the customer is satisfied. If performance exceeds expectations, the customer is highly satisfied or delighted.

Outstanding marketing companies go out of their way to keep important customers satisfied. Most studies show that higher levels of customer satisfaction lead to greater customer loyalty, which in turn results in better company performance. Smart companies aim to delight customers by promising only what they can deliver and then delivering more than they promise. Delighted customers not only make repeat purchases but also become willing marketing partners and "customer evangelists" who spread the word about their good experiences to others.

For companies interested in delighting customers, exceptional value and service become part of the overall company culture. For example, year after year, Ritz-Carlton ranks at or near the top of the hospitality industry in terms of customer satisfaction. Its passion for satisfying customers is summed up in the company's credo, which promises that its luxury hotels will deliver a truly memorable experience—one that enlivens the senses, instills well-being, and fulfills even the unexpressed wishes and needs of our guests."[21]

Check into any Ritz-Carlton hotel around the world, and you'll be amazed by the company's fervent dedication to anticipating even your slightest need. Without ever asking, they seem to know that you're allergic to peanuts and want a king-size bed, a nonallergenic pillow, extra body gel, the blinds open when you arrive, and breakfast with decaffeinated coffee in your room. Each day, hotel staffers—from those at the front desk to those in maintenance and housekeeping—discreetly observe and record even the smallest guest preferences. Then, every morning, each hotel reviews the files of all new arrivals who have previously stayed at a Ritz-Carlton and prepares a list of suggested extra touches that might delight each guest. For example, according to one Ritz-Carlton manager, if the chain gets hold of a picture of a guest's pet, it will make a copy, have it framed, and display it in the guest's room in whatever Ritz-Carlton the guest visits.

Once they identify a special customer need, Ritz-Carlton employees go to legendary extremes to meet it. For instance, when a businessman attending a conference at the Ritz-Carlton Orlando ordered his favorite soda during a dinner in a hotel ballroom, his banquet server told him that the hotel didn't serve that beverage but he would see what he could do. To no one's surprise, the server quickly returned with the requested beverage, and for the rest of the week he had the drink waiting for the guest. But here's the best part. A year later when the guest returned for the conference, as he sat in the ballroom waiting for dinner the first night, the same server walked up with his favorite drink in hand. As a result of such customer service heroics, an amazing 95 percent of departing guests report that their stay has been a truly memorable experience. More than 90 percent of Ritz-Carlton's delighted customers return.

A company doesn't need to have over-the-top service to create customer delight. For example, quick service restaurants Chick-fil-A and Raising Cane's have highly satisfied customers, as a result of the excellent products and the care their employees show for their customers. Thus, customer satisfaction comes not just from service heroics, but from how well a company delivers on its basic value proposition. "Most customers don't want to be 'wowed,'" says one marketing consultant. "They [just] want an effortless experience."[22]

Although a customer-centered firm seeks to deliver high customer satisfaction relative to competitors, it does not attempt to maximize customer satisfaction. A company can always increase customer satisfaction by lowering its prices or increasing its services. But this may result in lower profits. Thus, the purpose of marketing is to generate customer value profitably. This requires a very delicate balance: The marketer must continue to generate more customer value and satisfaction but not "give away the house."

Customer Relationship Levels and Tools

Beyond offering consistently high value and satisfaction, marketers can use specific marketing tools to develop stronger bonds with customers. For example, many companies offer frequency marketing programs that reward customers who buy frequently or in large amounts. Airlines offer frequent-flyer programs, hotels give room upgrades to frequent guests, and supermarkets give patronage discounts to "very important customers." These days almost every brand has a loyalty rewards program. However, some innovative loyalty programs offer members special benefits and create member communities.

Engaging Customers

Significant changes are occurring in the nature of customer brand relationships. Today's digital technologies—the Internet and the surge in online, mobile, and social media—have profoundly changed the ways that people on the planet relate to one another. In turn, these events have had a huge impact on how companies and brands connect with customers, and how customers connect with and influence each other's brand behaviors.

Customer Engagement and Today's Digital and Social Media

The digital age has spawned a dazzling set of new customer relationship-building tools, from Web sites, online ads and videos, mobile ads and apps, and blogs to online communities and the major social media, such as Twitter, Facebook, YouTube, Instagram, and Pinterest.

Yesterday's companies focused mostly on mass marketing to broad segments of customers at arm's length. By contrast, today's companies are using online, mobile, and social media to refine their targeting and to engage customers more deeply and interactively. The old marketing involved marketing brands to consumers. The new marketing is **customer-engagement marketing** fostering direct and continuous customer involvement in shaping brand conversations, experiences, and community. Customer-engagement marketing goes beyond just selling a brand to consumers. Its goal is to make the brand a meaningful part of consumers' conversations and lives.

The burgeoning Internet and social media have given a huge boost to customer-engagement marketing. Today's consumers are better informed, more

Customer-engagement marketing. Fosters direct and continuous customer involvement in shaping brand conversations, experiences, and community.

connected, and more empowered than ever before. Newly empowered consumers have more information about brands, and they have a wealth of digital platforms for airing and sharing their brand views with others. Thus, marketers are now embracing not only CRM but also customer-managed relationships, in which customers connect with companies and with each other to help forge their own brand experiences.

Greater consumer empowerment means that companies can no longer rely on marketing by intrusion. Instead, they must practice marketing by attraction—creating market offerings and messages that engage consumers rather than interrupt them. Hence, most marketers now augment their mass-media marketing efforts with a rich mix of online, mobile, and social media marketing that promote brand–consumer engagement and conversation.

For example, companies post their latest ads and videos on social media sites, hoping they'll go viral. They maintain an extensive presence on Twitter, YouTube, Facebook, Google+, Pinterest, Vine, and other social media to create brand buzz. They launch their own blogs, mobile apps, online microsites, and consumer-generated review systems, all with the aim of engaging customers on a more personal, interactive level.

Almost every company has something going on Facebook these days. Starbucks has more than 36 million Facebook "fans." And every major marketer has a YouTube channel where the brand and its fans post current ads and other entertaining or informative videos. Artful use of social media can get consumers involved with and talking about a brand. Rental car company Hertz uses a broad range of digital and social media to engage its customers and boost sales.[23] A recent Hertz study found that consumers who engage in social conversations about the brand are 30 percent more likely to make a purchase than those who don't. And customers who engage in Hertz-related social activity in early stages of the rental process are four times more likely to visit Hertz's Web site. So, Hertz now incorporates social media in almost all of its marketing, such as Twitter hashtags, links to major social media, and sharing features. For example, Hertz's Twitter feed is a 140-character customer service line that tends to each problem and question posted by members. On the brand's Facebook and Google+ pages, Hertz posts specials, such as waiving the young driver fee for car rentals during the spring break season. More than just creating conversations, Hertz also uses the social media to help build sales.

The key to engagement marketing is to find ways to enter consumers' conversations with engaging and relevant brand messages. Simply posting a humorous video, creating a social media page, or hosting a blog isn't enough. Successful engagement marketing means making relevant and genuine contributions to consumers' lives and conversations.

Consumer-Generated Marketing

A growing form of customer-engagement marketing is consumer-generated marketing, by which consumers themselves are playing a bigger role in shaping their own brand experiences and those of others. This might happen through uninvited consumer-to-consumer exchanges in blogs, video-sharing sites, social media, and other digital forums. But increasingly, companies themselves are inviting consumers to play a more active role in shaping products and brand content.

Some companies ask consumers for new product and service ideas. For example, at its My Starbucks Idea site, Starbucks collects ideas from customers on new products, store changes, and just about anything else that might make their Starbucks experience better. Starbucks realizes that the best way to see the business through the eyes of the customers is to ask its customers for ideas that will improve its operation. The site invites customers to share their ideas, vote on and discuss the ideas of others, and see which ideas Starbucks has implemented.[24]

Moreover, because consumers have so much control over social media content, inviting their input can sometimes backfire. For example, McDonald's famously launched a Twitter campaign using the hashtag #McDStories, hoping that it would inspire heartwarming stories about Happy Meals. Instead, the effort was hijacked by Twitter users, who turned the hashtag into a "bashtag" by posting less-than-appetizing messages about their bad experiences with the fast-food chain.

McDonald's pulled the campaign within only two hours, but the hashtag was still churning weeks, even months later.[25]

As consumers become more connected and empowered, and as the boom in digital and social media technologies continues, consumer brand engagement—whether invited by marketers or not—will be an increasingly important marketing force. Through a profusion of consumer-generated videos, shared reviews, blogs, mobile apps, and Web sites, consumers are playing a growing role in shaping their own and other consumers' brand experiences. Engaged consumers are now having a say in everything from product design, usage, and packaging to brand messaging, pricing, and distribution. Brands must embrace this new consumer empowerment and master the new digital and social media relationship tools or risk being left behind.

Partner Relationship Management

When it comes to creating customer value and building strong customer relationships, today's marketers know that they can't do it alone. They must work closely with a variety of marketing partners. In addition to being good at CRM, marketers must also be good at partner relationship management—working closely with others inside and outside the company to jointly engage and bring more value to customers.

Traditionally, marketers have been charged with understanding customers and representing customer needs to different company departments. However, in today's more connected world, every functional area in the organization can interact with customers. The new thinking is that—no matter what your job is in a company—you must understand marketing and be customer focused. Rather than letting each department go its own way, firms must link all departments in the cause of creating customer value.

Marketers must also partner with suppliers, channel partners, and others outside the company. Marketing channels consist of distributors, retailers, and others who connect the company to its buyers. The supply chain describes a longer channel, stretching from raw materials to components to final products that are carried to final buyers. Through supply chain management, companies today are strengthening their connections with partners all along the supply chain. They know that their fortunes rest more on than just how well they perform. Success at delivering customer value rests on how well their entire supply chain performs against competitors' supply chains.

▪▪▪ Capturing Value from Customers

The first four steps in the marketing process outlined in Figure 1–1 involve building customer relationships by creating and delivering superior customer value. The final step involves capturing value in return in the form of current and future sales, market share, and profits. By creating superior customer value, the firm creates highly satisfied customers who stay loyal and buy more. This, in turn, means greater long-run returns for the firm. Here, we discuss the outcomes of creating customer value: customer loyalty and retention, share of market and share of customer, and customer equity.

Customer Loyalty and Retention

Good CRM creates customer delight. In turn, delighted customers remain loyal and talk favorably to others about the company and its products. Studies show big differences in the loyalty of customers who are less satisfied, somewhat satisfied, and completely satisfied. Even a slight drop from complete satisfaction can create an enormous drop in loyalty. Thus, the aim of CRM is to create not only customer satisfaction but also customer delight.

Losing a customer means losing more than a single sale. It means losing the entire stream of purchases that the customer would make over a lifetime of

Lifetime value (LTV). The LTV of a customer is the stream of profits a customer will create over the life of his or her relationship to a business.

patronage. For example, here is a dramatic illustration of customer **lifetime value (LTV)**.

Stew Leonard, who operates a highly profitable four-store supermarket in Connecticut and New York, says he sees $50,000 flying out of his store every time he sees a sulking customer. Why? Because his average customer spends about $100 a week, shops 50 weeks a year, and remains in the area for about 10 years. If this customer has an unhappy experience and switches to another supermarket, Stew Leonard's has lost $50,000 in revenue. The loss can be much greater if the disappointed customer shares the bad experience with other customers and causes them to defect. To keep customers coming back, Stew Leonard's has created what the *New York Times* has dubbed the "Disneyland of Dairy Stores," complete with costumed characters, scheduled entertainment, a petting zoo, and animatronics throughout the store. From its humble beginnings as a small dairy store, Stew Leonard's has grown at an amazing pace. It has built 29 additions onto the original store, which now serves more than 300,000 customers each week. This legion of loyal shoppers is largely a result of the store's passionate approach to customer service. "Rule #1: The customer is always right. Rule #2: If the customer is ever wrong, re-read rule #1."[26]

Stew Leonard is not alone in assessing customer LTV. Ritz-Carlton Hotels put the LTV of a guest at more than $120,000. Domino's Pizza puts the LTV of a customer at more than $10,000.[27] A company can lose money on a specific transaction but still benefit greatly from a long-term relationship. This is one of the reasons successful companies empower employees to resolve customer complaints. The company wants to maintain the relationship with the customer. And that relationship keeps customers coming back.

Growing Share of Customer

Share of customer. The portion of the customer's purchasing that a company gets in its product categories.

Beyond simply retaining good customers to capture customer LTV, good CRM can help marketers increase their **share of customer**—the share they get of the customer's purchasing in their product categories. Thus, restaurants want to get more "share of stomach" and airlines want greater "share of travel." To increase share of customer, firms can offer greater variety to current customers, for example, a coffee house can expand its selection of flavored teas and add smoothies. Or they can create to cross-sell pastries and other snacks and/or up-sell from brewed coffee to blended drinks to market more products and services to existing customers.

We can now see the importance of not only acquiring customers but also keeping and growing them. One marketing consultant puts it this way: "The only value your company will ever create is the value that comes from customers—the ones you have now and the ones you will have in the future. Without customers, you don't have a business."[28]

Building Customer Equity

We can now see the importance of not only acquiring customers but also keeping and growing them. The value of a company comes from the value of its current and future customers. CRM takes a long-term view. Companies want to not only create profitable customers but also "own" them for life, earn a greater share of their purchases, and capture their customer LTV.

What Is Customer Equity?

Customer equity. The discounted lifetime values of all the company's current and potential customers.

The ultimate aim of CRM is to produce high customer equity.[29] **Customer equity** is the total combined customer LTVs of all of the company's current and potential customers. Therefore, it's a measure of the future value of the company's customer base. Clearly, the more loyal the firm's profitable customers, the higher its customer equity. Customer equity may be a better measure of a firm's performance than current sales or market share. Although sales and market share reflect the past, customer equity suggests the future.[30]

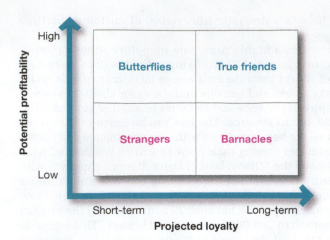

Figure 1–5
Customer relationship groups.
Source: Kotler, Philip; Armstrong, Gary, Principles of Marketing, 16th Ed., ©2016, pp. 12, 24, 50. Reprinted and Electronically reproduced by permission of Pearson Education, Inc., New York, NY.

Building the Right Relationships with the Right Customers

Companies should manage customer equity carefully. They should view customers as assets that must be managed and maximized. But not all customers, not even all loyal customers, are good investments. Surprisingly, some loyal customers can be unprofitable, and some disloyal customers can be profitable. Which customers should the company acquire and retain?

The company can classify customers according to their potential profitability and manage its relationships with them accordingly. One classification scheme defines four relationship groups based on potential profitability and projected loyalty: strangers, butterflies, true friends, and barnacles; see Figure 1–5.[31] Each group requires a different relationship management strategy. For example, "strangers" show low potential profitability and little projected loyalty. There is little fit between the company's offerings and their needs. The relationship management strategy for these customers is simple: Don't invest anything in them.

"Butterflies" are potentially profitable but not loyal. There is a good fit between the company's offerings and their needs. However, like real butterflies, we can enjoy them for only a short while and then they're gone. An example is stock market investors who trade shares often and in large amounts but who enjoy hunting out the best deals without building a regular relationship with any single brokerage company. Efforts to convert butterflies into loyal customers are rarely successful. Instead, the company should enjoy the butterflies for the moment. It should create satisfying and profitable transactions with them, capturing as much of their business as possible in the short time during which they buy from the company. Then it should cease investing in them until the next time around.

"True friends" are both profitable and loyal. There is a strong fit between their needs and the company's offerings. The firm wants to make continuous relationship investments to delight these customers and nurture, retain, and grow them. It wants to turn true friends into "true believers," those who come back regularly and tell others about their good experiences with the company.

"Barnacles" are highly loyal but not very profitable. There is a limited fit between their needs and the company's offerings. An example is smaller bank customers, who bank regularly but do not generate enough returns to cover the costs of maintaining their accounts. Like barnacles on the hull of a ship, they create drag. Barnacles are perhaps the most problematic customers. The company might be able to improve their profitability by selling them more, raising their fees, or reducing service to them. However, if they cannot be made profitable, they should be "fired."

The point here is an important one: Different types of customers require different relationship management strategies. The goal is to build the right relationships with the right customers.

■■■ The Changing Marketing Landscape

In this section, we examine the major trends and forces that are changing the marketing landscape and challenging marketing strategy. We look at five major developments: the digital age, the changing economic environment, the growth of not-for-profit marketing, rapid globalization, and the call for more ethics and social responsibility.

The Digital Age: Online, Mobile, and Social Media Marketing

The explosive growth in digital technology has fundamentally changed the way we live—how we communicate, share information, access entertainment, and shop. An estimated 3.2 billion people, over 40 percent of the world's population, are now online. More than two-thirds of American adults now own smartphones; 50 percent of those adults use their smartphones and other mobile devices to access social media sites. These numbers are similar to smartphone use in other countries and will only grow as digital technology rockets into the future.[32]

Most consumers are totally smitten with all things digital. For example, according to one study, more than half of Americans keep their mobile phone next to them when they sleep—they say it's the first thing they touch when they get up in the morning and the last thing they touch at night. Favorite online and mobile destinations include the profusion of Web sites and social media that have sprung up. People in the United States spent more time viewing digital media than viewing TV and the percentage of time spent on digital media is ever increasing, while the time spent on TV is decreasing. The time spent reading newspapers is only 3 percent of the time the average person spends with digital media.

The consumer love affair with digital and mobile technology makes it a fertile ground for marketers trying to engage customers. So it's no surprise that the Internet and rapid advances in digital and social media have taken the marketing world by storm. **Digital and social media marketing** involves using digital marketing tools such as Web sites, social media, mobile ads and apps, online video, e-mail, blogs, and other digital platforms that engage consumers anywhere, anytime via their computers, smartphones, tablets, Internetready TVs, and other digital devices. These days, it seems that every company is reaching out to customers with multiple Web sites, newsy tweets and Facebook pages, viral ads and videos posted on YouTube, rich-media e-mails, and mobile apps that solve consumer problems and help them shop.

At the most basic level, marketers set up company and brand Web sites that provide information and promote the company's products. Many of these sites also serve as online brand communities, where customers can congregate and exchange brand-related interests and information.

Beyond brand Web sites, most companies are also integrating social and mobile media into their marketing mixes.

Social Media Marketing

It's hard to find a brand Web site, or even a traditional media ad, that doesn't feature links to the brand's Facebook, Twitter, Google+, LinkedIn, YouTube, Pinterest, Instagram, or other social media sites. Social media provide exciting opportunities to extend customer engagement and get people talking about a brand. Nearly 90 percent of all U.S. companies now use social media as part of their marketing mixes, and 78 percent have dedicated social marketing teams. By various estimates, social media spending accounts for about 10 percent of marketing budgets and will rise to an estimated nearly 20 percent within the next five years.[33]

Some social media are huge—Facebook has more than 1.1 billion members, Twitter has more than 500 million, and Pinterest draws in 70 million. Instagram racks up an estimated 85 million unique monthly visitors. And Reddit, the online social news community, has nearly 70 million unique visitors a month from 174 countries.[34] Online social networks provide a digital home where people can connect and share important information and moments in their lives. Chili's, a causal restaurant chain, realizes the importance of social media. It is spending millions of dollars to make its food more shareable; this is not part of a program to reduce food waste; it relates to promoting its food products on social media. Food is difficult to photo; realizing this, Chili's is changing its recipes to make food that is more photogenic. It is brushing its hamburger buns with an

Digital and social media marketing. Using digital marketing tools such as Web sites, social media, mobile apps and ads, online video, e-mail, and blogs that engage consumers anywhere, at anytime, via their digital devices.

Social Media Managers are one of the fastest growing positions in the hotel industry. Courtesy of Rawpixel/Fotolia.

egg wash to make them shine in a photo, the ribs are stacked just so on a plate to make them attractive to an amateur photographer, and it now serves its fries in a basket. Chili's management realizes photos of its food will be shared and viewed by millions. It wants to make sure its food looks as good as possible in these photos.[35]

Mobile Marketing

Mobile marketing is perhaps the fastest-growing digital marketing platform. Twenty-nine percent of smartphone owners use their phones for shopping-related activities—browsing product information through apps or the mobile Web, reading online product reviews, finding and redeeming coupons, and more.[36] Smartphones are ever-present, always on, finely targeted, and highly personal. This makes them ideal for engaging customers anytime and anywhere, as they move through the buying process. For example, Starbucks customers can use their mobile devices for everything from finding the nearest Starbucks and learning about new products to placing and paying for orders.[37]

Starbucks has made use of mobile devices to promote its stores. Courtesy of siraphol/123RF.

Although online, social media, and mobile marketing offer huge potential, most marketers are still learning how to use them effectively. The key is to blend the new digital approaches with traditional marketing to create a smoothly integrated marketing strategy and mix. We will examine digital, mobile, and social media marketing throughout the text—they touch almost every area of marketing strategy and tactics. Then, after we've covered the marketing basics, we'll look more deeply into digital and direct marketing in Chapter 16.

The Changing Economic Environment

The Great Recession of 2008 to 2009 and its aftermath hit American consumers hard. After two decades of overspending, new economic realities forced consumers to bring their consumption back in line with their incomes and rethink their buying priorities.

In today's postrecession era, consumer incomes and spending are again on the rise. However, even as the economy has strengthened, rather than reverting to their old freespending ways, Americans are now showing an enthusiasm for frugality not seen in decades. Sensible consumption has made a comeback, and it appears to be here to stay. The new consumer-spending values emphasize simpler living and more value for the dollar. Despite their rebounding means, consumers continue to buy less, clip more coupons, swipe their credit cards less, and put more in the bank.

Many consumers are reconsidering their very definition of the good life. "People are finding happiness in old-fashioned virtues—thrift, savings, do-it-yourself projects, self-improvement, hard work, faith, and community," says one consumer behavior expert. "We are moving from mindless to mindful consumption." The new, more frugal spending values don't mean that people have resigned themselves to lives of deprivation. As the economy has improved, consumers are indulging in luxuries and bigger-ticket purchases again, just more sensibly.

In adjusting to the new economy, companies may be tempted to cut their marketing budgets and slash prices in an effort to coax more frugal customers into opening their wallets. However, although cutting costs and offering selected discounts can be important marketing tactics, smart marketers understand that making cuts in the wrong places can damage long-term brand images and customer relationships. The challenge is to balance the brand's value proposition with the current times while also enhancing its long-term equity. Thus, rather than slashing prices in uncertain economic times, many marketers hold the line on prices and instead explain why their brands are worth it. Restaurants will design menu items they can sell for a lower price, rather than reduce the size or quality of existing items.

Rapid Globalization

As they are redefining their customer relationships, marketers are also taking a fresh look at the ways in which they relate with the broader world around them. Today, almost every company, large or small, is touched in some way by global competition. A neighborhood florist supplies flowers for a wedding reception that came from Mexican nurseries, and major U.S. hotel companies compete with hotel companies based in Europe and Asia for a conference being held in Seoul.

McDonald's now serves 70 million customers daily in more than 36,000 local restaurants in 118 countries worldwide—71 percent of its corporate revenues come from outside the United States.[38] Thus, managers in countries around the world are increasingly taking a global, not just local, view of the company's industry, competitors, and opportunities. They are asking: What is global marketing? How does it differ from domestic marketing? How do global competitors and forces affect our business? To what extent should we "go global"?

Sustainable Marketing—the Call for More Environmental and Social Responsibility

Marketers are reexamining their relationships with social values and responsibilities and with the very Earth that sustains us. As the worldwide consumerism and environmentalism movements mature, today's marketers are being called on to develop sustainable marketing practices. Corporate ethics and social responsibility have become hot topics for almost every business. And few companies can ignore the renewed and very demanding environmental movement. Every company action can affect customer relationships. Today's customers expect companies to deliver value in a socially and environmentally responsible way.

The social responsibility and environmental movements will place even stricter demands on companies in the future. Some companies resist these movements, budging only when forced by legislation or organized consumer outcries. Forward-looking companies, however, readily accept their responsibilities to the world around them. They view sustainable marketing as an opportunity to do well by doing good. They seek ways to profit by serving immediate needs and the best long-run interests of their customers and communities.

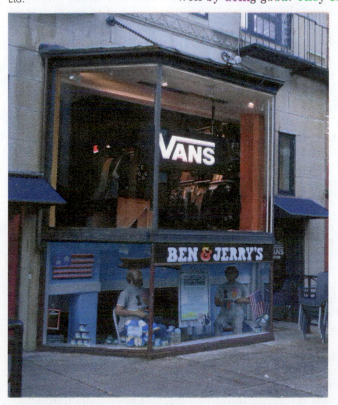

Ben & Jerry's three-part "linked prosperity" mission drives it to make fantastic ice cream (product mission), manage the company for sustainable financial growth (economic mission), and use the company "in innovative ways to make the world a better place" (social mission). Shown in the photo is a Ben & Jerry's in London, England. Courtesy of Dorling Tony Souter/Dorling Kindersley, Ltd.

Under its three-part mission, Ben & Jerry's wants to make fantastic ice cream (product mission), manage the company for sustainable financial growth (economic mission), and use the company "in innovative ways to make the world a better place" (social mission). Ben & Jerry's backs its mission with actions. For example, the company is committed to using wholesome, natural, non-GMO (genetically modified organism), fair trade-certified ingredients, and buys from local farms. It employs business practices "that respect the earth and the environment," investing in wind energy, solar usage, travel offsets, and carbon neutrality. Its Caring Dairy program helps farmers develop more sustainable practices on the farm (Caring Dairy means happy cows, happy farmers, and a happy planet). The Ben & Jerry's Foundation awards nearly $2 million annually in grassroots grants to community service organizations and projects in communities across the nation. Ben & Jerry's also operates 14 Partner Shops—scoop shops that are independently owned and operated by community-based not-for-profit organizations. The company waives standard franchise fees for these shops. Sustainable marketing presents both opportunities and challenges for marketers.[39]

Co-Creation

First time travelers are often not familiar with the offerings of a destination and sadly miss experiences that would have created lifelong positive memories for them. Co-creation involves the hospitality or travel company interacting with the guest to create experiences through this interaction. The interaction can be passive or active. Visit Houston provides an example of passive co-creation. The management of Visit Houston has grouped activities tourists can experience to create lifestyle itineraries, including "Girlfriends Getaway," "Guy's Weekend," several itineraries for families, and a tour of local breweries.[40] They have developed a total of 17 itineraries based on the interests of the visitor. Someone who enjoys craft beer could follow the itinerary set by Visit Houston or modify the itinerary based on their time and interests.

Withlocals.com is an organization that works across destinations. It is an application of the sharing economy co-creating experiences for tourists. For example, you can have lunch or dinner prepared by a local couple in their home in Vietnam. The write-up for the dinner states you can take a 10-minute taxi ride to our home, or we can pick you up on cycles, which takes more time but is more fun. If you want lunch, the hosts invite you to come to the local market with them and pick out the fresh food for lunch, then go back to their home and prepare food. Withlocals. com has a social responsibility focus; the goal is to provide sustainable income for locals through tourism.[41] At the same time it lets tourists cocreate experiences they will not forget. Destinations attracting international visitors who possess the self-confidence to spend time with locals will benefit from providing these experiences. The tourist will gain lifelong memories. Memories they will share with others on social media.

Two European researchers provide an example of active cocreation, which results in providing customized suggestions to an individual tourist or group of tourists in real time.[42] They provide an example of a traveler that is headed to a beach destination, planning to spend a week in the sun. As her vacation date approaches so do storms, ending her dream of spending her days on the beach. Through social media the DMO of the beach location is able to gain access to the dates the tourist will be in the city, the weather forecast for this period, and what the tourist enjoys besides going to the beach. Using this information the DMO can develop itineraries the tourist should enjoy. The ultimate goal of co-creation is to create memories. Memories the tourist will have for life and share with others face-to-face and on social media.

The Sharing Economy

The sharing economy is not new to the hospitality and travel industries. For example, fractional or shared ownership in vacation homes is a well-established form of shared ownership. The recent surge in the sharing economy has been in part to individuals sharing talents, time, and tangible assets they own to gain additional income and the Internet enabling them to connect with customers. For example, Airbnb created a distribution system allowing individuals to share a room in their house, their entire home, or their vacation home with travelers. Some people are willing to vacate their apartment during a citywide convention, as they can earn the equivalent of several months' rent during a week of high demand for accommodation in their city. Uber and Lyft have allowed individuals to share their time and their car with others by driving others around town. DogVacay is a service provided by people who like dogs and are willing to take care of other people's dogs, either in their home or the client's home. BonAppetour provides a platform for travelers to find locals who will host travelers for a meal in their home, or even cooking lessons on local cuisine. The sharing economy is creating new experiences and conveniences for the traveler and opportunities for income to the provider of the service.

The disruptive sharing economy is also creating challenges. Many hospitality industries such as the restaurant, hotel, and taxi sectors of the industry are highly regulated for the protection of travelers. They often have high taxes to support the promotion of tourism and tourism infrastructure. One source of controversy between conventional providers of hospitality and travel services is the sharing economy operates without regulation and thus has an unfair advantage. Despite these disputes, some established companies are now joining the sharing economy. Mercedes Benz has created a ride-sharing platform called Car2Go, and Avis recently brought the car sharing company Zipcar. Couchsurfing provides a platform for travelers to stay with others for free. It pairs people willing to host travelers with willingness to stay on a "couch," the same way they would if they were visiting a friend. As the sharing economy continues to grow, it will create threats and opportunities for the hospitality and travel industries. Managers will need to manage and minimize the threats and take advantage of the opportunities.

■■■ Marketing's Future

A technology executive stated, "The pace of change is so rapid that the ability to change has now become a competitive advantage." Rapid changes can quickly make yesterday's winning strategies out of date. As management thought leader Peter Drucker once observed, a company's winning formula for the last decade will probably be its undoing in the next decade. When we wrote the last edition, companies were trying to figure out how to use social media. Now social media has made an impact on marketing that has been a major driver of a new concept, marketing 3.0. Social media will forever change how we do marketing.

The worldwide growth of the travel industry has created a shortage of managers, as much so that in some regions projects are put on hold because the developer does not have and cannot acquire a management staff. These are truly great times for those entering the hospitality industry, but they are not without their challenges.

Baby boomers have long dominated the business travel market; in a few years the millennials will replace the baby boomers as the most important business travel market. Fast-food restaurants are seeing people who grew up on their food, now going to limited-service restaurants such as Jimmy Johns and Chipotle. In challenging times, good management is always sought.

This book is not just for students who desire a successful career in marketing; it is for students who desire a successful career. Marketing with its customer orientation has become the job of everyone and your passport to success.

Relationship marketing. Involves creating, maintaining, and enhancing strong relationships with customers and other stakeholders.

Customer touch point. Any occasion on which a customer encounters the brand and product—from actual experience to personal or mass communications to casual observation.

■■■ CHAPTER REVIEW

I. Customer Orientation. The purpose of a business is to create and maintain profitable customers. Customer satisfaction leading to profit is the central goal of hospitality marketing.

II. What Is Hospitality Marketing? Marketing is the art and science of finding, retaining, and growing profitable customers.

III. Importance of Marketing
   A. The entrance of corporate giants into the hospitality market and the marketing skills these companies have brought to the industry have increased the importance of marketing within the industry.
   B. Analysts predict that the hotel industry will consolidate in much the same way as the airline industry has, with five or six major chains dominating the market. Such consolidation will create a market that is highly competitive. The firms that survive this consolidation will be the ones that understand their customers.

   C. In response to growing competitive pressures, hotel chains are relying on the expertise of the marketing director.

IV. Travel Industry Marketing
   A. Successful hospitality marketing is highly dependent on the entire travel industry.
   B. Government or quasi-government agencies play an important role in travel industry marketing through legislation aimed at enhancing the industry and through promotion of regions, states, and nations.
   C. Few industries are as interdependent as the travel and hospitality industries.

V. Understanding the Marketplace and Customer Needs

The marketing process is a five-step model of the marketing process. In the first four steps, companies work to understand consumers, create customer value, and build strong customer relationships. In the final step, companies reap the rewards of creating superior customer value. By creating value for customers, they in turn capture value from customers in the form of sales, profits, and long-term customer equity.

A. Understand customers

1. **Needs.** Human beings have many complex needs. These include basic physical needs for food, clothing, warmth, and safety; social needs for belonging, affection, fun, and relaxation; esteem needs for prestige, recognition, and fame; and individual needs for knowledge and self-expression.

2. **Wants.** Wants are how people communicate their needs.

3. **Demands.** People have almost unlimited wants but limited resources. They choose products that produce the most satisfaction for their money. When backed by buying power, wants become demand.

4. **Market offerings.** Some combination of tangible products, services, information, or experiences that are offered to the market.

5. **Value, expectations, and satisfaction**
   a. **Customer value** is the difference between the benefits that the customer gains from owning and/or using a product and the costs of obtaining the product.
   b. **Customer expectations** are based on past buying experiences, the opinions of friends, and market information.
   c. **Satisfaction** with a product is determined by how well the product meets the customer's expectations for that product.

B. Exchange and relationships

1. **Exchange.** Exchange is the act of obtaining a desired object from someone by offering something in return.

2. **Relationship marketing.** Relationship marketing focuses on building a relationship with a company's profitable customers. Most companies are finding that they earn a higher return from resources invested in getting repeat sales from current customers than from money spent to attract new customers.

3. **Designing customer-driven marketing strategy.** Marketing management is the art and science of choosing target markets and building profitable relationships with them.
   a **Selecting customers to serve.** The company must select those market segments it wishes to serve.
   b **Choosing a value proposition.** The company must also decide how it will serve targeted customers—how it will differentiate and position itself in the marketplace. A company's value proposition is the set of benefits or values it promises to deliver to consumers to satisfy their needs.

VI. Designing a Customer Value-Driven Marketing Strategy

A. Choosing a value proposition. The company must also decide how it will serve targeted customers and how it will differentiate and position itself in the marketplace.

B. Marketing management orientation

1. **Production concept.** The production concept holds that customers will favor products that are available and highly affordable, and therefore management should focus on production and distribution efficiency.

2. **Product concept.** The product concept holds that customers prefer existing products and product forms, and the job of management is to develop good versions of these products.

3. **Selling concept.** The selling concept holds that consumers will not buy enough of the organization's products unless the organization undertakes a large selling and promotion effort.

4. **Marketing concept.** The marketing concept holds that achieving organizational goals depends on determining the needs and wants of target markets and delivering the desired satisfaction more effectively and efficiently than competitors.

5. **Societal marketing concept.** The societal marketing concept holds that the organization should determine the needs, wants, and interests of target markets and deliver the desired satisfactions more effectively and efficiently than competitors in a way that maintains or improves the consumer's and society's well-being.

VII. Prepare an Integrated Marketing Plan. The company's marketing strategy outlines which customers the company will serve and how it will create value for these customers. Next, the marketer develops an integrated marketing program that will actually deliver the intended value to target customers. The marketing program builds customer relationships by transforming the marketing strategy into action. It consists of the firm's marketing mix, the set of marketing tools the firm uses to implement its marketing strategy. The major marketing mix tools are classified into four broad groups, called the four Ps of marketing: product, price, place, and promotion.

VIII. Build Customer Relationships. Customer relationship management (CRM) involves managing detailed information about individual customers and carefully managing **customer "touch points"** in order to maximize customer loyalty.

IX. Capturing Value from Customers. We try to capture value from our customers in the form of current and future sales, market share, and profits. By creating superior customer value, the firm creates highly satisfied customers who stay loyal and buy more.

A. Customer loyalty and retention. The benefits of customer loyalty come from continued patronage of loyal customers, reduced marketing costs, decreased price sensitivity of loyal customers, and partnership activities of loyal customers. Loyal customers purchase from the business they are loyal to more often than non-loyal customers. They also purchase a broader variety of items. A manager who is loyal to a hotel brand is more likely to place his or her company's meetings with that hotel chain. Reduced marketing costs are the result of requiring fewer marketing dollars to maintain a customer than to create one and the creation of new customers through the positive word of mouth of loyal customers.

    B. Growing share of customer. Beyond simply retaining good customers to capture customer LTV, good CRM can help marketers to increase their share of customer—the share they get of the customer's purchasing in their product categories.

    C. Building customer equity. Customer equity is the discounted LTVs of all the company's current and potential customers. One builds customer equity by delivering products that create high customer satisfaction and have high perceived value.

X. The Changing Marketing Landscape

    A. The digital age: online, mobile, and social media marketing. The explosive growth in digital technology has fundamentally changed the way we live—how we communicate, share information, access entertainment, and shop.

    B. The changing economic environment. The new consumer spending values emphasize simpler living and more value for the dollar. Despite their rebounding means, consumers continue to buy less, clip more coupons, swipe their credit cards less, and put more in the bank.

    C. Rapid globalization. Today, almost every company, large or small, is touched in some way by global competition.

    D. Sustainable marketing. As the worldwide consumerism and environmentalism movements mature, today's marketers are being called on to develop sustainable marketing practices.

    E. Cocreation. Cocreation involves the hospitality or travel company interacting with the guest to create experiences through this interaction.

    F. The sharing economy. The recent surge in the sharing economy has been in part to individuals sharing talents, time, and tangible assets they own to gain additional income and the Internet enabling them to connect with customers.

■■■ DISCUSSION QUESTIONS

1. Discuss why you should study marketing.

2. Marketing can be defined in many ways. In your own words, describe marketing to someone who has not read this chapter.

3. Many managers view the purpose of business as making a profit, whereas some view the purpose as being able to create and maintain a customer. Explain how these alternative viewpoints could affect a company's interactions with its customers. If a manager views the purpose as being able to create and maintain a customer, does this mean that the manager is not concerned with profits?

4. Talk to two people and ask them to think about a hotel they stayed in that was a good value. Ask them what made the hotel a good value. Record a summary of their comments.

5. A restaurant has a great reputation as the result of providing consistent food for over 10 years. The restaurant is full every weekend and has above-average business during the week. The manager claims that the restaurant does not practice marketing because it does not need marketing; the restaurant has more than enough business now. Is it true that this restaurant does not practice marketing?

6. Look at Figure 1–2. Why do you think persons who give you 2 (a relatively high score) out of 7 are not likely to return?

7. What is customer equity? How can a company increase its customer equity?

8. Give several examples you have found of hospitality companies being socially responsible. Include in your discussion how being socially responsible helps the company.

■■■ EXPERIENTIAL EXERCISES

Do one of the following:

Restaurant

Visit two restaurants in the same class, such as two fast-food restaurants or two casual restaurants. Observe the cleanliness of the restaurants, in-house signage, and other physical features. Then order a menu item and observe the service and the quality of the food. Write up your observations, and then state which restaurant you feel is more customer oriented. Explain why.

Hotel

Call the central reservation number of two hotels. Request information on room availability, different room types, and price for a date one month from now. (Note: Do not make a reservation.) Write up your experience, including a description of how quickly the phone was answered, the customer orientation of information provided, and the friendliness of the employee. Based on your experiences, which hotels do you feel had the more customer-oriented reservation system?

Other Hospitality Companies

If you are interested in another area of the travel industry, you may compare two organizations in that area for their customer orientation using similar criteria, as mentioned earlier. For example, if you are interested in tourism, you may contact two tourism organizations regarding their destinations. This could be a city convention and tourist bureau or it could be a government tourist bureau.

■■■ INTERNET EXERCISES

Exercise 1

In only a few short years, *consumer-generated marketing* has increased exponentially. It's also known as *consumer-generated media* and *consumer-generated content*. More than 100 million Web sites contain user-generated content. You may be a contributor yourself if you've ever posted something on a blog, reviewed a product at Amazon.com, uploaded a video on YouTube, or sent a video from your mobile phone to a news Web site. This force has not gone unnoticed by marketers and with good reason. Nielsen, the TV ratings giant, found that most consumers trust consumer opinions posted online. As a result, savvy marketers encourage consumers to generate content. For example, Moe's restaurant has created a creative dance contest. These are the instructions for the contest. "To enter, create a dance video no longer than 30 seconds and upload it to www.ilovequeso.com any time before July 24, 2011." Moe's panel of judges will consider originality, video quality, dance moves, and the dance-off ranking to determine who will win the $10,000 grand prize (http://moes.com/). However, consumer-generated marketing is not without problems—just search "I hate (insert company name)" in any search engine!

1. Find two examples (other than those discussed in this chapter) of marketer-supported, consumer-generated content and two examples of consumer-generated content that is not officially supported by the company whose product is involved. Provide the Web link to each and discuss how the information impacts your attitude toward the companies involved.

2. Discuss the advantages and disadvantages of consumer-generated marketing.

Exercise 2

Choose three restaurant or hotel companies you have found on the Internet.

Based on information provided in each company's Web site:

A. Describe how each of these companies tries to satisfy a customer's wants.
B. How does each of these companies create value for the customer?
C. Do companies segment the market by offering pages for a specific market segment? For example, a hotel may provide information for meeting planners, and a restaurant may provide information for customers who are concerned about nutrition or families.
D. Select the company you would purchase from and state why.

■■■ REFERENCES

1   Denise Lee Yohn, "How Chipotle Changed American Fast Food Forever," *Fast Company*, March 14, 2014, www.fastcompany.com/3027647/lessons-learned/how-chipotle-changed American-fast-food-forever; Tim Nudd, "Chipotle Makes Magic Yet Again with Fiona Apple and a Dark Animated Film," *Adweek*, September 12, 2013, www.adweek.com/print/152380; Danielle Sacks, "Chipotle: For Exploding All the Rules of Fast Food," *Fast Company* (March 2012): 125–126; John Trybus, "Chipotle's Chris Arnold and the Food with Integrity Approach to Corporate Social Responsibility," *The Social Strategist*, March 22, 2012, https://blogs.commons.georgetown.edu/socialimpact/2012/03/22/the-social-strategist-part-xvi-chipotle%E2%80%99schris-arnold-and-the-food-with-integrity-approach-to-corporate-social-responsibility/; Emily Bryson York. "Chipotle Ups the Ante on Its Marketing," *Chicago Tribune* (September 30, 2011); Dan Mitchell, "Chipotle's Hilariously Scare Take on the Industrial Food System." *Fortune*, February 13, 2014, http://fortune.com/2014/02/13/chipotleshilariously-scary-take-on-the-industrial-food-system/; information from www.chipotle.com and www.chipotle.com/en-US/twi/fwi.aspx (accessed September 2014).

2   "International Tourism Generates US$ 1.4 trillion in Export Earnings, World Tourism Organization," May 14, 2014, http://media.unwto.org/press-release/2014-05-13/international-tourism-generates-us-14-trillion-export-earnings (accessed June 15, 2015).

3   "China Tourism in 2014," *TravelChinaGuide.com*, http://www.travelchinaguide.com/tourism/ (accessed June 16, 2015); Chien Li-hsin, "China's Domestic and Outbound Tourism to Keep Growing in 2014," *Want China Times*, June 1, 2014, http://www.wantchinatimes.com/news-subclass-cnt.aspx?id=20140106000006&cid=1202 (accessed June 15, 2016).

4   "2015 Travelors Choice TripAdvisor Top 25 Hotels – World," http://www.tripadvisor.com/TravelersChoice-Hotels-cTop-g1Airport of the year 2011 (accessed June 26, 2015); Skytrax world airport survey, http://www.worldairportawards.com/ (accessed June 27, 2015); Skytrax world airline survey, http://www.worldairlineawards.com/ (accessed June 27, 2015);

"The World's 50 Best Restaurants," http://www .theworlds50best.com/ (accessed June 27, 2015).

5 Accor 2001–2002 Asia Pacific Hotel Directory, p. 1.

6 Smashburger Website, http://smashburger.com/us/ company/story/ (accessed June 18, 2015).

7 Theodore Levitt, *Marketing Imagination* (New York: Free Press, 1986).

8 Patricia Sellers, "Getting Customers to Love You," *Fortune* (March 13, 1989): 38–49.

9 Frederick Reichheld, *The Loyalty Effect* (Boston, MA: Harvard Business School Press, 1996).

10 James L. Heskett, Jr., W. Earle Sasser, and W. L. Hart Chistopher, *Service Breakthroughs* (New York: Free Press, 1990).

11 Karl Albrecht, *At America's Service* (Homewood, IL: Dow Jones/Irwin, 1988), p. 23.

12 Peter F. Drucker, *Management: Tasks, Responsibility, Practices* (New York: Harper & Row, 1973), pp. 64–65.

13 "Cruise Forum," *Travel Agent* (May 2, 1994): B2.

14 "Specialty Promotions" *Manage My Restaurant,* and "Facts at a Glance," National Restaurant Association, retrieved July 10, 2011, from http://www.restaurant.org (accessed June 18, 2015).

15 Theodore Levitt, "Marketing Myopia," *Harvard Business Review* (July/August 1960): 45–46.

16 "The Changing Look of Tourism," Arts & Cultural Tourism. Speech given at Economic Summit 2004, May 26–27, 2004, Steamboat Springs, CO.

17 John T. Bowen and Shiang-Lih Chen, "The Relationship Between Customer Loyalty and Customer Feedback," *Modern Maturity*, 40, no. 4 (July/August 1997): 12.

18 "Best in Customer Service," *Fortune*, August 29, 2013, http://money.cnn.com/gallery/technology/2013/08/29/ social-media-all-stars.fortune/2.html; "JetBlue and Southwest's Net Rises on Gains From Capacity Expansion," *Forbes*, February 4, 2014, www.forbes. com/sites/greatspeculations/2014/02/04/ jetblue-southwest's-net-rises-on-gains-from-capacity-expan sion/; Kevin Randall, "Red, Hot, and Blue: The Hottest American Brand Is Not Apple," *Fast Company*, June 3, 2010, http://www.fastcompany.com/1656066/red-hot and-blue-hottest-american-brand-not-apple; "The American Customer Satisfaction Index: Benchmarks by Industry," www.theacsi.org/customer-satisfac- tion-benchmarkslbenchmarks-by-industry (accessed June 2014); Rupal Parekh, "The Newest Marketing Buzzword? Human," *Advertising Age*, September 20, 2013, http://adage.com/prinV244261/; http:// experience.jetblue.com/ and www.jetblue.com/abouV (accessed September 2014).

19 Sustainable Restaurant Association, The Discerning Diner, Sustainable Restaurant Association, 2013, http://www.thesra.org/wp-content/uploads/2012/01/ Consumer-Report.pdf (accessed June 25, 2015).

20 See Michael E. Porter and Mark R. Kramer, "Creating Shared Value," *Harvard Business Review* (January–February 2011): 63–77; Marc Pfrtzer, Valerie Bockstette, and Mike Stamp, "Innovating for Shared Value," *Harvard Business Review* (September 2013): 1D0–107; "About Shared Value," *Shared Value Initiative*, http://sharedvalue.org/about-shared-value (accessed September 2014); "Shared Value," www .fsg.org (accessed September 2014).

21 Based on information from Michael Bush, "Why You Should Be Putting on the Ritz," *Advertising Age* (June 21, 2010): 1; Julie Barker, "Power to the People," *Incentive* (February 2008): 34; Philip Kotler and Kevin Lane Keller, *Marketing Management*, 14th ed. (Upper Saddle River, NJ: Prentice Hall, 2012), p. 381; http://corporate.ritzcarltoncom/en/AbouVAwards.htm (accessed June 2014); "Stories That Stay with You," www.ritzcarlton.com/en/StoriesThatStay.htm (accessed June 2014).

22 "Delighting the Customer Doesn't Pay," *Sales & Marketing Management*, November 11, 2013, http://salesandmarketing.com/ contenVdelighting-customers-doesnt-pay.

23 Based on information from Noreen O'Leary, "Hertz Learns Value of Sharing in Purchase Cycle," *Adweek*, May 30, 2012; "Hertz Fans Share It Up! on Facebook," *PRNewswire*, April 11, 2012, www.prnewswire .com/ news-releaseslhertz-fans-share-it-up-on-face book-146987 185.html; "The Top 10 Social Media Success Stories of 2012 & What We Can Learn from Them,"· *Social Media Strategies Summit blog*, November 28, 2012, http://socialmediastrategies summit.com/blog/the-top-10-socialmedia-success- stories-of-2012-what-we-can-leam-from-them; "Hertz Moves with the High-Tech Times to Breathe New Life into the Brand," *Eye for Travel*, January 16, 2014, www.eyefort ravel.com/social-media and-marketing/ hertz-moves-high-tech-times-breathe-new-life-brand; www.Hertz.com (accessed September 2014).

24 See http://mystarbucksidea.force.com (accessed September 2014).

25 See "#Bashtag: Avoiding User Outcry in Social Media," *WordStream*, March 8, 2013, www.wordstream .com/blog/ws/2013103107 /bashtag avoiding-social- media-backlash; "What Is Hashtag Hijacking?" *Small Business Trends*, August 18, 2013, http://smallbiz- trends.corn/2013/08/what-is-hashtag-hijacking-2.html.

26 "Stew Leonard's," Hoover's Company Records, July 15, 2010, pp. 104–226; www.stew-leonards.com/html/ about.cfm (accessed August 2010).

27 Brad Rosenthal, "LTV Lifetime Value of a Customer," *Lincolnrose Blog*, May 10, 2011, retrieved July 14, 2011, from http://www.lincolnrosetrust.com/Blog .html?entry=ltv-lifetime-value-of-a.

28 Don Peppers and Martha Rogers, "Customers Don't Grow on Trees," *Fast Company* (July 2005): 26.

29 For more discussion on customer equity, see Roland T. Rust, Valerie A. Zeithaml, and Katherine A. Lemon, *Driving Customer Equity* (New York: Free Press, 2000); Rust, Lemon, and Zeithaml, "Return on Marketing:

Using Customer Equity to Focus Marketing Strategy," *Journal of Marketing* (January 2004): 109–127; Dominique M. Hanssens, Daniel Thorpe, and Carl Finkbeiner, "Marketing When Customer Equity Matters," *Harvard Business Review* (May 2008): 117–124; Thorsten Wiesel, Bernd Skieram, and Julian Villanueva, "Customer Equity: An Integral Part of Financial Reporting," *Journal of Marketing* (March 8, 2008): 1–14; V. Kumar and Denish Shaw, "Expanding the Role of Marketing: From Customer Equity to Market Capitalization," *Journal of Marketing* (November 2009): 119.

30   See Roland T. Rust, Valerie A. Zeithaml, and Katherine A. Lemon, *Driving Customer Equity* (New York: Free Press, 2000); Robert C. Blattberg, Gary Cetz, and Jacquelyn S. Thomas, *Customer Equity* (Boston, MA: Harvard Business School Press, 2001); Rust, Lemon, and Zeithaml, "Return on Marketing: Using Customer Equity to Focus Marketing Strategy," *Journal of Marketing* (January 2004): 109–127; James D. Lenskold, "Customer-Centered Marketing ROI," *Marketing Management* (January/February 2004): 26–32; Rust, Zeithaml, and Lemon, "Customer-Centered Brand Management," *Harvard Business Review* (September 2004): 110; Don Peppers and Martha Rogers, "Hail to the Customer," *Sales & Marketing Management* (October 2005): 49–51; Alhson Enright, "Serve Them Right," *Marketing News* (May 1, 2006): 21–22.

31   Werner Reinartz and V. Kumar, "The Mismanagement of Customer Loyalty," *Harvard Business Review* (July 2002): 86–94. Also see Stanley F. Slater, Iakki I. Mohr, and Sanjit Sengupta, "Know Your Customer," *Marketing Management* (February 2009): 37–44.

32   See Stuart Feil, "Mobile on the Cusp (Again)," *Adweek* (February 11, 2013): M1–M3+, "ITU Release Latest Tech Figures & Global Rankings," October 7, 2013, vrww.itu.inVneVpressoffice/ press_ releases/2013/41.aspx# .Uumujvad6cC; John Heggestuen, "One in Every 5 People in the World Own a Smartphone, One in Every 17 Own a Tablet," *Business Insider*, December 15, 2013, www.businessinsider.com/smartphone-and-table t-penetration-2013-10.

33   See Stuart Feil, "How to Win Friends and Influence People," *Adweek* (September 12, 2013): S1–S7; Joe Mandese, "Carat Projects Digital at One-Fifth of All Ad Spend, Beginning to Dominate Key Markets," *MediaPost News*, March 20, 2013, www.mediapost.com/publication s/article/196238/carat-projects-digitalat-one-fifth-of-all-ad-spen.html#axzz2PsYL9uFf; Julia McCoy, "A 2014 Social Media Guide: New Trends and Solutions to Uve By," *Social Media Today*, January 15, 2014, http://socialmediatoday.com/expresswriters/2066416/2014-social-media-guide-new-trendsand-solutions-live.

34   See Mai Erne, "Calculating Customer Lifetime Value," HaraParlners, www.haraparlners.com/blog/calculating-lifetime-value/ (accessed September 2014).

35   Michael Solomon, "Chili's Spends Millions to Make Food Look Good on Social Media, for a Millennial Customer Experience," *Forbes*, May 24, 2015 (accessed June 25, 2015) http://www.forbes.com/sites/micahsolomon/2015/05/24/chilis-spends-millions-to-make-food-look-good-on-social-for-a-millennial-customer-experience/

36   Michael Applebaum, "Mobile Magnetism," *Adweek* (June 25, 2012): S1–89; Bill Briggs. "M-Commerce Is Saturating the Globe," *Internet Retailer*. February 20, 2014, www.internet retailer.com/2014/02/20/m-commerce-saturating-globe.

37   See Applebaum, "Mobile Magnetism," p. S7; Brian Quintion, "2012 PRO Award Winner: Catapult Action Biased Marketing for Mars Petcare," *Chief Marketer*, August 3, 2012, www.chiefmarketer.com/agencies/2012-pro-award-winner-catapult-action-biasedmarketing-for-mars-petcare-03082012.

38   www.aboutmcdonalds.com/mcd and www.nikeinc.com (accessed June 2014).

39   See www.benjeny.com/values, www.benandjerrysfoundation.org/, and www.unilever.com/brands-in-action/detail/ben-and-jerrys/291995/ (accessed September 2014).

40   See http://www.visithoustontexas.com/travel-planning/itineraries-and-trip-ideas/

41   See Withlocals Web site https://www.withlocals.com/experiences/vietnam/ho%20chiminhcity/?guests=2&keywords=dinner&pagesize=20 (accessed December 15, 2015).

42   Buhalis, D., and Foerste, M. (2015). "SoCoMo Marketing for Travel and Tourism: Empowering Co-creation of Value." *Journal of Destination Marketing & Management*, 4: 151–161.

Objectives

After reading this chapter, you should be able to:

1. Describe a service culture.
2. Identify four service characteristics that affect the marketing of a hospitality or travel product.
3. Explain seven marketing strategies for service businesses.

Service Characteristics of Hospitality and Tourism Marketing

Starbucks

Starbucks opened in Seattle in 1971, when coffee consumption in the United States had been declining for a decade and rival brands used cheaper beans to compete on price. Howard Schultz came to Starbucks in 1982. While in Milan on business, he had walked into an Italian coffee bar and had an epiphany: "There was nothing like this in America. It was an extension of people's front porch. It was an emotional experience." To bring this concept to the United States, Schultz set about creating an environment that would blend Italian elegance with U.S. informality.

Customers: He envisioned Starbucks as a "personal treat" for its customers, a comfortable, sociable gathering spot bridging the workplace and home. Starbucks's success is often attributed to its high-quality products and services and its relentless commitment to providing consumers the richest possible sensory experience.

Employees: Starbucks gives back to its community in many ways starting with employees, called partners. Schultz believed that to exceed customers' expectations, the company must first exceed those of employees. Since 1990, it has provided comprehensive health care to all employees, including part-timers. (Health insurance now costs the company more each year than coffee.) In the United States a college graduate can expect to earn 66 percent more than a high-school graduate over a 40-year career. Starbucks found that more than 70 percent of its U.S. partners (employees) are students or aspiring students. Wanting to help employees achieve their ambitions, Starbucks is offering all partners, both full- and part-time, 100 percent tuition coverage to earn a bachelor's degree from Arizona State University's online program. Employees can seek opportunities within the company or with other companies when they graduate. A stock option plan allows employees to participate in the firm's financial success.

Suppliers: Starbucks collaborates with Conversation International (CI), a nongovernmental organization, and follows Coffee and Farmer Equity (C.A.F.E.) Practices, a comprehensive coffee-buying program, to purchase high-quality coffee from farmers who meet social, economic, and environmental standards. Of 396 million pounds of coffee Starbucks chased in 2013, 95 percent was ethically sourced. The company also works continuously with farmers to improve responsible methods of farming, such as by planting trees along rivers and using shade-growing techniques to help preserve forests. Over the years, Starbucks has invested more than $70 million in collaborative farmer programs and activities. Starbucks's social responsibility goes beyond the company. It includes the well-being of those who supply products to Starbucks, as well as helping the suppliers follow environmentally sound practices.

Community: Another critical component is its commitment to the communities in which it operates and to the environment. Starbucks established The Starbucks Foundation in 1997, "to create hope, discovery, and opportunity in communities," by supporting literacy programs for children and families in the United States and Canada and charities worldwide. The company has committed to hiring 10,000 veterans and military spouses over the next five years. In 2013, the foundation gave $8.7 million to 144 nonprofit organizations around the world. Starbucks has donated more than $11 million to the Global Fund through its partnership with PRODUCT (RED), a global initiative to help stop the spread of human immunodeficiency virus (HIV) in Africa. Starbucks's partners' social responsibility is consistent with Starbucks's. Its partners donated 1 million hours of community service.

Environment: Starbucks is considered a leader in green initiatives, building new Leadership in Energy and Environmental Design (LEED)-certified green buildings, reducing waste, and improving water conservation. The world's first recycled beverage cup made of 10 percent postconsumer fiber, 10 years in the making, and a new hot cup paper sleeve that requires fewer materials to make conserve approximately 100,000 trees a year. Now the team is working to ensure that customers recycle. Jim Hanna, Starbucks's director of environmental impact, explained, "[Starbucks] defines a recyclable cup not by what the cup is made out of but by our customers actually having access to recycling services." Starbucks's goal is to make 100 percent of its cups recycled or reused by 2015. Schultz believes Starbucks must retain a passion for coffee and a sense of humanity and continue to prove that the company "stands for something more than just profitability."[1] Starbucks exhibits the characteristics of a well-managed service business. It serves high-quality products. The *Starbucks Experience* strives to create a great experience for each customer. The physical environment is warm and inviting. So inviting that many people use Starbucks as a place to meet, study, or conduct business. Starbucks realizes that it must take care of its employees if they are to take care of their customers, and it creates lasting relationships with its customers and its suppliers. Starbucks also realizes the importance of social responsibility.

■■■ The Service Culture

Service culture. A system of values and beliefs in an organization that reinforces the idea that providing the customer with quality service is the principal concern of the business.

One of the most important tasks of a hospitality business is to develop the service side of the business, specifically, a strong service culture. The **service culture** focuses on serving and satisfying the customer. Creation of a service culture has to start with top management and flow down. The business mission discussed in Chapter 3 should contain a service vision. An organization should hire employees with a customer service attitude, and then it works with employees to instill the concept of service. The outcome of these efforts is employees who provide service to the customers. In well-run services, employees are taught to own the customer's request. For example, a guest requesting towels from the front desk is not just transferred to housekeeping. The request is taken by the employee at the front desk. He or she will then call housekeeping. But that is not the end of his or her involvement. He or she will check back with housekeeping in 10 minutes to make sure the towels were delivered. If they were, he or she will call the guest to make sure the guest got the towels and ask if there is anything else he or she can do for the guest. A service culture lets the employees know they are expected to deliver service to the guest and provides employees with the tools and support they need to deliver good service.

■■■ Characteristics of Service Marketing

Service marketers must understand the four characteristics of services: **intangibility**, **inseparability**, **variability**, and **perishability** (see Figure 2–1).

Intangibility. A major characteristic of services; they cannot be seen, tasted, felt, heard, or smelled before they are bought.

Inseparability. A major characteristic of services; they are produced and consumed at the same time and cannot be separated from their providers.

Variability. A major characteristic of services; their quality may vary greatly, depending on who provides them and when, where, and how they are provided.

Perishability. A major characteristic of services; they cannot be stored for later use.

Intangibility

Unlike physical products, intangible products cannot be seen, tasted, felt, heard, or smelled before they are purchased. Hospitality and travel industry products are experiential only, and we do not know the quality of the product until after we have experienced it. A restaurant customer will not know how good the meal is until after he or she has consumed it. Likewise, a family planning a vacation will not know if the destination for their vacation and the choice of their resort was a good one until they have had their vacation experience.

One implication of experiential products is that we take away only the memories of our experiences. Marriott Vacation Clubs International realizes this and has made a deliberate effort to create memorable guest experiences. Marriott realizes that a white-water rafting trip can create memories that a family visiting their Mountainside Resort in Utah will talk about for years. The fun the family experienced while white-water rafting, along with their other experiences at the resort, will make them want to return. As a result, the staff at the Mountainside Resort know they must promote the activities of the destination as well as the resort. Other resorts create memories. It might be champagne and music on the beach at sunset or the special and unexpected attention that an employee provides for a guest. The goal is to create experiences that result in positive experiences.

Because guests will not know the service they will receive until after they receive it, service marketers should take steps to provide their prospective customers with evidence that will help them evaluate the service.[2] This process is called providing tangible evidence. Promotional material, employees' appearance, and the service firm's physical environment all help tangibilize service. Hospitality companies today include virtual tours and pictures on their Web site. They also take advantage of Facebook, Instagram, and other social media to share photos and videos.

A banquet salesperson for a fine restaurant can make the product tangible by taking pastry samples on morning sales calls. This creates goodwill and provides the prospective client with some knowledge about the restaurant's food quality. The salesperson might also bring a photo album showing photographs of banquet setups, plate presentations for different entrees, and testimonial letters from past clients. For persons having a dinner as part of their wedding reception, some hotels prepare the meal for the bride's family before the wedding day. Thus the bride actually gets to experience the food before the reception so there are no surprises.

The salesperson may be the prospective customer's first contact with the hotel or restaurant.

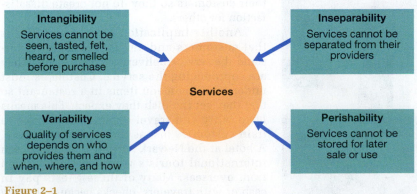

Figure 2–1
Four service characteristics.

A salesperson who is well groomed and dressed appropriately and who answers questions in a prompt, professional manner can do a great deal to help the customer develop a positive image of the hotel. Uniforms also provide tangible evidence of the experience. The uniforms worn by front-desk staff of the Hotel Nikko San Francisco are professional and provide tangible evidence that the guest is walking into a four-diamond hotel.

Everything about a hospitality company communicates something. The wrappers put on drinking glasses in the guest rooms serve the purpose of letting the guest know that the glasses have been cleaned. The fold in the toilet paper in the bathroom lets the guest know the bathroom has been tidied.

Physical Evidence

Physical evidence. Tangible clues such as promotional material, employees of the firm, and the physical environment of the firm. Physical evidence is used by a service firm to make its product more tangible to customers.

Physical evidence that is not managed properly can hurt a business. Negative messages communicated by poorly managed physical evidence include signs that continue to advertise a holiday special two weeks after the holiday has passed, signs with missing letters or burned-out lights, parking lots and grounds that are unkempt and full of trash, and employees in dirty uniforms at messy workstations. Such signs send negative messages to customers. Restaurant managers are trained to do a preopening inspection of the restaurant. One of the things they look for is that all light bulbs are working. A little thing like a burned-out bulb can give a guest sitting near it an impression that the restaurant does not pay attention to detail. Our customers notice details; this is why a consistent message from industry leaders is that managers must pay attention to detail.

A firm's communications should also reinforce its positioning. Ronald McDonald is great for McDonald's, but a clown would not be appropriate as the primary mascot of Four Seasons Hotels. All said, a service organization should review every piece of tangible evidence to make sure that each delivers the desired **organization image**—the way a person or group views an organization—to target customers.[3]

Organization image. The way a person or group views an organization.

Inseparability

Physical goods are produced, then stored, later sold, and still later consumed. In contrast, hospitality products are first sold and then produced and consumed at the same time. In most hospitality services, both the service provider and the customer must be present for the transaction to occur. Inseparability means both the employee and the customer are often part of the product. The food in a restaurant may be outstanding, but if the employee serving the food to the customer has a poor attitude or provides inattentive service, customers will not be satisfied with their experience.

A couple may have chosen a restaurant because it is quiet and romantic, but if other customers include a group of loud and boisterous conventioneers seated in the same room, these customers will spoil the couple's experience. Managers must manage their customers so they do not create dissatisfaction for others.

Another implication of inseparability is that customers and employees must understand the service-delivery system because they are coproducing the service. Customers must understand the menu items in a restaurant so that they get the dish they expect. This means hospitality and travel organizations have to train customers just as they train employees. A hotel at the Newark Airport is popular with international tourists who have just arrived from overseas. Many of these guests pay in cash or with travelers' checks because they do

The umbrellas, bright colors, and outside seating of the café in Perth, Australia, create an environment that attracts attention and is inviting to those who want informal dining. Courtesy of MNStudio/Fotolia.

not use credit cards. On more than one occasion, the front-desk clerk has been observed answering the phone of an upset guest who claims the movie system does not work. The clerk must explain that the guest did not establish credit because cash was paid for his or her room. He or she informs guests that they must come to the front desk and pay for the movie before it can be activated. Guests obviously become upset on receiving this information. The hotel could avoid this problem and improve customer relations by asking guests at arrival time if they would like to make a deposit for anything they might charge, such as in-room movies.

Casinos know they must train customers how to play certain table games such as blackjack or craps. Casinos provide booklets on how to play the games and also offer free lessons in the casino. This enables the guest to enjoy the casino resort and creates new customers for the casino.

Finally, we often ask customers to coproduce the service they are consuming. This means organizations must select, hire, and train customers.[4] Fast-food restaurants train customers to get their own drinks. This gives the customer something to do while waiting and reduces the need for employees to fill drink orders themselves. Hotels, restaurants, airlines, and rental car companies train customers to use the electronic check-in and the Internet to get information and to make reservations. The customer using these services is performing both the job of customer service agent and reservationist. The benefits provided to the guest by becoming an "employee" include increased value, customization, and reduced waiting time. The characteristic of inseparability requires hospitality managers to manage both their employees and their customers.

Variability

Services are highly variable. Their quality depends on who provides them and when and where they are provided. There are several causes of service variability. Services are produced and consumed simultaneously, which limits quality control. Fluctuating demand makes it difficult to deliver consistent products during periods of peak demand. The high degree of contact between the service provider and the guest means that product consistency depends on the service provider's skills and performance at the time of the exchange. A guest can receive excellent service one day and mediocre service from the same person the next day. In the case of mediocre service, the service person may not have felt well or perhaps experienced an emotional problem. Lack of communication and heterogeneity of guest expectations also lead to service variability. A restaurant customer ordering a medium steak may expect it to be cooked all the way through, whereas the person working on the broiler may define medium as having a warm pink center. The guest will be disappointed when he or she cuts into the steak and sees pink meat. Restaurants have solved this by developing common definitions of steak doneness and communicating them to the employees and customers. Sometimes the communication to the customer is verbal, and sometimes it is printed on the menu. Customers usually return to a restaurant because they enjoyed their last experience. When the product they receive is different and does not meet their expectations on the next visit, they often do not return. Variability or lack of consistency in the product is a major cause of customer disappointment in the hospitality industry.

When variability is absent, we have consistency, which is one of the key factors in the success of a service business.[5] Consistency means that customers receive the expected product without unwanted surprises. In the hotel industry, this means that a wake-up call requested for 7 A.M. always occurs as planned and that a meeting planner can count on the hotel to deliver coffee ordered for a 3 P.M. meeting break, which will be ready and waiting when the group breaks at that time. In the restaurant business, consistency means that the shrimp scampi will taste the same way it tasted two weeks ago, towels will always be available in the bathrooms, and the brand of vodka specified last week will be in stock next month. Consistency is one of the major reasons for the worldwide success of McDonald's.

Here are three steps hospitality firms can take to reduce variability and create consistency:

1. **Invest in good hiring and training procedures.** Recruiting the right employees and providing them with excellent training is crucial, regardless of whether employees are highly skilled professionals or low-skilled workers. Better-trained personnel exhibit six characteristics: *Competence*—they possess the required skill and knowledge. *Courtesy*—they are friendly, respectful, and considerate. *Credibility*—they are trustworthy. *Reliability*—they perform the service consistently and accurately. *Responsiveness*—they respond quickly to customers' requests and problems. *Communication*—they make an effort to understand the customer and communicate clearly. Excellent hospitality and travel companies such as Marriott and Southwest Airlines spend a great deal of time and effort making sure they hire the right employees. But their attention to employees does not end there. They also invest in their employees by providing ongoing training.

2. **Standardize the service-performance process throughout the organization.** Diagramming the service-delivery system in a service blueprint can simultaneously map out the service process, the points of customer contact, and the evidence of service from the customer's point of view. The guest's experience includes a series of steps he or she must enact while receiving the service. Behind the scenes, the service provider must skillfully help the guest move from one step to the next. By visually representing the service, a service blueprint can help one understand the process and see potential design flaws. Service blueprints include a line of interaction, line of visibility and line of internal support. The line of interaction represents the guest's contact with employees. The line of visibility represents those areas that will be visible to the guest and provide tangible evidence of the service. The line of internal interaction represents internal support systems that are required to service the guest.

3. **Monitor customer satisfaction.** Use suggestion and complaint systems, customer surveys, and comparison shopping. Hospitality companies have the advantage of knowing their customers. Companies also have the e-mail addresses of those who purchase from their Web sites. This makes it easy to send a customer satisfaction survey after a guest has stayed in a hotel or used its service. Travel intermediaries, such as Travelocity.com, contact guests to see how satisfied they were with a hotel they booked on their site. They realize if a customer had a bad experience they may not use their service again, even though they cannot control the service and quality of the hotels they represent. They try to create a consistent experience and set customer expectations by using a star rating system and publishing customer comments. Firms can also develop customer information databases and systems to permit more personalized, customized service, especially online.

Perishability

Services cannot be stored. A 100-room hotel that sells only 60 rooms on a particular night cannot inventory the 40 unused rooms and then sell 140 rooms the next night. Revenue lost from not selling those 40 rooms is gone forever. Because of service perishability, airlines and some hotels charge guests holding guaranteed reservations when they fail to arrive. Restaurants are also starting to charge a fee to customers who do not show up for a reservation. They, too, realize that if someone does not show up for a reservation, the opportunity to sell that seat may be lost.

Some hotels will often sell hotel rooms at a very low rate rather let them go unsold. Because of inseparability, this can cause problems. Oftentimes, the discounted rate brings in a different type of customer that is not compatible with the hotel's normal customer. For example, one luxury hotel that normally sold rooms for $300 placed rooms on Priceline's (opaque channel) for $80.* The guest paying $80 a night is not likely to use the food and beverage outlets, but instead will use less expense restaurants outside of the hotel or come back into the hotel carrying a bag of food from a nearby fast-food restaurant. Revenue managers must be careful that they maintain a brand's image while at the same time trying to reduce unsold inventory. We will discuss techniques for managing demand at the end of this chapter.

■■■ Service Management Concepts for the Hospitality Industry

The Service Profit Chain

In a service business, the customer and the frontline service employee *interact* to create the service. Effective interaction, in turn, depends on the skills of frontline service employees and on the support processes backing these employees. Thus, successful service companies focus their attention on *both* their customers and their employees. They understand the **service profit chain**, which links service firm profits with employee and customer satisfaction. This chain consists of the following five links:

Service profit chain. A model that shows the relationships between employee satisfaction, customer satisfaction, customer retention, value creation, and profitability.

1. **Internal service quality:** superior employee selection and training, a quality work environment, and strong support for those dealing with customers, which results in . . .

2. **Satisfied and productive service employees:** more satisfied, loyal, and hard-working employees, which results in . . .

3. **Greater service value:** more effective and efficient customer value creation and service-delivery, which results in . . .

Internal marketing. Marketing by a service firm to train effectively and motivate its customer-contact employees and all the supporting service people to work as a team to provide customer satisfaction.

4. **Satisfied and loyal customers:** satisfied customers who remain loyal, repeat purchase, and refer other customers, which results in . . .

5. **Healthy service profits and growth:** superior service firm performance.

Therefore, reaching service profits and growth goals begins with taking care of those who take care of customers.[6]

Three Types of Marketing

Service marketing requires more than just traditional external marketing using the four Ps. Figure 2–2 shows that service marketing along with external marketing also requires both internal marketing and interactive marketing.

Internal marketing means that the service firm must effectively train and motivate its customer-contact employees and all the supporting service people to work as a team to provide customer satisfaction. For the firm to deliver consistently high service quality, everyone must practice customer orientation. It is not enough to have a marketing department doing traditional marketing while the rest of the company goes its own way. Everyone else in the organization must also practice marketing. In fact, internal marketing must precede external marketing. Failure to practice internal marketing can be expensive.

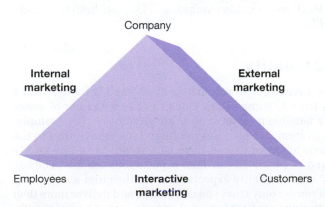

Figure 2–2
Three types of marketing in service industries.

---

* An opaque channel is a one where the customer knows the general location and class of the hotel, but does not know the specific name of the hotel he or she is purchasing. These channels are used by hotels to prevent loyal customers from purchasing at discounted rates.

Interactive marketing.
Marketing by a service firm that recognizes perceived service quality depends heavily on the quality of the buyer–seller interaction.

A study of 33 hotels showed that turnover costs averaged approximately $10,000 per employee for those with complex jobs.[7] In Chapter 10 we discuss internal marketing.

Interactive marketing means that perceived service quality depends heavily on the quality of the buyer–seller interaction during the service encounter. In product marketing, product quality often depends little on how the product is obtained. But in services of marketing, service quality depends on both the service deliverer and the quality of the delivery. The customer judges service quality not just on technical quality (the quality of the food) but also on its functional quality (the service provided in the restaurant). Service employees have to master interactive marketing skills or functions as well.[8]

Today as competition and costs increase and as productivity and quality decrease, more marketing sophistication is needed. Hospitality companies face the task of increasing three major marketing areas: their service differentiation, service quality, and service productivity.

■■■ Management Strategies for Service Businesses

Managing Service Differentiation

Service marketers often complain about the difficulty of differentiating their services from those of competitors. To the extent that customers view the services of different providers as similar, they care less about the provider than the price.

The solution to price competition is to develop a differentiated offering, rather than starting a price war. Competing by reducing price results leads to lowering expenses to offset the price reduction. Cuts to employee expenses result in reduced service levels. Cuts in maintenance result in a facility that becomes worn. The offer can include innovative features that set one company's offer apart from that of its competitors. See Marketing Highlight 2–1 to see how three companies were able to compete through creativity and innovation. Still, the service company that innovates regularly usually gains a succession of temporary advantages and an innovative reputation that may help it keep customers who want to go with the best.

Service companies can differentiate their service delivery in three ways: through people, physical environment, and process. The company can distinguish itself by having more able and reliable customer-contact people than its competitors, or it can develop a superior physical environment in which the service product is delivered. It can design a superior delivery process. Finally, service companies can also differentiate their images through symbols and branding. For example, a familiar symbol would be McDonald's golden arches, and familiar brands include Hilton, Shangri-La, and Sofitel.

Managing Service Quality

One of the major ways that a service firm can differentiate itself is by delivering consistently higher quality than its competitors. One can have a number of objective criteria for evaluating a tangible product such as an automobile. For example, how long does it take it to go from 0 to 60 miles per hour, how many miles to the gallon does it get, how much leg room does it have, and so on. With hospitality products, quality is measured by how well customer expectations are met. The key is to exceed the customers' service-quality expectations. As the chief executive at American Express puts it, "Promise only what you can deliver and deliver more than you promise!" These expectations are based on past experiences, word of mouth, and service firm advertising. If perceived service of a given firm exceeds expected service, customers are apt to use the provider again. Customer retention is perhaps the best measure of quality: A service firm's ability to retain its customers depends on how consistently it delivers value to them. A manufacturer's quality goal might be zero defects, but the service provider's goal is zero customer defections.

The service provider needs to identify the expectations of target customers concerning service quality. In Chapters 4, 5, and 6, we discuss how to obtain

Marketing HIGHLIGHT 2.1   JetBlue, Southwest, and Cirque du Soleil provide three examples of service differentiation

In an industry often characterized by bankruptcies and unhappy customers, two exceptions are Southwest Airlines and JetBlue. The companies have followed very different paths on their way to financial and marketplace success. Southwest, the older of the two, developed an unusual business model for an airline: short hauls only, no travel agents, no meals, no gates at major airports, and no fees. Although the carrier has changed some of those practices, it remains determined to avoid the bag, ticket change, and other fees adopted by competing airlines, believing it would lose $1 billion in revenue from lost bookings otherwise. A true discount airline, Southwest has been able to offer low fares by virtue of a disciplined cost structure that keeps planes in the air and seats filled, all with an informal, friendly style. The company hires employees with outgoing personalities who like to work with people and empowers them to do so.[9]

JetBlue also started with a very different business model from other airlines, primarily targeting leisure travelers at its John F. Kennedy (JFK) hub in New York City. Another discount carrier with a low-cost structure, the company had the advantage of offering comfy seats, live TV, and choice of snacks. It is building a $25 million lodge at JetBlue University in Orlando to foster culture and camaraderie among employees and exploring options for business travelers, including fancier more expensive seating on its transcontinental routes.[10]

In its more than 25-year history, Cirque du Soleil (French for "circus of the sun") has repeatedly broken loose from circus convention. The company takes traditional ingredients such as trapeze artists, clowns, muscle men, and contortionists and places them in a nontraditional setting with lavish costumes, new age music, and spectacular stage designs. And it eliminates other common circus elements—there are no animals. Each production is loosely tied together with a theme such as "a tribute to the nomadic soul" (Varekai) or "a phantasmagoria of urban life" (Saltimbanco). The group has grown from its Quebec street-performance roots to become a half-billion-dollar global enterprise, with 3,000 employees on four continents

entertaining audiences of millions annually. Part of its success comes from a company culture that encourages artistic creativity and innovation and carefully safeguards the brand. One new production is created each year—always in-house—and is unique: There are no duplicate touring companies. In addition to Cirque's mix of media and local promotion, an extensive interactive e-mail program to its million-plus-member Cirque Club creates an online community of fans—20 to 30 percent of all ticket sales come from club members, generating $800 million in revenue annually.[11]

Cirque du Soleil developed a unique form of entertainment by taking the traditional forms of circus entertainment such as trapeze artists and clowns and places them in a nontraditional setting. The result is a circus for adults that is popular with international audiences, as one does not have to understand the local language to enjoy the show. Courtesy of Renato Rovina/Fotolia.

information on your customers and how to understand your customers. Knowing your customer is a requisite for delivering quality. Once customer expectations are determined, managers need to develop a service-delivery system that will deliver a service that meets the guest's expectations. It is important that the service provider clearly define and communicate that level to its employees and customers what needs to be delivered to meet customer expectations. Investments in service usually pay off through increased customer retention and sales.

Studies of well-managed service companies show that they share a number of common virtues regarding service quality. First, top service companies are "customer obsessed." They have a philosophy of satisfying customer needs, which wins enduring customer loyalty. Second, well-managed service companies have a history of top management commitment to quality. Management at companies such as Six Senses Hotels and Resorts, Disney, and Chili's look not only at financial performance but also at service performance. Third, the best service providers set high service-quality standards. A 98 percent accuracy standard may sound good, but using this standard, the MGM Grand Hotel would send 50 guests a day to rooms that are already occupied, the Outback Steak House chain would have hundreds of miscooked steaks, and Accor Hotels would make hundreds of errors in its central reservation office every week. This level of errors is unacceptable for customer-directed companies. Top service companies do not settle merely for "good" service; they aim for 100 percent defect-free service.

Fourth, the top service firms watch service performance closely, both their own and that of competitors. They use methods such as comparison shopping, customer surveys, suggestions, and complaint forms. Good service companies also communicate their concerns about service quality to employees and provide performance feedback. Ritz-Carlton has daily meetings with its employees to go over customer feedback and to review the guest history of arriving guests. Many quick-service restaurant chains offer customers a chance to win prizes answering several service-related questions on an Internet-based questionnaire.

Managing Service Productivity

With their costs rising rapidly, service firms are under great pressure to increase service productivity. They can do so in several ways. They can train current employees better or hire new ones who will work harder or more skillfully. Or they can increase the quantity of their service by giving up some quality. The provider can "industrialize the service" by adding equipment and standardizing production, as in McDonald's assembly-line approach to fast-food retailing. Finally, a service provider can harness the power of technology. Although we often think of technology's power to save time and costs in manufacturing companies, it also has great— and often untapped—potential to make service workers more productive.

However, companies must avoid pushing productivity so hard that doing so reduces quality. Attempts to industrialize a service or cut costs can make a service company more efficient in the short run. But in making them more efficient, they can become less effective. For example, a restaurant that reduces kitchen payroll, may find that it cannot keep up with the orders resulting in long wait times for food and dissatisfied customers. Thus, in attempting to improve service productivity, companies must be mindful of how they create and deliver customer value. In short, they should be careful not to take the "service" out of service.

Resolving Customer Complaints

Many service companies have invested heavily to develop streamlined and efficient service-delivery systems. They want to ensure that customers will receive consistently high-quality service in every service encounter. Unlike product manufacturers, who can adjust their machinery and inputs until everything is perfect, service quality always varies, depending on the interactions between employees and customers. Problems inevitably occur. As hard as they try, even the best companies have an occasional late delivery, burned steak, or grumpy employee. A company cannot always prevent service problems, but it can learn from them. Good service recovery can turn angry customers into loyal ones. In fact, good recovery can win more customer purchasing and loyalty than if things had gone well in the first place. Therefore, companies should take steps not only to provide good service every time but also to recover from service mistakes.

To have effective complaint resolution, managers must empower frontline service employees—to give them the authority, responsibility, and incentives that they need to recognize, care about, and tend to customer needs. For example, Marriott places its employees in empowerment training, which encourages them to go beyond their normal jobs to solve customer problems. Empowered employees can act quickly and effectively to keep service problems from resulting in lost customers. The Marriott Desert Springs says the major goal for customer-contact employees is to ensure that "our guests experience excellent service and hospitality

Marketing HIGHLIGHT 2.2

Recommendations for Improving Service Quality

Berry, Parasuraman, and Zeithamil, pioneers in conducting academic service research, offer 10 lessons that they maintain are essential for improving service quality across service industries.

1. **Listening.** Understand what customers really want through continuous learning about the expectations and perceptions of customers and noncustomers (e.g., by means of a service-quality information system).

2. **Reliability.** The single most important dimension of service quality. Reliability must be a service priority.

3. **Basic service.** Service companies must deliver the basics and do what they are supposed to do: Keep promises, use common sense, listen to customers, keep customers informed, and be determined to deliver value to customers.

4. **Service design.** Develop a holistic view of the service while managing its many details.

5. **Recovery.** To satisfy customers who encounter a service problem, service companies should encourage customers to complain (and make it easy for them to do so), respond quickly and personally, and develop a problem-resolution system.

6. **Surprising customers.** Although reliability is the most important dimension in meeting customers' service expectations, process dimensions such as assurance, responsiveness, and empathy are most important in exceeding customer expectations (e.g., by surprising them with uncommon swiftness, grace, courtesy, competence, commitment, and understanding).

7. **Fair play.** Service companies must make special efforts to be fair, and to demonstrate fairness, to customers and employees.

8. **Teamwork.** Teamwork is what enables large organizations to deliver service with care and attentiveness by improving employee motivation and capabilities.

9. **Employee research.** Marketers should conduct research with employees to reveal why service problems occur and what companies must do to solve problems.

10. **Servant leadership.** Quality service comes from inspired leadership throughout the organization; from excellent service-system design; from the effective use of information and technology; and from a slow-to-change, invisible, all-powerful, internal force called corporate culture.[12]

while staying at our resort." Well-trained employees are given the authority to do whatever it takes, on the spot, to keep guests happy. They are also expected to help management ferret out the cause of guests' problems, and to inform managers of ways to improve overall hotel service and guests' comfort.

Resolving customer complaints is a critical component of customer retention. One study by the Technical Research Programs Institute found that if a customer has a major complaint, 91 percent will not buy from you again, but if it was resolved quickly, 82 percent of those customers will return. The complaint resolution drops the customer defection from 91 out of 100 to 18 out of 100. With resolution of minor complaints, the defection rate can be reduced to less than 5 out of 100.[13] In complaint resolution there are two important factors. First, if you resolve a complaint and do it quickly—the longer it takes to resolve, the higher the defection rate. Second, seek out customer complaints. If you are unaware of complaints, it is impossible to resolve them.

For example, a businesswoman had just returned from an overseas trip. After a good night's sleep in a New York hotel, she was ready for an American breakfast. She dialed room service, and her breakfast was delivered promptly. A cheerful waiter wheeled the table into the room and positioned it so that the woman could look out the window. He opened the heating compartment and pulled out the breakfast that the woman had been waiting for: a full hot American breakfast. The waiter handed the woman the bill, and she promptly signed the bill and added a handsome tip. Now she was ready to start her breakfast.

The waiter said, "I'm sorry, you will have to pay cash." She explained that she did not have any money with her and pulled out her credit cards, offering the American Express Card she had used to check in to the hotel. The waiter called on the phone and after five minutes it was resolved that the woman could use her credit card. The woman, now upset, sat down to a cold breakfast.[14] If the waiter had been empowered to resolve complaints, he would have been able to leave the room, go down to the front desk, and resolve the problem at the front desk while the woman was enjoying her breakfast.

Complaints that come in by letter should be responded to quickly by personal form of communication. This could be through responding to a complaint on social media, e-mail, Short Message Service (SMS), or telephone. When responding on social media, try to move the conversation off line and resolve the complaint. The worst thing a company can do is send out a form letter or e-mail that shows no empathy to the guest's problem or not respond at all. *Restaurant Business* had an employee contact 25 customer service representatives of restaurant chains, stating she had received poor service. Of the 25 companies contacted, only 15 responded to her complaint. One customer service representative told her, "I'm busy right now, can you call back in a half an hour?" When she called back, the customer service rep said, "Okay, I have a minute now. What's your problem—slow service, is that all? Okay, I can write up a report if you want." Of those restaurants that did respond, only 10 did a good or excellent job of resolving the complaint. The customer service representatives at these restaurants did a nice job of showing concern on the initial phone call and followed up with a letter and coupons. In one case, a regional vice president called the customer back to find out what went wrong.[15]

Another critical area in complaint resolution is that most customers do not complain. They do not give managers a chance to resolve their problem. They just leave and never come back. When a customer does complain, management should be grateful because it gives them a chance to resolve the complaint and gain the customer's repeat business. Most complaints come from loyal customers who want to return, but they also want management to fix the problem so it will not occur on their next visit. Managers must develop ways to encourage customers to complain. Methods to seek complaints include customer hotlines that encourage customers to call about problems they are having. Customer comment cards encourage customers to discuss problems that they had with the product. Managers can train employees to look out for guests who look dissatisfied and try to determine their problems. A service guarantee is another way of getting customers to complain; to invoke the guarantee, they have to complain. If we shift our perspective to see complaints as gifts, we can more readily use the information the complaints generate to grow our own business. Customer complaints are one of the most available yet underutilized sources of customer and market information.[16]

A club manager told us about a surprise the club had from a truly excellent Christmas party. The staff was proud of the way the evening went because everything went as planned. The manager was truly surprised when a member of many years said he wanted to set up a conference call with the food and beverage manager, chef, and the manager to discuss the shortcomings of the event. The call lasted an hour and a half, with many of the complaints considered frivolous by the management team. Through careful listening, the manager was able to separate the symptoms from the real problem. The manager asked his staff to reflect on the call and set a meeting for the next day. He also asked the food and beverage manager to develop a profile of who came to the event. What they discovered is that most of the people attending the event were older retired members who did not have family in the area and were alone during the holidays. Normally the club's parties attracted 45-year-old members and this party was planned for this group, not the 65 and older group who attended the party. This was the essence of the member's complaint: The menu and theme of the party were developed for a much younger group. By listening to what the member was saying and being open to the member's comments, the club's managers discovered the party was developed for the wrong target market. If the member had not complained or the club's managers were not open to the member's complaint, the holiday party would have continued to be developed for the wrong target audience.

Managing Employees as Part of the Product

In the hospitality industry employees are a critical part of the product and marketing mix. This means that the human resources and marketing departments must work closely together. In restaurants without a human resources department, the restaurant manager serves as the human resource manager. The manager must hire friendly and capable employees and formulate policies that support positive relations between employees and guests. Even minor details related to personnel policy can have a significant effect on the product's quality.[17]

In a well-run hospitality organization, there are two customers, the paying customers and the employees.[18] The task of training and motivating employees to provide good customer service is called internal marketing. In the hospitality industry, it is not enough to have a marketing department focused on traditional marketing to a targeted external market. The job of the marketing department includes encouraging everyone in the organization to practice customer-oriented thinking[19] (see Chapter 10). The following excerpt from *In Search of Excellence* illustrates the importance of well-trained employees in a hospitality operation:

> We had decided, after dinner, to spend a second night in Washington. Our business day had taken us beyond the last flight out. We had no reservations but were near the new Four Seasons, had stayed there once before, and liked it. As we walked through the lobby wondering how best to plead our case for a room, we brace for the usual chilly shoulder accorded to latecomers. To our astonishment, the concierge looked up, smiled, called us by name, and asked how we were. She remembered our names! We knew in a flash why in the space of a brief year the Four Seasons had become the "place to stay" in the District and was a rare first-year holder of the venerated four-star rating.[20]

Managing Perceived Risk

Customers who buy hospitality products experience some anxiety because they cannot experience the product beforehand.[21] This is one of the reasons customers rely on user-generated content on sites such as Yelp, TripAdvisor, and other social media they use. These sources are deemed to be credible sources.

Consider a salesperson whose sales manager asks him or her to set up a regional sales meeting. Suppose that the salesperson had never set up a meeting or worked with hotels. The salesperson is obviously nervous. If the meeting goes well, the sales manager will be favorably impressed; if it goes badly, the salesperson may be blamed. In arranging for the meeting place, the salesperson has to trust the hotel's salesperson. Good hotel salespeople alleviate client fears by letting them know that they have arranged hundreds of successful meetings. The salesperson's claims to professionalism can be affirmed through letters of praise from former clients and a tour of the hotel's facilities. A salesperson must reduce the client's fear and gain the client's confidence.

One way of combating concern is to encourage the client to try the hotel or restaurant in a low-risk situation. Hotels and resorts offer familiarization (or Fam) trips to meeting planners and travel agents. Airlines often offer complimentary flight tickets because they are also interested in creating business. Hotels provide rooms, food, beverage, and entertainment at no cost to the prospective client in the hope that this exposure will encourage him or her to recommend the hotel. Fam trips reduce a product's intangibility by letting the intermediary customer experience the hotel beforehand.

The high risk that people perceive when purchasing hospitality products increases loyalty to hotels, restaurants, and event companies that have provided them with a consistent product in the past. Salespeople must have patience and continue calling on prospective clients. At some point one of

User-generated content on TripAdvisor used by many travelers to choose hotels, restaurants, and activities when they travel. Courtesy of Antonioguillem/Fotolia.

their suppliers will make a mistake and they will be open to trying a new supplier. Hospitality companies must strive to satisfy every group, knowing if they make a mistake another company is waiting to take their business.

Managing Capacity and Demand

Managers have two major options for matching capacity with demand: change capacity or change demand. For example, airlines use dynamic capacity management to adjust capacity to match demand. The airlines swap small aircraft for larger aircraft on flights that are selling out faster than normal. The smaller aircraft are assigned to flights that are expected to have low load factors.[22] If a larger plane is not available, they can reduce demand by eliminating discounted fares and charging a higher fare. The higher fare means that some passengers, often pleasure travelers visiting friends and relatives, will decide not to make the trip or switch to another flight, thus reducing the overall demand. In this section we discuss capacity management, and in the next section we focus on demand management.

Capacity Management

Corporate management is responsible for matching capacity with demand on a long-term basis; unit managers are responsible for matching capacity with fluctuations in short-term demand. The techniques presented in this section assist in managing short-term demand.

INVOLVE THE CUSTOMER IN THE SERVICE-DELIVERY SYSTEM   Getting the customer involved in service operations expands the number of people that one employee can serve, thus increasing the capacity of the operation. The concept has wide acceptance in food and beverage operations, but modern technology is responsible for its increasing use in the accommodation sector.

Self-service technologies (SSTs) allow the customer to serve as the company's employee. The adoption of SSTs that increase customer satisfaction represents one of the biggest opportunities for the travel and hospitality industry. A common example is a self-service soft drink dispenser in a fast-food restaurant. Hilton Hotels has developed a system allowing guests to use their smartphone to make reservations, choose their room a day before they arrive, and then use it to access their room when they arrive. Through surveys and by following comments on social media, Hilton found guests valued the control they received when they were allowed to choose the location of their room and the bedding configuration in the room. There are no employees or employee interaction involved in the process. Hilton is now working on how they create positive interaction with guests in the future to replace the interaction they received with employees at the front desk.[23]

CROSS-TRAIN EMPLOYEES   In a hotel, the demand for all services does not rise and fall in unison. One outlet may experience sudden strong demand while other areas enjoy normal levels. When managers cross-train their employees, they can shift employees to increase the capacity. A hotel restaurant that does only 30 to 40 covers a night cannot justify more than two service people, even though it may have 80 seats. However, such low staffing levels mean that the restaurant may have a difficult time serving more than 60 guests, especially if they arrive at about the same time. Having front-desk staff and banquet staff trained in à la carte service means the restaurant manager has a group of employees that can be called on if demand for the restaurant on any particular night exceeds the capacity of two service people.

USE PART-TIME EMPLOYEES   Managers can use part-time employees to expand capacity during an unusually busy day or meal period or during the busy months of the year for seasonal businesses. Summer resorts hire part-time staff to work during the summer period. They reduce their staff during the slower seasons and either reduce staff further or close during the low season. Part-time employees allow a hotel or restaurant to increase or decrease its capacity efficiently. Part-time employees can also be used on an on-call basis. Hotels usually have a list of banquet waiters to call for large events. Part-time employees give an organization the flexibility to adjust the number of employees to the level required to meet demand.

RENT OR SHARE EXTRA FACILITIES AND EQUIPMENT   Businesses do not have to be constrained by space limitations or equipment limitations. A hotel with an opportunity to book a three-day meeting from Tuesday to Thursday may have to turn down the business because all the function space is booked Wednesday evening, and there is no space for the group's Wednesday evening dinner. Rather than lose the group, a creative solution would be to suggest the group go outside the hotel for a unique dinner experience. In Paris, the alternative might be a dinner cruise on the Seine. In Arizona, it might be an outdoor steak fry, and in Hong Kong, it could be a dinner at Jumbo, the famous floating restaurant.

Catering firms often purchase only the amount of equipment they use regularly. When they have a busy period, they rent equipment. Renting, sharing, or moving groups to outside facilities can increase capacity to accommodate short-term demand.

SCHEDULE DOWNTIME DURING PERIODS OF LOW DEMAND   Businesses in seasonal resorts have periods of high and low demand. The actions we have discussed so far enable a business to increase capacity to meet peak demand. One way to decrease capacity to match the lower demand is to schedule repairs and maintenance during the low season.

CHANGE THE SERVICE-DELIVERY SYSTEM   Because services are perishable, managing capacity and demand is a key function of hospitality marketing. For example, Mother's Day is traditionally a restaurant's busiest day of the year, with the peak time at lunch from 11 A.M. to 2 P.M. This three-hour period presents restaurateurs with one of their greatest sales opportunities. To take full advantage of this opportunity, restaurant managers must accomplish two things: First, they must adjust their operating systems to enable the business to operate at maximum capacity. Second, they must remember that their goal is to create satisfied customers.

Many restaurants feature buffets on Mother's Day to increase capacity. An attractive buffet creates a festive atmosphere, provides an impression of variety and value, and expedites service by eliminating the need to prepare food to order. Customers provide their own service, with the service staff providing the beverage and check, which frees the staff to wait on more customers. Buffets eliminate the time required for order taking and preparing the order. Food is available when customers arrive, allowing them to start eating almost immediately. This increases turnover of tables, further increasing the restaurant's capacity. The buffet also allows the restaurant to create a buffer inventory. Although three hours' worth of food cannot be kept on a steam table without a reduction in quality and attractiveness, the food can be cooked in batches that will last 20 to 30 minutes.

Restaurants and entertainment facilities can increase capacity by extending their hours. A hotel coffee shop that is full by 7:30 A.M. may find it useful to open at 6:30 A.M. instead of 7 A.M. If five tables arrive in the first half hour, these should be free in about a half hour, allowing the restaurant to have more tables available during the peak period. Leaps and Bounds, a children's entertainment center that is normally closed at night, offers all-night parties for groups of 20 or more. When the demand exists, the center supplies the capacity by opening at night. Many businesses can increase their capacity by expanding their hours of operation.

This rural banquet is set using bales of hay for seats and a table. The unique setting provides a memorable experience for guests, plus is an option for a hotel to add capacity when their banquet space is booked. Courtesy of Sirichai Raksue/123RF.

DEMAND MANAGEMENT In an ideal situation, managers simply expand capacity to meet demand. However, during a citywide convention, a hotel may receive requests for rooms that exceed its capacity. The Saturday before Christmas, a restaurant could book more banquets if it had space, and during a summer holiday a resort could sell more rooms if it had them. All successful hospitality businesses become capacity constrained. Capacity management allows a business to increase its capacity, but it does not prevent situations where demand exceeds capacity. The following are some ways to manage demand.

USE PRICE TO CREATE OR REDUCE DEMAND Pricing is one method used to manage demand. To create demand, restaurants offer specials on slow days. For example, some Subway restaurants, a submarine sandwich shop, offer two-for-one specials on Tuesdays. Port of Subs (a competitor) offers special discounts after 5 P.M., because most people do not eat sandwiches for the evening meal. Resorts lower prices during the off-season, and city hotels offer weekend specials. Managers must make sure that the market segments attracted by the lower price are their desired targets.

When demand exceeds capacity, managers raise prices to lower demand. On New Year's Eve, many restaurants and nightclubs offer set menus and packages that exceed the normal average check. They realize that even with higher prices, demand remains sufficient to fill to capacity.

USE RESERVATIONS Hotels and restaurants often use reservations to monitor demand. When it appears they will have more demand than capacity, managers can save capacity for the more profitable segments. Reservations can also limit demand by allowing managers to refuse any further reservations when capacity meets demand.

Although reservations in restaurants can help manage demand, they can also decrease capacity. This is the reason that high-volume mid-priced restaurants do not usually take reservations. A group may arrive 10 minutes late, or one couple of a two-couple party may arrive on time and wait 20 minutes at the table until the other couple shows up. The estimated times of customer arrival and departure may not fit precisely, resulting in tables remaining empty for 20 minutes or more. In high-priced restaurants, guests expect to reserve a table and have it ready when

Disney's FASTPASS helps manage demand. Courtesy of John Raoux/AP Images.

they arrive. Customers of mid-priced restaurants have different expectations, allowing popular restaurants to increase their capacity by having customers queue and wait for the next available table. Queues allow managers to inventory demand for short periods of time and fill every table immediately when it becomes available, eliminating dead time.

To maximize capacity, some restaurants accept reservations for seating at designated times. For example, they may have seating at 6, 8, and 10 P.M.. When customers call to make a reservation, the receptionist makes them aware of the seating times and lets them know that the table is theirs for up to two hours. After two hours, another party will be waiting to use the table. The use of seatings increases capacity by ensuring that the restaurant will have three turns and by shifting demand. As the 8 P.M. seating fills, managers can shift demand to either 6 or 10 P.M., depending on the customer's preference.

In cases where demand is greater than capacity, guests can be asked to prepay or make a deposit. For example, some New Year's Eve parties at hotels and restaurants require that guests purchase their tickets in advance. Resorts often require a nonrefundable deposit with a reservation. By requiring an advance payment, managers help ensure that revenue matches capacity. If a customer fails to arrive, the resort does not lose revenue.

Disneyland has come up with its own form of reservations, FastPass. Guests may go up to one of the rides offering the FastPass service and obtain a reservation to come at a certain time. When the guests come back, they bypass the waiting line and move to the FastPass line, often saving an hour or more in waiting. Guests are limited to one FastPass every four hours to ensure that the rides are able to accommodate both FastPass and regular guests. The beauty of FastPass is that rather than waiting in line, guests can now spend money in the restaurants and shops. By handling demand with FastPass, Disney has created a more satisfying customer experience and also created the opportunity for more sales.

Reservation systems can be very complex. It is not within the scope of this book to explore the variations of reservations for hotels, restaurants, and other hospitality organizations.

OVERBOOK   Not everyone who reserves a table or books a room shows up. Plans change and people with reservations become no-shows. Overbooking is another method that hotels, restaurants, trains, and airlines use to match demand with capacity. Hotel managers who limit reservations to the number of available rooms frequently find themselves with empty rooms. For example, at one hotel, 20 percent of guests holding nonguaranteed reservations and 5 percent of those holding guaranteed reservations typically do not honor those reservations. If this hotel has 80 guaranteed reservations and 40 nonguaranteed reservations, it will, on average, be left with 12 empty rooms. For a hotel with an average room rate of $150, this can mean a potential annual loss of more than $750,000 in room, food, and beverage revenue.

Overbooking must be managed carefully. Knowing the hotel's customers, past history of the event, availability of rooms at other hotels, and weather conditions are important factors to consider when overbooking. When a hotel fails to honor its reservations, it risks losing the future business of guests whose reservations are not honored and possibly the business of their companies and travel agents. Usually, it is better to leave a room unoccupied than to fail to honor a reservation.

Developing a good overbooking policy minimizes the chance of walking a guest. This requires knowing the no-show rate of different types of reservations. Groups who reserve rooms should be investigated to see what percentage of their room block they have filled in the past. One study found that reservations made one day before arrival and on the day of arrival had a higher no-show rate than reservations made much earlier.[24] Today with the help of well-designed software systems we can develop an accurate overbooking policy.

Some hotels do nothing for the traveler whose reservation is not honored. Well-managed hotels find alternative accommodations, pay for one night's stay at the new hotel, and provide transportation to the hotel. They may also give the guest a free phone to inform those back home of the new arrangements and keep the guest's name on their information rack so they can refer any phone calls the guest may receive to the hotel where the guest is staying. Smart managers try to get turned-away guests back by offering a free night's stay at their hotel the next day. Hotels that are careless in handling their reservations can be held liable. In one case a travel agent, Rainbow Travel Service, reserved 45 rooms with the Fontainebleau Hilton for clients going to a Miami–Oklahoma football game. The Fontainebleau walked a number of Rainbow's clients, and Rainbow sued for damage to its reputation. A jury awarded the travel agency $250,000. The jury believed that the Fontainebleau should have altered its policy of overbooking by 15 percent because of the demand created by the football weekend.[25]

Revenue management. A pricing method using price as a means of matching demand with capacity.

REVENUE MANAGEMENT   Overbooking is often part of a comprehensive **revenue management** system. Price is inversely related to demand for most products. Managers can create more demand for a product by lowering its price and lower demand by raising its price. With the help of computer programs, managers are using price, reservation history, and overbooking practices to develop a sophisticated approach to demand management called revenue management, a methodological approach to allocating a perishable and fixed inventory to the most profitable customers. For graduates of hospitality programs that enjoy numbers and marketing strategy, revenue management can be an interesting career. The ability to maximize revenue has become such an important management tool that today the position of corporate revenue manager has become a path to the position of corporate vice president of marketing. Well-designed revenue management bases pricing decisions on data and can increase revenue by 8 percent or more. A 200-room hotel was able to add $600,000 to its top line after implementing revenue management. Its system was designed to maximize RevPAR (revenue per available room). Revenue management techniques have also been designed for restaurants, where they are designed to maximize revenue per available seat (RevPASH). In restaurants, seat utilization along with off-peak pricing is among the tools used to maximize RevPASH.

Properly designed revenue management systems value the business or repeat customers. Thus a customer who stays at a hotel 11 times a year for two nights per stay is treated differently than a one-time convention guest. The frequent loyal guest's business is valued, and some hotel companies have developed corporate rates for these guests that do not fluctuate with the demand for business. They protect these guests. As one can see, the practice of revenue management for a hotel can be very complex. It takes an understanding of forecasting models and the hotel's customer base.[26]

USE QUEUING   When capacity exceeds demand and guests are willing to wait, queues form. Sometimes guests make the decision to wait; in other cases they have no choice. For example, a guest is told a restaurant has a 20-minute wait and he or she decides to wait. However, on occasion, hotel guests may find themselves waiting to check in to a hotel where they have made a reservation.

Voluntary queues, such as waits at restaurants, are a common and effective way of managing demand. Good management of the queue can make the wait more tolerable for the guest. Always overestimate the wait. When the estimated wait is 30 minutes, it is better to tell guests that it will be a 35-minute wait than to tell them they will have a 20-minute wait. Some managers fear that if the wait is too long they will lose guests, so they "shorten" the wait time. Once customers have accepted the wait time, they may sit down and have a drink, but they tend to keep their eyes on their watches. When their names have not been called after the allotted time, they run up to the host and ask where they are on the list. When guests wait longer than they were told they would, they go to their dining table upset and in a mood that makes them tend to look for other service failures. It can be difficult for the restaurant to recover from this initial failure, and many guests leave with memories of an unsatisfactory experience.

If the host tells guests it will be a 35-minute wait and then seats them in 30 minutes, the guests will be delighted. If a guest decides not to accept the wait, the host can suggest a time when the wait will be shorter.

In general, the higher the level of service, the longer the guest is willing to wait. Twenty minutes for sit-down service might be acceptable, whereas a five-minute wait at a fast-food restaurant will be unacceptable. Fast-food restaurants must raise their capacity to meet demand or lose customers.[27]

David Maister, a service expert, provides the following tips for the management of a waiting line:[28]

1. **Unoccupied time feels longer than occupied time.** Entertainment parks have characters who talk to kids in waiting lines, occupying time and making the wait pass faster. Restaurants send customers waiting for a dinner table into their cocktail lounge, where a cocktail and conversation make the time pass more quickly. The Rio Hotel places television monitors over the line for their buffet. The monitors promote different products that the resort has to offer, such as its entertainment and other food and beverage outlets. These are a few examples of how managers can occupy guests' time and make their wait more enjoyable.

2. **Unfair waits are longer than equitable waits.** Guests can become upset and preoccupied with a wait if they feel they are being treated unfairly. Restaurants with a limited number of large tables try to maximize the capacity of these tables. For example, rather than put a party of four at a table for six, the restaurant seats a party of six at the table, even if there are several parties of four in front of them. This sometimes leads to anger on the part of the guests in the passed-over party of four. Because they were next, they feel the host should seat them next. In such cases the host should explain what is going on to the next party in line. Another example of an unfair wait is when a guest who has been waiting for 20 minutes to check-in finally reaches the front of the line. Just as he or she is starting to give the details of his or her reservation to the front-desk clerk, the phone rings. The phone is answered promptly by the

clerk, who gets involved in a 10-minute conversation with the caller. Marriott has started a policy of removing phones from the front desk to avoid this distraction and eliminate unfair waits.

3. **Uncertain waits are longer than known, finite waits.** Most travelers have experienced a flight delay. If the agent states the flight will be delayed an hour, the traveler can get something to eat, shop in the stores, or find other activities to fill his or her time. However, if the traveler is just told there will be a delay and when he or she asks how long the agent says, I am not sure it's a mechanical problem, the person often becomes anxious. The anxiety is caused by the uncertain delay. He or she does not want to leave the gate for fear the plane will be promptly fixed and depart. He or she is too anxious to relax. The 30-minute delay will seem like an eternity. When possible we should tell guests the reason for the delay and the expected amount of time of the delay. The reason airlines sometimes do not give delays is because they do not know how long it will take to fix the plane and they do not want people leaving the area. However, they should keep people updated on the progress to reduce the uncertainty.

Maister states that the customer's sense of equity is not always obvious and needs to be managed. Whatever priority rules apply, the service provider must make vigorous efforts to ensure that these rules match with the customer's sense of equity, either by adjusting the rules or by convincing the client that the rules are appropriate.

SHIFT DEMAND It is often possible to shift the demand for banquets and meetings. A sales manager may want to set up a sales meeting for the end of October or the beginning of November and knows that when the hotel is called to check availability, a date must be given. Suppose that October 31 is picked, although it could have been October 24 or November 7 just as easily. Twenty rooms will be needed the night before and a meeting room the day of the event. The hotel is forecast to sell out on October 31 but presently has rooms available. The smart manager asks whether October 31 is a firm date. If the date is flexible, the manager shifts the date to a period when the hotel is not projected to sell out and needs the business.

CREATE PROMOTIONAL EVENTS An object of promotion is to increase demand or, as we will learn later, to shift the demand curve to the left. During slow periods, creative promotions can be an effective way of building business. We discuss promotions later in the book.

The four characteristics of services, intangibility, inseparability, variability, and perishability, create the need for marketing strategies and tactics that are different from goods-producing companies. In the rest of the book we will discuss those strategies and tactics and the principles that support them.

■■■ CHAPTER REVIEW

I. The Service Culture. The service culture focuses on serving and satisfying the customer. The service culture has to start with top management and flow down.

II. Four Characteristics of Services

A. Intangibility. Unlike physical products, services cannot be seen, tasted, felt, heard, or smelled before they are purchased. To reduce uncertainty caused by intangibility, buyers look for tangible evidence that will provide information and confidence about the service.

B. Inseparability. In most hospitality services, both the service provider and the customer must be present for the transaction to occur. Customer-contact employees are part of the product. Inseparability also means that customers are part of the product. The third implication of inseparability is that customers and employees must understand the service-delivery system.

C. Variability. Service quality depends on who provides the services and when and where they are provided. Services are produced and consumed simultaneously. Fluctuating demand makes it difficult to deliver consistent products during periods of peak demand. The high degree of contact between the service provider and the guest means that product consistency depends on the service provider's skills and performance at the time of the exchange.

D. Perishability. Services cannot be stored. If service providers are to maximize revenue, they must manage capacity and demand because they cannot carry forward unsold inventory.

III. Service Management Concepts
  A. Service profit chain
  B. Types of marketing
    1. Internal marketing
    2. External marketing
    3. Interactive marketing

IV. Management Strategies for Service Businesses
  A. Managing differentiation. The solution to price competition is to develop a differentiated offering. The offer can include innovative features that set one company's offer apart from that of its competitors.
  B. Managing service quality. With hospitality products, quality is measured by how well customer expectations are met.
  C. Manage service productivity
  D. Resolving customer complaints. Resolving customer complaints is a critical component of customer retention.

E. Managing employees as part of the product. In the hospitality industry, employees are a critical part of the product and marketing mix. The human resource and marketing department must work closely together. The task of internal marketing to employees involves the effective training and motivation of customer-contact employees and supporting service personnel.

F. Managing perceived risk. The high risk that people perceive when purchasing hospitality products increases loyalty to companies that have provided them with a consistent product in the past.

G. Managing capacity and demand. Because services are perishable, managing capacity and demand is a key function of hospitality marketing. First, services must adjust their operating systems to enable the business to operate at maximum capacity. Second, they must remember that their goal is to create satisfied customers. Research has shown that customer complaints increase when service firms operate above 80 percent of their capacity.

■■■ DISCUSSION QUESTIONS

1. Illustrate how a hotel, restaurant, or theater can deal with the intangibility, inseparability, variability, and perishability of the service it provides. Give specific examples.

2. Do you use consumer-generated content from a site like TripAdvisor or Yelp? If so explain why you think the information is credible. If not state how you choose a new restaurant. If other consumers acquire information the same way you do, how should managers attract new customers.

3. Discuss how the service person in a restaurant is part of the product the customer receives when purchasing a meal.

4. Look up several hotels or restaurants on TripAdvisor and review customer comments. Do you think the managers of the company responded to the comments appropriately? Explain the reasons for your answer.

5. What are internal and interactive marketing? Give an example of how a specific firm or organization might use these concepts to increase the effectiveness of its services. How might these concepts be linked to services differentiation?

■■■ EXPERIENTIAL EXERCISES

Do one of the following:

1. Perishability is very important in the airline industry; unsold seats are gone forever, and too many unsold seats mean large losses. With computerized ticketing, airlines can easily use pricing to deal with perishability and variations in demand.
   a. Go to the Web site of an airline and get a fare for an eight-day stay between two cities it serves. Get prices on the same route for 60 days in advance, two weeks, one week, and tomorrow. Is there a clear pattern to the fares?
   b. When a store is overstocked on ripe fruit, it may lower the price to sell out quickly. What are airlines doing to their prices as the seats get close to "perishing"? Why are tomorrow's fares often higher?

2. Visit a restaurant or a hotel. Observe and record how they manage their customers. This could include how they get them to move through the hotel, stand in line, or throw their trash away in a hotel. Write what you think the business does well and what it does poorly. Explain your answer.

3. Visit a restaurant or hotel and give an example of how they use tangible evidence to tell the customer what type of business they are and how they are run. Things to look at include the exterior of the business, the inside of the business, signage, and employee uniforms. Write what you think the business does well and what it does poorly. Explain your answer.

■■■ INTERNET EXERCISES

1. Visit the Web site of a hotel chain. What does the Web site do to make the product tangible for the customer? Does anything in the site deal with the characteristic of perishables, for example, specials at some of the properties?

2. Visit the Web site of a tourism destination; it can either be a city or be a country. Explain how the site provides tangible evidence relating to the experiences a visitor to the destination can expect.

■■■ REFERENCES

1 Howard Schultz, "Dare to Be a Social Entrepreneur," *Business 2.0* (December 2006): 87; Edward Iwata, "Owner of Small Coffee Shop Takes on Java Titan Starbucks," *USA Today*, December 20, 2006; "Staying Pure: Howard Schultz's Formula for Starbucks," *Economist* (February 25, 2006): 72; Diane Anderson, "Evolution of the Eco Cup," *Business 2.0* (June 2006): 50; Bruce Horovitz, "Starbucks Nation," *USA Today*, May 19, 2006; Theresa Howard, "Starbucks Takes Up Cause for Safe Drinking Water," *USA Today*, August 2, 2005; Howard Schultz and Dori Jones Yang, *Pour Your Heart into It: How Starbucks Built a Company One Cup at a Time* (New York: Hyperion, 1997); "At MIT Starbucks Symposium, Focus on Holistic Approach to Recycling; MIT," May 12, 2010, http://slice.mit.edu/2010/05/12/mit-starbucks/ (accessed July 2, 2015); Starbucks Global Responsibility Report 2013; Starbucks 2013 Annual Report, Starbucks Annual Report 2014, http://quote.morningstar.com/stock-filing/Annual-Report/2014/9/28/t.aspx?t=:SBUX&ft=10-K&d=baddadfea5e1c6d22c6423ef7b-8c2fe0 (accessed July 2, 2015); Starbucks College Achievement Plan, http://www.starbucks.com/careers/college-plan (accessed July 3, 2015).

2 G. Lynn Shostack, "Breaking Free from Product Marketing," *Journal of Marketing* (April 1977): 73–80.

3 Bernard H. Booms and Mary J. Bitner, "Marketing Services by Managing the Environment," *Cornell Hotel and Restaurant Administration Quarterly*, 23, no. 1 (1982): 35–39.

4 Robert C. Ford and Cherrill P. Heaton, "Managing Your Guest as a Quasi-Employee," *Cornell Hotel and Restaurant Administration Quarterly*, 42, no. 2 (2001): 46–61.

5 Diane Schanlensee, Kenneth L. Bernhardt, and Nancy Gust, "Keys to Successful Services Marketing: Customer Orientation, Creed, Consistency," in *Services Marketing in a Changing Environment*, ed. Thomas Bloch et al. (Chicago, IL: American Marketing Association, 1985), pp. 15–18.

6 See James L. Heskett, W. Earl Sasser, Jr., and Leonard A. Schlesinger, *The Service Profit Chain: How Leading Companies Link Profit and Growth to Loyalty, Satisfaction, and Value* (New York: Free Press, 1997); Heskett, Sasser, and Schlesinger, *The Value Profit Chain: Treat Employees Like Customers and Customers Like Employees* (New York: Free Press, 2003); Christian Homburg, Jan Wieseke, and Wayne D. Hoyer, "Social Identity and the Service-Profit Chain," *Journal of Marketing* (March 2009): 38–54; Rachael W. Y. Yee and others, "The Service-Profit Chain: A Review and Extension," *Total Quality Management & Business Excellence* (2009): 617–632.

7 Tracey J. Bruce and Timothy R. Hinkin, "The Costs of Employee Turnover: Where the Devil Is the Details?" *Cornell Hospitality Report*, 6, no. 15 (2006): 9.

8 For more reading on internal and interactive marketing, see Christian Gronroos, "A Service Quality Model and Its Marketing Implications," *European Journal of Marketing*, 18, no. 4 (1984): 36–44; Leonard Barry, Edwin F. Lefkowith, and Terry Clark, "In Services, What's in a Name?" *Harvard Business Review* (September/October 1988): 28–30.

9 Brad Tuttle, "One Airline That Stubbornly Refuses to Pile on the Fees (for Now)," *Time*, May 7, 2013; Jennifer Rooney, "Southwest Airlines CMO Kevin Krone Explains What's Behind the New Grown-Up Ads," *Forbes*, April 22, 2013; Brad Tuttle, "Southwest Airlines: We're Not Really about Cheap Flights Anymore," *Time*, March 26, 2013; David Whelan, "All Grown Up," *Forbes*, July 18, 2011.

10 Dan Tracy, "JetBlue Revives Plans for Trainee Hotel at Orlando Airport," *Orlando Sentinel*, August 19, 2013; Justin Bachman, "How JetBlue Aims to Grab Some High-Dollar Traffic," *Bloomberg*, June 13, 2013; Robin Farzad and Justin Bachman, "Once High-Flying, JetBlue Returns to Earth," *Bloomberg Businessweek*, April 5, 2012.

11 Dinah Eng, "The Rise of Cirque du Soleil," *Fortune* (November 7, 2011): 39–42; Matt Krantz, "Tinseltown Gets Glitzy New Star," *USA Today*, August 24, 2009; Linda Tischler, "Join the Circus," *Fast Company* (July 2005): 53–58; "Cirque du Soleil," America's Greatest Brands 3 (2004); Geoff Keighley, "The Factory," *Business 2.0* (February 2004): 102; Robin D. Rusch, "Cirque du Soleil Phantasmagoria Contorts," Brandchannel.com, December 1, 2003.

12 Adapted from Leonard L. Berry, A. Parasuraman, and Valarie A. Zeithaml, "The Lessons for Improving

Service Quality," *MSI Reports Working Paper Series, no. 03-Vol* (Cambridge, MA: Marketing Science Institute, 2003): 61–82. See also Leonard I. Berry's books, *On Great Service: A Framework for Action* (New York: Free Press, 2006), *Discovering the Soul of Service* (New York: Free Press, 1999), as well as his articles; Leonard L. Berry, Vankatesh Shankar, Janet Parish, Susan Cadwallader, and Thomas Dotzel, "Creating New Markets through Service Innovation," *Sloan Management Review* (Winter 2006): 56–63; Leonard L. Berry, Stephen H. Haeckel, and Lewis P. Carbone, "How to Lead the Customer Experience," *Marketing Management* (January–February 2003): 18–23; Leonard L. Berry, Kathleen Seiders, and Dhruv Grewal, "Understanding Service Convenience," *Journal of Marketing* (July 2002): 1–17.

13 *Feelings Consultant Marketing Manual* (Bloomington, MN: Better Than Money Corporation, n.d.). The Technical Research Programs Institute does studies on customer complaints and the success of complaint resolution.

14 Linda M. Lash, *The Complete Guide to Customer Service* (New York: Wiley, 1989), pp. 68–69.

15 Majorie Coeyman, "You Call This Service?" *Restaurant Business* (May 15, 1997): 93–104.

16 Janelle Barlow and Claus Moller, *A Complaint Is a Gift* (San Francisco, CA: Berrett-Koehler, 1996).

17 Richard Norman, *Service Management: Strategy and Leadership in Service Businesses* (New York: Wiley, 1984).

18 See Karl Albrecht, *At America's Service* (Homewood, IL: Dow Jones/Irwin, 1988).

19 See Leonard Berry, "Big Ideas in Services Marketing," in *Creativity in Services Marketing*, ed. M. Venkatesan et al. (Chicago, IL: American Marketing Association, 1986), pp. 6–8.

20 Thomas J. Peters and Robert H. Waterman, *In Search of Excellence* (New York: Warner Books, 1982), p. xv.

21 See Valarie A. Zeithaml, "How Consumer Evaluation Processes Differ Between Goods and Services," in *Marketing of Services*, ed. James H. Donnelly and William George (Chicago, IL: American Marketing Association, 1981), pp. 186–190.

22 Sanne de Boer, "The Impact of Dynamic Capacity Management on Airline Seat Inventory Control," *Journal of Revenue and Pricing Management*, 2, no. 4 (2004): 315–320.

23 "Hilton Revolutionizes Hotel Experience with Digital Check-In, Room Selection and Customization, and Check-Out across 650,000-Plus Rooms at More Than 4,000 Properties Worldwide," Hilton Worldwide, July 28, 2014, http://news.hiltonworldwide.com/index.cfm/news/hilton-revolutionizes-hotel-experience-with-digital-checkin-room-selection-and-customization-and-checkout-across-650000plus-rooms-at-more-than-4000-properties-worldwide (accessed June 30, 2015).

24 Carolyn U. Lambert, Joseph M. Lambert, and Thomas P. Cullen, "The Overbooking Question: A Simulation," *Cornell Hotel and Restaurant Administration Quarterly*, 30, no. 2 (1989): 15–20.

25 Mark Pestronk, "Finding Hotels Liable for Walking Guests," *Travel Weekly*, 49, no. 37 (1990): 371.

26 Sunmee Choi and Anna S. Mattila, "Hotel Revenue and Its Impact on Customer's Perceptions of Fairness," *Journal of Revenue and Pricing*, 2, no. 4 (2004): 303–314; Karyn Strauss and Jeff Weinstein, "Lesson in Revenue Management," *Hotels* (July 2003): 22; R. G. Cross, *Revenue Management: Hardcore Tactics for Market Domination* (New York: Broadway Books, 1997).

27 Carolyn U. Lambert and Thomas P. Cullen, "Balancing Service and Costs through Queuing Analysis," *Cornell Hotel and Restaurant Administration Quarterly*, 28, no. 2 (1987): 69–72.

28 David H. Maister, "The Psychology of Waiting Lines," in *Service Encounter*, ed. John A. Czepiel, Michael R. Solomon, and Carol F. Surprenant (Lexington, MA: D.C. Heath, 1985).

3

Objectives

*After reading this chapter,
you should be able to:*

1. Explain company-wide strategic planning.

2. Understand the concepts of stakeholders, processes, resources, and organization as they relate to a high-performing business.

3. Explain the four planning activities of corporate strategic planning.

4. Understand the processes involved in defining a company's mission and setting goals and objectives.

5. Discuss how to design business portfolios and growth strategies.

6. Explain the steps involved in the business strategy planning process.

The Role of Marketing in Strategic Planning

Red Robin Gourmet Burgers

Red Robin is a casual service restaurant chain with full alcoholic beverage service. At the beginning of this decade it had grown to a large chain with 445 restaurants and sales in excess of $1 billion. Despite this success, Red Robin's financial performance began to decline due in part to intense competitive pressure and significant increases in commodity and other operating costs, all of which contributed to declining restaurant margins and profits.

In September 2010, Red Robin appointed a new chief executive officer (CEO), Steve Carley. Carley had extensive experience in the restaurant industry, hospitality industry, and brand management. Red Robin's board felt he was the right person to return the chain to profitable and sustainable growth. When Carley arrived, the company's stock was trading at low multiples, and its valuation was depressed. This made the company a target for a takeover by another restaurant company or private equity firm. Carley needed to move quickly to improve Red Robin's business performance and increase shareholder value. His actions were deliberate, as he realized the importance of creating value for shareholders, but he did not want to do this at the expense of employees, which the company refers to as "Team Members," or customers, known at Red Robin as "guests." Carley had joined the company with a great deal of respect for Red Robin's previous four decades of success building a highly recognized restaurant brand. He also admired the strong Team Member culture at Red Robin and believed that there was considerable untapped potential within the company in terms of both talent and ideas. He knew that listening to his fellow Team Members would be an essential part of developing a plan that would improve business performance and create a "best-in-class" restaurant company that preserved the strong internal culture, served quality food and a great dining experience to guests, and delivered strong and consistent returns to shareholders.

Working with his management team and the company's board of directors, Carley led the development of Red Robin's long-term strategic plan, which the company named "Project RED." As Carley explained the plan's chosen shorthand, "RED, in addition to being a color that is almost universally associated with a sense of urgency, stands for Revenue growth, Expense management, and optimum Deployment of capital."

By way of example, before Carley's arrival, Red Robin teams developed an initiative to increase revenue called Red Royalty™, a loyalty program designed to not only increase frequency of guest visits but also establish true customer loyalty by understanding guest purchase behavior and preferences to tailor incentives for repeat visits. A trademark of any successful loyalty program is changing consumer behavior. For example, a guest who comes several times a year to a Red Robin might be offered only a free burger if he or she comes during the next month. A customer who comes in once a week, but never eats an appetizer, might be offered a free appetizer on their next visit. The program also features surprise offers that are designed to entice customers to try menu items they would not ordinarily order, such as appetizers or desserts. This creates an interesting and fun dining experience. Red Royalty™ had already been in a successful test phase in 45 restaurants. One of Carley's early moves to increase revenues was to accelerate rollout of the program to all company restaurants and begin a rollout to Red Robin's franchise system.

To address the "E" of Project RED, expense reduction, Carley directed his team's focus on three main areas of controllable costs: reducing administrative and restaurant-level expenses, reducing supply chain costs, and improving day-to-day business efficiencies and productivity. In addition to implementing a reduction in force at the company's home office, Carley challenged the company's operations teams to identify opportunities to improve restaurant operating margins by about 200 basis points, representing several million in annualized cost savings. Within the first year of the cost management directive, Red Robin's operations teams had identified more than 200 potential cost-saving opportunities, big and small and all across the business.

Finally, Carley's management team took a fresh look at how the company deploys capital, the "D" in Project RED. The goal was to establish capital deployment strategies that allow Red Robin to both grow the brand and maximize long-term shareholder value. Initiatives included continued efforts to improve the performance of new company-owned Red Robin® restaurants to maximize cash-on-cash returns for new restaurant development, and increased investment to overhaul systems and infrastructure to not only better serve the existing restaurant base but also support future growth.

While Carley and his team moved quickly to implement Project RED initiatives, it was also important to make sure that the company continued to live its core values, which included taking care of Team Members. For Carley, an important part of respecting and taking care of Team Members was open and consistent internal communication—making sure that he and his senior team created a culture that encouraged honest assessment and sharing facts about how the company is performing—"telling our people the score," Carley explained.

Instead of hiding bad news from employees, Carley held meetings with key employees to discuss precisely the financial and market share problems facing Red Robin. When asked about this, Carley said, "Employees in any company know the company's problems and how serious they may be. They appreciate straight talk and honest answers to their questions. When employees are told the facts and are given an opportunity to assist in correcting problems, they will respond in a positive way."

Carley also said that it is counterproductive to blame poor financial performance on external factors, circumstances beyond the company's control or bad decisions from former leadership, or to make Team Members feel they somehow failed. Instead, he said it is much better to start by recognizing the many years of dedication and hard work by Team Members in the past that led to Red Robin's many years of growth and prosperity. Carley needed to make sure Team Members were now focusing on making Red Robin the truly great company that everyone in the organization knew it could become.

If the company's goal was to become great, it was important for Team Members to understand what greatness looks like, Carley said. The management of Red Robin selected several restaurants they considered to be great performers, many of which performed considerably better than Red Robin, even when faced with the same macroeconomic challenges in recent years, and used them as "best-in-class" benchmarks. Carley said that without such external benchmarks, companies revert to measuring performance against their own prior results.

Carley also employed the balanced scorecard. This concept was originally developed by Professors Kaplan and Norton of Harvard University. It is used by management to cover the following:

1. **The Financial Perspective.** The financial objectives of an organization are viewed and managers can track financial success and shareholder value.

2. **The Customer Perspective.** Customer objectives such as customer satisfaction are covered. Market share goals are also considered.

3. **Internal Process Perspective.** Internal operational goals are covered, as well as key processes necessary to deliver customer objectives.

4. **Learning and Growth Perspectives.** Intangible drivers of success such as human capital and information capital including skills, training, leadership, systems, and databases are covered.

About half of the companies in the United States, Europe, and Asia use a balanced scorecard system.[1] In the absence of a measurable management tool such as balanced scorecard, Carley said that his experience has shown that companies would slowly develop internal silos and that Team Member discontent would follow.

Carley feels that Team Members perform best when they and management receive feedback from critical sources such as the customer. He also said that he wanted to prevent "churn" in which Team Members are moved from location to location to the detriment of the company. He gave an example of top managers from a restaurant being moved to a poorly performing one with a result of Team Member dissatisfaction and unsatisfactory financial results.

Instead of churn, Carley believes that greater return on investment (ROI) in Team Members is achieved by enhancing tenure with a property. Carley feels this is particularly important in the case of restaurant general managers. He believes in hiring talented people that are passionate about working for Red Robin and providing them with the direction and support that will enable them to perform well. If you do this, employees are self-motivating and will do their best to provide good serve to the customers, other employees, and the company.

As Carley talked about Red Robin Team Members, he continuously mentioned the importance of measurement metrics. Red Robin cannot be just a "feel-good" place, he said. It must be a company that continuously grows toward greatness. With that in mind, Carley said he wanted to ensure that transparency on all elements of the key operating metrics was available for Team Members. "Our people appreciate and deserve honesty," said Carley.[2]

Nature of High-Performance Business

The major challenge facing today's hospitality companies is knowing how to build and maintain healthy businesses in the face of a rapidly changing marketplace and environment. The consulting firm of Arthur D. Little proposed a model of the characteristics of a high-performance business.[3] It pointed to four factors: stakeholders, processes, resources, and organization. A review of these factors will help set the foundation for our study of strategic marketing.

Stakeholders

Stakeholder. Stakeholders include customers, employees, suppliers, and the communities where their business is located and other people or organizations that have an interest in the success of the business.

The starting point for any business is to define the **stakeholders** and their needs. Traditionally, most businesses focused on their stockholders. Today businesses recognize that there are many stakeholders, people and organizations that have an interest in their success. Stakeholders include customers, employees, suppliers, and the communities where their businesses are located. A business must at least strive to satisfy the minimum expectations of each stakeholder group just mentioned.

A dynamic relationship connects the stakeholder groups. The progressive company creates a high level of employee satisfaction, which leads employees to work on continuous improvements as well as breakthrough innovations. The result is higher-quality products and services, which create high customer and stakeholder satisfaction.

As a response to economic downturn, Hilton Hotels Corporation implemented a strategic goal of creating value for all its stakeholders—customers, owners and shareholders, employees (known as team members), strategic partners, and the communities—and a systematic business model to ensure consistency across properties. To do this, the company adopted the Hilton balance scorecard that measured Hilton's creation of value by integrating all aspects of the business—guest satisfaction, employee satisfaction, mystery shopper reports, financial and revenue management indexes, and brand standards. Over time, the balanced scorecard has been used widely by the Hilton Worldwide to reward teamwork and achieve customer service excellence. The performance measures have evolved to include total quality scorecard (TQS), loyalty score according to SALT (satisfaction and loyalty tracking), and the quality assurance (QA) score. Currently, best hotels are selected and recognized in an annual award ceremony based on these performance metrics.[4]

A critical and sometimes overlooked stakeholder group is that of owners of hotels managed by a hotel management company. Such a company may be one of the well-known flag companies or one that is unknown to the public. Many hotel owners are actually investors and do not wish to manage a property actively, so they contract with an experienced hotel management company.

Processes

Company work is traditionally carried on by departments. However, departmental organization poses some problems. Departments typically operate to maximize their own objectives, not necessarily the company's. Walls go up between departments creating silos, and there is usually less than ideal cooperation. Work is slowed down and plans often are altered as they pass through departments.

Companies are increasingly refocusing their attention on the need to manage processes even more than departments. They are studying how tasks pass from department to department as well as the impediments to creative output. They are now building cross-functional teams that manage core business processes.

Resources

To carry out processes, a company needs such resources as personnel, materials, machines, and information. Traditionally, companies sought to own and control most of the resources that entered the business. Now that is changing. Companies are finding that some resources under their control are not performing as well as those that they could obtain from outside. More companies today have decided to outsource less critical sources. However, they appreciate the need to own and nurture those core resources and competencies that make up the essence of their business. Smart companies are identifying their core competencies and using them as the basis for their strategic planning.

Table 3–1 provides a quick reference concerning organizational resources for use in strategic planning.

Hilton Hotels and Resorts use the balanced scorecard concept to manage its hotels. Shown in the picture is the Hilton Hawaiian Village. Courtesy of Steven Heap/123RF.

TABLE 3–1

Strategic Analysis: Questions That Generate Creative Ideas

1. How can this firm take advantage of changes that are expected to occur in society?
2. How can this firm use its relationships with customers to maximize its position in existing or future businesses?
3. Are there any stakeholders that should be seriously considered for partnerships?
4. Does the firm possess any resources or capabilities that are likely to lead to competitive advantage?
5. Are there any resources or capabilities the firm should consider developing to achieve competitive advantage?
6. Can the firm form joint ventures or other alliances with competitors or other stakeholders to acquire valuable knowledge, skills, or other resources?
7. Are there any resources or capabilities the firm does not possess, the absence of which might put it at a competitive disadvantage?
8. Are there any looming threats in the broad environment that the firm should consider in developing its strategy?

Source: Jeffrey S. Harrison, "Strategic Analysis for the Hospitality Industry," *Cornell Hotel and Restaurant Administration Quarterly*, 44, no. 2, April 2003, 152.

Organization

The organizational side of a company consists of its structure, policies, and culture, all of which tend to become dysfunctional in a rapidly changing company. Although structure and policies can be changed, the company's culture is the hardest to change. Successful hospitality companies work hard to maintain a service culture, which was introduced in Chapter 2. In addition to the service culture, they also have to align their organization's structure, policies, and culture to the changing requirements of business strategy. Sometimes structural change and policy change are created by mergers. Other times they are necessary to meet the changing environment. For example, one of the positions being added to organizational structures is that of social media manager. For marketing managers and general managers, it is important that policies and structure support a service culture.

Corporate Strategic Planning: Defining Marketing's Role

At the corporate level, the company starts the strategic-planning process by defining its overall purpose and mission (see Figure 3–1). This mission then is turned into detailed supporting objectives that guide the whole company. Next, headquarters decides what portfolio of business and products is best for the company and how much support to give each one. In turn, each business and product develops detailed marketing and other departmental plans that support the company-wide plan. This marketing planning occurs at the business unit, product, and market levels. It supports company strategic planning with more detailed plans for specific marketing opportunities.

Each company must find the game plan for long-run survival and growth that makes the most sense given its specific situation, opportunities, objectives, and resources. This is the focus of **strategic planning**, the process of developing and maintaining a strategic fit between the organization's goals and capabilities and its changing marketing opportunities.

Strategic planning sets the stage for the rest of the planning in the firm. Companies usually prepare

Strategic planning. The process of developing and maintaining a strategic fit between the organization's goals and capabilities and its changing marketing opportunities.

Figure 3–1
Steps in strategic planning.

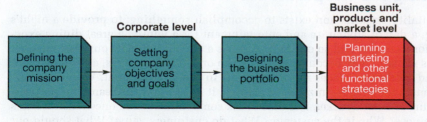

Managing the business portfolio: Most people think of Tommy Bahama as a clothing retailer, but they also have full-service restaurants attached to 15 of their stores in the United States, as well as a restaurant in Japan.

annual plans, long-range plans, and strategic plans. The annual and long-range plans deal with the company's current businesses and how to keep them going. In contrast, the strategic plan involves adapting the firm to take advantage of opportunities in its constantly changing environment.

Corporate headquarters has the responsibility for setting into motion the whole planning process. Some corporations give a lot of freedom to their business units but let them develop their own strategies. Others set the goals and get heavily involved in the individual strategies. For example, a key success factor for Outback Steakhouse in Korea was attributed to decentralized structure to adapt to local culture and supply procurement.[5] In the mid-1980s, Walt Disney Company set up a powerful, centralized strategic-planning group to guide its direction and growth. Over the next two decades, the strategic-planning group turned The Walt Disney Company into a huge and diverse collection of media and entertainment businesses. The sprawling company grew to include everything from theme resorts and film studios (Walt Disney Pictures, Touchstone Pictures, Pixar, and others) to media networks (ABC Television plus ESPN, Disney Channel, parts of A&E and the History Channel, and a half dozen others) to consumer products and a cruise line. To improve performance, Disney disbanded the centralized strategic-planning unit, decentralizing its functions to Disney division managers. Despite the recently weak economy, Disney's sound strategic management of its broad mix of businesses has helped it fare better than rival media companies.[6]

The hospitality industry faces the need for greater empowerment of employees, particularly at middle-management levels. It has been suggested that many of the traditions within the hospitality industry have experienced little change. "Most of its managers, for instance, were trained in the classical management style." This system ensured that "formal rules and regulations guide decision making and ensure organizational stability. Work is done by the book... one's rank in the hierarchy structure determines authority and decision making tends to be centralized, coming primarily from the top."[7] Increasingly, hospitality industry executives and researchers view this traditional approach as needing change.

The hospitality and tourism industries are international and multicultural. Attitudes and culture sometimes create sharp differences in management style and in the perceived importance of strategic planning, empowerment, and other concepts discussed in this chapter. A study of hospitality managers in Poland, France, and Austria demonstrated differences in risk taking and international vision. Interestingly, Polish managers were shown to have a greater international vision than those in France. The authors concluded that different attitudes of managers in the nations affected the degree of autonomy of the manager. The authors also believed that the strategy of a hospitality firm and its level of performance were affected by the differing attitudes of managers within the three nations.[8]

Defining the Corporate Mission

A hospitality organization exists to accomplish something: to provide a night's lodging, a day of adventure and entertainment for a family, a great dining experience for a couple, and so on. At first, it has a clear mission or purpose, but over time, its mission may become unclear as the organization grows, adds new products and markets, or faces new conditions in the environment. When management senses that the organization is drifting, it must renew its search for purpose. According to Peter Drucker, it is time to ask some fundamental questions.[9] What is our business? Who is the customer? What do customers value? What should our business be? These simple-sounding questions are among the most difficult the company will ever have to answer. Successful companies raise these questions continuously and answer them carefully and completely.

Many organizations develop formal mission statements that answer these questions. A mission statement is a statement of the organization's purpose— what it wants to accomplish in the larger environment. A clear mission statement acts like an "invisible hand" that guides people in the organization. Studies have shown that firms with well-crafted mission statements have better organizational and financial performance.[10]

Some companies define their missions myopically in product or technology terms ("We provide lodging" or "We are a hotel Internet reservations company"). However, a market-oriented mission statement defines the business in terms of satisfying customer needs. The following examples illustrate the difference between a product orientation and a market orientation. A product orientation for Disney would be "We run theme parks." A market orientation would be "We create fantasies—that enable the family to have a great time together and produce memories that will last a lifetime." A product-oriented mission statement for Ritz-Carlton would be "We rent luxury hotel rooms and have fine restaurants." A market-oriented mission statement would be "We create the Ritz-Carlton experience—one that enlivens the senses, instills well-being, and fulfills even the unexpressed wishes and needs of our guests." And Chipotle's mission isn't to sell burritos. Instead, the restaurant promises "Food with Integrity," highlighting its commitment to the immediate and long-term welfare of customers and the environment. To back its mission, Chipotle's serves only the very best natural, sustainable, local ingredients.[11]

Management should avoid making a mission too narrow or too broad. In many cases hospitality companies have gone into businesses that would not fit a marketing-oriented business statement. For example, a fast-food hamburger chain in Texas went into the cattle ranching business because their restaurants used thousands of pounds of beef. They felt they should cut out the middleman and produce their own beef. They soon found out that raising cattle and serving hamburgers took two different sets of business expertise. Mission statements should be realistic. Thai Airlines would be deluding itself if it adopted the mission to become the world's largest airline. However, it could provide excellent service and hospitality for persons flying from the cities that are Thailand's top source of business and/or tourist travelers.

The organization should base its mission on its distinctive competencies. McDonald's could probably enter the solar energy business, but that would not use its core competence.

The company's mission statement should be motivating. Employees need to feel that their work is significant and contributes to people's lives. Missions are at their best when they are guided by a vision, an almost impossible dream. Thomas Monaghan wanted to deliver hot pizza to any home within 30 minutes, and he created Domino's Pizza. Ruth Fertel wanted to provide customers with the finest steak dinners available, and she created Ruth's Chris Steakhouses. Phil Roberts wanted to bring back the warmth and passion of the immigrant southern Italian family-style neighborhood restaurant, so he created Buca di Beppo.[12] James Thomson wanted to create a truly unique and memorable dining experience and created the Witchery by the Castle in Edinburgh, Scotland—one of the United Kingdom's finest. Following that success, James and his team, who were experienced in renovating old buildings, conducted an extensive renovation of a seventeenth-century estate called Prestonfield. Within a short time Prestonfield had gained a reputation as Edinburgh's most opulent retreat, Scotland's most romantic hotel, and one of the top 100 hotels in the world. The restaurant "Rhubarb" within Prestonfield gained an equal reputation.[13] The **corporate mission statement** should stress major policies that the company wants to honor.

Some companies like Marriott and Wendy's have public vision statements, but no mission statements. Vision statements are short forwarded looking statements.

Corporate mission statement. A guide to provide all the publics of a company with a shared sense of purpose, direction, and opportunity, allowing all to work independently, yet collectively, toward the organization's goals.

Policies define how employees should deal with customers, suppliers, competitors, and other important groups.

The company's mission statement should provide a vision and direction for the company for the next 10 to 20 years. Missions are not revised every few years in response to every new turn in the economy. But a company must redefine its mission if that mission no longer defines an optimal course.[14]

Mandarin Oriental manages over 40 hotels across the globe in 26 countries. It is known for operating some of the finest hotels in the world. It describes its vision as delighting and satisfying its guests, and being committed to making a difference every day and continually improving to stay on top.

Finally, a company's mission should not be stated as making more sales or profits; profits are only a reward for creating value for customers. Instead, the mission should focus on customers and the customer experience the company seeks to create. Thus, the fast-growing Buffalo Wild Wings restaurant chain's mission isn't just to sell the most wings at a profit:

Customers do, in fact, come to Buffalo Wild Wings to eat wings and drink beer, but also to watch sports, trash talk, cheer on their sports teams, and meet old friends and make new ones—that is, a total eating and social experience. "We realize that we're not just in the business of selling wings," says the company. "We're something much bigger. We're in the business of fueling the sports fan experience." True to that broader mission, Buffalo Wild Wings creates in-store and online promotions that inspire camaraderie. "It's about giving them tools to not just be spectators but advocates of the brand," says the chain. For example, the brand's very active Web site draws 1.4 million visitors per month and its Facebook page has more than 12 million fans. Pursuing a customer-focused mission has paid big dividends for Buffalo Wild Wings. The wing joint's sales have quadrupled in the past eight years and the company brags that it's the number one brand in its industry for fan engagement.[16]

Corporate values. A set of corporate priorities and institutional standards of behavior.

Mission and vision statements are followed by articulation of **corporate values**, which are a set of corporate priorities and institutional standards of behavior. Increasing number of corporations embed social and environmental responsibility in the mission, vision, and values.[17] Hospitality corporations develop mission, vision, and value statements for social and environmental sustainability to communicate what they're doing toward creating a sustainable world and their seriousness on the sustainability front. The values of Shangri-La Hotels and Resorts are rooted in the triple bottom line—economic, environmental, and social: "We envision a community of responsible and educated citizens who are environmentally conscious, practice social responsibility in their daily lives and inspire others to do the same. We commit to operating in an economically, socially and environmentally responsible manner whilst balancing the interests of diverse stakeholders."[18] Starwood Hotels and Resorts briefly state: "At Starwood, we believe sustainable, responsible behavior is a priority—it benefits our business as well as society. And we act on that belief."[19] Marriott International defines their thoughts on sustainability and environment with "We recognize our responsibility to reduce consumption of water, waste and energy in our hotels and corporate offices and are focused on integrating greater environmental sustainability throughout our business," and provides global values and goals such as developing green hotels and inspiring employees and guests to partner with them on sustainability initiatives. The corporation also lists specific areas of focus such as sustainability in hotel kitchens through purchasing organic and responsibly sourced food, planting herb gardens, and sourcing seafood caught in a sustainable manner.[20]

These statements would appeal to minds, hearts, and spirits of younger generations. For example, millennials are very concerned about environmental issues and corporate responsibility. They are more likely to purchase from companies that engage in and commit to social and environmental sustainability.[21]

Setting Company Objectives and Goals

The company needs to turn its mission into detailed supporting objectives for each level of management. Each manager should have objectives and be responsible for reaching them. "The Ritz-Carlton experience enlivens the senses, instills well-being, and fulfills even the unexpressed wishes and needs of our guests." This broad mission leads to a hierarchy of objectives, including business objectives and marketing objectives. Ritz-Carlton's overall objective is to build profitable customer relationships by providing genuine care and comfort for its guests. It does this by understanding what its guests want. This is done by observing guests, seeing how they use the room, and getting employees to provide feedback on what the guests say about Ritz-Carlton and its competitors. Profits can be improved by increasing sales or reducing costs. Sales can be increased by improving the company's share of leisure, group, and transient business markets. These goals then become the company's current marketing objectives.[22]

Marketing strategies and programs must be developed to support these marketing objectives. To increase its market share, Ritz-Carlton may add sales-people to attract the incentive travel market. It may expand its presence in international markets. Ritz-Carlton also realizes that condominiums as part of a Ritz-Carlton hotel project increase the value by 35 percent over an unbranded condominium. Therefore, this becomes an option to provide the cash flow and thus gain financing for new properties.

Each broad marketing strategy must then be defined in greater detail. For example, increasing the incentive travel business may require more salespeople, advertising, and public relations efforts; if so, both requirements will need to be spelled out. In this way, the firm's mission is translated into a set of objectives for the current period.

Designing the Business Portfolio

Most companies operate several businesses. However, they often fail to define them carefully. Businesses are too often defined in terms of products. Companies are in the "hotel business" or the "cruise line business."[23] However, market definitions of a business are superior to product definitions. A business must be viewed as a customer-satisfying process, not a product-producing process. Companies should define their business in terms of customer needs, not products.

Ski resorts are no longer content to sell only ski tickets. Major ski resorts today offer children's programs, summer mountain biking, and rock concerts. Country clubs are no longer just for golfing and occasional dining. Today they are a lifestyle that includes health clubs, spas, and summer camps for children.

Management, of course, should avoid a market definition that is too narrow or too broad. Holiday Inns, Inc., the world's largest hotel chain, fell into this trap. There was a time when Holiday Inns broadened its business definition from the "hotel business" to the "travel industry." It acquired Trailways, Inc., then the nation's second-largest bus company, and Delta Steamship, Inc., but it did not manage these companies well and later divested the properties.[24] Today Holiday Inns is part of the Intercontinental Hotel Group and has refocused on the lodging industry.

Companies have to identify those of its businesses that they must manage strategically. These businesses are called **strategic business units (SBUs)**. An SBU has the following three characteristics:

Strategic business units (SBUs). A single business or collection of related businesses that can be planned separately from the rest of the company.

1. It is a single business or a collection of related businesses that can be planned for separately from the rest of the company.

2. It has its own set of competitors.

3. It has a manager who is responsible for strategic planning and profit performance and who controls most of the factors affecting profits.

The purpose of identifying the company's SBUs is to assign to these units strategic-planning goals and appropriate funding. These units send their plans to company headquarters, which approves them or sends them back for revision. Headquarters reviews these plans to decide which of its SBUs to build, maintain, harvest, and divest. Management cannot rely just on impressions. Analytical tools are needed for classifying businesses by profit potential.

Choice Hotels International has initiated a multifaceted plan to strengthen and revitalize its Comfort brand family, which includes Comfort Inn and Comfort

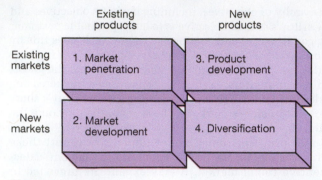

Figure 3–2
The product–market expansion grid is useful in helping managers visualize and identify market opportunities.

Ansoff product–market expansion grid. A matrix developed by cell, plotting new products and existing products with new products and existing products. The grid provides strategic insights into growth opportunities.

Market development strategy. Finding and developing new markets for your current products.

Product development. Offering modified or new products to current markets.

Concentric diversification strategy. A growth strategy whereby a company seeks new products that have technological or marketing synergies with existing product lines.

Horizontal diversification strategy. A product growth strategy whereby a company looks for new products that could appeal to current customers, which are technologically unrelated to its current line.

Suites, about 2,000 domestic hotels. The "Comfort: Redefined and Redesigned" plan focuses on three key strategies: removing underperforming properties, refreshing existing hotels, and adding new construction prototypical hotels.[25]

Developing Strategies for Growth

Companies need growth if they are to compete and attract top talent. "Growth is pure oxygen," states one executive. "It creates a vital, enthusiastic corporation where people see genuine opportunity.... In that way growth is more than our single most important financial driver; it's an essential part of our corporate culture." At the same time, a firm must be careful not to make growth itself an objective. The company's objective must be "profitable growth." Many would add that growth must be environmentally responsible. This is not unilaterally accepted, however.

Marketing has a responsibility to achieve profitable growth for the company. Marketing must identify, evaluate, and select opportunities and lay down strategies for capturing them. The **Ansoff product–market expansion grid** (Figure 3–2) offers a useful framework for examining growth.[26] Management first considers whether it could gain more market share with its current products in its current markets (market concentration strategy). Dunkin stores in the United States generate about 40 percent of their sales after 11 A.M. The chain started offering discounted menu items and coffee from 3 P.M. to 6 P.M. to increase afternoon business.[27] Starbucks focuses on its loyalty program and mobile payment applications to increase sales.

Next it considers whether it can find or develop new markets for its current products (**market development strategy**). Southwest Airlines began flying internationally to Mexico City and select Caribbean destinations such as Jamaica and Dominican Republic. Hooters' renovate their restaurants and update their menu as an attempt to draw younger generation and female consumers.[28]

Next, management should consider **product development**: offering modified or new products to current markets. By examining these three intensive growth strategies, management ideally will discover several ways to grow. Still, that may not be enough, in which case management must also examine diversification and integrative growth opportunities. For example, Starbucks developed packaged products that can be sold in supermarkets. McDonald's increases its consumer base through product expansion. For example, the introduction of McCafé directly targeted consumers in the booming coffee industry and stole share from companies like Starbucks and Dunkin' Donuts.[29] McDonald's also offers new products such as fruits, salads, and McWrap sandwiches to draw millennials as well as new breakfast menu items to increase coffee sales at its McCafé.[30] InterContinental Hotels Group (IHG) developed EVEN Hotels to target business and leisure travelers who are looking for a wellness experience in a hotel stay.

Diversification Growth

Diversification growth makes sense when good opportunities can be found outside the present businesses. A good opportunity is one where the industry is highly attractive and the company has the mix of business strengths to be successful. Three types of diversification can be considered. First, the company could seek new products that have technological or marketing synergies with existing product lines, even though the products may appeal to a new class of customers (**concentric diversification strategy**). In mid 2000s, Wyndham Worldwide entered into timeshare business by launching the brand Wyndham Vacation Ownership, to attract independent timeshare and hotel developers to participate in a franchise and affiliation arrangement under the Wyndham brand. The company now operates timeshare resorts throughout the United States, Canada, Mexico, the Caribbean, and the South Pacific.[31] Second, the company might search for new products that could appeal to its current customers, although technologically unrelated to its current product line (**horizontal diversification strategy**). Hotels, restaurants, cruise lines, and airlines all pursue this strategy when they sell gift items such as T-shirts, perfume, and luggage. Many restaurants, such as the Hard Rock Café franchise, have found that the sale of restaurant logo clothing in their restaurants is highly profitable and the clothing serves as an excellent advertising medium. Hilton Hotel and Resorts sell beds and in-room amenities online through Hilton to Home Web site.[32]

Diversification opportunities sometimes arise as a result of new technology. A new class of lightweight aluminum ferries can cruise at 55 miles per hour and carry hundreds of passengers. This new technology allows ferries to serve new routes: Opportunities for onboard food and beverage service as well as the ferry service itself will be available to the hospitality/tourism industries.[33]

Finally, the company might seek new businesses that have no relationship to the company's current technology, products, or markets (**conglomerate diversification strategy**). The restaurant we mentioned earlier in this chapter that went into the cattle ranching business is an example of conglomerate diversification.

The company Sodexo of Marseille, France, was experienced and successful in providing hospitality services on ocean liners and cruise ships.[34] The company's founder, Pierre Bellon, decided to expand into other industries with similar needs, such as health-care facilities and schools, and to seek international expansion. Within five years, the company was successful in Belgium, and then expanded to North and South America and went public on the Paris Bourse. In 2008 Sodexo's global expansion led to a name change to Sodexo from Sodexho because in some countries a "xh" is difficult to pronounce.

Companies that diversify too broadly into unfamiliar products or industries can lose their market focus. Thus we see that a company can systematically identify new business opportunities by using a marketing systems framework. Despite the risk, companies that started in one market often desire to enter others considered complimentary. The hospitality industry is witness to this phenomenon. This is by no means a secure strategy because different businesses often require different management style and practices.

Conglomerate diversification strategy. A product growth strategy in which a company seeks new businesses that have no relationship to the company's current product line or markets.

Marketing HIGHLIGHT 3.1   Starbucks Coffee: Where Growth Is Really Perking

In only three decades, Starbucks has grown at an astonishing pace, from a small Seattle coffee shop to a powerhouse with more than 21,800 retail stores in 65 countries. In the United States alone, Starbucks serves more than 70 million espresso-dependent customers each week. Growth is the engine that keeps Starbucks perking; Starbucks targets (and regularly achieves) amazing revenue growth exceeding 20 percent each year.

Starbucks's success, however, has drawn a full litter of copycats, ranging from direct competitors such as Caribou Coffee to fast-food merchants (such as McDonald's McCafé) and even the merger between Burger King and Tim Hortons, Canadian coffee chain. These days it seems that everyone is peddling his or her *own* brand of premium coffee. In the early 1990s, there were only 200 coffeehouses in the United States. Today there are more than 21,400. To maintain its phenomenal growth in an increasingly overcaffeinated marketplace, Starbucks has brewed up an ambitious, multipronged growth strategy. Let's examine the key elements of this strategy.

More Store Growth

Some 85 percent of Starbucks's sales come from its own stores. So, not surprisingly, Starbucks is opening new stores at a breakneck pace. Eighteen years ago, Starbucks had just 1,015 stores, total—that's about 1,400 fewer than it plans to build in a year alone. Starbucks's strategy is to put stores *everywhere*. In Seattle, there's a Starbucks for every 9,400 people; in Manhattan, there's one for every 12,000. One three-block stretch in Chicago contains six of the trendy coffee bars. In New York City, there are two Starbucks in one Macy's store. In fact, cramming so many stores close together caused one satirical publication to run this headline: "A New Starbucks Opens in the Restroom of Existing Starbucks." The company's ultimate goal is 40,000 stores worldwide. Starbucks focuses more on its loyalty program and mobile payment applications for market penetration.

Enhanced Starbucks Experience

Beyond opening new shops, Starbucks is adding in-store products and features that get customers to stop in more often, stay longer, and buy more. Its beefed-up menu added hot breakfast sandwiches plus lunch and dinner items, increasing the average customer purchase. To get customers to linger, Starbucks offers wireless Internet access in most of its stores. The chain also offers in-store music streaming and letting customers influence in-store playlists while sipping their lattes. Out of cash? No problem—just swipe your prepaid Starbucks card on the way out (a Starbucks store in your wallet) or use your Starbucks Card Duetto Visa (a credit card that also serves as a gift, stored-value, and rewards card). Starbucks is remodeling many of its stores to give them more of a neighborhood feel—with earth tones, wood counters, and handwritten menu boards.

New Retail Channels

The vast majority of coffee in the United States is bought in retail stores and brewed at home. To capture this demand, Starbucks has also pushed into U.S. supermarket aisles. It has a cobranding deal with Kraft, under which Starbucks roasts and packages its coffee and Kraft markets and distributes it. Beyond supermarkets, Starbucks has forged an impressive set of new ways to bring its brand to market. Some examples: Host Marriott operates Starbucks kiosks in U.S. airports, and several airlines serve Starbucks coffee to their passengers. Starbucks has installed coffee shops in most Barnes & Noble bookstores and many grocery stores. Starbucks also sells gourmet coffee, tea, gifts, and related goods through business and consumer catalogs. And its Web site, StarbucksStore.com, has become a kind of "lifestyle portal" on which it sells coffee, tea, coffee-making equipment, gifts, and collectibles.

New Products, Store Concepts, and Diversification

Starbucks has partnered over the years with several firms to extend its brand into new categories. For example, it joined with PepsiCo to stamp the Starbucks brand on bottled Frappuccino drinks and its DoubleShot espresso drink. Starbucks ice cream, marketed in a joint venture with Dreyer's, is now the leading brand of coffee ice cream. Starbucks has also diversified into the entertainment business. Starbucks Entertainment "selects the best in music, books, and film to offer Starbucks customers the opportunity to discover quality entertainment in a fun and convenient way as a part of their daily coffee experience." The company has also teamed with Apple to create a Starbucks Entertainment area on the Apple Tunes store. To increase business beyond the breakfast business, which still constitutes the bulk of the company's revenue, the chain has added an evening menu in some markets featuring wine, beer, and tapas such as "Warmed Rosemary and Brown Sugar Cashews" and "Bacon Wrapped Dates with Balsamic Glaze" (day-part diversification).

For more diversification growth, the company recently acquired Evolution Fresh, a boutique provider of super-premium fresh-squeezed juices. Starbucks intends to use Evolution as its entry into the "health and wellness" category, including stand-alone stores called Evolution By Starbucks. It recently entered the energy drink market with Starbucks Refreshers, a beverage that combines fruit juice and green coffee extract.

International Growth

Finally, Starbucks has taken its American-brewed concept global. In 1996 the company had only 11 coffeehouses outside North America. Today Starbucks has more than 8,000 stores in over 65 international markets, from Paris to Osaka to Oman to Beijing. Starbucks continues to open new international stores at a rate of close to 400 per year. Starbucks is now expanding swiftly in Asian markets. The company recently opened its thousandth store in Japan, expects to have 1,500 stores in China by 2015, and plans to more than double its number of stores in South Korea to 700 by 2016.

Although Starbucks's growth strategy so far has met with amazing success, many analysts are now expressing strong concerns. What's wrong with Starbucks's rapid expansion? Critics worry that the company may be overextending the Starbucks brand name and diluting the Starbucks experience. People pay $4.50 for a cafe latte, say the critics, because of the brand's coffee-brewing expertise, cozy ambiance, and exclusivity. When you see the Starbucks name plastered on everything from airport coffee cups to supermarket packages, you wonder.

When gasoline hit $4 a gallon in the United States in 2008, it had appeared that Starbucks had grown too fast. At least too fast for the deteriorating economic environment in the United States. The increase in gasoline process meant that consumers were paying $50 or more a month for gasoline. This cut into their morning coffee budget. Part of strategic planning is trying to predict the economic environment. In this case Starbucks's market penetration strategy was fine for a strong economy, but when the economy worsened, it closed 600 sites in 2008, mostly stores that were close together and fighting each other for customers. Starbucks's problems led to the ouster of CEO Jim McDonald, and its founder, Howard Schultz, came back as CEO. Schultz felt that Starbucks had developed too many products and had gotten away from creating a sense of community and the Starbucks experience. He eliminated the breakfast sandwiches whose smell interfered with the aroma of freshly brewing coffee. Starbucks's mission statement is, "Establish Starbucks as the premier purveyor of the finest coffee in the world while maintaining our uncompromising principles as we grow." Schultz also closed all the 7,100 stores for three hours to train the employees. He felt too many employees were no longer making the finest cup of coffee. Later in 2008, he realized a breakfast sandwich was drawing customers who wanted more than coffee and pastry for breakfast. Schultz added back breakfast sandwiches, but this time he developed ones that did not have an aroma that would interfere with the smell of fresh coffee. The moves that Howard Schultz in 2008 made were driven by his quest to move the company back to implementing its mission statement. The quest for growth moved Starbucks away from its mission. Starbucks provides a good example of the need to strategically plan growth and stay close to your mission.

Only time will tell whether Starbucks turns out to be the next McDonald's—it all depends on how well the company manages future growth. Schultz says, "We are in the second inning of a nine-inning game."[35]

Red Lobster uses backward integration by owning its supply chain. Courtesy of Philip Kotler.

Backward integration. A growth strategy by which companies acquire businesses supplying them with products or services (e.g., a restaurant chain purchasing a bakery).

Forward integration. A growth strategy by which companies acquire businesses that are closer to the ultimate consumer, such as a hotel acquiring a chain of travel agents.

Horizontal integration. A growth strategy by which companies acquire competitors.

Integrative Growth

Opportunities in diversification, market development, and product development can be seized through integrating backward, forward, or horizontally within that business's industry. A hotel company could select **backward integration** by acquiring one of its suppliers, such as a food distributor, or it could acquire tour wholesalers or travel agents (**forward integration**). MGM Resorts International set up its own tour wholesaler, MGM Resorts Vacations, to sell complete vacation packages of SBUs in its portfolio. Finally, the hotel company might acquire one or more competitors, provided that the government does not bar the move (**horizontal integration**). In 2013, Pinnacle Entertainment offered a $2.8 billion buyout of regional casino rival Ameristar Casinos. The Federal Trade Commission blocked the buyout because the merger would reduce competition, lead to higher prices, and lower quality for customers in the St. Louis, Missouri, and Lake Charles, Louisiana, areas. Pinnacle Entertainment and Ameristar Casinos have agreed to sell casino properties in St. Louis, Missouri, and Lake Charles, Louisiana, to settle and complete the transaction.[36] In 2015, IHG acquired Kimpton Hotels & Restaurants, a boutique hotel and food and beverage operator whose portfolio consisted of 62 hotels and 71 restaurants and bars.[37]

A company can systematically identify new business opportunities by using a marketing systems framework, looking at ways to intensify its position in current product markets, searching for profitable opportunities outside its current businesses, and considering ways to integrate backward, forward, or horizontally in relation to its current businesses.

Downsizing

Growth strategies are not the only strategies for a firm to consider. Sometimes downsizing will lead to the long-term viability of a company. There are many reasons a company may want to abandon products or markets. The firm may have grown too fast. In the United States restaurant chains with publicly traded stock are under intense pressure to grow their sales and net profits each quarter. Restaurant companies will sometimes expand beyond their capabilities to manage the quality across their rapidly growing chain. When this happens, sales per store start to decline and stock prices follow. When this happens they will reduce the number of stores they have and consolidate, hopefully moving back into an effective organization. Sometimes during economic downturns companies will be faced with pruning unprofitable units to focus their resources on the most profitable units. Sometimes the focus of the company will change and it will enter new markets and exit old ones.

Landry's restaurants sold a casual restaurant chain called Joe's Crab Shack. Landry's decided on focusing on casinos and upscale restaurants. The lower end Joe's Crab Shack no longer fit into their plans. The CEO of Landry's stated, "Joe's has been an important part of our growth over the years. We are now going in a different strategic direction . . . Joe's just does not fit well in our future plans."[38] Since divesting Joe's, Landry's has purchased Morton's, an upscale chain of steakhouses, and opened a major casino in Louisiana. When a firm finds brands or businesses that are unprofitable or that no longer fit its overall strategy, it must carefully prune, harvest, or divest them.

■■ Planning Marketing: Partnering to Build Customer Relationships

The company's strategic plan establishes what kinds of businesses the company will operate and its objectives for each. Then, within each business unit, more detailed planning takes place. The major functional departments in each unit—marketing, finance, accounting, purchasing, operations, information systems, human resources, and others—must work together to accomplish strategic objectives.

Marketing plays a key role in the company's strategic planning in several ways. First, marketing provides a guiding philosophy—the marketing concept—that suggests the company strategy should revolve around creating customer value and building profitable relationships with important consumer groups. Second, marketing provides inputs to strategic planners by helping to identify attractive market opportunities and assessing the firm's potential to take advantage of them. Finally, within individual business units, marketing designs strategies for reaching the unit's objectives. Once the unit's objectives are set, marketing's task is to help carry them out profitably.

Customer engagement and value are the key ingredients in the marketer's formula for success. However, as noted in Chapter 1, although marketing plays a leading role, it alone cannot produce engagement and superior value for customers. It can be only a partner in attracting, engaging, and growing customers. In addition to customer relationship management, managers must also practice partner-relationship management. They must work closely with partners in other company departments to form an effective internal value chain that serves customers. For example, most hotels outsource the cleaning of their laundry. They need a reliable supplier that will provide a clean, finished product and deliver it when it is needed. We now take a closer look at the concepts of a company value chain and a value delivery network.

Partnering with Other Company Departments

Value chain: The series of internal departments that carry out value-creating activities to design, produce, market, deliver, and support a firm's products.

Each company department can be thought of as a link in the company's internal **value chain**.[39] That is, each department carries out value-creating activities to design, produce, market, deliver, and support the firm's products. The firm's success depends not only on how well each department performs but also on how well the various departments coordinate their activities.

Ideally, then, a company's different functions should work in harmony to produce value for consumers. But, in practice, interdepartmental relations are full of conflicts and misunderstandings. The general manager takes the consumer's point of view. But when managers try to improve customer satisfaction, it can cause conflict if all the departments do not put the customer first. For example the sales department may want a late checkout for an important group, but house-keeping may not want to keep extra staff on to provide this service. If everyone has the interests of the guest and future business in mind then the departments will work together to provide great guest service.

Yet general managers must find ways to get all departments to "think consumer" and develop a smoothly functioning value chain. One marketing expert puts it this way: "True market orientation . . . means that the entire company obsesses over creating value for the customer and views itself as a bundle of processes that profitably define, create, communicate, and deliver value to its target customers. . . . Everyone must do marketing regardless of function or department." Says another, "Engaging customers today requires commitment from the entire company. We're all marketers now."[40] Thus, whether you're an accountant, an operations manager, a financial analyst, an IT specialist, or a human resources manager, you need to understand marketing and your role in creating customer value.

Partnering with Others in the Marketing System

In its quest to create customer value, the firm needs to look beyond its own internal value chain and into the value chains of its suppliers, distributors, and, ultimately, its customers. Consider McDonald's. People do not swarm to McDonald's only because they love the chain's hamburgers. Consumers flock to the McDonald's system, not only to its food products. Throughout the world, McDonald's finely tuned value delivery system delivers a high standard of QSCV—quality, service, cleanliness, and value. McDonald's is effective only to the extent that it successfully partners with its franchisees, suppliers, and others to jointly create "our customers' favorite place and way to eat."

More companies today are partnering with other members of the supply chain—suppliers, distributors, and, ultimately, customers—to improve the performance of the customer value delivery network. Competition no longer takes place only between individual competitors. Rather, it takes place between the entire value delivery networks created by these competitors.

■■■ Marketing Strategy and the Marketing Mix

The strategic plan defines the company's overall mission and objectives. Figure 3–3 shows marketing's role and activities and summarizes the major activities involved in managing a customer-driven marketing strategy and the marketing mix.

Marketing strategy. The marketing logic by which the company hopes to create this customer value and achieve these profitable relationships.

Consumers stand in the center. The goal is to create value for customers and build profitable customer relationships. Next comes **marketing strategy**, the marketing logic by which the company hopes to create this customer value and achieve these profitable relationships. The company decides which customers it will serve (segmentation and targeting) and how (differentiation and positioning). It identifies the total market and then divides it into caller segments, selects the most promising segments, and focuses on serving and satisfying customers in these segments.

Guided by marketing strategy, the company designs an integrated *marketing mix* made up of factors under its control—product, price, place, and promotion (the four Ps). To find the best marketing strategy and mix, the company engages in marketing analysis, planning, implementation, and control. Through these activities, the company watches and adapts to the actors and forces in the marketing environment. We now look briefly at each activity. Then, in later chapters, we discuss each one in more depth.

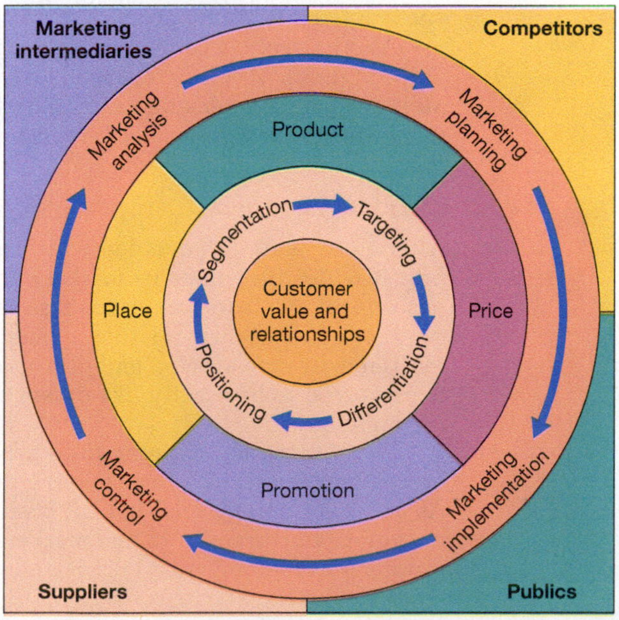

Figure 3-3
Managing marketing strategy and the marketing mix.
Source: Kotler, Philip; Armstrong, Gary, Principles of Marketing, 16th Ed., ©2016, pp. 12, 24, 50. Reprinted and Electronically reproduced by permission of Pearson Education, Inc., New York, NY.

Customer Value-Driven Marketing Strategy

As we emphasized throughout Chapter 1, to succeed in today's competitive marketplace, companies need to be customer centered. They must *win* customers from competitors and then keep and grow them by delivering greater value. But before it can satisfy consumers, a company must first understand their needs and wants. Thus sound marketing requires a careful customer analysis.

Companies know that they cannot profitably serve all consumers in a given market—at least not all consumers in the same way. There are too many different kinds of consumers with too many different kinds of needs. And most companies are in a position to serve some segments better than others. Thus each company must divide up the total market, choose the best segments, and design strategies for profitably serving chosen segments. This process involves *market segmentation, market targeting, differentiation*, and *positioning*.

Market Segmentation

The market consists of many types of customers, products, and needs. The marketer must determine which segments offer the best opportunities. Consumers can be grouped and served in various ways based on geographic, demographic, psychographic, and behavioral factors. The process of dividing a market into distinct groups of buyers who have different needs, characteristics, or behavior and who might require separate products or marketing programs is called **market segmentation**.

Market segmentation. The process of dividing a market into distinct groups of buyers who have different needs, characteristics, or behavior and who might require separate products or marketing programs.

Every market has segments, but not all ways of segmenting a market are equally useful. It would be difficult to make one car model that was the first choice of consumers in both segments. Companies are wise to focus their efforts on meeting the distinct needs of individual market segments.

Market Targeting

After a company has defined market segments, it can enter one or many of these segments. Market targeting involves evaluating each market segment's attractiveness and selecting one or more segments to enter. A company should target segments in which it can profitably generate the greatest customer value and sustain it over time. A company with limited resources might decide to serve only one or a few special segments or "market niches."

Alternatively, a company might choose to serve several related segments—perhaps those with different kinds of customers but with the same basic wants. Most companies enter a new market by serving a single segment, and if this proves successful, they add segments. Large companies eventually seek full market coverage.

Market Differentiation and Positioning

After a company has decided which market segments to enter, it must decide how it will differentiate its market offering for each targeted segment and what positions it wants to occupy in those segments. A product's *position* is the place the product occupies, relative to competitors' products, in consumers' minds. Marketers want to develop unique market positions for their products. If a product is perceived to be exactly like others on the market, consumers would have no reason to buy it.

Positioning is arranging for a product to occupy a clear, distinctive, and desirable place relative to competing products in the minds of target consumers. As one positioning expert puts it, positioning is "why a shopper will pay a little more for your brand."[41] Thus marketers plan positions that distinguish their products from competing brands and give them the greatest advantage in their target markets.

In positioning its product, the company first identifies possible customer value differences that provide competitive advantages on which to build the position. The company can offer greater customer value either by charging lower prices than competitors do or by offering more benefits to justify higher prices. But if the company *promises* greater value, it must then deliver that greater value. Thus effective positioning begins with differentiation, actually *differentiating* the company's market offering so that it gives consumers more value. Once the company has chosen a desired position, it must take strong steps to deliver and communicate that position to target consumers. The company's entire marketing program should support the chosen positioning strategy.

Developing an Integrated Marketing Mix

After deciding on its overall marketing strategy, the company is ready to begin planning the details of the marketing mix, one of the major concepts in modern marketing. The marketing mix is the set of controllable, tactical marketing tools that the firm blends to produce the response it wants in the target market. The marketing mix consists of everything the firm can do to influence the demand for its product. The many possibilities can be collected into four groups of variables known as the four Ps: *product, price, place*, and *promotion*.

Product means the goods-and-services combination the company offers to the target market. *Price* is the amount of money customers must pay to obtain the product. *Place* includes company activities that make the product available to target customers. *Promotion* means activities that communicate the merits of the product and persuade target customers to buy it.

An effective marketing program blends all of the marketing mix elements into an integrated marketing program designed to achieve the company's marketing objectives by delivering value to consumers. The marketing mix constitutes the company's tactical tool kit for establishing strong positioning in target markets.

Some critics think that the four Ps may omit or underemphasize certain important activities. For example, they ask, "Where are services?" Just because they don't start with a *P* doesn't justify omitting them. The answer is that services, such as banking, airline, and retailing services, are products too. We might call them *service products*.

"Where is packaging?" the critics might ask. Marketers would answer that they include packaging as just one of many product decisions. All said, as Figure 3–3 suggests, many marketing activities that might appear to be left out of the marketing mix are subsumed under one of the four Ps. The issue is not whether there should be 4, 6, or 10 Ps so much as what framework is most helpful in designing integrated marketing programs.

There is another concern, however, that is valid. It holds that the four Ps concept takes the seller's view of the market, not the buyer's view. From the buyer's viewpoint, in this age of customer value and relationships, the four Ps might be better described as the four Cs:[42]

4Ps	4Cs
Product	Customer solution
Price	Customer cost
Place	Convenience
Promotion	Communication

Thus, although marketers see themselves as selling products, customers see themselves as buying value or solutions to their problems. And customers are interested in more than just the price; they are interested in the total costs of obtaining, using, and disposing of a product. Customers want the product and service to be as conveniently available as possible. Finally, they want two-way communication. Marketers would do well to think through the four Cs first and then build the four Ps on that platform.

Figure 3-4
The relationship between analysis, planning, implementation, and control.

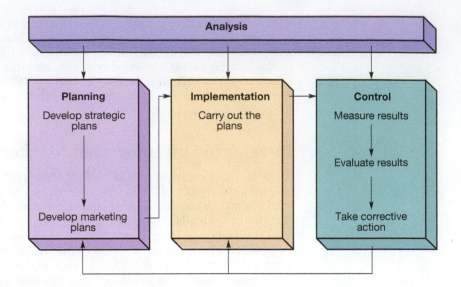

Managing the Marketing Effort

In addition to being good at the *marketing* in marketing management, companies need to pay attention to the *management*. Managing the marketing process requires the four marketing management functions shown in Figure 3–4: *analysis, planning, implementation*, and *control*. The company first develops company-wide strategic plans and then translates them into marketing and other plans for each division, product, and brand. Through implementation, the company turns the plans into actions. Control consists of measuring and evaluating the results of marketing activities and taking corrective action where needed. Finally, marketing analysis provides information and evaluations needed for all of the other marketing activities.

Marketing Analysis

SWOT analysis. Evaluates the company's overall strengths (S), weaknesses (W), opportunities (O), and threats (T).

Managing the marketing function begins with a complete analysis of the company's situation. The marketer should conduct a **SWOT analysis**, by which it evaluates the company's overall strengths (S), weaknesses (W), opportunities (O), and threats (T) (see Figure 3–5). Strengths include internal capabilities, resources, and positive situational factors that may help the company serve its customers and achieve its objectives. Weaknesses include internal limitations and negative situational factors that may interfere with the company's performance. Opportunities are favorable factors or trends in the external environment that the company may be able to exploit to its advantage. And threats are unfavorable external factors or trends that may present challenges to performance.

The company should analyze its markets and marketing environment to find attractive opportunities and identify environmental threats. It should analyze company strengths and weaknesses as well as current and possible marketing actions to determine which opportunities it can best pursue. The goal is to match the company's strengths to attractive opportunities in the environment while eliminating or overcoming the weaknesses and minimizing the threats.

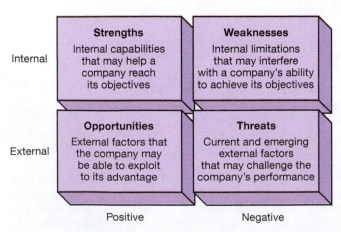

Figure 3-5
SWOT analysis: The goal of SWOT analysis is to match the company's strengths to attractive opportunities in the environment while eliminating or overcoming the weaknesses and minimizing threats.

Atlantis Resort on Paradise Island in the Bahamas gained access to Marriot's reservation system when it became part of Marriott's Autograph Collection. Courtesy of Worachat Sodsri/ Shutterstock.

Internal Environmental Analysis (Strengths and Weaknesses Analysis)

It is one thing to discern attractive opportunities in the environment and another to have the necessary competencies to succeed with these opportunities. Each business needs to evaluate its strengths and weaknesses periodically. Management or an outside consultant reviews the business's marketing, financial, manufacturing, and organizational competencies. Each factor is rated as to whether it is a major strength, minor strength, neutral factor, minor weakness, or major weakness. A company with strong marketing capability would probably show up with the 10 marketing factors all rated as major strengths.

In examining its pattern of strengths and weaknesses, clearly the business does not have to correct all its weaknesses or gloat about all its strengths. The big question is whether the business should limit itself to those opportunities for which it now possesses the required strengths or should consider better opportunities.

Many hospitality industry specialists believe that to compete effectively, companies such as hotels, resorts, and cruise lines need seamless connectivity within their computer reservation systems (CRS), including a global distribution system (GDS). If a hotel company wishes to increase its international business and its reservations through travel agents, the existence or development of such a system would surely be viewed as a strength.[43] Sometimes a business does poorly not because its department lacks the required strengths, but because employees do not work together as a team. In some hospitality companies, salespeople are viewed as overpaid playboys and playgirls who produce business by practically giving it away to customers. In turn, salespeople often view those in operations as incompetent dolts who consistently foul up their orders and provide poor customer service. It is therefore critically important to assess interdepartmental working relationships as part of the internal environmental audit.

Every company must manage some basic processes, such as new product development, raw materials to finished products, sales leads to orders, customer orders to cash payments, and so on. Each process creates value and each process requires interdepartmental teamwork.

External Environmental Analysis (Opportunity and Threat Analysis)

The business manager now knows the parts of the environment to monitor if the business is to achieve its goals. In general, a business unit has to monitor key **macroenvironmental forces** (demographic-economic, technological, political-legal, and social-cultural) and significant **microenvironmental forces** (customers, competitors, distribution channels, and supplies) that will affect its ability to earn profits in the marketplace. The business unit should set up a marketing intelligence system to track trends and important developments. For each trend or development, management needs to identify the implied opportunities and threats.

The terrorist attacks on September 11, 2001, brought a sudden awareness to the worldwide hospitality/tourism industry of the dramatic impact such events can have on business and pleasure travel. This has caused tourism promotion agencies, convention centers, transportation firms, and lodging companies to seriously consider alternative markets, new product design, increased security, emergency energy sources, and many other factors.

The emergence of China, India, and Eastern Europe as new industrial and political powers is seriously affecting hospitality/tourism in ways that were unforeseen. For example, the high quality of health care combined with the low cost in

Macroenvironmental forces. Demographic, economic, technological, political, legal, social, and cultural factors.

Microenvironmental forces. Customers, competitors, distribution channels, and suppliers.

countries such as India has created a new segment of tourism known as medical tourism. At the same time, the Texas Medical Center, one of the world's largest medical centers, has seen its medical tourism from the Middle East decline. In today's rapidly changing environment, external environmental threats and opportunities have taken on new importance in strategic planning.

Marketing opportunity. An area of need in which a company can perform profitably.

OPPORTUNITIES   A major purpose of environmental scanning is to discern new opportunities. We define a **marketing opportunity** as follows: an area of need that a company can perform profitably.

Opportunities can be listed and classified according to their attractiveness and the success probability. Success probability depends on whether its business strengths match the key success requirements for operating in the target market and exceed those of competitors. The best performing company will be the one that can generate the greatest customer value and sustain it over time.

The concept of incorporating health and recreation clubs into resorts has been an opportunity for some resorts. Programs are aimed at local markets, allowing members to enjoy the resort facilities and sometimes even stay in the rooms. Membership programs offer opportunities for increased revenue, but there is a negative side if they are not well managed. Resort guests who are paying to stay in the resort and use its facilities will not appreciate the competition for tennis or golf times from local residents.[44] The franchising of B&Bs (bed and breakfasts) might offer an opportunity for a franchise company that is able to overcome considerable obstacles. The B&B industry today is comparable to the hotel/motel industry in the 1950s. B&B owners do not view franchising favorably, yet they have specific needs that could be met through franchising under a well-planned strategic franchise program.[45]

Many opportunities lie in unmet needs of consumers. Recently, new boutique and lifestyle concepts have emerged to appeal to millennial generation, and environmentally and health conscious customers. The list includes Moxy and Edition by Marriott International; W, Aloft, and Element by Starwood Hotels & Resorts Worldwide; Indigo by IHG; and Andaz by Hyatt Hotels Corporation. For example, Element by Westin Hotels and Resorts, an extended hotel, positions itself as an eco-friendly concept offering a balanced experience where guests can "eat right, sleep well, exercise, and relax."[46] IHG has developed the EVEN Hotels brand in response to results from customer research that found both business and leisure guests were frustrated with hotels that did not meet their lifestyle and wellness needs. EVEN properties feature amenities in the following four pillars[47]:

Even properties feature amenities focusing on menus using fresh and organic ingredients, natural bath products, color LED mood lighting, exercise equipment such as yoga mats in guestrooms, and flexible work space.

THREATS   Some developments in the external environment represent marketing threats. We define an environmental threat as follows: A challenge posed by unfavorable trends or developments that would lead, in the absence of defensive marketing action, to sales or profit deterioration. Threats should be classified according to their seriousness and probability of occurrence. After assembling a picture of major threats and opportunities, the following four outcomes are possible:

1. An ideal business is high in major opportunities and low in major threats.
2. A speculative business is high in both major opportunities and threats.
3. A major business is low in major opportunities and threats.
4. A troubled business is low in opportunities and high in threats.

Traditional institutional food-service providers to hospitals, schools, government offices, and office buildings face the threat of competition from quick service restaurants (QSRs). Many QSRs such as Pizza Hut, Dunkin' Donuts, and Burger King have entered this market. Traditional institutional food-service firms such as Aramark cannot ignore this threat.[48]

Today, the impact of threats is so critical that all hospitality companies must study possible threats and build risk management systems. We have previously spoken of the effects of 9/11, but risks such as mad cow disease and microbial contamination are of vital concern to hospitality companies. Several years ago, "The Jack-in-the-Box QSR chain was linked to 400 illnesses and deaths of three children due to an outbreak of *Escherichia coli* in their hamburgers. The chain was accused of serious deception, irresponsibility, and poor communications."[49] Jack-in-the-Box suffered heavy financial loss for four years and nearly went out of business as a result of the problem.

Because microbial outbreaks are possible in any food establishment, they must be considered as risks with prescribed procedures to follow after an outbreak.

Goal Formulation

After the business unit has defined its mission and conducted a SWOT analysis, it can proceed to develop specific objectives and goals.

Very few businesses pursue only one objective. Most business units pursue a mix of objectives, including profitability, sales growth, market share improvement, and cost containment. The business unit sets these objectives and manages by objectives. The business unit should strive to arrange its objectives from most to least important. Where possible, objectives should be stated quantitatively. The objective "increase the return on investment" is not as satisfactory as "increase ROI [return on investment] to 15 percent" or even better, "increase ROI to 15 percent within two years." Objectives support measurable goals. A business should set realistic goals. The levels should arise from an analysis of the business unit's opportunities and strengths, not from wishful thinking.

Finally, the company's objectives need to be consistent. Objectives are sometimes in a tradeoff relationship. Here are some important tradeoffs:

- High profit margins versus high market share
- Deep penetration of existing markets versus developing new markets
- Profit goals versus nonprofit goals
- High growth versus low risk

The hotel industry is faced with unique challenges concerning goal formulation and performance measurement due to management agreements between hotel owners and hotel operating companies. Most industries such as manufacturing, construction, or retailing hire their own management staff rather than contracting with an independent operations management company. "Of all the issues addressed in the negotiation of a hotel management agreement, among the most difficult to resolve is establishing an appropriate performance test that is acceptable to both parties."[50]

Goals indicate what a business unit wants to achieve; strategy answers how to get there. Every business must tailor a strategy for achieving its goals. Although we can list many types of strategies, Michael Porter has condensed them into three generic types that provide a good starting point for strategic thinking.[51]

1. **Overall cost leadership.** Here the business works hard to achieve the lowest costs. The problem with this strategy is that other firms usually emerge with still lower costs. The real key is for the firm to achieve the lowest costs among those competitors adopting a similar differentiation or focus strategy. Red Lobster has its own seafood supply chain to help achieve its low-cost leadership in the market.

2. **Differentiation.** Here the business concentrates on achieving superior performance in an important customer benefit area valued by a large part of the market. The relative importance of customer benefits shifts as demographic and psychographic characteristics of market populations change. In-N-Out differentiates themselves from the big burger chains by using fresh ingredients. The meat is cooked to order and french fries are hand-cut from whole potatoes.

In-N-Out Burger offers freshly made burgers and fries to differentiate its product from the larger burger chains. Courtesy of Kent Nishimura/ Getty Images.

Although difficult, some firms have been successful by combining low-cost and differentiation strategy, a hybrid approach. Southwest Airlines designed a low-cost delivery system, but does not charge a change fee and bags fly for free.

3. **Focus.** Here the business focuses on one or more narrow market segments rather than going after a large market. The firm gets to know the needs of these segments and pursues either cost leadership or a form of differentiation within the target segments. Food trucks have become increasingly popular in major U.S. cities. They offer specialized and niche menus for those who seek authentic and regional dishes.

The online air travel industry has provided a good example of these three strategies: Travelocity has pursued a differentiation strategy by offering the most comprehensive range of services to the traveler, Lowestfare has pursued a lowest-cost strategy for the leisure travel market, and Last Minute has pursued a niche strategy by focusing on travelers who have the flexibility to travel on very short notice.[52]

Marketing Planning

Marketing planning involves deciding on marketing strategies that will help the company attain its overall strategic objectives. A detailed marketing plan is needed for each business, product, or brand. The plan begins with an executive summary, which quickly overviews major assessments, goals, and recommendations. The main section of the plan presents a detailed SWOT analysis of the current marketing situation as well as potential threats and opportunities. The plan next states major objectives for the brand and outlines the specifics of a marketing strategy for achieving them.

A *marketing strategy* consists of specific strategies for target markets, positioning, the marketing mix, and marketing expenditure levels. It outlines how the company intends to create value for target customers in order to capture value in return. In this section, the planner explains how each strategy responds to the threats, opportunities, and critical issues spelled out earlier in the plan. Additional sections of the marketing plan lay out an action program for implementing the marketing strategy along with the details of a supporting *marketing budget*. The last section outlines the controls that will be used to monitor progress, measure return on marketing investment, and take corrective action. As a manager or a director of sales of a hospitality business, you will be required to develop a marketing plan every year. A well-developed marketing plan is critical to the success of a business. This is why we have devoted the last chapter of this book to developing a marketing plan.

Implementation

Even a clear strategy and well-thought-out supporting program may not be enough. The firm may fail at implementation. Employees in a company share a common way of behaving and thinking. They must understand and believe in the company's strategy. The company must communicate its strategy to its employees and make them understand their part in carrying it out. To implement a strategy, the firm must have the required resources, including employees with the necessary skills to carry out that strategy.

Feedback and Control

All companies need to track results and monitor new developments in the environment. The environment will change. When it does, the company will need to review its strategies or objectives. Peter Drucker pointed out that it is more important to do the right thing (being effective) than to do things right (being efficient). Excellent companies excel at both.

Once an organization starts losing its market position through failure to respond to a changed environment, it becomes increasingly harder to retrieve market leadership. Organizations, especially large ones, have much inertia. Yet organizations can be changed through leadership, ideally in advance of a crisis.

The hotel-resort industry faces unique challenges in strategic planning. Most other members of the hospitality industry, such as airlines, cruise lines, and major restaurant chains, may approach strategic planning in much the same manner as a manufacturing company. These organizations have highly centralized management operations in which strategic decisions are made.

■■■ Measuring and Managing Return on Marketing Investment

Marketing managers must ensure that their marketing dollars are being well spent. In the past, many marketers spent freely on big, expensive marketing programs, often without thinking carefully about the financial returns on their spending. They believed that marketing produces intangible creative outcomes, which do not lend themselves readily to measures of productivity or return. But in today's more constrained economy, all that is changing.[53]

According to a recent study, as finances have tightened, marketers see return on marketing investment as the second biggest issue after the economy. "Increasingly, it is important for marketers to be able to justify their expenses," says one marketer. For a marketing program, says another, marketers need to ask themselves, "Do I have the right combination of strategy and tactics that will generate the most return in terms of share, revenue, and/or profit objectives from my investment?"[54]

In response, marketers are developing better measures of *marketing ROI*. **Return on marketing investment** or marketing ROI is the net return from a marketing investment divided by the costs of the marketing investment. It measures the profits generated by investments in marketing activities.

A recent survey found that although two-thirds of companies have implemented return on marketing investment programs in recent years, only 22 percent of companies report making good progress in measuring marketing ROI. Another survey of chief financial officers reported that 93 percent of those surveyed are dissatisfied with their ability to measure marketing ROI. The major problem is figuring out what specific measures to use and obtaining good data on these measures.[55]

A company can assess marketing ROI in terms of standard marketing performance measures, such as brand awareness, sales, or market share. Many companies are assembling such measures into *marketing dashboards*—meaningful sets of marketing performance measures in a single display used to monitor strategic marketing performance. Just as automobile dashboards present drivers with details on how their cars are performing, the marketing dashboard gives marketers the detailed measures they need to assess and adjust their marketing strategies.

There is commercial software that produces dashboards for both lodging and food-service operations. Searchview by TravelClickHotels is designed to give an instant update of one's online presence, including production by online travel agencies (OTAs), page presence of these agencies, your star ratings on the OTA, performance of pay-per-click (PPC) activities, and the individual customer ratings and comments. A company can also compare its site with its ratings with its competitors on sites such as travel click. Restaurant dashboards can include sales mix reports, reports on promotions, coupon redemption, information on each comp, payroll

Return on marketing investment (or marketing ROI). The net return from a marketing investment divided by the costs of the marketing investment. It measures the profits generated by investments in marketing activities.

Dashboards, such as Revinate Dashboard, organize and present data creating an effective way for managers to access and understand key data. Courtesy of Revinate.

costs, and costs of goods sold. Up until a few years ago intelligence would have been cost prohibitive for the individual property to collect.

A growing number of companies provide dashboards showing customer ratings of a business across selected social media sites and comparing them with those of competitors. These dashboards enhance a manager's ability to monitor user-generated content (UGC) and manage online branding.

Revinate, a Software as a Service (SaaS) tech company, provides such a platform built exclusively for hotels to track and manage their social media reviews and online reputation and to connect with their guests in real time. The company provides benchmarking dashboards including ratings across multiple social media sites, trend analysis to compare a property's performance to that of a competitive set, customer sentiment analysis summarizing positive and negative online reviews, performance reports (ADR, RevPAR [revenue per available room], and Occupancy), and monthly property report.

■■■ CHAPTER REVIEW

I. Nature of High-Performance Business
A. Stakeholder. Stakeholders include customers, employees, suppliers, and the communities where their business is located and other people or organizations that have an interest in the success of the business. A business must at least strive to satisfy the minimum expectations of each stakeholder group.
B. Processes. Companies build cross-functional teams that manage core business processes in order to be superior competitors.
C. Resources. Companies decide to outsource less critical resources. They identify their core competencies and use them as the basis for their strategic planning.
D. Organization. Companies align their organization's structure, policies, and culture to the changing requirements of business strategy.

II. Corporate Strategic Planning: Defining Marketing's Role
A. Defining the corporate mission. A mission statement is a statement of the organization's purpose—what it wants to accomplish in the larger environment.
B. Setting company objectives and goals. The company needs to turn its mission into detailed supporting objectives for each level of management. Marketing strategies and programs must be developed to support these marketing objectives.
C. Designing the business portfolio. Market definitions of a business are superior to product definitions. A business must be viewed as a customer-satisfying process, not a product-producing process. Companies should define their business in terms of customer needs, not products.
   1. Developing growth strategies. Companies need growth if they are to compete and attract top talent.
      a. Ansoff product–market expansion grid offers a useful framework for examining growth.
   2. Diversification growth. Makes sense when good opportunities can be found outside the present businesses
      a. Concentric diversification strategy. The company could seek new products that

have technological or marketing synergies with existing product lines, even though the products may appeal to a new class of customers.
      b. Horizontal diversification strategy. The company might search for new products that could appeal to its current customers, although technologically unrelated to its current product line.
      c. Conglomerate diversification strategy. The company might seek new businesses that have no relationship to the company's current technology, products, or markets.
   3. Integrative growth. Opportunities in diversification, market development, and product development can be seized through integrating backward, forward, or horizontally within that business's industry.
      a. Backward integration. Acquiring a supplier.
      b. Forward integration. For example, a hotel might acquire tour wholesalers or travel agents.
      c. Horizontal integration. Acquiring one or more competitors.
   4. Downsizing. When a firm finds brands or businesses that are unprofitable or that no longer fit its overall strategy. It must carefully prune, harvest, or divest them.

III. Partnering to Build Customer Relationships
A. Partnership with other company departments. The major functional departments in each unit—marketing, finance, accounting, purchasing, operations, information systems, human resources, and others—must work together to accomplish strategic objectives.
B. Partnering with others in the marketing systems. Competition no longer takes place only between individual competitors. Rather, it takes place between the entire value delivery networks created by these competitors.

IV. Marketing Strategy and the Marketing Mix
A. Customer value-driven marketing strategy. Before it can satisfy consumers, a company must first

understand their needs and wants. Thus sound marketing requires a careful customer analysis. Each company must divide up the total market, choose the best segments, and design strategies for profitably serving chosen segments.

1. **Market segmentation.** The market consists of many types of customers, products, and needs. The marketer must determine which segments offer the best opportunities. Consumers can be grouped and served in various ways based on geographic, demographic, psychographic, and behavioral factors.

2. **Market targeting.** Market targeting involves evaluating each market segment's attractiveness and selecting one or more segments to enter. A company should target segments in which it can profitably generate the greatest customer value and sustain it over time.

3. **Market differentiation and positioning.** After a company has decided which market segments to enter, it must decide how it will differentiate its market offering for each targeted segment and what positions it wants to occupy in those segments.

B. **Developing an integrated marketing mix.** The marketing mix is the set of controllable, tactical marketing tools that the firm blends to produce the response it wants in the target market. The marketing mix consists of everything the firm can do to influence the demand for its product.

1. **Product.** The goods-and-services combination the company offers to the target market.

2. **Price.** The amount of money customers must pay to obtain the product.

3. **Place.** Company activities that make the product available to target customers.

4. **Promotion.** Activities that communicate the merits of the product and persuade target customers to buy it.

V. **Managing the Marketing Effort**

A. **Marketing analysis.** Managing the marketing function begins with a complete analysis of the company's situation. The marketer should conduct a SWOT analysis, by which it evaluates the company's overall strengths (S), weaknesses (W), opportunities (O), and threats (T).

1. **Internal environmental analysis** (strengths and weaknesses analysis)

a. **Strengths.** Internal capabilities, resources, and positive situational factors that may help the company to serve its customers and achieve its objectives.

b. **Weaknesses.** Internal limitations and negative situational factors that may interfere with the company's performance.

2. **External environmental analysis** (opportunity and threat analysis)

a. **Opportunities.** Favorable factors or trends in the external environment that the company may be able to exploit to its advantage.

b. **Threats.** Unfavorable external factors or trends that may present challenges to performance.

B. **Goal formulation.** After the business unit has defined its mission and conducted a SWOT analysis, it can proceed to develop specific objectives and goals.

1. **Overall cost leadership.** The real key is for the firm to achieve the lowest costs among those competitors adopting a similar differentiation or focus strategy.

2. **Differentiation.** The business concentrates on achieving superior performance in an important customer benefit area valued by a large part of the market.

3. **Focus.** The business focuses on one or more narrow market segments rather than going after a large market.

C. **Marketing planning.** Marketing planning involves deciding on marketing strategies that will help the company attain its overall strategic objectives. A detailed marketing plan is needed for each business, product, or brand.

D. **Implementation.** To implement a strategy, the firm must have the required resources, including employees with the necessary skills to carry out that strategy.

E. **Feedback and control.** All companies need to track results and monitor new developments in the environment. The environment will change. When it does, the company will need to review its strategies or objectives.

VI. **Measuring and Managing Return on Marketing Investment.** Marketing managers must ensure that their marketing dollars are being well spent.

■■■ DISCUSSION QUESTIONS

1. Conduct a SWOT analysis for a hospitality company near your college.

2. From your earlier analysis, suggest a strategy from the product–market expansion grid and an appropriate marketing mix to implement the strategy.

3. What is a marketing dashboard and how is it useful to hospitality marketers?

4. Think about the shopping area near your campus. Assume that you wish to start a business here and are looking for a promising opportunity for a restaurant. Is there an opportunity to open a distinctive and promising business? Describe your target market and how you would serve it differently than current businesses do.

■■■ EXPERIENTIAL EXERCISES

Do one of the following:

1. Visit two hotels, restaurants, or other hospitality businesses. From your observations write down what you think are the strengths and weaknesses of the businesses. You will be able to observe elements such as location, physical facilities, employee attitude, quality of products, reputation of the brand (if it is a brand), and other factors.

2. Find a strategic alliance between a hotel company and another company (this can be for another hospitality organization or a company outside the hospitality industry). State what you think the benefits of the alliance are for each partner.

■■■ INTERNET EXERCISES

1. Find the mission statement of a hospitality or travel company on the Internet. Critique the mission statement against the guidelines for a mission statement, as stated in the text.

2. Visit the annual report of a hospitality organization (these can usually be accessed through the company's home page). What does the annual report tell you about the organization's strategy?

■■■ REFERENCES

1   What Is a Balanced Scorecard? Advanced Performance Institute, Buckinghamshire, MK12STS, United Kingdom.

2   Steve Coomes, *Nation's Restaurant News* (June 13, 2011): 32–33.

3   See Tamara J. Erickson and Everett Shorey, "Business Strategy: New Thinking for the 90s," *Prism* (4th Quarter 1992): 19–35.

4   Dieter Huckestein and Robert Duboff, "Hilton Hotels: A Comprehensive Approach to Delivering Value for All Stakeholders," *The Cornell HRA Quarterly* (August 28–38, 1999); http://www.bscdesigner.com/bsc-for-hotel-top-management.htm (accessed February 2015); http://news.hiltonworldwide.com/index.cfm/newsroom/detail/26370 (accessed February 2015).

5   Kyuho Lee, Mahmood A. Khan, and Jae-Youn Ko, "Outback Steakhouse in Korea: A Success Story," *The Cornell Hospitality Quarterly*, 49, no. 1 (2008): 62–72.

6   Lisa Richwine, "Disney Earnings Beat Despite Shaky Economy," Reuters.com, February 8, 2012, www.reuters.com/article/2012/02/08/us-disney-idUS-TRE8161TE20120208; http://corporate.disney.go.comlinvestors/annual_reports.html (accessed July 2013).

7   Bruce J. Tracey and Timothy R. Hinkin, "Transformational Leaders in the Hospitality Industry," *Cornell Hotel and Restaurant Administration Quarterly*, 35, no. 2 (1994): 18.

8   Patrick Legoherel, Philippe Callot, Karine Gallopel, and Mike Peters, "Personality Characteristics, Attitude Toward Risk and Decisional Orientation of the Small Business Entrepreneur: A Study of Hospitality Managers," *Journal of Hospitality and Tourism Research*, 28, no. 1 (2004): 117–118.

9   See Peter Drucker, *Management Tasks, Responsibilities and Practices* (New York: Harper & Row, 1973), Chapter 7.

10 For more on mission statements, see Frank Buytendijk, "Five Keys to Building a High-Performance Organization," *Business Performance Management* (February 2006): 24–29; Joseph Peyrefitte and Forest R. David, "A Content Analysis of Mission Statements of United States Firms in Four Industries," *International Journal of Management* (June 2006): 296–301; Jeffrey Abrahams, *101 Mission Statements from Top Companies* (Berkeley, CA: Ten Speed Press, 2007).

11 Ritz Carlton Website accessed September 16, 2012, http://corporate.ritzcarlton.com/en/About/GoldStandards.htm.

12 "Mission Statements for the Next Millennium," *Restaurant Hospitality* (December 1998): 46.

13 www.scotland-edinburgh.co.uh/hotel-home.asp, Prestonfield-Edinburgh's most indulgent retreat, 2008.

14 For more discussion, see Laura Nash, "Mission Statements: Mirrors and Windows," *Harvard Business Review* (March/April 1988): 155–156. See also Tom Feltenstein, "Strategic Planning for the 1990s: Exploiting the Inevitable," *Cornell Hotel and Restaurant Administration Quarterly*, 33, no. 3 (1994): 45.

15 Retrieved August 7, 2011, from http://www.mandarinoriental.com/.

16 Based on information from "Buffalo Wild Wings," a 22SQUARED case study, September 5, 2012, http://22squared.com/work/projec/buffalo-wild-wings-flavor-fanatics-case-study; Lauren Johnson, "Buffalo Wild Wings Mobile Campaign Increased Purchase Intent by 45pc," *Mobile Commerce Daily*, April 15, 2013, www.mobilecommercedaily.com/buffalo-wild-wings-mobile-campaign-increases-purchaseintent-by-45pc; Brandon Southward, "The Crowd Goes Wild," *Fortune* (July 22, 2013): 18; www.buffalowildwings.com/about/ (accessed September 2014). Buffalo Wild Wings® is a registered trademark of Buffalo Wild Wings, Inc.

17 Phillip Kotler, Hermawan Kartajaya, and Iwan Setiawan, *Marketing 3.0* (New Jersey: John Wiley & Sons, Inc., 2010).

18 See http://www.shangri-la.com/corporate/about-us/corporate-social-responsibility/sustainability/mission-statement/ (accessed March 2015).

19 See http://www.starwoodhotels.com/corporate/about/citizenship/index.htmⁱ (accessed February 2015).

20 See http://www.marriott.com/corporate-social-responsibility/corporate-environmental-responsibility.mi (accessed January 2015).

21 See http://www.chicagobusiness.com/article/20140325/OPINION/140329895/corporate-social-responsibility-is-millennials-new-religion (accessed March 2014).

22 See the BASF Innovations Web page, www.corporate.basi.comJenJinnovationenl7idZj-HA6MObcp4PX (accessed November 2007).

23 Theodore Levitt, "Marketing Myopia," *Harvard Business Review* (July/August 1960): 45–46.

24 See "Holiday Inns: Refining Its Focus to Food, Lodging, and More Casinos," *Business Week* (July 21, 1980): 100–104.

25 See http://www.hospitalitynet.org/news/4054592.html (accessed January 2012).

26 Igor H. Ansoff, "Strategies for Diversification," *Harvard Business Review* (September/October 1957): 113–124.

27 Leslie Patton, "Dunkin' Donuts Upgrades Stores to Be More Like Starbucks," *BusinessWeek*, June 13, 2013, http://www.businessweek.com/bw/articles/2013-06-13/dunkin-donuts-upgrades-stores-to-be-more-like-starbucks

28 Josh Sanburn, "Hooters' Big Experiment: New Menu, New Decor and a New Target Audience," August 2, 2012, http://business.time.com/2012/08/02/hooters-big-experiment-new-menu-new-decor-and-a-new-target-audience/; Erin Dostal, "Hooters Unveils Newly Built Restaurant Prototype," *Nation's Restaurant News*, June 20, 2013, http://nrn.com/operations/hooters-unveils-newly-built-restaurant-prototype.

29 See http://www.forbes.com/sites/greatspeculations/2014/10/03/mcdonalds-mccafe-to-face-stiff-competition-in-canada/; Emily Morgan, "McDonald's Loses Millennials to Fast-Casual Restaurants," August 25, 2014, http://www.hngn.com/articles/40192/20140825/mcdonald-s-loses-millennials-to-fast-casual-restaurants.htm.

30 Dan Moskowitz, "McDonald's New Menu Item Test Hints at the Company's Future Strategy", *The Motley Fool*, March 17, 2014, http://www.fool.com/investing/general/2014/03/17/mcdonalds-new-menu-item-test-hints-at-the-companys.aspx.

31 See http://www.wyndhamworldwide.com/about-wyndham-worldwide/wyndham-vacation-ownership.

32 See http://www.hiltontohome.com/index.aspx

33 John Ritter, "Full Speed Ahead for New Ferries," *USA Today* (April 12, 2004): 3A.

34 Dennis Reynolds, "Managed Services Companies," *Cornell Hotel and Restaurant Administration Quarterly*, 38, no. 3 (1997): 90.

35 Tess Steins, "Starbucks Details Plans for Energy Drink, International Expansion," *Wall Street Journal*, March 21, 2012, http://online.wsj.comlarticle/SB100014240527023046364045772956735574641 82.htrnl; U.S. Coffee Shops Still Simply Too Hot to Handle," www.marketresearchworld.net (retrieved August 8, 2007); Tess Steins, "Starbucks Details Plans for Energy Drink, International Expansion," *Wall Street Journal*, March 21, 2012, http://online.wsj.comlarticle/SB1000142405270230463640457729567355746 4182.html; David A. Kaplan, "Strong Coffee," *Fortune* (December 12, 2011): 101–115; Jon Carter, "Star Bucks: For Infusing a Steady Stream of New Ideas to Revise Its Business," *Fast Company* (March 2012): 112+; "Company Profile," January 2015, http://www.starbucks.com/about-us/company-information, Profile.pdf; "Starbucks Details Five-Year Plan to Accelerate Profitable Growth, December 4, 2014, http://news.starbucks.com/news/; Burt Helm, "Saving Starbucks' Soul," *Business Week* (April 9, 2007): 56–62; Curt Woodward, "Weak Coffee: Some Question If Starbucks Expansion May Dilute the Brand," *Marketing News* (May 15, 2007): 1; Land Starbucks annual reports and other information accessed at www.starbucks.com, July 2008; Mellisa Allison, "Starbucks Closing 5 Percent of U.S. Stores," *The Seattle Times* (July 2, 2008): 1–3, http://seattletimes.nwsource.com; Brian White, "Starbucks to Close Stores and Discontinue Breakfast Sandwiches," *BloggingStocks* (January 31, 2008): 1, www.bloggingstocks.com; Sarah Gilbert, "Starbucks Nationwide to Close for Emergency Re-training Feb. 26," *BloggingStocks* (February 13, 2008); 1; Venessa Wong, "What to Expect From Starbucks's New Booze Menu," March 20, 2014, http://www.bloomberg.com/bw/articles/2014-03-20/what-to-expect-from-starbucks-new-booze-menu.

36 See http://www.ftc.gov/news-events/press-releases/2013/08/ftc-requires-pinnacle-sell-two-casino-properties-condition

37 See http://www.ihgplc.com/index.asp?pageid=57&newsid=3362

38 "Landry's Reaches Deal to Sell Joe's Crab Shack," *Houston Chronicle*, October 10, 2006, http://www.chron.com/business/article/Landry-s-reaches-deal-to-sell-Joe-s-Crab-Shack-1905117.php (accessed July 5, 2015).

39 See Michael E. Porter, *Competitive Advantage: Creating and Sustaining Superior Performance* (New York: Free Press, 1985); Michael E. Porter, "What Is Strategy?" *Harvard Business Review* (November–December 1996): 61–78. Also see "The Value Chain," www.quickmba.com/strategy/value-chain (accessed July 2013); Philip Kotler and Kevin Lane Keller, *Marketing*

Management, 14th ed. (Upper Saddle River, NJ: Prentice Hall, 2012), pp. 34–35 and 203–204.

40 Nirmalya Kumar, "The CEO's Marketing Manifesto," *Marketing Management* (November–December 2008): 24–29; Tom French and others, "We're All Marketers Now," *McKinsey Quarterly*, July 2011, www.mckinseyquarterly/Were_all_marketers_now_2834.

41 Jack Trout, "Branding Can't Exist Without Positioning," *Advertising Age* (March 14, 2005): 28.

42 The four Ps classification was first suggested by B. Jerome McCarthy, *Basic Marketing: A Managerial Approach* (Homewood, IL: Irwin, 1960). For the 4Cs, other proposed classifications, and more discussion, see Robert Lauterborn, "New Marketing Litany: 4Ps Passé C-Words Take Over," *Advertising Age* (October 1, 1990): 26; Don F. Schulti, "New Definition of Marketing Reinforces Idea of Integration," *Marketing News* (January 15, 2005): 8; Phillip Kotler, "Alphabet Soup," *Marketing Management* (March–April 2006): 51.

43 Rita M. Emmer, Chuck Tauck, Scott Wilkinson, and Richard G. Moore, "Marketing Hotels Using Global Distribution Systems," *Cornell Hotel and Restaurant Administration Quarterly*, 34, no. 6 (1993): 80–89.

44 Michael P. Sim and Chase M. Burritt, "Enhancing Resort Profitability with Membership Programs," *Cornell Hotel and Restaurant Administration Quarterly*, 34, no. 4 (1993): 59–63.

45 Ali Poorani and David R. Smith, "Franchising as a Business Expansion Strategy in the Bed & Breakfast Industry: Creating a Marketing and Development Advantage," *Hospitality Research Journal*, 18, no. 2 (1994): 32–33.

46 Maria-Pia Intini, "Boutique Evolved: 5 Key Trends," November 14, 2011, http://www.hotelnewsnow.com/Article/6945/Boutique-evolved-5-key-trends.

47 See http://www.hotelnewsnow.com/Article/12455/Brands-focus-on-health-and-wellness-in-design (accessed October 2013).

48 H. G. Parsa and Mahmood A. Khan, "Quick Service Restaurants of the 21st Century: An Analytical Review of Macro Factors," *Hospitality Research Journal*, 17, no. 1 (1993): 164.

49 Dennis Reynolds and William M. Balinbin, "Mad Cow Disease: An Empirical Investigation of Restaurant Strategies and Consumer Response," *Journal of Hospitality and Tourism Research*, 27, no. 3 (2003): 361.

50 Jonathan Berger, "Applying Performance Tests in Hotel Management Agreements," *Cornell Hotel and Restaurant Administration Quarterly*, 38, no. 2 (1997): 25.

51 See Michael E. Porter, *Competitive Strategy: Techniques for Analyzing Industries and Competitors* (New York: Free Press, 1980), Chapter 2.

52 Philip Kotler and Kevin Lane Keller, *Marketing Management* (New York: Pearson Education, 2016): 52

53 Adapted from information found in Diane Brady, "Making Marketing Measure Up," *BusinessWeek* (December 13, 2004): 112–113; Gray Hammond, "You Gotta Be Accountable," *Strategy* (December 2008): 48; Kate Maddox, "Optimism, Accountability, Social Media Top Trends," *BtoB* (January 18, 2010): 1.

54 See Kenneth Hein, "CMOs Pressured to Show ROI," *Brandweek* (December 12, 2008): 6; Lance Richard, "The Paradox of ROI and Decreased Spending in the Ad Industry," *American Journal of Business* (Fall 2009), www.bsu.edu/mcobwin/majb/?p=599; Kevin J. Clancy and Peter C. Krieg, "Getting a Grip," *Marketing Management* (Spring 2010): 18–23.

55 See Hein, "CMOs Pressured to Show ROI": 6; Hammond, "You Gotta Be Accountable": 48; Lawrence A. Crosby, "Getting Serious about Marketing ROI," *Marketing Management* (May/June 2009): 10–11.

Developing Hospitality and Tourism Marketing Opportunities and Strategies

Objectives

After reading this chapter, you should be able to:

1. List and discuss the importance of the elements of the company's microenvironment, including the company, suppliers, marketing intermediaries, customers, and public.

2. Describe the macroenvironmental forces that affect the company's ability to serve its customers.

3. Explain how changes in the demographic and economic environments affect marketing, and describe the levels of competition.

4. Identify the major trends in the firm's natural and technological environments.

5. Explain the key changes that occur in the political and cultural environments.

6. Discuss how companies can be proactive rather than reactive when responding to environmental trends.

The Marketing Environment

Manna Restaurant: A Popular Community Restaurant Within the Castle Rock Adventist Hospital

Hospitality marketing is by no means confined to the for-profit sector. Today, many nonprofit organizations have embraced marketing concepts. Alumni returning to universities and colleges are often amazed at changes in recreational and eating facilities on campus. Many of these hospitals replicate designs used in the for-profit sector. Hospitals used to have very poor reputations for the quality and presentation of their food. Castle Rock Adventist Hospital in Castle Rock, Colorado, offers an example of a nonprofit organization that carefully developed a winning hospital and restaurant by paying close attention to environmental and societal concerns and blending them with their own lifestyle choices.

Castle Rock, Colorado, a community of over 50,000 residents, has a young (median age 33) and well-educated (45 percent college degrees) population with household incomes well above those for the state of Colorado in general.[1] Located south of Denver, this city looks west to the foothills and then the towering Rocky Mountain Range. Given their scenic location, residents are highly concerned about environmental issues.

Castle Rock Adventist Hospital opened in August 2013 and reflects the environmental and societal concerns of the community. It also reflects the values of its sponsor, the Adventist Health System (AHS), the largest not-for-profit Protestant health-care system in the United States with 38 hospitals, nursing homes, and in-home care agencies supporting 44,000 employees and serving over 4 million people each year. One of these values centers on supporting the community in living as healthy as possible through a wellness model called Creation Health.

The hospital was designed to provide patients with views of the nearby mountains. Research has shown that views of nature from a patients's

window create a positive healing environment. A community service the hospital provided is the Garden of Eatina, largest community in Colorado. Members of the community have access to the garden to grow fresh nutrious natural foods. Other hospital
features include a fitness program based on the Creation Health model for wellness based
on choice, rest, environment, activity, trust, interpersonal relationships, outlook, and
nutrition.

Within the hospital's environment, a new restaurant concept was planned by Chef
Dan Skay, a graduate of the Culinary Institute of America, who felt that the restaurant
should serve the community, not just hospital staff and patient visitors. Dan and the hospital's chief executive officer (CEO), Todd Folkenberg, believed that the nutrition department should provide healthy dining alternatives for the community. Manna Restaurant
was designed to be a destination, full-service restaurant complete with customer-oriented
service. Unlike many restaurants, Manna offers community cooking classes to encourage
the preparation of healthy meals.

Local sources of provisions are used when possible by Manna Restaurant. Honey
supplies are local as are vegetables from the Garden of Eatin. To help ensure a year-round
supply of fresh herbs, the hospital plans to build a hydroponic garden.

Initial challenges were convincing the leadership that a different model of meal service was possible to meet the needs of the staff, as well as guests and the community.
Concerns for quick service and staff meals were met by the addition of a c-store (Manna
Market) selling barista coffees, convenience items, salad bar, and carry out hot meals. In
addition to the Manna Market, the restaurant incorporated a call-ahead service for to-go
meals, called Manna on the Move, and patient food service called Bedside Manna.

Menus were designed to be "veggie centric" but not exclusively veggie. Forty to fifty
percent of the menu items are veggie. Meat is used in several dishes with quality as an
overriding concern. Thus, grass-fed beef and free-range chickens are used.

Project design was a critical factor to ensure customer satisfaction. It called for a
kitchen with a central circulation spine to accommodate traffic moving from receiving and
storage into the production areas. This allowed food to be delivered to specific areas without interfering with production. Ware washing facilities were strategically placed to allow for
delivery of soiled patient meal carts and restaurant dishes through two separate entrances
to avoid cross contamination.

Green design concepts were incorporated with dining and kitchen areas displaying
floor to ceiling windows allowing for natural sunlight, a water-efficient dish machine, utility
distribution system for equipment flexibility/modification with energy-efficient equipment,
and a computer hood system. Moving from a cafeteria model to a traditional restaurant
galley resulted in minimized food waste. Some by-products are composted for use in the
onsite community gardens. Since opening, wind turbines and solar panels have been
added on the roof. These supply up to 30 percent of the facilities' electricity.

Much of the kitchen's equipment was strategically placed to allow visibility from the
dining room, including the double-windowed hearth oven. Aesthetic consideration was
given to local influences of wood, stone, and iron structures within the restaurant's interior,
from local art work and handcrafted wood community table to the use of Rhyolite (a stone
native to Castle Rock) stonework.

Combining patient room service and restaurant kitchens allowed Manna to minimize
the amount of equipment needed as compared to normal cafeterias with separate production areas. As a result, a chef-inspired European-style cook island and high-end equipment were purchased to help drive functionality/efficiency and customer appreciation. The
design of the open chef exhibition window allowed patrons to dine and view the kitchen
while offering minimal intrusion to the chefs. Having a streamlined production area also
improved labor efficiency, team work, shared production, and ease of cross training. Separate expo lines and windows for room service and the restaurant allowed smooth delivery
of meals, again with customer needs in mind.

Without the need to duplicate production and service areas, the ability to purchase
high-end furnishings and kitchen equipment was possible. These additions resulted in
fewer repairs and less replacement cost. This efficient service model changed staff load.
Fewer cooks allowed more hospitality serving staff, resulting in significant cost savings and
high customer satisfaction. In turn, this permitted Manna Restaurant to pay above-market
wages to the wait staff.

Manna Restaurant exceeded expectations for the 50-bed hospital by generating an
average of $130,000 a month in restaurant revenue. With Manna's quick grab and go

market and eclectic contemporary lunch/dinner menu, Manna does approximately 350–400 covers daily with a check average of $9. Approximately 85 percent of traffic into the restaurant is community driven, helping Manna achieve high ratings on YELP for Castle Rock restaurants. Patrons do not have to tip, but often do. As a result, a Foundation was created from tips to fund many local nonprofit and community-wellness-related projects. Fund-related events and projects are communicated to restaurant guests and the community through various projects like FreeCycle, a free bike-rental program within the city.

The overall objective of this project was to meet the proactive health needs of the community by delivering innovative dishes to fuel health and wellness in a nurturing and restful atmosphere. With the chef-driven design and ease of flow from production to delivery, chances for success were enhanced. Like the game of tennis, if you can't serve well, you will never win. All aspects of this design allowed customers to be the ultimate winners!

A company's **marketing environment** consists of outside actors and forces that affect a company's ability to build and maintain successful relationships with its target customers. The marketing environment offers both opportunities and threats. Successful companies know the vital importance of constantly watching and adapting to the changing environment.

Managers who practice marketing will be the trend trackers and opportunity seekers. Good marketers have two special aptitudes. They have disciplined methods—marketing intelligence—for collecting information about the marketing environment. They also spend more time in the customer and competitor environments. By carefully studying the environment, marketers can adapt marketing strategies to meet new marketplace challenges and opportunities.

The marketing environment is made up of a microenvironment and a macroenvironment. The **microenvironment** consists of factors close to the company that affect its ability to serve its customers, the company itself, marketing channel firms, customer markets, and a broad range of publics. The **macroenvironment** consists of larger societal forces that affect the entire microenvironment, that is, demographic, economic, natural, technological, political, competitor, and cultural forces. We first examine the company's microenvironment and then its macroenvironment.

> **Marketing environment.** The actors and forces outside marketing that affect marketing management's ability to develop and maintain successful transactions with its target customers.
>
> **Microenvironment.** The forces close to a company that affect its ability to serve its customers: the company, market channel firms, customer markets, competitors, and the public.
>
> **Macroenvironment.** The larger societal forces that affect the whole microenvironment: competitive, demographic, economic, natural, technological, political, and cultural forces.

■■■ The Company's Microenvironment

Marketing management's job is to build relationships with customers by creating customer value and satisfaction. This requires working closely with the company's microenvironment. These actors are shown in Figure 4–1. They include supplier, market intermediaries, customers, and publics that combine to make up the company's value delivery system.

The Company

Marketing managers must work closely with top management and the various company departments. The finance department is concerned with finding and using funds required to carry out the company's plans. The accounting department has to measure revenues and costs to help marketing know how well it is achieving its objectives. Housekeeping is responsible for delivering clean rooms sold by the sales department. Top management sets the company's mission, objectives, broad strategies, and policies. Marketing decisions must be made within the strategies and plans made by top management.

Under the marketing concept, all managers, supervisors, and employees must "think consumer." They should work in harmony to provide superior customer

Figure 4–1
Major actors in the company's microenvironment.

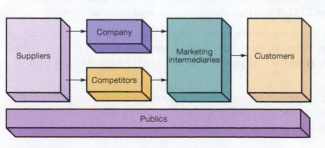

value and satisfaction. Together, all departments have an impact on the marketing department's plans and actions.

Existing Competitors

We include competitors in both the microenvironment and macroenvironment. Existing customers are part of the microenvironment. Every company faces a broad range of existing competitors. The marketing concept holds that a successful company must satisfy the needs and wants of consumers better than its competitors. It must also adapt to the strategies of other companies serving the same target markets. Companies must gain strategic advantage by strongly positioning their product in the minds of consumers.

No single competitive marketing strategy is best for all companies. Each firm must consider its size and industry position in relation to that of its competitors. Large firms with dominant positions in an industry can use strategies that smaller firms cannot afford. Small firms can also choose strategies that give them certain advantages. For example, a large restaurant chain can use its buying power to purchase national advertising, spreading the cost among hundreds or thousands of operations. But small individually owned restaurants are able to adjust quickly to local trends and can offer more menu variety because they do not have to worry about standardizing menu items across thousands of restaurants. Both large and small firms must find marketing strategies that give them specific advantages over competitors. A company should monitor market share when analyzing competitors. Market share is the portion of the target market held by each player.

Managers often fail to identify their competitors correctly. The manager of a Houston seafood restaurant said that his restaurant had no competition because there were no other seafood restaurants within several miles. Months later the restaurant was out of business. Customers decided to spend their money at competitors, either by driving farther to other seafood restaurants or by dining at non-seafood restaurants. Our research has shown that only about 40 percent of the customers that rate a hotel or restaurant as being good will return. The figure jumps to 90 percent when customers give a rating of excellent. Competitive forces are so strong in our industry that being good is no longer good enough. We must strive for excellence.

One of the authors found that although 78 percent of the customers came to a casino regularly and were considered loyal customers, only 34 percent were considered truly loyal. The other 44 percent he called spurious loyals. In addition to having the behavioral loyalty of coming to the casino regularly, true loyals exhibited attitudinal loyalty, and as a result they were more likely to recommend the casino to a friend. Spurious loyals are not emotionally attached to the casino and are likely to leave if a new casino opens. It is important for managers to understand how many of their customers might be at risk if a new competitor opens in their market area.[2]

Every company faces the following four levels of competitors (see Figure 4–2):

1. A company can view its competitors as companies that offer similar products and services to the same customers at a similar price. At this level, McDonald's views its competition as Burger King and Wendy's.

2. A company can see its competitors as all companies making the same product or class of products. Here McDonald's may see its competition as all fast-food restaurants, including KFC, Taco Bell, Jamba Juice, and Arby's.

3. A company can see its competitors more broadly as all companies supplying the same service. Here McDonald's would see itself competing with all restaurants and other suppliers of prepared food, such as the deli section of a supermarket.

4. A company can see its competitors even more broadly as all competitors that compete for the same consumer dollars. Here McDonald's would see itself competing with the self-provision of the meal by the consumer.[3]

Figure 4–2

Levels of competition. Source: Adapted from *Analysis for Market Planning*, Donald R. Lehmann and Russell S. Winer, p. 22, 1994, by Richard D. Irwin.

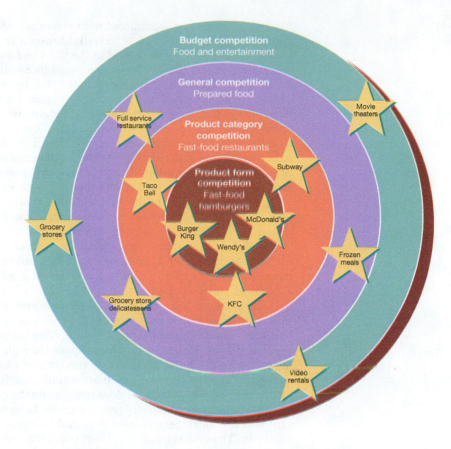

Putting this framework into action, Subway sandwich shops came out with advertising targeting second-level competition. The ads stressed the nutritional value of their sandwiches compared with other types of fast food, such as hamburgers. The McDonald's "You deserve a break today" advertising campaign was aimed at the fourth level of competition, telling people to give themselves a break from cooking. Carnival Cruise Lines viewed its competition at the third level, that is, as other vacation destinations, such as Hawaii and Las Vegas.

Suppliers. Firms and individuals that provide the resources needed by a company and its competitors to produce goods and services.

Inland seafood restaurants need to have reliable suppliers with whom they have developed a good relationship. Courtesy of David P. Smith/Shutterstock.

Suppliers

Suppliers are firms and individuals that provide the resources needed by the company to produce its goods and services. Trends and developments affecting suppliers can, in turn, seriously affect a company's marketing plan. Suppose that a restaurant manager decides to run a live lobster special for the weekend. The seafood supplier promises to supply 200 lobsters for the weekend promotion. Friday morning the supplier calls and reports that lobsters were shorted on the shipment from Boston, and they will not be delivered until Saturday morning. The manager must now find alternative sources or disappoint guests who have reservations for Friday night.

In another case, a restaurant chain wanted to add a new scallop seafood dish to its menu. The corporate office spent six months perfecting the scallop dish. During the development period, the price of scallops doubled. The restaurant would now have to charge a price higher than customers would pay. The project was scrapped. Management must pay attention to changes in supply availability (as affected by shortages and strikes) and supply costs.

Some hotels have contracted with restaurant companies to supply their food and beverage services. The W in Dallas brought in Craft, a famous restaurant in New York, to operate a restaurant in the W.[4] The New York-New York in Las Vegas contracted with ARC restaurants to manage its restaurants. These and other hotels are bringing branded restaurants to their hotels to create value for their guests and expose restaurant guests to the hotel. The outsourcing of food and beverage operations allows the hotel to concentrate on lodging while letting a food and beverage specialist handle this area within the hotel. There are several ways to partner with a celebrity chef or branded restaurant. One is paying a licensing fee or management fee for a celebrity chef to oversee a restaurant and put his or her name on the restaurant. The fees generally run from 4 to 7 percent of the gross revenue. The second is a partnering deal where the chef is an equity partner, usually taking a 30 to 50 percent share of the equity. Additionally, the chef gets a 3 to 6 percent management fee. This creates more of a commitment on the chef's part because the chef now shares directly in the profits of the restaurant.[5]

On paper this sounds like a great arrangement, and in real life it often works out well. However, the outsourcing is not as simple as it may seem. Focus groups of business travelers have told us that a coffee shop suitable for a business meeting is sometimes the deciding factor in the choice of a hotel. A problem for some hotels that have leased their operations to upscale operators is that upscale restaurant operators often are not interested in the coffee shop and room service operations, and these operations suffer as a result. Another problem is that the leasing of food-service operations ties up hotel space through lease agreements. This can be a problem if the hotel decides to renovate and change the design of the public spaces. When hotel guests complain about poor food service at the front desk, telling the guest that the hotel does not operate the restaurants is *not* an acceptable answer. Thus service recovery programs need to be worked out between the restaurant and the hotel. Suppliers of food and beverage for a hotel have to be chosen carefully. The concept works the best when the restaurant brought in for its brand name operates just the restaurant on an equity basis. The coffee shop, room service, and banquet operations are best left to the hotel to run.

Some restaurant chains have developed close relationships with selected suppliers. The Chick-fil-A chain teamed with THRIVE Farmers, a Costa Rica producer co-op, to provide specialty grade coffee to its restaurant patrons. Under this relationship, coffee farmers can earn as much as 10 times more income than by sales through traditional channels. David Farmer, vice president of Product Strategy and Development for Chick-fil-A, said, "Now we are able to serve our customers an amazing cup of coffee that will also improve the lives of the farmer who grows it."[6] This relationship also provided Chick-fil-A with many public relations opportunities such as through social media and in-store information on coffee cups and paper mats on serving trays.

Tourist destinations need suppliers. Airline service, hotels, restaurants, ground operations, meeting facilities, and entertainment are some of the components of a tourist destination. One of the roles of a regional convention and visitors' bureau (CVB) is to make sure there is a good selection of suppliers of tourist products in their area. They must recruit organizations to provide visitors with a variety of tourist activities and options. CVBs must also work to represent the interests of these suppliers to make sure they do well after they are recruited.

Marketing Intermediaries

Marketing intermediaries.
Firms that help the company to promote, sell, and distribute its goods to final buyers; they include middlemen, physical distribution firms, marketing service agencies, and financial intermediaries.

Disintermediation. The elimination of intermediaries.

Marketing intermediaries help the company promote, sell, and distribute its goods to the final buyers. Intermediaries are business firms that help hospitality companies find customers or make sales. They include travel agents, wholesale tour operators, hotel representatives, and online travel agencies (OTAs), such as Expedia, Travelocity, and Orbitz. The OTAs bundle airfare with hotel rooms, creating value for the customer.

The Internet has created both disintermediation and pricing transparency. **Disintermediation** is the elimination of intermediaries. Hotels have created their own Internet reservation systems, referred to as Brand.com (where the name of the company replaces "Brand," e.g., Hyatt.com). The brands are now less dependent on intermediaries, but still use them to provide extra demand. The demand cannot be filled through direct channels. Small hotels can now distribute their products worldwide over the Internet.

When hotels sell to intermediaries who use the Internet, they have to be careful of price transparency. For example, group rates for associations often include free rooms for the association directors, which are factored into the hotel room rate. The association is also required to book a set number of rooms to take advantage of the complimentary services. If the group is given a rate of $229 per night for a hotel room and members of the organization can book directly on the hotel's Web site for $209, then members may choose to book directly rather than going through the association's block. Hotel sales managers should either set the prices of groups the same as group prices or give the group credit toward meeting their room block with people who have booked directly through the hotel. The Internet has created many distribution opportunities, but it has also made interactions with intermediaries and end users more complex.

Thus, today's marketers recognize the importance of working with their intermediaries as partners rather than simply as channels through which they sell their products. For example, restaurants serve as intermediaries for soft drink companies when they sign an agreement to exclusively distribute the soft drink company's products to their customers. When Coca-Cola signs on as the exclusive beverage provider for a fast-food chain, such as McDonald's, Wendy's, or Subway, it provides much more than just soft drinks. It also pledges powerful marketing support.[7]

Coca-Cola assigns cross-functional teams dedicated to understanding the finer points of each retail partner's business. It conducts a staggering amount of research on beverage consumers and shares these insights with its partners. It analyzes the demographics of U.S. zip code areas and helps partners determine which Coke brands are preferred in their areas. Coca-Cola has even studied the design of drive-through menu boards to better understand which layouts, fonts, letter sizes, colors, and visuals induce consumers to order certain items. Based on such insights, the Coca-Cola Food Service group develops marketing programs and merchandising tools that help its retail partners improve their beverage sales and profits. Such intense partnering efforts have made Coca-Cola a leader in the U.S. fountain soft drink market. Coca-Cola and other major suppliers realize that they are your partners. If the restaurant does well, they sell their product.

Marketing services agencies are suppliers that help the firm formulate and implement its marketing strategy and tactics. These suppliers include public relations agencies, advertising agencies, and direct mail houses. They work directly with the company's marketing program and also include marketing research firms, media firms, and marketing consulting firms, which help companies target and promote their products to the right markets. These firms vary in creativity, quality, service, and price. The company should regularly review performance and replace service firms that no longer perform well.

Financial intermediaries include banks, credit companies, insurance companies, and other firms that help hospitality companies finance their transactions or insure the risks associated with the buying and selling of goods and services. Rising insurance costs, in particular liquor liability insurance, have forced some hospitality firms out of business. Because rising credit costs, limited credit, or both can seriously affect a company's marketing performance, the company has to develop strong relationships with important financial institutions. Small multiunit chains often feel the pressure to grow to keep their stock price up and their stockholders happy. This is what happened to Boston Market, Fuddrucker's, and Del Taco. These companies reorganized and recovered, but they went through hard times. Companies must be careful that they do not succumb to unmanageable growth expectations.

Marketing services agencies. Marketing research firms, advertising agencies, media firms, marketing consulting firms, and other service providers that help a company to target and promote its products to the right markets.

Financial intermediaries. Banks, credit companies, insurance companies, and other businesses that help finance transactions or insure against the risks associated with the buying and selling of goods.

Beverage companies provide marketing support for chain restaurants that distribute its products. Shown in the picture is a Subway Restaurant in Sibiu, Romania. Courtesy of jovannig/Fotolia.

Customers

The hospitality company needs to study five types of general customer markets closely. Consumer markets consist of individuals and households that purchase hospitality services for leisure activities, medical needs, and gatherings such as reunions, weddings, or funerals. Business markets buy hospitality services to facilitate their business. This can be individual rooms for travelers representing the company or for group meetings the company or organization may conduct. Companies have sales meetings, and associations have annual conventions. Resellers purchase a product and then resell it. For example, a tour operator may purchase airline seats, hotel rooms, ground transportation, and restaurant meals to package a tour, which will be resold to the consumer market. Government markets are made up of government agencies that purchase hospitality services for individual travelers and meetings. They often have room rates that are limited by government per diem rates. Finally, international markets consist of those buyers in other countries, including consumers, businesses, resellers, and governments. Each market type has special characteristics that call for careful study by the seller. We discuss these characteristics in Chapters 6 and 7.

Publics

Public. Any group that has an actual or potential interest in or impact on an organization's ability to achieve its objectives.

The company's marketing environment also includes various publics. A **public** is any group that has an actual or potential interest in or impact on an organization's ability to achieve its objectives. We identify the following seven types of publics:

- Financial publics. These influence the company's ability to obtain funds. Banks, investment houses, and stockholders are the major financial publics.

- Media publics. These carry news, features, and editorial opinions. They include newspapers, magazines, and radio and television stations.

- Government publics. Management must take government developments into account. Marketers often consult the company's lawyers on issues of product safety, truth in advertising, and other matters.

- Citizen-action publics. A company's marketing decisions may be questioned by consumer organizations, environmental groups, minority groups, and others. Its public relations department can help it stay in touch with consumer and citizen groups.

- Local publics. These include neighborhood residents and community organizations. Large companies usually appoint a community relations officer to deal with the community, attend meetings, answer questions, and contribute to worthwhile causes.

- General publics. A company needs to be concerned about the general public's attitude toward its products and activities. The public's image of the company affects its buying.

- Internal publics. These include workers, managers, volunteers, and the board of directors. Large companies use newsletters and other means to inform and motivate their internal publics. When employees feel good about their company, this positive attitude spills over to better customer service.

A company can prepare marketing plans for these major publics as well as for its customer markets. Suppose the company wants a specific response from a particular public, such as goodwill, favorable word of mouth, or donations of time or money. The company would need to design an offer to this public that is attractive enough to produce the desired response. For example, casino resorts in Las Vegas discuss how they are making efforts to conserve water when they announce plans for a new resort. They know that local residents and local government will be concerned about this issue.

■■■ The Company's Macroenvironment

The company and all of the other actors operate in a larger macroenvironment of forces. Figure 4–3 shows the seven major forces in the company's macroenvironment. In the remaining sections of this chapter, we examine these forces and show how they affect marketing plans.

Competitors

We consider future competitors as part of the macroenvironment. The entrance of future competitors is often difficult to predict and can have a major effect on existing businesses.

Barriers to Entry, Exit, and Competition

Two forces that affect competition are the ability of companies to enter and exit markets.[8] Entry barriers prevent firms from getting into a business, and barriers to exit prevent them from leaving. Low barriers to entry characterize the restaurant industry. It takes a relatively small amount of capital to get started in the restaurant business. This makes it hard to predict future competition. As a result, some restaurant managers open without direct competition and soon find themselves with four or five competitors in a year's time. This phenomenon demonstrates the importance of anticipating competition. Restaurant managers should manage a business as if there is strong competition even if there is none. By taking this approach, the manager will be prepared when competition does arrive.

Hotels have moderately high barriers of entry, due to the costs of building a hotel and the scarcity of good locations. High barriers to exit from the industry present a different set of competitive problems. The large capital investment required to build a hotel becomes a sunk cost. As a result, hotels that cannot meet all of their debt payments, taxes, and other fixed costs, but can produce enough gross profit to partially offset these fixed costs, may operate at a loss rather than close their doors. Thus when hotel demand plummets, room supply remains the same. With fewer customers bidding for the same number of hotel rooms in a marketplace, competition becomes intense.

The hotel's competitive environment is affected by another factor: Most hotels are planned during upswings in the business cycle when there is not enough supply to meet demand. But it can take four years or more from the planning stages to the opening of a hotel. By that time the economic cycle may have turned down. Sadly, new hotels often open their doors during a recessionary period.[9] So at a period when existing hotels are struggling to fill their rooms, it is not uncommon for competitors to enter the market.

Figure 4–3
Major forces in the company's macroenvironment.

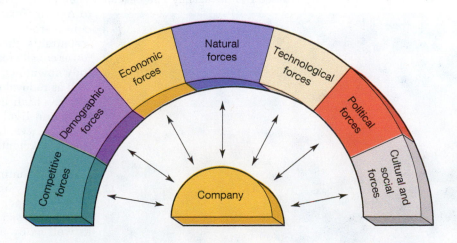

Marketing HIGHLIGHT 4.1   Visit Indy—Destination Digital Marketing

"Visit Indy is making a seismic shift in how we promote the destination to leisure visitors with a move into 100 percent digital and social marketing," said Mary Huggard, vice president of Tourism Development for Visit Indy, the publicly supported Destination Marketing Organization (DMO) for the city of Indianapolis, Indiana.

Like the majority of visitor destinations throughout the United States, and indeed, the world, destination promotion had been confined to traditional media such as television, radio, print, and outdoor. A new and creative agency, The Basement, specializing in digital marketing, was recently awarded the Visit Indy account. Changing markets accompanied by growth in Indianapolis called for a new marketing strategy away from messages carried in traditional media. Major reasons for the shift to digital marketing according to Visit Indy were as follows:

- The millennial generation will soon be #1 travel consumer, and they are the first full adopters of technology.

- Digital/social marketing gives Visit Indy the ability to microtarget consumers (right audience, right message, at the right time).

- Digital marketing offers more flexibility to alter advertising/messages based on testing and immediate feedback from audiences.

- Digital/social marketing (if done correctly) moves the consumer from passivity to interaction and engagement—hopefully leading to a higher level of loyalty and sharing with others.

- Tracking results is easier—Visit Indy can track Web analytics for its own purposes and for its co-op attraction partners.

- To locals, social and digital media will be the primary method used to engage them in Visit Indy's Tourism Master Plan process.

It is easy to see after reading this section that the competitive environment in the hospitality industry is unpredictable. This is why we include it as part of the macroenvironment. A wealthy person may decide to open a restaurant in your market area that is completely unfeasible, but he or she does it for ego reasons. A hotel company wants to have a presence in your city. The hotel on its own is not feasible, but by giving the company a presence in your city it is able to justify the investment, even though it adds rooms to an already weak market. A wealthy international businessperson wants to invest in real estate and chooses a hotel as a way to implement his or her investment. Although the project is not economically feasible in the short term, this investor is looking at long-term real estate gains. The projects just mentioned all bring capacity to markets that already have too much supply and not enough demand. If the projects were based on economic feasibility, they would not have been built. Investments in the hospitality industry are not always predictable.

The city of Indianapolis is rapidly changing. Brian Phillips, executive creative director of the agency The Basement, compared dynamic changes in Indianapolis to Austin, Texas. "Ten years ago few people considered visiting Indianapolis for great restaurants, theatre, and night life and even fewer considered living downtown."[10] Today, Indy downtown condo development is hot as well as redevelopment of formerly run-down areas, which now embrace trendy restaurants and lively "meet your friends over a drink" places. Like in Austin, truck eateries, interesting boutiques, and breweries are also flourishing.

Brian continued, "The management team of Visit Indy agreed that digital marketing offers an opportunity to reach micro-market segments based on traditional demographics as well as by psychographics. Digital also allows our client to develop a real interaction

Indianapolis has transited into an attractive tourist destination. Courtesy of f11photo/Fotolia.

with buyers and to understand their behavior. Measurement of the effectiveness of messages is now more precise which should lead to improved productivity in the dollars spent to promote the city. Imagine our ability to reach and influence all market segments including the visiting friend and relatives (VFR) segment and first time Indy visitors. We will be able to show our city block by block with a voice and digital message telling each buyer what he or she is looking for whether it is a Jewish deli, a salon, spa, a museum perhaps a public monument or a wine bar. The use of drones in the delivery of these messages is also under consideration." Brian continued by saying, "This will require great creative work combined with relevant and attention holding content to micro-market Indy individually to each person. Content will be king! Visitor marketing has often had a nearly indistinguishable look and message by city destinations. Digital based marketing by Visit Indy is intended to set it apart from competitors as we can now speak directly to each visitor and potential visitor. The intention is to create a voice and personality such as that which happens in an interaction between two people. Good conversations are not static. Digital will permit us to adjust and refine our message voice."

Chris Gahl, vice president of Marketing and Communications for Visit Indy, said, "Success will also depend upon 'buy in' by critical sectors of the city."[11] With this in mind, Visit Indy is preparing a Tourism Master Plan with the direct involvement of individuals from the traditional visitor industry as well as from public, quasi-governmental organizations, affected city departments, and the private sector. All participants have been asked to represent their interests, such as putting heads on the beds by the lodging sector, but also to think strategically with a macro view concerning how the city should grow and change to meet the needs of visitors and residents who may today be grade school students.

Mary Huggard spoke for Visit Indy and their agency, The Basement, when she said, "We know that digital marketing is no longer the future, it is the now. The time has come to move direction."

Demographic Environment

Demography. The study of human populations in terms of size, density, location, age, sex, race, occupation, and other statistics.

Demography is the study of human populations in terms of size, density, location, age, gender, race, occupation, and other statistics. The demographic environment is of major interest to marketers because it involves people, and people make up markets. The world population is growing at an explosive rate. It now exceeds 6.6 billion people and will grow to 8.1 billion by 2030.[12] The world's large and highly diverse population poses both opportunities and challenges.

Changes in the world demographic environment have major implications for business. For example, consider China. More than a quarter century ago, to curb its skyrocketing population, the Chinese government passed regulations limiting families to one child each. As a result, Chinese children have been showered with attention and luxuries under what's known as the "six-pocket syndromes." As many as six adults—two parents and four doting grandparents—may be indulging the whims of an only child. These children, now ranging in age from newborns to mid-twenties, are affecting markets for everything including restaurants and travel. Parents with only children at home spend about 40 percent of their income on their cherished child.[13]

Starbucks is targeting China's millennials, positioning itself as a new kind of informal but indulgent meeting place.[14] Instead of believing in traditional Chinese collective goals, these young people embrace individuality. "Their view of this world is very different," says the president of Starbucks Greater China. "They have never gone through the hardships of our generation."[15] Starbucks is in sync with that, he says, given its customized drinks, personalized service, and original music compilations. In the United States about 80 percent of Starbucks business is takeout. In China, Starbucks is a destination with about 90 percent of the consumption on premise. Young people flock to Starbucks to hang out with friends. Starbucks knows that China will become its largest market and is preparing for that day. In 2011 they established a coffee farm and processing facilities in China's southern Yunnan province.[16]

Marketers keep close track of demographic trends and developments in their markets, both at home and abroad. They track changing age and family structures, geographic population shifts, educational characteristics, and population diversity. Here, we discuss the most important demographic trends in the United States.

Changing Age Structure of the Population

The U.S. population is currently about 315 million and may reach almost 364 million by 2030.[17] The single most important demographic trend in the United States is the changing age structure of the population. The U.S. population contains several generational groups. The baby boomers, Generation X, and millennials have a strong impact on today's marketing strategies.

The Baby Boomers

Baby boomers. The 78 million people born between 1946 and 1964.

The post–World War II baby boom produced 78 million **baby boomers**, born between 1946 and 1964. Over the years, the baby boomers have been one of the most powerful forces shaping the marketing environment. Today's baby boomers account for nearly 25 percent of the population, spend about $2 trillion annually, and hold three-quarters of the nation's financial assets.[18] However, many baby boomers saw their retirement evaporate in the recession of 2008. As a result of the need for income and the desire to keep active, 70 percent of Americans between the ages of 45 and 74 plan on working in their retirement years.[19] This creates a new workforce for quick-service restaurants and hotels.

The youngest boomers are now in their mid-forties; the oldest are in their sixties. The maturing boomers are rethinking the purpose and value of their work, responsibilities, and relationships. As they reach their peak earning and spending years, the boomers constitute a lucrative market for travel and entertainment, eating out, spas, and other leisure activities. It would be a mistake to think of the boomers as aging and staid. Many boomers are rediscovering the excitement of life. For example, according to the Travel Industry Association of America, half of all U.S. adults took adventure vacations within the past five years. Some 56 percent of these travelers were boomers. Baby boomers do not feel old; one study found they feel 12 years younger than they actually are.[20] They will spend billions of dollars on travel, looking for active vacations where they can have adventure or explore. Through their continuing education departments, universities have developed educational tours that target the baby boomers. Butterfield and Robinson, agents for upscale biking tours, market two-week bike tours with overnight stays in luxury accommodations to the boomers. Boomers look for value and research their vacations. One of the reasons cruises are popular with boomers is because of the value of the all-inclusive vacation.

Generation X

Generation X. A generation of 45 million people born between 1965 and 1979; named Generation X because they lie in the shadow of the boomers and lack obvious distinguishing characteristics; other names include "baby busters," "shadow generation," or "yiffies"—young, individualistic, freedom-minded few.

The baby boom was followed by a "birth dearth," creating another generation of 49 million people born between 1965 and 1979. Author Douglas Coupland calls them **Generation X** because they lie in the shadow of the boomers and lack obvious distinguishing characteristics. Others call them the "baby busters" or the "generation caught in the middle" (between the larger baby boomers and later millennials).

The Generation Xers are defined as much by their shared experience as by their age. Having grown up during times of recession and corporate downsizing, they developed a more cautious economic outlook. They care about the environment and respond favorably to socially responsible companies. Hotel and restaurant companies that are taking initiatives to be environmentally responsible are attractive to this group. Although they seek success, they are less materialistic; they prize experience, not acquisition. For many of the 30 million Gen Xers who are parents, family comes first, career second.[21]

The Gen Xers are a more skeptical bunch. "Marketing to Gen Xers is difficult," says one marketer, "and it's all about word of mouth. You can't tell them you're good, and they have zero interest in a slick brochure that says so. They have a lot of 'filters' in place."[22] Another marketer agrees: "Sixty-three percent of this group will research products before they consider a purchase. They are also creating extensive communities to exchange information. The information swap is trusted and thus is more powerful than any marketing pitch."[23]

The Gen Xers have brought us the quality movement. Food-service operations such as Starbucks, Chipotle's, and Panera Bread are favorites of Gen Xers. They like to be intrigued by menus more than millennials or boomers. They enjoy menus that combine the familiar with the unique. When it comes to vacations, Gen Xers look for something different, which means they spend more than boomers. The Gen Xers have set a higher bar for casual dining, business travel, and mid-priced hotels."[24]

Hyatt is positioning Andaz as an unpretentious upscale hotel catering to customers looking for fresh, uncomplicated luxury that is timeless and gimmick free. Andaz is squarely aimed at the maturing Generation X market. Gen Xers are becoming the major market segment for business travel. Like all great demographic segments, they demand alternative brands to those patronized by their parents, the baby boomers. Xers are notoriously uncomfortable with general global brands and prefer to seek out local specialties and experiences. Although their parents might prefer hotels with identical bathrooms from Amsterdam to Zurich, Xers like to celebrate local differences. Andaz caters to this by allowing each of its hotels to celebrate its local autonomy through different designs and offerings. In fact, the word *Andaz* means personal style. Andaz will also cater to the Xer market by offering organic food and environmentally sound operating principles. Hyatt pitches the new hotel as a "luxury lifestyle brand" that "expresses individual style and personal independence in an environment of casual elegance. It offers local personality, innovative design, and a relaxed atmosphere, plus unpretentious, responsive, personalized service."[25]

The Virginia Tourism Corporation (VTC), the state's tourism DMO, is now targeting Gen X families. Virginia's 40-year romance with the baby-boomer generation is waning. The VTC, best known for its enduring "Virginia is for Lovers" campaign, is now wooing a new audience: Generation X. They're younger and more adventuresome, and they spend more money on travel in Virginia. VTC research showed that Generation X households contribute about 45 percent of the billions spent on travel in Virginia each year, whereas most boomers are done or almost done with raising their children and lean toward more exotic travel locations farther from home.[26]

Millennials

Both the baby boomers and Gen Xers will one day be passing the reins to the **millennials** (also called **Generation Y** or the **echo boomers**). Born between 1977 to 1980, these children of the baby boomers number 83 million, dwarfing the Gen Xers and are even larger than the baby-boomer segment. This group includes several age cohorts: teens (13 to 19) and young adults (20 to 35). With total purchasing power of more than $733 billion, Gen Y represents a huge and attractive market. One thing all of the millennials have in common is their fluency and comfort with computer, digital, and Internet technology.[27]

Marriott's Moxy and citizenM are two hotel brands designed specifically to attract millennials. Moxy makes use of its small room size by hanging folding furniture on pegs along one wall. This allows guests to design their room according to their need whether it is for entertainment or work.

Mix these ingredients for success with the Gen X millennial segment: adventure, meeting new friends, great exercise, tons of fun, great tacos, and even a chance to be on national television. This is the Taco Ride, a 9.6-mile, night bike ride that attracts 700 to 1500 millennial bike riders weekly.

The ride begins in Council Bluffs, Iowa, and ends in Mineola at the Mineola Steakhouse. The participants ride on the Wabash Trace Nature Trail, a converted railroad right of way. Not all riders complete the trip as many stop at a picnic area known as Margaritaville. Commercial firms aware of the promotional potential join the ride at the steakhouse. Recognizing the fun atmosphere and public interest in the ride, Jennie-O® provided turkey tacos to participants at the Mineola Steakhouse and filmed responses that were later used in advertisements on national television.

Millennials (also called Generation Y or the echo boomers.) Born between 1977 to 1980, these children of the baby boomers number 83 million, dwarfing the Gen Xers and larger even than the baby-boomer segment. This group includes several age cohorts: tweens (ages 8 to 12), teens (13 to 18), and young adults (the 20 somethings).

Generation Y. See millennials.

Echo boomers. See millennials. Born between 1977 and 1994, these children of the baby boomers now number 72 million, dwarfing the Gen Xers and almost equal in size to the baby-boomer segment. Also known as Generation Y.

Budweiser and Miller beers donated T-shirts to help raise funds for a cyclist injured on the ride.[28]

Generational Marketing

One way marketers can segment is by forming age-specific segments within each group. Defining people by their birth date may be less effective than segmenting them by their lifestyle, life stage, or the common values they seek in the products they buy. We discuss many other ways to segment markets in Chapter 8.

An Australian company, Green Getaways Australia, offers luxury ecotourism to a niche market that may cross demographics. Green Getaways further segments its niche market by budget or luxury and by type of experience as follows:

- Luxury Ecolodges
- Romantic Getaways
- Treehouse
- Glamping (luxury camping in glamorous tents)

This experience is designed for adults who wish to experience wilderness but wilderness with luxury. Green Getaways promotes sleeping on a latex bed with 1,000 thread count quality sheets.

Treehouse and Glamping are promoted as "not cheap." Will Green Getaways find that their product line is too broad? Will they find that appealing to both the luxury and budget markets is too difficult to maintain/manage at a profit? Experienced marketers would probably say yes to both questions but one must admire the entrepreneurship and product uniqueness of entrepreneurs like Green Getaways.[29]

Few industries have been affected more by changing demographics than the golf and ski industries. Of the approximately 34,000 worldwide golf courses, 45 percent are in the United States. However, the number of U.S. courses has been in steady decline. In 2015 the Associated Press reported there were 15,372 U.S. courses, down from a peak of 16,052.[30]

Jim Hinckley of Palmer Golf claims, "New golfers are different. They see the sport as entertainment, not competition. For the future, golf has to be thought of as a fun experience not a serious experience." While the play on golf courses is in decline, Topgolf created a rapidly growing golf business by responding to environmental changes. Using radio frequency identification (RFID) chips in their golf balls, Topgolf is able to track a player's balls. The players try to hit different targets on the driving range, and they receive points for how close they hit to the designated target. The games are designed so that novices as well as experienced golfers can enjoy them. A video screen keeps track of the scores. The golf bays were designed with seating. At a small table, a server will bring drinks and food. Topgolf's success in part is due to its food and beverage sales that are routinely more than the golf sales. People come to Topgolf to have a good time.

During a trade show by Snowsports Industries America (SIA), Bill Jensen, a ski industry executive, said, "The industry is facing huge challenges and predicted that 150 of the current U.S. ski resorts would fail." He said there are only 45 ski resorts with climbing revenues.[31] Reasons for this include the following:

- Warmer winter weather with new cycles.
- Demographics in which couples with infants and toddlers are less likely to take ski vacations.
- Financial pressures on the middle class.

Increasing Diversity

Countries vary in their ethnic and racial makeup. At one extreme is Japan, where almost everyone is Japanese. At the other extreme is the United States, with people from virtually all nations. The United States has often been called a melting pot.

Instead, the United States seems to have become more of a "salad bowl" in which various groups have mixed together but have maintained their diversity by retaining and valuing important ethnic and cultural differences.

Marketers are facing increasingly diverse markets, both at home and abroad as their operations become more international. The U.S. population is about 63 percent white, with Hispanics at 16 percent and African Americans at about 14 percent. More than 12 percent of the population was born in another country. The nation's ethnic populations are expected to explode in coming decades. By 2050 Hispanics will comprise an estimated 24 percent of the U.S. population, with Asians at 9 percent.[32]

Diversity goes beyond ethnic heritage. For example, there are more than 60 million disabled people in the United States—a market larger than African Americans or Hispanics—representing almost $200 billion in annual spending power. This spending power is likely to increase in the years ahead as the wealthier, freer-spending baby boomers enter the "age of disabilities." Julie Perez sees the difference when she goes to the Divi Hotels resort at Flamingo Beach on the Caribbean island of Bonaire. "It is famous for being totally accessible," she says. "The hotel brochures show the wheelchair access. The dive staff are trained and aware, really want to take disabled people diving. They're not afraid." Perez, aged 35, of Ventura, California, is an experienced scuba diver, a travel agent, and a quadriplegic.[33] People with disabilities appreciate products that work for them, explains Jim Tobias, president of Inclusive Technologies, a consultancy specializing in accessible products. Those with disabilities tend to be brand evangelists for products they love. They typically tell more friends about a favorite product, than a typical satisfied guest.[34]

According to one estimate, 6 to 7 percent of the population who identify themselves as lesbian, gay, bisexual, and transgender (LGBT) have buying power of $712 billion.[35] The British Tourist Authority (BTA) teamed up with British Airways and the London Tourist Board to target this market. The group worked with WinMark Concepts, a Washington marketing and advertising firm that specializes in advising mainstream companies, on how to target the gay and lesbian market. "We wanted something that was gay-specific and fun, but also extremely tasteful," says WinMark's president. "These are educated, savvy consumers." One recent magazine ad shows five young to early-middle-age men—the target age group is ages 35 to 50—posing in and around several of London's distinctive red phone booths. The headline reads, "One Call. A Rainbow of Choices."[36] The campaign was successful. "The magazine ads got the word out that Britain is gay and lesbian-friendly and also generated a database of 40,000 names across the country. Now, it's time for a more targeted direct mail and e-mail campaign to people we know are interested in our offer." Since BTA launched the campaign, both United Airlines and Virgin Airways have signed onto the program, as have the tourist boards of Manchester, Brighton, and Glasgow.[37]

As the population in the United States grows more diverse, successful marketers will continue to diversify their marketing programs to take advantage of opportunities in fast-growing segments. Warning—issues of race, religion, and politics can produce negative reactions. In March 2015, Starbucks initiated a campaign having U.S. workers write "Race Together" on beverage cups. Several companies had been tying their brands to social issues but the Starbucks campaign was ridiculed on social media by people who said it was opportunistic and inappropriate. Some went so far as to say that it used racial tensions within the United States to boost Starbucks bottom line. Following criticism, Starbucks reviewed this tactic and dropped it.

The Changing American Family

The "traditional household" consists of a husband, wife, and children (and sometimes grandparents). Yet the once American ideal of the two-child, two-car suburban family has lately been losing some of its luster.

In the United States, married couples with children make up only 22 percent of the nation's 117 million households, married couples without children make up

29 percent, and single parents comprise another 11 percent. A full 38 percent are nonfamily households—single person or adults living together composed of one or both sexes.[38]

More people are divorcing or separating, choosing not to marry, marrying later, or marrying without intending to have children. Marketers must increasingly consider the special needs of nontraditional households because they are now growing more rapidly than traditional households. For example, people in their thirties who are marrying for the first time are used to going out to eat frequently. When they have children they continue to dine out, taking their children with them.

The number of working women has also increased, growing up to 59 percent. Both husband and wife work in the majority of married couple families.[39] This has spawned the need for takeout food, prepared by someone else but eaten at the home dining table. Grocery stores are also preparing heat-and-serve entrees and side dishes. These grocery stores are now seeking graduates of culinary programs and hospitality programs as this business grows. Royal Caribbean targets time-crunched working mothers with budget-friendly family vacations that are easy to plan and certain to wow. Royal Caribbean estimates that, although vacations are a joint decision, 80 percent of all trips are planned and booked by women— who are pressed for time, whether they work or not. Royal Caribbean communicates to mothers that all their vacation will pay off by providing an excellent vacation for the whole family including themselves.[40]

Two decades ago, terms such as *guppies* and *dinks* were commonly discussed in sociological and marketing circles. As millennials have become adults, the terms PANKS (Professional Aunts, No Kids) was developed by Melanie Notkin, a New York marketing executive.

PANKS should be of interest to the hospitality/tourism industry since this group consists of college-educated women in their thirties who are unmarried and childless but devote love and attention to their nephews and nieces. Some of these women take these children on vacation trips, and this group is growing. In 1971, 35 percent of women this age were childless, but had increased to 47 percent by 2010.[41]

Geographic Shifts in Population

This is a period of great migratory movements between and within countries. Americans, for example, are a mobile people, with about 15 percent of all U.S. residents moving each year. Over the past two decades, the U.S. population has shifted toward the Sunbelt states. The West and South have grown, whereas the Midwest and Northeast have lost population.[42] As companies look for new locations, they need to understand both national and local geographic trends relating to shifting populations.

A Better-Educated, More White-Collar, More Professional Population

The U.S. population is becoming better educated. Moreover, nearly two-thirds of high-school graduates now enroll in college within 12 months of graduating.[43.] The rising number of educated people will increase the demand for quality products, including luxury hotels, travel, wine, and dining at restaurants that have interesting menus.

Economic environment. The economic environment consists of factors that affect consumer purchasing power and spending patterns. Markets require both power and people. Purchasing power depends on current income, price, saving, and credit; marketers must be aware of major economic trends in income and changing consumer spending patterns.

Economic Environment

Markets require buying power as well as people. The **economic environment** consists of factors that affect consumer purchasing power and spending patterns. Nations vary greatly in their levels and distribution of income. Some countries have subsistence economies: They consume most of their own agricultural and industrial output. These countries offer few market opportunities. At the other extreme are industrial economies, which constitute rich markets for many different kinds of goods. Marketers must pay close attention to major trends and consumer-spending patterns both across and within their world markets. Following are some of the major economic trends in the United States.

Changes in Income

Throughout the 1990s, American consumers fell into a consumption frenzy, fueled by income growth, a boom in the stock market, rapid increases in housing values, and other economic good fortune. They bought and bought, seemingly without caution, amassing record levels of debt. However, the free spending and high expectations of those days were dashed by the recession of the early 2000s. In fact, we are now facing the age of the "squeezed consumer." Along with rising incomes in some segments have come increased financial burdens. The collapse of the housing markets in 2008 eliminated the opportunity for many consumers to borrow home equity. They now face repaying debts acquired during earlier spending splurges, increased household and family expenses, and saving ahead for children's college tuition payments and retirement. This reduction in discretionary income created hard times for the restaurant industry as customers cut back both on the number of times they dined out and on the amount they spent when they did dine out.

Over the past three decades, the rich have grown richer, the middle class has shrunk, and the poor have remained poor. The top 1 percent of American families now controls 33.4 percent of the nation's net worth, up 3.3 points from 1989. By contrast, the bottom 90 percent of families now control only 30.4 percent of the net worth, down 3.5 points.[44]

The Super Rich

This presentation is not intended for political or sociological discussion. Instead it is included to introduce a group that is unfamiliar to most people but is a viable market segment for hospitality and tourism.

The world's Super Rich represents 0.5 percent of the world's population but over 38.5 percent of its wealth. Despite a recession, global wealth reached a high of $231 trillion in 2011.

Individuals with a net worth of $50 million or more are located primarily in North America, Europe, and Asia/Pacific. London has become a magnet for the Super Rich of the world (top 1 percent). There is a greater concentration of Super Rich in London than anywhere else on the planet. London has the distinction of having the largest concentration of Russian millionaires outside of Moscow.

Deluxe ultra-long vacations are in demand. Realizing this, Four Seasons offers four-week around-the-world, all-inclusive itineraries for $130,000 per person. All accommodations are at Four Seasons hotels/resorts, which are reached on the Four Seasons Private Jet, ground transportation, planned excursions, meals, and gratuities. According to Chris Norton, Four Seasons executive vice president, Global Products & Operations, these trips are consistently sold out.[45] In 2015, Cunard Lines offered 120 nights on the ocean liner RMS *Queen Mary 2* for $233,998 per person for accommodations in its 2,249-square-foot duplex suite.

The Global Economy

Today the travel industry operates in a global environment. When the exchange rate between the Euro and the U.S. dollar favors the Euro, fewer travelers from America go to Europe, and Americans divert their vacations to locations in the United States and South America.

One of the positive outcomes of currency devaluations in Argentina is that it is gaining as a destination for conventions and meetings. But when international meeting planners move meetings to Santiago, Sao Paulo, Rio de Janeiro, Buenos Aires, and other cities of South America, cities in Asia, Europe, and North America lose these conventions. Argentina, Chile, and Uruguay are all among tourist destinations, attracting over a million visitors. This is in part due to the economic consequences of currency exchange.

Natural Environment

The natural environment involves the natural resources that are needed as inputs by marketers or that are affected by marketing activities. Environmental concerns

Tango dancers are a popular tourist attraction in Agrentina, where favorable currency exchange has resulted in attracting more business meetings and tourists. Courtesy of vikiri/Shutterstock.

have grown steadily during the past three decades. In many cities around the world, air and water pollution have reached dangerous levels.

Marketers should be aware of several trends in the natural environment. The first involves growing shortages of raw materials including air and water. Air pollution chokes many of the world's large cities, and water shortages are already a big problem in some parts of the United States and the world. By 2030 more than one in three of the world's human beings will not have enough water to drink.[46] Renewable resources, such as forests and food, also must be used wisely. Nonrenewable resources, such as oil, coal, and various minerals, pose a serious problem. Shortages increase construction costs of new hotels, restaurants, and tourist attractions. A second environmental trend is increased pollution. Consider the disposal of garbage and sewage by resorts. In destinations where this is not managed, the groundwater has been polluted, damaging the water supply. Garbage can be seen on the beaches and back bays of some destinations. Hospitality companies must be good corporate citizens and embrace corporate responsibility.

The natural environment consists of many amenities that attract tourists, such as forests, clean beaches, pristine streams, wildlife, and clean air. The Maldives, an island nation south of Sri Lanka, has seen its coral reefs bleached by warm water from El Nino. With 60 percent of their visitors doing some form of diving, the coral reefs are an important attraction.[47] Anyone involved in tourism has an obligation to protect the environment and develop sustainable tourism. The concern for sustainability is increasing and has led to publications such as greenlodgingnews.com and organizations such as Green Restaurant Association.

A third trend is increased government intervention in natural resource management. The governments of different countries vary in their concern and efforts to promote a clean environment. Some, such as the German government, vigorously pursue environmental quality. Others, especially many poorer nations, do little about pollution, largely because they lack the needed funds or political will. Unfortunately, many of these countries often rely on tourism and suffer from the problems mentioned in the preceding paragraphs. The general hope is that companies around the world will accept more social responsibility, and less expensive devices can be found to control and reduce pollution.

Technological Environment

The most dramatic force shaping our destiny is technology, which has given us wireless access to the Internet. This has made it possible for individuals to have interactions with others involving both audio and visual connections using programs such as Skype and FreeConference.com. Many organizations now accept a document that has been signed, scanned, and e-mailed instead of a hard copy of the original document. The end result is that speed at which business is occurring has increased dramatically. Sites like LinkedIn and Facebook allow us to keep track of both our business and personal networks.

Technology has affected the hospitality industry in many ways. For example, Intelity has produced a product called ICE (Interactive Customer Experience) that can be accessed from a number of Web-enabled platforms, including smartphones and tablets. Guest services from the hotel such as room service, valet parking, dining room reservations, and spa services can be accessed from the tablet. External reservations at theatres, restaurants, golf courses, and airlines can also be accessed. To prevent theft, the equipment has tracking devices.[48] There are predictions that the front desk will be no longer necessary as guests check-in using their smartphone. The Hen-na Hotel in Japan has developed robots that will man the front desk. By reducing the cost of labor, the hotel intends to be the low-price leader in the area. The hotel is using facial recognition as a way for guests to access their rooms. The application of technology is changing how we do business in the hospitality industry.[49]

One of the most powerful changes is from social media. We will discuss social media in Chapter 14. The smartphone is a versatile tool for travelers. They can book and check on reservations, use it as a boarding pass for airlines, register at a hotel, and use it as a key access to the hotel room. These self-service technologies save the guest time and labor for the hospitality company. This also means that one's Web presence has to be formatted to work well on smartphones. Technology has also helped eliminate the theft of hotel products.[50]

Technology is also helping operations. Washable RFID chips are being embedded in towels, bathrobes, banquet linen, and other washable linens. This allows management to determine the inventory of linen in storage closets and on the hotel floors. Since it is becoming more common for full-service hotels to send their linen off premise to be cleaned, the RFID chips help the laundry to keep track of the linen and to locate missing items.[51] Panera had converted 400 of its cafes to an easy-order and fast-delivery model. Customers could place orders using iPads-equipped kiosks for delivery to their tables. This was in response to customer complaints about long order lines.[52]

Marketers must understand and anticipate changes in the technological environment. Because the guest is involved in the service delivery process, technology changes often mean we need to train the guest in how to use the new technology.

Political Environment

Political environment. Laws, government agencies, and pressure groups that influence and limit the activities of various organizations and individuals in society.

Marketing decisions are strongly affected by developments in the **political environment**. This environment consists of laws, government agencies, and pressure groups that influence and limit the activities of various organizations and individuals in society. We cite some current political trends and their implications for marketing management.

Increased Legislation and Regulation Affecting Business

As products become more complex, public concern about their safety increases. Governmental agencies have become involved in the investigation and regulation of everything from fire codes to food-handling practices. Employment and employee practices fall under government regulation, as do sales of alcohol, which vary from state to state and sometimes from precinct to precinct in the same county. Politicians also see travelers as good sources of revenue because nonresidents pay taxes on hotel rooms, rental cars, and many other purchases but cannot vote against them. Hotel taxes are supposed to be used to support tourism; however, the spending of this money has sometimes been used for questionable purchases, such as statues for suburban parks. The hospitality industry must make sure that taxes designed to promote tourism are used effectively. Managers must also work with hotel and restaurant associations to ensure that taxes do not become oppressive. New York City hiked its hotel tax to over 21.25 percent for rooms costing over $100 in 1990. Many meeting and convention planners avoided New York because of the unfriendly tax. Convention business plunged by 37 percent during the next three years, and tax revenues declined despite the tax increase. The real loser was New York City's hospitality industry. New York has since reduced its hotel tax in line with other cities.[53]

Government regulation aims at protecting consumers from unfair business practices. Various government units define unfair consumer practices and offer remedies. Businesses can minimize government intervention through active self-regulation. Such associations as the American Hotel and Motel Association and the National Restaurant Association (NRA) define and encourage good trade practices.

Government regulation also aims to protect society's interests. Profitable business activity does not always improve the quality of life. Thus regulations are passed to discourage smoking, littering, polluting, over-congestion of facilities, and others in the name of protecting society's interests. Regulation aims to make firms responsible for the social as well as private costs of their activities.

Government regulation and enforcement are likely to increase. Business executives must know the major laws protecting competition, consumers, and society when planning their products and marketing programs.

Changing Government Agency Enforcement

To enforce laws, Congress established federal regulatory agencies: the Federal Trade Commission, the Food and Drug Administration, the Interstate Commerce Commission, the Federal Communications Commission, the Federal Power Commission, the Civil Aeronautics Board, the Consumer Products Safety Commission, the Environmental Protection Agency, and the Office of Consumer Affairs. These agencies can have a major impact on a company's marketing performance. Government agencies have discretion in enforcing the laws, and from time to time, they appear to be overly eager. Lawyers and economists, who often lack a practical sense of marketing and other business principles, frequently dominate the agencies. In recent years, the Federal Trade Commission has added marketing experts to its staff to gain a better understanding of complex issues.

International Politics

Sometimes hospitality companies and products are boycotted or worse because of political differences between countries or groups with in a country. McDonald's has become an icon of the United States worldwide and has been the victim of boycotts, bomb threats, and on rare occasions bombs. Here are some of the actions that targeted companies can take:

- Emphasize the company's connections to the local community. In Indonesia, McDonald's launched television ads showing some of the staff of the local franchise owners wearing traditional clothing. In Argentina where McDonald's entrances were blocked by protestors, the restaurant chain launched a campaign showing a Big Mac with the words "Made in Argentina" stamped on it.

- Adopt a low profile. Avoid conflicts and even press interviews with reporters known to be against your product or company.

- Counter lies and misinformation with professional public relations and advertising. Select a well-versed and believable spokesperson. Do not allow random staff members to be spokespeople.

- Be patient. These kinds of things usually have a life of their own and fade away as protestors and the public lose interest.[54]

Cultural Environment

The cultural environment includes institutions and other forces that affect society's basic values, perceptions, preferences, and behaviors. As a collective entity, a society shapes the basic beliefs and values of its members. The following cultural characteristics can affect marketing decisions.

Persistence of Cultural Values

People in any society hold certain persisting core beliefs and values. For example, most Americans believe in working, getting married, giving to charity, and being honest. Core beliefs and values are passed from parents to children and are reinforced by schools, churches, business, and government. Secondary beliefs and values, however, are more open to change. Believing in marriage is a core belief; believing that people should get married early is a secondary belief.

The hospitality industry is worldwide. Chances are very good that many of you will find yourselves serving in a foreign setting sometime during your career. Cultural norms and cultural prohibitions may affect your managerial roles in ways quite different from those in your native country. For example, hoteliers in Israel are expected to understand and observe the rules of kashruth, or keeping kosher. These are complicated and require constant supervision. Hotels in Israel must have two kitchens, one for meat and one for dairy products. Because kosher meat is expensive in Israel, hotel food costs are higher.[55]

A practice widely followed in China, Hong Kong, and Singapore (and that has also spread to Japan, Vietnam, and Korea), feng shui means wind and water. Practitioners of feng shui, or geomancers, recommend the most favorable conditions for any venture, particularly the placement of office buildings and the arrangement of desks, doors, and other items. To have good feng shui, a building should face the water and be flanked by the mountains. It should not block the view of the mountain spirits. The Hyatt Hotel in Singapore was designed without feng shui in mind and had to be redesigned to boost business. Originally, the front desk was parallel to the doors and road, which was thought to lead to wealth flowing out. Furthermore, the doors were facing northwest, which gave easy access to undesirable spirits in. The geomancer recommended designed alterations so that wealth could be retained and undesirable spirits kept out.[56]

Increased Emphasis on Socially Responsible Actions and Ethics

Written regulations cannot possibly cover all potential marketing abuses, and existing laws are often difficult to enforce. Beyond written laws and regulations, business is also governed by social codes and rules of professional ethics.

SOCIALLY RESPONSIBLE BEHAVIOR.   Enlightened companies encourage their managers to look beyond what the regulatory system allows and simply "do the right thing." These firms actively seek out ways to protect the long-run interests of their consumers and the environment.

Today, almost every aspect of marketing involves ethical and societal issues. These issues usually involve conflicting interests and well-meaning people can honestly disagree about the right course of action in a given situation. Companies are now developing policies, guidelines, and other responses to complex social issues.

The boom in Internet marketing has created a new set of social and ethical issues. Critics worry about online privacy issues. There has been an explosion in the amount of personal digital data available. Users, themselves, supply some of it. They voluntarily place highly private information on social-networking sites, such as Facebook or LinkedIn, or on genealogy sites that are easily searched by anyone with a computer or a smartphone.

Information is systematically developed by businesses seeking to learn more about their customers, often without consumers realizing that they are under the microscope. Legitimate businesses plant cookies on consumers' PCs and collect, analyze, and share digital data from every move consumers make at their Web sites. Critics are concerned that companies may now know too much and might use digital data to take unfair advantage of consumers. Although most companies fully disclose their Internet privacy policies and use data to benefit their customers, abuses do occur.

The number of public-interest groups has increased. These groups take on issues of social responsibility. Cindi Lamb and her five-month-old daughter, Laura, were on their way home from a grocery store when a drunk driver slammed into their car. The accident left the baby paralyzed from the waist down. Cindi was outraged when she discovered the drunk driver was a chronic offender. She set out to change the way judges, police officers, and politicians handled drunk driving. Joining together with her friends and other victims, she formed what is now known as MADD (Mothers Against Drunk Driving). MADD has had a major impact on the hospitality industry by demanding that restaurants be more responsible in their serving of alcohol. MADD is helping push stronger legislation against drinking and driving.

One expert who follows People for the Ethical Treatment of Animals (PETA) states that the organization would like to see all fast-food outlets that serve meat closed. Nishiki Sushi in Sacramento used to serve "Dancing Shrimp," a popular menu item in Japan. The shrimp are served live. Customers are instructed to squeeze lemon juice on the shrimp to make them "dance." PETA asked the restaurant to remove the shrimp from the menu. The restaurant voluntarily removed the shrimp. Certainly, improved treatment of animals would be good, but the complete elimination of animals from human diets is something that the majority of people would not embrace.

The cultural eating practice in Chinese restaurants using shark fins to flavor soup resulted in the near disappearance of some shark populations including hammerhead, mahu, and tiger. Fortunately, a report by the wildlife protection group Wild Aid indicated that demand is declining for shark fins. In Southern China, sales dropped by 82 percent from 2012 to 2015.

Many nations have banned "finning," the practice of catching a shark, cutting off its fins, and then throwing the dismembered animal into the ocean to die.

CAUSE-RELATED MARKETING.   To exercise social responsibility and build positive images, many companies are now linking themselves to worthwhile causes. Cause-related marketing has become a primary form of corporate giving. It lets companies "do well by doing good" by linking purchases of the company's products or services with fund-raising for worthwhile causes or charitable organizations. Companies sponsor dozens of cause-related marketing campaigns each year. For example, BJ's Restaurants, through its "Cookies for Kids" program, donates a portion of the sale of every signature "Pizookie" dessert to the Cystic Fibrosis Foundation.

Cause-related marketing has stirred controversy. Critics worry that cause-related marketing is more a strategy for selling than a strategy for giving—that "cause-related" marketing is really "cause-exploitative" marketing. Thus, companies using cause-related marketing might find themselves walking a fine line between increased sales and facing charges of exploitation. However, if handled well, cause-related marketing can benefit the company and the cause. The company gains an effective marketing tool while building a positive public image. The charitable organization or cause gains visibility and important new sources of funding and support.

■■■ Linked Environmental Factors

When the millennials became teenagers, the total expenditures on food in restaurants and food-service operations exceeded food expenditures in grocery stores for the first time. In 1996 people in the United States purchased more meals outside the home than they ate home-prepared meals. One of the forces behind this change is that both heads of the household are working in many families. The average time spent preparing meals is currently 15 minutes and dropping. No longer is the woman expected to prepare home-cooked meals for the man. Many people prefer to eat at home; they just do not have time to cook. The "home-meal replacement" restaurant developed as a result of these trends. Robert Del Grande's Café Express restaurants in Texas and Arizona and Foodies Kitchen in Metairie, Louisiana, are examples of restaurant concepts creating quality meals with the convenience of self-service.

Grocery stores provide competition to restaurants. According to David Audrian, vice president of the Texas Restaurant Association, the number one trend in the food-service industry today is the growth of food service in supermarkets and convenience stores.[57] Most grocery stores have a food display near the deli counter of microwaveable freshly prepared meals. These entries include pot roast, teriyaki chicken, and pasta dishes. The Hy-Vee grocery store at 14th and Park Avenue in Des Moines, Iowa, has a drive-through window.[58]

These examples show how the elements of the environment are linked. Economic forces result in families with both heads of the household working. This is a demographic statistic that can be tracked over time. Women are also able to build careers and take management positions once reserved for men. We have seen a cultural change where men now participate in home duties and no one member of the household is expected to prepare all meals. Technology has also made it easier to reconstitute food and to warm prepared meals at home. Finally, the competitive environment between grocery stores and quick-service restaurants is expected to heat up. Grocery stores are building elaborate delicatessens with a variety of prepared meals; they have fresh microwaveable meals to go, and the drive-through window on the Hy-Vee store may become commonplace in the future. The change in food consumption patterns relates to economic, demographic, technological, cultural, and competitive trends.

Responding to the Marketing Environment

Many companies view the marketing environment as an "uncontrollable" element to which they must adapt. They passively access the marketing environment. They analyze environmental forces and design strategies that will help the company avoid the threats.

Environmental management perspective. A management perspective in which a firm takes aggressive actions to affect the publics and forces in its marketing environment rather than simply watching and reacting to it.

Other companies take an **environmental management perspective**.[59] Rather than simply watching and reacting, these firms take aggressive action to affect the publics and forces in their marketing environment. Lobbyists are hired to influence legislation affecting their industries and to stage media events to gain favorable press coverage. They run advertorials to shape public opinion and press lawsuits and file complaints. They form contractual agreements to control their distribution channels.

One of the elements of the macroenvironment that can be influenced is the political environment. Companies join trade organizations such as the American Hotel and Lodging Association (AH & LA), the American Society of Travel Agents (ASTA), the Hotel and Catering International Management Association (HCIMA), and the NRA. Trade associations hire lobbyists and form political action committees (PACs) to represent and communicate their industry's concerns to government officials.

Marketing management cannot always affect environmental forces; in many cases, it must settle for simply watching and reacting to the environment. For example, a company would have little success trying to influence geographic population shifts, the economic environment, or major cultural values. But whenever possible, marketing managers take a proactive rather than a reactive approach to the publics and forces in their marketing environment.

Environmental Scanning

Use of an environmental scanning plan has proved beneficial to many hospitality companies. The following steps are involved: (1) Determine the environmental areas that need to be monitored; (2) Determine how the information will be collected, including information sources, the information frequency, and who will be responsible; (3) Implement the data collection plan; and (4) Analyze the data and use them in the market planning process. Part of the analysis is weighing the importance of the trends so the organization can keep the trends in proper perspective.

It is never sufficient simply to collect data about the environment. Managers must turn the data into useful information that will help them make decisions. The information used to make decisions must be reliable, timely, and used in decision making. William S. Watson, senior vice president of Best Western Worldwide Marketing, offered advice on this subject: "Collecting data for its own value is like collecting stamps. It is a nice hobby but it does not deliver the mail."[60]

■■■ CHAPTER REVIEW

I. Microenvironment. The microenvironment consists of actors and forces close to the company that can affect its ability to serve its customers. The actors in the microenvironment include the company, suppliers, market intermediaries, customers, and publics.

  A. The company. Marketing managers work closely with top management and the various company departments.

  B. Existing competitors. They are part of the microenvironment and must be monitored closely.

  C. Suppliers. Firms and individuals that provide the resources needed by the company to produce its goods and services.

  D. Marketing intermediaries. Firms that help the company promote, sell, and distribute its goods to the final buyers.

  E. Disintermediation. The elimination of intermediaries.

  F. Marketing services agencies. Marketing research firms, advertising agencies, media firms, and marketing consulting firms help companies to target and promote their products to the right market.

  G. Financial intermediaries. Include banks, credit companies, insurance companies, and other firms that help hospitality companies to finance their transaction or insure risks associated with the buying and selling of goods and services.

  H. Customers. Managers must understand the different types of customers: consumers, business markets, government markets, resellers, and international markets.

  I. Publics. A public is any group that has an actual or potential interest in or impact on an organization's ability to achieve its objectives.

II. Macroenvironment. The macroenvironment consists of the larger societal forces that affect the whole microenvironment: demographic, economic, natural, technological, political, competitor, and cultural forces. Following are the seven major forces in a company's macroenvironment.

  A. Competitive environment. Each firm must consider its size and industry position in relation to its competitors. A company must satisfy the needs and wants of consumers better than its competitors do in order to survive.

  B. Demographic environment. Demography is the study of human populations in terms of size, density, location, age, sex, race, occupation, and other statistics. The demographic environment is of major interest to marketers because markets are made up of people.

  C. Economic environment. The economic environment consists of factors that affect consumer purchasing power and spending patterns. Markets require both power and people. Purchasing power depends on current income, price, saving, and credit; marketers must be aware of major economic trends in income and changing consumer spending patterns.

  D. Natural environment. The natural environment consists of natural resources required by marketers or affected by marketing activities.

  E. Technological environment. The most dramatic force shaping our destiny today is technology.

  F. Political environment. The political environment is made up of laws, government agencies, and pressure groups that influence and limit various organizations and individuals in society.

  G. Cultural environment. The cultural environment includes institutions and other forces that affect society's basic values, perceptions, preferences, and behaviors.

III. Linked Environment Factors

IV. Responding to the Marketing Environment. Many companies view the marketing environment as an "uncontrollable" element to which they must adapt. Other companies take an environmental management perspective. Rather than simply watching and reacting, these firms take aggressive actions to affect the publics and forces in their marketing environment. These companies use environmental scanning to monitor the environment.

■■■ DISCUSSION QUESTIONS

1. How has the McDonald's concept changed since the 1960s? What environmental forces were behind these changes? How will the McDonald's concept change in the next decade, given the new forces operating in the environment?

2. What environmental trends will affect the success of a first-class hotel chain, such as Hyatt or Sofitel, over the next 10 years? If you were corporate director of marketing for this type of hotel, what plans would you make to deal with these trends?

3. The 78 million members of the baby-boomer generation are aging, with the oldest members in their early sixties. List some marketing opportunities and threats associated with this demographic trend for the hospitality and travel industry.

4. How have environmental trends affected the design of hotels?

5. Mobile marketing involves any type of marketing message—voice, text, image, or video—delivered to a handheld device such as a cell phone, iPhone, or BlackBerry. Learn more about mobile marketing and discuss the current applications and the potential for future applications in the travel and hospitality industries.

6. If we have little control over the macroenvironment, why should we be concerned with it?

7. What environmental trends will affect the success of the Walt Disney Company in the next five years? If you were in charge of marketing at Disney, what plans would you make to deal with these trends?

■■■ EXPERIENTIAL EXERCISES

Do one of the following:

1. View the annual reports of several hospitality companies. How did you find out about how they might be changing their business to fit the environment from their annual report? If you do not have access to an annual report, visit the book's Web site for electronic access to annual reports.

2. Choose and visit a restaurant, club, or hotel you feel is designed for one of the generations discussed in the book (e.g., baby boomers, Generation X, echo boomers). After doing some research on the generation, state what the business you chose has done to cater to its target generation.

■■■ INTERNET EXERCISES

Support for these exercises can be found on the Web site for Marketing for Hospitality and Tourism, www.prenhall.com/kotler.

1. On the Internet, find how ecotourism is being used to attract tourists by different organizations.

2. From information you can find on the Internet, when do you think space tourism will be a viable form of tourism? What organizations are working to develop space tourism?

3. Go to Web sites of travel or hospitality companies and find examples of how they are taking measures to sustain and improve the natural environment. Which companies that you examined do you think have the best programs? Explain your answer.

■■■ REFERENCES

1 Castle Rock (Town) Colorado, U.S. Census Bureau, State and County Quick Facts, February 5, 2015, http://quickfacts.census.gov

2 Seyhmus Baloglu, "Dimensions of Customer Loyalty, Separating Friends from Well Wishers," *Cornell Hotel and Restaurant Administration Quarterly*, 43, no. 1 (2002): 47–59.

3 Philip Kotler, *Marketing Management* (Upper Saddle River, NJ: Prentice-Hall, 1988); Donald R. Lehmann and Russel S. Winer, *Analysis for Marketing Planning* (Plano, TX: Business Publications, 1988).

4 Craft web site, www.craftrestaurant.com (accessed August 1, 2008).

5 Tejal Rao, "The New Hotel Cuisine: Don't Bite the Brand That Feeds You," StarChefs.com, May 2007, http://www.starchefs.com/features/trends/concept/index.shtml (accessed August 2, 2008).

6 Chick-fil-A Looks to Perk Sales by Offering First-Ever Specialty Grade Coffee in QSR Industry, Chick-fil-A.com 2014 CFA Properties, Inc.

7 Information from Robert J. Benes, Abbie Jarman, and Ashley Williams, "2007 NRA Sets Records," at www.chefmagazine.com (accessed September 2007); www.thecoca-colacompany.com/presscenter/press-kit_fs.html and www.cokesolutions.com (accessed November 2010).

8 Michael Porter, Competitive Strategy (New York: Free Press, 1980).

9 Melinda Bush, "The Critical Need to Know," *Cornell Hotel and Restaurant Administration Quarterly*, 26, no. 3 (1985): 1.

10 From Brian Phillips, Executive Creative Director of the agency. Copyright © by Visit Indy. Reprinted by permission.

11 From Chris Gahl, Vice President of Marketing and Communications for Visit Indy. Copyright © by Visit Indy. Reprinted by permission.

12 World POPClock, U.S. Census Bureau, www.census.gov (accessed September 2007). This Web site provides continuously updated projections of the U.S. and world populations.

13 See Clay Chandler, "Little Emperors," *Fortune* (October 4, 2004): 138–150; "China's Little Emperor's," *Financial Times* (May 5, 2007): 1; "Me Generation Finally Focuses on US," *Chinadaily.com.cn* (August 27, 2008), www.chinadaily.com.cn/china/2008-08/27/content_6972930.htm; Melinda Varley, "China: Chasing the Dragon," *Brand Strategy* (October 6, 2008): 26; Clifford Coonan, "New Rules to Enforce China's One Child Policy," *Irish Times* (January 14, 2009): 12; David Pilling, "Reflections of Life in China's Fast Lane," *Financial Times* (April 19, 2010): 10.

14 Adapted from information in Janet Adamy, "Different Brew: Eyeing a Billion Tea Drinkers, Starbucks Pours It On in China," *Wall Street Journal* (November 29, 2006). Also see, "Where the Money Is," *Financial Times* (May 12, 2007): 5; Laurie Burkitt, "Starbucks Menu Expands in China," *Wall Street Journal*, March 9, 2011.

15 Janet Adamy, "Different Brew: Eyeing a Billion Tea Drinkers, Starbucks Pours It On in China," *Wall Street Journal*, November 29, 2006.

16 Laurie Burkitt, "Starbucks Menu Expands in China," *Wall Street Journal* (March 9, 2011): B.7.

17 U.S. Census Bureau projections and POPClock Projection, U.S. Census Bureau, www.census.gov (accessed September 2007).

18 Louise Lee, "Love Those Boomers," *Business Week* (October 24, 2005): 94–102; Tom Ramstack, "The New Gray: Boomers Spark Retirement Revolution," *Washington Tones*, December 29, 2005; "Baby Boomers in the United States Have an Estimated Annual Spending Power of over $2 Trillion," *Business Wire*, April 27, 2007.

19 Noreen O'Leary, "Squeeze Play," *Adweek* (January 12, 2009): 8–9; David Court, "The Downturn's New Rules for Marketers," *The McKinsey Quarterly* (December 2008), accessed at www.mckinseyquarterly.com/the_down-town_new_rules_for_marketers_2262; Emily Brandon, "Planning to Retire: 10 Things You Didn't Know About Baby Boomers," USNews.com (January 15, 2009), accessed at http://money.usnews.com; Iris Taylor, "Impact of Baby Boomers Delaying Retirement Explored," *McClatchy-Tribune Business News* (April 5, 2010).

20 See Simon Hudson, "Wooing Zoomers: Marketing to the Mature Travelers," *Marketing Intelligence & Planning*, 28, no. 4 (2010): 444–461.

21 Scott Schroder and Warren Zeller, "Get to Know Gen X and Its Segments," *Multichannel News* (March 21, 2005): 55; Jim Shelton, "When Children of Divorce Grow Up," *Knight Ridder Tribune Business News* (March 4, 2007): 1.

22 "Mixed Success: One Who Targeted Gen X and Succeeded – Sort Of," *Journal of Financial Planning*, 17, no. 2 (February 2004): 15.

23 Paul Greenberg, "Move Over, Baby Boomers; Gen Xers Want Far More Collaboration with Companies, Both as Consumers and Employees," *CIO* 70 (March 1, 2006): 1.

24 Scott Hume, "Consumer Insights: The Leading Edge, Give Generation X the Credit It Is Due for Revolutionizing the American Dining Experience," Restaurants and Institutions online (www.rimag.com/article/CA6556319.html), May 1, 2008 (accessed July 28, 2008).

25 Adapted from information found in Mark Ritson, "Have You Got the Gen X Factor?" *Marketing* (April 25, 2007): 25; "75 Wall Street to Be a Hyatt Andaz Property" (April 25, 2007), www.hotelchatter.con0taghkndax%20Hotels.

26 Based on information found in Donna C. Gregory, "Virginia Tourism Corp. Marketing to Generation X" (December 29, 2009), www.virginiabusiness.com/index.php/news/article/romancing-generation-x. Also see www.virginia.org/home.asp (accessed November 2010).

27 Deirde van Dyk, "The Generation Y Hotel," *Time* online (www.time.com), June 12, 2008 (accessed August 3, 2008); R. K. Miller and Kelli Washington, *Consumer Behavior* 2009; Piet Levy, "The Quest for Cool," *Marketing News* (February 28, 2009): 6.

28 "Taco Ride Sets New Record," August 18, 2008, http://www.bikeiowa.com/news/334/taco-ridesets-newrecord; Wabash Trace Nature Trail, http://www.traillink.com/trail/Wabash-trace-nature-trail.aspx; Taco Ride – Wabash Trace Weekly Ride Hosted by Taco Ride, Wabash Trace Nature Trail, Council Bluffs, Iowa, https://www.bikeiowa.com/eventpop/7165/taco-ride-wabash-trace-weekly-ride?lightbox%.

29 Green Getaways Australia, site built with help from Rapid Websites, http://www.greengetawaysaustralia.com.au

30 U.S. Golf Courses in Steady Decline, Associated Press, www.espn.go.com/golfstory.id12461331/, March 11, 2015.

31 Megan Barber, "Ski Industry Expert Says 31% of Today's Ski Areas Are Dying," http://ski.curbed.com/archives/2015. See also Tom Ross, "Era of the Super Pass: Ski Resorts Forced to Adapt and Change with Demographic Cycles," SteamboatToday.com, December 7, 2014.

32 See U.S. Census Bureau, "U.S. Population Projections," www.census.gov/population/www/projections/summarytables.html (accessed August 2010); "Characteristics of the Foreign-Born Population by Nativity and U.S. Citizenship Status," www.census.gov/population/www/socdemo/foreign/cps2008.html

33 Dan Fost, "The Fun Factor: Marketing Recreation to the Disabled," *American Demographics*, 20, no. 2 (February 1998): 54–58.

34 Joan Voight, "Accessibility of Disability," *Adweek*, March 27, 2006, 20.

35 For these and other statistics, see Witeck-Combs Communications, "Buying Power of Gay Men and Lesbians in 2008," www.rivendellmedia.com/ngng/executive_summary/NGNG PPT and www.gaymarket.com/ngng/ngng_reader.html (accessed April 2009); Paul Morrissette, "Market to LGBT C," *American Agent and Broker* (July 2010): 50.

36 Robert Sharoff, "Diversity in the Mainstream," *Marketing News* (May 21, 2001): 1, 13.

37 For these and other examples, see Laura Koss-Feder, "Out and About," *Marketing News* (May 25, 1998): 1, 20; Jennifer Gilber, "Ad Spending Booming for Gay-Oriented Sites," *Advertising Age* (December 6,

1999): 58; John Fetto, "In Broad Daylight," *American Demographics* (February 2001): 16, 20; Robert Sharoff, "Diversity in the Mainstream," *Marketing News* (May 21, 2001): 1, 13; David Goetzl, "Showtime, MTV Gamble on Gay Net," *Advertising Age* (January 14, 2002): 4; Kristi Nelson, "Canada's Gay TV Network Gets Ready for U.S.," *Electronic Media* (Chicago, May 6, 2002).

38 See U.S. Census Bureau, "Families and Living Arrangements: 2009," at www.census.gov/population/www.socdemo/hh-fam.html (accessed May 2010).

39 U.S. Census Bureau, "Families and Living Arrangements: 2009"; "Census Bureau News – 2009 America's Families and Living Arrangements," *PR Newswire*, January 15, 2010; U.S. Census Bureau, "Facts for Features," March 2010, accessed at https://www.census.gov/newsroom/releases/archives/facts_for_features_special_editions/cbs0-ff03.html

40 See Marissa Miley and Ann Mack, "The New Female Consumer: The Rise of the Real Mom," *Advertising Age* (November 16, 2009): A1.

41 Kelly Spors, "The Two Hottest Niche Markets You've Probably Never Heard Of," April 2014, Open Forum, https://www.americanexpress.com

42 U.S. Census Bureau, "Geographical Mobility/Migration," www.census.gov/population/www/socdemo/migrate.html (accessed April 2010).

43 U.S. Census Bureau, "Educational Attainment," www.census.gov/population/www/socdemo/educ-attn.html (accessed April 2010).

44 Bradley Johnson, "Recession's Long Gone, But America's Average Income Isn't Budging," *Advertising Age* (April 17, 2006): 22. See also Jeremy Siegel, "Why the Rich Got Richer," *Kiplinger's Personal Finance* (July 2007): 532; Frederic L. Pryor, "The Anatomy of Increasing Inequity of U.S. Family Incomes," *Journal of Socio-Economics* (August 2007): 595.

45 Carrie Coolidge, "Trend Spotting: Grand Tours for Highfliers Between Jobs," *Barron's*, Penta, March 2, 2015, 8.

46 Andrew Zolli, "Business 3.0," *Fast Company* (March 2007): 64–70.

47 Mohammadi Kamin, "Calling Robinson Crusoe," *Geographical Magazine*, responsibletravel.com (October 18, 2004); "Maldive Islands Could Be Sinking" (October 5, 2004), http://news.bbc.co.uk/cbbcnews/hi/world/newsid_3715000/3715928.stm (accessed October 18, 2004.

48 See www.intelitycorp.com (accessed August 18, 2010).

49 Robert Loos, "Robots to Staff Hotel in Japan," *Robotics Today*, February 3, 2015, http://www.roboticstoday.com/news/hotel-androids-robots-to-staff-hotel-in-japan-3106 (accessed July 10, 2015).

50 "Mobile Phones Replace Room Keys in Stockholm Hotel, Check In and Check Out Without Ever Stopping by the Front Desk," November 2, 2010, http://news.discovery.com/tech/mobile-phones-replace-hotel-keys.html (accessed August 18, 2011).

51 Roger Yu, "Hotels Use RFID Chips to Keep Linens from Checking Out," (July 31, 2011), http://abcnews.go.com/travel/hotels-rfid-chips-linens-checking/story?id=14179579 (accessed August 18, 2011).

52 Machan Dyron, "Flour on His Shoes," CEO Spotlight, Ron Shaich, Panera Bread, Barron's: *The Dow Jones Business and Financial Weekly*, XCV, no. 8 (February 23, 2015): 38–39.

53 Gene Sloan, "Restaurant Taxes Gain Weight in Cash-Strapped Cities," *USA Today*, International Edition (Asia) (September 28, 1994): B7.

54 Salah Al Shebil, Adbul A. Rasheed, and Hussam Al-Shammari, "Battling Bigots," *Wall Street Journal* (April, 28, 2007): R6, R11.

55 Kenneth J. Gruber, "The Hotels of Israel: Pressure and Promise," *Cornell Hotel and Restaurant Administration Quarterly*, 28, no. 4 (1988): 42.

56 J.S. Perry Jobson, "Feng Shui: Its Impacts on the Asian Hospitality Industry," *International Journal of Contemporary Hospitality Management*, 6, no. 6 (1994): 21–26; Bernd H. Schmitt and Yigang Pan, "In Asia, the Supernatural Means Sales," *New York Times* (February 19, 1995): sec. 3, 11.

57 Richard L. Papiernik, "Foodservice – Food Market Lines Blur, But Focus Is on the Big $650 Billion Pie," *Nation's Restaurant News* (September 1, 1997): 57.

58 Matthew Schifrin and Bruce Upton, "Crab Rangoon to Go," *Forbes* (March 24, 1997): 124–128.

59 Carl P. Zeithami and Valarie Zeithami, "Environmental Management: Revisiting the Marketing Perspective," *Journal of Marketing* (Spring 1984): 46–53.

60 William S. Watson, "Letters, the New Research Responsibility," *Cornell Hotel and Restaurant Administration Quarterly*, 34, no. 5 (1993): 7.

Aerial view of Caesar's Palace, Las Vegas. Courtesy of Charles Zachritz/Shutterstock.

Managing Customer Information to Gain Customer Insights

Joseph, a 30-something New Yorker, recently went on a weekend trip to Atlantic City, New Jersey, where he hoped to stay at one of his favorite Caesars Entertainment resorts and enjoy some gaming and entertainment. Unfortunately for Joseph, he picked a weekend when all hotels were booked solid. But after swiping his Caesars Entertainment Total Rewards card to play the tables, the pit boss came by and directed him to the front desk. He was told that a room had become available, and he could stay in it for a reduced rate of $100 a night. When he checked out two nights later, Joseph was told that all the room charges were on the house.

Was this sudden vacancy a case of lady luck smiling down on an Atlantic City visitor? Or was it a case of a company that knows what managing customer relationships truly means? If you ask any of Caesars Entertainment Total Rewards program members, they will tell you without hesitation that it's the latter. "They are very good at upgrading or in some cases finding a room in a full hotel," Joseph reported later. "And I always liked the fact that no matter where I gambled, Atlantic City, Vegas, Kansas City, or New Orleans, or which of their hotels I gambled in, I was always able to use my [Total Rewards card]."

Caesars Entertainment customers like Joseph aren't the only ones praising its customer relationship management (CRM) capabilities. In fact, Caesars Entertainment's program is considered by CRM experts to set the gold standard. With the Total Rewards program at the center of its business and marketing strategies, Caesars Entertainment has the ability to gather data, convert that data into customer insights, and use those insights to serve up a customer experience like no other.

Gathering Data

One thing that makes Total Rewards so effective is that Caesars Entertainment has a customer relationship culture that starts at the top with president and chief executive officer (CEO) Gary Loveman. In 1998, Loveman joined the company and turned its existing loyalty program into Total Rewards. The program worked well from the start. But through smart investments and a continued focus, Caesars Entertainment has hit the CRM jackpot.

The mechanics of the program go something like this: Total Rewards members receive points based on the amount they spend at Caesars Entertainment facilities. They can then redeem the points for a variety of perks, such as cash, food, merchandise, rooms, and hotel show tickets. The simplicity of Total Rewards gains power in volume and flexibility. Through numerous acquisitions over the past decade, Caesars Entertainment has grown to more than 50 properties under several brands across the United States, including Harrah's, Caesars Palace, Bally's, Planet Hollywood, the Flamingo, and Showboat. Total Rewards members swipe their card every time they spend a dime at one of these properties: checking into 1 of 40,000 hotel rooms, playing 1 of 60,000 slot machines, eating at 1 of 390 restaurants, picking up a gift at 1 of 240 retail shops, or playing golf at 1 of its 7 golf courses. Over 80 percent of Caesars Entertainment customers—40 million in all—use a Total Rewards card. That's roughly one out of six adults in the United States. That's a big pile of data points. Added to this, Caesars Entertainment regularly surveys samples of its customers to gain even more details.

Customer Insights

Analyzing all this information gives Caesars Entertainment detailed insights into its casino operations. For example, "visualization software" can generate a dynamic "heat map" of a casino floor, with machines glowing red when at peak activity and then turning blue and then white as the action moves elsewhere. More importantly, Caesars Entertainment uses every customer interaction to learn something new about individuals—their characteristics and behaviors, such as who they are, how often they visit, how long they stay, and how much they gamble and entertain. "We know if you like gold ... chardonnay, down pillows; if you like your room close to the elevator, which properties you visit, what games you play, and which offers you redeemed," says David Norton, Caesars Entertainment senior vice president and chief marketing officer.

From its Total Rewards data, Caesars Entertainment has learned that 26 percent of its customers produce 82 percent of revenues. And these best customers aren't the "high-rollers" that have long been the focus of the industry. Rather, they are ordinary folks from all walks of life—middle-aged and retired teachers, assembly line workers, and even bankers and doctors who have discretionary income and time. Caesars Entertainment "low-roller" strategy is based on the discovery that these customers might just visit casinos for an evening rather than staying overnight at the hotel. And they are more likely to play the slots than the tables. What motivates them? It's mostly the intense anticipation and excitement of gambling itself.

Kris Hart, vice president of brand management for Caesars Entertainment, reports on a survey of 14,000 Total Rewards members. "We did a lot of psychographic segmenting—looking at what were the drivers of people's behavior. Were they coming because of the location? Were they coming because there were incented to do so with a piece of direct mail? Were they coming because they have an affinity for a loyalty program? And that allowed us to look at segments that clumped around certain drivers ... and it enabled us to construct our brands and messaging ... in a way that would capitalize on those drivers."

Customer Experience

Using such insights, Caesars Entertainment focuses its marketing and service development strategies on the needs of its best customers. For example, the company's advertising reflects the feeling of exuberance that target customers seek. Caesars Entertainment sends out over 250 million pieces of direct mail and almost 100 million e-mails to its members every year. A good customer can receive as many as 150 pieces of mail in a given year from one or all of its properties. From the customer's perspective, that might sound like a nightmare. But Caesars Entertainment has tested customer sentiment on receiving multiple mailings from multiple locations, and they actually like it. The reason is that the information that any given customer receives is relevant to him or her, not annoying. That's why Caesars Entertainment has a higher-than-average direct mail response rate.

Caesars Entertainment is certainly concerned about metrics, such as response rates, click-through rates, revenue, and customer profitability. But Caesars Entertainment's program is one of the best because it places emphasis on knowing how all the outcomes are linked. And because Caesars Entertainment CRM culture extends from the IT department to frontline employees, the gaming giant has an uncanny ability to translate all its data into an exceptional customer experience.

Marilyn Winn, the president of three Las Vegas resorts, lives and breathes Caesars Entertainment CRM culture. "My job is to make money for Caesars Entertainment by creating a great climate for customers and employees." She focuses on what goes on inside the hotel properties. She spot-checks details on casino floors and in gift shops. She attends weekly employee rallies that are not only a party but also a communications tool. Winn points out how Caesars Entertainment motivates its employees to do their best. "Every week, we survey our customers. Customer service is very specific at Caesars Entertainment's systematic." Based on customer service scores, employees have their own system for accumulating points and redeeming them for a wide variety of rewards, from iPads to pool equipment. "Every property has the goal to improve service. This is just one way we do it. We also use mystery shoppers to verify we are getting the service we want and we train our employees to our standards."[1]

Caesars Entertainment combines its service culture with the brain center of Total Rewards. After a day's gaming, Caesars Entertainment knows which customers should be rewarded with free show tickets, dinner vouchers, or room upgrades. In fact, Caesars Entertainment processes customer information in real time, from the moment customers swipe their rewards cards, creating the ideal link between data and the customer experience. Caesars Entertainment chief information officer calls this "operational CRM." Based on up-to-the-minute customer information, "the hotel clerk can see your history and determine whether you should get a room upgrade, based on booking levels in the hotel at that time and on your past level of play. A person might walk up to you while you're playing and offer you $5 to play more slots, or a free meal, or perhaps wish you a happy birthday."

Caesars Entertainment is constantly improving its technology so that it can better understand its customers and deliver a more fine-tuned experience. Most recently, Total Rewards gained the ability to track and reward nongaming spending. This is good for people who don't view themselves as big gamblers. "We wanted to make it relevant to them as well because they could spend a couple of hundred dollars on a room, the spa, food, and shows and not be treated any better than a $50-a-day customer," Norton said. This demonstrates the "total" part of Total Rewards. It isn't a program about getting people into casinos. It's a program designed to maximize the customer experience, regardless of what that experience includes.

Hitting Twenty-One

Caesars Entertainment's CRM efforts have paid off in spades. The company has found that happy customers are much more loyal. Although customer spending decreases by 10 percent based on an unhappy casino experience, it increases by 24 percent with a happy experience. And Caesars Entertainment Total Rewards customers appear to be a happier bunch. Compared with nonmembers, member customers visit the company's casinos more frequently, stay longer, and spend more of their gambling and entertainment dollars in Caesars Entertainment rather than in rival casinos. Since setting up Total Rewards, Caesars Entertainment has seen its share of customers' average annual gambling budgets rise 20 percent, and revenue from customers gambling at Caesars Entertainment rather than their "home casino" has risen 8 percent.

Although Caesars Entertainment and the entire gaming industry were hit hard by the Great Recession, things are turning back around; through its acquisitions and the success of its Total Rewards pro-ram, Caesars Entertainment is the biggest in its industry, with over

$10 billion revenue in 2010. Loveman calls Total Rewards "the vertebrae of our business," and says "it touches, in some form or fashion, 85 percent of our revenue."[2] David Norton, senior vice president and chief marketing officer, says, "We know if you like golf … chardonnay, down pillows, if you like your room close to the elevator which properties you visit, what games you play and which offers you redeemed. We not only use these things on the front end of marketing but for the service experience." Mr. Norton said it's a mixture of good customized messaging and a strong loyalty program that sets Caesars Entertainment's program apart.[3]

Caesars Entertainment shows us how marketers can use information to gain powerful market insights. Caesars Entertainment harnesses marketing information to gain customer insights while customers have been gaming, booking rooms, making travel arrangements, dining, and enjoying other activities at the company's properties. All this information is stored, analyzed, and used for enhancing customer satisfaction, experience, and loyalty.

▪▪▪ Marketing Information and Customer Insights

To create value for customers and to build meaningful relationships with them, marketers must first gain fresh, deep insights into what customers need and want. Companies use such customer insights to develop competitive advantage. Such insights come from the good marketing information.[4]

But although customer and market insights are important for building customer value and relationships, these insights can be very difficult to obtain. Customer needs and buying motives are often anything but obvious—consumers themselves usually can't tell you exactly what they need and why they buy. To gain good customer insights, marketers must effectively manage marketing information from a wide range of sources.

Marketing Information and Today's "Big Data"

Big Data presents companies with big opportunities to gain rich and timely customer insights. Courtesy of Monty Rakusen/Cultura/Getty Images.

Today's marketers have ready access to plenty of marketing information. With the recent explosion of information technologies, companies can now generate information in great quantities.

Consumers themselves are now generating tons of marketing information. Through e-mail, text messaging, blogging, and social media, consumers now volunteer a tidal wave of bottom-up information to companies and to each other.

Far from lacking information, most marketing managers are overloaded with data and often overwhelmed by it. This problem is summed up in the concept of **Big Data**. The term *Big Data* refers to the huge and complex data sets generated by today's sophisticated information generation, collection, storage, and analysis technologies. Every day, the people and systems of the world generate an amazing 2.5 quintillion bytes of new data—about a trillion gigabytes of information each year. Put in perspective, that's enough data to fill 2.47 trillion

good old CD-ROMs, a stack tall enough to go to the moon and back four times. If every word uttered by every human being who ever lived were written down and digitized, it would equal only two days' worth of the data being generated at today's rate.[5]

Big Data is characterized by three Vs: volume (large amounts of information from hundreds of terabytes to petabytes and beyond), velocity (the increasing rate at which data flows into an organization including real-time delivery), and variety (encompassing structured and unstructured formats: text from social networks, data from apps, Web services, images, GPS [global positioning system] signals, and readings from sensors).

Industry experts believe Big Data will be the primary basis of competitive advantage. Whoever unlocks the reams of data and uses it strategically for value creation and delivery will win. However, when a company designs its own databases, the information is organized and structured. The Big Data, on the other hand, is mostly external, less structured, and often incompatible with the company's own data systems. It is very challenging to store a photo, a sound bite, a video clip, or a Facebook status update in a way that it can be combined with other data and mined for useful insights.

In fact, most marketing managers are overloaded with data and often overwhelmed by it. Still, despite this data glut, marketers frequently complain that they lack enough information of the right kind. They don't need *more* information—they need *better* information. And they need to make better *use* of the information they already have. Says another marketing information expert, "Transforming today's vast, ever-increasing volume of consumer information into actionable marketing insights … is the number-one challenge for digital-age marketers."[6]

Managing Marketing Information

Thus, a company's marketing research and information system must do more than simply generate lots of information. The real value of marketing research and marketing information lies in how it is used—in the customer insights that it provides. "The value of the market research department is not determined by the number of studies that it does," says the marketing expert, "but by the business value of the insights that it produces and the decisions that it influences."[7]

Based on such thinking, many companies are now restructuring and renaming their marketing research and information functions. They are creating "customer insights teams," headed by a vice president of customer insights and made up of representatives from all of the firm's functional areas. For example, the head of marketing research at Kraft Foods is called the director of consumer insights and strategy.

Customer insight groups collect customer and market information from a wide variety of sources—ranging from traditional marketing research studies to mingling with and observing consumers to monitoring consumer social media conversations about the company and its products. They mine Big Data from variety of sources. Then they use the marketing information to develop important customer insights from which the company can create more value for its customers. For example, one customer insights group states its mission simply as "getting better at understanding our consumers and meeting their needs."

Marketing information system (MIS). A structure of people, equipment, and procedures to gather, sort, analyze, evaluate, and distribute needed, timely, and accurate information to marketing decision makers.

■■■ The Marketing Information System

A **marketing information system (MIS)** consists of people, equipment, and procedures to gather, sort, analyze, evaluate, and distribute needed, timely, and accurate information to marketing decision makers. Figure 5–1 illustrates the

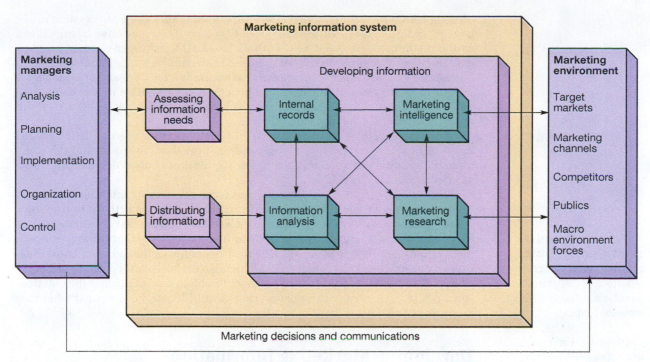

Figure 5-1
Marketing information
system.

MIS concept. The MIS begins and ends with marketing managers, but managers throughout the organization should be involved in the MIS. First, it interacts with managers to assess their information needs. Next, it develops needed information from internal company records, marketing intelligence activities, and the marketing research process. Information analysts process information to make it more useful. Finally, the MIS distributes information to managers in the right form and at the right time to help in marketing planning, implementation, and control.

We now take a closer look at the functions of a company's MIS.

Assessing Information Needs

A good MIS balances information that managers would like to have against that which they really need and is feasible to obtain. A company begins by interviewing managers to determine their information needs. For example, Mrs. Field's Cookies provides its managers with sales forecasts with updates each hour. When sales are falling behind, the computer suggests merchandising techniques such as sampling in the mall to pick up sales.[8]

Some managers ask for whatever information they can get without thinking carefully about its cost or usefulness. Too much information can be as harmful as too little. Other busy managers may fail to ask for things they need to know, or managers may not ask for some types of information that they should have. For example, managers might need to know about surges in favorable or unfavorable consumer discussions about their brands on blogs or online social media. Because they do not know about these discussions, they do not think to ask about them.

For example, managers need to anticipate new competitive product offerings. However, competitors withhold information to prevent their competition from knowing about the product. During KFC's development of one of its sandwiches, only a few corporate managers knew of the project. KFC had developed ingredient specifications for the making of the sandwich, and its suppliers had to sign secrecy agreements. KFC did not want competitors to learn about the new product offering before its test marketing. Yet competitors with a good MIS system might have picked up clues in advance about KFC's plans. They may have heard a bread supplier commenting about KFC's orders for small hamburger-style buns. They may have heard an executive stating how KFC would be strengthening its lunch business. Even with secret agreements, news inadvertently leaks out. Managers who keep their eyes and ears open can pick up on competitive moves using legal and ethical sources of information such as speeches by company executives and trade publications.

The company must estimate the value of having an item of information against the costs of obtaining it. The value depends on how it will be used, and this judgment is highly subjective. Similarly, estimating the cost of obtaining a specific item of information may be difficult.

The costs of obtaining, processing, storing, and delivering information can add up quickly. Sometimes additional information contributes little to improving a manager's decision. Its cost may exceed its benefit. Suppose that a restaurant manager estimates that launching a new menu item without further information will yield a lifetime profit of $500,000. The manager believes that additional information will improve the marketing mix and increase the company's profit to $525,000. It would be foolish to pay $30,000 or more to obtain the additional information. A good MIS balances the information users would like to have against what they really need and what is feasible to offer.

Developing Marketing Information

Information needed by marketing managers can be obtained from **internal data**, **marketing intelligence**, and **marketing research** (see Figure 5–2).

Internal Data

Many companies build extensive internal databases, electronic collections of consumer and market information obtained from data sources within the company network. Marketing managers can readily access and work with information in the database to identify marketing opportunities and problems, plan programs, and evaluate performance. The answers to the questions in Table 5–1 will help managers assess their marketing information needs.

Internal data. Internal data consist of electronic databases and nonelectronic information and records of consumer and market information obtained from within the company.

Marketing intelligence. Everyday information about developments in the marketing environment that helps managers prepare and adjust marketing plans.

Marketing research. The systematic design, collection, analysis, and reporting of data and findings relevant to a specific marketing situation facing a company.

Figure 5–2
Three sources of marketing information.

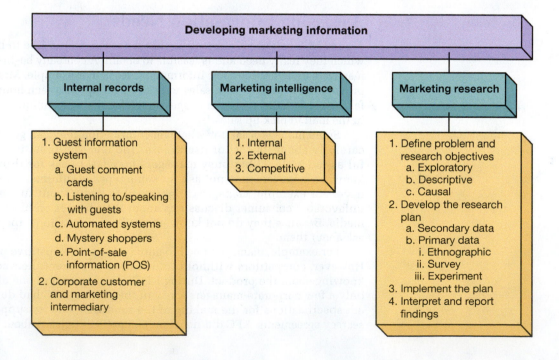

Developing marketing information		
Internal records	**Marketing intelligence**	**Marketing research**
1. Guest information system 　a. Guest comment cards 　b. Listening to/speaking with guests 　c. Automated systems 　d. Mystery shoppers 　e. Point-of-sale information (POS) 2. Corporate customer and marketing intermediary	1. Internal 2. External 3. Competitive	1. Define problem and research objectives 　a. Exploratory 　b. Descriptive 　c. Causal 2. Develop the research plan 　a. Secondary data 　b. Primary data 　　i. Ethnographic 　　ii. Survey 　　iii. Experiment 3. Implement the plan 4. Interpret and report findings

TABLE 5–1
Questions for Assessing Marketing Information Needs

1. What types of decisions do you make regularly?
2. What types of information do you need to make these decisions?
3. What types of useful information do you get regularly?
4. What social media sites can provide useful information?
5. What types of information would you like to get that you are not getting now?
6. What types of information do you get now that you don't really need?
7. What information would you want daily? weekly? monthly? yearly?
8. What topics would you like to be kept informed about?
9. What databases would be useful to you?
10. What types of information analysis programs would you like to have?
11. What would be the four most helpful improvements that could be made in the present information system?

Information in the database can come from many sources. The marketing department furnishes information on customer transactions, demographics, psychographics, and buying behavior. The customer service department keeps records of customer satisfaction or service problems. The accounting department prepares financial statements and keeps detailed records of sales, costs, and cash flows. Operations reports on production schedules, shipments, and inventories. The sales force reports on reseller reactions and competitor activities, and marketing channel partners provide data on point-of-sale (POS) transactions. Marketing managers should take advantage of the information that is currently being generated by various departments. Harnessing such information can provide powerful customer insights and competitive advantage.

Here is an example of how one company uses its internal database to make better marketing decisions:

Pizza Hut's database contains detailed customer data on 40 million U.S. households, gleaned from phone orders, online orders, and POS transactions at its more than 6,600 restaurants around the nation. Pizza Hut also uses Facebook to get customers to register for deals, collecting their e-mail, phone number, zip code, and other information. The company can slice and dice the data by favorite toppings, what you ordered last, and whether you buy a salad with your cheese and pepperoni pizza. It then uses all this data to enhance customer relationships, sending customers deals that will create another order. Says one blogger, "So who is always on my mind when I feel like pizza? Who is sending me coupons and free things that make me want to get pizza rather than make dinner? You got it, Pizza Hut. They had me buy in and now they'll have my loyalty. They make it so easy that I wouldn't want to bother getting it anywhere else."[9]

Internal databases usually can be accessed more quickly and cheaply than other information sources, but they also present some problems. Because internal information was often collected for other purposes, it may be incomplete or in the wrong form for marketing decisions. For example, sales and cost data used by the accounting department for preparing financial statements must be adapted for use in evaluating the value of specific customer segment, sales force, or channel performance. Data also ages quickly; keeping the database current requires a major effort. In addition, a large company produces mountains of information, which must be well integrated and readily accessible so managers can find it easily and use it effectively. Managing that much data requires highly sophisticated equipment and techniques.

Every company contains more information than any manager can possibly know or analyze. The information is scattered in countless databases, plans, and records, and in the heads of many longtime managers. The company must somehow bring order to its information gold mine, so that its managers can more easily find answers to questions and make informed decisions. Increasingly, companies are creating **data warehouses** to house their customer data in a single, more accessible location. Then, using powerful data mining techniques, they search for meaningful patterns in the data and communicate them to managers. For example, a hotel can use data to examine profiles of customers who respond positively to particular types of promotions and events invitations. Then, the hotel marketing department can identify customers with the same profiles and target them for similar promotions and events.

Useful marketing information is contained in kitchen production schedules and sales reports, front-desk reports, sales call reports, and functions. Managers can use information gathered from these and other sources to evaluate performance and detect problems and opportunities. Here are some examples of how companies use internal records to make marketing decisions:[10]

- Hotel managers use reservations records and registration information to aid in timing their advertising and sales calls. If most vacationers book February reservations in November, advertising in December will be too late.

- Reservation records also provide information concerning the hotel's top-producing travel agents. Hotel representatives can phone, fax, or visit travel agents to inform them of hotel-sponsored promotional activities in an effort to generate a higher volume of room sales.

- Louisiana found through visitors' studies that most families plan for their summer vacations in the spring. They now advertise to the family market January through May, so their message will be in front of prospective visitors while they are making the vacation decision.

GUEST HISTORY INFORMATION   The single most important element in any hospitality MIS is to have a process for capturing and using information concerning guests. Guest information is vital to improving service, creating effective advertising and sales promotion programs, developing new products, improving existing products, and developing marketing and sales plans and to the development and use of an effective revenue management program. Unfortunately, far too many hospitality firms have only a vague idea of who their guests are.

Specific guest information needs may include any or all of the information shown in Table 5–2. At first appearance this list undoubtedly seems overbearing and unduly inquisitive. The fact is that hospitality companies increasingly collect and use this type of information. Obviously, a hotel, resort, cruise line, or other hospitality company must be very careful not to infringe on the privacy rights of guests or to disturb them. An amazing amount of this information is available from internal records. This requires interfacing with other departments, such as reservations and accounting.

GUEST INFORMATION TRENDS   Information concerning guest trends is vital to planning and revenue/yield management. Types of guest trend information used by hotels, airlines, cruise lines, and auto rental companies include the following:

- Booking patterns
- Cancellations
- Conversion percentages (percentage of inquiries to reservations)
- Overbooking patterns
- Historical trends on occupancy for prime, shoulder, and low seasons
- Yield patterns by season

Data warehouses. Collect data from a variety of sources and store it in an accessible location.

TABLE 5–2

Specific Guest Information That Might Be Collected

Personal guest information	Type of primary product/service purchased
Name	Examples for a hotel:
Address	Regular sleeping room
Postal code	Suite
E-mail address	Deluxe suite
Phone numbers	Other purchases (cross-purchases)
Home	Examples for a hotel:
Work	Long-distance phone
Cell	Laundry
E-mail	Room service
Number in party	Minibar
Reason for trip	Hotel restaurants
Business	Health club
Pleasure	Recreational facilities
Emergency	Retail products charged to bill
Person who made reservation	Length of stay
Self-days stayed	Specific dates as guest
Employer	Method of arrival
Source of reservation	Personal auto
Name of employer	Rental auto
Address of employer	Tour bus
Title/position	Train
Method of payment	Taxi or limo
Credit card	Member of frequent guest programs
Which?	This hotel (number)
Cash	Others presented for credit
Check	Airline (number)
Bill to company	Company (number)

Guest history records enable hotel marketers to identify repeat guests and their individual needs and preferences. If a guest requests a particular newspaper delivered during one stay, a notation entered into the guest's file will ensure that the newspaper is received during all future visits. If a luxury hotel upgrades its guests to a better room on their fifth visit, its managers are increasing guest satisfaction. Frequent guests appreciate the free upgrade, and many request the higher-priced room on the next visit.

GUEST INFORMATION MANAGEMENT   Acquisition of this critical information cannot be left to chance or the whims of department managers. A system for obtaining guest information may include any or all of the techniques discussed next.

Guest Comment Cards   Guest comment cards are often found on dining room tables and in guest rooms or are handed to departing customers. They provide useful information and can provide insights into problem areas in departments and service delivery system to take corrective actions. A problem with guest comment cards is that they may not reflect the opinions of the majority of guests. Commonly, only about 1 to 2 percent of the people who are very angry or very pleased take the time to complete a card.[11] Thus comment cards can be useful in spotting problem areas, but they are not a good indication of overall guest satisfaction. Also, if the distribution and control of comment cards is not well thought out, employees may selectively distribute comment cards to guests they feel will give a positive response. Employees may also discard negative comment cards if they have the opportunity to do so. Many companies have the card mailed to a corporate office to avoid this problem.

Listening to and Speaking with Guests   Many organizations have developed formal ways of interacting with guests. Hotels offer free receptions in the afternoon for their frequent guests. This not only is a way of saying thank you to the guests but also provides an opportunity for managers to speak with guests. Sea World in Australia requires that managers take several customer surveys every week. This is an excellent way to find out what guests think, and it lets management hear it firsthand. Wyndham hotels now call all guests five minutes before their room service order will arrive. This procedure was developed as a result of a guest's comment. The female business traveler said she often orders room service, takes a shower, gets dressed, and then eats breakfast. The call lets her know when the service person will arrive so she does not get caught in the shower. Wyndham found that all business travelers appreciated this thoughtfulness, and they were able to create a better service based on talking with their customers. Gaining information from your guests lets them know you are interested in them and can help create trust and customer loyalty.[12] Trump Hotel Collection has created a guest preferences program across its brands, named Trump Attaché, to treat every guest like a VIP, with a tenet "No stay should feel like the first." A personal "concierge" is assigned to guests to take care of their individual needs. The company collects and stores every request and all the individual preferences their employees observe about each guest during their stay. The Attaché team contacts the guests prior to their arrival and after their departure to know their likes and dislikes and their preferences, which are also recorded in the database for future visits. The company has observed that this program creates significant and enduring guest loyalty.[13]

If employees are trained to listen to guest comments and feed them back to management, this can be a powerful source of information. Your employees can be like microphones recording guest comments. For this listening to work, management has to feed back to the employees how it is using the information, and there must be trust between the employees and management. Ritz-Carlton makes excellent use of the "listening posts" concept. Horst Schulze, former president of Ritz-Carlton, said, "Keep on listening to customers because they change. And if you want to have 100% satisfied customers then you have to make sure that you listen and change—just in case they change their expectations that you change with them."[14]

Automated Systems   The decreasing cost and increasing capacity of automated guest history systems will allow hotels to create close relationships with their customers once again.[15]

Obviously, any hotel property or hospitality company, such as a large cruise line, must use automated systems. A variety of systems are available and should be examined carefully and tested before purchasing. Remember that an automated guest information system is part of broader systems such as database marketing and yield/revenue management.

An automated guest history system can be of great benefit to the sales force. Salespeople can pull guest histories by a specific geographic area, such as a city. This information can greatly assist in a sales blitz by identifying frequent guests who can receive top priority in the blitz. The guest history can also identify former frequent guests who are no longer using the hotel. Salespeople will want to call on these former clients to see if they can regain their business.

An automated guest history system offers a real competitive advantage to a chain, particularly a smaller chain. "By means of a centralized system or network, a group of hotels could share guest information. Imagine how impressed a guest would be if he or she requested a suite, champagne, and a hypoallergenic pillow when staying at a hotel in Boston, then received the same services at a chain affiliate in Maui without even having to ask."[16]

Mystery shoppers. Hospitality companies often hire disguised or mystery shoppers to pose as customers and report back on their experience.

Mystery Shoppers Mystery shopping is estimated to be more than a $1.5 billion industry. Hospitality companies often hire disguised or **mystery shoppers** to pose as customers and report back on their experience. Mystery shoppers are used in all types of operations. McDonald's uses a mystery shopping program to make sure their stores are performing to their standards. They post the results on the Web, making them accessible to local managers and corporate managers.[17] Companies hire mystery shoppers to examine their competitors, as well.

A mystery shopper works best if there is a possibility for recognition and reward for good job performance. This is the concept of positive reinforcement. The most effective mystery shopping systems provide the employees with a list of the items the mystery shoppers will be checking. If employees feel that the only purpose of a disguised shopper program is to report poor service and reprimand them, the program will not fulfill its full potential.

Point-of-Sale Information For restaurants, the POS register will undoubtedly offer opportunities to compile and distribute, through a computer, information that is currently entered into reports manually. A POS system could collect information about individual restaurant patrons where credit cards are used.

Some observers of the fast-food industry believe that future POS systems will use expert systems that employ computers using artificial intelligence. One possible scenario is the "computaburger." Data concerning customer preference, order size, and volume will be taken from a POS machine and provided to an expert system. The expert system will then predict and possibly even order a volume of hamburger and the accompanying condiments for specific times in each day.[18]

The casino industry has displayed a high interest in POS systems and their increasing sophistication. Some slot machines are now capable of recording the numbers of play and the win–loss record of frequent players who activate the machines through use of a magnetic card. The player receives points based on the amount of play, and the casino is able to track the playing habits of players using the slot club cards. Systems are also in place in most casinos to track players who are brought to the casino by junket reps. Tracking of these players is the responsibility of the pit boss in each gaming area, such as blackjack.

The need to develop and use reliable guest information, particularly guest satisfaction data, has been examined by researchers within the restaurant industry, who observed that "restaurant failures are partly a result of management's lack of strategic orientation in measuring and focusing on customer satisfaction."[19]

CORPORATE CUSTOMER AND MARKETING INTERMEDIARY INFORMATION A database of customers/prospects is of great value to a professional sales force. The sales force of Benchmark Hospitality Conference Resorts is trained to go beyond demographic studies and to target prospects by geography and industry segment. Benchmark's salespeople monitor the health of specific industries and qualify prospects. Before arranging a sales meeting with any corporate meeting planner, the salesperson obtains marketing information concerning the prospect, such as the following:

- The industry standing and strategic outlook for growth
- Profit and loss statements from annual reports
- Debt-to-equity ratios
- Corporate culture information
- Data concerning how this company uses meetings

This information can be obtained from annual reports, financial analyses of public companies, and articles on the company, and by talking with company employees. In addition to detailed information concerning prospects, Benchmark expects sales force members to be regular readers of the business press, such as the *Wall Street Journal* and the *New York Times*.[20]

Marketing Intelligence

Marketing intelligence includes everyday information about developments in the marketing environment that helps managers prepare and adjust marketing plans and short-run tactics. Marketing intelligence systems determine the needed intelligence, and they collect and deliver it in a useful format to marketing managers.

INTERNAL SOURCES OF MARKETING INTELLIGENCE   Marketing intelligence can be gathered by a company's executives, front-desk staff, service staff, purchasing agents, and sales force. Employees, unfortunately, are often too busy to pass on important information. The company must sell them on their role as intelligence gatherers and train them to spot and report new developments. Managers should debrief contact personnel regularly.

Hotel owners and managers are essential parts of a marketing intelligence system. John F. Power, the general manager of the New York Hilton and Towers, served in this role on a trip to Japan. "I realized how different a Japanese breakfast is from our own," said Power, "and while most people like to sample the cuisine of the country they are visiting, everyone prefers to eat familiar food for breakfast."

As a result of marketing intelligence gathered on Power's trip, the New York Hilton now serves miso soup, nori (dried seaweed), yakizanaka (grilled fish), raw eggs, natto (fermented beans), oshiako (pickled vegetables), and rice as an authentic Japanese breakfast buffet.[21]

EXTERNAL SOURCES OF MARKETING INTELLIGENCE   A hospitality company must encourage suppliers, convention and tourist bureaus, and travel agencies to pass along important intelligence. It is worthwhile for a hospitality company to encourage the gathering of this information by treating vendors, salespeople, and potential employees in a friendly and receptive manner. Members of management should be encouraged to join community and professional organizations where they are likely to obtain essential marketing information.

Hotel and restaurant managers are in a particularly good position to acquire excellent information by entertaining key information sources in their properties. Sales force members are excellent conduits of information.

Sometimes rival companies offer you the information. For example, Bob Ayling, ex-chief executive of British Airways, accomplished such a mission when he visited the offices of the recently launched EasyJet. Ayling approached the company's founder, Stelios Haji-Ioannou, to ask whether he could visit, claiming to be fascinated as to how the Greek entrepreneur had made the budget airline formula work. Haji-Ioannou not only agreed, but allegedly he showed Ayling his business plan. A year later, British Air announced the launch of Go. "It was a carbon copy of EasyJet," says EasyGroup's director of corporate affairs. "Same planes, same direct ticket sales, same use of a secondary airport, and same idea to sell on-board refreshments. They succeeded in stealing our business model—it was a highly effective spying job."[22]

SOURCES OF COMPETITIVE COMPETITION   Competitive intelligence is available from competitors' annual reports, trade magazine articles, speeches, press releases, brochures, and advertisements. Hotel and restaurant managers should also visit their competitors' premises periodically. As mentioned in Chapter 4, a major consideration in any competitive information system is clearly defining the competition. Marketing intelligence techniques range from benchmarking competitors' products to researching on the Internet and monitoring social media buzz.

Social media companies such as Revinate provide hotel reputation benchmarking reports based on hotel review scores in social media sites and services to monitor your competition performance in social media on daily basis. Benchmarking allows hotels to track their performance against the competition and take actions.[23]

Monthly Performance at a Glance—My Property vs. Competitive Set

Upper Upscale Urban Hotel 555 Central Ave Any City, ST 12345-1234 Phone: (555) 121-1212 STR # 1234 ChainID: MgtCo: None Owner: None
For the Month of December 2012   Date Created: January 18, 2013   Monthly Competitive Set Data Excludes Subject Property

| | December 2012 | | | | | | | | |
| | Occupancy (%) | | | ADR | | | RevPAR | | |
	My Prop	Comp Set	Index (MPI)	My Prop	Comp Set	Index (ARI)	My Prop	Comp Set	Index (RGI)
Current Month	51.3	54.0	95.0	124.26	126.44	98.3	63.73	68.28	93.3
Year to Date	66.8	71.6	93.3	147.67	158.47	93.2	98.64	113.40	87.0
Running 3 Month	59.4	66.8	88.9	149.58	159.19	94.0	88.86	106.40	83.5
Running 12 Month	66.8	71.6	93.3	147.67	158.47	93.2	98.64	113.40	87.0

| | December 2012 vs. 2011 Percent Change (%) | | | | | | | | |
| | Occupancy | | | ADR | | | RevPAR | | |
	My Prop	Comp Set	Index (MPI)	My Prop	Comp Set	Index (ARI)	My Prop	Comp Set	Index (RGI)
Current Month	-22.7	-16.2	-7.8	-0.8	-2.8	2.0	-23.4	-18.6	-5.9
Year to Date	-8.5	1.2	-9.5	4.4	5.8	-1.3	-4.4	7.0	-10.7
Running 3 Month	-16.6	-2.7	-14.2	-0.5	6.5	-6.5	-17.0	3.6	-19.8
Running 12 Month	-8.5	1.2	-9.5	4.4	5.8	-1.3	-4.4	7.0	-10.7

SMITH TRAVEL RESEARCH, Inc.

The Star report allows a hotel to compare how it is doing compared to a competitive set the management selects. The competitive set statistics are always shown as group data so the hotel is never able to determine the actual statistics for the different members of the competitive set. The Star report is a commonly used tool to provide competitive intelligence in the hotel industry. Provided with permission for Smith Travel Research Monthly Performance at a Glance—My Property vs. Competitive Set. Courtesy of Smith Travel Research.

"In today's information age, companies are leaving a paper trail of information online," says an online intelligence expert. Today's managers "don't have to simply rely on old news or intuition when making investment and business decisions."[24] Using Internet search engines, marketers can search specific competitor names, events, or trends and see what turns up. Intelligence seekers can also pore through any of thousands of online databases. Some are free. For example, the U.S. Securities and Exchange Commission's database provides a huge stockpile of financial information on public competitors. And for a fee, companies can subscribe to more than 3,000 online databases and information search services such as Dialog, DataStar, LEXIS-NEXIS, Dow Jones News Retrieval, UMI ProQuest, and Dun & Bradstreet's Online Access. Hospitality managers can also subscribe to newsletters such as HotelMarketing.com, National Restaurant Association Smart Brief, and HotelOnline.net. One news service, HotelOnline.com, has editions by country, including Brazil, Germany, China, Poland, and Romania. To get your country's edition, add your country's Internet abbreviation to the URL, for example, www.HotelOnline.com.br for Brazil.

Associations sometimes collect data from member companies, compile it, and make it available to members for a reasonable fee. Information of this nature can often be misleading because member companies frequently provide incorrect data or may refuse to contribute any statistics if they have a dominant market share.

Marketing Research

Managers cannot always wait for information to arrive in bits and pieces from the marketing intelligence system. They often require formal studies of specific situations. When McDonald's decided to add salads to its menu, its planners needed to research customers' preferences for types of vegetables and dressings.

Ben's Steakhouse in Palm Beach, Florida, would like to know what percentage of its target market has heard of Ben's, how they heard about Ben's, what they know, and how they feel about the steakhouse. This would enable Ben's Steakhouse to know how effective their marketing communications have been. Casual marketing intelligence cannot answer these questions. Managers sometimes need to commission formal marketing research.

Marketing research is a process that identifies and defines marketing opportunities and problems, monitors and evaluates marketing actions and performance, and communicates the findings and implications to management.[25] Marketing researchers engage in a wide variety of activities. Their 10 most common activities are measurement of market potentials, market-share analysis, the determination of market characteristics, sales analysis, studies of business trends, short-range forecasting, competitive product studies, long-range forecasting, MIS studies, and testing of existing products.

A company can conduct marketing research by employing its own researchers or hiring outside researchers. Most large companies—in fact, more than 73 percent—have their own marketing research departments. But even companies with their own departments hire outside firms to do fieldwork and special tasks.

Frank Camacho, a former vice president of corporate marketing services for Marriott, listed Marriott's research priorities as follows:[26]

- Market segmentation and sizing
- Concept development and product testing
- Price-sensitivity assessment
- Advertising and promotions assessment
- Market tracking
- Customer satisfaction

Figure 5–3
Marketing research process.

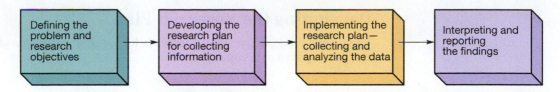

Defining the problem and research objectives → Developing the research plan for collecting information → Implementing the research plan—collecting and analyzing the data → Interpreting and reporting the findings

Small hotels or restaurants can obtain research help from nearby universities or colleges with business or hospitality programs. College marketing classes can be used to do exploratory research, find information about prospective customers, and conduct customer surveys. Instructors often arrange for their classes to gain marketing research experience in this way.

The marketing research process consists of four steps (see Figure 5–3): defining the problem and research objectives, developing the research plan, implementing the research plan, and interpreting and reporting the findings.

Defining the Problem and Research Objectives

Managers must work closely with marketing researchers to define the problem and the research objectives. The manager best understands the problem or decision for which information is needed, and the researcher best understands marketing research and how to obtain the information.

Managers must know enough about marketing research to interpret the findings carefully. If they know little about marketing research, they may accept the wrong information, draw the wrong conclusions, or request much more information than they need. Marketing researchers can help the manager define the problem and use the findings correctly.

In one case a restaurant manager hired a researcher to determine the restaurant's level of awareness among the target market. The manager felt that lack of awareness explained low patronage. The researcher found, to the contrary, that many people were aware of the restaurant but thought of it as a special-occasion rather than an everyday restaurant. The manager had misdefined the problem and the research objective.

Assuming the problem is well defined, the manager and researcher must set research objectives. A marketing research project can have one of three types of objectives: **exploratory research**, to gather preliminary information that will help define the problem and suggest hypotheses; **descriptive research**, to describe the size and composition of the market; and **causal research**, to test hypotheses about cause-and-effect relationships. Managers often start with exploratory research and later follow with descriptive and/or causal research.

A sad example of the need for marketing research was a self-help project initiated on U.S. Indian reservations. A total of 52 hotels were built as a result of promoting and anticipating tourism. Only two survived because of poorly conceived plans. In several cases, hotels were built in seldom-visited remote areas. Marketing research could have provided valuable information, such as visitor trends to the areas, identification of possible market segments, plus their size and travel preferences.[27]

Exploratory research.
Marketing research to gather preliminary information that will help to better define problems and suggest hypotheses.

Descriptive research.
Marketing research to better describe marketing problems, situations, or markets, such as the market potential for a product or the demographics and attitudes of consumers.

Causal research. Marketing research to test hypotheses about cause-and-effect relationships.

A cruise in Victoria Harbor is a popular tourist activity in Hong Kong. Tourist authorities such as the Hong Kong Tourist Association use research to determine who comes to their cities and what tourist attractions create value for them. Courtesy of Norman Chan/Shutterstock.

Developing the Research Plan

The second marketing research step calls for determining the needed information and developing a data-collection plan.

Determining Specific Information Needs

Research objectives must be translated into specific information needs. When Marriott decided to research a new lower-priced hotel system, it had two goals: to pull travelers away from competitors and to minimize cannibalization of its own existing hotels. This research might call for the following specific information:[28]

- What features should the hotel offer?

- How should the new hotels be priced?

- Where should the hotels be located? Can they safely be located near existing Marriott hotels without incurring cannibalization?

- What are the probable sales and profits?

Gathering Secondary Information

Secondary data. Information that already exists somewhere, having been collected for another purpose.

Primary data. Information collected for the specific purpose at hand.

To meet a manager's information needs, researchers can gather secondary data, primary data, or both. **Secondary data** consist of information already in existence somewhere, having been collected for another purpose. **Primary data** consist of information collected for the specific purpose at hand.

Researchers usually start by gathering secondary data. Secondary data are usually obtained more quickly and at a lower cost than primary data. For example, Restaurants USA, published by the National Restaurant Association, provides a yearly projection of sales for food-service establishments, presenting the projections by state and by industry segment. A company has the options of paying a research firm to develop this information or of joining the National Restaurant Association and receiving this information through its publication. The latter is more cost effective. Groups on social media sites can also be good sources of secondary information. LinkedIn, for example, has groups that include hotel sales, revenue management, event management, and lodging, food, and beverage trends.

Basing decisions on secondary data, however, can also present problems. The required information may not exist. Even when it exists, it might not be very relevant, accurate, current, and impartial. For example, a trade magazine wanted to identify the best hotel chains in the minds of corporate travel managers and travel agents. It distributed its survey as inserts in its magazine. The response rate was less than 0.05 percent. Yet the magazine issued a ranking based on this unreliable response rate.[29] Additionally, if research of this type is not properly designed, it can favor the companies with the most hotels or restaurants because they will be more familiar to the respondent.

Secondary data provide a good starting point for marketing research. However, when secondary sources cannot provide all the needed information, the company must collect primary data.

Planning Primary Data Collection

Some managers collect primary data by developing a few questions and finding people to interview. But data collected casually can be useless or, even worse, misleading. Table 5–3 shows that designing a plan for primary data-collection calls for decisions about research approaches, contact methods, a sampling plan, and research instruments.

TABLE 5–3
Planning Primary Data Collection

Research Approaches	Contact Methods	Sampling Plan	Research Instruments
Observation	Mail	Sampling unit	Questionnaire
Survey	Telephone	Sample size	Mechanical instruments
Experiment	Personal	Sampling procedure	
	Online		

Observational research. The gathering of primary data by observing relevant people, actions, and situations.

RESEARCH APPROACHES   Three basic research approaches are observations, surveys, and experiments. **Observational research** is the gathering of primary data by observing relevant people, actions, and situations. For example, a multiunit food-service operator sends researchers into competing restaurants to learn menu item prices, check portion sizes and consistency, and observe point-of-purchase merchandising. Another restaurant evaluates possible new locations by checking the locations of competing restaurants, traffic patterns, and neighborhood conditions. A hotel chain sends observers posing as guests into its coffee shops to check on cleanliness and customer service. Marriott International choose bathroom amenities based on observational research. The design and development team has tested 52 brands of shampoo, conditioner, body gel, lotion, and soap before choosing the ideal one for Marriott brands. The team observes how frequently guests use in-room amenities and whether they take any amenity with them, indicating they have liked the product.[30]

Observational research can yield information that people are normally unwilling or unable to provide. Observing numerous plates containing uneaten portions of the same menu item indicates that the food is not satisfactory. But feelings, beliefs, and attitudes that motivate buying behavior cannot be observed. Long-run or infrequent behavior is also difficult to observe. Because of these limitations, researchers often supplement observation with survey research.

A wide range of companies now use **ethnographic research**, which involves sending trained observers to watch and interact with consumers in their "natural habitat."

Ethnographic research. Trained observers interact with and/or observe consumers in their natural habitat.

Hotel companies will send researchers into hotel rooms after the guest has checked out to see how the guest has changed the furniture and accessories in the room to fit their wants. For example, did the guest move the TV around so they could see it while working at the desk? Did he or she move furniture next to the desk to create additional work space, to put materials on while they were working? By observing how the customer uses the room, ethnographers can help designers create rooms and furniture that meet the needs of the guest. Ethnographers have also helped in the design of hotel lobbies to make them more social. Rather than working, reading, watching television, or spending time on social media in the confines of his or her room, the guest can now come to the lobby and engage in these activities in an inviting and open environment.

Marriott design and development team continuously experiments with bathroom amenities. Courtesy of ismagination/ Shutterstock.

Ethnographic research often yields the kinds of details that just don't emerge from traditional research questionnaires or focus groups. Although traditional quantitative research approaches seek to test known hypotheses and obtain answers to well-defined product or strategy questions, observational research can generate fresh customer and market insights. The beauty of ethnography is that it provides a richer understanding of consumers than traditional research.[31] This is especially important in hotels and restaurants and all hospitality products where there is social interaction between the customers. One problem with customer research is consumers cannot always tell you what they want, especially if the product has not been developed. Ethnography gives us insight into how consumers use a product that they may not be able to articulate.

Beyond conducting ethnographic research in physical consumer environments, many companies now routinely conduct "Webnography" research—observing consumers in a natural context on the Internet. Observing people as they interact online can provide useful insights into both online and off-line buying motives and behavior.[33]

Marketing HIGHLIGHT 5–1
Ethnographic Research: Watching What Consumers Really Do

girl walks into a bar and says to the bartender, "Give me a Diet Coke and a clear sight line to those guys drinking Miller Lite in the corner." If you're waiting for a punch line, this is no joke. The "girl" in this situation is Emma Gilding, corporate ethnographer at ad agency Ogilvy & Mather. In this case, her job is to hang out in bars around the country and watch groups of guys knocking back beers with their friends. No kidding. This is honest-to-goodness, cutting-edge marketing research—ethnography style.

As a videographer filmed the action, Gilding kept tabs on how close the guys stood to one another. She eavesdropped on stories and observed how the mantle was passed from one speaker to another, as in a tribe around a campfire. Back at the office, a team of trained anthropologists and psychologists pored over more than 70 hours of footage from five similar nights in bars from San Diego to Philadelphia. One key insight: Miller is favored by groups of drinkers, while its main competitor, Bud Lite, is a beer that sells to individuals. The result was a hilarious series of ads that cut from a Miller Lite drinker's weird experiences in the world—getting caught in the subway taking money from a blind musician's guitar case or hitching a ride in the desert with a deranged trucker—to shots of him regaling friends with tales over a brew. The Miller Lite ads got high marks from audiences for their entertainment value and emotional resonance.

Today's marketers face many difficult questions: What do customers *really* think about a product and what do they say about it to their friends? How do they *really* use it? Will they tell you? *Can* they tell you? All too often, traditional research simply can't provide accurate answers. To get deeper insights, many companies use ethnographic research, watching and interacting with consumers in their "natural environments."

Ethnographers are looking for "consumer truth." In surveys and interviews, customers may state (and fully believe) certain preferences and behaviors, when the reality is actually quite different. Ethnography provides an insider's tour of the customer's world, helping marketers get at what consumers *really* do rather than what they *say* they do. "That might mean catching a heart-disease patient scarfing down a meatball sub and a cream soup while extolling the virtues of healthy eating," observes one ethnographer, "or a diabetic vigorously salting his sausage and eggs after explaining how he refuses jelly for his toast."[32]

By entering the customer's world, ethnographers can scrutinize how customers think and feel as it relates to their products. Ethnographic research often yields the kinds of intimate details that just don't emerge from traditional focus groups and surveys. For example, focus groups told the Best Western hotel chain that it's men who decide when to stop for the night and where to stay. But videotapes of couples on cross-country journey showed it was usually the women. And observation can often uncover problems that customers don't even know they have. By videotaping consumers in the shower, plumbing fixture maker Moen uncovered safety risks that consumers didn't recognize—such as the habit some women have of shaving their legs while holding on to one unit's temperature control. Moen would find it almost impossible to discover such design flaws simply by asking questions.

Experiencing firsthand what customers experience can also provide powerful insights. Thus more and more marketing researchers are getting up close and personal with consumers—watching them closely as they act and interact in natural settings or stepping in to observe firsthand how they behave.

Sources: Adapted excerpts and other information from Brooks Barnes, "Disney Expert Uses Science to Draw Boy Viewers," *New York Times* (April 14, 2009): A1; Linda Tischler, "Every Move You Make," *Fast Company* (April 2004): 73–75; Ellen Byron, "Seeing Store Shelves Through Senior Eyes," *Wall Street Journal* (September 14, 2009): B1; Spencer E. Ante, with Cliff Edwards, "The Science of Desire," *Bloomberg Businessweek* (June 5, 2006), http://www.businessweek.com/magazine/content/06_23/b3987083.htm (accessed August 25, 2011).

Observational and ethnographic research often yields the kinds of details that just don't emerge from traditional research questionnaires or focus groups. Yes, companies are still using focus groups, surveys, and demographic data to glean insights into the consumer's mind. But closely observing people where they live and work allows companies to zero in on their customers' unarticulated desires.[34] Agrees another researcher, "Classic market research doesn't go far enough. It can't grasp what people can't imagine or articulate. Think of the Henry Ford quote: 'If I had asked people what they wanted, they would have said faster horses.'"[35]

Survey research is the approach best suited to gathering descriptive information. Survey research can be structured or unstructured. Structured surveys use formal lists of questions asked of all respondents in the same way. Unstructured surveys let the interviewer probe respondents and guide the interview according to their answers.

Survey research may be direct or indirect. In the direct approach, the researcher asks direct questions about behavior or thoughts, for example, "Why don't you eat at Arby's?" Using the indirect approach, the researcher might ask: "What kinds of people eat at Arby's?" From the response, the researcher may be able to discover why the consumer avoids Arby's. In fact, it may suggest factors the consumer is not consciously aware of.

The major advantage of survey research is its flexibility. It can be used to obtain many different kinds of information in many different marketing situations. Depending on the survey design, it may also provide information more quickly and at lower cost than can be obtained by observational or **experimental research.**

Survey research also has some limitations. Sometimes people are unable to answer survey questions because they cannot remember or never thought about what they do and why. Or they may be reluctant to answer questions asked by unknown interviewers about things that they consider private. Busy people may not want to take the time. Respondents may answer survey questions even when they do not know the answer in order to appear smart or well informed. Or they may try to help the interviewer by giving pleasing answers. Careful survey design can help minimize these problems.

The most scientifically valid research is experimental research, designed to capture cause-and-effect relationships by eliminating competing explanations of the observed findings. If the experiment is well designed and executed, research and marketing managers can have confidence in the conclusions.

Experiments call for selecting matched groups of subjects, subjecting them to different treatments, controlling extraneous variables, and checking whether observed response differences are statistically significant. If we can eliminate or control extraneous factors, we can relate the observed effects to the variations in the treatments or stimuli. American Airlines might introduce in-flight Internet service on one of its regular flights from Chicago to Tokyo and charge $15 one week and $10 the next week. If the plane carried approximately the same number of first-class passengers each week and the particular weeks made no difference, the airline could relate any significant difference in the number of passengers using the service to the different prices charged. Marketers using direct mail often will test different pricing levels when they send out an offer.

Experimental research is best suited for gathering causal information. Researchers at Arby's might use experiments before adding a new sandwich to the menu to answer such questions as the following:

- By how much will the new sandwich increase Arby's sales?

- How will the new sandwich affect the sales of other menu items?

- Which advertising approach would have the greatest effect on sales of the sandwich?

- How would different prices affect the sales of the sandwich?

For example, to test the effects of two different prices, Arby's might set up the following simple experiment. The company could introduce the new sandwich

Survey research. The gathering of primary data by asking people questions about their knowledge, attitudes, preferences, and buying behavior.

Experimental research. The gathering of primary data by selecting matched groups of subjects, giving them different treatments, controlling related factors, and checking for differences in group responses.

at one price in its restaurants in one city and at another price in restaurants in a similar city. If the cities are very similar and if all other marketing efforts for the sandwich are identical, differences in sales volume between the two cities should be related to the price charged.

CONTACT METHODS.   Information can be collected by mail, telephone, or personal interview.

Mail questionnaires have many advantages. They can be used to collect large amounts of information at a low cost per respondent. Respondents may give more honest answers to personal questions on a mail questionnaire than they would to an unknown interviewer in person or over the phone. No interviewer is involved to bias respondents' answers. Mail questionnaires are convenient for respondents, who can answer the survey when they have time. It is also a good way to reach people who often travel, such as meeting planners.

Mail questionnaires also have some disadvantages. They are not very flexible, they require simple and clearly worded questions, all respondents answer the same questions in a fixed order, and the researcher cannot adapt the questionnaire based on earlier answers. Mail surveys usually take longer to complete than telephone or personal surveys, and the response rate (the number of people returning completed questionnaires) is often very low. When the response rate is low, respondents may not be typical of the population being sampled. Also, the researcher has little control over who answers the questionnaire in the household or office.

Telephone interviewing provides a method for gathering information quickly. It also offers greater flexibility than mail questionnaires. Interviewers can explain questions that are not understood; they can skip some questions and probe more on others, depending on respondents' answers. Telephone interviewing allows greater sample control. Interviewers can ask to speak to respondents who have the desired characteristics or can even request someone by name, and response rates tend to be higher than with mail questionnaires.

Customer intercept surveys collected from people in a shopping mall can be a good way to access respondents for a survey. The survey often begins with screening questions to eliminate people who are not part of the target market of the hospitality firm conducting the research. Courtesy of Pearson Education.

Telephone interviewing also has drawbacks. The cost per respondent is higher than with mail questionnaires, and some people may not want to discuss personal questions with an interviewer. Using an interviewer increases flexibility but also introduces interviewer bias. The interviewer's manner of speaking, small differences in the way interviewers ask questions, and other personal factors may affect respondents' answers. Different interviewers may interpret and record responses in a variety of ways, and under time pressures, there is the possibility that some interviewers may record answers without actually asking the questions.

One growing use of telephone surveys is when the customer volunteers to take the survey and calls into a toll-free number. The customer is told at the time of purchase that he or she has been selected to take part in a survey and will receive an incentive for taking part in it. Usually these incentives range from $3 to $5 off on their next visit. Some of these surveys are automated, which reduces the cost of the survey. Phil Friedman, CEO of McAlister's Deli, states that McAlister's uses a customer call-in system, which works well. McAlister's has over 150 restaurants, mainly in the midwestern and southwestern regions of the United States. The results of the survey are posted every day on the Web. They can be searched by location, date of survey, and survey question. McAlister's shows how companies are taking advantage of technology to develop low-cost customer feedback systems that provide easy access to information.[36]

Ritz-Carlton measures the success of its customer service efforts through Gallup phone interviews, which ask both functional and emotional questions. Functional questions include: "How was the meal?" or "Was your bedroom clean?" while emotional questions reveal the customer's sense of well-being. The hotel uses these findings as well as day-to-day experiences to continually enhance and improve the experience for its guests.[37]

Unfortunately, the general public has become increasingly reluctant to participate in telephone surveys. Many unethical companies have misled respondents into believing that legitimate research is being conducted when in fact this was a ruse for a sales call. Thieves have also used this approach to find out when homeowners are likely to be away and even to determine the contents of the house.

Personal interviewing takes two forms: individual (intercept) and group interviewing. The later methods are called qualitative methods. *Individual (intercept) interviewing* involves talking with people in their homes, offices, on the street, or in shopping malls. For InterContinental Hotel Group's new fitness and wellness-themed brand, EVEN Hotels, designers conducted personal interviews by visiting travelers at their homes to ask them about their eating and exercise habits, what helps put them to sleep and how their bathrooms look.[38] The interviewer must gain the interviewee's cooperation, and the time involved can range from a few minutes to several hours. For longer surveys, a small payment is sometimes offered to respondents in return for their time.

Intercept interviews are widely used in tourism research. For instance, Las Vegas Convention and Visitors Authority uses this technique to interview 3,600 visitors annually. Interviewing is conducted at different locations and different times of the day. Upon completion of the interview, visitors are given souvenirs as "thank you's." Intercept interviews allow the research sponsor to reach known visitors in a short period of time. There may be few or no alternative methods of reaching visitors whose names and addresses are unknown. Intercept interviews generally involve the use of judgmental sampling. The interviewer may be given guidelines as to whom to "intercept," such as 20 percent under age 20 and 40 percent over age 60. This always leaves room for error and bias on the part of the interviewer, who may not be able to correctly judge age, race, and even sex from appearances. Interviewers may also be uncomfortable talking to certain ethnic or age groups.

The main drawbacks to personal interviews are cost and sampling. Personal interviews may cost three to four times as much as telephone interviews. Because group interview studies generally use small sample sizes to keep time and costs down, it may be difficult to generalize from the results. In addition, because interviewers have more freedom in personal interviews, however, interview bias is a greater problem.

A common type of group interviewing is a focus group. *Focus group interviewing* is usually conducted by inviting 6 to 10 people to gather for a few hours with a trained moderator to talk about a product, service, or organization. The moderator needs objectivity, knowledge of the subject and industry, and some understanding of group and consumer behavior. Participants normally receive a small sum or gift certificates for attending. The meeting is held in a pleasant place, and refreshments are served to create a relaxed environment. The moderator starts with broad questions before moving to more specific issues, encouraging open and easy discussion to foster group dynamics that will bring out true feelings and thoughts. At the same time, the interviewer focuses the discussion, hence the name "focus group" interviewing. Comments are recorded through note taking or on videotape and studied later to understand consumers' buying process. In many cases, a two-way mirror separates respondents from observers, who commonly include personnel from the ad agency and the client.

Focus group interviewing is rapidly becoming one of the major marketing research tools for gaining insight into consumers' thoughts and feelings. This method is especially suited for use by managers of hotels and restaurants, who have easy access to their customers. For example, some hotel managers often invite a group of hotel guests from a particular market segment to have a free breakfast with them. During the breakfast the manager gets a chance to meet the guests and discuss what they like about the hotel and what the hotel could do to make their stay more enjoyable and comfortable. The guests appreciate this recognition, and the manager gains valuable information. Restaurant managers use the same approach by holding discussion meetings with guests at lunch or dinner.

Here are examples of how restaurants have used group interviews:

- A steakhouse suffering from declining sales went to its customers to gain insight into the causes of its problem. Two focus groups were conducted, one composed of customers who indicated they would return and another composed of those who said they would not. From these sessions, the owners learned that patrons considered the restaurant a fun place but thought the food was boring. The problem was solved by expanding and upgrading the menu.[39]

- Focus groups provided critical information to Andy Reis of Café Provincial in Evanston, Illinois. He found that his clientele wanted valet parking. Reis had assumed because on-street parking and a nearby parking garage were available that parking was not a problem. He also found that his diners felt uncomfortable in the restaurant's Terrace Room. This was a casual dining room with glass tables and porch furniture. Apparently, it was too casual for his diners. The Terrace Room was remodeled, and valet parking was added. Now people request to sit in the Terrace Room. Reis states that focus groups are worthwhile if you listen carefully.[40]

Hotels have always used focus groups to provide input on service and initiatives. Social media has empowered guests to inform hotels of their likes and dislikes in real time. Hyatt recently hosted what it called "The World's Largest Focus Group," involving Hyatt employees around the world leading discussions with guests via Twitter and Facebook. In the second phase, the company conducted more than 40 focus group discussions around the world to redefine guest experience, which led to discovering new amenities like deodorant, curling irons, and healthier menu items.[41]

In-depth interviews are another form of qualitative personal interviewing. As the name states, these are individual interviews using open-ended questions. They allow the researcher to probe and gain insight into consumer behavior. For example, if someone recalls one of his or her more memorable hotel stays involved a luxurious hotel suite, the researcher can probe to see what made the hotel suite luxurious. In-depth surveys can be used instead of focus groups when it is difficult to put together a focus group. For example, we wanted to probe a number of concepts with luxury hotel guests. It was impossible to get six or more travelers to participate in a focus group at a specific time. We were able to gain interviews of individuals during breakfast.[42] One popular technique to understand consumers' thoughts and feelings about a brand or program is **Zaltman Metaphor Elicitation Technique (ZMET)** (see Marketing Highlight 5–2).

Qualitative research is useful to gain insight into definitions and concepts. A good understanding of concepts is critical to designing a survey instrument; thus, focus groups and in-depth surveys are often done as part of the survey development process. Qualitative research is also useful to gain insight into survey results. For example, quick-service restaurant customers may tell us that speed of service is important. As managers, we need to know how customers measure and define speed of service. This information can be gained through qualitative research.

Choice Hotels International initiated a "Redefined and Redesigned" plan to give a new look to Comfort brand family that includes 2,000 domestic Comfort Inn and Comfort Suites. To redesign elements and identify the amenities appealing most to the guest, the corporation has conducted extensive consumer testing that included surveying 1,500 guests in addition to in-depth interviews with developers.[43]

Online marketing research. Collecting primary data online through Internet surveys, online focus groups, Web-based experiments, or tracking of consumers' online behavior.

ONLINE MARKETING RESEARCH The growth of the Internet has had a dramatic impact on how marketing research is conducted. Increasingly, researchers are collecting primary data through **online marketing research**: Internet surveys, online panels, experiments, and online focus groups and brand communities. There are so many ways to

Marketing HIGHLIGHT 5-2 | ZMET: Getting into the Heads of Consumer

What is the meaning of a brand to consumers? How do consumers feel about a brand? Why are consumers loyal to a particular brand? Standard methods such as surveys do not address these issues at a deep level. Former Harvard Business School marketing professor Gerald Zaltman, with colleagues, developed an in-depth methodology to uncover what consumers think and feel about products, services, brands, and other things. The basic assumption behind the Zaltman Metaphor Elicitation Technique (ZMET) is that most thoughts and feelings are unconscious and shaped by a set of universal deep metaphors, basic orientations toward the world that shape everything consumers think, hear, say, or do. In other words, ZMET assumes that much of subconscious content is based in images, not words.

The ZMET technique works by first asking participants in advance to select a minimum of 12 images from their own sources (magazines, catalogs, family photo albums) to represent their thoughts and feelings about a particular issue or brand. In a one-on-one interview, the study administrator uses advanced interview techniques to explore the images with the participant and reveal hidden meanings. Finally, the participants use a computer program to create a collage with these images that communicates their subconscious thoughts and feelings about the topic. The results often significantly influence marketing actions, as the following example illustrates:

After a ZMET study of slot club members of both local and visitor at a mega resort casino, the property made significant changes in its slot club and gave the players control over their comps. Club members have started to use their cash-back points in exchange for cash, promotional credits, or gift cards at different exchange rates. The events were augmented with greater entertainment and higher prizes. To improve the slot club human aspects, the casino also provided training for managing customer interactions.

Sources: Gerald Zaltman and Lindsay Zaltman, "What Deep Metaphors Reveal About the Minds of Consumers," *Marketing Metaphoria* (Boston: Harvard Business School Press, 2008); Glenn L. Christensen and Jerry C. Olson, "Mapping Consumers' Mental Models with ZMET," *Psychology & Marketing*, 19 (June 2002): 477–502; Emily Eakin, "Penetrating the Mind by Metaphor," *New York Times*, February 23, 2002; Flavia Hendler and Kathryn A. LaTour, "A Qualitative Analysis of Slot Clubs as Drivers of Casino Loyalty," *The Cornell Hospitality Quarterly*, (May 2008): 105–121; Gerald Zaltman, *How Customers Think*. (Cambridge, MA: Harvard Business School Press, 2003).

Internet surveying is growing in popularity. It offers quick and inexpensive access to many samples. The data are also automatically tabulated, eliminating errors and time. Courtesy of mama_mia/ Shutterstock.

use the Internet to do research. A company can include a questionnaire on its Web site or social media sites or use e-mail invitation and offer an incentive to answer it, or it can place a banner on a frequently visited site such as Yahoo!, inviting people to answer some questions and possibly win a prize. One theme park management company has developed a survey panel of 11,000 guests. It surveys the members of the panel on a regular basis through the Internet. The company's research director claims Internet surveying saves him at least $30,000 over telephone surveying and provides good information.[44]

A company can also conduct online experiments. It can experiment with different prices, headlines, or product features on different Web or mobile sites or at different times to learn the relative effectiveness of their offers.

As response rates for traditional survey approaches decline and costs increase, the Internet is quickly replacing mail and the telephone as the dominant data-collection methodology. Yet, as popular as online research methods are, smart companies are choosing to use them to augment rather than replace more traditional methods. A director of marketing states, "Online is not a solution in and of itself to all of our business challenges but it does expand our toolkit."

Even smaller companies can use online survey services such as Snap Surveys (www.snapsurveys.com) and SurveyMonkey (www.surveymonkey.com) to create, publish, and

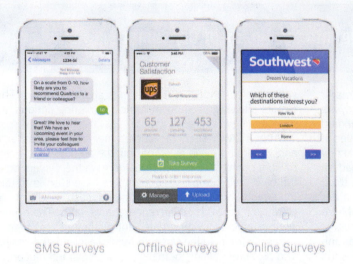

SMS Surveys   Offline Surveys   Online Surveys

Qualtrics is a survey platform provider, helping organizations collect, analyze, and act on customer, employee, and market insights. Courtesy of Qualtrics, LLC.

Online focus groups. Gathering a small group of people online with a trained moderator to chat about a product, service, or organization and gain qualitative insights about consumer attitude and behavior.

distribute their own custom online or mobile surveys in minutes. Jacob Brown, a marketing researcher specializing in Internet-based surveys, has these suggestions. As with other surveys, always do a pretest. If you have a limited number of names in your database and don't want to waste them on a pretest, buy a list with similar characteristics and use this list for your pretest.

This is a much better alternative to not pretesting. Look at the number of people who drop out after each question. If there is a high dropout rate after one question, this could indicate problems with that question. If the completion rate is low, but no one question has a high dropout rate, this could indicate the survey is too long. Using simple technology for a consumer market is critical. Don't expect respondents to wait for graphics to load or to reset their monitor's resolution. Internet surveys are quick and can be inexpensive. The response rate can be a problem if they are not properly designed and targeted.[45]

Marketing Highlight 5–3, "Pros and Cons of Online Research," outlines some of the advantages and disadvantages of online research. Online researchers have also begun to use instant messaging (IM) in various ways—to conduct a chat with a respondent, to probe more deeply with a member of an online focus group, or to direct respondents to a Web site.[47] IM is also a useful way to get teenagers to open up on topics.

Just as marketing researchers have rushed to use the Internet for quantitative surveys and data collection, they are now also adopting qualitative Internet-based research approaches, such as online focus groups, blogs, and social networks. The Internet can provide a fast, low-cost way to gain qualitative customer insights. A primary qualitative Web-based research approach is **online focus groups**. Such focus groups offer many advantages over traditional focus groups. Participants can log in from anywhere; all they need is a laptop and a Web connection. Thus, the Internet works well for bringing together people from different parts of the country or world, especially those in higher-income groups who can't spare the time to travel to a central site. Also, researchers can conduct and monitor online focus groups from just about anywhere, eliminating travel, lodging, and facility costs. Finally, although online focus groups require some advance scheduling, results are almost immediate.

Online focus groups can take any of several formats. Most occur in real time, in the form of online chat room discussions in which participants and a moderator sit around a virtual table exchanging comments. Alternatively, researchers might set up an online message board on which respondents interact over the course of several days or a few weeks. Participants log in daily and comment on focus group topics.

Although low in cost and easy to administer, online focus groups can lack the real-world dynamics of more personal approaches. To overcome these shortcomings, some researchers are now adding real-time audio and video to their online focus groups. For example, online research firm Channel M2 "puts the human touch back into online research" by assembling focus group participants in people-friendly "virtual interview rooms."[48] Participants are recruited using traditional methods and then sent a Web camera so that both their verbal and nonverbal reactions can be recorded. Participants receive instructions via e-mail, including a link to the Channel M2 online interviewing room and a toll-free teleconference number to call. At the appointed time, when they click on the link and phone in, participants sign on and see the Channel M2 interview room, complete with live video of the other participants, text chat, screen or slide sharing, and a whiteboard. Once the focus group is under way, questions and answers occur in "real time" in a

Marketing HIGHLIGHT 5–3   Pros and Cons of Online Research

Advantages

- *Online research is inexpensive.* A typical e-mail survey can cost between 20 and 50 percent less than what a conventional survey costs, and return rates can be as high as 50 percent.

- *Online research is fast.* Online surveys are fast because the survey can automatically direct respondents to applicable questions and transmit results immediately. One estimate says that 75 to 80 percent of a survey's targeted response can be generated in 40 hours using online methods compared to a telephone survey that can take 70 days to obtain 150 interviews.

- *People tend to be honest online.* Britain's online polling company YouGov.com surveyed 250 people via intercom in a booth and the other half online asking questions such as "Should there be more aid to Africa?" Online answers were deemed much more honest. People may be more open about their opinions when they can respond privately and not to another person whom they feel might be judging them, especially on sensitive topics.

- *Online research is versatile.* Increased broadband penetration offers online research even more flexibility and capabilities. For instance, virtual reality software lets visitors inspect 3D models of products such as cameras, cars, and medical equipment and manipulate product characteristics. Even at the basic tactile level, online surveys can make answering a questionnaire easier and more fun than paper-and-pencil versions.

- *Data are more accurate.* Online interviewing programs enable the survey responses to be tabulated as the respondent is entering them. As in any form of computer-aided interviewing, the next question automatically comes up in branching questions or skip sequences. For example, if a business traveler is to answer one set of questions and a pleasure traveler another set, when asked if you were traveling for business or pleasure, the proper set will come up.

Disadvantages

- *Samples can be small and skewed.* Some 33 percent of households are without Internet access in the United States; the percentage is even higher among lower-income groups, in rural areas, and in most parts of Asia, Latin America, and Central and Eastern Europe, where socioeconomic and education levels also differ. Although people older than 65 are one of the fastest growing segments of Internet users, they have been light users. Thus, one could expect to get a younger sample through an Internet survey. Tourism research has found significant differences in responses received from pen-and-paper surveys and Internet surveys, including demographic differences.[46] Although it's certain that more and more people will go online, online market researchers must find creative ways to reach population segments on the other side of the "digital divide." One option is to combine off-line sources with online findings. Providing temporary Internet access at locations such as malls and recreation centers is another strategy.

- *Online market research is prone to technological problems and inconsistencies.* Because online research is relatively new, many market researchers have not gotten survey designs right. Others overuse technology, concentrating on the bells and whistles and graphics while ignoring basic survey design guidelines. Problems also arise because browser software varies. The Web designer's final product may look very different on the research subject's screen.

Sources: "Survey: Internet Should Remain Open to All," www.consumeraffairs.com (accessed January 25, 2006); "Highlights from the National Consumers League's Survey on Consumers and Communications Technologies: Current and Future Use," www.nclnet.org/ (accessed July 21, 2005); Catherine Arnold, "Not Done Net; New Opportunities Still Exist in Online Research," *Marketing News* (April 1, 2004): 17; Louella Miles, "Online, on Tap," *Marketing* (June 16, 2004): 39–40; Suzy Bashford, "The Opinion Formers," *Revolution* (May 2004): 42–46; Nima M. Ray and Sharon W. Tabor, "Contributing Factors; Several Issues Affect e-Research Validity," *Marketing News* (September 15, 2003): 50; Bob Lamons, "Eureka! Future of B to B Research Is Online," *Marketing News* (September 24, 2001): 9–10.

remarkably lively setting. Participants comment spontaneously—verbally, via text messaging, or both. Researchers can "sit in" on the focus group from anywhere, seeing and hearing every respondent. Or they can review a recorded version at a later date.

The Internet has become an important new tool for conducting research and developing customer insights. But today's marketing researchers are going even further on the Web—well beyond structured online surveys, focus groups, and

Web communities. Increasingly, they are listening to and watching consumers by actively mining the rich veins of unsolicited, unstructured, "bottom-up" customer information already coursing around the Web. This might be as simple as scanning customer reviews and comments on the company's brand site or shopping sites such as zagat.com or tripadvisor.com. Or it might mean using sophisticated Web-analysis tools of data and text mining to deeply analyze Big Data involving consumer comments and messages found in blogs or on social networking sites, such as Facebook or Twitter. Listening to and watching consumers online can provide valuable insights into what consumers are saying or feeling about brands. As one information expert puts it, "The Web knows what you want."[49]

Perhaps the most explosive issue facing online researchers concerns consumer privacy. Some critics fear that unethical researchers will use the e-mail addresses and confidential responses gathered through surveys to sell products after the research is completed. They are concerned about the use of technologies that collect personal information online without the respondents' consent. Failure to address such privacy issues could result in angry, less-cooperative consumers and increased government intervention. For example, Dunkin' Donuts regularly eavesdrops on consumer online conversations as an important input to its customer relationship building efforts. Take the case of customer Jeff Lerner, who recently tweeted about a loose lid that popped off his Dunkin' Donuts drive-through coffee and soaked his white shirt and new car. Within minutes, Dunkin' picked up Lerner's tweet, sent him a direct message asking for his phone number, called him to apologize, and sent him a $10 gift card. Lerner found Dunkin's actions laudable. "This is social media. This is listening. This is engagement," he stated in a later blog post. However, some disconcerted consumers might see Dunkin's Twitter monitoring as an invasion of their privacy.[50]

SAMPLING PLAN Marketing researchers usually draw conclusions about large consumer groups by taking a sample. A **sample** is a segment of the population selected to represent the population as a whole. Ideally, the sample should be representative and allow the researcher to make accurate estimates of the thoughts and behaviors of the larger population.

Sample. (1) A segment of a population selected for marketing research to represent the population as a whole; (2) offer of a trial amount of a product to consumers.

Designing the sample calls for the following four decisions:

1. *Who will be surveyed?* This is not always obvious. For example, to study the decision-making process for a family vacation, should the researcher interview the husband, wife, other family members, the travel agent, or all of these? The researcher must determine what type of information is needed and who is most likely to have it.

2. *How many people should be surveyed?* Large samples give more reliable results than small samples. However, it is not necessary to sample the entire target market or even a large portion to obtain reliable results. If well chosen, samples of less than 1 percent of a population can give good reliability.

3. *How should the sample be chosen?* Sample members might be chosen at random from the entire population (a probability sample), or the researcher might select people who are easiest to obtain information from (a convenience sample). The researcher might also choose a specified number of participants from each of several demographic groups (a quota sample). These and other ways of drawing samples have different costs and time limitations and varying accuracy and statistical properties. The needs of the research project will determine which method is most effective. Table 5–4 lists the various kinds of samples.

4. *When will the survey be given?* This is particularly important in personal surveys. The days and hours should be representative of the flow of traffic. For example if 70 percent of the customers come after 7 P.M., then the data-collection needs to be heavier in the evening. The type of guest may change depending on the day or time. People working in the area may visit a restaurant at lunch, whereas people living in the area visit the restaurant for dinner. Businesspersons stay at a hotel Sunday through Thursday, and pleasure

TABLE 5–4

Types of Samples

Probability Samples	
Simple random sample	Every member of the population has a known and equal chance of selection.
Stratified random sample	The population is divided into mutually exclusive groups (e.g., age groups), and random samples are drawn from each group.
Cluster (area) sample	The population is divided into mutually exclusive groups (e.g., blocks), and the researcher draws a sample of the groups to interview.
Nonprobability Samples	
Convenience sample	The researcher selects the easiest population members from which to obtain information.
Judgment sample	The researcher uses his or her judgment to select population members who are good prospects for accurate information.
Quota sample	The researcher finds and interviews a prescribed number of people in each of several categories.

travelers are heavier users on weekends. Thus, if the population of interest is business travelers, there should be heavier sampling during the week. Failure to match the time the data is collected with business patterns can result in invalid survey results.

RESEARCH INSTRUMENTS In collecting primary data, marketing researchers have a choice of two main research instruments: the questionnaire and mechanical devices.

You can usually spot several errors in a carelessly prepared questionnaire (see Marketing Highlight 5–4).

Questionnaires The questionnaire is by far the most common instrument, whether administered in person, by phone, by e-mail, or online. Questionnaires are very flexible—there are many ways to ask questions. Closed-end questions include all the possible answers, and subjects make choices among them. Examples include multiple-choice questions and scale questions. Open-end questions allow respondents to answer in their own words. In a survey of airline users, Southwest Airlines might simply ask, "What is your opinion of Southwest Airlines?" Or it might ask people to complete a sentence: "When I choose an airline, the most important consideration is ...." These and other kinds of open-end questions often reveal more than closed-end questions because they do not limit respondents' answers.

Open-end questions are especially useful in exploratory research, when the researcher is trying to find out *what* people think but is not measuring *how many* people think in a certain way. Closed-end questions, on the other hand, provide answers that are easier to interpret and tabulate.

Researchers should also use care in the *wording* and *ordering* of questions. They should use simple, direct, and unbiased wording. Questions should be arranged in a logical order. The first question should create interest if possible, and difficult or personal questions should be asked last so that respondents do not become defensive.

In preparing a questionnaire, the marketing researcher must decide what questions to ask, what form the questions should take, and how to word and sequence the questions. Questionnaires too often omit questions that should be answered and include questions that cannot, will not, or need not be answered. Each question should be examined to ensure that it contributes to the research objectives. Questions that are merely interesting should be dropped. You can usually spot several errors in a carelessly prepared questionnaire (see Marketing Highlight 5–4).

Researchers in the hospitality industry must be extremely careful in developing questions and selecting the sample not to offend respondents unwittingly. This problem is less pervasive with many products, such as building

Marketing HIGHLIGHT 5–4   A "Questionable" Questionnaire

Suppose that the following questionnaire has been prepared by a restaurant manager to build a profile of his or her potential market. How do you as a consumer feel about each question?

1. What is your income to the nearest hundred dollars?
   People don't necessarily know their income to the nearest hundred dollars, nor do they want to reveal their income that closely. Furthermore, a questionnaire should never open with such a personal question. Personal questions should be placed at the end of the survey.

2. How often do you go out to eat?
   The question is ambiguous. To provide useful information one would need to know, at a minimum, the meal period and type of restaurant.

3. During the business week, how often do you eat breakfast?
   1 _____ 2 _____ 3 _____ 4 _____ 5 _____
   The responses are not collectively exhaustive. That is, they do not provide all responses possible. What if a person never eats breakfast? The addition of a sixth response, 0 _____, would solve the problem.

4. On average, how much do you spend for lunch?
   _____ 0 to $2   _____ $2 to $4
   _____ $4 to $6   _____ $6 to $8
   The choices are overlapping. If someone spent $2, $4, or $6, he or she could mark his or her

response in one of two spots. Also, the response choices are not collectively exhaustive. If someone spends more than $8, there is nowhere to mark this response.

5. Would you like (name of restaurant) to have live bands on Friday and Saturday night?
   Yes ( )   No ( )
   The word *like* does not indicate purchase behavior. Many respondents would answer yes because it offers them an entertainment option, but they would not come out on a regular basis. Also, many times there is a cost to adding an extra feature. If the respondent is going to pay for the cost through a cover charge or higher drink prices, it should be addressed. Finally, the question does not specify the type of band. Someone who wants a country-and-western band may answer yes and then be disappointed when the manager puts in a heavy metal band.

6. Did you receive more restaurant coupons this April or last April?
   Who can remember this?

7. What are the most salient and determinant attributes in your evaluation of restaurants?
   What are "salient and determinant attributes"? Don't use big words that the respondent may not understand.

tile or brass fittings. A classic example of a marketing research mistake was made by a U.S. airline. This company offered a special companion price for business travelers with the idea that the companion would be the executive's spouse. Following the promotion, questionnaires were sent to the spouse, not the executive. These innocently asked, "How did you like the recent companion trip?" In several cases the answer was, "What trip? I didn't go!" The airline received angry calls and threats of suits for invasion of privacy or contribution to the breakup of a marriage (Table 5–5).

Mechanical Instruments   Researchers also use mechanical instruments to monitor consumer behavior. These methods are as simple as recording how much customers consume to measuring how brain activities change when exposed to different marketing stimuli. Restaurant managers use POS systems to track the sales of menu items. Managers can look for increases in sales of promotional items, to measure the success of a promotion. Customer loyalty programs track the purchasing habits of customers and use this information to offer loyalty rewards. If customers never buy an appetizer, they may be offered an appetizer as a loyalty bonus since this free item is not likely to reduce the customer's check average. Keeping track of what customers consume is a very simple yet very effective way of understanding customer behavior.

Researchers are applying "neuromarketing," measuring brain activity to learn how consumers feel and respond. Marketing scientists using magnetic resonance

TABLE 5-5
Types of Questions

A. Closed-End Questions

Name	Description	Example
Dichotomous	A question offering two answer choices.	"In arranging this trip, did you personally phone Delta?" Yes ☐ No ☐
Multiple choice	A question offering three or more answer choices.	"With whom are you traveling on this flight?" No one ☐ Children only ☐ Spouse ☐ Business associates/friends/relatives ☐ Spouse and children ☐ An organized tour group ☐
Likert scale	A statement with which the respondent shows the amount of agreement or disagreement.	"Small airlines generally give better service than large ones." Strongly disagree ☐ 1 Disagree ☐ 2 Neither agree nor disagree ☐ 3 Agree ☐ 4 Strongly agree ☐ 5
Semantic differential	A scale is inscribed between two bipolar words, and the respondent selects the point that represents the direction and intensity of his or her feelings.	*Delta Airlines* Large X : __ : __ : __ : __ : __ : Small Experienced __ : __ : __ : __ : X : __ : Inexperienced Modern __ : __ : __ : X : __ : __ : Old-fashioned
Importance scale	A scale that rates the importance of some attribute from "not at all important" to "extremely important."	"Airline food service to me is" Extremely important 1 Very important 2 Somewhat important 3 Not very important 4 Not at all important 5
Rating scale	A scale that rates some attribute from "poor" to "excellent."	"Delta's food service is" Excellent 1 Very good 2 Good 3 Fair 4 Poor 5
Intention-to-buy scale	A scale that describes the respondent's intentions to buy.	"If in-flight telephone service were available on a long flight, I would" Definitely buy 1 Probably buy 2 Not certain 3 Probably not buy 4 Definitely not buy 5

(continued)

TABLE 5–5 (continued)
Types of Questions

B. Open-End Questions

Completely unstructured	A question that respondents can answer in an almost unlimited number of ways.	"What is your opinion of Delta Airlines?"
Word association	Words are presented, one at a time, and respondents mention the first word that comes to mind.	"What is the first word that comes to your mind when you hear the following?" Airline _____ Delta _____ Travel _____
Sentence completion	Incomplete sentences are presented, one at a time, and respondents complete the sentence.	"When I choose an airline, the most important consideration in my decision is _____"
Story completion	An incomplete story is presented, and respondents are asked to complete it.	"I flew Delta a few days ago. I noticed that the exterior and interior of the plane had very bright colors. This aroused in me the following thoughts and feelings." *Now complete the story.*
Picture completion	A picture of two characters is presented, with one making a statement. Respondents are asked to identify with the other and fill in the empty balloon.	*Fill in the empty balloon.*
Thematic apperception tests (TATs)	A picture is presented, and respondents are asked to make up a story about what they think is happening or may happen in the picture.	*Make up a story about what you see.*

imaging (MRI) scans and electroencephalography (EEG) devices have learned that tracking brain electrical activity and blood flow can provide companies with insights into what turns consumers on and off regarding their brands and marketing. "Companies have always aimed for the customers heart, but the head may make a better target," suggests one neuromarketer. "Neuromarketing is reaching consumers where the action is: the brain."[51] A neuromarketing study in Germany has suggested that Starbucks's coffee prices are too low, underpriced by a third, which leaves profits on the table.[52]

PepsiCo's Frito-Lay unit uses neuromarketing to test commercials, product designs, and packaging. Recent electroencephalogram (EEG) tests showed that, compared with shiny packages showing pictures of potato chips, matte beige bags showing potatoes and other healthy ingredients trigger less activity in an area of the brain associated with feelings of guilt. Needless to say, Frito-Lay quickly switched away from the shiny packaging. Although neuromarketing techniques can measure consumer involvement and emotional responses second by second, such brain responses can be difficult to interpret. Thus, neuromarketing is usually used in combination with other research approaches to gain a more complete picture of what goes on inside consumers' heads.[53]

PRESENTING THE RESEARCH PLAN The final stage of developing the research plan is to put the plan in writing so the plan can be reviewed by those involved in the implementation of the plan and those involved in using the results of the research can review the plan. The plan should cover the management problems addressed, the research objectives, information to be obtained, sources of secondary information and/or methods for collecting primary data, and how the results will aid in management decision making. The plan should also include research costs and expected benefits. A written research plan helps ensure that management and researchers have considered all the important aspects of the research and they agree on why and how the research will be done. The manager should review the proposal carefully before approving the project.

Implementing the Research Plan

The researcher puts the marketing research plan into action by collecting, processing, and analyzing the information. Data collection can be done by the company's marketing research staff, which affords the company greater control of the collection process and data quality, or by outside firms. Outside firms that specialize in data collection can often do the job more quickly at lower cost.

The data-collection phase of the marketing research process is generally the most expensive and the most subject to error. The researcher should watch the fieldwork closely to ensure that the plan is implemented correctly and to guard against problems with contacting respondents who refuse to cooperate or who give biased or dishonest answers, and interviewers who make mistakes or take shortcuts.

The collected data must be processed and analyzed to pull out important information and findings. Data from questionnaires are checked for accuracy and completeness and coded for computer analysis. The researcher applies standard computer programs to prepare tabulations of results and to compute averages and other measures for the major variables.

Interpreting and Reporting the Findings

The researcher must now interpret the findings, draw conclusions, and report the conclusions to management. The researcher should avoid overwhelming managers with numbers, complex statistical techniques, and focus. Instead, management desires major findings that will be useful in decision making.

Interpretation should not be left entirely to the researcher. Findings can be interpreted in different ways, and discussions between researchers and managers will help point to the best interpretations. The manager should also confirm that the research project was executed properly. After reviewing the findings, the manager may raise additional questions that can be answered with research data. Researchers should make the data available to marketing managers, so that they can perform new analyses and test relationships on their own.

Interpretation is an important phase of the marketing process. The best research is meaningless if a manager blindly accepts wrong interpretations. Similarly, managers may have biased interpretations. They sometimes accept research results that show what they expected and reject those that did not provide expected or hoped-for answers. Thus, managers and researchers must work closely together when interpreting research results. Both share responsibility for the research process and resulting decisions.

Interpreting and reporting findings is the last step of the four-step research process. It is important for managers to remember that research is a process and that the researcher must proceed through all steps of the process. Marketing Highlight 5–5 explains some of the problems that can occur during a research project.

Information gathered by the company's marketing intelligence and marketing research systems can often benefit from additional analysis to help interpret the findings. This might include advanced statistical analysis to learn more about the relationships within a set of data. Such analysis allows managers to go beyond means and standard deviations in the data and answer such questions as the following:

- What are the major variables affecting sales, and how important is each?

- If the price is raised 10 percent and advertising is increased 20 percent, what will happen to sales?

- What are the best predictors of who are likely to come to my hotel versus my competitor's hotel?

- What are the best variables for segmenting my market, and how many segments exist?

Mathematical models might also help marketers to make better decisions. Each model represents a real system, process, or outcome. These models can help answer the questions "what if" and "which is best." In the past 20 years, marketing scientists have developed a great number of models to help marketing managers make better marketing mix decisions, design sales territories and sales call plans, select sites for retail outlets, develop optimal advertising mixes, and forecast new product sales.[54]

Marketing information has no value until managers use it to make better decisions. The information gathered must reach the appropriate marketing managers at the right time. Large companies have centralized MISs that provide managers with regular performance reports, intelligence updates, and reports on the results of studies. Managers need these routine reports for making regular planning, implementation, and control decisions. But marketing managers also need nonroutine information for special situations and on-the-spot decisions. For example, a sales manager having trouble with an important customer needs a summary of the account's sales during the past year. Or a restaurant manager whose restaurant has stocked out of a best-selling menu item needs to know the current inventory levels in the chain's other restaurants. In companies with centralized information systems, these managers must request the information from the MIS staff and wait. Often, the information arrives too late to be useful.

Recent developments in information handling have led to a revolution in information distribution. With recent advances in microcomputers, software, and communications, many companies are decentralizing their MISs and giving managers direct access to information stored in the systems. In some companies, marketing managers can use a desk terminal to tie into the company's information network. Without leaving their desks, they can obtain information from internal records or outside information services, analyze the information, prepare reports on a word processor, and communicate with others in the network through telecommunications. The Internet is an excellent source of marketing information (see Marketing Highlight 5–6).

Marketing HIGHLIGHT 5—5   Research Problem Areas

1. **Making assumptions.** A restaurant was considering adding a piano bar. Researchers developed a customer survey. One question asked customers if they would like entertainment in the lounge, without mentioning the type of entertainment. The customers could answer this question positively, thinking of a dance band. The manager, seeing the positive responses, would put in the piano bar and then wonder why so many customers did not respond to the piano bar. Luckily, this question was modified during a pretest of the survey.

    A country club asked its members if they felt the club needed a renovation. Most members said "yes." The club then paid consultants to draw up designs for the renovations. When these, along with the proposed dues increase, were presented, the members expressed outrage at the higher dues. If the original survey had addressed the costs associated with the renovation, it could have saved thousands of dollars in consulting fees.

2. **Lack of qualitative information.** Most surveys reported in trade magazines provide descriptive information. For example, a study done by Procter & Gamble found that the most important attribute in the decision of frequent travelers to return to a hotel was a clean appearance. To use this information, management needs to know how its guests judge clean appearance. Through focus groups, managers can learn what guests look for to determine whether the room is clean, what irritants there are concerning cleanliness, and other more specific information.

3. **Failing to look at segments within a sample.** Survey results should be analyzed to determine difference between customer groups. Often, the arithmetic means (averages) for each question are calculated, and the survey is analyzed based on this information, which can mask important differences between segments. For example, a club surveyed its membership on how satisfied the members were with the lunches purchased in the dining room. The average of all responses was 2, with 1 being very satisfied, 3 being satisfied, and 5 being not satisfied. However, when the total sample was divided into membership classes, it was found that one category of members had a high level of satisfaction 1.5, whereas another class gave an average rating of 2.7. This information is more useful to management than the overall mean of 2. Management now had to decide whether to invest additional money to build satisfaction for the members who gave the dining room a lower rating or promote its food and beverage room to the satisfied segment.

4. **Improper use of sophisticated statistical analysis.** One researcher reported that faculty size explained a remarkable 96 percent of the enrollment in hospitality management programs housed in business schools. He then presented a formula for projecting student enrollment based on the number of faculty, implying that if a school had three faculty members it would have 251 students, but if two more faculty were hired, it would have 426 students. Schools that base decisions on this formula might be disappointed.

    The researcher claimed that adding a professor would increase enrollment. What happens at most universities is professors are added to meet an increase in student enrollment. The number of faculty and students are positively correlated; however, students create faculty positions, not the other way around.

5. **Failure to have the sample representative of the population.** A sample is a segment of the population selected to represent the population as a whole. Ideally, the sample should be representative so that the researcher can make accurate estimates of the thoughts and behaviors of the larger population. It is common for hotel managers to receive a bonus based on a customer satisfaction score. Sometimes segments of the population give ratings that are lower than other segments, even though they seem satisfied with the service. For example, in one customer satisfaction survey, respondents between 26 and 35 years of age rated the service attributes of the company lower than other segments. However, they also rated the competition lower, making the company's relative satisfaction compared with the competition the same as other segments. This segment did not appear to be displeased with the service; they just tended to rate lower on the scale. When segments like this are present in the population, they can skew the results of the survey if they are overrepresented or underrepresented. If they are underrepresented, the overall satisfaction will increase; if they are overrepresented, the overall satisfaction score will decrease.

Such systems offer exciting prospects. They allow managers to obtain needed information directly and quickly, and tailor it to their needs. As more managers become skilled in using these systems and as improvements in technology make them more economical, hospitality companies will increasingly use decentralized MISs.

Marketing HIGHLIGHT 5-6   HSMAI's Knowledge Center: A Great Source of Marketing Information

The Hospitality Sales and Marketing Association International (HSMAI) has refined its Knowledge Center Web site over the last 10 years. HSMAI has done a great job of cataloging hospitality marketing information from a variety of sources.

This searchable portal, which delivers global information and resources on a variety of hospitality marketing topics, is a great resource for marketing professionals and students of hospitality marketing. One can also subscribe to news from the HSMAI Knowledge Center.

The portal features major sections on sales, marketing, and revenue management. The sales section includes articles, presentations, and tools for sales professionals. The marketing section contains information on everything from job descriptions to marketing plans. It also offers insights from industry marketing leaders. Revenue section offers

resources to optimize revenue, including presentations, expert articles, and revenue management templates. Like the other sections, these sections feature a blog, allowing members to have a dialogue with each other. Hotels are now hiring managers in the areas of revenue management and social media marketing at the individual property level. Students wishing to obtain a position in this area can keep up-to-date by reading the information and postings on knowledge center.

A wealth of marketing information has been gathered into one searchable site. Knowledge Center can be accessed through www.hsmai.org. HSMAI offers special membership rates for students and faculty members. Students interested in hospitality marketing should become familiar with the HSMAI Web site and take advantage of the resources it offers.

◼◼◼ International Marketing Research

International marketing researchers follow the same steps as domestic researchers, from defining the research problem and developing a research plan to interpreting and reporting the results. However, these researchers often face more and different problems. Although domestic researchers deal with fairly homogeneous markets within a single country, international researchers deal with markets in many different countries. These different markets often vary dramatically in their levels of economic development, cultures and customs, and buying patterns.

In many foreign markets, the international researcher has a difficult time finding good secondary data. Although U.S. marketing researchers can obtain reliable secondary data from dozens of domestic research services, many countries have almost no research services at all. Even the largest international research services operate in only a relative handful of countries. For example, A. C. Nielsen, the world's largest marketing research company, has offices in many countries outside the United States.[55] Thus, even when secondary information is available, it usually must be obtained from many different sources on a country-by-country basis, making the information difficult to combine or compare.

Because of the scarcity of good secondary data, international researchers often must collect their own primary data. Here researchers face problems not encountered domestically. For example, they may find it difficult simply to develop appropriate samples. Although U.S. researchers can use current telephone directories, census tract data, and any of several sources of socioeconomic data to construct samples, such information is largely lacking in many countries. Once the sample is drawn, the U.S. researcher usually can reach most respondents easily by telephone or mail or in person. Reaching respondents is often not so easy in other parts of the world. For example, although there are 79 Internet users per 100 people in the United States, there are only 36 Internet users per 100 people in Mexico. In Madagascar, the number drops to 2 Internet users per 100 people. In other countries, the postal system is notoriously unreliable. In Brazil, for instance, an estimated 30 percent of the mail is never delivered; in Russia, mail delivery can take several weeks. In many developing countries, poor roads and transportation systems make certain areas hard to reach, making personal interviews difficult and expensive.[56]

Differences in cultures from country to country cause additional problems for international researchers. Language is the most obvious culprit. For example, questionnaires must be prepared in one language and then translated into the languages of each country researched. Responses then must be translated back into the original language for analysis and interpretation. This adds to research costs and increases the risks for error.

Translating a questionnaire from one language to another is far from easy. Many points are "lost" because idioms, phrases, and statements mean different things in different cultures. A Danish executive observed, "Check this out by having a different translator put back into English what you've translated from the English. You'll get the shock of your life. I remember [an example in which] 'out of sight, out of mind' had become 'invisible things are insane.'"[57]

Buying roles and consumer decision processes vary greatly from country to country, further complicating international marketing research. Consumers in different countries also vary in their attitudes toward marketing research. People in one country may be very willing to respond; in other countries, nonresponse can be a major problem. For example, customs in some Islamic countries prohibit people from talking with strangers—a researcher simply may not be allowed to speak by phone with women about brand attitudes or buying behavior. High functional illiteracy rates in many countries make it impossible to use a written survey for some segments. In addition, middle-class people in developing countries often make false claims in order to appear well off. For example, in a study of tea consumption in India, over 70 percent of middle-income respondents claimed that they used one of several national brands. However, the researchers had good reason to doubt these results; more than 60 percent of the tea sold in India is unbranded generic tea.

Despite these problems, the recent growth of international marketing has resulted in a rapid increase in the use of international marketing research. Global companies have little choice but to conduct such research. Although the costs and problems associated with international research may be high, the costs of not doing it—in terms of missed opportunities and mistakes—might be even higher. Once recognized, many of the problems associated with international marketing research can be overcome or avoided.

■■■ Marketing Research in Smaller Organizations

Managers of small businesses often believe that marketing research can be done only by experts in large companies with large research budgets. But many marketing research techniques can be used by smaller organizations and at little or no expense.

Managers of small businesses can obtain good marketing information by observing what occurs around them. Thus, restaurateurs can evaluate their customer mix by recording the number and type of customers in the restaurant at different times during the day. Competitor advertising can be monitored by collecting advertisements from local media.

Managers can conduct informal surveys using small convenience samples. The manager of a travel agency can learn what customers like and dislike about travel agencies by conducting informal focus groups, such as inviting small groups to lunch. Restaurant managers can talk with customers; hospital food-service managers can interview patients. Restaurant managers can make random phone calls during slack hours to interview consumers about where they eat out and what they think of various restaurants in the area. Managers can also conduct simple experiments. By changing the design in regular direct mailings and watching results, a manager can learn which marketing tactics work best. By varying newspaper advertisements, a manager can observe the effects of ad size and position, price coupons, and media used.

Small organizations can obtain secondary data. Many associations, local media, chambers of commerce, and government agencies provide special help to small organizations. The U.S. Small Business Administration offers dozens of free publications giving advice on topics ranging from planning advertising to ordering business signs. Local newspapers often provide information on local shoppers and their buying patterns.

Sometimes volunteers and colleges carry out research. Many colleges are seeking small businesses to serve as cases for projects in marketing research classes. Sales management classes are eager to do sales blitzes for hotels.

Thus, secondary data collection, observation, surveys, and experiments can be used effectively by small organizations with small budgets. Although informal research is less complex and costly, it must still be done carefully. Managers must think through the objectives of the research, formulate questions in advance, and recognize the biases systematically. If planned and implemented meticulously, low-cost research can provide reliable information for improving marketing decision making.

▪▪▪ CHAPTER REVIEW

I. Marketing Information and Customer Insights. To create value for customers and to build meaningful relationships with them, marketers must first gain fresh, deep insights into what customers need and want.

II. The Marketing Information System (MIS). An MIS consists of people, equipment, and procedures to gather, sort, analyze, evaluate, and distribute needed, timely, and accurate information to marketing decision makers.

  A. Assessing information needs. A good MIS balances information that managers would like to have against that which they really need and is feasible to obtain.

  B. Developing information. Information needed by marketing managers can be obtained from internal company records, marketing intelligence, and marketing research. The information analysis system processes this information and presents it in a form that is useful to managers.

    1. **Internal data.** Internal data consist of information gathered from sources within the company to evaluate marketing performance and to detect marketing problems and opportunities.

    2. **Guest information management.** A set of procedures and processes for collecting data about guest experience and distributing them within the company.

  C. Marketing intelligence. Marketing intelligence includes everyday information about developments in the marketing environment that helps managers prepare and adjust marketing plans and short-run tactics. Marketing intelligence can come from internal sources or external sources.

    1. **Internal sources.** Internal sources include the company's executives, owners, and employees.

    2. **External sources.** External sources include competitors, government agencies, suppliers, trade magazines, newspapers, business magazines, trade association newsletters and meetings, and databases available on the Internet.

    3. **Sources of competitive information.** They include competitors' annual reports, trade magazine articles, speeches, press releases, brochures, and advertisements.

III. Marketing Research. Marketing research is a process that identifies and defines marketing opportunities and problems, monitors and evaluates marketing actions and performance, and communicates the findings and implication to management. Marketing research is project oriented and has a beginning and an ending. It feeds information into the MIS that is ongoing. The marketing research process consists of four steps: defining the problem and research objectives, developing the research plan, implementing the research plan, and interpreting and presenting the findings.

  A. Defining the problem and research objectives. There are three types of objectives for a marketing research project:

    1. **Exploratory.** To gather preliminary information that will help define the problem and suggest hypotheses.

    2. **Descriptive.** To describe the size and composition of the market.

    3. **Causal.** To test hypotheses about cause-and-effect relationships.

  B. Developing the research plan for collecting information

    1. **Determining specific information needs.** Research objectives must be translated into specific information needs. To meet a manager's information needs, researchers can gather secondary data, primary data, or both. Secondary data consist of information already in existence somewhere, having been collected for another purpose. Primary data consist of information collected for the specific purpose at hand.

    2. **Gather secondary information.** To gather information already in existence somewhere, having been collected for another purpose.

    3. **Research approaches.** Three basic research approaches are observations, surveys, and experiments.

a. **Observational research.** Gathering of primary data by observing relevant people, action, and situations.

b. **Ethnographic research.** A form of observational research that involves sending trained observers to watch and interact with consumers in their "natural environments."

c. **Survey research (structured/unstructured, direct/indirect).** Best suited to gathering descriptive information.

d. **Experimental research.** Best suited to gathering causal information.

4. **Contact methods.** Information can be collected by mail, telephone, or personal interview.

a. **Sampling plan.** Marketing researchers usually draw conclusions about large consumer groups by taking a sample. A sample is a segment of the population selected to represent the population as a whole. Designing the sample calls for four decisions: (1) Who will be surveyed? (2) How many people should be surveyed? (3) How should the sample be chosen? (4) When will the survey be given?

b. **Research instruments.** In collecting primary data, marketing researchers have a choice of primary research instruments: the interview (structured and unstructured), mechanical devices, and structured models such as a test market. Structured interviews make the use of a questionnaire.

c. **Presenting the research plan.** At this stage the marketing researcher should summarize the plan in a written proposal.

C. **Implementing the research plan.** The researcher puts the marketing research plan into action by collecting, processing, and analyzing the information.

D. **Interpreting and reporting the findings.** The researcher must now interpret the findings, draw conclusions, and report them to management.

1. **Information analysis.** Information gathered by the company's marketing intelligence and marketing research systems can often benefit from additional analysis. This analysis helps to answer the questions related to "what if" and "which is best."

2. **Distributing information.** Marketing information has no value until managers use it to make better decisions. The information that is gathered must reach the appropriate marketing managers at the right time.

IV. **International Marketing Research.** International marketing researchers follow the same steps as domestic researchers, from defining the research problem and developing a research plan to interpreting and reporting the results. However, these researchers often face more and different problems.

V. **Marketing Research in Smaller Organizations.** Managers of small businesses can obtain good marketing information by observing what occurs around them.

■■■ DISCUSSION QUESTIONS

1. What role should marketing research play in helping a firm to implement the marketing concept?

2. You own an elegant, high-priced restaurant in your area and want to improve the level of service offered by your 30-person staff. How could observational research help you accomplish this goal?

3. Compare and contrast internal databases, marketing intelligence, and marketing research as a means for developing marketing information.

4. Researchers usually start the data-gathering process by examining secondary data. What secondary data sources would be available to the manager of a full-service restaurant that wanted to research consumer trends?

5. Discuss the advantages and disadvantages of using guest comment cards in a restaurant.

6. Which type of research would be most appropriate in the following situations, and why?
   a. A fast-food restaurant wants to investigate the effect that children have on the purchase of its products.

b. A business hotel wants to gather some preliminary information on how business travelers feel about the menu variety, food, and service in its restaurants.

c. A casual restaurant is considering locating a new outlet in a fast-growing suburb.

d. A fast-food restaurant wants to test the effect of two new advertising themes for its roast beef sandwich sales in two cities.

e. The director of tourism for your state wants to know how to use his or her promotion dollars effectively.

7. Focus group interviewing is both a widely used and a widely criticized research technique in marketing. What are the advantages and disadvantages of focus groups? What are some kinds of questions that are appropriate for focus groups to investigate?

8. What is *Big Data* and what opportunities and challenges does it provide for marketers?

■■■ EXPERIENTIAL EXERCISES

Do one of the following:

1. You have been asked to find out how the campus community feels about the food service on campus.
   a. Who is the population for this study?
   b. Develop a sampling plan, including times and places that will provide you with a sample that is representative of the population of interest.

2. Get a customer comment card from a local hospitality company. What, if any, design changes would you make to the form? If you were the manager, how would you use the information collected from the comment cards?

■■■ INTERNET EXERCISES

1. You are asked to develop a loyalty program for a hotel or restaurant. Go on the Internet and find out what information you can find out about loyalty programs, including existing hotel or restaurant loyalty programs. Write up a summary of your findings. The book's Web site has some suggestions on how to set up your search.

2. Perform an Internet search on "social media marketing" to find companies that specialize in monitoring social media. Discuss two of these companies. Then find two more sites that allow free monitoring and discuss how marketers can use these to monitor their brands. Write a brief report of your findings.

■■■ REFERENCES

1 Reprinted by permission from Richard Abowitz.

2 Neil A. Martin, "A Tempting Wager," *Barron's*, 86, no. 15 (April 10, 2006): 28, 30.

3 Michael Bush, "Why Harrah's Loyalty Effort Is Industry's Gold Standard," *Advertising Age* (October 5, 2009).

4 Unless otherwise noted, quotes in this section are from the excellent discussion of customer insights found in Mohanbir Sawhney, "Insights into Customer Insights," www.mohansawhney.com/registered/content/Trade Article/Insights%20into%20Customer%20Insights.pdf (accessed March 15, 2007). The Apple iPod example is also adapted from this article.

5 See "Big Data," Wikipedia, http://en.wikipedia.org/wiki/Big_data (accessed February 2014); and Yuyu Chen, "Marketers Still Struggle to Harness Power of Big Data," ClickZ, November 12, 2013, www.clickz.com/clickz/news/2303229/marketers-still-struggle-to-harness-power-of-big-data-study.

6 Helen Leggatt, "IBM: Marketers Suffering from Data Overload," *BizReport*, October 12, 2011, www.bizreport.com/2011/10/ibm-marketers-suffering-data-overload.html#; Michael Fassnacht, "Beyond Spreadsheets," *Advertising Age* (February 19, 2007): 15.

7 Mohanhir Sawhney, "Insights into Customer Insights," p. 3.

8 Tom Richman, "Mrs. Field's Secret Ingredient" (October 1987), as cited in *Managing Services* by Christopher Lovelock (Upper Saddle River, NJ: Prentice Hall, 1992): 365–372.

9 See "Pizza Hut and Its Local Agency Win Direct Marketing Association Award," *Pegasus Newswire*, November 18, 2006, www.pegasusnews.com; Jennifer Brown, "Pizza Hut Delivers Hot Results Using Data Warehousing," *Computing Canada* (October 17, 2003): 24; http://newspapergrl.wordpress.com/2006103/22lpizza-hut%E2%80%99s-vip-elub/; www.yum.com/investors/fact/asp (accessed March 2007).

10 John Bowen, "Computerized Guest History: A Valuable Marketing Tool," in *The Practice of Hospitality Management II*, ed. Robert C. Lewis et al. (Westport, CT: AVI, 1990).

11 Mark Lynn, "Making Customer Feedback a Priority—A Key to Inducing Demand and Maximizing Value," *Hospitality Net*, June 28, 2004, http://hospitalitynet.org.

12 Rick Hendrie, "Hear Me Out: Talking, Listening to Current Guests May be the Best Way to Get More Through the Door," *Nation's Restaurant News* (January 20, 2003): 28+; Cary Jehl Broussard, "Inside the Customer-Focused Company," *Harvard Business Review* (May 2000): S20.

13 See Donald Trump Jr. and Suzie Mills, "Valuing Customer Loyalty – The 76% Factor," http://hotelexecutive.com/business_review/2702/valuingcustomerloyalty-the76factor (accessed February 2015).

14 James L. Heskett, W. Earl Sasser, Jr., and Leonard A. Schlesinger, *The Service Profit Chain* (New York: Free Press, 1997), p. 67.

15 Chekitan S. Dev and Bernard O. Ellis, "Guest Histories: An Untapped Service Resource," *Cornell Hotel and Restaurant Administration Quarterly*, 32, no. 2 (1991): 31.

16 Tammy P. Bieber, "Guest History Systems: Maximizing the Benefits," *Cornell Hotel and Restaurant Administration Quarterly*, 30, no. 3 (1989): 22.

17 Carolyn Taschner, "Commentary: Mystery Shopping Is Booming Business," *The Daily Record* (Baltimore)

(May 15, 2004); Allison Perlik, "If They're Happy, Do You Know It," *Restaurants and Institutions* (October 15, 2002): 65–70.

18 Joseph F. Durocher and Neil B. Neiman, "Technology: Antidote to the Shakeout," *Cornell Hotel and Restaurant Administration Quarterly*, 31, no. 1 (1990): 35.

19 Laurette Dubé, Leo M. Renaghan, and Jane M. Miller, "Measuring Customer Satisfaction for Strategic Management," *Cornell Hotel and Restaurant Administration Quarterly*, 35, no. 1 (1994): 39.

20 Burt Cabanas, "A Marketing Strategy for Resort Conference Centers," *Cornell Hotel and Restaurant Administration Quarterly*, 33, no. 3 (1992): 47.

21 "Making Them Feel at Home," *Cornell Hotel and Restaurant Administration Quarterly*, 30, no. 3 (1989): 4.

22 James Curtis, "Behind Enemy Lines," *Marketing* (May 24, 2001): 28–29.

23 http://www.revinate.com/blog/2015/02/2014-hotel-reputation-benchmark-report/ (accessed February 2014).

24 "Company Sleuth Uncovers Business Info for Free," *Link-Up* (January–February 1999): 1, 8.

25 *American Marketing Association*, officially adopted definition (1987).

26 Frank E. Camacho and D. Matthew Knain, "Listening to Customers: The Market Research Function at Marriott Corporation," *Marketing Research* (March 1989): 5–14.

27 "The Entrepreneurial Approach to Indian Affairs," *Cornell Hotel and Restaurant Administration Quarterly*, 29, no. 2 (1988): 5.

28 Jerry Wind, Paul E. Green, Douglas Shifflet, and Marsha Scarbrough, "Courtyard by Marriott: Designing a Hotel Facility with Consumer-Based Marketing," *Interfaces*, 19, no. 1 (1989): 25–47.

29 Robert C. Lewis and Richard E. Chambers, *Marketing Leadership in Hospitality: Foundations and Practices* (New York: Van Nostrand Reinhold, 1989), p. 518.

30 See Halah Touryalai, "Hotel Science: How Marriott & Starwood Hotels Choose Your Room Amenities," *Forbes*, August 6, 2014, http://www.forbes.com/sites/halahtouryalai/2014/08/06/hotel-science-how-marriott-starwood-hotels-choose-your-room-amenities/

31 Linda Tischler, "Every Move You Make," *Fast Company* (April 2004): 73–75.

32 Spencer E. Ante, "The Science of Desire," *Business Week* (June 5, 2006): 99–106.

33 See Pradeep K. Tyagi, "Webnography: A New Tool to Conduct Marketing Research," *Journal of American Academy of Business* (March 2010): 262–268.

34 Spencer E. Ante, "The Science of Desire," *Business Week* (June 5, 2006): 100. Also see Jan Fulton and Suzanne Gibbs Howard, "Going Deeper, Seeing Further: Enhancing Ethnographic Interpretations to Reveal

More Meaningful Opportunities to Design," *Journal of Advertising Research* (September 2006): 246–250.

35 Spencer E. Ante, "The Science of Desire," *BusinessWeek* (June 5, 2006): 100; Rhys Blakely, "You Know When It Feels Like Somebody's Watching You …," *Times* (May 14, 2007): 46; Jack Neff, "Marketing Execs: Researchers Could Use a Softer Touch," *Advertising Age* (January 27, 2009), http://adage.com/article7article_id=134144.

36 Allison Perlik, "If You Are Happy, Do You Know It," *Restaurants and Institutions* (October 15, 2002): 65–70.

37 Robert Reiss, "How Ritz-Carlton Stays at Top," Forbes, October 30, 2009, http://www.forbes.com/2009/10/30/simon-cooper-ritz-leadership-ceonetwork-hotels.html.

38 Nancy Trejos, "Guests Help Design the Hotel of the Future," *USA Today*, November 15, 2013, accessed http://www.usatoday.com/story/travel/hotels/2013/11/14/hotel-guests-millennials-design-marriott-holiday-inn/3538573/.

39 Joe L. Welch, "Focus Groups for Restaurant Research," *Cornell Hotel and Restaurant Administration Quarterly*, 26, no. 2 (1985): 78–85.

40 Dorothy Dee, "Focus Groups," *Restaurants USA*, 10, no. 7 (1990): 30–34.

41 Nancy Trejos, "Guests Help Design the Hotel of the Future," *USA Today*, November 15, 2013, http://www.usatoday.com/story/travel/hotels/2013/11/14/hotel-guests-millennials-design-marriott-holiday-inn/3538573/.

42 Robert J. Kwortnik, "Clarifying 'Fuzzy' Hospitality-Management Problems with Depth Interviews and Qualitative Analysis: Properly Conducted Depth Interviews Can Dig to the Sometimes-Confusing Heart of Consumers' Motivation for Hospitality Purchases," *Cornell and Hotel Restaurant Administration Quarterly* (April 2003): 117–129.

43 See "Choice Hotels Launches Plan to Redefine and Redesign its Comfort Brand Family," http://www.hospitalitynet.org/news/4054592.html (accessed January 25, 2012).

44 Anne Chen, "Customer Feedback Key for Theme Park," *eWeek* (December 15, 2003): 58.

45 Jacob Brown, "Survey Metrics Ward Off Problems," *Marketing News* (November 11, 2003) accessed online via Business Source Premier, October 12, 2004.

46 Stephen W. Litvin and Goh Hwai Kar, "E-Surveying for Tourism Research: Legitimate Tool or a Researcher's Fantasy?" *Journal of Travel Research* (2001): 308–314.

47 Deborah L. Vence, "In an Instant: More Researchers Use IM for Fast, Reliable Results," *Marketing News* (March 1, 2006): 21.

48 Based on information found at www.channelm2.com/HowOnlineQualitativeResearch.html (accessed December 2010).

49 Stephen Baker, "The Web Knows What You Want," *BusinessWeek* (July 27, 2009): 48.

50 Tina Sharkey, "Who Is Your Chief Listening Officer?" *Forbes*, March 13, 2012, www.forbes .com/sites/tinasharkey/2012/03/13/who-is-your-chief-listening-officer/.

51 Jessica Tsai, "Are You Smarter than a Neuromarketer?" *Customer Relationship Management* (January 2010): 19–20.

52 See Roger Dooley, "Is Starbucks Coffee Too Cheap?" *Forbes*, October 14, 2013, http:// www.forbes.com/sites/rogerdooley/2013/10/14/ is-starbucks-coffee-too-cheap/.

53 This and the other neuromarketing examples are adapted from Laurie Burkitt, "Neuromarketing: Companies Use Neuroscience for Consumer Insights," *Forbes*, November 16, 2009, www.forbes.com/ forbes/2009/1116/marketing-hyundai-neurofocus-brain-waves-battle-for-the-brain.html.

54 For further reading, see Gary L. Lilien, Philip Kotler, and K. Sridhar Moorthy, *Marketing Models* (Upper Saddle River, NJ: Prentice Hall, 1992).

55 Jack Honomichl, "Top Marketing/Ad/Opinion Research Firms Profiled," *Marketing News* (June 2, 1992): H2.

56 For these and other examples, see "From Tactical to Personal: Synovate's Tips for Conducting Marketing Research in Emerging Markets," *Marketing News* (April 30, 2011): 20–22. Internet stats are from http://data.worldbank.org/indicator/IT.NET.USER.P2 (accessed February 2014).

57 Jain, *International Marketing Management*, p. 338.

Objectives

After reading this chapter, you should be able to:

1. Explain the model of buyer behavior.

2. Outline the major characteristics affecting consumer behavior, and list some of the specific cultural, social, personal, and psychological factors that influence consumers.

3. Explain the buyer decision process and discuss need recognition, information search, evaluation of alternatives, the purchase decision, and postpurchase behavior.

Consumer Markets and Consumer Buying Behavior

Years ago, Taco Bell practically invented the fast-food "value menu," with its "59¢-79¢-99¢" pricing structure. With slogans such as "The Cure for the Common Meal," "Make a Run for the Border," and "Think Outside the Bun," Taco Bell firmly established its affordable Mexican-inspired fare as a unique "more-for-your-money" alternative to the mostly burgers and fries offered by dominant McDonald's and other fast-food competitors. Taco Bell grew rapidly into a $6-billion-a-year international brand.

In the early 2000s, however, consumer tastes began to change. Americans were looking for fresher, better tasting, healthier eating options, and more contemporary fast-casual atmospheres. Taco Bell's "food-as-fuel" marketing philosophy—its "fill them up, move them out" thinking—made the chain seem out of step with the times. After three straight years of flat sales, Taco Bell ended 2011 with a 1.4 percent decline in system-wide revenues. These dire results called for a shift in Taco Bell's strategy.

The shift began with the realization that customers want more from a fast-food restaurant than just lots of food that is cheap. More than "calories per dollar," they are seeking a food-eating experience, one that fits with and enhances their lifestyles. So in early 2012, Taco Bell shifted its positioning from "food as fuel" to "food as experience and lifestyle." It launched a new, innovative lifestyle marketing campaign called "Live Mas" ("mas" is Spanish for "more"). Backed by a $280 million annual budget, the "Live Mas" slogan is designed as a lifestyle rallying cry for Taco Bell's target customers, millennials—young adults who consume a disproportionate share of fast and fast-casual food.

Taco Bell's aspirational "Live Mas" message is crafted to inspire millennials to try new things and to live life to the fullest. The first "Live Mas" ad, called "Pockets," showed a hip, 20-something man coming into a dim apartment as dawn breaks. He empties his pockets onto a table as he thinks back over the night he's had. Along with the standard wallet, keys, and smartphone, he tosses out a concert ticket stub, a matchbook from a 24-hour psychic, a pair of Kanji dice, and a strip of photo-booth images of himself with a young woman. The last item he pulls out is a blister pack of Taco Bell Fire Sauce, adorned with the new "Live Mas" logo and the message, "You have chosen wisely." It's this last item that brings a smile to his face.

The "Live Mas" lifestyle marketing campaign goes well beyond just advertising. For example, it includes new menu items aimed to please millennial lifestyles. For example, in early 2012, Taco Bell unveiled cobranded Doritos Locos Tacos, like a standard Taco Bell taco or Taco Supreme, but wrapped in a tasty shell made from Nacho Cheese Doritos. Hungry millennials gobbled up 100 million Doritos Locos Tacos in just the first 10 weeks, making it the most successful new product launch in the company's 50-year history. The brand quickly added Cool Ranch and Fiery versions.

Recognizing that customers who want to "Live Mas" might be looking to eat at just about any time of the day, Taco Bell is focusing on more day parts. For example, after a long absence from morning hours, Taco Bell is now rolling out a 7 to 11 A.M. breakfast menu. Options include breakfast burritos, the A.M. Cruchwrap, waffle tacos, and bite-size Cinnabon Delights. Similarly, Taco Bell's "Happier Hour" initiative targets between-meal snack appetites from 2 to 5 P.M. daily featuring new Mountain Dew frozen beverages and $1 loaded Grillers. And for the late-night "Live Mas" crowd, there's Fourthmeal, as in "You're out. You're hungry. You're doing Fourthmeal." In one ad—titled "After-Wedding Party"—a newlywed couple feasts on Taco Bell fare in the back of a limo, along with their groomsmen and maids of honor. The announcer concludes, "Fourthmeal—sometimes the best dinner is after the dinner."

To better engage targeted millennials, Taco Bell now reaches them where they hang out—online, digital, and mobile. Befitting the millennial lifestyle, a significant portion of the "Live Mas" promotion budget goes to social media, digital tools, and other nontraditional channels. Beyond the usual Facebook, Twitter, and Pinterest, Taco Bell uses social media such as Vine, Pheed, and Snapchat for buzz-building announcements, limited-time promotions, and sneak peeks at new products. The revitalized chain watches and participates in online brand conversations with its "Fish-bowl"—Taco Bell's own command center for monitoring social media and generating digital dialogue. For example, the brand achieved more 2 billion social media impressions for Cool Ranch Doritos Locos Tacos alone, before the product even launched.

Some analysts suggest that with "Live Mas," Taco Bell is stretching too far beyond its core affordable fast-food positioning. "They're trying to suggest a lifestyle aspiration, but this seems an overreach for Taco Bell," says one restaurant-marketing consultant. "A tagline should embrace the DNA of the brand, which for Taco Bell is extraordinary value." Not so, says Taco Bell. Rather than abandoning the brand's "value" roots, says the company, the new tagline and other elements of the "Live Mas" campaign underscore brand values dating back to its founding—"value, quality, relevance, and an exceptional experience." The "value" message still resonates in the campaign, but "Live Mas" also energizes the "relevance" and "experience" aspects of Taco Bell's long-standing value proposition.

The early results suggest that Taco Bell is right on track with "Live Mas" and the new lifestyle positioning. The year following the introduction of the campaign, sales soared 8 percent, more than twice the gain of industry leader McDonald's. And last year, ad industry magazine *Advertising Age* named Taco Bell its Marketer of the Year, for going "into innovation overdrive, churning out a string of hot new products, game-changing menus, and an aggressive mix of traditional, social, and digital media that's hitting the mark with Millennials."

In addition to the menu changes, Taco Bell has also made other changes based on changes in consumer behavior. In 2015 it began a process of replacing additives and artificial preservatives with natural ingredients. In the same year Taco Bell began a delivery service. Taco Bell realized that most of the food it serves is not eaten in the restaurant;

about 70 percent is served through the drive-through window. Mary Chapman, a restaurant consultant, said the move into delivery could be a smart move by Taco Bell as it tests the waters in more urban areas and looks to continue to serve millennials. Many millennials use car sharing, such as ZipCars, rather than own their own car. She states, "If you look at the long-term trend, particularly in urban markets, well maybe the drive thru isn't where to look for growth."

Taco Bell provides an example of how a company changes to keep up with changes and anticipated changes in consumer behavior. Understanding consumer behavior is an essential component of effective marketing.[1]

■■■ A Model of Consumer Behavior

Today's marketplace has become very competitive with thousands of hotels and restaurants. In addition, during recent years the hospitality and travel industries have undergone globalization. Hotel companies headquartered in nations as diverse as Germany, the United States, and Hong Kong compete aggressively in markets such as Singapore and Japan. The result is a fiercely competitive international market with companies fighting for their share of consumers. To win this battle, they invest in research that will reveal what customers want to buy, which locations they prefer, which amenities are important to them, how they buy, and why they buy.

This is the central question: How do consumers respond to the various marketing stimuli that a company might use? The company that really understands how consumers will respond to different product features, prices, and advertising appeals has a great advantage over its competitors. As a result, researchers from companies and universities are constantly studying the relationship between marketing stimuli and consumer response. Their starting point is the model of buyer behavior shown in Figure 6–1. This figure shows that marketing and other stimuli enter the consumer's "black box" and produce certain responses. Marketers must determine what is in the buyer's black box.

On the left side of Figure 6–1, the marketing stimuli consist of the four Ps: product, price, place, and promotion. Other stimuli include major forces and events in the buyer's environment: economic, technological, political, and cultural. All these stimuli enter the buyer's black box, where they are turned into the set of observable buyer responses shown on the right: product choice, brand choice, dealer choice, purchase timing, and purchase amount.

Marketers must understand how the stimuli are changed into responses inside the consumer's black box. The black box has two parts. First, a buyer's characteristics influence how he or she perceives and reacts to the stimuli. Second, the buyer's decision process itself affects outcomes. In this chapter we look first at buyer characteristics that affect buying behavior and then examine the buyer decision process.

Figure 6–1
Model of buyer behavior.

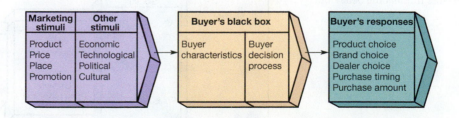

◼◼◼ Personal Characteristics Affecting Consumer Behavior

Consumer purchases are strongly influenced by cultural, social, personal, and psychological characteristics. These factors are shown in Figure 6–2. For the most part, they cannot be controlled by the marketer, but they must be taken into account.

Cultural Factors

Cultural factors exert the broadest and deepest influence on consumer behavior. We examine the role played by the buyer's culture, subculture, and social class.

Culture. The set of basic values, perceptions, wants, and behaviors learned by a member of society from family and other important institutions.

Culture is the most basic determinant of a person's wants and behavior. It comprises the basic values, perceptions, wants, and behaviors that a person learns continuously in a society. Today, most societies are in a state of flux. Determinants of culture learned as a child are changing in societies from Chile to California. Culture is expressed through tangible items such as food, architecture, clothing, and art. Culture is an integral part of the hospitality and travel business. It determines what we eat, how we travel, where we travel, and where we stay. Culture is dynamic, adapting to the environment.

Marketers try continuously to identify cultural shifts in order to devise new products and services that might find a receptive market. For example, the cultural shift toward greater concern about health and fitness has resulted in many hotels adding exercise rooms or health clubs or developing an agreement with a local health club so that their guests can have access to it. The shift toward lighter and more natural food has resulted in menu changes in restaurants. The shift toward lighter-colored and simpler home furnishings is reflected in new restaurant designs.

At the same time, a significant number of consumers seem to be rebelling against foods that are good for them, preferring good taste. Restaurants face a consumer who orders broiled flounder and a light salad only to top it off with high-butterfat ice cream for dessert.

Subculture

Subculture. A group of people with shared value systems based on common life experiences and situations.

Each culture contains smaller **subcultures**, or groups of people with shared value systems based on common life experiences and situations. Subcultures include nationalities, religions, racial groups, and geographic regions. Many subcultures make up important market segments, and marketers often design products and marketing programs tailored to their needs. Examples of three such important subculture groups are Hispanic, African American, and Asian consumers. As we discuss them, it is important to note that each major subculture is, in turn, made of many smaller subcultures, each with its own preferences and behavior.

HISPANIC CONSUMERS. The U.S. Hispanic market consists of Americans of Cuban, Mexican, Central American, South American, and Puerto Rican descent. The population of Hispanics is over 55 million. Hispanic consumers have a buying power of more than $1.5 trillion.[2]

Figure 6–2
Factors influencing behavior.

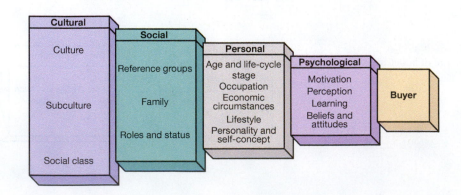

Although Hispanic consumers share many characteristics and behaviors with the mainstream buying public, there are also distinct differences. They tend to be deeply family oriented and make shopping a family affair; children have a big say in what brands they buy. Perhaps more important, Hispanic consumers, particularly first-generation immigrants, are very brand loyal, and they favor brands and sellers who show special interest in them. Younger Hispanics, however, have shown increasing price sensitivity in recent years and a willingness to switch brands. Hispanics are more active on mobile and social networks than other segments, making digital medium ideal for reaching this segment.[3]

To make people aware of their purchasing power, as well as provide continuing education opportunities, the Hispanic meeting planners have formed the International Association of Hispanic Meeting Planners (IAHMP). Its membership includes meeting planners from the United States, Puerto Rico, Mexico, Portugal, Costa Rica, Panama, Guatemala, and Spain. In the United States, IAHMP is establishing chapters in the states and major cities where Hispanics are in the majority.[4]

Papa John's pizza restaurants understood the importance of the Hispanic market and shifted a larger portion of their marketing dollars toward the market, resulting in a 43 percent increase in Hispanic sales. Another example of a company increasing their marketing to Hispanics is Denny's. It increased not only its budget for Spanish language television but also its bilingual social media presence.[5]

Even within the Hispanic market, there exist many distinct subsegments based on nationality, age, income, and other factors. For example, a company's product or message may be more relevant to one nationality over another, such as Mexicans, Costa Ricans, Argentineans, or Cubans. Companies must also vary their pitches across different Hispanic economic segments.

Thus, companies often target specific subsegments within the larger Hispanic community with different kinds of marketing effort.

AFRICAN AMERICAN CONSUMERS. The U.S. African American population is growing in affluence and sophistication. The 45 million African American consumers have more than $1 trillion in buying power. Although more price conscious than other segments, blacks are also strongly motivated by quality and selection. Brands are important. So is shopping. Black consumers seem to enjoy shopping more than other groups, even for something as mundane as groceries. Black consumers are also the most fashion conscious of the ethnic groups.[6]

One of the objectives of the National Coalition of Black Meeting Planners (NCBMP) is to develop a collaborative network of African Americans professionals that plan, provide meeting space or support the planning of meetings. The coalition helps bring together members that are suppliers and meeting planners to create business opportunities. The network also facilitates career development for its members.[7] The NCBMP realizes that African American meeting planners are an important force in the hospitality industry.

With American markets becoming more diverse, companies are seeking managers who are members of a subculture that is a target market of their business. Courtesy of Rob Marmion/123RF.

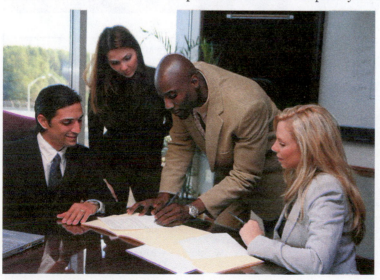

ASIAN AMERICAN CONSUMERS. Asian Americans are the most affluent U.S. demographic segment. They now number more than 18 million with annual buying power that approaches $1 billion in annual spending power. They are the second fastest-growing population subsegment after Hispanics. Chinese Americans constitute the largest group, followed by Filipinos, Asian Indians, Vietnamese, Korean Americans, and Japanese Americans. The U.S. Asian American population is expected to double by 2050, when it will make up more than 9 percent of the U.S. population. Asian consumers may be the most tech-savvy segment; more than 90 percent of Asian Americans go online regularly and are most comfortable with Internet technologies such as online banking.[8]

As a group, Asian consumers shop frequently and are the most brand conscious of all the ethnic groups. They can be fiercely brand loyal. As a result, many firms are now targeting the Asian American market. For example, among its many other Asian American targeting efforts, McDonald's has built a special Web site for this segment (www.myinspirasian.com), offered in both English and Asian languages. The community-oriented site highlights how McDonald's is working with and serving the Asian American community.

Cross-Cultural Marketing

Cross-cultural marketing.
This is the practice of including ethnic themes and cross-cultural perspectives within the mainstream marketing of the organization.

Beyond targeting segments such as Hispanics, African Americans, and Asian Americans with specially tailored efforts, many marketers now embrace **cross-cultural marketing**. This is the practice of including ethnic themes and cross-cultural perspectives within the mainstream marketing of the organization. An example is a general-market commercial for Cheerios that featured an interracial family.[9] Cross-cultural marketing appeals to consumer similarities across subcultural segments rather than differences.

Many marketers are finding that insights gleaned from ethnic consumers can influence their broader markets. For example, today's youth-oriented lifestyle is influenced heavily by Hispanic and African American entertainers. So it follows that consumers expect to see many different cultures and ethnicities represented in the advertising and products they consume. For instance, McDonald's takes cues from African Americans, Hispanics, and Asians to develop menus and advertising in hopes of encouraging mainstream consumers to buy smoothies, mocha drinks, and snack wraps as avidly as they consume hip-hop and rock 'n' roll. "The ethnic consumer tends to set trends," says McDonald's chief marketing officer. "So they help set the tone for how we enter the marketplace." Thus, McDonald's might take an ad primarily geared toward Africa Americans and run it in general-market media. "The reality is that the new mainstream is multicultural," concludes one cross-cultural marketing expert.[10]

Understanding consumer behavior is difficult enough for companies marketing within the borders of a single country. For companies operating in many countries, however, understanding and serving the needs of consumers can be daunting. Although consumers in different countries may have some things in common, their values, attitudes, and behaviors often vary dramatically. International marketers must understand such differences and adjust their products and marketing programs accordingly. Table 6–1 shows how McDonald's adapts its menu to fit the consumer wants of different cultures.

TABLE 6–1

McDonald's Global Menu Variations

Country	Noteworthy Menu Items
United States	Big Mac, Chicken McNuggets, Filet-o-Fish, Egg McMuffin, Fries
India	McVeggle, Chicken Maharaja-Mac, McSpIcy Paneer
France	Le McBaguette, Le Croque McDo, Le Royal Cheese
Egypt	Beef N Pepper, McArabia (grilled kofta), McFalafel
Israel	McKebab, McFalafel, Big New York and Big Texas (hamburgers)
Japan	Ebi Filet-O, MegaTeriyakl Burger, Bacon Egg and Lettuce Wrap, Shaka Shaka Chicken
China	Prosperity Burger, Taro Pie, McWIngs, McNuggets with Chili Garlic sauce
Brazil	Banana Pie, McNIfIco Bacon, Cheddar McMelt, Big Tasty
Mexico	Big Mac, McChicken, Fries, etc.

Sources: "Discover McDonald's Around the World," www.aboutmcdonalds.com/mcd/country/map.html, accessed May 20, 2014; David Griner, "McDonald's 60-Second Meals in Japan Aren't Going So Well," *Adweek*, January 7, 2013; Richard Vines and Caroline Connan, "McDonald's Wins Over French Chef with McBaguette Sandwich," www.bloomberg.com, January 15, 2013; Segolene Poirier, "McDonald's Brazil Has Big Plans," *We Rio Times*, April 8, 2012; Susan Postlewaite, "McDonald's McFalafel a Hit with Egyptians, *Advertising Age*, June 19, 2001.

Social Class

Social classes. Relatively permanent and order divisions in a society whose members share similar values, interests, and behaviors.

Almost every society has some form of social class structure. **Social classes** are relatively permanent and ordered divisions in a society whose members share similar values, interests, and behaviors. Social scientists have identified the seven American social classes: upper uppers (1 percent), lower uppers (2 percent), upper middles (12 percent), middle (32 percent), working (38 percent), upper lowers (9 percent), and lower lowers (7 percent).[11]

Social class in newer nations such as the United States, Canada, Australia, and New Zealand is not indicated by a single factor such as income but is measured as a combination of occupation, source of income, education, wealth, and other variables. In many older nations, social class is something into which one is born. Bloodlines often mean more than income or education in such societies. Marketers are interested in social class because people within a given class tend to exhibit similar behavior, including buying behavior. Social classes show distinct product and brand preferences in such areas as food, travel, and leisure activity. There are also language differences between social classes, which means advertisers must compose copy and dialogue that will be familiar to the social class being targeted.

Social Factors

Consumer behavior is also influenced by social factors, including the consumers' groups, family, social roles, and status.

Groups and Social Networks

Group. Two or more people who interact to accomplish individual or mutual goals.

Reference groups. Groups that have a direct (face-to-face) or indirect influence on a person's attitude or behavior.

Many small **groups** influence a person's behavior. Groups that have a direct influence and to which a person belongs are called membership groups. In contrast, **reference groups** serve as direct (face-to-face) or indirect points of comparison or reference in forming a person's attitudes or behavior. People often are influenced by reference groups to which they do not belong. For example, an aspirational group is one to which the individual wishes to belong, as when a young basketball player hopes to someday emulate basketball star Lebron James and play professionally.

Marketers try to identify the reference groups of their target markets. Reference groups influence consumers in at least three ways: (1) They expose the person to new behaviors and lifestyles; (2) they influence the person's attitudes and self-concept; and (3) they create pressures to conform that may affect the person's product, brand, and vendor choices.

Membership groups. Groups that have a direct influence on a person's behavior and to which a person belongs.

Groups to which the person belongs that have a direct influence are called **membership groups**. They include primary groups, such as family, friends, neighbors, and coworkers—specifically, those with whom there is regular but informal interaction. Secondary groups are more formal and have less regular interaction; they include religious groups, professional associations, and trade unions. In some societies, secondary groups may be membership groups. Members of the Mormon faith, for example, are greatly influenced by their religious affiliation. Mormons do not drink alcoholic beverages and, therefore, would not be buyers of wine at a fine restaurant.

Aspirational group. A group to which a person wishes to belong.

People can also be influenced by **aspirational groups** to which they do not belong but would like to. For example, a college freshman may aspire to be part of Hyatt's management team and may identify with this group even though not a member.

The importance of group influence varies by product and brand. It tends to be strongest when the product is visible to others whom the buyer respects. Purchases of products that are used privately are not greatly affected by group influence. Certain nightclubs can be associated with reference groups, attracting people who belong or wish to belong to the groups who frequent the nightclubs. Country clubs and city clubs tend to attract members who want to affiliate with their type of members.

Word-of-Mouth Influence and Buzz Marketing

Word-of-mouth influence can have a powerful impact on consumer buying behavior. The personal words and recommendations of trusted friends, associates, and other consumers tend to be more credible than those coming from commercial sources, such as advertisements or salespeople. One study found that 92 percent of consumers trust recommendations from family and friends above any form of advertising.[12] Most word-of-mouth influence happens naturally: Consumers start chatting about a brand they use or brands they have strong positive or negative feelings toward. Often, however, rather than leaving it to chance, marketers can help create positive conversations about their brands.

Marketers of brands subjected to strong group influence must figure out how to reach **opinion leaders**—people within a reference group who, because of special skills, knowledge, personality, or other characteristics, exert social influence on others. Some experts call this group *the influentials* or *leading adopters*. When these influentials talk, consumers listen. Marketers try to identify opinion leaders for their products and direct marketing efforts toward them. For example, the guest list for the grand opening of a restaurant or the first anniversary of a hotel should include opinion leaders.

Buzz marketing involves enlisting or even creating opinion leaders to serve as "brand ambassadors," who spread the word about a company's products. Many companies now create brand ambassador programs in an attempt to turn influential but everyday customers into brand evangelists. A recent study found that such programs can increase the effectiveness of word-of-mouth marketing efforts by as much as 50 percent.[13] For example, JetBlue's CrewBlue program employs real customers to create buzz on college campuses.[14]

Over the past few years, the JetBlue CrewBlue program has recruited a small army of college student ambassadors—all loyal JetBlue lovers. CrewBlue representatives advise JetBlue on its campus marketing efforts, talk up the brand to other students, and help organize campus events, such as JetBlue's BlueDay. Held each fall on 21 campuses, the highly successful event urges students to wear outlandish blue costumes (and, on occasion, blue skin and hair). Students with the best costumes are each given a pair of free airline tickets.

The CrewBlue ambassadors are crucial to the success of JetBlue's campus marketing efforts: "Students know what kinds of activities are important to other kids, what we should say to them in our marketing, and how we should say it," says a JetBlue marketing executive. You might think that such brand ambassadors would be perceived as best avoided. Not so, says the executive. "Our brand ambassadors are seen by their college friends as entrepreneurial, creative people." What they aren't, he adds, are the supercool people on campus who are typically thought of as influentials. The best ambassadors, says the executive, are "friendly, everyday brand loyalists who love to talk to people."[15]

Online Social Networks

Over the past few years, a new type of social interaction has exploded onto the scene—online social networking. **Online social networks** are online communities where people socialize or exchange information and opinions. Social networking media range from blogs (Consumerist, Gizmodo, and Zenhabits) and message boards (Craigslist) to social media sites (Facebook, Twitter, YouTube, Pinterest, and Foursquare) and virtual worlds (Second Life and Everquest). This new form of consumer-to-consumer and business-to-consumer dialogue has big implications for marketers.

Marketers are working to harness the power of these new social networks and other "word-of-Web" opportunities to promote their products and build closer customer relationships. Instead of throwing more one-way commercial messages at consumers, they hope to use the Internet and social networks to *interact* with consumers and become a part of their conversations and lives.

For example, brands ranging from Burger King to the Chicago Bulls are tweeting on Twitter. Southwest Airlines employees share stories with each other and customers on the company's "Nuts about Southwest" blog. And Hilton developed H360 to connect Hilton employees from across the globe, allowing them to connect and share best practices.[16] Other companies, including Marriott, McDonald's, and Chipotle, regularly post ads or custom videos on video-sharing sites such as YouTube. McDonald's ad featuring former National Basketball Association (NBA) basketball players Larry Bird and Michael Jordan has recorded almost 7 million visits.

Opinion leaders. People within a reference group who, because of special skills, knowledge, personality, or other characteristics, exert influence on others.

Buzz marketing. Cultivating opinion leaders and getting them to spread information about a product to others in their community.

Online social networks Online social communities— blogs, social networking, Web sites, or even virtual worlds—where people socialize or exchange information and opinions.

But marketers must be careful when tapping into online social networks. Results are difficult to measure and control. Ultimately, the users control the content, so social network marketing attempts can easily backfire. We will dig deeper into online social networks as a marketing tool in Chapter 15.

Family

Family members have a strong influence on buyer behavior. The family remains the most important consumer buying organization in American society and has been researched extensively. Marketers are interested in the roles and influence of the husband, wife, and children on the purchase of different products and services. Husband–wife involvement varies widely by product category and by stage in the buying process. Buying roles change with evolving consumer lifestyles. In the United States, the wife traditionally has been the main purchasing agent for the family, especially in the areas of food, household products, and clothing. But with 70 percent of women holding jobs outside the home and the willingness of husbands to do more of the family's purchasing, all this is changing. For example, women now make or influence up to 80 percent of car-buying decisions and men account for about 40 percent of food-shopping dollars.[17]

Children may also have a strong influence on family buying decisions. The 36 million children of the United States aged 9 to 13 influence the spending of $43 billion in disposable income. They also influence an additional $200 billion that their families spend on them, such as food, clothing, entertainment, and personal items. One study found that kids significantly influence family decisions about everything from where they take vacation and what cars and cell phones they buy.[18]

To encourage families to take their child out to eat, casual restaurants feature children eat-free nights during the week. These promotions are set up to bring business into the restaurant on slower nights. For example, there usually has to be an adult meal purchased for every free children's meal and they are held on week nights when the restaurant is less busy. At Roy's Restaurants, as soon as children are seated, the Roy's server learns their names. "We want them to get excited and happy immediately," says a Roy's executive. Other kids' perks at Roy's include portable DVD players with movies and headphones on request and sundaes with kids' names written in chocolate. "They love seeing their name in chocolate," says a Roy's executive. Roy's big-hearted commitment to children's happiness is a no-brainer. Happy children equal happy parents.[19]

In Asia children are also becoming more influential. One study found that 66 percent of Asia's teens were influenced by television advertising and 20 percent by the Internet. This is significant because research conducted in Taiwan found that 98 percent of the children have a say in what programs they watch on television. Children all over the world are having an influence on where the family dines when they go out to eat. In the United States the food industry spends $14 billion advertising to children. A study by Mintel found that before the age of 12, children's eating habits are influenced primarily by their parents, but after 12 there is a shift to peer influence.[20]

Roles and Status

Role. The activities that a person is expected to perform according to the persons around him or her.

A person belongs to many groups: family, clubs, and organizations. An individual's position in each group can be defined in terms of role and status. A **role** consists of the activities that a person is expected to perform according to the persons around him or her. Common roles include son or daughter, wife or husband, and manager or worker.

Each role influences buying behavior. For example, college students dining with their parents may act differently than when they are dining with peers. A person purchasing a banquet for his church's men's club may be more price conscious than usual if he believes church activities call for frugality. The same person might be more interested in detail and quality than in price when purchasing a banquet for his company. Thus, a person's role at that time significantly affects his or her purchasing behavior.

Our roles are also influenced by our surroundings. People dining at an elegant restaurant behave differently than when they dine at a fast-food restaurant. They

Businesspeople will behave according to the role they are in and act differently during a business meal compared to when they are enjoying a casual dining experience with friends. Courtesy of Ryan McVay/ Photodisc/Getty Images.

also have expectations about the roles that employees in different establishments should play. Failure to meet these role expectations creates dissatisfaction.[21] For example, diners at an elegant restaurant might expect waiters to hold their chairs during seating. The same diners would be surprised and possibly offended if a person cleaning tables at a fast-food hamburger restaurant assisted with seating.

Each role carries a status reflecting the general esteem given to it by society. People often choose products that show their status in society. For example, a business traveler became upset when all first-class seats were sold on a desired flight. The traveler was forced to fly economy class. When questioned about his concern over flying economy class, the traveler's main concern was what people he knew might think if they saw him sitting in the economy section. He did not seem to be concerned over the lower level of service or the smaller seating space provided by the economy section. These illustrations show that role and status are not constant social variables. Many marketing and sales professionals have made serious judgmental errors relative to the role and status of prospective customers.

Personal Factors

A buyer's decisions are also influenced by personal characteristics, such as age and life-cycle stage, occupation, economic situation, lifestyle, personality, and self-concept.

Age and Life-Cycle Stage

The types of goods and services people buy change during their lifetimes. Preferences for leisure activities, travel destinations, food, and entertainment are often age related. Important age-related factors are often overlooked by marketers. This is probably due to wide differences in age between those who determine marketing strategies and those who purchase the product/service. A study of mature travelers showed that this segment places great importance on grab bars in bathrooms, night lights, legible visible signs in hallways, extra blankets, and large printing on menus. Despite the logical importance of the factors, researchers found that this information "is not usually included in advertising and information listings."[22]

Successful marketing to various age segments may require specialized and targeted strategies. This will almost certainly require segmented target publications and database marketing. It may also require a marketing staff and advertising agency with people of varying ages and cultural backgrounds.

Family life cycle. The stages through which families might pass as they mature.

Buying behavior is also shaped by the **family life-cycle** stages. Young unmarried persons usually have few financial burdens, and they spend a good portion of their discretionary income on entertainment. Young married people without children have high discretionary incomes and dine out frequently. In fact, they have a higher frequency of dining out than any other group. Once they have children, their purchases from restaurants can change to more delivery and carryout. A study by the National Restaurant Association found couples with no children spent 60 percent more on food away from home as did married couples with children at home. When the children leave home, the discretionary income can jump, and expenses on dining out increases for people aged 55 to 74. Marketers often define their target markets in life-cycle terms and develop appropriate products and marketing plans.[23]

One of the leading life-stage segmentation systems is the Nielsen PRIZM Lifestage Groups system. PRIZM classifies every American household into one of 66 distinct life-stage segments, which are organized into 11 major life-stage

Many aging baby boomers still have an active lifestyle and choose to stay at resorts offering outdoor activities. Courtesy of Spotmatik Ltd/Shutterstock.

groups, based on affluence, age, and family characteristics. The classifications consider a host of demographic factors such as age, education, income, occupation, family composition, ethnicity, and housing; and behavioral and lifestyle factors, such as purchases, free-time activities, and media preferences.

The major PRIZM Lifestage Groups carry names such as "Striving Singles," "Midlife Success," "Young Achievers," "Sustaining Families," "Affluent Empty Nests," and "Conservative Classics," which in turn contain subgroups such as "Brite Lites, Li'l City," "Kids & Cul-de-Sacs," "Gray Power," and "Big City Blues." The "Young Achievers" group includes seven subsegments, with names like "Young Digerati," "Bohemian Mix," and "Young Influentials." The "Young Achievers" group consists of hip, single 20-somethings who rent apartments in or close to metropolitan neighborhoods. Their incomes range from working class to well-to-do, but the entire group tends to be politically liberal, listen to alternative music, and enjoy lively nightlife.[24]

Different life-stage groups exhibit different buying behaviors. Life-stage segmentation provides a powerful marketing tool for marketers in all industries to better find, understand, and engage consumers. Armed with data about the makeup of consumer life stages, marketers can create actionable, personalized campaigns based on how people consume and interact with brands and the world around them.

Occupation

A person's occupation affects the goods and services bought. For example, construction workers often buy their lunches from industrial catering trucks that come out to the job site. Business executives purchase meals from a full-service restaurant, whereas clerical employees may bring their lunch or purchase lunch from a nearby quick-service restaurant. Employees of some consulting firms are not allowed to eat in fast-food restaurants. The managers of these companies do not think it creates a proper image to have their clients see $300-an-hour consultants eating in a fast-food restaurant. Marketers try to identify occupational groups that have an above-average interest in their products.

Economic Situation

A person's economic situation greatly affects product choice and the decision to purchase a particular product. Consumers cut back on restaurant meals, entertainment, and vacations during recessions. They trade down in their choice of restaurants and/or menu items and eat out less frequently, looking for a coupon or deal when they do go out. Marketers need to watch trends in personal income, savings, and interest rates. If economic indicators point to a recession, they can redesign, reposition, and reprice their products. Restaurants may need to add lower-priced menu items that will still appeal to their target markets.

Conversely, periods of economic prosperity create opportunities. Consumers are more inclined to buy expensive wines and imported beers, menus can be upgraded, and air travel and leisure expenditures can be increased. Companies must take advantage of opportunities caused by economic upturns and take defensive steps when facing an economic downturn. Managers sometimes react too slowly to changing economic conditions. It pays to remain continuously aware of the macroenvironment facing customers. Regular reading of publications such as the *Wall Street Journal*, the business section of the local press, and regional economic reports by local and regional banks help to keep managers informed.

Lifestyle

Lifestyle. A person's pattern of living as expressed in his or her activities, interests, and opinions.

People coming from the same subculture, social class, and occupation may have quite different lifestyles. A **lifestyle** is a person's pattern of living as expressed in his or her activities, interests, and opinions. Lifestyle portrays the "whole person" interacting with his or her environment. Marketers search for relationships between their products and people who are achievement oriented. A chef may then target his or her restaurants more clearly at the achiever lifestyle. A study of tourists who purchase all-inclusive travel packages versus those who make travel arrangements independently revealed that lifestyle characteristics varied. All-inclusive travel purchasers were "more socially interactive, solicitous, and take their vacations mainly to relax." Tourists who preferred independent travel arrangements were more self-confident and often sought solitude.[25]

The San Diego Padres, like many baseball teams in the United States, have difficulty filling the stadium during day games that are held during the work week and when they play weak teams. Through marketing research the team's management was able to identify a market segment composed of retired couples, with a low income that were very loyal to the Padres. These fans enjoyed seeing the Padres play, didn't care who they were playing, and preferred day games. By identifying and marketing to this lifestyle segment who wanted to go to day games, the Padres were able to fill seats in games where they had excess capacity.

Personality and Self-Concept

Personality. A person's distinguishing psychological characteristics that lead to relatively consistent and lasting responses to his or her environment.

Self-concept. Self-image, the complex mental pictures people have of themselves.

Each person's personality influences his or her buying behavior. By **personality** we mean distinguishing psychological characteristics that lead to relatively consistent and enduring responses to the environment.

Personality can be useful in analyzing consumer behavior for some product or brand choices. For example, a beer company may discover that heavy beer drinkers tend to rank high in sociability and aggressiveness. This information can be used to establish a brand image for the beer and to suggest the type of people to show in an advertisement.

Stanley Paskie, the 72-year-old head bartender at the Drake Hotel in Chicago's Gold Coast, said, "It's imperative that a bartender possess the human touch. Unfortunately, human relations isn't a required course at the nation's bartending schools where most bartenders now learn the craft. I've had conversations with customers in which I never said a word. I remember one customer who, as he was leaving, said 'thanks for listening to me, fella.'"[26] Paskie believed that a good bartender is part father, part philosopher, part confessor, and part devil's advocate. These traits are undoubtedly important in many areas of hospitality and travel marketing.

Many marketers use a concept related to personality: a person's **self-concept** (also called self-image). Each of us has a complex mental self-picture, and our behavior tends to be consistent with that self-image.[27] People who perceive themselves as outgoing and active will be unlikely to purchase a cruise vacation if their perception of cruises is one of elderly persons lying on lounge chairs. They would be more likely to select a scuba-diving or skiing vacation. The cruise line industry has been quite successful in changing its "geriatric" image and now attracts outgoing and active consumers.

The role of self-concept obviously has a strong bearing on the selection of recreational pursuits, including golf, sailing, dirt bike riding, fishing, and hunting. Anyone who enjoys boating will testify to the difference between boaters who use sails and those who use engines. Yachters/sail boaters refer to those who use engines as "stink potters." Stink potters think of the sailing crowd as stuffy, pretentious, and generally not much fun.

Cruise lines, led by Carnival, changed cruising to include night clubs and family activities to attract a younger clientele. Courtesy of icholakov/Fotolia.

Psychological Factors

A person's buying choices are also influenced by four major psychological factors: motivation, perception, learning, and beliefs and attitudes.

Motivation

A person has many needs at any given time. Some are biological, arising from hunger, thirst, and discomfort. Others are psychological, arising from states of tension, such as the need for recognition, esteem, or belonging. Most of these needs are not strong enough to motivate a person to act at a given point in time. A need becomes a **motive** when it is aroused to a sufficient level of intensity. Creating a tension state causes the person to act to release the tension. Psychologists have developed theories of human motivation. Two of the most popular, the theories of Maslow and Herzberg, have quite different meanings for consumer analysis and marketing.

Motive. A need that is sufficiently pressing to direct a person to seek satisfaction of that need.

MASLOW'S THEORY OF MOTIVATION. Abraham Maslow sought to explain why people are driven by particular needs at particular times.[28] Why does one person spend much time and energy on personal safety and another on gaining the esteem of others? Maslow's answer is that human needs are arranged in a hierarchy, from the most pressing to the least pressing. Maslow's hierarchy of needs in order of importance are physiological needs, safety needs, social needs, esteem needs, and self-actualization needs. A person tries to satisfy the most important need first. When that important need is satisfied, it will stop being a motivator, and the person will then try to satisfy the next most important need. For example, a starving man (need 1) will not take an interest in the latest happenings in the art world (need 5), or in how he is seen or esteemed by others (need 3 or 4), or even in whether he is breathing clean air (need 2). But as each important need is satisfied, the next most important need will come into play.

Normally, needs are prioritized. For example, a college student with $500 to pay for incidental and recreational expenses during the term is unlikely to spend $400 on a trip to Florida over spring break. Instead, the money will probably be spent on smaller purchases of entertainment throughout the semester. If the student unexpectedly receives $2,000, there might be a strong temptation to satisfy a higher-order need.

HERZBERG'S THEORY. Frederick Herzberg developed a *two-factor theory* that distinguishes dissatisfiers (factors that cause dissatisfaction) and satisfiers (factors that cause satisfaction). The absence of dissatisfiers is not enough; satisfiers must be actively present to motivate a purchase. For example, a computer that does not come with a warranty would be a dissatisfier. Yet the presence of a product warranty would not act as a satisfier or motivator of a purchase because it is not a source of intrinsic satisfaction with the computer. Ease of use would be a satisfier.

Herzberg's theory has two implications. First, sellers should do their best to avoid dissatisfiers (e.g., a poor training manual or a poor service policy). Although these things will not sell a product, they might easily unsell it. Second, the manufacturer should identify the major satisfiers or motivators of purchase in the market and then supply them. These satisfiers will make the major difference as to which brand the customer buys.

Perception

A motivated person is ready to act. How that person acts is influenced by his or her perception of the situation. In the same situation, two people with the same motivation may act quite differently based on how they perceive conditions. One person may perceive the waiters at T.G.I. Friday's as casual and unsophisticated, whereas another person may view them as spontaneous with cheerful personalities. Friday's is targeting those in the second group.

Why do people have different perceptions of the same situation? All of us experience a stimulus by the flow of information through our five senses: sight, hearing, smell, touch, and taste. However, each of us receives, organizes, and interprets this sensory information in an individual way. A person receives a great deal of information every day. For example, individuals are exposed an estimated 3,000 to 5,000 messages every day. The cluttered digital environment adds 5.3 trillion online display ads shown every year, 400 million tweets sent daily, 144,000 hours of video uploaded daily, and 4.75 billion pieces of information shared on Facebook every day.[29] It is impossible for people to pay attention to all the stimuli surrounding them. This means perception is the process by which an individual selects, organizes, and interprets information to create a meaningful picture of the world.[30] From a marketing standpoint an individual's perception is reality to them. One can have an excellent restaurant, but if the appearance of the restaurant from the street is that of a very ordinary restaurant many people who would have enjoyed the restaurant will never try it because of their perception, based on the street appearance of the restaurant.

The key word in the definition of perception is *individual*. One person might perceive a fast-talking salesperson as aggressive and insincere; another, as intelligent and helpful. People can emerge with different perceptions of the same object because of three perceptual processes: selective attention, selective distortion, and selective retention.

SELECTIVE ATTENTION. People are exposed to a tremendous amount of daily stimuli: The average person may be exposed to over 1,500 ads a day. Because a person cannot possibly attend to all of these, most stimuli are screened out—a process called selective attention. Selective attention means that marketers have to work hard to attract consumers' notice. The real challenge is to explain which stimuli people will notice. Here are some findings:

- People are more likely to notice stimuli that relate to a current need. A person who is motivated to buy a computer will notice computer ads; he or she will probably not notice stereo-equipment ads.

- People are more likely to notice stimuli that they anticipate. You are more likely to notice computers than radios in a computer store because you do not expect the store to carry radios.

- People are more likely to notice stimuli whose deviations are large in relation to the normal size of the stimuli. You are more likely to notice an ad offering $100 off the list price of a computer than one offering $5 off.

SELECTIVE DISTORTION. Ever noticed stimuli do not always come across in the way the senders intended? Selective distortion is the tendency to twist information into personal meanings and interpret information in a way that will fit our preconceptions. Unfortunately, marketers can't do much about selective distortion.

SELECTIVE RETENTION. People forget much of what they learn but tend to retain information that supports their attitudes and beliefs. Because of selective retention, we are likely to remember good points mentioned about competing products. Selective retention explains why marketers use drama and repetition in sending messages to their target market.

The retail space of the Venetian Macau is consistent with a guests perception of luxury resort retail space. Courtesy of korkorkusung/Fotolia.

Marketing HIGHLIGHT 6.1

Sensory Marketing—A Powerful Tool for Hospitality Businesses

Sensory marketing has been defined as "marketing that engages the consumers' senses and affects their perception, judgment, and behavior." In other words, sensory marketing is an application of the understanding of sensation and perception to the field of marketing. All five senses may be engaged with sensory marketing: sight, sound, smell, taste, and feel. In a 2012 *Journal of Consumer Psychology* article, Aradhna Krishna offers an excellent review of the rapidly accumulating academic research on this topic.

In doing so, she notes, "Given the gamut of explicit marketing appeals made to consumers every day, subconscious 'triggers' which may appeal to the basic senses may be a more efficient way to engage consumers." In other words, consumers' own inferences about a product's attributes may be more persuasive, at least in some cases, than explicit claims from an advertiser.

Krishna argues that sensory marketing's effects can be manifested in two main ways. One, sensory marketing can be used subconsciously to shape consumer perceptions of more abstract qualities of a product or service (say, different aspects of its brand personality such as its sophistication, ruggedness, warmth, quality, and modernity). Two, sensory marketing can also be used to affect the perceptions of specific product or service attributes such as its color, taste, smell, or shape.

Marketers certainly appreciate the importance of sensory marketing. Many hotels, retailers, and other service establishments use signature scents to set a mood and distinguish themselves. Westin's White Tea scent was so popular it began to sell it for home use. Although NBC, Intel, and Yahoo! have trademarked their brand jingles (or yodels), Harley-Davidson was unsuccessful in trademarking its distinctive engine roar. In packaging, companies try to find shapes that are pleasing to the touch, and in food advertising, visual and verbal depictions try to tantalize consumers' taste buds.

Based on Krishna's review of academic research in psychology and marketing, we next highlight some key considerations for each of the five senses.

Touch

Touch is the first sense to develop and the last sense we lose with age. People vary in their need for touch. One study found that when a server touched a customer with her hand on the customer's shoulder for 2–3 seconds, sales increased when compared to customers who did not receive the touch.[31]

Smell

Scent-encoded information has been shown to be more durable and last longer in memory than information encoded with other sensory cues. People can recognize scents after very long lapses of time, and using scents as reminders can cue all kinds of autobiographical memories. Most travelers in the United States will recognize the scent of Cinnabon as they pass by the restaurant in the airport. Pleasant scents have also been show to enhance evaluations of products and stores. Consumers also take more time and engage in more variety seeking in the presence of pleasant scents.

Sound

Marketing communications by their very nature are often auditory in nature. Even the sounds that make up a word can carry meanings. One study showed that Frosh-brand ice cream sounded creamier than Frish-brand ice cream. Language too can have its own associations. In bilingual cultures where English is the second language—such as Japan, Korea, Germany, and India—use of English in ads signals modernity, progress, sophistication, and a cosmopolitan identity. Ambient music in a store has also been shown to influence consumer mood, time spent in a location, perception of time spent in a location, and spending.

Taste

Humans can distinguish only five pure tastes: sweet, salty, sour, bitter, and umami. Umami comes from Japanese food researchers and stands for "delicious" or "savory" as it relates to the taste of pure protein or monosodium glutamate (MSG). Taste perceptions themselves depend on all the other senses—the way a food looks, feels, smells, and sounds to eat. Thus many factors have been shown to affect taste perceptions, including physical attributes, brand name, product information (ingredients, nutritional information), product packaging, and advertising. Foreign-sounding brand names can improve ratings of yogurt, and ingredients that sound unpleasant (balsamic vinegar or soy) can affect consumers' taste perceptions if disclosed before product consumption.

Vision

Visual effects have been studied in detail in an advertising context. Many visual perception biases or illusions exist in day-to-day consumer behavior. For example, people judge tall thin containers to contain more volume than short fat ones, but after drinking from the containers, people actually feel they have consumed more from short fat containers than tall thin containers, over-adjusting their expectations. Even something as simple as the way a mug is depicted in an ad can affect product evaluations. A mug photographed with the handle on the right side was shown to elicit more mental stimulation and product purchase intent from right-handed people than if shown with the handle on the left side.[32]

Learning

When people act, they learn. **Learning** describes changes in an individual's behavior arising from experience. Most human behavior is learned. Learning theorists say that learning occurs through the interplay of drives, stimuli, cues, responses, and reinforcement.

When consumers experience a product, they learn about it. Members of the site-selection committee for a convention often sample the services of competing hotels. They eat in the restaurants, note the friendliness and professionalism of the staff, and examine the hotel's features. Based on what they have learned, a hotel is selected to host the convention. During the convention, they experience the hotel once again. Based on their experience and those of the attending conventioneers, they will be either satisfied or dissatisfied.

Hotels should help guests learn about the quality of their facilities and services. Luxury hotels give tours to first-time guests and inform them of the services offered. Repeat guests should be updated on the hotel's services by employees and by letters and literature.

Beliefs and Attitudes

Through acting and learning, people acquire beliefs and attitudes, which, in turn, influence their buying behavior. A **belief** is a descriptive thought that a person holds about something. A customer may believe that Novotel has the best facilities and most professional staff of any hotel in the price range. These beliefs may be based on real knowledge, opinion, or faith. They may or may not carry an emotional charge.

Marketers are interested in the beliefs that people have about specific products and services. Beliefs reinforce product and brand images. People act on beliefs. If unfounded consumer beliefs deter purchases, marketers will want to launch a campaign to change them.

Unfounded consumer beliefs can severely affect the revenue and even the life of hospitality and travel companies. Among these beliefs might be the following:

- A particular hamburger chain served ground kangaroo meat.
- A particular airline has poor maintenance.
- A particular country has unhealthy food-handling standards.

People have attitudes about almost everything: religion, politics, clothes, music, and food. An **attitude** describes a person's relatively consistent evaluations, feelings, and tendencies toward an object or an idea. Attitudes put people into a frame of mind for liking or disliking things and moving toward or away from them. Companies can benefit by researching attitudes toward their products. Understanding attitudes and beliefs is the first step toward changing or reinforcing them.

Attitudes are very difficult to change. A person's attitudes fit into a pattern, and changing one attitude may require making many difficult adjustments. It is easier for a company to create products that are compatible with existing attitudes than to change the attitudes toward its products. There are exceptions, of course, where the high cost of trying to change attitudes may pay off.

There is a saying among restaurateurs that a restaurant is only as good as the last meal served. Attitudes explain in part why this is true. A customer who has returned to a restaurant several times and on one visit receives a bad meal may begin to believe it is impossible to count on having a good meal at that restaurant. The customer's attitudes toward the restaurant begin to change. If this customer again receives a bad meal, negative attitudes may be permanently fixed and prevent a future return. Serving a poor meal to first-time customers can be disastrous. Customers develop an immediate negative attitude that prevents them from returning.

Attitudes developed as children often influence purchases as adults. Children may retain negative attitudes toward certain vegetables, people, and possibly places. Chances are equally good that they may retain very positive images toward McDonald's and Disneyland. Hospitality and travel companies are particularly

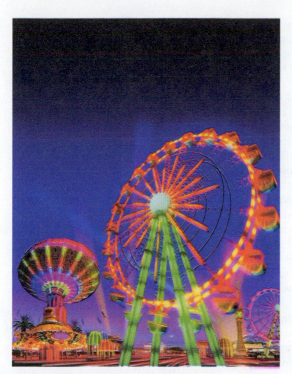

Amusement parks view children as lifelong customers. They want them to come back as parents, aunts, uncles, and grandparents Courtesy of Fei Wong/123RF.

subject to lifelong consumer attitudes that result from positive or negative childhood experiences. Harsh words from the manager of a miniature golf course or air sickness on a commercial flight in which the flight attendant showed little sympathy are negative attitude-building experiences.

Disney and McDonald's both view children as lifelong customers. They want children to return as teenagers, parents, aunts, uncles, and grandparents and treat them in a manner to ensure future business. Many hospitality and travel companies have still not learned from McDonald's and Disney.

Once negative attitudes are developed, they are hard to change. New restaurant owners often want quick cash flow and sometimes start without excellent quality. A new restaurateur complained that customers are fickle. When his restaurant first opened, there were lines of people waiting for a seat. A few months later, he had plenty of empty seats every night. Obviously, he had not satisfied his first guests. Even though he may have subsequently corrected his early mistakes, his original customers had been disappointed, were not returning, and probably were reporting negative comments to their friends.

We can now appreciate the many individual characteristics and forces influencing consumer behavior. Consumer choice is the result of a complex interplay of cultural, social, personal, and psychological factors. Many of these cannot be influenced by the marketer; however, they help the marketer to better understand customers' reactions and behavior.

The Buyer Decision Process

We are now ready to look at how consumers make buying decisions. Figure 6–3 shows that the buyer decision process consists of five stages: need recognition, information search, evaluation of alternatives, purchase decision, and postpurchase behavior. This model emphasizes that the buying process starts long before and continues long after the actual purchase. It encourages the marketer to focus on the entire buying process rather than just the purchase decision.

The model appears to imply that consumers pass through all five stages with every purchase they make. But in more routine purchases, consumers skip or reverse some of these stages. A customer in a bar purchasing a glass of beer may go right to the purchase decision, skipping information search and evaluation. This is referred to as an *automatic response loop*.[33] The dream of every marketer is to have customers develop an automatic response to purchase its products. However, this does not typically happen. The model in Figure 6–3 shows the considerations that arise when a consumer faces a new and complex purchase situation.

To illustrate this model, we follow Rosemary Martinez, a college student. She has just remembered that next Saturday is her boyfriend's birthday.

Need Recognition

The buying process starts when the buyer recognizes a problem or need. The buyer senses a difference between his or her actual state and a desired state. The need can be triggered by internal stimuli. From previous experience, the person has learned how to cope with this need and is motivated toward objects that he or she knows will satisfy it.

Figure 6–3
Buyer decision process.

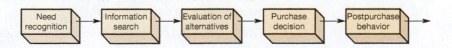

Need recognition → Information search → Evaluation of alternatives → Purchase decision → Postpurchase behavior

Needs can also be triggered by external stimuli. Rosemary passes a restaurant, and the aroma of freshly baked bread stimulates her hunger; she has lunch with a friend who just came back from Bali and raves about her trip; or she watches a television commercial for a Hyatt resort. All these stimuli can lead her to recognize a problem or need.

At this stage, marketers must determine the factors and situations that trigger consumer problem recognition. They should research consumers to find out what kinds of needs or problems led them to purchase an item, what brought these needs about, and how they led consumers to choose this particular product.

Rosemary might have mentioned that she passed a card shop and noticed birthday cards, which reminded her that her boyfriend's birthday was approaching. She knew he liked German food, so she decided to take him to a German restaurant.

By gathering such information, marketers can identify stimuli that most often trigger interest in the product and develop marketing programs that involve these stimuli. Marketers can also show how their product is a solution to a problem. For example, T.G.I. Friday's advertised its gift certificates as a solution to Christmas shopping. Friday's food and atmosphere attracts a broad range of people; the gift certificates are easy to buy, avoiding the need to go to crowded shopping centers; and they can be bought in denominations that fit with planned expenditures. Friday's promoted gift certificates as a solution to a common problem experienced before Christmas.

When looking for a hotel, "business travelers want a hotel to give them the tools to get their work done efficiently, which includes having competent staff members on duty, more than they want personalized services and fancy surroundings."[34] Hotels have responded to this by good work spaces in the rooms and by creating lobbies that support a work environment, through computer spaces, free Wi-Fi, and tables in the food and beverage area where one can enjoy a meal or snack while checking e-mails or conducting work.

The Travel Industry Association of America found that families with both heads of the household employed were finding it difficult to find a week when everyone was free. As a result, this segment needed three- and four-day getaways that could be booked at the last minute because 42 percent of this group makes plans within two weeks of the actual vacation.[35] These examples show that businesses must understand the needs of their customers and how these needs are translated into wants.

Information Search

An aroused consumer may or may not search for more information. If the consumer's drive is strong and a satisfying product is near at hand, the consumer is likely to buy it at that moment. If not, the consumer may simply store the need in memory and search for relevant information.

How much searching a consumer does will depend on the strength of the drive, the amount of initial information, the ease of obtaining more information, the value placed on additional information, and the satisfaction one gets from searching.

Rosemary asked several of her friends if they knew of a good German restaurant. Then she scanned a city magazine's restaurant listings. Finally, she looked in the Yellow Pages to see if she could find additional German restaurants. As a result of her search, Rosemary identified three German restaurants. She then tried to find friends and acquaintances who had been to one or more of the restaurants to get their impressions. She also looked in the *Zagat Restaurant Guide* for her city to see how the restaurants were rated.

The consumer can obtain information from several sources. These include the following:

- *Personal sources:* Family, friends, neighbors, acquaintances
- *Commercial sources:* Advertising, salespeople, dealers, packaging, displays
- *Public sources:* Restaurant reviews, editorials in the travel section, consumer-rating organizations
- *The Internet:* the company's Web site and comments from previous guests

With hospitality and travel products, personal and public sources of information are more important than advertisements. This is because customers do not know what they are going to receive until they have received it. People often ask others—friends, relatives, acquaintances, professionals—for recommendations concerning a product or service. Thus, companies have a strong interest in building such *word-of-mouth sources*. These sources have two chief advantages. First, they are convincing: Word of mouth is the only promotion method that is *of* consumers, *by* consumers, and *for* consumers.[36] Having loyal, satisfied customers who brag about doing business with you is the dream of every business owner. Not only are satisfied customers repeat buyers, but they are also walking, talking billboards for your business. Second, the costs are low. Keeping in touch with satisfied customers and turning them into word-of-mouth advocates cost the business relatively little. A customer cannot try out an intangible product before he or she purchases it. For example, people may hear of a restaurant through advertising but ask their friends about the restaurant before they try it. Responses from personal sources have more impact than advertising because they are perceived to be more credible. Christopher Lovelock lists these sources of information as ways customers can reduce the risk of purchasing a service:

- Seeking information from respected personal sources (family, friends, peers)
- Relying on a firm that has a good reputation
- Looking for guarantees and warranties
- Visiting service facilities or trying aspects of the service before purchasing
- Asking knowledgeable employees about competing services
- Examining tangible cues or other physical evidence
- Using the Internet to compare service offerings

By gathering information, consumers increase their awareness and knowledge of available choices and product features. A company must design its marketing mix to make prospects aware of and knowledgeable about the features and benefits of its products or brands. If it fails to do this, it has lost its opportunity to sell the customer. A company must also gather information about competitors and plan a differentiated appeal.

Marketers should carefully identify consumers' sources of information and the importance of each source. Consumers should be asked how they first heard about the brand, what information they received, and the importance they place on different information sources. This information is helpful in preparing effective communication.

Evaluation of Alternatives

We have seen how the consumer uses information to arrive at a set of final brand choices. But how does the consumer choose among the alternatives? How does the consumer mentally sort and process information to arrive at brand choices? Unfortunately, there is no simple and single evaluation process used by all consumers or even by one consumer in all buying situations. There are several evaluation processes.

Rosemary Martinez preferred a restaurant with good food and service. However, she believed that all the restaurants under consideration offered these attributes. She also wanted to patronize a restaurant with entertainment and a romantic atmosphere. Finally, she had a limited amount of money, so price was important. If several restaurants met her criteria, she would choose the one with the most convenient location.

Certain basic concepts help explain consumer evaluation processes. First, we assume that each consumer sees a product as a bundle of product attributes. For restaurants, these attributes include food quality, menu selection, and quality of service, atmosphere, location, and price. Consumers vary as to which of these attributes they consider relevant. The most attention is paid to attributes connected

Brand image. The set of beliefs consumers hold about a particular brand.

with their needs. Second, the consumer attaches different degrees of importance to each attribute. That is, each consumer attaches importance to each attribute according to his or her unique needs and wants. Third, the consumer is likely to develop a set of beliefs about where each brand stands on each attribute. The set of beliefs held about a particular brand is known as the **brand image**. The consumer's beliefs may vary from true attributes because of the consumer's experience and the effects of selective perception, selective distortion, and selective retention. Fourth, the consumer is assumed to have a utility function for each attribute. A utility function shows how the consumer expects total product satisfaction to vary with different levels of different attributes. Fifth, the consumer arrives at attitudes toward the different brands through some evaluation procedure. One or more of several evaluation procedures are used, depending on the consumer and the buying decision.

When it was evaluated against its competitors, Domino's was known by many customers for the speed of its delivery, but not as the best-tasting pizza. Domino's decided to address negative perceptions about its taste head on. A major communication program featured documentary-style TV ads that opened with Domino's employees at corporate headquarters reviewing written and videotaped focus group feedback from customers. The feedback contained biting and vicious comments, such as, "Domino's pizza crust to me is like cardboard" and "The sauce tastes like ketchup." After President Patrick Doyle is shown on camera stating these results were unacceptable, the ads proceeded to show Domino's chefs and executives in their test kitchens proclaiming that its pizza was new and improved with a bolder, richer sauce; a more robust cheese combination; and an herb- and garlic-flavored crust. Many critics were stunned by the admission of the company that their number 2 ranked pizza, in effect, had been inferior for years. Others countered by noting that the new product formulation and unconventional ads were addressing a widely held, difficult-to-change negative belief that was dragging the brand down and required decisive action. Doyle summed up consumer reaction as "Most really like it, some don't. And that's OK."[37]

Purchase Decision

In the evaluation stage, the consumer ranks brands in the choice set and forms purchase intentions. Generally, the consumer buys the most preferred brand, but two factors can come between the purchase intention and the purchase decision. These factors are shown in Figure 6–4.

Attitudes of others represent the first. Rosemary Martinez selected a German restaurant because her boyfriend likes German food. Rosemary's choice depended on the strength of another person's attitudes toward her buying decision and on her motivation to comply with those wishes. The more intense the other person's attitude and the closer that person is to the decision maker, the more influence the other person will have. Nowhere is this better identified than in the case of children. Children do not hide their desires and parents and grandparents are affected intensely.

Purchase intention is also influenced by unexpected situations. The consumer forms a purchase intention based on factors such as expected family income, expected price, and expected benefits from the product. When the consumer is about to act, unexpected situations may arise to change the purchase intention. Rosemary Martinez may have an unexpected car problem that will cost $200 for repairs. This may cause her to cancel dinner reservations and select a less expensive gift.

Figure 6–4
Steps between evaluation of alternatives and a purchase decision.

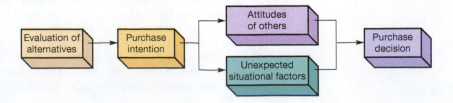

Because customers do not know what the experience will be until after the purchase, managers must remember that first-time customers are really trying the product. While customers are in the purchase act, employees must do everything possible to ensure that they will have a good experience and the postpurchase evaluation will be favorable.

Postpurchase Behavior

The marketer's job does not end when the customer buys a product. Following a purchase, the consumer will be satisfied or dissatisfied and will engage in postpurchase actions of significant interest to the marketer. What determines postpurchase satisfaction or dissatisfaction with a purchase? The answer lies in the relationship between consumer expectations and perceived product performance.[38] If the product matches expectations, the consumer will be satisfied. If it falls short, the consumer will experience dissatisfaction.

Consumers base expectations on past experiences and on messages they receive from sellers, friends, and other information sources. If a seller exaggerates the product's likely performance, the consumer will be disappointed. The larger the gap between expectations and performance, the greater the consumer's dissatisfaction. This suggests that sellers must faithfully represent the product's performance so that buyers are satisfied. For example, Bermuda enticed tourists to enjoy the island during the off season at a lower price. It called this period "Rendezvous Time" and advertised that all the island's amenities would be available. When tourists arrived, they found that many facilities and attractions were closed. Hotels had shut down many of their food and beverage facilities, leaving tourists disappointed. Advertising claims initially brought tourists, but the truth got out and hotel occupancy dropped by almost 50 percent over a period of six years.[39]

Cognitive dissonance. Buyer discomfort caused by postpurchase conflict.

Almost all major purchases result in **cognitive dissonance**, or discomfort caused by postpurchase conflict. Every purchase involves compromise. Consumers feel uneasy about acquiring the drawbacks of the chosen brand and losing the benefits of the rejected brands. Thus consumers feel some postpurchase dissonance with many purchases, and they often take steps after the purchase to reduce dissonance.[40]

Marketing HIGHLIGHT 6.2   Unique Aspects of Hospitality and Travel Consumers

Valarie Zeithaml, a marketing consultant, published a classic article describing how the consumer evaluation process differs between goods and services. Persons purchasing hospitality and travel services rely more on information from personal sources. When looking for a good restaurant, people ask friends or people familiar with the town, such as front-desk employees or the concierge. Restaurants should attempt to affect positively those persons whom potential customers may contact. In larger cities there is a concierge association. Smart restaurateurs seek to host this club, letting their members experience the restaurants.

Postpurchase evaluation of services is important. The intangibility of services makes it difficult to judge the service beforehand. Consumers may seek advice from friends but use the information they receive from actually purchasing the service to evaluate it. The first-time customer is on a trial basis. If the hotel or restaurant satisfies the customers, they will come back.

When purchasing hospitality and travel products, customers often use price as an indication of quality. A business executive who has been under a lot of pressure decides to take a three-day vacation now that the project is complete. She wants luxury accommodations and good food service. She is prepared to pay $175 a night for the room. She calls a hotel that offers a special rate of $85. This hotel may be able to satisfy her needs and has simply dropped its rate to encourage business. In this case, the hotel has dropped its rate too low to attract this customer. Because she has never visited the hotel, she will perceive that the hotel is below her standard. Similarly, a person who enjoys fresh seafood and sees grilled red snapper on the menu for $7.99 will assume that it must be a low-quality frozen product because fresh domestic fish usually costs at least twice as much. When using price to create demand, care must be taken to ensure that one does not create the wrong consumer perceptions about the product's quality.

When customers purchase hospitality and travel products, they often perceive some risk in the purchase. If customers want to impress friends or business associates, they usually take them to a restaurant they have visited previously. Customers tend to be loyal to restaurants and hotels that have met their needs. A meeting planner is reluctant to change hotels if the hotel has been doing a good job.

Customers of hospitality and travel products often blame themselves when dissatisfied. A man who orders scampi may be disappointed with the dish but not complain because he blames himself for the bad choice. He loves the way his favorite restaurant fixes scampi, but he should have known that this restaurant would not be able to prepare it the same way. When the waiter asks how everything is, he replies that it was okay. Employees must be aware that dissatisfied customers may not complain. They should try to seek out sources of guest dissatisfaction and resolve them. A waiter noticing someone not eating his or her food may ask if he or she could replace it with an alternative dish and suggest some items that could be brought out very quickly.[41]

Dissatisfied consumers may take any of several actions. They may return the product or complain to the company and ask for a refund or exchange. They may initiate a lawsuit or complain to an organization or group that can help them get satisfaction. Buyers may also simply stop purchasing the product and discourage purchases by family and friends. In each of these cases, the seller loses.

Marketers can take steps to reduce consumer postpurchase dissatisfaction and help customers to feel good about their purchases. Hotels can send a letter to meeting planners congratulating them on having selected their hotel for their next meeting. They can place ads featuring testimonials of satisfied meeting planners in trade magazines. They can encourage customers to suggest improvements.

Understanding the consumer's needs and buying process is the foundation of successful marketing. By understanding how buyers proceed through problem recognition, information search, evaluation of alternatives, the purchase decision, and postpurchase behavior, marketers can acquire many clues as to how to better meet buyer needs. By understanding the various participants in the buying process and major influences on buying behavior, marketers can develop a more effective marketing program.

CHAPTER REVIEW

I. Model of Consumer Behavior. The company that really understands how consumers will respond to different product features, prices, and advertising appeals has a great advantage over its competitors. As a result, researchers from companies and universities have heavily studied the relationship between marketing stimuli and consumer response. The marketing stimuli consist of the four Ps: product, price, place, and promotion. Other stimuli include major forces and events in the buyer's environment: economic, technological, political, and cultural. All these stimuli enter the buyer's black box, where they are turned into a set of observable buyer responses: product choice, brand choice, dealer choice, purchase timing, and purchase amount.

II. Personal Characteristics Affecting Consumer Behavior
   A. Cultural factors
      1. **Culture.** Culture is the most basic determinant of a person's wants and behavior. It compromises the basic values, perceptions, wants, and behaviors that a person learns continuously in a society.
      2. **Subculture.** Each culture contains smaller subcultures, groups of people with shared value systems based on common experiences and situations.
      3. **Social classes.** These are relatively permanent and ordered divisions in a society whose members share similar values, interests, and behaviors. Social class in newer nations such as the United States, Canada, Australia, and New Zealand is not indicated by a single factor such as income but is measured as a combination of occupation, source of income, education, wealth, and other variables.
   B. Social factors
      1. **Groups.** Groups that have a direct influence and to which a person belongs are called membership groups. In contrast, reference groups serve as direct (face-to-face) or indirect points of comparison or reference in forming a person's attitudes or behavior.
      2. **Word-of-mouth influence and buzz marketing.** The personal words and recommendations of trusted friends, associates, and other

consumers tend to be more credible than those coming from commercial sources. Buzz marketing involves enlisting or creating opinion leaders to serve as "brand ambassadors," who spread the word about a company's products.

3. **Online social networks.** These networks are online communities where people socialize or exchange information and opinions. Social networking media range from blogs to social networking Web sites, such as Facebook.com and YouTube, to entire virtual worlds, such as Second Life.

4. **Family.** Family members have a strong influence on buyer behavior. The family remains the most important consumer buying organization in American society.

5. **Role and status.** A role consists of the activities that a person is expected to perform according to the persons around him or her. Each role carries a status reflecting the general esteem given to it by society. People often choose products that show their status in society.

C. **Personal factors**
1. **Age and life-cycle stage.** The types of goods and services people buy change during their lifetimes. As people grow older and mature, the products they desire change. The makeup of the family also affects purchasing behavior. For example, families with young children dine out at fast-food restaurants.
2. **Occupation.** A person's occupation affects the goods and services bought.
3. **Economic situation.** A person's economic situation greatly affects product choice and the decision to purchase a particular product.
4. **Lifestyle.** Lifestyles profile a person's whole pattern of acting and interacting in the world. When used carefully, the lifestyle concept can help the marketer understand changing consumer values and how they affect buying behavior.
5. **Personality and self-concept.** Each person's personality influences his or her buying behavior. By personality we mean distinguishing psychological characteristics that disclose

a person's relatively individualized, consistent, and enduring responses to the environment. Many marketers use a concept related to personality: a person's self-concept (also called self-image). Each of us has a complex mental self-picture, and our behavior tends to be consistent with that self-image.

D. **Psychological factors**
1. **Motivation.** A need becomes a motive when it is aroused to a sufficient level of intensity. Creating a tension state causes a person to act to release the tension.
2. **Perception.** Perception is the process by which a person selects, organizes, and interprets information to create a meaningful picture of the world.
3. **Learning.** Learning describes changes in a person's behavior arising from experience.
4. **Beliefs and attitudes.** A belief is a descriptive thought that a person holds about something. An attitude describes a person's relatively consistent evaluations, feelings, and tendencies toward an object or an idea.

III. **Buyer Decision Process**
A. **Need recognition.** The buying process starts when the buyer recognizes a problem or need.
B. **Information search.** An aroused consumer may or may not search for more information. How much searching a consumer does will depend on the strength of the drive, the amount of initial information, the ease of obtaining more information, the value placed on additional information, and the satisfaction one gets from searching.
C. **Evaluation of alternatives.** Unfortunately, there is no simple and single evaluation process used by all consumers or even by one consumer in all buying situations. There are several evaluation processes.
D. **Purchase decision.** In the evaluation stage, the consumer ranks brands in the choice set and forms purchase intentions. Generally, the consumer buys the most preferred brand.
E. **Postpurchase behavior.** The marketer's job does not end when the customer buys a product. Following a purchase, the consumer will be satisfied or dissatisfied and will engage in postpurchase actions of significant interest to the marketer.

■■■ DISCUSSION QUESTIONS

1. Explain why marketers study buyer behavior and discuss characteristics affecting consumer behavior. Which characteristics do you think would have the greatest impact on your decision to select a restaurant to celebrate a special occasion, such as a birthday or anniversary?

2. Choose a restaurant concept that you would like to take overseas. How will the factors shown in Figure 6–2 work for or against the success of this restaurant?

3. Discuss when the family can be a strong influence on buying behavior regarding the choice of restaurants.

4. Apply the five stages in the decision process to your selection of a destination for your next vacation.

5. An advertising agency president says, "Perception is reality." What does he mean by this? How is perception important to marketers?

■■■ EXPERIENTIAL EXERCISE

Do one of the following:

1. Choose a hospitality or travel organization. You are in charge of designing a consumer advertisement for that organization. How would you determine the message of the advertisement?

2. Talk to several people about how they would choose a hotel in a city they have never been to before, a restaurant for a special occasion, or a place to vacation. What did you learn about the buyer decision process from these discussions?

■■■ INTERNET EXERCISES

Choose a restaurant, tourist destination, or hotel near where you live. Go to a Web site that has user-generated content such as TripAdvsior.com or Expedia.com. As a manager

of the organization you have chosen, what actions would you take based on the information you gathered from the reviews?

■■■ REFERENCES

1 Aamer Madhani, "Taco Bell Begins Testing Delivery Service at 200 Stores," *USA TODAY*, July 8, 2015, http://www.usatoday.com/story/money/2015/07/08/taco-bell-to-test-delivery-california-texas/29832469/ (accessed July 10, 2015); Chelsey Dulaney, "Taco Bell, Pizza Hut to Remove Artificial Flavors, Coloring," *Wall Street Journal*, May 26, 2015, http://www.wsj.com/articles/taco-bell-to-remove-artificial-flavors-coloring-1432638320 (accessed July 10, 2015); Maureen Morrison, "Sales Are Going Loco at Taco Bell, Ad Age's Marketer of the Year," *Advertising Age* (September 2, 2013): 2; Shirley Brady, "Taco Bell Promotes New 'Live Mas' Tagline in New Campaign," *Brand Channel*, February 24, 2012, www.brandchannel.com/home/post/2012/02/24/Taco-Beii-Uve-Mas-Doritos-Locos-Tacos-Spots-022412.aspx; Maureen Morrison, "Taco Bell to Exchange 'Think Outside the Bun' for 'Live Mas,'" *Advertising Age*, February 21, 2012, adage.corn/print/232849/; Mark Brandau, "Yum Plans to Double U.S. Taco Bell Sales," *Restaurant News*, May 22, 2013, nrn.corn/quick-service/analysts-yum-plans-double·us-taco-bell-sales; Mark Brandau, "Taco Bell NBA Sponsorship to Emphasize Digital, Social Media," *Restaurant News*, October 18, 2013, nm.corn/social-media/taco-bell-nba-sponsorship-emphasize-digital-social-media; and various pages at www.tacobell.com (accessed September 2014).

2 Robert J. Benes, Abbie Jarman, and Ashley Williams, "2007 NRA Sets Records," www.chefmagazine.com (accessed September 2007); www.cokesolutions.com (accessed September 2014).

3 "Hispanics Lead as Web Users Who Are Truly Mobile-First," *eMarketer*, October 8, 2013, http://www.emarketer.com/Article/Hispanics-Lead-Web-Users-Who-Truly-Mobile-First/1010280 (accessed July 15, 2010).

4 http://www.iahmp.org/ (accessed August 29, 2011).

5 Hernan Tagliani, "3 Ways to Keep Success on a Restaurant's Menu," *Orlando Business Journal*, April 20, 2015, http://www.bizjournals.com/orlando/ blog/2015/04/3-ways-to-keep-success-on-a-restaurants-menu.html (accessed July 10, 2015)

6 See Todd Wasserman, "Report Shows Shifting American Population," *Brandweek* (January 11, 2000): 6; R. Thomas Umstead, "BET: African-Americans Grow in Numbers, Buying Power," (January 26, 2010), www.multichannel.com/article/446028-BET_African_Americans_Grow_in_Numbers_Buying_Power.php; Mark Dolliver, "How to Reach Affluent African Americans," *Adweek* (February 2, 2010), www.adweek.com/aw/content_display/news/strategy/e3i8decb5ca03594f57dadfad445ed35524; U.S. Census Bureau reports, www.census.gov (accessed February 2010).

7 http://www.ncbmp.com/about/ (accessed August 29, 2010).

8 See Lynn Russo Whylly, "Marketing to Asian Americans," advertising supplement to *Brandweek* (May 26, 2008): S1–S3; Jeffrey M. Humphreys, *The Multicultural Economy 2008*; U.S. Census Bureau reports, www.census.gov (accessed October 2010).

9 See Stuart Elliott, "New Ad Organization to Promote Cross Cultural Marketing," *New York Times*, August 30, 2013, http://www.nytimes.com/2013/08/31/business/media/new-ad-organization-to-promote-cross-cultural-marketing.html?_r=0 (accessed July 15, 2015); "Just Checking," https://www.youtube.com/watch?v=1QnsLRzwuv0 (accessed July 15, 2015).

10 See Eleftheria Parpis, "Goodbye Color Codes," *Adweek* (September 27, 2010): 24–25; "Ethnic Marketing: McDonald's Is Lovin' It," *Bloomberg BusinessWeek* (July 18, 2010): 22–23; Alex Frias, "5 Tips to Refresh Your Multicultural Marketing Strategy in 2013," *Forbes*, February 8, 2013, www.forbes.com/sites/theyec/2013/02/08/5-tips-to-refresh-your-multicultural-marketingstrategy-in-2013/; Stuart Elliott, "New Ad Organization to Promote Cross-Cultural Marketing," *New York Times*, August 30, 2013, http://www.nytimes.com/2013/08/31/business/media/new-ad-organization-to-promote-cross-cultural-marketing.

html and The Cross-Cultural Marketing & Communications Association, "Total Market," www.theccmca.org/?page_id=3631 (accessed September 2014).

11 See Richard P. Coleman, "The Continuing Significance of Social Class to Marketing," *Journal of Consumer Research* (December 1983): 264–280; Leon G. Shiffman and Leslie Lazar Kanuk, *Consumer Behavior*, 6th ed. (Upper Saddle River, NJ: Prentice Hall, 1997), p. 388.

12 Adam Bluestein, "Make Money in 2013 (and Beyond)," *Inc.*, December 2012/January 2013, pp. 58–65, here p. 64.

13 "Research Reveals Word-of-Mouth Campaigns on Customer Networks Double Marketing Results," *Business Wire* (October 27, 2009).

14 See "JetBlue Lovers Unite to Share Brand Perks with Peers," WOOMA Case, www.womma.org/case-study/examples/create-an-evangelism-program/jet-blue-lovers-unite-to-share/ (accessed March 2010); Joan Voigt, "The New Brand Ambassadors," *Adweek* (December 31, 2007): 18–19, 26; Rebecca Nelson, "A Citizen Marketer Talks," *Adweek* (December 31, 2007): 19; Holly Shaw, "Buzzing Influencers," *National Post* (March 13, 2009): FP 12; information from www.repnation.com (accessed October 2010).

15 Joan Voigt, "The New Brand Ambassadors," *Adweek* (December 31, 2007): 18–19.

16 See Brian Morrissey, "Social Rings," *Brandweek* (January 18, 2010): 20.

17 See Darla Dernovsek, "Marketing to Women," *Credit Union Magazine* (October 2000): 90–96; Sharon Goldman Edry, "No Longer Just Fun and Games," *American Demographics* (May 2001): 36–38.

18 See "Tweens 'R Shoppers: A Look at the Tween Market & Shopping Behavior." *POPAI*, March 7, 2013, www.popai.com/store/downloads/POPAIWhitePaper-Tweens-R-Shoppers-2013.pdf; Michael R. Solomon, *Consumer Behavior*, 10th ed. (Upper Saddle River, NJ: Pearson Publishing, 2013), Chapter10.

19 Ron Ruggless, "Casual Chains Cater to Kids as Way to Lure *Back* Families," *Nation's Restaurant News* (July 13, 2009): 1, 29–30.

20 Linda Abu-Shalback Zid, "What's for Dinner," *Marketing Management* (September/October 2004): 6; David Evans and Olivia Toth, "Parents Buy, But Kids Rule," *Media Asia* (November 14, 2003): 22+.

21 John E. G. Bateson, *Managing Services Marketing* (New York: Dryden, 1989), pp. 291–300.

22 Richard M. Howey, Ananth Mangala, Frederick J. De Micco, and Patrick J. Moreo, "Marketplace Needs of Mature Travelers," *Cornell Hotel and Restaurant Administration Quarterly*, 33, no. 4 (1992): 19–20.

23 *Consumer Spending in Restaurants 2014*, National Restaurant Association, Washington, D.C., 2015.

24 For more on the PRIZM lifestage segmentation, see "MyBestSegments: Nielsen PRIZM Lifestage Groups," www.claritas.com/MyBestSegments/Default.jsp?ID=7010&menuOption=learnmore&pageName=PRIZM%2BLifestage%2BGroups&segSystem=PRIZM (accessed September 2014).

25 Jihwan Yoon and Elwood L. Shafer, "An Analysis of Sun-Spot Destination Resort Market Segments: All Inclusive Package Versus Independent Travel Arrangements," *Journal of Hospitality and Tourism Research*, 21, no. 1 (1997): 157–158.

26 Edmund O. Lawler, "50 Years Behind the Bar," *F&B Magazine*, 2, no. 1 (1994): 44.

27 James U. McNeal, *Consumer Behavior: An Integrative Approach* (Boston, MA: Little, Brown, 1982), pp. 83–90.

28 Abraham H. Maslow, *Motivation and Personality*, 2nd ed. (New York: Harper & Row, 1970), pp. 80–106.

29 See "Air on the Side of Humanity," September 17, 2013, www.mullen.com/air-on-the-side-of-humanity/; "The Newest Marketing Buzzword? Human," *Advertising Age*, September 20, 2013, www.adage.com/prinV244261; www.jetblue.com/corporate-social-responsibility/ (accessed September 2014).

30 M. Joseph Sirgy, "Self-Concept in Consumer Behavior: A Critical Review," *Journal of Consumer Research* (December 1982): 287–300.

31 Douglas Kaufman and John Mahoney, "The Effect of Waitresses' Touch on Alcohol Consumption in Dyads," *The Journal of Social Psychology*, 139, no. 3 (1999): 261–267.

32 Sources: Aradhna Krishna, *Sensory Marketing: Research on the Sensuality of Products* (New York: Routledge, 2010); Aradhna Krishna, "An Integrative Review of Sensory Marketing: Engaging the Senses to Affect Perception, Judgment and Behavior," *Journal of Consumer Psychology*, 22 (July 2012): 332–351; Joann Peck and Terry L. Childers, "To Have and to Hold: The Influence of Haptic Information on Product Judgments," *Journal of Marketing*, 67 (April 2003): 35–48; Joann Peck and Terry L. Childers, "Individual Differences in Haptic Information Processing: On the Development, Validation, and Use of the 'Need for Touch' Scale," *Journal of Consumer Research*, 30 (December 2003): 43D-42; Joann Peck and Terry L. Childers, "Effects of Sensory Factors on Consumer Behaviors," Frank Kardes, Curtis Haugtvedt, and Paul Herr, eds., *Handbook of Consumer Psychology* (Mahwah, NJ: Erlbaum, 2008), pp. 193–220; Aradhna Krishna, May Lwin, and Maureen Morrin, "Product Scent and Memory," *Journal of Consumer Research*, 37 (June 2010): 57–67; Eric Yorkston and Geeta Menon, "A Sound Idea: Phonetic Effects of Brand Names on Consumer Judgments," *Journal of Consumer Research*, 31 (June 2004): 43–45; Aradhna Krishna and Rohini Ahluwalia, "Language

Choice in Advertising to Bilinguals: Asymmetric Effects for Multinationals Versus Local Firms," *Journal of Consumer Research*, 35 (December 2008): 692–705; Richard F. Yalch and Eric R. Spangenberg, "The Effects of Music in a Retail Setting on Real and Perceived Shopping Times," *Journal of Business Research*, 49 (August 2000): 139–147; France Leclerc, Bernd H. Schmitt, and Laurette Dube, "Foreign Branding and Its Effect on Product Perceptions and Attitudes," *Journal of Marketing Research*, 31 (May 1994): 263–270; Priya Raghubir and Aradhna Krishna, "Vital Dimensions: Antecedents and Consequences of Biases in Volume Perceptions," *Journal of Marketing Research*, 36 (August 1994): 313–326; Ryan S. Elder and Aradhna Krishna, "The 'Visual Depiction Effect' in Advertising: Facilitating Embodied Mental Simulation through Product Orientation," *Journal of Consumer Research*, 38 (April 2012): 988–1003.

33 McNeal, *Consumer Behavior*, p. 77.

34 Anna Mattila, "Consumers' Value Judgments," *Cornell Hotel and Restaurant Administration Quarterly*, 40, no. 1 (1999): 40.

35 "TIA Study: Weekend Trips Increasing in Popularity," *Travel Weekly* (July 2, 2001): 4.

36 For more on word-of-mouth sources, see Philip Kotler, *Marketing Management*, 11th ed. (Upper Saddle River, NJ: Prentice Hall, 2003), pp. 574–575.

37 Seth Stevenson, "Like Cardboard," *Slate* (January 1, 2010); Ashley M. Heher, "Domino's Comes Clean Wit! New Pizza Ads," *Associated Press* (January 11, 2010); Bob Garfield, "Domino's Does Itself a Disservice by Coming Clean About Its Pizza," *Advertising Age* (January 11, 2010); *Domino's Pizza*, www.pizzaturnaround.com.

38 Priscilla A. LaBarbara and David Mazursky, "A Longitudinal Assessment of Consumer Satisfaction/Dissatisfaction: The Dynamic Aspect of the Cognitive Process," *Journal of Marketing Research* (November 1983): 393–404.

39 Thomas Beggs and Robert C. Lewis, "Selling Bermuda in the Off Season," in *The Complete Travel Marketing Handbook* (Lincolnwood, IL: NTC Business Books, 1988).

40 Leon Festinger, *A Theory of Cognitive Dissonance* (Stanford, CA: Stanford University Press, 1957); Leon G. Schiffman and Leslie Lazar Kanuk, *Consumer Behavior* (Upper Saddle River, NJ: Prentice Hall, 1991), pp. 304–305.

41 Valarie Zeithaml, "How Consumer Evaluation Processes Differ Between Goods and Services," in *Marketing of Services*, ed. James Donnelly and William R. George (Chicago: American Marketing Association, 1981), pp. 186–190.

Courtesy of Viacheslav Lopatin/Shutterstock.

Objectives

After reading this chapter, you should be able to:

1. Understand the organizational buying process.
2. Identify and discuss the importance of the participants in the organizational buying process.
3. Identify the major influences on organizational buyers.
4. List the eight stages of the organizational buying process.
5. Identify and describe the group markets in the hospitality industry.

Organizational Buyer Behavior

Picture this: A multiunit casual restaurant company in the United States is getting an increasing number of international inquires from organizations that want to gain franchising rights for the restaurant brand in their respective countries. The company recently promoted a regional manager, Frank Jones, to director of international development. It dispatches Mr. Jones to Europe, Asia, and Africa to follow up on inquiries from these areas. Mr. Jones stops first in London on his way to Paris. He calls his potential franchises on the phone from an airport business lounge. Mr. Jones handles Parisians with confidence after securing a table at the prestigious restaurant, La Tour d'Argent. He greets his luncheon guest, the president of a large French real estate development company, with the words, "Just call me Frank, Jacques." In Germany, Mr. Jones is a powerhouse. Whisking through a flashy multimedia presentation, showing his prospective clients that he knows how to sell the restaurant concept. Mr. Jones next swings through Saudi Arabia, where he coolly presents a potential client with a proposal in a classy pigskin binder. Heading on to Moscow, Frank strikes up a conversation with a Japanese businessman sitting next to him on the plane. Frank complements the man on his cuff links several times, recognizing him as a man of importance. As the two say good-bye, the man gifts his cuff links to Frank, presents his business card with both hands, and bows at the waist. Frank places his hand firmly on the man's back to express sincere thanks, and then slips his own business card into the man's shirt pocket.

Frank takes Russia by storm as he meets with the chief executive officer (CEO) of an energy company that wants to diversify into real estate development. Feeling very at ease with the Russian executive, Frank sheds his suit coat, leans back, crosses one foot over the other knee, and slips his hands into his pockets.

At his next stop in Beijing, China, Frank talks business over lunch with a group of Chinese executives. After completing the meal, he drops his chopsticks into his bowl of rice and presents each guest with a gift, an elegant Tiffany clock, as a gesture of his desire to do business.

When he arrived back in the United States, Mr. Jones felt he would be very busy following up with his international clients and working on closing deals with them. He was surprised that he heard nothing from them; even after following up with them there was still no response. Frank has nothing to show for the extended trip but a stack of bills. Before he left on his international trip it looked like there was a promising future for international expansions. Frank was not sure why this interest had evaporated.

This hypothetical case has been exaggerated for emphasis. Americans are seldom such dolts. But experts say success in international business has a lot to do with knowing the territory and its people. By learning English and extending themselves in other ways, the world's business leaders, in non-English speaking countries, have met Americans more than halfway. In contrast, Americans too often do little except assume that others will march to their music. "We want things to be 'American' when we travel. Fast, Convenient, Easy. So we become 'ugly Americans' by demanding that others change," says one American world trade expert. "I think more business would be done if we tried harder."

Poor Frank tried, all right, but in all the wrong ways. The British do not, as a rule, make deals over the phone as much as Americans do. It's not so much a "cultural" difference as a difference in approach. A proper Frenchman neither likes instant familiarity nor refers to strangers by their first names. "That poor fellow, Jacques, probably wouldn't say anything, but he'd not be pleased," explains an expert on French business practices. Frank's flashy presentation would likely have been a flop with the Germans, who dislike overstatement and showiness. And to the Saudi Arabians, the pigskin binder would have been considered vile. An American salesperson who actually presented such a binder was unceremoniously tossed out of the country, and his company was blacklisted from working with Saudi businesses. Frank also committed numerous faux pas with his new Japanese acquaintance. Because the Japanese strive to please others, especially when someone admires their possessions, the executive likely felt obligated rather than pleased to give up his cuff links. Frank's "hand on the back" probably labeled him as disrespectful and presumptuous. Japan, like many Asian countries, is a "no contact culture" in which even shaking hands is a strange experience. Frank made matters worse with his casual treatment of the business cards. Japanese people revere the business card as an extension of self and as an indicator of rank. They do not hand it to people; they present it—with both hands. Things didn't go well in Russia, either. Russian business people maintain a conservative, professional appearance, with dark suits and dress shoes. Taking one's coat off during negotiations of any kind is taken as a sign of weakness. Placing hands in one's pockets is considered rude, and showing the bottoms of one's shoes is a disgusting gesture. Similarly, in China, Frank casually dropping his chopsticks could have been misinterpreted as an act of aggression. Stabbing chopsticks into a bowl of rice and leaving them signifies death to the Chinese. The clocks Frank offered as gifts might have confirmed such dark intentions. To "give a clock" in Chinese sounds the same as "seeing someone off to his end." Thus, to compete successfully in global markets, or even to deal effectively with international firms in their home markets, companies must help their managers to understand the needs, customs, and cultures of international business buyers. Several companies now offer smartphone apps that provide tips to international travelers and help prevent them from making embarrassing mistakes while abroad. Cultures around the world differ greatly, and marketers must dig deeply to make certain they adapt to these differences. "When doing business in a foreign country and a foreign culture … take nothing for granted," advises an international business specialist. "Turn every stone. Ask every question. Dig into every detail."[1]

The hospitality business has become a global business. Companies are sending managers around the globe to find locations for their businesses, sell meetings, and source products. The opening vignette discusses some of the cultural differences one has to be aware of when they conduct business with representatives of international business. One does not have to travel internationally to find differences between business and consumer markets. Business markets differ in many ways from consumer markets. The differences are in market structure and demand, the nature of the buying unit, the types of decisions, and the decision process involved. This chapter will help you understand more efficiently your ability to sell to other businesses as well as your ability to make more effective purchases by understanding the process. We will also discuss group markets that generate business for the hospitality and travel industry.

■■■ The Organizational Buying Process

Market Structure and Demand

Derived demand.
Organizational demand that ultimately comes from (derives from) the demand for consumer goods.

Organizational demand is **derived demand**; it comes ultimately from the demand for consumer goods or services. It is derived or a function of the businesses that supply the hospitality and travel industry with meetings, special events, and other functions. Las Vegas hosts two conventions for products people add to their cars. These providers include audio systems, special tires, navigation systems, and similar products. These shows attract a combined attendance of over 100,000 people. If car sales fall, the demand for these products will fall. Companies that sell and install the products will cut their spending on travel. Attendance at the conventions will fall, causing a loss of revenue to the hotels, casinos, restaurants, and shows in Las Vegas.

Through good environmental scanning, marketers can identify emerging industries, companies, and associations. They screen these organizations to find good business partners. Hotel managers need to understand the financial health of the corporations and associations they serve. If clients fall on hard times, managers need to look for industries that are healthy to replace the lost business, before it affects the revenue per available room (RevPAR).

Compared with consumer purchases, a business purchase usually involves more decision makers and a more professional purchasing effort. Corporations that frequently use hotels for meetings may hire their own meeting planners. Professional meeting planners receive training in negotiating skills. They belong to associations such as Meeting Planners International (MPI), which educates its members in the latest negotiating techniques. A corporate travel agent's job is to find the best airfares, rental car rates, and hotel rates. Therefore, hotels must have well-trained salespeople to deal with well-trained buyers, creating thousands of jobs for salespeople. Additionally, once the meeting is sold, the account is turned over to a convention service manager who works with the meeting planner to make sure the event is produced according to the meeting planner's expectations. Outside the hotel, jobs relating to meetings include corporate meeting planners, association meeting planners, independent meeting planners, and convention and visitor bureau salespersons.

Types of Decisions and the Decision Process

Organizational buying process.
The decision-making process by which formal organizations establish the need for purchased products and services and identify, evaluate, and choose among alternative brands and suppliers.

Organizational buyers usually face more complex buying decisions than consumer buyers. Their purchases often involve large sums of money, complex technical features (room sizes, room setups, breakout rooms, audiovisual [AV] equipment, and the like), economic considerations, and interactions among many people at all levels of the organization. The **organizational buying process** tends to be more formalized than the consumer process and a more professional purchasing effort. The more complex the purchase, the more likely it is that several people will participate in the decision-making process. The total bill for a one-day sales meeting for 75 people can be tens of thousands of dollars. If a company is having a series of sales meetings around the country, it will be worthwhile to get quotes from several hotel chains and spend time analyzing the bids.

Finally, in the organizational buying process, buyer and seller are often very dependent on each other. Sales is a consultative process. The hospitality organization's staff develops interesting and creative menus, theme parties, and coffee breaks. The staff works with meeting planners to solve problems and works. They also have a close working relationship with their corporate and association customers to find customized solutions to satisfy their needs. Hotels and catering firms retain customers by meeting their current needs and thinking ahead to meet their future needs.

◼◼◼ Participants in the Organizational Buying Process

Buying center. All those individuals and groups who participate in the purchasing and decision-making process and who share common goals and the risks arising from the decisions.

The decision-making unit of a buying organization, sometimes called the **buying center**, is defined as "all those individuals and groups who participate in the purchasing decision-making process, who share common goals and the risks arising from the decisions."[2]

The buying center includes all members of the organization who play any of the six roles in the purchase-decision process:[3]

1. **Users.** Users are those who use the product or service. They often provide recommendations to those directly involved in the purchase decision, either directly or through user-generated comments on Web sites.

2. **Influencers.** Influencers directly influence the buying decision but do not make the final decision themselves. They often help define specifications and provide information for evaluating alternatives. Past presidents of trade associations may exert influence in the choice of a meeting location. Executive secretaries, a spouse, regional managers, and many others can and do exert considerable influence in the selection of sites for meetings, seminars, conferences, and other group gatherings.

3. **Deciders.** Deciders select product requirements and suppliers. For example, a company's sales manager for the Denver area selects the hotel and negotiates the arrangements when the regional sales meeting is held in that area.

4. **Approvers.** Approvers authorize the proposed actions of deciders or buyers. Although the Denver sales manager arranges the meeting, the contracts may need to be submitted to the corporate vice president of marketing for formal approval.

5. **Buyers.** Buyers have formal authority for selecting suppliers and arranging the terms of purchase. Buyers may help shape product specifications and play a major role in selecting vendors and negotiating.

6. **Gatekeepers.** Gatekeepers have the power to prevent sellers of information from reaching members of the buying center. For example, a hotel salesperson calling on a meeting planner may have to go through an administrative assistant. This administrative assistant can easily block the salesperson from seeing the meeting planner. This can be accomplished by failing to forward messages, telling the salesperson the meeting planner is not available, or simply telling the meeting planner not to deal with the salesperson.

Buying centers vary by number and type of participants. Salespersons calling on organizational customers must determine the following:

*   Who are the major decision participants?
*   What decisions do they influence?
*   What is their level of influence?
*   What evaluation criteria does each participant use?

When a buying center includes multiple participants, the seller may not have the time or resources to reach all. Smaller sellers concentrate on reaching the key buying influencers and deciders. It is important not to go over the decider's

It is important to have good relationships with administration assistants; they can help you gain an appointment and may influence the purchase decision. Courtesy of Andresr/Shutterstock.

head. Most deciders like to feel in control of the purchasing decision; going over a decider's head and working with the boss will be resented. In most cases the boss will leave the decision up to the decider and the ill will created by not dealing with the decider directly will result in the selection of another company. Larger sellers use multilevel, in-depth selling to reach as many buying participants as possible. Their salespeople virtually "live" with their high-volume customers.

Special Importance of International Companies

The growth of international tourists has led to the growth of international commerce. Sheer numbers of visitors are impressive. The U.S. National Tourism and Travel Office has forecasted 88.3 million foreign visitors by 2019 with the largest growth from the following countries[4]:

China	172%
Columbia	72%
India	47%
Brazil	43%
Mexico	38%

Other countries showed similar trends. The United Kingdom experienced a record of 32.8 million visitors in 2013.[5]

Visitor numbers alone do not reflect the equally important worldwide trend of foreign companies locating in one's home nation. Montreal, Canada, has over 2,800 foreign subsidiaries with expenditures of $26 billion. Many of these companies are from the high-tech sector: aerospace, life sciences, health technology, and information/communications technology.

In the United States, over 1,500 German companies are located in Georgia. South Carolina automotive business now ranks high as an industry sector with many representing foreign companies.

The entrance of foreign companies provides new opportunities and challenges for the local hospitality industry. It also poses unique learning opportunities. Foreign companies like to bring visitors to their locations from the home country.

A local conference center, resort, or hotel desiring the meeting business of these companies must be familiar with any unusual needs such as cuisine. This may require the addition of a chef experienced in this cuisine or other client needs unfamiliar to the local hospitality industry.

Major Influences on Organizational Buyers

Organizational buyers are subject to many influences as they make their buying decisions. Some vendors assume that the most important influences are economic. They see buyers as favoring the supplier who offers the lowest price, best product, or most service. This view suggests that hospitality marketers should concentrate on price and cost variables.

Others believe that buyers respond to personal factors such as favors, attention, or risk avoidance. A study of buyers in 10 large companies concluded that emotions and feelings play a part in the decision process of corporate decision makers.

Figure 7–1
Major influences on business buying behavior.

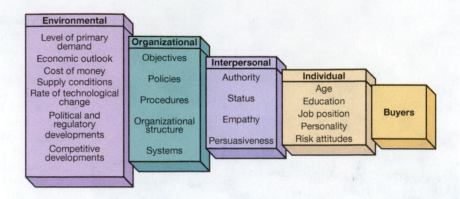

They respond to "image," buy from known companies, and favor suppliers who show them respect and personal consideration. They "overreact" to real or imagined slights, tending to reject companies that fail to respond or delay in submitting bids.[6]

In reality, organizational buyers commonly respond to both economic and personal factors. Where there is substantial similarity in supplier offers, price becomes an important determinant.

The various influences on organizational buyers may be classified into four main groups: environmental, organizational, interpersonal, and individual, see Figure 7–1.[7]

Environmental Factors

Organizational buyers are heavily influenced by the current and expected economic environment. Factors such as the level of primary demand, the economic outlook, and the cost are important. In a recession, companies cut their travel budgets, whereas in good times, travel budgets are usually increased.

Organizational Factors

Each organization has specific objectives, policies, procedures, organizational structures, and systems related to buying. The hospitality marketer has to be familiar with them and must know the following: How many people are involved in the buying decision? Who are they? What are the evaluation criteria? What are the company's policies and constraints on the buyers?

Interpersonal Factors

The buying center usually includes several participants, with differing levels of interest, authority, and persuasiveness. Hospitality marketers are unlikely to know the group dynamics that take place during the buying decision process. Salespeople commonly learn the personalities and interpersonal factors that shape the organizational environment and provide useful insight into group dynamics.

Individual Factors

Each participant in the buying decision process has personal motivations, perceptions, and preferences. Buyers definitely exhibit different buying styles. Hospitality marketers must know their customers and adapt their tactics to known environmental, organizational, interpersonal, and individual influences.

■■■ Organizational Buying Decisions

Organizational buyers do not buy goods and services for personal consumption. They buy hospitality products to provide training, to reward employees and distributors, and to provide lodging for their employees. Eight stages of the organizational buying process have been identified and are called *buyphases*.[8] This model is called *buygrid framework*. The eight steps for the typical new-task buying situation are as follows:

1. Problem Recognition

The buying process begins when someone in the company recognizes a problem or need that can be met by acquiring a good or a service. **Problem recognition** can occur because of internal or external stimuli. Internally, a new product may create the need for a series of meetings to explain the product to the sales force. A human resource manager may notice a need for employee training and set up a training meeting. A CEO may feel that the executive team would benefit from a weekend retreat to reformulate the firm's strategy. Externally, the buyer sees an ad or receives a call from a hotel sales representative who offers a favorable corporate program. Marketers can stimulate problem recognition by developing effective ads and calling on prospects.

Recently Walmart announced it would spend $1 billion on employee raises and on training. Hospitality chains should have automatically asked for appointments at Walmart to determine travel and lodging needs. A corporate-wide strategy should then have been devised to earn Walmart's business.

2. General Need Description

Having recognized a need, the buyer goes on to determine the requirements of the product and to formulate a general need description. For a training meeting, this would include food and beverages, meeting spaces, AV equipment coffee breaks, and sleeping room requirements. The corporate meeting planner works with others—the director of human resources, the training manager, and potential participants—to gain insight into the requirements of the meeting. Together, they determine the importance of the price, meeting space, sleeping rooms, food and beverages, and other factors.

The hotel marketer can render assistance to the buyer in this phase. Often, the buyer is unaware of the benefits of various product features. Alert marketers can help buyers define their companies' needs and show how their hotel can satisfy them.

3. Product Specification

Once the general requirements have been determined, the specific requirements for the meeting can be developed. For example, a meeting might require 20 sleeping rooms, a meeting room for 25 set up classroom style with a whiteboard and overhead projector, and a separate room for lunch. For larger meetings with an exhibit area, the information need becomes more complex. Information often required includes availability of water, ceiling heights, door widths, security, and procedures for receiving and storing materials prior to the event. Salespersons must be prepared to answer their prospective client's questions about their hotel's capabilities to fulfill the **product specification**. Today, these needs are certain to include technology, including portals for computers, the latest AV equipment, and others.

4. Supplier Search

The buyer now conducts a **supplier search** to identify the most appropriate hotels. The buyer can examine trade directories, do a computer search, or phone familiar hotels. Hotels that qualify may receive a site visit from the meeting planner, who eventually develops a short list of qualified suppliers. Personal recommendations from individuals such as members of management, consultants, lawyers, and others often are seriously considered in the search process.

5. Proposal Solicitations

Once the meeting planner has drawn up a short list of suppliers, qualified hotels are invited to submit proposals. Thus hotel marketers must be skilled in researching, writing, and presenting proposals. These should be marketing-oriented, not simply technical, documents. They should position their company's capabilities and resources so that they stand out from the competition. Many hotels have developed videos for this purpose. Unfortunately, far too many videos are look-alikes and do not effectively differentiate one hotel/resort from another.

6. Supplier Selection

Supplier selection. The stage of the industrial buying process in which a buyer receives proposals and selects a supplier or suppliers.

In this stage, members of the buying center review the proposals and move toward **supplier selection**. They conduct an analysis of the hotel, considering physical facilities, the hotel's ability to deliver service, and the professionalism of its employees. Frequently, the buying center specifies desired supplier attributes and suggests their relative importance. In general, meeting planners consider the following attributes in making their selection of a location:

- Sleeping rooms
- Meeting rooms
- Food and beverage
- AV staff and equipment
- Billing procedures
- Check-in/checkout
- Staff
- Availability of online information

Technology has made it possible for meeting planners to take a visual tour of the meeting space. Companies such as eMarketing 360 specialize in capturing video images of meeting space and making it accessible to buyers on the Web. Meeting Matrix provides a Web site with meeting information, including room diagrams, and videos of meeting space. This helps meeting planners narrow their selection or even make their selection without visiting the site. The later would likely be made up of buyers who have a lot of faith in the brand. Regardless of the sophistication of communication devices, nothing can substitute for on-site visits. These should be an integral part of the selection process.

The organization may attempt to negotiate with preferred supplies for better prices and terms before making the final selection. There are several ways the hotel marketer can counter the request for a lower price. For example, the dates can be moved from a high-demand period to a need period for the hotel, or menus can be changed. The marketer can cite the value of the services the buyer now receives, especially where services are superior to competitors.

7. Order-Routine Specification

Order-routine specification. The stage of the industry buying process in which a buyer writes the final order with the chosen supplier(s), listing the technical specifications, quantity needed, expected time of delivery, return policies, warranties, and so on.

The buyer now writes the final order with the chosen hotels, listing the technical **order-routine specifications** of the meeting. The hotel responds by offering the buyer a formal contract. The contract specifies cutoff dates for room blocks, the date when the hotel will release the room block for sale to other guests, and minimum guarantees for food and beverage functions. Many hotels and restaurants have turned what should have been a profitable banquet into a loss by not having or enforcing minimum guarantees.

8. Performance Review

Performance review. The stage of an industrial buying process in which a buyer rates its satisfaction with suppliers, deciding whether to continue, modify, or drop the relationship.

The buyer does a postpurchase **performance review** of the product. During this phase the buyer determines if the product meets the buyer's specifications and if the buyer will purchase from the company again. It is important for hotels to have

The Hong Kong Convention Center is a popular site for major international conventions. Attendees enjoy coming to Hong Kong and its easy accessibility makes it a popular spot for association meetings. Courtesy of estherpoon/Shutterstock.

at least daily meetings with a meeting planner to make sure everything is going well and to correct those things that did not go well. This manages the buyer's perceived service and helps to avoid a negative postpurchase evaluation by the buyer.

■■■ Group Markets

One of the most important types of organizational business is group business. It is important for marketing managers to understand the differences between a group market and a consumer market. The group business market is often more sophisticated and requires more technical information than the consumer market. Many group markets book more than a year in advance. During this time, cognitive dissonance can develop; thus, marketers must keep in contact with buyers to assure them that they made the right decision in choosing the seller's hotel.

The four main categories of group markets are conventions, association meetings, corporate meetings, and SMERF (social, military, educational, religious, and fraternal organizations) groups. Conventions attract large numbers, but meetings occur much more frequently than conventions. The attendance at an association's annual convention can number in the tens of thousands, while a training session put on by an association may have only 20 participants. Thus, associations provide convention centers as well as smaller hotels with business. Corporations can put on large events, such as Hilton's Annual General Managers Conference or smaller regional conferences. When choosing a hotel, an important consideration for a meeting planner is whether the hotel can house the participants. Group business is a very important segment for most hotels. Successful hotels know which groups to attract, how to use group business to fill need dates, and how to sell groups on the hotel's benefits rather than just price.

The Convention Industry Council (CIC) is made up of 30 member organizations that represent both buyers and suppliers to the meetings industry. CIC developed the Accepted Practices Exchange (APEX), which brings a set of standards and best practices to all parties involved in the creation and implementation of a meeting. APEX's event specifications provide a template of a checklist for planning an event, and its glossary brings a common meaning to terms used in the meetings industry. APEX is a great tool for those involved in selling or planning meetings.[9]

Convention. A specialty market requiring extensive meeting facilities. It is usually the annual meeting of an association and includes general sessions, committee meetings, and special-interest sessions.

Conventions

Conventions are a specialty market requiring extensive meeting facilities. These are usually the annual meeting of an association and include general sessions, committee meetings, and special-interest sessions. Hotels with convention facilities, such as the Chicago Hyatt or the Atlanta Marriott Marquis, can house small and midsized conventions. Conventions that use a major facility, such as the Jacob Javitts Convention Center in New York, often have tens of thousands of delegates. They are called citywide conventions because hotels throughout the city house their delegates. In the United States there are about 2 million meetings held annually with 113 million people attending those meetings; 60 million attended conventions, conferences, and congresses; and 30 million attended trade shows.[10] With this size of market, it is no wonder that this industry attracts the interest of developers, city planners, and various levels of government.

There are 256 convention centers in the United States. California has the most at 23 and Florida and Texas have 20 each. The largest convention center in the United States in McCormick Place in Chicago with 2.6 million square feet but the largest convention center in the world is the Hannover Messegelände.[11]

Associations usually select convention sites two to five years in advance, with some large conventions planned 10 to 15 years before the event. October is the most popular month for conventions, followed by November, September, and April.[12]

Some associations prefer to have their conventions in the same city year after year, whereas others prefer to move to a different area of the country each year.

A convention can be a major source of income for the sponsoring organization. Registration fees from attendees and sales of exhibition space in the trade show are major sources of revenue. A trade show gives suppliers a chance to show and sell their products to the association's members. Companies such as GES Exposition Services work with the association and conference center to provide electrical hookups, booth setup, and other services to make sure the trade show exhibitors have the resources they need to set up their exhibits. The price that can be charged for exhibition space is related to the number of attendees. When choosing a convention location, an association looks for sites that will be both accessible and attractive to members. The annual convention is one of the main sources of revenue for many associations, thus balancing the annual budget depends on a good turnout.

Many hotels contract with independent AV companies to supply and maintain this equipment. The AV company can pool its equipment and staff within the city. So, when a group has special AV requirements, the company can bring the equipment and staff needed to produce the event. In large hotels, AV companies have an office in the hotel to store equipment and house technicians. For large meetings, AV companies have on-site technicians to remain with the group during the meeting to correct problems as they occur, thus ensuring that speaker presentations proceed as planned. Under this arrangement, the hotel bills the client for the AV and then pays the AV company an agreed-upon percentage of the charges; for example, 60 percent often goes to the AV company, with the hotel keeping 40 percent.

Billing procedures are also important to convention planners. Billing can create problems for hotels that take it for granted and do not have a customer-oriented accounting department. Professional meeting planners want a bill that is understandable, accurate, and delivered in a timely manner. Without these characteristics, the bill can be a nightmare. Important attributes for a convention planner other than facilities and rates are food quality, billing procedures, and the professionalism and attention of the hotel's staff.

Convention Bureaus

Convention bureaus are nonprofit marketing organizations that help hotels sign conventions and meetings. These organizations are often supported by a hotel or by sales tax and are run by chamber of commerce, visitor bureaus, or city and county governments. They are often one of the first sources of information for a convention or meeting planner. A hotel relying on meeting business for a significant portion of its occupancy should have a good working relationship with the convention bureau, which includes active membership in the organization.

■■■ Association Meetings

The most important attributes of a destination for an association meeting planner are availability of hotel and facilities, ease of transportation, distance from attendees, and transportation costs. Climate, recreation, and cultural activities are not as important as they are to the convention market because the meeting itself is the major draw. In selecting a hotel, the association meeting planner looks for food quality, rates, meeting rooms, billing procedures, and attributes similar to the convention planner except for exhibition space.[13] Notice that for the association meeting planner, food and beverage are the most important attributes in the selection of the hotel.

Convene polled a group of successful and well-respected meeting planners, to determine what they looked for when they selected a meeting location. The top 10 criteria were as follows:

1. Location and accessibility

2. Meeting room capacity

3. Flow and layout of space

4. Quality and capability of AV equipment

5. Room flexibility
6. Decor
7. Intelligent staff, from sales to service
8. Price flexibility
9. Quality of food
10. Participant experience[14]

The need for a location that will be desirable and accessible to their attendees was at the top of the list. The next six items relate to having the proper physical facilities—AV and staff to put on a successful meeting. Although quality of food is number 9, a reputation for serving poor food can eliminate a venue from consideration. When we discuss small groups we will state some hotels offer a fixed price package, with seasoned meeting planners there was a need to show their value to their companies. They wanted to develop a customized price package, rather than accept a set price. Surveys like the one mentioned earlier will give overall results, but it is also important to realize that meeting planners are different. A successful salesperson will develop a package that will meet the wants of the meeting planner.

Membership in the American Society of Association Executives (ASAE) is beneficial for hotels actively pursuing association business. It provides an opportunity to network with association executives and is a source of information on national and local associations. Many of the hotel's corporate clients are also members of trade associations. These customers can become ambassadors for the hotel at their trade association meetings.

Members attend association meetings voluntarily. The hotel should work with meeting planners to make the destination seem as attractive as possible. Making sure that the meeting planner is aware of local attractions, offering suggestions for spousal activities, and assisting in the development of after-convention activities can be useful to the hotel and the meeting planner. It is important to market both the destination and the hotel.

Corporate Meetings

Corporate meeting. A meeting held by a corporation for its employees.

For employees of a company, a **corporate meeting** is a command performance. They are directed to attend the meeting without choice. One implication of required attendance is a short lead time. Because corporations do not have to develop and implement a marketing plan to gain attendees, they often plan meetings with a few weeks' lead time. Corporate meetings can range in size from a board meeting for 10 to 12 people to a sales meeting for several hundred people. Overall, 35 percent of corporate meetings are for 10 to 24 people, 29 percent have 25 to 49 attendees, 18 percent have 50 to 99 people, and 18 percent are for over a hundred attendees.[15]

Many corporate meetings are set up by mega agencies, such as American Express, Carlson Wagonlit, and Consortia. These agencies provide travel management services for companies. Thus, when seeking business from corporations, a hotel manager must understand who has the responsibility for booking meetings.[16]

The corporation's major concern is that the meeting be productive and accomplish the company's objectives. Types of corporate meetings include training, management, and planning. Another type of corporate meeting is the incentive meeting, which will be discussed later.

To a corporate meeting planner, the most important attributes in the choice of a destination are the availability of hotels, ease of transportation, transportation costs, and distance from the location to the attendees.

Full service hotels have a number of meeting facilities ranging from a large ballrooms to small meeting rooms. Courtesy of KAL Hotel Jeju.

Corporate meeting planners want to ensure that meetings are productive and the corporation gets good value for the money it spends. Their success depends on planning smooth-running meetings. Hotels interested in capturing and retaining corporate meeting business must make sure that meeting rooms are adequate and set up properly. Because meeting planners want attendees to be comfortable, sleeping rooms are important to them. They are also concerned about the quality of food. Recreation and modern indoor exercise facilities may also be important. In a multiday technical meeting, the interaction of the participants outside the formal meetings is valuable. Golf or tennis can be used to encourage participants to interact socially and break up the monotony of the classroom sessions. Similarly, an evening outing to an area restaurant, sporting, or cultural event can serve as an enjoyable break for participants.

Warning: Convention/Conference Center Exuberance

Many communities believe that constructing a convention center is essential to develop a visitor/tourism industry. From 1990 to 2015, the amount of square footage available for exhibitions increased from 40.4 million square feet to over 70 million. Many communities believed that if they had more space they would attract more visitors and generate more revenue. Unfortunately, the concept "if you build it they will come" is too often dangerous and faulty. During that same period, demand did not sufficiently grow to meet the supply.[17]

In some cases, communities are stuck with debt service that may continue 15 to 25 years and can result in negative economic impacts. The National Council for Urban Economic Development (CUED) warned that meeting facilities often lose money and stated that "even in rare cases where revenues cover operating costs in meeting facilities, they never cover debt service."

Unrealistic projections are often accepted by city councils and others who genuinely want a conference center, and, in their exuberance, overlook faulty planning. This does not imply that conference/convention centers never serve the needs of a community. Instead it is a warning of the difficulties in attracting sufficient visitors on a regular basis who will provide revenues required to support these facilities.[18]

Retreats

Retreat centers are commonly owned and operated by nonprofit organizations such as religious groups, Young Men's Christian Association (YMCA), Boy Scouts, and others. Each year thousands of people participate in retreats worldwide but very little if any of their business is arranged by professional intermediaries. Instead, members of the organization or a professional director and staff arrange accommodations.

Small Groups

The small corporate meeting, less than 50 rooms, has gained the attention of hotel chains. Although small in terms of number of participants, thousands of small meetings are held every month. Many hotels have developed a marketing effort toward small groups. A consistent message is your small group is important to us and will not get lost at our hotel. Some hotels, such as Kimpton Hotels, a collection of boutique hotels, have developed a small group desk designed to help someone planning a small group function. Larger hotels also seek small group functions, the large resorts that are 2,000 rooms plus in Las Vegas, also value small groups. The Aria has a small group page focusing on leisure customers coming to Las Vegas for a family reunion, wedding, and bachelor or bachelorette party.

Many hotels offer a set price per person for a small group. The price includes meals,

African photo safaris have become a popular incentive travel destination. There are a number of luxury facilities, such as this one, that attract incentive groups. Courtesy of GTS Productions/Shutterstock.

breaks, meeting room, AV, and sleeping rooms. The set price makes it easy for meeting planners to understand their costs. Simplifying small meeting arrangements is critical because those who plan small meetings are often not meeting planners.

Incentive Travel

Incentive travel. A reward that participants receive for achieving or exceeding a goal.

Incentive travel, a unique subset of corporate group business, is a reward participants receive for achieving or exceeding a goal. Companies give awards for both individual and team performance. A hotel salesperson selling incentives must be able to help his or her client justify the expenditure. Reminding the meeting planner of the value of the sales to the company created by the attendees is an excellent way to do this.

Participants must perceive the destination and the hotel as something special. Climate, recreational facilities, and sightseeing opportunities are high on an incentive meeting planners' list of desired attributes.[19] The Caribbean, Hawaii, Europe, and resort destinations within the continental United States are common incentive travel destinations. The right location and excellent facilities are important. Brian Jones, senior vice president sales at Morgans Hotel Group, states, "It is also about creating unique experiences that motivate, celebrate, or educate. The more we speak to these issues the more successful we will be."

Incentive trips used to last from three to seven days; however, the current trend is to keep the trips short and get the participants back to their jobs. Scott Walker, director of incentive and promotion certificates for Hyatt Hotels, states, "I am hearing, 'let's change it from five nights to four, but add extras.' These extras include meals, spa treatments, a round on the golf course, or Hyatt Cheque certificates that they can spend any way they want."[20] The average expenditure per room is high. Winners of incentive trips sometimes receive a cash deposit to their account that can be used for charges to their account or services provided through the hotel, such as rental cars. For example, participants in an incentive trip sponsored by Revlon for the best regional sales performance received a $500 credit on their hotel bill that could be spent as they wished. In such cases the participants spend freely in the hotel's restaurants and bars, often supplementing the credit with their own money. Thus, incentive travel can be very profitable for a hotel.

Incentive travel is handled in-house or by incentive houses, travel agencies, consultants, and travel fulfillment firms that handle only the travel arrangements. The trend is moving away from in-house planners to incentive houses, fulfillment houses, and travel agencies. One reason for the shift is that outside organizations specializing in incentive travel often buy blocks of airline seats and hotel rooms. As a result, they can put together packages more efficiently than in-house planners. Incentive houses usually provide a choice of several locations to the company, so the ultimate choice of location is made by the company, even when it uses an incentive house. Travel destinations and their service suppliers such as resorts must work with both the incentive house and the decision makers within the company.

Destination Choice Factors

Maritz Travel, a company with substantial experience in incentive travel, developed an International Certification Index that reflects travel preferences among 1,000 U.S.-based employees who were eligible to earn incentive travel. The results demonstrated the following:

- Visiting new destinations that seem otherwise unattainable is a key motivator.
- Luxurious trips to sun and sand destinations are preferred.
- Long-haul destinations do not mean lower motivational value. Travel time is considered luxurious.

Negative factors affecting travel incentives are as follows:

- General lack of interest in the destination.
- Previous visit to the destination.
- Safety concerns regarding the destination.

The Maritz study also showed that the motivational level of travel increases for those who earned previous trips. However, 70 percent want to go someplace new and interesting. This means that incentive planners must continuously offer new destinations to this important group as they clearly represent very important employees or clients for a sponsoring company or organization.[21]

SMERFs

SMERF. SMERF stands for social, military, educational, religious, and fraternal organizations. This group of specialty market has a common price-sensitive thread.

SMERF stands for social, military, educational, religious, and fraternal organizations. On a broader scale, this meeting classification includes smaller specialty organizations that are price sensitive. The individual pays for the majority of the functions sponsored by these organizations, and sometimes the expenses are not

---

Marketing HIGHLIGHT 7.1 Green Meetings—The Right Thing to Do for the Environment and Business

The CIC provides this definition of a green meeting. A green meeting or event incorporates environmental considerations to minimize its negative impact on the environment. Green or environmental considerations are one aspect of sustainability. Sustainability takes a "triple bottom line" approach that seeks to balance the social, environmental, and economic concerns against business needs.

The APEX, an initiative of the CIC, is creating standards for environmentally sustainable meetings. It has developed standards for nine sectors of a meeting: accommodations, AV, communications and marketing, destinations, exhibits, food and beverage, meeting venue, on-site offices, and transportation.

New meeting facilities can be built to meet green standards. The Leadership in Energy and Environmental Design (LEED) Green Building Rating System provides design guidelines for environment-friendly buildings. A good environmental plan begins with the construction of the building.

A second area of sustainability is general facility management. Even for buildings that were not built with sustainability in mind, there are still ways to make the building greener. These include changing incandescent light bulbs to light-emitting diodes (LEDs) or compact fluorescent light bulbs, recycling programs, and the efficient management of room temperatures, which are just a few ways one can minimize the negative effect of the meeting venue on the environment.

The third component relates to the meeting. For example, boxed lunches using a disposable cardboard box with packaged chips and cookies have been an industry standard. Often the chips and cookies are thrown away by those on a diet. A green way to do boxed lunches is to set up a sandwich buffet, with chips, salads, and desserts. This eliminates the package material and waste, since people are likely to take what they will eat. It also saves labor, as packing box lunches is labor intensive. Some hotels and restaurants have installed water purification systems, so they can serve bottled water quality from pitchers or

carafes, eliminating the need to use water in disposable plastic or glass bottles and the shipping of water to the hotel from faraway places. Hotels and restaurants serve the water in elegant carafes. Some provide the water free of charge and others charge banquet customers for the water, similar to a charge for imported water. Recycling name badges reduces solid waste and can save the planner 75 cents per recycled badge. Serving bulk sugar and cream for coffee and tea breaks reduces solid waste from sugar wrappers and cream containers, while cutting the food cost by over 50 percent on those items.

A researcher found that 90 percent of the 140 largest companies in the United States believe that adapting environmentally responsible practices is important for their reputation. This group also feels that the importance of environmental sustainability will continue to grow. The Travel Industry Association of America found that over 80 percent of the customers surveyed were willing to spend 6.5 percent more on products and services provided by environmentally friendly companies. Green meeting practices can enhance reputation, save money, increase revenue, and are the right thing to do for the planet.

For more information on green meetings, see the following Web sites:[22]

Coalition for Environmentally Responsible Economies	www.ceres.org
Environmental Protection Agency—Green Meetings Initiative	www.epa.gov/oppt/greenmeetings
The Green Meeting Industry Council (GMIC)	http://www.gmicglobal.org
Council International Association of Conference Centers	http://www.iacconline.org/environmental-initiatives
Meeting Professionals International Corporate Social Responsibility	http://www.mpiweb.org/Portal/CSR

tax deductible. As a result, participants are usually price conscious. They want a low room rate and often find the food and beverage within the hotel too expensive, preferring to eat elsewhere or purchase food and eat in their rooms. Because attendees are price sensitive, one of the biggest challenges is to get the attendees to book within the room block.[23] Hotels often provide concessions, such as free rooms or a free or reduced food and beverage function based on the number of room nights in the groups' block. If the block does not materialize, the meeting planner is responsible for extra charges.

On the positive side, SMERFs are willing to be flexible to ensure a lower room rate. They are willing to meet during the off season or on weekends. Weekends are often preferred because most participants attend meetings during their free time. Also, the size of these segments should not be overlooked. In the United States, over 50,000 religious organizations have group travel programs.[24] Thus, SMERFs provide good filler business during off-peak times. If you decide to go into hotel sales upon graduation, there is a good chance you will be assigned to the SMERF market, as it is usually assigned to the most junior sales person.

Segmentation of Group Markets by Purpose of the Meeting

Besides dividing group markets into convention, association, corporate, and SMERF, they also can be broken into the purpose of the meeting. Four major purposes are conventions, conferences, seminars, and meetings. Table 7–1 shows a matrix describing some of the critical sales decision variables for these types of gatherings. This matrix reflects the general nature of sales decision variables within the group market. Exceptions can and do exist.

Restaurants as a Meeting Venue

Restaurants are designing their space so they can take advantage of meetings such as using a room off the main room that can be closed for meetings, giving the restaurant the option of using it as part of the public dining space on Saturday night or as a

TABLE 7–1
Decision Variable Matrix: Group Markets

Sales Decision Variables	Conventions	Conferences	Seminars	Meetings
Decision makers	Many: committees, chapter presidents, high-ranking officers	Conference organizer, meeting planner	Seminar organizer, boss, secretary	Boss, secretary, regional manager, meeting planner
Decision influencers	Many	Limited	Limited	Few
Degree of politicalization	Highly political	Somewhat political	Personal	Highly personal
Decision time	Years	One year or less	Months	Short time; sometimes one day
Customer price sensitivity	Very	Somewhat	Somewhat	Not highly sensitive
Personal service sensitivity	Low	Moderate	High	Extreme
Opportunity for upsell	Low	Moderate	Moderate	High
Team selling opportunity	Definitely	Sometimes	Probably not	No
Special advertising promotion	Definitely	Usually no	No	No
International	Definitely	Possible	Probably not	Usually not, but opportunities exist (board of directors)
Repeat sales opportunity	Long time, poor	Moderate time	Yes	Definitely
Need for personal sales call (travel)	Probably yes	Probably no	Probably no	Depends on the situation

Traditional Chinese restaurants have private meeting rooms. Courtesy of xy/Fotolia.

a meeting room during a weekday. According to a meeting research firm, meetings held in space of 700 square feet or less (20 feet by 35 feet) increased by over 25 percent in the past two years. Meetings of 50 people or less can be a great source of business for a restaurant. Many times they are held at off-peak times, such as during a weekday. Restaurant Dante in Boston does a great private events business, with 70 percent of its business coming from small corporate meetings, and it has its own marketing and events manager. Many restaurants are adding private rooms and hiring salespeople to gain their share of the meetings market.[25] Civic organizations such as Rotary, Kiwanis, and Lion Clubs International are important sources of business for restaurants.

Dealing with Meeting Planners

Discussions over price can either drive the meeting planner and the hotel sales executive apart or bring them together. One successful technique for negotiating with a meeting planner is to determine the group's requirements in detail and work out a package based on needs and budget. Some meeting planners try to negotiate every item separately, starting with the room rate. Then they choose a $65 banquet and try to negotiate the price to $45. In this scenario, every line item becomes a point of contention between the meeting planner and the hotel salesperson.

Taking a consultative approach is much more effective. If the hotel knows that the meeting planner wants to spend $50 for dinner, the chef can develop alternatives within this price range, suggesting something the attendees will enjoy, and the hotel can produce the meal at a profit and sell it for $50. The hotel gains a profitable meeting, and the meeting stays within the planner's budget. Debra Kaufman, an association meeting planner, states that if attendees are able to get work done while they are at the conference they will stay longer.[26] If space is available, the hotel can offer a small meeting room set up with business services, including Internet access, computers, and printers. Given the space is available, this can be a low-cost item to the hotel, which has a high value to the meeting planner.

Most group rates are noncommissionable. Meeting planners sometimes turn meetings over to travel agents. If the meeting planner does so without understanding that the rate is noncommissionable, problems can arise when the travel agent tries to collect a commission. If the rates are commissionable, it should be determined during the negotiation process. It is also common for hotels to give one complimentary room night for every 50 room nights that the group produces—another point of negotiation. Suites are usually counted as two rooms. Thus, a suite for three nights would be the equivalent of six room nights. When a hotel has a smaller meeting room that it will not be able to sell during a proposed meeting, it can be used in the negotiation process as a space for the meeting manager to work. The hotel salesperson must look for items that will create value for the meeting planner without creating costs or sacrificing revenue for the hotel.

Many associations have a president, elected from the membership, and a professional executive vice president. The executive vice president usually sets up the meeting. In larger associations there may be a paid executive director, a convention manager, and one or more meeting managers who handle the association's meetings. In some associations the elected officers also like to get involved in the selection of sites and hotels for meetings or conventions. To further complicate matters, the previous year's president usually becomes the chairman of the association's board of directors and therefore can hold great power in the association. It is important for the salesperson to find out who is involved in the decision-making process, both officially and unofficially.

When the vice president of sales asks a junior salesperson to organize a sales meeting, the salesperson is usually unsure of how to proceed with newly assigned and unfamiliar tasks. However, meeting administrators often know the business as well as the hotel salesperson. Salespeople should listen to the meeting administrator to understand his or her requirements. Sometimes meeting administrators know exactly what they want and simply desire a quote for the meeting according to their specifications. If this is the case, a salesperson trying to alter their specifications arbitrarily can appear unprofessional and lose the meeting administrator's business. For example, a hotel salesperson altered the meeting administrator's menu and developed a quotation based on the altered menus. The meeting administrator was planning a series of training sessions to be presented at various locations throughout the United States and had developed menus to meet group needs. This uninvited intrusion by the hotel salesperson infuriated the meeting administrator, who then proceeded to a competitive hotel.

Most meeting planners maintain a history of the group for the purpose of planning future meetings. This includes past dates, locations, and attendance figures. They also have evaluations of past meetings. A salesperson can gain valuable information by asking questions about past conferences. These questions can provide insight into room pickups, attendance at banquets, past problems with a hotel, and what their members have enjoyed. The salesperson should also interview hotels that hosted the conference in past years.

Consider the following expectations of meeting planners.[27] Meeting planners want their calls or e-mails returned the same day they are received. When they ask about the availability of meeting space, they expect a response the same day and a complete proposal in five days. They want check-in and checkout to last no more than four minutes. Most meeting planners want their bill within one week of the event, and 25 percent want it within 2 days. Planners feel that hotel management should empower the convention service manager to solve their problems. They do not want to wait while the convention service manager checks with a superior. Ultimately, when dealing with group business, the hotel has to please both the meeting planner and the meeting planner's clients. These clients include those attending the conference, association executives, and the president or senior officer of a corporation. Jonathan Tisch, president and CEO of Loews Hotels, states, "What we're looking to do is to create a win–win situation. If the senior officer is happy, then the planner's happy, and if the planner's happy we've done our job."[28]

One of the most important aspects creating a successful function is a prefunction meeting between the hotel staff and the meeting planner. The bell captain should know if a gratuity for his or her staff is included in the package. If it is, Renee Goetz, a meeting planner, states that the staff should be instructed to say, "Thank you, that's been taken care of," when a guest offers a tip. The concierge needs to know the meeting has open nights with no banquets because this will allow the concierge to set aside tables at local restaurants. If garage space is limited, arrangements need to take place to make sure there is adequate space for the group. The hotel staff who will be receiving questions about the event should be briefed. Reservation agents should know the names of the group's VIPs and who should get early check-in privileges. Those responsible for receiving packages for the meeting should know how to store them properly. A prefunction meeting can go a long way to creating a successful event.[29]

Career Opportunities

It is estimated there are 94,200 meeting planners in the United States. Some may be called convention or event planners. In 2012, median pay was $45,810 per year. A bachelor's degree is usually required with a preference for those with degrees in hospitality or tourism management. Demand is expected to increase by over 30 percent.

These individuals spend most of their time in offices. They also work on site at hotels or convention centers and often travel to attend events and visit properties.[30]

■■■ The Corporate Account and Corporate Travel Manager

A nongroup form of organizational business is the individual business traveler. Most hotels offer a corporate rate, which is intended to provide an incentive for corporations to use the hotel. Because of competitive pressures, most hotels have dropped the qualification requirements for their basic corporate rate, offering it now to any businessperson who requests the corporate rate. To provide an incentive system for heavy users, hotels developed a second set of corporate rates. The basic corporate rate is about 10 to 15 percent below the hotel's rack rate. The contract rate is a negotiated rate below the hotel's rack rate.[31] It often includes other benefits such as morning newspapers, upgrades when available, use of the hotel's fitness center, early check-ins, and late checkouts.[32] When negotiating a corporate contract, it is important to understand what creates greater value to the client.

The corporate business traveler is a sought-after segment. Although the corporate contract rate is a discounted rate, it is higher than the group rate. The business traveler is on an expense account and makes use of the hotel's restaurants, health club, laundry, and business center facilities.

The competition for business travelers, once limited to mid-class and luxury hotels, has spread to limited-service hotels. Limited-service hotels now have a 35 percent market share of business traveler rooms. The strong showing of limited-service hotels can be attributed to the upgrading of amenities found in these hotels and at a lower price. Companies that would not consider putting their people in a limited-service hotel a few years ago are now using them. These companies realize they can save thousands of dollars by purchasing less expensive accommodations and yet meet quality standards of guests.

Larger companies have corporate traveler management programs run by the company or in-house branches of a travel agency. These managers negotiate the corporate hotel contracts. The following are the most important attributes when negotiating a hotel contract:

- A favorable image of the hotel's brand by the company's travelers
- Guaranteed availability of negotiated rate (focus groups have told us that a quick way to lose their business is to charge them a higher rate during citywide conventions or tell them rooms are not available during these conventions)
- Location
- Reputation of the hotel's brand
- Negotiated rate
- Flexibility on charges for late cancellation of room reservations

In addition to developing corporate hotel contracts, the travel managers set per diem rates, specifying the amount a company traveler can spend on food and beverage. Often these rates increase as one moves up in the corporation. It is important to find out what a company's per diem rates are to determine whether the hotel is in the company's price range. If the per diem for a company's salespeople is in the hotel's rate range, the hotel can expect more volume than it could expect if only the executive management falls within the price range.

Some corporations use in-house travel agencies, or in-plants, that also represent other corporations, providing the advantage of negotiating leverage. A business represented through an in-plant may have only 100 room nights a year in New York, but the travel agency represented by the in-plant may service 10 companies with a total of 1,500 room nights in New York. The travel agency can negotiate a rate based on the 1,500 room nights and pass this rate along to the individual companies. The hotel compensates in-plants by straight commissions, monthly fees, or a combination of a fee and commission.[33]

Wedding Planners

The wedding market worldwide is of great importance to many sectors of the travel/hospitality industry. The Wedding Report estimates the U.S. wedding market generates $57 billion from over 2 million weddings.[34] The site puts the average wedding at $26,000, with the average attendance 130 guests. Las Vegas is usually considered the number one city in the United States for weddings. Wedding expenditures vary by nationality. Japanese brides are often considered the largest spenders with estimates over $70,000 per wedding. (Please be aware that estimates may actually be guesstimates). For U.S. weddings as many as one in ten may be destination weddings, meaning that the wedding is held somewhere that is home to neither the bride nor the groom.

Many weddings are complex and are served by professional wedding consultants who take responsibility for all details. Others may serve in an advisory capacity. It is important for resorts, hotels, cruise lines, airlines, conference centers, and others to understand the complexities of the wedding market and work closely with wedding planners. The salesforce of hospitality industry vendors often have a dedicated salesperson or group whose sole responsibility is to know and work with wedding planners.

Other Planners

Today, travel and meeting planners exist for a wide variety of groups, including ethnic, alumni, religious, outdoor, hobby interests, and many more. A word of caution: Many of these individuals may be unregulated and not members of a professional trade association. Therefore it is critical to perform background checks and ask for references prior to accepting business from those who are unknown to the vendor.

■■■ CHAPTER REVIEW

I. The Organizational Buying Process. Their purchases often involve large sums of money; complex technical, economic considerations; and interactions among many people at all levels of the organization. Buyer and seller are often very dependent on each other.
  A. Market structure and demand
  B. Types of decisions and the decision process

II. Participants in the Organizational Buying Process
  A. Users. Users are those who use the product or service.
  B. Influencers. Influencers directly influence the buying decision but do not themselves make the final decision.
  C. Deciders. Deciders select product requirements and suppliers.
  D. Approvers. Approvers authorize the proposed actions of deciders or buyers.
  E. Buyers. Buyers have formal authority for selecting suppliers and arranging the terms of purchase.
  F. Gatekeepers. Gatekeepers have the power to prevent sellers or information from reaching members of the buying center.

III. Major Influences on Organizational Buyers
  A. Environmental factors. Organizational buyers are heavily influenced by the current and expected economic environment.
  B. Organizational factors. Each organization has specific objectives, policies, procedures, organizational structures, and systems related to buying.
  C. Interpersonal factors. The buying center usually includes several participants with different levels of interest, authority, and persuasiveness.
  D. Individual factors. Each participant in the buying decision process has personal motivations, perceptions, and preferences. The participant's age, income, education, professional identification, personality, and attitudes toward risk all influence the participants in the buying process.

IV. The Organizational Buying Decisions
  A. Problem recognition. The buying process begins when someone in the company recognizes a problem or need that can be met by acquiring a good or service.
  B. General needs description. The buyer goes on to determine the requirements of the product.
  C. Product specifications. Once the general requirements have been determined, the specific requirements for the product can be developed.
  D. Supplier search. The buyer now tries to identify the most appropriate suppliers.
  E. Proposal solicitation. Qualified suppliers are invited to submit proposals. Skilled research, writing, and presentations are required.

F.   **Supplier selection**. Once the meeting planner has drawn up a short list of suppliers, qualified hotels are invited to submit proposals.

G.   **Order-routine specification**. The buyer writes the final order, listing the technical specification. The supplier responds by offering the buyer a formal contract.

H.   **Performance review**. The buyer does postpurchase evaluation of the product. During this phase the buyer determines if the product meets the buyer's specifications and if the buyer will purchase from the company again.

V.   **The Group Business Markets**

A.   **Conventions**. Conventions are usually the annual meeting of an association and include general sessions, committee meetings, and special-interest sessions. A trade show is often an important part of an annual convention.

B.   **Association meetings**. Associations sponsor many types of meetings, including regional, special-interest, educational, and board meetings.

C.   **Corporate meetings**. A corporate meeting is a command performance for employees of a company. The corporation's major concern is that the meeting be productive and accomplishes the company's objectives.

D.   **Small groups**. Meetings of less than 50 rooms are gaining the attention of hotels and hotel chains.

E.   **Incentive travel**. Incentive travel, a unique subset of corporate group business, is a reward participants receive for achieving or exceeding a goal.

F.   **SMERF groups**. SMERF stands for social, military, educational, religious, and fraternal organizations. This group of specialty markets has a common price-sensitive thread.

G.   Segmentation of group markets by purpose of meeting.

H.   Restaurants as a meeting venue.

VI.   **Dealing with Meeting Planners.** When negotiating with meeting planners, it is important to try to develop a win–win relationship. Meeting planners like to return to the same property.

VII.   **The Corporate Account and Travel Manager.** A nongroup form of organizational business is the individual business traveler. Most hotels offer a corporate rate, which is intended to provide an incentive for corporations to use the hotel.

■■■ DISCUSSION QUESTIONS

1.   What is derived demand? Give an example of derived demand for a hotel in your town.

2.   The buying center costs of six roles. Why is it important for marketers to understand these roles?

3.   Discuss the major environmental influences that affect the purchase meeting space by IBM (or another corporation of your choice) for its sales meetings.

4.   How would a catering sales manager handle a mother and daughter making arrangements for the daughter's wedding differently from a meeting planner from a major corporation wishing to get a quote on a regional sales meeting, which he or she has already done in five other cities?

5.   How can a hotel sales representative identify who is responsible for purchasing meeting space, banquets, and rooms for corporate travelers in the corporate headquarters of an insurance company?

■■■ EXPERIENTIAL EXERCISE

Do the following:

Talk with persons who travel for business. Ask them if they can choose their own hotel and airlines when they travel for their company. If they can choose their own hotels and airlines, ask if they have any restrictions or guidelines. If they are not able to choose their own hotels and airlines, ask if they have any input into where they stay. How would this information help you market travel products to their organization?

■■■ INTERNET EXERCISE

Go to the Internet site of a travel organization (e.g., a hotel, cruise line, travel agency, large restaurant). Does it have a separate section for group or organizational purchases? If so, how does the information in the section differ from the organization's consumer site? If it does not have a separate site, go to another organization until you find one that has a separate site for group or organizational purchases.

■■■ REFERENCES

1 Portions adapted from Susan Harte, "When in Rome, You Should Learn to Do What the Romans Do," *The Atlanta Journal-Constitution* (January 22, 1990): 1, 6. Additional information and examples can be found in Susan Adams, "Business Etiquette Tips for International Travel," *Forbes*, June 6, 2012, www .forbes.com/sites/susanadams/2012/06/15/business-etiquette-tips-for-international-travel; Janette S. Martin and Lillian H. Cheney, *Global Business Etiquette* (Santa Barbara, CA: Praeger Publishers, 2013); "Learn Tips to Do Business in China," *The News-Sentinel*, February 9, 2012, www.news-sentinel .com; and www.cyborlink.com (accessed September 2014).

2 Frederick E. Webster, Jr. and Yoram Wind, *Organizational Buying Behavior* (Upper Saddle River, NJ: Prentice-Hall, 1972), pp. 33–37.

3 Ibid, pp. 78–80.

4 "U.S. Department of Commerce Forecasts Continued Strong Growth for International Travel to the U.S. 2014–2019," International Trade Administration, International Business, National Tourism and Travel Office, October 22, 2014, p. 1.

5 Visit Britain, Inbound Tourism, updated May 2014, www.VisitBrittain.

6 See Edward G. Brierty, Robert W. Eckles, and Robert R. Reeder, *Business Marketing*, 3rd ed. (Upper Saddle River, NJ: Prentice-Hall, 1998), Chapter 3; Murray Harding, "Who Really Makes the Purchasing Decision?" *Industrial Marketing* (September 1966): 76; This point of view is further developed in Ernest Dichter, "Industrial Buying Is Based on Same Only Human Emotional Factors That Motivate Consumer Market's Housewife," *Industrial Marketing* (February 1973): 14–16.

7 Frederick Webster and Yoram Wind, *Organizational Buying Behavior*, Prentice Hall, 1972.

8 See Tom Reilly, "All Sales Decisions Are Emotional for the Buyer," *Selling* (July 2003): 13; Patrick J. Robinson, Charles W. Faris, and Yoram Wind, *Industrial Buying Behavior and Creative Marketing* (Needham Heights, MA: Allyn & Bacon, 1967), p. 14.

9 conventionindustry.org/apex, Lynn McCullough, "APEX: A Playbook for the Meetings Industry," *Hotel Business Review* (September 19, 2007), www .acomonline.org.APEXHotelExec91907.pdf (accessed July 20, 2015).

10 Sarah J. F. Braley, "The Big Picture," *Meetings and Conventions* (October 1998): 2–35; Sarah J. F. Braley, "Meetings Market Report 2008-Associations," *Meeting and Convention Magazine*, "2008 Meetings Report" (August 2008), www.ncmag.com (accessed August 17, 2008).

11 Statista, "The Statistics Portal, Statistics and Facts on the Exhibition, Convention and Meeting Industry in the U.S.," http://www.statista.com,support@statista.com

12 Sarah J. F. Braley, "The Big Picture," *Meetings and Conventions* (October 1998): 2–35; Sarah J. F. Braley, "Meetings Market Report 2008-Associations," *Meeting and Convention Magazine*, "2008 Meetings Report" (August 2008), www.ncmag.com (accessed August 17, 2008)

13 Julie Barker, "The State of the Industry Report," *Successful Meetings* (January 1999): 35–47.

14 Top 10 Factors to Consider When Selecting a Meeting Location (Meeting Planner Forum Session One Recap), Convene, February 3, 2014, http://convene .com/top-10-factors-to-consider-when-selecting-a-meeting-location-meeting-planner-forum-session-one-recap/ (accessed July 20, 2015).

15 Sarah J. F. Bailey, "Corporate Meetings Market Report," *Meetings and Conventions* (December 1, 2010), http://www.meetings-conventions.com/articles/corporate-meeitngs-market-report/a37846/aspx ?page=3 (accessed September 9, 2011).

16 HSMAI econnect, www.hsami.org (accessed October 24, 2001).

17 Jeff Jacoby, "The Convention Center Follies," http:// townhall.com, February 17, 2015, p. 2.

18 Steven E. Spickard, "Economic Impact of Convention and Conference Centers, Economic Research Associates, Ideas and Trends," http://hotel-online.com, 1998, p. 5.

19 Sarah J. F. Braley, "The Big Picture," *Meetings and Conventions* (October 1998): 2–35.

20 Andrea Graham, "Companies Add Perks to Individual Travel Awards," *Corporate Meetings and Incentives* (October 1, 2004), www.cmi.meetingsnet.com (accessed October 24, 2004).

21 Travel White Paper, April 2013, Making Destination Choice Go the Distance, Maritz Travel, www .maritztravel.com, 877-4-MARITZ.

22 Sources: "Green Meetings" Convention Industry Council, http://www.convention/industry.org/ StandardsPractices/GreenMeetings.aspx (accessed September 8, 2011); Green Meetings, www.mpiweb .com (accessed September 9, 2011); www.green meetings.info/goodforbusiness.htm (accessed August 23, 2008); "Green Meetings Policy," The National Recycling Coalition (accessed August 23, 2008); www .ceres.org (accessed August 23, 2008).

23 Regina McGee, "Getting a Fix on SMERF," *Association Meetings* (April 1, 2004), www.meetingsnet.com (accessed June 18, 2004).

24 "Special Report on the Religious Group Travel Market," http://www.premiertourismmarketing.com/fyi/religious .html (accessed October 24, 2004).

25 Naomi Kooker, "Small Meetings Driving Big Hotel, Restaurant Business," *Boston Business Journal* (November 9, 2007).

26 Barker, "The State of the Industry Report," pp. 35–47.

27 Howard Feiertag, "New Survey Reveals Meeting Planners' Priorities," *Hotel and Motel Management* (November 23, 1992).

28 James P. Abbey, *Hospitality Sales and Advertising* (East Lansing, MI: Educational Institute of the American Hotel and Motel Association, 1993), p. 569.

29 See Jonathan Vatner, "Inside Track," *Meetings and Conventions*, www.meetings-conventions.co/printarticles .aspx?pageid=4366 (accessed June 7, 2004).

30 Occupational Outlook Handbook, Meeting, Convention and Event Planners, U.S. Bureau of Labor Statistics, Office of Occupational Statistics and Employment Projections, PSB Suite 2135, 2 Massachusetts Avenue, Washington, DC, 20212, www.bls.gov/ooh

31 Lisa Casey Weiss, "How Different Hotel Rate Programs Stack Up," *Business Travel News* (July 26, 1993): 9–16.

32 Days Inn, http://www.daysins.com/ctg/cgi-bin/DaysInn/ incentives/AAksrACwAAANxAAO (accessed April 20, 2000).

33 Robert Lewis and Richard E. Chambers, *Marketing Leadership in Hospitality: Foundations and Practices* (New York: Wiley, 2000).

34 The Wedding Report, https://www.theweddingreport .com/index.cfm/action/wedding_statistics/view/market/ id/00/idtype/s/location/united_states/ (accessed July 20, 2015).

8

Objectives

*After reading this chapter,
you should be able to:*

1. Define the major steps in designing a customer-driven marketing strategy: market segmentation, targeting, and positioning.

2. List and distinguish among the requirements for effective segmentation: measurability, accessibility, substantiality, and actionability.

3. Explain how companies identify attractive market segments and choose a market-targeting strategy.

4. Illustrate the concept of positioning for competitive advantage by offering specific examples.

Customer-Driven Marketing Strategy: Creating Value for Target Customers

A few years back, Dunkin' Donuts paid dozens of faithful customers in Phoenix, Chicago, and Charlotte, North Carolina, $100 a week to buy coffee at Starbucks instead. At the same time, the no-frills coffee chain paid Starbucks customers to make the opposite switch. When it later debriefed the two groups, Dunkin' says it found them so polarized that company researchers dubbed them "tribes," each of whom loathed the very things that made the other tribe loyal to their coffee shop. Dunkin' fans viewed Starbucks as pretentious and trendy, whereas Starbucks loyalists saw Dunkin' as plain and unoriginal. Most Dunkin' customers were just looking for a good cup of coffee and didn't want an upholstered chair to sit in when they drank their coffee. They did not understand the sense of community Starbucks's was trying to create.

Dunkin' Donuts is rapidly expanding into a national coffee powerhouse, on par with Starbucks, the nation's largest coffee chain. But the research confirmed a simple fact: Dunkin' is not Starbucks. In fact, it doesn't want to be. To succeed, Dunkin' must have its own clear vision of just which customers it wants to serve and how. Dunkin' and Starbucks target very different customers, who want very different things from their favorite coffee shops. Starbucks is strongly positioned as a sort of highbrow "third place," with (the first two being the home and office) couches, eclectic music, and art-splashed walls. Dunkin' has a decidedly more lowbrow, "everyman" kind of appeal.

Dunkin' Donuts built itself on serving simple fare at a reasonable price to working-class customers. It gained a reputation as a morning pit stop where everyday folks could get their daily donut and caffeine fix. But recently, to broaden its appeal and fuel expansion, the chain has been moving upscale a bit, but not too far. It has spiffed up its stores and added new menu items, such as lattes and non-breakfast items such as breaded chicken sandwiches with barbeque sauce. Dunkin' has also made dozens of store and atmosphere redesign changes, big and small, ranging from adding free Wi-Fi, digital menu boards, and more electrical outlets for laptops and smartphones to playing relaxing background music. Dunkin' franchisees can now redecorate in any of four Starbucks-esque color schemes, including "Dark Roast," "Cappuccino Blend," and "Jazz Brew," which features "dark orange and brown cozy booth seating, as well as hanging light fixtures that lend a soft glow to wall murals printed with words such as 'break,' 'fresh' and 'quality'."

However, as it inches upscale, Dunkin' Donuts is being careful not to alienate its traditional customer base. There are no couches in the remodeled stores. Dunkin' even renamed a new hot sandwich a "stuffed melt" after customers complained that calling it a "panini" was too fancy; it then dropped it altogether when faithful customers thought it was too messy. "We're walking [a fine] line," says the chain's vice president of consumer insights. "The thing about the Dunkin' tribe is, they see through the hype."

Dunkin' Donuts's research showed that, although loyal customers want nicer stores, they were bewildered and turned off by the atmosphere at Starbucks. They groused that crowds of laptop users made it difficult to find a seat. They didn't like Starbucks's "tall," "grande," and "venti" lingo for small, medium, and large coffees. And they couldn't understand why anyone would pay so much for a cup of coffee. It was clear the Dunkin' customers not only felt uncomfortable going to a Starbucks's, but they did not understood the concept. The Starbucks customers that Dunkin' paid to switch were equally uneasy in Dunkin' shops. "The Starbucks people couldn't bear that they weren't special anymore," says the ad executive.

Such opposing opinions aren't surprising, given the differences in the two stores' customers. Dunkin's customers include more middle-income blue- and white-collar workers across all age, race, and income demographics. By contrast, Starbucks targets a higher income, more professional group. But Dunkin's researchers concluded that it was more the ideal, rather than income, that set the two tribes apart: Dunkin's tribe members want to be part of a crowd, whereas members of the Starbucks's tribe want to stand out as individuals. Over the past several years, both Dunkin' Donuts and Starbucks have grown rapidly, each targeting its own tribe of customers and riding the wave of America's growing thirst for coffee. Now, both are looking for more growth by convincing "grab-and-go" morning customers to visit later in the day and stick around longer. Although still smaller than Starbucks—which captures a 33 percent U.S. market share versus Dunkin's 16 percent share—Dunkin' is currently the nation's fastest-growing snack and coffee chain. It hopes that the recent repositioning and upgrades will help keep that momentum going. Dunkin' plans to double its number of U.S. stores by 2020.

However, in refreshing its stores and positioning, Dunkin' Donuts has stayed true to the needs and preferences of the Dunkin' tribe. So far so good. For seven years running, Dunkin' Donuts has ranked number one in the coffee category in a leading customer loyalty and engagement survey, ahead of number two Starbucks. According to the survey, Dunkin' Donuts was the top brand for consistently meeting or exceeding customer expectations with respect to taste, quality, and customer service.

Dunkin' Donuts's targeting and positioning are pretty well summed up in its popular ad slogan "America Runs on Dunkin'." No longer just a morning pit stop, Dunkin' now bills itself as America's favorite all-day, everyday stop for coffee and baked goods. Nothing too fancy—just meeting the everyday, all-day needs of the Dunkin' tribe.[1]

▪▪▪ Markets

Companies today recognize that they cannot appeal to all customers in the marketplace, or at least not all customers the same way. Customers are too numerous, too widely scattered, and too varied in their needs and buying processes. Moreover, the companies themselves vary widely in their abilities to serve different segments of the market. Instead, like Dunkin' Donuts, a company must identify the parts of the

Figure 8–1
Steps in segmentation, targeting, and positioning.

market that it can serve best and most profitably. It must design customer-driven marketing strategies that build the right relationships with the right customers.

Most companies have moved away from mass marketing and toward target marketing—identifying market segments, selecting one or more of them, and developing products and market programs tailored to each. Instead of scattering their marketing efforts (the "shotgun" approach), firms are focusing on the buyers who have great interest in the values they create well (the "rifle" approach).

Figure 8–1 shows the three major steps in target marketing. The first is **market segmentation**, dividing a market into distinct groups that might require separate products and/or marketing mixes. The company identifies different ways to segment the market and develops profiles of the resulting market segments. The second step is **market targeting**, evaluating each segment's attractiveness and selecting one or more of the market segments. The third step is **market positioning**, developing competitive positioning for the product and an appropriate marketing mix.

Market segmentation.
Dividing a market into direct groups of buyers who might require separate products or marketing mixes.

Market targeting. Evaluating each market segment's attractiveness and selecting one or more segments to enter.

Market positioning.
Formulating competitive positioning for a product and a detailed marketing mix.

◾◼◻ **Market Segmentation**

Buyers in any market differ in their wants, resources, locations, buying attitudes, and buying practices. Because buyers have unique needs and wants, each is potentially a separate market. Ideally, a seller might design a separate marketing program for each buyer. For example, a caterer can customize the menu, entertainment, and the setting to meet the needs of a specific client.

However, most companies are unable to offer complete segmentation because of cost. Companies, therefore, look for broad classes of buyers who differ in their product needs or buying responses. For example, married adults who vacation with small children have different needs than young single adults.

The restaurant industry offers many examples of segmentation by a variety of variables. The type of service varies from quick service to fine dining. One-segment retail host restaurants are restaurants located in retail outlets such as a Walmart or gas station. This segment now accounts for over $41 billion in the United States.[2] The target market for these restaurants are people who are in the store or are traveling, hungry, and want to make one stop for food and gas. The main benefit is convenience. One of the fastest-growing restaurant segments is the fast-casual segment. These restaurants offer excellent food, but require the customer to order the food themselves and then a server brings it to their table, lowering the labor cost for the restaurant and both the cost of the meal and amount of the tip for the customer. Segmenting restaurants by type of service and location are just two of the many ways of segmenting a restaurant.

There is no single way to segment a market. A marketer has to try different segmentation variables. Table 8–1 outlines major variables that might be used

TABLE 8–1
Major segmentation variables for consumer markets.

Segmentation Variable	Examples
Geographic	Nations, regions, states, counties, cities, neighborhoods, population density (urban, suburban, rural), climate
Demographic	Age, life-cycle stage, gender, income, occupation, education, religion, ethnicity, generation
Psychographic	Social class, lifestyle, personality
Behavioral	Occasions, benefits, user status, usage rate, loyalty status

Source: Kotler, Philip; Armstrong, Gary, *Principles of Marketing*, 16th Ed., ©2016, p. 199. Reprinted and Electronically reproduced by permission of Pearson Education, Inc., New York, NY.

in segmenting consumer markets. Here we look at the geographic, demographic, psychographic, and behavioristic variables used in segmenting consumer markets.

Geographic Segmentation

Geographic segmentation calls for dividing the market into different geographic units, such as nations, states, regions, counties, cities, or even neighborhoods. A company decides to operate in one or several geographic areas by paying attention to geographic differences in customer preferences. For example, within the Central American countries, beans are a dietary staple, yet in one nation consumers prefer red beans while in another black beans are preferred.

Restaurants use geographic data about their customers to determine the extent of their market reach, which could be 2 miles for a fast-food restaurant to 50 miles or more for a specialty restaurant. Information on where customers are coming from can be collected by simply asking customers for their zip code or come from more sophisticated studies that create customer databases that include other customer data in addition to the geographic information. The customer origin information can be used to show the decay of a customer base over distance, the effect of competition, and the placement of media.[3]

Multiunit restaurant chains will often focus on a geographic region containing customers that they understand. The geographic focus also creates an opportunity for effective management and promotion. For example, Port of Sub, a sandwich restaurant that started in Nevada, has expanded into a chain that has over 140 restaurants. All of their units are in the west, with the majority in Nevada and the states adjacent to Nevada—Arizona, California, and Utah.

Companies that cover a wide geographic area are localizing their products, services, advertising, promotion, and sales efforts to fit the needs of individual regions, cities, and neighborhoods. For example, Domino's Pizza, the nation's largest pizza delivery chain, keeps its marketing and customer focus decidedly local. Hungry customers anywhere in the nation can use the Domino's online platform or tablet and smartphone apps to track down local coupon offers, locate the nearest store with a global positioning system (GPS) store locator, and even use Domino's Pizza Tracker to follow their pies locally from store to door.[4]

Similarly, one of Marriott International lifestyle brands, Renaissance Hotels, has rolled out its Navigator program, which hyper-localizes guest experiences at each of its 155 lifestyle hotels around the world.[5] Renaissance Hotels' Navigator program puts a personal and local face on each location by "micro-localizing" recommendations for guests' food, shopping, entertainment, and cultural experiences at each destination. The program is anchored by on-site "Navigators" of Renaissance Hotels at each location. Whether it's Omar Bennett, a restaurant-loving Brooklynite at the Renaissance New York Times Square Hotel, or James Elliott at the St. Pancras Renaissance London Hotel, a history buff and local pub expert, Navigators are extensively trained locals who are deeply passionate about the destination and often have a personal connection to the locale. Based on their own personal experiences and ongoing research, they work with guests personally to help them experience "the hidden gems throughout the neighborhood of each hotel through the eyes of those who know it best."

In addition, Renaissance Hotels engage locals in each city to participate by inviting them to follow their local Navigator via social media, as well as adding their own favorites to the system, creating each hotel's own version of Yelp. Navigators then cull

The St. Pancras Renaissance Hotel in London is located in a building that formerly housed railway offices. Courtesy of richie0703/Fotolia.

through submitted tips and feature the best recommendations alongside their own, for sharing within the hotel lobby or on its Web site and social media channels. Since introducing the hyper-localized Navigator program as part of Renaissance Hotels' "Live Life to Discover" campaign two years ago, the hotel's Web site traffic has grown more than 80 percent, Facebook likes have exploded from 40,000 to more than 915,000, and Twitter followers have surged from 5,000 to 61,000.

Demographic Segmentation

Demographic segmentation. Dividing the market into groups based on demographic variables such as age, gender, family size, family life cycle, income, occupation, education, religion, race, and nationality.

Demographic segmentation divides the market into segments based on variables such as age, life-cycle stage, gender, income, occupation, education, religion, ethnicity, and generation. Demographic variables are the most popular bases for segmenting customer groups. One reason is that consumer needs, wants, and usage rates often vary closely with demographic variables. Another is that demographic variables are easy to measure. Even when market segments are first defined using other bases, such as personality or behavior, demographic characteristics must be known to assess the size of the market and to reach it efficiently. Now we show you how certain demographic factors have been used in market segmentation.

Age and Life-Cycle Stage

Consumer preferences change with age. Some companies offer different products or marketing strategies to penetrate various age and life-cycle segments. Other companies focus on the specific age of life-stage groups. For example, although consumers in all age segments love Disney cruises, Disney Cruise Lines focuses primarily on families with children, large and small. Most of its destinations and shipboard activities are designed with parents and their children in mind. On board, Disney provides trained counselors who help younger kids join in hands-on activities, teen-only spaces for older children, and family-time or individual-time options for parents and other adults. It's difficult to find a Disney Cruise Lines ad or Web page that doesn't feature a family full of smiling faces. In contrast, Viking River Cruises, the deluxe smaller-boat cruise line that offers tours along the world's great rivers, primarily targets older-adult couples and singles. It states on its Web site, "Due to the nature of our cruise itineraries, Viking Cruises does not maintain facilities or services for children aboard cruise vessels."[6]

Marketers must be careful to guard against stereotypes when using age and life-cycle segmentation. Although some 80-year-olds fit the doddering stereotype, others play tennis. Similarly, whereas some 40-year-old couples are sending their children off to college, others are just beginning new families. Thus, age is often a poor predictor of a person's life cycle, health, work or family status, needs, and buying power. Companies marketing to mature consumers usually use positive images and appeals. For example, Disney's "The Grand Adventure," promotes Disney's amusement as a great place for active grandparents to take their grandkids.

The onboard activities of European River cruises are designed for the adult traveler. Courtesy of peteri/Fotolia.

Gender

Gender marketing is by no means simplistic. A "typical" male or female does not exist, yet droves of companies have erred in trying to develop and market a product or service for such an individual. It is natural for each of us to think of typical as someone in our respective age, income, and lifestyle. This is always wrong. Gender marketing is most effective when combined with lifestyle and demographic information.

According to the Lipstick Economy, a Web Site communicating the purchasing power of woman, "The average adventure traveler is not a male but a 47-year-old female." The author cites a growing segment of single women that are traveling. She cites one of the reasons for this growth is the growth of indies, a term for women over 30 years that are not living with a partner and are without children. Jamie Dunham, president of the branding and marketing company Brandwise, states indies account for almost a third of all adult women. She states they have high discretionary income as they do not have the expense of a family household.[7]

Income Segmentation

Income segmentation.
Dividing a market into different income groups.

Income segmentation has long been used by marketers of products and services. The lodging industry is particularly effective in using income segmentation. Upper-income guests and corporations serve as targets for country clubs, boxes at sports stadiums, and upscale hotels and resorts. The Four Seasons Miami recently offered a Five Diamond package that included a two-carat Graff diamond eternity band (or another diamond piece designed to your specifications) and a stay in the presidential suite with a bottle of 1990 Dom Perignon Oenotheque champagne, caviar for two, and an 80-minute in-suite couples massage using a lotion infused with real ground diamonds. The price tag: "From $50,000."[9]

Seadream Yacht Club, a small-ship luxury cruise line, calls select guests after every cruise and offers to have the chief executive officer (CEO) fly out to their home and host, at Seadream's expense, a brunch or reception for a dozen of the couple's best friends. The brochure rate of Sundream cruises averages over $2,500 per day per couple. The CEO of a cruise line visiting your home is an impressive gesture. The customers have no trouble getting a group of friends together, many of whom are corporate executives like the visiting CEO. The CEO offers a great rate to the guests and sells several cruises that night as well as more sales are generated in the future through the couple telling their friends about the cruise. One of these visits could generate $100,000 or more in short-term sales, as well as the value of repeat cruises

Marketing HIGHLIGHT 8–1   Targeting Families by Targeting Kids

Friendly's is a casual restaurant originally known for its ice cream. Friendly's was known for sandwiches and ice cream, but not somewhere where a family would go for dinner. Friendly's management wanted to reposition the restaurant as a place where customers would go for lunch and dinner. Research had shown that when determining where a family will eat, kids have a major influence. In fact, children influenced over $125 billion in restaurant spending. Families with children account for 56 percent of all dollars spent on food away from home. Management realized that parents are pressed for time, and they often feel bad about not spending more time with their children. If Friendly's could make a dining experience that the children would enjoy, the family would have fun together and everyone would be a winner.

To find out what would make a good dining experience for children, Friendly's held focus groups with children. One of the things that came out of the focus groups was that children wanted "real" menus, like their parents' menus. They didn't want placemat menus. The kids also told them what kind of food they wanted, and how they wanted it presented. Besides talking to kids, it is also useful to talk to their parents. At the Kids' Marketing Conference, parents told restaurant managers that comfortable seating was important; kids squirm in hard seats. They also said they did not like play areas in sit-down-service restaurants; they want to be with their kids. They also expect more nutritious meals in a sit-down-service restaurant than they do in a fast-food restaurant.

Friendly's put a kids' coordinator on each shift to make sure the wants of the children were being met. Parents mentioned that having servers who can deal with kids is important. According to image research done before and after the program, Friendly's effort to reposition as a family restaurant was successful, and its image as a good place for kids jumped 50 percent. Notice how Friendly's used marketing research to find out about the market it wanted to target. The marketing information it gathered helped it understand the consumer behavior of the family market, namely, that kids play a major role in where the family dines. Knowing this, Friendly's created a program to make Friendly's a place where children would want to come.[8]

from the newly recruited customer. This has been so successful for Seadream that it has abandoned most traditional advertising.[10] Carnival cruises target the much larger middle-income market. Its cruises start at around $150 per day per couple. Both cruise lines have been successful targeting their chosen target markets.

Fractional ownership is a product clearly designed for the upscale income market. Fractional ownership is partial ownership of a property. For instance, Hotel companies such as Hyatt, Ritz-Carlton, Four Seasons, and Starwood will sell one-fourth, one-eighth, or one-sixteenth interest in condominiums built adjacent to one of their hotels. This allows an upper-middle-class person to have access to a multimillion dollar condo. The marketing of fractional ownership (also called residence clubs) is essentially a high-end real estate function, with the sales of the condominiums used to support the financial viability of multi-use development, which also includes the hotel. The concept also spread to exotic car, yacht, and jet ownership.[11]

Income does not always predict which customers will buy a given product or service. Some upscale urban restaurateurs opened branches in upper-middle-class suburbs. They were attracted by high suburban household incomes. But many had to close their doors. Why? Urban dwellers tend to be singles and couples without children. A large portion of their income is discretionary and their lifestyle includes dining out frequently. According to the National Restaurant Association, singles spend more than half of their food budget dining out, whereas married couples spend only 37 percent of their food budget eating out. On the other hand, families in the suburbs often have a high household income, but spend a heavy percentage of their money on housing, automobiles, and children. Singles represent a prime market segment for the restaurant industry.[12]

Psychographic Segmentation

Psychographic segmentation.
Dividing a market into different groups based on social class, lifestyle, or personality characteristics.

Psychographic segmentation divides buyers into different segments based on social class, lifestyle, or personality characteristics. People in the same demographic group can have very different psychographic characteristics. In Chapter 6, we discussed how the products people buy reflect their lifestyles. As a result, marketers often segment their markets by consumer lifestyles and base their marketing strategies on lifestyle appeals. For example, car-sharing nicher Zipcar rents cars by the hour or the day. But it doesn't see itself as a car-rental company. Instead it sees itself as enhancing its customer's urban lifestyles and targets accordingly. "It's not about cars," says Zipcar's CEO, "it's about urban life." In New York, the rental of a parking place for a car can be as expensive as an apartment in other cities. New York also has good public transportation. Many people living in Manhattan do not have a car. Zipcar becomes their car.[13]

Marketers also use personality variables to segment markets. For example, cruise lines target adventure seekers. Royal Caribbean appeals to high-energy couples and families by providing hundreds of activities, such as rock wall climbing and ice skating. Its commercials urge travelers to "declare your independence and become a citizen of nation—Royal Caribbean, The Nation of Why Not." By contrast, the Regent Seven Seas Cruise Line targets more serene and cerebral adventurers, mature couples, seeking a more elegant ambiance and exotic destinations such as the Orient. Regent invites them to come along as "luxury goes exploring."[14]

Social Class

In Chapter 6, we described the six social classes and explained that social class has a strong effect on preferences for cars, clothes, home furnishings, leisure activities, reading habits, and retailers. Afternoon tea at the Ritz-Carlton is aimed at the upper middle and upper classes. A neighborhood pub near a factory targets the working class. The customers of each of these establishments would probably feel uncomfortable in the other establishments.

Lifestyle

Chapter 6 also showed the influence of people's lifestyles on the goods and services that they buy. Marketers are increasingly segmenting the markets by

Marketing HIGHLIGHT 8–2   W Hotels: A Lifestyle Hotel

You approach the glitzy, contemporary building in London, a 10-story structure encased in a translucent glass veil. Cameras mounted on the roof capture the surrounding skyline and project it onto the building's surface, creating a seamless blend of the building with its setting. Inside, you're greeted by thumping hip-hop music, large mirrored glitter balls, open fires, and a huge Chesterfield sofa that snakes around the lounge bar. You're in a nightclub perhaps, or the latest trendy restaurant. No, you're in the W London, a hotel that offers much more than just rooms for the night.

Starwood Hotels and Resorts operate nine different hotel chains—something for everyone, you might say. But its W Hotels brand stands out from all the rest. In fact, W Hotels doesn't really think of itself as just a hotel chain. Instead, it positions itself as "an iconic lifestyle brand." More than just rooms, W Hotels prides itself on "offering guests unprecedented insider access to a world of 'Wow' through contemporary cool design, fashion, music, nightlife, and entertainment." W Hotels exudes a youthful, outgoing, jet-setting lifestyle that fits its ultra-hip, trendsetter clientele—mostly from the media, music, fashion, entertainment, and consulting industries. For these patrons, W provides an unmatched sense of belonging.

W Hotels' lifestyle positioning starts with unique design. Although most hotel chains churn out cookie-cutter locations in search of a consistent brand image, W Hotels' 54 properties worldwide look nothing alike. W's patrons view themselves as unique, so they demand the same from the hotels they choose. Every W Hotel projects a common "energetic, vibrant, forward-thinking attitude," and an appreciation for fashion, art, and music befitting its lifestyle image. But in terms of design, each W Hotel is "uniquely inspired by its destination, mixing cutting-edge design with local influences."

For example, the W Taipei in Taiwan, located in the Xinyi district near Taipei 101, the city's tallest skyscraper, is designed around the theme of "nature electrified," blending soft wooden walls; geometric, box-shaped shelves; and lighting inspired by Chinese lanterns. The W Koh Samui (in Thailand), an all-villa beach resort, treats guests to the concept of "day and night"—relaxing by the pool by day and partying by night with modern interiors accented by bright flashes of red, off-white terrazzo floors, and wooden decks for private guest pools. The W Bali features an "inside and outside" theme, with grass-like green pillows that bring a bit of outdoors into the rooms and bed headboards made from the skin of stingrays.

With each unique design, however, W maintains a consistent ambiance that leaves no question in guests' minds that they are living the W lifestyle. The W Paris, for example, blends the facade of its historic and elegant 1870s building with the theme of Paris as the "City of Light," all wrapped in W's signature contemporary energy. The hotel design revolves around an oversized backlit digital undulating wall that defines the central core of the building and weaves through the public and private spaces. "Our design feeds off the elegance, richness, and radiance of Paris and W's DNA for infusing a sense of energy," says the head of the hotel's design group. In true W fashion, it brings the historic building to life with a glowing vibrancy.

Under the direction of a global music director, W's long-running Symmetry Live concert series offers guests access to exclusive performances by some of the world's hottest entertainers, such as Cee Lo Green, Janelle Monae, Ellie Goulding, and Theophilus London. This year, W is sponsoring an exclusive traveling exhibition of the photography of Madonna, curated by Rock Paper Photo and sponsored by vitaminwater. The exhibit features never seen before photos of pop star Madonna from the 1980s. The exclusive exhibition celebrates music and fashion, two of the W brand's core passions.

Another constant at W Hotels is first-class service—what W calls "Whatever-Whenever" service. "We aim to provide whatever, whenever, as long as it is legal—something that is very much consistent throughout the W brand," explains one W Hotel manager. W Hotels don't have concierges; instead, they have "W Insiders." The Insiders go a step beyond. Rather than waiting to be asked for advice, they proactively seek out things they can do to enhance the stay of each guest. In keeping with the brand's lifestyle positioning, insiders stay in tune with special need-to-know happenings and advise guests on all the latest places to see and be seen.

Staying at a W Hotel isn't cheap. The basic W room runs about $450 a night, with top suites running up to five figures. But a W Hotel isn't just a place where you rent a room and get a good night's sleep. It's the design of the place, the contemporary ambiance, what's hanging on the walls, the music that's playing, the other guests who stay there—all of these things contribute mightily to the W's lifestyle positioning and allure to its young, hip, upscale W clientele. It's not just a room—it's part of an entire trendsetter lifestyle.[15]

consumer lifestyles. For example, many bars/watering holes are designed for young singles wanting to meet the opposite sex, singles wanting to meet the same sex, and couples wanting to avoid the entire singles scene and enjoy each other's company.

Personality

Marketers use personality variables to segment markets, endowing their products and personalities. For example, cruise lines target adventure seekers. Royal Caribbean appeals to high-energy couples and families with hundreds of activities such as rock climbing walls and ice skating. By contrast, the Regent Seven Seas Cruise Line targets mature couples seeking a more elegant ambiance and exotic destinations, such as Asia. Regent invites them to come along as "luxury goes exploring."[16]

Behavioral Segmentation

Behavioral segmentation.
Dividing a market into groups based on consumers' knowledge, attitude, use, or response to a product.

In **behavioral segmentation**, buyers are divided into groups based on their knowledge, attitude, and use or response to a product. Many marketers believe that behavioral variables are the best starting point for building market segments.

Occasion Segmentation

Buyers can be grouped according to occasions when they make a purchase or use a product. Occasion segmentation helps firms build product use. For example, air travel is triggered by occasions related to business, vacation, or family. Airline advertisements aimed at the business traveler often incorporate service, convenience, and on-time-departure benefits in the offer. Airline marketing aimed at the vacation traveler uses price, interesting destinations, and prepackaged vacations. Airline marketing aimed at the family market often shows children traveling alone to visit a relative, under the watchful eye of an airline employee. A message of this nature is particularly relevant to the single-parent segment.

Occasion segmentation can help firms build product use. For example, Mother's Day has been promoted as a time to take your mother or wife out to eat. St. Patrick's Day has been promoted as a night of celebration. Monday holidays, such as Labor Day and Memorial Day, have been promoted as times to enjoy a mini vacation. These are examples of occasion marketing.

The honeymoon market represents an occasion with excellent potential for the hospitality industry. In many cultures, the honeymoon trip is paid for by parents or other family members. As a gift, the honeymoon package may contain upscale products and services such as a hotel suite and first-class airfare. The Japanese honeymoon market is particularly important to the hospitality industry of Guam, Hawaii, New Zealand, and Australia. Group honeymoon tours have proved to be successful, in which several Japanese newlyweds participate in a tour of one or more destinations.

Marketing HIGHLIGHT 8-3 The VFR Traveler Segment

One of the largest traveler segments for many visitor destinations, city, state, region, or nation, is the VFR (visiting friends and relatives) market. This market is sometimes overlooked in destination marketing because VFR travelers often stay in private homes and eat many of their meals in the home.

A U.S. study of this market showed that "VFR travelers were highly homogeneous in terms of their travel party composition, demographic characteristics, and decision-making mode." This was the largest segment to stop at a travel information center (TIC). The majority of VFR travelers preferred to obtain information from TICs about hotels and attractions.

Contrary to some opinions that rate the VFR segment low in terms of market appeal, the study showed, "This segment performed well on profitability measurements, having the highest number of travelers, the highest average expenditures per person, and the highest expenditure on shopping."[17]

The author recommended the following:

- Tourism/hospitality marketers should take advantage of advertising and promotion opportunities available through TICs.

- Public tourism promotion agencies should allocate a significant amount of space in their travel guides to special events and festivals because the VFR segment wants this information.

- Destination marketers should implement strategies to enhance local residents' knowledge about things of interest to the VFR traveler because local residents are a prime source of information for this travel segment.[18]

Benefits Sought

Buyers can also be grouped according to the product benefits they seek. After studying patrons and nonpatrons of three types of restaurants—family popular, atmosphere, and gourmet—one researcher concluded that there are five major appeal categories for restaurant customers.[19] The relative importance of food quality, menu variety, price, atmosphere, and convenience factors across each group was studied. It was found that patrons of family-service restaurants sought convenience and menu. Variety patrons of atmosphere restaurants ranked food quality and atmosphere as the top attributes. Patrons of gourmet restaurants valued quality.

Knowing the benefits sought by customers is useful in two ways. First, managers can develop products with features that provide the benefits their customers are seeking. Second, managers communicate more effectively with their customers if they know what benefits customers seek.

At their W hotels, guests who indicate they are traveling with a pet receive a pet toy and treat at check-in. In the room they will find pet food and water bowls and a bed for their pet. The pet even receives a special treat as part of their turn-down service.[20] Those traveling with pets will place a high value on this feature, while it will have no value to those who do not travel with pets.

Thus, a benefit is a positive outcome received from a product feature. Those product features that create positive outcomes for guests create value. Features that do not offer positive outcomes for the guest will have no value.

User Status

Many markets can be segmented into nonusers, former users, potential users, first-time users, and regular users of a product. High-market-share companies such as major airlines are particularly interested in keeping regular users and attracting potential users. Potential users and regular users often require different marketing appeals.

Usage Rate

Markets can also be segmented into light, medium, and heavy product users. Heavy users are often a small percentage of the market but account for a high percentage of total consumption. For example, researchers discovered that 4.1 percent of airline travelers account for 70.4 percent of airline trips, and thus airlines were eager to capture this lucrative market.[21] Clearly marketers are eager to identify heavy users and build a marketing mix to attract them. Many hospitality firms spread their marketing resources evenly across all potential customers. Seasoned marketers identify heavy users and focus marketing strategies toward them.

Loyalty Status

A market can also be segmented on the basis of consumer loyalty. Consumers of hospitality products can be loyal to brands, such as Courtyard by Marriott, or to companies, such as Qantas Airlines. Others are only somewhat loyal. They may be loyal to two or three brands or favor one brand but buy others. Still other buyers show no brand loyalty at all. They want variety or simply buy whichever brand is cheapest or most convenient. These people will stop at a Hilton Garden Inn or Courtyard by Marriott, depending on which they see first when looking for a motel.

A major reason for increasing customer loyalty is that "loyal customers are price insensitive compared to brand-shifting patrons."[22] In the hospitality and travel industries, marketers attempt to build brand loyalty through relationship marketing. Although manufacturing companies often lack direct contact with their customers, most hospitality and travel marketers do have direct contact. They can develop a guest history database and use this information to customize offers and customer communications.

Millennials do not want to stay 20 times before they get significant rewards. They rate "ability to value me" and "ability to understand my needs" as the most important attributes in creating loyalty.[23] A challenge for hotel and airline marketers will be transitioning the tiered loyalty programs, developed for the baby boomers, to programs that will be meaningful for millennials. They want to feel special from the moment they arrive at the hotel for the first time; they desire experiences that are customized for them.[24] The traditional tier-based programs that require the guest to stay a number of nights before they receive their rewards are, therefore, less effective.[25] citizenM, a hotel brand targeted at millennials, has a one-level loyalty program called "citizen," and when you join, you instantly get 15 percent off the room rates and a more liberal cancellation policy.

Using Multiple Segmentation Bases

Marketers rarely limit their segmentation analysis to only one or a few variables. Rather, they often use multiple segmentation bases in an effort to identify smaller, better-defined target groups. Several business information services—such as Nielsen, Acxiom, and Experian—provide multivariable segmentation systems that merge geographic, demographic, lifestyle, and behavioral data to help companies segment their markets down to zip codes, neighborhoods, and even households.

One of the leading consumer segmentation systems is Experian's Mosaic USA system. It classifies U.S. households into one of 71 lifestyle segments and 19 levels of affluence, based on specific consumer demographics, interests, behaviors, and passions. Mosaic USA segments carry exotic names such as Birkenstocks and Beemers, Bohemian Groove, Sports Utility Families, Colleges and Cafes, Hispanic Harmony, Rolling the Dice, Small Town Shallow Pockets, and True Grit Americans.[26] Such colorful names help bring the segments to life.

For example, the Birkenstocks and Beemers group is located in the Middle Class Melting Pot level of affluence and consists of 40- to 65-year-olds who have achieved financial security and left the urban rat race for rustic and artsy communities located near small cities. They enjoy cruises and warm weather vacations. They enjoy cooking at home and going out to casual restaurants. Promotions to these restaurants will attract this group.[27]

Bohemian Groove consumers, part of the Significant Singles group, are urban singles aged 45 to 65 living in apartments in smaller cities such as Sacramento, California, and Harrisburg, Pennsylvania. They tend to be laid back, maintain a large circle of friends, and stay active in community groups. They enjoy music, hobbies, and the creative arts. When they go out to eat, they choose places such as the Macaroni Grill or Red Robin.

Mosaic USA and other such systems can help marketers to segment people and locations into marketable groups of like-minded consumers. Each segment has its own pattern of likes, dislikes, lifestyles, and purchase behaviors. Using the Mosaic system, marketers can paint a surprisingly precise picture of who you are and what you might buy. Such rich segmentation provides a powerful tool for marketers of all kinds. It can help companies identify and better understand key customer segments, reach them more efficiently, and tailor market offerings and messages to their specific needs.

Requirements for Effective Segmentation

Although there are many ways to segment a market, all are not equally effective. For example, buyers of restaurant meals could be divided into blond and brunette customers. But hair color does not affect the purchase of restaurant meals. Furthermore, if all restaurant customers buy the same number of meals each month and believe all restaurant meals are of equal quality and are willing to pay the same price, the company would not benefit from segmenting this market.

To be useful, market segments must have the following characteristics:

- *Measurability:* The degree to which the segment's size and purchasing power can be measured. Certain segmentation variables are difficult to measure, such as the size of the segment of teenagers who drink beer primarily to rebel against their parents.

- *Accessibility:* The degree to which segments can be assessed and served. One of the authors found that 20 percent of a college restaurant's customers were frequent patrons. However, frequent patrons lacked any common characteristics. They included faculty, staff, and students. There was no usage difference among part-time, full-time, or class year of the students. Although the market segment had been identified, there was no way to access the heavy-user segment.

- *Substantiality:* The degree to which segments are large or profitable enough to serve as markets. A segment should be the largest possible homogeneous group economically feasible to support a tailored marketing program. For example, large metropolitan areas can support many different ethnic restaurants, but in a smaller town, Thai, Vietnamese, and Moroccan food restaurants might not survive.

- *Actionability:* The degree to which effective programs can be designed for attracting and serving segments. A small airline, for example, identified seven market segments, but its staff and budget were too small to develop separate marketing programs for each segment.

■■■ Market Targeting

Marketing segmentation reveals a company's market-segment opportunities. The firm has to evaluate the various segments and decide how many and which ones to target. We now look at how companies evaluate and select target markets.

Evaluating Market Segments

When evaluating different market segments, a firm must look at three factors: segment size and growth, segment-structured attractiveness, and company objectives and resources.

Segment Size and Growth

A company must first collect and analyze data on current segment sales growth rates and expected profitability for various segments. It will be interested in segments that have the right size and growth characteristics, but "right size and growth" is a relative matter. Some companies want to target segments with large current sales, a high growth rate, and a high profit margin. However, the largest, fastest-growing segments are not always the most attractive ones for every company. Smaller companies often find they lack the skills and resources needed to serve the larger segments or that these segments are too competitive. Such companies may select segments that are smaller but are potentially more profitable.

Segment Structural Attractiveness

A segment might have desirable size and growth and still not offer attractive profits. The company must examine several major structural factors that affect long-run segment attractiveness. For example, a segment is less attractive if it already contains many strong and aggressive competitors. The existence of many actual or potential substitute products may limit prices and profits. For example, supermarkets have entered the take-away-meals market that has had an impact on the fast-food restaurant market. The relative power of buyers also affects segment attractiveness. If the buyers in a segment possess strong bargaining power relative to sellers, they will force prices down, demand more quality services, and set competitors against one another. Large buyers, such as an airline with a hub in Dallas that needs 50 rooms a night for flight crews, will be able to negotiate a low price. Finally, a segment may not be attractive if it contains powerful suppliers who control prices or reduce the quality of ordered goods and services. Suppliers tend to be powerful when they are large and concentrated, when few substitutes exist, or when the supplied product is an important input. In certain areas, restaurants specializing in fresh seafood are limited to a few suppliers.

Landry's Inc. decided to sell Joe's Crab Shack, popular casual seafood restaurant chain, to concentrate on higher end restaurants. Courtesy of Philip Kotler.

Company Objectives and Resources

All companies must consider their own objectives and resources in relation to available segments. Some attractive segments can be dismissed quickly because they do not mesh with the company's long-run objectives. Although such segments might be tempting in themselves, they might divert a company's attention and energies away from its main goal. Or they might be a poor choice from an environmental, political, or social responsibility viewpoint. In Chapter 3 we mentioned that Landry's decided to sell Joe's Crab Shack restaurants because it wanted to focus on higher end restaurants.

If a segment fits the company's objectives, it must then decide whether it possesses the skills and resources to succeed in that segment. If the company lacks the strengths needed to compete successfully in a segment and cannot readily obtain them, it should not enter the segment. A company should enter segments only where it can gain sustainable advantages over competitors.

Selecting Market Segments

After evaluating different segments, the company must decide which and how many segments to serve. This is a problem of target-market selection. A target market consists of a set of buyers who share common needs or characteristics that the company decides to serve. Figure 8–2 shows that a firm can adopt one of three market-coverage strategies: undifferentiated marketing, differentiated marketing, and concentrated marketing.

Undifferentiated Marketing

Using an undifferentiated marketing strategy, a company ignores market segmentation differences and goes after the entire market with one market offer. It focuses on what is common in the needs of consumers rather than on differences. It designs a marketing plan that will reach the greatest number of buyers. Mass distribution and mass advertising serve as the basic tools to create a superior image in consumers' minds.

Undifferentiated marketing provides cost economies. The narrow product line keeps down production, inventory, and transportation costs. An undifferentiated advertising program holds down advertising costs. The neglect of segmentation holds down marketing research costs and product development costs.

Figure 8–2
Three alternative market-coverage strategies.

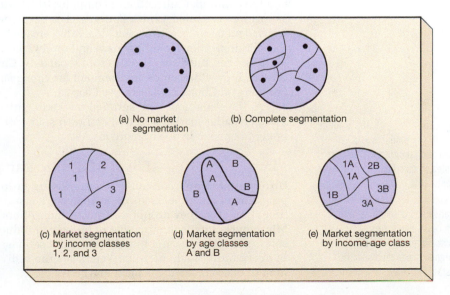

(a) No market segmentation

(b) Complete segmentation

(c) Market segmentation by income classes 1, 2, and 3

(d) Market segmentation by age classes A and B

(e) Market segmentation by income-age class

Public cafeterias sometimes believe they fit this model, but in fact, observation of their customer mix usually reveals a disproportionate number of middle-age and older customers.

Most contemporary marketers have strong doubts about the strategy in today's competitive environment. It is difficult to develop a product and brand that will satisfy all or even most consumers. When several competitors aim at the largest segments, the inevitable result is heavy competition. Small companies generally find it impossible to compete directly against giants and are forced to adopt market-niche strategies. Larger segments may become less profitable because of heavy marketing costs, including the possibility of price cutting and price wars.

Differentiated Marketing

Using a differentiated marketing strategy, a company targets several market segments and designs separate offers for each. Accor Hotels, a French company, has 18 brands of hotels. Included in its brands are international luxury hotels (Sofitel), three-star hotels (Novotel), two-star hotels (Ibis), limited-service hotels (Formula One), and extended-stay hotels featuring served apartments (The Sebel). This segmentation has allowed Accor to become one of the world's foremost hotel groups.

Differentiated marketing typically produces more total sales than undifferentiated marketing. Accor gets a higher hotel room market share with three different brands in one city than if it only had one brand in a city. Sofitel attracts the upscale business traveler. Novotel attracts the mid-scale traveler, whereas Formula One attracts families and the budget traveler. Accor offers a different marketing mix to each target market. At the same time, it has to have marketing plans, marketing research, forecasting, sales analysis, promotion planning, and advertising for each brand.

Concentrated Marketing

Concentrated marketing is especially appealing to companies with limited resources. Instead of going for a small share of a large market, the firm pursues a large share of one or a few small markets.

There are many examples of concentrated marketing. Four Seasons Hotels, Six Senses, and Rosewood Hotels concentrate on the high-priced hotel room market. Through concentrated marketing, hospitality companies achieve a strong market position in the segments that they serve, thanks to their greater knowledge of those segments' needs. The company also enjoys many operative economies. If the segment is well chosen, the company can earn a high rate of return on investment.

Chuck E. Cheese is a restaurant that targets families with young children. It is difficult to take young children to a table service restaurant, as they get bored easily. Many restaurants provide crayons and paper placemats with games to entertain the children. Chili's offers a computer tablet with games to keep adults as well as children occupied. Chuck E. Cheese has developed an entire restaurant concept focused on families with young kids. It has arcade type games and offers basic food that children enjoy including pizza and sandwiches. Some meals come with tokens for the games, the tokens are also sold separately. Children love coming to Chuck E. Cheese. It provides a nice environment for young families to spend time together.[28] For more on Chuck E. Cheese, see Case 21.

At the same time, concentrated marketing involves higher than normal risks. The particular market segment can turn sour. For this reason, many companies prefer to operate in two or more markets.

Micromarketing—Local Marketing and SoLoMo

Micromarketing. The practice of tailoring products and marketing programs to suit the tastes of specific individuals and locations.

Local marketing. Tailoring brands and promotions to the needs and wants of local customer groups—cities, neighborhoods, and specific restaurant/hotel/store locations.

Differentiated and concentrated marketers tailor their offers and marketing programs to meet the needs of various market segments and niches. At the same time, however, they do not customize their offers to each individual customer. **Micromarketing** is the practice of tailoring products and marketing programs to suit the tastes of specific individuals and locations. Rather than seeing a customer in every individual, micromarketers see the individual in every customer. One form of micromarketing is **local marketing**.

Local marketing involves tailoring brands and promotions to the needs and wants of local customer groups—cities, neighborhoods, and specific restaurant/hotel/store locations. For example, Omni Hotels and Resorts develop its restaurants to reflect the local culinary offering of the community where the hotel is located.

Advances in communications technology have given rise to new high-tech versions location-based marketing. Thanks to the explosion of net-connected smartphones with GPS capabilities and location-based social networks, companies can now track consumers' whereabouts closely and gear their offers accordingly. Using location-based social media check-in services such as Foursquare or and local-marketing deal-of-the-day services such as Groupon, retailers can engage consumers with local deals and information.

SoLoMo (social+local +mobile). Marketing that targets on-the-go consumers as they come and go in key local market areas.

Increasingly, location-based marketing is going mobile, reaching on-the-go consumers as they come and go in key local market areas. It's called **SoLoMo (social+local+mobile).**[29] For example, a local restaurant can decide to implement SoLoMo marketing, using platforms such as Foursquare, Yelp, and Facebook, to offer deals only to those located in your neighborhood or city. There are also new sites being developed for SoLoMo marketing, including Kapture, SidewalkAd, and LocalBox.[30] Professor Bill Carroll states, "The Mark Hotel in New York City uses Foursquare's list functionality as a virtual extension of its concierge services." Guests looking for local dining and sightseeing suggestions can follow The Mark on Foursquare. The hotel benefits by promoting its own food and beverage options in its recommendations.[31]

When using deals of local marketing, one has to be careful that the business generated by the promotion is profitable. The promotion should be priced so the restaurant makes money on the promotion after paying promotional costs. Also, do promotions only when you have excess capacity to handle the promotion. For example, if you are busy on Friday and Saturday night exclude these periods from the promotion.

Choosing a Market-Coverage Strategy

Companies need to consider several factors in choosing a market-coverage strategy. One factor is the company's resources. When the company's resources are limited, concentrated marketing makes the most sense. Another factor is the **degree of product homogeneity**. Undifferentiated marketing is more suited for homogeneous products. Products that can vary in design, such as restaurants and hotels, are more suited to differentiation or concentration. The product's life-cycle stage must also be considered. When a firm introduces a new product, it may be practical to launch only one version, so undifferentiated or concentrated marketing makes the most sense. For example, the early McDonald's had a very limited selection compared with their present menu selection. In the mature stage of the product life cycle, differentiated marketing becomes more feasible. Another factor is **market homogeneity**. If buyers have the same tastes, buy a product in the same amounts, and react the same way to marketing efforts, undifferentiated marketing is appropriate. Finally, **competitors' strategies** are important. When competitors use segmentation, undifferentiated marketing can be suicidal. Conversely, when competitors use undifferentiated marketing, a firm can gain an advantage by using differentiated or concentrated marketing.

Degree of product homogeneity. Undifferentiated marketing is more suited for homogeneous products. Products that can vary in design, such as restaurants and hotels, are more suited to differentiation or concentration.

Market homogeneity. If buyers have the same tastes, buy a product in the same amounts, and react the same way to marketing efforts, undifferentiated marketing is appropriate.

Competitors' strategies. When competitors use segmentation, undifferentiated marketing can be suicidal. Conversely, when competitors use undifferentiated marketing, a firm can gain an advantage by using differentiated or concentrated marketing.

Socially Responsible Target Marketing

Smart targeting helps companies become more efficient and effective by focusing on the segments that they can satisfy best and most profitably. Targeting also benefits consumers; companies serve specific groups of consumers with offers carefully tailored to their needs. However, target marketing sometimes generates controversy and concern. The biggest issues usually involve the targeting of vulnerable or disadvantaged consumers with controversial or potentially harmful products.

For example, fast-food chains have generated controversy over the years by their attempts to target inner-city minority consumers. They've been accused of pitching their high-fat, salt-laden fare to low-income, urban residents who are much more likely than suburbanites to be heavy consumers.

Children are seen as an especially vulnerable audience. Marketers have been criticized for their marketing efforts directed toward children. Critics worry that enticing premium offers and high-powered advertising appeals will overwhelm children's defenses. In recent years, for instance, McDonald's has been criticized by various health advocates and parent groups concerned that its popular Happy Meals offers—featuring trinkets and other items tied in with children's movies—create a too powerful connection between children and the often fat- and calorie-laden meals. McDonald's has responded by putting the Happy Meal on a diet, cutting the overall calorie count by 20 percent, adding fruit to every meal, and promoting Happy Meals only with milk, water, and juice.[32]

Today's marketers are also using sophisticated analytical techniques to track consumers' digital movements and to build detailed customer profiles containing highly personal information. Such profiles can then be used to hypertarget individual consumers with personalized brand messages and offers. Hypertargeting can benefit both marketers and consumers, getting the right brand information into the hands of the right customers. However, if taken too far or used wrongly, hypertargeting can harm consumers more than benefit them. Marketers must use these new targeting tools responsibly.

■■■ Market Positioning

Once a company has chosen its target-market segments, it must decide on a value proposition—how it will create differentiated value for targeted markets and what positions to occupy in those segments. A product's position is the way the product is defined by consumers on important attributes—the place the product occupies in consumers' minds relative to competing products. Consumers are overloaded with information about products and services. They cannot reevaluate products every time they make a buying decision. To simplify buying decisions, consumers organize products into categories—they "position" products and companies in their minds.

Marketers do not want to leave their products' positions to chance. They plan positions that will give their products the greatest advantage in selected target markets and then design marketing mixes to create the planned positions. In the fast-food hamburger business, Wendy's promotes never-frozen meat, hot off the grill; Burger King is known for its flame-broiled food; and Smashburger smashes its burger on the grill to sear it. Smashburger hopes the customer will perceive it to have a better quality burger, as it charges more than Wendy's or Burger King.

A hotel brand's position can be viewed from two perspectives—that of the brand's management and that of the guests. The brand's management must have a clear concept of the hotel's intended position. Its promotional efforts must articulate not only what the brand offers, but how its offerings are different from those of other brands. In the final analysis, a brand's position is determined by its customers.

Positioning Strategies

Specific product attributes.
Price and product features can be used to position a product.

Marketers can follow several positioning strategies. They can position their products based on **specific product attributes**. Product attribute positioning can be dangerous. The attribute has to create a benefit for the consumer. Subway has been successful in positioning its sandwiches as a healthy alternative to fried foods and hamburgers. It features eight sandwiches that have six grams of fat or less. Its "Fresh Fit for Kids" program is aimed at parents. The following message is found on its Web site: "You no longer have to sacrifice nutrition or flavor when you're short on time. Choose a Mini sub (Black Forest Ham, Turkey Breast or Roast Beef) and pair it with a delicious side, like fresh apple slices. Then select from 1 percent low fat white milk or 100% juice for a tasty, better-for-them meal that kids will love."[33] Subway has been effective in promoting nutrition, without sacrificing flavor, as nutrition is an important food attribute to many people. Not all companies are successful in selecting meaningful product attributes. The Stamford

Hotel in Singapore advertised that it is the world's tallest hotel (now the tallest in Southeast Asia). Most people are interested in service, location, and other attributes when choosing a hotel, but height is not a product attribute that is valued by many people. In fact hotel guests often prefer to stay on lower floors as they perceive they will have a better chance of survival in case of emergency. If one promotes a product attribute that is not usually associated as a benefit, the benefits must be communicated. The Marina Bay Sands Singapore has done a good job at promoting the benefit of height for its swimming pool and SkyBar with these messages: "Imagine swimming in the clouds, overlooking Singapore's skyline. At 200m in the sky, the 150m swimming pool is the world's largest infinity and outdoor pool at that height. Hotel guests can indulge in this ultimate experience now." "Savour the view from Singapore's most iconic bar. The SkyBar is perched above the Marina Bay Sands SkyPark observation deck, the perfect hangout from which to survey the world below. Take in the vista of the city spread out before you and the panoramic view of the Singapore Strait as you sip on cocktail creations by KU DÉ TA mixologists."[34] Notice how the messages from the Marina Bay Sands have an emotional appeal, whereas simply stating you are the tallest hotel is an unemotional fact. In the hospitality industry, appealing to emotions is important.

Finally, products can be positioned against another product class. Cruise ships positioned themselves against other vacation alternatives such as destination resorts, and bed and breakfast (B&Bs) are positioned as a home-like alternative to other forms of lodging. Airbnb provides a marketplace for individuals to rent their house, apartment, or room to a traveler. Airbnb positions itself as providing unique travel experiences through the diversity of its offerings. These offerings include a lighthouse in Croatia, castles, underground homes, and John Steinbeck's writers' studio. It also includes a room in a common home. Airbnb offers some very inexpensive places to stay in most cities; however, it does not want to position itself as an inexpensive place to stay. Instead Airbnb states, "Airbnb connects people to unique travel experiences."[35]

Choosing and Implementing a Positioning Strategy

Some firms find it easy to choose a differentiation and positioning strategy. For example, a firm well known for quality in certain segments will go after this position in a new segment if there are enough buyers seeking quality. But in many cases, two or more firms will go after the same position. Then each will have to find other ways to set itself apart. Each firm must differentiate its offer by building a unique bundle of benefits that appeals to a substantial group within the segment.

Above all else, a brand's positioning must serve the needs and preferences of well-defined target markets. For example, as discussed previously, although both Dunkin' Donuts and Starbucks are coffee and snack shops, they target very different customers, who want very different things from their favorite coffee seller. Starbucks targets more upscale professionals with more highbrow positioning. In contrast, Dunkin' Donuts targets the "average Joe" with a decidedly more lowbrow, "everyman" kind of positioning. Yet each brand succeeds because it creates just the right value proposition for its unique mix of customers.

The differentiation and positioning task consists of three steps: identifying a set of differentiating **competitive advantages** on which to build a position, choosing the right competitive advantages, and selecting an overall positioning strategy. The company must then effectively communicate and deliver the chosen position to the market.

Competitive advantage. An advantage over competitors gained by offering consumers greater value either through lower prices or by providing more benefits that justify higher prices.

Differentiating Competitive Advantages

A hospitality company or a visitor destination must differentiate its products/services from those of its competitors. Differentiation can occur by physical attributes, service, personnel, location, or image.

Physical Attribute Differentiation

Classic hotels such as the Waldorf-Astoria in New York, Palmer House in Chicago, Brown Palace in Denver, and Raffles in Singapore.

The Raffles Hotel is one of the most recognized buildings in San Antonio. Courtesy of Bildagentur Zoonar GmbH/Shutterstock.

The five-star Casa Santo Domingo Hotel in Antigua, Guatemala, was built into the ruins of a sixteenth-century monastery partially destroyed in an earthquake. The architects and interior designers masterfully blended new construction with the remains of the old monastery, including a crypt. The roofless remains of the sanctuary, surrounded by thousands of blazing candles, serves as a popular site for evening weddings.

Unfortunately, many hotels, restaurants, and airlines lack physical differentiation. Motels in particular follow a standard architectural look that provides no differentiation. When this happens, price becomes the primary differentiating factor.

Restaurants such as Chez Panisse in Berkeley, Lidia's in Kansas City, and the chain Chipotle Mexican Grill use natural/organic foods to differentiate themselves. These restaurants have developed a network of farmers to provide fresh products produced to each restaurant's standards.[36]

Differentiation that excites the consumer and offers something new can lead to excellent public relations opportunities, customer loyalty, and greater profits.

Service Differentiation

Hospitality companies differentiate themselves on service. For example, Hilton offers Hilton Huanying, as a point of service differentiation for the growing Chinese market in 110 of its hotels in markets heavily frequented by Chinese travelers. Huanying takes its name from the Chinese word for "welcome." Hilton conducted market research to determine preferences and needs of Chinese travelers. The service includes a welcome note in simplified Chinese upon arrival, at least one television channel in Mandarin, tea kettles in the room, and a Chinese breakfast.[37]

Unwanted differentiation occurs when a company consistently provides a horrible level of guest service. Such a reputation often requires a change in management or ownership to correct. It is strange that so many members of service industries ignore good customer service. The basics of good customer service are comparable to the Golden Rule: "Do unto others as you would have them do unto you."

Mature consumers place special value on friendly staff, guest name recognition by staff, assistance in making a product decision, opportunities to socialize, and no pressure to leave. These simple services can reap large rewards for members of the hospitality industry.[38] Because so many companies overlook the importance of good service, those who truly emphasize service will achieve positive differentiation.

Personnel Differentiation

Companies can gain a strong competitive advantage through hiring and retaining better people than their competitors. Thus, Singapore Airlines enjoys an excellent reputation largely because of the grade of its flight attendants. Southwest Airlines claimed that a competitor could replicate its low-cost system but would find it more difficult to create the spirit of Southwest's employees.

Personnel differentiation requires that a company select its customer-contact people carefully and train them well. These personnel must be competent and must possess the required skills and knowledge. They need to be courteous, friendly, and respectful. They must serve customers with consistency and accuracy, and they must make an effort to understand their customers, communicate clearly with them, and respond quickly to customer requests and problems. We will discuss how to create personnel differentiation in Chapter 10.

Location Differentiation

Location can provide a strong competitive advantage. For example, hotels facing Central Park in New York City have a competitive advantage over hotels a

These restaurants along the River Walk in San Antonio have a competitive advantage over restaurants located a block away. Courtesy of Brandon Seidel/Shutterstock.

block away. Motels located right off a freeway exit can enjoy double-digit advantages in percentage of occupancy over hotels a block away. Hotels along the River Walk in San Antonio, Texas, have a strong advantage over hotels located off the river. International airlines often use their location as a point of differentiation in their home markets. For example, Qantas promotes itself as Australia's airline and has a strong following in its home market. Hospitality and travel firms should look for benefits created by their location, keeping in mind that this advantage is subject to chance. Factors such as a new highway bypass or criminal activity in a neighborhood can quickly turn an advantage into a problem.

Taco John's 425 quick-service restaurants are located in 25 states. However, their strength has been what the company calls "the Heartland of America." The company started in Cheyenne, Wyoming, and then expanded to places like Scottsbluff, Nebraska, and Rapid City, South Dakota. Most of its locations are still in small to midsized midwestern towns where it has obviously been successful. It is questionable if this success could be duplicated in towns such as San Antonio, Texas, or Los Angeles. Hospitality companies are well advised to seriously consider what geographic factors may have created their success before expanding too widely. Perhaps the sauces or something else in the product are perfect for people in Nebraska or Minnesota but might not be acceptable in other geographic regions.[39]

Image Differentiation

Even when competing offers look the same, buyers may perceive a difference based on company or brand image. Thus, hospitality companies need to work to establish images that differentiate them from competitors. A company or visitor destination image should convey a singular or distinctive message that communicates the product's major benefits and positioning. In the case of visitor destinations such as tropical locations, it is often impossible to distinguish the advertising of one from another. Most seem to employ beaches, clear water, and other features that do not provide any differentiation from other beach resorts. Developing a strong and distinctive image calls for creativity and hard work. A positive image must be earned. Chili's developed an image as a casual and fun neighborhood restaurant. This image must be supported by everything that the company says and does.

A common mistake made by new owners/operators of a property is to implement a new image/positioning strategy before fully understanding the property, the community, and the market. New owners of the Telluride Ski and Golf Resort announced they would not make this mistake. Instead of announcing grand changes, the new owners said, "Our intentions are to honor unique characteristics that define Telluride. We want to preserve Telluride's authenticity, charm, and casual atmosphere." They further said that they would seek input from the community to develop a shared vision of what the resort should look like.[40]

One of the leading hotel and leisure companies in the world, Starwood Hotels & Resorts Worldwide, has 1,200 properties in more than 95 countries and 180,000 employees at its owned and managed properties. Starwood has differentiated its hotels, creating an image along emotional, experiential lines. Consumer research suggested these positions for some of the brands:

Sheraton. With the tagline "You don't stay here, you belong," Sheraton—the largest brand—is about warm, comforting, and casual. Its core value centers on "connections," an image aided by the hotel's alliance with Yahoo!, which cofounded the Yahoo! Link@Sheraton lobby kiosks and cyber cafes.

Four Points by Sheraton. For the self-sufficient traveler, Four Points strives to be honest, uncomplicated, and comfortable. The brand is all about providing a high level of comfort and little indulgences like free high-speed Internet access and bottled water. Its ads feature apple pies and talk about providing guests with "the comforts of home."

W. With a brand personality defined as flirty, for the insider, and an escape, W offers guests unique experiences around the warmth of cool.

Westin. Westin's emphasis on "personal, instinctive, and renewal" has led to a new sensory welcome featuring a white tea scent, signature music and lighting, and refreshing towels. Each room features Westin's own "Heavenly Beds," sold exclusively in the retail market through Nordstrom, further enhancing the brand's upscale image.[41]

Choosing the Right Competitive Advantages

Suppose that a company is fortunate enough to discover several potential competitive advantages. It must now choose the ones on which it will build its positioning strategy.

How Many Differences?

Many marketers think that companies should aggressively promote only one benefit to the target market. Adman Rosser Reeves, for example, said a company should develop a unique selling proposition (USP) for each brand and stick to it. Each brand should pick an attribute and tout itself as number one on that attribute. Buyers tend to remember number one better, especially in an overcommunicated society. Thus, Motel 6 consistently promotes itself as the lowest-priced national chain, and Ritz-Carlton promotes itself as a value leader. What are some number-one positions to promote? The major ones are best quality, best service, lowest price, best value, and best location. A company that hammers away at a position that is important to its target market and consistently delivers on it probably will become the best known and remembered.

Other marketers think that companies should position themselves on more than one differentiating factor. A restaurant may claim that it has the best steaks and service. A hotel may claim that it offers the best value and location. Today, in a time when the mass market is fragmenting into many small market segments, companies are trying to broaden their positioning strategies to appeal to more segments. For example, the Boulders in Arizona promotes itself as a top golf resort and as a luxury resort, giving guests a chance to experience the flora and fauna of the Sonoran Desert. By doing this, the Boulders can attract both golfers and nongolfers.

However, as companies increase the number of claims for their brands, they risk disbelief and a loss of clear positioning. In general, a company needs to avoid three major positioning errors. The first is **underpositioning**, or failing ever to position the company at all. Some companies discover that buyers have only a vague idea of the company or that they do not really know anything special about it. Many independent hotels trying to capture an international market are underpositioned. The Seoul Plaza Hotel, a luxury hotel in Seoul, Korea, is not well known in Europe or North America. To establish positions in distant markets, hotels like the Seoul Plaza are affiliating with marketing groups such as "Leading Hotels of the World" and "Preferred Hotels." The second positioning error is **overpositioning**, or giving buyers too narrow a picture of the company. Finally, companies must avoid **confused positioning**, leaving buyers with a confused image of a company. Good positioning helps build brand loyalty. In the case of hotels, it may not be enough to simply satisfy guests. Satisfied customers do not repurchase unless they are also attitudinally brand loyal.[42]

Underpositioning. Failing ever to position the company at all.

Overpositioning. Giving buyers a too-narrow picture of the company.

Confused positioning. Leaving buyers with a confused image of a company.

Which Differences?

Not all brand differences are meaningful or worthwhile. Not every difference makes a good differentiator. Each difference has the potential to create company costs as well as customer benefits. Therefore, a hospitality company or a visitor

Casino resorts, such as the Marina Bay Sands in Singapore, need to gain the trust of their customers and establish an emotional bond with them. Courtesy of Marina Ignatova/Fotolia.

destination must carefully select the ways in which it will distinguish itself from competitors. A difference is worth establishing to the extent that it satisfies the following criteria:

- *Important.* The difference delivers a highly valued benefit to target buyers. In the case of a visitor destination, personal safety has become a top benefit.

- *Distinctive.* Competitors do not offer the difference, or the company can offer it in a more distinctive way.

- *Superior.* The difference is superior to other ways that customers might obtain the same benefit.

- *Communicable.* The difference is communicable and visible to buyers.

- *Preemptive.* Competitors cannot easily copy the difference.

- *Affordable.* Buyers can afford to pay for the difference.

- *Profitable.* The company can introduce the difference profitability.

Some competitive advantages may quickly be ruled out because they are too slight, too costly to develop, or too inconsistent with the company's profile. Suppose that a company is designing its positioning strategy and has narrowed its list of possible competitive advantages to four. The company needs a framework for selecting the one that makes the most sense to develop.

Customers of casinos exhibit two critical reasons for maintaining a long-term relationship and recommending a particular casino to others. These are trust and emotional ties.[43] A positioning statement that emphasizes game payout will not succeed if customers don't believe this statement. Likewise, a positioning statement that emphasizes the latest technology may not succeed if customers feel the casino is cold and mechanical rather than a place to which they can relate.

Selecting an Overall Positioning Strategy

Value proposition. The full mix of benefits on which a brand is differentiated and positioned.

The full positioning of a brand is called the brand's **value proposition**, the full mix of benefits on which a brand is differentiated and positioned. It is the answer to the customer question, "Why should I buy your brand." Value Place is a low-priced hotel with a full kitchen and a low weekly rate. Sometimes low-priced hotels attract persons who do not have the credit or money to rent an apartment, drug dealers, and prostitutes. This can create an unsafe atmosphere. Value Place stresses safety as a point of differentiation in their value proposition. They stress the affordability, cleanliness and safety of their properties. Fairmont, an upscale hotel chain, values providing exceptional service experiences that will create favorable memories for its guests. Firehouse subs uses "Piping hot and piled high for maximum deliciousness." Red Lobster uses "Sea Food Differently." Through these value propositions these companies strive to influence the perception prospective customers have of their brand.

Communicating and Delivering the Chosen Position

Having chosen positioning characteristics and a positioning statement, companies must communicate their positions to targeted customers. All of a company's marketing mix efforts must support its positioning strategy. If a company decides to build service superiority, for example, it must hire service-oriented employees, provide training programs, reward employees for providing good service, and develop sales and advertising messages to broadcast its service superiority.

Building and maintaining a consistent positioning strategy is not easy; many counterforces are at work. Advertising agencies hired by the company may not like a selected position and may overtly or covertly work against it. New management may not understand the positioning strategy. Budgets may be cut for critical support programs such as employee training or sales promotion. The development of an effective position requires a consistent, long-run program with continuous support by management, employees, and vendors.

Olive Garden opened a restaurant in Tuscany, Olive Garden Riserva di Fizzano, and developed the Culinary Institute of Tuscany. It added Tuscan dishes to its menu, sent its chefs to the Culinary Institute of Tuscany, and developed a Tuscan farmhouse design for its restaurants. It also included recipes and cooking tips on its Web site. The restaurant and Culinary Institute in Italy help communicate Olive Garden's position as an authentic Italian restaurant. Its advertisements enforced this by featuring Italian families dining at Olive Garden.[44]

A company's positioning decisions determine who its competitors will be. When selecting a positioning strategy, a company should review its competitive strengths and weaknesses and select a position that places it in a superior position against its competitors.

Positioning is enhanced and supported by creating memorable customer experiences. Hospitality companies provide many services throughout the day. Most of these become routine and are indistinguishable from competitors. The key to creating memorable and differentiating customer experiences is not simply to improve them but to layer an enjoyable/memorable experience on top.[45]

Positioning Measurement: Perceptual Mapping

In planning their differentiation and positioning strategies, marketers often prepare perceptual positioning maps that show consumer perceptions of their brand versus those of competing products on important dimensions. Figure 8–3 is a perceptual positioning map of hotels plotted on the attributes of price and perceived service.

Figure 8–3
Positioning map of service level versus price.
Source: Lovelock, Christopher H; Wirtz, Jochen, Services Marketing: People, Technology, Strategy, 7th Ed., ©2011, p. 74. Reprinted and Electronically reproduced by permission of Pearson Education, Inc., New York, NY.

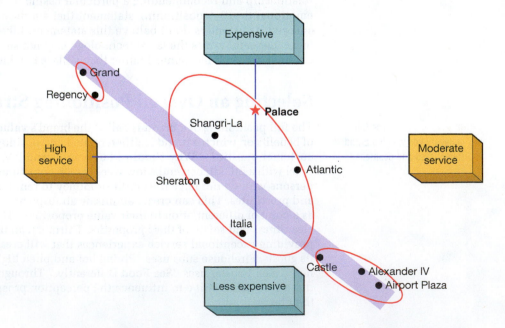

On this map we see there is a correlation between service and price; as price goes up, so does service.

Some hotels appear to offer a better value than others. For example, Italia offers a little higher level of service than the Palace but is less expensive. Two-by-two perceptual maps provide an easy-to-read picture, but one often has to study multiple maps plotting different attributes to obtain a good feel of the marketplace. Perceptual maps can also be developed using consumers' perceptions of a number of product attributes. Increased competition or an ineffective positioning strategy can make repositioning necessary. Perceptual maps provide data supporting the need for repositioning.

■■■ CHAPTER REVIEW

I. Market. A market is the set of all actual and potential buyers of a product.

II. Three Steps of the Target Marketing Process
  A. Market segmentation is the process of dividing a market into distinct groups of buyers who might require separate products and/or marketing mixes.
  B. Market targeting is the process of evaluating each segment's attractiveness and selecting one or more of the market segments.
  C. Positioning is the process of developing competitive positioning for the product and an appropriate marketing mix.

III. Market Segmentation
  A. Bases for segmenting a market. There is no single way to segment a market. A marketer has to try different segmentation variables, alone and in combination, hoping to find the best way to view the market structure.
    1. Geographic segmentation calls for dividing the market into different geographic units, such as nations, states, regions, counties, cities, or neighborhoods.
    2. Demographic segmentation consists of dividing the market into groups based on demographic variables such as age, gender, family life cycle, income, occupation, education, religion, race, and nationality.
    3. Psychographic segmentation divides buyers into different groups based on social class, lifestyle, and personality characteristics.
    4. Behavior segmentation divides buyers into groups based on their knowledge, attitude, use, or response to a product.
  B. Requirements for effective segmentation
    1. Measurability. The degree to which the segment's size and purchasing power can be measured.
    2. Accessibility. The degree to which segments can be accessed and served.
    3. Substantiality. The degree to which segments are large or profitable enough to serve as markets.
    4. Actionability. The degree to which effective programs can be designed for attracting and serving segments.

IV. Evaluating Market Segments
  A. Segment size and growth. Companies analyze the segment size and growth and choose the segment that provides the best opportunity.
  B. Segment structural attractiveness. A company must examine major structural factors that affect long-run segment attractiveness.
  C. Company objectives and resources. The company must consider its own objectives and resources in relation to a market segment.

V. Selecting Market Segments. Segmentation reveals market opportunities available to a firm. The company then selects the most attractive segment or segments to serve as targets for marketing strategies to achieve desired objectives.
  A. Market-coverage alternatives
    1. Undifferentiated marketing strategy. An undifferentiated marketing strategy ignores market segmentation differences and goes after the whole market with one market offer.
    2. Differentiated marketing strategy. The firm targets several market segments and designs separate offers for each.
    3. Concentrated marketing strategy. Concentrated marketing strategy is especially appealing to companies with limited resources. Instead of going for a small share of a large market, the firm pursues a large share of one or more small markets.
    4. Micromarketing—local marketing and SoLoMo. Micromarketing is the practice of tailoring products and marketing programs to fit the tastes of specific individuals and locations. Local marketing and SoLoMo (social, local, mobile) marketing are forms of micromarketing.
    5. Choosing a market-coverage strategy. Companies need to consider several factors in choosing a market-coverage strategy.
      a. Company resources. When the company's resources are limited, concentrated marketing makes the most sense.
      b. Degree of product homogeneity. Undifferentiated marketing is more suited for homogeneous products. Products that can

vary in design, such as restaurants and hotels, are more suited to differentiation or concentration.

    c. **Market homogeneity.** If buyers have the same tastes, buy a product in the same amounts, and react the same way to marketing efforts, undifferentiated marketing is appropriate.

  6. **Socially responsible target marketing.** As marketers gain more information on customers, they must use this information responsibly.

VI. **Market Positioning.** A product's position is the way the product is defined by consumers on important attributes—the place the product occupies in consumers' minds relative to competing products.

  A. **Positioning strategies**
    1. **Specific product attributes.** Price and product features can be used to position a product.
    2. **Needs products fill or benefits products offer.** Marketers can position products by the needs that they fill or the benefits that they offer. For example, a restaurant can be positioned as a fun place.

  B. **Choosing and implementing a positioning strategy.** The positioning task consists of three steps: identifying a set of possible competitive advantages on which to build a position, selecting the right competitive advantages, and effectively communicating and delivering the chosen position to a carefully selected target market.

  C. **Product differentiation**
    1. Physical Attributes
    2. Service
    3. Personnel
    4. Location
    5. Image

  D. **Choosing the right competitive advantage**
    1. How many differences?
    2. Which differences?

  E. **Selecting an overall positioning strategy.** The full positioning of a brand is called the brand's value proposition.

  F. **Communicating and delivering the chosen position.** Once having chosen positioning characteristics and a positioning statement, a company must communicate its position to targeted customers. All of a company's marketing mix efforts must support its positioning strategy.

  G. **Perceptual mapping.** A map of consumer perceptions of competing brands.

■■■ DISCUSSION QUESTIONS

1. Explain the process of market segmentation, market targeting, and market positioning.

2. Choose a hospitality business, for example, a hotel or restaurant. Explain some of the segments in its overall market (in this case, the hotel market or restaurant market), one of these markets that it targeted, and how it differentiated itself from its competitors to position itself in the market.

3. Identify a restaurant or hotel market segment in your community that you feel would be a good market segment to target. Explain the marketing mix you would put together to go after this market segment.

4. Some restaurateurs want to develop a restaurant with something for everyone. Why is this idea a dangerous policy?

5. What roles do product attributes and perceptions of attributes play in the positioning of a product? Can an attribute common to several competing brands contribute to a successful positioning strategy?

6. Provide an example (other than one given in this chapter) of the use of SoLoMo marketing by a hospitality company.

■■■ EXPERIENTIAL EXERCISE

Find an advertisement from a hospitality or travel company that targets a specific segment, such as children, young adults, seniors, or upper-income customers. Then visit a location of that company. What does the company do at the location with its marketing mix to attract the segment that it targeted in the advertisement? This can include sales promotions, signage, product mix, location of the company, and pricing of products.

■■■ INTERNET EXERCISE

Go to the Web site of a major brand of hospitality or travel company. Explain how it appeals to different segments through the Web site. Give specific examples.

■■■ REFERENCES

1   Leslie Patton, "Dunkin' Donuts Adds Jazz to Get Less Pij and More Stop,"·*Bloomberg Businessweek*, June 7, 2013, www.bloomberg.com/news/2013-06-07/dunkin·donuts·adds·jazz·to·get·less·ptt·and·more·stop.html; Leslie Patton, "Starbucks Turns to Happy Hour to Bring in More Traffic," *Bloomberg Businessweek*, February 1, 2012, www.businessweek.corn/news/2012-0201/starbucks-turns-tohappy-hour-tobringin-more-traffic·retail.html; Janet Adamy, "Battle Brewing: Dunkin' Donuts Tries to Go Upscale, But Not Too Far," *Wall Street Journal* (April 8, 2006): A1; 'Brand Keys Ranks Dunkin' Donuts Number One in Coffee Customer Loyalty and Packaged Coffee Customer Loyalty: February 19, 2013, http://news.dunkindonuts.com; www.dunkindonuts.com (accessed September 2014).

2   "Forecast of Retail Sales in the Foodservice Industry in the United States in 2014, by Venue Segment," statista, http://www.statista.com/statistics/288612/retail-sales-us-foodservice-industry-by-venue-category/ (accessed July 22, 2015).

3   Elisabeth A. Sullivan, "Customer Spotting," *Marketing News* (March 15, 2008): 10.

4   https://order.dominos.com/en/pages/content/content.jsp?page=apps&so=hpnf&panelnumber=3&panel-name=apps (accessed September 2014).

5   See Joan Voight, "Marriott Chain Adds Some Local Flavor," *Adweek* (January 7, 2013): 9; "Renaissance Hotels Launches New Navigator Program to Help Guests Discover 'Hidden Gems' of Various Cities around the World," January 8, 2013, www.adweek.com/prit/146321; http://renaissance-hotels.marriott.com/r-navigator (accessed September 2014).

6   Viking Cruises Web site, http://www.vikingcruises.com/terms-conditions/index.html (accessed July 28, 2015).

7   Paula Froelich, "Advertising's Untapped Market: Single Women," *Newsweek*, February 26, 2014, http://www.newsweek.com/2014/02/28/advertisings-untapped-market-single-women-245588.html (accessed July 25, 2015); Jamie Dunham, "Marketing Travel to Women: Eight New Trends You Need to Know," *The Lipstick Economy*, July 16, 2013, https://jamiedunham.wordpress.com/2013/07/16/marketing-travel-to-women-eight-new-trends-you-need-to-know/ (accessed July 25, 2015).

8   "Young Family Travelers," http://www.youngfamily-travelers.com/europe/novotel/novotel.htm (accessed October 31, 2004); "Family Adventure Traveler," http://www.colorado.com/family/default.asp; "Family Friendly" (accessed October 31, 2004); *Restaurant Hospitality* (June 1998): 48; Katie Smith, "Kiddin' Around," *Restaurant Hospitality* (April 2001): 52–64.

9   Peter Coy, "Why Price Is Rarely Right," *Bloomberg Business Week* (February 1 and 8, 2010): 77–78.

10 Richard Baker, "Retail Trends—Luxury Marketing: The End of a Mega-Trend," *Retail* (June/July 2009): 8–12, http://www.seadream.com/voyages/ (accessed July 24, 2015).

11 Les Christie, CNNMoney.com, June 23, 2006.

12 Chris Reynolds, "Me, Myself and I," *American Demographics* (November 2003): 1; Gary M. Stern, "Solo Diners," *Restaurants USA*, 10, no. 3 (1990): 15–16; www.unmarriedamerica.org (accessed August 23, 2008).

13 See Kunur Patel, "Zipcar: An America's Hottest Brands Case Study," *Advertising Age* (November 16, 2009): 16; Paul Keegan, "Zipcar: The Best New Idea in Business," *Fortune* (August 27, 2009), www.fortune.com; Elizabeth Olson, "Car Sharing Reinvents the Company Wheels," *New York Times* (May 7, 2009): F2; Stephanie Clifford, "How Fast Can This Thing Go, Anyway?" *Inc* (March 2008), www.inc.com; www.zipcar.com (accessed October 2010).

14 Information from www.rssc.com, http://nationof-whynot.com (accessed November 2010).

15 Janet Hanner, "W London-A Hotel That Dares to Be Different," *Caterer & Hotelkeeper*, (March 4–10, 2011): 26–28; Nancy Keates, "The Home Front: His Hotel, His Hangout," *Wall Street Journal* (June 3, 2011): D6; Christina Binkley, "Putting the Hot Back in Hotel," *Wall Street Journal* (August 18, 2011), http://online.wsj.com/article/SB10001424053111903596904576514293384502896.html; "W Hotels Unveils Innovative Design Concept of the Soon-to-Open W Paris-Opera by Acclaimed Rockwell Group Europe," Starwood Press Release, December 14, 20 II, http://development.Starwoodhotels.coml news/7/336-w_hotels_unveils_innovative_design_concept_of_the_soon-to-open_w_paris-opera_by_acclaimed_rockwell_group_europe; information and press releases from www.starwoodhotels.com/whotels/about/index.html (accessed September 2013).

16 www.smarttravel, www.rssc.com, www.royalcaribbean.com (accessed November 2007).

17 Soo K. Kang, Cathy H. C. Hsu, and Kara Wolfe, "Family Traveler Segmentation by Vacation Decision-Making Patterns," *Journal of Hospitality and Tourism Research*, 27, no. 4 (2003): 464–465.

18 Soo K. Kang, Cathy H. C. Hsu, and Kara Wolfe, "Family Traveler Segmentation by Vacation Decision-Making Patterns," *Journal of Hospitality and Tourism Research*, 27, no. 4 (2003): 464–465.

19 Robert C. Lewis, "Restaurant Advertising: Appeals and Consumers' Intensions," *Journal of Advertising Research*, 21, no. 5 (1981): 69–75.

20 From Starwood Hotel and Resorts, www.starwood.com/promotion/promo_landing.html?category=pets (accessed October 24, 2004); Elaine Sciolino, "Versailles Hotel Treats Dog Royally," *Denver Post* (December 4, 2003): 31A.

21 Victor J. Cook, Jr., William Mindak, and Arch Woodside, "Profiling the Heavy Traveler Segment," *Journal of Travel Research*, 25, no. 4 (1987).

22 Jiang Weizhong, Chekitan S. Dev, and Vithala R. Rao, "Brand Extension and Customer Loyalty," *Cornell Hotel and Restaurant Administration Quarterly*, 43, no. 4 (2002): 15.

23 A. Weissenberg, A. Katz, and A. Narula, "A Restoration in Hotel Loyalty – Developing a Blueprint for Reinventing Loyalty Programs," 2013, www.deloitte.com/view/en_US/us/Industries/travel-hospitality-leisure/72ce4f52478ab310VgnVCM1000003256f70aRCRD.htm (accessed July 23, 2014).

24 P. Mayock, "Personalization Equals Loyalty for Millennials," *Hotel News Now*, 2014, www.hotelnewsnow.com/article/13067/Personalization-equals-loyalty-for-millennials (accessed October 10, 2014).

25 John T Bowen and Shiang-Lih Chen McCain, "Transitioning Loyalty Programs," *International Journal of Contemporary Hospitality Management*, 27, no. 3 (2015): 415–430.

26 For this and other information on Experian's Mosaic USA system, see www.experian.com/marketing-services/consumer-segmentation.html and http://classic.demographicsnow.com/Templates/static/mosaicPDF/K40%20Bohemian%20Groove.PDF (accessed September 2014).

27 Type H 27: Birkenstocks and Beemers http://library.demographicsnow.com/custom/img/mosaicPDF/H27%20Birkenstocks%20and%20Beemers.pdf (accessed July 27, 2015).

28 Eric Jackson, "Forget Kids, Investors Can Go for Chuck E. Cheese," *Breakout Performance*, Thursday, March 4, 2010, http://breakoutperformance.blogspot.com/2010/03/forget-kids-investors-can-go-for-chuck.html (accessed November 22, 2011).

29 Based on information found in Samantha Murphy, "SoLoMo Revolution Picks Up Where Hyperlocal Search Left Off," *Mashable*, January 12, 2012, http://mashable.com/2012/01/12/solomo-hyperlocal-search/; "Localeze/15miles Fifth Annual comScore Local Search Usage Study Reveals SoLoMo Revolution Has Taken Over: Business Wire," February 29, 2012; Joe Ruiz, "What Is So-Mole and Why Is It Important to Marketers?" *Business2Community*, February 1, 2013, www.business2community.com/marketing/what-is-somolo-and-why-is-it-important-to-marketers-039528; www.shopkick.com (accessed April 2014). For examples of successful retailer and brand SoLoMo efforts; see Jennifer Unger-felt, "What Airlines and Hotels Can Learn from Starbucks, Coca-Cola and Sephora's Approach to SoLoMo," *Joyalty360*, May 18, 2013; http://loyalty360.org/loyalty-today/article/what-airlines-and-hotels-can-learn-from-starbucks-coca-cola-and-sephoras-ap.

30 Ashtyn Douglas, "Go SoLoMo: Connecting with Your Local Customers," business.com, January 6, 2014, http://www.business.com/online-marketing/solomo-important-marketing-technique-local-businesses/ (accessed July 27, 2015).

31 Bill Carroll, "SoLoMo: Still Going Strong," *eCornell Blog*, April 9, 2013 (accessed July 27, 2015).

32 See "McDonald's Introduces New Automatic Offerings of Fruit in Every Happy Meal," *PRNewswire*, January 20, 2012; "Judge Dismisses Happy Meal Lawsuit," *Advertising Age*, April 4, 2012, http://adage.corn/print/233946; Allison Aubrey, "McDonald's Says Bye-Bye to Sugary Sodas in Happy Meals," *NPR*, September 26, 2013, www.npr.org/blogs/the-salt/2013/09/26/226564560/mcdonalds-says-bye-bye-to-sugary-sodas-in-happy-meals.

33 http://www.subway.com/Menu/Product.aspx?CC=USA&LC=ENG&MenuTypeId=1&MenuId=41 (accessed September 1, 2011).

34 http://www.marinabaysands.com/ (accessed September 11, 2011).

35 Airbnb, https://www.airbnb.com/about/about-us (accessed July 27, 2015).

36 Dean Houghton, "Close to the Consumer," *The Furrow* (September/October 2003): 12, John Deer Agricultural Marketing Center, 1145 Thompson Avenue, Lenexa, KS 66219–2302.

37 Hilton offers global program for Chinese travelers, Fact Sheet, Hilton Worldwide, undated, http://hiltonglobal-mediacenter.com/assets/HILT/docs/factsheets/HuanyingFactSheetEnglish.pdf (accessed July 27, 2015).

38 George Moschis, Carolyn Folkman Curasi, and Danny Bellinger, "Restaurant Selection Preferences of Mature Consumers," *Cornell Hotel and Restaurant Administration Quarterly*, 44, no. 4 (2003): 59–60.

39 "Taco Johns—the Fresh Taste of West-Mex," www.TacoJohn.com.

40 Chris Walsh, "New Partners to Preserve Old Charm of Telluride Ski," *Rocky Mountain News* (February 19, 2004): 7B.

41 Christopher Hosford, "A Transformative Experience," *Sales & Marketing Management*, 158 (June 2006): 32–36; Mike Beirne and Javier Benito, "Starwood Uses Personnel to Personalize Marketing," *Brandweek* (April 24, 2006): 9.

42 Back Ki-Joon and Sara C. Parks, "A Brand Loyalty Model Involving Cognitive, Affective and Cognitive Brand Loyalty and Customer Satisfaction," *Journal of Hospitality and Tourism Research*, 27, no. 4 (2003): 431.

43 Sui Jun Jian and Seyhmus Baloglu, "The Role of Emotional Commitment in Relationship Marketing: An Empirical Investigation of a Loyalty Model for Casinos," *Journal of Hospitality and Tourism Research*, 27, no. 4 (2003): 483.

44 Nancy Brumback, "Room at the Table," *Restaurant Business* (March 15, 2001): 71–82.

45 James H. Gilmore and B. Joseph Pine, II, "Differentiating Hospitality Operations vis Experiences," *Cornell Hotel and Restaurant Administration Quarterly*, 43, no. 3 (2002): 88.

Developing the Hospitality and Tourism Marketing Value-Driven Strategy and Mix

III

9

Designing and Managing Products and Brands: Building Customer Value

When you hear someone mention Las Vegas, what comes to mind? Sin City? Wholesome entertainment for the entire family? An indulgent luxury vacation? Or perhaps a value-oriented reward for hard-working Americans? If you answered "all of the above," you wouldn't necessarily be wrong. The truth: All of these have been characteristics associated with Las Vegas over the years. In recent times, the Las Vegas Convention and Visitors Authority (LVCVA) fielded several national ad campaigns. Tourism is Vegas's biggest industry, and the LVCVA is charged with maintaining the city's brand image and keeping visitors coming to one of the world's most famous cities.

Although the positioning of the Vegas brand has changed from time to time, the town will probably never entirely lose the "Sin City" label. That title was born when Las Vegas was young—an anything-goes gambling town full of smoke-filled casinos, bawdy all-girl revues, all-you-can-eat buffets, Elvis impersonators, and no-wait weddings on the Vegas Strip.

But as the 1990s rolled around, many Las Vegas officials felt that the town needed to broaden its target audience. So they set out to appeal to—of all things—families. Some of the biggest casinos on the Las Vegas Strip built roller coasters and other thrill rides, world-class water parks, and family-friendly shows like Treasure Island's live-action swashbuckler spectacle, visible to everyone passing by on the street. Although this strategy seemed effective for a brief time, marketers came to realize that the family image just didn't sync well with casino gambling—the high-profit product that built Las Vegas.

Objectives

After reading this chapter, you should be able to:

1. Define the term *product*, including the core, facilitating, supporting, and augmented product.

2. Explain how accessibility, atmosphere, customer interaction with the service delivery system, customer interaction with other customers, and customer coproduction are all critical elements to keep in mind when designing a product.

3. Understand branding and the conditions that support branding.

4. Discuss branding strategies and decisions companies make in building and managing their brands.

5. Explain the new-product development process.

6. Understand how the product life cycle can be applied to the hospitality industry.

As the LVCVA started to consider its options, the terrorist attacks of September 11, 2001, gave Las Vegas tourism one of its worst blows ever. Declining tourism led to 15,000 lost jobs. The LVCVA decided that it was time to unabashedly proclaim that Las Vegas was a destination for adults. That didn't just mean a return to the classic vices. The LVCVA engineered an image of Vegas as a luxury destination oozing with excess and indulgence. The theme parks were replaced by five-star resorts, high-rise condos, expansive shopping malls filled with the world's top luxury brands, and restaurants bearing the names of world-renowned chefs. A new breed of expensive stage shows for adult audiences replaced family-friendly entertainment. This change of strategy worked. Even as Las Vegas struggled through economic recovery in the post-9/11 world, visitors returned in record numbers.

However, to Rossi Ralenkotter, CEO of the LVCVA, it soon became apparent that the town was much more than just an assortment of facilities and amenities. "We talked to old customers and new customers to determine the essence of the brand of Las Vegas," he said.[1] The LVCVA found that to the nearly 40 million who flocked to the city each year, Vegas is an emotional connection—a total brand experience.

And just what is the "Las Vegas experience"? Research showed that when people come to Las Vegas, they're a little naughtier—a little less inhibited. They stay out longer, eat more, do some gambling, and spend more on shopping and dining. "We found that [the Las Vegas experience] centered on adult freedom," says Ralenkotter. "People could stay up all night and do things they wouldn't normally do in their own towns."[2]

Based on these customer insights, the LVCVA coined the now-familiar catchphrase—"Only Vegas: What happens here, stays here." The phrase captured the essence of the Las Vegas experience—that it's okay to be a little naughty in Vegas. That simple phrase became the centerpiece of what is now deemed one of the most successful tourism campaigns in history. The campaign transformed Las Vegas's image from the down-and-dirty "Sin City" to the enticing and luxurious "Only Vegas."

The $75 million ad campaign showed the naughty nature of people once they arrive in Las Vegas. In one ad, a woman spontaneously married a visibly younger man in a Las Vegas wedding chapel. Then, ignoring his ardent pleas, she kissed him goodbye and pulled herself away, insisting that she had to get back to her business convention. In another ad, an outgoing young woman is shown introducing herself to various men, each time giving a different name. In a third ad, a sexy woman hops into a limo, flirts with the driver, and emerges from the car at the airport for her trip home as a conservative business woman. At the end of each ad was the simple reminder, "What happens here, stays here."

The LVCVA continued investing heavily in the bold and provocative campaign and in a variation on the theme, "Your Vegas is showing." All the while, Las Vegas experienced its biggest growth boom in history. Hotel occupancy rates hovered at an incredible 90 percent, visitors came in ever-increasing numbers, and there was seemingly no end to the construction of lavish new luxury properties. To top it off, Las Vegas was dubbed the number two hottest brand by respected brand consultancy Landor Associates, right behind Google. It seemed that the LVCVA had found the magic formula and that Vegas had found its true identity. With everything going so well, what could possibly go wrong?

Then in 2008, Las Vegas suffered two more punches. First, the worst recession since the Great Depression had consumers scaling back on unnecessary expenses. Second, in the wake of government bailouts and a collapsing financial industry, company CEOs and executives everywhere came under scrutiny for lavish expenses. Suddenly, Las Vegas's carefully nurtured, naughty, indulgent image made even prudent, serious company conferences held there look bad. It didn't help matters when President Obama delivered a statement that Las Vegas's mayor, Oscar Goodman, perceived as the straw that broke the camel's back. Obama scolded Wall Street executives by saying, "You can't get corporate jets; you can't go take a trip to Las Vegas or go down to the Super Bowl on the taxpayer's dime." As a result of the new economic realities, both leisure travel and the convention industry—two staples in Las Vegas's success—took a big hit.

As a result, 2008 and 2009 were some of the worst years ever for Las Vegas. In 2009, the total number of visitors dropped to 36.4 million, 7 percent less than the 2007 peak of 39.1 million. This translated into a 24 percent decrease in convention attendance, a 22 percent drop in room occupancy, and a 10 percent decline in gambling revenues. "People aren't coming in the numbers they used to, and those that are bet on the cheaper tables," said Steven Kent, an analyst for Goldman Sachs. Nevada's unemployment rate climbed to one of the highest in the United States. The Las Vegas hospitality industry responded by chopping prices. Rooms on the Las Vegas Strip could be had as cheaply as $25 a night. Gourmet meals were touted for half price. The town was practically begging for visitors.

After years of successfully pedaling Vegas naughtiness as the primary selling point, the LVCVA realized it had to make a shift. So in the mid of the economic carnage, with so much to offer and great deals to be had, it focused on the value and affordability of a Vegas vacation. A new ad campaign, "Vegas Bound," urged hard-working Americans to take a well-deserved break in Las Vegas to recharge their batteries before returning home to brave the tough economy. A series of Vegas Bound ads and online mini-documentaries showed average Americans in high-end nightclubs, spas, and restaurants. One grinning 81-year-old woman was even shown giving a thumbs-up after an indoor skydiving session.

"We had to think how we should address our customers during this financial crisis when they're reluctant to make big financial commitments," said Ralenkotter at the start of the campaign. "We're appealing to Americans saying, 'You're working hard. It's OK to take a break.'" The campaign didn't eliminate glamour and luxury. Rather, it repackaged these traits in an "affordable" and "well-deserved" wrapper.

But after so many years of hearing about Las Vegas as a guilt-free adult playground, no matter what the ad campaign said, consumers had a hard time seeing Vegas as prudent. Research showed that even in a painful recession, consumers still saw Vegas for what it was: a place they could go to for simple pleasures not available at home. It took the LVCVA only five months to pull the plug on "Vegas Bound" and resurrect "What happens here, stays here." In a near 180-degree flip, Ralenkotter said, "We feel it is time to get back to our brand messaging."

Goldman analyst Kent expresses confidence in the brand. "For the long-term, we believe in Vegas and its ability to transform itself and attract more customers." R&R Partners, the ad agency handling the Las Vegas marketing campaigns, made an important discovery that supports Kent's point of view. It found through its research that, especially during hard economic times, people wanted to know that the same Vegas they've known and loved is still there.

Just as the needle started to budge, MGM Resorts International opened the most ambitious project Las Vegas had ever seen. In fact, its $8.5 billion CityCenter was said to be the largest privately funded construction project in U.S. history. A pedestrian-friendly resort, CityCenter, was designed as a small city in and of itself with four luxury hotels, two residential condo towers, and a 500,000-square-foot high-end shopping and dining center.

Adding 6,000 rooms and 12,000 jobs to the Las Vegas Strip has met with mixed reactions. Some speculate that this game-changing property will put an exclamation point on Las Vegas's image and provide additional oomph in a time of crisis. "History has shown that new properties increase visitation across the board," said Ralenkotter.

But even as such major signs of life are sprouting up along the Las Vegas Strip, there's an air of caution. Jim Murren, CEO for MGM, believes his company is not yet out of the woods. When asked if he thought CityCenter was in the clear, he responded emphatically. "Absolutely not. We're not declaring victory at all. We are a year or two away from even having a chance to consider that." That is probably the best attitude to take. After all, the Las Vegas Monorail filed for bankruptcy. Two other major projects that were expected to boost the Vegas economy have been shelved. Cheap (i.e., inexpensive) rooms are still available on the Las Vegas Strip. And although tourist visits are on the rise, the additional hotel room supply means it will be awhile, before 2007 occupancy rates are reached.[3] Between 2010 and 2014, giant boutique and luxury lifestyle hotels have been sprouting up in Las Vegas. In 2010, the Cosmopolitan of Las Vegas, with 2,995 rooms, opened its doors to public. In 2013, Caesars Entertainment opened 181-room Nobu Hotel and co-branded it with Caesars Palace. In 2014, SLS Las Vegas, another high-end hotel, was added to Las Vegas hotel inventory, with 1600 rooms, nightclubs, restaurants, and luxury shopping.

Although there is rarely a magic bullet in a situation like the one Las Vegas faced, the LVCVA's return to its core brand message seems to be working. From 2010 to 2013, the visitor volume climbed from 37.3 million to 39.7 million. As 2014 unfolded, the city attracted 41.2 million visitors, a 3.7 percent growth.

Las Vegas has certainly had its share of ups and downs. The recovery is shaping up and times may be brightening now. LV has a long history of reinvigorating itself and bringing in new consumers. But the city faces new challenges in the months and years to come. Kevin Bagger, the director of marketing for the LVCVA, said that his agency's latest studies pinpointed the reason for concern. "Before the recession, the average consumer coming to Las Vegas put aside $650 to spend on gambling. Now, it is closer to $480." Las Vegas also aims to attract more international visitors and set a goal of making international travelers 30 percent of the Las Vegas total visitors. In 2014, 19 percent of the 41.2 million tourists were international visitors, or about 8 million.[4]

A~s~ the Las Vegas example shows, in their quest to create customer relationships, marketers must build and manage products and brands that connect with customers. This change begins with a deceptively simple question: What is a product?

■■■ What Is a Product?

A room at the Four Seasons in Toronto, a Hawaiian vacation, McDonald's french fries, a vacation package in Bali, a catered luncheon, a bus tour of historic sites, and a convention in a modern convention center with group rates in a nearby hotel are all products. Consider the variety of products in a typical casino hotel.

We define the term *product* as follows: *A product is anything that can be offered to a market for attention, acquisition, use, or consumption that might satisfy a want or need. It includes physical objects, services, places, organizations, and ideas.*

This definition refers to the planned component of the product that the firm offers. Besides the planned component, the product also includes an unplanned component. This is particularly true in hospitality and travel products, which are often heterogeneous. For example, a consumer entered a restaurant in Dallas and was greeted by the hostess, who presented him with a menu. When he opened his menu, he saw a dead roach stuck to the inside on the menu. After receiving this unexpected bonus, the consumer decided to leave the restaurant. The restaurant certainly did not plan on having a dead roach in the menu. The product the customer receives is not always as management plans. Managers of service organizations need to work hard to eliminate unexpected negative surprises and make sure guests get what they expect.

Today, as products and services become more commoditized, many companies are moving to a new level in creating value for their customers. To differentiate their offers, they are creating and managing customer *experiences* with their brands and companies. Many hospitality companies have developed brands—Moxy and Edition by Marriott International; W, Aloft and Element by Starwood Hotels & Resorts Worldwide; Indigo by InterContinental Hotels Group; and Andaz by Hyatt Hotels Corporation —to deliver a personalized and lifestyle experience: an eco-friendly, wellness, authentic, and/or local experience.

The Hotel Le Royal is an MGallery Collection property of Accor Hotels, and situated right in the heart of Lyon, between the Saône and the Rhône rivers. Its value proposition is traditional elegance in a convenient location, with proximity to attractions to experience and feel the city. Courtesy of Philip Kotler.

Experiences have always been an important part of marketing for some companies. Disney has long produced dreams and memories through its theme parks. It wants theme park cast members to deliver a thousand "small wows" to every customer.

■■■ Product Levels

Hospitality managers need to think about the product on four levels: the core product, the facilitating product, the supporting product, and the augmented product (Figure 9–1). When developing products, marketers first must identify the core benefit that consumers seek from the product. They must then design the actual product and find ways to augment it to create customer value and a satisfying brand experience.

Core Products

Core product. Answers the question of what the buyer is really buying. Every product is a package of problem-solving services.

The most basic level is **core product**, which answers the following question: *What is the buyer really buying?*

A four-day holiday in Dublin, Ireland, isn't a plane ride, hotel room, taxis, and meals. Depending on the visitor, it might be cultural enrichment, a return to one's roots, safe adventure, or even romance.

As all good steakhouses know, "Don't sell the steak, sell the sizzle." Marketers must uncover the core benefit to the consumer of every product and sell these benefits rather than merely selling features. A highway motel sells a good night's sleep, whereas a casino resort sells entertainment.

Facilitating Products

Facilitating products. Those services or goods that must be present for the guest to use the core product.

Facilitating products are services or goods that must be present for the guest to use the core product. A first-class corporate hotel must have check-in and checkout services, a business center, a restaurant, and valet service, for instance. In an

Figure 9–1
Product levels.
Source: Adapted from C. Gonroos, "Developing the Service Offering—A Source of Competitive Advantage," in *Add Value to Your Service*, ed. C. Surprenant (Chicago, IL: American Marketing Association 1987), p. 83.

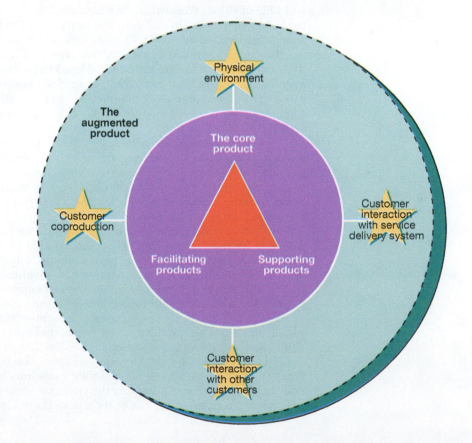

economy hotel, facilitating services might be no more than check-in and checkout service. Product design requires an understanding of the target markets and the facilitating services that they require.

A state park might not come to mind for customer service, but Chadron State Park in western Nebraska offers security for campers and cabin guests through a security station at the entrance. Late arrivals are welcomed by the security officer and given a key (cabins) as well as a map and instructions on how to find their location. Chadron State management knows that guests travel many miles to reach the park, and often arrive late at night.

Supporting Products

Supporting products. Extra products offered to add value to the core product and to help differentiate it from the competition.

Core products require facilitating products but do not require supporting products. **Supporting products** are extra products offered to add value to the core product and help differentiate it from the competition. In a corporate hotel, an iPad in the room or a full-service health spa is a supporting product that exists to help draw and retain customers. The distinction between facilitating and supporting products is not always clear. Facilitating products for one market segment may be supporting products for another. For example, although families may not require restaurants and valet service when staying at a hotel, business travelers depend on them. Hyatt was among the first chains to offer a broad line of bathroom amenities, including shampoo, conditioners, and several choices of soap. When hotels first introduced these amenities, they were supporting the core product. Today, amenities have become facilitating products.

In 2014, Hilton Worldwide announced the launch of Canopy by Hilton, a new lifestyle brand built on extensive market research. Capitalizing on growing consumer interest in locally focused travel, each Canopy property will uniquely reflect its neighborhood and local culture through its design, food and beverage, and art. Designed for today's leisure and business travelers, the hotel emphasizes open lobbies and comfortable spaces. "We saw an opportunity to not only enter the lifestyle space by developing a new brand, but also to redefine this category by creating a more accessible lifestyle brand," says Christopher J. Nassetta, president and CEO of Hilton Worldwide. "We identified the need to take the emphasis off of capital-intensive design and deliver exactly what the target consumer desires: an energizing, comfortable stay with more included value."

The more included value contains free Wi-Fi, a complimentary breakfast delivered to the room or to go, artisanal breakfast option, a local welcome gift, and evening tastings of local beer, wine, or spirits. Canopy aims to provide excellent service with its employees or "enthusiasts" in a "positively yours" service culture. Canopy properties will also offer guests the option of mobile straight-to-room arrival.[5]

In Aloft Hotels, a robot, nicknamed "Botlr" is being used to deliver items such as smartphone chargers, newspapers, or snacks from the front desk to guestrooms on request. The goal is to differentiate from competitors and create a value proposition. A futuristic Japanese hotel, named "Henn-na Hotel"—meaning "Evolve Hotel," will be run almost entirely by robots to perform duties such as manning the front desk, acting as porter, and cleaning.[6]

Hospitality firms should choose supporting products that are not easily matched by the competition. They should also be able to deliver supporting services in a professional manner. For example, some midscale hotels offer room service because they see it as a competitive advantage to attracting the business traveler. However, unprofessional delivery of supporting products can do more harm than good. Many mid-priced hotels offering room service lack a designated area in the kitchen for room-service carts, a room-service coordinator to answer the phone and write up the tickets, and designated room-service waiters. Necessary equipment and personnel are assembled at the time of the order, and as one might imagine, the results are sometimes disastrous. The person answering the phone lacks the proper training to ask the right questions (e.g., how the steak is to be cooked, the type of salad dressing the customer would like, and the type of potatoes desired). After taking the order, the next step is to find someone to set up the cart and take the order to the room. Likely candidates are the bell person, bus person, or a service person from the dining room. Personnel in the first two categories are not properly trained but may jump at the opportunity to gain a tip. Because they are not trained, the bell person and bus person may forget such essential items as salt and pepper, sugar, forks, and napkins when setting up the cart. To damage the hotel's image further, the guest puts the tray in the hallway after finishing the meal where it will sit until housekeeping picks it up the next morning.

Jogging is a popular means of exercise. Hotels are now offering jogging maps as well as bottles of water in the lobby for joggers. The Swiss Hotel in Boston provides serve-yourself coffee for early-morning flight crews. Some hotels place cold bottles of water as well as a note thanking the guest for staying at the hotel in the guest's car as the valet returns it to them after they have checked out of the hotel. These are examples of low-cost supporting products that add value.[7]

Increasing number of hotel brands provide amenity program for health- and wellness-conscious guests. Kimpton hotels have offered a brand-wide bicycle-share program for guests interested in experiencing outdoors while burning calories. The company made in-room yoga mats a nationwide standard in every guestroom and complimentary "Roll Out" service, which provides flavored water and fresh fruit in rooms. To meet the health and wellness needs of female guests, Omni Hotels & Resorts provide its select loyalty program members with a Fit Kit that includes complimentary weights and a yoga or stretch mat. JW Marriott Hotels & Resorts incorporated healthy living and sleep into its turndown service with amenities such as an aromatherapy oil and bedtime snack bar developed by a known nutritionist.[8]

In summary, supporting products offer a competitive advantage, only if they are properly planned and implemented. They must meet or exceed customer expectations to have a positive effect.

Augmented Product

Augmented products.
Additional consumer services and benefits built around the core and actual products.

The **augmented product** includes accessibility, atmosphere, customer interaction with the service organization, customer participation, and customers' interaction with each other. These elements combine with the core facilitating and supporting products to provide the augmented product.

From a managerial standpoint, the core product provides a focus for the business; it is the reason for being. Facilitating products are those that are essential for providing the core product to the target market. Supporting products can help position a product. According to Christian Gronroos, a services marketing expert, the core, facilitating, and supporting products determine what customers receive but not how they receive it.[9] The delivery of the service affects the customer's perception of the service, illustrated by the room-service example earlier. The augmented service offering combines what is offered with how it is delivered.

The augmented product is an important concept because hospitality and travel services require customer coproduction of the service. For most hospitality products, the customer comes to the service delivery system and has to interact with the service delivery system. For example, guests have to check in at the front desk, get to the room, and understand how to use the television and telephone systems. They also have to interact with other customers and employees. Because guests come to the service, atmosphere is an important part of the product. The augmented product captures the key elements that must be managed when the customer comes to the service factory (e.g., the hotel, restaurant, country club, conference center, amusement park). We now take a look at some of the elements of the augmented product.

Accessibility

If a product is not accessible, it has no value. Two barriers to accessibility are hours of operation and lack of knowledge. A hotel health club or a swimming pool that opens at 7 A.M. does not help the businessperson who wants to work out at 6 A.M., eat breakfast, and get to an 8 A.M. business appointment. A restaurant that opens at 7 A.M. becomes an irritant to a guest who has to leave at 6 A.M. for the airport.

International hotels housing guests suffering from jet lag may find that opening the restaurant earlier in the morning would provide both a valued service and additional revenue. If there is a line of guests waiting for the restaurant to open in the morning, it may indicate that the hours need to be adjusted to make the restaurant more accessible.

The Palms Casino Resort in Las Vegas recently announced a 24-hour checkout policy for all guests at no extra cost. Guests can choose their departure time when they book rooms directly on the hotel's Web site.

Atmosphere: The Physical Environment

Atmosphere is a critical element in services. It can be the customer's reason for choosing to do business with an establishment. Burgundy's restaurant in Houston lacked street appeal and went out of business. The restaurant was located in a strip shopping center with a glass panel exterior and wall, common in many strip centers. The owners carpeted the concrete floor, put in booths, installed a sign over the door, and opened the restaurant. Perhaps they felt that their food quality and service would attract customers. But few ever reached the restaurant. The restaurant's exterior lacked identity or character and was not inviting to potential customers. People who saw Burgundy's simply did not come into the restaurant. Conversely, BJs Restaurant and Brewhouse has used atmosphere effectively. It builds all of its restaurants, rather than move into existing locations, to give them a common look inside and out. This also ensures they operate efficiently. The exterior is modern and inviting; the interior is casual and promotes a relaxed and fun environment.

Atmosphere is appreciated through the senses. Sensory terms provide descriptions for the atmosphere of a particular set of surroundings.

Visual. The dimension of atmosphere relating to color, brightness, size, and shape.

Aural. The dimension of atmosphere relating to volume and pitch.

Olfactory. The dimension of atmosphere relating to scent and freshness.

Tactile. The dimension of atmosphere relating to softness, smoothness, and temperature.

- The main **visual** dimensions of atmosphere are color, brightness, size, and shape.

- The main **aural** dimensions of atmosphere are volume and pitch.

- The main **olfactory** dimensions of atmosphere are scent and freshness.

- The main **tactile** dimensions of atmosphere are softness, smoothness, and temperature.

When a strong atmosphere is created through the senses, it can set expectations for the fifth sense, taste. If loyal customers walk into a Starbucks, the atmospherics set the taste expectations for a cup of their favorite Starbucks beverage. As they taste their beverage, the consistency of the product does not disappoint them.

Atmosphere can affect purchase behavior in at least four ways. First, atmosphere may serve as an attention-creating medium. The Casa Bonita Mexican Restaurant in Denver, Colorado, features an 85-foot bell tower to attract one's attention to the building. It has expanded the Mexican theme to include artificial volcanoes and a replica of the diving cliffs of Acapulco from which divers perform for dinner patrons. It has used atmospherics to develop an experiential product. People come to Casa Bonita not only for the food but also for an experience.

Second, atmosphere may serve as a message-creating medium to potential customers. The modern style of Aloft Hotels is evident from the exterior design of the hotel. When one enters the lobby, one gets the sense of an urban loft environment, consistent with the exterior. This is how the Aloft Web site describes its public space: The Aloft Web site describes its public space as one where walls have been knocked down to create an open space and where energy flows and personalities mingle.[10] According to this Aloft guest, the atmosphere of Aloft achieves its desired effect, "When you come down to the lobby, you always see an activity. It's like a car wreck: You have to stop and watch the scene."[11]

Third, atmosphere may serve as an effect-creating medium. Colors, sounds, and textures directly arouse visceral reactions that stimulate the purchase of a product. In Harrah's casino in Las Vegas, an area on the slot floor was infused with a pleasant odor over several weekends. The revenue from the scented floor exceeded the non-scented area by 45 percent. Today most large casinos follow similar strategies. When things are slow, a popcorn attendant at Disney World turns on a machine that produces a popcorn smell and a line for popcorn quickly forms.[12]

Finally, environment can be a mood-creating medium. An environmental psychologist has described environments as high load and low load. High and low refer to the information that one receives from the environment. Bright colors, bright lights, loud noises, crowds, and movement are typical elements of a high-load environment, whereas their opposites are characteristic of a low-load environment.[13] A high-load environment creates a playful, adventurous mood, whereas low-load environments create a relaxing mood. Vacationers going to Las Vegas or Branson, Missouri, are likely to react positively to a high-load environment that offers the excitement they were expecting. The front desk of the Flamingo Hilton is adjacent to the hotel's casino. While waiting to check in, guests hear the sounds of the casino, watch the players, and feel the excitement. In contrast, Courtyard by Marriott creates a relaxing, home-like low-load environment for business travelers who wish to relax after a busy day.

Le Méridien created a group of cultural innovators and artists who define and enrich the guest experience at Le Méridien.[14] The group comprises a global array of visionaries, from artists to photographers, musicians to designers, and chefs to architects. Some members of the group appointed to develop a unique atmosphere for Le Méridien include Andrea Illy, of Illy Coffee, Chef Jean-Georges Vongerichten, and perfume creators Fabrice Penot and Eddie Roschi, of Le Labo. Penot commented, when someone stays at a hotel they want to feel the comfort and safety of their home, but they still want to experience a new environment, they want to know they are not at home. The scent, LM01™, created by Le Labo to capture this feeling is the first thing one notices when you walk into any of Le Méridien's 120 hotels.[15]

Atmosphere must be considered when creating hospitality products. As marketers, we should understand what the customer wants from the buying experience and what atmospheric variables will fortify the beliefs and emotional reaction the buyers are seeking or, in some cases, escaping. Will the proposed atmosphere compete effectively in a crowded market?[16]

Customer Interaction with the Service Delivery System

The customer participates in the delivery of most hospitality and travel products. There are three phases to this involvement: joining, consumption, and detachment.[17] In the **joining stage**, the customer makes the initial inquiry contact. When designing products we must make it easy for people to learn about the new product. This information must be delivered in a professional way.

The joining phase is often enhanced through sampling. Visitors to foreign countries are often reluctant to order a full meal of native foods. The Inter-Continental Hotel of Jakarta, Indonesia, took steps to introduce visitors to the local cuisine by selling sample plates of selected native foods from a typical native pushcart in the afternoon cocktail area of the hotel adjacent to the lobby. This innovation created excitement and enhanced the atmosphere, introduced guests to native foods served in the hotel's restaurant, and served as a profit-making product line.

Unfortunately, some hospitality companies attempt to manage service variability by standardizing service behavior. "Adopting systems to increase organizational efficiency by constraining or scripting employee behavior may lead to counterproductive service outcomes."[18] A well-trained and knowledgeable employee can greatly assist customers in the joining stage without following a script or acting like an android.

As a consideration during the joining phase organizations must make it easy for customers to purchase the product. Pei Wei restaurants, a popular limited-service Asian restaurant, have a separate cash register and entrance for take-out orders. This enables the person who has made an order online to bypass the line of dine-in customers waiting to order.

The **consumption phase** takes place when the service is consumed. In a restaurant it occurs when the customer is dining, and in a hotel when an individual is a guest. Designers of hospitality products must understand how guests will interact with the product. The employees, customers, and physical facilities are

Joining stage. The product life-cycle stage when the customer makes the initial inquiry contact.

Consumption phase. Takes place when the customer consumes the service.

all part of the product. A business hotel that opens a concierge floor aimed at the luxury market must train its employees to meet the expectations of this new class of traveler. In addition to employee–customer interaction, hospitality firms have to consider how customers will interact with one another during the consumption stage. A business hotel near a large amusement park developed a package for the summer family market. The package proved to be so popular that some of the hotel's main market, business travelers, was driven away. The noise of the children in the hallways and the lobby changed the atmosphere. Gone was the comfortable atmosphere desired by the business traveler.

Physical features, layout, and signage can also be used to help customers interact with the product. In many hotels, finding your way to a meeting can be frustrating. This problem can be overcome by proper attention to directional signage. Signage can also be used to make customers aware of the existence of supporting products. Guests may leave a hotel not realizing that it had a health club or a business center. It does no good to invest in supporting products if guests aren't aware of their existence.

Occasionally, even the best-designed signage is not observed or understood. Guests who appear lost in the Orlando Peabody Hotel are very apt to discover an employee, including the general manager, who will personally escort them to their destination. This does not occur by accident. Training and positive reinforcement in hotels such as the Peabody ensure that this type of service is an integral part of the hotel's product.

Detachment phase. When the customer is through using the product and departs.

The **detachment phase** is when the customer is through using a product and departs. For example, hotel guests may need a bell person to help with the bags. They will need to settle their account and acquire transportation to the airport. International travelers may need an airport departure tax stamp.

Guests in a roadside motel may need to know directions, road conditions, the hours of check services, and other information. The manager of a Super 8 motel in Benson, Arizona, prides himself on serving guests with this information. Unfortunately, this is not the case at many motels as front-desk clerks are often part-time employees, feel harassed by a line of guests, and give abrupt answers such as "I don't know; why don't you check the Internet?"

Thinking through these three stages helps management understand how the customer will interact with the service delivery system, resulting in a product designed to fit the needs of the customer. Well-managed international hotels ask guests if they have their passports and airline tickets and if they have cleared their safety deposit box when they are checking out. Managers should think through and then experience the joining, consumption, and detachment phases of their guests.

Destination marketers have a special responsibility to carefully plan and help manage each of these phases. Tourism promotion organizations sometimes feel their responsibility is solely to bring "heads to beds," in other words, to increase the number of visitors. This simplistic thinking has resulted in a mix-match of attracting the wrong visitor to the community. It also ignores the organization's responsibility to use part of its funding for crime awareness and prevention programs, service-sector personnel training, signage, language instruction, beautification, and many other support activities to help ensure visitor satisfaction.

Customer Interaction with Other Customers

An area that is drawing the interest of hospitality researchers is the interaction of customers with one another. An airline flight on Friday afternoon from Dallas to Houston was sold out with a number of people on standby. Some on standby were construction workers returning home from their job sites. The airline's ground crew, in an effort to maximize revenue, put a construction worker in an empty first-class seat. The passenger paying a premium to sit in first class did not appreciate a worker in dirty construction clothes in the next seat. Hospitality organizations must manage the interaction of customers to ensure that some do not negatively affect the experience of others.

The issue of customer interaction is a serious problem for hotels and resorts. The independent nontour guest consistently objects to the presence of large group-inclusive tours (GITs). This problem is magnified if the GIT guests represent a different culture, speak a foreign language, or are from an age group years different from that of independent nontour guests.

The Shangri-La Hotel of Singapore dealt successfully with this problem by constructing three different hotel properties on the same grounds. The tower hotel serves GIT and lesser-revenue, independent nontour guests. The Bougainvillea section serves a more upscale guest, and a third executive property is for the exclusive use of very upscale guests. Interaction among the three groups is limited to the common outdoor swimming pool.

Ski resorts are facing a serious problem of guest interaction. Traditionally, skiers have been a fairly homogeneous group with common cultural norms, even though they arrive from widely separated geographic areas. German, French, Japanese, American, and Mexican skiers tended to have societal commonalities, despite differences in language.

The arrival of the snowboard changed this congenial mix of guests. Skiers began to complain that they must share the slopes with people dressed in counterculture clothing who often show blatant disregard for slope-side courtesy. The management of ski resorts was suddenly faced with a serious problem. Taos responded by refusing entry to snowboarders and positioned itself as "Skiing for Purists." Others turned part of the ski areas into terrain peaks with half pipes and other physical attractions popular with "riders."

Many hotels such as Embassy Suites provide free wine and cheese for guests during a set time period in the evening. These hotels commonly report that this act of hospitality has an added benefit of bringing guests together. Lasting friendships and business deals have resulted from the evening wine and cheese.

More and more hotels transform their lobbies into places to work, surf the Web, or meet friends for a drink. Aloft hotels by Starwood embraced this idea by creating the "social lobby" and XYZ Bar with a much younger vibe that appeals to millennials and draws them to socialize in the lobby. Moxy hotels by Marriott have adopted multi-zone lobbies that shift from quiet areas to social zones around the lobby bar. "Here's what we're hearing [from Millennials]: What I want is to be able to get out and see the city," says Indy Adenaw, VP of brand consulting at Marriott Hotels, and continues, "What I want is to be able to go downstairs and have a very lively and energetic bar experience. I want to meet people, I want to be communal. I want to be fiercely independent when I want to be, but also part of a larger community when it's active and when it's social."

Hotel Indigo by Intercontinental Hotel Group positions itself as a brand to deliver a local cultural experience. Director of brand management for Hotel Indigo brand says about their target market: "They want to sit in the lobby. They want to have local coffee, or they want to have local craft beer. They want to experience the neighborhood even if they don't get to leave the hotel."

Several hotels, such as Novotel by Accor, have taken the social lobby concept one step further with the use of LobbyFriend, an app that encourages hotel guests to meet and greet fellow guests and access a relevant and mobile stream of information about happenings within their hotel or city location. It also enables hotels to communicate with guests during their stay and connect hotel guests and hotel employees together.[19]

Customers as Employees

Customers often help hospitality organizations coproduce the product. Involving the guest as an employee can increase capacity, improve customer satisfaction, and reduce costs. Wait staff are not needed when guests help themselves.

The Las Vegas Sports Club used to have an attendant handing out keys and towels to members. The club installed a device that releases the locker key when the membership card is placed in a slot. Then someone observed that members could get their own towels if they were neatly stacked on shelves. The club no longer needed the space for the towel attendant in both the women's and men's locker rooms. It reconfigured the locker rooms and created a spa. The processes given to the customer resulted in considerable labor savings for the club and additional revenue for the spa. The members received a new amenity and gained control over their locker room experience.

Chili's has installed tabletop iPad-like tablets in its restaurants that allow customers to place orders and pay their bill at the table. Courtesy of Philip Kotler.

Self-service technologies (SSTs) are a rapidly growing means for increasing customer coproduction in food-service experiences. For example, managers at Disney noticed guests at one of Walt Disney World's water parks standing in line at a snack bar just to get their refillable drink mug filled. This process cost the customer valuable time, added additional people to the queue, and required employees to take the drink order and refill mugs. The solution was an SST that saved time for the guest and labor. Management developed a drink-dispensing system that was activated by a bar code on the mug. The customer holds the mug in front of a scanner, which scans the bar code on the mug and activates the drink machine long enough for him or her to fill the mug. To prevent misuse of the system, Disney changes bar codes each day of the week.[20]

Chili's has installed tabletop computer screens in its restaurants so customers can order directly and pay by credit card. The restaurant found users of the service spend more per check, in part because they buy more desserts and coffee when the screen is present.[21] You can add an app like WaitAway to your cell phone and be contacted by text message when your table is ready at a restaurant—and monitor the length of the line in the process.[22]

■■■ Branding Strategy

Building Strong Brands

Brand. A name, term, sign, symbol, design, or a combination of these elements that is intended to identify the goods or services of a seller and differentiate them from competitors.

A **brand** is a name, term, sign, symbol, design, or a combination of these elements that is intended to identify the goods or services of a seller and differentiate them from competitors. Some analysts see brands as the major enduring asset of a company, outlasting the company's specific products and facilities. A former CEO of McDonald's declared, "If every asset we own, every building, and every piece of equipment were destroyed in a terrible natural disaster, we would be able to borrow all the money to replace it very quickly because of the value of our brand. . . . The brand is more valuable than the totality of all these assets."[23]

Branding. The process of endowing products and services with the power of a brand. It's all about creating differences between products.

Branding is the process of endowing products and services with the power of a brand. It's all about creating differences between products. This process must be carefully developed and managed. In this section, we examine the key strategies for building and managing brands (Table 9–1).

Brand Equity

Brands are more than just names and symbols. They are a key element in the company's relationships with consumers. Brands represent consumers' perceptions and feelings about a product and its performance—everything that the product means to consumers. In the final analysis, brands exist in the heads of consumers. Adds Jason Kilar, CEO of the online video service Hulu, "A brand is what people say about you when you're not in the room."[24]

Brand equity. The added value endowed on products and services. It may be reflected in the way consumers think, feel, and act with respect to the brand, as well as in the prices, market share, and profitability the brand commands for the firm.

A powerful brand has high brand equity. **Brand equity** is the added value endowed on products and services. It may be reflected in the way consumers think, feel, and act with respect to the brand, as well as in the prices, market share, and profitability the brand commands for the firm. It's a measure of the brand's ability to capture consumer preference and loyalty. A brand has positive brand equity when consumers react more favorably to it than to a generic or unbranded version

TABLE 9-1

Marketing Advantages of Strong Brands

Improved perceptions of product performance
Greater loyalty
Less vulnerability to competitive marketing actions
Less vulnerability to marketing crises
Larger margins
More inelastic consumer response to price increases
More elastic consumer response to price decreases
Greater cooperation and support from suppliers
Greater support from marketing intermediaries
Increased marketing communications effectiveness
Brand extension opportunities

of the same product. It has negative brand equity if consumers react less favorably than to an unbranded version.

Brands vary in the amount of power and value they hold in the marketplace. Some brands—such as Hilton, Marriott, and McDonald's—become larger-than-life icons that maintain their power in the market for years, even generations. Other brands create fresh consumer excitement and loyalty, such as NYLO, Aloft, Westin, Red Mango, YouTube, and Twitter. These brands win in the marketplace not simply because they deliver unique benefits or reliable service. Rather, they succeed because they forge deep connections with customers.

Ad agency Young & Rubicam's Brand Asset Valuator measures brand strength along four consumer perception dimensions: *differentiation* (what makes the brand stand out), *relevance* (how consumers feel it meets their needs), *knowledge* (how much consumers know about the brand), and *esteem* (how highly consumers regard and respect the brand). Brands with strong brand equity rate high on all four dimensions. The brand must be distinct, or consumers will have no reason to choose it over other brands. But the fact that a brand is highly differentiated doesn't necessarily mean that consumers will buy it. The brand must stand out in ways that are relevant to consumers' needs. But even a differentiated, relevant brand is far from a shoe-in. Before consumers will respond to the brand, they must first know about and understand it. And that brand recognition must lead to a strong, positive consumer–brand connection.[25] Thus, positive brand equity derives from consumer feelings about and connections with a brand. Consumers sometimes bond very closely with specific brands.

High brand equity provides a company with many competitive advantages. A powerful brand enjoys a high level of consumer brand awareness and loyalty. Because consumers are loyal to strong brands, the brand has more leverage in bargaining with the consumer and the members of the distribution channel. Because a brand name carries high credibility, the company can more easily launch line and brand extensions. A powerful brand offers the company some defense against fierce price competition.

Above all, however, a powerful brand forms the basis for building strong and profitable customer relationships. The fundamental asset underlying brand equity is customer equity—the value of customer relationships that the brand creates. A powerful brand is important, but what it really represents is a profitable set of loyal customers. The proper focus of marketing is building customer equity, with brand management serving as a major marketing tool. Companies need to think of themselves not as portfolios of products but as portfolios of customers.

Brand Positioning

Marketers need to position their brands clearly in target customers' minds. They can position brands at any of three levels.[26] At the lowest level, they can position the brand on *product attributes*. For example, a hamburger restaurant can state that it uses only Angus beef. In general, however, attributes are the least desirable level for brand positioning. Competitors can easily copy attributes. More importantly, customers are not interested in attributes; they are interested in what the attributes will do for them.

A brand can be better positioned by associating its name with a desirable *benefit*. In the hospitality and travel industry, these benefits often relate to customer service or experience. Fleming's Prime Steakhouse and Wine Bar targets an upscale market that enjoys great wine, food, and service and has the resources to dine at a top restaurant. Fleming's positions the restaurant as a place where you can experience the celebration of exceptional food and wine.

The strongest brands go beyond attribute or benefit positioning. They are positioned on strong *beliefs and values*. Even a seemingly mundane brand such as Amtrak can be positioned this way. Recent Amtrak ads suggest that an Amtrak train ride does more than just get you from point A to point B. The moment you come on board Amtrak the journey begins. With more ways to relax on your journey, including plenty of legroom, spectacular views, and a unique dining experience, your state of mind will transform just like the land you're passing through.

Successful brands engage customers on a deep, emotional level. According to Stengel, "Marketing inspires life, and life inspires marketing."[27] Fleming's knows that its core customer enjoys wine. In order for a guest to try all one-hundred wines it has on its wine list, known as the Fleming's 100, a term it has trademarked, Fleming's provided a tasting of 25 wines each starting Friday at 5:30 P.M. for five consecutive weeks. It charged a nominal $25 for the tasting and sold small plates of food for those who wanted a snack.

Brand promise. The marketer's vision of what the brand must be and do for consumers.

When positioning a brand, the marketer should establish a mission for the brand and a vision of what the brand must be and do. The **brand promise** is the marketer's vision of what the brand must be and do for consumers. The brand promise must be simple and honest. Motel 6, for example, offers clean rooms, low prices, and good service but does not promise expensive furnishings or large bathrooms. In contrast, The Ritz-Carlton offers luxurious rooms and a truly memorable experience but does not promise low prices.

Virgin America's brand promise is to enter categories where customers' needs are not well met, do different things, and do things differently, all in a way that better meets those needs. After flying for only a few years, Virgin America became an award-winning airline that passengers adore. It is not unusual for the company to receive e-mails from customers saying they actually wished their flights lasted longer!

Virgin America set to reinvent the entire travel experience, starting with an easy-to-use and friendly Web site and check-in. In flight, passengers revel in Wi-Fi, spacious leather seats, mood lighting, and in-seat food and beverage ordering through touch-screen panels. Some passengers remark that Virgin America is like "flying in an iPod or nightclub." The brand is seeking to be positioned as "an established player featuring discount pricing and a hip, stylish customer experience for travelers." Without a national TV ad campaign, Virgin America has relied on PR, word of mouth, social media, and exemplary customer service to create that customer experience and build the brand. To get customers more involved with the brand, Virgin America launched a digital marketing campaign offering the opportunity to upload a photo to Instagram from the flight. By tweeting the company's Twitter account, travelers can also upload their photo onto Virgin America's Times Square billboard or share it via their own social media accounts.[28]

Brand Name Selection

A good name can add greatly to a product's success. However, finding the best brand name is a difficult task. It begins with a careful review of the product and its benefits, the target market, and proposed marketing strategies. After that, naming a brand becomes part science, part art, and a measure of instinct.

Desirable qualities for a brand name include the following: (1) It should suggest something about the product's benefits and qualities: Luxury Collection, Sleep Inn, and Comfort Suites. (2) It should be easy to pronounce, recognize, and remember: Motel 6, Four Seasons, and JetBlue. (3) The brand name should be distinctive: Aloft, Moxy, and Element. (4) It should be extendable: Marriott began as a lodging company but chose a name that would allow expansion into other categories such as vacation ownership. (5) The name should translate easily into foreign languages. (6) It should be capable of registration and legal protection. A brand name cannot be registered if it infringes on existing brand names.

Many hotel corporations often market many different brands in a given product category. *Multibranding* offers a way to establish different features that appeal to different customer segments and capture a larger market share. If a hospitality company decides to brand its multiple concepts, it must choose which brand names to use. Hotel chains take various approaches to naming their brands.[29]

Individual Brand Names

Hospitality companies may choose to brand different products by different names. Starwood and Choice Hotels International use individual branding without including the family or corporate name. A major advantage of separate family brand names is that if a product fails or appears to be of low quality, the company has not tied its reputation to it.[30]

Corporate Umbrella (Family) or Sub-branding

Hospitality companies may use their corporate brand as an umbrella brand across their entire range of products. Corporate-image associations of innovativeness, expertise, and trustworthiness have been shown to directly influence consumer evaluations. Marriott International used to include its corporate family name on majority of its brands. A sub-brand strategy, falling somewhere between, combines two or more of the corporate brand, family brand, or individual product brand names. For example, Hilton and Wyndham have used both individual and family branding. Marriott International now uses both umbrella branding (e.g., Courtyard by Marriott, AC Hotels by Marriott) and individual branding (e.g., Moxy, Edition, Renaissance Hotels). Recently, Marriott created Moxy Hotels aimed at price-conscious and millennial consumers.

Leveraging Brands

Companies can leverage an existing brand by employing co-branding and ingredient branding.

Co-branding, or *dual branding*, can take advantage of the complementary strengths of two brands. For example, the Tim Hortons coffee chain is establishing co-branded Tim Hortons-Cold Stone Creamery shops. Tim Hortons is strong in the morning and midday periods, with coffee and baked goods, soups, and sandwiches. By contrast, Cold Stone Creamery's ice cream snacks are strongest in the afternoon and evening, which are Tim Hortons's nonpeak periods. The co-branded locations offer customers a reason to visit morning, noon, and night.[31] Taco Bell and Doritos teamed up to create the Doritos Locos Taco. Taco Bell sold more than 100 million of the tacos in just the first 10 weeks and quickly added Cool Ranch and Fiery versions.[32] Caesars Palace, the megaresort with 3,950 rooms, co-branded with the world's first Nobu Hotel, a luxury boutique hotel branded around celebrated Chef Nobu Matsuhisa. Co-branding enhances the credibility of the hotel's brand by borrowing credibility from other brands.[33]

Another form of co-branding is *same-company* or *retail co-branding* in which two

Co-branding: Four Seasons Hotel Las Vegas is located on floors 35 to 39 of the Mandalay Bay. Courtesy of Philip Kotler.

In response to guest demand for healthy travel options, "Stay Well" rooms at MGM Grand Hotel and Casino, in addition to private registration and lounge, include over 20 health and wellness features that allow business and leisure guests to maintain their healthy lifestyle practices. Courtesy of MGM Resorts International.

retail establishments use the same location to optimize space and profits, such as jointly owned Pizza Hut, KFC, and Taco Bell restaurants. In 2012, Choice Hotels International unveiled a new dual-brand combination hotel prototype for its Sleep Inn and MainStay Suites brands. The new combo unit features a shared front desk, lobby and community room, fitness centers, and laundry facilities.[34] The main advantage of co-branding is that a product can be convincingly positioned by virtue of the multiple brands. Co-branding can generate greater sales from the existing market and open opportunities for new consumers and channels. It can also reduce the cost of product introduction because it combines two well-known images and speeds adoption.

Ingredient branding is a special case of co-branding. Ingredient brands can provide differentiation and important signals of quality. Many hotels use well-known brands for their in-room amenities such as care products, healthy meal options, and coffee. An interesting take on ingredient branding is self-branded ingredients that companies advertise and even trademark.[35] Westin Hotels advertises its own "Heavenly Bed"—a critically important ingredient to a guest's good night's sleep. The brand has been so successful that Westin now sells the bed, pillows, sheets, and blankets via an online catalog, along with other "Heavenly" gifts, bath products, and even pet items. The success of the bed has also created a halo for the Westin brand as a whole. Heavenly Bed enthusiasts are more likely to rate other aspects of their room or stay as more positive.[36] If it can be done well, using self-branded ingredients makes sense because firms have more control over them.

Hotels often have brands within a brand. Delos Living—a wellness design company—has observed a consumer demand for maintaining their health-conscious and wellness-oriented lifestyle while on the road, and designed a health and wellness hotel room concept—the "Stay Well" rooms. The company partnered with MGM Resorts International to convert 42 rooms of the MGM Grand in Las Vegas to Stay Well rooms. After receiving positive feedback, MGM Grand expanded the concept to 171 Stay Well suites, encompassing the entire 14th floor of the hotel's main tower. Among the numerous health and wellness features in the rooms are showers with vitamin C–infused water, an air-purification system, room lighting designed to combat jet lag and regulate levels of melatonin, aromatherapy, healthy menu options, and bedside lighting designed to enhance sleep.[37]

Brand Portfolios

A brand can only be stretched so far, and all the segments the firm would like to target may not view the same brand equally or favorably. Marketers often need multiple brands in order to pursue these multiple segments. Some other reasons for introducing multiple brands in a category include:[38]

1. attracting consumers seeking variety who may otherwise have switched to another brand;

2. increasing internal competition within the firm;

3. yielding economies of scale in advertising, sales, merchandising, and physical distribution.

The brand portfolio is the set of all brands and brand-particular category or market segment.

Recently, to target millennials and health- and well-being-sensitive customers, hotel chains have diversified their portfolio with lifestyle or boutique brands such as Moxy and Edition by Marriott International; W, Aloft and Element by Starwood

Hotels & Resorts Worldwide; Indigo by InterContinental Hotels Group; and Andaz by Hyatt Hotels Corporation. For example, Element by Westin Hotels and Resorts, an extended stay hotel concept, positions itself as an eco-friendly hotel offering a balanced experience where guests can "eat right, sleep well, exercise and relax."[39]

InterContinental Hotels Group has gone beyond providing in-room health and wellness amenities and created a single brand, the Even Hotels, targeting health- and wellness-conscious travelers. Even properties features elements based on four pillars:

- Eat well. Menus are focused on fresh, organic ingredients; food is clearly labeled; and free flavored filtered water is always available.

- Rest easy. Guestrooms feature natural eucalyptus fiber, high thread count linens; natural bath products; antibacterial wipes; and color LED mood lighting.

- Keep active. Exercise equipment such as yoga mats are provided in guestrooms.

- Accomplish more. Flexible space is provided for guests to work.[40]

One of the leading hotel and leisure companies in the world, Starwood Hotels & Resorts Worldwide, has 1,200 properties in more than 100 countries and 181,400 employees at its owned and managed properties. In its rebranding attempt to go "beyond beds," Starwood has differentiated its hotels along emotional, experiential lines. Its hotel and call center operators convey different experiences for the firm's different chains, as does the firm's advertising. Starwood has nine distinct lifestyle brands in its portfolio. This strategy emerged from a major 18-month positioning project, started in 2006, to find positions for the portfolio of brands that would establish an emotional connection with consumers. Consumer research suggested these positions for some of the brands:[41]

> **Sheraton** With the tagline "You don't stay here, you belong," Sheraton—the largest brand—is about warm, comforting, and casual. Its core value centers on "connections," an image aided by the hotel's alliance with Yahoo!, which cofounded the Yahoo! Link@Sheraton lobby kiosks and cyber cafes.

> **Four Points by Sheraton** For the self-sufficient traveler, Four Points strives to be honest, uncomplicated, and comfortable. The brand is all about providing a high level of comfort and little indulgences like free high-speed Internet access and bottled water. Its ads feature apple pies and talk about providing guests with "the comforts of home."

> **W** With a brand personality defined as flirty, for the insider, and an escape, W offers guests unique experiences around the warmth of cool. W's "Whatever/Whenever" service complements the stylish designs in its lobby gathering places and signature bars and restaurants.

> **Westin** Westin's emphasis on "personal, instinctive, and renewal" has led to a new sensory welcome, featuring a white tea scent, signature music and lighting, and refreshing towels. Each room features Westin's own "Heavenly Beds," sold exclusively in the retail market through Nordstrom, further enhancing the brand's upscale image.

The hallmark of an optimal brand portfolio is the ability of each brand in it to maximize equity in combination with all the other brands in it. Marketers generally need to trade off market coverage with costs and profitability. If they can increase profits by dropping brands, a portfolio is too big; if they can increase profits by adding brands, it's not big enough. The basic principle in designing a brand portfolio is to maximize market coverage so no potential customers are being ignored, but minimize brand overlap so brands are not competing for customer approval. Each brand should be clearly differentiated and appealing to a sizable-enough marketing segment to justify its marketing and production costs.[42]

Marketers carefully monitor brand portfolios over time to identify weak brands and kill unprofitable ones.[43] Brand lines with poorly differentiated brands are likely to be characterized by much cannibalization and require pruning.[44]

Marketing HIGHLIGHT 9–1 Extending Your Brand to China: What Name Do You Use?

You are delegated with extending your brand to China. Your brand is well known and has a positive image. However, will you benefit from the brand's strong image in China? Do you use your foreign language brand name in China or do you adapt it to Mandarin or create a new name in Mandarin? Below are some considerations to help answer these questions, and some examples of what others have done.

Some names do not translate in Mandarin. Haagen-Dazs is an example of this category. The name does not have any meaning but because of the association with Denmark, it suggests high quality and a premium price can be charged. The name Haagen-Dazs was successfully used in China. In fact although it is an American company many Chinese view it as a Danish company. Hilton does not translate; however, Hilton decided to use a phonetic translation, Xi er dun; it hopes its strong worldwide brand name will carry over to China. Hyatt, realizing its name had no meaning in China, decided to use the name Yue, which translates into imperial. It used the name Kai Yue for Hyatt Regency, Juri Yue for Grand Hyatt, and Bo Yue for Park Hyatt.

Some brand names translate well into Mandarin. For example Coca-Cola translates to Ke Kou Ke Le, which means tasty fun. Marriott Hotels is Wan hao, which translate to 10,000 wealthy elites. These brands and others have the benefit of being able to use their own brand name, which have a translated name that has a positive image.

Today for products appealing to a broader market, another important question is how the name will be searched online. Research shows that for that for many consumer products, the Chinese name is used to search online, not the international name. Also, the acronym can be a more frequently used search term than the full name. This should benefit a company like KFC, which changed its name from Kentucky Fried Chicken to KFC in 1991. In this age of digital marketing, it is important to know how your name will be used online, including how customers will try to find you online.

Chinese local brands have learned from observing how the brand names of multinational firms were accepted in China. For examples, a local company Paris Baguette and Croissants de France knows France is known for quality baked goods and uses a name that associates it with France. These shops are local but use foreign verbal elements to portray an association with a foreign culture. Such associations confer the brand some credibility and allow it to charge a premium. Chinese companies have also modified those names of multinational companies. Examples of this include Pizza Huh, KFG, and McDnoald.

Sources: Philip Kotler, Kevin Keller, Swee Ang, Siew Leong, Chin Tan, *Marketing Management: An Asian Perspective*, 2013, Pearson, Singapore; Carly Chalmers, "12 Amazing Translations of Chinese Brand Names," *Today Translations*, September 27, 2013, http://www.todaytranslations.com/blog/12-amazing-translations-of-chinese-brand-names/ (accessed August 20, 2015); Michael Winesnov, "Picking Brand Names in China Is a Business Itself," *New York Times*, November 12, 2011, http://www.nytimes.com/2011/11/12/world/asia/picking-brand-names-in-china-is-a-business-itself.html?_r=3&partner=rss&emc=rss&pagewanted=all (accessed August 210, 2015); Clarissa Ward, "China's Logo Ripoffs: KFG, Pizza Huh and McDnoalds," ABC News, July 22, 2011, http://abcnews.go.com/Business/counterfeit-logos-hit-groupon-apple-pizza-hut-kfc/story?id=14131984 (accessed August 20, 2015); Daniel Guo and Kevin Gentle, "Cultural Naming," *Lab Report*, 13, no. 4, Lab Brand, 12/2010 http://www.labbrand.com/sites/default/files/reports/pdf/en/1012Labreport_En_OK.pdf (accessed August 20, 2015); "Understanding Chinese Brand Names Online," *Lab Brand* http://www.labbrand.com/brand-source/understanding-chinese-brand-names-online (accessed August 20, 2015).

Managing Brands

Companies must manage their brands carefully. First, the brand's positioning must be continuously communicated to consumers. Major brand marketers often spend huge amounts on advertising to create brand awareness and build preference and loyalty.

Brand identity is about positioning a brand in the minds of consumer. Brand image is about perceptions of the brand and differentiation by consumers, both features and feelings. Brand integrity is fulfilling the promise and delivering the experience claimed, connecting brand identity and brand image. It establishes the credibility and trust that consumers will establish after their actual brand experience. Companies should deliver experiences that they promise. Losing credibility will result in losing the community (online and offline) of potential buyers.[45]

Advertising campaigns can help create name recognition, brand knowledge, and perhaps even some brand preference. However, the fact is that brands are not maintained by advertising but by customers' *brand experiences*. Today, customers come to know a brand through a wide range of contacts and touch points. These include not only advertising but also personal experience with the brand, word of mouth, social media sites, and company Web pages. The company must put as much care into managing these touch points as it does into producing its ads. "Managing each customer's experience is perhaps the most important ingredient in building [brand] loyalty," states one branding expert. "Every memorable interaction . . . must be completed with excellence and . . . must reinforce your brand essence." A former Disney top executive agrees: "A brand is a living entity, and it is enriched or undermined cumulatively over time, the product of a thousand small gestures."[46] The brand's positioning will not take hold fully unless everyone in the company lives the brand. Therefore, the company needs to train its people to be customer centered. Even better, the company should carry on internal brand building to help employees understand and be enthusiastic about the brand promise. Many companies go even further by training and encouraging their distributors and dealers to serve their customers well.

Finally, companies need to periodically audit their brands' strengths and weaknesses.[47] They should ask: Does our brand excel at delivering benefits that customers truly value? Is the brand properly positioned? Do all of our customer touch points support the brand's positioning? Do the brand's managers understand what the brand means to customers? Does the brand receive proper, sustained support? The brand audit may turn up brands that need more support, brands that need to be dropped, or brands that must be rebranded or repositioned because of changing customer preferences or new competitors.

■■■ The New-Product Development

A company can obtain new products in two ways. One is through acquisition—by buying a whole company or a license to use someone else's product. The other is through the company's own new-product development efforts. To create successful new products, a company must understand its consumers, markets, and competitors and develop products that deliver superior value to customers. It must carry out strong new-product planning and set up a systematic, customer-driven *new-product development process* for finding and growing new products. Figure 9–2 shows the eight major steps in this process.

In 2004, Panda Restaurants developed a new retail line in partnership with Overall Farms of Texas, a supplier of frozen foods to the food-service industry. Panda placed two frozen entrees, beef with broccoli and mandarin chicken, into a test market within Costco and Sam's Clubs. "Consumers are ready to try our new frozen products because they feel a familiarity with the entrees and our company," said David Landsberg, vice president of business planning.[48]

Perhaps so, but other restaurant chains such as El Chico have also tried this form of product expansion and experienced severe problems. If consumers view the retail product the same as the restaurant one, they may question why they need to visit the restaurant. In some cases, consumers believe that the restaurant serves frozen rather than freshly prepared products. Two years after launching its fast-food line, Panda announced that it was discontinuing the line.[49]

Thus, companies face a problem: They must develop new products but the risk of failure is high. The solution lies in strong new-product planning and in setting up a systematic new-product development process for finding and nurturing new products.

Figure 9–2
Major stages in new-product development.

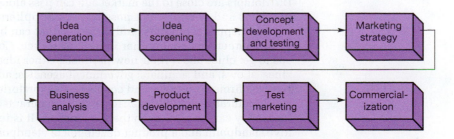

Idea Generation

New-product development starts with idea generation—the systematic search for new-product ideas. A company typically generates hundreds of ideas, even thousands, to find a few good ones. Major sources of new-product ideas include internal sources and external sources such as customers, competitors, and distributors and suppliers.

Awareness of External Environment

All members of the hospitality industry are highly dependent on the external environment. Recession, inflation, economic growth, terrorists, an aging population, and other external factors all directly affect this industry. Ideas for new products should come from a familiarity with what is happening in the external world. As an example, hotel security is of foremost importance, particularly to single women and other segments. A study of 930 hotel guests revealed a high acceptance of certain security measures. Guests younger than 40 said they would pay more for added security, including a first-aid kit in the room.[50]

Internal Sources

Using internal sources, the company can find new ideas through formal R&D. However, in one survey, 750 global CEOs reported that only 14 percent of their innovation ideas came from traditional R&D. Instead, 41 percent came from employees, and 36 percent came from customers.[51] Thus, beyond its internal R&D process, companies can pick the brains of its employees—from executives to scientists, engineers, and manufacturing staff to salespeople. Many companies have developed successful "intrapreneurial" programs that encourage employees to envision and develop new-product ideas.

Increasingly, restaurant chains are creating formal research and development facilities at their corporate headquarters staffed by a chef or team of chefs. For example, T.G.I. Friday's and Whataburger have these centers with kitchens replicating those found in their restaurants. The vice president of brand development for Whataburger states, "When it comes to menu development, having your own facility offers convenience, accessibility, and confidentiality." Quick-service chains such as Whataburger add around five items annually, whereas casual dining restaurants add 15 to 60 items. Usually new items are introduced as special promotions, with about 25 percent making it to the permanent menu.[52]

Within the hotel industry, new-product decisions are made at both the corporate and the property levels. New-product decision makers at the corporate level include mid-level to top management. In some cases, people not employed directly by the company but closely affiliated with it, such as bankers, lawyers, and consultants, become involved in this process.

Decision makers at the property level often include the owner if a chain does not own the hotel. In some cases, someone, such as a president, represents the owner. Others involved in the process are the general manager, department managers, and directors of various areas. Often a corporate vice president from the chain may participate in the process. A danger with this source is that managers and employees may say, "Yes the idea is good" when in fact they believe it is bad.

External Idea Sources

Companies can also obtain good new-product ideas from any of a number of external sources. For example, distributors and suppliers can contribute ideas. Distributors are close to the market and can pass along information about consumer problems and new-product possibilities. Suppliers can tell the company about new concepts, techniques, and materials that can be used to develop new products. Competitors are another important source. Companies watch competitors' ads to get clues about their new products. Other idea sources include trade magazines, shows, and seminars; government agencies; advertising agencies; marketing research firms; university and commercial laboratories; and inventors.

Restaurant and hotel managers visit restaurants when they travel, looking for ideas they can bring back to their businesses. It is important from both a competitive standpoint and a product development standpoint to visit the competition.

Perhaps the most important source of new-product ideas is *customers* themselves. The company can analyze customer questions and complaints to find new products that better solve consumer problems. Or it can invite customers to share suggestions and ideas. For example, Starbucks sponsors My Starbucks Idea, a Web site that invites customers to share, discuss, and vote on new product and service ideas.[53]

Crowdsourcing

Crowdsourcing. An open-innovation new-product idea program.

More broadly, many companies are now developing **crowdsourcing** or open-innovation new-product idea programs. Jeff Howe is credited with developing the term. He defines *crowdsourcing* as "the application of open source principles to fields outside of software."[54] Crowdsourcing throws the innovation doors wide open, inviting broad communities of people—customers, employees, independent scientists and researchers, and even the public at large—into the new-product innovation process. The idea, says one analyst, is that when it comes to helping to improve "your products, services, Web site, or marketing efforts . . . two heads—or 2,000 or 20,000—are better than one."[55]

Hospitality companies embrace the trend of crowdsourcing or "co-creation" and consider it a viable way to engage customers and generate new product ideas and innovative designs in a social-media-driven world. They can use crowdsourcing in many different ways such as building hotel bar menus, voting on logos and room key designs, recommending names for new hotel spaces and concepts, and selecting games and entertainment options for lobbies.[56]

In 2013, Marriott International opened a new 10,000-square-foot Innovation Lab located beneath the company's headquarters in Bethesda, Maryland. The Innovation Lab is a place where employees, customers, and hotel owners brainstorm, design, and refine their ideas for the hotel of the future. Marriott invites frequent guests to its Innovation Lab to provide input on ideas and initiatives and "co-create" their next brand innovation.

Social media has empowered guests to let hotels know about their likes and dislikes in real time. Marriott Hotels and Resorts also turned to digital crowdsourcing and launched a "Travel Brilliantly" campaign aimed at millennials. The company solicited ideas from travelers on everything from design to technology to food and beverage on its Web site (travel-brilliantly.marriott.com). Among the 700 submissions, a panel of judges awarded the grand prize to the idea of a vending machine with healthful options.

Chris Baer, senior director of insight, strategy, and innovation at Marriott International, says, "There is no creation anymore except co-creation. To build any idea in a vacuum is more of a risk than building it with the insight of your guests and your associates."[57]

InterContinental Hotels Group's (IHG) partnered with Chase to develop a Priority Club Rewards Select Visa. This was targeted at members of its IHG's loyalty program. It hired Communispace, a provider of private online communities, to gather 300 current Priority Club Visa cardholders willing to share their opinions on the proposed card benefits and current card features. Based on the comments of this group, benefits were expanded to provide points on products other than IHG hotels. 4Food, a restaurant in New York, is using crowdsourcing to develop menu items. The restaurant serves hamburgers with a hole in the middle that is filled with the customer's choice of 40 different vegetarian dishes, including humus, salsa, and vegetarian chili. Customers can develop their own combination of these ingredients to create unique burgers and give them a name. If 4Food can get others to order "its" hamburger, it will get 20 cents for each burger sold. 4Food is using crowdsourcing to develop menu items and promote its restaurant.[58]

Marriott International has opened a 10,000-square-foot Innovation Lab, located beneath the company's headquarters, to promote innovation and collaboration. Architects, designers, employees, and customers are invited to explore new concepts and product testing. Upon entry to the Innovation Lab, guests will traverse a gallery filled with projected images and presentations on walls, setting the scene for Marriott's newest designs. Courtesy of Marriott International, Inc.

REO Eats in Lansing, Michigan, used crowdsourcing to gain ideas for its concepts. So, what does this mean? It means REO wants customers' input on everything, including its logo, interior design, exterior design of the building, menu ideas and pricing, and promotional strategy. It also used crowdsourcing to find investors and employees.[59] Crowdsourcing can produce a flood of innovative ideas. In fact, opening the floodgates to anyone and everyone can overwhelm the company with ideas—some good and some bad. "Even a small crowdsourcing event can generate a few hundred ideas. If I told you next year you're going to get 20,000 ideas from your customers, how would you process that?"[60]

Truly innovative companies don't rely only on one source or another for new-product ideas. Instead, according to one expert, they create "extensive networks for capturing inspiration from every possible source, from employees at every walk of the company to customers to other innovators and myriad points beyond."[61]

Idea Screening

The purpose of idea generation is to create a large number of ideas. The purpose of screening is to spot good ideas and drop poor ones as quickly as possible. Product development costs rise greatly in later stages, so the company wants to proceed only with ideas that will turn into profitable products. Marriott's healthy vending machine mentioned earlier is an example. Most companies require their executives to write up new-product ideas on a standard form that can be reviewed by a new-product committee. The executives describe the product, the target market, and the competition. They make some rough estimates of market size, product price, development time and costs, manufacturing costs, and rate of return. They also answer the following questions: Is this idea good for our particular company? Does it mesh well with the company's objectives and strategies? Do we have the people, skills, equipment, and resources to make it succeed? Many companies have well-designed systems for rating and screening new-product ideas.

The idea or concept screening stage is the appropriate time to review carefully the question of product line compatibility. A common error in new-product development is to introduce products that are incompatible with the company. The following describes major compatibility issues. How will the product assist us to:

- Fulfill our mission?
- Meet corporate objectives?
- Meet property objectives?
- Protect and promote our core business?
- Protect and please our key customers?
- Better use existing resources?
- Support and enhance existing product lines?

Concept Development and Testing

Product idea. Envisioning a possible product that company managers might offer to the market.

Product concept. A detailed version of a product idea stated in meaningful consumer terms.

Product image. The way that consumers picture an actual or potential product.

Surviving ideas must now be developed into product concepts. It is important to distinguish between a product idea, a product concept, and a product image. A **product idea** envisions a possible product that company managers might offer to the market. A **product concept** is a detailed version of the idea stated in meaningful consumer terms. A **product image** is the way that consumers picture an actual or potential product.

Major restaurant chains cannot afford to place an untested menu in all their restaurants. Burger King, like others, uses test market restaurants in selected cities. The Piedmont area of North Carolina was used as a test market for American fries. Apparently, the product performed poorly because it disappeared from the menus. Hotels commonly introduce new-product ideas to selected floors and to selected properties. Guests are sometimes invited to an afternoon product screening.

Concept Development

In the late 1970s, Marriott recognized that the urban market for its current hotel products was becoming saturated. It needed a hotel concept that would work in secondary sites and suburban locations. Marriott decided to focus its assets on the company's core business, lodging, through the development of a new product.

This was a product idea. Customers, however, do not buy a product idea; they buy a product. The marketer's task is to develop this idea into alternative product concepts, determine how attractive each is to customers, and choose the best one.

The concept for the new product was called Courtyard by Marriott. Marriott selected persons from different areas of the company to manage the development of this new product. The company conducted extensive competitor and market analysis and, as a result of this research, developed the following conceptual framework for the project:[62]

1. It would be tightly focused for the transient market.

2. It would house fewer than 150 rooms.

3. It would project a residential image. (Through its research Marriott identified a major segment of hotel users who did not like hotels. These consumers preferred homelike settings.)

4. It would not have significant cannibalization of Marriott's other hotels.

5. It would have a limited-menu restaurant.

6. Public and meeting space would be limited.

7. It would be a standardized product with five to eight in a region.

8. The name Marriott would be attached for recognition and a halo effect. ("Halo" or "umbrella effect" refers to the carryover of a corporate or brand name to other products. The name Disney has a halo effect for many products, from movies to a cruise ship.)

Concept Testing

Concept testing occurs within a group of target consumers. New-product concepts may be presented through word or picture descriptions. Marriott tested its concept for the Courtyard Motel using a statistical technique called *conjoint analysis*. This involved showing potential target guests different motel configurations and having them rank the configurations from the most to the least desirable. The rankings were statistically analyzed to determine the optimal motel configuration.[63]

In most cases, however, simpler consumer attitude surveys are used. Suppose that 10 percent of the consumers said they "definitely" would buy and another 5 percent said "probably." The company would project these figures to the population size of this target group to estimate sales volume. But the estimate would be uncertain because people do not always carry out their stated intentions.

Unfortunately, the Marriott example is far too rare within the hospitality industry. The corporate headquarters of major hotel, resort, and restaurant chains do engage in professional concept testing, but smaller chains and individual properties often pass over this critical stage. They often move directly from product idea to full implementation.

In some cases, intuition or luck proves to be correct, and the new product is a winner, thus placing the company well ahead of competition. However, the history of the hospitality industry has proved that in many cases the idea needed concept testing because the product proved to be a disastrous mistake. In the case of a tactical product decision, such as a hotel room amenity or a new room service beverage, there may be relatively little damage from an incorrect new-product decision. This is not true of new-product decisions involving heavy capital expenditures, such as a new ship for a cruise line or a new destination resort. These decisions involve millions of dollars and have sometimes proved so disastrous that hospitality companies have been forced into bankruptcy. The expenditure of a few thousand dollars and a few extra months for concept testing might prove invaluable in the long run.

Marketing Strategy

The next step is marketing strategy development: designing an initial marketing strategy for introducing the product into the market. The marketing strategy statement consists of three parts. The first part describes the target market, the planned product positioning, and the sales, market share, and profit goals for the first few years. The target markets for Courtyard by Marriott were business travelers who wanted moderately priced, high-quality rooms and pleasure travelers who wanted a safe, comfortable room.

The second part of the marketing strategy statement outlines the product's planned price, distribution, and marketing budget for the first year. Statistical software enabled Marriott to build sophisticated models. These models provided information on pricing and expected market share based on these prices. The segmentation information gave Marriott the information it needed for marketing the hotels.

The third part of the marketing strategy statement describes the planned long-run sales, profit goals, and marketing mix strategy.

Business Analysis

Once management decides on the product concept and marketing strategy, it can evaluate the business attractiveness of the proposal. Business analysis involves a review of the sales, costs, and profit projections to determine whether they satisfy the company's objectives. If they do, the product can move to the product development stage.

Many communities view arenas and conference centers as essential products to serve the needs of the local populace and to attract out-of-town visitors. Unfortunately, many have suffered from a lack of sound business analysis. Political and emotional pressures often prevail in the planning stage. "This town needs a baseball team and that means we must have a new multimillion-dollar arena." Sentiments such as these often prevail. In the movie *Field of Dreams*, it was "If you build it, they will come." Sadly this has proven to be untrue for many arenas and convention centers.

The Generals from Greensboro, North Carolina, play in the minor-league East Coast Hockey League. To keep the team from folding, thus further affecting the coliseum's revenue, the City of Greensboro took over the day-to-day operations of the Generals. The team's coach became a city employee. The coliseum's authority assumed responsibility for marketing ticket sales, resulting in a loss of about $300,000 from operating the team.[64] Sports arenas brand their product with the name of corporate sponsors, such as Coors Field in Denver. This does not guarantee a long life for the brand because sponsoring companies have declared bankruptcy, including some involved in great corporate scandals.

Visitor products supported by tax money such as coliseums, convention centers, museums, and zoos should be developed only after careful and unbiased business analysis, including a professional marketing plan.

Product Development

If the product concept passes the business test, it moves into product development and into a prototype. Up to now it existed only as a word description, a drawing, or mockup. The company develops one or more physical versions of the product concept. Restaurants can develop prototypes of menu items and run them as specials; hotels build guest room prototypes. It hopes to find a prototype that meets the following criteria:

1. Consumers perceive it as having the key features described in the product concept statement.

2. It performs safely under normal use.

3. It can be produced for the budgeted costs.

Developing a successful prototype can take days, weeks, months, or even years. Marriott built a Courtyard room prototype with portable walls. It developed three room types: a standard, a short, and a narrow configuration. The consumers liked the overall concept. They rejected the narrow version but not the short version, which Marriott estimated would result in substantial cost savings.

One problem with developing a prototype is that the prototype is often limited to the core product. Many of the intangible aspects of the product, such as the performance of the employees, cannot be included.

Test Marketing

If the product passes functional and consumer tests, the next step is market testing in which the product and marketing program are introduced into realistic market settings.

Market testing allows the marketer to gain experience in marketing the product, to find potential problems, and to learn where more information is needed before the company goes to the great expense of full introduction. Market testing evaluates the product and the entire marketing program in real market situations. The product and its positioning strategy, advertising, distribution, pricing, branding, packaging, and budget levels are evaluated during market testing. Market testing results can be used to make better sales and profit forecasts.

The amount of market testing needed varies with each new product. Market testing costs can be enormous, and market testing takes time, during which competitors may gain an advantage. When the costs of developing and introducing the product are low or when management is already confident that the new product will succeed, the company may do little or no market testing. Minor modifications of current products or copies of successful competitor products might not need testing.

The costs of market tests are high but are often small compared with the costs of making a major mistake. When the risks are high, or when management is not sure of the product or its marketing program, a company may do a lot of test marketing. For instance, KFC conducted more than three years of product and market testing before rolling out its major new Kentucky Grilled Chicken product. The fast-food chain built its legacy on serving crispy, seasoned fried chicken but hopes that the new product will lure back health-conscious consumers who dropped fried chicken from their diets. "This is transformational for our brand," says KFC's chief food innovation officer. Given the importance of the decision, "You might say, 'what took you so long,'" says the chain's president. "I've asked that question a couple of times myself. The answer is we had to get it right."[65]

Commercialization

Market testing gives management the information it needs to make a final decision about whether to launch a new product. If the company goes ahead with commercialization, it will face high costs. It may have to spend several million dollars for advertising and sales promotion alone in the first year. For example, McDonald's spent $100 million on an advertising blitz to introduce its McCafe coffee in the United States. The media spend included TV, print, radio, outdoor, the Internet, events, public relations, and sampling.[66]

When?

The first decision is whether it is the right time to introduce the new product. In Marriott's case the test market hotel experienced occupancy of 90 percent.

Where?

The company must decide whether to launch the new product in a single location, a region, several regions, the national market, or the international market. Few companies have the confidence, capital, and capacity to launch new products into full national distribution. Instead, they develop a planned market rollout over time. Small companies in particular tend to select an attractive city and put on a blitz campaign to enter the market. They may enter other cities one at a time. Large companies may decide to introduce their product into one region and then move to the next. Marriott decided to introduce the Courtyard in regional markets.

To Whom?

Within the rollout markets, the company must target its promotion to the best prospect groups. Management should have determined profiles of prime prospects during earlier market testing. It must now fine-tune its market identification, looking for early adopters, heavy users, and opinion leaders.

How?

The company must develop an action plan for introducing the new product into the selected markets and spend the marketing budget on the marketing mix.

■■■ Product Development Through Acquisition

Large companies such as McDonald's sometimes buy a small restaurant chain such as Chipotle rather than develop their own new concepts. They are able to watch the fledgling chain grow. They sit back and observe its customer base, volume of sales per unit, and how easy or difficult it is to open new stores. When they are convinced that the new chain looks like a winner and makes a good strategic fit with their organization, the large company simply buys the chain. This is what Brinker International did when it purchased Romano's Macaroni Grill and PepsiCo purchased California Pizza Kitchen. This method of product development reduces the risk considerably for large companies that have the assets to purchase and then develop the chain. This acquisition strategy has a new class of restaurant entrepreneurs, those who try to develop a chain with the specific purpose of selling it to a large chain.

Another technique is to purchase distressed chains. The mismanagement of a chain and resulting poor performance can drive the market value of the chain down. These chains become attractive targets for companies that believe they can turn them around.

■■■ Product Life-Cycle Strategies

After launching a new product, management wants the product to enjoy a long and lucrative life. Although the product is not expected to sell forever, managers want to earn enough profit to compensate for the effort and risk. To maximize profits, a product's marketing strategy is normally reformulated several times. Strategy changes are often the result of changing market and environmental conditions as the product moves through the product life cycle (PLC).

The PLC (Figure 9–3) is marked by five distinct stages:

1. **Product development** begins when the company finds and develops a new-product idea. During product development, sales are zero and the company's investment costs add up.

2. **Introduction** is a period of slow sales growth as the product is being introduced into the market. Profits are nonexistent at this stage because of the heavy expenses of product introduction.

3. **Growth** is a period of rapid market acceptance and increasing profits.

4. **Maturity** is a period of slowdown in sales growth because the product has achieved acceptance by most of its potential buyers. Although sales are still high, profits level off or decline because of increased marketing outlays to defend the product against competition.

5. **Decline** is the period when sales fall off quickly and profits drop.

Product development. Developing the product concept into a physical product to ensure that the product idea can be turned into a workable product.

Introduction. The product life-cycle stage when a new product is first distributed and made available for purchase.

Growth. The product life-cycle stage when a new product's sales start climbing quickly.

Maturity. The stage in a product life cycle when sales growth slows or levels off.

Decline. The period when sales fall off quickly and profits drop.

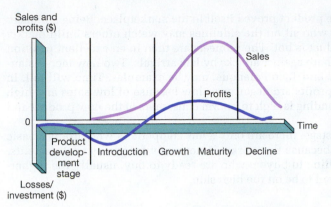

Sales and profits ($)

0

Time

Sales

Profits

Product development stage

Introduction Growth Maturity Decline

Losses/ investment ($)

Figure 9–3
Sales and profits over the product's line from inception to demise.

The PLC concept can describe a product class (fast-food restaurants), a product form (fast-food hamburgers), or a brand (Popeyes). The PLC applies differently in each case. Product classes have the longest life cycles. The sales of many product classes stay in the mature stage for a long time. Product forms, in contrast, tend to have the standard PLC shape. Product forms such as the drive-in restaurant and roadside tourist court pass through a regular history of introduction, rapid growth, maturity, and decline. A specific brand's life cycle can change quickly because of changing competitive attacks and responses.

The PLC concept is a useful framework for describing how products and markets work. But using the PLC concept for forecasting product performance or for developing marketing strategies presents some practical problems. For example, managers may have trouble identifying a product's current life-cycle stage, determining when it has moved into the next stage, and enumerating the factors that affect how it will move through the stages. In practice, it is very hard to forecast the sales level at each PLC stage, the length of each stage, and the shape of the PLC curve.

Most marketing texts feature the PLC, yet very few managers claim that they use it in the development of marketing strategy. There are two explanations for this. First, managers make strategic decisions based on the characteristics of each stage of the PLC, without using the PLC itself as a tool. The second reason is that accurate prediction of the shape of the PLC is impossible. Many products do not follow the typical curve.

The PLC is not a predictive tool to determine the length of a product's useful life. It is, instead, a means of conceptualizing the effect of the market, the environment, and competition and understanding how that product may react to various stimuli.[67] Recognizing that products have life cycles with identifiable stages can provide insights into how to manage the cycle to extend its life. Unmanaged products travel along the life cycle with little resistance. Environmental and competitive changes move a product through its life cycle, and companies must react to keep their products salable. McDonald's has been able to extend by modifying the product concept. The McDonald's of today is a different concept than the McDonald's of the 1960s. The menu and the store design are different. McDonald's has evolved from stands with no seating into fast-food restaurants with attractive indoor seating areas and playgrounds for children. The company also changed its location strategy. In addition to its traditional suburban locations, McDonald's developed international, urban, and institutional locations such as hospitals and colleges. Often, when a product begins to peak in sales, management assumes that it has started its decline. The downturn could be attributable to many factors: ineffective marketing support, competition, economic conditions, or lack of market development. If managers wearing "PLC blinders" do not investigate these reasons, they risk seeing the PLCs as the cause of the slowdown.[68]

Using the PLC concept to develop marketing strategy can be difficult. Strategy is both a cause and a result of the product's life cycle. The product's current PLC position suggests the best marketing strategies, and the resulting marketing strategies affect product performance in later life-cycle stages. Yet when used carefully, the PLC concept can help in developing good marketing strategies for different stages of the PLC.

We looked at the product development stage of the PLC earlier. We now examine strategies for each of the other life-cycle stages.

Introduction Stage

The introduction stage starts when the new product is first made available for purchase. Introduction takes time, and sales growth is apt to be slow. Some products may linger in the introduction stage for many years before they enter a stage of rapid growth; suite hotels followed this pattern. Many companies watch others go into the market as pioneers. When suite hotels were introduced, many players sat on the sidelines until the product proved itself in the marketplace. Being a pioneer involves risk, but those who sit on the sidelines may watch others build market share quickly if the product is hot. The pioneers are then in an excellent position to defend their market share against attacks by late arrivals. Two new taco restaurant concepts, Taco Tote and Taco Palenque, may be examples. Time will tell. In the introductory stage, profits are negative or low because of low sales and high expenses. Promotion spending is high to inform consumers of the new product and encourage them to try it.

In the introductory stage, there are only a few competitors who produce basic versions of the product because the market is not ready for product refinements. Companies focus on selling to buyers who are ready to buy, usually the higher-income groups. Prices tend to be on the high side.

Growth Stage

If the new product satisfies the market, it enters the growth stage and sales start climbing quickly. The early adopters continue to buy, and later buyers start following their lead, especially if they hear favorable word of mouth. Competitors enter the market, attracted by the opportunity for profit. They introduce new product features, which expand the market.

Prices remain the same or fall only slightly. Companies keep their promotion spending at the same or at a slightly higher level to meet competition and continue educating the market. Profits increase during this growth stage, as costs are spread over a large volume and more efficient systems are developed.

Companies use several strategies to sustain rapid market growth as long as possible:

1. Product quality is improved and new product features and models are introduced.
2. New market segments are entered.
3. Advertising is shifted from building product awareness to building product conviction and purchase.
4. Prices are lowered to attract more buyers.

In the growth stage, a company faces a trade-off between high market share and high current profit. By investing heavily in product improvement and promotion, it can capture and dominate a position. But it sacrifices maximum current profit in the hope of making it up in the next stage.

Maturity Stage

At some point a product's sales growth slows down, and the product enters the maturity stage. This stage normally lasts longer than the previous two stages, and it poses strong challenges to marketing management. Most producers are in the maturity stage of the life cycle, and therefore, most marketing management deals with mature products.

The slowdown in sales growth causes supply to exceed demand. This overcapacity leads to greater competition. Competitors begin lowering prices, and they increase their advertising and sales promotion. "Burger wars" and "pizza wars" are the result of these products being in the mature stage. Real sales growth is about the same as population growth. The only way to increase sales significantly is to steal customers from the competition. Price battles and heavy advertising are often the means to do this. Both result in a drop in profits. Weaker competitors start dropping out. The industry eventually contains only well-established competitors in the main market segments, with smaller competitors pursuing the niche markets.

Applebee's restaurant chain has experienced product maturity. Things were not good when the founder, T. J. Palmer, said, "It doesn't have anything that would make me come back." In 2007, Applebee's found itself with falling profits, a lagging stock, and restless investors. According to the *Wall Street Journal*, "Applebee's didn't change quickly enough while a raft of competitors copied it. Applebee's stayed too long with a formula that had worked for it in the past."[69]

While Applebee's failed to change, U.S. customers were more exposed to ethnic cuisine and cooking shows. They also expressed concern about overprocessed foods and disliked the decor of high school sports paraphernalia and dark wood. In response, Applebee's made several product changes such as a high-low price strategy of offering a $14.95 New York strip steak on the front of the menu and a $5.99 soup and salad on the back. These did not stop the sales slide. In November 2007, Applebee's was bought by IHOP. The combination of IHOP and Applebee's resulted in the formation of DineEquity.

DineEquity was able to increase same store sales in 2010 for the first time since 2005, albeit the increase was only about 0.3 percent. DineEquity created new promotions such as "Sizzling Entrees," "Great Tasting Items Under 550 Calories," "2 for $20" (a shared appetizer and two entrees), and an advertising promotion called "There's No Place Like the Neighborhood." DineEquity through menu development, operating efficiencies, and effective advertising was able to create positive momentum. The Applebee's case shows how hard it is to create momentum in a mature product. It took DineEquity three years to change the direction of Applebee's. DineEquity's battle is not over; each year in a mature product is a battle to keep the product relevant and gain or maintain market share.[70]

In addition to old decor and an old menu, some blamed the lack of destination items. These are specialty items that diners seek out and are willing to go out of their way to purchase.

Market Modification

At this point, the aggressive product manager tries to increase consumption of the product. The manager looks for new users and market segments and ways to increase use among present customers. McDonald's added breakfast, salads, desserts, and chicken sandwiches in its efforts to attract new users and increase use. Product managers may also reposition the brand to appeal to a larger or faster-growing segment. When anti-drunk-driving campaigns reduced alcoholic beverage consumption, Bennigan's emphasized its food.

Product Modification

The product manager can also change product characteristics, product quality, features, or style to attract new users and stimulate more usage. A strategy of quality improvement aims at increasing the performance of the product—its durability, reliability, speed, or taste. This strategy is effective when quality can be improved, when buyers believe the claim of improved quality, and when enough buyers want higher quality.

Wendy's has remodeled its restaurants to give them a modern and fact-casual look. The exterior features a contemporary design with large windows while the interior showcases open, bright dining areas, with multiple seating options. The restaurant has new menu items and a new customer ordering process, digital menu boards, and a high-definition television. Wendy's hopes to rejuvenate its image as a higher-end fast-food chain with the new design and changes.[71]

Responding to declining same-store sales, McDonald's pilot tested and expanded a custom-built burger program, which lets customers skip the counter and head to touch-screen tablet kiosks where they can customize their bun, cheese, toppings, and sauces, and pay for the orders. Dine-in customers can choose from 22 different ingredients, including caramelized onions, grilled mushrooms, red onions, pepper jack cheese, apple-wood smoked bacon, and sliced jalapenos.[72]

Wendy's has been rebranded to rejuvenate its image as a higher-end fast-food chain, with a sleek new look and new menu items such as premium Dave's Hot 'N Juicy burger. Courtesy of Philip Kotler.

Marketing Mix Modification

The product manager can also try to improve sales by changing one or more marketing mix elements. Prices can be cut to attract new users and competitors' customers. A better advertising campaign can be developed. The company can also offer new or improved services to buyers.

Instead of just making cosmetic changes, hospitality companies may choose to *rebrand* the whole concept, with new marketing strategies. In 2005, Caesars Entertainment purchased the Imperial Palace, a 33-year run-down property offering lowest rates on the Strip, and changed the name to the Quad after limited renovation in 2012. Two years later, Caesars Entertainment invested $223 million toward revamping the 2,256-room Quad Resort & Casino, rebranded it as the Linq Hotel & Casino, and connected it with its newly developed outdoor dining, nightlife, and entertainment district. The resort now provides a social and connected environment and takes advantage of restaurant and shops and the High Roller (550-foot-tall observation wheel). The Linq Hotel offers new amenities such as spa, pool deck, a lobby bar for social hub to attract younger crowd, and automated check-in to reduce wait times.[73]

Decline Stage

Sales of most product forms and brands eventually decline. The decline may be slow or rapid, as in the case of Minnie Pearl Chicken. Sales may plunge to zero, or they may drop to a low level and continue there for many years.

Sales decline for many reasons, such as technological advances, shifts in consumer tastes, and increased competition. Carrying a weak product can be very costly to the firm and not just in terms of reduced profit but also in terms of hidden costs such as wasted management and sales force time and tarnished brand image in the future.

Companies must pay close attention to their aging products. Regularly reviewing sales, market share, costs, and profit trends for each of its products will help identify products in the decline stage.

Management has to decide whether to maintain, harvest, or drop weak products. Management may decide to harvest the product, which means reducing various costs. Successful harvesting may increase a company's profits in the short run. Management may also decide to drop the product.

Destination and hospitality marketers must be aware of the PLC as it affects retailers. Hotels are often located near centers of shopping. In fact, the giant mall in Edmonton, Alberta, contains a hotel. Restaurants have found malls to be excellent locations, but the PLC is changing.

Shopping malls are in the decline stage in many parts of the United States.[74] Crime, teenagers hanging around, huge parking lots, confusing layouts, fear of terrorism, and expensive rents are among the reasons for this decline. Stores such as JC Penney, Sears, and the May Company served as anchors in malls but are now moving to free-standing locations. This decline will make malls less attractive locations for restaurants.

Shopping remains one of the primary activities of travelers, particularly pleasure travelers. Additionally, thousands, if not millions, of travelers throughout the world plan overnight trips primarily for shopping. This includes international travelers. The motor coach industry in many nations derives a heavy percentage of income from shopping tours.

Table 9–2 summarizes the key characteristics of each stage of the PLC. The table also lists the marketing objectives and strategies for each stage.

Product Deletion

As we have seen, the PLC illustrates that most products will become obsolete and have to be replaced. Thus, understanding the product deletion process is just as important as understanding product development. A successful restaurant

TABLE 9–2
Summary of Product Life-Cycle Characteristics, Objectives, and Strategies

	Introduction	Growth	Maturity	Decline
Characteristics				
Sales	Low sales	Rapidly rising sales	Peak sales	Declining sales
Costs	High cost per customer	Average cost per customer	Low cost per customer	Low cost per customer
Profits	Negative	Rising profits	High profits	Declining profits
Customers	Innovators	Early adopters	Mainstream adopters	Lagging adopters
Competitors	Few	Growing number	Stable number beginning to decline	Declining number
Marketing objectives	Create product engagement and trial	Maximize market share	Maximize profit while defending market share	Reduce expenditure and milk the brand
Strategies				
Product	Offer a basic product	Offer product extensions, service, and warranty	Diversify brand and models	Phase out weak items
Price	Use cost-plus	Price to penetrate market	Price to match or beat competitors	Cut price
Distribution	Build selective distribution	Build intensive distribution	Build more intensive distribution	Go selective: phase out unprofitable outlets
Advertising	Build product awareness among early adopters and dealers	Build engagement and interest in the mass market	Stress brand differences and benefits	Reduce to level needed to retain hard-core loyals
Sales Promotion	Use heavy sales promotion to entice trial	Reduce to take advantage of heavy consumer demand	Increase to encourage brand switching	Reduce to minimal level

Source: Adapted from Philip Kotler and Kevin Lane Keller, *Marketing Management*, 14th ed. (Upper Saddle River, NJ: Prentice Hall, 2012), p. 317. © 2012. Printed and Electronica Reproduced by permission of Pearson Education, Inc., Upper Saddle River, New Jersey.

Phase-out. The ideal method of removing an unpopular or unprofitable product; it enables a product to be removed in an orderly fashion.

Run-out. Removing a product after existing stock has been depleted; used when sales for an item are low and costs exceed revenues, such as the case of a restaurant serving a crabmeat cocktail with sales of only one or two items per week.

Drop. The action taken toward a product that may cause harm or customer dissatisfaction.

in Houston served a chicken breast topped with sautéed mushrooms. This dish enjoyed success for more than 10 years. When sales started to drop and the decline continued, it appeared that the product was no longer in favor with the restaurant's customers. Customers were asked about the dish, and they responded that it was too greasy. When the sautéed mushrooms were poured over the chicken breast, the butter collected at the bottom of the plate. When the product was first introduced, butter sauces were in vogue, but preferences changed. The restaurant removed the sautéed mushrooms and garnished the chicken with fresh sliced mushrooms. If management of the Strawberry Patch had been wearing life-cycle blinders, it would have deleted the product.

The deletion analysis is a systematic review of a product's projected sales and estimated costs associated with those sales. If a product no longer appears to be profitable, the analysis looks at possible ways to make modifications and return it to profitability. If the analysis indicates that the product should be deleted, there are three choices: phase-out, run-out, or drop it immediately.[75]

Phase-out is the ideal method; it enables a product to be removed in an orderly fashion. For example, a menu item would be replaced on the next revision of the menu. A **run-out** would be used when sales for an item are low and costs exceed revenues, such as the case of a restaurant serving a crabmeat cocktail with sales of only one or two items per week. If the restaurant decides to delete the product, it may choose to deplete its existing stock of crabmeat rather than reorder. The last option is an immediate **drop**. This option is usually chosen when the product may cause harm or complaints; it is best to drop the item rather than continuing to create unhappy customers.

The issue of dropping a product is particularly complex in the case of the properties of a hotel or restaurant chain. Management is usually quite aware of individual properties that should be dropped from the chain affiliation due to deterioration of the property or the neighborhood in which the property is located.

In many cases, it is impossible or impractical to close the property quickly or drop it from chain affiliation:

- Contracts may prohibit a quick close.

- The property may have sentimental attachments to the community and to management.

- Closure might have a negative effect on the community.

- A buyer may not be readily available.

- Special relationships may exist between the franchisee and the franchisor.

Despite difficulties in closing hotels or disassociating properties from a chain, eventually the inevitable must occur. As in the earlier example of menu items, it is best to make this difficult decision as quickly as possible.

International Product and Service Marketing

International product and services marketers face special challenges. First, they must figure out what products and services to introduce and in which countries. Then, they must decide how much to standardize or adapt their products and services for world markets.

On the one hand, companies would like to standardize their offerings. Standardization helps a company develop a consistent worldwide image. It also lowers the product design and marketing costs of offering a large variety of products. On the other hand, markets and consumers around the world differ widely. Companies must usually respond to these differences by adapting their product offerings. For example, by carefully adapting its menu and operations to local tastes and eating styles, YUM! Brands—parent company of quintessential fast-food restaurants KFC, Pizza Hut, and Taco Bell—has become the largest restaurant company in mainland China. Consider KFC.[76]

A typical Kentucky Fried Chicken meal in the United States features original, extra crispy, and a Pepsi. What do you get at a KFC in China? Of course, you can get some good old Kentucky fried, but more popular items include chicken with Sichuan spicy sauce and rice, egg soup, or a "dragon twister" (KFC's version of a traditional Beijing duck wrap), all washed down with some soybean milk. Also on the menu: egg tarts, fried dough sticks, wraps with local sauces, fish and shrimp burgers on fresh buns, and congee, a popular rice porridge that is KFC's number one seller at breakfast. The Chinese menu also offers a large selection—some 50 items compared with 29 in the United States—meant to appeal to the Chinese style of eating, in which groups of people share several dishes. And although KFC outlets in the United States are designed primarily for takeout and eating at home, outlets in China are about twice the size of their U.S. counterparts, providing more space for eat-in diners, who like to linger with friends and family. Through such adaptation, KFC and YUM!'s other brands in China have positioned themselves not as a foreign presence but as a part of the local community. As a result, YUM! Brands has achieved finger lickin' good success in China. Its 4,000 KFC restaurants in more than 800 cities in China earned more revenue than all 19,000 of its restaurants in the United States combined, including KFC, Pizza Hut, and Taco Bell.

Many hotel chains—Marriott, Starwood, and IHG—have also globalized. The trend toward international growth of hospitality companies will continue. Today, hospitality companies are no longer simply following their manufacturing counterparts. Instead, they are taking the lead in international expansion.

Global product adaptation: By adapting to local tastes and eating styles, KFC has achieved finger-lickin' good success in China. Courtesy of Chen Chao/ Dorling Kindersley, Ltd.

■■■ CHAPTER REVIEW

I. What Is a Product? A product is anything that can be offered to a market for attention, acquisition, use, or consumption that might satisfy a want or need. It includes physical objects, service, places, organizations, and ideas.

II. Product Levels

A. Core product. It answers the question of what the buyer is really buying. Every product is a package of problem-solving services.

B. Facilitating products. These are services or goods that must be present for the guest to use the core product.

C. Supporting products. These are extra products offered to add value to the core product and to help differentiate it from the competition.

D. Augmented products. These include accessibility (geographic location and hours of operation), atmosphere (visual, aural, olfactory, and tactile dimensions), customer interaction with the service organization (joining, consumption, and detachment), customer participation, and customers' interactions with one another.

  1. Accessibility. This refers to how accessible the product is in terms of location and hours of operation.

  2. Atmosphere. Atmosphere is a critical element in services. It is appreciated through the senses. Sensory terms provide descriptions for the atmosphere as a particular set of surroundings. The main sensory channels for atmosphere are sight, sound, scent, and touch.

  3. Customer interactions with the service system. Managers must think about how the customers use the product in the three phases of involvement: joining, consumption, and detachment.

  4. Customer interactions with other customers. Customers become part of the product you are offering.

  5. Coproduction. Involving the guest in service delivery can increase capacity, improve customer satisfaction, and reduce costs.

III. Branding Strategy. Brand is a name, term, sign, symbol, design, or a combination of these elements that is intended to identify the goods or services of a seller and differentiate them from those of competitors.

A. Building strong brands. Brands are powerful assets that must be carefully developed and managed. In this section, we examine the key strategies for building and managing brands (see Table 9–1).

B. Brand equity. It is the added value endowed on products and services. It may be reflected in the way consumers think, feel, and act with respect to the brand, as well as in the prices, market share, and profitability the brand commands for the firm.

C. Brand positioning. Companies can position brands at any of three levels. At the lowest level, they can position the brand on product attributes. A brand can be better positioned by associating its name with a desirable benefit. The strongest brands go beyond attribute or benefit positioning. They are positioned on strong beliefs and values.

D. Brand name selection. A good name can add greatly to a product's success. However, finding the best brand name is a difficult task. It begins with a careful review of the product and its benefits, the target market, and proposed marketing strategies.

E. Leveraging brands. Companies can leverage an existing brand by employing co-branding and ingredient branding.

F. Brand portfolios. The brand portfolio is the set of all brands and brand-particular category or market segment. Marketers often need multiple brands in order to pursue these multiple segments.

G. Managing brands. Companies must manage their brands carefully. First, the brand's positioning must be continuously communicated to consumers. The company should carry on internal brand building to help employees understand and be enthusiastic about the brand promise. Finally, companies need to periodically audit their brands' strengths and weaknesses.

IV. New-Product Development

A. New-product development process

  1. Idea generation. Ideas are gained from internal sources, customers, competitors, distributors, and suppliers.

  2. Idea screening. The purpose of screening is to spot good ideas and drop poor ones as soon as possible.

  3. Concept development and testing. Surviving ideas must now be developed into product concepts. These concepts are tested with target customers.

  4. Marketing strategy development. There are three parts to the marketing strategy statement. The first part describes the target market, the planned product positioning, and the sales, market share, and profit goals for the first two years. The second part outlines the product's planned price, distribution, and marketing budget for the first year. The third part describes the planned long-run sales, profit, and the market mix strategy over time.

  5. Business analysis. Business analysis involves a review of the sales, costs, and profit projections to determine whether they satisfy the company's objectives.

  6. Product development. Product development turns the concept into a prototype of the product.

  7. Market testing. Market testing is the stage in which the product and marketing program are introduced into more realistic market settings.

  8. Commercialization. The product is brought into the marketplace.

V. Product Development Through Acquisition. Large companies such as McDonald's sometimes buy a small restaurant chain such as Chipotle rather than develop their own new concepts. Another technique is to purchase distressed chains. The mismanagement of a chain and resulting poor performance can drive the market value of the chain down. These chains become attractive targets for companies that believe they can turn them around.

VI. Product Life-Cycle Stages
   A. Product development. It begins when the company finds and develops a new-product idea.

   B. Introduction. It is a period of slow sales growth as the product is being introduced into the market. Profits are nonexistent at this stage.
   C. Growth. It is a period of rapid market acceptance and increasing profits.
   D. Maturity. It is a period of slowdown in sales growth because the product has achieved acceptance by most of its potential buyers.
   E. Decline. It is the period when sales fall off quickly and profits drop.

■■■ DISCUSSION QUESTIONS

1. Given all the changes in the branding strategy for Las Vegas over the years, has the Vegas brand had a consistent meaning to consumers? Is this a benefit or a detriment to the city as it moves forward?

2. Use a product from the hospitality or travel industry to explain the following terms (provide an example in your explanation): (a) facilitating product, (b) supporting product, and (c) augmented product.

3. ARAMARK, a large-contract food-service company, is introducing branded food as part of its campus feeding. Why would ARAMARK pay a royalty to Burger King when it is capable of making its own hamburgers very efficiently?

4. As a hotel or restaurant manager, how would you gain new-product ideas?

5. Less than a third of new-product ideas come from the customer. Does this percentage conflict with the

marketing concept's philosophy of "find a need and fill it"? Why or why not?

6. If you were the director of new-product development for a national fast-food chain, what factors would you consider in choosing cities for test marketing a new sandwich? Would the place where you live be a good test market? Why or why not?

7. Give examples of co-branding and ingredient branding practices in hotel and restaurant industry. What are the advantages and disadvantages of these practices?

8. Explain why many people are willing to pay more for branded products than for unbranded products. What does this tell you about the value of branding?

9. Apply the concept of the product life cycle to a hotel. How does a company keep its products from going into the decline stage?

■■■ EXPERIENTIAL EXERCISES

Do one of the following:

1. Visit a hospitality or travel company. Look around at the physical facilities and the atmosphere of the company. Things you should look at include the exterior appearance, cleanliness, employees, atmosphere, and signage. Does the physical atmosphere support the image of the company or communicate to prospective customers and existing customers? Explain your answer.

2. Visit two locations of the same brand, such as two restaurants or two hotels. Does each location portray the same brand image? Explain your answer. If the images are inconsistent, how could this affect prospective customers?

3. Visit http://www.brandme.jobs/en/. Explain how you would apply branding principles to brand yourself for job applications.

■■■ INTERNET EXERCISE

Go to the Internet site of a hospitality or travel company. Think about the company's target market and the brand image it should portray. Does the company's Web site reinforce this brand image? Why or why not? What suggestions do you have for enhancing the image that the site portrays?

◼◼◼ REFERENCES

1 Damon Hodge, "Tourism Chief Aims to Continue Vegas' Hot Streak," *Travel Weekly* (February 12, 2007): 64.

2 Damon Hodge, "Tourism Chief Aims to Continue Vegas' Hot Streak," *Travel Weekly* (February 12, 2007): 64.

3 *Sources:* Jeff Delong, "After a Down Year, Vegas Hoping for a Rebound," *USA Today* (May 21, 2010): 2A; Nancy Trejos, "Las Vegas Bets the Future on a Game-Changing New Hotel Complex," *Washington Post* (January 31, 2010): F01; Tamara Audi, "Vegas Plans a New Push to Attract More People," *Wall Street Journal* (January 7, 2008): B2; John King, "Luck Running Low in Las Vegas—Will It Turn Around," *CNN.com* (May 22, 2009), www.cnn.com; Tamara Audi, "Vegas Tries Luck with Old Slogan," *Wall Street Journal* (May 13, 2009): B5; Damon Hodge, "Tourism Chief Aims to Continue Vegas' Hot Streak," *Travel Weekly* (February 12, 2007): 64; Tamara Audi, "Las Vegas Touts Its Affordability," *Wall Street Journal* (February 4, 2009): B5.

4 *Sources:* Adam Nagourney, "Crowd Returns to Las Vegas but Gamble Less," July 31, 2013, http://www.nytimes.com/2013/08/01/us/as-las-vegas-recovers-new-cause-for-concern.html?_r=0;AnnFriedman, "Latest Trend in Las Vegas Is Boutique Hotels," *Las Vegas Business Press* (November 24, 2014): 7; Alison Gregor, "As Las Vegas Evolves, Boutique Hotels Gain," *The New York Times* (April 17, 2013): B10; Steve Green, "New Nobu Hotel at Caesars Palace Could Help Define Las Vegas as a City for Boutique Hotels," July 6, 2012, http://www.vegasinc.com/business/real-estate/2012/jul/06/new-nobu-hotel-caesars-palace-could-help-define-la/; Laura Carrol, "Las Vegas Aims to Benefit From Surge in Foreign tourism," *Las Vegas Review Journal*, January 8, 2012, http://www.reviewjournal.com/business/tourism/las-vegas-Aims-Benefit-Surge-Foreign-Tourism; http://www.lvcva.com/stats-and-facts/visitor-statistics (accessed January 2016).

5 "Say Hello to Canopy by Hilton," October 15, 2014, http://news.hiltonworldwide.com/index.cfm/newsroom/detail/27567; "Hilton Launches 'Canopy' Lifestyle Hotel Brand," *TravelAgent*, November 3, 2014: P11; "Hilton Lifts Lid on its New Lifestyle Brand," boutiqedesign.com (accessed November 2014).

6 Elliot Mest, "Robots Make Their Way into Hotels," June 17, 2015, http://www.hotelmanagement.net/technology/robots-make-their-way-into-hotels-31575; Junvi Ola, "Hotels Engaging Social Media-Savvy Guests with Perks and Prizes," February 23, 2014, http://hospitality.cvent.com/blog/junvi-ola/hotels-engaging-social-media-savvy-guests-with-perks-and-prizes.

7 Joseph A. Michelli, *The New Gold Standard* (New York: McGraw-Hill, 2008).

8 See "Creating a Balance: Help Guests Stay Healthy," April 9, 2014, *Hotel Business*, http://www.hotelbusiness.com/Amenities/Creating-a-Balance-Help-Guests-Stay-Healthy-While-Traveling/47108; "Brands Focus on Health and Wellness Design," http://www.hotelnewsnow.com/Article/12455/Brands-focus-on-health-and-wellness-in-design (accessed October 15, 2013).

9 Christian Gronroos, *Service Management Marketing* (New York: Lexington Books, 1990), p. 69.

10 http://www.starwoodhotels.com/alofthotels/about/index.html (accessed September 17, 2011).

11 Andrea Sachs, "Aloft Hotels: A Hip Addition to the Inn Crowd," *Washington Post*, July 15, 2009, http://www.washingtonpost.com/wp-dyn/content/-article/2009/07/14/AR2009071403194.html (accessed September 24, 2011).

12 Martin Lindstrom, *Brand Sense* (New York: Free Press, 2005).

13 Bernard Booms and Mary J. Bitner, "Marketing Services by Managing the Environment," *Cornell Restaurant and Hotel Administration Quarterly* (May 1992): 35–39.

14 See Le Méridien LM 100, http://www.starwoodhotels.com/lemeridien/lm100/index.html (accessed September 25, 2011).

15 Britt Aboutaleb, "Le Labo's Scent for Le Meridien Smells of Libraries and the Little Prince, *Elle* (September 23, 2011), http://fashion.elle.com/life-and-love/ (accessed September 24, 2011).

16 Philip Kotler, "Atmospherics as a Marketing Tool," *Journal of Retailing*, 49, no. 4 (1973–1974): 48–64.

17 Gronroos, *Service Management and Marketing*.

18 Karthik Namasivayam and Timothy R. Hinkin, "The Customer's Role in the Service Encounter," *Cornell Hotel and Restaurant Administration Quarterly*, 44, no. 3 (2003): 34.

19 See Scott Mayerowitz, "Making the Hotel Lobby a Place to See and Be Seen," September 4, 2013, http://news.yahoo.com/making-hotel-lobby-place-see-seen-070232759.html; Alissa Ponchione, "Millennial Mind," hospitalitydesign.com, May 2014, p. 132; Greg Oates, "Marriott Wants Moxy to Deliver the

Millennial Customer, with Help from Ikea," February 3, 2014, http://skift.com/2014/02/03/marriott-wants-moxy-to-deliver-the-millennial-customer/#1; Nancy Trejos, "Marriott Debuts Hotel Brand for Millennials," *USA Today*, December 8, 2014, http://www.usatoday.com/story/travel/hotels/2014/12/08/marriott-ac-hotels-millennials-new-orleans/20066811/.

20 T. O'Brien, "Disney Looks to Fill Needs of Guests with Refill Soft Drink Mugs," *Amusement Business*, 114, no. 34 (2002): 7.

21 Sarah Nassauer, "Chili's to Install Tabletop Computer Screens," *Wall Street Journal*, September 15, 2013, http://www.wsj.com/articles/SB10001424127887323342404579077453886739272.

22 Sarah Turcotte, "The Wait Is Over," Fast Company, September 2012.

23 See "McAtlas Shrugged," *Foreign Policy* (May–June 2001): 26–37; Philip Kotler and Kevin Lane Keller, *Marketing Management*, 13th ed. (Upper Saddle River, NJ: Prentice Hall, 2009), p. 254.

24 Quotes from Jack Trout, "'Branding' Simplified," *Forbes* (April 19, 2007), www.forbes.com; a presentation by Jason Kilar at the Kenan-Flagler Business School, University of North Carolina at Chapel Hill, Fall 2009.

25 For more on Young & Rubicam's Brand Asset Valuator, see "Brand Asset Valuator," Value Based Management.net, www.valuebasedmanagement.net/methods_brand_asset_valuator.html (accessed May 2010); www.brandassetconsulting.com (accessed May 2010); W. Ronald Lane, Karen Whitehill King, and Tom Reichert, *Kleppner's Advertising Procedure*, 18th ed. (Upper Saddle River, NJ: Pearson Prentice Hall, 2011), pp. 83–84.

26 See Scott Davis, *Brand Asset Management*, 2nd ed. (San Francisco, CA: Jossey-Bass, 2002). For more on brand positioning, see Philip Kotler and Kevin Lane Keller, *Marketing Management*, 13th ed., Chapter10.

27 See www.jimstengel.com (accessed June 2010).

28 Lara O' Reilly, "Virgin America Bids to Banish Command Culture," *Marketing Week*, September 20, 2012; Joan Voight, "Where's the Party? At 30,000 Feet Virgin America Marketing Chief: 'What Would Richard Do?'" *Adweek*, February 5, 2013; Michael Bush, "Virgin America," *Advertising Age*, November 16, 2009, p. 12.

29 John W. O'Neill and Anna S. Matilla, "Hotel Brand Strategy," *Cornell Hospitality Quarterly*, 51 (February 2010), 27–34.

30 Jing Lei, Niraj Dawar, and Jos Lemmink. "Negative Spillover in Brand Portfolios: Exploring the Antecedents of Asymmetric Effects." *Journal of Marketing*, 72 (May 2008): 111–123.

31 "Tim Hortons and Cold Stone: Co-Branding Strategies," *BusinessWeek* (July 10, 2009), www.businessweek.com/smallbiz/content/jul2009/sb20090710_574574.htm; Steve McKee, "The Pros and Cons of Co-Branding," *BusinessWeek* (July 10, 2009), www.businessweek.com/smallbiz/content/jul2009/sb20090710_255169.htm.

32 See Austin Carr, "The Hard Sell at Taco Bell," *Fast Company*, July/August 2013, pp. 36–38; www.tacobell.com/food/menuitem/Doritos-Locos-Tacos-Supreme (accessed September 2014).

33 Steve Green, "New Nobu Hotel at Caesars Palace Could Help Define Las Vegas as a City for Boutique Hotels," July 2012, *VegasInc*, http://www.vegasinc.com/business/real-estate/2012/jul/06/new-nobu-hotel-caesars-palace-could-help-define-la/.

34 http://www.smartbrief.com/05/17/12/choice-unveils-new-fb-program-dual-brand-hotel-concept#.VRrqVnF_1Y; Mark Chesnut, "New Food, New Look at Choice Hotels Properties," June 7, 2012, http://www.orbitz.com/blog/2012/06/new-food-new-look-at-choice-hotels-properties/.

35 Philip Kotler and Waldermar Pfoertsch, *Ingredient Branding: Making the Invisible Visible* (Heidelberg, Germany: Springer-Verlag, 2011); Kalpesch Kaushik Desai and Kevin Lane Keller, "The Effects of Brand Expansions and Ingredient Branding Strategies on Host Brand Extendibility," *Journal of Marketing*, 66 (January 2002): 73–93.

36 Martin Bishop, "Finding Your Nemo: How to Survive the Dangerous Waters of Ingredient Branding," *Chief Executive*, March 15, 2010.

37 See http://www.mgmgrand.com/hotel/stay-well.aspx for MGM Stay Well suites features; "MGM Grand Hotel & Casino to Expand Stay Well Program to 171 Guestrooms," http://newsroom.mgmgrand.com/ (accessed September 17, 2013).

38 David A. Aaker, *Brand Portfolio Strategy: Creating Relevance, Differentiation, Energy, Leverage, and Clarity* (New York: Free Press, 2004).

39 Maria-Pia Intini, "Boutique Evolved: 5 Key Trends," November 14, 2011, http://www.hotelnewsnow.com/Article/6945/Boutique-evolved-5-key-trends.

40 Alicia Hoisington, "Brands Focus on Health and Wellness in Design," October 15, 2013, http://www.hotelnewsnow.com/Article/12455/Brands-focus-on-health-and-wellness-in-design; http://www.evenhotels.com/hotels/us/en/reservation.

41 Christopher Hosford, "A Transformative Experience," *Sales and Marketing Management*, 158 (June 2006): 32–36; Mike Beirne and Javier Benito, "Starwood Uses Personnel to Personalize Marketing," *Brandweek* (April 24, 2006): 9.

42 Jack Trout, *Differentiate or Die: Survival in Our Era of Killer Competition* (New York: Wiley, 2000); Kamalini Ramdas and Mohanbir Sawhney, "A Cross-Functional Approach to Evaluating Multiple Line Extensions for Assembled Products," *Management Science*, 47 (January 2001): 22–36.

43 Nirmalya Kumar, "Kill a Brand, Keep a Customer," *Harvard Business Review* (December 2003): 87–95.

44 For a methodological approach for assessing the extent and nature of cannibalization, see Charlotte H. Mason and George R. Milne, "An Approach for Identifying Cannibalization Within Product Line Extensions and Multibrand Strategies," *Journal of Business Research*, 31 (October–November 1994): 163–170.

45 Phillip Kotler, Hermawan Kartajaya, and Iwan Setiawan. *Marketing 3.0* (New Jersey: John Wiley & Sons, Inc., 2010).

46 Stephen Cole, "Value of the Brand," *CA Magazine* (May 2005): 39–40.

47 See Kevin Lane Keller, *Strategic Brand Management* (Upper Saddle River, NJ: Prentice Hall, 2008), Chapter10.

48 "Panda Restaurants Goes into Retail," *American City Business Journal* (February 2004).

49 Howard Riell, "High Expectations," *Kahiki*, July 12, 2006, http://kahiki.blogspot.com/2006/09/frozen-food-age-article.html (accessed September 19, 2011).

50 Julie Feickert, Rohit Verma, Gerhart Plaschka, and Cheikitan Dev, "Safeguarding Your Customers," *Cornell Hotel and Restaurant Administration Quarterly* (August 2006): 224.

51 John Peppers and Martha Rogers, "The Buzz on Customer-Driven Innovation," *Sales and Marketing Management* (June 2007): 13.

52 Kate Leahy, "Discovery Zone," *Restaurants and Institutions* (July 15, 2007): 49.

53 http://mystarbucksidea.force.com/apex/idealist?lsi=1 (accessed December 16, 2015).

54 Joseph Mackenzie, "Can Hotels Use Crowdsourcing," February 5, 2009, http://www.hotelmarketingstrategies.com/can-hotels-use-crowdsourcing/ (accessed September 19, 2011).

55 Elisabeth A. Sullivan, "A Group Effort: More Companies Are Turning to the Wisdom of the Crowd to Find Ways to Innovate," *Marketing News* (February 28, 2010): 22–29.

56 Kristin Boyd, "Crowdsourcing Is Changing Hotel Design and Marketing," *Lodging*, May 5, 2014, http://lodgingmagazine.com/crowdsourcing-is-changing-hotel-design-and-marketing/.

57 Nancy Trejos, "Guests Help Design the Hotel of the Future," *USA Today*, November 15, 2013, http://www.usatoday.com/story/travel/hotels/2013/11/14/hotel-guests-millennials-design-marriott-holiday-inn/3538573/; "Designs on the Future – Big Ideas Become Reality at Marriott Hotels' New 'Underground' Innovation Lab," May 30, 2013, http://news.marriott.com/2013/05/designs-on-the-future-big-ideas-become-reality-at-marriott-hotels-new-underground-inno-vation-lab.html; Kristin Boyd, "Crowdsourcing Is Changing Hotel Design and Marketing," *Lodging*, May 5, 2014, http://lodgingmagazine.com/crowdsourcing-is-changing-hotel-design-and-marketing/.

58 Lauren McKay, "300 current Priority Club Visa Cardholders Willing to Share Their Opinions on What Card Benefits and Services Are Important," December 8, 2010, http://www.emarketer.com/blog/index.php/case-study-using-online-community-crowd-source-customer-loyalty-strategies/ (accessed September 17, 2011); Amanda Kludt, "4Food, the Bonkers Techie Resto Coming Soon to Midtown," May 26, 2010, http://ny.eater.com/archives/2010/05/meet_4food_the_most_bonkers_restaurant_to_ever_hit_midtown.php (accessed September 17, 2010).

59 "The REO Eats Project," http://www.reoeatsproject.com/about-the-project/ (accessed September 17, 2010).

60 Guido Jouret, "Inside Cisco's Search for the Next Big Idea," *Harvard Business Review* (September 2009): 43–45.

61 Kevin O'Donnell, "Where Do the Best Ideas Come From? The Un-likeliest Sources," *Advertising Age* (July 14, 2008): 15.

62 The Marriott example and this list were drawn from Christopher W. L. Hart, "Product Development: How Marriott Created Courtyard," *Cornell Hotel and Restaurant Administration Quarterly*, 27, no. 3 (1986): 68–69; Jerry Wind, Paul E. Green, Douglas Shifflet, and Marsha Scarborough, "Courtyard by Marriott: Designing a Hotel Facility with Consumer Based Marketing," *Interfaces*, 19, no. 1 (1989): 25–47.

63 J. L. Heskett and R. Hallowell, "Courtyard by Marriott," *Harvard Case* 9-693-036 (Boston, MA: Harvard Business School Publishing, 1993).

64 Michael Lowrey, "Poor Attendance Plagues N. C. Arenas," *Carolina Journal*, 11, no. 3 (March 2004): 15.

65 Anonymous, "KFC Serves Up a Second Secret Recipe: Kentucky Grilled Chicken," *PR Newswire* (April 14, 2009).

66 See Emily Bryson York, "McD's Serves Up $100M McCafe Ad Blitz," *Cram's Chicago Business* (May 4, 2009), www.chicagobusiness.com; John Letzing, "Bing's Share Rises Again," *Wall Street Journal* (June 18, 2009), http://online.wsj.com; Rita Chang, "With $100M Saturation Campaign, Droid Will Be Impossible to Avoid," *Advertising Age* (November 9, 2009): 3.

67 Theodore Levitt, *The Marketing Imaginization* (New York: Free Press, 1986), p. 173.

68 Christopher W. Hart, Greg Casserly, and Mark J. Lawless, "The Product Life Cycle: How Useful?" *Cornell Hotel and Restaurant Administration Quarterly*, 25, no. 3 (November 1984): 54–63.

69 Janet Adamy, "A Shift in Dining Scene Nicks a Once-Hot Chain," *Wall Street Journal* (June 29, 2007): A1 and A3.

70 *Momentum!*, DineEquity Annual Report 2010.

71 Candice Choi, "Wendy's Outlines Airier, Modern Restaurant Look," *USA Today*, March 1, 2012, http://usatoday30.usatoday.com/money/companies/earnings/story/2012-03-01/wendys/53315420/1; Hank Hayes, "New-Look Wendy's Restaurant Opens on West Stone

Drive," October 9, 2013, http://www.timesnews.net/article/9068456/new-look-wendys-restaurant-opens-on-west-stone-drive#ixzz3Ua3brTKg.

72 Bruce Horovitz, "McDonald's Expands Custom Sandwich Option," December 7, 2014, http://www.usatoday.com/story/money/business/2014/12/07/mcdonalds-fast-food-restaurants-create-your-taste-millennials/19943987/; Alexandria Fisher, "McDonald's Expands 'Build-Your-Own-Burger,'" September 11, 2014, http://www.nbcchicago.com/blogs/inc-well/McDonalds-Expands-Build-Your-Own-Burger-Test-274815801.html.

73 Richard N. Velotte, "Caesars to Spend $223 Million on Revamping Quad, Rebranding It as Linq Hotel," *Las Vegas Review-Journal*, July 1, 2014, http://www.review-journal.com/business/casinos-gaming/caesars-spend-223-million-revamping-quad-rebranding-it-linq-hotel;

Leo Jakobson, "Outdoors Is In," *Successful Meetings*, January 15, 2015, pp. 56, 58.

74 Kortney Stringer, "Abandoning the Mall," *Wall Street Journal* (March 24, 2001): B1.

75 William Pride and O. C. Ferrell, *Marketing* (Boston, MA: Houghton-Mifflin Publishing, 1995), pp. 312–313.

76 Based on information found in Celia Hatton, "KFC's Finger Lickin' Success in China," *CBS News*, March 6, 2011, www.cbsnews.com/2100-3445_162-20039783.html; Maggie Starvish, "KFC's Explosive Growth in China," *HBS Working Knowledge*, June 17, 2011, http://hbswk.hbs.edu/cgi-bin/print/6704.html; David E. Bell and Mary L. Shelman, "KFC's Radical Approach to China," *Harvard Business Review*, November 2011, pp. 137–142; www.yum.com/brands/china.asp (accessed October 2013).

Internal Marketing

Objectives

After reading this chapter, you should be able to:

1. Understand why internal marketing is an important part of a marketing program.
2. Explain what a service culture is and why it is important to have a company where everyone is focused on serving the customer.
3. Describe the three-step process involved in implementing an internal marketing program.
4. Explain why the management of nonroutine transactions can create the image of being an excellent service provider.

Other exclusive resorts pamper their guests, but Four Seasons has perfected the art of high-touch, carefully crafted service. Whether it's at the elegantly "re-imagined" Four Seasons London, the regally attentive Four Seasons Hotel Riyadh in Saudi Arabia, the tropical island paradise at the Four Seasons Resort Mauritius, or the luxurious Sub-Saharan "camp" at the Four Seasons Safari Lodge Serengeti, guests paying $1,000 or more a night expect to have their minds read. For these guests, Four Seasons doesn't disappoint. Its mission is to perfect the travel experience through the highest standards of hospitality.

As a result, Four Seasons has a cult-like customer clientele, making it one of the most-decorated hotel chains in the world. As one Four Seasons Maui guest recently told a manager, "If there's a heaven, I hope it's run by Four Seasons."

But what makes Four Seasons so special? It's really no secret. Just ask anyone who works there. From the CEO to the doorman, they'll tell you it's the quality of the Four Seasons staff. Its people are responsible for the success of the organization, states Four Seasons founder Isadore Sharp. Just as it does for customers, Four Seasons respects and pampers its employees. It knows that happy, satisfied employees make for happy, satisfied customers.

The Four Seasons customer service legacy is deeply rooted in the company's culture, which in turn is grounded in the Golden Rule. In all of its dealings with both guests and staff, the luxury resort chain seeks to treat others as it wishes to be treated. If you expect your employees to treat your customers well, you must treat them well.

Most important, once it has the right people in place, Four Seasons treats them as it would its most important guests. Compared with the competition, Four Seasons salaries are in the 75th to 90th percentile, with generous retirement and profit-sharing plans. All employees—from the maids who make up the rooms to the general manager—dine together (free of charge) in the hotel cafeteria. Perhaps best of all, every employee receives free stays at other Four Seasons resorts, starting at three free nights per year after six months with the company, then six free nights or more after one year.

The room stays make employees feel as important and pampered as the guests they serve, and they motivate employees to achieve even higher levels of service in their own jobs. Kanoe Braun, a pool attendant at the Four Seasons Maui, has visited several other Four Seasons resorts in his 10 years with the company "I've been to the one in Bali. That was by far my favorite," he proclaims. You walk in and they say, "How are you, Mr. Braun. 'Yeah I'm somebody!'" Adds another Four Seasons staffer, "You're never treated like just an employee. You're a guest. You come back from those trips on fire. You want to do so much for the guests."

As a result, the Four Seasons staff loves the hotel just as much as customers do. Although guests can check out anytime they like, employees never want to leave. The annual turnover for full-time employees is only 18 percent, half the industry average. Four Seasons has been included for 17 straight years on *Fortune* magazine's list of 100 Best Companies to Work For. And that's the biggest secret to Four Seasons' success. Creating customer satisfaction and value involves more than just crafting a lofty competitive marketing strategy and handing it down from the top. At Four Seasons, creating customer value is everybody's business. And it all starts with taking care of those who take care of customers.[1]

■■■ Internal Marketing

Internal marketing. Involves marketing to the firm's internal customers, its employees.

Moment of truth. Occurs when an employee and a customer have contact.

Marketing in the hospitality and travel industries must be embraced by all employees; it cannot be left to the marketing or sales department. Marketing must be part of the philosophy of the organization, and the marketing function should be carried out by all line employees. In manufacturing firms, the marketing function is often carried out by a marketing department because many employees do not interact with customers. In service industries, the line employees carry out a majority of the marketing function (see Figure 10–1). **Internal marketing** involves marketing to the firm's internal customers, its employees.

Danny Meyer stated in *Setting the Table*, "Virtually nothing is as important as how one is made to feel in any business transaction. Hospitality is present when something happens *for* you. It is absent when something happens *to* you; these two propositions *for* and *to* express it all."[2]

A study by the American Society for Quality Control found that when consumers were asked what quality in services meant, the largest group of responses cited employee contact skills such as courtesy, attitude, and helpfulness.[3] In studies we have conducted in luxury hotels and/or large elaborate casinos, employees play a large role in whether the guests intend to return. No matter how much one spends on the physical environment, the human environment has to be warm, friendly, and caring for guests to return. Because employees are an important part of our product, we must make sure they are excited about our product and care about their customers. The importance of employees and internal marketing is supported by a study that found that internal marketing is one of the top three determinants of a company's financial performance.[4]

Richard Normann, a former management consultant for SAS Airlines, stated that a key ingredient in almost all service companies is some innovative arrangement or formula for mobilizing and focusing human energy.[5] Normann along with Denis Boyle, an SAS strategy consultant, developed the term *moments of truth*. A **moment of truth** occurs when employee and customer have contact. Normann states that when this occurs, what happens is no longer directly influenced by the company. It is the skill, motivation, and tools employed by the firm's representative and the expectations and behavior of the client together that create the service delivery process.[6] Normann borrowed the idea from bullfighters, who used the term to describe the moment when the bullfighter faces the bull in the ring. Despite all his training and preparation, a wrong move by the bullfighter or an unanticipated move by

Figure 10–1
The relationship between the marketing function and the marketing department. In hospitality organizations employees perform much of the marketing function. Adapted from Christian Gronroos, "Designing a Long Range Marketing Strategy for Services," *Long Range Planning*, 40 (April 1980).

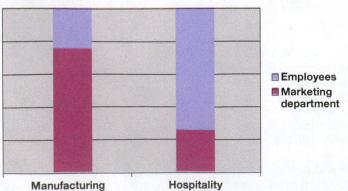

Employees
Marketing department

Manufacturing   Hospitality

the bull can result in disaster. Similarly, when employees and customers interact, a careless mistake by an employee or an unanticipated request by a guest can result in a dissatisfied guest.

Post Face-to-Face Guest Relations

Guest satisfaction does not end when the guest pays the bill and leaves. The concept of "a moment of truth" continues with public reviews and comments on social media.

Today it is important for members of the hospitality and tourism industry to review all comments, favorable and unfavorable, by former guests. A recent study of the impact of negative reviews by guests provides excellent advice.

"Responses (to guests who give negative reviews) should be empathetic and include a strong signal that hotels (or other hospitality/tourism members) are reading the complaints, typically with a paraphrase of the complaint rather than repeatedly duplicating generic responses."[7] Unfortunately, negative reviews may sometimes be fostered or supported by employees who receive complaints from guests but either feel they are helpless to correct the problems or don't care. In these cases, an employee may state something such as "You can always complain through social media."

On the positive side, excellent reviews from a guest should be rewarded with a personal letter from a member of management. There are mixed opinions as to whether the guest should also be rewarded with something such as free drink coupons.

The hospitality industry is unique in that *employees are part of the product*. The hotel must have a staff that will perform well during moments of truth. When people think of marketing, they usually think of efforts directed externally toward the marketplace, but a hotel or restaurant's first marketing efforts should be directed internally to employees. Managers must make sure that employees know their products and believe they are a good value. Employees must be excited about the company they work for and the products they sell. Otherwise, it will be impossible for guests to become excited. All managers must understand marketing and its customer orientation. External marketing brings customers, but it does little good if the employees do not perform to the guest's expectations. It is often hard to differentiate the tangible part of the product of competing companies. Steak dinners and hotel rooms in the same price range tend to be similar. Product differentiation often derives from the people who deliver the service. It is the employees' delivery of the service that brings customers back. This explains why a study by the National Restaurant Association found the most important issue facing food-service managers was employees.[8] As Christine Andrews, vice president of human resources for Hostmark Hospitality, states, "If your people don't perform, your property won't perform."[9]

Marketing HIGHLIGHT 10–1 Pinehurst Resort & Country Club "Do What's Right"

Pinehurst Resort & Country Club is known as the foremost golf resort and spa in the United States and shares international prominence with Saint Andrews of Scotland. Scott Bruton, general manager of Pinehurst, attributes much of this success to its loyal and motivated employees. "About half of our 1,200 employees were born near Pinehurst and many of the others moved here because of golf and Pinehurst. The parents and grandparents of many also worked here at Pinehurst so obviously there is tremendous employee loyalty and a love of golf."

Don Padgett, president of Pinehurst, has a simple philosophy of "Do What's Right." With 1,200 employees, many top executives would have chosen to introduce themselves in a huge meeting with a formal speech. Shortly after Don was appointed president, he held 29 small meetings where he chatted with employees informally. Both Don and Scott believe it is important not to "hard sell" employees. They believe that employees are the face of Pinehurst to its customers. "Anybody can run a resort when things go well," said Scott, but "the moment of truth occurs when

The Carolina Hotel at the Pinehurst Resort. Courtesy of Gary Newkirk/ Getty Images.

employees are confronted with unhappy guests or an emergency such as a sick guest."

Employees at Pinehurst are not allowed to hide behind corporate policy or the fact that they are not in top management. Employees are taught to fix a problem personally when it occurs. Employees must use ethical and moral behavior. They are guided by the knowledge that they will not be disciplined if they honestly tried to fix a customer problem but failed. Management may review the situation and coach the employee in better ways to handle customer problems, but they will not discipline the employee.

Pinehurst believes in rapid recognition of positive acts by employees. Instead of waiting for scheduled meetings, all managers carry "CHATSKYS," which are instant rewards such as gift certificates at Wal-Mart or Chick-fil-A or the local car wash. If a manager observes or is informed of a positive guest action, he or she thanks the employee and gives that person a Chatsky.

Employee news is changed every five to seven days and may be seen on e-mail in any of the 400 computers on the property. This prevents unfounded rumors and provides rapid employee peer recognition.

Pinehurst offers a unique employee assistance plan (EAP). This is administered by a board of employees, not management. Loans are made to employees who may have missed a mortgage payment, need to purchase an airplane ticket to attend a funeral, or have other unexpected financial needs. These are loans—not gifts.

Each year Pinehurst donates the use of its most famous course "No. 2" for one day to support the EAP. Players pay $200 per person to play the course, earning $20,000 for the EAP.

The employee cafeteria is another employee benefit with a small charge of only $2 per meal. Employees compare this price to a fast-food meal and know they receive a bargain. Members of management also eat in the cafeteria as well as the chef. This has an added benefit of encouraging management to mingle with employees.

Scott said that employee satisfaction depends on all managers. "Managers can't lead their staff if they can't motivate them. Managers can have great technical skills and a great education, but if they can't relate to their employees, they won't last long at Pinehurst."

Pinehurst believes strongly in the lifetime value of a customer. Guest records show that many guests first came to Pinehurst as kids with their parents or grandparents. Children are important guests at Pinehurst as witnessed by the summer golf schools for kids and the "Kids U.S. Open."

All of the employees know that Pinehurst respects kids as important guests. That sense of caring for the youngest guests is part of the culture of Pinehurst. Employees appreciate this because many are parents and grandparents and understand that an employer who cares for kids also cares for them.

■■■ The Internal Marketing Process

Techniques and procedures must be developed to ensure that employees are able and willing to deliver high-quality service. The internal marketing concept evolved as marketers formalized procedures for marketing to employees. Internal marketing ensures that employees at all levels of the organization experience the business and understand its various activities and campaigns in an environment that supports customer consciousness.[10] The objective of internal marketing is to enable employees to deliver satisfying products to the guest. As Christian Gronroos notes, "The internal marketing concept states that the internal market of employees is best motivated for service-mindedness and customer-oriented performance by an active, marketing-like approach, where a variety of activities are used internally in an active, marketing-like and coordinated way."[11] Internal marketing uses a marketing perspective to manage the firm's employees.[12]

Internal marketing is aimed at the firm's employees. Internal marketing is a process that involves the following steps:

1. Establishment of a service culture

2. Development of a marketing approach to human resource management

3. Dissemination of marketing information to employees

Establishment of a Service Culture

An internal marketing program flows out of a service culture. A service marketing program is doomed to fail if its organizational culture does not support serving the customer. An article in *The Australian*, a national newspaper, reported that four firms had pumped $2 million into customer service programs with little result.[13] One reason these customer service efforts failed was that the companies' cultures were not service oriented. The companies carried out the customer service programs because they thought they would produce satisfied customers and make the firm more money. These firms soon discovered that a good customer service program involves much more than working with line employees. *An internal marketing program requires a strong commitment from management.*

A major barrier to most internal marketing programs is middle management. Managers have been trained to watch costs and increase profits. Their reward systems are usually based on achieving certain cost levels. Imagine a hotel's front-desk clerks returning from a training session, eager to help the guests. They may take a little extra time with the customers or perhaps give away a health club visit to help a dissatisfied guest recover from an unsatisfactory experience at the hotel. The front-office manager, who has not been through similar training, may see the extra time spent as unproductive and the services given away as wasteful.

If management expects employees' attitudes to be positive toward the customer, management must have a positive attitude toward the customer and the employees. Too often, organizations hire trainers to come in for a day to get their customer-contact employees excited about providing high-quality customer service. The effect of these sessions is usually short lived, however, because the organizations do little to support the customer-contact employees. Managers tell receptionists to be helpful and friendly, yet often the receptionists are understaffed. The greeting developed to make receptionists sound sincere and helpful—"Good morning, Plaza Hotel, Elizabeth speaking, how may I help you," becomes hollow when it is compressed into three seconds with a "Can you please hold?" added to the end. The net result from the guest's perspective is to wait 14 rings for the phone to be answered and then receive a cold, rushed greeting. Management must develop a **service culture**: a culture that supports customer service through policies, procedures, reward systems, and actions.

An **organizational culture** is the pattern of shared values and beliefs that gives members of an organization meaning, providing them with the rules for behavior in the organization.[14] In well-managed companies, everyone in the organization embraces the culture. A strong culture helps organizations in two ways. First, it directs behavior. Culture is important to service organizations because every customer and each experience is different. The employee must have some degree of discretion over the creation and delivery of the experience to ensure the customer's differing needs and expectations are met.[15] Second, a strong culture gives employees a sense of purpose and makes them feel good about their company.[16] They know what their company is trying to achieve and how they are helping the company achieve that goal.

Here is how Kimpton hotels describes its culture.

> At Kimpton, we believe a culture of care will be established when every employee is on the alert, fully aware of all the opportunities to form an emotional connection with each guest. When we provide care, our guests experience comfort.[17]

Culture serves as the glue that holds an organization together. When an organization has a strong culture, the organization and its employees act as one. But a company that has a strong culture may not necessarily have a service culture. A strong service culture influences employees to act in customer-oriented ways and is the first step toward developing a customer-oriented organization.

The Company Story

Coleen Reinhart, a professional business writer, advises that it is important for employees to understand the history of a company. She states that writing the history of your business will make your employees seem like they are the part of

Service culture. A system of values and beliefs in an organization that reinforces the idea that providing the customer with quality service is the principal concern of the business.

Organizational culture. The pattern of shared values and beliefs that gives members of an organization meaning and provides them with the rules for behavior in that organization.

something larger. It is important to include the values on which the company was founded. One can also explain the positioning opportunity they saw when they founded the company. This will help the employees understand the organization and how its culture was formed.[18]

Developing a customer-oriented organization requires a commitment from management of both time and financial resources. The change to a customer-oriented system may require changes in hiring, training, reward systems, and customer complaint resolution, as well as **empowerment** of employees. When a firm empowers employees, it moves the authority and responsibility to make decisions to the line employees from the supervisor.

The results of a recent study concerning front-line service employees in the hospitality industry concluded, "Front line service employees (respondents) often felt unsatisfied or stressed when serving customers because they were unable to make decisions independently without prior consultation with their supervisor. They felt that to act independently could potentially jeopardize the subordinates' career."[19]

Employee empowerment requires that managers spend time talking to both customers and customer-contact employees. Management must be committed to these changes. A service culture does not result from a memorandum sent by the chief executive officer (CEO). It is developed over time through the actions of management. For example, a hotel manager who spends time greeting guests and inquiring about their welfare during morning checkout and afternoon check-in demonstrates caring about guests.[20]

In some companies, including Hyatt, McDonald's, and Hertz, management spends time working alongside customer-contact employees serving customers. This action makes it clear to employees that management does not want to lose touch with operations and that managers care about both employees and customers. A service culture and internal marketing program cannot be developed without the support of management. Organizations cannot expect their employees to develop a customer-oriented attitude if it is not visibly supported by company management.

Empowerment. When a firm empowers employees, it moves the authority and responsibility to make decisions to the line employees from the supervisor.

Weak Service Culture Compared to a Strong Service Culture

In firms that have weak corporate cultures, there are few or no common values and norms. Employees are often bound by policies and regulations; sometimes these policies may make no sense from a customer service perspective. In this environment, employees become insecure about making decisions outside the rules and regulations.[21] Because there are no established values, employees do not know how the company wants them to act, and they spend time trying to figure out how to behave. When they do come up with a solution, they must get their supervisor's permission before applying it to the problem. Supervisors, in turn, may feel the need to pass the responsibility upward. During the decision process, the guest is kept waiting. In a company with a strong service culture, employees know what to do, and they do it.

When you come into contact with an organization that has a strong service culture, you recognize it right away. There is a difference in the feeling a guest receives from an employee who has a genuine interest in guests and communicates this personally and an employee who does not care.

The following example from the Viceroy Hotel Group demonstrates how a hotel group tells its employees, suppliers, and guests how this organization thinks and behaves based on its accolades. The Viceroy

Four Seasons Hotels are known for their strong service culture. This is the Beverly Wilshire Hotel, a Four Seasons Hotel. Courtesy of jc/Fotolia.

Hotel Group's positioning statement focuses on delivering unique lifestyle experiences.[22]

One of the distinguishing factors of Viceroy hotels is their legendary location designed to provide the guest a one-of-the-kind experience. However, location and physical facilities alone are not enough to create an excellent hotel. Viceroy has combined their excellent physical facilities with exceptional service. Their hotels have been recognized as some of the best in the world. This would have not been possible without employees that met or exceeded the expectations of the guest and a corporate culture that supported service.

Turning the Organizational Structure Upside Down

The conventional organizational structure is a triangular structure. For example, in a hotel the CEO (chief executive officer) and COO (chief operating officer) are at the peak of the triangle. The general manager is on the next level, followed by department heads, supervisors, line employees, and the customers (Figure 10–2). Ken Blanchard, author of *One Minute Manager*, states that the problem with a conventional organizational structure is that everyone is working for his or her boss. Employees want to do well in the organization. Thus, line employees are concerned with what their supervisors think of their performance, department heads are concerned with how the general manager views them, and the general managers want the corporate office to think highly of them. The problem with this type of organization is that everyone is concerned with satisfying people above them in the organization, and very little attention is paid to the customer.[23]

When a company has a service culture, the organizational chart is turned upside down. The customers are now at the top of the organization, and corporate management is at the bottom of the structure. In this type of organization, everyone is working to serve the customer. Corporate management is helping its general managers to serve the customer, general managers are supporting their departments in serving the customer, department heads are developing systems that will allow their supervisors to better serve the customer, and supervisors are helping line employees serve the customer.

A bell person at a Ritz-Carlton hotel delivered baggage to a guest about an hour after he had checked in due to an error. After he had delivered the luggage, he told his supervisor. The supervisor apologized to the guest and noted in the hotel's

Figure 10–2
Turning the organizational structure upside down.

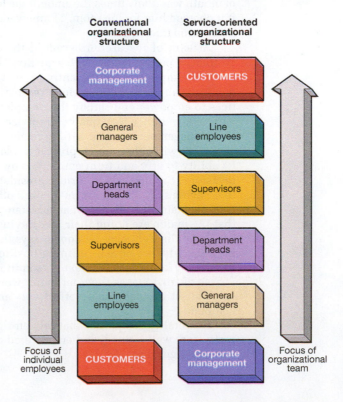

Conventional organizational structure

| Corporate management |
| General managers |
| Department heads |
| Supervisors |
| Line employees |
| CUSTOMERS |

Focus of individual employees

Service-oriented organizational structure

| CUSTOMERS |
| Line employees |
| Supervisors |
| Department heads |
| General managers |
| Corporate management |

Focus of organizational team

computer that this guest had experienced a problem and should receive exceptional service during the rest of his stay.[24] This seems like a rational way to handle the problem, but it is really an extraordinary event. In a hotel with a conventional organizational structure, if employees make a mistake, they hope their supervisor never finds out about it; they may even try to cover it up. They know that if their supervisor does find out about a mistake, they may be reprimanded. The Ritz-Carlton has a service culture; it has turned the organizational structure upside down. The bell person was concerned about the guest and knew his supervisor would take action that would enable the hotel to recover from his mistake. The supervisor was not afraid to communicate the department's mistake to other departments. When you turn the organization upside down, everyone works to serve the guest. When you have a conventional organizational structure, everyone works to please the boss. What is ironic is that when everyone works for the boss, the company loses. When everyone works for the customer, the financial performance is greater.

Nonroutine Transactions

An advantage of a strong culture is that it prepares employees to handle nonroutine transactions. A nonroutine transaction is a guest transaction that is unique and usually experienced for the first time by employees. The number of possible nonroutine transactions is so great that they cannot be covered in a training manual or in training programs. One benefit of a service culture is that it provides employees with the right attitude, knowledge, communication skills, and authority to deal with nonroutine transactions. The ability to handle nonroutine transactions separates excellent hospitality companies from mediocre ones.

An example of a nonroutine transaction is a guest who requested a late checkout so he could hold a business meeting in his room. Unfortunately, the hotel was fully booked, and the room was needed for guests arriving that afternoon. The policy manual would have said to tell the guest that he could not be accommodated in this situation. A service culture creates a desire to service the guest. The manager made provisions for him to use a vacant conference room free of charge. The guest offered to pay, but the hotel refused. The room would have never been rented at the last minute, so there was no lost revenue. The future business the hotel received from the guest who was a business consultant and the positive word of mouth was many times the amount the hotel would have received from the guest if it charged him for the room.[25] Empowered and innovative employees can handle nonroutine transactions.

A team of researchers studied the effect of employee empowerment on customers' perception of service quality. They found, "Ultimately, empowered and satisfied employees significantly influence how customers perceive the service quality of a restaurant. Therefore, restaurants must establish excellent HRM practices to empower and satisfy their employees, who in turn will deliver what the customer wants—a high quality of service."[26]

Management must be willing to give employees the authority to make decisions that will solve guests' problems. Management should exhibit confidence in its ability to hire and train employees by trusting the employees' ability to make decisions. Simon Cooper, former president of Delta Hotels and Resorts, believes that having staff do nothing but control other staff reflects poorly on the organization. He states that the job of an assistant housekeeper is to go around and check that the maids are doing their job. Having that position is an admission that we can't hire the right people. Cooper says that Delta has only a few assistant housekeepers, who are now in training positions. When their housekeepers finish a room, they know that the next person in it will be a guest. Cooper states that the degree of trust makes them far better workers.[27] When we trust employees, they solve guest problems more effectively and create fewer causes for the guest to complain.

Hospitality companies that rely on rigid policies and procedures rather than motivated, well-trained, and empowered employees have little hope of achieving maximum guest satisfaction.

The issue of nonroutine transactions will become increasingly important in the future. Hospitality firms are now using technology to serve routine customer transactions. This use of technology will become even more pervasive. Computerized check-in, video checkout, and robotics will be adapted to the hospitality industry, so employees will find themselves dealing more frequently with nonroutine tasks. Self-confident guests will take advantage of technology designed to enhance and hasten guest service. The uncertain guest or guests with problems will wish to deal with an employee. As the workplace becomes more automated, employees will take a greater role in answering questions and solving guests' problems. They must also be prepared to handle nonroutine transactions.

As Parasuraman says, "Customer service earned through several satisfactorily performed routine transactions can be badly damaged by just one botched attempt at processing a nonroutine transaction. No amount of written procedures, guidelines, or specifications can prevent the occurrence of such botched attempts; only true organizational dedication to customer satisfaction can."[28] A strong service culture enables employees to make decisions required to handle nonroutine transactions.

Development of a Marketing Approach to Human Resources Management

Creating Jobs That Attract Good People

Managers must use the principles of marketing to attract and retain employees. They must research and develop an understanding of their employees' needs, just as they examine the needs of customers. Not all employees are the same. Some employees seek money to supplement their incomes; others are looking for work that will be their sole source of income. Marketers can use marketing research techniques to segment the employee market, choosing the best segments for the firm and developing a marketing mix to attract those segments. For employees, the marketing mix is the job, pay, benefits, location, transportation, parking, hours, and intangible rewards, such as prestige and perceived advancement opportunities. Just as customers look for different attributes when they purchase a product, employees look for different benefits. Some may be attracted by flexible working hours, others are attracted by good health insurance benefits, and still others may be attracted by child-care facilities. Flexible working hours for office or housekeeping positions, cafeteria-style benefit programs in which employees design their own benefit package, and child care can all be used to attract a certain type of employee. Advertising should be developed with prospective employees in mind, building a positive image of the firm for present and future employees and customers. Employees choose employers and leave them the same way that guests select certain hotels and then decide to switch. It is expensive to lose both guests and employees.[29] Using a marketing approach to develop positions and company benefits helps attract and maintain good employees. A reduction in turnover can result in hundreds of thousands of dollars in savings.[30]

Within the United Kingdom, turnover for the hospitality industry is estimated at 30 percent and higher in London. Recruitment and training is estimated at £1500 per employee making the total cost about £886 million.[31]

The Hiring Process

The service product, at least in part, is the attitude the employee displays as he or she delivers the service experience. It is unlikely that the service provider can teach the service attitude that all its customer-contact employees need. Service organizations need to hire for attitude and train for skills.[32] "Service characteristics like intangibility and customer contact require service employees to display more initiative, to cope more effectively with stress, to be more interpersonally flexible and sensitive, and to be more cooperative than their colleagues who work in manufacturing."[33] This idea means that service firms place more emphasis on personality, energy, and attitude than on education, training, and experience in their recruitment, selection, and training strategies. Finding employees who are good at creating a service experience is a vital goal and major hiring criterion of service organizations.

Several service marketing experts have stated there are lessons hospitality organizations can learn from theater. Dramaturgy (the craft of theatrical production) includes selecting people for a customer service role similar to casting people for roles in a theatrical production. The costumes help put some into character, just as uniforms do in a hospitality organization. The actors, stagehands, and theater attendants need to work together, just as the hostess, cooks, servers, and bus help do in a restaurant. Good actors know how to get into character and leave any personal problems at home so they can produce a great performance for the audience. Finally, they know the audience and work to please the audience. Dramaturgy also involves the setting for the theatrical production, something we have discussed in previous chapters.[34] The study of theater can provide useful insights for service marketers.

Swissair carefully screens its applicants, selects candidates for personal interviews, and puts them through a five- to six-hour selection process. The airline then puts successful applicants on probation for a three-month period. It invests a great deal in each candidate because it realizes it is better to spend money choosing the right employee than trying to repair mistakes caused by poor employees. Swissair understands the importance of hiring the right employees.[35]

Southwest Airlines strongly believes inherent attitudes cannot be changed in people. To test for behaviors such as a sense of humor, ability to work with others, and friendliness, Southwest's interview process includes group interviews where applicants tell jokes and role-play a variety of situations to demonstrate teamwork and the capacity to act spontaneously. Southwest can afford to be very selective because it receives an extremely large number of job applications with little active advertising, thanks to its reputation for being a unique and excellent place to work.

Southwest places special emphasis on preparing its people to perform and on teamwork. It considers employee training to be a continuous process rather than a single event. Throughout their careers, employees are cross-trained on multiple jobs to enrich every employee's work experience and to prepare them to perform flexibly in different positions as needed. In addition, employees are specifically assigned to work with a senior employee who serves as a mentor to provide a clear demonstration of Southwest's service quality and to be available to answer questions.[36] Colleen Barrett, president emeritus of Southwest Airlines, states that Southwest's real business is customer service; their product just happens to be air transportation.[37]

Cast members. A term used for employees. It implies that employees are part of a team that is performing for their guests.

The craft of theater productions provides principles that apply to the hospitality industry. Courtesy of maslovskiy.com/ Fotolia.

Disney World allows its best employees, its star "**cast members**," to pick future employees. Disney gives cast members who will be used in the selection process three weeks of training. They are then turned loose in a 45-minute interview session to select potential new employees. James Poisant, a former manager at Disney World, explains that employees choose employees who mirror their own values. "In 45 minutes the cast members pick up on who is fooling and who's genuine."[38]

Careful selection can also have a positive effect on the employees who are hired because they feel special. Adam Hassan, a Ritz-Carlton boiler operator, explains, "When people take so much time to select you, you really want to prove they made the right choice. So if I see anything unusual I take care of it."[39]

Danny Meyer, New York restaurateur and author of *Setting the Table*, sums up the essence of hiring in the hospitality industry by stating that he looks for people who have good technical skills, but more importantly they must also have good emotional skills. The emotional skills include optimistic warmth, a curiosity to learn new things coupled with the intelligence that enables one to learn, a work ethic that includes attention to detail, empathy, and self-awareness, and integrity.[40]

Selection methods that identify customer-oriented candidates must be used as part of the hiring process. Employee's attitude, appearance, and willingness to handle the guest's requests help form a first impression of a hotel or a restaurant. Hiring and training, traditionally the responsibility of human resources management, are key areas in any internal marketing program. A marketing-like approach to human resources management starts with hiring the right employees.

Teamwork

If a company hires the right people, they will be team players. In companies that practice internal marketing, if one employee makes an error, other employees try to correct it before the guest notices. In these organizations, guests do not have to understand the hotel's organization and business to ensure that their needs are met. The front desk handles most requests, relaying the guest's desire to the appropriate department. In restaurants that have used internal marketing to create a service culture, staff members cover for each other. Employees who see that a guest needs something will serve the guest, even though it may not be their table.

Organizations that lack teamwork create an uncomfortable environment for the guest. For example, a guest called the front desk of a five-star resort and asked for extra towels. The front-desk clerk answering the telephone acted puzzled. Surely a guest would know to call housekeeping for towels. The operator stated that this was the front desk, not housekeeping, told the guest to call housekeeping, and hung up. Many restaurant guests have asked for a drink while they are sitting at their tables looking over the dinner menu. The response to some of these guests is that they have mistaken the food-service person for a cocktail-service person. The food serviceperson then tells the customers to redirect their requests to cocktail service and departs, leaving the guests' needs unfilled. In both of these incidents, the first employee contacted should have taken care of the customer's request and passed it along to the appropriate person. This is referred to as *ownership of the problem*. Customers should not have to learn the hotel or restaurant's organizational chart. They should not have to redirect their request for service to another employee. Hiring procedures need to identify those employees who are team players.

Older employees were one group that surprised some managers by their willingness to support other employees. Some managers believed the elderly might not be willing to cooperate with much younger workers or to accept direction from a youthful supervisor. KFC and McDonald's were among the first hospitality firms to prove the invalidity of these assumptions. A survey of National Restaurant Association members demonstrated that older workers were regarded to have better relations with guests and fellow employees than the "average employees."[41]

Coworker Support

The support or denial of support from coworkers may be the difference between a service-directed employee or an unhappy one whose negative feelings are transmitted to guests.

A study concerning the importance of coworkers concluded that, "It is important to train frontline employees concerning the critical role of co-worker support. Since such individuals have intense face-to-face or voice-to-voice interactions with customers, they are likely to be faced with various problems they may not be able to handle. Therefore, they need the support of co-workers. The availability of co-worker support appears to be essential, because co-worker support alleviates turnover intentions."[42]

"Fun in the workplace has both beneficial and potentially negative effects (if not carefully carried out) on employees in the hospitality industry." The authors of this statement recommended productive fun events such as productivity contests and social events. Fun may be an antidote to turnover challenge. Most individuals want more from work than financial compensation.[43]

The Importance of Initial Training

A guest overheard a conversation between a guest and the dining-room hostess of a hotel. The guest asked for a recommendation concerning a good place to eat in the area. Managers would hope that the hostess first would suggest the hotel's restaurant and then mention other restaurants in the area. Instead, the hostess said she had just moved to the area and had not yet found a good place to eat. Too often, employees know nothing about the hotel they work for or its products and other items of interest to guests. If employees are not enthusiastic about the company they work for and the products they sell, it will be difficult to create enthusiastic customers.

At the other extreme, a guest checked into the Quality Suites Tech Center South in Denver, Colorado, on a Saturday night and asked the front-desk clerk if he knew where the closest Catholic Church was for Mass the next morning. The clerk replied that he was not of that faith and did not know but would find out. Five minutes after the guest was in his room, the phone rang. It was from the front-desk clerk who said he had found three Catholic churches and Mass times and had personally called a Catholic friend to see which of the three he would recommend. At the same time the desk clerk asked if the guest had eaten yet and when the answer was no, he proceeded to tell him of the great Mexican food in the hotel's restaurant and then offered to make a reservation. The guest enjoyed the Mexican food. If we hire the right employees and provide good training, we will be well on the way to having enthusiastic employees create repeat guests.

When we spend a great deal of time and effort selecting employees, we want to keep them. Consultant Jeanne d'Orleans provides some suggestions on how to make employees feel welcome during their first week.

Day One
- Ask employees to arrive at a time when someone has time to greet them.
- Make the team aware they are coming so *everyone* can welcome them.
- Use bulletin boards or even marquees to say "Welcome Robert!"
- Give them a basic tour and introduce them to as many people as possible.

Within Week One
- Make sure employees participate in an organized orientation.
- Provide them with a partner/mentor during those first tenuous days.
- Have a skills training program for them.
- Tailor training to the level of expertise they bring.[44]

To be effective, employees must receive information regularly about their company. The company's history, current businesses, and its mission statement and vision are important for employees to know. They must be encouraged to feel proud of their new employer. Desire to contribute to the company's success must be instilled in them. At Disney all new employees take a course called "Traditions," in which they learn about the company, its founder, and its values and beliefs. Employees then receive specific training for their particular assignments. Disney trains its ticket takers for four days because the company wants them to be more than ticket takers; it wants them to be cast members. The term *cast members* implies they are members of a team. Like other Disney cast members, they are putting on a performance. While they work in the ticket booths, guests will ask many questions. They must know the answers to these questions or be able to find them quickly. Disney understands the importance of these moments of truth. It provides its staff with extensive training before the first moment of truth is faced.[45] Disney has become so well known for its training and human resources management that it now conducts courses for other companies.

Opryland Hotel has developed a training program that begins with an orientation for new employees, designed to instill pride in the history, culture, and stature of the hotel. The purpose of the orientation process is to create an inspiring atmosphere and build a solid work commitment that helps reduce turnover. According to Marc Clark, former director of training at Opryland, "The new employee orientation program and all employee policies are built on a foundation of a sincere service attitude. If employees, particularly managers, are not serving guests directly, then they should be serving those who are."[46]

Continuous Training

Isadore Sharp, founder of Four Seasons Hotels and Resorts, told his managers, "Our competitive edge is service, service delivered by frontline employees we expect you to develop." "Your role then will be a leader, not a boss. Your job will be to bring out the best in all individuals and weld them into a winning team."[47]

Cross-training. Training employees to do two or more jobs within the organization.

Two principal characteristics have been identified in companies that lead their industries in customer service: They emphasize **cross-training**, and they insist that everybody share certain training experiences. Most hotel training programs for college graduates rotate new employees through all departments in the hotel. This gives the trainees an insight into the importance of each department and how they work together to provide customer service. James Coney Island, a fast-food restaurant chain, cross-trains its employees so that they understand all the positions in the restaurant. Embassy Suites Hotels goes a step further, providing employees an opportunity to increase their wages based on the number of positions they have mastered.

Companies must make sure that their employees are familiar with all the products they sell. For example, all restaurant employees should be prepared to tell guests about the restaurant's Sunday brunch. A restaurant service person in a hotel should be able to give directions to the hotel's health club. Often, employees do not have knowledge of products in their own areas because they have never been given the opportunity to sample them. When a service person does not know how an item tastes, it promotes the perception that the employee or management does not care about the customer.

Truthful Training

It should not be necessary to place this warning in a textbook but feedback from embarrassed and angry employees indicates that in some cases individuals in responsible management positions purposely lie to employees. An actual example occurred to a daughter of one of the authors. The daughter acquired a part-time waitress position at an upscale restaurant. She was told that the pork roast featured that day would be served pink since it was from Durok hogs and their flesh was pink when fully cooked.

The new waitress took an order of roast pork to a customer who immediately summoned her back and complained that his roast pork was not sufficiently cooked. The waitress then told him what she had been trained to say about Durok hogs. At this, the customer became very angry and said, "Young lady, I am a farmer of Durok hogs and what you said is a bold face lie. The meat in this breed should be white when cooked properly, not pink. My meat is not cooked, and I refuse to eat it." The waitress returned the order to the chef and told him he was a liar, that she was embarrassed, and furthermore she would no longer work for a restaurant where the chef was a liar.

A front-desk clerk in a large casino resort said she felt uneasy when guests asked her about the show in the casino's showroom. The hotel had stressed the importance of promoting it favorably but did not give the front-desk employees an opportunity to see the show. As a result, the front-desk clerk would tell the guest that it was a great show. Sometimes, the guest would start asking specific questions about the show. When this happened, her answers usually reflected her lack of firsthand knowledge about the show and made her feel foolish. It would have been wise for the hotel to provide an opportunity for front-desk employees to see the show. They could have enthusiastically promoted the show with firsthand knowledge instead of cringing when someone asked about it. They may even have promoted the show on their own rather than waiting for a guest to ask about it.

In well-managed restaurants, employees know the menu. They are trained to direct guests to the menu selections that will best suit their taste and instructed in how to sell the choices on the menu. Every restaurant should have tastings where employees sample the products they are selling. Product training is a continuous learning process; it should be part of every company's employee training.

The Olive Garden brand promise is "the idealized Italian family meal" characterized by "fresh, simple, delicious Italian food," "complemented by a great glass of wine," served by "people who treat you like family," "in a comfortable home-like setting." To live up to that brand promise, the Olive Garden has sent more than 1,100 restaurant general managers and team members on cultural immersion trips to Italy, launched the Culinary Institute of Tuscany in Italy to inspire new dishes and teach general managers and team members authentic Italian cooking techniques, conducts wine training workshops for team members and in-restaurant wine sampling for guests, and is remodeling restaurants to give them a Tuscan farmhouse look. Communications include in-store, employee, and mass media messages that all reinforce the brand promise and ad slogan, "When You're Here, You're Family."[48]

Product training sometimes must extend into the visual arts. The Grand Hyatt of Hong Kong is a magnificent hotel with caring and well-trained personnel. The Grand Hyatt is truly an art museum within a hotel. The decor features sculpture, paintings, and other fine works of visual art. If exquisite art is part of the product, it should be part of the training. Guests will be impressed, and employees will gain pride in the hotel.

This results in the circular effect of creating satisfied and proud employees who in turn create satisfied guests. The results of a study of this circular effect clearly demonstrated that "as employees' job satisfaction, job involvement, and job security improve, their customer focus also improves."[49]

Insurance executives checking out of the Sheraton Boca Raton locked their keys in their car. The car was blocking traffic, and the executives had a plane to catch. The bellman telephoned the car's make and serial number to a nearby locksmith, and the hotel staff rolled the car out of traffic. Fifteen minutes after the bellman's call, the locksmith arrived with replacement keys.[50] The employees were successful in handling the problem because they were prepared for such an incident. They knew that a car blocking the entrance could cause problems, so they stored a car jack attached to a dolly nearby. The bell staff contacted nearby locksmiths. They also understood the importance of keeping guests informed to relieve anxiety. Throughout this event, they kept the insurance executives apprised of what was going on. Leaving the Sheraton Boca Raton could have been a disaster; instead, it provided an exciting incident that enabled the staff to show their professionalism and to further convince the guests that they had indeed chosen the right hotel.

The Hyatt Sanctuary Cove in Australia has adjusted its training programs. Training is now conducted by each department instead of by a trainer from the human resources department. Departments decide what their training needs are and develop programs to fill those needs. The hotel also allows any employee to attend any training session and posts all training sessions on the employee bulletin board so every employee can review the hotel's training program for the coming month. During a visit to the Hyatt, an accounting department employee was observed training a food-service waiter on the hotel's computerized food and beverage accounting system. It became obvious from their conversation that each was learning about the other's department and how the departments could better support each other.

The development of a good training program can start organizations on an upward spiral. A research study found that service quality is related inversely to staff turnover. Properly trained employees can deliver quality service, which helps the image of the firm, attracting more guests and employees to the organization.

Employee turnover rates of 100 percent or more are common in the hospitality industry. For example, limited-service restaurants have a turnover rate of

123 percent, whereas full-service restaurants have a turnover rate of 88 percent for hourly employees.[51] Firms with high turnover often ask why they should spend money training employees if they are just going to leave. This can turn into a self-fulfilling prophecy for firms that have this attitude. The employees are not properly trained and thus are not capable of delivering quality service. Not being able to deliver good service, they will feel uncomfortable in their jobs and quit. Unfortunately, this reinforces employers' beliefs that they should not spend money training their employees, but not investing in employee training programs leads to a cycle of high employee turnover and guest dissatisfaction.

Hospitality companies with a strong commitment to employee training are well advised to make this philosophy well known to all employees in action and in word. The Centennial Hotel Management Company of Canada has a written statement of a human resources philosophy that includes orientation and training. This statement is an excellent internal marketing tool:

Orientation

- The purpose of Centennial Hotel orientation is to assure the new employee that he or she has made the right decision and to build a strong sense of belonging to the company, the team, and the industry.

- Orientation assures the employees that the company provides the support they require to be successful. It is also a time to share the values of Centennial Hotel and to introduce the facilities of the hotel.

Training

- Centennial Hotel is committed to providing consistent basic training throughout the company, as well as continuous upgrading. Training is for everyone and must be planned, systematic, and comprehensive. The success of training must be measurable.[52]

Part-Time Seasonal Help

One of the worst mistakes any hospitality firm can make is to hire part-time help and then fail to make them part of the team or properly train them.

Customers expect the same level of service from these people as from full-time employees. If large numbers of part-time and seasonal employees are used, it may be necessary to place one or more individuals in charge of making certain that they are given clear instructions concerning what is expected of them. When possible, consider using a working buddy system where full-time employees are asked to watch out and assist part-time ones. Good seasonal employees must be encouraged to remain for the full term of their contract (whether written or handshake). Consider an incentive program that both rewards them for excellent performance and gives them a bonus for remaining the full season. Nonmonetary motivations such as the promise of a positive letter of recommendation, planned parties, picnics, theater events, and other social gatherings with full-time and part-time/seasonable employees are generally winners.

Managing Emotional Employees

Just as we try to understand the needs of our customers, we need to understand the needs of our employees. One of these needs is the ability to manage their emotions. According to Zeithaml and Bitner, two services marketing experts, friendliness, courtesy, empathy, and responsiveness directed toward customers all require huge amounts of emotional labor from frontline employees who shoulder this responsibility.[53] The term **emotional labor** was first used by Hochschild and has been defined as the necessary involvement of the service provider's emotions in the delivery of the service.[54] The display of emotions can strongly influence the customer's perception of service quality. To manage emotional labor, managers must hire employees who can cope with the stress caused by dealing with customers. Then emotional labor must be managed on a day-to-day basis. Some common techniques used to manage emotional labor include monitoring overtime and avoiding double shifts, encouraging work breaks, and support from fellow workers and managers. Managers are sometimes the cause of emotional stress, for

Emotional labor. The necessary involvement of the service provider's emotions in the delivery of the service.

example, by yelling at an employee before a shift and then sending the employee out to work with customers.

One of the biggest causes of emotional stress is long hours. Employees often find it hard to manage their emotions after working 10 hours straight. At this point, the employees are tired and often care little about the customer. We have all been in that position or observed service providers who were rude or uncaring after working a long shift. The cause of such behavior is that the employee is emotionally drained. The story is told of a waitress who was having a particularly hard day when a customer complained about the food. The customer shouted that his baked potato was bad. The waitress picked up the potato, slapped it a couple of times, yelling, "Bad potato, bad potato," put the potato back on the customer's plate, and walked away. Although this is a humorous story, the customer was not amused. When employees are overworked emotionally, service suffers.

Implementation of a Reward and Recognition System

To sustain a service culture, human resource policies must create a system that rewards and recognizes employees and managers that provide good customer service. Professors Sturman and Way state, "If you want to improve employee performance in the hospitality industry, ensure that the employees accurately perceive the practices, procedures, and behaviors that are rewarded, supported, and expected of them by your company."[55] Employees must receive feedback on how they are doing to perform effectively. Communication must be designed to give them feedback on their performance. An internal marketing program includes service standards and methods of measuring how well the organization is meeting these standards. The results of any service measurement should be communicated to employees. Major hotel companies survey their guests to determine their satisfaction level with individual attributes of the hotel. One researcher found that simply communicating information collected from customers changed employee attitudes and performance.[56] Customer service measurements have a positive effect on employee attitudes if results are communicated and recognition is given to those who serve the customer. If you want customer-oriented employees, seek out ways to observe them serving the customer and reward and recognize them for making the effort.[57]

Reward systems in the hospitality and travel industry used to be based only on meeting financial objectives such as achieving a certain labor cost or food cost or increasing revenue. Now well-managed companies are giving rewards based on customer satisfaction. If companies want to have customer-oriented employees, they must reward them for servicing the customer. Reward systems and bonuses based on customer satisfaction scores are one method of rewarding employees.

Unless an individual has taken a vow of poverty and wishes to live a communal spiritual life or is very wealthy, the rest of society is very concerned about monetary income. The subject of employee compensation is one that requires serious and continuous planning and sometimes modification. Professionals in the field should be retained or hired to work with members of management, particularly those in the Human Resources Department to ensure that all compensation programs provide incentives to excel. There is a subject that is not widely understood but has been proven in the hospitality industry and others to offer ongoing opportunities to provide earned financial rewards above the traditional financial programs. The purpose is to increase loyalty and longevity for employees and managers. This is an Employee Stock Ownership Plan (ESOP) and Phantom Stock.

One of the hospitality companies that successfully uses an ESOP program for managers and staff is the Waffle House. Many employees of the Waffle House have found that by retirement time their ESOP has grown to a position to provide financial assistance in retirement. Managers in many companies have an opportunity to participate in stock options or other programs but employees such as counter and grill staff may not have such opportunities. Conversations with counter employees at the Waffle House who have been in their ESOP for many years reveal that it has resulted in making a positive difference in their retirement funds.

An ESOP is generally used by privately held companies in which their stock is not traded on the stock market. The basic concept is to encourage managers and employees to dedicate effort to make certain that the company is successful so that their employment is secure and their stock value grows.

Phantom Stock is also a stock-based incentive program used by companies (public) whose stock is traded on an exchange. In this case, management may wish to offer employees an opportunity to participate in the value of the company's stock without providing actual equity ownership. This involves establishing a separate stock program (a phantom program) that tracks the company's stock price in the marketplace and rewards participating employees who own shares in the phantom stock with the price tied to the price of the actual stock. A record is maintained of the number of phantom shares an employee has earned and the current price.

Companies commonly establish conditions for participation in stock ownership programs including:

Number of years' employed

Ranking of the position held by the employee

Special stock incentives such as winning employee of the year

Professional council should be sought and used in the development of either an ESOP or a Phantom Stock program.

Nondiscrimination—Gender Gap

It is surprising in this era but apparently there still exist cases of wage discrimination. A recent study of "Gender Gap Wages" concluded, "It is clear that women still experience considerable wage discrimination in the U.S. hospitality sector." The researcher concluded, "The hospitality industry could expect to see higher turnover among women as several studies have shown that fair compensation is an important element contributing to career commitment among current students and graduates of hospitality programs."[58]

Dissemination of Marketing Information to Employees

Often, the most effective way of communicating with customers is through customer-contact employees. They can suggest additional products, such as the hotel's health club or business center, and they can upsell when it is to the guest's benefit. Employees often have opportunities to solve guest problems before they become irritants. To do this, employees need information. Unfortunately, many companies leave customer-contact employees out of the communication cycle. The director of marketing may tell managers and supervisors about upcoming events, ad campaigns, and new promotions, but some managers may feel employees do not need to know this information.

Beth Lorenzini, a restaurant trade magazine editor, states, "Promotions designed to generate excitement and sales can do just the opposite if employees aren't involved in planning and execution." Monica Kass, a former sales and marketing coordinator for Lawry's the Prime Rib, Chicago, says that employees and marketing people who develop promotions must communicate. Lawry's increased its Thanksgiving Day sales by 48 percent through employee involvement. Lawry's invited all the "wait staff" to a Thanksgiving dinner a week before Thanksgiving. This was the same meal it was serving to guests on Thanksgiving Day. The dinner not only was a festive affair to get everybody into the Thanksgiving holiday mood, but it also served as a training tool. Employees knew exactly what was going to be served on Thanksgiving Day, including wines. The management of Lawry's also asked the staff for their input as to how to make the promotion run smoothly. On Thanksgiving Day, each wait person was given a corsage or a boutonniere. Like the employees at Lawry's, all staff should be informed about promotions. They should hear about promotions and new products from management, not from advertisements meant for external customers.[59]

The actions of management are one way that an organization communicates with its employees. Management at all levels must understand that employees are watching them for cues about expected behavior. If the general manager picks a piece of paper off the floor, other employees will start doing the same. A manager who talks about the importance of employees working together as a team can reinforce the desire for teamwork through personal actions. Taking an interest in employees' work, lending a hand, knowing employees by name, and eating in the employee cafeteria are actions that will give credibility to the manager's words.

Hospitality organizations should use printed publications as part of their internal communication. Most multiunit companies have an employee newsletter, and larger hotels usually have their own in-house newsletters. Besides mass communication, personal communication is important to spread the word effectively about new products and promotional campaigns. Leonard Berry suggests

Marketing HIGHLIGHT 10–2   Internal Marketing in Action: Lewis Hotels

Burt and Andria Lewis of Boulder, Colorado, purchased second-rate failing hotels and turned them into award-winning properties with good rates and exceptionally high occupancy with strong guest and employee loyalty. The Golden Hotel in Golden, Colorado, was bought out of receivership. The Lewises were able to turn the hotel around and within two and a half years the property's occupancy was so high that even friends of the owners had difficulty acquiring a room. This hotel received awards from Choice hotels, including the Platinum Award, Best in Brand, and a nomination for Inn of the Year.

Although Burt has been in the hotel business for over 40 years, Andria joined the company eight years ago with no hotel experience. How was this accomplished by this husband/wife team from two very different backgrounds?

They used sound management practices and picked hotels in quality locations with limited potential for the development of new hotels. For example, they chose a city center hotel such as the Golden Hotel, where the availability and cost of a similar location would serve as a barrier to entry for other hotels. They also maintained their hotels.

One of the characteristics of their management was internal marketing. They created a quality product with amenities that created value for their guests. But they also wanted their employees to be able to say, "I am proud to work for this hotel." They also followed these internal marketing principles.

Hire Quality People Who Want to Succeed

Many employees are self-selected. They know about the Lewis Hotels and want to work there. Why?

- Each employee receives a thorough orientation in which the topic of personal and hotel success is foremost and accompanied by clear guidelines as to what is expected.
- Employees participate in analyzing costs and for all areas of their work such as the cost of silverware and glasses. Expense and profit information is shared with employees; thus, they feel part of the management of the operation and continuously learn.

A Quality Management Team

Lewis Hotels calls this its SWAT Team. "Best investment in this hotel," Andria said of this team. In addition to assuming responsibility for critical areas such as food and beverage operations, the team is prepared to open new properties as Lewis Hotels expands.

Food and Beverage Director Connie Laslow is representative of the quality of the SWAT Team. Connie speaks five languages and has extensive experience working for a variety of hospitality companies, including upscale restaurants and hotels. Connie is so customer focused that she can often recall what customers ordered a year later. Connie says, "You are only as successful as your staff" and works closely with them while allowing them to be creative. "You can put your fingerprints on many exciting things in the Lewis Hotels," says Connie.

Employee Empowerment

They empower employees and encourage staff to think creatively and not be bound to standardized rules. The Lewises believe that this is probably not possible for a company like McDonald's, but it is highly possible and desirable for Lewis Hotels and has much to do with providing a quality guest experience.

Managers Create a Service Culture and Show They Care About Guest Satisfaction

If a guest is dissatisfied and has left the hotel, Andria personally calls the person. Guests are often stunned that the owner has contacted them to resolve a problem. This has led to repeat business by otherwise angry guests who would select another hotel.

Burt and Andria Lewis realize that physical facilities, guest amenities, and a sound business plan are important. But they also realize customer-oriented employees are responsible for their guests returning. They use their physical environment and the warmth created by their employees to cause both guests and employees to say "wow" on a continual basis. This is accomplished by striving to exceed guest expectations at all times.

having two annual reports, one for stockholders and one for employees. Many firms are now implementing his suggestion.[60]

Snowshoe Mountain in Snowshoe, West Virginia, embarked on a marketing program to better brand the ski resort with a promise of an "authentic, rustic and engaging wilderness experience." In launching a branding initiative to define their goals and articulate what they wanted the Snowshoe Mountain brand to represent to visitors, the resort's marketers started inside. They incorporated the new brand promise in a 40-page brand book that contained the history of the resort and a list of seven attitude words that characterized how employees should interact with guests. On-mountain messaging and signs also reminded employees to deliver on the brand promise. All new hires received a brand presentation from the director of marketing to help them better understand the brand and become effective advocates.[61]

Ongoing communication between management and employees is essential—not just group meetings but regular individual meetings between the employee and management. Every customer-contact employee communicates with hundreds of customers. Managers should meet with these employees to gain customer need insights and determine how the company can make it easier for the employee to serve the customer.

DAILY BRIEFINGS   Many managers and consultants believe that daily briefings should be held at the beginning of each work day. As the name implies, these briefings must be short in duration. Ten or fifteen minutes are generally sufficient to inform staff about:

- Special guests
- New menu items
- Possible disruption of power during the day
- Special hospitality events such as a kitchen tour complete with appetizers
- Anything else that could affect the staff and guests in a positive or negative way

It has often been said that such briefings need to occur even on the busiest days since that is when problems usually occur.

EMPLOYEES WHO DO NOT UNDERSTAND YOUR LANGUAGE   The worldwide hospitality industry hires thousands of employees who are not familiar with the language spoken by management. If employees do not fully understand what management tells them, problems will occur and customer service will be negatively affected. Companies who hire large numbers of foreign employees must have a program to effectively communicate with them, including translation services and on-the-job training in the spoken language.

Research in this area showed that organizational practices do indeed influence manager's communication satisfaction with subordinates and specifically with those who have limited English skills.[62]

Front-desk clerks are the communication center of the hotel, yet they frequently do not know the names of entertainers or the type of entertainment featured in the hotel's lounges. They may also be unaware of special marketing promotions. Hotels can use technology and training to provide employees with product knowledge. Technology can be used to develop a database. Information can be readily accessible to employees, who should then be trained in the hotel's products and services. Finally, employees can be encouraged to try the company's products. They can eat in the restaurants, stay overnight in the hotel, and receive special previews of lounge entertainment. It is much more convincing if the front-desk employee can give a potential guest firsthand information rather than reading a description.

Employees should receive information on new products and product changes, marketing campaigns, and changes in the service delivery process. All action steps in the marketing plan should include internal marketing. For example, when a company introduces a new mass media campaign, the implementation plan should include actions to inform employees about the campaign. The first time that most employees see company advertisements is in the media in which the advertisement is placed. Before the advertisements appear in the media, the company

Managers should involve employees in the choice of uniforms. Courtesy of erwinova/ Fotolia.

should share the ad with its employees. Managers should also explain the objective of the campaign and the implications.

One of the authors once worked in a restaurant whose owner decided to install a computer system without discussing it with the staff. The system was first used during a busy lunch period, and the restaurant had given the staff almost no prior training. The system did not perform well, and the staff grew determined to get rid of it. They found that the system was sensitive to grease spots on the check. If a service person got butter on a check, the guest would be charged for all sorts of extra items. Some staff would deliberately put grease spots on their checks to develop false charges for the customer. When the customer complained about the bill, the server would explain to the guest the problems they were having with the new system. Customers quickly sided with the service personnel, and within three months the owner was forced to eliminate the new system. If management had consulted the employees before installation, the employees might have supported the computer. Management could have shown the employees how the system would help them better serve the guest by adding their tickets automatically and keeping them current. This would have created employee support. Instead, without the proper information and training, employees were determined from the beginning to get rid of the computer.

Employee Involvement in Uniform Selection

Employees should be involved in the selection of the uniforms they wear every day. Selecting uniforms is often left to designers and managers, with little input from the service worker. Uniforms are important because employee dress contributes greatly to the guest's encounter with customer-contact employees. Uniforms also become part of the atmospherics of a hospitality operation or travel operation; they have the ability to create aesthetic, stylish, and colorful impressions of the property.[63] They distinguish employees from the general public, making employees accessible and easily identified. In cases where uniforms are lacking, guests may become frustrated because they have difficulty identifying employees when they need help. Uniforms have the ability to create attitudes about an employee's job. Employees dressing in formal wear state that they feel and behave differently once they put on their uniform. This anecdotal evidence has been supported by research. Clothing has been found to be a contributing factor in role-playing, acting as a vivid cue that can encourage employees to engage in the behaviors associated with the role of the employee.[64] Putting on the costume can mean putting on a role and shedding other roles. Employees' dress can direct employees' behavior to be more consistent with the goals and standards of behavior established by the organization. A study of resort employees found a significant relationship between employees' perceptions of their uniforms and their overall job attitude. The higher the employees' perception of the uniform, the more positive was their rating of their overall attitude toward their job.[65]

Uniforms should be functional and accepted by the employees. Management often looks for uniforms that represent the property, acting as a marketing tool— enhancing the image of the organization. It is paramount to allow employees to be involved in uniform choices regarding both function and projected image. For example, food servers at a pirate-themed restaurant complained about the loose-fitting sleeves on their shirts and blouses. The uniforms looked great until the servers began working. The sleeves dragged across plates when they were being cleared or when trays were being unloaded at the dishwasher. In a few hours the sleeves were stained with food. The employees stated that the problem embarrassed them when they approached a guest, and they became less outgoing in their dealings with guests. Other problems with functionality include uniforms that are designed without pockets and uniforms that are uncomfortable. The selection of uniforms can have an impact on both the employees' attitude and their ability to serve the customers well. Managers need to consider the employees and involve them in uniform decisions.

Isadore Sharp claims that customer service provided by employees of Four Seasons could be a point of distinction for the brand. Some managers replied that all good hotels gave good service. They said, "Look at their ads they all promoted smiling employees and great service." Sharp replied. "Your right they all do. By *their* standards. But we are going to do it differently. Do it so it is something we are known for." Creating an internal marketing program that produces distinctive service takes years to establish. Once one has created a competitive advantage based on employee service it creates a sustainable advantage. The competition may be aware of the advantage, but it will take them years to match the service levels—if they can.

▪▪▪ CHAPTER REVIEW

I. Internal Marketing
A. The hospitality industry is unique in that employees are part of the product.
B. Marketers must develop techniques and procedures to ensure that employees are able and willing to deliver quality service.
C. Internal marketing is marketing aimed at the firm's employees.
D. Employee satisfaction and customer satisfaction are correlated.
E. The behavior of employees can be monitored through reading reviews on social media and Online Travel Agency (OTA) sites.

II. The Internal Marketing Process
A. **Establishment of a service culture**
1. A **service culture** is an organizational culture that supports customer service through policies, procedures, reward systems, and actions.
2. An **organizational culture** is a pattern of shared values and beliefs that gives members of an organization meaning, providing them with the rules for behavior in the organization.
3. Weak culture (not sure if this is a part of service/organization).
4. **Turning the organizational chart upside down.** Service organizations should create an organization that supports those employees who serve the customers.
5. Empower and train employees to handle non-routine transactions.
B. **Development of a marketing approach to human resources management**
1. Create positions that attract good employees.
2. Use a hiring process that identifies and results in hiring service-oriented employees.
3. Use hiring procedures that identify those employees who are team players.
4. Provide initial employee training designed to share the company's vision with the employee and supply the employee with product knowledge.
5. Provide continuous employee training programs.
6. Make sure employees maintain a positive attitude. Managing emotional labor helps maintain a good attitude.
7. Reward and recognize customer service and satisfaction.
C. **Dissemination of marketing information to employees**
1. Often, the most effective way of communicating with customers is through customer-contact employees.
2. Employees should hear about promotions and new products from management, not from advertisements meant for external customers.
3. Management at all levels must understand that employees are watching them for cues about expected behavior.
4. Hospitality organizations should use printed publications as part of their internal communication.
5. Hotels can use technology and training to provide employees with product knowledge.
6. Employees should receive information on new products and product changes, marketing campaigns, and changes in the service delivery process.
D. **Employee involvement in uniform selection**

■■■ DISCUSSION QUESTIONS

1. Why are employees called internal customers?
2. What is a service culture? Why is it a requirement for an internal marketing program?
3. Discuss the possible ways that marketing techniques can be used by human resources managers.
4. What are the benefits of explaining advertising campaigns to employees before they appear in the media?
5. The handling of nonroutine transactions separates excellent hospitality companies from mediocre ones. Discuss this statement.

■■■ EXPERIENTIAL EXERCISES

Do one of the following:
Visit a hospitality or travel company. Ask some questions about its products. For example, at a restaurant you may ask about the hours it is open and about menu items. You may state you are looking for a good steak restaurant and ask about its steaks. At a hotel you may ask about its rooms or restaurants. The idea is to have enough dialogue with its employees to be able to judge the customer orientation of the employees. Write your findings supporting how the employees demonstrated they had a customer orientation and ideas you have on how they could have been more customer oriented.

■■■ INTERNET EXERCISE

Go to the site of an OTA such as Expedia, Travelocity, Priceline or a social media site such as Yelp or Urban Spoon. For those outside of the United States you may use your local OTAs and social media sites. Find 10 reviews where employee actions resulted in either a positive review or a negative review. Make a log of these employee actions.

■■■ REFERENCES

1. *Sources:* Based on information from Jeffrey M. O'Brien, "A Perfect Season," *Fortune*, January 22, pp. 62–66; "The 100 Best Companies to Work For," *Fortune*, February 4, 2013, p. 85; Micah Solomon, "Four Seasons Hotels: Building Hospitality and Customer Service Culture," *Forbes*, September 1, 2013, www.forbes.com/sites/micahsolomon/201four-seasons-ho-tels-building-a-hospitality-service-cluture-without-start-ing-from-scratch/; http://jobs.fourseasons.com/Pages/Home.aspx and www.fourseasons.com/about_us/ (accessed September 2014).

2. Danny Meyer, *Setting the Table* (New York: HarperCollins, 2006), p. 11.

3. Joseph W. Benoy, "Internal Marketing Builds Service Quality," *Journal of Health Care Marketing*, 16, no. 1 (1996): 54–64.

4. Julia Chang, "From the Inside Out," *Sales and Marketing Management* (August 2005): 14.

5. Richard Normann, *Service Management: Strategy and Leadership in Service Businesses* (New York: Wiley, 1984), p. 33.

6. Ibid., p. 9.

7. Hyounae Min, Yumi Lin, and Vincent P. Magnini, "The Impact of Empathy, Professionalism and Speed, Factors Affecting Customer Satisfaction," *Cornell Hospitality Quarterly*, 58 (May 2015).

8. Bill Heatly, "Operators Who Make Staff Satisfaction a Top Priority Will Get Results on Bottom Line," *Nation Restaurant News* (May 17, 2004): 24.

9. John P. Walsh, "Employee Training Leads to Better Service, More Profits," *Hotel and Motel Management* (January 12, 2004): 14.

10. William R. George and Christian Gronroos, "Developing Customer-Conscious Employees at Every Level: Internal Marketing," in *The Handbook of Marketing for the Service Industries*, ed. Carole A. Congram (New York: American Management Association, 1991), pp. 85–100.

11. Christian Gronroos, *Strategic Management and Marketing in the Service Sector* (Cambridge, MA: Marketing Science Institute, 1983), as cited in C. Gronroos, *Service Management and Marketing* (Lexington, MA: Lexington Books, 1990), p. 223.

12. Ibid., p. 85.

13. *The Australian* (October 10, 1990).

14. S. M. Davis, *Managing Corporate Culture* (Cambridge, MA: Ballinger, 1985).

15. John Bowen and Robert Ford, "Service Organizations— 'Does Having a Thing Make a Difference,'" *Journal of Management*, 28, no. 3 (2002): 447–469.

16. Terrence E. Deal and Allan A. Kennedy, *Corporate Cultures* (Reading, MA: Addison-Wesley, 1982), pp. 15–16.

17. http://www.kimptonhotels.com/hr/cul_moments.aspx (accessed September 21, 2011).

18. Coleen Reinhart, "Organizational Culture in the Hospitality Industry," *Small Business Chronicle*,

Houston Chronicle, http://smallbusiness.chron.com/organizational-culture-hospitality-industry-12969.html (accessed July 27, 2015).

19 Flora F. T. Chiang, Thomas A. Birtch, and Zhenyao Cai, "Front Line Service Employees Job Satisfaction in the Hospitality Industry," *Cornell Hospitality Quarterly*, 55, no. 4 (November 2014).

20 A. Parasuraman, "Customer-Oriented Corporate Cultures Are Crucial to Services Marketing Success," *Journal of Services Marketing*, 1, no. 1 (Summer 1987): 39–46.

21 Ibid.

22 Viceroy Hotel Group Web Site, http://www.viceroyhotelgroup.com/en/about_us (accessed July 27, 2015).

23 Ibid., p. 107; Nathan Tyler, *Service Excellence*, Tap. 2 (videotape) (Boston, MA: Harvard Business School Management Productions, 1987).

24 James L. Heskett, W. Earl Sasser, and Leonard A. Schlesinger, *Saving Customers with Service Recovery* (videotape) (Boston, MA: Harvard Business School Management Productions, 1994).

25 Karl Albrecht and Ron Zemke, *Service America!: Doing Business in the New Economy* (Homewood, IL: Dow Jones-Irwin, 1985), pp. 127–128.

26 Gabriel Gazzoil, Murat Hancer, and Yumi Park, "The Role and Effect of Job Satisfaction and Empowerment on Customers' Perception of Service Quality: A Study in the Restaurant Industry," *Journal of Hospitality and Tourism Research*, 34, no. 1 (February 2010): 70.

27 Carla B. Furlong, *Marketing for Keeps* (New York: Wiley, 1993), pp. 79–80.

28 A. Parasuraman, "Customer-Oriented Corporate Cultures," pp. 33–40.

29 Leonard L. Berry, "The Employee as Customer," *Journal of Retail Banking*, 3, no. 1 (1981): 33–40.

30 John J. Hogan, "Turnover and What to Do About It," *Cornell Hotel and Restaurant Administration Quarterly*, 33, no. 1(February 1992), p. 41.

31 Caroline Cooper and Lacy Whittington, *Hotel Success Handbook: How to Achieve Great Customer Service*, Part 2, August 27, 2012, www.hotelsuccesshandbook.com.

32 Bowen, John, and Robert C. Ford. "Managing Service Organizations: Does Having a "Thing" Make a Difference?." *Journal of management* 28, no. 3 (2002): 447–469.

33 B. Schneider and D. Bowen, *Winning the Service Game* (Boston, MA: HBS Press, 1995).

34 C. R. Bell and K. Anderson, "Selecting Super Service People," *HR Magazine*, 37, no. 2 (1992): 52–54; Stephen J. Grove, and Raymond P. Fisk, "The Dramaturgy of Services Exchanges: An Analytical Framework for Services Marketing" in *Emerging Perspectives on Services Marketing*, G. Lynn Shostack, Leonard L. Berry, and Gregory D. Upah, ed. (Chicago, IL: American Marketing Association, 1983), pp. 45–49.

35 Miliand Lele, *The Customer Is Key* (New York: Wiley, 1987), p. 252.

36 Andrew J. Czaplewski, Jeffery M. Ferguson, and John F. Milliman, "Southwest Airlines: How Internal Marketing Pilots Success," *Marketing Management* (September/October 2001): 14–17.

37 Steve Fisher, "Flying Off into the Sunset," *Costco Connection*, 22, no. 9 (2007): 17.

38 Tschohl, *Achieving Excellence*, Through Customer Service (Englewood Cliffs, Prentice Hall, 1991), p. 113.

39 Joseph A. Michelli, *The New Gold Standard* (New York: McGraw-Hill, 2008), p. 77.

40 Danny Meyer, *Setting the Table* (New York: Harper Collins, 2006), p. 143.

41 Ibid., p. 58.

42 Osman M. Karatepe, "The Effects of Co-Worker and Perceived Organizational Support on Hotel Employee Outcomes," *Journal of Hospitality and Tourism Research*, 36, no. 4 (November 2012): 511.

43 Timothy R. Hinkin and J. Bruce Tracey, "What Makes it So Great," *Cornell Hospitality Quarterly*, 51, no. 2 (May 2015): 158–170.

44 Jeanne d'Orleans, "It's Basic Customer Service," *Hotel & Motel Management*, December 6, 2007, www.hotelmotel.com (accessed June 8, 2008).

45 N. W. Pope, "Mickey Mouse Marketing," *American Banker* (July 25, 1979), as included in W. Earl Sasser, Jr., Christopher W. L. Hart, and James L. Heskett, *The Service Management Course: Cases and Reading* (New York: Free Press, 1991), pp. 649–654.

46 Marc Clark, "Training for Tradition," *Cornell Hotel and Restaurant Administration Quarterly*, 31, no. 4 (1991): 51.

47 Isadore Sharp, *Four Seasons: The Story of a Business Philosophy* (Canada: Toronto, Penguin), p. 110.

48 Drew Madsen, "Olive Garden: Creating Value Through an Integrated Brand Experience," presentation at Marketing Science Institute Conference, *Brand Orchestration*, Orlando, Florida, December 4, 2003.

49 John R. Dienhart and Mary B. Gregoire, "Job Satisfaction, Job Involvement, Job Security and Customer Focus of Quick Service Restaurant Employees," *Hospitality Research Journal*, 16, no. 2 (1993): 41.

50 Christopher W. L. Hart, James L. Heskett, and W. Earl Sasser, Jr., *Service Breakthroughs* (New York: Free Press, 1990), p. 109.

51 Bruce Grindy, "The Restaurant Industry: An Economic Powerhouse," *Restaurants USA* (June/July 2000): 40–45.

52 Michael K. Haywood, "Effective Training: Toward a Strategic Approach," *Cornell Hotel and Restaurant Administration Quarterly*, 33, no. 6 (1992): 46.

53 Valarie A. Zeithaml and Mary Jo Bitner, *Services Marketing* (New York: McGraw-Hill, 1996).

54 A. R. Hochschild, *The Managed Heart* (Berkeley, CA: University of California Press, 1983); definition from

Gunther Berghofer, "Emotional Labor," Working Paper (Bond University, Robina, Queensland, Australia, 1993).

55 Michael C. Sturman and Sean A. Way, "Questioning Conventional Wisdom: Is a Happy Employee a Good Employee, or Do Attitudes Matter More?" The Center for Hospitality Research, Cornell University, March 2008.

56 Albrecht, Karl, and Ron Zemke. *Service America! (Homewood, Ill.* Dow Jones-Irwin, 1985).

57 Chip R. Bell and Ron Zemke, *Managing Knock Your Socks Off Service* (New York: American Management Association, 1992), p. 169.

58 Susan S. Fleming, "Déjà Vu? An Updated Analysis of the Gender Wage Gap in the U.S. Hospitality Sector," *Cornell Hospitality Quarterly*, 56, no. 2 (May 2015).

59 Beth Lorenzini, "Promotion Success Depends on Employee's Enthusiasm," *Restaurants and Institutions* (February 12, 1992): 591.

60 Berry, Leonard L. "The employee as customer." *Journal of retail banking* 3, no. 1 (1981): 33–40.

61 Paula Andruss, "Employee Ambassadors," *Marketing News* (December 15, 2008): 26–27.

62 Mary Dawson, Juan Madera, Jack Neal, and Jue Chen, "The Influence of Hotel Communication Practices on Manager's Satisfaction with Limited English-Speaking Employees," *Journal of Hospitality and Tourism Research*, 38, no. 4 (November 2014): 558.

63 M. R. Solomon, "Dress for Effect," *Psychology Today*, 20, no. 4 (1986): 20–28.

64 A. Rafaeli and M. G. Pratt, "Tailored Meanings: On the Meaning and Impact of Organizational Dress," *Academy of Management Review*, 18, no. 1 (1993): 32–55.

65 Kathy Nelson and John Bowen, "The Effect of Employee Uniforms on Employee Satisfaction," *Cornell Hotel and Restaurant Administration Quarterly*, 41, no. 2 (2000): 86–95.

11

Pricing: Understanding and Capturing Customer Value

Successful pricing at Wild Dunes® Resort requires coordinated planning and strategy. Located on the Isle of Palms near Charleston, South Carolina, Wild Dunes offers a mix of lodging, golf, tennis, dining, and family activities. This product mix combined with seasonal and special-occasion demand means that multiple factors must be considered in pricing decisions. Responsibility for planning and coordination of pricing is under the direction of the Director of Sales and Marketing.

Lodging at Wild Dunes involves three distinct properties. The first is the Boardwalk Inn, a 93-room hotel, with a private pool, billiards room, and the resort's fine dining restaurant option, the Sea Island Grill. The property is owned and operated by the resort.

The Village at Wild Dunes is the resort's newest offering, with 166 identically furnished rooms and suites and a family-style restaurant, fitness center, and day spa. Studios to three-bedroom suites and four-bedroom penthouses that were newly constructed were all sold to private owners who placed their units into the property rental program, and share in the revenues.

Additional lodging is available in nearby private homes, which Wild Dunes also manages for absentee owners. Property owners are free to use other booking and property management firms. The revenue management team must price these units to compete with them and also provide a good return to Wild Dunes and the property owners.

Wild Dunes also has other product lines—strategic business units (SBUs). These include two 18-hole golf courses, 17 tennis courts ranked in the top 10 by *Tennis Magazine*, and several tennis programs, including professional clinics and exhibitions. Island Adventures® offers recreational programs for preteen kids, teenagers, and adults. Each requires different pricing, such as the Pirate Adventure Pass and the VIP Club Pass for kids. Weekly entertainment events such as the Low Country Luau and the Blue Crabbing Expedition require price planning. Wellness programs such as group yoga, water aerobics, and spa services must also be price managed.

One of the major activities at any destination resort is dining, and Wild Dunes offers a variety in four restaurants, ranging from the Dunes Deli and Pizzeria to luxury dining at the Sea Island Grill. Dinner Delivered is another food and beverage (F&B) product that has become very popular with guests who rent condos or homes. Complete dinners are delivered to the guests' homes. Prices range from $145 to $220, but these also require careful price planning, particularly in times of increased competition and rising food costs.

Package pricing is a critical marketing responsibility. Golf is a major attraction for guests, and packages must be developed for commercial groups, groups such as a group of salespeople, and for individuals with varying abilities and interest in golf. Packages typically include accommodations, golf, and breakfast. Specialty packages also include additional items such as a 50-minute massage in the Ladies Golf Package. Packages must be priced to be competitive with other destination resorts, but success also depends on creativity in packaging. For instance, would guests prefer breakfast on the links or a lunch following golf? "Dudes on the Dunes" is a creative package designed for men that includes poker in a guest room with snacks and beer. The "Romance Package" was designed for those celebrating an anniversary or perhaps just reconnecting.

Packages offer excellent opportunities for cross-merchandising and upselling, both of which are important factors in revenue management. Participation by employees in building packages is important since these people "know the guests" better than management.

Wild Dunes employs three full-time revenue management professionals and a director of revenue optimization with responsibility for budgeting, forecasting, and helping correctly positioning Wild Dunes and its product line.

Lodging revenue is the most important part of the product line and also the most variable. Golf and tennis lessons remain relatively stable, but the price of rooms is dependent on many variables. Therefore, the revenue optimization team, including the reservations manager, meets every Wednesday.

During the meeting, the team carefully examines room inventory at all price segments and also looks at the prices of two competitive sets: one in the Charleston area and another among a group of luxury destination resorts. According to the season and anticipated demand, Wild Dunes may decide to be the price leader and at other times to follow competitors.

Like most destination resorts, Wild Dunes faces prime, shoulder, and trough periods. Eight weeks during summer is prime and demand has been increasing 15 percent for this peak period. Rooms during this period were $295 per night but the same room sold for $495 earlier during Memorial Day in May.

The revenue optimization team is instructed to let the quality of the products drive price whenever they can. Sunday is traditionally a low-demand day. Package deals are often used to fill Sunday rooms.

The reservations sales team is also focused on increasing ancillary spending for products such as bike rentals, the spa, and excursions. This means cross-selling and creative packaging and promotions. Hotel guests are reminded of daily activities and items through a guest newsletter, the on-resort television channel, and the resort's magazine and vacation planner, which is the comprehensive resource for events and activities.

Wild Dunes has found that guests crave the ability to plan their vacation their way. The Wild Dunes Web site allows guests to plan their experience through their online concierge. The concierge is a Web page that shows a calendar with all possible activities. Guests can select their itinerary and submit it through the Web site, where it will be received by the reservations call center. A pre-arrival concierge staff member from Wild Dunes responds to the inquiry and confirms the requests if available. Users of the online concierge indicate whether they prefer a response by telephone or e-mail. Guest satisfaction with this has been high and ancillary spending has increased.

Upselling has improved as guests are encouraged to custom design their own packages. This allows guests to create their ideal experience. When guests build their own package, they commonly upgrade much like buyers of a car who add more accessories or a kid in an ice cream store who orders a double scoop with "the works" on top.

Menu prices for each F&B outlet are also regularly examined against a competitive set.

The head of revenue management states his position is complex. He states he is fortunate to have three areas that absolutely must work together report to him: reservations, group sales, and catering and marketing. All of these department heads participate in the development of the marketing plan. All new associates in these areas are required to spend one and a half days in orientation and two weeks in training. During this time, concepts such as teamwork, cross-selling, upselling, and revenue optimization are stressed.

He feels those responsible for revenue management must understand the needs of the hotel's departments and how pricing and occupancy will affect these departments. In order to do this the person managing revenue must take an active role in the executive team.

■■■ Price

Price is the only marketing mix element that produces revenue. All others represent cost. Some experts rate pricing and price competition as the number-one problem facing marketing executives. Pricing is the least understood of the marketing variables, yet pricing is controllable in an unregulated market. Pricing changes are often a quick fix made without proper analysis. The most common mistakes include pricing that is too cost oriented, prices that are not revised to reflect market changes, pricing that does not take the rest of the marketing mix into account, and prices that are not varied enough for different product items and market segments. A pricing mistake can lead to a business failure, even when all other elements of the business are sound. Every manager should understand the basics of pricing.

Simply defined, **price** is the amount of money charged for a good or service. More broadly, price is the sum of the values consumers exchange for the benefits of having or using the product or service.

Marketers and managers must have an understanding of price. Charging too much chases away potential customers. Charging too little can leave a company without enough revenue to maintain the operation properly. Equipment wears out, carpets get stained, and painted surfaces need to be repainted. A firm that does not produce enough revenue to maintain the operation eventually goes out of business. In this chapter, we examine factors that hospitality marketers must consider when setting prices, general approaches, pricing strategies for new products, product mix pricing, initiating and responding to price changes, and adjusting prices to meet buyer and situational factors.

Price. The amount of money charged for a product or service, or the sum of the values that consumers exchange for the benefits of having or using the product or service.

■■■ Factors to Consider When Setting Prices

Internal and external company factors affect a company's pricing decisions. Figure 11–1 illustrates these. Internal factors include the company's marketing objectives, marketing mix strategy, costs, and organizational considerations. External factors include the nature of the market, demand competition, and other environmental elements.

Figure 11–1
Factors affecting price decisions.

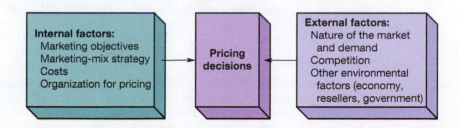

Internal factors:
Marketing objectives
Marketing-mix strategy
Costs
Organization for pricing

Pricing decisions

External factors:
Nature of the market and demand
Competition
Other environmental factors (economy, resellers, government)

Internal Factors Affecting Pricing Decisions

Marketing Objectives

Before establishing price, a company must select a product strategy. If the company has selected a target market and positioned itself carefully, its marketing mix strategy, including price, will be more precise. For example, Four Seasons positions its hotels as luxury hotels and charges a room rate that is higher than most. Motel 6 and Formula One have positioned themselves as limited-service motels, providing rooms for budget-minded travelers. This market position requires charging a low price. Thus, the strategic decisions on market positioning have a major influence on price.

SURVIVAL Companies troubled by too much capacity, heavy compensation, or changing consumer preferences set survival as their objective. In the short run, **survival** is more important than profit. Hotels often use this strategy when the economy slumps. A manufacturing firm can reduce production to match demand. During a recession, a 300-room hotel still has 300 rooms to sell each night, although the demand has dropped to 140 a night. The hotel tries to ride out the slump in the best way possible by cutting rates and trying to create the best cash flow possible under the conditions. This strategy directly affects immediate competitors and sometimes the entire industry. Competitors in the hospitality industry are highly cognizant of price changes and usually respond if they feel threatened. This results in soft markets: Not only does occupancy fall, room rates and profits also fall.

Observers of the hospitality industry have sometimes suggested that competition using a survival pricing strategy should be monitored carefully but not necessarily emulated. If the hotel is one of two in a market such as a small town, the effect of price discounting could be considerable. In contrast, if the hotel is in Orlando, Florida, it is one of many and represents a fraction of the total room supply. In this case competitors with a strong marketing program may want to use their marketing skills to gain customers rather than cut their price. Also, for a hotel with good marketing it can make sense to allow a competitor to lower prices and skim off the budget-conscious customers, leaving more profitable business for them, particularly if the hotel using a survival strategy has a small market share.

CURRENT PROFIT MAXIMIZATION Many companies want to set a price that will maximize current profits. They estimate what demand and costs will be at different prices and choose the price that will produce the maximum current profit, cash flow, or return on investment (ROI), seeking current financial outcomes rather than long-run performance. For example, a company may purchase a distressed hotel at a low price. The objective becomes to turn the hotel around, show an operating profit, and then sell. If the hotel owners can achieve a successful turnaround, they may receive a good capital gain.

Some entrepreneurs develop a restaurant concept with the objective of selling the concept to a major chain. They realize that the concept's viability must be proved through a small chain that produces a high net profit. If they can do this, they may attract the attention of a major corporation. The pricing objective in this case is current profit maximization. The success of Steve Ells with Chipotle Mexican Grill and its sale to McDonald's is a prime example.

A study of a Restaurant in Arizona demonstrated that gross revenue could be increased 5 percent by carefully analyzing revenue factors and making appropriate changes. This study showed it is important to establish a measure of baseline revenue performance known as RevPASH, which is the revenue per available seat hour. The increase in revenue came from an improved table mix and improved service delivery. "Seat occupancy and RevPASH increased, dining duration and variation in that duration increased, and revenue and profitability increased."[1]

MARKET-SHARE LEADERSHIP Some companies want to obtain a dominant market-share position. They believe that a company with the largest market share will eventually enjoy low costs and high long-run profit. Thus, prices are set as low as possible. Marriott strives to be the market-share leader in its class. When it opens a new hotel,

---

Survival. A technique used when a company's or business unit's sales slump, creating a loss that threatens its existence. Because the capacity of a hotel or restaurant is fixed, survival often involves cutting prices to increase demand and cash flow. This can disrupt the market until the firm goes out of business or the economy improves.

Marriott builds market share as quickly as possible. For example, Marriott opened its resort on Australia's Gold Coast with rates well below market. Low opening rates created demand. A great hotel with good service created repeat customers and strong positive word of mouth. Six months after opening, the hotel moved its rates up to market rates. Such a strategy uses price and other elements of the marketing mix to create the awareness of better value than the competition.

PRODUCT-QUALITY LEADERSHIP The Ritz-Carlton chain has a construction or acquisition cost per room that can exceed $1,000,000. Besides a high capital investment per room, luxury chains have a high cost of labor per room. Their hotels require well-qualified staff and a high employee-to-guest ratio to provide luxury service. They must charge a high price for their luxury hotel rooms' product.

Groen, a manufacturer of food-service equipment, is known for its high-quality steam-jacketed kettles. Kitchen designers specify Groen equipment because of its known quality, enabling the company to demand a high price for its equipment. To maintain its quality, Groen must have a well-engineered product composed of high-quality materials. It also must have the budget to ensure that it maintains its position as a quality leader.

Quality leaders such as Ritz-Carlton and Groen charge more for their products, but they also have to reinvest in their operations continuously to maintain positions as quality leaders.

OTHER OBJECTIVES A company also might use price to attain other, more specific objectives. A restaurant may set low prices to prevent competition from entering the market or set prices at the same level as its competition to stabilize the market. Fast-food restaurants may reduce prices temporarily to create excitement for a new product or draw more customers into a restaurant. Thus, pricing may play an important role in helping accomplish the company's objective at many levels.

Marketing Mix Strategy

Price is only one of many marketing mix tools that a company uses to achieve its marketing objectives. Price must be coordinated with product design, distribution, and promotion decisions to form a consistent and effective marketing program. Decisions made for other marketing mix variables may affect pricing decisions. For example, resorts that plan to distribute most of their rooms through wholesalers must build enough margin into their room price to allow them to offer a deep discount to the wholesaler. Owners usually refurbish their hotels every five to seven years to keep them in good condition. Prices must cover the costs of future renovations.

A firm's promotional mix also influences price. A restaurant catering to conventioneers receives less repeat business than a neighborhood restaurant and must advertise in city guides targeted to conventioneers. Managers of restaurants who do not consider promotional costs when setting prices experience revenue/cost problems.

Companies often make pricing decisions first. Other marketing mix decisions are based on the price a company chooses to charge. For example, Marriott saw an opportunity in the economy market and developed Fairfield Inns, using price to position the motel chain in the market. Fairfield Inns' target price defined the product's market, competition, design, and product features. Companies should consider all marketing mix decisions together when developing a marketing program.

Costs

Costs set the floor for the price a company can charge for its product. A company wants to charge a price that covers its costs for producing, distributing, and promoting the product. Beyond covering these costs, the price has to be high enough to deliver a fair rate of return to investors. Therefore, a company's costs can be an important element in its pricing strategy. Many companies work to become the low-cost producers in their industries. McDonald's has developed systems for producing fast food efficiently. A new hamburger franchise would have a hard time competing with McDonald's *on cost*. Effective low-cost producers achieve cost savings through efficiency rather than cutting quality. Companies with lower costs can set lower prices that result in greater market share. Lower costs do not always mean lower prices. Some companies with low costs keep their prices the same as competitors, providing a higher ROI.

Fixed costs. Costs that do not vary with production or sales level.

Variable costs. Costs that vary directly with the level of production.

Total costs. Costs that are the sum of the fixed and variable costs for any given level of production.

Costs take two forms, fixed and variable. **Fixed costs** (also known as *overhead*) are costs that do not vary with production or sales level. Thus, whatever its output, a company must pay bills each month for rent, interest, and executive salaries. Fixed costs are not directly related to production level. **Variable costs** vary directly with the level of production. For example, a banquet produced by the Hyatt in San Francisco has many variable costs; each meal may include a salad, rolls and butter, the main course, a beverage, and a dessert. In addition to the food items, the hotel provides linen for each guest. These are called variable costs because their total varies with the number of units produced. **Total costs** are the sum of the fixed and variable costs for any given level of production. In the long run, management must charge a price that will at least cover total costs at a given level of sales.

Managers sometimes forget that customers are not concerned with a business's operating costs; they seek value. The company must watch its costs carefully. If it costs the company more than competitors to produce and sell its product, the company must either charge a higher price or make less profit.

Many hospitality companies are developing sophisticated models and software to better understand costs and their relations to price. Embassy Suites recognizes this relationship and believes the most valuable guest is not necessarily the one who pays the highest price for a suite. A contribution model developed by Embassy Suites now examines costs to acquire and service guests, such as room labor costs, advertising, special promotions, and associated costs.

Cost Subsidization

Destination ski resorts such as Steamboat Springs, Colorado, and Sun Valley, Idaho, depend upon air transportation to bring guests from distant markets. In many cases these ski resorts are served by only one commuter airline during the nonski season. This is insufficient for the ski season when the resorts depend upon daily flights by major carriers.

Revenue management.
Forecasting demand to optimize profit. Demand is managed by adjusting price. Fences are often built to keep all customers from taking advantage of lower prices. For example, typical fences include making a reservation at least two weeks in advance or staying over a Saturday night.

Royal Caribbean Cruises has developed a revenue management department with the responsibility for price, including coordinating with other departments that influence price. Courtesy of ozphotoguy/Fotolia.

Major carriers are unwilling to assume the entire financial risk of serving resort locations for only a few months each year. Therefore, the resorts and the nearby towns that profit from ski visitors are asked to help ensure that flights will be profitable by guaranteeing an agreed-to revenue base for the airlines. Steamboat Springs Local Marketing District (LMD) guaranteed $4.8 million to airlines for one ski season.[2]

Organizational Considerations

Management must decide who within the organization should set prices. Companies handle pricing in a variety of ways. In small companies, top management, rather than the marketing or sales department, often sets the prices. In large hospitality companies, pricing is typically handled by a revenue management department under guidelines established by corporate management. A hotel develops a marketing plan that contains monthly average rates and occupancies for the coming year. Regional or corporate management approves the plan.

Many corporations within the hospitality industry now have a **revenue management** department with responsibility for pricing and coordinating with other departments that influence price. Airlines, cruise lines, auto rental companies, and many hotel chains have developed revenue management departments.

The potential rewards are enormous from professional revenue management in a large hospitality company. According to Brian Rice, Director of Revenue Planning and Analysis for Royal Caribbean Cruise Line, "If the average yield at Royal Caribbean goes up by $1 a day, it is worth $5.5 million and 100 percent of it goes to the

bottom line." Brian conservatively estimated the monetary benefits of "baby-sitting" the revenue on a day-to-day basis at Royal Caribbean at over $20 million per day.[3]

External Factors Affecting Pricing Decisions

External factors that affect pricing decisions include the nature of the market and demand, competition, and other environmental elements.

Market and Demand

Although costs set the lower limits of prices, the market and demand set the upper limit. Both consumer and channel buyers such as tour wholesalers balance the product's price against the benefits it provides. Thus, before setting prices, a marketer must understand the relationship between price and demand for a product.

Rudy's was one of the finest restaurants in Houston. It prospered during Houston's boom, but when Houston moved into recession due to low oil prices, the demand for fine dining fell and Rudy's suffered. Its lunches were just breaking even. Management considered a price increase as a way to push revenue above the break-even (BE) point. On the surface this may have seemed like a good idea: Just charge each customer $5 more, and the revenue would move above BE. This tactic assumed that the market was price inelastic.

Sales dropped at Rudy's because business expense accounts were being cut. An increase in price would have further reduced the size of the market that could afford the restaurant's prices. Another restaurant in Houston, La Colombe d'Or, adapted its pricing tactics to fit the recession. The restaurant booked many business luncheons. The host of a business luncheon generally does not force guests to order the cheapest item on the menu and may even encourage them to order wine, which is a high-margin menu item. As a result, La Colombe d'Or not only sold meals at regular prices but also enjoyed higher margin sales from business lunches.

Cross-Selling and Upselling

Cross-selling. The company's other products that are sold to the guest.

The owner of La Colombe d'Or used **cross-selling**, one of the basics of effective revenue management. Cross-selling opportunities abound in the hospitality industry. A hotel can cross-sell F&B, exercise room services, and executive support services, and it can even sell retail products ranging from hand-dipped chocolates to terry-cloth bathrobes. A ski resort can cross-sell ski lessons and dinner sleigh rides.

Upselling. Training sales and reservation employees to offer continuously a higher-priced product that will better meet the customers' needs, rather than settling for the lowest price.

Upselling, also part of effective revenue management, involves training sales and reservations employees to continuously offer a higher-priced product, rather than settling for the lowest price. One proponent of upselling believes that any hotel can increase its catering revenue by 15 percent through upselling.[4] Las Vegas resorts train front desk personnel and incentivize them to upsell guests into suites and premium rooms.

Hundreds of upselling opportunities exist. They must be recognized and programs developed and implemented to ensure their success. The common practice of offering after-dinner coffee can be turned into an upselling opportunity by offering high-image upgraded presentations of coffee and tea rather than the standard pot of coffee. Price changes are easy to make and are often seen as a quick fix to a complex problem. Although it is easy to increase or decrease prices, it is hard to change a perception that your price is incorrect.

In this section we look at how the price–demand relationship varies for different types of markets and how buyer perceptions of price affect pricing decisions. We also discuss methods for measuring the price–demand relationship.

Consumer Perceptions of Price and Value

In the end, it is the consumer who decides whether a product's price is right. When setting prices, management must consider how consumers perceive price and the ways that these perceptions affect consumers' buying decisions. Like other marketing decisions, pricing decisions must be buyer oriented.

"We can't see the value of our product," explains Carlos Talosa, senior vice president of operations at Embassy Suites. "We can only set price. The market value is set by our customers and our ability to sell to it." According to Talosa,

"Even in recessionary times, consumers aren't necessarily buying the cheapest options, but they are demanding value for their dollars and rightly so. If you aren't value-selling, then you are giving away precious assets."[5]

Pricing requires more than technical expertise. It requires creative judgments and awareness of buyers' motivations. Effective pricing opens doors. It requires a creative awareness of the target market, why they buy, and how they make their buying decisions. Recognition that buyers differ in these dimensions is as important for pricing as it is for effective promotion, distribution, or product policy.

Marketers must try to look at the consumer's reasons for choosing a product and set price according to consumer perceptions of its value. Because consumers vary in the values that they assign to products, marketers often vary their pricing strategies for different segments. They offer different sets of product features at different prices. For example, a quarter-pound hamburger might cost $6 at McDonald's, $12 at a sit-down service restaurant, and $20 in an exclusive city club.

Buyer-oriented pricing means that the marketer cannot design a marketing program and then set the price. Good pricing begins with analyzing consumer needs and price perceptions. Managers must consider other marketing mix variables before setting price. Most hotel and restaurant concepts are designed by identifying a need in the marketplace. The product concept usually contains a price range that the market is willing to pay. Limited-service hotels identified a market segment that did not value many amenities found in a full-service motel. These guests did not use cocktail lounges, hotel restaurants, and banquet and meeting facilities. By eliminating these features, owners of limited-service hotels saved money in both construction and operating costs. They passed these savings along to the customer as lower prices, offering a sleeping room at a lower price than that of midscale hotels.

Consumers tend to look at the final price and then decide whether they received a good value. For example, two people dining in a restaurant receive their bill and see that it is $80. The diners then decide whether they were satisfied during the postpurchase evaluation. Rather than going over each item on the menu individually and judging its value, they judge the entire dining experience against the cost of that experience. If a restaurant offers good value on food but poor value on wine—charging $14 a glass for house wine, for instance—a couple who consume six glasses of wine may feel the check total is too high when $56 for wine is added to the bill.

Melvyn Greene, a hotel marketing consultant, once interviewed guests immediately after they had paid their bills and were leaving the hotel. Only about a fifth could remember the room rate they had just paid. They could, however, state whether they had received good value. Most of the guests had stayed for more than one day, used the Internet, and dined in the hotel's F&B outlets. The room rate was only one part of the charges on their total bill. They tended to accept the charges and sign their charge card.[6] The guests based their perception of value on the total dollar amount of the bill, the products they had received, and their satisfaction with those products.

Different market segments evaluate products differently. Managers must provide their target markets with product attributes that the target market will value and eliminate those features that do not create value. Then they have to price the product so it will be perceived to be good value by the desired target market. For some markets, this means modest accommodations at a low price; for other markets, this means excellent service at a high price. Perceived value is a function of brand image, product attributes, and price.

Analyzing the Price–Demand Relationship

Each price a company can charge leads to a different level of demand. The demand curve illustrates the relationship between price charged and the resulting demand. It shows the number of units the market will buy in a given period at different prices that might be charged. In the normal case, demand and price are inversely related; that is, the higher the price, the lower the demand (Figure 11–2). Thus, the company would sell less if it raised its price from P_1 to P_2. Consumers with limited budgets usually buy less of something if the price is too high.

Most demand curves slope downward in either a straight or a curved line. But for prestige goods, the demand curve sometimes slopes upward. For example, a

Figure 11–2
Two hypothetical demand schedules.

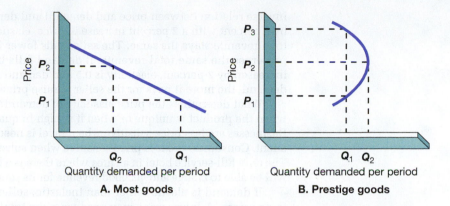

A. Most goods

B. Prestige goods

luxury hotel may find that by raising its price from P_1 to P_2, it sells more rooms rather than fewer: Consumers do not perceive it as a luxury hotel at the lower price. However, if the hotel charges too high a price, (P_3), the level of demand will be lower than at P_2.

Most company managers understand the basics of a demand curve, but few are able to measure their demand curves. The type of market determines the type of demand curve. In a monopoly, the demand curve shows the total market demand resulting from different prices. But if the company faces competition, its demand at different prices will depend on whether competitors' prices remain constant or change with the company's own prices.

Estimating demand curves requires forecasting demand at different prices. For example, a study by the Economic Intelligence Unit (EIU) estimated the demand curve for holiday travel in Europe. Its findings suggested that a 20 percent reduction in the price of visiting a holiday destination increases demand by 35 percent, whereas a 5 percent decrease results in a 15 percent increase in demand.[7] The EIU study used vacation destinations in the Mediterranean and assumed that other variables were constant.

Researchers can develop models that assume other variables remain constant. For managers, it's not that simple. In normal business situations, other factors affect demand along with price. These factors include competition, the economy, advertising, and sales effort. If a resort cut its price and then advertised, it would be hard to tell what portion of the increased demand came from the price decrease and what portion came from the advertising. Price cannot be isolated from other factors.

Economists show the impact of nonprice factors on demand through shifts in the demand curve rather than movement along it. Suppose that the initial demand curve is D_1 (Figure 11–3), the seller is charging P and selling Q_1 units. Now suppose that the economy suddenly improves or the seller doubles the advertising budget. Higher demand is reflected through an upward shift of the demand curve from D_1 to D_2. Without changing the price, P, the demand has increased.

Price Elasticity of Demand

Marketers also need to understand the concept of price elasticity, how responsive demand will be to a change in price. Consider the two demand curves in Figure 11–4. In Figure 11–4A, a price increase from P_1 to P_2 leads to a small drop in demand from Q_1 to Q_2. In Figure 11–4B, however, the same price increase leads to a large drop in demand from Q_1 to Q_2. If demand hardly varies with a small change in price, we say that the demand is inelastic. If demand changes greatly, we say the demand is elastic.

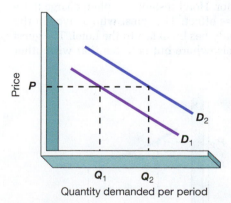

Figure 11–3
Effects of promotion and other nonprice variables on demand through shifts of the demand curve.

$$\frac{\% \text{ Change in Quality Demanded}}{\text{Price Elasticity of Demand}} = \% \text{ Change in Price}$$

Suppose that demand falls by 10 percent when a seller raises its price by 2 percent. Price elasticity of demand is therefore –5 (the minus sign confirms the inverse relation between price and demand) and demand is elastic. If demand falls by 2 percent with a 2 percent increase in price, elasticity is 1. In this case the seller's total revenue stays the same: The seller sells fewer items but at a higher price that preserves the same total revenue. If demand falls by 1 percent when the price is increased by 2 percent, elasticity is 0.5 and demand is inelastic. The less elastic the demand, the more it pays for the seller to raise price.

What determines the price elasticity of demand? Buyers are less price-sensitive when the product is unique or when it is high in quality, prestige, or exclusiveness. Businesses are less price-sensitive when travel is needed to serve a client or potential client. Consumers are less price-sensitive when substitute products are hard to find. The only full-service hotel in an area where there is a high demand for four-star hotels will be able to charge and get good revenue for its rooms until competition arrives.

If demand is elastic rather than inelastic, sellers generally consider lowering their prices. A lower price may produce more total revenue. This practice makes sense when the extra costs of producing and selling more products do not exceed the extra revenue.

Factors Affecting Price Sensitivity[8]

We now look at some factors that affect price sensitivity. These include the unique value effect, the substitute awareness effect, the business expenditure effect, the end-benefit effect, the total expenditure effect, the shared cost effect, and the price quality effect.

UNIQUE VALUE EFFECT   In Houston, the Pappas family has converted failed locations into successful restaurants, taking what had been dead restaurants and turning them into businesses with a one-hour wait on weeknights. The Pappas family did not have to use coupons or other price discounts to sell its food. It created a perception of value by giving large portions of food at a moderate price, which appealed to the upper lower class and the middle class.

Creating the perception that your offering is different from those of your competitors avoids price competition. In this way, the firm lets the customer know it's providing more benefits and offering a value that is superior to that of competitors, one that will attract either a higher price or more customers at the same price.

The guests may not always be able to describe what they mean by "value" but they certainly recognize it when they see or experience it. Price is a reflection of value and occasionally guests are highly offended by paying five-star prices for a three-star product. The Internet offers photos of properties and even menu offerings but staged photos may not accurately reflect reality.

SUBSTITUTE AWARENESS EFFECT   The existence of alternatives of which buyers are unaware cannot affect their purchase behavior. Hotel restaurants often charge more for meals based on the substitute awareness effect. The guest who arrives in the evening, being unfamiliar with the city, usually has breakfast in the hotel. The guest knows that a better value probably exists elsewhere but is unfamiliar with other

Figure 11–4
Inelastic and elastic demand.

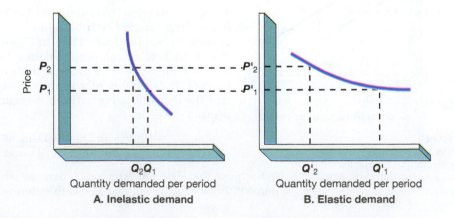

restaurants in the city. Although the breakfast in the hotel may cost twice as much as a meal in a nearby restaurant, the search costs, the time it would take to find the restaurant, and the travel time to it are greater than the dollar savings of the meal.

Restaurants that target the convention market or out-of-town guests use the substitute awareness effect to their advantage. These restaurants have large advertisements in the city's entertainment magazines that are distributed in the hotels. They are often not the choice of the local resident, who perceives them as overpriced, but they do attract hotel guests who are unaware of alternatives.

When consumers discover products offering a better value, they switch to those products. Many hotel restaurants are empty in the evening. They are perceived as overpriced by the local market. Hotel guests have time during the day to find alternatives. These hotels often view F&B as a required amenity rather than an opportunity to compete for local business. A better philosophy is to use F&B as a means to attract customers. This requires unique offerings and concepts that provide realized value for the guest.

BUSINESS EXPENDITURE EFFECT When someone else pays the bill, the customer is less price-sensitive. This person will prefer to stay in an upscale hotel, and enjoy a good breakfast. When setting rates, management needs to know what the market is willing to pay. If a hotel can attract people traveling for business who have a generous travel allowance and are willing to pay high room rates, the hotel is leaving money on the table by offering discounts.

Airlines have been known to offer a second business-class ticket at a discount when one is purchased at full price. Hotels have been known to offer bonus frequent-flyer miles. Both of these promotions are taking advantage of the business expenditure effect. The airline knows that the employer or client will pick up the full-fare ticket, and the business traveler will be able to take a companion along at a discount. The hotel knows that because the traveler's company will pay for the hotel room, cutting prices by a few dollars might not bring in extra business travelers, but giving the business traveler bonus frequent-flyer miles that they can use for vacation trips will be effective. The business expenditure effect has numerous applications in the hospitality and travel industry.

END-BENEFIT EFFECT Customers are more price-sensitive when the price of the product accounts for a large share of the total cost of the end benefit. For example, a Japanese couple paying $3,000 in airfare to travel to Australia will pay $350 a night for a luxury ocean-front hotel. The $350 is a small cost of the end benefit (their vacation). Many families driving to the Gold Coast from Sydney (a 500-mile trip) are looking for less expensive accommodations. These families are often on a limited budget and prefer a less expensive motel a few blocks from the ocean.

When the Japanese couple goes to Dreamworld (a theme entertainment park), they pay the full per-person entrance fee without hesitation. The admission fee is a small portion of the price of their vacation. However, the local family of four looking for weekend entertainment may view the charges as high. In this case, the entry fee amounts to a large portion of their entertainment expenses for the month. To attract the local customer, Dreamworld offers yearly passes for just twice the single admission charge. Dreamworld knows that if it were to raise its prices by 20 percent, it would lose more local customers than international travelers. Thus, it is important for Dreamworld to know its customer mix. If 75 percent of Dreamworld's customers are local residents, Dreamworld must be cautious about its price increases. It is common for tourist attractions to provide special rates for local residents.

Upscale hotels can use the end-benefit effect as a tool to convince potential customers

International visitors to the Gold Coast are less price-sensitive than local visitors. Courtesy of jodie777/Fotolia.

to pay an additional amount for hotel rooms. A company holding a two-day sales meeting may spend $750 in airfare, pay $500 in salary per day, and spend $100 in speaker fees per participant. A smart hotel salesperson may convince the meeting planner to upgrade by pointing out that the hotel costs are a small portion of the total costs. The sales presentation might be structured like this:

> And the difference between our luxury accommodations and the hotel accommodations you're considering is only $75 per night or $150 per participant, which is a small portion of your total cost per participant. Don't you think it's worth $150 to instill pride in your employees and show them that you care enough about them to put them in one of the best hotels in the city? Surely, the attitude difference this will create in the participants will play a significant role in the total success of the conference. Let's get the contracts drawn up for your sales meeting right now while we still have the space.

When working with price, the end-benefit price is an important concept to consider. The end-benefit price identifies price-sensitive markets and provides opportunities to overcome pricing objections when the product being sold is a small cost of the end benefit. To take full advantage of this effect, remember that many purchases have nonmonetary costs. For example, a mother planning the wedding of her daughter wants everything to be perfect to avoid embarrassing moments. High emotional involvement often makes the buyer less price-sensitive.

TOTAL EXPENDITURE EFFECT   The more someone spends his or her own money on a product or service, the more sensitive that person is to the product's price. For example, limited-service chains such as Hampton Inns, Red Roof Inns, and La Quinta have made a successful effort to appeal to salespersons. The travel expenses of a salesperson can be significant, especially for those who average two to three days a week away from home. A salesperson that saves just $20 a night can realize annual savings of more than $2,000. This savings adds to the profit of salespeople on straight commission. Companies that pay the expenses of their salespeople can save $2,000 times the number of salespeople that they employ. Thus, a company with 12 salespeople can save $24,000.

The total expenditure effect is useful in selling lower-price products or products that offer cost savings to volume users. The hotel concepts mentioned earlier provide salespeople with the benefits that they seek in a hotel: clean, comfortable rooms; security; free telephone calls; and a coffee shop nearby.

The total expenditure effect is a dominant decision-making force for thousands of travelers who are provided with a set figure per trip. Many truckers are given a predetermined amount of cash, such as $500 for a trip. Expenditures over that level are not reimbursed. Not all motels desire the business of truckers, but those who do are highly cognizant of the fixed expenditures of their guests. They realize that ample parking for a 16- or 18-wheeler, a clean room with two beds, and a reasonable price will attract business.

Hotels that cater to upscale travelers frequently feature one king-size bed in a room because few people on unlimited or high-expense accounts wish to share a room. Quite the opposite is true of truckers or pipeline construction teams with fixed-expenditure travel budgets. A $70 room shared by two extends a fixed budget.

PRICE QUALITY EFFECT   Consumers tend to equate price with quality, especially when they lack any prior experience with the product. For example, a friend may recommend that you stay at the Grand Hotel on your trip to Houston. If you call to make reservations and the reservationist offers you a $69 weekend rate, you may perceive this rate as too low for the class of hotel that you want and select another. The Grand Hotel may have met all your needs, but because of the low price, you assumed it would not.

A high price can also bring prestige to a product because it limits availability. Restaurants where the average check is more than $100 per person for dinner would lose many of their present customers if they lowered their prices. In cases where price is perceived to relate to quality or where price creates prestige, a positive association between price and demand may exist with some market segments. For example, the Gosforth Park Hotel, an upscale hotel in Newcastle, England, found that occupancy increased as its rates increased.[9]

HIDDEN FEES The hospitality industry is known for charging hidden fees or fees that a guest has to pay to use the product that are not included in the basic price. Resorts often add a resort fee that can be $30 or more. This fee usually covers items such as Internet connection and the health club whether or not the guest uses these services. Many airlines charge baggage fee that can be from $25 to $100 per bag. Budget airlines will charge extra for an aisle or window seat. Some cruise lines add a $20–30 per day gratuity charge to the final bill on the cruise. In addition to alcoholic drinks some also charge for carbonated soft drinks. This charge is about $5 a day for children and $7 a day for adults. These charges allow the hotel, airline, or cruise to post a lower base rate, attracting price-sensitive customers and then collecting these hidden fees from the guest. These fees are unlikely to ever disappear from the hospitality industry. However, to avoid angry guests and embarrassment, it is important to keep such fees transparent to the guest before reaching the point of paying for the bill. If guests inquire at any time about extra fees, they should be given clear and direct answers.[10]

Competitors' Prices and Offers

Competitors' prices and their possible reactions to a company's own pricing moves are other external factors affecting pricing decisions. A meeting planner scheduling a meeting in Chicago will check the price and value of competitive hotels.

Once a company is aware of its competitors' prices and offers, it can use this information as a starting point for deciding its own pricing. For example, if a customer perceives that the Sheraton in Singapore is similar to the Hilton, the Sheraton must set its prices close to those of the Hilton or lose that customer. This is called a competitive set. The Star Report is a popular tool provided by STR. It compares a hotel with a set of competitors (usually 4), which they select. The Star Report compares price, occupancy, and RevPAR of your hotel with an aggregate of the competitive set.

Price-Rate Compression

During periods of weak demand, very few competitors escape the effect of a weak market. Those with a strong and loyal customer base are best suited to "ride out" such a market. In many cases, competitors are inclined to lower prices as a response rather than seek other strategies. Under these conditions, "price compression" may occur.

Price (rate) compression occurs when the difference between room rates for three- to four- and five-star properties is not significant. This occurs when higher-priced hotels lower rates to maintain occupancy and become direct competitors to lower-rated hotels. This creates margin problems for economy sector hotels, which may have less ability to lower rates.

Other External Elements

When setting prices, the company must also consider other factors in the external environment. Economic factors such as inflation, boom, or recession and interest rates affect pricing decisions. For example, when gasoline prices went from $2.40 a gallon to $3.80 a gallon, many families were paying $50 to $100 more a month for gasoline. This money reduced their discretionary budget, reducing the money they had to spend on restaurants. Many restaurants had to reduce their prices to maintain customer counts. Most cannot offer the same product at a lower price and survive. The restaurants create new menus with lower-cost items that can be sold at a lower price.

■■■ General Pricing Approaches

The price the company charges is somewhere between one that is too low to produce a profit and one that is too high to produce sufficient demand. Product costs set a floor for the price; consumer perceptions of the product's value set the ceiling. The company must consider competitors' prices and other external and internal factors to find the best price between these two extremes.

Companies set prices by selecting a general pricing approach that includes one or more of these sets of factors. We look at the following approaches: the cost-based approach (**cost-plus pricing**, BE analysis, and target profit pricing), the value-based approach (perceived-value pricing), and the competition-based approach (going rate).

Cost-plus pricing. Adding a standard markup to the cost of the product.

Cost-Based Pricing

The simplest pricing method is cost-plus pricing, adding a standard markup to the cost of the product. F&B managers often use the cost-plus method to decide wine prices. For example, a bottle of wine that costs $14 may sell for $42, or three times the cost.

Cost as a percentage of selling price is another commonly used pricing technique in the restaurant industry. Some restaurant managers target a certain food cost and then price their menu items accordingly. For example, a manager wanting a 40 percent food cost prices the items 2.5 times greater than their cost. The multiplicand is found by dividing the desired food cost percentage by 100. A manager desiring a 30 percent food cost would multiply the cost by 3.33. Managers using this type of pricing should realize that a restaurant is not 100 percent efficient. To make up for spoilage, shrinkage, and mistakes, managers usually have to price three or four percentage points below their desired food cost. Thus, a manager wanting a 40 percent food cost would need to price the menu at 36 to 37 percent. The adjustment figure varies depending on the volume and efficiency of the operation. In high-volume, limited-menu operations, it is lower.

For managers using this technique, it is advisable to use prime cost, the cost of labor and food, when determining menu prices. There is often a tradeoff between labor and food costs; thus, prime cost is a truer reflection of the cost of producing a menu item. For example, if a restaurant makes its own desserts, the cost of the ingredients is usually cheaper than that of buying a similar product from a bakery; however, there are no labor costs for the preparation of the purchased product. It is better to look at both labor and food costs to determine prices.

Does using standard markups to set prices make logical sense? Generally, no. Any pricing method that ignores current demand and competition is not likely to lead to the best price. Some items with high costs such as steaks may have a lower markup, whereas signature desserts or appetizers have a high markup. Most managers who use cost as a percentage of selling price to determine menu prices use this technique to develop a target price. They adjust individual prices for menu items based on factors such as what the market will bear, psychological pricing, and other techniques discussed in this chapter.

Wine was typically sold in restaurants at about three times cost. A growing trend is to reduce the markup as the price increases. For example, at three times markup, the sales price for bottles of wine costing $8, $25, and $75 would be $24, $75, and $225. A more rational approach is to sell less expensive bottles for three to four times markup and gradually reduce the cost multiplier on higher-priced bottles to 1.5 times cost. Using this model, the price of bottles that cost $8, $25, and $75 could be $28, $65, and $150. This type of pricing also attracts guests who enjoy finer wines and also tend to enjoy fine dining, increasing the overall check average.[11] In the case of exceptional wines, some establishments prefer to reserve them for a special gourmet dinner involving many courses and several wines. The price per person for such a dinner can easily exceed $200 per guest. The Steamboat Inn, situated 38 miles north of Roseburg, Oregon, on the Umpqua River, has built a strong reputation with such diners.

Markup pricing remains popular for many reasons. First, sellers are more certain about costs than about demand. Tying the price to cost simplifies pricing, and managers do not have to adjust as demand changes. Second, because many F&B operations tend to use this method, prices are similar, and price competition is minimized.

Break-Even Analysis and Target Profit Pricing

Another cost-oriented pricing approach is BE pricing, in which the firm tries to determine the price at which it will break even. Some firms use a variation of BE pricing called *target profit pricing*, which targets a certain ROI.

Target profit pricing uses the concept of a BE chart (Figure 11–5). For example, a buffet restaurant may want to make a profit of $200,000. Its BE chart shows the total cost and total revenue at different levels of sales. Suppose that fixed costs are $300,000, and variable costs are $10 per meal. Variable costs are added to fixed costs to find total costs, which rise with volume. Total revenue starts at zero and rises with each unit sold. The slope of the total revenue reflects the price. If the restaurant sells 50,000 meals at a price of $20, for example, the company's revenue is $1 million.

At the $20 price, the company must sell at least 30,000 meals to break even; that is, at this sales level, total revenues will equal total costs of $600,000. If the company wants a target profit of $200,000, it must sell at least 50,000 meals, or 137 meals a day. This level of sales will provide $1 million of revenue to cover costs of $800,000, plus $200,000 in target profits. In contrast, if the company charges a higher price, say $25 per meal, it will need to sell only 33,334 meals, or 92 a day, to meet its target profit. The higher the price, the lower the company's BE point. The selling price less the variable cost represents the gross profit or contribution that the sale makes toward offsetting fixed costs. Here is the formula for the BE point:

BE = Fixed Costs/Contribution (Selling Price – Variable Cost)

In the previous example,

BE = $300,000/$10 ($20 Selling Price – $10 Variable Cost) = 30,000 meals

Hotels use this concept of contribution margin to set rates when demand drops. Hotels set low rates, rationalizing that at least they are covering their variable costs.

Figure 11–5
Break-even chart for determining target price.

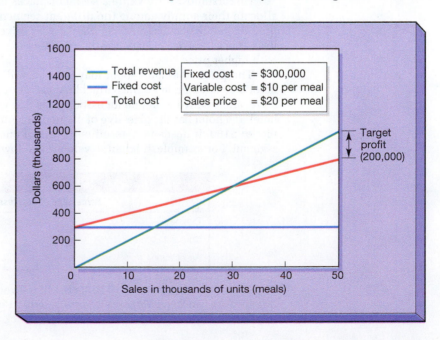

This can be effective if it creates additional demand. However, some hotels try to steal business during good times by cutting rates. This is a difficult strategy to manage, as recuperating from any substantial cut in prices in an inelastic market is not easy. A hotel that is 60 percent occupied with a room rate of $120 and a fixed cost of $40 per room and that cut its rates to $95 would have to increase its occupancy rate to 87 percent to BE on rooms profit. The fixed cost includes the cost of laundry, amentias, utilities, and cleaning of the room.[12]

Much depends on the relationship between price and demand. For example, suppose a company calculates that given its current fixed and variable costs, it must charge a price of $30 for the product to earn its desired target profit. But marketing research shows that few customers will pay more than $25 for the product. In this case, the company must trim its costs to lower the BE point so it can charge the lower price that consumers expect.

Value-Based Pricing

Value-based pricing. Uses the buyer's perceptions of value, not the seller's cost, as the key to pricing.

An increasing number of companies are basing their prices on the products' perceived value. **Value-based pricing** uses the buyers' perceptions of value, not the seller's cost, as the key to pricing. Value-based pricing means that the marketer cannot design a product and marketing program and then set the price. Price is considered along with other marketing mix variables before the marketing program is set. The company uses the nonprice variables in the marketing mix to build perceived value in the buyers' minds, setting price to match the perceived value.

Any company using perceived-value pricing must learn the value in the buyers' minds for different competitive offers. Sometimes researchers ask consumers how much they would pay for each benefit added to the offer. One method of identifying how much customers are willing to pay involves using a technique called *tradeoff analysis*. Researchers ask buyers how much they would pay for a hotel room with and without certain amenities. This information provides an idea of which features add more value than the cost. If the seller charges more than the buyers' perceived value, its sales will suffer.

Jack Welch, the former CEO of General Electric, stated, "The best way to hold your customers is to constantly figure out how to give them more for less."[13] More and more marketers have adopted value-pricing strategies. They strive to offer just the right combination of quality and good service at a fair price. This can result in redesigning existing brands to provide more quality or offer the same amount of quality for a lower price.

Understanding the value a segment places on a product can help marketers allocate their supply among the different segments. A study of meeting planners provided evidence that meeting planners perceived a greater value in paying $200 for a room than $175. Apparently, planners, like many guests, associate quality with higher price.[14]

The price of a hotel room may vary according to the type of customer. The hotel may have a rate for individual business guests, a group rate for groups of 10 or more, and a convention rate for associations that want to hold large functions at the hotel. If a hotel has the objective of maintaining 60 percent occupancy at an average rate of $180, it needs to determine its mix of customers and the average rate per segment. For example, it might develop the following mix to achieve a $180 rate:

	Percentage of Business	Average Rate ($)
Business	30	200
Corporate group	40	180
Association	30	160

To achieve its target rate of $180, the hotel would have to sell above the average rate in peak times to compensate for discounted prices during off-peak times. It is important to develop target rates and keep on track toward meeting these goals. If the hotel offers a group 100 rooms for three nights at a rate of $150, it will need to make up $4,500 [(100 rooms × 3 nights × $90 target rate) − (300 × $75 actual rate)] in revenue. It must sell to other groups above the $90 target rate, sell more business rooms at the $100 rate, or increase the targeted occupancy rate and sell additional rooms.[15]

A successful guest price mix depends on careful study of the behavior profiles of major guest segments. For most hospitality companies, this begins with a separation of guests into leisure and business segments. Subsegmentation of each category may occur, providing greater information about these major guest categories. Undoubtedly, the most important distinguishing profile characteristics of these two major segments are their relative degree of price elasticity. In general, business travelers exhibit inelastic price behavior and leisure travelers an elastic price response.

Competition-Based Pricing

Going-rate pricing. Setting price based largely on following competitors' prices rather than on company costs or demand.

A strategy of **going-rate pricing** is the establishment of price based largely on those of competitors, with less attention paid to costs or demand. The firm might charge the same, more, or less than its major competitors. Some firms may charge a bit more or less, but they hold the amount of difference constant. For example, a limited-service hotel chain may charge $25 more than Motel 6 in markets where they compete. This form of pricing is quite popular.

■■■ Pricing Strategies

New-Product Pricing Strategies

Pricing strategies usually change as a product passes through its life cycle. The introductory stage is especially challenging. Several options exist for pricing new products: prestige pricing, market-skimming pricing, and market-penetration pricing.

Prestige Pricing

Hotels or restaurants seeking to position themselves as luxurious and elegant enter the market with a high price to support this position. Nightclubs may charge a cover charge to attract a certain type of clientele and create an image of exclusiveness. In each of these cases, lowering the price would reposition the business, resulting in a failure to attract the target market.

Market-Skimming Pricing

Price skimming is setting a high price when the market is price-insensitive. Price skimming can make sense when lowering the price will create less revenue. For

The Hotel Vier Jahreszeiten Kempinski, built in 1858, is situated on Maximilianstrasse, regarded as Munich's most desirable street. Kempinski operates luxury hotels. It has a prestigious name and is often the price leader in the markets it serves. Courtesy of Mariusz Jarymowicz/Dorota Jarymo/Dorling Kindersley, Ltd.

example, the owner of the only motel in a small town in South Dakota during pheasant hunting season can set high prices if there is more demand than rooms. Price skimming can be an effective short-term policy. However, one danger is that competition will notice the high prices that consumers are willing to pay and enter the market, creating more supply and eventually reducing prices. The hospitality industry is particularly affected by this because market entry by competitors is relatively easy.

Market-Penetration Pricing

Rather than setting a high initial price to skim off small but profitable market segments, other companies set a low initial price to penetrate the market quickly and deeply, attracting many buyers and winning a large market share. Theodore Zinck's, a cocktail lounge, opened in a new market with prices about 20 percent lower than the competition. Management had negotiated a low lease, giving Zinck's a competitive advantage. Competitors could not match Zinck's lower prices because of the higher overhead. The policy allowed Zinck's to attract many customers quickly.

Several conditions favor setting a low price: (1) The market must be highly price-sensitive so that a low price produces more market growth, (2) there should be economics that reduce costs as sales volume increases, and (3) the low price must help keep out competition.

Existing-Product Pricing Strategies

The strategies just described are used primarily when introducing a new product. However, they can also be useful with existing products. The following strategies are ones that can be used with existing products.

Product-Bundle Pricing

Sellers who use product-bundle pricing combine several of their products and offer the bundle at a reduced price. For example, hotels sell specially priced weekend packages that include room, meals, and entertainment or offer commercial rates that include breakfast and a newspaper. Product bundling can promote the sales of products that consumers might not otherwise buy, but the combined price must be low enough to convince them to buy the bundle. The items added to the core service must hold more value to the customer than they cost to provide.

Product-bundle pricing is a strategy that has been well developed by cruise lines, tour wholesalers, and casinos. Cruise lines typically offer fly-cruise or fly-drive cruise packages in which the services of an auto rental company, airline, cruise line, and hotel are combined at a price well under the cost of purchasing each separately. The Internet has increased the use of product bundling by allowing companies to sell related products over their sites, such as airlines selling hotel rooms, rental cars, and vacation packages on their Web sites. Online travel agencies (OTAs) (Orbitz.com and Expedia.com), tour operators (Carlsontravel.com), destinations (Lasvegas.com), travel-related search engines (Kayak.com), travel agency consortia (Vacation.com), and global distribution systems (GDSs) (Amadeus and Sabre) all sell packages. With the Internet as the distribution system, product bundles are expected to continue to grow in popularity.[16]

Price bundling has two major benefits to hospitality and travel organizations. First, customers have different maximum prices or reservation prices they will pay for a product. Thus, by packaging products, we can transfer the surplus reservation price on one component to another component of the package. For example, customer "A" may be willing to pay $280 for two nights in a hotel room near Disneyland and $350 for two 3-day passes to Disneyland. Customer "B" is willing to pay $325 for two nights in a hotel room and $300 for two 3-day passes. If a hotel that wants to get $160 for a night for its rooms is able to get discounted three-day passes to Disneyland and offer a package that includes a room for two for two nights and two 3-day passes for $620, both customers will take advantage of the package. Even though the room price of $20 a night is above what the one customer wanted to pay, when the room and tickets are packaged together, the components are below the reservation price. In this case, the three-day pass was $50 below customer A's reservation price for the pass and the hotel price was $20 a night above what customer A wanted to pay. When they were packed together, the passes and the room were $10 less than customer A's reservation price for the package. Customers have different reservation prices; by bundling we can transfer surpluses from one component to another to expand the market.

A second benefit of price bundling is that the price of the core product can be hidden to avoid price wars or the perception of having a low-quality product. For example, a Las Vegas hotel that normally has an average rate above $120 may sell rooms to airlines for $55 to help fill the hotel. The airline bundles the hotel with a round-trip air ticket. The airline's package includes two nights in the hotel and airfare from Los Angeles for $299. This creates a much better perception for the hotel than if it ran an advertisement pushing $55 room rates. The $55 rates give a message to some that the hotel is desperate for business, to others who do not know the hotel it will give a perception of a hotel of the $55 quality level, and guests who had paid $129 for a room may ask for a refund. By selling the rooms to an airline and creating a bundled product, the hotel avoided the image problems that can come with low rates. Hotels can also create their own bundles. For example, the Royal Palms Hotel and Spa in Phoenix offered a "Royal Romance Package." The package included champagne, chocolate-covered strawberries, a rose-petal turn-down, dinner for two, and a room for $456. The rack rate was $439 for a room for the same date. Rather than cut rates to try to attract guests, the exclusive resort bundled a number of products that have value to a couple wanting to get away.[17]

Dynamic packaging. A package vacation on a single Web site in which buyers can put together airline flights, lodging, car rental, entertainment, and tours in their own customer-designed packages.

Dynamic packaging is a relatively new term that refers to an old practice. Today it refers primarily to a package vacation on a single Web site in which buyers can put together airline flights, lodging, car rental, entertainment, and tours in their own customer-designed packages.

Price-Adjustment Strategies

Companies usually adjust their basic prices to account for various customer differences and changing situations. We look at the following adjustment strategies: discount pricing and allowances and discriminatory pricing.

VOLUME DISCOUNTS   Most hotels have special rates to attract customers who are likely to purchase a large quantity of hotel rooms, either for a single period or throughout the year. Hotels usually offer special prices or provide free goods for association and corporate meeting planners. As an example, suppose that a convention held by an industry association is attended by people who pay their own room charges. The association may prefer to receive a free room night for every 20-room nights booked, rather than a lower room rate. It can use the free nights for its staff and invited speakers, reducing the association's total costs. Hotels offer corporate rates to companies that will guarantee their use of the hotel for an agreed-upon number of room nights per year.

DISCOUNTS BASED ON TIME OF PURCHASE   Seasonal discounts allow the hotel to keep demand steady during the year. Hotels, motels, and airlines offer seasonal discounts during selling periods that are traditionally slower. Airlines often offer off-peak prices, based on the time of day or the day of the week that the passenger flies. International flights adjust the price according to seasonal demand. Restaurants offer early-bird specials to attract customers before their normal rush. Unfortunately, the various discount rates offered by a company sometimes clash to negate the desired positive effects. For example, restaurants that offer seniors 10 percent discounts have more difficulty offering early-bird specials. Seniors often feel no reason to accept the early-bird special because they will qualify for a discount at peak hours.

Discriminatory pricing. Refers to segmentation of the market and pricing differences based on price elasticity characteristics of the segments.

DISCRIMINATORY PRICING   The term *discriminatory pricing* often invokes mental images of discrimination on the basis of ethnicity, religion, gender, or age. **Discriminatory pricing**, from the vocabulary of economics, refers to segmentation of the market and pricing differences based on price elasticity characteristics of these segments. Price discrimination as used in this chapter is legal and viewed by many as highly beneficial to the consumer.

Companies often adjust basic prices to allow for differences in customers, products, and locations. In discriminatory pricing, the company sells a product or service at two or more prices, although the difference in price is not based on differences in cost.

Suppose, for example, that a steak dinner has a menu price of $40, and the demand is 100 dinners at this price. If the restaurant lowers the price to $28, demand increases to 200 dinners. If the variable costs for preparing and serving the dinner are $16, the gross profit in each case will be $2,400. Price discrimination, a microeconomic concept, theoretically tries to capture the maximum amount someone would pay from each customer. From a practical standpoint, we might have several different prices to try to capture additional customers above the BE point.

In the case illustrated, we would charge $40 to customers willing to pay $40. Those who are willing to pay only $28 would be charged $28. How do we do this? We can't ask the customer, "Would you like to pay $40 or would you like to pay $28?" Obviously, everyone would say $28. Instead, we give different prices to different segments, offering the highest price to those segments that are less price-sensitive. For example, our standard price is $40 for the dinner. We offer an early-bird special of $28 to diners arriving before 6 P.M. A person who works until 5 P.M. probably is unwilling to rush home and rush to the restaurant to take advantage of the discount. This customer prefers to relax at home after work and arrive at the restaurant at 7 P.M. However, retired persons who may be more price-sensitive, but less time-sensitive, would be attracted by this special. The restaurant could also choose to send a coupon in a direct-mail package to prospective customers. The price-sensitive customers keep the coupon and use it the next time they go out to eat. Other people who receive the coupon throw it away. These customers do not want to be bothered with filing the coupon and then looking for it when they want to dine out. To these customers, the $12 savings is not worth the hassle of using the coupon. Price discrimination discriminates in favor of the price-sensitive customer.

The supersaver fares on airlines usually require an advance purchase and minimum stay. These criteria are both designed to eliminate business travelers, whereas the advance purchase eliminates business trips made on short notice. Airlines know that business travelers are less price-sensitive; that is, they exhibit inelastic price behavior. Airlines offer low fares with the leisure traveler in mind. The leisure traveler uses discretionary income to pay for travel and as a result is more price-sensitive than the business traveler. A reduction in price often results in additional demand from the leisure segment.

A flight between Detroit and Los Angeles provides an example of airline pricing. The flight had economy fares that ranged from $629 to $129, with 11 different fare categories. The least expensive fare was a special fare for seniors. Like the airlines, many hotels discriminate between the leisure and business segments. Business hotels in central business districts often suffer low occupancy on weekends. Many of these hotels have developed lower-priced weekend packages to entice the leisure traveler.

Low variable costs combined with fluctuations in demand make price discrimination a useful tool for smoothing demand and bringing additional revenue and profits to most businesses. This form of pricing uses lower prices to attract additional customers, without lowering the price for everyone.

Major sectors of the hospitality industry, such as airlines, hotels, cruise lines, and railroads, are faced with enormous fixed costs. Companies in these sectors are faced with the need to fill seats or beds. Richard Hanks, vice president of revenue management for the Marriott Corporation, believes that "our greatest opportunity cost is an empty room." Marriott and other hotel chains employ a pricing system based on discriminatory pricing to fill rooms and maximize revenue opportunities using fencing to keep price-inelastic customers from using rates designed for price-elastic segments.[18]

Fencing at Marriott is accomplished by establishing restrictions that allow customers to self-select price discriminatory rates that are best for them. Such fences include advance reservations and nonrefundable advance purchases. These policies permit price-sensitive customers to enjoy lower rates and inelastic segments to pay full fare without restrictions.

To price-discriminate successfully, the following criteria must be met:[19]

1. Different groups of consumers must have different responses to price; that is, they must value the service differently.

2. The different segments must be identifiable and a mechanism must exist to price them differently.

3. There should be no opportunity for persons in one segment who have paid a lower price to sell their purchases to other segments.

4. The segment should be large enough to make the exercise worthwhile.

5. The cost of running the price discrimination strategy should not exceed the incremental revenues obtained. This is partly a function of criterion 4.

6. The customers should not become confused by the use of different prices.

■■■ Revenue Management

One application of discriminatory pricing is revenue management. Revenue management involves upselling, cross-selling, and analysis of profit margins and sales volume for each product line. Revenue management systems are used to maximize a hospitality company's yield or contribution margin. In the case of hotels, this is done by the rates that a hotel will charge and the number of rooms available for each rate based on projected occupancies for a given period. These systems help hotels achieve the maximum contribution margin based on the demand for hotel rooms. The concept behind revenue management is to manage revenue and inventory effectively by pricing differences based on the elasticity of demand for selected customer segments.

Hotel companies are placing a great deal of emphasis on revenue management because the extra revenue it generates is pure profit that drops to the bottom line. However, at a meeting of revenue managers, half of the respondents indicated that their senior management did not understand revenue management.[20] If you are going into the hospitality industry, an understanding of revenue management is essential.

Marketing HIGHLIGHT 11–1 Segmented Pricing: The Right Product to the Right Customer at the Right Time for the Right Price

In most hospitality, travel and entertainment products capacity is fixed, but demand varies. In these situations, a common price may result in many people not being able to access the product during prime times and empty seats during off-peak periods. In some products such as airline transportation and events, all seats many not be the same. Live performances, including sporting events, theater, and concerts, will charge more for seats with great views and less for seats father away from the event. Some airlines charge more for aisle and window seats. Customers wanting better seats with the capacity to pay for these seats will have the opportunity to purchase the seats they want. Those who want to see the event or want to get to a certain destination but want to spend less can purchase less expensive seats. Susan Greco gives an example of an opera company, which went from a single price for all seats to pricing based on the location of the seat, increasing the price for better seats and lowering the price for seats in the back. Seat prices on the weekends were increased and those during the week were reduced. The variety of prices allowed the customers to choose what they would pay and the opera company increased its overall revenue by 9 percent. Some customers who previously could not afford to attend now had the opportunity to attend by selecting tickets further from the stage on weekday nights.

The opera company had introduced a simple form of revenue management. Airlines, hotels, and restaurants call it revenue management and practice it religiously. Robert Cross, a longtime consultant to the airlines, states there are opportunities for all companies to gain from revenue management. He states, "This will allow you to attract customers by having the right product at the right price for the right customer."

Segmented pricing and yield management aren't really new ideas. For instance, Marriott Corporation used seat-of-the-pants yield-management approaches long before it installed its current sophisticated system. Back when J. W. "Bill" Marriott was a young man working at the family's first hotel, the Twin Bridges in Washington, DC, he sold rooms from a drive-up window. As Bill tells it, the hotel charged a flat rate for a single occupant, with an extra charge for each additional person staying in the room. When room availability got tight on some nights, Bill would lean out the drive-up

Theaters often apply revenue management by charging more for seats with better views and during times when demand is higher.
Courtesy of Richard Cummins/Corbis.

window and assess the cars waiting in line. If some of the cars were filled with passengers, Bill would turn away vehicles with just a single passenger to sell his last rooms to those farther back in line who would be paying for multiple occupants. He might have accomplished the same result by charging a higher rate at peak times, regardless of the number of room occupants.

It is important to understand the demand cycles of your product and the motivation of your customers. For example, many resorts in Las Vegas will show their prices by day of the month. This provides transparency and lets the traveler who has flexibility in his or her travel dates to choose a date when there is less demand and prices are lower. For example, a retired couple driving to Las Vegas from the Los Angeles area will benefit by choosing lower-rated dates without reducing the benefits they receive from the trip. Shifting demand by charging higher prices when rooms are needed for convention delegates creates the ability to

provide rooms for those who want to be in Las Vegas during the higher demand dates and are willing to pay the price for these dates. The transparency of the prices is important so that guests understand when a number of conventions are in town and the delegates to the convention will need rooms, the room rates will be higher.

Greco provides an example of a Cafe in Boston, which always had a wait over the lunch period but was empty by 3 P.M. until closing. The owner offered a 20 percent discount in the morning and after 2 P.M. By shifting some demand away from the lunch hour, he still remained full at lunch but was able to increase the off-peak business. He was able to increase overall revenue and even with the 20 percent discount he was still able to make a profit on the increased revenue.

These examples show that understanding your customers, what they value, and the demand for your product can create pricing that will allow you to create value for your customers and increase your revenue and profits.[21,22]

Revenue management involves the development and use of different rate classes based on the projected demand for the service. These rates are used to maximize yield. This is the formula for yield:

$$\frac{\text{room} - \text{nights sold}}{\text{room} - \text{nights available}} \times \frac{\text{actual average room rate}}{\text{room rate potential}} = \text{yield}$$

A hotel with sufficient history can project occupancy based on current booking patterns. If low occupancy is projected, the hotel keeps lower rate classes open to increase occupancy. The lower rates typically use price discrimination techniques that favor the leisure traveler. For example, a hotel may offer advance supersaver rates. The idea is to create extra demand with low rates, attracting guests that the hotel would not otherwise have. If the projected occupancy is high, the lower rates will be closed, and only the higher rate classes will be accepted. Today, several computerized systems are available that automatically project occupancy levels for a given date and suggest pricing levels for each day. It is common for a revenue-management system to increase revenues by at least 5 percent. Reservations for Hyatt's Regency Club concierge floors climbed 20 percent after Hyatt implemented revenue management. One Hilton hotel increased its average transient rate by $7.50 with no reduction in occupancy the first month after installing a revenue-management system.[23]

Three important concepts in revenue management are RevPAR, GopPAR, and RevPASH. RevPAR is revenue per available room. It takes into consideration both occupancy and average rate, by determining the average rate per available room. A 100-room hotel that sold 60 rooms at an average rate of $200 would have a RevPAR of $120 (60/100 × $200). GopPAR is the gross operating profit (Gop) per available room. Gop is equal to total revenue minus total departmental and operating expenses. GopPAR does not indicate the mix of a hotel property but it does provide a clear indication of a hotel's profit potential. GopPAR can reflect management's efficiency.[24]

RevPASH is the revenue per available seat hour. It is tracked hourly because we do not sell a seat for a day, like we do hotel rooms. For example, it identifies peak periods and periods of less demand. It supplies data to track the effectiveness of the promotions to fill the low-demand periods. For many restaurants, increasing RevPASH can be as easy as getting the right table configurations. Seating a deuce at a four-top results in zero revenue for two seats. Thus, having two-tops that combined to seat a party of four is a nonprice method of increasing revenue. The County Inn and Suites uses RevPAR measurements to compare renovated hotels in the chain to those it views as stabilized. An analysis of renovated rooms revealed a

5.7 percent favorable RevPAR, which equated to an additional $140,000 in annual revenue for an average 80-room hotel.[25]

This chain also uses a RevPAR index as a measurement to gauge nonperforming hotels. Terminated hotels had a RevPAR score that was far below others in the chain.

Another use of RevPAR by this chain is to compare its RevPAR improvement against that of competitive hotels. As an example, if RevPAR increased 10 percent for this chain but 13 percent for competitors, then the conclusion was that it was not performing as well as competitors. RevPASH can also provide data to help us with revenue management.[26]

Revenue management systems must be based on sound marketing. They should be developed with the long-term value of the customer in mind. One early yield-management system cut off reservations from travel agents when projected occupancy for a given date was high. This was done to eliminate travel agency commissions when the hotel could sell the rooms. This system saved money in the short term by saving travel agency commissions. However, in the long term, the hotel could lose a significant portion of its travel agency business. Think of the person who wants to stay at the Regal Hotel in Orlando and fly to Orlando on Delta. The travel agent informs the client that the airline is confirmed, but no rooms are available at the Regal, so a reservation was made at the Gator Hotel. The client calls the Regal only to find that rooms are available. The client now thinks the travel agent is pushing the Gator Hotel and gets upset with the travel agent. The travel agent becomes upset with the Regal and refuses to book future business with them. The Regal gains short-run extra revenue but loses the travel agent's business in the long term. Revenue management programs should focus on long-term profitability, not just the maximization of one day's revenue.

With some revenue management systems, customers staying a longer period can be charged more than those staying only a few nights. Normally, one might expect a concession for longer stays. Sometimes the longer stay may take the guest into a period of high occupancy. These systems average the occupancy over the guest's stay. For example, based on the occupancy levels in the following table, a guest checking in on May 8 and checking out on May 10 would be quoted a $65 rate as the lowest available rate. A guest checking in on May 8 and checking out on May 12 would be quoted $85 as the lowest available rate because the hotel can sell more rooms for May 10 and 11 at a minimum of $105 a night. Under this system, the staff must be well trained to explain rate differences to the guest.

Projected Occupancy (%)	
May 8	60
May 9	60
May 10	85
May 11	90

Revenue management systems can be useful in managing the number of rooms available for transient demand. Most hotels have a base of transient demand composed of individual guests who pay a high rate. Some of these transient guests are businesspersons who may stay in the hotel several times during the year. Groups make their reservations well in advance of the transients. When group business displaces transient business, the average rate drops, and some displaced transient guests may never return, deciding to stay at an alternative hotel. Revenue management systems help eliminate the problem of displaced transient guests by projecting the number of transient rooms that will be used on any given date.

If used properly, revenue management systems can provide extra revenue. A good revenue management system benefits both the hospitality company and the guest. It opens low-rated rooms for the leisure traveler during times of low occupancy and saves rooms during periods of peak demand for the business traveler willing to pay full rates. The company gains because revenue management focuses on maximizing revenue, not cutting costs.

A revenue management system requires the availability of good data. This has forced many hospitality companies to go back to the basics and develop sound information-retrieval systems for internal data, such as booking patterns, and to develop and use better forecasting methods. The end result is that without even using revenue management, the company is in a far better position to make intelligent management decisions.

An effective revenue management system depends on several variables.[27] These are the ability to segment markets, perishable inventory, ability to sell product in advance, fluctuating demand, low-marginal sales costs, high-marginal production costs (can easily add another room), booking pattern data, information on demand pattern by market segment, an overbooking policy, knowledge of effect of price changes, a good information system for internal and external data, and ability to fence customer segments.

Use of revenue management within the hospitality industry is expanding to new sectors. The Dalmahoy Golf and Country Club Resort near Edinburgh, Scotland, implemented a revenue-management program for its golf course operation. This tied the costs of an annual membership to the time and day that the purchaser used the golf course.[28]

Hotel guests commonly realize that different prices are charged for similar rooms for a specific night. To offset customer perceptions of this being unfair, one study showed that if customers were given information about how the system works, the feelings of unfair prices were reduced. Specifically, when customers were told that rates vary according to day of the week, length of stay, and how far in advance the reservation was made, perceptions of fairness improved.[29]

Dynamic Pricing

Dynamic pricing. Continually adjusting prices to meet the characteristics and needs of the marketplace.

A popular tool used by revenue managers is **dynamic pricing**. Dynamic pricing continually adjusts prices to meet the characteristics and needs of the marketplace. When demand increases or capacity is reduced due to previous sales, prices increase and the reverse is also true.

Airlines, cruise lines, and hotels use dynamic pricing. Dynamic pricing is different from price discrimination. Dynamic pricing does not put up fences to restrict certain customers from taking advantage of lower prices. It raises or lowers prices based on demand for the hotel on a particular day, a particular flight, or cruise. It will raise the price of the lowest fare or rate available to leisure customers based on demand. Airlines change their rates several times if the demand for a flight keeps increasing and is predicted to be sold out. Prices will be lowered if the flight is predicted to leave with empty seats. Although dynamic pricing is different than price discrimination, often a revenue manager will use both techniques; they are not mutually exclusive.

Uber is an international app-based car dispatch service that lets customers summon cars from their app or by SMS. Uber uses a form of dynamic pricing called *surge pricing*. Under normal circumstances, Uber customers pay reasonable fares. However, using Uber in periods of surging demand can result in shocking price escalations, for example, on a stormy Saturday night in New York City. Uber knew that people would not want to walk in stormy weather, and demand would be high. Fares were eight times its average fare. On Uber's Web site, there is an explanation of Surge pricing. They want to be able to provide service their customers can rely on whenever they need a driver.[30] Thus, the increase in prices is to encourage more drivers to be available. However, despite this explanation on their Web site and the fact that Uber's app warned customers of heightened fares before processing their requests, many customers were still outraged. They commented, e-mailed, and tweeted their displeasure with messages charging the company with price gouging. One customer shared an Instagram photo of a taxi receipt for $415. However, despite the protests, Uber experienced no subsequent drop in demand in New York. Uber's policy is working. Its higher fares offered to drivers attracted more drivers and increased capacity. The high fares reduced capacity, with some potential riders deciding to stay home. The end result was capacity and demand approached equilibrium. Thus, dynamic pricing can help sellers optimize sales and profits. [31]

BAR Pricing

Best available rate (BAR) pricing is a relatively new pricing technique used for guests who stay several nights. Instead of charging a single rate for a multiple-night stay, such as $100 per night, BAR pricing charges different rates for each night. Thus, some nights might be priced below $100 and others above the rate. These daily rates are determined through revenue management.

BAR pricing originated with the Internet intermediaries Hotels.com, Expedia, Priceline, and Orbitz. The practice then spread to hotel companies. To assure customers that they are receiving the BARs for any date, price guarantees are often given. These vary in terms between firms offering them.[32] BAR is sometimes referred to as nonblended pricing.

Rate Parity

Hotel Rate Parity is a controversial strategy that has been challenged in court and survived. However, pressure against this strategy remains.

Rate Parity is essentially a strategy in which hotel chains agree to allow their product (rooms) to be shown and sold by OTAs provided the prices they offer are the same and are not lower than the hotel's BAR. The OTAs refer to these hotels as merchant model suppliers. Consumers are unlikely to find a rate lower than the BAR rate set by the hotel.

The OTAs ask for assurances of rate parity since they are assured that the hotel will not offer lower rates than what the OTAs can offer and make a profit. Rate Parity applies only to "public rates"—those available to the general public. It does not apply to affinity rates for special segments such as ministerial or military rates.

The hotel industry knows that many travelers search for a hotel room online first. With this price knowledge in hand, they then call the 800 number for one of the hotel chains for which they have price information. The hotel will quote a BAR as well as others. At this point, the hotel has an advantage over the OTAs since the hotel can offer a special *topper* (add-on offering) such as a meal or drink package.

In a particularly hot market, hotels do not need OTAs and could tell them they will not honor rate parities nor will they not pay commissions. However, when demand becomes weak, most hotels need the OTAs. "In down markets, many properties can't even break even without the steady flow of traffic from Expedia, Orbitz, and Travelocity and their subsidiaries."[33]

Nonuse of Revenue Management

Some members of the hospitality industry have chosen not to use a revenue management system. However, researchers on this subject concluded, "Waiting is part of life and particularly part of an experience with a restaurant. Having long waits for tables in a restaurant does not necessarily mean there is a problem. Demand in restaurants like Cheesecake Factory, Houston's, and Outback Steakhouse far exceeds supply on most days."[34]

Instead of using price discrimination and fencing, Outback Steakhouse sets a menu price but offers a streamline takeaway service to assist those who don't wish to wait for table service (uncaptured demand).

For popular restaurants like the Cheesecake Factory demand far exceeds capacity on some days. Courtesy of Peter Wilson/Dorling Kindersley.

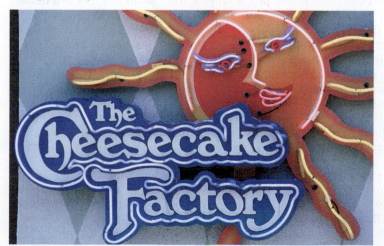

Overbooking

Revenue management continues to provide great service to the hospitality industry.

Nevertheless, occasionally there are problems with overbooking, which can create guest/passenger dissatisfaction. When overbooking occurs, the supplier has an ethical and legal responsibility to compensate the buyer and/or find alternative flights, hotels, and so on.

Airlines offer to pay passengers to give up their seats and accept an alternative flight. Guests of hotels are not interested in accepting a hotel room the next day or even hours later. The management of the hotel must, therefore, "walk" the guest, meaning the guest will be forced to accept a room in a different hotel. In fact, very few, if any, guests are expected to walk to a different hotel despite the name. Transportation is generally provided. In addition to providing an equal room elsewhere, some hotels follow the airline practice of providing extra compensation. This extra compensation may be in the form of vouchers or cash, as both seem to have about equal positive responses with the guest.[35]

■■■ Psychological Pricing

Psychological pricing considers the psychology of prices, not simply the economics. Earlier in this chapter, we discussed the relationship between price and quality. Prestige can be created by selling products and services at a high price.

Another aspect of psychological pricing is reference prices; these are prices that buyers carry in their minds and refer to when they look at a given product. A buyer's reference price might be formed by noting current prices, remembering past prices, or assessing the buying situation. Popular products often have reference prices. For a given type of restaurant, most consumers have a preconceived idea about the price or price range of certain items, such as a cup of coffee, a strip steak, or a hamburger. For example, a pizza chain may advertise its medium pizza for a price it knows is $2 less than the competition to establish a reference price for pizza eaters. But its price for beverages and extra items will be the same as that of the competition. The reference item creates the perception of value; consequently, little would be gained by cutting the price of the other items.

Price Endings

A study of hotel price-ending strategies demonstrated that "just under pricing strategies are utilized intentionally to signal value while round price endings of 0 and 5 are utilized to signal quality."[36] While dollar pricing is most commonly used by hotels, in the case of lower-rated hotels, odd ending prices are more common.

Customers tend to simplify price information by ignoring end figures. For instance, there is greater perceived distance between $0.69 and $0.71 than there is between $0.67 and $0.69. Consumers also tend to round figures. One restaurant study found that consumers round prices ranging from $0.86 to $1.39 to a dollar, from $1.40 to $1.79 to a dollar and a half, and from $1.80 to $2.49 to two dollars. If this is the case, there may be little change in demand caused by a price increase of $0.30 from $1.45 to $1.75, but there may be a significant decrease in demand if we raise the price by $0.40 to $1.85.[37]

The length of the field is another consideration. The jump from $0.99 to $1.00 or the jump from $9.99 to $10.00 can be perceived as a significant increase, although it is only $0.01. Taco Bell's value prices were all under $1, and therefore only two digits. Some psychologists argue that each digit has symbolic and visual qualities that should be considered in pricing. For example, because the number 8 is round, it creates a soothing effect, whereas 7 is angular, creating a jarring effect.

Perhaps the most interesting finding in this study was from a hotel management company of upscale, full-service hotels that added $0.95 to all of its managed properties. They reported no customer complaints but instead said that the practice added significant amounts to their EBITDA.

Promotional Pricing

When companies use promotional pricing, they temporarily price their products below list price and sometimes even below cost. Promotional pricing takes several forms. Fast-food restaurants price a few products as loss leaders to attract customers to the store in the hope that they will buy other items at normal markups. Donut shops may offer coffee for 75 cents, knowing a customer will usually buy at least one donut. Jack-in-the-Box offers special prices on its tacos because it often sells a soft drink with the order. During slow periods, hotels may offer special promotional rates to increase business. Rather than just lower prices, well-managed hotels create special events: a Valentine's weekend special, including a room, champagne upon arrival, a dinner for two, and a breakfast in the room, or a theater package, including a room, tickets to a play, dinner for two, and breakfast for two. These promotions give the guest a reason to come; the bundle of products adds value for the customer. The promotion creates a positive image, whereas straight price discounting can create a negative image.

The gaming industry is particularly aware of the importance of product bundling and promotional pricing. A casino executive stated, "We are in the adult entertainment business; our main product offering is gambling and there are many components that support it, such as hotels, entertainment facilities, and restaurants." Casino managers view hotel rooms as a means to entice and enable customers to gamble. Casinos must ensure that rooms are readily available for the most profitable gaming customers.[38] Hotel pricing reflects the fact that the company's main product offering is gaming, and a hotel room is only a supporting product for gaming.

Opaque pricing is a form of promotional pricing and used by some OTAs such as Priceline and Hotwire. Opaque offers do not identify the name of the supplier but usually give a general location and a rating such as a four-star hotel in the central business district offered at a very attractive price. Once the booking has been completed, the name and exact location of the property will be revealed to the buyer. Often exceptional price deals may be obtained in this manner.

Value Pricing—Low Price Approach

The term *value pricing* is confusing. It could be argued that anytime a product/service is purchased, at any price, the buyer must have perceived value in that product. Value pricing has become synonymous with the term *everyday low prices (EDLP)*. It has been used as a marketing strategy by some members of the hospitality industry, such as Taco Bell and Southwest Airlines.

"Value pricing can be extremely risky. Properly conceived and executed, it can earn positive results." It can also be disastrous.[39] In its simplest form, value pricing means offering a price below competitors permanently, which differs from promotional pricing, in which price may be temporarily lowered during a special promotion.

Value pricing is risky if a company does not have the ability to cut costs significantly. It is usually most appropriate for companies able to increase long-run market share through low prices (Taco Bell) or niche players with a lower-cost operating basis who use price to differentiate their product (Southwest Airlines). A study of value pricing in retail stores showed that "retailers can be profitable charging low prices but only when they have low costs."[40]

Prior to initiating a strategy of value pricing, managers must ask themselves these questions:

- What will happen if this starts a price war?

- Can our company significantly lower costs or increase productivity to compensate for lower prices?

- What is the price elasticity of our products?

- Can we gain significant market share or ensure a strong market niche position with this strategy?

- Can we reverse this strategy if it doesn't work, or will we create price levels that can't be sustained and can't easily be raised?

Marketing HIGHLIGHT 11–2   Ryanair Uses Value Pricing to Attract Customers and Gains Revenue from Extra Sales

Profits for discount European air carrier Ryanair have been sky-high thanks to its revolutionary business model. The secret? Founder Michael O'Leary thinks like a retailer, charging passengers for almost everything—except their seat. A quarter of Ryanair's seats are free, and O'Leary wants to double that within five years, with the ultimate goal of making all seats free. Passengers currently pay only taxes and fees of about $10 to $24, with an average one-way fare of roughly $52. Everything else is extra: checked luggage ($9.50 per bag), snacks ($5.50 for a hot dog, $4.50 for chicken soup, $3.50 for water), and bus or train transportation into town from the secondary airports Ryanair uses ($24). Flight attendants sell a variety of merchandise, including digital cameras ($137.50) and iPocket MP3 players ($165). Onboard gambling and cell phone service are projected new revenue sources. Other strategies cut costs or generate outside revenue. Seats don't recline, window shades and seat-back pockets have been removed,

and there is no entertainment. Seat-back trays carry ads, and the exteriors of the planes are giant revenue-producing billboards for Vodafone Group, Jaguar, Hertz, and others. More than 99 percent of tickets are sold online. The Web site also offers travel insurance, hotels, ski packages, and car rentals. Only Boeing 737-800 jets are flown to reduce maintenance costs, and flight crews buy their own uniforms. O'Leary has even discussed the possibility of pay toilets and 10 rows of standing room with handrails like a New York City subway car (to squeeze 30 more passengers aboard), though both suggestions drew much public concern and skepticism. Although his ideas may seem unconventional, the formula works for Ryanair's customers; the airline flies 58 million people to more than 150 airports each year. All the extras add up to 20 percent of revenue. Ryanair enjoys net margins of 25 percent, more than three times Southwest's 7 percent. Some industry pundits even refer to Ryanair as "Walmart with wings"!

■■■ Price Changes

Initiating Price Changes

After developing their price structures and strategies, companies may face occasions when they want to cut or raise prices.

Initiating Price Cuts

Several situations may lead a company to cut prices. One is excess capacity. Unable to increase business through promotional efforts, product improvement, or other measures, a hotel may resort to price cutting. As the airline, hotel, rental car, and restaurant industries have learned, cutting prices in an industry loaded with excess capacity generally leads to price wars as competitors try to regain market share.

Companies may also cut prices in a drive to dominate the market or increase market share through lower costs. Either the company starts with lower costs than its competitors or it cuts prices in the hope of gaining market share through larger volume. Price cutting to increase revenue must be carefully planned. Studies conducted across hotel sectors and in the United States and Asia have shown that in most mature markets, price cutting increases occupancy but the RevPAR decreases. Thus, the increased occupancy does not overcome the decrease in average rate. For an established hotel, the best tactic is to maintain prices slightly above the competitive rate.[41] Exceptions include hotels, such as casino hotels where high non-room expenditures, such as casino gaming or F&B, would offset the decrease in room revenue.

Initiating Price Increases Inevitably

Many companies must eventually raise prices. They do this knowing that price increases may be resented by customers, dealers, and their own sales force. However, a successful price increase can greatly increase profits. For example, if the company's profit margin is 3 percent of sales, a 1 percent price increase improves profits by 33 percent if sales volume is unaffected.

A major factor in price increases is cost inflation. Increased costs squeeze profit margins and lead companies to regular rounds of price increases. Companies often raise their prices by more than the cost increase in anticipation of further inflation. Companies do not want to make long-run price agreements with customers. They fear that cost inflation will reduce profit margins. For example, hotels prefer not to quote a firm price for conventions booked three years in advance. Another factor leading to price increases is excess demand. When a company cannot supply all its customers' needs, it raises its prices, rations products to customers, or it does both. When a city hosts a major convention, hotels may charge rates that are twice the average room rate. They know that demand for hotel rooms will be great, and they can take advantage of this demand.

Raising prices in the hospitality industry can be dangerous even when caused by inflation. It must be remembered that with the exception of some travel such as business or to attend funerals, the demand for travel generally faces an elastic demand curve. A couple may plan to celebrate their wedding anniversary with friends and relatives at a restaurant or resort, but if prices dramatically increase they may switch to a gathering at home or even a nearby park shelter. The travel industry has learned that much business travel can be postponed or conducted through electronic means, including the use of software such as GoToMeeting and Skype, which allow two-way audio-video using personal computers.

Cross substitutability of demand is a reality that always faces members of the hospitality industry, for example, the use of electronic communication rather than an airline trip.

In passing price increases on to customers, the company should avoid the image of price gouger. It is best to increase prices when customers perceive the price increase to be justified. Restaurants had an easier time implementing increased menu prices after the price of beef jumped because their customers noticed this price increase in the supermarket. If food prices are going down while the other costs of operating a restaurant are going up, it is difficult to gain customer acceptance of the need for a price increase. Restaurant managers should try to time price increases so they will be perceived as justified by customers, such as when increases in the price of food receive media attention, after an increase in the minimum wage, or when inflation is in the news. Price increases should be supported with a company communication program informing customers and employees why prices are being increased.

Buyer Reaction to Price Changes

Whether the price is raised or lowered, the action affects buyers, competitors, distributors, and suppliers. Price changes may also interest the government. Customers do not always put a straightforward interpretation on price changes. They may perceive a price cut in several ways. For example, what would you think when you see a restaurant advertising a buy-one-meal-get-one-free special? If you know the restaurant and have a positive feeling, you might be attracted. Someone who doesn't know the restaurant may feel it is having trouble attracting customers or something is wrong with the food or service. Or you might wonder if portion size has been reduced or inferior-quality food was being served. Remember, buyers often associate price with quality when evaluating hospitality products they have not experienced directly.

Similarly, a price increase that would normally lower sales may have a positive meaning for buyers. A nightclub that increases its cover charge from $5 to $10 might be perceived as the "in place" to go.

Competitor Reactions to Price Changes

A firm considering a price change has to worry about competitors' reactions. Competitors are most likely to react when the number of firms involved is small, when the product is uniform, and when buyers are well informed.

One problem with trying to use price as a competitive advantage is that competitors can neutralize the price advantage by lowering their prices. In a competitive market where supply exceeds demand, this often sets off price wars in which the industry as a whole loses. In the United States, Burger King and McDonald's are locked in a battle for market share. When one of these fast-food giants cuts its price, the other usually follows.

Competitors may choose to retaliate in different markets. For example, when Southwest Airlines cut prices on its Houston-to-San Antonio flights, its competitors reacted by cutting prices on their Houston-to-Dallas flights. The Houston-to-Dallas flights were Southwest's bread and butter. By hitting here, the competition hurt Southwest more than they could have by matching prices on the Houston-to-San Antonio route. Competitors may also react to a price cut with nonprice tactics. When Continental Airlines offered a "chicken-feed" discount fare, the competition responded by not booking their connecting passengers on Continental's flights. Continental was forced to rescind its price cuts. Before cutting prices, it is essential to consider competitive reactions. As we mentioned at the beginning of this chapter, price is a very flexible element of the marketing mix. It can easily be matched by the competition. A firm that lowers its price and has it matched by competition loses both its competitive advantage and profit.[42]

Responding to Price Changes

Here, we reverse the question and ask how a firm should respond to a price change by a competitor. The firm needs to consider several issues. Why did the competitor change the price? Was it to gain more market share, to use excess capacity, to meet changing cost conditions, or to lead an industry-wide program change? Does the competitor plan to make the price change temporary or permanent? What will happen to the company's market share and profits if it does not respond? Are other companies going to respond? What are the competitors' and other firms' responses likely to be to each possible reaction?

In addition to these issues, the company must make a broader analysis. It must consider its own product's stage in the life cycle, its importance in the company's product mix, the intentions and resources of the competitor, and possible consumer reactions to price changes.

When Marriott's Fairfield Inns was just getting started, it offered a special discounted rate that was 40 percent less than its average daily rate. Its competitors decided not to match the rate because Fairfield had only 30 hotels at the time. Joan Ganje-Fischer, vice president of Super 8, said that if a major chain such as Super 8, Econo Inns, or Days Inn matched the discount, it would catch the attention of the other organizations. A price war would be the likely result of such a cut by a major chain. But because Fairfield Inns consisted of only 30 units, major competitors were unwilling to reduce rates across their 100-plus motel chains. Fairfield Inns used size to its advantage, recognizing that the larger chains would be unwilling to give up revenue from hundreds of hotels and thousands of rooms to match the price of a 30-unit chain.[43]

These examples show how companies can avoid competitive reactions to price changes by planning those changes carefully.

■■■ CHAPTER REVIEW

I. Price. Simply defined, price is the amount of money charged for a good or service. More broadly, price is the sum of the values consumers exchange for the benefits of having or using the product or service.

II. Factors to Consider When Setting Price
  A. Internal factors
    1. Marketing objectives
      a. Survival. It is used when the economy slumps or a recession is going on. A manufacturing firm can reduce production to match demand and a hotel can cut rates to create the best cash flow.

b. Current profit maximization. Companies may choose the price that will produce the maximum current profit, cash flow, or ROI, seeking financial outcomes rather than long-run performance.

c. Market-share leadership. When companies believe that a company with the largest market share will eventually enjoy low costs and high long-run profit, they set low opening rates and strive to be the market-share leader.

    d. **Product-quality leadership.** Hotels like the Ritz-Carlton chain charge a high price for their high-cost products to capture the luxury market.

    e. **Other objectives.** Stabilize market, create excitement for new product, and draw more attention.

2. **Marketing mix strategy.** Price must be coordinated with product design, distribution, and promotion decision to form a consistent and effective marketing program.

3. **Costs**

    a. **Fixed costs.** Costs that do not vary with production or sales level.

    b. **Variable costs.** Costs that vary directly with the level of production.

4. **Cost subsidization**

5. **Organization considerations.** Management must decide who within the organization should set prices. In small companies, this will be top management; in large companies, pricing is typically handled by a corporate department or by a regional or unit manager under guidelines established by corporate management.

B. **External factors**

1. **Nature of the market and demand**

    a. **Cross-selling.** The company's other products are sold to the guest.

    b. **Upselling.** Sales and reservation employees are trained to offer continuously a higher-priced product that will better meet the customer's needs, rather than settling for the lowest price.

2. **Consumer perception of price and value.** It is the consumer who decides whether a product's price is right. The price must be buyer oriented. The price decision requires a creative awareness of the target market and recognition of the buyers' differences.

3. **Analyzing the price–demand relationship.** Demand and price are inversely related; the higher the price, the lower the demand. Most demand curves slope downward in either a straight or a curved line. The prestige goods demand curve sometimes slopes upward.

4. **Price elasticity of demand.** If demand hardly varies with a small change in price, the demand is inelastic; if demand changes greatly, the demand is elastic. Buyers are less price-sensitive when the product is unique or when it is high in quality, prestige, or exclusiveness. Consumers are also less price-sensitive when substitute products are hard to find. If demand is elastic, sellers generally consider lowering their prices to produce more total revenue. The following factors affect price sensitivity.

5. **Factors Affecting Price–Demand Relations**

    a. **Unique value effect.** Creating the perception that your offering is different from those of your competitors avoids price competition.

    b. **Substitute awareness effect.** Lack of the awareness of the existence of alternatives reduces price sensitivity.

    c. **Business expenditure effect.** When someone else pays the bill, the customer is less price-sensitive.

    d. **End-benefit effect.** Consumers are more price-sensitive when the price of the product accounts for a large share of the total cost of the end benefit.

    e. **Total expenditure effect.** The more someone spends on a product, the more sensitive he or she is to the product's price.

    f. **Price quality effect.** Consumers tend to equate price with quality, especially when they lack any prior experience with the product.

6. **Competitors' price and offers.** When a company is aware of its competitors' price and offers, it can use this information as a starting point for deciding its own pricing.

    a. **Price-rate compression.** This occurs when higher-priced hotels lower these rates to maintain occupancy and become direct competitors to lower-rated hotels.

7. **Other environmental factors.** Other factors include inflation, boom or recession, interest rates, government purchasing, and birth of new technology.

III. General Pricing Approaches

A. **Cost-based pricing.** Cost-plus pricing: a standard markup is added to the cost of the product.

B. **Break-even analysis and target profit pricing.** Price is set to break even on the costs of making and marketing a product, or to make a desired profit.

C. **Value-based pricing.** Companies base their prices on the product's perceived value. Perceived-value pricing uses the buyers' perceptions of value, not the seller's cost, as the key to pricing.

D. **Competition-based pricing.** Competition-based price is based on the establishment of price largely against those of competitors, with less attention paid to costs or demand.

IV. Pricing Strategies

A. **New product pricing strategies.** Pricing strategies usually change as a product passes through its life cycle. The introductory stage is especially challenging.

1. **Prestige pricing.** Hotels or restaurants seeking to position themselves as luxurious and elegant enter the market with a high price that supports this position.

2. **Market-skimming pricing.** Price skimming is setting a high price when the market is price-insensitive. It is common in industries with high research and development costs, such as pharmaceutical companies and computer firms.

3. **Marketing-penetration pricing.** Companies set a low initial price to penetrate the market quickly and deeply, attracting many buyers and winning a large market share.

4. **Product-bundle pricing.** Sellers using product-bundle pricing combine several of their products and offer the bundle at a reduced price. Most used by cruise lines.

B. **Existing-product pricing strategies.** The strategies just described are used primarily when introducing a new product. However, they can also be useful with existing products. The following strategies are ones that can be used with existing products.

1. **Price-adjustment strategies.** Companies usually adjust their basic prices to account for various customer differences and changing situations.

   a. **Volume discounts.** Hotels have special rates to attract customers who are likely to purchase a large quantity of hotel rooms, either for a single period or throughout the year.

   b. **Discounts based on time of purchase.** A seasonal discount is a price reduction to buyers who purchase services out of season when the demand is lower. Seasonal discounts allow the hotel to keep demand steady during the year.

   c. **Discriminatory pricing.** Segmentation of the market and pricing differences based on price elasticity characteristics of the segments. In discriminatory pricing, the company sells a product or service at two or more prices, although the difference in price is not based on differences in cost. It maximizes the amount that each customer pays.

2. **Revenue management.** A yield-management system is used to maximize a hotel's yield or contribution margin.

3. **Psychological pricing.** Psychological aspects such as prestige, reference prices, round figures, and ignoring end figures are used in pricing.

4. **Promotional pricing.** Hotels temporarily price their products below list price, and sometimes even below cost, for special occasions, such as introduction or festivities. Promotional pricing gives guests a reason to come and promotes a positive image for the hotel.

5. **Value pricing.** Value pricing means offering a price below competitors permanently, which differs from promotional pricing, in which price may be temporarily lowered during a special promotion.

V. **Price Changes**

A. **Initiating price cuts.** Reasons for a company to cut price are excess capacity, inability to increase business through promotional efforts, product improvement, follow-the-leader pricing, and desire to dominate the market.

B. **Initiating price increases.** Reasons for a company to increase price are cost inflation or excess demand.

C. **Buyer reactions to price changes.** Competitors, distributors, suppliers, and other buyers associate price with quality when evaluating hospitality products they have not experienced directly.

D. **Competitor reactions to price changes.** Competitors are most likely to react when the number of firms involved is small, when the product is uniform, and when buyers are well informed.

E. **Responding to price changes.** Issues to consider are reason, market share, excess capacity, meeting changing cost conditions, leading an industry-wide program change, temporary versus permanent.

■■■ DISCUSSION QUESTIONS

1. One way of increasing revenue is through upselling. Give examples from the hospitality or travel industries of when upselling can result in a more satisfied guest.

2. You have just been hired as the dining room manager at a local hotel. The manager asks you to evaluate the menu prices to see if they need to be adjusted. How would you go about this task?

3. A number of factors affecting price sensitivity are discussed in this chapter. Provide some examples of the application of these factors in the hospitality or travel businesses.

4. Give an example of an effective use of price discrimination. Support your reasons for thinking that it is a good example.

5. Can a hotel or restaurant increase or maintain customer satisfaction after implementing its first revenue management program? Explain your answer.

6. Airlines and hotels give bonus frequent-flyer miles, gifts, and free companion tickets to attract the business traveler. These promotions are often provided in lieu of a price cut. The traveler benefits personally, although his or her company does not get the benefit of lower rates. Is this ethical?

■■■ EXPERIENTIAL EXERCISE

Do the following:

Conduct a price comparison of several hotels or restaurants in the same class. What price differences did you find? Do you feel the companies that had the higher prices could justify those higher prices by offering additional features or a higher-quality product?

■■■ INTERNET EXERCISE

You are going on a three-day business trip for your company to Pittsburgh, Pennsylvania. You have up to $300 a day to spend on lodging and food. If you do not spend the money you save money for your company; you do not get to keep the unspent money. You will check in on October 18 and check out on October 21. Choose the hotel where you would stay; what Web site would you use to pick the hotel? What did your search process involve? How many Web sites did you use to make your selection? What criteria did you make in choosing the hotel? (Note: Look up the hotel rates, but please do not make an actual reservation.)

■■■ REFERENCES

1 Sheryl E. Kimes, "Restaurant Revenue Management at Chevys Arrowhead," *Cornell Hotel and Restaurant Administration Quarterly*, 45, no. 1 (2004): 52–56.

2 Tom Ross, "Steamboat Airline Program Still Pursuing Service for Cities like Phoenix, Charlotte, Detroit," *Steamboat Today*, Friday, July 18, 2014.

3 Ibid., p. 6.

4 Howard Feiertag, "Up Your Property's Profits by Upselling Catering," *Hotel and Motel Management*, 206, no. 14 (1991): 20.

5 "Embassy's Suite Deal," *Scorecard: The Revenue Management Quarterly* (Second Quarter, 1993), 3.

6 Melvyn Greene, *Marketing Hotels and Restaurants into the 90's* (New York: Van Nostrand Reinhold, 1987).

7 Anthony Edwards, "Changes in Real Air Fares and Their Impact on Travel," *EIU Travel and Tourism Analyst*, 2 (1990): 76–85.

8 This section draws on Thomas T. Nagle, *The Strategy and Tactics of Pricing* (Upper Saddle River, NJ: Prentice Hall, 1987).

9 Melvyn Greene, *Marketing Hotels and Restaurants into the 90's*, p. 47.

10 Sarah Schlicter, "Hidden Hotel Fees," *Independent Traveler*, May 6, 2015; Erica Silverstein, Senior Editor, and Carolyn Spencer, "The 10 Hidden Costs of Cruising and How to Fight Back."

11 Juliet Chung, "Cracking the Code of Restaurant Wine Pricing," *Wall Street Journal*, 1–4, online.wsj.com (accessed August 15, 2008).

12 *The Horwath Accountant*, 47, no. 7 (1967): 8.

13 Philip Kotler and Gary Armstrong, *Principles of Marketing* (Upper Saddle River, NJ: Prentice Hall, 2001), p. 387.

14 Leo M. Renaghan and Michael Z. Kay, "What Meeting Planners Want: The Conjoint Analysis Approach," *Cornell Hotel and Restaurant Administration Quarterly*, 28, no. 1 (1987): 73.

15 Melvyn Greene, *Marketing Hotels and Restaurants in the 90's*, p. 42.

16 William J. Carroll, Robert J. Kwortnik, and Norman L. Rose, "Cornell Hospitality Report: Travel Packaging: An Internet Frontier," *The Center for Hospitality Research*, 7, no. 17 (2007): 7.

17 Royal Palms Resort and Spa Web site, http://www.royalpalmshotel.com (accessed January 23, 2009).

18 Richard O. Hanks, Robert G. Cross, and Paul R. Noland, "Discounting in the Hotel Industry: A New Approach," *Cornell Hotel and Restaurant Administration Quarterly*, 33, no. 1 (1992): 23.

19 John E. G. Bateson, *Managing Services Marketing* (Fort Worth, TX: Dryden Press, 1992), p. 339.

20 "Survey Findings on Hotel Revenue Management," Hotelmarketing.com, September 16, 2008 (accessed September 25, 2008).

21 Sources, Susan Greco, "Are Your Prices Right?" *INC.* (January 1997): 88–89. Copyright 1997 by Goldhirsh Group, Inc., 38 Commercial Wharf, Boston, MA 02110. Other information from Robert G. Cross, *Revenue Management: Hard Core Tactics for Market Domination* (New York: Broadway Books, 1998); William J. Quain, Michael Sansbury, and Dennis Quinn, "Revenue Enhancement, Part 3: Picking Low-Hanging Fruit—A Simple Approach to Yield Management," *Cornell Hotel and Restaurant Administration Quarterly* (April 1999): 76–83. Also see Plumrao Desiraju and Steven M. Shugan, "Strategic Service Pricing and Yield Management," *Journal of Marketing* (January 1999): 44–56.

22 Portions adapted with permission from Susan Greco, "Are Your Prices Right?" *INC.* (January 1997): 88–89. Copyright 1997 by Goldhirsh Group, Inc., 38 Commercial Wharf, Boston, MA 02110. Other information from Robert G. Cross, *Revenue Management: Hard Core Tactics for Market Domination* (New York: Broadway Books, 1998); William J. Quain, Michael Sansbury, and Dennis Quinn, "Revenue Enhancement, Part 3: Picking Low-Hanging Fruit—A Simple Approach to Yield Management," *Cornell Hotel and Restaurant Administration Quarterly* (April 1999): 76–83. Also see Plumrao Desiraju and Steven M. Shugan, "Strategic Service Pricing and Yield Management," *Journal of Marketing* (January 1999): 44–56.

23 Eric B. Orkin, "Boosting Your Bottom Line with Yield Management," *Cornell Hotel and Restaurant Administration Quarterly*, 28, no. 4 (1988): 52–56.

24 Elie Younen and Russel Kett, GopPAR, A Derivative of RevPAR, March 2003, HVS International.

25 *Hotline: The Magazine of Carlson Hotels*, GBC, 2011, Vision in Action, pp. 38 and 41.

26 Gary M. Thompson and Heeju (Louise) Sohn, "Cornell Hospitality Report: Accurately Estimating Time-Based Restaurant Revenues Using Revenue per Available Seat-Hour," *The Center for Hospitality Research*, 8, no. 9 (2008).

27 Zvi Schwartz and Eli Cohen, "Hotel Revenue Management Forecasting: Evidence of Expert-Judgment Bias," *Cornell Hotel and Restaurant Administration Quarterly*, 45, no. 1 (2004): 49.

28 William H. Kaven and Myrtle Allardyce, "Dalmahoy's Strategy for Success," *Cornell Hotel and Restaurant Administration Quarterly*, 35, no. 6 (1994): 87–88.

29 Sunmee Choi and Anna S. Mattila, "Impact of Information on Customer Fairness Perceptions of Hotel Revenue Management," *Cornell Hotel and Restaurant Administration Quarterly*, 46, no. 4 (2005): 444–445.

30 "What Is Surge Pricing," Uber Web site, https://help .uber.com/h/6c8065cf-5535-4a8b-9940-d292ff-dce119 (accessed August 3, 2015).

31 Jessi Hempel, "Why the Surge-Pricing Fiasco Is Great for Uber," Fortune.com, December 30, 2013, http://fortune.com/2013/12/30/why-the-surge-pricing-fiasco-is-great-for-uber/ (accessed August 3, 2015); Victor Fiorillo, "Will Everyone Please Shut Up About Uber Surge Pricing?" December 18, 2013. *Philadelphia Magazine*, http://www.phillymag .com/news/2013/12/18/uber-surge-pricing/#rhT8X-23vORdjS8Jd.99 (accessed August 15, 2015); Alison Griswald, "Everybody Hates Surge Pricing, So Why Does the D.C. Taxicab Commission Want to Introduce It?" *Slate*, http://www.slate.com/articles/business/moneybox/2014/04/uber_style_surge_pricing_does_the_system_make_sense_for_d_c_cabs.html (accessed August 3, 2015).

32 Kristin V. Rohlfs and Sheryl E. Kimes, "Customers' Perceptions of Best Available Hotel Rates," *Cornell Hotel and Restaurant Administration Quarterly*, 46, no. 2 (2007): 151.

33 Hotel Revenue Tools, Rate Parity, Definition and Strategies, Hotel Revenue Tools.com, 1-702-703-4511, May 6, 2015; Sean O'Neill, Marriott, Expedia, Priceline and Other Brands Escape Hotel Rate Parity Suit, *TNooz*, February 19, 2014.

34 Alex M. Susskind, Dennis Reynolds, and Eriko Tsuchiya, "An Evaluation of Guests' Preferred Incentives to Shift Time-Variable Demand in Restaurants," *Cornell Hotel and Restaurant Administration Quarterly*, 45, no. 1 (2004): 82.

35 Buffie Noone and Chung Hun Lee, "Hotel Overbooking: The Effect of Over-Compensation on Customers' Reactions to Denied Service," *Journal of Hospitality and Tourism Research*, 35, no. 3 (August 2011): 334.

36 Michael Collins and H.G. Paisa, "Pricing Strategies to Maximize Revenues in the Lodging Industry," *Hospitality Management*, 25 (2006): 91–107.

37 JoAnn Carmin and Gregory X. Norkus, "Pricing Strategies for Menus: Magic or Myth," *Cornell Hotel and Restaurant Administration Quarterly*, 31, no. 3 (1990): 50.

38 "High Stakes at Harrah's," *Scorecard: The Revenue Management Quarterly* (First Quarter, 1993), 3.

39 David K. Hayes and Lynn M. Huffman, "Value Pricing: How Long Can You Go?" *Cornell Hotel and Restaurant Administration Quarterly* (February 1995): 51–56.

40 Stephan J. Hock, Xavier Drge, and Mary E. Park, "EDLP, Hi-Low, and Margin Arithmetic," *Journal of Marketing*, 58 (1994): 27.

41 Linda Canina and Cathy Enz, "Pricing for Revenue Enhancement in Asian Pacific Region Hotels: A Study of Relative Pricing Strategies," *Cornell Hospitality Report*, 8, no. 3 (February 2008).

42 Nagle, *The Strategy and Tactics of Pricing*, pp. 95–96.

43 "Fairchild Cuts Rates to Gain Stronger Presence," *Hotel and Motel Management* (June 19, 1989): 11.

12

Distribution Channels Delivering Customer Value

Sunflower Travel of Wichita, Kansas, and Belair/Empress Travel in Bowie, Maryland, typify the kind of business most threatened by the advent of new marketing channels, particularly the surge in Internet selling. Like other traditional travel agencies, they face some scary new-age competitors. In recent years, they have seen a flurry of online competitors, ranging from giant travel superstars such as Expedia, Travelocity, Priceline, and Orbitz to newcomers like Trip.com that let consumers surf the Web for rock-bottom travel deals. To make matters worse, the airlines themselves now sell more than half of their own tickets online and no longer pay travel agencies commissions on ticket sales. Hotels are also aggressively promoting booking on their Web sites to avoid paying 10 percent commissions to travel agents. Travel ranks as the number-one product sold over the Internet.

These new channels give customers more choices, and they threaten the very existence of many travel agencies. During the 1990s, the number of U.S. travel agents dropped by 18 percent, and some studies suggest that another 25 percent will go out of business during the next few years. This is a worldwide trend. In the United Kingdom, the number of leisure travelers booking through travel agents has dropped by 12 percent over the last three years and the number of travel agents who were members of the Association of British Travel Agents (ABTA) dropped by 14 percent.

There is a fancy word to describe this phenomenon: *disintermediation*. Strictly speaking, *disintermediation* means the elimination of a layer of intermediaries from a marketing channel. More broadly, disintermediation includes not only the elimination of channel levels through direct marketing but also the displacement of traditional sellers by radically new types of intermediaries. Disintermediation works only when a new channel form succeeds in bringing greater value to consumers. The success of Internet-based travel distributors suggests they are bringing value to the customer.

If travel agents are to survive, they will have to counter the lower prices offered by the Internet distribution of travel products with another form of value: personal service. Sunflower Travel has added a number of value-added products. These include adventure and active travel such as white-water rafting, safaris, houseboat rental, and trips to remote fishing lodges. Many consumers are likely to seek the advice of an expert when purchasing these travel products. Ciclismo Classico is a tourist agency specializing in bicycling tours of eight regions around the world, including the northeastern United States and Italy. The agency is located in Arlington, Massachusetts. It sells travel personally through its office, over the phone, and over the Internet. It targets adventure tourists by offering a unique product. It has selected the tour routes, arranged for rental bikes, and packaged the lodging and food and beverage. It has created value through its knowledge of the product and incorporating this knowledge into the products it sells. Travel agents that add personalized service and unique or customized products will be able to survive disintermediation.[1]

■■■ Supply Chains and the Value Delivery Network

Supply Chain. Upstream and downstream partners. Upstream from the company is a set of firms that supply raw materials, components, parts, information, finances, and expertise needed to create a product. Downstream marketing channel partners, such as wholesalers and retailers, form a vital connection between the firm and its customers.

Producing a product and making it available to buyers requires building relationships not just with customers but also with key suppliers and resellers in the company's **supply chain**. This supply chain consists of "upstream" and "downstream" partners. Upstream from the company is the set of firms that supply the raw materials, components, parts, information, finances, and expertise needed to create a product or service. Marketers, however, have traditionally focused on the "downstream" side of the supply chain—on the *marketing channels* (or *distribution channels*) that look toward the customer. Downstream marketing channel partners, such as wholesalers and retailers, form a vital connection between the firm and its customers.

Both upstream and downstream partners may also be part of other firms' supply chains. But it is the unique design of each company's supply chain that enables it to deliver superior value to customers. An individual firm's success depends not only on how well *it* performs but also on how well its entire supply chain and marketing channel compete with competitors' channels.

The term *supply chain* may be too limited: It takes a make-and-sell view of the business. A better approach is a value delivery network made up of the company, suppliers, distributors, and ultimately customers who "partner" with each other to improve the performance of the entire system. For example, Red Lobster does more than just serve seafood dinners. It manages a network of seafood producers, suppliers, and a transportation system. Red Lobster has a team that regularly inspects its seafood producers to make sure the product is safe and meets all its other quality standards. In this age of globalization, both seafood and other products are sourced from throughout the globe. Seafood may come from farms in Central America, furniture for a hotel comes from China with a six-month order to delivery time, and a company's call center may be in India. Managing the participants in an organization's supply chain is both an important and a complex task.

This chapter focuses on marketing channels, the downstream side of the value delivery network. However, remember that this is only part of the full-value network. In creating customer value, companies need upstream supplier partners just as they need downstream channel partners. Red Lobster working with seafood producers is an example of a company with upstream suppliers. Increasingly, marketers are participating in and influencing their company's upstream activities as well as downstream activities. More than marketing channel managers, they are becoming full-value network managers.

■■■ Nature and Importance of Distribution Systems

If we view properties as the heart of a hotel company, distribution systems can be viewed as the company's circulatory system.[2] Distribution systems provide a steady flow of customers. A well-managed distribution system can make the difference between a market-share leader and a company struggling for survival. Many hospitality companies are making greater use of the marketing channels available to them. For example, Ritz-Carlton receives a significant share of business from travel agents because of aggressive development of this channel. Marriott entered a marketing alliance with New Otani Hotels, giving Marriott exposure to Japanese travelers in North America. In return, New Otani gained Marriott's marketing expertise to help reach Americans traveling to Japan.[3] Enterprise Rent-A-Car built locations next to auto dealers and repair facilities, realizing these facilities create a demand for rental cars. In today's competitive environment, companies must develop increasingly complex distribution networks.

Competition, a global marketplace, electronic distribution techniques, and a perishable product have increased the importance of distribution. Innovative ways of approaching new and existing markets are needed. Globalization has meant that many hotel companies must choose foreign partners to help them market or distribute their products. Sheraton built an alliance with the Welcome Group in India, which manages Sheraton Hotels on the Indian subcontinent. New electronic distribution methods have resulted in the growth of international reservation systems such as Utell. Finally, the importance of distribution has increased because hospitality products are perishable. RCI, a time-share exchange company, uses its large membership base to negotiate special hotel rates for its members. The agreement works well for both parties: Hotels have a chance to sell rooms during a soft period, and RCI can offer its members a benefit.

■■■ Nature of Distribution Channels

A distribution channel is a set of independent organizations involved in the process of making a product or service available to the consumer or business user.[4] Development of a distribution system starts with the selection of channel members. Once members are selected, the focus shifts to managing the channel. Distribution networks in the hospitality industry consist of contractual agreements and loosely organized alliances between independent organizations.[5] In marketing, distribution systems are traditionally used to move goods (tangible products) from the manufacturer to the consumer. In the hospitality and travel industries, distribution systems are used to move the customer to the product: the hotel, restaurant, cruise ship, or airplane.

We first look briefly at traditional distribution systems. These systems provide the framework for the development of hospitality distribution networks. The products used by hospitality and travel companies come through distribution channels; thus, it is important to understand their structure. Graduates of hospitality and tourism programs often work for companies that distribute products. Graduates with restaurant experience may find themselves working for a company that distributes food or beverages to restaurants. They may sell food-service equipment or tabletop items to restaurants and hotels.

Some graduates have taken jobs as food brokers. The food **broker** works as an **agent** for the manufacturer, trying to create demand for a product. For example, if Mrs. Smith's pies develops a new no-bake pie for the food-service industry, brokers representing Mrs. Smith's pies would introduce the product to food-service managers they think will be interested in using it. The hospitality and travel industries use billions of dollars' worth of products, all moved through distribution channels. These distribution channels create thousands of jobs.

Broker. A wholesaler who does not take title to goods and whose function is to bring buyers and sellers together and assist in negotiations.

Agent. A wholesaler who represents buyers or sellers on a more permanent basis, performs only a few functions, and does not take title to goods.

Why Are Marketing Intermediaries Used?

Why does Syracuse China sell its chinaware to restaurants through an intermediary? Although doing so means giving up control over pricing the products, Syracuse does gain advantages from selling through an intermediary. The company does not have to maintain several display rooms and a large sales force in every major city. Instead, a restaurant supply company displays, promotes, and makes personal sales calls. The restaurant supply house sells hundreds of other items. Its large assortment makes it a convenient supplier to the restaurant industry. The sales potential from its product assortment allows it to make personal sales calls, send catalogs, and provide other support for the products that it represents. Selling through wholesalers and retailers usually is much more efficient than direct sales.

A restaurant manager can make one call to a restaurant supply house and order a French knife, a dozen plates, a case of candles, a dozen oyster forks, a case of wine glasses, and a case of cocktail napkins. A different manufacturer produces each of these items, but they are all available through one distributor. To the purchaser, this means access to small quantities of products because these become part of a large order. This reduces inventory requirements, number of deliveries, and number of processed invoices. Figure 12–1 shows one way that intermediaries can provide economies. Without distribution systems, the restaurateur would have to call individual manufacturers, such as a knife manufacturer, a china company, and a paper company. Each of these manufacturers would receive thousands of calls from individual restaurants. This would create unnecessary work and shipping costs for both the manufacturer and the customer, as represented in Figure 12–1A. Figure 12–1B shows the efficiencies created by a distribution system. The restaurants or customers call one distributor and get all of their supplies. The manufacturers can reach many restaurants through one distributor.

Distribution Channel Functions

A distribution channel moves goods from producers to consumers. It overcomes the major time, place, and possession gaps that separate goods and services from those who would use them. Members of the marketing channel perform many key functions:

1. **Information:** Gathering and distributing marketing research and intelligence information about the marketing environment

2. **Promotion:** Developing and spreading persuasive communications about an offer

3. **Contact:** Finding and communicating with prospective buyers

Figure 12–1
How a distributor reduces the number of channel transactions.

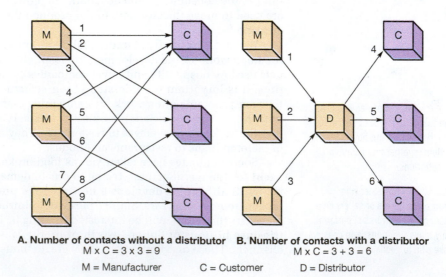

A. Number of contacts without a distributor
M x C = 3 x 3 = 9

B. Number of contacts with a distributor
M x C = 3 + 3 = 6

M = Manufacturer   C = Customer   D = Distributor

4. **Matching:** Shaping and fitting the offer to the buyer's needs, including such activities as manufacturing, grading, assembling, and packaging

5. **Negotiation:** Agreeing on price and other terms of the offer so that ownership or possession can be transferred

6. **Physical distribution:** Transporting and storing goods

7. **Financing:** Acquiring and using funds to cover the costs of channel work

8. **Risk taking:** Assuming financial risks such as the inability to sell inventory at full margin

The first five functions help complete transactions. The last three help fulfill the completed transactions.

All these functions have three things in common: They use scarce resources, they can often be performed better through specialization, and they can be shifted among channel members. Shifting functions to the intermediary may keep producer costs and prices low, but intermediaries must add a charge to cover the cost of their work. To keep costs low, functions should be assigned to channel members who can perform them most efficiently. For example, a cruise is an expensive purchase with many options for the traveler. Travel representing all the major cruise lines answers questions about cruise lines, itineraries, activities in the ports of call, and the many other questions a guest may have about the selection of a cruise. Online travel agents specializing in cruise products allow customers to browse through the different products and talk to an agent when they have questions or are ready to purchase. The online travel agencies as well as the agents with physical locations provide a broad distribution network for this infrequently purchased and complex product. This is why the majority of cruise ship bookings are made through travel agents. Frequently purchased products such as hotel rooms are less complex. Once people find a brand they like, they often prefer to book directly with the brand.

Number of Channel Levels

Channel level. A level of middleman that performs some work in bringing the product and its ownership closer to the final buyer.

Direct marketing channel. A marketing channel that has no intermediary levels.

Retailer. Business whose sales come primarily from retailing.

Wholesaler. Firms engaged primarily in wholesaling activity.

Distribution channels can be described by the number of **channel levels**. Each layer that performs some work in bringing the product and its ownership closer to the final buyer is a channel level. Because the producer and the final consumer both perform some work, they are part of every channel. We use the number of intermediary levels to show the length of a channel. Figure 12–2 shows several consumer distribution channels.

Channel 1, called a **direct marketing channel**, has no intermediary level. It consists of a manufacturer selling directly to consumers. For example, a restaurateur may buy produce directly from the grower at a farmers' market. Channel 2 contains one level. In consumer markets, this level is typically a **retailer**. The Fisherman's Pier restaurant in Geelong, near Melbourne, Australia, purchases its fish from a fisherman's cooperative. The cooperative markets the fish, allowing the fishers to specialize in fishing, not marketing.

Many of the agricultural products purchased by the hospitality industry come from cooperatives. In the United States, Sunkist, Diamond Walnuts, and Land O'Lakes butter are all producer cooperatives. New Zealand Milk Products Company is also a cooperative and sells dried milk and cheese throughout Southeast Asia and Latin America.

Channel 3 contains two levels. In consumer markets, these are typically a **wholesaler** and a retailer. Smaller manufacturers use this type of channel. Channel 4 contains three levels. The jobber buys from wholesalers and sells to smaller firms that are not served by larger wholesalers. From the producer's point of view, a greater number of intermediaries in the channel means less control, more complexity, and more cost.

All the institutions in the channel are connected by several types of flows. These include the physical flow of products, the flow of ownership, payment flow, information flow, and promotion flow. These flows can make channels with only one or a few channels very complex.

Figure 12–2
Business-to-consumer and business-to-business marketing channels.

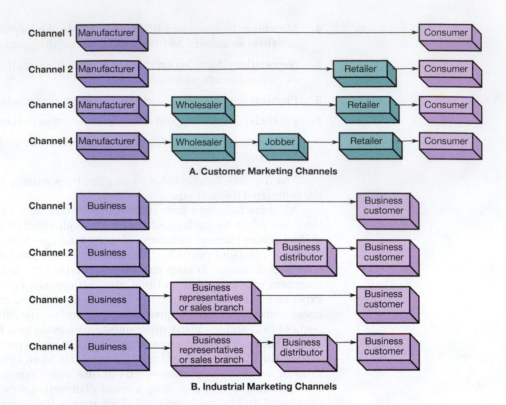

A. Customer Marketing Channels

B. Industrial Marketing Channels

Many specialized channels are available to hospitality and travel organizations. We discuss the following components of a hospitality or travel distribution system: travel agents; tour wholesalers; specialists; hotel representatives; national, state, and local tourist agencies; consortia and reservation systems; global distribution systems (GDSs); the Internet; and concierges. A manager must choose the intermediaries that will make up the distribution system and the number of levels that the distribution system will have.

■■■ Hospitality Distribution Channels

Major Hospitality Distribution Channels

The largest number of reservations, 33 percent, comes to a hotel through brand.com. Brand.com is a term used for the brands reservation system. For example, for Hilton it would be www.hilton.com. About 24 percent come from direct bookings, and 13 percent come from the calls into the central reservation office (CRO).[6] Twenty-nine percent come from third parties: online travel agencies and global distribution systems. The cost of these different channels varies greatly. The least expensive way is when the guest makes a reservation through the brand's Web site. However, when a hotel has rooms to fill, OTAs can help sell the rooms. A revenue manager has to manage the channels, knowing when to open and close different channels. See Table 12–1.

Direct Booking

Managers often like to encourage direct booking because of the low transaction costs. However, front-desk personnel are usually not trained in revenue management. Front-desk staff also develop a personal relationship with repeat guests. Thus, a repeat guest who is making a future reservation and is quoted a $189 rate by a front-desk clerk quickly asks for the $139 rate he paid during his last stay. The front-desk clerk is unable to explain why there is such a price difference and quickly acquiesces to the lower rate. The Hilton University of Houston found that

TABLE 12–1
Comparison of Channel Costs

	Rate ($)	Commission	Transaction Fee ($)	Total Cost ($)	Net Rate ($)
Brand.com	209	0	0	0	209.00
Brand.com*	209	$17.77 (8.5%)	$0	$17.77	$191.23
CRO—Phone	209	0%	$3.00	$3.00	$206.00
GDS	209	$20.90 (10%)	$0	$20.90	$188.10
OTA	209	$37.62 (18%)	$0	$37.62	$171.38

Brand.com accessed through a search engine (Google, Bing, etc.).

Source: John Bowen based on charges for a branded property. The rate for OTAs will vary by the agency. Through negotiations large brands receive better pricing with some OTAs than independent hotels. The brand.com and CRO rates will vary across brands; these are indicative rates.

reservations booked through the front desk were approximately 15 percent less than reservations booked through the CRO or Hilton.com. Hotels are advised to refer nongroup customers to brand.com or the brand's toll-free number, rather than to take nongroup reservations at the hotel. Together the Web and the brand's 800# account for about 36 percent of a hotel's reservations. It is important that the photos, wording, and packages on the brand.com Web site are accurate and do a good job of promoting the hotel. In addition to hotels, restaurants also receive most of their reservations through direct booking.

Online Travel Agency

Online travel agencies (OTAs) conduct business through the Internet with no physical locations or stores. OTAs account for about 14 percent of a hotel's reservation. One way of dividing OTAs is into opaque and nonopaque. The nonopaque OTAs include merchant, retail, and referral models. The most popular nonopaque sites are merchant agencies that collect payment from the customer and include well-known names like Hotels.com, Travelocity, and Expedia. Although they only produce 14 percent of a hotel's reservations, it is estimated that 75 percent of U.S. online hospitality shoppers are on OTA sites prior to booking.[7] They are popular booking channels for younger travelers making under $75,000.[8] One important feature of an OTA is people often search through hotel choices and then go to brand .com to book the reservation. Cindy Estess Green calls this the Billboard Effect. It is important that the hotel have a good presence in terms of photos and description on the OTA sites.

Opaque sites reduce cannibalization of brand.com by not disclosing the brand and specific hotel one is purchasing until it is purchased in a nonrefundable transaction with the consumer. For example, Hotwire will describe a hotel as a 3½ star hotel in the Ohio State University area for $99. Priceline also uses a general location within the city and stars to categorize its hotels. Priceline uses an auction system where the buyer "names" the price he or she will pay; if the buyer's price is high enough, he or she will get the room; if not, he or she may bid again after waiting 24 hours, changing hotel category and/or location within the city. People who are loyal to a certain brand or want to stay at a specific brand are not attracted to opaque agencies since they have no guarantee they will get the brand or hotel they want. Some hotels will give excess inventory to opaque merchants at deeply discounted prices to attract additional guests. When using opaque OTAs, one should consider that OTAs could reduce the perceived value for those who purchase through brand.com, if people in the same hotel discuss what they paid for the room. It can also bring in price-sensitive guests who will not spend money on food and beverage.

Another type of OTA is a retail agency, which is similar to a conventional travel agency; the hotel pays a commission to the agent and collects the room rental directly from the guest. OTAs also sell rental cars, airplane flights, ground transportation, cruises, and tours.

Persons who purchase from a third party on the Internet pay the third party. Thus, if hotels want to capture guests for their database, they need to collect the guests' names and addresses when they register. Guests who are new to Internet booking are often anxious and call the hotel to confirm the booking after making the reservation. The hotel may have no record, and the reservationist has to spend valuable time trying to sort out the status of the reservation. By simply asking guests how they made the reservation, the hotel employee can identify those who book with a third party and inform them that the reservation has not been transferred from the OTA, and advise them when to check back.

Southwest Airlines books 80 percent of its revenues through its brand.com sites.[9] Recently, Lufthansa Airlines added an $18 fee for tickets purchased through an OTA to discourage travelers from using this channel.[10] Airlines are less dependent on OTAs as they control their inventory. The hotel industry is a very fragmented industry, in terms of ownership. Hotel brands have little control over their inventory. Many hotel brands do not own their hotels and may have hundreds of franchisees and developers that own the hotels and control the inventory. This creates an opportunity for OTAs to provide a channel for hotels that need to sell their rooms, and are willing to pay a high price to sell them rather than have them sit vacant. This in turn creates competitive environment where other hotels turn to OTAs to compete. To encourage customers to book through brands.com, hotel brands did not give loyalty points or benefits for guests booking through OTAs. OTAs countered by developing their own loyalty program, allowing a traveler to stay across multiple brands and still gain rewards.[11]

Metasearch engines such as Kayak, Trivago, and Google Hotel Finder search across a number of OTAs to compare prices. The line between metasearch sites and OTAs has become blurred with popular sites like TripAdvisor becoming OTAs, both searching across sites for pricing information and providing booking through TripAdvisor. The fragmentation of the hotel industry, the perishability of travel products, and the transition of metasearch sites into OTAs ensure that in the near-term OTAs will continue to expand their share of hotel bookings.

In some hotels commissions and fees paid to OTAs can represent one-third or more of the net profits of the hotel. A major discussion among hotel owners is how to reduce the dependence on and the amount paid to OTAs. To illustrate the power of OTAs in August 2015, Priceline was worth $66 billion and Marriott was worth $19 billion.

Global Distribution Systems

GDSs are computerized reservation systems that serve as a product catalog for travel agents and other distributors of hospitality products. These reservation systems were originally developed by the airlines to promote sales. Before the Internet, GDSs offered a way for suppliers and end users to connect globally. As the Internet evolved, they developed Internet solutions for their customers. A distribution service provider provides the connection between a hotel's CRS and the GDS. Smaller hotel chains or independent hotels may link through a reservation service. There are four main GDSs: Amadeus, Sabre, Galileo, and Worldspan. Amadeus is the largest producer of travel bookings. It has a network that includes 75,000 travel agencies, 500 airlines, and 78,000 hotels. It also has an interest in vacations .com, the leading OTA for vacation travel. Travelport is a distribution system that owns Galileo and Worldspan. It produces 1.1 billion travel transactions per day. Additionally, Travelport has an interest in four OTAs, including Gulliver's Travel Associates. Sabre is the other major GDS. It has also expanded into the OTA business and is the owner of Travelocity as well as a number of other brands.[12]

Travel Agents

One way of reaching a geographically diverse marketplace is through travel agents.[13] The number of travel agents has been decreasing in recent years due to the growth of direct booking and customers self-booking travel on the Internet. Today, the majority of airline reservations are booked directly on the airline's Web site.

Almost all airlines have discontinued paying commissions to travel agents.[14] This has led agencies to charge a $25 to $50 fee for issuing tickets. In addition to selling airline tickets, travel agents book hotel sales, and nearly all cruise travel.[15] Hotels typically pay 10 percent commission to travel agents, and cruise lines can pay up to 15 percent. The combination of reduced commissions and growth of direct sales from hotels and airlines to the consumer has led to a steady decrease of travel agents in the United States.

Hotels interested in travel agency business are listed in airline reservation systems and hotel guides. Hotels also send information packages to travel agents that include collateral material and hotel news, including updates about hotel packages, promotions, and special events. Travel agents are also invited to visit hotel property on familiarization tours (fam trips). Airlines sometimes assist with these trips by providing free airfare. It is important that fam trips be well organized.[16] Finally, promotional campaigns can be directed at travel agents through travel agent publications such as *Travel Weekly, Travel Trade*, and *Travel Agent*. The use of promotional campaigns targeted at travel agents is discussed in Chapter 14.

Hotels seeking travel agent business must make it easy for agents to make reservations. Providing toll-free reservation numbers is essential. Hotels that generate many bookings from travel agents have a separate number dedicated to business travel. Travel agents like to be paid quickly. Hotels that want travel agent business process commissions rapidly. Hyatt guarantees payment within one week of the guest's departure.[17] Foreign chains are now paying commissions in the travel agent's local currency, eliminating the need for the agent to go through the costly process of converting a commission check. On a $50 commission foreign currency check, the travel agent stands to lose nearly the full amount because most banks charge a minimum of $30 to $40 per transaction for processing and converting checks drawn on a foreign bank.

Hospitality providers who serve travel agents must remember that agents entrust the hotel with their customers. In a travel agency market survey, travel agents rated reputation for honoring reservations, reputation for good service, ease of collecting commission, and room rates as the most important factors in choosing a hotel.[18] Hotels must do everything possible to make a favorable impression on guests booked through travel agents to ensure future business from that agent. When business is obtained through an intermediary, the hospitality provider, such as a hotel or cruise line, has two customers, the guest and the intermediary. The majority of cruise lines do not sell directly to the ultimate consumer but insist that bookings be made through travel agents or tour operators.

Corporate travel agents are one of the strongest areas of the travel agency business. Companies are a major source of travel bookings. U.S. corporations spend over $310 billion on travel.[19] Each dollar of that amount represents a cost that corporations would like to reduce. Consequently, companies make arrangements with travel agents and in some cases set up their own travel agency. Many organizations sign an exclusive agreement with one travel agency, and employees are required to book through this firm. The travel agency assumes responsibility for locating the least expensive travel alternatives for the company.

Travel Wholesalers and Tour Operators

Travel wholesalers assemble blocks or rooms and airline seats and sometimes create packages usually targeted at the leisure market. These packages are sold through travel agents or tour operators to the traveler. Tour operators create packages and sell them to travel agents or directly to the consumer.[20] These packages generally include transportation and accommodations but may include meals, ground transportation, and entertainment. In developing a package, a tour operator contracts with airlines and hotels for a specified number of seats and rooms, receiving a quantity discount. The operator also arranges transportation between the hotel and the airport. Retail travel agents sell these packages. The tour operator has to provide a commission for the travel agent and give consumers a package that is perceived to be a better value than what they could arrange on their own. Additionally, tour operators have to make a profit for themselves. The profit margin on each package is small. Generally, operators and wholesalers must sell 85 percent of the packages available to break even.[21] This high break-even point leaves little room for error. As a result, it is not uncommon for a tour wholesaler to go broke. Thus, it is important that hospitality providers check the history of the tour operator, receive a deposit, and get paid promptly. Additional security is provided by dealing with tour operators who are members of the U.S. Tour Operators Association (USTOA). USTOA requires its members to post a $100,000 indemnity bond for its consumer payments protection program. This ensures refund of tour deposits and payments in the event of financial failure of any of its members.[22]

With the increased number of international resorts, tour wholesalers are becoming a powerful member of the distribution channel. It is impossible for travel agents to know every resort. Instead, they rely on catalogs provided by tour wholesalers. If a couple wants to holiday on Saipan, they are given the catalog of a tour operator covering Micronesia. The catalog contains a selection of several luxury hotels, four-star hotels, three-star hotels, and tourist hotels. The wholesaler writes a description of each. The hotel may provide information, but the tour operator decides on the description of the hotel that goes in the brochure.

If a couple wants to stay at a luxury hotel, the brochure may include only three luxury hotels. Others are eliminated from consideration and will not be part of the couple's awareness set. The couple chooses a resort that seems to offer the best value based on the information provided by the tour wholesaler. So the tour wholesaler exerts a powerful force over resorts, especially remote international markets.

The Caribbean resort industry is particularly dependent on tour wholesalers, who provide over half the business. One effect of the power of tour wholesalers in this area is the existence of substantial discounts to them regardless of seasonal demand. This seriously affects the ability of Caribbean hotel managers to control pricing through tools such as yield management (see Chapter 11). It also affects cash flow. Caribbean wholesalers collect payment from customers three to six months before they arrive at a hotel, but most hotels have to wait 60 days after guest arrival for payment from wholesalers.

Airlines may also serve as tour operators. Almost all major airlines have vacation packages promoted through brochures and their Web sites. An airline such as Air New Zealand offers farm/ranch or bed and breakfast packages for the foreign independent traveler (FIT) market. Visitors to New Zealand can book auto rentals or camper rentals and reservations with these specialized lodging providers through the tour desk of Air New Zealand.

Specialists: Tour Brokers, Motivational Houses, and Junket Reps

Motivational houses. Provide incentive travel offered to employees or distributors as a reward for their efforts.

Colonial Williamsburg and other historical sites often rely on bus tours as a source of guests. Courtesy of Jiawangkun/Shutterstock.

Tour brokers sell motor coach tours, which are attractive to a variety of markets. Tours through New England to view the fall foliage, trips to college and sporting events, tours built around Mardi Gras, and regularly scheduled tours of the Washington, DC, area are examples of popular motor coach trips. Some motor coach tours are seasonal, some are based on one event, and others are year round. For hotels on their routes, motor coach tours can provide an important source of income.[23]

Motor coach tours are very important to museums and historic restorations such as historic Colonial Williamsburg in Virginia. Hospitality providers such as historic restorations, hotels, and destination cities usually participate in a travel conference sponsored by the American Bus Association. Booth space is rented, and salespeople representing these providers scramble to make appointments with bus tour companies that serve their area.

Motivational houses provide incentive travel offered to employees or distributors as a reward for their efforts. Companies often use incentive travel as a prize for employees who achieve sales goals or for the sales team achieving the highest sales. The incentive trip is usually to a resort area and includes first-class or luxury properties. For resorts or upmarket properties in destination cities, such as New York, San Francisco, Chicago, or Boston, motivational houses represent an effective distribution channel. Ways of reaching tour brokers and incentive houses include trade magazines and trade associations, such as the National Tour Association and the Society of Incentive Travel Executives.[24]

Junket reps. Serve the casino industry as intermediaries for premium players.

Junket reps serve the casino industry as intermediaries for premium players. Junket reps maintain lists of gamblers who like to visit certain gaming areas, such as Reno, Las Vegas, or Atlantic City, and they work with one or a few casinos rather than the entire industry. They are paid a commission on the amount the casino earns from the players or in some cases on a per-player basis. Members of a junket receive complimentary or low-cost hospitality services, including air transportation, ground transportation, hotel lodging, food and beverage, and entertainment. The amount of complimentary services received depends on the amount that players gamble in the casino.

Hotel Representatives

Hotel representatives sell hotel rooms and hotel services in a given market area. It is often more effective for hotels to hire a hotel representative than to use their own salesperson. This is true when the market is a distant one and when cultural differences may make it hard for an outsider to penetrate the market. For example, a corporate hotel in Houston may find it is more effective to hire a hotel representative in Mexico City than to send a sales manager there. Hotel sales representatives should represent noncompeting hotels. They receive a straight commission, a commission plus a salary, or a combination of both. It takes time for a hotel representative to learn a company's products and inform the market about them. The choice of a hotel representative should not be taken lightly. They represent your hotel, as your sales staff. As with any member of your sales team, frequent changes in hotel representatives can be disruptive.

National, State, and Local Tourist Agencies

National, state, and local tourist agencies are an excellent way to get information to the market and gain room bookings. National associations promote tourism within their own countries. Their impact can be important to hotel chains that have locations throughout the country. State agencies promote the state resources and attractions overseas, nationally, and in the state itself. State tourist agencies usually have tourist information centers strategically located throughout the state, often at entrance points. Regional associations can also help the independent and chain operators.

The Sydney Convention and Visitors Bureau (SCVB) has offices in London, Melbourne, and New York, in addition to its main office in Sydney. The staff members in these offices work to bring meetings and conventions to Sydney by making them aware of the facilities and amenities the city has to offer. The SCVB also provides materials for organizations to help promote their meeting in Sydney. For example, it provides promotional videos of Sydney, postcards for teaser campaigns, slides for presentations, and brochure shells with images of Sydney that can be overprinted with the program, registration material, or other information. The SCVB also helps event planners match their needs with what the city has to offer, including venues for meeting, lodging accommodations, and ideas for unique activities. One suggestion is a private breakfast on Shark Island in the middle of Sydney Harbor, with the sunrise over the Opera House and the harbor bridge. Another is having an Australian bush theme party in a five-star hotel complete with live kangaroos, koalas, and sheep shearing. The SCVB, like other convention and visitors' bureaus, serves as a channel to bring business to its city or region.[25]

Consortia and Reservation Systems

Reservation systems such as Global Hotel Alliance and Leading Hotels of the World are expanding their services. Reservation systems provide a CRS for hotels.

They usually provide the system for small chains or provide an overseas reservation service, allowing international guests to call a local number to contact the hotel.

A consortium is a group of hospitality organizations that is allied for the mutual benefit of the members. Marketing is often the reason why consortia are formed. The consortium allows a property to be independent in ownership and management while gaining the advantages of group marketing. An example of a consortium is Leading Hotels of the World. The distinction between consortia and reservation services is becoming blurred, as reservation services such as Supranational also provide marketing activities. It is a natural evolution for reservation systems to add additional services once they have a critical number of hotels as subscribers.

Regions are also developing consortia to promote their area as a tourism attraction. For example, tourist attractions in the Bath area of the United Kingdom have formed the Association of Bath and District Leisure Enterprises (ABLE). This type of cooperative allows smaller hospitality organizations to develop and distribute promotional material. Travel agents have formed consortia to negotiate lower rates for hotel rooms, airlines, and other tourist products. One of the larger travel agent consortia is Woodside Management Systems. Consortia can also develop vertical marketing systems by negotiating special prices on supplies that members may use. Consortia and reservation systems combined with OTAs have allowed nonbranded hotels to compete effectively with branded properties.[26]

Distribution Systems in the Sharing Economy

Companies like Airbnb and Uber have created distribution systems that allow individuals to share the cooking skills, knowledge of wine, transportation, and/or lodging with others. Airbnb requests potential lodging suppliers to list anything from their Seaside Villa to an air mattress in their living room on their Web site.[27] The renting of unused lodging space by individuals has created increased competition for the lodging industry. It has also created controversy as facilities rented on Airbnb often do not pay hotel tax, and often do not meet the life safety requirements provided by hotels and requirements for persons with disabilities. Uber is an international ride service that recruits local drivers to use their car to provide transportation for others, both local residents needing a ride and tourists. Uber competes directly with taxi services. Uber's Web site claims if you own a car you can make money.[28] Sites like cookening.com and eatwith.com serve as distribution channels for cooks who will prepare meals for guests in their homes or at the guest's home. These channels are creating distribution channels allowing part-time provision of hospitality products by people who may have full-time jobs.

Airbnb lists accommodations in over 190 countries. In Cuba, it offers an ocean front home for $1100 a day to youth hostels for $10 a night. Courtesy of David Paul Morris/Bloomberg/Getty Images.

Restaurant Distribution Channels

Online Reservations—OpenTable

There are a number of online reservation systems for restaurants. The largest one, OpenTable owned by Priceline, serves over 30,000 worldwide restaurants. OpenTable charges $1 for each reservation received from its Web site and $0.25 for every reservation that the customer books directly with the restaurant after linking through OpenTable. OpenTable is linked with a number of sites that provide restaurant reviews, allowing the customer review restaurant choices and then make a reservation through OpenTable.[29] OpenTable also has become an important database, housing dining habits on millions of dinners. It has also developed a mobile app, allowing the bill to automatically be charged to a stored credit card with a predetermined tip added.[30]

OpenTable's $1 fee per person for reservation over its site can be high for some restaurants. An independent restaurant may make only 5 to 10 percent profit; thus, a $1 fee can be the profit from $20 in sales. Restaurants with low-check averages may want to look at other online options. Also, a restaurant that has meal periods with low-check averages, such as breakfast, may want to close this meal period off to reservations from OpenTable.

Delivery, Take-Out, Drive-Through Window

Restaurants produce a tangible product, allowing it to be delivered to a customer's home. Most restaurants will manage this process by hiring drivers. There are also services such as Eat24, owned by Yelp, that will deliver for restaurants, gaining fees from both the restaurant and customer. Delivery is becoming almost a necessity for restaurants in Urban areas, where people may not have cars. For restaurants that do start a delivery program, management should make sure they have proper insurance coverage. Some guests will prefer to come to the restaurant to pick up food. Many restaurants will have a separate area for guests to order and pick-up to take out. An app for a mobile phone makes it easy for guests to place pick-up orders. For quick service restaurants, drive-through windows make it convenient for guests to get food to go. Approximately two-thirds of a fast-food hamburger restaurant's sales will come from a drive-through window. This number drops to about 40 percent for chicken and Mexican Food fast-food restaurants.[31]

Food Trucks

Food trucks have been around for decades, primarily serving construction sites by providing hot meals for workers. In recent years, they have served as a way for a chef to start his or her own business. The attraction is the low start-up cost. The start-up cost, including the purchase of a used food truck is $75,000 to $100,000.[32] The mobility of the food truck is also a benefit. This allows the truck to move to where the customers are, such as festivals, parks, business districts, colleges, and train stations. In addition to entrepreneurs, major companies such as Starbucks are getting into the food truck business. The J.W. Marriott San Antonio Country Resort and Spa uses food trucks to provide an interesting food option for its convention guests and to serve outdoor functions.

The number of used food trucks on the market is evidence that food trucks are a business and like other businesses if you are not competitive you will not survive. Social media is important to the success of food trucks. Letting customers know where you are through Foursquare, which is linked to your Facebook and Twitter accounts, will help generate business from your regulars and their friends.[33] Food trucks have a small cooking area; many food trucks use a commissary to do their prep work. Also, food truck owners tend to go out and pick up their provisions on a daily basis. At the end of the day, the truck has to be cleaned, often back at a commissary that serves food trucks. Local health departments and city/county ordinances also regulate food trucks. Those considering starting a food truck should understand the hours involved and the local permits and requirements for starting this business.

Concierges

Concierges, bell staff, and front-desk employees can be good sources of business for local hospitality products and travel, such as restaurants, tours, and fishing guides. Concierges will be a source of business for those restaurants they think their guests will enjoy. Restaurants wishing to cultivate a relationship with concierges usually invite them for a complimentary meal so they can experience the restaurant firsthand and supply them with copies of menus, they can show their guests. The restaurant's management may also volunteer the restaurant as a site for the local concierge association meetings if the restaurant has meeting space. Finally, the restaurant instructs the staff on how to handle calls from a concierge. For example, even though concierges know there is no chance of getting a reservation at a popular restaurant on a Saturday night, they are still obliged to call because the guest has requested it and is standing at their side. Thus, when such requests do come, the person answering the phone at the restaurant should be courteous and understand the situation.

■■■ Channel Behavior and the Organization

Distribution channels are more than simple collections of firms tied together by various flows. They are complex behavioral systems in which people and companies interact to accomplish goals. Some channel systems consist of formal interactions among loosely organized firms. Others consist of formal interactions guided by strong organizational structures. Channel systems do not stand still. New types surface and new channel systems evolve. We now look at channel behavior and how members organize to do the work of the channel.

Channel Behavior

A distribution system consists of dissimilar firms that have banded together for their common good. Each channel member is dependent on the others, playing a role in the channel and specializing in performing one or more functions.

Ideally, because the success of individual channel members depends on general channel success, all channel firms should work together. They should understand and accept their roles, coordinate their goals and activities, and cooperate to attain overall channel goals. By cooperating, they can understand and serve the target market more effectively.

But individual channel members rarely take such a broad view. They are usually more concerned with their own short-run goals and their dealings with the firms operating closest to them in the channel. Cooperating to achieve overall channel goals sometimes means giving up individual company goals. Although channel members depend on each other, they often act alone in their own short-run best interests. They frequently disagree on the roles each should play or who should do what for which rewards. Such disagreements over goals and roles generate **channel conflict**.

Horizontal conflict is conflict between firms at the same level of the channel. For example, some Pizza Inn franchisees may complain about other Pizza Inn franchisees cheating on ingredients and giving poor service, thereby hurting the overall Pizza Inn image.

Vertical conflict, conflicts between different levels of the same channel, is even more common. In recent years, for example, Burger King has had a steady stream of conflicts with its franchised dealers over everything from increased ad spending and offensive ads to the prices it charges for cheeseburgers. At issue is the chain's right to dictate policies to franchisees.

The price of a double cheeseburger has generated a lot of heat among Burger King franchisees. In an ongoing dispute, the burger chain insisted that the sandwich be sold for no more than $1—in line with other items on its "Value Menu." Burger King saw the value price as key to competing effectively in the current economic environment. But the company's franchisees claimed that they would lose money at that price. After months of public wrangling, Burger King finally

Channel conflict.
Disagreement among marketing channel members on goals and roles—who should do what and for what rewards.

Horizontal conflict. Conflict between firms at the same level.

Vertical conflict. Conflict between different levels of the same channel.

Vertical marketing systems (VMSs). Distribution channel structures in which producers, wholesalers, and retailers act as a unified system: Either one channel member owns the others, or has contracts with them, or has so much power that they all cooperate.

Corporate VMS. A vertical marketing system that combines successive stages of production and distribution under single ownership. Channel leadership is established through common ownership.

Administered VMS. A vertical marketing system coordinates successive stages of production and distribution, not through common ownership or contractual ties, but through the size and power of one of the parties.

let franchisees have it their way. It introduced a double-patty burger with just one slice of cheese, instead of two, cutting the cost of ingredients and the price on Value Menu was increased to $1.19.[34] Burger King was not alone; McDonald's had a similar dispute with some of its franchisees. When sales per store slowed, it wanted to increase items on its Dollar Menu to drive sales. McDonald's was also upset with its franchisees over low customer service scores and wanted the franchisees to improve these scores. Customer satisfaction was not the only thing that was at a low, McDonald's franchisee relations scores dropped to an all-time low, 1.99 out of 5.00. That could be why the employees were not smiling; one restaurant management consultant stated there is a correlation between franchisee satisfaction and customer satisfaction.[35]

Some conflict in the channel takes the form of healthy competition. Such competition can be good for the channel; without it, the channel could become passive and noninnovative. For example, McDonald's conflict with its franchisees might represent normal give-and-take over the respective rights of the channel partners. But severe or prolonged conflict can disrupt channel effectiveness and cause lasting harm to channel relationships. Franchisors should manage the channel conflict carefully to keep it from getting out of hand.

Vertical Marketing Systems

For the channel as a whole to perform well, each channel member's role must be specified, and channel conflict must be managed. The channel will perform better if it includes a firm, an agency, or a mechanism that provides leadership and has the power to assign roles and manage conflict.

Historically, *conventional distribution channels* have lacked such leadership and power, often resulting in damaging conflict and poor performance. One of the biggest channel developments over the years has been the emergence of **vertical marketing systems (VMSs)** that provide channel leadership. Figure 12–3 contrasts the two types of channel arrangements.

A conventional distribution channel consists of one or more independent producers, wholesalers, and retailers. Each is a separate business seeking to maximize its own profits, perhaps even at the expense of the system as a whole. No channel member has much control over the other members, and no formal means exist for assigning roles and resolving channel conflict.

In contrast, a VMS consists of producers, wholesalers, and retailers acting as a unified system. One channel member owns the others, has contracts with them, or wields so much power that they must all cooperate. The producer, the wholesaler, or the retailer can dominate the VMS.

We now look at the three major types of VMSs. Each type uses a different means for setting up leadership and power in the channel. In a **corporate VMS**, coordination and conflict management are attained through common ownership at different levels in the channel. In an administered VMS, one or a few dominant channel members assume leadership. In a contractual VMS, leadership and power are attained through contractual agreements among channel members.

A corporate VMS combines successive stages of production and distribution under single ownership. For example, Red Lobster has its own food-processing plants and distributes food products to its restaurants. Craft breweries often open their own pubs serving or at least featuring their own beer.

An **administered VMS** coordinates successive stages of production and distribution not through common ownership or contractual ties but through the size and power of the parties. The world's airline industry has been affected by administered VMSs since the birth of the industry. Many nations continue to cling to a subsidized national carrier known as a flag carrier. These airlines, and the government, often exert an inordinate amount of power over reservation systems, tour operators, and travel agencies within their respective nations.

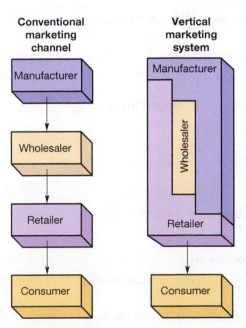

Conventional marketing channel

Manufacturer → Wholesaler → Retailer → Consumer

Vertical marketing system

Manufacturer / Wholesaler / Retailer → Consumer

Figure 12–3
Comparison of conventional marketing channel with vertical marketing system.

Contractual VMS. A vertical marketing system in which independent firms at different levels of production and distribution join together through contracts to obtain more economies or sales impact than they could achieve alone.

Franchise. A contractual vertical marketing system in which a channel member called a franchiser links several stages in the production distribution process.

The third type of VMS is contractual. A **contractual VMS** consists of independent firms at different levels of production and distribution who join through contracts to obtain economies or sales impact. A contract with a hotel representative would be an example of a contractual VMS. An important form of contractual VMS is franchising.

Franchising

Franchising is a method of doing business by which a franchisee is granted the right to engage in offering, selling, or distributing goods or services under a marketing format, which is designed by the franchisor. The franchisor permits the franchisee to use its trademark, name, and advertising.

Franchises have been popular forms of distribution for both hotels and restaurants. Some of the most popular brands are franchised, including Holiday Inn Express, Hilton Garden Inn, and Fairfield Inn by Marriott, McDonald's, and KFC. Franchises have been responsible for shifting the restaurant business from individual operators to multiunit chains

For the right to use the name, methods of operation, and other benefits that come with a franchise, the franchisee pays an initial fee, a royalty, and a marketing fee to the franchise organization. In the case of hotels, there is a reservation fee and a fee for the loyalty program; for an overview of hotel franchise fees see *Hotel Franchise Fee Guide*, published by HVS. Royalty is based on gross room revenue, as are the other total revenue-based fees. The franchisor can verify gross receipts through tax reports. A contentious area with franchisees is the marketing fee. It is administered by the brand, but uses the fees paid by franchisees. If the use of the marketing fee is not communicated well, it can create conflict with franchisees. To avoid this and other forms of conflict, franchisors should encourage the formation of a franchisee association and work through issues with the association.

The initial fee and the royalty depend on the brand equity of the franchise. For example, McDonald's is recognized as a fast-food restaurant around the world. People in London, Paris, Hong Kong, and New York recognize McDonald's. The stronger the market position, the more valuable is the brand name. Thus, a McDonald's franchise offers more value than a Mr. Quick Hamburger franchise. These are the advantages of the franchise to the franchisee (person or organization buying the franchise):

- Recognition of brand
- Less chance of a business failure
- National advertising, premade advertisements, and marketing plans
- Faster business growth
- Help with site selection
- Architectural plans
- Operational systems, software, and manual to support the systems
- National contracts with suppliers
- Product development
- Consulting
- Help with financing

The disadvantages of purchasing a franchise are as follows:

- Fees and royalties are required.
- It limits the products sold and the recipes used.
- The franchisee is often required to be open a minimum number of hours and offer certain products.
- A poorly operated company can affect the reputation of the entire chain.
- The franchisor's performance affects the profitability of franchisees.
- Some franchisees may not benefit from national advertising as much as other franchisees—often a source of conflict.

One of the reasons that companies decide to franchise is that it allows for increased distribution of their products. The franchisee's money expands the business while the franchisor collects an initial fee and royalties. Franchising is not effective for all companies. The company must be able to offer the operational systems, management support, and a good business concept. For new businesses, it requires time and money to provide a good franchisee package. Smaller chains often franchise to people who are close to the business. For example, franchising is used in smaller restaurant chains to help them retain managers. It is difficult for a small chain to compete with opportunities that a large chain offers its managers. Some small chains combat the career opportunities of the large chains by helping their best managers get their own store through franchising. This allows the chain to keep managers who might otherwise grow bored and unchallenged. The advantages of franchising for the franchisor are as follows:

- Receives a percentage of gross sales

- Expands brand

- Gets support for national advertising campaign

- Is able to negotiate support for national contracts with suppliers

The disadvantages of a franchise for a franchisor are as follows:

- There are limits on other options of expanding distribution; for example, the ability to develop alliances may be limited if the alliances violate the territorial agreements of the franchisees.

- Franchisees must be monitored to ensure product consistency.

- There is limited ability to require franchisees to change operations; for example, Pizza Hut had a difficult time getting franchisees to add delivery when Domino's was developing the delivery market.

- Franchisees want and need to have an active role in decision making.

Alliances. Alliances are developed to allow two organizations to benefit from each other's strengths.

Alliances, another form of contractual agreement, are developed to allow two organizations to benefit from each other's strengths. In the beginning of this chapter, we mentioned the alliance between the Welcome Group and Sheraton Hotels. It would be difficult, if not impossible, for Sheraton to go into India by itself because of India's regulation of foreign-owned businesses. The Welcome Group offered Sheraton an Indian partner. Additionally, the Welcome Group had a good reputation in India and understood how to do business there. Sheraton offered the Welcome Group a name that was known to the international business traveler. Sheraton offered training and management support systems. Thus, both partners benefited from the alliance.

Restaurants are expanding their locations through alliances with hotel chains. This provides the restaurant with a good location and access to the hotel's guests. The hotel gains the value of the brand name of the restaurant. For example, Trader Vic's, one of the first restaurants to align with hotels, has locations in several Hiltons, the Anantara Bangkok Hotel, and the New Otani hotel in Tokyo. Ruth's Chris Steak Houses has locations in hotels operated by Marriott and Hyatt. Las Vegas resorts are famous for bringing nationally and internationally known chefs to open restaurants in their resorts. Additionally, many resorts have food courts similar to those in the malls, featuring branded fast-food outlets. The use of branded restaurants is attracting the attention of hotel management and creating opportunities for restaurants to expand their distribution.

Airlines are developing alliances to access customers in other parts of the world and to provide their customers with new destination opportunities. For example, SAS developed an alliance with Continental Airlines to give it access to the U.S. market. Before the alliance, SAS served only a handful of U.S. cities. Since the alliance, Continental's U.S. flights can be used to feed into SAS's flights to Europe. Continental gained the SAS passengers flying into Newark and other U.S. gateways, who will now use Continental to reach their final destination in the United States.

The National Motor Coach Network, a marketing consortium of motor coach operators, has developed a partner program to bring charter business to preferred hotels. Now tour operators sometimes extend their trips to include an overnight stay. In the past, operators preferred a day trip to staying overnight in an unfamiliar hotel. A network representative visits all participating hotels before they are accepted. The alliance brings business to the hotels and provides motor coach operators with negotiated rates at hotels that meet their standards.[36]

Growth of Horizontal Marketing Systems

Horizontal marketing system (HMS). Two or more companies at one level join to follow new marketing opportunities. Companies can combine their capital, production capabilities, or marketing resources to accomplish more than what one company can accomplish working alone.

Another channel development is **horizontal marketing systems (HMSs)**, in which two or more companies at one level join to follow a new marketing opportunity.[37] By working together, companies can combine their capital, production capabilities, or marketing resources to accomplish more than what one company can accomplish working alone. Seaworld offers tickets at a discount to an automobile club, which promotes these discount tickets as one benefit for its members. In return, Seaworld gains access to several hundred thousand automobile club members. Such symbiotic marketing arrangements have increased in number in recent years, and the end is nowhere in sight.

American Express, the Coeur d'Alene resort, and K2 Skis worked together to offer a free pair of skis at check-in if the guest booked an American Express "Ski Week Holiday."

Growth of Multichannel Marketing Systems

Multichannel marketing distribution. Multichannel distribution, as when a single firm sets up two or more marketing channels to reach one or more customer segments.

In the past, many companies used a single channel to sell to a single market or market segment. Today, with the proliferation of customer segments and channel possibilities, more companies have adopted **multichannel marketing distribution**. Such multichannel marketing occurs when a single firm sets up two or more marketing channels to reach one or more customer segments.[38] For example, McDonald's sells through a network of independent franchisees but owns more than a fourth of its outlets. Thus, the wholly owned restaurants compete to some extent with those owned by McDonald's franchisees.

The multichannel marketer gains sales with each new channel but also risks offending existing channels. Existing channels can cry "unfair competition" and threaten to drop the marketer unless it limits competition or repays them in some way. For example, franchisees have brought lawsuits against franchisors that have developed competing operations in their market area.

■■■ Selecting Channel Members

Selecting channel members involves a number of factors, including customer needs, the company's ability to attract channel members, the economic feasibility of the channel member, and the control that might be given up to gain a channel member.

Food-service distributors used to be primarily confined to selling to all types of sit-down restaurants ranging from college cafeterias and fast-food places to exquisite dining establishments. Today, these companies serve a relatively new food-service outlet known as convenience stores.

Customer Needs

Selecting channel members starts with determining the services that consumers in various target segments want. Independent hotels need OTAs to help sell their products. Booking.com for example represents hotels in Europe that may only have a dozen rooms, giving the small hotel international exposure.

A large resort such as the Fiesta Americana in Puerto Vallarta, Mexico, might consider aligning with a wholesaler. The wholesaler would put together a package that includes airfare, rooms, and ground transportation and distribute it through travel agents in the United States. In doing so, the wholesaler provides a package that gives guests everything they need to go on a vacation in Puerto Vallarta, eliminating the worry of finding their way around a foreign country. To design an effective channel, the company must understand the services its customers require and then balance the needs of those customers against the feasibility and costs of meeting them.

Marketing HIGHLIGHT 12–1 Restaurant Franchising

These days, it's nearly impossible to stroll down a city block or drive on a suburban street without seeing a Wendy's, a McDonald's, a Pizza Hut, or a Starbucks. One of the best-known and most successful franchisers, McDonald's, has more than 35,000 stores in more than a hundred countries. Subway is one of the fastest-growing franchises, with more than 45,000 shops in over a hundred countries.

How does a franchising system work? The individual franchises are a tightly knit group of enterprises whose systematic operations are planned, directed, and controlled by the operation's innovator, called a franchisor. The franchisee is required to pay for the right to be part of the system. Yet this initial fee is only a small part of the total amount that franchisees invest when they sign a franchising contract. Start-up costs include rental and lease of equipment and fixtures and sometimes a regular license fee. McDonald's franchisees invest as much $1 to $2 million in initial start-up costs. Subway's success is partly due to its low start-up cost of $100,000 to $300,000, which is lower than most other franchises. However, Subway franchisees pay an 8 percent royalty on gross sales, one of the highest in the food franchise industry, plus a 4.5 percent advertising fee.

The franchiser provides its franchisees with marketing and operations system for doing business. McDonald's requires franchises to attend its "Hamburger University" in Oak Brook, Illinois, for three weeks to learn how to manage the business; franchisees must also adhere to certain procedures in buying materials.

In the best cases, franchising is mutually beneficial to both franchisor and franchisee. Franchisers can cover new territory in little more than the time it takes the franchisee to sign a contract. They can achieve enormous purchasing power. Franchisers also benefit from the franchisees' familiarity with local communities and conditions and from the motivation and hard work of employees who are entrepreneurs rather than "hired hands." Similarly, franchisees benefit from buying into a proven business with a well-known and accepted brand name. And they receive ongoing support in areas ranging from marketing and advertising to site selection, staffing, and financing.

As a result of the franchise explosion in recent years, some fast-food franchisers are facing worrisome market saturation. One indication is the number of franchisee complaints filed with the Federal Trade Commission against parent companies. The most common complaint is that franchisers "encroach" on existing franchisees' territory by bringing in another store. For example, McDonald's franchisees in California and other states recently complained when the company decided to open new company-owned stores in their areas. Franchisees may object to parent company marketing programs that may adversely affect their operations. Franchisees often strongly resist value promotions in which the company reduced prices on menu items in an effort to revive stagnant sales. Many franchisees believe that the value promotion cheapens the image of the chain and unnecessarily reduces their profit margins. Another complaint is higher-than-advertised failure rates. Subway, in particular, has been criticized for misleading its franchisees by telling them that it has only a 2 percent failure rate when the reality is much different. In addition, some franchisees feel that they've been misled by exaggerated claims of support, only to feel abandoned after the contract is signed and money has been invested.

International expansion is delivering both franchisor growth and franchisee earnings. Fast-food franchises have become very popular throughout the world. Domino's has entered Japan with master franchisee Ernest Higa, who owns 106 stores in Japan with combined sales of $140 million. Part of Higa's success can be attributed to adapting Domino's product to the Japanese market, where food presentation is everything. Higa carefully charted the placement of pizza toppings and made cut-mark perforations in the boxes for perfectly uniform slices.

It appears franchise fever will not cool down soon. Experts estimate franchises capture 50 percent of all U.S. retail sales. Of the top 12 franchisees in worldwide sales, 10 are related to the travel and hospitality industry. These franchises include McDonald's, Carlson Wagonlit Travel, Burger King, KFC, Pizza Hut, Wendy's, Marriott Hotels, Subway Restaurants, Sheraton, and Taco Bell.[39]

Through franchising, Subway has grown to become the largest restaurant chain. Courtesy of Jovannig/Fotolia.

Attracting Channel Members

Companies vary in their ability to attract qualified intermediaries. Well-known hotel companies that have a reputation for paying commissions promptly and honoring the reservations of travel agents have no trouble gaining the support of intermediaries.

When contracting with a hotel sales representative, the hotel company should investigate the number and type of other hotels that the firm represents. It will also want to investigate the size and quality of its workforce. Just as a company carefully chooses its employees, it should carefully choose channel members. These firms will represent the company and will be partially responsible for the company's image.

Evaluating Major Channel Alternatives

Economic Feasibility of the Channel Member

Each channel produces different levels of sales and costs. The business that channel members bring must offset the cost of paying and supporting the channel member. These costs are measured in two ways: directly and by opportunity costs. For example, some casinos use bus operators to bring customers to them. The bus operator is paid a fee for each bus, plus the riders get an incentive, such as a free roll of quarters from the casino. Some casinos found that the cost of bringing a bus customer to the casino was greater than the casino's win from the bus customer. Previous management felt good because the buses brought hundreds of customers to the casino. However, when the buses were evaluated from an economic standpoint, they were found to be unprofitable because they did not cover their direct costs. Another direct cost of working with intermediaries is the support they will need from the company. Intermediaries require brochures and other collateral material, training, familiarization trips, and regular communication. A company should limit the size of its distribution system to one that it is able to support.

When the MGM Grand hotel opened, it used tour operators to fill many of its rooms. This business brought a low room rate, but the room rate more than covered the variable cost of the room, creating an operating profit. As demand for the MGM Grand's rooms grew, MGM could sell its rooms directly through travel agents and receive a higher room rate. At this point, there was an opportunity cost associated with the tour operator, that is, the difference between the tour operator's rate and the higher rate that could be received through travel agents. An opportunity cost is created when we sell a product for a lower price than its market value. Opportunity costs are created when we discount products, only to find out that we could sell them for a higher price. In the example, the hotel decreased its allocation of rooms to tour operators and increased its allocation to travel agents to reduce the opportunity cost of selling rooms to tour operators.

A company must regularly evaluate the performance of its intermediaries. As business changes, the value of an intermediary may change, as was the case with MGM. The intermediary may not perform as expected. In this case, the company must work with the intermediary to try to bring about the desired performance or eliminate the intermediary if it becomes unprofitable.

Checking on intermediaries is a delicate business. Sometimes problems may be due to improper support from the supplier. Companies need to evaluate the support they are giving to their channel members and make the necessary adjustments. Underperforming intermediaries need to be counseled. They may need more training or motivation. If they do not shape up, it might be better to terminate them.

Control Criteria

An important consideration in the choice of channels is control. Using sales representatives offers less control than building your own sales force. Sales representatives may prefer to sell rooms in other hotels because it requires less effort. They may avoid smaller customers, preferring instead to call on larger companies who can use most of the hotels they represent.

In this example, it could be that the smaller customers are actually more profitable than the larger ones. This points out the importance of having data that show the degree of profit or loss from different customer groups and from all intermediaries. In the absence of the information, marketing/sales managers are forced to make decisions based on the assumptions or guesses or personal preferences. None of these is the basis for sound decision making.

Unfortunately, the accounting departments of most hospitality companies do not offer this kind of assistance. Therefore, it may be necessary for the marketing department to hire its own analyst to provide this vital information.

Control is also an important consideration in franchising and choosing multiple channel members. One problem with franchising is that a company sacrifices some control to gain wider distribution. The company may have trouble getting franchisees to add new products or to participate in promotions. Some companies have problems getting their franchisees to meet quality control standards.

When a firm adds multiple channels, it must consider the rights of existing channel members. Often, existing channel members limit their activities with new channel members. For example, earlier in this chapter we talked about the promotion between Embassy Suites Hotel and Hertz. The promotion was modified because it went against the interests of another channel member, the travel agent.

Each channel involves a long-term commitment and loss of flexibility. A hotel firm using a sales representative in Mexico City may have to sign a five-year contract. During this five-year period, the hotel company may develop an alliance with an airline or hotel company based in Mexico. The sales representative in Mexico City may become unnecessary, but the company will be unable to end the relationship until the contract has ended. There is often a tradeoff between the benefits created by developing a long-term alliance and the loss of flexibility that often comes with such alliances. Understanding the tradeoffs and how the marketplace might change in the future can help a manager make decisions regarding the length of contractual agreements with channel members.

■■■ Responsibilities of Channel Members and Suppliers

The company and its intermediaries must agree on the terms and responsibilities of each channel member. For instance, hotels make it clear to travel agents which rates are commissionable and the amount of commission to be paid, and they often guarantee to pay the commission within a certain number of days. Wendy's and other companies provide franchisees with promotional support, a record-keeping system, training, and general management assistance. In turn, franchisees must meet company standards for physical facilities, cooperate with new promotional programs, provide requested information, and buy specified food products. To avoid disputes, it is important that companies have an explicit arrangement in writing with their channel members.

After the selection of the channel members, a company must continuously motivate its members. Just as a firm must market to its employees, it must also market to its intermediaries. Most firms use positive incentives during times of slow demand. For example, during slow periods, hotel or rental car companies often increase the percentage of commission that they pay. Keeping channel members informed about the company's products is another way to motivate channel members. Hotels with sales representatives must keep them informed about changes in facilities and new products. A company must provide communication and support for its channel members.

■■■ Business Location

One of the most important aspects of distribution for hospitality organizations is location. For businesses whose customers come to them, the business must be conveniently located. Many retailers say the three secrets of successful retailing are "location, location, and location." There is no single formula for location. A good location for a Ritz-Carlton Hotel is different from that of a Motel 6 or a Burger King.

The Fairmont Copley Plaza has an excellent location in Boston on Copley Square and near the convention center. Courtesy of SuzyM/Fotolia.

Restaurant sites tend to be evaluated on the ability of the local area to provide business. Hotel sites are evaluated on the attractiveness of their location to persons coming to that destination. In both cases, location depends on the firm's marketing strategy. Each firm has its own set of location evaluation characteristics.

In general, there are four steps in choosing a location. The first is understanding the marketing strategy and target market of the company. La Quinta motels cater to the traveling salesperson and other midclass hotel guests arriving primarily by automobiles. Locations are typically along freeways outside major metropolitan areas. They are close enough to the central business district to offer convenient access, yet far enough away to allow economic purchase of the site. Hyatt, in contrast, caters to groups and the businessperson who often arrive by plane. Hyatt hotels are often located in the heart of the central business district. The location decision, like other marketing decisions, cannot be separated from the marketing strategy.

The second step of the selection is regional analysis, which involves the selection of geographic market areas.[40] A restaurant chain may plan to expand into a new metropolitan market. It may need to find a region that will support at least five new stores. This allows the company to split the marketing costs and costs of management support across five restaurants. A business hotel chain expanding into Southeast Asia may target key cities such as Singapore, Bangkok, Kuala Lumpur, and Jakarta. The chain wants to have a presence in major cities of the region so that business travelers can stay in the chain as they travel throughout the region.

A firm would want to make sure a region has sufficient and stable demand to support the hotel(s) or restaurant(s). A growing area with a diverse economic base is attractive. Areas based on one industry are often attractive when that industry is in favor but are highly vulnerable when that industry suffers.

This is equally true when tourism and hospitality are the primary industries. Miami Beach experienced industry problems when some European tourists were assaulted or killed. The ski industry and ski resort towns depend on the whims of nature. Too little or too much snow can create major economic problems.

Once the firm has chosen a geographic region, the next step is to select an area within that region. If a restaurant chain wants to open five restaurants in a metropolitan area, it must choose favorable sites. The chain will look at the demographic and psychographic characteristics of the area. Competition and growth potential of the different areas will be evaluated. The result will be a choice of five areas within the region that seem most promising.

Finally, the firm will choose individual sites. A key consideration in site analysis is compatible businesses. A restaurant or hotel will look for potential demand generators. For a hotel, these can be major office complexes, airports, or integrated retail, residential, and business complexes. A restaurant may look for residential communities, shopping centers, or motels without food and beverage facilities. Demand generators vary depending on the target markets of the business. It is important for firms to have a good profile of their customers when they look for customer sources within a given area.

In addition to demand generators, a firm looks at competitors. If there is an adequate supply of similar restaurants or hotels, the site is usually rejected. Hotels have entered saturated markets just to gain a presence in that city. Competition is not always a negative factor. Restaurants often tend to be clustered, creating a restaurant row. This can be beneficial. Customers going to one restaurant are exposed to a selection of others.

Site evaluation includes accessibility. Is the site easily accessible by traffic going in different directions, or do uncrossable medians create a barrier? Is the site visible to allow drivers to turn? Speed of traffic is also a factor. The slower the traffic is, the longer the visibility. Restaurant sites at intersections with a stoplight have the benefit of exposure to waiting drivers. The desirability of the surroundings is another consideration. Is the area attractive? If the site is in a shopping center, is the center well maintained? Other considerations for the site include drainage, sewage, utilities, and size.

Often, companies develop a profile of preferred sites. For example, Carl's Jr. Restaurant, a fast-food hamburger restaurant, developed this profile:[41]

- Free-standing location in a shopping center
- Free-standing corner location (with a signal light at the intersection)
- Inside lot with 125-foot minimum frontage
- Enclosed shopping mall
- Population of 12,000 or more in a one-mile radius (growth areas preferred)
- Easy access of traffic to location
- Heavy vehicular/pedestrian traffic
- An area where home values and family income levels are average or above
- Close to offices and other demand generators
- A parcel size of 30,000 to 50,000 square feet
- No less than two or three miles from other existing company locations

A checklist, statistical analysis, or a combination of both often determines the choice of a site. A checklist usually contains items such as those listed in the profile and specific building requirements. Items such as building codes, signage restrictions, availability of utilities, parking, and drainage are also included in a checklist. A common type of statistical analysis used in site selection is regression analysis. The dependent variable in the equation is sales, and the independent variables are factors that contribute to sales. Typical independent variables might include population within the market area, household income of the market, competitors, and attributes of the location.

Restaurants have been downsizing to allow access to smaller markets and new types of locations. This makes the unit feasible in locations that do not have room for a full-size unit or cannot support the sales the larger unit would require. McDonald's was one of the first chains to develop smaller units that made it feasible for the franchise to go into smaller towns and inside retail outlets. Chili's, a casual service restaurant, has developed a smaller version with a reduced menu called Chili's Too for airport and other nontraditional locations. As good locations become more difficult to find, restaurants are looking for nontraditional locations and building units that will fit these sites. They are then using the strength of their brand name as a competitive advantage. Location is a key attribute for a hotel or restaurant. The location must not only be favorable at the present time but also continue to be good throughout the life of the business.

Chain operations generally have a real estate department that is responsible for selecting locations and negotiating leases or contracts to purchase successful properties. Commercial real estate agencies can be extremely helpful to hospitality companies desiring to locate in a new market. These firms should be expected to participate in multiphases from planning to acquisition of properties. They should offer services to assist in many or all of the tasks previously described that are associated with locating and acquiring new properties.

▪▪▪ CHAPTER REVIEW

I. Supply Chains and the Value Delivery Network

II. Nature and Importance of Distribution Systems. A distribution channel is a set of independent organizations involved in the process of making a product or service available to the consumer or business user.

  A. Reasons that marketing intermediaries are used. The use of intermediaries depends on their greater efficiency in marketing the goods available to target markets. Through their contacts, experience, specialization, and scale of operation, intermediaries normally offer more than a firm can on its own.

  B. Distribution channel functions

    1. **Information.** Gathering and distributing marketing research and intelligence information about the marketing environment.

    2. **Promotion.** Developing and spreading persuasive communications about an offer.

    3. **Contact.** Finding and communicating with prospective buyers.

    4. **Matching.** Shaping and fitting the offer to the buyers' needs.

    5. **Negotiation.** Agreeing on price and other terms of the offer so that ownership or possession can be transferred.

6. **Physical distribution.** Transporting and storing goods.
7. **Financing.** Acquiring and using funds to cover the cost of channel work.
8. **Risk taking.** Assuming financial risks, such as the inability to sell inventory at full margin.

C. **Number of channel levels.** The number of channel levels can vary from direct marketing, through which the manufacturer sells directly to the consumer, to complex distribution systems involving four or more channel members.

III. Hospitality Distribution Channels
A. **Major hospitality distribution channels**
1. Direct booking
2. Online travel agencies
3. Global distribution systems
4. Travel agents
5. Travel wholesalers and tour operators
6. Specialists: tour brokers, motivational houses, and junket reps
7. Hotel representatives
8. National, state, and local tourist agencies
9. Consortia and reservation systems
10. Restaurant distribution systems
   a. Online reservation systems—OpenTable
   b. Delivery, take-out, drive-through window
   c. Concierge

IV. Channel Behavior
A. **Channel conflict.** Although channel members depend on each other, they often act alone in their own short-run best interests. They frequently disagree on the roles each should play on who should do what for which rewards.
1. **Horizontal conflict.** Conflict between firms at the same level.
2. **Vertical conflict.** Conflict between different levels of the same channel.

V. Channel Organization. Distribution channels are shifting from loose collections of independent companies to unified systems.
A. **Conventional marketing system.** A conventional marketing system consists of one or more independent producers, wholesalers, and retailers. Each is a separate business seeking to maximize its own profits, even at the expense of profits for the system as a whole.
B. **Vertical marketing system.** A vertical marketing system consists of producers, wholesalers, and retailers acting as a unified system. VMSs were developed to control channel behavior and manage channel conflict and its economies through size, bargaining power, and elimination of duplicated services. The three major types of VMSs are corporate, administered, and contractual.

1. **Corporate.** A corporate VMS combines successive stages of production and distribution under single ownership.
2. **Administered.** An administered VMS coordinates successive stages of production and distribution, not through common ownership or contractual ties, but through the size and power of the parties.
3. **Contractual.** A contractual VMS consists of independent firms at different levels of production and distribution who join through contracts to obtain economies or sales impact.
   a. **Franchising.** Franchising is a method of doing business by which a franchisee is granted the right to engage in offering, selling, or distributing goods or services under a marketing format that is designed by the franchisor. The franchisor permits the franchisee to use its trademark, name, and advertising.
   b. **Alliances.** Alliances are developed to allow two organizations to benefit from each other's strengths.
C. **Horizontal marketing system.** Two or more companies at one level join to follow new marketing opportunities. Companies can combine their capital, production capabilities, or marketing resources to accomplish more than what one company can accomplish working alone.
D. **Multichannel marketing system.** A single firm sets up two or more marketing channels to reach one or more customer segments.

VI. Selecting Channel Members
A. Customer needs
B. Attracting channel members
C. Evaluating major channel alternatives
1. Economic feasibility of channel member
2. Control criteria

VII. Responsibilities of Channel Members and Suppliers. The company and its intermediaries must agree on the terms and responsibilities of each channel member. According to the services and clientele at hand, the responsibilities are formulated after careful consideration.

VIII. Business Location. There are four steps in choosing a location:
A. **Understanding the marketing strategy.** Know the target market of the company.
B. **Regional analysis.** Select the geographic market areas.
C. **Choosing the area within the region.** Demographic and psychographic characteristics and competition are factors to consider.
D. **Choosing the individual site.** Compatible business, competitors, accessibility, drainage, sewage, utilities, and size are factors to consider.

▪▪▪ DISCUSSION QUESTIONS

1. Discuss how you think technology will change distribution channels in the hospitality and travel industries over the next five years.

2. Explain how international travel changed distribution channels in the hospitality and travel industries.

3. What are the major differences between a distribution channel for a business making tangible products and a firm producing hospitality and travel products?

4. Can a business have too many channel members? Explain your answer.

5. Explain the difference between a tour wholesaler and a travel agent.

6. Why is franchising such a fast-growing form of retail organization?

7. According to the International Franchising Association, between 30 and 50 percent of all new franchise applicants are people who formerly worked in large corporations and who lost their jobs as a result of corporate downsizing. How do you think these midlevel, midcareer corporate executives will adapt to life as franchise owners? How will their previous corporate experience help them? How will it hurt them?

■■■ EXPERIENTIAL EXERCISES

Do one of the following:

1. Visit a restaurant that offers take-out service. What has it done to facilitate take-out service? For example, does it have a special order and pickup area; does it have paper menus to take home; does it accept phone, fax, or Internet orders; and does it have special packaging for take-out? Report on what you find and any suggestion that you might have.

2. Investigate franchises available in the hospitality or travel business. Select a franchise you feel would be a good business investment based on what the franchise offers and the fees the franchisor charges. Support your findings in a two- to three-page report.

■■■ INTERNET EXERCISES

Find a hospitality or travel company that allows customers to make reservations directly through its Web site. What customer segment do you think will make reservations through this site, and do you think the design of the site is effective? Explain your answer.

■■■ REFERENCES

1 "Not all Gloom and Doom," *Travel Weekly* (October 1, 2004): 12; Juliet Dennis, "Survey Finds Market Share Is Diminishing," *Travel Weekly* (October 1, 2004): 12; Alan Ching-biu Tse, "Disintermediation of Travel Agents in the Hotel Industry," *International Journal of Hospitality Management*, 22 (2003): 453–460; Bill Anckar, "Consumer Intentions in Terms of Electronic Travel Distribution, *eService Journal* (Winter 2003): 68–86; Paulette Thomas, "Case Study: Travel Agency Meets Technology's Threats," *Wall Street Journal* (May 21, 2002): B4.

2 E. Raymond Corey, Frank V. Cespedes, and V. Kasturi Rangan, *Going to Market* (Boston, MA: Harvard Business School Press, 1989), p. xxvii; Sunflowertravel.com, Ciclismoclassico.com.

3 Amy Ricciardi, "Marriott, Otani Enter Marketing Pact," *Travel Weekly*, 51, no. 12 (1992): 3.

4 Louis W. Stern and Adel I. El-Ansary, *Marketing Channels*, 3rd ed. (Upper Saddle River, NJ: Prentice Hall, 1988), p. 3.

5 Corey, Cespedes, and Rangan, *Going to Market*.

6 Danielle DeVoren and Andrew Herweg, "Hoteliers Continue to See Growth in Bookings via Online Channels," February 17, 2015, http://www.travelclick.com/en/news-events/press-release/hoteliers-continue-see-growth-bookings-online-channels (accessed August 3, 2015).

7 Patrick Mayock, "Consumer booking behavior in the age of comparison shopping," *HotelNewsNow.Com*, January 15, 2011, http://www.hotelnewsnow.com/ Articles.aspx/4861/Consumer-booking-behavior-in-the-age-of-comparison-shopping (accessed August 5, 2012); Stacey Mieyal Higgins, " Researchers: Distribution ROI closer to reality," *HotelNewsNow.Com*, June 15, 2011, http://www.hotelnewsnow.com/Articles.aspx/5760/Researchers-Distribution-ROI-closer-to-reality (accessed August 5, 2012).

8 Arnie Weissmann, "Widening 'advantage gap' bodes well for agents," TravelWeekly.com, August 11, 2014, http://www.travelweekly.com/Travel-News/Travel-Agent-Issues/2014-Consumer-Trends (accessed August 4, 2015).

9 Southwest Airlines Web site, http://swamedia.com/channels/Corporate-Fact-Sheet/pages/corporate-fact-sheet#funfacts (accessed August 4, 2015).

10 Trefis Team, "Airlines To Thwart Air Ticket Sales Through OTAs: The Possible Ramifications," Forbes.com, June 23, 2015, http://www.forbes.com/sites/greatspeculations/2015/06/23/airlines-to-thwart-air-ticket-sales-through-otas-the-possible-ramifications/3/ (accessed August 4, 2015).

11 Liz Weiss, "The Booking Battle: OTAs Break Into the Loyalty Market," USNEWS.com, August 4, 2014, http://travel.usnews.com/features/The-Booking-Battle-OTAs-Break-into-the-Loyalty-Market/ (accessed August 4, 2015).

12 Stowe Shoemaker and Margaret Shaw, *Marketing Essentials in Hospitality and Tourism: Foundations and Practices* (Upper Saddle River, NJ: Pearson Education,

2008); www.sabre-holdings.com; www.Travelport.com; www.amadeus.com (accessed September 29, 2008).

13 *Frequently Asked Questions: Travel Agents by the Numbers*, http://www.astanet.com/about/faq.asp#many (accessed November 28, 2004).

14 *Airline Commissions*, http://www.traveltrade.com/generic_page.jsp?articleID=1335 (accessed November 28, 2004).

15 Robert C. Lewis, *Marketing Leadership in Hospitality: Foundations and Practices*, 3rd ed. (New York: Wiley, 2000).

16 For more information on familiarization trips, see *How to Plan and Program Travel Agent Familiarization Tours* (Washington, DC: Hotel Sales and Marketing Association, undated).

17 James R. Abbey, *Hospitality Sales and Advertising* (East Lansing, MI: Educational Institute of the American Hotel and Motel Association, 1989).

18 Fran Golden, "Room for Growth," *Travel Weekly*, 53, no. 65 (1994): 118.

19 The Global Business Travel Association (GBTA) U.S. Business Travel Spending Projected to Top $310 Billion in 2015, January 13, 2015, http://www.gbta.org/PressReleases/Pages/rls_011215.aspx (accessed August 4, 2015).

20 Cathy Salustri, "Tour Operators and Travel Wholesalers Key Terms," Busines.com, February 18, 2010, http://www.business.com/hotels/tour-operators-and-travel-wholesalers-key-terms/ (accessed August 4, 2015).

21 Michael M. Coltman, *Tourism Marketing* (New York: Van Nostrand Reinhold, 1989).

22 Chuck Y. Gee, James C. Makens, and Dexter J. L. Choy, *The Travel Industry* (New York: Van Nostrand Reinhold, 1989).

23 For more information on tour brokers, see *HSMA/Group Tour Information Manual* (Washington, DC: Hotel Sales and Marketing Association, undated).

24 Coltman, *Tourism Marketing*.

25 *Sydney Convention and Visitors Bureau*, http://www.scvb.com.au (accessed November 28, 2004).

26 See J. C. Holloway and R. V. Plant, *Marketing for Tourism* (London: Pitman, 1992), pp. 124–126.

27 "How to Host," https://www.airbnb.com/help/getting-started/how-to-host (accessed August 5, 2015).

28 "Uber Needs Partners Like You," https://get.uber.com/drive/ (accessed August 5, 2015).

29 Matt Marshall, "OpenTable Seats 3M Diners a Month, Releases a Mobile Version," June 29, 2008, www.VentureBeat.com (accessed September 25, 2008).

30 Kat Kane, "Thanks, OpenTable, But I Like Being an Anonymous Diner," Wired.com, May 24, 2015, http://www.wired.com/2015/05/opentable-diner-anonymity/ (accessed August 4, 2015).

31 Steve McDonnell, "What Percentage of Sales Are from Drive Through Windows at Fast Food Restaurants?" Chron.com, http://smallbusiness.chron.com/percentage-sales-drive-through-windows-fast-food-restaurants-75713.html (accessed August 4, 2015).

32 Rich Mintzer, "Food Trucks 101: How to Start a Mobile Food Business," *Entrepreneur Press*, July 21, 2011, http://www.entrepreneur.com/article/220060 (accessed August 13, 2015).

33 Kianta Key, "4 Social Media Lessons from a Successful Food Truck," Forbes.com, January 30, 2012, http://www.forbes.com/sites/dailymuse/2013/01/30/4-social-media-lessons-from-a-successful-food-truck/print/SuccessfulFoodTruck201 (accessed August 13, 2015).

34 Example adapted from Richard Gibson, "Burger King Franchisees Can't Have It *Their* Own Way," *Wall Street Journal* (January 21, 2010): Bl; with additional information from Emily Bryson York, "BK Swears Off Sex in Ads to Quell Franchisee Freak Out," *Advertising Age* (July 13, 2009): 1; York, "Burger King, Franchisees Start Making Nice," *Advertising Age* (February 17, 2010), http://adage.com/article?article_id=142158.

35 Joe Cahill, "Mind Your Franchisees. Mayor McCheese," *Crain's Chicago Business*, April 26, 2013, www.chicagobusiness.com/article/20130426/BLOGS10/130429841 (accessed August 9, 2015; "McDonald's Customer Service Push Irritates Some Franchisees," *Chicago Business Journal*, April 17, 2014, www.bizjournals.corn/chicago/news/2013/04/17/mcdonalds-riding-flne-line-francnisees.html (accessed August 9, 2015).

36 Bill Poling, "Motor Coach Network Launches Partner Program for Hotels," *Travel Weekly*, 51, no. 83 (1992): 7.

37 See Lee Adler, "Symbiotic Marketing," *Harvard Business Review* (November/December 1966): 59–71; P. Varadarajan and Daniel Rajaratnam, "Symbiotic Marketing Revisited," *Journal of Marketing* (January 1986): 7–17.

38 See Robert Weigand, "Fit Products and Channels to Your Markets," *Harvard Business Review* (January/February 1977): 95–105.

39 www.mcdonalds.com (accessed December 5, 2004); www.subway.com (accessed December 5, 2004); "The Top 200," *Franchise Times* (October 2003); Norman D. Axelrad and Robert E. Weigand, "Franchising—A Marriage of System Members," in *Marketing Managers Handbook* (3rd ed.), ed. Sidney Levy, George Frerichs, and Howard Gordon (Chicago, IL: Dartnell, 2004), pp. 919–934; Andrew E. Sewer, "McDonald's Conquers the World," *Fortune* (October 17, 1994): 103–116; Roberta Maynard, "The Decision to Franchise," *Nation's Business* (January 1997): 49–53; Cliff Edwards, "Campaign '55 Flop Shows Power of Franchisees," *Marketing News* (July 7, 1997): 9; Richard Behar, "Why Subway Is the Biggest Problem in Franchising," *Fortune* (March 16, 1998): 126–134; Patrick J. Kaufman and Sevgin Eroglu, "Standardization and Adaptation in Business Format Franchising," *Journal of Business Venturing* (January 1999): 69–85.

40 See Avijit Gosh, *Retail Management* (Fort Worth, TX: Dryden Press, 1990), pp. 216–249.

41 Donald E. Lindberg, *The Restaurant from Concept to Operation* (New York: Wiley, 1985), p. 35.

13

Engaging Customers and Communicating Customer Value and Advertising

Nearly two decades ago, regional fast-food chain Chick-fil-A set out in search of a promotion strategy that would set it apart from big—three fast-food competitors—burger joints McDonald's, Burger King, and Wendy's. Chick-fil-A's strength had always been its signature fried chicken sandwich—you still won't find anything but chicken on the menu. But somehow, just saying we make good chicken sandwiches wasn't enough. Chick-fil-A needed a creative big idea—something memorable that would communicate the brand's unique value proposition.

What it came up with—of all things—was an improbable herd of renegade black-and-white cows that couldn't spell. Their message: "Eat Mor Chikin." Their goal: to convince consumers to switch from hamburgers to chicken. Acting in their own self-interest, the fearless cows realized that when people eat chicken, they don't eat beef. So in 1995, the first mischievous cow, with paintbrush in mouth, painted "Eat Mor Chikin" on a billboard. From that first billboard, the effort has now grown to become one of the most consistent and enduring **integrated marketing communications** (IMC) campaigns in history, a full multimedia campaign that has forever changed the burger-eating landscape.

The key to the "Eat Mor Chikin" campaign's success lies in its remarkable consistency. As industry publication *Advertising Age* pointed out when it recently crowned Chick-fil-A as its runner-up marketer of the year, "Often, the smartest marketing is the most patient marketing." And few promotion campaigns have been more persistently patient than this one. For nearly 20 years, Chick-fil-A has

Integrated marketing communications. Under this concept, the company carefully integrates its many communication channels to deliver a clear, consistent, and compelling message about the organization and its brands.

stuck steadfastly to its simple but potent "Eat Mor Chikin" message, and the brand's rascally cows have now become pop culture icons.

Building on the basic "Eat Mor Chikin" message, Chick-fil-A keeps the campaign fresh with an ever-changing mix of clever message executions and innovative media placements. Today, you find the cows just about anywhere and everywhere, from traditional television, print, and radio ads, to imaginative sales promotions and event sponsorships, to online social media and smartphone apps, with an occasional water tower still thrown in.

For example, in a TV ad promoting Chick-fil-A's growing breakfast menu, the pesky cows set off car alarm after car alarm, awakening an apartment building full of tenants to the message, "Wake up—itz chikin time." In print ads, the cows promote menu staples with taglines like "Milk shakes—the after chikin dinner drink." Billboards sport quotes such as "Lose that burger belly." During election years, the cows show their nonpartisanship with phrases like "Vote chikin. Itz not right wing or left." The ubiquitous cows even pull zany stunts, such as parachuting into football stadiums with signs reading "Du the wave. Eat the chikin."

Although the "Eat Mor Chikin" campaign has made plentiful use of the traditional media, it is perhaps the nontraditional promotional tactics that have won the cows a special place in the hearts of Chick-fil-A's fiercely loyal customers. Shortly after the start of the campaign, the company began its now-packed promotional merchandise catalog with an annual cow-themed calendar. A few years ago, it offered the first ever digital calendar. Today, Chick-fil-A loyalists snap up large quantities of cow-themed mugs, T-shirts, stuffed animals, refrigerator magnets, laptop cases, and dozens of other items. These promotional items not only generate revenue, they also help strengthen company–customer engagement while at the same time spreading the brand's "Eat Mor Chikin" message.

Chick-fil-A further engages customers through an assortment of in-store promotional events. Every July, for example, the company promotes "Cow Appreciation Day ('cow bells welcome')," on which customers who show up at any Chick-fil-A store dressed as a cow get a free meal. Nearly 600,000 cow-clad customers show up for this event. And when a new Chick-fil-A restaurant opens, under the chain's "First 100" promotion, fans who camp out for 24 hours in advance of the opening get a chance to be one of the lucky 100 who win free Chick-fil-A meals for a year. While waiting, they'll likely meet Chick-fil-A CEO Dan Cathy—known for his customer-centered leadership style—who often camps out overnight with customers, signing T-shirts, posing for pictures, and ultimately handing out those vouchers for a free year's worth of Chick-fil-A. The uniqueness of this event, with scores of people sleeping in the parking lot the night before the opening, catches the attention of local media, creating publicity for the opening,

Most recently, Chick-fil-A has taken its "Eat Mor Chikin" message to social media, including Facebook, YouTube, Pinterest, and Twitter. When the company first plotted its social media strategy a few years back, it discovered that it already had a robust Facebook fan page with some 25,000 fans. Customer Brandy Bitzer, a true Chick-fil-A brand evangelist, created the page. In a genuine gesture of customer appreciation, Chick-fil-A joined forces with Bitzer, who continues to administer the page while the company provides assets to fuel enthusiasm for the brand. The strategy is working. Today, the Chick-fil-A Facebook page boasts more than 7.4 million fans. It's packed with information, customer-engaging communications, and plenty of cow advice like "Eat chikin or I'll de-friend u."

These days, you never know where the quirky cows will show up next. But no matter where you see them—on TV, in a sports arena, on your smartphone, or in your local Chick-fil-A restaurant—the long-standing brand message remains consistent. Over the years, the "Eat Mor Chikin" campaign has racked up a who's who list of major advertising awards and honors. More important, the campaign has helped engage customers and communicate Chick-fil-A's personality and positioning, making it one of the nation's most successful quick-service chains.

Chick-fil-A's more than 1,900 restaurants rang up almost $6 billion. Since the first Chick-fil-A store opened, the company has posted revenue increases for 46 straight years. Since the "Eat Mor Chikin" campaign began, Chick-fil-A sales have increased more than 7.5-fold. The average Chick-fil-A restaurant pulls in more sales per year than the average McDonald's, despite being open only six days a week (all Chick-fil-A stores are famously closed on Sundays for both practical and spiritual reasons). Chick-fil-A is now America's number-one chicken chain, and its phenomenal growth has contributed greatly to number-two KFC's falling market share in the category.

In all, Chick-fil-A's now classic but still contemporary IMC campaign "has been more successful than we ever imagined it could be," concludes the company's senior vice president of marketing. "The Cows started as part of our advertising campaign, and now they have become part of our passion and our brand." Who knows what the cows can accomplish in yet another 5 or 10 years. Whatever the future brings, the Chick-fil-A message will still be loud and clear: Eat Mor Chikin![1]

Building good customer relationships calls for more than just developing a good product, pricing it attractively, and making it available to target customers. Companies must also *communicate* their value propositions to customers, and what they communicate should not be left to chance. All of their communications must be planned and blended into carefully integrated marketing communication programs. Just as good communication is important in building and maintaining any kind of relationship, it is a crucial element in a company's efforts to build profitable customer relationships.

■■■ The Promotion Mix

Promotion mix. The specific mix of advertising, personal selling, sales promotion, and public relations a company uses to pursue its advertising and marketing objectives.

Personal selling. Personal presentation by the firm's sales force to make sales and build customer relationships.

Direct-marketing. Connections carefully targeted at individual consumers to both obtain an immediate response and cultivate lasting customer relationships: the use of direct mail, the telephone, direct-response television, e-mail, the Internet, and other tools to communicate directly with specific consumers.

A company's total **promotion mix**—also called its marketing communications mix—consists of the specific blend of advertising, public relations, **personal selling**, sales promotion, and **direct-marketing** tools that the company uses to communicate customer value and build customer relationships persuasively. Definitions of the five major promotion tools follow:[2]

Advertising: Any paid form of nonpersonal presentation and promotion of ideas, goods, or services by an identified sponsor

Sales promotion: Short-term incentives to encourage the purchase or sale of a product or service

Personal selling: Personal presentation by the firm's sales force for the purpose of making sales and building customer relationships

Public relations: Building good relations with the company's various publics by obtaining favorable publicity, building up a good corporate image, and handling or heading off unfavorable rumors, stories, and events

Direct and digital marketing: Engaging directly with carefully targeted individual consumers and customer communities to both obtain an immediate response and build lasting customer relationships

Each category involves specific promotional tools used to communicate with consumers. For example, *advertising* includes broadcast, print, Internet, outdoor, and other forms. *Sales promotion* includes discounts, coupons, displays, and demonstrations. *Personal selling* includes sales presentations, trade shows, and incentive programs. *Public relations* includes press releases, sponsorships, special events, and Web pages. And *direct and digital marketing* includes direct mail, catalogs, online and social media, and mobile marketing.

At the same time, marketing communication goes beyond these specific promotion tools. The salesperson's manner and dress, the place's decor, and the company's stationery—all communicate something to the buyers. Every brand contact delivers an impression that can strengthen or weaken a customer's view of the company. The whole marketing mix must be integrated to deliver a consistent message and strategic positioning.

■■■ Integrated Marketing Communications

Marketers perfected the art of mass marketing: selling highly standardized products to masses of customers. In the process, they developed effective mass media communications techniques to support these strategies. Large companies now routinely invest millions or even billions of dollars in television, magazine, or other mass media advertising, reaching tens of millions of customers with a single ad. Today, however, marketing managers face some new marketing communications realities. Perhaps no other area of marketing is changing so profoundly as marketing communications, creating both exciting and scary times for marketing communications.

The New Marketing Communications Model

Several major factors are changing the face of today's marketing communications. First, consumers are changing. In this digital, wireless age, consumers are better informed and more connected. Rather than relying on marketer-supplied information, they can use the Internet, social media, and other technologies to seek out information on their own. More than that, they can more easily connect with other consumers to exchange brand-related information or even to create their own marketing messages.

Second, marketing strategies are changing. As mass markets have fragmented, marketers are shifting away from mass marketing. More and more, they are developing focused marketing programs designed to build closer relationships with customers in more narrowly defined micromarkets.

Finally, sweeping advances in digital technology are causing remarkable changes in the ways in which companies and customers communicate with each other. The digital age has spawned a host of new information and communication tools—from smartphones and tablets to satellite and cable television systems to the many faces of the Internet (e-mail, social media, blogs, brand Web sites, the mobile web, and much more). These explosive developments have had a dramatic impact on marketing communications. Just as mass marketing once gave rise to a new generation of mass media communications, the new digital and social media have given birth to a more targeted, social, and engaging marketing communications model.

Although television, magazines, newspapers, and other mass media remain very important, their dominance is declining. In their place, advertisers are now adding a broad selection of more specialized and highly targeted media to reach smaller customer segments with more personalized, interactive messages. The new media range from specialty cable television channels and made-for-the-Web videos to Internet catalogs, e-mail, blogs, mobile coupons, and social media content such as Twitter, Facebook, Google+, and Pinterest. Such new media have taken the industry by storm.

Some advertising industry experts even predict that the old mass media communications model will soon be obsolete. Mass media costs are rising, audiences are shrinking, ad clutter is increasing, and viewers are gaining control of message exposure through technologies such as video streaming or digital video recordings (DVRs) that let them skip past disruptive television commercials. As a result, they suggest, marketers are shifting ever-larger portions of their marketing budgets away from old-media mainstays and moving to digital and social media.

As the marketing communications environment shifts, so will the role of marketing communicators. Rather than just creating and placing "TV ads" or "print ads" or "Facebook display ads," many marketers now view themselves more broadly as content marketing managers. As such, they create, inspire, and share brand messages and conversations with and among customers across a fluid mix of paid, owned, earned, and shared communication channels. These channels include media that are both traditional and new, and controlled and not controlled.

The Need for Integrated Marketing Communications

The shift toward a richer mix of media and brand content approaches poses a problem for marketers. Consumers today are bombarded by brand content from a broad range of sources. But consumers don't distinguish between content sources the way marketers do. In the consumer's mind, brand content from different sources—whether it's a Super Bowl ad, in-store display, mobile app, or a friend's social media post—all become part of a single message about the brand or company. Conflicting content from these different sources can result in confused company images, brand positions, and customer relationships.

All too often, companies fail to integrate their various communication channels. The result is a hodgepodge of brand content to consumers. Mass media ads say one thing, whereas an in-store promotion sends a different signal, and the company's Internet site, e-mails, social media pages, or videos posted on YouTube say something altogether different. The problem is that these communications often come from different parts of the company. Advertising messages are planned and implemented by the advertising department or an ad agency. Other company departments or agencies are responsible for public relations (PR), sales promotion events, and online or social media content. However, although companies may have separated their communications tools, customers don't. Mixed content from these sources results in blurred brand perceptions by consumers.

The new world of online, mobile, and social media marketing presents not only tremendous opportunities but also big challenges. It can "give companies increased access to their customers, fresh insights into their preferences, and a broader creative palette to work with," says one marketing executive. But "the biggest issue is complexity and fragmentation ... the amount of choice out there," says another. The challenge is to "make it come together in an organized way."[3]

To that end, more companies today are adopting the concept of IMC. Under this concept, as illustrated in Figure 13–1, the company carefully integrates its many communication channels to deliver a dear, consistent, and compelling message about the organization and its brands.

IMC calls for recognizing all touch points where the customer may encounter content about the company and its brands. Each contact with the brand will deliver a message—whether good, bad, or indifferent. The company's goal should be to deliver a consistent and positive message at each contact. IMC ties together all of the company's messages and images. Its television and print ads have the same brand message as its e-mail and personal selling communications. And its PR materials are consistent with Web site, online, social media, and mobile marketing content.

Often, different media play unique roles in engaging, informing, and persuading consumers. For example, a recent study showed that more than two-thirds of advertisers and their agencies are planning video ad campaigns that stretch across multiple viewing platforms, such as traditional TV and digital, mobile, and social media. Such digital video ad convergence, as it's called, combines TV's core strength—vast reach—with digital's better targeting, interaction, and engagement.[4]

Figure 13–1
Integrated marketing communications.

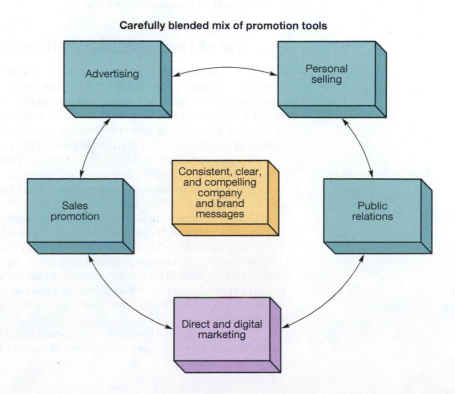

Carefully blended mix of promotion tools

Advertising

Personal selling

Consistent, clear, and compelling company and brand messages

Sales promotion

Public relations

Direct and digital marketing

These varied media and roles must be carefully coordinated under the overall marketing communications plan.

A great example of a well-integrated marketing communications effort is Coca-Cola's recent "Mirage" campaign. Built around two Super Bowl XLVII ads, the campaign integrated the clout of traditional big-budget TV advertising with the interactive power of social media to create real-time customer engagement with the Coke brand.[5]

Coca-Cola's "Mirage" tells the story of three bands of desert vagabonds—Cowboys, Showgirls, and Mad Max-inspired "Badlanders"—as they trek through the blazing-hot desert pursuing the same elusive mirage—a frosty bottle of Coca-Cola. The Mirage campaign began two weeks before the Super Bowl with a 30-second teaser ad on American Idol and posted on YouTube and other online destinations inviting fans to visit CokeChase.com to get to know the story and teams. Then, during the big game, a 60-second Mirage ad set up the exciting chase, with a cliff-hanging close that urged viewers to visit CokeChase.com, where they could help decide the outcome by casting votes for their favorite team and throwing obstacles in front of rival teams. During the rest of the game, Coca-Cola listening teams monitored related activity on major social media, and put fans in the middle of the action by posting real-time chase updates on Facebook, YouTube, and Twitter and chase photos on Tumblr and Instagram. After the end of the game, a second Mirage ad announced the chase team with the most viewer votes—the Showgirls, in their glam pink and silver outfits, won the Coke. But the real winner was Coca-Cola. The Mirage campaign exceeded all expectations. In addition to the usual huge Super Bowl audience numbers, during the game, the campaign captured an eye-popping 8.2 million online and social media interactions and 910,000 votes, far exceeding the brand's internal goals of 1.6 million interactions and 400,000 votes. Contributing to these interactions was 4.5 million views of the ad on YouTube. Instead of fast-forwarding this ad, people are going to YouTube to watch it!

In the past, no one person or department was responsible for thinking through the communication roles of the various promotion tools and coordinating the promotion mix. To help implement IMC, some companies have appointed a marketing communications director who has overall responsibility for the company's communications efforts. This helps produce better communications consistency and greater sales impact. It places the responsibility in someone's hands—where none existed before—to unify the company's image as it is shaped by thousands of company activities.

A View of the Communication Process

IMC involves identifying the target audience and shaping a well-coordinated promotional program to obtain the desired audience response. Too often, marketing communications focus on immediate awareness, image, or preference goals in the target market. But this approach to communication is too shortsighted. Today, marketers are moving toward viewing communications as managing ongoing customer engagement and relationships with the company and its brands.

Because customers differ, communications programs need to be developed for specific segments, niches, and even individuals. And, given the new interactive communications technologies, companies must ask not only "How can we reach our customers?" but also "How can we let our customers reach us?"

Thus, the communications process should start with an audit of all the potential touch points that target customers may have with the company and its brands. For example, looking for a good restaurant may include talking to others, reading articles and ads in newspapers and magazines, and visiting various Web sites for prices and reviews. The marketer needs to assess what influence each communication experience will have at different stages of the buying process. This understanding helps marketers allocate their communication dollars more efficiently and effectively.

To communicate effectively, marketers need to understand how communication works. Communication involves the nine elements shown in Figure 13–2.

Figure 13–2
Elements in the communications process.

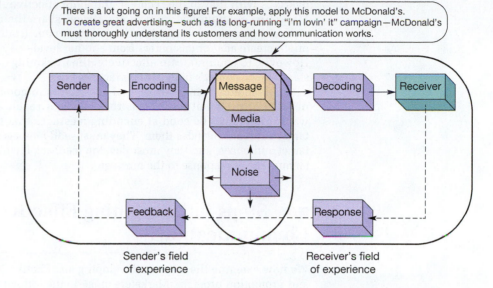

There is a lot going on in this figure! For example, apply this model to McDonald's. To create great advertising—such as its long-running "i'm lovin' it" campaign—McDonald's must thoroughly understand its customers and how communication works.

Sender — Encoding — Message / Media — Decoding — Receiver

Noise

Feedback — Response

Sender's field of experience   Receiver's field of experience

Two of these elements are the major parties in a communication—the *sender* and the *receiver*. Another two are the major communication tools—the *message* and the *media*. Four more are major communication functions—*encoding, decoding, response*, and *feedback*. The last element is *noise* in the system. Definitions of these elements follow and are applied to a McDonald's "i'm lovin' it" television commercial.

- *Sender: The party sending the message to another party*—here, McDonald's.

- *Encoding:* The process of *putting thought into symbolic form*—for example, McDonald's ad agency assembles words, sounds, and illustrations into a TV advertisement that will convey the intended message.

- *Message:* The *set of symbols* that the sender transmits—the actual McDonald's ad.

- *Media:* The *communication channels* through which the message moves from the sender to the receiver—in this case, television and the specific television programs that McDonald's selects.

- *Decoding:* The process by which the receiver *assigns meaning to the symbols* encoded by the sender—a consumer watches the McDonald's commercial and interprets the words and images it contains.

- *Receiver:* The *party receiving the message* sent by another party—the customer who watches the McDonald's ad.

- *Response:* The *reactions of the receiver* after being exposed to the message— any of hundreds of possible responses, such as the consumer likes McDonald's better, is more likely to eat at McDonald's next time, hums the "i'm lovin' it" jingle, or does nothing.

- *Feedback:* The part of the *receiver's response communicated back to the sender*—McDonald's research shows that consumers are either struck by and remember the ad or they write or call McDonald's, praising or criticizing the ad or its products.

- *Noise:* The *unplanned static or distortion* during the communication process, which results in the receiver getting a different message than the one the sender sent—the consumer is distracted while watching the commercial and misses its key points.

For a message to be effective, the sender's encoding process must mesh with the receiver's decoding process. The best messages consist of words and other symbols that are familiar to the receiver. The more the sender's field of experience overlaps with that of the receiver, the more effective the message is likely to be. Marketing communicators may not always share their customer's field of experience. For example, an advertising copywriter from one socioeconomic level might create ads for customers from another level—say, wealthy business owners. However, to communicate effectively, the marketing communicator must understand the customer's field of experience.

This model points out several key factors in good communication. Senders need to know what audiences they wish to reach and what responses they want. They must be good at encoding messages that take into account how the target audience decodes them. They must send messages through media that reach target audiences, and they must develop feedback channels so that they can assess an audience's response to the message.

■■■ Steps in Developing Effective Communications

We now examine the steps in developing an effective integrated communications and promotion program. Marketers must do the following: identify the target audience, determine the communication objectives, design the message, select the communication channels, select the message source, and collect feedback.

Identifying the Target Audience

A marketing communicator starts with a clear target audience in mind. The audience may be potential buyers or current users, those who make the buying decision, or those who influence it. The audience may be individuals, groups, special publics, or the general public. The target audience heavily affects the communicator's decision on what will be said, how it will be said, when it will be said, where it will be said, and who will say it. To create effective communication, a marketer must understand the target audience by creating a message that will be meaningful to them in a media they will understand. Managers need to understand their target markets before they can communicate with them.

Determining the Communication Objective

Once a target audience has been defined, the marketing communicator must decide what response is sought. Of course, in most cases, the final response is purchase. But purchase is the result of a long process of consumer decision making. The marketing communicator needs to know where the target audience stands in relation to the product and to what state it needs to be moved.

The Indian tribes of South Dakota wished to significantly increase tourist visitation to their reservations. These were their objectives:

- To provide guests for B&B operations

- To increase the market for Indian products

- To participate in other tourism-related incomes

- To correct misconceptions about the American Indian; it was deemed important to show that the Lakota, Dakota, and Nakota people are living cultures

This combination of economic and cultural education objectives led to the development of the Alliance of Tribal Tourism Advocates (ATTA) as a communication vehicle. Instead of depending on the South Dakota Department of Tourism or other organizations, Indians would promote themselves. "If you want to visit an Indian, the best person to talk with is a Native American," said Ronald L. Neiss, acting director of ATTA and a member of the Rosebud Sioux Tribal Council.[6]

The target audience may be in any of six buyer readiness states: awareness, knowledge, liking, preference, conviction, or purchase, which are shown in Figure 13–3.

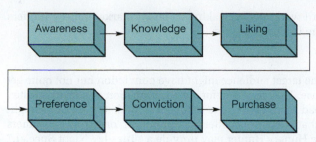

Figure 13–3
Buyer readiness stage.

Awareness

First, the communicator must be able to gauge the target audience's awareness of the product or organization. The audience may be totally unaware of it, know only its name, or know one or a few things about it. If most of the target audience is unaware, the communicator tries to build awareness, perhaps by building simple name recognition. This process can begin with simple messages repeating the name. Even then, building awareness takes time. Suppose that an independent restaurant named the Hungry Hunter opens in a northern suburb of Houston. There are 50,000 people within a three-mile radius of the restaurant. Initially, the restaurant has little name recognition. The Hungry Hunter may set an objective of making 40 percent of the people living within three miles of the restaurant aware of its name.

Red Roof Inns use the color of its roofs and locations with good visibility (near freeways) to create awareness. Another Red Roof strategy is to develop several properties in an area simultaneously. This has a "mushroom" effect, as motorists suddenly see Red Roof Inns everywhere. People forget names of other people, places, and products. Thus, awareness communication is a never-ending responsibility. A product must have top-of-mind awareness.

Knowledge

The target audience might be aware of the company or product but know little else. The Hungry Hunter specializes in wild game, but the market may not be aware of this. The restaurant may decide to select product knowledge as its first communication objective.

The chain of Ruth's Chris Steak House restaurants uses a simple slogan and advertises on a quarter page in airline in-flight magazines. The message is directed at frequent flyers who deserve a "sizzling reward." The advertisement features a color photo of a very thick steak, a list of restaurant addresses, and the slogan of Ruth's Chris Steak House, "Home of Serious Steaks." This simple message quickly gives the reader knowledge of restaurant location, size of the steak, and seriousness of the restaurant as a steakhouse.

Liking

If target audience members know the product, how do they feel about it? We can develop a range of preference, such as a Likert scale covering degrees of liking, for example, "dislike very much," "dislike somewhat," "indifferent," "like somewhat," and "like very much." If the market is unfavorable toward the Hungry Hunter, the communicator must learn why and then develop a communication campaign to create favorable feelings. If unfavorable feelings are based on real problems, such as slow service, communication alone cannot do the job. The Hungry Hunter has to fix its problems and then communicate its renewed quality.

Preference

A target audience might like the product but not prefer it to others. In this case, the communicator must try to build consumer preference. The communicator promotes the product's quality, value, performance, and other features. The communicator can check on the campaign's success by measuring audience preferences after the campaign. If the Hungry Hunter finds that many area residents like the name and concept but choose other restaurants, it will have to identify those areas where its offerings are better than competing restaurants. It must then promote its advantages to build preference among possible customers.

Conviction

A target audience might prefer the product but not develop a conviction about buying the product. Marketers have a responsibility to turn favorable attitudes into conviction because conviction is closely linked with purchase. Communication from the Hungry Hunter will work toward making its target market believe it offers the best steaks at a fair value in its market area.

Purchase

Finally, some members of the target audience might have conviction but not quite get around to making the purchase. They may wait for more information or plan to act later. The communicator must lead these consumers to take the final step. Actions might include offering the product at a low price, offering a premium, or letting consumers try it on a limited basis. The Hungry Hunter may provide a "Tuesday Night Special," offering prime rib or its seafood of the day for $24.95 instead of the usual price of $29.95.

Designing the Message

Having defined the desired audience response, the communicator turns to developing an effective message. Ideally, the message should get attention, hold interest, arouse desire, and obtain action (a framework known as the AIDA model). In practice, few messages take the consumer all the way from awareness to purchase, but the AIDA framework does suggest the desirable qualities of a good message.

In putting the message together, the marketing communicator must solve three problems: what to say (message content), how to say it logically (message structure), and how to say it symbolically (message format).

It's a fair statement to say that Americans like Australia and everything Australian. Outback Steakhouse built on that positive image. The company says, "Outback Steakhouse is an Australian steakhouse" (actually it's a member of an American multi-restaurant chain, but who cares?).

Outback offers what it describes as a "no worry zone." This too is typical of Australia where people commonly say, "No worry, mate." Outback's commercial says,

"Kick back for the moment. Toss all your worries in the air cause you'll forget them when you're here. Let's go outback tonight."
Source: Michael Carey, Laurie Garnier & Robin Schwarz for Lyrics and Music.

Message Content

The communicator has to figure out an appeal or theme that will produce a desired response. The three types of appeals are rational, emotional, and moral.

Rational appeals relate to audience self-interest. They show that the product will produce desired benefits. Occasionally, rational appeals are overlooked.

Emotional appeals attempt to provoke emotions that motivate purchase. These include fear, guilt, and shame appeals that entice people to do things that they should (brush their teeth, buy new tires) or stop doing things they shouldn't (smoke, drink too much, or overeat).

Emotional appeals are widely used by resorts and hotels to stimulate cross-purchases:

- Commercials on in-room television, posters, and desktop tents promote the health center and the need to reduce stress and work off "pounds gained from eating in the hotel."

- The "Think of the Spouse and Kids at Home" theme is widely used to promote a myriad of products available in the hotel, from hand-dipped chocolates to stuffed animals. This appeal is also used to convince business guests to purchase a vacation for the family at one of the chain's resort properties.

Moral appeals are directed to the audience's sense of what is right and proper. They are often used to urge people to support such social causes as a cleaner environment, better race relations, equal rights, and aid to the needy.

Go RVing created a series of lifestyle ads promoting RVing. This one shows a father and daughter spending time together. Courtesy of Go RVing

Message Structure

The communicator must also decide how to handle three message structure issues. The first is whether to draw a conclusion or leave it to the audience. Early research showed that drawing a conclusion was usually the most effective. More recent research, however, suggests that in many cases the advertiser is better off asking questions and letting buyers come to their own conclusions.

The second message structure issue is whether to present a one- or two-sided argument. Usually, a one-sided argument is more effective in sales presentations except when audiences are highly educated and negatively disposed.

The third message structure issue is whether to present the strongest arguments first or last. Presenting them first creates strong attention but may lead to an anticlimactic ending.[7]

"World's Largest Outdoor Swimming Pool" is the first message presented by the San Alfonso del Mar Resort in Chile. The accommodation and food actually take a second seat to the beauty and immensity of the 1-km-long salt water swimming pool, 115 feet deep and holding 66 million gallons of water.

Message Format

The communicator also needs a strong format for the message. In a print ad, the communicator has to decide on the headline, copy, illustration, and color. To attract attention, advertisers can use novelty and contrast, eye-catching pictures and headlines, distinctive formats, message size, position, color, shape, and movement. If the message is to be carried over the radio, the communicator has to choose words, sounds, and voices.

If the message is to be carried on television or in person, all these elements, plus body language, must be planned. Presenters plan their facial expressions, gestures, dress, posture, and hairstyle. If the message is carried on the product or its package, the communicator has to watch texture, scent, color, size, and shape. For example, color plays a major communication role in food preferences. When consumers sampled four cups of coffee that had been placed next to brown, blue, red, and yellow containers (all the coffee was identical, but the consumers did not know this), 75 percent felt that the coffee next to the brown container tasted too strong, nearly 85 percent judged the coffee next to the red container to be the richest, nearly everyone felt that the coffee next to the blue container was mild, and the coffee next to the yellow container was perceived as weak.

Selecting Communication Channels

The communicator must now select channels of communication. The two broad types of communication channels are personal and nonpersonal.

Personal Communication Channels

In personal communication channels, two or more people communicate directly with each other. They might communicate face to face, on the phone, via mail or e-mail, or even through an Internet "chat." Personal communication channels are effective because they allow for personal addressing and feedback.

Some personal communication channels are controlled directly by the company. For example, company salespeople contact business buyers. But other personal communications about the product may reach buyers through channels not directly controlled by the company. These channels might include independent experts—consumer advocates, bloggers, and others—making statements to buyers. Or they might be neighbors, friends, family members, and associates talking to target buyers in person or via social media. This last channel, word-of-mouth influence, has considerable effect in many product areas.

Personal influence carries great weight for products that are expensive, risky, or highly visible. Hospitality products are often viewed as being risky because they cannot be tried out beforehand. Therefore, personal sources of information are often sought before someone purchases a travel package, selects a restaurant, or stays at a hotel.

Marketing HIGHLIGHT 13–1   Thank You—A Great Personal Communication

Two of the most powerful words in any language are *thank you*. That's a sales manager for a limited service hotel in Indianapolis, Indiana, decided to initiate a special thank-you program for guests.

The manager's objectives were to increase corporate business and let guests know that the inn appreciated their patronage and wanted them to return. She felt that a handwritten note would be appreciated in this high-tech world of e-mail, Internet, and voice-mail communications.

Names and addresses were obtained from business cards left by guests in a fish bowl qualifying them for a monthly drawing. After the drawing was held, any one of the three desk clerks would write thank-you notes during slow times on the desk. Each desk clerk is provided with personalized business cards that are included with the handwritten note.

The manager has spoken with many guests who were amazed that the inns took time to write a personal note to them. One client mentioned that he really liked having the business card sent from a front-desk associate rather than a general manager or salesperson. Because the desk associates are usually the ones to make reservations, guests like having the name of someone to ask for when they call back for future reservations.

The thank-you notes help build a relationship between the guests and the hotel. They let the guests know that the staff appreciates their business and cares about them as individuals. The manager's support of the program lets the employees know that creating positive guest relations is important to the hotel.

Online recommendations have become a powerful influence on consumers. One survey found that recommendations from friends and family are far and away the most powerful influence on consumers worldwide. More than 50 percent of consumers said friends and family are the number one influence on their awareness and purchase. Another study found that 90 percent of the customers trust recommendations from people they know and 70 percent trust consumer opinions posted online, whereas trust in advertisements runs from a high of 62 percent to a low of 24 percent, depending on the medium.[8]

The power of online ratings means that it is important to provide great service, to help eliminate negative reviews. It also means that one must monitor and respond to both negative and positive reviews. For negative reviews, it is best to take the conversation off-line. This can be done by apologizing online and asking the reviewer that had a problem to contact the manager directly by e-mail.

Companies can take steps to put personal communication channels to work for them. They can create *opinion leaders* for their brands—people whose opinions are sought by others—by supplying influencers with the product on attractive terms or by educating them so that they can inform others. **Buzz marketing** involves cultivating opinion leaders and getting them to spread information about a product or service to others in their communities.

Social marketing firm BzzAgent takes a different approach to creating buzz. It creates customers for a client brand, and then turns them into influential brand advocates.[9]

BzzAgent has assembled a volunteer army of natural-born buzzers, millions of actual shoppers around the world who are highly active in social media and who love to talk about and recommend products. Once a client signs on, BzzAgent searches its database and selects "agents" that fit the profiles of the product's target customers. Selected volunteers receive product samples, creating a personal brand experience. BzzAgent then urges the agents to share their honest opinions of the product through face-to-face conversations and via tweets, Facebook posts, online photo and video sharing, blogs, and other social sharing venues. If the product is good, the positive word of mouth spreads quickly. If the product is not so good, that's worth learning quickly as well. BzzAgent advocates have successfully buzzed the brands of hundreds of top marketing companies, including Disney and Dunkin' Donuts. BzzAgent's appeal is its authenticity. The agents aren't scripted. Instead, the company tells its advocates, "Here's the product; if you believe in it, say whatever you think. Bzz is no place for excessive, repetitive, or unauthentic posts."

Buzz marketing. Cultivating opinion leaders and getting them to spread information about a product to others in their community.

Nonpersonal Communication Channels

Media. Nonpersonal communication channels, including print media (newspapers, magazines, direct mail), broadcast media (radio, television), and display media (billboards, signs, posters).

Atmosphere. Designed environments that create or reinforce a buyer's leanings toward consumption of a product.

Events. Occurrences staged to communicate messages to target audiences, such as news conferences or grand openings.

Nonpersonal communication channels are media that carry messages without personal contact or feedback. They include media, atmospheres, and events. Major **media** consist of print media (newspapers, magazines, direct mail), broadcast media (radio and television), display media (billboards, signs, posters), and online media (e-mail, Web sites, and online social and sharing networks). **Atmospheres** are designed environments that create or reinforce the buyer's leanings toward purchasing a product. The lobby of a five-star hotel contains a floral display, original works of art, and luxurious furnishings to reinforce the buyer's perception that the hotel is a five-star hotel. **Events** are occurrences staged to communicate messages to target audiences. PR departments arrange press conferences, grand openings, public tours, and other events to communicate with specific audiences.

The Scanticon Princeton (a conference center) used its lobby as a gallery for original artworks by members of the Princeton Artists Alliance. This resulted in excellent publicity, including a full-page story with pictures and the address of Scanticon Princeton in the Sunday edition of a major Philadelphia newspaper.

Nonpersonal communication affects buyers directly. In addition, using mass media often affects buyers indirectly by causing more personal communication. Mass communications affect attitudes and behavior through a two-step flow of communication. In this process, communications first flow from television, magazines, and other mass media to opinion leaders and then from these opinion leaders to others. Thus, opinion leaders step between mass media and their audiences and carry messages to people who are less exposed to media.

Selecting the Message Source

The message's impact on the audience is also affected by how the audience views the sender. Messages delivered by highly credible sources are persuasive. What factors make a source credible? The three factors most often found are expertise, trustworthiness, and likability. Expertise is the degree to which the communicator appears to have the authority needed to back the claim. Doctors, scientists, and professors rank high on expertise in their fields. Trustworthiness is related to how objective and honest the source appears to be. Friends, for example, are trusted more than salespeople. Likability is how attractive the source is to the audience. People like sources who are open, humorous, and natural. Not surprisingly, the most highly credible source is a person who scores high on all three factors: expertise, trustworthiness, and likability.

Memphis used prominent people to promote that city as a convention and meeting site. A video was produced in which convention planners, tour wholesalers, and association officials endorsed the city as an ideal convention location. Messages delivered by attractive sources achieve higher attention and recall. Advertisers often use celebrities as spokespeople, such as Michael Jordan for McDonald's. Celebrities are likely to be effective when they personify a key product attribute. But what is equally important is that the spokesperson must have credibility.

The use of living personalities to serve as spokespeople for a company or product carries inherent problems:

- Celebrities are often difficult to work with and may refuse to participate in important media events or to pose under certain conditions.

- Living personalities are sometimes publicly embarrassed.

The message source in this ad, a young girl having a great time at the beach, will appeal to parents or grandparents with young children. Courtesy of Pettus Advertising, Inc. Courtesy of The Corpus Christi Convention & Visitors Bureau

CORPUS CHRISTI
MUSTANG & PADRE ISLANDS

MEMORIES MADE HERE

It's smiles & sunglasses season!

You're just a hop, skip, and a jump away from the pristine beaches of Corpus Christi and the Texas Coastal Bend. Come curl your toes in the sand, take a dip in the salty sea, or race your kids down the beach. Exuberance never felt so good! While you're here, stand atop the landing deck of the USS Lexington Aircraft Carrier, get a kiss from a dolphin at the Texas State Aquarium, eat just-caught flounder, and float the Torrent Tidal Wave River at the new Schlitterbahn waterpark opening this summer. Plan your trip online and find the perfect lodging, restaurants, and activities to fit your family *and* your budget. Don't forget the flip flops and a camera, because memories are made here.

VisitCorpusChristiTX.org
or 800.766.BEACH (2322)

The Hilton Hotels and Resorts' logo is used in their advertising campaigns to increase awareness of the brand. Courtesy of Philip Kotler

Qantas Airlines has been successful using a kangaroo and a koala bear as symbols. For decades, McDonald's has effectively used the imaginary Ronald McDonald. Cartoon characters and animals are dependable and unlikely to create negative publicity. An increasingly popular Web site design for luxurious hotels, such as Grand Hotel Villa Feltrinelli (www.villafeltrinelli.com), is to use a minimum of written words but instead depend on mood music and beautiful scenes of the hotel, furnishings, and grounds to create the image of luxury.

Collecting Feedback

After sending the message, the communicator must research its effect on the target audience. This involves asking the target audience whether they remember the message, how many times they saw it, what points they recall, how they felt about the message, and their past and present attitudes toward the product and company. The communicator would also like to measure behavior resulting from the message: How many people bought a product, talked to others about it, or visited the store.

After not using television advertising for seven years, Sheraton Hotels and Resorts started an aggressive mass media campaign that included television, radio, and print media. The objective of the ad was to tell travelers about Sheraton's upgraded services and amenities. Sheraton's iconic "S" was featured in its advertisements to reestablish the identity of the icon. A test found that the Sheraton "S" has an unaided recall of 93 percent. It is called unaided recall if there is no prompting with elements of the ads or commercials being examined. With prompting, the results are called aided recall.[10] After the campaign, Web bookings also increased by 20 percent.[11]

Figure 13–4 shows an example of feedback measurement. Looking at hotel brand A, we find that 80 percent of the total market was aware of it, 20 percent of those who were aware had tried it, but only 20 percent of those who tried it were satisfied. These results suggest that although the communication program created awareness, the product failed to give consumers the satisfaction expected. The company should, therefore, try to improve the product while continuing the successful communication program. With hotel brand B, the situation was different: Only 40 percent of the total

Figure 13–4
Feedback measurement for two brands.

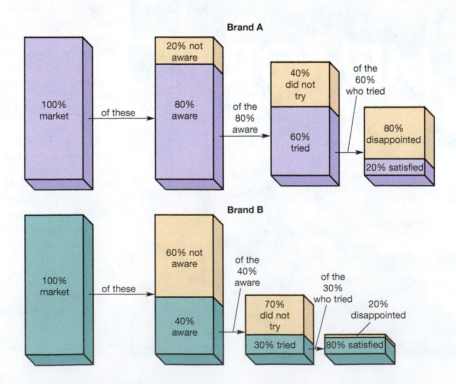

market was aware of it. Only 10 percent of those had tried it, and 80 percent of those who tried it were satisfied. In this case, the communication program needed to be stronger to take advantage of the brand's power to create satisfaction.

■■■ Setting the Total Promotion Budget and Mix

We have looked at the steps in planning and sending communications to a target audience. But how does the company determine its total promotion budget and the division among the major promotional tools to create the promotion mix? By what process does it blend the tools to create IMC? We now look at these questions.

Setting the Total Promotional Budget

One of the hardest marketing decisions facing companies is how much to spend on promotions. John Wanamaker, the department store magnate, once said, "I know that half of my advertising is wasted, but I don't know which half. I spent $2 million for advertising, and I don't know if that is half enough or twice too much."

How do companies determine their promotion budget? Four common methods are used to set the total budget for advertising: (1) the affordable method, (2) the percentage of sales method, (3) the competitive parity method, and (4) the objective and task method.[12]

Affordable Method

Many companies use the affordable method: They set a promotion budget at what they think the company can afford. One executive explained this method as follows: "Why, it's simple. First, I go upstairs to the controller and ask how much they can afford to give this year. He says a million and a half. Later, the boss comes to me and asks how much should we spend and I say 'Oh, about a million and a half.'"[13]

Unfortunately, this method of setting budgets completely ignores the effect of promotion on sales volume. It leads to an uncertain annual promotion budget, which makes long-range marketing planning difficult. Although the affordable method can result in overspending on advertising, it more often results in underspending.

Percentage of Sales Method

Many companies use the percentage of sales method, setting their promotion budget at a certain percentage of current or forecasted sales, or they budget a percentage of the sales price. Some firms use this method because it is easy. For example, some restaurateurs know that the mean expenditure for promotion for restaurants is 4 percent; therefore, they set their promotion budget at 4 percent.

A number of advantages are claimed for the percentage of sales method. First, using this method means that promotion spending is likely to vary with what the company can "afford." It also helps management think about the relationship between promotion spending, selling price, and profit per unit. Finally, it supposedly creates competitive stability because competing firms tend to spend about the same percentage of their sales on promotion.

However, despite these claimed advantages, the percentage of sales method has little justification. It wrongly views sales as the cause of promotion rather than as the result. The budget is based on availability of funds rather than on opportunities. It may prevent increased spending, which is sometimes needed to turn around falling sales. Because the budget varies with year-to-year sales, long-range planning is difficult. Finally, the method does not provide a basis for choosing a specific percentage, except past actions or what competitors are doing.

Competitive Parity Method

Other companies use the competitive parity method, setting their promotion budgets to match competitors' outlays. They watch competitors' advertising or get industry promotion spending estimates from publications or trade associations and then set their budgets based on the industry average. For example, the advertising expenditure for the average hotel is 1 percent of sales, and the marketing budget is 5 percent. However, for limited-service hotels, the advertising expenditure is 2 percent of sales and the marketing budget.[14]

Two arguments are used to support this method. First, competitors' budgets represent the collective wisdom of the industry. Second, spending what competitors spend helps prevent promotion wars. Unfortunately, neither argument is valid. There are no grounds for believing that competition has a better idea of what a company should be spending on promotion. Companies differ greatly, and each has its own special promotion needs. Furthermore, no evidence indicates that budgets based on competitive parity prevent promotion wars.

Objective and Task Method

The most logical budget setting method is the objective and task method. Using this, marketers develop their promotion budgets by (1) defining specific objectives, (2) determining tasks that must be performed to achieve these objectives, and (3) estimating the costs of performing them. The sum of these costs is the proposed promotional budget.

The objective and task method forces management to spell out its assumptions about the relationship between dollars spent and promotional results. It is also the most difficult method to use because it can be hard to determine which tasks will achieve specific objectives. Management must consider such questions even though they are difficult to answer. With the objective and task method, the company sets its promotion budget based on what it wants to accomplish.

■■■ Shaping the Overall Promotion Mix

The concept of IMC suggests that the company must blend the promotion tools carefully into a coordinated *promotion mix*. But how does it determine what mix of promotion tools to use? Companies within the same industry differ greatly in the design of their promotion mixes. We now look at factors that influence the marketer's choice of promotion tools.

The Nature of Each Promotion Tool

Each promotion tool has unique characteristics and costs. Marketers must understand these characteristics in shaping the promotion mix. Often one promotional tool must be used to promote another. Thus, when McDonald's decides to run a million-dollar sweepstakes in its fast-food outlets (a sales promotion), it has to run ads to inform the public. Many factors influence the marketer's choice of promotion tools. Each promotional tool, advertising, personal selling, sales promotion, PR, and direct marketing, has unique characteristics and costs. Marketers must understand these characteristics to select their tools correctly.

Advertising

Because of the many forms and uses of advertising, generalizing about its unique qualities as a part of the promotion mix is difficult. Yet several qualities can be noted. Advertising's public nature suggests that the advertised product is standard and legitimate. Because many people see ads for the product, buyers know that purchasing the product will be publicly understood and accepted. Advertising also allows the seller to repeat a message many times. Large-scale advertising by a seller says something positive about the seller's size, popularity, and success. Advertising can be used to build a long-term image for a product (e.g., Four Seasons or McDonald's ads) and also stimulate quick sales (as when Embassy Suites in Phoenix advertises a promotion for the Fourth of July holiday). Advertising can reach masses of geographically dispersed buyers at a low cost per exposure.

Advertising also has shortcomings. Although it reaches many people quickly, advertising is impersonal and cannot be as persuasive as a company salesperson. Advertising is able to carry on only a one-way communication with the audience, and the audience does not feel it has to pay attention or respond. In addition, advertising can be very costly. Although some forms, such as newspaper and radio advertising, can be done on small budgets, other forms, such as network TV advertising, require very large budgets.

For hotels, restaurants, and other hospitality companies that cater to traveling visitors in private vehicles, the use of advertising (billboards) represents the largest expenditure item in their advertising budgets.

The Little America group of hotels has used a theme that all parents recognize with their tired and bored children: "Are we there yet?" In some cases, these hotels also advertise very inexpensive ice cream cones at the next exit, at Little America.

A critical challenge faced by hotel marketers is creating an immediate awareness of brand name to ensure that their properties are included in the traveler's evoked set of lodging choices. The evoked set of brand preferences and the relative impact of advertising and prior stay were investigated in a study of frequent travelers. It was found that chains whose names were well established in the traveler's evoked set most often won the traveler's business. There was little influence on chain name recall of prior stay without ad exposure or influence on ad exposure without prior stay. The combined effect of ad exposure and prior stay was an important influence on brand selection.[15]

Personal Selling

Personal selling is the most effective tool at certain stages of the buying process, particularly in building buyer preference, conviction, and purchase. Compared with advertising, personal selling has several unique qualities. It involves personal interaction between two or more people, allowing each to observe the other's needs and characteristics and make quick adjustments. Personal selling also lets all kinds of relationships spring up, ranging from a matter-of-fact selling relationship to a deep personal friendship. The effective salesperson keeps the customer's interests at heart to build a long-term relationship. Finally, with personal selling, the buyer usually feels a greater need to listen and respond, even if the response is a polite "no thank you."

These unique qualities come at a cost. A sales force requires a longer-term company commitment than advertising; advertising can be turned on and off, but sales force size is harder to vary. Personal selling is the company's most expensive promotion tool, costing industrial companies an average of $225 per sales call.[16] American firms spend up to three times as much on personal selling as they do on advertising.

Personal selling by members of the hospitality industry is used primarily for large key customers, travel intermediaries, and meeting planners and others with responsibility for group sales.

Sales Promotion

Sales promotion includes an assortment of tools, coupons, contests, cents-off deals, premiums, and others, and these tools have many unique qualities. They attract consumer attention and provide information that may lead the consumer to buy the product. Sales promotions offer strong incentives to purchase by providing inducements or contributions that give additional value to consumers, and they invite and reward quick response. Advertising says "buy our product." Sales promotion says "buy it now."

A well-managed personal selling program is effective for hotels and restaurants with banquet space. Courtesy of Michaelcourtney/Fotolia.

Companies use sales promotion tools to create a stronger and quicker response. Sales promotion can be used to dramatize product offers and to boost sagging sales. Its effects are usually short lived, however, and are not effective in building long-run brand preference.

Public Relations

PR offers several advantages. One is believability. News stories, features, and events seem more real and believable to readers than do ads. PR can reach many prospects who avoid salespeople and advertisements. The message gets to the buyers as news rather than as a sales-directed communication. Like advertising, PR can dramatize a company or product.

A relatively new addition to the promotion mix is the infomercial, a hybrid between advertising and PR. Companies provide interesting stories on videotape for use on television during periods of light viewing, such as early morning. Infomercials provide enough information to keep the attention of viewers, combined with a "soft" approach to product or brand advertising.

Hospitality marketers tend to underuse PR or use it only as an afterthought. Yet a well-thought-out PR campaign used with other promotion mix elements can be very effective and economical.

Direct and Digital Marketing

Direct and digital marketing connections carefully targeted individual consumers to both obtain an immediate response and cultivate lasting customer relationships: the use of direct mail, the telephone, direct-response television, e-mail, online, mobile and social media, and other tools to communicate directly with specific consumers. Although there are many forms of direct marketing, they all share four distinctive characteristics. Direct marketing is *nonpublic*: The message is normally directed to a specific person. Rather than advertise reduced fares or room rates, airlines and hotels will send a direct marketing message to offering these promotions to their best customers. Direct marketing is *immediate* and *customized*: Messages can be prepared very quickly and can be tailored to appeal to specific consumers. Finally, direct marketing is *interactive*: It allows a dialogue between the marketing team and the consumer, and messages can be altered depending on the consumer's response. Thus, direct marketing is well suited to highly targeted marketing efforts and to building one-to-one customer relationships. Online, mobile, and social media marketing range from nonpublic text messages to Facebook sites and is one of the fastest growing areas of marketing.

Promotion Mix Strategies

Companies consider many factors when developing their promotion mix, including the following: type of product and market, push versus pull strategy, buyer readiness state, and product life-cycle stage.

Type of Product and Market

The importance of different promotion tools varies among consumers and commercial markets. When hospitality firms market to consumer markets, they spend more on advertising and sales promotion and often very little on personal selling. Hospitality firms targeting commercial organizations spend more on personal selling. In general, personal selling is used more heavily with expensive and risky goods and in markets with fewer and larger sellers. A meeting or convention is customized for the organization putting on the event. It takes a skilled salesperson to put together a package that will give clients what they want at an appropriate price that will provide good revenue for the company.

Push Versus Pull Strategy

The promotional mix is heavily affected by whether a company chooses a push or pull strategy. The two strategies are contrasted in Figure 13–5. A push strategy involves "pushing" the product through distribution channels to final consumers. The manufacturer directs its marketing activities (primarily personal selling and trade promotion) at channel members to induce them to order and carry the product and to promote it to final consumers. For example, Dollar Rent-A-Car offered travel agents a 15 percent commission instead of 10 percent to persuade them to order its brand for clients. Continental Plaza Hotels and Resorts developed a promotion that gave travel agents an extra $10 in addition to their normal commission for bookings. A push strategy provides an incentive for channel members to promote the product to their customers or push the product through the distribution channels.

Using a pull strategy, a company directs its marketing activities (primarily advertising and consumer promotion) toward final consumers to induce them to buy the product. For example, Sheraton placed an ad for its Hawaiian properties

Figure 13–5
Push versus pull promotion strategy.

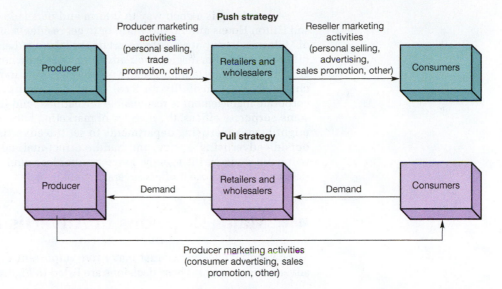

in the Phoenix, Arizona, paper. Interested readers were instructed to call their travel planner or Sheraton. If the strategy is effective, consumers will purchase the product from channel members, who will, in turn, order it from producers. Thus, under a pull strategy, consumer demand "pulls" the product through the channels.

Buyer Readiness State

Promotional tools vary in their effects at different stages of buyer readiness. Advertising, along with PR, plays a major role in the awareness and knowledge stages, more important than that played by cold calls from salespeople. Customer liking, preferences, and conviction are more affected by personal selling, which is closely followed by advertising. Finally, closing the sale is accomplished primarily with sales calls and sales promotion. Only personal selling, given its high costs, should focus on the later stages of the customer buying process.

Product Life-Cycle Stage

The effects of different promotion tools also vary with stages of the product life cycle. In the introduction stage, advertising and PR are good for producing high awareness, and sales promotion is useful in product early trial. Personal selling must be used to get the trade to carry the product in the growth stage; advertising and PR continue to be powerful while promotion can be reduced because fewer incentives are needed. In the mature stage, sales promotion again becomes important relative to advertising. Buyers know the brands, and advertising is needed only to remind them of the product. In the decline stage, advertising is kept at a reminder level, PR is dropped, and salespeople give the product only a little attention. Sales promotion, however, may continue to be strong.[17]

■■■ Advertising

The remainder of this chapter examines advertising in more detail. Subsequent chapters deal with personal selling, sales promotion, and direct and digital marketing. We define **advertising** as any paid form of nonpersonal presentation and promotion of ideas, goods, or services by an identified sponsor.

The fast-food industry in the United States has reached the mature stage, and fast-food companies are fighting for market share. McDonald's, Yum Brands, Burger King, and Wendy's are stepping up their campaigns and trying to take market share from each other. Marketing wars such as the burger wars and pizza wars are fought with advertising dollars. Marketing wars break out in mature markets where growth of the market is slow. To increase their sales, companies must try to steal market share from their competitors.

Advertising. Any paid form of nonpersonal presentation and promotion of ideas, goods, or services by an identified sponsor.

Advertising is a good way to inform and persuade, whether the purpose is to sell Hilton Hotels around the world or to get residents of Kuala Lumpur, the capital of Malaysia, to stay at a nearby resort on the island of Langkawi. Organizations have different ways of managing their advertising. The owner or the general manager of an independent restaurant usually handles the restaurant's advertising. Most hotel chains give responsibility for local advertising to the individual hotels, whereas corporate management is responsible for national and international advertising. In some corporate offices, the director of marketing handles advertising. Other firms might have advertising departments to set the advertising budget, work with an outside advertising agency, and handle direct-mail advertising and other advertising not done by the agency. Large companies commonly use an outside advertising agency because it offers several advantages.

■■■ Major Decisions in Advertising

Marketing management must make five important decisions in developing an advertising program. These decisions are listed in Figure 13–6 and discussed next.

Setting the Objectives

The first step in developing an advertising program is to set advertising objectives, which should be based on information about the target market, positioning, and marketing mix. Marketing positioning and mix strategies define the role that advertising must perform in the total marketing program.

An advertising objective is a specific communication task to be accomplished with a specific target audience during a specific period of time. Advertising objectives can be classified by their aim: to *inform, persuade*, or *remind*. **Informative advertising** is used heavily when introducing a new product category and when the objective is to build primary demand. When an airline opens a new route, its management often runs full-page advertisements informing the market about the new service. Junior's Deli, in the Westwood section of Los Angeles, uses direct-mail campaigns to create new customers. New residents in the neighborhood receive a gift certificate for a Deli Survival Kit, which contains a chunk of beef salami, two types of cheese, a loaf of fresh rye bread, and a home-baked dessert. The kit is absolutely free, with no purchase required, but the certificate must be redeemed at the restaurant. More than a 1,000 new neighbors come in to claim their kits each year. Thus, the kit not only informs potential customers about the restaurant but also results in visits to the restaurant by customers who sample its products.[18]

Persuasive advertising becomes more important as competition increases and a company's objective becomes building selective demand. Some persuasive advertising has become comparison advertising, which compares one brand directly or indirectly with one or more other brands. For example, Dunkin' Donuts ran a TV and Web campaign comparing the chain's coffee to Starbucks's brews. "In a recent national blind taste test," proclaimed the ads, "more Americans preferred the taste of Dunkin' Donuts coffee over Starbucks. It's just more proof it's all about the

Informative advertising.
Advertising used to inform consumers about a new product or feature to build primary demand.

Figure 13–6
Major advertising decisions.

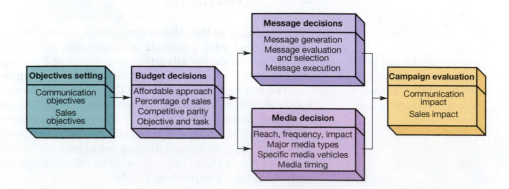

coffee (not the couches or music)." Dunkin' Donuts ran a TV and Web campaign comparing the chain's coffee to Starbucks's brews. "Try the coffee that won," the ads concluded.

Advertisers should use comparative advertising with caution. All too often, such ads invite competitor responses, resulting in an advertising war that neither competitor can win. Upset competitors might take more drastic action, such as filing complaints with the self-regulatory National Advertising Division of the Council of Better Business Bureaus or even filing false-advertising lawsuits. An unwritten rule of using comparison ads is that the prestige brands and market-share leaders should never use this tactic because it draws attention to competitors and causes the customer to question the value of the market-share leader or prestige brand.

Reminder advertising is important for mature products because it keeps consumers thinking about the product. Expensive McDonald's ads on television are designed to remind people about McDonald's, not to inform or persuade them.

Reminder advertising.
Advertising used to keep consumers thinking about a product.

Advertising is not a substitute for poor products. For an advertising campaign to create long-term sales, the product advertised must create satisfied customers. One mistake frequently made by the owners of new restaurants is advertising before the operation has gone through a shakedown period. Eager to get a return on their investment, the owners advertise before the restaurant's staff is properly trained and the restaurant's systems are tested under high-demand situations.

Because most people look forward to trying a new restaurant, advertising campaigns are usually effective, resulting in waits during peak periods. However, success can be short lived when restaurateurs deliver poor-quality food, poor service, or poor value. Dissatisfied customers quickly spread negative word of mouth to potential customers, who are eager to find out about the new restaurant. Frequently, advertising a noncompetitive product quickens the product's death through negative word. The owner of a restaurant in Houston who went through this experience and ultimately went out of business blamed his loss on fickle customers. In his words, "The restaurant used to have waits every night of the week. Now, the restaurant is empty. I can't believe how fickle customers are." The customers weren't fickle; in fact, they knew exactly what they wanted: good food and good service. These were things the restaurant did not offer.

The president of a hospitality marketing, advertising, and PR firm believes that the implementation of an effective advertising campaign is one of the fastest ways to jeopardize the performance of a mediocre property. You must first be sure the property can live up to the promises your advertising makes. If your property or service is inconsistent with the claims made, the money you spend to generate additional business will probably do little more than increase the number of dissatisfied guests.[19]

Even highly satisfied customers need frequent reminders. Ski and scuba-diving resorts share a common problem. Satisfied guests often fail to return because they wish to experience new slopes and new dive areas. Years may pass before the guest is ready to return. Reminder advertising may shorten that period of time.

Setting the Advertising Budget

After determining advertising objectives, a company can establish an advertising budget for each product. The role of advertising is to affect demand for a product. The company wants to spend the amount needed to achieve the sales goal. Four commonly used methods for setting the promotional budget were discussed earlier in this chapter. These methods—the affordable method, the percentage of sales method, the competitive parity method, and the objective and task method—are also often used when determining the advertising budget. The advertising budget also has some specific factors that should be considered when setting a budget:

- *Stage in the product life cycle.* New products typically need large advertising budgets to build awareness and gain consumer trial. Mature brands usually require lower budgets as a ratio to sales. For example, a casual neighborhood restaurant may want to budget heavily for advertising in its first year of operation and less per month after its first year. By the end of the first year, it should have established a clientele. After this point, it will need to maintain its existing customers and gain new customers (albeit at a lower rate than the first year). Its loyal customers should be spreading positive word of mouth by the end of the first year.

- *Competition and clutter.* In a market with many competitors and heavy advertising support, a brand must be advertised more frequently to be heard above the noise of the market.

- *Market share.* High-market-share brands usually require greater advertising expenditures as a percentage of sales than do low-share brands. Building a market or taking share from competitors requires larger advertising budgets than maintaining current share. For example, McDonald's spends about 5 percent of its sales on advertising.

- *Advertising frequency.* Larger advertising budgets are essential when many repetitions are needed to present the brand's message.

- *Product differentiation.* A brand that closely resembles others in its product class (pizza, limited-service hotels, air travel) requires heavy advertising to set it apart. When a product differs greatly from those of competitors, advertising can be used to communicate differences to consumers.

How much impact does advertising really have on consumer purchases and brand loyalty? One study found that advertising increased purchases by loyal users but was less effective in winning new buyers. The study found that advertising appears unlikely to have a cumulative effect that leads to loyalty. Features, displays, and especially price have a stronger impact on response than advertising.[20]

Most advertising takes many months or even years to build strong brand positions and consumer loyalty. Long-run effects are difficult to measure. This debate underscores the fact that the measurement of sales results from advertising remains in its infancy.

Strategic Versus Tactical Budgets

The last three areas deal with strategic issues, building brand awareness, and brand image. Another budget decision is deciding how much will be spent for strategic advertising and how much will be spent on tactical advertising. Tactical advertising deals with sales promotions and often includes price discounts. Thomson, the United Kingdom's largest tour operator, divides its advertising budget equally between tactical and strategic advertising. It refers to its strategic advertising as advertising to build brand awareness for Thomson and holiday destinations.[21]

Overall Promotional Budget

Another factor in planning the advertising budget is the overall promotional budget. To gain synergy between the different elements of the promotional mix, money should be available for training employees about new promotions, in-house sales promotion materials, collateral material, and PR.

Consistency

In his book *Guerrilla Advertising*, Jay Conrad Levinson states that the advertising budget should be viewed like rent, something that has to be paid each month.[22] When times are tough, there is often a tendency to cut the advertising budget. The rent, employees, utilities, and suppliers all have to be paid; the advertisements for the coming month are seen as discretionary. This view of advertising can lead to continued poor sales and the eventual decline of the business.

Opportunities to Stretch the Budget

Hospitality companies often have ways they can stretch their advertising dollars. Tradeouts are one of these ways. Tradeouts involve trading advertising for products the media company can use, such as rooms, food, or travel. A tradeout can be a good way of getting advertising without using cash. To be a good deal, the target market of the media gained through the trade must match the target market of the restaurant, hotel, or travel company. Second, the advertisements should be played when the market will be exposed to them. Another way of expanding the budget is through cooperative advertising, that is, two or more companies getting together to pay for an ad. For example, a credit card company may pay for a portion of an advertisement if it is mentioned in the ad, and cruise lines will provide cooperative advertising for their top agents. Travel agents can also use tagging, that is, placing their ad below a wholesaler's, resort's, or cruise line's advertisement, so that those reading the ad and interested in the product come to the travel agent's ad immediately after reading the main advertisement.

The Final Budget

The advertising budget is a subset of the marketing budget. It depends on the objectives of the marketing plan and the promotional plan. Setting an advertising budget becomes a complex process. It must consider the other uses of the marketing budget. It must balance the objectives of the advertising plan against the money available from the company. The method most effective for setting a budget is the objective and task method: determining what needs to be done and then developing a budget to accomplish the task, as long as the expense results in positive returns. However, often the budget is dictated by the corporate office. In this case, the marketing manager has to defend his or her case for a higher budget or make do with a lower budget. If a lower budget is required, the budget must be reviewed and prioritized, with the lower priority items being eliminated.

The final advertising budget makes effective use of the funds allocated to the budget. It takes into account funds needed for other areas of the promotional mix. Finally, it provides funds for promotional campaigns throughout the year.

Developing Advertising Strategy

Advertising strategy consists of two major elements: creating advertising messages and selecting advertising media. In the past, companies often viewed media planning as secondary to the message-creation process. The creative department first created good advertisements, and then the media department selected and purchased the best media for carrying those advertisements to desired target audiences. This often caused friction between creatives and media planners.

Today, however, soaring media costs, more-focused target marketing strategies, and the blizzard of new digital and interactive media have promoted the importance of the media-planning function. The decision about which media to use for an ad campaign—television, newspapers, magazines, cell phones, a Web site or an online network, or e-mail—is now sometimes more critical than the creative elements of the campaign. As a result, more and more advertisers are orchestrating a closer harmony between their messages and the media that deliver them. In fact, in a really good ad campaign, you often have to ask, "Is that a media idea or a creative idea?"

Creating the Advertising Message

No matter how big the budget, advertising can succeed only if advertisements gain attention and communicate well. Good advertising messages are especially important in today's costly and cluttered advertising environment. Today, the average household receives more than 180 channels, and consumers have more than 20,000 magazines from which to choose.[23] Add in the countless radio stations and a continuous barrage of catalogs, direct mail, e-mail and online ads, out-of-home media, mobile and social media exposures, and consumers are being bombarded with ads at home, work, and all points in between. For example, Americans are exposed to a cumulative 5.3 trillion online and ad impressions each year and a daily diet of 400 million tweets, 144,000 hours of uploaded YouTube video, and 4.75 billion pieces of shared content on Facebook.[24]

Breaking Through the Clutter

If all this advertising clutter bothers some consumers, it also causes huge headaches for advertisers. Take the situation facing network television advertisers. They pay an average of $354,000 to make a single 30-second commercial. Then, each time they show it, they pay an average of $122,000 for 30 seconds of advertising time during a popular prime-time program. They pay even more if it's an especially popular program, such as *American Idol* ($355,000), *Sunday Night Football* ($594,000), *The Big Bang Theory* ($317,000), or a mega-event such as the *Super Bowl* (nearly $4 million per 30 seconds!).[25] Then their ads are sandwiched in with a clutter of other commercials, announcements, and network promotions, totaling nearly 20 minutes of nonprogram material per prime-time hour, with commercial breaks coming every six minutes on average. Such clutter in television and other ad media has created an increasingly hostile advertising environment.

According to one recent study, more than 70 percent of Americans think there are too many ads on TV, and 62 percent of national advertisers believe that TV ads have become less effective, citing clutter as the main culprit.[26]

Until recently, television viewers were pretty much a captive audience for advertisers. But today's digital wizardry has given consumers a rich new set of information and entertainment choices. With the growth in cable and satellite TV, the Internet, video streaming, tablets, and smartphones, today's viewers have many more options.

Digital technology has also armed consumers with an arsenal of weapons for choosing what they watch or don't watch. Increasingly, thanks to the growth of DVR systems, consumers are choosing not to watch ads. Half of American TV households now have DVRs, and an estimated 67 percent use them to skip commercials. At the same time, video downloads and streaming are exploding, letting viewers to watch programming on their own time terms—with or without commercials.[27]

Thus, advertisers can no longer force-feed the same old cookie-cutter ad messages to captive consumers through traditional media. Just to gain and hold attention, today's advertising messages must be better planned, more imaginative, more entertaining, and more emotionally engaging. Simply interrupting or disrupting consumers no longer works. Instead, unless ads provide information that is interesting, useful, or entertaining, many consumers will simply skip them.

Merging Advertising and Entertainment

To break through the clutter, many marketers have subscribed to a new merging of advertising and entertainment, dubbed "Madison & Vine." You've probably heard of Madison Avenue, the New York City street that houses the headquarters of many of the nation's largest advertising agencies. You may also have heard of Hollywood & Vine, the intersection of Hollywood Avenue and Vine Street in Hollywood, California, long the symbolic heart of the U.S. entertainment industry. Now, Madison Avenue and Hollywood & Vine have come together to form a new intersection—Madison & Vine—that represents the merging of advertising and entertainment in an effort to create new avenues for reaching consumers with more engaging messages.

This merging of advertising and entertainment takes one of two forms: advertainment or branded entertainment. The aim of advertainment is to make ads themselves so entertaining, or so useful, that people want to watch them. There's no chance that you'd watch ads on purpose, you say? Think again. For example, the Super Bowl has become an annual advertainment showcase. Tens of millions of people tune in to the Super Bowl each year, as much to watch the entertaining ads as to see the game. And ads posted online before and after the big game draw tens of millions of views.

These days, it's not unusual to see an entertaining ad or other brand content on YouTube before you see it on TV. And you might well seek it out at a friend's suggestion rather than having it forced on you by the advertiser. Moreover, beyond making their regular ads more engaging, advertisers are also creating new content forms that look less like ads and more like short films or shows. A range of new brand messaging platforms, from Webisodes and blogs to online videos and apps, now blur the line between ads and entertainment.

For example, The Palm Restaurant created a series of Webisodes, which were promoted on its Web site, Facebook page, and were available through YouTube. These Webisodes were also promoted to the 100,000 members of the Palm's Loyalty program, 837 Club. The Webisodes featured "Chef Bruce," Bruce Bozzi, EVP of The Palms, and great grandson of the cofounder of the Palms, in a series of cooking demonstrations.[28] One of the most successful uses of Webisodes is McDonald's "Our Food, Your Questions," series. The series features Grant Imahara, who portrays an investigative reporter asking questions about McDonald's food and going to the food production facilities. The videos promote the quality of the production facility as well as the food ingredients that go into McDonald's products. The videos are promoted on the Web site and available on YouTube. Many of the videos have over a million views with some videos approaching 10 million views.

Another use of entertainment for promoting products is placement of products in movies or television shows. This is referred to as branded entertainment. For example, it might be showing Starbucks' coffee products on the television show, *Morning Joe* on MSNBC. In an episode of *The Apprentice*, participants were required to design a promotional campaign for the Blizzard. Dairy Queen is reported to have paid over $1,000,000 for this placement.[29]

So, Madison & Vine is now the meeting place for the advertising and entertainment industries. The goal is for brand messages and content to become a part of the entertainment rather than interrupting it. As advertising agency JWT puts it, "We believe advertising needs to stop interrupting what people are interested in and be what people are interested in. However, advertisers must be careful that the new intersection itself doesn't become too congested. With all the new ad formats and product placements, Madison & Vine threatens to create even more of the very clutter that it was designed to break through. At that point consumers might decide to take yet a different route."

Message Strategy

The first step in creating effective advertising messages is to plan a message strategy—the general message that will be communicated to consumers. The purpose of advertising is to get consumers to think about or react to the product or company in a certain way. People will react only if they believe they will benefit from doing so. Thus, developing an effective message strategy begins with identifying customer benefits that can be used as advertising appeals.

Ideally, the message strategy will follow directly from the company's broader positioning and customer value strategies. Message strategy statements tend to be plain, straightforward outlines of benefits and positioning points that the advertiser wants to stress. The advertiser must next develop a compelling creative concept—or "big idea"—that will bring the message strategy to life in a distinctive and memorable way. At this stage, simple message ideas become great ad campaigns. Usually, a copywriter and an art director will team up to generate many creative concepts, hoping that one of these concepts will turn out to be the big idea.

The creative concept may emerge as a visualization, a phrase, or a combination of the two. The creative concept will guide the choice of specific appeals to be used in an advertising campaign. Advertising appeals should have three characteristics. First, they should be meaningful, pointing out benefits that make the product more desirable or interesting to consumers. Second, appeals must be believable. Consumers must believe that the product or service will deliver the promised benefits. However, the most meaningful and believable benefits may not be the best ones to feature. Appeals should also be distinctive. They should tell how the product is better than competing brands.

Message Execution

The impact of the message depends on what is said and how it is said: message execution. The advertiser has to put the message across in a way that wins the target market's attention and interest. Advertisers usually begin with a statement of the objective and approach of the desired ad.

The advertising agency's creative staff must find a style, tone, words, and format for executing the message. Any message can be presented in different execution styles, such as the following:

1. **Slice of life** shows one or more people using the product in a normal setting. Restaurants may show friends and family enjoying an evening together at their restaurant.

2. **Lifestyle** shows how a product fits with a lifestyle. For example, an airline advertising its business class featured a businessperson sitting in an upholstered chair in the living room, having a drink, and enjoying the paper.

The other side of the ad featured the same person in the same relaxed position with a drink and a paper in one of the airline's business-class seats.

3. **Fantasy** creates a wonder world around the product or its use. For instance, Cunard's *Sea Goddess* featured a woman lying in a raft in the sea, with the luxury liner anchored in the background. A cocktail server in a tuxedo is walking through the ocean carrying a drink for the woman.

4. **Mood or image** builds a mood or image around the product, such as beauty, love, or serenity. No claim is made about the product except through suggestion. Bally's resort in Las Vegas developed an advertisement designed to change its image after its renovation. The headlines in the ad were "To them a watch does more than tell time, a car is not merely transportation, and their resort is Bally's in Las Vegas."

5. **Musical** shows one or more people or cartoon characters singing a song about the product. Many cola ads have used this format. Certain cultures seem particularly receptive to the use of theme songs and sing-along melodies in advertisements. Australians often use simple but catchy melodies in their advertisements. Brazilians often use adaptations of samba music, particularly music that is popular during carnival.

6. **Personality** symbol creates a character that represents the product. The character might be created by the company; for example, Jack in The Box Restaurants uses the character Jack, a business person with a clown head, as their spokesperson.

7. **Technical expertise** shows the company's expertise with the product. Trivago claims to be able to find great hotel prices for its users.

8. **Scientific evidence** presents survey or scientific evidence that the brand is better or better liked than one or more other brands.

9. **Testimonial evidence** features a highly believable or likable source endorsing the product (e.g., sports personalities, such as Peyton Manning and Phil Mickelson).

Emirates first-class features your own cabin, a shower spa, and a lounge. The first-class cabin fits the lifestyle of the wealthy, who are willing and capable of paying for the service. Courtesy of Emirates.

emirates.com

Make friends in high places

Rub shoulders with some of the most interesting people on the planet at 40,000 ft. Enjoy good company, sparkling conversation, and surprising service in our A380 Onboard Lounge.

Hello Tomorrow   Emirates

The advertiser must choose a tone for the ad. Hyatt uses a positive tone, with ads that say something very positive about its own products. Hyatt ads avoid humor that might take attention away from the message or be misunderstood by its many international guests. By contrast, Taco Bell ads have used humor. To promote their new breakfast offering, they recruited and paid 20 people named Ronald McDonald. The Ronald McDonalds appeared in television ads and on YouTube. Taco Bell did include a disclaimer saying the Ronald McDonalds were not affiliated with McDonald's restaurants, but added "but man, they sure did love it."[30]

Finally, format elements make a difference in an ad's impact and cost. A small change in design can make a big difference in an ad's effect. The illustration is the first thing the reader notices. It must be strong enough to draw attention. Then the headline must effectively entice the right people to read the copy. The copy, the main block of text in the ad, must be simple but strong and convincing. These three elements must effectively work together. Even then, a truly outstanding ad is noted by less than 50 percent of the exposed audience. An even smaller percentage, about 30 percent, can recall the main point of the headline. Only 25 percent will remember the advertiser's name, and fewer than 10 percent read most of the body copy. Less-than-outstanding ads do not even achieve these results.

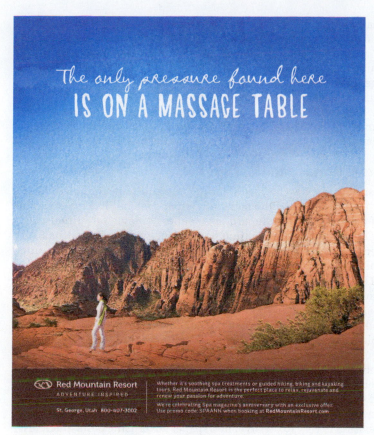

The Red Mountain resort shows what people come to a resort for in its ad: relaxation and rejuvenation. Courtesy of Red Mountain Resort.

Consumer-Generated Messages

Taking advantage of today's interactive technologies, many companies are now tapping consumers for message ideas or actual ads. They are searching existing video sites, setting up their own sites, and sponsoring ad-creation contests and other promotions. Sometimes the results are outstanding; sometimes they are forgettable. If done well, however, user-generated content can incorporate the voice of the customer into brand messages and generate greater consumer brand involvement.

Many brands develop brand Web sites or hold contests that invite consumers to submit ad message ideas and videos. Not all consumer-generated advertising efforts, however, are successful. As many big companies have learned, ads made by amateurs can be well, pretty amateurish. Done well, however, consumer-generated advertising efforts can produce new creative ideas and fresh perspectives on the brand from consumers who actually experience it. Such campaigns can boost consumer involvement and get consumers talking and thinking about a brand and its value to them.[31]

Selecting Advertising Media

The major steps in media selection are (1) deciding on reach, frequency, and impact; (2) choosing among major media types; (3) selecting specific media vehicles; and (4) deciding on media timing.

Deciding on Reach, Frequency, and Impact

To select media, the advertiser must decide what reach and frequency are needed to achieve advertising objectives. Reach is a measure of the percentage of people in the target market who are exposed to the ad campaign during a given period of time. For example, the advertiser might try to reach 70 percent of the target market during the first year. Frequency is a measure of how many times the average person in the target market is exposed to the message. For example, the advertiser might want an average exposure frequency of three. The advertiser must also decide on desired media impact, the qualitative value of message exposure through a given medium. For products that must be demonstrated, television messages using sight and sound are more effective. The same message in one magazine (*Newsweek*) may be more believable than in another (*National Enquirer*).

Suppose that the advertiser's product has the potential to appeal to a market of 1 million consumers. The goal is to reach 700,000 consumers (70 percent of 1 million). Because the average consumer will receive three exposures, 2.1 million exposures (700,000 × 3) must be bought. If the advertiser wants exposures of 1.5 impact (assuming that 1.0 impact is the average), a rated number of exposures of 3.15 million (2.1 million × 1.5) must be bought. If 1,000 exposures with this impact cost $10, the advertising budget must be $31,500 (3,150 ×10). In general, the more reach, frequency, and impact that the advertiser seeks, the larger the advertising budget has to be.

Gross rating points (GRPs) show the gross coverage or duplicated coverage of an advertising campaign. GRPs are determined by multiplying reach times frequency. In the preceding example, an ad with a reach of 700,000 and frequency of three exposures would produce 210 GRPs if the market was 1 million. Each GRP is equal to 1 percent of the market.

Waste is the part of the medium's audience not in the firm's target market.[32] An entrepreneur owning a single restaurant in Worthington, Ohio (north of Columbus), will find that only about 20 percent of those reading the *Columbus Dispatch* will be in that entrepreneur's market area. Thus, he or she will probably advertise in other media. A travel agency may advertise in a newspaper targeted at seniors knowing that only 50 percent of the readers will spend more than $1,000 on travel annually. The travel agency factored this in when they purchased the media. Despite the waste, the medium still offered a good value. In choosing media, the circulation aimed at your target market is the important factor, not the total circulation.

Choosing Among Major Media Types

The media planner has to know the reach, frequency, and impact of each major media type. Table 13–1 summarizes the major advertising media. The major media types, in order of advertising volume, are newspapers, television, direct mail, radio, magazine, and outdoor. Each medium has advantages and limitations. For example, more than 75 percent of Holiday Inn Express guests arrive by car. Jennifer Ziegler, director of marketing for Holiday Inn Express, said, "Billboards serve as a reinforcement. They create top-of-mind awareness that make a difference when last-minute decisions about lodging are being made."[33]

Media planners consider many factors when making their media choices, including the media habits of target consumers. The nature of the product also affects media choices. Resorts are best shown in color magazines. Fast-food ads targeted at young children are best on television. Different types of messages may require different media. A message announcing a Mother's Day buffet would be conveyed effectively on radio or in newspapers. A message that contains technical data, such as an ad explaining the details of a travel package, might be disseminated most effectively in magazines or through direct mail. Cost is also a major factor in media choice. Television is very expensive; newspaper advertising costs much less. The media planner looks at both the total cost of using a particular medium and at the cost per 1,000 exposures, that is, the cost of reaching a 1,000 people.

Ideas about media impact and cost must be reexamined regularly. For many years, television and magazines dominated the media mixes of national advertisers while other media were neglected. Recently, costs and clutter (competition from competing messages) have increased, and audiences have dropped. As a result, many marketers have adopted strategies targeted at narrower segments, and TV and magazine advertising revenues have leveled off or declined. Advertisers have increasingly turned to alternative media, including cable TV, outdoor

TABLE 13–1
Profiles of Major Media Types

Medium	Advantages	Limitations
Newspapers	Flexibility; timeliness; good local market coverage; broad acceptance; high believability	Short lift; poor reproduction quality; small pass-along audience
Television	Combines sight, sound, and motion; appealing to the senses; high attention; high reach; appeals to the senses	High absolute cost; high clutter; fleeting exposure; less audience selectivity
Direct mail	High audience selectivity; flexibility; no ad competition within the same medium; personalization	Relatively high cost; junk mail image
Radio	Good local acceptance; high geographic and demographic selectivity; low cost	Audio only; lower attention ("the half-heard medium") fragmented audiences, music stations being replaced by personal devices
Magazines	High geographic and demographic selectivity; credibility and prestige; high-quality reproduction; long life; good pass-along readership	Long ad purchase lead time; some waste circulation; no guarantee of position
Outdoor	Flexibility; high repeat exposure; low cost; low message competition	Little audience selectivity; creative limitations
Digital and social media	Audience selectivity; low cost; personalization; immediacy, interactive capabilities	Potentially low impact; high audience control of content and exposure

advertising, specialty advertising, and Internet advertising. Given these and other media characteristics, the media planner must decide how much of each type of media to buy.

Selecting Specific Media Vehicles

The media planner must now choose the best specific media vehicles within each general media type. A comparison of the top television shows in the United States with younger (ages 18 to 34) and older audiences (age 35 to 54) found there were no shows that appeared on the top 10 list for both groups. Each group had a unique set. Thus, advertising must know the favorite media of its target market. Magazine vehicles include *Newsweek*, *Conde Nast Traveler*, *The New Yorker*, and *Town and Country*. If advertising is placed in magazines, the media planner must look up circulation figures and the costs of different ad sizes, color options, ad positions, and frequencies for various specific magazines. The planner then evaluates each magazine on such factors as credibility, status, reproduction quality, editorial focus, and advertising submission deadlines. The media planner decides which vehicles give the best reach, frequency, and impact for the money.

Media planners also compute the cost per thousand persons reached by a vehicle. If a full-page, four-color advertisement in the U.S. national edition of *Forbes* costs $148,000 and *Forbes*'s readership is 900,000 people, the cost of reaching a 1,000 persons is $164. The same advertisement in *Bloomberg Businessweek* may cost only $48,100 but reach only 155,000 persons, at a cost per 1,000 of about $310.[34] The media planner would favor magazines with the lower cost per 1,000 for reaching target consumers. In addition to the cost of the ad, the costs of producing ads for different media must also be considered. Although newspaper ads can cost very little to produce, flashy television ads may cost millions.

The media planner must thus balance media cost measures against several media impact factors. First, costs should be balanced against the media vehicle's audience quality. For a corporate hotel brand, business magazine would have high exposure to audience that use their product, whereas *People* magazine would have a low-exposure value. Second, the media planner should consider audience attention. Readers of *Vogue*, for example, typically pay more attention to ads than do readers of *Newsweek*. Third, the planner assesses the vehicle's editorial quality; *Time* and the *Wall Street Journal* are more believable and prestigious than the *National Enquirer*.

Media planners are increasingly developing more sophisticated measures of effectiveness and using them in mathematical models to arrive at the best media mix. Many advertising agencies use computer programs to select the initial media and then make further media schedule improvements based on subjective factors not considered by the media section model.[35]

Deciding on Media Timing

The advertiser must also decide how to schedule advertising over the course of a year. For a hotel or resort, effective advertising requires knowledge of the origin of its guests and how far in advance they make their reservations. If guests living in Connecticut make their reservations in November to go to a Caribbean resort in January, it will not be effective for a resort to advertise in December after consumers have already made their vacation plans. Mauritius launched a major campaign in the United Kingdom in October to create demand for the December holiday season.[36] Restaurants with a strong local demand may decide to vary their advertising to follow the seasonal pattern, to oppose the seasonal pattern, or to be the same all year. Most firms do some seasonal advertising.

Continuity. Scheduling ads evenly within a given period.

Pulsing. Scheduling ads unevenly over a given period.

Finally, the advertiser must choose the pattern of the ads. **Continuity** means scheduling ads evenly within a given period. **Pulsing** means scheduling ads unevenly over a given period. Thus, 52 ads could either be scheduled at one per week during the year or pulsed in several bursts. Those who favor pulsing feel that the audience will learn the message more completely and that money can be saved. However, some media planners believe that although pulsing achieves awareness, it sacrifices depth of advertising communications.

Road Blocking

Advertisers can sometimes use a tactic known as *road blocking* to help ensure that an intended audience receives the advertising message. The tropical island resort Great Keppel in Queensland, Australia, knew that its audience in Brisbane, Sydney, and Melbourne listened to certain FM rock stations. Great Keppel purchased drive-time radio spots for exactly the same time on all rock stations in the three markets. This prevented listeners from switching stations to avoid the advertisement.

Evaluating Advertising Effectiveness and the Return on Advertising Investment

Managers of advertising programs should regularly evaluate the communication and sales effects of advertising.

Measuring the communication effect reveals whether an ad is communicating well. Called **copy testing**, this process can be performed before or after an ad is printed or broadcast. There are three major methods of advertising pretesting. The first is **direct rating**, in which the advertiser exposes a consumer panel to alternative ads and asks them to rate the ads. Direct ratings show how well the ads attract attention and how they affect consumers. Although it is an imperfect measure of an ad's actual impact, a high rating indicates a potentially effective ad. In **portfolio tests**, consumers view or listen to a portfolio of advertisements, taking as much time as they need. The interviewer then asks the respondent to recall all the ads and their contents. The recall can be either aided or unaided by the interviewer. Recall level indicates the extent to which an ad stands out and how well its message is understood and remembered. **Laboratory tests** use equipment to measure consumers' physiological reactions to an ad: heartbeat, blood pressure, pupil dilation, and perspiration. The tests measure an ad's attention-getting power but reveal little about its impact on beliefs, attitudes, or intentions.

There are two popular methods of posttesting ads. Using **recall tests**, the advertiser asks people who have been exposed to magazines or television programs to recall everything they can about the advertisers and products that they saw. Recall scores indicate the ad's power to be noticed and retained. In **recognition tests**, the researcher asks readers of, for instance, a given issue of a magazine to point out what they have seen. Recognition scores can be used to assess the ad's impact in different market segments and to compare the company's ads with those of competitors.

Measuring the Sales Effect

What quantity of sales is caused by an ad that increases brand awareness by 20 percent and brand preference by 10 percent? The sales effect of advertising is often harder to measure than the communication effect. Sales are affected by many factors besides advertising, such as product features, price, and availability. One way to measure sales effect is to compare past sales with past advertising expenditures. Another is through experiments.

Measuring the Awareness Effect

If the objective of the advertising is to inform, then conducting a pretest and a posttest of the target markets' awareness of the product or brand is often used as a method of measuring the effect of an advertising campaign. For example, in Figure 13–4, we saw that 60 percent of the market is not aware of the product of brand B. The objectives of brand B's advertising campaign are to increase awareness to 50 percent and increase trail from 30 to 50 percent of those who were aware of brand B. By replicating the research that produced the data for Figure 13–4, they could see if the campaign met its goals.

To spend a large advertising budget wisely, advertisers must define their advertising objectives, develop a sound budget, create a good message, make media decisions, and evaluate the results.

Copy testing. A process performed before or after an ad is printed or broadcast.

Direct rating. The advertiser exposes a consumer panel to alternative ads and asks them to rate the ads.

Portfolio tests. Consumers view or listen to a portfolio of advertisements, taking as much time as they need.

Laboratory test. This test uses equipment to measure consumers' physiological reactions to an ad: heartbeat, blood pressure, pupil dilation, and perspiration.

Recall tests. The advertiser asks people who have been exposed to magazines or television programs to recall everything they can about the advertisers and products that they saw.

Recognition tests. The researcher asks readers of, for instance, a given issue of a magazine to point out what they have seen.

◾◾◾ CHAPTER REVIEW

I. Promotion Mix

A. Advertising. Any paid form of nonpersonal presentation and promotion of ideas, goods, or services by an identified sponsor.

B. Sales promotion. Short-term incentives to encourage the purchase or sale of a product or service.

C. Personal selling. Personal presentation by the firm's sales force for the purpose of making sales and building customer relationships.

D. Public relations. Building good relations with the company's various publics by obtaining favorable publicity, building up a good corporate image, and handling or heading off unfavorable rumors, stories, and events.

E. Direct and digital marketing. Engaging directly with carefully targeted individual consumers and customer communities to both obtain an immediate response and build lasting customer relationships.

II. Integrated Marketing Communications. The company carefully integrates its many communication channels to deliver a clear, consistent, and compelling message about the organization and its brands.

A. The new marketing communications landscape

The digital age has spawned a host of new information and communication tools.

B. The Shifting Marketing Communications Model

1. Consumers are changing. Communication through digital, mobile and social media are becoming more important.

2. Marketers are shifting away from mass marketing to targeted communication.

3. The digital age has spawned new communication tools including smartphones and tablets.

C. The need for integrated marketing communications

1. Integrated marketing communications calls for recognizing all touch points where the customer may encounter content about the company and its brands.

2. As mass markets have fragmented, marketers are shifting away from mass marketing to narrowly defined micromarkets.

3. The digital age has spawned a host of new information and communication tools, from smartphones and tablets to the Internet and cable and satellite television systems.

D. A view of the communications process

1. IMC calls for recognizing all contact points where the customer may encounter the company and its brands. The company wants to deliver a consistent and positive message with each contact.

2. IMC ties together all the company's messages and images. The company's television and print advertisements have the same message,

look, and feel as its e-mail and personal selling communications. And its public relations materials project the same image as its Web site.

3. Four more are major communication functions—*encoding*, *decoding*, *response*, and *feedback*. The last element is *noise* in the system.

III. Steps in Developing Effective Communications

A. Identify the target audience. A marketing communicator starts with a clear target audience in mind.

B. Determine the communication objective. The six buyer readiness states are awareness, knowledge, liking, preference, conviction, and purchase.

C. Design a message

1. **AIDA model.** The message should get attention, hold interest, arouse desire, and obtain action.

2. **Three problems that the marketing communicator must solve:**

   a. **Message content (what to say).** There are three types of appeals:

      i. Rational appeals relate to audience self-interest. They show that the product will produce desired benefits.

      ii. Emotional appeals attempt to provoke emotions that motivate purchase.

      iii. Moral appeal is directed to the audience's sense of what is right and proper.

   b. **Message structure (how to say it)**

      i. Whether to draw a conclusion or leave it to the audience.

      ii. Whether to present a one- or two-sided argument.

      iii. Whether to present the strongest arguments first or last.

   c. **Message format (how to say it symbolically)**

      i. Visual ad: using novelty and contrast, eye-catching pictures and headlines, distinctive formats, message size and position, color, shape, and movement.

      ii. Audio ad: using words, sounds, and voices.

D. Select communication channels

1. **Personal communication channels.** Used for products that are expensive and complex. It can create opinion leaders to influence others to buy.

2. **Nonpersonal communication channels.** Include media (print, broadcast, and display media), atmospheres, and events.

E. Message source. Using attractive sources to achieve higher attention and recall, such as using celebrities.

F. Measure the results of the communication. Evaluate the effects on the targeted audience.

IV. Setting the Total Promotion Budget and Mix

A. Setting the total promotional budget

1. **Affordable method.** A budget is set based on what management thinks it can afford.
2. **Percentage of sales method.** Companies set promotion budget at a certain percentage of current or forecasted sales or a percentage of the sales price.
3. **Competitive parity method.** Companies set their promotion budgets to match competitors.
4. **Objective and task method.** Companies develop their promotion budget by defining specific objectives, determining the tasks that must be performed to achieve these objectives, and estimating the costs of performing them.

B. Shaping the Overall Promotion Mix

C. The nature of each promotional tool

1. **Advertising** suggests that the advertised product is standard and legitimate; it is used to build a long-term image for a product and to stimulate quick sales. However, it is also considered impersonal one-way communication.
2. **Personal selling** builds personal relationships, keeps the customers' interests at heart to build long-term relationships, and allows personal interactions with customers. It is also considered the most expensive promotion tool per contact.
3. **Sales promotion** includes an assortment of tools: coupons, contests, cents-off deals, premiums, and others. It attracts consumer attention and provides information. It creates a stronger and quicker response. It dramatizes product offers and boosts sagging sales. It is also considered short lived.
4. **Public relations** has believability. It reaches prospective buyers and dramatizes a company or product.
5. **Direct and digital marketing** are more targeted, immediate and personalized. It includes direct mail, mobile, and social media.

D. Promotion mix strategies

1. **Type of product and market.** The importance of different promotional tools varies among consumers and commercial markets.
2. **Push versus pull strategy**
   a. **Push strategy.** The company directs its marketing activities at channel members to induce them to order, carry, and promote the product.
   b. **Pull strategy.** A company directs its marketing activities toward final consumers to induce them to buy the product.
   c. **Buyer readiness state.** Promotional tools vary in their effects at different stages of buyer readiness.
   d. **Product life-cycle stage.** The effects of different promotion tools also vary with stages of the product life cycle.

V. Advertising.
We define advertising as any paid form of nonpersonal presentation and promotion of ideas, goods, or services by an identified sponsor.

VI. Major Decisions in Advertising

A. Setting objectives.
Objectives should be based on information about the target market, positioning, and market mix. Advertising objectives can be classified by their aim: to inform, persuade, or remind.

1. **Informative advertising.** Used to introduce a new product category or when the objective is to build primary demand.
2. **Persuasive advertising.** Used as competition increases and a company's objective becomes building selective demand.
3. **Reminder advertising.** Used for mature products because it keeps the consumers thinking about the product.

B. Setting the advertising budget.
Factors to consider in setting a budget are the stage in the product life cycle, market share, competition and clutter, advertising frequency, and product differentiation.

1. Strategic versus tactical budgets
2. Overall promotional budget
3. Consistency
4. Opportunity to stretch the budget
5. The final budget

C. Developing the advertising strategy

D. Creating the advertising message

1. **Breaking through the clutter**
2. **Merging advertising and entertainment**
3. **Message strategy**
4. **Message execution.** The impact of the message depends on what is said and how it is said.
5. **Consumer-generated messages**
6. **Message evaluation and selection.** Messages should be meaningful, distinctive, and believable.

E. Selecting advertising media

1. **Deciding on reach, frequency, and impact.** Reach is a measure of how many people in the target market are exposed to the ad. Frequency is the number of times the average person in the target market will see the ad. Impact is a qualitative measure of the value of the message exposure through a given medium.
2. **Choosing among major media types.** Choose among newspapers, television, direct mail, radio, magazines, and outdoor.
3. **Selecting specific media vehicles.** Costs should be balanced against the media vehicles: audience quality, ability to gain attention, and editorial quality.
4. **Deciding on media timing.** The advertiser must decide on how to schedule advertising over the course of a year based on seasonal fluctuation in demand, lead time in making reservations, and if they want to use continuity in their scheduling or use a pulsing format.
5. **Road blocking.**

F. **Evaluating advertising effectiveness and the return on advertising investment.** There are three major methods of advertising pretesting and two popular methods of posttesting ads.
1. **Measuring the communication effect**—copy testing
   a. **Direct rating.** The advertiser exposes a consumer panel to alternative ads and asks them to rate the ads.
   b. **Portfolio tests.** The interviewer asks the respondent to recall all ads and their contests after letting the respondent listen to a portfolio of advertisements.
   c. **Laboratory tests.** Equipment is used to measure consumers' physiological reactions to an ad.

2. **Posttesting**
   a. **Recall tests.** The advertiser asks people who have been exposed to magazines or television programs to recall everything that they can about the advertisers and products they saw.
   b. **Recognition tests.** The researcher asks people exposed to media to point out the advertisements they have seen.
   c. **Measuring the sales effect.** The sales effect can be measured by comparing past sales with past advertising expenditures and through experiments.
   d. **Measuring the awareness effect.** The target market's awareness of the brand or product is measured before and after the advertising.

■■■ DISCUSSION QUESTIONS

1. Explain the difference between promotion and advertising.
2. Explain the concept of integrated marketing communications.
3. Recently, a number of restaurants have shifted some of their promotional budget from advertising to public relations. What benefits does public relations offer that would make the restaurants spend more?
4. The percentage of sales method is one of the most common ways of setting a promotional budget. What are some advantages and disadvantages of this method?

5. Apply the five major tools in the marketing communication mix to a hospitality or travel company by showing how a company can use all these tools.
6. According to advertising expert Stuart Henderson Britt, good advertising objectives spell out the intended audience, the advertising message, the desired effects, and the criteria for determining whether the effects were achieved (e.g., not just "increase awareness" but "increase awareness 20 percent"). Why should these components be part of the advertising objective? What are some effects that an advertiser wants a campaign to achieve?

■■■ EXPERIENTIAL EXERCISES

Do one of the following:

1. Provide an example of a communication from a hospitality or travel company that does a good job of communicating with a specific market segment. The example can be any form of communication (e.g., an advertisement, a sales promotion, or publicity).

2. Find an example of a promotion for a hospitality company that uses the push promotion strategy. Explain how the company is using the strategy.
3. Provide evidence that a hospitality company is using integrated marketing communications, by finding two communications by the firm that have the same message, look, and feel.

■■■ INTERNET EXERCISE

Find a print advertisement or a commercial on YouTube that includes socially responsible advertising. Do the examples you found seem authentic? Explain your answer.

■■■ REFERENCES

1 Based on information from "The Cow Campaign: A Brief History," www.chick-fil-a.com/Cows/Campaign-History (accessed June 2014); "Company Fact Sheet," www.chick-fil-a.com/Company/HighlightsFact-Sheets (accessed June 2014); Thomas Pardee, "Armed with a Beloved Product and a Strong Commitment to Customer Service, Fast Feeder Continues to Grow," *Advertising Age*, October 18, 2010, http://adage.com/prinV146491/; Brian Morrissey, "Chick-fil-A's Strategy: Give Your Fans Something to Do," *AdWeek*, October 3, 2009, www.adweek.com/prinV106477; Information from various other pages and press releases at www.chick-fil-a.com and www.chick-fil-a.com/Pressroom/Press-Releases (accessed September 2014).

2 These definitions, except for sales promotion, are from *Marketing Definitions: A Glossary of Marketing Terms* (Chicago, IL: American Marketing Association, 1995). Other definitions can be found on www.marketingpower.com/live/mg-dictionary.php.

3 See Jon Lafayette, "4A's Conference: Agencies Urged to Embrace New Technologies," *Broadcasting & Cable*, March 8, 2011, www.broadcastingcable.com/news/advertising-and-marketing/4asconference-agencies-urged-embrace-new-technologies/52550; David Gelles, "Advertisers Rush to Master Fresh Set of Skills," *Financial Times*, March 7, 2012, www.ft.com/intl/cms/s/0/8383bbae-5e20-11e1-b1e9-00144feab-dc0.html#axzz1xUrmM3KK.

4 See "Advertisers Blend Digital and TV for Well-Rounded Campaigns," *eMarketer*, March 12, 2014, www.emarketer.com/Article/Advertisers-Blend-Digital-TV-Well-Rounded-Campaigns/1010670.

5 See "Thrill of the Chase: Coca-Cola Invites Fans to Shape Storyline of Big Game Ad," *Coca Cola Journey*, January 25, 2013, www.Coca-colacompany.com/stories/thrill-of-the-chase-coca-colainvites-fans-to-shape-storyline-of-big-game-ad; Dale Buss, "Super Bowl Ad Watch: Crowdsourcing Peaks with Coke's 'Mirage' Campaign, *BrandChannel*, January 22, 2013, www.brandchannel.com/home/posV2013/01/22/SuperBowl-Coke-012213.aspx; Natalie Zmuda, "Watching the Super Bowl from Coca-Cola's War Room(s)," *Advertising Age*, February 4, 2013, http://adage.com/ prinV239582/.

6 Konnie Le May, "South Dakota Tribes Beating Tom-toms to Drum Up Increased Tourist Trade," *Star-Ledger* (May 8, 1994): Sec. 8, 6.

7 For more on message content and structure, see Leon G. Schiffman and Leslie Lazar Kanuk, *Consumer Behavior*, 4th ed. (Upper Saddle River, NJ: Prentice Hall, 1991), Chapter 10; Frank R. Kardes, "Spontaneous Inference Processes in Advertising: The Effects of Conclusion Omission and Involvement on Persuasion," *Journal of Consumer Research* (September 1988): 225–233.

8 Jonah Bloom, "The Truth Is: Consumers Trust Fellow Buyers Before Marketers," *Advertising Age*, February 13, 2006, p. 25; "Jack Morton Publishes New Realities 2012 Research," press release, January 26, 2012, www.jackmorton.com/news/article.aspx?itemiD=106.

9 www.bzzagent.com and http://about.bzzagent.com/ (accessed September 2014).

10 *Marketing Glossary Dictionary*, American Marketing Association, http://www.marketingpower.com/mgdictionary.php?Searched=1&SearchFor=recall%20test (accessed December 12, 2004).

11 "Sheraton Wakes Up," *Hotels* (January 2004): 20.

12 For a more comprehensive discussion on setting promotion budgets, see Michael L. Rothschild, *Advertising* (Lexington, MA: D.C. Heath, 1987), Chapter 20.

13 Quoted in Daniel Seligman, "How Much for Advertising?" *Fortune* (December 1956): 123.

14 The Hospitality Research Group of PKF Consulting, as cited in *Hotel and Motel Management* (May 15, 2000): 44.

15 Michael S. Morgan, "Traveler's Choice: The Effects of Advertising and Prior Stay," *Cornell Hotel and Restaurant Administration Quarterly*, 32, no. 4 (1991): 40–49.

16 "The Rise (and Fall) of Cost per Call," *Sales and Marketing Management* (April 1990): 26.

17 For more on advertising and the product life cycle, see John E. Swan and David R. Rink, "Fitting Market Strategy to Product Life Cycles," *Business Horizons* (January/February 1982): 60–67.

18 Leslie Ann Hogg, *50 More Promotions That Work for Restaurants* (New York: Walter Mathews Associates, 1989), p. 11.

19 Peter C. Yesawich, "Execution and Measurement of Programs," *Cornell Hotel and Restaurant Administration Quarterly*, 29, no. 4 (1989): 89.

20 Gerald J. Tellis, "Advertising Exposure, Loyalty, and Brand Purchase: A Two-Stage Model of Choice," *Journal of Marketing Research* (May 1988): 57–70.

21 Scheherazade Daneshkhu, "Media: A Trade in Dreams of Escape," *Financial Times* (February 10, 1997): 15.

22 Jay Conrad Levinson, *Guerrilla Advertising* (New York: Houghton Mifflin, 1994).

23 Justin Bachman, "The Ugly Numbers Behind Unbundled Cable," *Bloomberg Businessweek*, December 6, 2013, www.businessweek.com/articles/2013-12-06/the-ugly-numbers-behindunbundled-cable-tv; Thad McIlroy, "The Future of Magazines," *The Future of Publishing*, July 10, 2013, http://thefutureofpublishing.com/industries/the- future-of-magazines/.

24 Kelsey Ubert and Kristen Tynski, "Research: The Emotions that Make Marketing Campaigns Go Viral," HBR Slog Network, October 24, 2013, http://blogs.hbr.org/2013/10/research-the-emotions-that-make-marketing-campaigns-go-viral/ (accessed August 17, 2015).

25 "Results of 4A's 2011 Television Production Cost Survey," January 22, 2013, www.aaaa.org/news/bulletins/pages/tvprod_01222013.aspx; Sam Thielman, "The New Hour Is 43 Minutes Long," *Adweek*, June 24, 2013, p. 12; Jeanine Poggi, "TV Ad Prices," *Advertising Age*, October 20, 2013, http://adage.com/prinV244832; "Who Bought What in Super Bowl XLVIII," *Advertising Age*, February 3, 2014, http://adage.com/prinV244024.

26 "Advertising in the U.S.: Synovate Global Survey Shows Internet, Innovation and Online Privacy a Must" (December 3, 2009), http://www.synovate.com/news/article/2009/12/advertising-m-the-us-synovate-global-survey-shows-internet-innovation-and-on-line-privacy-a-must.html; Katy Bachman, "Survey: Clutter Causing TV Ads to Lack Effectiveness," *MediaWeek* (February 8, 2010).

27 Caleb Garling, "How Television Advertising Deals with DVRs Destroying Their Business," *SFGate*, December 27, 2013, http://blog.sfgate.com/

techchron/2013/12/27/dvr-advertisements/; "No Hardware, No Problem: VOD Lets Users Time-Shift with Ease," September 9, 2013, www.nielsen.com/us/en/newswire/2013/no-hardware--no-problem--vod-lets-users-time-shift-with-ease.html.

28 Amanda Baltazar, The Palm Connects Through Webisodes, *Full Service Restaurant Magazine*, July 23, 2012, http://www.fsrmagazine.com/content/palm-connects-through-webisodes (accessed August 14, 2015).

29 Product Placement, *Emerging-Advertising-Media*, undated, https://emerging-advertising-media.wikispaces.com/Product+Placement (accessed August 14, 2015).

30 Real Ronald McDonalds to Launch Its New Breakfast Errol Morris finds 25 subversive spokesmen By David Griner, Adweek.com, March 27, 2014, http://www.adweek.com/news/advertising-branding/ad-day-taco-bell-recruits-real-ronald-mcdonalds-launch-its-new-breakfast-156571 (accessed August 14, 2015).

31 For more on consumer-generated advertising, see Emma Hall, "Most Winning Creative Work Involves Consumer Participation," *Advertising Age* (January 6, 2010), http://adage.com/print?article_id=141329; Stuart Elliott, "Do-It-Yourself Super Ads," *New York Times* (February 8, 2010), www.nytimes.com; Michael Learmonth, "Brands Team Up for User-Generated-Ad Contests," *Advertising Age* (March 23, 2009): 8; Rich Thomaselli, "If Consumer Is Your Agency, It's Time for Review," *Advertising Age* (May 17, 2010): 2.

32 Joel R. Evans and Barry Berman, *Principles of Marketing* (Upper Saddle River, NJ: Prentice Hall, 1995), p. 432.

33 Jeff Higley, "Hoteliers Emphasize Importance of Billboard Marketing," *Hotel and Motel Management* (November 3, 2003): 76.

34 *Forbes and Bloomberg Businessweek* cost and circulation data found online at www.bloombergmedia.com/magazine/businessweeklrates/ and www.forbesmedia.com/forbes-magazine-rates/ (accessed September 2014).

35 See Roland T. Rust, *Advertising Media Models: A Practical Guide* (Lexington, MA: Lexington Books, 1986).

36 "Mauritius launches 1 m ad Campaign," *Travel Trade Gazette* (October 29, 2004): 60.

Promoting Products: Public Relations and Sales Promotions

With only two weeks left before the opening of the 2013 Calgary Stampede, the worst flood the city of Calgary, Alberta, Canada had ever witnessed submerged much of the Stampede's park area.

Each July, Calgary hosts over 1 million visitors during the 10-day Stampede. This not-for-profit event is an integral part of Western Canada. The principal event—a world-class rodeo—is accompanied by musical events, exhibitions, and a myriad of food vendor booths with offerings ranging from hamburgers to scorpion pizza.

Visitor expenditures during the Stampede exceed $300 million for hotels, restaurants, and other local businesses. Additionally, the Stampede serves as a major unifying event.

The flood in Alberta had attracted the attention of worldwide media creating doubt about the future of the 2013 Stampede. Then an unexpected event occurred that initiated a dramatic marketing program.

The following was reprinted with the written permission of the Calgary Stampede:

Social Media Initiative—"Hell or High Water"

In the early afternoon of Saturday, June 22, an image appeared on Twitter featuring the Calgary Stampede name and the words "Hell or High Water." Very quickly the image was shared across social media. Developed by an unknown person, the popularity of the phrase was immediate and became a tagline to the optimism, power, and resiliency of the community to get the job done no matter what obstacles we faced. Unfortunately at that point in time, Stampede Park was still in a state of emergency and as an organization we could not be so bold.

Objectives
After reading this chapter, you should be able to:

1. Understand the different public relations activities: press relations, product publicity, corporate communications, lobbying, and counseling.

2. Understand the public relations process: research, establishing marketing objectives, defining the target audience, choosing the PR message and vehicles, and evaluating PR results.

3. Explain how companies use public relations to communicate and influence important publics.

4. Explain how sales promotion campaigns are developed and implemented.

5. Implement a crisis management program in a hospitality business.

While we couldn't be certain there would be a Stampede, we could be certain of our support to our community and neighborhood. We adopted the phrase and the rallying spirit behind it and by the end of the day decided to design a t-shirt fitting within the already established Stampede brand. The shirt would be a tangible way to show individuals' support for Calgary and tell the world that this flood would not break the spirit of our community.

On Sunday, June 23, the t-shirt was posted for sale online at the Stampede Store, with proceeds donated to the Canadian Red Cross Alberta Floods Fund.

Target Audience

The Hell or High Water campaign was social in the truest sense of the word. It emerged from our social media community, was embraced by the Stampede and promoted exclusively through our social and digital channels so our main target audience really was our social media community. While we thought the shirt would mainly resonate in Calgary, Alberta and across Canada, we didn't expect how far the shirt would reach—truly showing the power of social media.

Execution

The shirt was promoted exclusively through social media and digital properties because of timing, costs and to connect to the online purchase more quickly. We used Facebook, Twitter, Instagram, as well as our website to link directly to the online store. As demand for the shirts exceeded all expectations, we communicated daily updates through these channels and kept the interest in the shirts high which helped push sales. When our community asked if kids' sizing would be available we went one step further and created a Heck or High Water version for the little ones that had adult-size attitude, with kid-friendly language!

From a logistics perspective, several partners and numerous volunteers assisted us in the packaging and distribution of shirts so that we could get them on people's backs in time for Stampede. To get some perspective on the scope of the project, the following were required to fulfill the overwhelming number of Hell/Heck or High Water shirts ordered:

1 cargo plane	10 warehouse and customer service
2 warehouses	staff
2 shirt distributors	25 WestJet employees
3 volunteer sign up sites	40 volunteers working 2 shifts per
4, 24-hour silk screeners	day, 7 days a week
5 data specialists	80 giant Canada Post containers
5 distribution managers	100 rolls of packing tape
6 companies offering workers	35,000+ labels, bags and boxes
9 courier companies	160,000+ black t-shirts

Results

Beyond individual sales, many corporations took the message to heart and jumped onboard as well. Canadian airline, WestJet bought thousands of shirts for their staff around the country. Bennett Jones' law firm sent shirts to their associates in firms around the world. The Canadian Tourism Commission placed two orders as demand from tourism partners to support the cause continued to grow.

Calgary's media-savvy Mayor, Naheed Nenshi, sang the praises of the campaign and the spirit it defined whenever he had the chance. Both local and national media picked up on the groundswell of support, referencing the defiance of the campaign in their broadcasts. Sales of shirts spiked with more than 19,000 shirts being sold just one day. Shirts were shipped around the world to destinations including Australia, Switzerland, Denmark, Ireland, Japan, Norway, Sweden, New Zealand, Russia, and the United States. When sales were finally closed on July 14, just 21 days after they began, the Calgary Stampede presented a check to the Canadian Red Cross Alberta Floods Fund for $2.1 million. It was the largest single donation to the Fund, more than $1 million more than the next highest donation.

With the Hell or High Water campaign such a success, an even bigger accomplishment was opening our gates for Stampede 101 on July 5. Expectations were modest, after all, more than 10,000 people were still displaced from their homes and much of the city was weeks or months away from returning to normal. Despite bad weather for much of the opening weekend, once again we welcomed more than 1.1 million people to Stampede Park.

Attendance figures were down slightly from 2012 and 2011, yet still spoke to the draw of the Stampede as a gathering place for the community. Comments on social channels were overwhelmingly positive with many people posting that they would be coming to Stampede Park to show off their shirts. Thousands of shirts were seen on-Park, tens of thousands more were sold on-Park and Hell or High Water was a phrase that was heard in every corner of the Park.

Results from our 2013 guest experience survey showed that the flood had no real impact on guest experience on Park but did drive overall goodwill towards the event—46% cited their main reason for attending was to show their support of the community while 32% attended as support towards the efforts of rebuilding Stampede Park in time to open up the gates on July 5. Ninety-three percent of the guests indicated they would return, with 65% saying they definitely would return.

The local tourism industry was obviously affected by the floods as well. Calgary's hotel industry saw a slight drop in occupancy in June but it rebounded in July with rates higher than 2012 when the Stampede celebrated its Centennial. The spirit of Hell or High Water would not be lost on the rest of the city as Tourism Calgary's marketing campaign soon after the flood assured everyone that Calgary was open for business.[1]

◾◾◾ Public Relations

"Public relations, perhaps the most misunderstood part of marketing communications, can be the most effective tools."[2] Definitions for public relations differ widely. We think that this definition by Hilton best fits the hospitality industry: "The process by which we create a positive image and customer preference through third-party endorsement."[3]

Public relations. The process by which a positive image and customer preference are created through third-party endorsement.

Public relations (PR) is an important marketing tool that until recently was treated as a marketing stepchild. PR is moving into an explosive growth stage. Companies are realizing that mass marketing is no longer the answer to some of their communication needs. Advertising costs continue to rise while audience reach continues to decline. Advertising clutter reduces the impact of each ad. Sales promotion costs have also increased as channel intermediaries demand lower prices and better commissions and deals. Personal selling can cost over $500 a call. In this environment, PR holds the promise of a cost-effective promotional tool. The creative use of news events, publications, social events, community relations, and other PR techniques offers companies a way to distinguish themselves and their products from competitors.[4]

The PR department of cruise lines, restaurant chains, airlines, and hotels is typically located at corporate headquarters. Often, its staff is so busy dealing with various publics—stockholders, employees, legislators, and community leaders—that PR support for product marketing objectives tends to be neglected. Many four- and five-star hotel chains have corrected this deficiency by hiring local PR managers.

In the past, it was common for the marketing function and PR function to be handled by two different departments within the firm. Today, these two functions are increasingly integrated. There are several reasons for this integration. First, companies are calling for more market-oriented PR. They want their PR departments to manage PR activities that contribute toward marketing the company and improving the bottom line. Second, companies are establishing marketing PR groups to support corporate/product promotion and image-making directly. Thus, marketing PR serves the marketing department.

Social Media

Social media has proven to be a great way to reach thousands of customers and potential customers. Today, most PR campaigns use Internet: Web sites, blogs, and social networks such as YouTube, Facebook, and Twitter are providing interesting new ways to reach more people. "The core strengths of public relations—the ability to tell a story and spark conversation—play well into the nature of such social media," says a PR expert. Consider the Papa John's "Camaro Search" PR campaign.[5]

During a road trip to find his long-lost Camaro, John Schnatter, the "Papa John" of Papa John's pizza, set a record for the world's highest pizza delivery (at the Willis Tower's Sky deck in Chicago), rang the closing bell at the NASDAQ stock exchange, and visited a children's hospital. The road trip got solid pickup in the media, with stories in the *New York Times*, the *Wall Street Journal*, and *USA Today*. ABC World News Tonight, CNBC, and CNN also covered the story, which included a $250,000 reward for the person reuniting Schnatter with his beloved Camaro Z28. These were all traditional pre-Web kinds of PR moves.

But unlike the old days, online social media was a key to getting word out about this Papa John's journey. A Web site dedicated to the trip drew 660,000 visitors. On the day of the media conference announcing Schnatter's reunion with his old Chevy classic—Kentuckian Jeff Robinson turned up with the car and took home the cash—there were more than 1,000 tweets about him finding his car, with links galore. In addition, hundreds of people posted photos of themselves on Facebook (in their own Camaros) picking up the free pizza Papa John offered to all Camaro owners as part of the celebration. In all, the Web was buzzing about the Camaro Search story. Pre-Web, "there were different techniques used for PR—speeches, publicity, awards," says a PR executive. "Now we're applying the same mindset to social media to build relationships."

PR Changes Due to Social Media

Social media has increasingly become mainstream media, particularly for younger consumers of hospitality and tourism. This has created challenges for PR professionals and was summed up by Michael Ni, a digital strategist for the Hawaii Visitors and Convention Bureau (CVB).[6]

Ni started his career in PR before social media gained its current importance. His position at CVB now involves working on paid advertising, a new function for travel destinations. Ni states it is important to make sure both PR and advertising align with the CVB's messaging. He points out that communication must be integrated to make sure it gets the intended message across to the audience." "According to Skift.com, Destinations now approach instagrammars and other social influencers to get publicity through those accounts. Research shows the general public sees these regular people as being like them and are more trusted as information sources today than in the past," said Brittani Wood, an account supervisor at DCI.[7]

Other tourism professionals expressed similar opinions. These opinions came from PR/communications managers in Dallas, Seattle, and Chicago.

1. Media familiarization trips are now more about journalists sharing their experiences instantly to their audiences.

2. There is now more networking and pitching with journalists via social media across all platforms.

3. Social media has affected communication with international journalists. A personal relationship is developed.

■■■ Major Activities of PR Departments

PR departments perform five activities discussed next, not all of which feed into direct product support.

Press Relations

Press relations. Placing newsworthy information into the news media to attract attention

The aim of **press relations** is to place newsworthy information into the news media to attract attention to a person, product, or service. One reason for the growth of press relations in the hospitality industry is its credibility. Most types of publicity are viewed by the consumer as third-party information. A favorable write-up of a restaurant in the local newspaper by the food editor has more impact than an advertisement written by the restaurant's management.

Product Publicity

Product publicity. Various efforts to publicize specific products.

Product publicity involves various efforts to publicize specific products. Special events such as food festivals, redesigned products such as a newly renovated hotel, and products that are popular because of current trends, such as nonfat desserts, are all potential candidates for publicity.

Tokyo's Narita International Airport transformed Terminal 3 walkways into a promotion for the 2020 Summer Olympic Games. The transformation also changed walking lanes into useful running tracks for travelers on a tight schedule to catch their flights. The running tracks look and feel like the shock absorbing tracks used in Olympic events. The architect chose not to install traditional moving sidewalks but instead decided to provide a change that would promote Olympics, promote good health, and assist in meeting tight schedules.[8]

New Products

New products are the lifeblood of any industry, including tourism/hospitality. Unfortunately, some communities and companies are slow to recognize trends in consumer preferences. Picnics by a lake remain popular but they are not an attractive substitute for the outdoor adventure needs of younger segments.

Mountain bike riding does not depend upon the existence of nearby mountains. Today, most consumers live in urban/suburban environments. Urban cities and countries have developed facilities for most sports with an oversupply of some such as golf courses in some locations. Mountain bikes and skateboard parks are exceptions.

Progressive bike ramps can be constructed in urban areas. These provide recreation and practice for mountain bike riders. Companies such as PBR (Progressive Bike Ramps) offer planning and construction assistance.[9]

A vital factor holding back the construction of bike ramps by city councils and private entrepreneurs is lack of knowledge and fear of injury and lawsuits. The mountain bike sector appears to lack a sufficient ongoing publicity program aimed at the public and decision makers.

A mountain bike association (IMBA) has grown to over 150 chapters with 35,000 members in 30 countries who are reached through Twitter. Over 800 retail and corporate supporters include Bell Helmets, Specialized Bicycle Components, Trek Bicycle Corporation, SCRAM Corporation, Shimano-American Corporation, and Subaru.[10] Given the appeal of mountain biking, great publicity opportunities exist.

Corporate Communication

Corporate communication. This activity covers internal and external communications and promotes understanding of an organization.

Corporate communication covers internal and external communications and promotes understanding of the organization. One important marketing aspect of corporate communication is directed toward employees, such as company newsletters. Companies also need to manage their communication with stockholders to make sure they understand the company's goals and objectives.

Lobbying

Lobbying. Dealing with legislators and government officials to promote or defeat legislation and regulation.

Lobbying involves dealing with legislators and government officials to promote or defeat legislation and regulation. Large companies employ their own lobbyists, whereas smaller companies lobby through their local trade associations.

Counseling

Counseling. Involves advising management about public issues and company positions and image.

Counseling involves advising management about public issues and company positions and images.[11] Counseling is important when there may be sensitive

Marketing HIGHLIGHT 14–1 Extreme Sports Bring Publicity and Tourists

Today, a version of many outdoor sports known as Extreme Sports has built a following. These were formerly reserved for professional stunt people or highly advanced experts in a particular sport. Today, advocates exist within each sport such as frozen waterfall climbing or snowboarding and skiing on extremely dangerous terrain.

In some cases, a growth in tourism/hospitality has occurred as a result of these activities. Each of them offers opportunities for publicity and promotion. An example is the seaside town of Nazare, Portugal, and the beach of the Praia do Norte.

Garret McNamara, an American who is a champion in the sport of Jet Ski Surfing (a surfing sport in which a jet ski takes a surfer and board to a giant wave and then quickly gets out of the way), came to the attention of Dino Casimiro, a Portuguese surfer. Senor Casimiro knew of the town Nazare and the beach Praia do Norte and contacted Garret to visit and see for himself the size of the waves. Dino also convinced the town's development group to promote the waves as a visitor/surfer attraction.

Garret was intrigued and visited Nazare and quickly became hooked on the waves and the area. In 2011, McNamara broke the world's large wave record by surfing the biggest wave in the world at 78 feet. News of this event was carried by media throughout Europe. The French newspaper *Le Parisien* carried a headline, "Il Surfe la Plus Haute Vague du Monde" announcing McNamara's accomplishment. Garret was becoming a world celebrity and a near icon for Nazare.

Today, Nazare has attracted scores of surfers from all over the world to try their luck at surfing these giant waves. Several have surfed what are said to be 100-foot waves; however, none of these rides have been officially recognized. The town attracts thousands of visitors who were made aware of the town by the publicity it received from suffers riding the big waves. These visitors discover the beaches, great views from the cliffs above the beaches, seafood restaurants, and other attractions of the town while hoping to see a Jet Ski surfer riding a wave reaching 120 feet in height. In the meantime, Portugal and the town of Nazare benefit from observer and participant interest in this extreme sport at Praia do Norte. If you put Nazare into the search function in YouTube, you will be able to watch some of these surfers.[12]

Nazare, Portugal's, 100 feet plus waves have attracted Jet Ski surfers from around the world. Courtesy of ataly/Fotolia.

issues associated with the business. For example, water is a scarce commodity in Las Vegas. Major resorts with water displays, such as the Mirage, counsel their managers on the resort's water conservation efforts, such as recycling the hotel's wastewater to be used in the hotel's fountains.

■■■ Publicity

Publicity is a direct function of PR. Publicity is the task of securing editorial and news space, as opposed to paid space, in print and broadcast media to promote a product or a service. Publicity is a popular PR tool used in the activities just described.

One of the uses of publicity is to assist in the launch of new products. For example, when the Hard Rock Café announced it was going into the hotel business with the development of the first Hard Rock Hotel, the media covered the event during the initial announcement and the ground breaking ceremonies. Later, when the hotel opened, a concert at the hotel featuring Sheryl Crow was broadcast on MTV.

This concert, the uniqueness of the hotel, and a concert the following day by the Eagles and Sheryl Crow ensured that the opening of the hotel received worldwide publicity.

Press release. Information released to the media about certain new products or services.

Publicity is also used with special events. To be successful, the **press release** developed to gain the publicity must be of interest to the target audience of the media the company is targeting. For example, a food editor is interested in recipes and food history. A travel editor is interested in unique aspects of the destination, not just the hotel's features. A business editor is interested in the financial success of the operation. A press release should be written for a target audience and have value for the media's audience. We now look at some ways publicity can be used to enhance an organization's image.

Tourist destinations are particularly influenced by negative publicity. When disaster hits a region or city, tourists instantaneously learn of the problem and quickly find alternative destinations. Tourism recovery depends on the reintroduction of a tourism destination. The reintroduction must overcome the adverse publicity resulting from the natural disaster. It may take several years to rebuild business to pre-disaster levels. The speed of recovery depends on these factors:[13]

1. The extent of damage caused by the disaster. In some cases such as the wreck of the cruise ship *Costa Concordia*, no level of publicity would have helped.

2. The efficiency with which tourism partners bring their facilities back online.

3. An effective marketing message that clearly states the destination is once again open (or still is) and ready for business.

Publicity builds corporate image in a way that is congruent with the organization's communication strategy. Olive Garden restaurants developed a charity program that tied in its sponsorship of a team entering the "Olive Garden Rafanelli V-10" in the American Le Mans races. The company worked with America's Second Harvest to help fill the food banks in its "Drive Against Hunger" program. The "Drive Against Hunger" was linked to race car "driving" by donating eight truckloads of food in the eight cities where the Le Mans races were held. By tying the two events together, Olive Garden was able to create synergy across the events in its PR efforts. This example illustrates the benefits of planning and integrating marketing communications.[14]

■■■ The Public Relations Process

Effective PR is the result of a process. This process must be integrated with the firm's marketing strategy. One common misconception about PR and publicity is that quantity is more important than quality. Some PR firms measure success by the number of articles placed in media. As in other marketing efforts, PR should be meaningful to the target market.

The PR process consists of the following steps: conducting research, establishing the marketing objectives, defining the target audience, choosing the PR messages and vehicles, implementing the PR plan, and evaluating the results.

Pamela Parseghian, a chef and food writer, provides a great example of the importance of using the PR process. She discusses a chef who proposed writing a column in a major newspaper. She states the chef had developed no previous relations with the newspaper and the newspaper had not even reviewed his restaurant. Thus, there was no chance that it was going to let a "stranger" write a column in its paper. She says that if you want to get a story in a publication, first research and read the publication. She states she has people calling her asking if *Nation's Restaurant News* publishes articles on restaurants! Obviously these people have never seen the publication, but they are ready to send in an article. Once you know the media, you match their objectives and target market with your objectives. Then choose some news stories they will likely publish, such as recipes for new dishes, unique backgrounds, and themed dinners. She also states that making the story exclusive adds value. Once you get some articles placed, then you can decide whether writing regular columns makes sense based on the results the other articles created for your business.[15]

Research

Before a company can develop a PR program, it must understand the company's mission, objectives, strategies, and culture. It should know the vehicles that will be effective in delivering messages to the target audience. Much of the information needed by a PR manager is contained in a well-written marketing plan. Ideally, the PR manager should be involved in the formation of the marketing plan.

The firm's environmental scanning system is another important source of information for the PR manager. Analysis of this information should identify trends and give the firm insights into how to react to these trends. For example, many hotel and restaurant companies are now showing what they are doing to save and protect the natural environment.

Establishing Marketing Objectives

Once the PR manager has identified opportunities through product experiment and research, priorities can be established and objectives set. Marketing PR can contribute to the following objectives:

- *Build awareness.* PR can place stories in the media to bring attention to a product, service, person, organization, or idea.

- *Build credibility.* PR can add credibility by communicating the message in an editorial context. Credibility can be enhanced through positive associations with respected institutions, companies, and individuals. Cabela's is a highly respected outdoor sporting goods company with several stores in many states. Hunting, fishing, and boating enthusiasts in these areas are very familiar with Cabela's and have faith in the products and services that Cabela's offers. Oak Tree Lodge in Clark, South Dakota, offers pheasant, duck, and goose hunting packages on 8,000 acres of hunting land at prices ranging from $750 to $1000 per day per hunter. These packages include upscale lodging and meals as well as the actual hunting experience. Oak Tree is a Cabela's certified hunting lodge. This designation gave the lodge great publicity, enhanced its image, and served as another channel of distribution. To receive this designation, the owner and staff of Oak Tree Lodge had to work closely with Cabela's and demonstrate that the lodge was indeed worthy of this designation and would maintain high standards.

  III Forks restaurant has received favorable reviews from Independent Retail Cattlemen's Association and Zagat. III Forks integrated these reviews into an advertisement which was used to provide evidence that its selection of top-quality meat helped earn the positive reviews.

- *Stimulate the sales force and channel intermediaries.* PR can help boost sales force and franchisee enthusiasm. Positive stories about a new menu item will make an impression on the customers, employees, and franchisees of a restaurant chain. The publicity Ritz-Carlton receives from winning the Baldridge Award provides its sales force with great ammunition when it makes a sales call.

- *Lower promotion costs.* PR costs less than direct mail and media advertising. The smaller the company's promotion budget, the stronger the case is for using PR to gain share of mind.

Specific Objectives Should Be Set for Every PR Campaign

The Wine Growers of California hired the PR firm of Daniel J. Edelman, Inc., to develop a publicity campaign to convince Americans that wine drinking is a pleasurable part of good living and to improve the image and market share of California wines. The following publicity objectives were established: (1) develop magazine stories about wine and place them in top magazines and in newspapers

Park City Utah is known for its skiing. Like most ski resorts, it has developed events to attract people during the summer. The Park City Food and Wine Classic is held every summer. Courtesy of kgrif/Fotolia.

(food columns, feature sections); (2) develop stories about wine's many health values and direct them to the medical profession; and (3) develop specific publicity for the young adult market, college market, governmental bodies, and various ethnic communities. These objectives were refined into specific goals so that final results could be evaluated.

The Homestead of Hot Springs, Virginia, conducts special weekends that serve as a part of that hotel's promotion mix. These weekends bring members of the media to the resort and give them an event to write about in addition to the resort's amenities. The resort features events around long-weekend holidays such as Martin Luther King Jr. Day and President's Day. It has also created events for women. For example, "Just for Women" features a number of classes and seminars, including nutrition, financial advice, and organizing your life. It also includes luxurious spa treatments and a Friday night fashion show. Another feature has wine experts giving wine seminars and offering a special gourmet dinner on Saturday evening.[16]

The restaurant association in many cities sponsors a Taste of the Town. This event features food from the city's restaurants. Restaurants have a chance for exposure to many potential customers in one evening. The association usually charges an admission fee, which helps ensure that those attending are interested in restaurant fare rather than obtaining a free dinner. One of the largest of these events is the Taste of Chicago billed as "The Nation's Premier Food Festival." The Taste hosts upward of three million participants with many from out-of-town. The event features hundreds of menu items served from truck vendors and pop-up-booths along with concerts, musical acts from local artists, and rides such as a Ferris Wheel.[17]

Defining the Target Audience

A relevant message delivered to a target audience by the appropriate vehicle is crucial to the success of any PR campaign. Effective PR practitioners carefully identify the publics they wish to reach. They study these publics and find media that can be used to deliver their message. They identify issues that will be important to the public and form the message so it will seem natural and logical to the target audience.

Choosing the PR Message and Vehicles

The PR practitioner is now ready to identify or develop interesting stories about the product or service. If the number of stories is insufficient, the PR practitioner should propose newsworthy events that the company can sponsor. Here the challenge is to create news rather than find it. PR ideas include hosting major academic conventions, inviting celebrity speakers, and developing news conferences. Each event is an opportunity to develop a multitude of stories directed at different audiences.

Publications

Companies rely extensively on communication materials to reach and influence their target markets. These include annual reports, brochures, cards, articles, audiovisual materials, e-mail, social media, and company newsletters and magazines. Brochures can play an important role in informing target customers about a product, how it works, and how it is to be assembled. McDonald's developed a series of brochures discussing the quality ingredients that it uses, the actions that it has taken to help protect the environment, and the nutritional content of its products. Thoughtful articles written by company executives can draw attention to the company and its products. Company newsletters and magazines can help build the company's image and convey important news to target markets. Audiovisual materials are very useful as promotional tools. The cost of audiovisual materials is usually greater than that of printed material, but so is the impact. Many resort destinations use DVDs to promote their properties. Disney World created a 20-minute DVD aimed at families considering it as a vacation site.

McDonald's developed a creative and trendsetting annual report for stockholders that contained statements by members of top management as well as commercials. Publicly traded hospitality corporations with thousands of stockholders should consider the annual report and other stockholder communication as opportunities to promote the company's products and services, not simply as information required by law.

Events

Hospitality companies can draw attention to new products or other company activities by arranging special events, such as the Homestead Wine and Food Festival mentioned earlier. Events include news conferences, seminars, outings, exhibits, contests, and competitions, anniversaries, and sport and cultural sponsorships that will reach the target publics.

The Gaylord Palms Resort and Convention Center in Orlando created "Christmas at the Palms" to provide a demand for rooms in December. The festive event created a reason to stay at the Gaylord Palms, turning it into a destination. The result was articles in the media about the resort. The event gave the media a reason to discuss the resort. The outcome for the hotel was 135,000 visitors and increased room occupancy.[18]

A less elaborate event is Little Woodrow's Turtle Race. The weekly event features turtles with numbers on their backs starting from an elevated spot in the center of the race circle. The event creates excitement for the customers and helps create word of mouth. If you go on YouTube, you are likely to see several videos of the event, with some having thousands of hits.

New York's Vista Hotel decided to offer a Cajun dinner, but needed a "hook" to make the event authentic and newsworthy. That hook was Paul Prudhomme, the colorful Cajun chef. The Vista arranged to host a publication party for Paul's Cajun cookbook at the hotel during the Cajun dinner. This type of creative thinking creates a great PR event from an otherwise interesting but not particularly newsworthy event.[19]

News

A major task of PR professionals is to find or create favorable news about the company, its products, and its people. News generation requires skill in developing a story concept, researching it, and writing a press release. But the PR person's skill must go beyond preparing news stories: getting the media to accept press releases and attend press conference calls for marketing and interpersonal skills. A good PR media director understands press needs for stories that are interesting and timely and for releases that are well written and attention getting. The media director needs to gain the favor of editors and reporters. As the press is cultivated, it is increasingly likely to provide better coverage to the company.

Bad News/Good News PR

Occasionally, a bad news story about a hospitality or tourism organization will occur that accidentally works for the company's benefit. Such an example occurred with the "Cruffins" when a thief stole the recipe for Cruffins and 230 other recipes from Mr. Holmes Bakehouse Kitchen in San Francisco. The Cruffin, a muffin-croissant hybrid, was so popular that customers lined up early to buy them.

The thief stole only recipes, not money, baking equipment, or computers. News of the theft was carried by national media. This inspired even more customers to try Cruffins. "If someone stole the recipe, it's got to be good," said the manager of a restaurant who was waiting in line. Fortunately, copies of the recipe were in the owner's computer.[20]

Despite thousands of vineyards throughout the world, Bordeaux continues to hold a prestigious position. The quality of this wine has been recognized by wine connoisseurs for many years but the continuation of worldwide publicity also assists in maintaining the premium reputation. Publicity aimed at a knowledgeable and high-income market target can be found in publications such as the *Wall Street Journal*.[21]

Not all this publicity contains glowing reports. An article titled "Is Betting on Bordeaux Pushing Your Luck" in which it was reported that a case of the 2010 harvest of Chateau Lafite Rothschild had sold for 11,900£ but had fallen to 5,700£ by November 2014. Certainly, the vineyard would have preferred a report showing a great appreciation in the price of its wine but experienced wine enthusiasts know that prices for quality wine like those for original art or beach-side properties can rise and fall. A full-page story in the *Wall Street Journal* keeps Bordeaux in the minds of the knowledgeable target market. In the meantime, restaurants and wine bars can benefit from the lower price and the publicity.

A proven technique for writing a good press release is to use the Hey-You-See-So technique. Imagine that a teenager saw a friend in front of the high school. The teenager might yell, "Hey (attention getter) Bill and Helen (you), look what I have, three tickets for Saturday's rock concert (see). Let's plan to go (so)." When this simple technique is followed in a press release, effectiveness is increased.

Another journalistic technique is to write a press release in an inverted pyramid form. Think of a pyramid standing on its point, and remember that editors can and do shorten a press release to serve space requirements. A press release should be written so that the bulk of the information the company wishes to transmit is contained in the first paragraph. Each additional paragraph simply adds to the original and is less and less damaging to the story if clipped by an editor.

Speeches are another tool for creating product and company publicity. Increasingly, company executives must field questions from the media or give talks at trade associations or sales meetings. These appearances can build or hurt the company's image. Companies are choosing their spokespersons carefully and using speech writers and coaches to help improve the speaking ability of those selected.

The creation of a high-quality speech is costly for any company. A considerable amount of staff and executive time must be devoted to the project. It therefore makes sense to obtain maximum PR mileage from each speech. This is accomplished by printing copies of the speech or excerpts for distribution to the press, stockholders, employees, and other publics. A speech that is given but not distributed represents a wasted PR opportunity.

Because publicity's goal is reach, not frequency, it would be useful to know the number of unduplicated exposures. It is also important for publicity to reach target markets. A common weakness of publicity is that the persons exposed to it are not part of the company's target market.

Public Services Activities

Part of social responsibility is to give back to the community. Many companies will support a cause and not only donate money to support the activities but also get their employees to volunteer their time. Millennials look at a company's public service activities when choosing a company. Companies realize that through public service activities they can create goodwill with the community and their employee. Some companies, including Choice Hotel, provide paid leave for public service activities.[22] Restaurant and hotel chains donate so much of each sale to a charitable cause for a given amount of time. For example, a fast-food restaurant may donate five cents from every sandwich purchased on a certain day to the Muscular Dystrophy Association. Applebee's restaurant sponsors a special recognition program for the students of Lee School. Every month, each teacher nominates two students who have displayed one of the following six pillars of character: trustworthiness, respect, responsibility, fairness, caring, or citizenship. A drawing is held to pick three nominated students and one teacher who will go to Applebee's restaurant to eat lunch together. The restaurant receives free publicity on the school's Web site for this promotion.[23]

Identity Media

Normally, a company's PR material acquires separate looks, which creates confusion and misses an opportunity to create and reinforce corporate identity. In a society subject to overcommunication, companies must compete for attention. They should strive to create a visual identity that the public immediately recognizes. The visual identity is carried by the company's logos, stationery, brochures, signs, business forms, business cards, buildings, uniforms, dress codes, and rolling stock.

Implementing the Marketing PR Plan

Implementing publicity requires care. Consider the matter of placing information in the media. Exciting information is easy to place. However, most press releases are less than great and might not get the attention of busy editors. A chief asset of publicists is their personal relationship with media editors. PR practitioners are often former journalists who know many media editors and what they want. PR people look at media editors as a market to satisfy so they will continue to use the company's press releases.

Publicity requires extra care when it involves staging special events, such as testimonial dinners, news conferences, and national contests. PR practitioners need a good head for detail and for coming up with quick solutions when things go wrong. Most hotel corporations have a crisis plan included as part of their PR plan. In this plan, they state who can talk to the media and who should not. These plans usually state that staff should not speak to media but instead direct inquiries to the director of PR.

Evaluating PR Results

The contribution of PR is difficult to measure because it is used along with other promotion tools. If it is used before other tools come into action, its contribution is easier to evaluate.

Exposures

The easiest measure of PR effectiveness is the number of exposures created in the media. Publicists supply the client with a clipping book showing all the media that carried news about the product and a summary statement, such as the following:

Media coverage included 3,500 column inches of news and photographs in 350 publications with a combined circulation of 79.4 million; 2,500 minutes of air time on 290 radio stations and an estimated audience of 65 million; and 660 minutes of air time on 160 television stations with an estimated audience of 91 million. If this time and space had been purchased at advertising rates, it would have amounted to $1,047,000.[24]

This exposure measure is not very satisfying. There is no indication of how many people actually read, heard, or recalled the message and what they thought afterward. There is no information on the net audience reached because publications overlap in readership. Because publicity's goal is reach, not frequency, it would be useful to know the number of unduplicated exposures. It is also important that publicity reach target markets. A common weakness of publicity is that the persons exposed to it are not part of the company's target market.

Awareness/Comprehensive/Attitude Change

A better measure is the change in product awareness/comprehension/attitude resulting from the campaign (after allowing for the effect of other promotional tools). For example, how many people recall hearing the news item? How many told others about it (a measure of word of mouth)? How many changed their minds after hearing it? The Potato Board learned, for example, that the number of people who agreed with the statement "Potatoes are rich in vitamins and minerals" went from 36 percent before the campaign to 67 percent after the campaign, a significant improvement.

Sales and Profit Contribution

Sales and profit impact is the most satisfactory measure, if obtainable. A well-planned PR campaign is usually part of an integrated promotional campaign. This makes it very difficult to isolate the impact of the PR campaign.

Overwhelming Negative Publicity

Amendment 64 was approved by Colorado voters legalizing the possession and sales of marijuana. This news was carried by virtually every form of media imaginable. Residents of foreign countries who had never been to Colorado knew what had happened.

A company or an organization facing a tidal wave of bad publicity has little choice but to wait and see. Colorado's negative publicity continued with stories of increases in marijuana use by underage smokers and traffic deaths attributed to the use of marijuana.

Angry correspondence was sent to various offices and people in Colorado announcing that the sender would not return to Colorado as a visitor. While the Colorado visitor industry braced for the worst, those who wished to mount a strategy to counteract the negativity were advised to wait and see. In the meantime, planned advertising and other marketing programs to increase tourist visits to Colorado would continue.

■■■ PR Opportunities for the Hospitality Industry

Individual Properties

PR is by far the most important promotional tool available to entrepreneurs and individual properties, such as a single restaurant, tourist attraction, bed and breakfast (B&B), tour operator, or hotel. Seldom can these enterprises afford costly advertising. Successful PR programs by individual operators have demonstrated winning strategies that can be emulated by others.

Employees should be trained to look for PR opportunities. For example, a convention service manager developed a story about 200 chinchilla breeders who were meeting at the hotel, a bell person heard that a famous person would be a speaker at a dinner in the ballroom, and a room clerk found out that one of the hotel guests was 104 years old. All these stories resulted in positive exposure for the employees' hotels.[25]

Build PR Around the Owner/Operator

The owner/operator and the enterprise itself often become one and the same in the minds of customers. Obviously, this strategy holds dangers, such as the death of the owners, but benefits usually exceed risks. The success of a restaurant operator named Joe is an example. The name of this restaurant—not surprisingly—was Joe's. Joe used to drive a Cadillac, with two magnetic signs advertising his restaurant. Everyone in the community knew Joe and watched for his car as it rolled about town. Joe built his own personal image by wearing white cook's pants, a starched white shirt, and big comfortable black shoes that squeaked. Joe wore this uniform everywhere. If people failed to see Joe coming, they knew by the aroma of his big cigar that he was near. Joe knew the power of visibility and built a gigantic window so that passersby could look directly into the kitchen. He had a team of "trained chefs" who knew the value of show biz. They stirred, flipped, and flamed dishes to the delight of all. Joe knew the value of show biz, but most of all he realized the value of "Joe." Joe's most powerful PR asset was that he was always at the restaurant. He called this personal goodwill. Customers came to see Joe. In turn, he knew them by name and greeted each with a firm handshake. Joe was a pro at "selling Joe."[26]

The owner/operator of a fishing lodge in Costa Rica had been a circus trapeze artist before retiring to the jungles of Costa Rica. Each year, U.S. and Canadian TV and radio talk shows featured this entrepreneur and his fishing lodge. This owner/operator knew the media is always hungry for a good human interest story.

Individuals successful at promoting themselves often use theatrical costumery such as Joey's squeaky shows or General MacArthur's corncob pipe. Ken Hamblin, an African American columnist and talk show host, is never seen without a hat. Obesity, a wart on the nose, a bony appearance, a limp, a mustache, and dozens of other personal characteristics have been used successfully to build memorable personalities.

Build PR Around a Product or Service

Wall Drug Store is a major tourist stop and tourist attraction for the state of South Dakota. Located in a town of less than 1,000 residents, Wall Drug attracts 15,000 or more visitors daily during tourist season. Wall Drug's reputation was built on free ice water. Before the days of air-conditioned cars, Mr. and Mrs. Ted Hustead, the owners, saw tourists passing by on their way to the Black Hills. These folks looked thirsty and indeed they were. Ted hand-painted a few signs reading "Free Ice Water—Wall Drug" and placed them along the highway. Before Ted returned from planting these signs, tourists had already found their way to Wall Drug. They have never stopped coming. Today, word of mouth and PR have replaced many of the road signs, but Wall Drug remains the free ice-water stop.

The Raffles Hotel in Singapore has a colorful and long history, but most visitors know it as the birthplace of the drink called the Singapore Sling. Today, the renovated bar serves thousands of Singapore Slings. Even the empty glasses are sold and serve as a PR vehicle throughout the world. Hospitality enterprises everywhere have built a solid and long-lasting image around a drink, a dessert, a special entrée, fireplaces in the guest rooms, and even ducks. The Peabody Hotel of Memphis became well known for a flock of ducks that waddled daily from the rooftop via the elevator to a foundation in the lobby. When the Peabody opened their Orlando property, the Peabody ducks became one of the features of the property, creating publicity for the new hotel.

The town of Luckenbach, Texas, has a handful of residents and only a saloon, general store, dance hall, and a former post office. However, it attracts thousands of visitors. How did this happen? First, in 1973, country singer Jerry Jeff Walker and the Lost Gonzo Band appeared there and sang Viva Terlinga, which became a popular recording. Second, four years later, Waylon Jennings and Willie Nelson sang and recorded *Back to the Basics of Love*, which featured Luckenbach. Finally in 2009, a fundraising "Pickin for the Record" was held in Luckenbach. This broke a record for the *Guinness Book of World Records* for the most guitars gathered at one time to play.

The popularity of Luckenbach with country and western music fans has now transcended to wine enthusiasts. It is located near the town of Fredericksburg, center of the Texas Wine Country. Luckenbach provides an alternative to wine tours with regularly scheduled entertainment attracting a number of the tourists staying in nearby Fredericksburg or visiting the wineries near Luckenbach.

■■■ Crisis Management

An important area of PR is crisis management. Not all publicity is good. Hotels are open 24 hours a day, major airline companies have thousands of flights a day, and fast-food companies serve millions of customers each day. There are times when

Marketing HIGHLIGHT 14–2   Cheshire's Best Kept Stations, Cheshire, United Kingdom

In an era of jet travel and theme parks catering to millions, tourism and trains in a sleepy village in the heart of the English countryside surrounded by green fields and milk cows might seem to have little or no publicity value. John Hulme, a self-trained expert in publicity, would strongly disagree.

Although only 20 minutes away from Liverpool, home of the Beatles, and half an hour from the world famous Manchester United Football Club, Cheshire is a world apart. With its lush countryside, waterways, public gardens, and heritage, it has a lifestyle to aspire to and is a relaxing place where the visitor can discover and indulge in fine food and the better things in life. It is also the home of John Hulme, an UK entrepreneur, who following a brainstorming session at a business retreat repositioned his training-based company into a hospitality and tourism program and then successfully built up the brand based on PR. One part of his repositioning strategy was to move the business into a restored village railway station, theme his training center with railway memorabilia, and upgrade his catering to fine dining for the trainees, and suddenly he had a brand that could be sold by positive PR.

John differentiated his brand in his customer's minds so much that he was able to sell the business to a national competitor. This enabled him to retire and turn his attention to Cheshire and its railway stations.

Railway stations, for many visitors, provide first and last impressions when visiting Cheshire. In the United Kingdom, many railway lines have community rail partnerships to build cooperation between the rail operator and community served. They arrange events like music trains and establish groups at the stations to look after flower beds and keep the stations tidy.

To further promote the development of improved stations, John created a brand, "Cheshire's Best Kept Stations," that encouraged volunteers to improve the stations and culminated in a prestigious annual awards evening that recognized the work by the rail operators and the community. The guest list included local mayors, town hall officials, railway executives, and the local business community. With 16 annual awards presented each year, the result was 16 different storylines going into 16 newspapers, all supported by photos and comments from the invited guests. This became a PR bonanza.

In reviewing the success of the annual awards evening, John said, "Opportunities for awards ceremonies are endless. It is possible to transform a small private event into an overblown public affair resulting in a PR gravy train." For one awards evening, John invited Her Majesty's Representative for Cheshire, the Lord Lieutenant, as his guest speaker. A special postcard was produced in memory of the event. This allowed those in attendance to tell others about the evening, providing a chain-letter type of PR.

John also made certain that throughout the year endless positive stories were sent to newspapers and magazines. Four color spreads appear in glossy magazines. These remained in doctors' and dentists' waiting rooms for years.

John owned a 60-foot canal barge, the Bilbo Baggins, and entertained many people, including the editor of the local paper, onboard. During this social event, he persuaded the editor to run a weekly column, The Baggin Man, which talked about the picturesque Cheshire countryside with the story always starting from the railway station.

The local tourist office was coaxed into using his column in a 36-page full-color booklet promoting the local area. This was such a success that John wrote three different booklets, which resulted in a national circulation of 30,000 copies.

Ten years prior to the rash of publicity for Cheshire and the railway stations, the passenger trains serving the area had many spare seats and the line was always under the threat of reduced service. Through years of positive PR, today there are usually no spare seats and the UK government is under pressure to permit the train service to increase.

Tourism in Cheshire is not only increasing but is dramatically outperforming its targets.

John is convinced that for the hospitality and tourism industries PR/publicity including well-planned and managed events can provide excellent returns to the members and their community.

Cheshire has some great attractions for tourists; however, like any tourist destination, there must be good access. Through publicity Cheshire was able to increase the number of visitors and maintain its rail access, which was under the threat of being cut. Courtesy of John Hulme.

things go wrong: sometimes it is management's fault and sometimes it is beyond management's control. Managers must realize that things do go wrong: people are poisoned by tainted or spoiled restaurant food, thieves rob guests, planes crash, and flooding occurs somewhere every spring. A crisis management program will reduce the negative effects of these events.

The first step in crisis management is to take all precautions to prevent negative events from occurring. As a communications consultant, Eric Bergman states that in crisis management we should concentrate more on the management and communication and less on the crisis.[27] Robert Irvine divides crises into two main categories—a sudden crisis and a smoldering crisis.[28] A sudden crisis is the one that comes without any warning. These can be natural disaster, such as earthquakes and floods, workplace or domestic violence, an outbreak of food poisoning, and fires. Smoldering crises can include sexual harassment by supervisors, safety violations that could result in fines or illegal actions, health code violations, and fire code violations.

Sudden crises need to be anticipated. Crisis management is a series of ongoing, interrelated assessment or audits of kinds of crises and forces that can pose a major problem to a company.[29] Companies and their management need to determine those crises that have a chance of occurring and develop plans in case they do occur. Hotels should have fire plans, and employees should know what to do in case of a fire. Hotels in areas where earthquakes are prevalent should have an earthquake plan. For example, Deborah Roker, PR director for Sonesta International Hotels, designed a crisis-communication program for each of the hotels in the 18-property chain. She conducts a half-day training session annually at each property, going over crisis management plans with department heads. Part of this training includes a session at which managers are asked challenging questions that may be asked by guests or the media.[30]

Smoldering crises can often be eliminated with good management. Smoldering crises give warning before they occur. It may be a drop in grades on a health report, an informal claim that a supervisor is practicing sexual harassment, grease dripping from exhaust ducts, or strangers walking the property. Good sanitation practices reduce the risk of serving poisoned food. Strict policies regarding sexual harassment create a climate where sexual harassment is not tolerated. Regular cleaning of kitchen ducts and employee training can eliminate grease fires in the kitchen. Hotels that train all their employees to look out for suspicious actions and report them to security can reduce the risk of crimes against guests. A well-managed property is the best form of crisis management.

The Internet is an area where major crises are being spawned. A damaging message about your organization (whether true or not) can be spread over the Internet to millions of people. This has two important implications for management. First, the stakes of crisis management have been raised. It is very important to reduce the risk of a crisis occurring. Second, managers should monitor chat groups on the Internet to find out what they are saying about their organization. For example, a hotel in Miami should monitor the various chat groups for tourists to Miami.

"In the online era, it becomes critical for the business of any size to have a social media crisis management plan—or even better, a crisis prevention plan in place for those times when things go wrong, and it is truly the matter of when vs if."[31]

When a crisis does occur, having a crisis management plan will help an organization retain its reputation. The first step is to have emergency plans in place for events that might occur such as fire, weather emergencies, loss of water, loss of electricity, robbery, and terrorists or shooters. Second, train your staff in the procedures for these plans. Have a contact list so the appropriate staff can be notified when a crisis occurs. To have effective crisis management, the company should appoint a spokesperson. Other employees should be instructed to refer media to this person. This ensures that the company is giving a consistent story based on facts. Second, this person should gather the facts and speak only from fact. This person needs to make timely statements and keep the press updated. The spokesperson should never use the term *no comment* because it raises suspicion. Using the term *I don't know at this time* is a better response.

The message about the event should be factual and transparent; this will reduce the impact of negative publicity. For example, a fire in a guest room resulting in no injuries could result in negative or positive publicity. If the hotel provides no information to the press, the headline might read, "Regal Hotel Fire Forces Evacuation of 360 Guests." If the hotel contacts the press, the hotel has a chance to tell its story. In this case, the hotel could state that there was a hotel fire. "The smoke alarm went off at 12:33 a.m. setting the hotel's fire plan into action. The fire department was called and employees conducted an orderly evacuation of the hotel as a precautionary measure. No one was injured and all guests were able to return to their rooms within thirty minutes. Ms. Roberta Dominquez, the general manager of the Regal, praised the quick action of the employees. She stated that as a result of the hotel's monthly fire drills, all employees knew exactly what to do." The headline from this story might read, "Well-Trained Employees Quickly Move Guests to Safety."

If the hotel has a PR agency, the agency should be contacted. In a major crisis, it is a good idea to seek the help of a PR firm. Every company should have a crisis management plan and instruct employees in crisis management as part of their initial training.

◼◼◼ Sales Promotion

Sales promotion. Consists of short-term incentives to encourage the purchase of sale of a product or service.

Sales promotion consists of short-term incentives to encourage the purchase or sales of a product or service. Sales promotion includes a variety of promotional tools designed to stimulate early or strong market response. It includes consumer promotion (samples, coupons, rebates, price-off, premiums, contests, and demonstrations), trade promotion-buying allowances (free goods, cooperative advertising, and push money), and sales force promotion (bonuses and contests). A well-planned sales promotion can result in publicity. The Omni San Antonio Hotel offered a Teacher's Appreciation Special in recognition of their contributions as educators. This sales promotion created goodwill among the teachers and the community and generated publicity for the hotel. It also generated room sales during a soft period. Applebee's gives a free meal to students who earn an A. This rewards students with good grades and provides the school with a no-cost way of recognizing students who have done well. In addition to the PR benefits, it brings the child's parents and siblings to Applebee's when the free meal is redeemed. Thus, Applebee's generates profitable sales from the promotion.

Sales promotion tools are used by most organizations. Estimates of annual sales promotion spending run as high as $100 billion. Spending has increased rapidly in recent years. Formerly, the ratio of advertising to sales promotion spending was about 60:40. Today, in many consumer packaged goods companies, the picture is reversed, with sales promotion often accounting for 60 to 70 percent of all marketing expenditures. Sales promotions are most effective when they are used with advertising or personal selling. Consumer promotions must normally be advertised and can add excitement and pulling power to ads. Trade and sales force promotions support the firm's personal selling process. In using sales promotions, a company must set objectives, select the right tools, develop the best program, pretest and implement it, and evaluate the results. These steps are discussed next.

Setting Sales Promotion Objectives

Sales promotion objectives vary widely. Consumer promotions can increase short-term sales or they can be used to help build long-term market share. The objective may be to entice consumers to try a new product, lure consumers away from competitors, or hold and reward loyal customers. Sales force objectives include building stronger customer relations and obtaining new accounts.

Sales promotions should build consumer franchise; that is, they should promote the product's positioning and include a sales message. Ideally, the objective is to build long-run consumer demand rather than to prompt temporary brand switching. If properly designed, every sales promotion tool has consumer franchise-building potential.

Consumer Promotion Tools

Many tools can be used to accomplish sales promotion objectives. The promotion planner should consider the type of market, the sales promotion objectives, the competition, and the costs and effectiveness of each tool. The main consumer promotion tools include samples, packages, coupons, premiums, patronage rewards, point-of-purchase displays, contests, sweepstakes, and games.

Samples

Sample. Offers of a trial amount of a product.

Samples are offers of a trial amount of a product. Some samples are free. For others, the company charges a small amount to offset its cost. McDonald's offered a cup of coffee and an apple-bran muffin for $1. The promotion was designed to get customers to try the muffin. Some people do not eat bran muffins, and by charging a small price for the muffin, McDonald's avoided giving the muffin away to customers who would never buy one in the future.

Sampling by the staff who are employed by a hospitality firm such as a hotel, restaurant, or ski resort can be a very useful educational and promotional device. Thorough knowledge of the product is particularly beneficial to upselling. It is difficult for anyone to recommend a premium-priced Bordeaux or California merlot if he or she has no idea how the wine tastes. The sales and reservation staff of a hotel or resort can more convincingly sell a prospect on the idea of upgrading to a poolside cabana or suite if they have a personal knowledge of the product.

How does the staff obtain personal knowledge of the product or service of a company? Several successful approaches have been used to accomplish staff product knowledge:

1. Provide continuous training programs and invite suppliers such as vintners, cheese producers, and gourmet coffee distributors to provide samples and assist with product training.

2. Offer sales and performance incentives that include prizes on the property, such as a five-course meal, a month's use of the health club, or a weekend in the deluxe suite.

3. Create an employee's day in which the staff has full use of the facility. Country clubs often provide a special day in which employees and sometimes their families are treated to exclusive use of the pool, the golf course, the restaurant, and even the ballroom for an evening dance.

4. Share product information with employees through newsletters or product brochures. Often, product information brochures remain only in the offices of the purchasing department, the food and beverage manager, or some other executive office.

5. Talk continuously about the company's products and services in a positive and upbeat manner. People have a tendency to forget the many positive attributes of the facilities and the services that surround us daily.

Preston L. Smith, the president and CEO of S-K-I Limited, regularly sends memos to company managers urging them to hit the slopes. Smith personally manages to ski over 60 times each season. "Everyone skis here. It's a way of sharing the customer's experience. It's also a way to achieve personal growth because skiing is exhilarating and exciting."[32]

Packages

Packages can involve either bundling a number of a company's products or packaging a resort's products with attractions from the area. Ideally, the package creates a great experience for the guest and produces business for the hospitality or travel business. During a slow period in Las Vegas, two resorts of the same reputation took two different approaches to generating sales. One resort gave a discount on rooms and increased its projected occupancy. The other resort produced a package that included a room, dining, and show tickets. Like its neighbor across the price of the components of the package was greatly reduced, but the overall price was similar to what the resort would receive for the room during a busy period. The package sold well and the resort also increased occupancy over what was projected. The difference between the two resorts was that the one selling the package achieved greater gaming revenue. The higher price of the package attracted a wealthier clientele, who also realized what they were saving by purchasing the package. They had the means to spend more and they did.

The Ritz-Carlton in Tyson's Corner developed a Fine Art of Cuisine weekend.[33] The weekend features gourmet meals matched with the appropriate wines. The hotel developed packages around the meals, tasting, and demonstrations. Guests received a room, tickets to the Grand Wine Tasting, and the Chef's brunch. Packages can also be developed around local events. The Best Western Palm Beach, Florida, created a three-night package that included a room for three nights, tickets to two baseball games (several teams and spring training near the hotel), and a continental breakfast.[34] Packages such as these bring in business during a slow period and create a memorable experience for the guest.

Coupons

Coupons. Certificates that offer buyers savings when they purchase specified products.

Coupons are certificates that offer buyers savings when they purchase specified products. In the United States, coupon redemption peaked at 3.5 billion in 2011, with 2.75 being redeemed in 2014.[35] Digital coupons could help the growth continue as 100 million digital coupons were redeemed in 2015. Forty percent of smartphone users will redeem at least one coupon using their phone.[36] Overall, mobile and online coupon redemption exceeds traditional newspaper coupon redemption. Coupons can be mailed, available through the Internet, included with other products, or placed in ads. Coupons are most popular in the restaurant industry; however, hotel, rental car companies, tourist attractions, and cruise lines also use coupons.

Some restaurants have suffered from overcouponing. In the "pizza wars," the major chains fought for marketing share by distributing coupons at least once a week. Some pizza restaurants posted signs saying that they would honor competitors' coupons to neutralize the impact of competitor advertising. During the pizza wars, the price of pizza dropped to the discounted coupon price for most customers. These customers felt they were getting poor value if they purchased a pizza without a coupon. Overcouponing should be avoided because it lowers the price so the coupon no longer offers a competitive advantage.

Besides stimulating sales of a mature product, coupons are also used to promote the trial of a new product. For example, when a fast-food chain develops a new product, it often introduces the product in print advertisements featuring a coupon. The coupon provides an incentive and reduces the risk for customers trying the new product.

Cellfire (cellfire.com) distributes digital coupons to the cell phones of consumers nationwide who sign up for its free service.[37] Cellfire's list of clients includes Domino's Pizza, TGI Friday, and Hardee's restaurants. Cellfire sends an ever-changing assortment of digital coupons to users' cell phones. To use the coupons, users simply call up the stored coupon list, navigate to the coupon they want, press the "Use Now" button, and show the digital coupon to the store cashier. Domino's even permits consumers holding the mobile coupons to simply click on a link to have their cell phones dial the nearest Domino's store to place an order.

Coupons distributed through Cellfire offer distinct advantages to both consumers and marketers. Consumers don't have to find and clip paper coupons or print out Web coupons and bring them along when they shop. They always have their cell phone coupons with them. For marketers, mobile coupons allow more careful targeting and eliminate the costs of printing and distributing paper coupons.

Many professional marketing consultants and observers of marketing and sales practices feel that too much promotion creates a commodity out of a differentiated product. It is argued that companies spend millions of dollars and years of effort to develop a distinct image and a high level of product differentiation in the minds of consumers, only to have it destroyed by promotions.

Groupon launched a couponing business in 2008 to help businesses leverage the Internet and e-mail to use promotions as a form of advertisement. Specifically, the company sends its large base of subscribers a humorously worded daily deal, a specific percentage or dollar amount off the regular price for a specific client's branded product or service. Through these e-mailed discounts, Groupon offers client firms three benefits: increased consumer exposure to the brand, the ability to price discriminate, and the creation of a "buzz factor." Groupon takes 40 percent to 50 of the revenues in each deal in the process. Many promotions are offered on behalf of local retailers such as spas, concerts, resorts, and restaurants.

Some businesses complained that Groupon attracts only deal-seekers and is not as effective in converting regular customers. One study found that 32 percent of companies lost money and 40 percent said they would not utilize such a promotion again, with restaurants faring the worst among service businesses and spas being the most successful. Groupon has tried to innovate in several ways. Leveraging its massive sales force to sell Groupon Now, the company enlists local businesses to offer time- and location-specific deals via the Web or smartphones. The iPhone app for the new service has two buttons, "I'm Bored" and "I'm Hungry," to trigger deals in real time. The service is a way to boost business at slow times. Even a popular restaurant might consider midday and midweek discounts to boost business at slow periods.[38]

In the hospitality industry where demand varies greatly by time period, coupons should have blackout periods during those times when a person using a coupon may displace a regular guest. For example, restaurants are typically busy on Fridays and Saturdays, so a new restaurant that is using coupons to attract customers should make the coupons good Sunday through Thursday. Coupons can serve an important part of a communications program, but their use should be part of an integrated communications plan.

Premiums

Premiums are goods offered either free or at low cost as an incentive to buy a product. For example, fast-food restaurants often offer a free promotional glass instead of their normal paper cup. A self-liquidating premium is a premium sold to consumers who request it. For example, McDonald's in Australia offered Batman figures for 95 cents with the purchase of a burger.

Many restaurants, such as the Hard Rock Café, have discovered that promotional items such as caps, T-shirts, and sweatshirts can be sold at a good profit, thus creating another profit center for the company. Others offer a premium-priced drink or dessert that is served with a special glass or plate. Guests actually pay for the glass or plate in the price of the product, take the "gift" home with them, and are reminded of a pleasant restaurant experience. Pat O'Brien's in the French Quarter of New Orleans serves a Hurricane cocktail in a commemorative glass. These glasses can be seen in homes throughout the world. The name recognition developed through its Hurricane glasses has helped make Pat O'Brien's a major tourist attraction in the French Quarter.

Marco Polo cruises gave a free flight to Europe for passengers from Sydney taking one of its Mediterranean cruises. The booking had to be made in the previous year and was restricted to Sydney, an area where the cruise line was trying to build additional business.[39]

The Hard Rock Café is known for its logo shops selling T-shirts and other items, which promote Hard Rock Cafes around the world. Courtesy of dabldy/Fotolia.

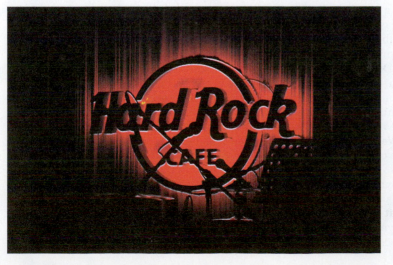

Patronage Rewards

Patronage rewards are cash or other rewards for regular use of a company's products or services. For example, most airlines offer frequent-flyer plans that award points for miles traveled. Most of the hotel chains have a frequent-stay program and many restaurants have frequent-dining programs. These programs reward loyal customers, gather guest information, and hopefully create a positive change in the consumer behavior of the member.

Often a dilemma for hotels, consumers feel that hotel frequent guest programs are worth less than those of airlines. Even so, a hotel company without a loyalty program may risk losing guests. Nevertheless, the majority of hotel guest program points are never redeemed. Starwood Hotels developed a program without blackout dates on free stays, instant online redemption, and the right to convert hotel points into airline miles. This proved so popular that Starwood signed 5 million new users or 50,000 each week.[40] Loyalty programs will be discussed in Chapter 16.

Hotels or restaurants can also create events to show their appreciation of loyal customers. For example, a casino invited 25,000 of its best customers to come to "Free Hug Friday." Five thousand players showed up to get a mug of Hershey's chocolate kisses and a hug from the company's executives. The players thought it was great, and the casino attracted 5,000 of its best players in one night.[41]

Another type of patronage rewards are specials for repeat customers. The Elephant Walk restaurants in Massachusetts are constantly looking for fine wines. Often their finds are wines that have limited availability. From their search for fine wines, they feature six wines each month. These are usually wines that do not have enough availability to put on their regular wine list. Customers are e-mailed information about the wines and can reserve a bottle for lunch or dinner. The restaurants sell these wines at normal retail levels, but half what a restaurant would normally charge. This promotion creates goodwill with frequent customers and gives them another reason to dine at the restaurants. The unique promotion has also generated publicity for the restaurants.[42]

Point-of-Purchase (POP) Promotions

Point-of-purchase (POP) promotions. Include displays and demonstrations that take place at the time of sale.

Point-of-purchase (POP) promotions include displays and demonstrations that take place at the point of purchase or sale. For example, a representative of Richmond Estate Wines might offer a taste of the estate's wines in the Robina Tavern package store.

The value of POP has long been recognized by the retailing industry and is making rapid inroads in restaurants, hotels, auto rental companies, and other hospitality industry firms. Hospitality firms have discovered that POP may be used (1) to disseminate information about the company's products or services and (2) to sell additional products and services, thus adding to gross revenue.

Hotels use display racks in the lobby to promote other hotels in the chain and additional services, from valet parking to sleigh rides. Restaurants such as Perkins, the Village Inn, and Denny's use the space near the cash register to create eye-catching displays of bakery items and desserts to be taken home by the guests.

Contests, Sweepstakes, and Games

Contests, sweepstakes, and games. Give consumers a chance to win something, such as cash or a trip.

Contests, sweepstakes, and games give consumers a chance to win something, such as cash or a trip. Viking River Cruises offers a chance to win a free trip on Viking by completing information online. This helps Viking to build a prospect list. A contest calls for consumers to submit an entry—a jingle, guess, or suggestion—to be judged by a panel. A sweepstakes calls for consumers to submit their names for a drawing. A game presents consumers with something every time they buy such as bingo numbers. A sales contest urges dealers or the sales force to increase their efforts, with prizes going to the top performers.

Dunkin' Donuts launched an integrated campaign to remind people of its roots as a doughnut maker and not just a coffee brand. From TV to Internet to in-store displays, "you can't walk in the door without thinking about donuts," says Dunkin's vice president of consumer engagement. At the heart of the "donut domination" campaign was a "Create Dunkin's Next Donut" contest that urged people to visit the contest Web site and design their own doughnuts. "Put on your apron and get creative," the campaign urged. At the site, entrants selected from a list of approved ingredients to create the new doughnut, give it a name, and write a 100-word essay about why they think their doughnut creation was the best. Twelve semifinalists were selected, who cooked their creations at a bake-off in the company's test kitchen at Dunkin' Donuts University in Braintree, Massachusetts. The grand winner received $12,000 and the winning doughnut—Toffee for Your Coffee—was added to the company's everyday value menu. In all, contestants submitted nearly

130,000 creations online. "We were absolutely amazed at the number of entries in our contest," said Dunkin' marketing executive.[43]

Tom Feltenstein, a restaurant marketing consultant, suggests a program where loyal customers are sent a $20 gift certificate. They can use $10 toward the purchase of their meal and the other $10 they give to an employee who provides them with the best service. Thus, the employee tries to earn as much money as possible by providing exceptional service.[44]

Finding Creative Ideas

The Internet makes it possible to see what sales promotion activities other companies are doing. If they are outside your market area, it is a good chance you can adapt the ideas to fit your needs. For example, at the Hilton Gaithersburg, Maryland, new Washington, DC, the chef prepares Maryland crab cake sliders presented on soft mini rolls to accentuate a perfect combination of spices and sauces. Accompanying this scrumptious local dish is a collection of to-go crab flavors, including Crab chips, Old Bay crab cake classic mix, Gordon's Chesapeake Classics Maryland-style red crab soup, and spicy Chesapeake peanuts.

The Ritz-Carlton at Powerscourt in Ireland put together a package that included its regular offerings. However, by packaging the items, it created value for the guest and produced additional revenue. The package included:[45]

- Two nights' accommodation in a deluxe room

- Daily breakfast in the restaurant

- Dinner for two in Gordon Ramsay at Powerscourt for one night (excluding beverages)

- A one-hour aromatherapy massage

Friday's in the United Kingdom offered a twist on restaurant birthday clubs. Instead of telling persons celebrating their birthday what they will get, they can sign up for their gift when they join the birthday club. They can choose from free cocktails, champagne, or desserts for their party. Many people celebrate their birthday by dining out; thus, a well-designed birthday club can provide a reason for the birthday celebration to be held at your restaurant.[46]

Another reason to celebrate is with a dining experience on Father's Day. Mother's Day is the busiest day of the year for restaurants in the United States. So why not encourage families to eat out on Father's Day as well? That is exactly what Outback did. For anyone bringing their husband or father to Outback on Father's Day, Outback gave a $10 certificate valid on their next visit. This type of certificate is called a bounce-back certificate because it encourages diners to return. However, Outback went one step further by collecting information about who came on Father's Day. Dads activated the certificate online at http://outback.com/. The certificate was valid for five weeks and had to be used with a purchase of $25 or more. Thus, Outback was encouraging a quick return visit, and the minimum purchase of $25 ensured that Outback would at least break even on the bounce-back visit.[47]

Chick-fil-A is a master of promotions. One of its promotions is giving away 52 Chick-fil-A meal coupons to the first 100 people when it opens a new restaurant. Dan Cathy, president of Chick-fil-A, states that he could not believe it when fans showed up 18 hours in advance of the opening the first time it started the promotion.[48] The store opening creates local publicity. Newspapers, radio stations, and television stations cover the unique event and interview people who sleep in the parking lot so they can claim their free meals. The cost of the meals is more than offset by the publicity.

Consulting companies also give ideas online as a way to attract potential clients. One firm lists 10 promotional tactics for restaurants. One of these is partnering with a business or social organization to expose the restaurant to potential customers. They state that if you select the right group as partner, you can leverage resources to promote your restaurant, and you can also target your core audience. Partnering with a business or charitable organization works on many levels and can help stretch your marketing budget while delivering higher returns on investment than can be achieved with traditional advertising.[49] There is no end to the types of promotions one can do. But managers must remember to fit the promotion to the operation.

Developing the Sales Promotion Program

The third step in developing a sales promotion is to define the full sales promotion program. This step calls for marketers to make other decisions. First, they must decide on the size of the incentive. A certain minimum incentive is necessary if the promotion is to succeed. A larger incentive produces more sales response. The marketer must also set conditions for participation. Incentives might be offered to everyone or only to select groups.

The marketer must decide how to promote and distribute the promotion program. Each distribution method involves a different level of reach and cost. The length of the promotion is also important. If the sales promotion period is too short, prospects will be unable to take advantage of it. If the promotion runs too long, the deal will lose some of its "act now" force.

Restaurant promotions often consist of cards, flyers, coupons, and other devices featuring two-for-one specials, 20 percent off, free drinks, and other "hooks." Normally, these bear a date at which the promotion becomes ineffective. In theory, this should work well, but in actuality, customers often present coupons months or even years old and become enraged when they are told the promotion is no longer in effect. A prospective new owner or buyer of any hospitality company should ask if there are outstanding promotions in the community. Many new owners have been shocked to witness a flood of promotional coupons that negatively affected cash flow.

Other problematic media used by hospitality companies include hot air balloons bearing the company's logo that crash on freeways or atop buildings, road signs that end up in strange places such as the mayor's lawn, and sponsored bicycle races in which a rider crashed through a competitor's storefront. In today's "I'll sue you" environment, it is wise to discuss proposed promotions with an attorney and with the company's insurance agent prior to initiation.

Finally, the marketer has to decide on the sales promotion budget. It can be developed in two ways. The marketer can choose the promotions and estimate total cost. However, the more common way is to use a percentage of the total budget for sales promotion. One study found three major problems in the way that companies budget for sales promotion. First, they do not consider cost effectiveness. Second, instead of spending to achieve objectives, they simply extend the previous year's spending, take a percentage of expected sales, or use the "affordable approach." Finally, advertising and sales promotion budgets are too often prepared separately.[50]

Partnerships can stretch a budget. The Palm, a national upscale steakhouse, developed a promotion with a Chicago car dealer to promote its Chicago restaurant.[51] The car dealer offered a $50 gift certificate for the Palm to all who test drove its luxury model car. The cost of the certificate was split equally between the partners. Partnerships can also be used to acquire prizes in sweepstakes. Companies often discount or provide merchandise in exchange for advertising exposure.

Pretesting and Implementing the Plan

Whenever possible, sales promotion tools should be pretested to determine if they are appropriate. Consumer sales promotions can be pretested quickly and inexpensively, yet few promotions are ever tested ahead of time. Seventy percent of companies do not test sales promotions before initiating them. To test sales promotions, researchers can ask consumers to rate or rank different promotions. Promotions can also be tried on a limited basis in selected geographic test areas.

Companies should prepare implementation plans for each promotion, covering lead time and sell-off time. Lead time is the time necessary to prepare the program. Sell-off time begins with the launch and ends when the promotion ends.

Evaluating the Results

Many companies fail to evaluate their sales promotion programs. Various evaluation methods are available; the most common is sales comparisons before, during, and after a promotion. Suppose that a company has a 6 percent market share before the promotion, which jumps to 10 percent during the promotion, falls to 5 percent immediately after, and rises to 7 percent later. The promotion appears to have attracted new customers and more purchases from current customers. After the promotion, sales fell as consumers used inventories or moved purchases forward. For example, a person planning on traveling to see relatives in New York in June may move the trip forward to April to take advantage of an airline promotion that expires on April 30. The long-run rise to 7 percent means that the airline gained some new users, but if the brand's share returned to the pre-promotion level, the promotion changed only the timing of demand rather than total demand.

Surveys can provide information on how many consumers recall the promotion, what they thought of it, how many accepted it, and how it affected their buying patterns.

Clearly, sales promotion plays an important role in the total promotion mix. To use it well, the marketers must define objectives; select the best tools; design the sales promotion program; and pretest, implement, and evaluate the results.

■■■ Local Area Marketing (Neighborhood Marketing)

Local area marketing or neighborhood marketing is defined as a low-cost, hands-on effort to take advantage of all opportunities within the immediate trading area to promote and market a business.[52] Although all areas of the promotional mix are used, PR is the heart of any local area marketing program. Local area marketing is used by both small and large companies. Independently owned businesses, such as restaurants or travel agencies, have an advantage over large companies because the owners become permanent fixtures of the community, whereas large companies tend to replace store managers every two or three years. Research has shown that 75 percent of a restaurant's customers come from within a 10-minute drive. With fast-food restaurants, the radius shrinks to three to five minutes' drive time.[53]

Examples of PR activities included in local area marketing are providing tours of your facility. Primary schools look for places to take their students on field trips. A restaurant or hotel can be an exciting venue. A short tour, followed by tasting and providing the students with a coupon (so that they can show their parents where they went), can be a good way to create business and goodwill. (As a result of worldwide terrorism, many companies in all industries have stopped allowing tours.) Many suburban and rural areas have weekly papers, providing a weekly or monthly article on travel, food, or wine. If articles are well written, the paper will appreciate the free articles, and the writer will gain exposure and credibility in the local market. Being a speaker at meetings of local social and service clubs is another way to gain exposure. During the holiday season, a business can become a depository for charities collecting toys for disadvantaged children. But don't accept this task passively. For example, if the local firefighters ask you to collect toys for their campaign, suggest that the campaign be started with a kickoff drive, including fire engines, sirens, and firefighters in uniform in your parking lot on a Saturday. If they agree, call the local news station for television coverage.[54]

Organizations such as the school band, girl scouts, and the local little league team are always looking for fundraisers. Many restaurants will give a portion of their proceeds to these groups if they refer business. For example, at Sweet Tomatoes restaurant, the organization must hand out flyers redeemable at the restaurant on a specific night designated for that organization, resulting in a 15 percent donation to the organization. Sweet Tomatoes offers an alternative program. That organization sells script that can be used at face value at the restaurant. The group receives the script at a 10 percent discount and sells it at face value. Merchants, including restaurants, receive many requests to assist local groups with fundraising by donating merchandise or meals. Some restaurants have a policy of donating only products such as coffee mugs or T-shirts with the restaurant's logo/name.

Cause-related promotions are another local area marketing tactic. These promotions bring business to the hotel or restaurant and help the community. Rock Bottom Restaurant and Brewery frequently creates promotions that are cause related. For example, one of the beers the brew pub creates is Firechief Ale. The company developed a fiery line of appetizers and teamed them with its Firechief Ale to create a promotion that helps local firehouses. Through its CraftWorks Foundation, it develops and supports local charity partnerships.[55]

El Torito restaurants, based in California, had a television campaign that was based almost exclusively in Los Angeles because the chain could not afford to advertise in multiple markets. As a result, restaurants outside Los Angeles gained little benefit from the ads. Joe Herrera, the restaurant's manager, decided to scrap the television ads and build a local area marketing campaign. Its ad dollars went into local papers and community marketing. Now El Torito has a presence in all its markets, and Herrera stated the managers were happy to have the marketing help.[56]

A good local area marketing campaign creates goodwill in the community and exposure for the restaurant, which translates into increased business and customer loyalty. Successful local marketers should not give products or money away freely. They evaluate every opportunity and make sure the effort will be worthwhile. By being creative, managers can ensure that their local marketing efforts will be noticed.

■■■ CHAPTER REVIEW

I. Public Relations. The process by which a positive image and customer preference are created through third-party endorsement. Social media has become an important tool for public relations.

II. Major Activities of PR Departments
- **A. Press relations.** The aim of press relations is to place newsworthy information into the news media to attract attention to a person, product, or service.
- **B. Product publicity.** Product publicity involves efforts to publicize specific products.
- **C. Corporate communication.** This activity covers internal and external communications and promotes understanding of the organization.
- **D. Lobbying.** Lobbying involves dealing with legislators and government officials to promote or defeat legislation and regulation.
- **E. Counseling.** Counseling involves advising management about public issues and company positions and image.

III. Publicity. Publicity is a direct function of PR. Publicity is the task of securing editorial and news space, as opposed to paid space, in print and broadcast media to promote a product or a service. Publicity is a popular PR tool used in the five activities described earlier. Three other popular uses of publicity are new product launches, special events, and crisis management.

IV. The Public Relations Process
- **A.** Researching to understand the firm's mission, culture, and target of the communication.
- **B.** Establishing marketing objectives
  1. Build awareness
  2. Build credibility

3. Stimulate the sales force and channel intermediaries
4. Lower promotion costs
- **C.** Defining the target audience
- **D.** Choosing the PR message and vehicles
  1. **Publications.** Companies can reach and influence their target market via annual reports, brochures, cards, articles, audiovisual materials, and company newsletters and magazines.
  2. **Events.** Companies can draw attention to new products or other company activities by arranging special events.
  3. **News.** PR professionals cultivate the press to increase better coverage to the company.
  4. **Speeches.** Speeches create product and company publicity. The possibility is accomplished by printing copies of the speech or excerpts for distribution to the press, stockholders, employees, and other publics.
  5. **Public service activities.** Companies can improve goodwill by contributing money and time to good causes, such as supporting community affairs.
  6. **Identity media.** Companies can create a visual identity that the public immediately recognizes, such as with company's logos, stationery, signs, business forms, business cards, buildings, uniforms, dress code, and rolling stock.
- **E.** Implementing the marketing PR plan
- **F.** Evaluating PR results
  1. Exposures
  2. Awareness/comprehension/attitude change
  3. Sales-and-profit contribution

V. PR Opportunities for the Hospitality Industry
  A. Individual properties. Public relations is by far the most important promotional tool available to entrepreneurs and individual properties, such as a single restaurant, tourist attraction, bed and breakfast (B&B), tour operator, or hotel. Seldom can these enterprises afford costly advertising or other promotional programs.
  B. Build PR around the owner/operator
  C. Build PR around the location. For instance, the isolation and obscurity of an enterprise can be used as a PR tactic.
  D. Build PR around a product or service
VI. Crisis Management
  A. Take all precautions to prevent negative events from occurring.
  B. When a crisis does occur:
    1. **Appoint a spokesperson.** This ensures that the company is giving a consistent story based on facts.
    2. **Contact the firm's public relations agency if it has one.**
    3. **The company should notify the press when a crisis happens.**
VII. Sales Promotion
  A. Setting sales promotion objectives. Sales promotion objectives vary widely and can include increasing short-term sales, increasing long-term sales, getting consumers to try a new product, luring customers away from competitors, or creating loyal customers.

  B. Selecting sales promotion tools. Many tools can be used to accomplish sales promotion objectives. The promotion planner should consider the type of market, the sales promotion objectives, the competition, and the costs and effectiveness of each tool. Common sales promotion tools include samples, coupons, premiums, patronage rewards, point-of-purchase (POP) displays, contests, sweepstakes, and games.
  C. Finding creative ideas
  D. Developing the sales promotion program. The following steps are involved in developing a sales promotion program:
    1. Decide on the size of the incentive
    2. Set the conditions for participation
    3. Decide how to promote and distribute the promotion program
    4. Set promotion dates
    5. Decide on the sales promotion budget
  E. Pretesting and implementing the plan. The marketer should pretest to determine if sales promotion tools are appropriate and the incentive size is efficient and effective.
  F. Evaluating the results. The company should evaluate the results against the objectives of the program.
VIII. Local Store Marketing. A good local store marketing campaign is an effective way for both a chain and an individually owned restaurant or hotel to gain goodwill and exposure in the community.

▪▪▪ DISCUSSION QUESTIONS

1. What is meant by the term *public?* Can a company have more than one public?
2. Why might it make sense for a hotel chain to shift some of its advertising dollars to public relations?
3. Give some examples of how a hospitality organization might be able to gain publicity.

4. Is publicity free?
5. Compare and contrast publicity with advertising. What are the benefits and drawbacks of each?
6. How can being socially responsible enhance a company's position in the community?

▪▪▪ EXPERIENTIAL EXERCISE

Do the following:

Find a good example of publicity in a print medium that has been linked to a social medium such as Facebook.

Explain how the print and electronic media complement each other.

▪▪▪ INTERNET EXERCISE

Find two Web sites of hospitality or travel organizations that offer PR support. This could be corporate announcements, a "press room section," or a gallery of photos that one can download for publicity purposes. Report on the sites you found and the support they offered for persons wanting to write a story about the organization.

■■■ REFERENCES

1   Reprinted with permission of The Calgary Stampede, Calgary, Alberta, Canada. Original—Social Media Initiative. Hell or High Water, Division 4.0, Inspiring Collaboration, Calgary Stampede.

2   Jessica Miller, "Marketing Communications," *Cornell Hotel and Restaurant Administration Quarterly*, 34, no. 5 (1993): 49.

3   Ibid.

4   Philip Kotler, "Public Relations Versus Marketing: Dividing the Conceptual Domain and Operational Turf" (paper presented at the Public Relations Colloquium 1989, San Diego, CA, January 24, 1989).

5   Adapted from information in "PR in the Driver's Seat," *Advertising Age* (October 26, 2009), S6–S7.

6   "Tourism PR Professionals Say How Social Media Changed Their Jobs," http://skift.com/2014/10/23, p. 3.

7   "According to Skift.com, Destinations now approach instagrammars and other social influencers to get publicity through those accounts. Research shows the general public sees these regular people as being like them and are more trusted as information sources today than in the past," said Brittani Wood, an account supervisor at DCI.

8   Shandrow Kim Lachance, "Tokyo Airport Terminal 3 Walkways Transformed into Racetrack Lanes," Fortune.com, April 13, 2015.

9   "Progressive Bike Ramps," product catalog, www.progressivebikeramps.com, 1-855-727-7267.

10 IMBA 2013 Annual Report, pp. 6, 8, and 9. 4888 Pearl East Circle, Suite 200D, Boulder, CO 80301.

11 Adapted from Scott M. Cutlip, Allen H. Center, and Glen M. Brown, *Effective Public Relations*, 6th ed. (Upper Saddle River, NJ: Prentice-Hall, 1985), pp. 7–17.

12 Eric Benson and Gotz Goppert, "A Good Break," *United Hemispheres*, January 2015, pp. 62–67, 98, 103; Damien Fletcher, "Surf's up to 100ft: Daredevil Breaks World Record for Largest Wave Ever Ridden," *Mirror*, January 30, 2013, http://www.mirror.co.uk/news/world-news/garrett-mcnamara-rides-100ft-wave-1563121 (accessed August 10, 2015); Chris Chase, "Watch: Surfer Nails Massive 100-Foot Wave," USA Today.com, October 29, 2013, http://www.usatoday.com/story/sports/2013/10/29/surf-big-wave-portugal/3296883/ (accessed August 10, 2015).

13 Joe Durocher, "Recovery Marketing: What to Do After a Natural Disaster," *Cornell Hotel and Restaurant Administration Quarterly*, 35, no. 2 (1994): 66.

14 "Olive Garden's Drive Against Hunger Raises More Than $1M," *Nation's Restaurant News* (June 25, 2001): 30.

15 Pamela Parseghian, "Chefs Looking for New Recipe to Drum Up Publicity Should Serve Up Side of Smarts," *Nation's Restaurant News* (September 6, 2004): 42.

16 The Homestead Resort Web site, http://www.thehomestead.com/welcome/calendar.asp (accessed December 18, 2004); Karen Weiner Escalera, "How to Get News Out of Nothing," *Lodging* (March 1992): 25–26.

17 http://www.choosechicago.com/event/tasteof Chicago18479..

18 Christine Blank, "Driving Revenue," *Hotel and Motel Management* (October 4, 2004): 3.

19 Arthur M. Merims, "Marketing's Stepchild: Product Publicity," *Harvard Business Review* (November/December 1972): 111–112; see also Katharine D. Paine, "There Is a Method for Measuring PR," *Marketing News* (November 7, 1987): 5.

20 Carol Rogash, "Recipe That Launched Cruffin Craze Stole from Bakery," *The New York Times*, March 6, 2015, pp. 1–6, www.seattletimes.com/news/recipe-for-cruffins-a-hot-new treat stolen from bakery.

21 Will Lyons, "Eating and Drinking, Is Betting on Bordeaux Pushing Your Luck?" *The Wall Street Journal* (Friday–Sunday, November 21–23, 2014): W3.

22 Choice Hotels Web site, http://careers.choicehotels.com/benefits/paid-leave.html (accessed August 20, 2015).

23 Lee Elementary School Web site, http://lee.usd383.org/LeeSchool/leeschool.htm (accessed December 18, 2004).

24 Arthur M. Merims, "Marketing's Stepchild: Product Publicity," *Harvard Business Review* (November–December 1972): 111–112. For more on evaluating public relations effectiveness, see Katharine D. Paine, "There Is a Method for Measuring PR," *Marketing News* (November 6, 1987): 5; Eric Stoltz and Jack Torobin, "Public Relations by the Numbers," *American Demographics* (January 1991): 42–46.

25 Tom McCarthy, "Add Publicity in the Mix," *Lodging Hospitality* (October 1999): 17.

26 Michael M. Lefever, "Restaurant Advertising: Coupons, Clauses and Cadillac's," *Cornell Hotel and Restaurant Administration Quarterly*, 29, no. 4 (1989): 94.

27 Eric Bergman, "Crisis? What Crisis?" *Communications World*, 11, no. 4 (1994): 19–23.

28 Robert Irvine, "What's a Crisis Anyway?" *Communications World*, 14, no. 7 (1997): 36–41.

29 Ian Mitroff, "Crisis Management and Environmentalism: A Natural Fit," *California Management Review*, 36, no. 2 (1994): 101–114.

30 Julie Miller, "Crisis to Calm," *Hotel and Motel Management* (August 11, 1997): 261.

31 Ekaterina Walter, "10 Tips for Reputation and Crisis Management in the Digital World," *Forbes*, www.forbes.com/sites/ekaterinawalter/2013/11/12/10

32 David H. Freeman, "An Unusual Way to Run a Ski Business," *Forbes* (December 7, 1992): 28.

33 Jennifer Coleman, "The Fine Art of Fine Dining," *Travel Agent* (September 18, 2000): 96.

34 David Cogswell and Sara Perez Webber, "Spring Flings," *Travel Agent* (February 21, 2000): 108.

35 Statista, "Total Number of Redeemed Consumer Packaged Goods (CPG) Coupons in the United States from 2007 to 2014," 2015, http://www.statista.com/statistics/247546/total-number-of-redeemed-consumer-packaged-goods-coupons-in-the-us/ (accessed August 10, 2015).

36 Trueship, "One-Click Savings: A Quick Look at 2015 Mobile Coupon Statistics," March 24, 2015, http://www.trueship.com/blog/2015/03/24/one-click-savings-a-quick-look-at-2015-mobile-coupon-statistics/#.VckNAVy-XA4 (accessed August 10, 2015).

37 Cellfire, www.google.com/cellfirecoupons.2015, Cellfire, Inc.

38 Nathan Vardi, "Groupon and Zynga Are the Worst-Performing Stocks of the Year," *Forbes* (October 8, 2012); Cassie Lancellotti-Young, "Groupon Case" (Glassmeyer/McNamee Center for Digital Strategies, Dartmouth College, 2011); Brad Stone and Douglas MacMillan, "Are These Four Words Worth $25 Billion," *Bloomberg BusinessWeek* (March 27, 2011); "Is Groupon a Good Deal?" *Entrepreneur* (March 2011): 61. For relevant academic research, see Xueming Luo, Michelle Andrews, Yiping Song, and Jaakko Aspara, "Group-Buying Deal Popularity," *Journal of Marketing*, 78 (March 2014): 20–33.

39 "Free-Flying Offer to Join Marco Polo Cruises," *Travel-trade* (October 20, 2004).

40 Ibid.

41 Tricia Campbell, "Cozying Up to Customers," *Sales & Marketing Management* (December 1999): 15.

42 Mary Ewing-Mulligan and Ed McCarthy, "Wine Lists Used Creatively Are Vintage Opportunity to Attract New Customers," *Nation's Restaurant News* (July 23, 2001): 43–46.

43 Based on information found in "Dunkin' Donuts Returns to Its Roots – Doughnuts – in $10 Million Campaign," *Promo* (March 18, 2009), http://promomagazine.com/contests/dunkindonutscampaign/; "Time to Judge the Donuts," *PR Newswire* (May 18, 2009); Steve Adams, "Dunkin Donuts Contest Finalists Cook Their Unique Creations in Bake-Off," *Patriot Ledger* (May 29, 2009), http://www.patriotledger.com/businessx1594716181/doughnut-design-101; www.dunkindonuts.com/donut/ (accessed August 2010).

44 Tom Feltenstein, "Slay the Neighborhood Goliath," *Restaurant Hospitality* (October 1999): 38.

45 http://www.hilton.com/en/hi/promotions (accessed October 4, 2008).

46 https://www.tgigreattimes.co.uk/ (accessed October 5, 2008).

47 https://outback.com; http://www.thefashionable-house-wife.com/?p=3907 (accessed October 5, 2008).

48 https://www.reuters.com/article/pressRelease/idUS80974_06-Aug-2008+MW20080806 (accessed October 5, 2008).

49 https://www.quantifiedmarketing.com/learning_center/restaurant-promotions.php (accessed October 5, 2008).

50 Roger A. Strang, "Sales Promotion Fast Growth, Faulty Management," *Harvard Business Review* (July/August 1976): 98.

51 Steve Weiss, "Promotions Trend: Get Yourself a Partner," *Restaurants and Institutions*, 103, no. 26 (1993): 78–93.

52 National Restaurant Association, *Promoting the Neighborhood Restaurant: A Local Store Marketing Manual* (Chicago, IL: National Restaurant Association, 1988).

53 Tom Feltenstein, "Wily Underdogs with Fewer Resources Still Have Bite in Competitive Foodservice Industry," *Nation's Restaurant News* (May 7, 2001): 40.

54 Tom Felterstein, *Restaurant Profits Through Advertising and Promotion* (New York: Van Nostrand Reinhold, 1983).

55 CraftWorks Foundation Web site, http://www.craftworksfoundation.org/signature-programs/ (accessed August 11, 2015); Theresa Howard, "Charitable Promos Can Be Profitable Market Strategy," *Nation's Restaurant News* (June 9, 1997): 18.

56 Scott Hume, "Taking It to the Streets," *Restaurants and Institutions* (October 15, 1999): 101–108.

1. Explain the role and nature of personal selling and the role of the sales force.

2. Describe the basics of managing the sales force, and explain how to set sales force strategy, how to pick a structure—territorial, product, customer, or complex—and how to ensure that sales force size is appropriate.

3. Identify the key issues in recruiting, selecting, training, and compensating salespeople.

4. Discuss supervising salespeople, including directing, motivation, and evaluating performance.

5. Apply the principles of the personal selling process, and outline the steps in the selling process: prospecting and qualifying, preapproach and approach, presentation and demonstration, negotiation, overcoming objections, closing, and follow-up.

Professional Sales

The city of Grapevine, Texas, became an important tourism destination without the benefit of beaches or mountains or a Grand Canyon. Sales planning and team sales work brought this about. What Grapevine had was available land for development and access to seven major highways, the Dallas-Fort Worth (DFW) airport, and a team of salespeople consisting of a mayor, city council, and the city manager's office "Go Team" who sold Grapevine to prospective hospitality companies.

Situated just north of the DFW metroplex and the DFW airport, Grapevine decided that tourism and hospitality were the industries it wanted. While many Texas communities continued to seek manufacturing industries, Grapevine decided that tourism, hospitality, and shopping would create thousands of jobs and would attract out-of-area visitors as well as day shoppers and restaurant patrons from the DFW metroplex. It was felt that these were complementary to the historic nature of the community and would assist in preserving the culture of a small town.

The mayor, city council, and the city manager's office believed in the value of tourism and the hospitality industry. Tommy Hardy, assistant city manager, was charged to promote the destination and tourism economic development of Grapevine. Tommy decided that to be successful, he would need to fully understand tourism and the hospitality industry. This meant knowing the major players in the hospitality industry and understanding their language, such as ADR and RevPAR. It also meant that Grapevine would need to develop a marketing plan with desired target hospitality companies to become members of the Grapevine community and then pursue them with professional marketing/sales strategies.

Tommy and staff members attended hospitality industry conventions as well as the huge ICSC (International Council of Shopping Centers) show in Las Vegas. This permitted them to build a database, determine new trends, and establish contacts with executives who might bring a new hospitality company to Grapevine.

The city of Grapevine worked closely with developers, architects, and the financial community. Tommy Hardy and staff made sales calls on targeted companies. They conducted tours, hosted receptions for prospects to meet members of the community, and, most important, provided continuous follow-up to "close the sale." Tommy said that he and staff were never afraid to go to the private sector for assistance in planning and marketing. "We always took big steps," he said, and "the private community supported us. Our responsibility is to bring prospect companies together with brokers and developers. Once that has been accomplished, we walk out of the room."

The mayor of Grapevine was born and raised in the community and has great civic pride in Grapevine. Unlike some desk-bound mayors, he worked aggressively with Tommy and staff to bring desired hospitality and retailing companies to the community. He also has a reputation as a great "closer" and personally clinched many deals.

Developing and building a visitor infrastructure is critical, but all this must be supported by advertising and promotion. Sales and bed taxes generated by the complex support the Grapevine Convention and Visitors Bureau, which organizes visitor events such as GrapeFest, one of the top 100 festivals in the United States, provides promotional materials, conducts familiarization tours, and helps coordinate and promote activities with other organizations. Events have proven very popular with the local community and with day visitors from the metroplex, adding to tourism revenue.

■■■ Results

An area in northeast Grapevine was targeted for commercial tourism/hospitality development. One of the earliest companies was the Gaylord Texan mega-resort, which opened 1,511 hotel rooms and a 400,000-square-foot convention center. Nine additional hotels were located in the development area, including Great Wolf Lodge, a 402 all-suite hotel with a 50,000-square-foot indoor water park and a conference center. Great Wolf then decided to add 203 more rooms and more meeting space. A typical Great Wolf water park is shown in the chapter opening picture.

Despite the growth in Grapevine hotel rooms, performance comparisons with other metroplex areas are excellent, as seen in the following table. Restaurant sales also increased during this time period by $3 to $5 million per year.

Attraction	Annual Visitors
Grapevine Mills Mall	13 million
Bass Pro Shops Outdoor World	2 million
Lake Grapevine	1.5 million
Festivals/events/historic district	1.15 million
Hotel guests	532,000
Grapevine Winery visitors	235,000
Heritage/information centers	150,000
Grapevine Vintage Railroad	80,000

Source: Based on Grapevine Convention and Visitors Bureau.

Tourism development planners know the importance of retail shopping, and a huge retail shopping area was developed, including Grapevine Mills Mall, an indoor mall of over 2 million square feet that annually attracts 15 million shoppers from a five-state region. The spectacular Bass Pro Shops Outdoor World with 200,000 square feet of space was built in proximity and by itself attracts 2 million visitors per year.

Success attracts others, including the Glass Cactus, a 26,000-square-foot entertainment center, and Lone Star Crossing, a 120,000-square-foot shopping center.

Tourism development also occurred outside the destination corridor within the historic downtown Grapevine area and other areas of Grapevine. The Grapevine Vintage Railroad connects Grapevine with the renovated Fort Worth Stockyards. A complex of upscale restaurants known as the Epicenter was developed on South Main Street in Grapevine. This complex complemented other downtown retailers, restaurants, and art galleries.

Tourism in Grapevine means 13 million visitors annually. Thousands of individuals are directly employed in the industry, providing a healthy economy. Tourism has allowed downtown Grapevine to flourish as contrasted to the dying centers of many Texas towns. It has also encouraged historical preservation and cultural growth in the arts. Grapevine also saw over a 22 percent increase in its RevPAR, over twice the rate of its competitors.

None of this would have been possible without the teamwork between the private sector and the public. Nor would it have been possible without sales planning and strategy by a dedicated team of the mayor, city council, and city staff who wanted to see Grapevine grow in a desired and beneficial manner.

■■■ Management of Professional Sales

Success or failure within the hospitality industry ultimately rests on the ability to sell. A roadside motel at an intersection of major highways or a popular restaurant with waiting lines is sometimes viewed as being above the need "to sell." No member of the hospitality industry can accept this as a long-run viewpoint.

Discourteous front-desk clerks and cashiers who would impress Grumpy of the Seven Dwarfs are part of one's sales force. These and all others who face the public can drive away or attract business. In the best cases, they can upsell through suggestive desserts, special drinks, and even a gift certificate for a friend. Higher-margin suites can be sold instead of the lowest priced room.

Successful owners and managers know that they must sell continuously. County commissioners, tax evaluation officials, planning boards, the press, bankers, and the local visitor center must all be sold on one's hospitality business. The city of Grapevine, Texas, in the opening vignette clearly demonstrates the need to sell and the research that follows.

Libraries could be filled with tales of lost sales or needlessly fractured guest relationships because of a curt response or an unsavory attitude on the part of support staff who mistakenly believe that sales is not their responsibility.

Everyone must sell, but a few individuals have the specific responsibility for ensuring that payrolls can be met, invoices can be paid, and a fair return on investment (ROI) can be achieved. These are the professional salespeople.

In this chapter we focus on seven major areas:

1. Nature of hospitality sales

2. Sales force objectives

3. Sales force structure and size

4. Organizing the sales department

5. Recruiting and training a professional sales force

6. Managing the sales force

7. Managing strategic client relationships

■■■ Nature of Hospitality Sales

Sales personnel serve as the company's personal link to customers. The sales representative *is* the company to many customers and in turn brings back much-needed customer intelligence. Personal selling is the most expensive contact and communication tool used by the company. If managed effectively it can produce great returns.

Hotels are known for having a sales staff. However, other areas of the industry use salespeople. Newly designed restaurants increasingly include areas that can be closed off for private parties. Rental car companies maintain sales staff, and the suppliers to industry hire salespeople. As a result of the importance of personal

Many restaurants have private rooms and a banquet sales person to sell these rooms. Courtesy of Andrew Bayda/ Fotolia.

Communicating. Sales representatives communicate information about the company's products and services.

Information gathering. Sales representatives conduct market research and intelligence work and fill in a call report.

selling in our industry and the opportunities in selling, many graduate of hospitality programs find themselves in careers with personal selling.

Cost estimates for making a personal sales call vary depending on the industry and the company, but one conclusion remains constant. However measured, the cost is high! Add to this the fact that sales orders are seldom written on the first call and often require five or more calls, particularly for larger orders. The cost of obtaining a new client thus becomes enormously high, as depicted in Table 15–1. Despite the high cost, personal selling is often the most effective tool available to a hospitality company. Sales representatives perform one or more of the following tasks for their companies:

- **Prospecting.** Sales representatives find and cultivate new customers.

- **Targeting.** Sales representatives decide how to allocate their scarce time among prospects and customers.

- **Communicating.** Sales representatives communicate information about the company's products and services.

- **Selling.** Sales representatives know the art of salesmanship: approaching, presenting, answering objections, and closing sales.

- **Servicing.** Sales representatives provide various services to the customers—consulting on their problems, rendering technical assistance, arranging financing, and expediting delivery.

- **Information gathering.** Sales representatives conduct market research and intelligence work and fill in call reports.

- **Allocating.** Sales representatives decide which customers to allocate scarce products during product shortages.

- **Maintaining strategic partnerships.** Senior salespeople, including the sales manager, provide valuable planning assistance to clients.

The sales representative's mix of tasks varies with the state of the economy. During product shortages, such as a temporary shortage of hotel rooms during a major convention, sales representatives find themselves with nothing to sell. Some companies jump to the conclusion that fewer sales representatives are then needed.

TABLE 15–1
Cost of Obtaining a New Client

Number of Calls Needed to Close a Sale	Total Cost to Obtain a New Client at Various Estimates of Cost of Sales Call ($)		
	AT 250	AT 500	AT 700
1	250	500	700
2	500	1,000	1,400
3	750	1,500	2,100
4	1,000	2,000	2,800
5[a]	1,250	2,500	3,500
6	1,500	3,000	4,200
7	1,750	3,500	4,900
8	2,000	4,000	5,600
9	2,250	4,500	6,300
10	2,500	5,000	7,000

Canadian resorts like the Fairmont Hotel Lake Louise attract international visitors to Canada. Courtesy of Tupungato/ Fotolia.

Allocating. Sales representatives decide on which customers to allocate scarce products.

But this thinking overlooks the salesperson's other roles: **allocating** the product, counseling unhappy customers, and selling the company's other products that are not in short supply. It also ignores the long-run nature of hospitality sales.

Many conventions and conferences are planned years in advance, and hospitality salespeople must often work with meeting and convention planners two to four years in advance of the actual event. Resorts in the United States have concentrated much of their selling efforts on meetings and conferences, which by now represent 35 percent or more of their customers.[1] This was not achieved by viewing professional sales as a short-run tactic. A senior analyst with Tourism Canada demonstrated that Canadian resort salespeople are effective in reaching foreign markets. Guests in Canadian resorts are 60 percent Canadian and 40 percent foreign. By comparison, U.S. resorts have a mix of 91 percent American and 9 percent foreign.[2] Again, penetrating foreign markets is not accomplished in the short run.

As companies move toward a stronger market orientation, their sales forces need to become more market focused and customer oriented. The traditional view is that salespeople should worry about volume and sell, sell, sell, and the marketing department should worry about marketing strategy and profitability. The newer view is that salespeople should know how to produce customer satisfaction and company profit. They should know how to analyze sales data, measure market potential, gather market intelligence, develop marketing strategies and plans, and become proficient at the use of sales tactics.

This has become very clear as micro marketing, including database marketing, online distribution, social media, marketing dashboards, and competitive information are readily available within the hospitality industry; salespeople need to understand how to analyze and effectively use the information.

After viewing the importance of marketing information to sales, a hospitality industry writer with *Hotel and Motel Management* magazine concluded the following:[3]

- Closing sales has more to do with professionalism than anything else.

- Understanding the identity of real prospects increases sales productivity.

- Sales force members can save hours of time by having information about prospect group clients.

- It is critical to know what groups have a history of booking rooms in your type of hotel.

Competitive Analysis and Competitive Sets

Sales managers within the hospitality industry are often held accountable for the performance of their properties against members of a competitive set. The selection of a comparable competitive set is, therefore, critical to meaningful comparative sales analysis.

Small bed and breakfasts (B&Bs) usually have no difficulty defining their competitive set. However, restaurants may not find this task an easy one. As an example, should a family-owned-and-run catfish restaurant be grouped with seafood restaurants such as Red Lobster? Perhaps it should be grouped with family-owned restaurants, but does this make sense to place it with Italian and Greek restaurants?

In the case of hotels, three common approaches are used to determine which competitive set or cluster is most appropriate.

ADR: The basis for average daily rate (ADR) clusters is that properties which are similar tend to sell for similar prices in a competitive market.

Product type: Properties may be grouped as luxury, resort, or in other ways such as the AAA diamond rating system or Mobil-star system. Whatever factors are selected to form a competitive set, there are certain to be inequalities.[4]

Management company set: Professional management companies may have contracts with a variety of hotels operating under different flags. It is tempting to use these hotels as a competitive set, but this practice is subject to criticism.

Hotels operating under the direction of an independent management company may have few competitive characteristics. Therefore, comparisons between these properties can be highly misleading.

Sales managers who focus on the actions and results of competitors may be focusing on the wrong variables. A study of customer orientation versus competitor orientation by management showed that "a customer orientation has a greater effect on a hotel's performance than does a competitor orientation." "A customer orientation that concentrates on acquisition, satisfaction and retention of customers is superior to a competitor orientation focused on monitoring, managing and outflanking competitors."[5]

■■■ Sales Force Objectives

Hospitality companies typically establish objectives for the sales force. Sales objectives are essential for two reasons:

1. Objectives ensure that corporate goals are met. Goals may include revenue, market share, and improved corporate image.

2. Objectives assist sales force members to plan and execute their personal sales programs. Objectives also help ensure that a salesperson's time and company-support resources such as personal computers are used efficiently.

Sales force objectives must be custom designed annually for each company. Individual sales objectives are established to support corporate goals and marketing and sales objectives. Annual marketing and sales objectives are normally broken into quarterly and monthly objectives. Sales force members break them down further into personal objectives by day and week.

It is the responsibility of the sales manager to establish and assign objectives to individual salespeople. These are often developed after consultation with the salesperson. An experienced salesperson is in the best position to understand what is happening in the marketplace and to assist the sales manager in formulating realistic objectives.

Occasionally, annual objectives must be changed before year end. This is generally due to a dramatic occurrence, such as the outbreak of war or a natural disaster.

Although sales objectives are custom designed, there are general objectives commonly employed by members of the hospitality industry.

Sales Volume

Occupancy, passenger miles, and total covers are common measures of sales volume within the hospitality industry. They all mean the same thing: Bring in as many customers as possible. An emphasis on volume alone inevitably leads to price discounting, attracting undesirable market segments, and cost cutting.

Sales Volume by Selected Segments

Prospecting. The process of searching for new accounts.

Exclusive resorts, charter flight services, and upper-end cruises tend to operate with the philosophy that if one establishes volume objectives but restricts **prospecting** to highly selective segments, price and profits will take care of themselves. Although appropriate for a few niche players, this thinking cannot be applied to the majority of the hospitality industry. Nevertheless, the concept of establishing sales objectives by specific market segment is feasible and basic to effective sales. Sales strategies must be analyzed and reviewed continuously in view of quantitative sales results.

Canadian resort operators targeted the meeting and convention market, with the result that this segment made up 25 percent of their customer mix, compared with 35 percent for U.S. resorts. This led to questions of whether the differences were the result of the sales techniques employed in the two nations.[6]

Sales Volume and Price/Margin Mix

Establish sales volume objectives by product lines to ensure a desired gross profit. This system is the basis for revenue management. Salespeople often criticize the system as restrictive and unrealistic. The fact is it works. British Airways, Hertz, Sheraton Hotels, and Royal Caribbean Cruises are representative of the firms that use this system. Whether a revenue management system is in place, establishing objectives by volume and by price/margin segments leads to improved revenue.

Upselling and Second-Chance Selling

Excellent profit opportunities exist for hospitality companies, particularly hotels and resorts, to upgrade price and profit margins by selling higher-priced products such as suites through upselling. A related concept is second-chance selling, in which the sales department contacts a client who has already booked an event such as a two-day meeting. Opportunities exist to sell additional services, such as airport limousine pickup and delivery or to upgrade rooms or food and beverage (F&B) from chicken to prime rib. Second-chance selling encourages cooperation and teamwork between departments, such as catering, F&B, and sales.

Market Share or Market Penetration

Airlines, cruise lines, major fast-food chains, and rental car companies are highly concerned with market share and market penetration. These concepts have considerably less meaning to many restaurants, hotels, resorts, and other members of the hospitality industry.

The management of most hotels is concerned primarily with measures such as occupancy, average room rate, yield, and customer mix. The corporate marketing department of a chain, however, is likely to be concerned about market share, particularly if it is a dominant chain in a market such as Hawaii. Hilton, Sheraton, Aston, Outrigger Hotels, Marriott, and others actively compete for market share in that market.

Evidence indicates that hotel management companies are increasingly held accountable for clearly defined performance standards. Among these is the level of market penetration. This is a clear departure from the past when contracts between owners and hotel management companies contained vague references to standards of performance.[7]

As a result, it is very possible that the sales department of hotels and resorts will increasingly be required to measure market potential and will be held accountable for a predetermined level of market penetration. Independent measures of market penetration such as STAR will undoubtedly assume increased importance in the measurement of hotel sales. STAR is a joint project of Smith Travel Research and PricewaterhouseCoopers. It provides information on average rate, occupancy, and RevPAR for Asia/Pacific, the Americas, Europe, the Middle East, and Africa.

Product-Specific Objectives

Occasionally, a sales force is charged with the specific responsibility to improve sales volume for specific product lines. This objective may be associated with upselling and second-chance selling but may also be part of the regular sales duties of the sales force. A sales force may be asked to sell more suites, higher-margin coffee breaks, holiday packages, honeymoon packages, and other product lines.

Excellent opportunities for enhanced revenues exist within many hotels and resorts from nonroom sales. Recreation club memberships, including children's programs, are sometimes sold to local residents. A properly designed club membership can generate substantial income from membership fees, dues, and F&B revenues. The Boca Raton Resort initiated a Premier Club Membership program that produced membership sales in excess of $40 million the first three years. The club gave residents access to its beach, spa, golf course, tennis course, children's activities, and concierge services. Additionally, special events were planned for career club members.[8]

■■■ Sales Force Structure and Size

The diverse nature of the hospitality industry means that different sales force structures and sizes have evolved. The structure of a sales force within the airline industry is different from that of a hotel or cruise line. In general, most restaurants do not use a sales force but depend on other parts of the marketing mix, such as advertising and sales promotion.

The hotel/resort industry traditionally uses a functional, hierarchical structure. Within this structure, hotel departments are organized around particular functions, such as housekeeping or sales. Department managers, including the sales manager, report to a GM. In smaller hotels such as roadside motels, the GM usually serves as sales manager because the organization is not large enough to support functional departments. Within large hotels and resorts, the sales department may have directors of specialized sales such as a convention and meetings sales director or a corporate accounts sales director.

The structure of a hotel sales department depends on the culture of the organization, size of the property, nature of the market, and type of hotel. A casino hotel might contain the same number of rooms as a ski resort hotel yet have a somewhat different organizational structure. Some casino hotels have sales directors who are responsible for working with junket reps and premium players. A resort hotel might have a sales director responsible for working with travel agents and tour wholesalers, or with nationwide ski clubs.

The sales force structures commonly used in the hospitality industry today are described next.

Territorial-Structured Sales Force

In the simplest sales organization, each sales representative is assigned an exclusive territory to represent the company's full line. This sales structure has a number of advantages. First, it results in a clear definition of the salesperson's responsibilities. As the only salesperson working the territory, he or she bears the credit or blame for area sales to the extent that personal selling effort makes a difference. Second, territorial responsibility increases the sales representative's incentive to cultivate local business and personal ties. These ties contribute to the sales representative's selling effectiveness and personal life. Third, travel expenses are relatively small because each sales representative travels within a small geographic area.

A territorial sales organization is often supported by many levels of sales management. Each higher-level sales manager takes on increasing marketing and administration work. Sales managers are paid for their management skills rather than their selling skills. The new sales trainee, in looking ahead, can expect to become a sales representative, then a district manager, and then a regional manager, and, depending on his or her ability and motivation, may move to still higher levels of sales or general management.

Territory Size

Territories can be designed to attempt to provide either equal sales potential or equal workload. Each principle offers certain advantages. Territories of equal potential provide each sales representative with the same income opportunities and provide the company with a means to evaluate performance. Persistent differences in sales yield by territory are assumed to reflect differences in ability or effort of individual sales representatives. Customer density varies by territory, and territories with equal potential can vary widely in size. The potential for selling cruises in Chicago is larger than in several Rocky Mountain states. A sales representative assigned to Chicago can cover the same sales potential with much less effort than the sales representative who sells in the Rocky Mountain West. The sales representative assigned to the larger and sparser territory is going to end up with either fewer sales and less income for equal effort or equal sales through extraordinary effort. A common solution is to acknowledge that territories differ in attractiveness and assign the better or more senior sales representatives to the better territories.

Alternatively, territories might be designed to equalize the sales workload. Each sales representative could then cover his or her territory adequately. This principle results in some variation in territory sales potential. This does not concern a sales force on straight salary, but when sales representatives are compensated partly on commission, territories vary in their attractiveness.

Territory Shape

Territories are formed by combining smaller units, such as counties or states, until they add up to a territory of a given sales potential or workload. Territorial design must take into account the location of natural barriers, the adequacy of transportation, and so on. Many companies prefer a certain territory shape because the shape can influence the cost and ease of coverage and the sales representatives' job satisfaction.

The territorial structure is most commonly used by airlines, cruise lines, and rental car companies, and at the corporate level by hotel chains. It is not frequently used by individual hotel/resort properties that instead seem to organize their sales departments by function or type of customer.

Market-Segment-Structured Sales Force

Companies often specialize their sales forces along market segment lines. Separate sales forces can be set up by different industries for the convention/meeting segment, the incentive travel market, and other major segments. This is the most common type of structure within the hotel industry. For example, associations have different needs than corporations; thus, one salesperson may be assigned to the association market, while another is assigned to the corporate market.

Market-Channel-Structured Sales Force

The importance of marketing intermediaries, such as wholesalers, tour operators, travel agencies, and junket reps, to the hospitality industry has created sales force structures to serve different marketing channels.

Targeting. Sales representatives decide how to allocate their scarce time among prospects and customers.

The cruise line industry has historically depended on travel agents for the bulk of its sales. A study by Claritas, the marketing support company, showed that 96 percent of cruise line passengers purchased tickets through a travel agency. This company developed thematic maps **targeting** the areas in which the best prospects for a cruise line were concentrated. The cruise line then used these maps in presentations by its sales force to travel agents.[9]

A segment of the cruise line industry, cargo freighters are ships that carry freight everywhere in the world and offer a few berths to travelers. They lack the glamour and service of cruise ships but appeal to travelers with time. Highly specialized travel agents sell this product. Information is also available at www .freightword.com or www.traveltips.com.

Some hotels such as those near historical sites receive substantial bookings through motor coach tour brokers. The location, size, and type of hospitality companies greatly affect the relative importance of travel intermediaries. This in turn affects whether a company designs its sales force structure by travel intermediary.[10]

Customer-Structured Sales Force

A customer-structured sales force recognizes that specific customers who are critical to the success of the organization exist. The sales force is usually organized to serve these accounts through a key or national account structure.

Key Accounts

Large accounts (called key accounts, major accounts, or national accounts) are often singled out for special attention and handling. If the account is a large company with divisions operating in many parts of the country, it is likely to be handled as a national account and assigned to a specific individual or sales team. If the company has several such accounts, it is likely to organize a national account management (NAM) division.

NAM is growing for a number of reasons. As buyer concentration increases through mergers and acquisitions, fewer buyers account for a larger share of a company's sales. Another factor is that many buyers are centralizing their purchases instead of leaving them to the local units. This gives buyers more bargaining power. Still another factor is that as products become more complex, more groups in the buyer's organization become involved in the purchase process, and the typical salesperson might not have the skill, authority, or coverage to be effective in selling to the large buyer.

Sheraton Hotels noted that business travelers were not shifting from one hotel chain to another as much as in the past. In response, Sheraton developed a reservations system that allowed the establishment of national accounts.

In organizing a national account program, a company faces a number of issues, including how to select national accounts; how to manage them; how to develop, manage, and evaluate a national account manager; how to organize a structure for national accounts; and where to locate NAM in the organization.

Combination-Structured Sales Force

Some hotels and resorts have a sales force structured by product, market segment, market channel, and customer. A large hotel might have a catering/banquet sales force (product), a convention/meeting sales force (market segment), a tour wholesale sales force (marketing intermediary), and a national accounts sales force (customer). Proponents of such a sales force believe it encourages the sales force to reach most available customers. They also contend it is impossible for a single salesperson to understand and effectively sell all the hotel's products to all available customer segments through all marketing channels. Sales specialists can become familiar with major customers, understand trends that affect them, and plan appropriate sales strategies and tactics.

Opponents of this system feel that in many cases this sales force structure indicates the hotel is trying to be all things to all people in the absence of long-run goals and strategies. They contend that such a structure is difficult to manage and can be confusing to the sales force and the customer because the same customer may be classified in different areas and thus be handled by more than one salesperson.

Regardless of which structure is used by a hotel or resort, a particular market segment neglected by many North American hoteliers is local markets. Many local markets offer potential for F&B and function room sales. Although a resort such as the Greenbriar in a rural area of West Virginia might not have a large local market, it is scarcely the case for most hotels. The Japanese seem to be particularly adept at penetrating local markets; 40 to 50 percent of Japanese hotel sales are accounted for by parties and other events from local companies.[11] Sales managers must be aware of the local market and develop a sales force structure appropriate for penetrating this market.

Seven months after opening, the Dalmahoy Golf and Country Club Resort near Edinburgh, Scotland, recognized the need for a strong sales effort in the local market and for a combination-structured sales force. Dalmahoy was experiencing low occupancy and less-than-desirable membership growth. Many factors were involved, such as a poor economy and almost no awareness by Edinburgh area golfers. As a member of the U.K.-based Country Club Hotel Group, Dalmahoy had the assistance of this company's national sales force. The management of Dalmahoy knew that a strong property-level sales effort was also needed and employed two salespersons to serve the local market, plus a travel trade manager to work with intermediaries to attract overseas business.[12]

Sales Force Size

Once the company clarifies its sales force strategy and structure, it is ready to consider sales force size. After determining the type and number of desired customers, a workload approach can be used to establish sales force size. This method consists of the following steps:

1. Customers are grouped into size classes according to their annual sales volume.

2. The desirable call frequencies (number of sales calls on an account per year) are established for each class.

3. The number of accounts in each size class is multiplied by the corresponding call frequency to arrive at the total workload for the country in sales calls per year.

4. The average number of calls a sales representative can make per year is determined.

5. The number of sales representatives needed is determined by dividing the total annual calls required by the average calls made by a sales representative.

Suppose that the company estimates its national market consists of 1,000 A accounts and 2,000 B accounts. A accounts require nine calls a year, whereas B accounts require six calls a year. This means that the company needs a sales force that can make 21,000 sales calls a year. Suppose that the average sales representative can make 1,000 calls a year. The company would need 21 full-time sales representatives.

The size of a sales force is determined by changes in the market, competition, and corporate strategies and policies. The sales process also directly affects decisions concerning sales force size. The following describes several of the factors that influence the size of a hotel's sales force:

*   *Corporate/chain sales support.* Several major hotel chains have employed a corporate sales force to reach the meeting/convention/conference market. The concept behind this sales force is that individual hotel properties may not be in a position to search out and track this important market and that a sales force representing the chain can recommend and sell all appropriate hotels within the chain, not simply a single property. In recent years, some chains have begun to question the value of this sales force and may drop this area of sales support. If this occurs, individual properties may find it necessary to employ one or more additional sales force members to ensure coverage of this important segment.

*   *Use of overseas independent sales reps.* Sales reps have traditionally been used by hotels and resorts to serve foreign countries. With the growing importance of many foreign markets, several companies are rethinking the use of independent reps and may substitute salaried sales staff in these markets.

*   *Team selling.* Team selling has proved to be an effective and powerful tactic to reach and retain key customers. Its opportunities and limitations are only beginning to be realized in the hospitality industry.

*   *Corporate selling.* Members of the travel industry sometimes join sales/marketing efforts to reach selected market segments. An example is the Luxury Hotel and Resort Collection—2015 by Chase Card Services and United Airlines through an agreement with Signature Travel Network.

    A program offering 750 luxury properties in 85 countries was offered only through selected Chase credit cards, in this case the Chase Mileage Plus® Explorer Card membership program. This program offered guest privileges such as a buffet breakfast and available upgrades. An attractive color brochure was sent to members. It was apparent based on the location and rates of the hotel/resort properties that above-average income travelers were selected. Opportunities for cooperative sales programs in the travel industry are limited only by creativity and willingness of two or more companies/organizations to work together for their mutual benefit.

- *Electronic and telephone sales.* Electronic sales are now firmly entrenched as an important sales tool for the hospitality industry. Even local restaurants use a Web site as an informational and sales tool. This tool is particularly effective in international sales where customers and providers such as B&Bs can quickly interface. The majority of hospitality firms do not depend solely on this tool but have instead found that electronic sales is most effective when used as part of a marketing/sales mix, including database marketing, telephone (800 numbers), personal sales, and a carefully selected blend of media.

- *Search engine marketing sales.* Search engine marketing (SEM) focuses on using the Internet effectively to market your hotel, restaurant, or tourism product. The importance of SEM has steadily increased over time as more travelers make reservations online. Hotel companies are putting more resources into SEM to help counter the need to pay commissions to online travel agencies (OTAs) to book their rooms. Some of the tactics used in SEM include the purchase of ads online and search engine optimization (SEO). SEO is a technique where the message on the Web is designed to catch the attention of search engines, so when a customer types in "Hotels in Vancouver" a company's hotel in Vancouver will come up on the first page of the search. Good SEM can be used to generate individual bookings as well as booking and leads for groups.[13]

- *Proprietary Web sites* —Effective SEM requires careful planning, including the development of a Web site.

A few strategies to create effective sales results from proprietary Web sites include the following:

A. Conduct data mining of potential guest profiles through information collected from frequent guest program databases or from guests at check-in.

B. Complement and support Web sites through direct mail sent to past guests inviting them to return and to use the company's Web site.

C. Provide Best Rate Guarantees that prices available on the Web site will match any price offered by an OTA.

D. Advertise on Google by "pay by click" to entice Google or another search engine to encourage the company's Web site to appear higher on the search.

Acquire the services of a Web page consultant to optimize key words that help locate a Web page higher on the search.

E. Entice customers to use a company's call center or on-site toll-free telephone number by offering "freebies," such as parking, breakfast, movies, and WiFi.

Experts in the field recognize that the use of toll-free numbers and call centers is labor intensive, but they say that the cost is less than paying commissions to OTAs.

The size of a sales force may need to increase to support new marketing strategies. The sales manager then has the responsibility to "sell" top management because a budgetary increase will almost certainly be necessary. Similarly, a professional sales manager must be aware of changing trends and new technology. Rather than tenaciously support a larger-than-necessary sales force, the sales manager must be prepared to downsize and substitute technology when appropriate.

Organizing the Sales Department

As discussed previously, hospitality companies traditionally design departments along functional lines. It is common to find hotels with several marketing-related departments, such as a sales department, a guest relations department, and an advertising and public relations department, but not a "marketing" department. In recent years, some hotels have given the title "sales and marketing" to the previously named sales department but with limited training in marketing for the sales manager.

Today's sales managers may have two types of salespeople within their departments: an inside sales force and a field sales force. The term *inside sales* can be misleading because many field salespeople spend a great deal of their time inside the hotel calling clients and prospects, meeting with them, making arrangements with other departments, answering mail, and performing many other duties, such as completing sales reports.

Inside Sales Force

Inside salespeople include three types. There are technical-support persons, who provide technical information and answers to customers' questions. There are sales assistants, who provide clerical backup for the field salespersons. They call ahead and confirm appointments, carry out credit checks, follow up on deliveries, and answer customers' questions when they cannot reach the outside sales rep. There are also telemarketers, who use the phone, Internet, and social media to find new leads, qualify them, learn about their business, and sell to them. Telemarketers can contact up to 50 customers per day compared with the four or five that an outside salesperson can contact. They can be effective in the following ways: cross-selling the company's other products, upgrading orders, introducing new company products, opening new accounts and reactivating former accounts, giving more attention to neglected accounts, and following up and qualifying leads.

Telemarketing has found a role in the hospitality industry. Some members of the cruise industry use a telemarketing sales force to reach individual guest prospects. Telemarketing has found disfavor among many recipients of these calls. Within the hospitality industry, meeting planners are besieged by hotel sales reps who have done no research concerning the planner. Instead, they commonly begin a conversation with the question, "Do you plan meetings?" Busy meeting planners find this disruptive and frustrating, particularly if frequently called by the same hotel but different sales reps.[14]

A more successful outcome has occurred in hospitality enterprises that employ a specialist to do prospecting and qualifying. This can provide the sale force with background information on the prospective client. The local Chamber of Commerce, Internet, and local news sources are all good sources of information. This information prioritizes the salesperson's time and the time of the prospective clients as the salesperson understands their needs.

Information Needed by the Sales Force

At the least, salespeople need a database of their customers/clients. This helps them prepare for sales calls and also to answer questions while talking with customers.

Basic Database Needs

- List of clients alphabetically and by key client listing
- Sales history of client
- Volume of sales by client
- Seasonality of sales by client
- Products/services purchased by client
- Profitability of client (many companies will not release this to the sales force)
- Buyer contact information
    - Name
    - Title
    - Address (both mailing, courier and post office)
    - E-mail
- Special needs of client
- Past problems of/with client

This is a partial list of the type of information that may be provided to sales force members. The purpose is not to overwhelm the sales force with data but instead to assist them to better serve the client and in turn realize sales success.

Reservations Department

The reservations department is a very important inside sales area for many hospitality companies because reservationists may speak with 80 percent of a company's customers. This department is sometimes not viewed as part of the sales team. It is sometimes a separate department, and unfortunately, the reservations and sales departments may have little communication. In worst-case scenarios, they may actually find themselves at odds. This is not the case at Hyatt Hotels, where reservations are under sales/marketing.

A study of reservations departments at a hotel company, airline, and cruise line revealed that much can be done to improve the effectiveness of this critical inside sales force.[15] The results of this study showed that reservations training is critical. The training program prescribed was remarkably similar to that for any sales position. Hyatt focuses on technical aspects, including how to sell. Hyatt's philosophy is that the skills necessary to be an effective salesperson can be taught.

Reservationist candidates at American Airlines are interviewed and hired for their sales ability. Days Inns has a program to hire the elderly and the physically challenged and through training turn them into reservation salespeople. Training your reservationists to be good company representatives and teaching them how to sell will pay big dividends in the long run.[16]

Field Sales Force

Today, sales managers face an increasingly complex marketplace, which has created the need to review the organizational design of the field sales force. We next discuss different types of field sales forces currently used by hospitality companies.

Commissioned Reps

Hotels and resorts commonly use commissioned sales representatives in distant markets where the market potential does not justify employing a salaried salesperson. A Los Angeles hotel may contract with commissioned sales reps in New York or Miami to reach companies and associations that are known to the local sales reps. Commissioned sales reps normally represent several different properties or chains but attempt not to represent competing clients. This is sometimes difficult in the case of chains, which have competing properties.

It is important to follow a few simple rules when working with commissioned sales reps.

1. **Select markets with care.** Distant markets should be selected to match corporate goals and marketing/sales objectives, not simply to have someone represent the company in a location.

2. **Visit the market personally.** Meet with prospective sales reps, examine their offices, check out references, note their personal appearance, ask for a list of current clients, ask for a credit report, and clear the rep through the police and the Better Business Bureau or the equivalent. In general, it is important to be as careful or even more careful in hiring a sales rep to cover distant markets as in hiring salaried sales force members. In some developing nations, a commissioned sales rep is considered to be a member of the client company's workforce and is dependent on that company for livelihood. Local courts often decide in favor of the rep and may award the rep large financial settlements in cases such as dismissal for failure to meet performance standards.

3. **Include the sales rep as part of the hotel's sales force.** It is important to visit the offices of distant sales reps occasionally. This requires an adequate budget for travel and may entail considerable effort to convince the GM that such an expenditure of time and money is worthwhile.

Salaried Sales Force

Most hospitality industry sales force members are paid a salary plus benefits. Additional compensation is sometimes available through commissions, bonuses, profit sharing, or other financial remuneration. In some nations, a sales force, by law, is paid an additional month's salary at Christmas or New Year's and may qualify for benefits unknown to North American companies, such as a month of paid vacation each year.

Team Sales

Team sales have become a necessity in many industries. The hospitality industry is no exception. The concept of a sales team is two or more persons working in concert toward a common sales objective. These persons are not necessarily from the same company. The purpose for a team sales approach is to accomplish objectives through the synergism of two or more people that would be impossible or unduly costly through individual sales efforts.

In addition to traditional objectives, such as to increase occupancy in a hotel, other nonquantifiable objectives are sometimes established for teams. These generally deal with enhancing image and goodwill. People from various disciplines and departments are sometimes brought together to improve morale, teach teamwork, and cross-educate.

Teams within the hospitality industry have traditionally been used for specific tasks, which include but are not limited to the following:

- Sales blitz

- Travel mission

- Charity promotions

- Community improvement programs

Although teams are used for many purposes, the primary purpose for team sales should be to improve sales competitive position. Teams are best used when the needs of the customer or prospect are complex and require the input of specialists. An example might be a large conference that requires the expertise and cooperation of an airline, a golf resort, and a ground transportation company.

Today, the concept of team sales is moving beyond occasional use, such as during a sales blitz, to the allied concepts of relationship marketing and strategic alliances.

■■■ Relationship Marketing and Strategic Alliances

The goal of personal selling traditionally was viewed as a specific contract with a customer. But in many cases the company is not seeking simply a one-time sale. It has targeted a major customer account that it would like to serve for a long period of time. The company would like to demonstrate that it has the capabilities to serve the account's needs in a superior way. The type of selling to establish a long-term collaborative relationship is more complex than a short-run, one-time sales approach. Obtaining long-run commitment involves many more agreements than simply closing the sale.[17]

More companies today are moving their emphasis from transaction marketing to relationship marketing. Today's customers are large and often global. They prefer suppliers who can sell and deliver a set of products and services to many locations, and who can work closely with customer teams to improve products and processes.

McDonald's offers a special example of the value of building trust with suppliers. Unlike some restaurant chains, McDonald's supply chain is 100 percent outsourced as opposed to vertically integrated suppliers. Agreements with suppliers are done on a handshake basis. *McDonald's noncontractual agreements with suppliers, both large and small, are built on trust.*

When McDonald's expands into overseas markets, most of the cost is absorbed by suppliers such as McCain Foods, J.R. Simplot, and ConAgra. As McDonald's expands, its suppliers also expand into the same markets. These companies make investments in the hundreds of millions of dollars once McDonald's says it is entering a market such as India. In the case of India, McCain Foods (Toronto, Canada) purchased 8,000 acres to grow french fry potatoes assuring McDonald's of sufficient supply.[18]

Companies recognize that sales teamwork increasingly is the key to winning and maintaining accounts. They recognize that asking their people for teamwork doesn't provide it. They need to revise their compensation system to give credit for work on shared accounts; they must set up better goals and measures for their sales forces; and they must emphasize the importance of teamwork in their training programs while honoring the importance of individual initiative.

Relationship marketing is based on the premise that important accounts need focused and continuous attention. Salespeople working with customers under relationship marketing must do more than call when they think customers might be ready to place orders. They should monitor key accounts, know their problems, be ready to serve them in a number of ways, and strive to become part of the client's team.

When a relationship management program is implemented properly, the organization begins to focus as much on managing its customers as on managing its products. At the same time, companies should realize that although there is a strong move toward relationship marketing, it is not effective in all situations. Hospitality companies must determine which customers will respond profitably to relationship marketing.

The Boca Raton Resort and Club provides an example of the benefits that can accrue from relationship marketing. The resort took the approach that they could no longer confine themselves to selling rooms, conference space, and banquets. They focused on how the resort could partner with the client to help them achieve the goals of the conference.[19] To provide a competitive advantage, companies are using consultative selling as a way of helping their clients and differentiating their product.

Strategic alliances are a highly developed form of relationship marketing that are common between vendor and buyer or between noncompeting vendors and a common buyer. "Alliances are relationships between interdependent parties that agree to cooperate but still retain separate identities."[20] A strategic alliance may involve sharing a combination of any of the following: confidences, database, market knowledge, planning resources, risks, security, and technology.

Strategic alliances have become a necessity due to a variety of factors: globalization, complicated customer needs, large customers with multiple locations, the need for technology, highly interdependent vendor/buyer relationships, intensified competition, and low profitability within the hospitality industry.

Strategic alliances directly affect the nature of the professional sales function within hospitality companies. The need for professional sales is dramatically enhanced.

Large customers may require services, such as assistance with planning, extended financing, and equity participation. In turn, these needs affect the policies and procedures of suppliers. A buyer who demands that all invoices be sent and settled through electronic data interchange (EDI) may create a need for new investment in hardware and software on the part of the suppliers.

Salespeople must be able to understand increasingly sophisticated buyer needs and communicate them to management. In many cases, the real test of a salesperson's skills comes in the ability of that person to convince his or her own management of the need to change policies and procedures.

The remainder of this chapter discusses the process of sales management. The topics selected are basic to sales managers of virtually all hospitality companies. Although these concepts have application to the management

Hotels, resorts, and meeting venues hosting meetings should work with their clients to ensure the organization's desired outcome of the meeting is met. Courtesy of Kasto/Fotolia.

of an inside sales force, a commission sales force, and team selling, they were developed primarily for the management of a traditional sales force composed of individual salaried salespeople. The majority of the remaining examples in this chapter refer to this traditional form of sales force.

■■■ Recruiting and Training a Professional Sales Force

Importance of Careful Selection

At the heart of a successful sales force operation is the selection of effective sales-people. The performance difference between an average and a top sales person can be considerable. One survey revealed that the top 27 percent of the sales force brought in over 52 percent of the sales. Beyond the differences in sales productivity are the great wastes entailed in hiring the wrong person. When a salesperson quits, the cost of finding and training a new salesperson plus the cost of lost sales can be substantial. Additionally, a sales force with many new people is generally less productive.[21]

Characteristics of a Good Sales Person?

Selecting salespeople would be simple if we knew what traits to look for. Most customers say they want sales representatives to be honest, reliable, knowledge-able, and helpful.

Look for traits common to the most successful salespeople in the company. A study of superachievers found that super sales performers exhibit the following traits: risk taking, powerful sense of mission, problem-solving bent, care for the customer, and careful planning.[22] Effective salespeople have two basic qualities: empathy, the ability to feel as the customer does, and ego drive, a strong personal need to make the sale.[23]

Establishing a Profile of Desired Characteristics Matching the Corporate Culture

The management of each hospitality company has a responsibility to determine a desired sales force profile. The GM, vice president marketing/sales, and others may help determine the preferred characteristics for a sales force.

The person who should first exemplify these is the sales manager. Management selects this person and then empowers him or her with the primary responsibility for recruiting, training, motivating, and controlling the sales force.

The rhetoric of most hospitality companies regarding a desired sales force is much the same, but actually putting words into action varies. This is due to the fact that managers sometimes overlook the importance of their unique corporate culture and simply adopt a generic profile description. All hotels are not alike, nor are all cruise lines, nor are the members of any hospitality company.

The corporate culture within some organizations is formal and authoritarian. In others, such as Southwest Airlines, fun is encouraged. Substantial differences exist among hospitality firms. Both the employer and the salesperson need to fully recognize that success cannot be realized if the two parties are incompatible. A salesperson might be very successful with InterContinental or Four Seasons Hotels but unable to adapt to the culture of Ramada or Novotel Hotels.

In service encounters, customers perform roles and employees perform roles. Satisfaction of both parties is likely when the customer and service provider engage in behaviors that are consistent with each other's role expectations. Ritz-Carlton realizes that its customers expect to be treated professionally and with a degree of formality. It communicates to its employees that they are ladies and gentlemen to prepare them for the role of providing professional service to their customers, who are also ladies and gentlemen.[24]

Matching Career Acquisitions with Corporate Objectives

The aspirations of a salesperson must first be clearly understood by that person and clearly communicated to the potential employer. The hospitality industry does not generally offer sales positions that allow a person to become wealthy from commissions or bonuses. Salespeople seeking great wealth are advised to seek careers in commercial real estate or securities. Despite this, the hospitality industry does offer many advantages to a salesperson:

- The industry is fun. Unlike selling funeral plots or cancer insurance, the product is by nature fun and even exciting.

- Clients are generally personable and willing to listen, unlike industries in which the client has little time to talk and exhibits an aggressive knock-you-over attitude.

- Fellow salespeople and other colleagues are generally people oriented, gregarious, and enjoyable.

- Opportunities for travel exist, particularly in sales of airlines, cruise lines, travel agencies, and travel wholesalers.

- Opportunities for movement within the hospitality industry exist. Considerable career movement occurs within the industry. Salespeople move among the various industry members, such as from a hotel or resort to a cruise line or rental car firm.

- Management opportunities exist. Career growth to positions of sales manager is quite feasible. Career growth to vice presidency of sales or marketing is also possible.

It should be recognized that career promotion to GM within hotels and resorts from sales historically has not often occurred but is beginning to happen. These positions generally call for individuals with broader experience and training, including F&B, front desk, and other operational areas.

Sales Force Training

Sales training is vital to success, yet unfortunately it remains a weak link within the hospitality industry. This is particularly problematic for recent graduates with little or no workplace experience. Fortunately, the situation is improving, and several hospitality companies now have training programs.

Sales training is not a one-time process but instead a career-long endeavor. Continuous training is part of the written philosophy of Singapore Airlines. This company believes that all employees must be trained and retrained continuously.

Types of Training Required

Members of a sales force require three types of training:

1. **Product/service training.** Technology creates continuous change within the hospitality industry. Reservation systems, equipment such as airplanes or cruise ships, and entire operational systems change. Service delivery systems, menus, branch locations, and other changes require regular and frequent training.

2. **Policies, procedures, and planning training.** As organizations increase in size and complexity, the need for formalized systems and procedures increases. Training is essential to ensure that all policies and procedures are understood.

   Effective salespeople continuously wink at some policies and procedures. This is generally done in an effort to satisfy customer needs and close the sale quickly. Unfortunately, a chronic failure to do things the "company way" leads to problems.

   Hospitality salespeople receive much criticism for their lack of attention to detail in the barrage of paperwork they must complete. Failure to complete paperwork correctly, on time, and in detail leads to costly errors, customer dissatisfaction, and ill will among other departments.

3. **Sales techniques training.** An age-old debate centers on the wisdom of attempting to teach techniques of selling. One camp firmly believes that salespeople are determined by genetics, personality, and motivation. The other side generally not only agrees that only a small percentage of individuals make effective salespeople but also contends their effectiveness can be enhanced by learning sales basics such as the following:

- Prospecting
- Obtaining the initial sales call (setting the appointment)
- Conducting the sales dialog
  - Becoming acquainted
  - Asking questions and probing for prospects' needs
  - Listening to what the prospect says and doesn't say
  - Presenting benefits of product/service features to match prospects' needs
  - Overcoming objections
  - Further probing if necessary to determine needs
  - Closing the sale
- Follow-up
  - To continue sales dialog if prospect did not buy
  - To say thank-you for the order
  - To assure client that this was the correct thing to do
  - To look for opportunities to upsell or cross-sell
  - To ask for leads and testimonials
  - To ask for another appointment or ask for another sale when client is again ready to purchase

Although sales training is most effective when customized, general factors that contribute to the success or failure of a salesperson should be considered when developing a sales training program.

Six factors have been determined to contribute to sales failure. Each is relevant to salespeople within the hospitality industry.[25]

1. Poor listening skills[26]
2. Failure to concentrate on top priorities
3. Lack of sufficient effort
4. Inability to determine customer needs
5. Lack of planning for sales presentations
6. Inadequate product/service knowledge

Sales training is a responsibility of the sales manager. It has been suggested that hotel sales management should spend 50 percent of their time selling; 30 percent supervising and training staff; and the remaining 20 percent with paperwork, meetings, and reviewing marketing plans.[27]

Members of upper management often assist in training by presenting an overview of the company and its history, culture, and norms. This sends a clear message to the sales force and helps establish an effective learning attitude.

Sales managers often invite people from other departments, such as the chef or reservations manager, to attend selected sales meetings for the purpose of discussing product improvements. It is also important for salespeople to experience the company's service. Salespeople for a cruise line cannot effectively sell the excitement of sailing if they have never left dry land.

Harrah's Cherokee Casino in North Carolina is connected with other casinos through its total rewards program. Courtesy of PR Newswire/AP Images

The hospitality industry has historically offered free or low-cost "fam trips" (familiarization trips) to travel agents and wholesalers. This may be considered as training of sales intermediaries. Other benefits, such as free flight privileges and expense accounts to entertain guests in the company's lounge and restaurants, also enhance product knowledge. These perks are often viewed with suspicion by employees and managers from other departments. It is essential that they be used judiciously.

Training Materials and Outside Training Assistance

Formal training may sometimes be necessary in which technical details must be memorized. The use of interactive video for this kind of training has proved effective. Some fast-food chains use such systems to help train operational employees.

Today, many companies are adding digital e-learning to their sales training programs. Online training may range from simple text- and video-based product training and Internet-based sales exercises that build sales skills to sophisticated simulations that recreate the dynamics of real-life sales calls. One of the most basic forms is virtual instructor-led training (VILT). Using this method, a small group of salespeople at remote locations log on to an online conferencing site, where a sales instructor leads training sessions using online video and interactive learning tools.

Training online instead of on-site can cut travel and other training costs, and it takes up less of a salesperson's selling time. It also makes on-demand training available to salespeople, letting them train as little or as much as needed, whenever and wherever needed. Although most e-learning is Web based, many companies now offer on-demand training from anywhere via almost any mobile digital device.

Many companies are now using imaginative and sophisticated e-learning techniques to make sales training more efficient—and sometimes even more fun. For example, some are creating a role-playing simulation video game to train its sales force.[28] Ultimately, all training is perfected on the job. Some managers continue to believe that effective training consists solely of learning from one's trials and errors while selling. What is overlooked is that this is costly. For many, this sink-or-swim system creates unnecessary turnover and morale problems.

As the new salesperson learns through experience, it is critical for the sales manager to monitor progress and offer encouragement and suggestions for improving areas of weakness. Effective sales managers are effective teachers. Individuals who do not enjoy teaching or coaching may find that their own management careers are limited.

All teachers dread a moment of truth. That is the time when grades must be given. Granting an "A" is pleasurable and easy, but placing an "F" on someone's record requires soul searching. The same is true for a sales manager, who must eventually come to the conclusion that no amount of training will create a professional salesperson of an individual.

Once this decision has been reached after serious study and thought, the sales manager has no alternative other than to release the salesperson promptly. Those who rescind this decision in the face of emotion-laden pleas for a second chance only postpone the inevitable.

■■■ Managing the Sales Force

The research and study dedicated to this subject clearly indicate that successful sales management is not the result of following a formula.

Successful sales managers cannot be described by a narrow profile. Successful sales managers come in all sizes, shapes, colors, and backgrounds. Perhaps, if a universal truth exists, it is that long-run successful sales managers exhibit a strong affinity for their subordinates, are willing to learn, and are reasonably bright. Even these conclusions sometimes seem to be disputed by observing some sales managers who meet objectives and please upper management, yet seem weak in virtually every skill and talent normally accorded to successful sales managers.

The fact is that market conditions often have an inordinate influence over a sales manager's failure or success. An economic climate in which guests are begging for hotel rooms versus three years of deep economic recession with a surplus of hotel rooms can produce very different results.

Hospitality sales management is neither a precise science nor a formula-based work procedure. Nevertheless, certain functions or processes have historically been associated with the management of a professional sales force.

Selecting Sales Strategies

Sales successes within the hospitality industry are not the result of a hit-and-run sales mentality. Success depends on the development of excellent long-run relationships with clients or accounts. The 80/20 rule prevails within the hospitality industry. A B&B, a highway motel, or a discount airline may find no relevance, but major hotels and major airlines know the phenomenon well. This concept says that a majority of a firm's business comes from a minority of its customers. These are commonly referred to as key, national, or major accounts. Certain corporate clients and travel intermediaries, such as OTAs, generally serve as key accounts. These companies provide large numbers of customers.

Based on the concept of key customers, six general sales strategies must be recognized by members of the hospitality industry:

1. **Prevent erosion of key accounts.** It does little good to attract new customers if key customers are lost. Companies operating on this kind of treadmill inevitably have higher than average sales force turnover and experience employee morale problems. Determine reasons why key customers leave and initiate corrective steps. Initiate and carefully manage programs that treat key customers as royalty. A single sales/service person may be assigned to work with only a handful of key accounts. Unless these accounts are provided highly personal service, the risk of loss to a competitor is great.

   The CEO of a large hotel chain reportedly once told franchisees that they should view their properties as buckets with holes in the bottom. From these holes escape large numbers of customers. The message was that franchises must place even greater efforts into sales to attract new customers. Some who attended this meeting reported that the message had a depressing effect on the audience, who viewed themselves on a treadmill that regularly increased in speed. This was undoubtedly not the desired effect of the analogy. Instead, the message should have been that each of us has holes in our respective buckets, but it is our responsibility to close or lessen the size of these holes so we retain more of our customers.

   Harrah's Casinos introduced a loyalty card program known as "Total Rewards." This allowed each Harrah's casino to track the gaming and purchasing activities of its customers. Data collected from this system were fed into an information system called "WINet," which linked all Harrah's properties, allowing the company to collect company-wide customer information.

   This changed the corporate culture of Harrah's from an individual property focus to a chain-wide collaborative customer focus. The WINet system analyzes information such as gender, age, place of residence, and types of casino games played. Key customers and potential key customers are then identified, and promotional strategies are custom designed for them.

   Harrah's discovered that 30 percent of its customers generated 80 percent of company revenues. Use of this information resulted in a $100 million increase in revenue from key customers in the first two years.[29]

2. **Grow key accounts.** As Harrah's clearly demonstrated, key accounts usually offer more sales potential than is currently realized. Key accounts may split their businesses between several provider companies. A hotel property or a

hotel chain seldom obtains all or even a majority of a company's business. Increasing evidence indicates that companies are willing to reduce the number of hotel providers, and to give more of their business to a few hotels, if these companies meet their requirements for service and price.

Sometimes the sales force of a hotel becomes enamored with what appears to be a sales opportunity gold mine. Unfortunately, when this happens, traditional customers and traditional marketing channels that have consistently produced for the hotel are momentarily forgotten. This is the old and familiar phenomenon of "the grass is always greener on the other side of the fence."

The sales departments of many U.S. hotels thought they had discovered a "sure-fire" client that would fill their hotel rooms. Organizers of soccer's World Cup convinced hotels to reserve large quantities of rooms for thousands of anticipated fans. Some luxury hotels blocked off up to 1,000 room nights only to find that demand did not materialize, thus requiring them to release 50 to 80 percent of the reserved rooms.

Hyatt International Sales Vice President Craig Parsons later described previous demand predictions as ludicrous. He claimed that by the time they were notified the World Cup was reducing the block, there was not enough time to sell them to summer tourists. Most of the summer tourists had already booked their rooms or chose an alternate destination because they could not find a room at a price they wanted to pay.[30]

In addition to negating probable sales, hotels blocking rooms may have infuriated good customers who were unable to book reservations and probably selected another hotel. It is possible that some of the guests may be difficult to recapture, particularly if they liked the competitor's hotel.

3. **Grow selected marginal accounts.** Selected marginal accounts can become key accounts if given sufficient time and a consistent level of service. They are currently marginal accounts for a variety of reasons, such as the following:

- Experimenting or sampling your product or service. If they like it, they might provide substantially more business.

- Have received poor service in the past and therefore use your services only when necessary.

- Account manager changes have resulted in splitting the business between various hospitality firms.

- Comfortable with your service but competitors have acquired the bulk of their business through better follow-up.

4. **Eliminate selected marginal accounts.** Unfortunately, some accounts result in net losses for a hospitality company. These negative-yield customers should be identified and eliminated whenever possible. It may be difficult to eliminate these customers due to an inability to identify them when the order of reservation is placed. A professional sales force has the responsibility to remove these customers from its list of prospects or active accounts, and refrain from future sales calls or sales promotions directed to them.

5. **Retain selected marginal accounts but provide lower-cost sales support.** Many accounts represent infrequent purchases or low-yield business. These accounts cannot bear the cost of personalized sales calls or expensive promotions. A common method of dealing with these accounts is to assign them to an inside sales force. These salespeople don't make field calls but instead interact with customers via telephone, telemarketing, catalogs, direct mail, and fax machines.

6. **Obtain new business from selected prospects.** The process of obtaining new accounts is costly and time consuming. Experienced salespeople know that it often requires five or more sales calls to obtain the business of a prospect. The cost of making a single sales call may be several hundred dollars when all costs are considered, such as travel expenses, salary, and benefits to the salesperson. The high cost of obtaining a new customer dictates that this person must have the potential to contribute significantly to profits. It is inefficient and nonproductive to pursue sales prospects who have little or no likelihood of ever providing significant returns to the company.

Sales Force Tactics: Principles of Personal Selling

We turn now to the purpose of a sales force: to sell. Personal selling is an ancient art. Effective salespersons have more than instinct. They are trained in tactics to achieve sales success. Selling today is a profession that involves mastering and applying a set of principles.

Today's companies spend hundreds of millions of dollars each year to train their salespeople in the art of selling. All the sales training approaches try to convert a salesperson from being a passive order taker to an active order getter.

In training salespeople to acquire signed orders (contracts), there are two basic approaches: a sales-oriented approach and a customer-oriented approach. The first trains the salesperson in high-pressure selling techniques, such as those often used in selling automobiles. The techniques include exaggerating the product's merits, criticizing competitive products, using a slick presentation, selling yourself, and offering some price concession to get the order on the spot. This form of selling assumes that customers are not likely to buy except under pressure, that they are influenced by a slick presentation and ingratiating manners, and that they will not be sorry after signing the order, or if they are, it doesn't matter.

The other approach trains salespeople in customer problem solving. The salesperson learns how to listen and question in order to identify customer needs and come up with good product solutions. Presentation skills are made secondary to customer-need analysis skills. The approach assumes that customers have latent needs that constitute company opportunities, that they appreciate constructive suggestions, and that they will be loyal to sales representatives who have their long-term interests at heart. The problem solver is a much more congruent concept for the salesperson under the marketing concept than the hard seller or order taker.

We examine briefly eight major aspects of personal selling.

Prospecting and Qualifying

The first step in the selling process is to identify prospects. Although the company will try to supply leads, sales representatives need skill in developing their own. Leads can be developed in the following ways:

- Through call-ins
- Having a booth at appropriate travel or trade shows
- Participating in international travel missions
- Asking current customers for the names of prospects
- Cultivating other referral sources, such as suppliers, dealers, noncompeting sales representatives, bankers, and trade association executives
- Through leads generated by the chain
- Joining organizations to which prospects belong
- Engaging in speaking and writing activities that will draw attention
- Examining data sources (newspapers, directories) in search of names
- Using the telephone and mail to find leads
- Dropping in unannounced on various offices (cold canvassing)
- Conducting a sales blitz

It is important not to overlook leads from internal sources. For example, working with the accounts payable department, a salesperson can find suppliers that may be sources of business. The reservations department should be trained to make inquiries of guests representing companies to find out if more business exists from those companies. Front-desk staff should talk with guests representing new companies and pass sales leads to the sales department. Prospecting internally and externally should be done daily. Once prospects have been identified, they need to be qualified.[31]

Sales representatives need skill in screening out poor leads. Prospects can be qualified by examining their financial ability, volume of business, special requirements, location, and likelihood of continuous business. The salesperson might phone or write to prospects before deciding whether to visit them.

Preapproach

Preapproach. The step in which the salesperson or company identifies qualified potential applicants.

The salesperson needs to learn as much as possible about the prospect company (what it needs, who is involved in the purchase decision) and its buyers (their personal characteristics and buying styles). The salesperson should set call objectives, which might be to qualify the prospect or gather information, or to make an immediate sale. Another task is to decide on the best approach, which might be a personal visit, a phone call, or a letter. Do not depend solely on e-mail as many e-mail messages are ignored. The best timing should be thought out because many prospects are busy at certain times.

Approach

Approach. The step in which the salesperson meets the customer for the first time.

The salesperson should know how to greet the buyer to get the relationship off to a good start. This involves the salesperson's appearance, the opening lines, and the follow-up remarks. The opening line should be positive, for example, "Mr. Smith, I am Alice Jones from the ABC Hotel Company. My company and I appreciate your willingness to see me. I will do my best to make this visit profitable and worthwhile for you and your company." This might be followed by key questions and active listening to understand the buyer and his or her needs.

Presentation and Demonstration

Presentation. The sales step in which the sales persons tells the "value story" to the buyer showing how the company's offer solves the customer's problems.

The salesperson now tells the product "story" to the buyer, following the AIDA formula of gaining attention, holding interest, arousing desire, and obtaining action. During the **presentation**, the salesperson emphasizes customer benefits throughout, bringing in product features as evidence of these benefits. A benefit is any advantage, such as lower cost, less work, or more profit for the buyer. A feature is a product characteristic, such as weight or size. A common selling mistake is to dwell on product features (a product orientation) instead of customer benefits (a market orientation).

A need-satisfaction approach to selling starts with a search for the customer's real needs by encouraging the customer to do most of the talking. This approach calls for good listening and problem-solving skills. The salesperson takes on the role of a knowledgeable business consultant, hoping to help the customer save money or make more money.

Negotiation

Much of business-to-business selling involves negotiating skills. The two parties need to reach agreement on the price and other terms of sale. Salespersons need to win the order without making deep concessions that will hurt profitability.

Although price is the most frequently negotiated issue, other issues include quality of goods and services offered, purchase volume, and responsibility for financing, risk taking, and promotion. The number of negotiation issues is virtually unlimited.

Unfortunately, far too many hotel salespeople rely almost exclusively on price as their negotiating tool. Even worse, they often begin negotiating from an already discounted price rather than from rack rates. Negotiations should always begin with rack rates, and price concessions should be given only when absolutely essential. Numerous bargaining tools exist, such as upgrades, complimentary tickets for the ski lift or golf courses, first-class coffee breaks instead of coffee and soft drinks, airport pickup, and use of hotel services such as the fitness center. A hotel sales force might package these amenities into bundles of services and give them names such as the President's Package, the Connoisseur's Package, and the Executive Package.

Sales force members should be taught to negotiate using services or bundled services as the primary negotiating tool rather than price. Table 15–2 shows the possible difference in service package negotiations versus price negotiation. It is easy to see that the hotel benefits by offering a package of services rather than a price discount at all levels other than a 10 percent discount. Sales force members

TABLE 15–2

Hotel Negotiation Cost Comparison: Offering a Service Package Versus Price

	50 Guests at 3 Nights Each	
	Cost/Guest	**Total Cost**
President's Package		
Airport pickup and delivery limousine service	$20	$1,000
Bottle of champagne in room	$25	$1,250
AV technician for meeting	2½ days at $50/hour × 20 hours	$1,000
		$3,250
Price Discounts	**Total Revenue Potential**	
Rack rate ($200/night; 50 guests at three nights each)	$3,000	
Price Cut (%)	**Revenue Lost ($)**	
10	3,000	
20	4,500	
30	6,750	
40	9,000	
50	11,250	

must understand the economic value of these kinds of tradeoffs before they enter into the negotiation process.

Salespeople who find themselves in bargaining situations need certain traits and skills to be effective. The most important traits are preparation and planning skills, knowledge of subject matter being negotiated, ability to think clearly and rapidly under pressure and uncertainty, ability to express thoughts verbally, listening skills, judgment and general intelligence, integrity, ability to persuade others, and patience. These will help the salesperson to know when and how to negotiate.[32]

WHEN TO NEGOTIATE   Consider the following circumstances in which negotiation in the hospitality industry is an appropriate procedure for concluding a sale:[33]

1.   When many factors bear not only on price but also on quality and service.

2.   When business risks cannot be accurately predetermined.

Negotiation is appropriate wherever a zone of agreement exists.[34] A zone of agreement exists when there are simultaneously overlapping acceptable outcomes for the parties.

FORMULATING A BARGAINING STRATEGY   Bargaining involves preparing a strategic plan before bargaining begins and making good tactical decisions during the bargaining sessions. A bargaining strategy can be defined as a commitment to an overall approach that has a good chance of achieving the negotiator's objectives. For example, some negotiators pursue a hard strategy with opponents, whereas others maintain that a soft strategy yields more favorable results.

The sales force of a hotel or resort is in a position to use negotiating skills nearly every day of their professional lives. Their negotiation process can be enhanced by understanding the negotiating strengths and weaknesses of the client, as shown in Table 15–3.

TABLE 15–3

Examples of Hotel Customer's Negotiation Strengths and Weaknesses

Strengths	Weaknesses
1. Provide many guests.	1. Provide few guests.
2. Come in low or shoulder seasons.	2. Come in prime season.
3. Stay low-occupancy nights.	3. Stay high-occupancy nights.
4. Bring quality guests.	4. Bring undesirable guests.
5. Provide cross-purchase potential.	5. Provide little or no cross-sale potential.
6. Purchase upscale rooms.	6. Purchase lowest priced rooms.

BARGAINING TACTICS DURING NEGOTIATIONS Negotiators use a variety of tactics when bargaining. Bargaining tactics can be defined as maneuvers to be made at specific points in the bargaining process. Threats, bluffs, last-chance offers, hard initial offers, and other tactics occur in bargaining.

Experts in negotiation have offered advice that is consistent with their strategy of principles negotiation. Their first piece of tactical advice concerns what should be done if the other party is more powerful. By identifying your alternatives if a settlement is not reached, it sets a standard against which any offer can be measured. It protects you from being pressured into accepting unfavorable terms from a more powerful opponent.[35]

Another tactic comes into play when the opposing party insists on arguing his or her position instead of his or her interests and attacks your proposals or person. Although the tendency is to push back hard when pushed, the better tactic is to deflect the attack from the person and direct it against the problem. Look at the interests that motivated the opposing party's position and invent options that can satisfy both parties' interests. Invite the opposing party's criticism and advice ("If you were in my position, what would you do?").

Another set of bargaining tactics involves opposition tactics that are intended to deceive, distort, or otherwise influence the bargaining. What tactic should be used when the other side uses a threat, or a take-it-or-leave-it tactic, or seats the other party on the side of the table with the sun in his or her eyes? A negotiation should recognize the tactic, raise the issue explicitly, and question the tactic's legitimacy and desirability—in other words, negotiate over it. Negotiating the use of the tactic follows the same principled negotiation procedure: Question the tactic, ask why the tactic is being used, or suggest alternative courses of action to pursue. If this fails, resort to your best alternative to a negotiated agreement and terminate the negotiation until the other side ceases to employ these tactics. Meeting these tactics by defending principles is more productive than counterattacking with tricky tactics.

Overcoming Objections

Handling objections. The sales step in which the salesperson seeks out, clarifies and overcomes any customer objections to buying.

Customers almost always pose objections during the presentation or when asked for the order. Their resistance can be psychological or logical. Psychological resistance includes resistance to interference, preference for established hotel or airline, apathy, reluctance to giving up something, unpleasant associations about the other person, predetermined ideas, dislike of making decisions, and neurotic attitude toward money. Logical resistance might consist of objections to the price or certain product or company characteristics. To handle these objections, the salesperson maintains a position approach, asks the buyer to clarify the objection, denies the validity of the objection, or turns the objection into a reason for buying. The salesperson needs training in the broader skills of negotiation, of which **handling objections** is a part.

Closing

Closing. The sales step in which a salesperson asks the customer for an order.

Now the salesperson attempts to close the sale. Some salespeople do not get to this stage or do not do it well. They lack confidence or feel uncomfortable about asking for the order or do not recognize the right psychological moment to close the sale. Salespersons need to know how to recognize closing signals from the buyer, including physical actions, statements or comments, and questions. Salespersons can use one of several closing techniques. They can ask for the order, recapitulate the points of agreement, offer to help the secretary write up the order, ask whether the buyers want A or B, get the buyer to make minor choices, or indicate what the buyer will lose if the order is not placed now. The salesperson might offer the buyer specific inducements.

Follow-Up/Maintenance

Follow-up. The sales step in which the salesperson follows up after the sale to ensure customer satisfaction and repeat business.

This last step is necessary if the salesperson wants to ensure customer satisfaction and repeat business. Immediately after closing, the salesperson should complete any necessary details on delivery time, purchase terms, and other matters. "Follow-up or foul-up" is a slogan of most successful salespeople. The salesperson should develop an account maintenance plan to make sure that the customer is not forgotten or lost.

Motivating a Professional Sales Force

Selling. Sales representatives know the art of salesmanship: approaching, presenting, answering objections, and closing sales.

Some sales representatives put forth their best effort without any special coaching from management. To them, **selling** is the most fascinating job in the world. They are ambitious and self-starters. But the majority of sales representatives require encouragement and special incentives to work at their best level. This is especially true of field selling, for the following reasons:

- *Nature of the job.* The selling job is one of frequent frustration. Sales representatives usually work alone, their hours are irregular, and they are often away from home. They confront aggressive, competing sales representatives; they have an inferior status relative to the buyer; they often do not have the authority to do what is necessary to win an account; and they lose large orders that they have worked hard to obtain.

- *Human nature.* Most people operate below capacity in the absence of special incentives, such as financial gain or social recognition.

- *Personal problems.* Sales representatives are occasionally preoccupied with personal problems, such as sickness in the family, marital discord, or debt.

  Here is a basic model of motivating sales representatives:[36]

  motivation → effort → performance → rewards → satisfaction

  The model implies the following:

1. Sales managers must be able to convince salespeople that they can sell more by working harder or by being trained to work smarter.

2. Sales managers must be able to convince salespeople that the rewards for better performance are worth the extra effort.

Sales Force Compensation

To attract and retain sales representatives, the company has to develop an attractive compensation package. Sales representatives would like income regularity, extra reward for an above-average performance, and fair payment for experience and longevity. Management would like to achieve control, economy, and simplicity. Management objectives, such as economy, conflict with sales representatives' objectives, such as financial security.

The level of compensation must bear some relation to the going market price for the type of sales job and required abilities. If the market price for salespeople is well defined, the individual firm has little choice but to pay the going rate. The market price for salespeople, however, is seldom well defined. Data on the average take-home pay of competitors' sales representatives can be misleading because of significant variations in the average seniority and ability levels of the competitors' sales forces.

The company must next determine the components of compensation: a fixed amount, a variable amount, expenses, and fringe benefits. The fixed amount, which might be salary, is intended to satisfy the sales representatives' need for income stability. The variable amount, which might be commissions, bonuses, or profit sharing, is intended to stimulate and reward greater effort. Expense allowances enable the sales representatives to meet the expenses involved in travel, lodging, dining, and entertainment; fringe benefits such as paid vacation, sickness or accident benefits, pensions, and life insurance are intended to provide security and job satisfaction. Fixed and variable compensations give rise to three basic types of sales force compensation plans: straight salary, straight commissions, and combination salary and commission.

Many companies in the hospitality industry suffer from high sales force turnover. A variety of reasons have been given to explain this situation, such as burnout. A survey of college graduates preparing to enter the hospitality industry ranked salary as number 10 among variables relating to what they wanted in a job.[37] A different study of young managers who left hospitality careers demonstrated that money was indeed important. Pay-related issues were the second most common reason for leaving, following long hours and inconvenient scheduling as the primary reason. One respondent wrote, "I had poor pay, high stress, low praise and recognition, and worked 75 to 80 hours a week, all for the chance to be a GM in 10 or 15 years with the same job characteristics."[38]

The importance of monetary rewards to a hospitality sales force must not be minimized. These people are expected to maintain a large fashionable wardrobe, to work long hours, experience stress, and often give up family experiences for the sake of their career. Under these circumstances, monetary reward becomes very important.

Supplementary Motivators

Companies use additional motivators to stimulate sales force effort. Periodic sales meetings provide a social occasion, a break from routine, a chance to meet and talk with "company brass," and a chance to air feelings and to identify with a larger group. Sales meetings are an important communication and motivational tool.[39] They can also be used for training in subjects such as how to make effective presentations.[40] Thus, the sales meeting can and should assume increased importance to the sales force.

Companies also sponsor sales contests to spur the sales force to a special selling effort above what would normally be expected. The contest should present a reasonable opportunity for salespeople to win. If only a few salespersons can win or almost everyone can win, it will fail to spur additional effort. The sales contest period should not be announced in advance or else some salespersons will defer some sales to the beginning of the period; also, some may pad their sales during the period with customer promises to buy that do not materialize after the contest period ends.

Sales managers of hotels and resorts sometimes offer vacations at sister properties for winners of a sales contest. When the winners visit a sister property, they are introduced to the sales department and often learn new techniques. In turn, this information is transmitted to others when the winners return and give a report in the next sales meeting.

Evaluation and Control of a Professional Sales Force

Sales Quotas

Many companies set sales quotas prescribing what their sales representatives should sell during the year. Compensation is often tied to the degree of quota fulfillment. Sales quotas are developed from the annual marketing plan. The company first prepares a sales forecast. This forecast becomes the basis for planning production, workforce size, and financial requirements. Then management establishes sales quotas for its regions and territories, which typically add up to more than the sales forecast. Sales quotas are often set higher than the sales forecast in order to stretch sales managers and salespeople to perform at their best level.

The sales manager assigns the area's quota to each of the area's salespeople. There are three schools of thought on quota setting. The high-quota school sets quotas that are higher than what most sales representatives will achieve but are attainable. Its adherents believe that high quotas spur extra effort. The modest-quota school sets quotas that a majority of the sales force can achieve. Its adherents feel that the sales force will accept the quotas as fair, attain them, and gain confidence. The variable-quota school thinks that individual differences among sales representatives warrant high quotas for some and modest quotas for others.

Developing Norms for Salespeople

New sales representatives should be given more than a territory, a compensation package, and training. They need supervision.

Companies vary in how closely they direct their sales representatives. Those who are paid mostly on commission generally receive less supervision. Those who are salaried and must cover definite accounts are likely to receive substantial supervision.

The number of calls that an average salesperson makes during a day has been decreasing. The downward trend is due to the increased use of technology. It is also due to difficulties in reaching prospects because of traffic congestion, busy prospect schedules, and other complexities of contemporary business.

Companies often decide how many calls to make a year on particular-sized accounts. Most companies classify customers into A, B, and C accounts, reflecting the sales volume, profit potential, and growth potential of the account. A accounts might receive nine calls a year; B, six calls; and C, three calls. The call norms depend on expected account profitability.

Regardless of how a sales force is structured, individual salespeople must classify their customer base. A salesperson responsible for channel intermediaries, such as tour operators and travel agents, quickly learns that not all are capable of producing the same sales volume/profit. This is equally true for a salesperson who has responsibility for the conference/meeting segment and for those responsible for national accounts.

Omni International Hotels emphasizes account planning with its sales force. A former president, Jon Canas, told a Harvard professor in a taped interview that not all prospects may be contacted in a particular year because they do not qualify as the best target customers. However, it is important to know the second- and third-tier prospects so that they can be contacted if a slowdown occurs within the top targeted groups.[41]

Companies often specify how much time their sales force should spend prospecting for new accounts. Companies set up prospecting standards for a number of reasons. If left alone, many sales representatives spend most of their time with current customers. Current customers are better-known quantities. Sales representatives can depend on them for some business, whereas a prospect might never deliver any business. Unless sales representatives are rewarded for opening new accounts, they might avoid new account development.

Using Sales Time Efficiently

Sales representatives need to know how to use their time efficiently. One tool is the annual call schedule, showing which customers and prospects to call on in which months and which activities to carry out.

Actual face-to-face selling time can amount to as little as 25 percent of total working time.[42] Companies are constantly seeking ways to improve sales force productivity. Their methods take the form of training sales representatives in the use of "phone power," simplifying record-keeping forms, and using the computer to develop call and routing plans and to supply customer and competitive information.

Managing Trade Shows

Trade shows are commonly used as a means of generating sales leads, keeping in touch with commercial customers, and writing business. Members of the hospitality industry participate in many trade shows, ranging from local/regional ones to international travel missions sponsored by visitor destinations, travel associations, and government departments or ministries of tourism.

Unfortunately, the cost/return effectiveness of trade shows is often placed in peril or disregarded through lack of effective planning and control. The conclusions of a study of hospitality trade show exhibitors were that "it is likely that the true marketing potential of trade shows is not being realized. Commitments to more effective planning would enhance the productivity of trade shows for most companies."[43]

Six steps were suggested to improve trade show effectiveness:

1. Construct a mailing list of prospects.

2. Identify potential leads and communicate with them before the show.

3. Promote the show with incentives that reflect the company's theme, products, and services.

4. Send letters to prospective buyers, inviting them to make a personal contact at the show or at an alternative location.

5. Keep good records of visitor contacts made during the show.

6. Follow up with qualified prospects after the show.

Sales force control and training are also needed to ensure success. The following are items a sales manager should implement before a trade show:

1. Review trade show objectives with the sales force before the show.

2. Designate a trade show captain responsible for managing sales activities.

3. Designate times when certain salespersons are expected to work the booth.

4. Prohibit smoking, drinking, eating, and bunching together in the trade booth.

5. Show sales force members how to deal with complaining/difficult visitors, greet customers/prospects (particularly key ones), develop prospects, identify nonprospects, and process and use leads, business cards, competitive data, and customer/prospect information acquired at the show.

Other Control Techniques

Management obtains information about its sales representatives in several ways. One important source is sales reports. Additional information comes through personal observation, customers' letters and complaints, customer surveys, and conversations with other sales representatives.

Sales reports are divided between activity plans and write-ups of activity results. The best example of the former is the salesperson's work plan, which sales representatives submit a week or month in advance.

The plan describes intended calls and routing. This report leads the sales force to plan and schedule their activities, informs management of their whereabouts, and provides a basis for comparing their plans and accomplishments. Sales representatives can be evaluated on their ability to "plan their work and work their plan."

Many hospitality companies require their sales representatives to develop an annual territory marketing plan in which they outline their program for developing new accounts and increasing business from existing accounts. This type of report casts sales representatives into the role of marketing managers and profit centers. Sales representatives write up their completed activities on call reports. Call reports inform sales management of the salesperson's activities, indicate the status of specific customer accounts, and provide useful information for subsequent calls. Sales representatives also submit expense reports, new business reports, lost business reports, and reports on local business and economic conditions.

These reports provide raw data from which sales managers can extract key indicators of sales performance. The key indicators are (1) average number of sales calls per salesperson per day, (2) average sales call time per contact, (3) average revenue per sales call, (4) average cost per sales call, (5) entertainment cost per sales call, (6) percentage of orders per 100 sales calls, (7) number of new customers per period, (8) number of lost customers per period, and (9) sales force cost as a percentage of total sales. These indicators answer several useful questions. Are sales representatives making too few calls per day? Are they spending too much time per call? Are they spending too much on entertainment? Are they closing enough orders per 100 calls? Are they producing enough new customers and holding on to the old customers?

Formal Evaluation of Performance

The sales force's reports along with other observations supply the raw materials for evaluating members of the sales force. Formal evaluation procedures lead to at least three benefits. First, management has to communicate its standards for judging sales performance. Second, management needs to gather comprehensive information about each salesperson. Third, sales representatives know that they will have to sit down one morning with the sales managers and explain their performance or failure to achieve certain goals.

SALESPERSON-TO-SALESPERSON COMPARISONS One type of evaluation is to compare and rank the sales performance of a company's sales representatives. Such comparisons, however, can be misleading. Relative sales performance is meaningful only if there are no variations in territory market potential, workload, competition, company promotional effort, and so on. Furthermore, current sales are not the only success indicator. Management should also be interested in how much each sales representative contributes to current net profits.

CUSTOMER SATISFACTION EVALUATION A salesperson might be very effective in producing sales but not rate high with customers. An increasing number of companies are measuring customer satisfaction not only with their product and customer-support service but also with their salespeople. Company salespeople who score high on satisfying their customers can be given special recognition, awards, or bonuses.

QUALITATIVE EVALUATION OF SALES REPRESENTATIVES Evaluations can also assess the salesperson's knowledge of the company, products, customers, competitors, territory, and responsibilities. The sales manager should also review any problem in motivation or compliance. The sales manager should check that the sales representatives know and observe company policies. Each company must develop its own evaluation procedure. Whatever procedure is chosen, it must be fair to the salesperson and the company. If members of a sales force feel they are being judged against incorrect norms, they will quickly become dissatisfied.

Hospitality sales is a profession and must be treated as such. It is very much to the advantage of any hospitality company to develop a professional, loyal, and contented sales force. Measurement of a salesperson's value and contribution must not be left to the last minute or to inappropriate standards and measures. No aspect of sales management is more important than developing and using the correct appraisal system for members of a professional sales force.

Regardless of what evaluation system is used, it must be tied to performance. Sales performance and company performance are inherently married. Professor Bill Quain has said, "I believe it is getting harder and harder to find employees who have the drive to sell, the drive to create profits, and the drive to satisfy customers by filling more of their needs with ever improving products and services."[44]

Peer-to-Peer Sales

The rise of shared use or peer-to-peer sales within the travel/hospitality industry is in part due to the difficulty finding good salespeople as described by Professor Quain. The concept of allowing others to temporarily use one's auto, home, apartment, boat, or RV for a fee is not a new concept but technology such as iPhones and social media has certainly facilitated the process.

Other facilitating factors include (1) the high cost of buying and maintaining assets such as an automobile or second home, (2) increasing urbanization in which residents have few good choices for storing equipment, (3) high cost of alternative choices such as hotels or taxis, and (4) desire for increased socialization such as that available in a private home rental through a company such as Home Way, VRBO, or Airbub or ground transportation available through Uber or Lyft.

Statistics concerning the size of this expanding industry are estimated to be in the billions of dollars. One thing is certain: Most entrepreneurs in this industry are young, technologically capable, and also families with social media. This industry will undergo change as governments pass legislation that directly affect the sales process as well as safety, security, and tax reporting issues. While there is little current concern that this industry will soon replace traditional hotels, train and bus service and asset ownership, it is obvious that peer-to-peer companies have discovered a profitable market niche.

Networking

One of the most effective sales tools anywhere in the world is networking. This is especially true for small hospitality members such as B&Bs, inns, fishing lodges, farm/ranch lodging, and many more. However, it remains important to all members of this industry.

The basis for networking is simple. Continuously contact members of the community. Tell these people what your enterprise offers and enthusiastically welcome them to visit and see for themselves.

Networking may at times (particularly for new hospitality members) require "cold calls" in which the owner/manager salesperson drops in without an appointment. In the case of a lodging owner, these calls are generally made on companies/organizations that might have clients or guests who need lodging. Sometimes assumptions are made that a particular business is not worth visiting but such assumptions are often wrong. One of the authors accompanied the owner of a new B&B during a day of cold calls. The owner said it was not worthwhile to call on government entities such as the Forest Service since they had low per diem rates available to them.

Nevertheless a call was made. Upon talking with the Forest Service people in the office, it was discovered that they have several overnight visitors during the year such as consultants, reporters, outdoor enthusiasts, and others who were not limited to low rates. Additionally, it was discovered that the Forest Service had raised their per diem rates and that regional meetings were held at that site during times of the year which were low-occupancy periods for the B&B.

Later, a competitor B&B and a small motel were seen and once again the owner accompanying the author did not wish to visit them. Once again they went anyway and the competitors were welcoming and said they were delighted to know about the quality of the new B&B since they occasionally were overbooked and needed a reliable place to send their guests. Never accept assumptions.

Good contacts for networking can be made through membership in a service club, church, school activities, community theatre, and other organizations. One can never predict the positive results of networking. Sales, of course, are the objective but other results occur such as publicity through interviews on radio or TV or offers to speak at community gatherings.

Never stop networking and always revisit members of the community with something new to tell them even if it is something seemingly trite such as repaving the driveway or planting a new bed of roses. Always extend a warm welcome for all to visit your enterprise. Many successful enterprises have used words such as "The coffee is always on" or as Tom Bodet, spokesman for Motel 6 used to say, "We'll leave a light on for you."

Remember that the most important product you will ever sell is yourself. Never rely on a resume or an e-mail to sell that important a product. Networking will serve you well throughout your life.

■■■ Social Selling: Online, Mobile, and Social Media Tools

Social selling. The use of online, mobile, and social media to engage customers, build stronger customer relationships and augment sales performance.

The fastest-growing sales trend is the explosion in **social selling**—the use of online, mobile, and social media to engage customers, build stronger customer relationships, and augment sales performance. New digital sales force technologies are creating exciting new avenues for connecting with and engaging customers in the digital and social media age. Some analysts even predict that the Internet will mean the death of person-to-person selling, as salespeople are ultimately replaced by Web sites, online social media, mobile apps, video and conferencing technologies, and other tools that allow direct customer contact.[45] Used properly, social media technologies won't make salespeople obsolete; they will make salespeople more productive and effective.

The new digital technologies are providing salespeople with powerful tools for identifying and learning about prospects, engaging customers, creating customer value, closing sales, and nurturing customer relationships. Social selling technologies can produce big organizational benefits for sales forces. They help conserve salespeople's valuable time, save travel dollars, and give salespeople new vehicles for selling and **servicing** accounts. Social selling hasn't really changed the fundamentals of selling. Sales forces have always taken the primary responsibility for reaching out to and engaging customers and managing customer relationships. Now, more of that is being done digitally. However, online and social media are dramatically changing the customer buying process. As a result, they are also changing the selling process. In today's digital world, many customers no longer rely as much as they once did on information and assistance provided by salespeople. Instead, they carry out more of the buying process on their own, especially the early stages. Increasingly, they use online and social media resources to analyze their own problems, research solutions, get advice from colleagues, and rank buying options before ever speaking to a salesperson. A recent study of business buyers found that 92 percent of buyers start their searches online and that, on average, buyers completed nearly 60 percent of the buying process before contacting a supplier.[46]

Servicing. Sales representatives provide various services to the customers: consulting on their problems, rendering technical assistance, arranging financing, and expediting delivery.

Thus, today's customers have much more control over the sales process than they had in the days when brochures, pricing, and product advice were only available from the salesperson. Customers can now browse Web sites, blogs, and YouTube videos to identify and qualify potential locations for their conference or meeting. They can hobnob with other buyers on social media such as LinkedIn, Google+, Twitter, or Facebook to share experiences, identify solutions, and evaluate products they are considering. As a result, if and when salespeople do enter the buying process, customers often know almost as much about a company's products as the salespeople. "It's not just that buyers start the sales process without you," says an analyst, "the typically complete most of the purchase journey before having any contact with sales. And by that point they are far more informed about your business than you are about theirs."[47]

In response to this new digital buying environment, sellers are reorienting their selling processes around the new customer buying process. They are "going where customers are; social media, Web forums, online communities, blogs, in order to engage customers earlier. They are engaging customers not just where and when they are buying, but also where and when they are learning about and evaluating what they will buy."

Salespeople now routinely use digital tools that monitor customer social media exchanges to spot trends, identify prospects, and learn what customers would like to buy, how they feel about a vendor, and what it would take to make a sale. They generate lists of prospective customers from online databases and social networking sites. They use Internet conferencing tools such as WebEx or GoToMeeting live with customers.

Ultimately, social selling technologies are helping make sales forces more efficient, cost effective, and productive. However, social selling is not without its drawbacks. It is not cheap, it can intimidate low-tech salespeople, and some features cannot be shown over the Internet. For example, the service orientation and culture of a meeting venue is hard to experience online. Social selling can be important sales tools, but it does not replace face-to-face selling for major clients.

■■■ CHAPTER REVIEW

I. Management of Professional Sales

II. Nature of Hospitality Sales
  A. Competitive analysis and competitive sets

III. Sales Force Objectives
  A. Sales volume
    1. **Sales volume by selected segments**
    2. **Sales volume and price/margin mix**
  B. Upselling and second-chance selling. Excellent profit opportunities exist for hospitality companies, particularly hotels and resorts, to upgrade price and profit margins by selling higher-priced products such as suites through upselling. A related concept is second-chance selling.
  C. Market share or market penetration. These are two important objectives.
  D. Product-specific objectives. Occasionally, a sales force is charged with the specific responsibility to improve sales volume for specific product lines.

IV. Sales Force Structure and Size
  A. Territorial-structured sales force. Each sales representative is assigned an exclusive territory in which to represent the company's full line.
    1. **Territory size.** Territories are designed to provide either equal sales potential or equal workload.
    2. **Territory shape.** Territories are formed by combining smaller units until they add up to a territory of a given sales potential or workload.
  B. Market-segment structured sales force. Company structures its sales force based on market segments.
  C. Market-channel structured sales force. The importance of marketing intermediaries, such as wholesalers, tour operators, travel agencies, and junket reps, to the hospitality industry has created sales force structures to serve different marketing channels.
  D. Customer-structured sales force. A sales force is organized by market segment, such as the association market and the corporate market or by specific key customers.
  E. Combination-structured sales force. A large hotel might have a catering/banquet sales force (product), a convention/meeting sales force (market segment), a tour wholesales sales force (marketing intermediary), and a national accounts sales force (customer).
  F. Sales force size
    1. Customers are grouped into size classes according to their annual sales volume.
    2. The desirable call frequencies (number of sales calls on an account per year) are established for each class.
    3. The number of accounts in each size class is multiplied by the corresponding call frequency to arrive at the total workload for the country in sales calls per year.
    4. The average number of calls a sales representative can make per year is determined.
    5. The number of sales representatives needed is determined by dividing the total annual calls required by the average annual calls made by a sales representative.

V. Organizing the Sales Department
  A. Inside sales force. The inside sales force includes technical support persons, sales assistants, and telemarketers.
  B. Field sales force. The field sales force includes commissioned reps, salaried reps, and sales team.
  C. Team sales

VI. Relationship Marketing and Strategic Alliances. The art of creating a closer working relationship and interdependence between the people in two organizations.
  A. Strategic alliances. Alliances are relationships between independent parties that agree to cooperate but still retain separate identities.
  B. Why strategic alliances are necessary. Globalization, complicated customer needs, large customers with multilocations, the need for technology, highly interdependent vendor/buyer relationship, intensified competition, and low profitability within the hospitality industry.

VII. Recruiting and Selecting Sales Representatives. The effective salesperson has two basic qualities: (1) empathy, the ability to feel as the customer does, and (2) ego drive, a strong personal need to make the sales.
  A. Importance of careful selection. Effective salespeople have two basic qualities: empathy, the ability to feel as the customer does; and ego drive, a strong personal need to make the sale.
  B. Establish a profile of desired characteristics matching the corporate culture.
  C. Matching career acquisitions with corporate objectives.
  D. Sales force training. There are three types of training: product/service training; policies, procedures, and planning training; and sales techniques training.

VIII. Managing the Sales Force
  A. Selecting sales strategies. The following are six general sales strategies:
    1. Prevent erosion of key accounts
    2. Grow key accounts
    3. Grow selected marginal accounts
    4. Eliminate selected marginal accounts
    5. Retain selected marginal accounts, but provide lower-cost sales support
    6. Obtain new business from selected prospects
  B. Sales force tactics: principles of personal selling. These are prospecting and qualifying, preapproach, approach, presentation and demonstration, negotiation, overcoming objections, closing, and follow-up/maintenance.
  C. Motivating a professional sales force
    1. Sales force compensation
    2. Supplementary motivators
  D. Evaluation and control of a professional sales force. There are several means of formal evaluation of

performance: sales-to-salesperson comparisons, customer satisfaction evaluation, qualitative evaluation of sales representatives, peer-to-peer sales, networking, and salesmanship.

IX. Social Selling: Online, Mobile, and Social Media Tools. The use of online, mobile, and social media to engage customers, build stronger customer relationships, and augment sales performance.

■■■ DISCUSSION QUESTIONS

1. Why should companies be concerned about key or national accounts?

2. What are the most common methods of structuring a sales force?

3. Discuss the importance of establishing sales objectives and the various kinds of sales force objectives common to the hospitality industry.

4. Many people feel they do not have the ability to be successful salespeople. What role does training play in helping someone develop selling ability?

5. Discuss the process of negotiation and how sales force members can use it effectively.

6. Good salespeople are familiar with their competitors' products as well as their own. What would you do if your company expected you to sell a product that you thought was inferior to the competition's? Why?

7. It has been said there are two parts to every sale: the part performed by the salesperson and the part performed for the salesperson by his or her organization. What should the company provide for the salesperson to help increase total sales? How does the sales manager's job differ from the sales rep's job?

8. A district sales manager voiced the following complaint at a sales meeting: "The average salesperson costs our company $40,000 in compensation and expenses. Why can't we buy a few less $40,000 full-page ads in *Time* magazine and use the money to hire more people? Surely one individual working for a year can sell more products than a one-page ad in one issue of *Time*." Evaluate this argument.

■■■ EXPERIENTIAL EXERCISES

Do the following:

Conduct an interview with a salesperson for a hospitality or tourism organization. Ask the salesperson about the job. Find out what a typical day is like, and what they like and dislike about the job. Ask how they feel technology will affect the sales department in the future. You may of course ask other questions that are of interest to you. Write up your finding in a report.

■■■ INTERNET EXERCISE

Find a hotel Web site that has a section for meeting planners. Does this site appear to be taking the place of a salesperson or offering assistance to the sales department? Include the names of the sites you have visited in your response.

■■■ REFERENCES

1 Donna J. Owens, "To Offset Their Seasonality, Canada's Resorts Should Stretch Their Seasons by Appealing to Multiple Market Segments," *Cornell Hotel and Restaurant Administration Quarterly*, 35, no. 5 (1994): 29.

2 Ibid., p. 30.

3 Howard Feiertag, "Database Marketing Proves Helpful in Group Sales," *Hotel and Motel Management* (March 8, 1993): 14.

4 Jin-Young Kim and Linda Canina, "Competitive Sets for Lodging Properties," *Cornell Hospitality Quarterly*, 52, no. 1 (February 2011): 20–32.

5 Chekitan Dev, Kevin Zheng Zhou, Jim Brown, and Sanjeev Agarwal; "Customer Orientation or Competitor Orientation," *Cornell Hospitality Quarterly*, 50, no. 1 (February 2009): 25.

6 Owens, "To Offset Their Seasonality."

7 Peter Rainsford, "Selecting and Monitoring Hotel Management Companies," *Cornell Hotel and Restaurant Administration Quarterly*, 35, no. 3 (1994): 34.

8 Boca Raton Resort, http://www.bocaresort.com/PremierClub/PremierClubFeatures.aspx (accessed December 20, 2004); Michael P. Sim and Burritt M. Chase, "Enhancing Resort Profitability with Membership Programs," *Cornell Hotel and Restaurant Administration Quarterly*, 34, no. 8 (1993): 59–62.

9 "Cruise Lines, Boosting Bookings with Segmentation, Case Studies and Clients," www.claritas.com (August 2004).

10 Christopher Schulz, "Hotel and Travel Agents: The New Partnership," *Cornell Hotel and Restaurant Administration Quarterly,* 35, no. 2 (1994): 45.

11 Taketosh Yamazaki, "Tokyo Hotel Construction Push Roger On," *Tokyo Business Today,* 59, no. 3 (1991): 50–51.

12 William A. Kaven and Myrtle Allardyce, "Dalmahoy's Strategy for Success," *Cornell Hotel and Restaurant Administration Quarterly,* 35, no. 6 (1994): 86–89.

13 Alexandra Paraskevar, Ioannis Katsogridakis, Rob Law, and Dimitros Buhalis, "Search Engine Marketing: Transforming Search Engines into Hotel Distribution Channels," *Cornell Hospitality Quarterly,* 52, no. 2 (May 2011): 200.

14 Phillip R. Mogle, "Planner Under Siege," *Successful Meetings* (September 1990): 76.

15 Barbara Jean Ross, "Training: Key to Effective Reservations," *Cornell Hotel and Restaurant Administration Quarterly,* 31, no. 3 (1990): 71–79.

16 Ibid., p. 79.

17 See Neil Rackham, *SPIN Selling* (New York: McGraw-Hill, 1988); Frank V. Cespedes, Stephen X. Doyle, and Robert J. Freedman, "Teamwork for Today's Selling," *Harvard Business Review* (March/April 1989): 44–54, 58.

18 Shanna Asti, "2 Stealth Drivers of McDonald's Global Margins," *The Motley Food,* June 24, 2013.

19 Fred Conner, "Resorts Makeup Means Sweet Smell of Success for Long-Term Client," *Cornell Hotel and Restaurant Administration Quarterly,* 35, no. 3 (1994): 9.

20 S. Dev Chekitan and Saul Klein, "Strategic Alliances in the Hotel Industry," *Cornell Hotel and Restaurant Administration Quarterly,* 34, no. 1 (1993): 43.

21 George H. Lucas, Jr., A. Parasuraman, Robert A. Davis, and Ben M. Enis, "An Empirical Study of Salesforce Turnover," *Journal of Marketing* (July 1987): 34–59.

22 See Charles Garfield, *Peak Performers: The New Heroes of American Business* (New York: Avon Books, 1986; "What Makes a Supersalesperson?" *Sales and Marketing Management* (August 23, 1984): 86; "What Makes a Top Performer?" *Sales and Marketing Management* (May 1989); Timothy J. Trow, "The Secret of a Good Hire: Profiling," *Sales and Marketing Management* (May 1990): 44–55.

23 David Moyer and Herbert A. Greenberg, "What Makes a Good Salesman?" *Harvard Business Review* (July/August 1964): 119–125.

24 K. Douglas Hoffman and John E. G. Bateson, *Essentials of Services Marketing* (Fort Worth, TX: Dryden Press, 1997), pp. 92–93.

25 Thomas N. Ingram, Charles H. J. Sobuepher, and Don Hutson, "Why Salespeople Fail," *Industrial Marketing Management,* 21, no. 3 (1992): 225–230.

26 Judi Brownell, "Listening: The Toughest Management Skills," *Cornell Hotel and Restaurant Administration Quarterly,* 27, no. 4 (1987): 64–71.

27 Howard Feiertag, "Sales Directors Build Productivity and Profitability," *Hotel and Motel Management,* 207, no. 19 (1992): 14.

28 Based on information found in Sara Donnelly, "Staying in the Game," *Pharmaceutical Executive* (May 2008): 158–159; Bayer Healthcare Pharmaceuticals, Inc., "Improving Sales Force Effectiveness: Bayer's Experiment with New Technology," 2008 , www.icmrindia.org/casestudies/catalogue/Marketing/MKTG200.htm; Tanya Lewis, "Concentric," *Medical Marketing and Media,* July 2008, p. 59, www.hydraframe.com/mobile/project_reprace.htm (accessed July 2012); Andrew Tolve, "Pharma Sales: How Simulation Can Help Reps Sell," *Eye for Pharma,* March 28, 2012, http://social.eyeforpharma.com/sales/pharma-sales-how-simulation-can-help-reps-sell; Krishna Depura, "Online Sales Training for Busy Sales Representatives," *MindTickle,* www.mindtickle.com/blog/online-sales-trainingfor-busy-sales-representative/#more-1474 (accessed June 2014).

29 Vincent P. Magnini, Earl D. Honeycutt, Jr., and Sharon K. Hodge, "Data Mining for Hotel Firms: Use and Limitations," *Cornell Hotel and Restaurant Administration Quarterly,* 44, no. 2 (2003): 97.

30 "U.S. Hoteliers Fail to Net Enough World Cup Trade," *Travel Trade Gazette,* U.S. and Ireland (June 1, 1994): 32.

31 Howard Feiertag, "Different People Should Perform Sales and Marketing Jobs," *Hotel and Motel Management* (February 4, 2002): 24.

32 For additional reading, see Howard Raiffa, *The Art and Science of Negotiation* (Cambridge, MA: Harvard University Press, 1982); Samuel B. Bacharach and Edward J. Lawler, *Bargaining Power, Tactics, and Outcome* (San Francisco, CA: Jossey-Bass, 1981); Herb Cohen, *You Can Negotiate Anything* (New York: Bantam Books, 1980); Gerald I. Nierenberg, *The Art of Negotiating* (New York: Pocket Books, 1984).

33 Lamar Lee and Donald W. Dobler, *Purchasing and Materials Management* (New York: McGraw-Hill, 1977), pp. 146–147.

34 This discussion of zone of agreement is fully developed in Raiffa, *Art and Science of Negotiation.*

35 Roger Fisher and William Ury, *Getting to Yes: Negotiating Agreement Without Giving In* (Boston, MA: Houghton Mifflin, 1981).

36 See Gilbert A. Churchill, Jr., Neil A. Ford, and Orville C. Walker, Jr., *Sales Force Management: Planning, Implementation, and Control* (Homewood, IL: Richard D. Irwin, 1985).

37 See Ken W. McCleary and Pamela A. Weaver, "The Job Offer: What Today's Graduates Want," *Cornell Hotel and Restaurant Administration Quarterly,* 28, no. 4 (1988): 28–31.

38 David V. Pavesic and Robert A. Brymer, "Job Satisfaction: What's Happening to Young Managers," *Cornell Hotel and Restaurant Administration Quarterly,* 30, no. 4 (1990): 90–96.

39 Richard Cavalier, *Sales Meetings That Work* (Homewood, IL: Dow Jones-Irwin, 1983).

40 See Joyce I. Nies and Richard F. Tas, "How to Add Visual Impact to Your Presentations," *Cornell Hotel and Restaurant Administration Quarterly,* 32, no. 1 (1991): 46–51.

41 Dunfey Hotels Corporation, "An Interview with Jon Canas, President," video case number 9-833-502 (Boston, MA: Harvard Business School, 1996).

42 "Are Salespeople Gaining More Selling Time?" *Sales and Marketing Management* (July 1986): 29.

43 Ali A. Poorani, "Trade-Show Management: Budgeting and Planning for a Successful Event," *Cornell Hotel and Restaurant Administration Quarterly,* 37, no. 4 (1996): 77–84.

44 Bill Quain, "No One Ever Made Money by Discouraging Their Customers from Spending It," *Cornell Hotel and Restaurant Administration Quarterly,* 4, no. 5/6 (2003): 172.

45 Lain Chroust Ehmann, "Sales Up!," *Selling Power,* January/February 2011, p. 40. Also see Scott Gillum, "The Disappearing Sales Process," *Forbes,* January 7, 2013, www.forbes.com/sites/gyro/2013/01/07/the-disappearing-sales-process/; Matt Dixon and Steve Richj3rd, "Solution Selling Is Dead: Why 2013 Is the Year of B2B Insight Selling," Openview,http://labs.openviewpartners.com/solution-selling-is-dead-2013-year-of-b2b-insight-selling/.

46 See "The Digital Evolution in B2B Marketing," Marketing Leaderships Council, December 2, 2012, p. 3; Scott Gillum, "The Disappearing Sales Process," *Forbes,* January 7, 2013, www.forbes.com/sites/gyro/2013/01/07/the-disappearing-sales-process/; Alice Myerhoff, "How Selling Has Gone Social in the Last 15 Years," *Salesforce Blog,* March 13, 2014, http://blogs.salesforce.com/ company/2014/03/social-selling-15-years-gp.html.

47 See Barbara Giamanco and Kent Gregoire, "Tweet Me, Friend Me, Make Me Buy," *Harvard Business Review* (July–August 2012): 88–94; John Bottom, "Research: Are B2B Buyers Using Social Media?" *Slideshare,* September 10, 2013, www.slideshare.net/basebot/b2b-buyer-behaviour.

Direct, Online, Social Media, and Mobile Marketing

16

Objectives

After reading this chapter, you should be able to:

1. Define direct marketing and discuss its benefits to customers and companies.

2. Identify and discuss the major forms of direct marketing.

3. Explain how companies have responded to the Internet and other powerful new technologies with online marketing strategies.

4. Discuss how companies go about conducting online marketing to profitably deliver more value to customers.

5. Understand how databases can be used to develop direct-marketing campaigns.

For decades, Southwest Airlines has communicated directly with customers through traditional direct-marketing approaches. And the company still uses lots of direct mail, sending promotional messages directly to customers through the good old U.S. Postal Service. But in recent years, Southwest has expanded its direct-marketing strategy to take advantage of the surging digital opportunities for direct, up-close-and-personal interactions with customers. Today, Southwest's new-age direct-marketing capability makes the passenger-centered company the envy of its industry.

When it comes to building direct customer relationships, Southwest Airlines is "the undisputed ruler of the social atmosphere," declares one travel expert. In addition to standard direct-marketing tools, such as direct mail and its Web site, Southwest's broad-based direct-marketing strategy uses a wide range of cutting-edge digital tools to engage customers. Consider the following examples:

- DING! Available as a desktop widget or a smartphone app, DING! offers exclusive, limited-time airfare deals. When an enticing new deal becomes available, DING! emits the familiar in-flight seatbelt-light bell-dinging sound. The deep discounts last only 6 to 12 hours and can be accessed only online through the application. DING! lets Southwest Airlines bypass the reservations system and pass bargain fares directly to interested customers. Eventually, DING! may even allow Southwest Airlines to customize fare offers based on each customer's unique characteristics and travel preferences.

- Smartphone app. In addition to the DING! app, Southwest's regular smartphone app lets customers book reservations directly, arrange car rentals, check in for flights, check flight status, access their Rapid Rewards accounts, and view flight schedules at any time from any location. "You asked for it," says the company. "The Southwest Airlines app is here to make traveling with Southwest Airlines even more convenient."

- E-mail. With their high response rates, Web and mobile e-mail are effective ways to build long-term, one-to-one relationships with carefully targeted customers. Working from its huge opt-in database, Southwest tailors e-mails—the design, message, offer, and even copy length—to the characteristics and needs of specific customers. Most important, Southwest's e-mails offer real value. For example, recent Southwest mobile ads in smartphone apps such as Pandora and Draw with Friends promised, "Only people who sign up get the e-mails—Click 'N Save." The enticing message worked and customers signed up in droves to start saving money by receiving e-mails from Southwest.

- Texting. With more than 3,200 flights every day, some of those flights are bound to be delayed, rescheduled, or canceled because of weather or other unforeseen circumstances. Because most of its customers carry a mobile device when they travel, Southwest now communicates with customers via text messaging to save them time, ensure they get important information, and provide them with peace of mind. "As more passengers adopt mobile devices, [they] are starting to expect information at their fingertips, and waiting in line to speak to customer service agents is not always acceptable," says Fred Taylor, senior manager of proactive customer service communications at Southwest. By providing customers with up-to-date information instantly, Southwest has created sky-high customer awareness, satisfaction, and loyalty.

- Nuts About Southwest blog. Written by Southwest employees, this creative blog allows for a two-way customer–employee dialogue that gives customers a look inside the company's culture and operations. At the same time, it lets Southwest talk directly with and get feedback from customers.

- The social networking media. Finally, of course, Southwest's customers interact directly with the company and with each other at the airline's many Web and mobile-based **social media** sites, from Facebook, Twitter, and YouTube to Pinterest and Flickr. "Southwest is an incredibly social company," says a social media analyst. "Its Twitter feed, which abounds with 'thank you' tweets and @mentions, has [more than 1.5 million] followers. More than [3.8 million] people 'like' the airline's comment-packed Facebook page, and its Nuts About Southwest blog is an industry standard." Another analyst states social media marketing fits Southwest's culture. Southwest has always been a leader in customer communication.

Social media. Independent and commercial online communities where the people congregate, socialize, and exchange views and information.

Southwest's creative, energetic, and super-friendly employees have long been an important competitive advantage. You might worry that with all of these new digital direct-marketing tools, Southwest might lose some of its human touch. Not at all. First, the digital touch points are only one option–customers are still only a phone call away from a human voice, and they still interact face-to-face with Southwest employees during flights. More important, the new digital approaches actually enhance customer contact with Southwest's people rather than substitute for it. In many of its direct-marketing efforts, Southwest lets its employees do the talking. For example, at its Nuts About Southwest blog, flight attendants, pilots, mechanics, and other employees armed with Flip cams tell insider stories. The company also encourages employees to create local Facebook pages to connect with their communities and lets them be creative in their approaches. As a result, Southwest's direct-marketing communications are loaded with employee personality. "You should sound like you're talking to a person," says a Southwest direct marketer. "People brace our quirkiness."

Mobile marketing. Marketing promotions, messages, and other content delivered to on-the-go consumers through mobile phones, smartphones, tablets, and other mobile devises.

Thus, Southwest's high-tech direct-marketing strategy hasn't changed the company's people orientation. In fact, digital direct marketing brings Southwest's people and customers closer together than ever.[1]

Many of the marketing and promotion tools that we've examined previously were developed in the context of mass marketing: targeting broad markets with standardized messages and offers distributed through intermediaries. Today, however, with the trend toward narrower targeting and the surge in digital and social media technologies, many companies are adopting direct marketing, either as a primary marketing approach or as a supplement to other approaches. In this section, we explore the exploding world marketing and its fastest-growing form, digital marketing, using online, social media and **mobile marketing** channels.

■■■ Direct and Digital Marketing

Direct and digital marketing involve engaging directly with carefully targeted individual consumers and customer communities to both obtain an immediate response and build lasting customer relationships. Companies use **direct marketing** to tailor their message to the needs and interests of narrowly defined segments or individual buyers. In this way, they build customer engagement, brand community, and sales.

Direct marketing. Direct communications with carefully targeted individual consumers to obtain an immediate response and cultivate lasting customer relationships.

For example, hotel hospitality companies have built apps, which help them interact with their customers. Marriott's app allows users to check in and out using their app. Before they arrive, customers can make special requests over the app, such as extra towels or restaurant reservations.[2] Presently, they receive their key at a special desk for app users, but before long guests should be able to use their phone as a key. Marriot requires customers to become a member of their rewards program, in order to sign up for the app. Thus, they collect customer information when they sign up, as well as track the guest's consumer behavior during their stay. Domino's has embraced the digital age, allowing customers to order by phone, smart television (TV), car using Ford Sync, and smart watch. By setting up a profile Domino's customers can order their favorite order by text or tweet.[3] These are just two examples of the many ways hospitality companies are using digital media.

The New Direct-Marketing Model

Today spurred by the surge in Internet usage and buying, and by rapid advances in digital technologies, from smartphones, tablets, and other digital devices to the spate of online social and mobile media, direct marketing has undergone a dramatic transformation.

In previous chapters, we discussed direct marketing as channels that contain no intermediaries. We also included direct and digital marketing elements of the promotion mix—as an approach for engaging consumers directly and creating brand community. In actuality, direct marketing is both of these things and much more.

Most companies still use direct marketing as a supplementary channel or medium.

However, for many companies, direct and digital marketing are more than just supplementary channels or advertising media; they constitute a complete model for doing business. Firms employing this direct model use it as the only approach. For example, online travel agencies (OTAs) such as Priceline.com have successfully built their entire approach to the marketplace around direct and digital marketing. Priceline.com sells its services exclusively through online, mobile, and social media channels. Priceline.com, along with other OTAs, has driven many traditional off-line travel agencies into extinction.

Rapid Growth of Direct and Digital Marketing

According to the Direct Marketing Association (DMA), U.S. companies spent almost \$133 billion on direct and digital marketing last year. As a result, direct-marketing–driven sales now amount to more than $2 trillion, accounting for 13 percent of the U.S. economy. The DMA estimates that direct-marketing sales will grow at an annual rate of 4.9 percent.[4]

Direct marketing continues to become more Internet-based, and digital direct marketing is claiming a surging share of marketing spending and sales. For example, U.S. marketers spent an estimated $43 billion per year on digital advertising, an amount increasing at double-digit rates. These efforts generated more than $260 billion in online consumer spending. Total digital advertising spending, including online and search advertising, video, social media, mobile, e-mail, and other, now accounts for the second-largest share of media spending, behind only TV.[5]

Benefits of Direct and Digital Marketing to Buyers and Sellers

For buyers, direct and digital marketing are convenient, easy, and private. They give buyers anywhere, anytime access to an almost unlimited assortment of goods and a wealth of product and buying information. Meta-search travel sites such as Kayak, TripAdvisor, and Trivago give the traveler a great deal of information and reviews on hotels as well as travel destinations. Zomato, Yelp, and OpenTable are common sites used by consumers to find reviews and information on restaurants. Through direct marketing, buyers can interact with sellers by phone or on the seller's Web site or app to create the exact configuration of information, or products they want and then order them on the spot. Finally, for consumers who want it, digital marketing through online, mobile, and social media provides a sense of brand engagement and community, a place to share brand information and experiences with other brand fans.

For sellers, direct marketing often provides low-cost, efficient, speedy alternative for reaching their markets. Today's direct marketers can target small groups of individual customers. Because of the one-to-one nature of direct marketing, companies can interact with customers by phone or online, learn more about their needs, and personalize products and services to specific customer tastes. In turn, customers can ask questions and volunteer feedback.

Direct and digital marketing also offer sellers greater flexibility. They let marketers make ongoing adjustments to prices and programs, or create immediate, timely, and personal engagement and offers. Especially in today's digital environment, direct marketing provides opportunities for real-time marketing that links brands to important moments and trending events in customers' lives. It is a powerful tool for moving customers through buying process and for building customer engagement, community, and personalized relationships.

■■■ Forms of Direct and Digital Marketing

The major forms of direct and digital marketing are shown in Figure 16–1. Traditional direct-marketing tools include face-to-face selling, direct-mail marketing, catalog marketing, telemarketing, direct-response TV marketing, and kiosk marketing. In recent years, however, a dazzling new set of digital direct-marketing tools has burst onto the marketing scene, including online marketing, social media marketing, and mobile marketing. We'll begin by examining the new direct digital and social media marketing tools that have received so much attention lately. Then, we'll look at the still heavily used and very important traditional direct-marketing tools. As always, however, it's important to remember that all of these tools—both the new digital and the more traditional forms—must be blended into a fully integrated marketing communications program.

We'll begin with the exciting new digital forms of direct marketing. But remember that the traditional forms are still heavily used, and that the new and old must be integrated for maximum impact.

Digital and social media marketing
Online marketing
(Web sites, online advertising,
e-mail, online videos, blogs)
Social media marketing
Mobile marketing

Build direct customer engagement and community

Traditional direct marketing
Face-to-face selling
Direct-mail marketing
Catalog marketing
Telemarketing
Direct-response TV marketing
Kiosk marketing

Figure 16–1
Forms of direct and digital marketing.
Source: Kotler, Philip T; Armstrong, Gary, Principles of Marketing, 16th Ed., ©2016, p. 515. Reprinted and Electronically reproduced by permission of Pearson Education, Inc., New York, NY.

Digital and Social Media Marketing

As noted earlier, digital and social media marketing is the fastest-growing form of direct marketing. It uses digital marketing tools such as Web sites, online video e-mail, blogs, social media, mobile ads and apps, and other digital platforms to directly engage consumers anywhere, anytime via their computers, smartphones, tablets, Internet-ready TVs, and other digital devices. The widespread use of the Internet and digital technology has a dramatic impact on both buyers and the marketers who serve them.

Marketing, the Internet, and the Digital Age

Much of the world's business today is carried out over digital networks that connect people and companies. These days, people connect digitally with information, brands, and each other at almost any time and from almost anywhere. The digital age has fundamentally changed customers' notions of convenience, speed, price, product information, service, and brand interactions. As a result, it has given marketers a whole new way to create customer value, engage customers, and build customer relationships.

Digital usage and impact continues to grow steadily. More than 85 percent of all U.S. adults use the Internet, and the average U.S. Internet user spends more than five hours a day using digital media. Moreover, more than 60 percent of smartphone owners access the Internet via their devices. In fact, Americans now use their smartphone and tablet apps more than their PCs to go online. Worldwide, 40 percent of the population have Internet access. And 22 percent have access to the mobile Internet, a number that's expected to double over the next five years as mobile becomes an ever-more-popular way to get online.[6]

Younger consumers embrace digital technology. A study by the National Restaurant Association (NRA) found that over two-thirds of the consumers aged 18 to 44 used phone apps for full-service restaurants, compared to less than one-third for those aged 55 and above. This shows the bifurcation of digital markets. Having a digital presence is critical for reaching younger consumers, but for those businesses that attract consumers over 55 years, it is important to maintain conventional means of accessing the business, such as phone and in-person. Also, more education will be required on the benefits and how to use digital access for older customers. Companies such as Amazon and OTAs are helping to both educate and getting customers used to using digital technology for information and purchases.

Young consumers embrace digital technology. Courtesy of Boggy/Fotolia.

Because of the popularity of digital media, it's hard to find a company that doesn't have a substantial online presence. Even companies that have traditionally operated off-line have now created their own online sales, marketing, and brand community channels. A study by the NRA found that over 80 percent of the restaurants they surveyed had a presence on social media. Direct digital and social media marketing take any of the several forms shown in Figure 16–1. These forms include online marketing, social media marketing, and mobile marketing. We discuss each in turn, starting with online marketing.

Online Marketing

Online marketing. Company efforts to market products and services and build customer relationships over the Internet.

Online marketing refers to marketing via the Internet using company Web sites, online advertising and promotions, e-mail marketing, online video, and blogs. Social media and mobile marketing also take place online and must be closely coordinated with other forms of digital marketing. However, because of their special characteristics, we discuss the fast-growing social media and mobile marketing approaches in separate sections.

Web Sites and Branded Web Communities

Marketing Web site. Web sites designed to engage consumers in an interaction that will move them closer to a purchase or other marketing outcome.

For most companies, the first step in conducting online marketing is to create a Web site. Web sites vary greatly in purpose and content. Some Web sites are primarily **marketing Web sites**, designed to engage customers and move them closer to a direct purchase or other marketing outcome. A new trend is to create a community of brand fans on the Web site, by providing content that will engage the consumer and create customer-branded loyalty. Such sites typically offer a rich variety of brand information, videos, blogs, activities, and other features that build closer customer relationships and generate engagement with and between the brand and its customers.

For example, on Chipotle's Web site there is a section called What's Happening. In the past this site has included a video showing how tofu is made and information on Cultivate, a festival with sites across the country featuring sustainable food through cooking demos and sales, as well as art and live music.

Creating a Web site is one thing; getting people to visit the site is another. To attract visitors, companies aggressively promote their Web sites in off-line print and broadcast advertising through ads and links on other sites. But today's Web users are quick to abandon any Web site that doesn't measure up. The key is to create enough engaging and valued content to get consumers to come to the site, stick around, and come back again.

At the very least, a Web site should be easy to use and visually appealing. Ultimately, however, Web sites must also be useful. When it comes to online browsing and shopping, most people prefer substance over style and function over flash. Effective Web sites contain deep and useful information, interactive tools that help find and evaluate content of interest, links to other related sites, changing promotional offers, and entertaining features that lend relevant excitement.

Convention and visitors bureaus' Web sites typically promote all aspects of the destination, including restaurants, hotels, and attractions. For example, visithoustontexas.com is a site designed for visitors to Houston by the Convention and Visitors Bureau. The site contains information that will not only answer the questions that most visitors will have, but it also offers a number of suggestions on things to do and see. The management of Visit Houston has grouped some of these activities together to create lifestyle itineraries, including "Girlfriends Getaway," "Guy's Weekend," several itineraries for families, and a tour of local breweries. They have developed a total of 17 itineraries based on the interests of the visitor. Of course it also has links allowing visitors to book their choices of hotels, restaurants, and attractions mentioned in the itineraries.

Online Advertising

Online advertising. Advertising that appears while consumers are surfing the Web, including display ads, search-related ads, and online classifieds.

As consumers spend more and more time online, companies are shifting more of their marketing dollars to **online advertising** to build brand sales or attract visitors to their Internet, mobile, and social media sites. Online advertising has become a major promotional medium. The main forms of online advertising are display ads and search-related ads. Together, display and search-related ads account for the largest portion of firms' digital marketing budgets, capturing 30 percent of all digital-marketing spending.[7]

Online display ads might appear anywhere on an Internet user's screen and are often related to the information being viewed. For instance, while browsing vacation packages on Travelocity.com, you might encounter a display ad offering a free upgrade on a rental car from Enterprise Rent-A-Car. Online display ads have come a long way in recent years in terms of attracting and holding consumer attention. Today's rich-media ads incorporate animation, video, sound, and interactivity.

Search-related advertising (or contextual advertising).
Text-based ads and links that appear alongside search engine results on sites such as Google and Yahoo!

The largest form of online advertising is **search-related advertising (or contextual advertising)**, which accounted for nearly half of all online advertising spending last year. In search advertising, text- and image-based ads and links appear atop or alongside search engine results on sites such as Google, Yahoo!, and Bing. For example, search Google for "New York hotels"; at the top and side of the resulting search list, you'll see ads for 10 or more advertisers, ranging from OTAs, to hotel brands. Ninety-six percent of Google's $50 billion in revenues last year came from ad sales. Search is an always-on kind of medium, and the results are easily measured.[8] A search advertiser buys search terms from the search site and pays only if consumers click through to its site.

E-Mail Marketing

E-mail marketing remains an important and growing digital marketing tool. "Social media is the hot new thing," says one observer, "but e-mail is still the king."[9] By one estimate, 91 percent of all U.S. consumers use e-mail every day. Sixty-five percent of all e-mails are now opened on mobile devices. Not surprisingly, then, a recent study found that e-mail is 40 times more effective at capturing customers than Facebook and Twitter combined. Marketers sent an estimated more than 838 billion e-mails last year. Despite all the e-mail clutter, thanks to its low costs, e-mail marketing still brings one of the highest marketing returns on investment. According to the DMA, marketers get a return of $44.25 on every $1 they spend on e-mail.[10]

Spam. Unsolicited, unwanted, commercial e-mail messages.

When used properly, e-mail can be the ultimate direct-marketing medium. Most blue-chip marketers use it regularly and with great success. E-mail lets these marketers send highly targeted, tightly personalized, relationship-building messages. And today's e-mails are anything but the staid, text-only messages of the past. Instead, they are colorful, inviting, personalized, and interactive. But there's a dark side to the growing use of e-mail marketing. The explosion of **spam**—unsolicited, unwanted commercial e-mail messages that clog up our e-mail boxes—has produced consumer irritation and frustration. According to one research company, spam now accounts for 70 percent of all e-mail sent worldwide.[11] E-mail marketers walk a fine line between adding value for consumers and being intrusive and annoying.

To address these concerns, most legitimate marketers now practice permission-based email marketing, sending e-mail pitches only to customers who "opt in." Some companies use configurable e-mail systems that let customers choose what they want to get. For example, a restaurant may ask if you want to receive e-mails on wine dinners. The idea is to send e-mails that will be welcomed by the receiver. For example, Fleming's sends e-mails that promote its wine tastings, special dinner, discounted prime rib dinners, and a $50 coupon. For those who like Fleming's, these e-mails are interesting and provide value. They also are used to promote sales during down periods. The prime rib dinner is on Monday night, one of the slowest nights of the week. The $50 dollar coupon is for August, when many of Fleming's customers are traveling on vacation. The coupon also followed the principles we discussed in the pricing chapter. To get the certificate one had to book online through the Web site linked to the coupon. Thus, not everyone was given the discount, only those who booked online. The coupon also required a $150 purchase excluding alcohol. To a Fleming's regular this was good value, $50 less than they would normally spend. To Fleming's this generated good sales during a slow period.

Janet Logan, an e-mail marketing expert, has these suggestions for effective e-mail marketing. Make the e-mail event-driven and related to events that will be of interest to the person receiving the e-mail.[12] For example, a person who has expressed interest in a Caribbean cruise will receive an e-mail on a Caribbean cruise promotion or a guest who likes jazz receives information on a jazz brunch. She also suggests integrating e-mail with Web marketing, as when an inquiry about a skiing vacation in the Alps on the Web can trigger a request to send the inquirer information on ski packages. E-mails can include Web links, allowing the receiver to go directly to a Web site to receive more information. Travel wholesalers often send travel agents messages about promotions with a link to their Web site. This reduces the size of the e-mail, and it allows agents to get the detailed information they will need to sell the travel package. E-mail marketing can be both low cost and effective. Red Lobster developed an e-mail program for members of its loyalty program, the Overboard Club. Red Lobster's goal was to focus on sweepstakes and members-only programs, such as gift cards and having live lobsters delivered to your home. Red Lobster wanted to avoid coupons because it believed couponing was not a good way to develop long-term relationships. Red Lobster sent out e-mails about once every four weeks, and the mailings are coordinated with the restaurant's promotions.[13]

Digital Alchemy, a service provider to the hospitality industry, has created a software program that captures e-mail address from guests making a reservation on a third party. It maintains the hotel's database and includes guest history and solicits guest comments via an electronic comment card during their stay. Using its service, the general manager gets negative comments sent to his or her smartphone, with the name, e-mail address, the room the guest stayed in, and when the guest checked out. It allows him or her to respond to the guest quickly, apologizing for the poor experience and providing an offer to bring the guest back to the hotel. The manager states, "A positive healing response counts more than a rotten experience."[14] New smartphone technology coupled with advances in software and the Internet will ensure that e-mail will continue to be an important way to communicate with guests and prospective guests. Like any other form of direct marketing, the e-mail must be relevant to the sender. For example, a resort can send a golf special to everyone in its database who lives within 200 miles, has stayed at the resort four times, played golf at least two times, and had an average daily rate of at least $395.

Online Videos

Another form of online marketing is posting digital video content on brand Web sites or social media sites such as YouTube, Facebook, and others. Some videos are made for the Web and social media. Such videos range from public relations (PR) pieces to brand promotions and brand-related entertainment. Other videos are ads that a company makes primarily for TV and other media but posts online before or after an advertising campaign to extend their reach and impact.

Good online videos can engage consumers by the millions. The online video audience is soaring, with over 60 percent of the U.S. population now streaming video.[15] Marketers hope that some of their videos will go viral. **Viral marketing**, the digital version of word-of-mouth marketing, involves creating videos, ads, and other marketing content that is so infectious that customers will seek them out or pass them along to their friends. Because customers find and pass along the message or promotion, viral marketing can be very inexpensive. And when video or other information comes from a friend, the recipient is much more likely to view or read it.

Companies also have to be aware of videos that are negative toward them posted by a third party. Oftentimes when one searches a company name, there will be more videos poking fun at the company than those that were posted by the company. Chili's posted all its videos in a company site, which is the first site to open when one does a search for Chili's on YouTube.

In one simple but honest McDonald's video, the director of marketing at McDonald's Canada answers an online viewer's question about why McDonald's products look better in ads than in real life by conducting a behind-the-scenes tour of how a McDonald's ad is made. The award-winning 3.5-minute video pulled almost 15 million views and 15,000 shares, earning the company praise for its honesty

Viral marketing. The Internet version of word-of-mouth marketing—Web sites, videos, e-mail messages, or other marketing events that are so infectious that customers will want to pass them along to friends.

and transparency.[16] Evian, called by one reporter "the master of online video," has long reaped huge viral video rewards. Evian's "Amazing Baby & Me," which showed adults breakdancing with baby-fied reflections of themselves in city store windows, became one the most-watched YouTube videos, pulling down an amazing 139 million (and counting) views in more than 80 countries, and generating over 120,000 tweets, more than 1 million shares, and over 289,000 Facebook comments. The digital director of Evian's parent company, Danone, stated, "Digital formats allow us to tell a great brand story with enthusiasm and excitement."[17]

However, marketers usually have little control over where their viral messages end up. They can seed content online, but that does little good unless the message itself strikes a chord with consumers. Says one creative director: "You hope that the creative is at a high enough mark where the seeds grow into mighty oaks. If they don't like it, it ain't gonna move. If they like it, it'll move a little bit; and if they love it, it's gonna move like a fast burning fire through the Hollywood hills."[18]

Blogs and Other Online Forums

Brands also conduct online marketing through various digital forums that appeal to specific special-interest groups. Blogs (or Web logs) are online journals where people and companies post their thoughts and other content, usually related to narrowly defined topics. Blogs can be about anything, from politics or baseball to haiku, car repair, brands, or the latest TV series. According to one study, there are now more than 31 million blogs in the United States. Many bloggers use social networks such as Twitter, Facebook, and Instagram to promote their blogs, giving them huge reach. Such numbers can give blogs—especially those with large and devoted followings—substantial influence.[19]

Most marketers are now tapping into the blogosphere with brand-related blogs that reach their customer communities. For example, the Disney Parks Blog is a place to learn about and discuss all things Disney, including a Behind the Scenes area with posts about dance rehearsals, sneak peeks at new construction sites, interviews with employees, and more. Beyond their own brand blogs, many marketers use third-party blogs to help get their messages out. For example, McDonald's systematically reaches out to key "mommy bloggers," those who influence the nation's homemakers, who in turn influence their families' eating-out choices.[20]

McDonald's recently hosted 15 bloggers on an all-expenses-paid tour of its headquarters in Oak Brook, Illinois. The bloggers toured the facilities (including the company's test kitchens), met McDonald's U.S. president, and had their pictures taken with Ronald at a nearby Ronald McDonald House. McDonald's knows that these mommy bloggers are very important. They have loyal followings and talk a lot about McDonald's in their blogs. So McDonald's is turning the bloggers into believers by giving them a behind-the-scenes view. McDonald's doesn't try to tell the bloggers what to say in their posts about the visit. It simply asks them to write one honest recap of their trip. However, the resulting posts (each acknowledging the blogger's connection with McDonald's) were mostly very positive. Thanks to this and many other such efforts, mommy bloggers around the country are now more informed about and connected with McDonald's. "I know they have smoothies and they have yogurt and they have other things that my kids would want," says one prominent blogger. "I really couldn't tell you what Burger King's doing right now," she adds. "I have no idea."

Bill Marriott, chairman of the Board of Marriott International, has become well known for his blog, which he writes once or twice a month. A hotel online marketing consultant claims all Web sites should include a blog. He states that search engines often look for activity on a site. Having a dynamic site helps with search engine optimization; posting a blog on a regular basis helps make the site dynamic.[21] Blogs can offer a fresh, original, personal, and cheap way to enter consumer online and social media conversations. Although companies can sometimes leverage blogs to engage customers in meaningful relationships, blogs remain largely a consumer-controlled medium. Whether or not they actively participate in the blogs, companies should monitor and listen to them.

Social Media Marketing

As we've discussed throughout the text so far, the surge in Internet usage and digital technologies and devices has spawned a dazzling array of online social media and digital communities. Countless independent and commercial social networks have arisen that give consumers online places to congregate, socialize, and exchange views and information. These days, it seems, almost everyone is buddying up on Facebook or Google+, checking in with Twitter, tuning into the day's hottest videos on YouTube, pinning images on social scrapbooking site Pinterest, or sharing photos with Instagram and Snapchat. And, of course, wherever consumers congregate, marketers will surely follow. Most marketers are now riding the huge social media wave. According to one survey, nearly 90 percent of U.S. companies now use social media networks as part of their marketing mixes.[22]

For travel products, it can be argued that social media entails a change from one-to-one recommendations from individuals to many-to-many conversations. In the past, these personal sources often came from talking with a friend, relative, or local resident. Social media has now expanded the conversation, in terms of both breadth and depth. On their fact sheet, TripAdvisor mentions it has over 200 million posts and 29 million user-generated images (UGIs).[23] Marketers can use insights from consumer online conversations to improve their marketing programs.

Millennials will account for over half of all travel spending by 2020.[24] As the millennials graduate from university and/or advance in their careers, their spending will increase over the next four decades.[25] Millennials share their personal experiences with products and learned from others' reviews through social media. They also use pricing information on these sites before making purchases.[26] For millennials, social media offers a means of connection, as they crave social interaction and want to share everything.[27] A large percentage of millennials, over 88 percent, visit social networking sites.[28] They also use these sites to obtain information before reserving hotel rooms.[29] The growing importance of millennials as consumers of travel products combined with their ability to use and their attraction to social media means that social media will grow in importance over the coming years.

Using Social Media

Marketers can engage in social media in two ways: They can use existing social media or they can set up their own. Using existing social media seems the easiest. Thus, most brands, large and small, have set up shop on a host of social media sites. Check the Web sites of hospitality brands and you'll find links to each brand's Facebook, Twitter, YouTube, Pinterest, Instagram, or other social media pages. Some multinational hotel chains also have links to Chinese social media including Tudou (video-sharing) and Weibo (microblogging). Some of the major social networks are huge. More than 1.2 billion people access Facebook every month, 3.4 times the combined populations of the United States and Canada. Similarly, Twitter has more than 645 million registered users, and more than 1 billion unique users visit YouTube monthly, watching more than 6 billion hours of video. The list goes on: Weibo has over 500 million users, Google+ has 400 million active users, LinkedIn 240 million, and Pinterest 70 million.[30]

Although these large social media networks grab most of the headlines, countless niche social media have also emerged. Niche online social networks cater to the needs of smaller communities of like-minded people, making them ideal vehicles for marketers who want to target special-interest groups. There's at least one social media network for just about every interest, hobby, or group.

Social Media Marketing Advantages and Challenges

Using social media presents both advantages and challenges. On the plus side, social media are targeted and personal—they allow marketers to create and share tailored brand content with individual consumers and customer communities. Social media are interactive, making them ideal for starting and participating in customer conversations and listening to customer feedback. For example, some companies use Tweetchat, Tweeter's platform that allows conversations in real time, to hold digital conversations to engage customers and obtain immediate input on everything from product features to creating ads. One marketing executive states regular Twitter chats are "creating good conversations." "People enjoy being part of [the process]."[31]

Social media are also immediate and timely. They can be used to reach customers anytime, anywhere with timely and relevant marketing content regarding brand happenings and activities. As discussed earlier in the chapter, the rapid growth in social media usage has caused a surge in real-time marketing, allowing marketers to create and join consumer conversations around situations and events as they occur. Marketers can now watch what's trending and create content to match.

Social media can be very cost effective. Although creating and administering social media content can be costly, many social media are free or inexpensive to use. Thus, returns on social media investments are often high compared with those of expensive traditional media such as TV or print. The low cost of social media puts them within easy reach of even small businesses and brands that can't afford the high costs of big-budget marketing campaigns.

Perhaps the biggest advantage of social media is their engagement and social sharing capabilities. Social media are especially well suited to creating customer engagement and community for getting customers involved with the brand and with each other. More than any other channels, social media can involve customers in shaping and sharing brand content and experiences.

Social media marketing is an excellent way to create brand communities, places where brand loyalists can share experiences, information, and ideas. For example, if you visit Buffalo Wild Wings Facebook page, you get a sense of the community the brand has created. They post videos, as well as pictures of customers and their food. One video was of a party they provided as a gift to one of their customers. It showed the unique delivery of the invitation to the party, which included a visit by a professional football player. In the first two months of posting, the video had over 1.3 million visits. In addition to the Buffalo Wild Wings content the site-contained UGC; much of it is positive but some is negative, which is certainly expected for a company that has over 1,100 stores. The negative postings allow both the local management and corporate management to have a feel for the problem areas in the operations. Buffalo Wild Wings responds to the negative comments. This is the characteristic of a well-managed social media site.

Social media marketing also presents challenges. First, many companies are still experimenting with how to use them effectively, and results are hard to measure. Second, such social networks are largely user controlled. The company's goal in using social media is to make the brand a part of consumers' conversations and their lives. However, marketers can't simply muscle their way into consumers' digital interactions—they need to earn the right to be there. Rather than intruding, marketers must become a valued part of the online experience by developing a steady flow of engaging content.

Managing User-Generated Social Media Content

UGC is valuable, whether it is positive or negative. The positive comments create community and encourage others to use the product. The negative comments provide feedback on what customers do not like and how we did not meet their expectations. These comments help us improve the service delivery system. They also remind us of the importance of consistently delivering a great product.

Customers view information posted on social media as credible. One study found that almost 80 percent of those surveyed said that UGC on social media was trustworthy.[32] Electronic word of mouth (eWOM) has the ability to influence thousands of people. First-time travelers are heavier users of UGC on social media sites, than repeat visitors.[33] A Nielsen survey found that 52 percent of those that searched social media before traveling modified their plans and 33 percent switched hotels.[34] The reviews on social media of tourism products, including the destinations, can lead to purchase or non-purchase of products including the selection of the destination. Thus tourism and travel marketers must monitor and respond to what visitors are saying about the different components of their destination.

Research has found that people post reviews for a number of reasons. One of the most common reasons is that they want to help other people, including helping people avoid mistakes they have made. Revenge is also a commonly cited reason. Consumers realize they have power. If service recovery is poor, they will let others know about their problems. As a manager it is important to monitor social media, both on their own sites and third-party sites such as TripAdvisor, Yelp, and Zomato. Ideally, there should be a response to both negative and positive responses. Researchers from Texas Tech found that hotel managers tended to respond to positive comments, but not negative comments.[35] One of their conclusions was hotels should have a dedicated person responsible for monitoring social media. Besides resolving customer complaints, responding to negative complaints lets others know you care about your customers. When resolving service failure, managers should remember that UGC content is public. They should try to take the resolution of a complaint off-line, to avoid the conversation continuing to be public.

Starwood employs a group of 30 social media managers spread across six centers in different time zones so they can respond to a guest at any time of the day. Many of the questions that guests ask are about local questions and attractions. Providing guests with information about the destination can increase their experience and result in their desire to return.[36] The social media manager's job is one of the fastest-growing positions in the hotel industry.

Listening to Customers on Social Media

One of the goals of a company's social media plan should be to engage its customers and create a conversation. Try to be unique and use engagement, which fits your brand. For example, Adventures by Disney, a company that provides group tours for families, has an "Ask Our Mom" tab on its Facebook page. Moms who have traveled with Disney personally answer the question of mothers thinking about taking their family on a trip. Disney has engaged former travelers to answer the questions of future travelers. Many restaurants use Foursquare, a location-based social media smartphone application. It is a great engagement tool for restaurants relying on local customers. For example, managers can create unique specials for customers who check in five times during a month. Carnival Cruises asked its Facebook fans to comment on the favorite port they have experienced on a Carnival Cruise. Carnival received 479 likes and 700 comments. Most of them promoted Carnival Cruises.[37]

Listening to what people are saying about a company is one of the benefits social media provides. Managers can find out what people are saying about their company as well as what they are saying about competitors. The following sites provide consumer reviews of your hotel or restaurant: TripAdvisor.com, HotelChatter.com, local.yahoo.com, CitySearch.com, yelp.com, ChowHound.com, OpenTable.com, and most of the OTAs such as Expedia.com. Listening to the conversation customers are having about one's company can provide valuable information and free marketing intelligence. Companies like Lodging Interactive provide Internet marketing and consultative Web site management services and offer a number of effective online tools and services to listen and even engage in the conversation with guests and potential guests online. In Chapter 5 we mentioned the importance of getting employees to feedback information they heard from customers to management: the listening post concept. With social media, we can monitor what customers are saying after they leave your business or travel destination. For example, one manager put TripAdvisor comments into a spreadsheet. This allowed the comments to be analyzed across segments and by rating. One of the findings was that the lowest ratings came from couples that stated this is not a luxury resort. In some media the resort advertised

It is important to not create expectations you cannot meet on social media as well as other media. A resort that is not a luxury resort should not promote itself as a luxury resort. Courtesy of Petrik Fotolia.

itself as a luxury resort, setting expectations it could not meet. Needless to say, the resort stopped marketing itself as a luxury resort.

Listening to your customers is good, but engaging in the conversation is better. It is often possible to participate in service recovery when someone posts a complaint. Managers I have talked to often avoid responding to negative comments. One manager stated that they know everyone at the resort is working hard to deliver good service and it makes them angry when someone posts a complaint. Others complain that they simply do not have time. This is why the position of social media manager is emerging. We should remember that social media amplifies the conversation. Whether the comment is good or bad, it will be communicated to hundreds, thousands, or perhaps hundreds of thousands of people. Ideally, one should respond to all comments, but those that are extremely good or negative deserve attention.

Holly Zoba, senior vice president of sales for the Hospitality Division of Signature Worldwide, provides this advice on how to respond online to a guest's comments. First remember others are viewing the comments, so be professional and avoid being defensive. When someone complains, apologize and show empathy for his or her situation. Don't use the response as a way to sell the hotel or restaurant's features. Respond to both negative and positive reviews; remember you want to engage in the conversation. Her final comment is to be proactive. If a guest says he or she had a great experience, ask him or her to go online and let others know about his or her experience.

A customer named Judy posted a comment on Jimmy John's (a popular sandwich shop) Facebook page. It seems Judy is a loyal customer; however, she writes that the last several times she came to Jimmy John's, her sandwich was not the way she ordered it and she is not sure if she will be back. The following is the response from Jimmy John's: "I'm all over it Judy. Send me your address and phone number to facebook@jimmyjohns.com so I can gain your trust again."

The response was posted within 12 hours of the customer's post. It let Judy and other customers know Jimmy John's was interested in resolving customer problems. Finally, she took the conversation off-line. Rather than get into a public conversation with dissatisfied customers, managers should take them off-line and resolve the problem. Judy's response was prompt, but it may not be fast enough. The average time for a hospitality company to respond to UGC on social media is 11.5 hours. Twenty-five percent of those posting UGC expect a response in an hour and only about 10 percent get a response at all! There is a huge opportunity for the industry to do a better job of conversing with customers and potential customers on social media.[38]

Affinia Hotels, with hotels in New York and Washington, D.C., was one of the first groups to link comments about its hotels from TripAdvisor to each hotel's home page. This includes all comments, both positive and negative. For a well-managed chain, this is a great marketing tactic. It spreads positive word of mouth and also provides feedback to the employees. Affinia's chief marketing officer states he plans to post video and audio testimonials to the Web site along with written comments provided by guests. He states, "My desire is to have a hotel company where the employees and the customers work together to create a better hotel."[39] One reservation company is working on a method that will extract all positive comments and place them on the hotel's Web site. Although at first this may seem like a clever way to promote your product, it goes against the social media revolution, which calls for transparency, integrity, authenticity, and trust. Social networks are about engagement and relationships. The most important attribute of a relationship is trust. If you lose the trust of your customers or employees, social media can destroy your personal reputation and your business.

International Social Media

One of the growth areas for the hospitality industry is China. Some of the most popular social media sites in the United States are not available in China. Multinational companies wanting to have a social media presence in China will have to familiarize themselves with a new set of social media. Some of the more popular sites are Wechat, Weibo, and Youku. These sites are used like Facebook,

Twitter, and YouTube, respectively. The popularity of social media will vary across countries. Social media managers working internationally will need to find out which sites are most effective as they move around the world.

Integrated Social Media Marketing

Using social media might be as simple as posting some messages and promotions on a brand's Facebook or Twitter pages or creating brand buzz with videos or images on YouTube or Pinterest. However, most large companies are now designing full-scale social media efforts that blend with and support other elements of a brand's marketing strategy and tactics. More than making scattered efforts and chasing "Likes" and tweets, companies that use social media successfully are integrating a broad range of diverse media to create brand-related social sharing, engagement, and customer community.

Managing a brand's social media efforts can be a major undertaking. For example, Starbucks, one of the most successful social media marketers, manages 51 Facebook pages (including 43 in other countries); 31 Twitter handles (19 of them international); 22 Instagram names (14 international); plus Google+, Pinterest, YouTube, and Foursquare accounts. Managing and integrating that entire social media content is challenging, but the results are worth the investment. Customers can engage with Starbucks digitally without ever setting foot in a store, and they do engage. With more than 36 million fans on its main U.S. page alone, Starbucks is the sixth-largest brand on Facebook. It ranks fifth on Twitter with 88.5 million followers.

But more than just creating online engagement and community, Starbucks's social media presence also drives customer into its stores. For example, in its first big social media promotion four years ago, Starbucks offered a free pastry with a morning drink purchase. A million people showed up. Its more recent "Tweet-a-Coffee" promotion, which let customers give a $5 gift card to a friend by putting both #tweetacoffee and the friend's handle in a tweet, resulted in $180,000 in purchases within little more than one month. Social media through engaging and telling a story connect with customers and have a positive impact on business.[40]

Marketing HIGHLIGHT 16–1   How Hospitality Companies Use Social Media

aco Bell had a class action lawsuit filed against it in January 2011, claiming its taco beef contained only 35 percent beef. Taco Bell used a blend of social media and traditional media to quickly respond to the suit. Full-page newspaper ads were run saying, "Thank you for suing us." The ad went on to say, "Here's the truth about our seasoned meat." Taco Bell also responded with Facebook postings and a YouTube video. The president of Taco Bell told YouTube viewers that the company's taco mixture contained 88 percent as opposed to the 35 percent claimed in the suit.

Taco Bell fought hard by bringing the key words "taco," "bell," "lawsuit" on Yahoo!, Google, and Bing search engines ensuring that the company's official remarks would appear first during a search. The *Wall Street Journal* said, "The episode is a reminder of the power of social media in mounting an aggressive defense." Taco Bell's president, Greg Creed, said that "customer response on Facebook and Twitter were positive." Taco Bell was able to quickly restore the trust of its customers and the lawsuit was dropped.

RIU Hotels and Resorts is a collection of over 100 properties concentrated around the Caribbean and Mediterranean Seas. At the beginning of 2010, it had only about 400 fans on its Facebook page. That was before it started a competition called the "Ultimate Fan." Guests were asked to send in their best photos and videos of the resorts and share their experiences at the resorts. At the end of the competition, more than 350 photos and 8 videos were uploaded. The fan base grew to 1,350. But that was just the start. After the competition, fans continued to post photos that were viewed by their friends and relatives. This created traffic for the Facebook page as well as drove customers to the resort. Today RIU has over 800,000 fans.

Eric's Restaurant in Houston uses Foursquare to drive happy-hour business. Eric's offers reduced prices on its appetizers as a reward for those who check in at Eric's on Foursquare. The promotion drives people to the restaurant, as well as encourages their friends to stop by the restaurant. Most people do not want to go into a bar after work where they do not know anyone. By checking in on Foursquare they can see who is at Eric's. Guests can draw their friends just by checking in on Foursquare.

Gunstock Mountain Resort near Boston developed a promotional strategy to promote on-mountain specials to increase incremental revenue. Customers were asked to text JitterGram 1091 to receive up to four on-mountain specials a day. Signs were displayed around the ski slopes, lifts, and lodges. Staff also told guests about the "Text to Save" club and encouraged them to sign up. Gunstock also used the database to text short-term promotions such as 2 for 1 ski tickets for tomorrow only. Since you had to receive the text to receive the promotion, the price was not lowered for everyone—just those redeeming the "JitterGram" promotion. The 2 for 1 promotion created almost $1,000 in incremental revenue with almost no incremental marketing expense.

Sunda is a Chicago restaurant featuring Asian food including sushi. It has an active Facebook page, which features both photos and videos of its food. It uses its downtown location and Twitter to let people who are taking part in downtown events know they can receive a 20 percent discount by showing a ticket stub or other evidence of participation. Tweeter is also used to tweet current specials. Those that check in on Foursquare can receive rewards. For example, the restaurant might offer a free appetizer on the third check-in or a special flash sale discount for the first 10 check-ins. Sunda has developed an integrated approach to social media. This creates followers, keeps the restaurant at the top of mind of its customers, keeps its customers engaged, and promotes business.[41]

Mobile Marketing

Mobile marketing features marketing messages, promotions, and other marketing content delivered to on-the-go consumers through their mobile devices. Marketers use mobile marketing to engage customers anywhere, anytime during the buying and relationship-building processes. The widespread adoption of mobile devices and the surge in mobile Web traffic have made mobile marketing a must for most brands.

Social media accounts for 66 percent of the time spent on mobile devices.[42] Facebook witnessed its mobile-only users grow by 34 percent in one year, twice the rate of its overall user growth, providing evidence of the mobile's popularity. In the United States, 90 percent of people owning mobile devices use these to engage in travel media, and in the United Kingdom, the rate is 66 percent.[43] The mobile penetration rates for the United States are similar to those in Asia, Latin America, and Europe.[44] Mobile devices allow travelers to find information in real time.

One reason for the mobile's popularity is that it allows travelers to change their itinerary during the trip. In the United States, 25 percent of travel booking is made on mobile devices, with the value of these bookings exceeding U.S. $25 billion.[45] As mobile users walk down the street in a city center, they can log on to a social media site to obtain information on nearby restaurants. Smartphones connected to Wi-Fi make it easy for international travelers to find information; recent statistics showed that 85 percent of them used smartphones during their trip.[46] Facebook now has over a third of its users accessing the site exclusively by mobile devices.[47] The number of Americans using mobile devices to book hotel rooms is approaching 50 percent.[48] The rapid adoption of mobile devices means that consumers will have access to social media in their pockets or purses. Travelers can find out what to do, where to stay, or where to dine as they move through their itinerary.

Travel companies will need to be mobile friendly. When a potential guest finds a business on a social media site by using a mobile device, he or she will probably access the travel company's site through the same device. If the site is mobile friendly, the traveler will receive information from it. Otherwise, he or she will likely exit the site and look somewhere else.[49]

Companies use mobile marketing to stimulate immediate buying, make shopping easier, enrich the brand experience, or all of these. It lets marketers provide consumers with information, incentives, and choices at the moment they are expressing an interest or when they are in a position to make a buying choice. For example, McDonald's uses mobile marketing to promote new menu items, announce special promotions, and drive immediate traffic at its restaurants. One recent interactive ad on Pandora's mobile app read, "Taste buds. Any size soft drink or sweet tea for $1. Tap to visit site." A tap on the mobile ad took customers to a mobile site promoting McDonald's ongoing summer promotion. Another McDonald's mobile campaign used a word scrabble game to entice customers to try the fast feeder's dollar menu items. Such efforts create both customer engagement and store traffic. Using a game "inside a mobile campaign is all about finding and maintaining engagement," says a McDonald's marketer.[50]

Today's rich-media mobile ads can create substantial engagement and impact. For example, JetBlue recently created a voice-activated mobile ad that interacts with customers and talks back. It starts with a JetBlue mobile banner ad that says, "Click here to learn how to speak pigeon." A click expands the ad, which then instructs users by voice to repeat words on the screen, such as "coo, coo, coo." When they've completed two full sentences in pigeon, users receive a virtual medal and the option to play again. Hitting "Learn more" takes users to the JetBlue Landing Perch, where they can explore and send messages to friends via digital carrier pigeons. The mobile ad is part of JetBlue's "Air on the Side of Humanity" campaign, which features pigeons—the ultimate frequent fliers. Rather than making direct sales pitches, the voice ad aims simply to enrich the JetBlue experience. The airline hopes people will "watch the ads, play with the pigeons, and remember us when they want to book tickets," says JetBlue's advertising manager.[51]

Many marketers have created their own mobile online sites, optimized for specific phones and mobile service providers. Others have created useful or entertaining mobile apps to engage customers with their brands and help them shop. Starbucks's mobile app lets customers use their phones as a Starbucks card to make fast and easy purchases.

As with other forms of direct marketing, however, companies must use mobile marketing responsibly or risk angering already ad-weary consumers. Most people don't want to be interrupted regularly by advertising, so marketers must be smart about how they engage people on mobiles. The key is to provide genuinely useful information and offers that will make consumers want to engage. And many marketers target mobile ads on an opt-in-only basis.

In all, digital direct marketing—online, social media, and mobile marketing—offers both great promise and many challenges for the future. Its most ardent apostles still envision a time when the Internet and digital marketing will replace magazines, newspapers, and even stores as sources for information engagement and buying. Most marketers, however, hold a more realistic view. For most companies, digital and social media marketing will remain just one important approach to the marketplace that works alongside other approaches in a fully integrated marketing mix.

Although the fast-growing digital marketing tools have grabbed most of the headlines lately, traditional direct-marketing tools are very much alive and still heavily used. We now examine the traditional direct-marketing approaches shown on the right side of Figure 16–1.

Customer Databases and Traditional Direct Marketing

Customer database. An organized collection of comprehensive data about individual customers or prospects, including geographic, demographic, psychographic, and behavioral data.

Effective direct marketing begins with a good customer database. A **customer database** is an organized collection of comprehensive data about individual customers or prospects, including geographic, demographic, psychographic, and behavioral data. A good customer database can be a potent relationship-building tool. The database gives companies "a snapshot of how customers look and behave." Says one expert, "A company is no better than what it knows [about its customers]."[52]

In consumer marketing, the customer database might contain a customer's demographics (age, income, family members, birthdays), psychographics (activities, interests, and opinions), and buying behavior (buying preferences and the recency, frequency, and monetary value—RFM—of past purchases). In business-to-business marketing, the customer profile might contain the products and services the customer has bought, past volumes and prices, key contacts (and their ages, birthdays, hobbies, and favorite foods), competing suppliers, status of current contracts, estimated customer spending for the next few years, and assessments of competitive strengths and weaknesses in selling and servicing the account.

Some of these databases are huge. For example, casino operator Harrah's Entertainment has built a customer database containing 30 terabytes worth of customer information, roughly three times the number of printed characters in the Library of Congress.[53]

Database Uses

Companies use their databases in many ways. They use databases to locate good potential customers and to generate sales leads. They can mine their databases to learn about customers in detail and then fine-tune their market offerings and communications to the special preferences and behaviors of target segments or individuals. In all, a company's database can be an important tool for building stronger long-term customer relationships.

Data warehouse. A central repository of an organization's customer information.

If a hotel has multiple databases, this can cause problems if they are not integrated. A **data warehouse** stores the information the company receives in a central repository of customer data.[54] Integrating all data collection systems into one central database created challenges. The consolidation that has occurred in the hotel industry has created the need for companies to build one centralized data warehouse for all their brands. Hilton Hotels has developed OnQ, a technology platform that will allow it to use information on its guests across all its brands.[55] Hilton's chief information officer stated, "OnQ allows employees to be put on stage in front of customers to perform 'on cue.' They will have access through OnQ to information that will allow them to deliver the most efficient service."[56]

Once the data are stored in a warehouse, companies use the relational database to look at relationships in the data. For example, if a resort hotel was projecting a low occupancy for the weekend after next, managers could query the database, asking for all guests who came to the resort on a weekend and lived within 250 miles. This would produce a list of guests who enjoyed the resort on weekends and could drive to the resort. Thus, they would not have to worry about higher last-minute airfares. A restaurant could query the database for all persons who spent over $50 on a bottle of wine if it wanted to develop a potential list for a special event pairing wine and food. The development of relational data warehouses has created a powerful marketing tool to assist their direct-marketing effort.

In the example just cited, the manager formed the query for the database; his or her results might have been better if the computer developed the query. Data mining is the exploration and analysis of a database by automatic or semiautomatic means to discover patterns or rules.[57] It is the process of automating information discovery.[58] Data mining is used to predict which customers are most likely to respond to an offer, to segment a market, and to identify a company's most loyal customers. Data mining software uses a variety of methods, including regression analyses and neural networks, to find the best solution. One of the major benefits of data mining is that it is not limited to the relationships that the marketing manager may think exists. Rather, it explores all relationships with a variety of techniques. Data mining has increased the effectiveness and efficiency of direct marketing in the hospitality and travel industries.

We have all heard the expression "garbage in, garbage out." To be useful, the data stored in a database must be accurate. Errors are usually a result of data entry. It is important that everyone using the database understand the importance of accurate data. For example, a guest whose last name is Smith and is entered into the database as Smyth will now have two files. The resort will not know his or her real value because it is divided between the two files. If the resort sends direct mail, he or she could receive two pieces, one under both names. This shows him or her that the resort staff does not really know him or her because they think he or she is two separate people. To

Employees of the Hilton Hawaiian Village's Rainbow Tower have access to OnQ that helps them deliver great service. Courtesy of Steheap/Fotolia.

be effective, duplicate files have to be combined, and addresses must be accurate. A clean database starts with accurate entry. There are also software packages that can identify potential duplicate files, check addresses, and make corrections.

Sometimes employees use empty fields in the database for their own personal notes. Training the employees in the use and importance of the database will correct this problem. For example, a desk clerk typed under the guest's name in the address file, "This guy is a jerk." He wanted to alert the other employees that the guest had the potential of creating problems. What the clerk did not realize is the address was used for direct mail. You can imagine the response of the guest when he received a letter from the hotel addressed to him with "This guy is a jerk" under his name. Employee training to ensure that the database is clean is a critical and ongoing part of an effective database system.

Like many other marketing tools, database marketing requires a special investment. Companies must invest in computer hardware, database software, analytical programs, communication links, and skilled personnel. The database system must be user friendly and available to various marketing groups, including those in product and brand management, new-product development, advertising and promotion, direct mail, telemarketing, Web marketing, field sales, order fulfillment, and customer service. However, a well-managed database should lead to sales and customer relationship gains that will more than cover its costs.

Finally, you should answer the question, "If you were a customer, why would you want to be in our database?" By answering this question, you find out whether your database has a strategic focus or is mainly used for tactical purposes.[59] Most marketers use their database tactically. For example, one of the most frequent uses of database marketing is in direct marketing. Direct-marketing campaigns often target recent customers, inviting them to return or offering incentives, as well as encouraging loyal customers to come during soft periods. There is nothing wrong with this use of database marketing, if the offers have value to the customer. A person who always orders wine with dinner will appreciate a notice promoting a half-price wine evening at the restaurant. However, if a customer does not drink alcoholic beverages and never has ordered them at the restaurant, this customer will view the promotion as a nuisance. If most of the promotions have no value, all communication from the restaurant will be viewed as junk and never opened.

For a customer to want to be in your database, it must provide the customer with benefits they would not receive if they were not on it. Database marketers must remember that only promotions relevant to the customer are those that will create value for the customer. A casino in Las Vegas sent a 2 for 1 buffet coupon to everyone on its database. Not only was the promotion not relevant for the best players who could get comp meals in the casino's finest restaurant, but it was also an insult because it communicated to them that the casino did not know them.

Let us return to the original question: Why would a customer want to be on your database? Vail Associates, operators of skiing facilities, is an example of what can happen when you provide answers to this question. It knew its customers wanted a hassle-free experience, and Vail Associates wanted to maximize their time on the slopes. Vail Associates set about implementing a database system that would give its customers the experience they desired. If you rented skis at Vail Associates in the past, it has your information on file. Renting skis a second time then becomes a hassle-free experience. It wasn't always this way. Everyone was asked for his or her boot size, what type of skis they wanted, and a number of other questions. Guests often spent a good deal of time waiting in line, instead of skiing. Now, if you are staying in one of Vail Associates' lodges, it delivers the skis to the lodge, so skis are ready when the guests arrive. The guests avoid the lines and the questions! Its upscale dining rooms are usually booked on weekends; if a lodging customer usually dines in one of these restaurants, the reservationist is prompted to ask if the customer would like to make a restaurant reservation when he or she books his or her room to avoid disappointment later. By using its database strategically, Vail Associates has created a competitive advantage. It is providing its customers with a better product, one that offers more benefits than the competitors' products.[60]

Several other examples of strategic databases are provided by Ritz-Carlton and Brennan's restaurant. Ritz-Carlton's database receives input from the frontline employees. They update the database based on information received from guests during the normal course of their work activities. For example, if a room service waiter finds out that a guest likes a certain type of mineral water, the mineral water is placed in the guest's refrigerator. The database is also used for service recovery. If a guest has encountered a problem, all departments in the hotel are notified, and everyone works to regain the guest's confidence and loyalty. Brennan's in Houston developed a database that included the customer's favorite table, captain, and wine. This information is used to provide the guest with a great experience. These companies, like Vail Associates, have used their database to create a competitive advantage. Companies that use a database to provide the guest with a better experience are gaining a major benefit. They are creating a competitive advantage based on the knowledge of their customers. They know what the customer likes and how to create messages that will be relevant to the customer. One of the uses of a database is to develop contact lists for direct marketing. No direct-marketing campaign can be successful if the list is poor. Thus, lists are a critical component of a successful direct-marketing campaign.[61] In conclusion, companies need to provide benefits to customers for being in their database.

■■■ Relationship Marketing and Loyalty Programs

The goal of relationship marketing is to build long-term relationships with customers by delivering value on a consistent basis, resulting in an organization customers can trust. Relationship marketing requires that all the company's departments work together with marketing as a team to serve the customer. It involves building relationships at many levels: economic, social, technical, and legal, resulting in high customer loyalty.

What specific marketing tools can a company use to develop stronger customer bonding and satisfaction? It can adopt any of three customer value-binding approaches.[62] The first relies primarily on adding financial benefits to the customer relationship. For example, airlines offer frequent-flyer programs, hotels give room upgrades to their frequent guests, and restaurants have frequent-diner programs. Although these reward programs and other financial incentives build customer preference, they can be imitated easily by competition and thus may fail to differentiate the company's offer permanently. Frequency programs often use tiered programs to encourage guests' preference for one hotel brand. For example, Marriott has silver (10 nights), gold (50 nights), and platinum (75 nights). Hilton has silver (10 nights), gold (40 nights), and diamond (60 nights). As guests move up into higher tiers, they gain more benefits.[63]

The second approach is to add social benefits, as well as financial benefits. Here company personnel work to increase their social bonds with customers by learning individual customers' needs and wants and then individualizing and personalizing their products and services. They turn their customers into clients: Customers may be nameless to the institution; clients cannot be nameless. Customers are served as part of the mass or as part of larger segments; clients are served on an individual basis. Customers are served by anyone who happens to be available; clients are served by the professional assigned to them.[64] For example, a server recognizes repeat guests and greets them by name. A salesperson develops a good relationship with his or her clients. Both these people have developed social bonds with their clients. This keeps the client coming back, but it also often means clients will follow that person when he or she changes jobs. Managers of hospitality and travel organizations want to make sure that their key clients have social bonds with multiple people in the organization. The general manager, front-desk manager, food and beverage manager, convention services manager, banquet manager, and restaurant manager should all know key clients. In fact, general managers should go on sales calls to key clients. If this is done, when the salesperson leaves, the client feels that he or she still knows key people in the hotel and is not dependent on the salesperson.

The third approach to building strong customer relationships is to add structural ties, as well as financial and social benefits. Structural changes require a change in business operations. For example, some hotels offer their best customers a 9 A.M. check-in. This means that the rooms of early checkouts must be turned around quickly.

After traveling on an overnight flight from Los Angeles to New York, this traveler will be glad to be able to check into his hotel room at 9 A.M. to rest before his 1 P.M. meeting. Courtesy of nenetus/Fotolia.

Housekeeping schedules and procedures had to be changed. It does provide a great benefit to customers arriving on overnight flights. It cannot be offered to all guests, but if it is offered to the top 10 percent of your guests, and only 25 percent of those arriving before noon, it is a manageable amenity to provide your best guests. Structural changes are difficult to implement, but they are harder for competitors to match. Thus structural changes can create a lasting competitive advantage until they are matched.

When it comes to relationship marketing, you don't want a relationship with every customer. A company should develop customer relationships selectively: Figure out which customers are worth cultivating because you can meet their needs more effectively than anyone else.[65] Then plan and implement a program that will develop a relationship with your target market. Table 16–1 breaks customers down into categories based on their frequency of purchase and profitability. Those customers that are high on frequency and profitability deserve management attention.

Benefits of Customer Relationship Management

The benefits of customer relationship management (CRM) stem from building continued patronage of loyal customers, reduced marketing costs, decreased price sensitivity of loyal customers, and partnership activities of loyal customers. Loyal customers purchase from the business they are loyal to more often than nonloyal customers. They also purchase a broader variety of items. A manager loyal to a hotel brand is more likely to place his or her company's meetings with that hotel chain. Reduced marketing costs are the result of requiring fewer marketing dollars to maintain a customer than to create one and the creation of new customers through the positive word of mouth of loyal customers. When asked what leads them to new restaurants, the number-one response (48 percent) was that friends or relatives took them or recommended the restaurant.[66] Loyal customers are less likely to switch because of price, and loyal customers make more purchases than do similar, nonloyal customers.[67] They state that they will perform partnership activities, such as business referrals, providing references, publicity, and serving on advisory boards. The combination of these attributes of loyal customers means that a small increase in loyal customers can result in a major increase in profitability. Riechheld and Sasser found that a 5 percent increase in customer retention resulted in a 25 to 125 percent increase in profits in nine service industry groups they studied.[68] As a result, the researchers claim that building a relationship with customers should be a strategic focus of most service firms.

Loyalty Programs

Loyalty programs were developed as a way to attract and maintain a company's best customers. The early loyalty programs were financial based, giving away free

TABLE 16–1
Types of Customers.

	Low Frequency	High Frequency
High Profitability	Try to get these customers to come more often.	These are your best customers, reward them.
Low Profitability	These customers follow promotions. Make sure your promotions make money.	Some of these guests have the potential to become more profitable.

products. They were easily replicated by competition. Over time they have become more strategic. One of the first changes was to create tiered systems, encouraging customers to spend more money with one company to increase the benefits they receive as the advance through the tiers. Another change is companies, such as United Airlines, are changing to reward customers for dollars spent, not just miles traveled. Business, customers booking closer to travel time, and paying high fares are recognized for the revenue they bring to the company. Reward systems are also becoming more strategic.

Some hotel programs offer early check-ins, most offer late checkouts, and they have special service access by phone or e-mail for their best customers. United Airlines and other companies have developed ultra-elite programs. United's Global Services has entrance requirements that are unpublished and not communicated to the public. People who fly 200,000 miles with United are members of their top tier loyalty program, 1K (for 100,000 miles), but many are not Global Services members. It is felt Global Services is based in part on total dollars spent with United. For example, it may be those who fly over 100,000 miles and always book in business class or higher. United has 400 employees across 60 airports to take care of this elite group. Flights of Global Services members are tracked to ensure smooth connections. One Global Services member was met after deplaning from her small commuter plane and taken in a Mercedes to the gate of her next flight.[69]

In developing a loyalty program, the objective is to change behavior, including purchasing more frequently, purchasing a higher dollar amount, and spreading positive word of mouth. A card punch program, where after getting your card punched 10 times, you get a free item, is the simplest form of loyalty program and the least effective form. These programs track behavior but do not change it. The most effective restaurant programs are those that offer a coupon for a discount that is good for two weeks to a customer that comes in every three to four weeks. This changes behavior. A free appetizer to a loyal customer that normally does not purchase appetizers does not give away revenue, but gives the guest a new experience, one he or she may continue without the coupon.

One of the advantages of a loyalty program is that companies also gain information that will develop systems and products to better serve their guests. This information can come from tracking the member's expenditures. It can also come from asking your best customers about their experiences and what they would like. For example, luxury hotel guests were asked which hotel features would cause them to be more loyal to a hotel. A total of 18 possible benefits developed from in-depth interviews were listed. The hotel customers were asked to rate each feature on a scale from 1, "would have no impact on loyalty," to 7, "would have a great impact on loyalty." In a separate area of the questionnaire, they were asked which of these features were offered currently at hotels to which they were loyal. If one considers what hotels are actually doing and compares this information with what customers would like hotels to do, one is easily able to see where hotels are either meeting the needs of guests or falling short. This is denoted as a gap (performance importance). Table 16–2 shows the gap for loyalty features.

The table shows there is tremendous opportunity to increase loyalty further. Interestingly, the top two features where the largest gaps occur should be very easy and inexpensive for luxury hotels to implement. This type of analysis helps managers identify areas of opportunity for creating more customer-delivered value. In this case they see those attributes that create loyalty or value. They also see those areas that most hotels do not offer, giving them a chance to create a competitive advantage. Finally, they can cost out the price of providing the features. For example, giving guests unexpected periodic upgrades can be inexpensive if you are using unsold suites for this program. Gaining this information would not have been possible without a database that enabled the questionnaires to be sent out to selected frequent users of luxury hotels.[70]

Harrah's, an operator of casino resorts, provides an example of how companies can benefit from a loyalty program. Harrah's developed a loyalty program called Total Rewards. Before starting the program, its research revealed that its customers spent only about 36 percent of their gaming budget with Harrah's. Today that number has increased to 44 percent, meaning Harrah's is getting almost 25 percent more revenue from existing customers. This revenue came by getting customers to

TABLE 16–2

Gap Analysis of Loyalty Features

Feature	Performance (%)	Importance (%)	Gap
The hotel provides upgrades when available.	18.7	69.4	50.7
You can request a specific room.	4.9	44.7	39.8
If the hotel is likely to be sold out at a time you normally visit, someone from the hotel will call you to ask if you would like to make a reservation.	3.0	37.7	34.7
The hotel uses information from your prior stays to customize services for you.	24.3	57.7	33.4
The staff recognizes you when you arrive.	15.1	38.3	23.2
Employees communicate the attitude that your problems are important to them.	24.0	42.6	18.6

Source: John Bowen, University of Houston and Stowe Shoemaker, University of Nevada, Las Vegas.

visit casinos near their home more frequently and trying to increase cross-market play by getting them to visit Harrah's casinos when they traveled. The increase in cross-market play has resulted in hundreds of millions of dollars in additional revenue for Harrah's. The object of any customer loyalty program is to change customer behavior. The programs are designed to get customers to shorten their purchase cycles, that is, to come back in two weeks instead of three or to purchase more when they do visit their restaurants or hotels. Harrah's Total Rewards is a great example of a loyalty program that has changed consumer behavior.[71]

Most of the current loyalty programs were developed by airlines and hotel brands in the 1980s for baby boomers and appear to be less effective for the millennials. These programs reward customers for their past loyalty; the more you stay, the higher your loyalty stays and the more benefits you receive. However, millennials rated "ability to value me" and "ability to understand my needs" as the most important attributes in creating loyalty.[72] In the same study, millennials ranked loyalty programs sixteenth. Millennials want to feel special from the moment they arrive at the hotel for the first time; they desire experiences that are customized for them.[73] A travel expert claims millennials look at the platinum level of a brand's loyalty program and choose the benefits they would like to receive. These choices are benefits they would like to receive on their first stay! The traditional tier-based programs that require the guest to stay a number of nights before they receive their rewards are therefore less effective.

Not surprisingly, the baby boomers and Gen-Xers who hold the bulk of memberships in travel programs continue to drive the expectations in those sectors. The challenge for marketers will be to evolve the design of loyalty programs to maintain the loyalty of baby boomers and Gen-Xers, while also adding features to attract millennials. Millennials now account for the highest percentage of members in retail store programs.

Many of these programs provide instant rewards when the customer or cashier swipes the loyalty card at the checkout, and discounts are applied immediately to the cardholder's invoice.

Millennials want instant rewards. Omni Hotels, a well-known upscale brand in North America, has developed a loyalty program where everyone becomes a Gold Member and earns free Wi-Fi when they sign up. After the first stay, they receive benefits that compare with or exceed the legacy hotel brands' for guests who achieved the first tier of a loyalty program. This loyalty program then becomes a traditional tier-based system that provides additional benefits. Omni's loyalty program is an example of how traditional travel loyalty programs can be modified to be more attractive to millennials. citizenM, a hotel brand

Most frequency programs were developed for baby boomers. Transforming these programs so they will be attractive to millennials is a challenge many companies are facing. Courtesy of stevecuk/Fotolia.

that targeted millennials, has a one-level loyalty program called "citizen," and when you join you instantly get 15 percent off the room rates and a more liberal cancellation policy. The biggest change for North American hotel loyalty programs is the shift in the importance of generational trends, with millennials trending and baby boomers fading.

■■■ Traditional Forms of Direct Marketing

The traditional forms of direct marketing used in the hospitality industry are direct-mail marketing, telephone marketing, and kiosk marketing.

Direct-Mail Marketing

Direct-mail marketing. Direct marketing through single mailings that include letters, ads, samples, foldouts, and other "salespeople with wings" sent to prospects on mailing lists.

Direct-mail marketing involves sending an offer, announcement, reminder, or other item to a person at a particular address. Using highly selective mailing lists, direct marketers send out millions of mail pieces each year: letters, catalogs, ads, brochures, samples, DVDs, and other "salespeople with wings." Direct mail is by far the largest direct-marketing medium. The DMA reports that direct mail (including both catalog and noncatalog mail) drives more than almost a third of all U.S. direct-marketing sales.[74]

Direct mail is well suited to direct one-to-one communication. It permits high target market selectivity, can be personalized, is flexible, and allows easy measurement of results. Although direct mail costs more than mass media, such as TV or magazines, per 1,000 people reached, the people it reaches are much better prospects. Some analysts predict a decline in the use of traditional forms of direct mail in coming years, as marketers switch to newer digital forms, such as e-mail and mobile (cell phone) marketing. E-mail, mobile, and other newer forms of direct mail deliver direct messages at incredible speeds and lower costs compared to the post office's "snail mail" pace.

However, even though the new digital forms of direct mail are gaining popularity, the traditional form is still by far the most widely used. Mail marketing offers some distinct advantages over digital forms. It provides something tangible for people to hold and keep. E-mail is easily screened or trashed. "[With] spam filters and spam folders to keep our messaging away from consumers' inboxes," says one direct marketer, "sometimes you have to lick a few stamps."[75] Traditional direct mail can be used effectively in combination with other media, such as company Web sites.

Telephone Marketing

Telephone marketing. Using the telephone to sell directly to customers.

Telephone marketing involves using the telephone to sell directly to consumers and business customers. Telephone marketing now accounts for 19 percent of all direct-marketing–driven sales. We're all familiar with telephone marketing directed toward consumers, but business-to-business marketers also use telephone marketing extensively, accounting for more than 55 percent of all telephone marketing sales.[76]

Properly designed and targeted telemarketing provides many benefits, including purchasing convenience and increased product and service information. However, the explosion in unsolicited outbound telephone marketing over the years annoyed many consumers, who objected to the almost daily "junk phone calls" that pull them away from the dinner table or fill the answering machine.

U.S. lawmakers responded with a National Do-Not-Call Registry, managed by the Federal Trade Commission (FTC). The legislation bans most telemarketing calls to registered phone numbers (although people can still receive calls from nonprofit groups, politicians, and companies with which they have recently done business). Delighted consumers have responded enthusiastically. To date, they have registered more than 191 million phone numbers at www.donotcall.com or by calling 888-382-1222. Businesses that break do-not-call laws can be fined up to $11,000 per violation. As a result, reports an FTC spokesperson, the program "has been exceptionally successful."[77]

Airport kiosks allow travelers to find information; choose seats; and purchase tickets, food, and beverages. Courtesy of Fizkes/Fotolia.

Do-not-call legislation has hurt the telemarketing industry, but not all that much. Two major forms of telemarketing—inbound consumer telemarketing and outbound business-to-business telemarketing—remain strong and growing. Telemarketing also remains a major fundraising tool for nonprofit groups. However, many telemarketers are shifting to alternative methods for capturing new customers and sales, from direct mail, direct-response TV, and live-chat Web technology to sweepstakes that prompt customers to call.

In fact, do-not-call appears to be helping most direct marketers more than it's hurting them. Many of these marketers are shifting their call-center activity from making cold calls on often resentful customers to managing existing customer relationships. They are developing "opt-in" calling systems, in which they provide useful information and offers to customers who have invited the company to contact them by phone or e-mail. These "sales tactics have [produced] results as good—or even better—than telemarketing," declares one analyst. "The opt-in model is proving [more] valuable for marketers [than] the old invasive one."[78]

Kiosk Marketing

As consumers become more and more comfortable with computer and digital technologies, many companies are placing information and ordering machines—called kiosks (in contrast to vending machines, which dispense actual products)—in stores, airports, and other locations. Kiosks are popping up everywhere these days, from self-service hotel and airline check-in devices to in-store ordering kiosks that let you order merchandise not carried in the store.

At JetBlue's Terminal Five at New York's John F. Kennedy Airport, more than 200 screens throughout the terminal allow passengers to order food and beverages to be delivered to their gate. Business marketers also use kiosks. For example, at trade shows, kiosks are used to collect sales leads and to provide information on products. The kiosk system reads customer data from encoded registration badges and produces technical data sheets that can be printed at the kiosk or e-mailed to the customer. The system has resulted in up to a 400 percent increase in qualified sales leads.[79]

Interactive TV

Interactive TV (iTV) lets viewers interact with TV programming and advertising using their remote controls. In the past, iTV was slow to catch on. However, the technology now appears poised to take off as a direct-marketing medium. Research shows that the level of viewer engagement with iTV is much higher than with 30-second spots. A recent poll indicated that 66 percent of viewers would be "very interested" in interacting with commercials that piqued their interest.[80]

iTV gives marketers an opportunity to reach targeted audiences in an interactive, more involving way. During the ads, a bar at the bottom of the screen lets viewers use their remotes to choose additional content and offers, such as on-demand free product samples, brand channels, or video showcases. For example, in an early test last year, the Disney Travel Channel allowed subscribers to browse information about Disney theme parks and then request a call from an agent. The booking rate for people requesting a call was 25 percent.

■■■ Online Privacy and Security

E-commerce. The general term for a buying and selling process that is supported by electronic means, primarily the Internet.

Online privacy is perhaps the number-one **e-commerce** concern. Most e-marketers have become skilled at collecting and analyzing detailed consumer information. Marketers can easily track Web site visitors, and many consumers who participate in Web site activities provide extensive personal information. This may leave consumers open to information abuse if companies make unauthorized use of the information in marketing their products or exchanging databases with other companies. Many consumers and policy makers worry that marketers have stepped over the line and are violating consumers' right to privacy.[81] A recent survey found that seven out of ten consumers are concerned about online privacy.

Many consumers also worry about *online security*. They fear that unscrupulous snoopers will eavesdrop on their online transactions or intercept their credit card numbers and make unauthorized purchases. In turn, companies doing business online fear that others will use the Internet to invade their computer systems for the purposes of commercial espionage or even sabotage. There appears to be an ongoing competition between the technology of Internet security systems and the sophistication of those seeking to break them.

In response to such online privacy and security concerns, the federal government is considering legislative actions to regulate how Web operators obtain and use consumer information. Congress is considering an online privacy bill that would require online service providers and commercial Web sites to get customers' permission before they disclose important personal information. That would include financial, medical, ethnic, religious, and political information, along with Social Security data and sexual orientation. The bill would also direct the FTC to enact rules imposing similar requirements on both online and off-line data collection. "I think this subject of privacy is a ticking time bomb because people do not want their personally identifiable medical and financial information spread all over every place," says one senator. "A doctor needs to know what ails you. But those ailments, your mortgage banker doesn't need to know that."

Of special concern are the privacy rights of children. In 1998, the FTC surveyed 212 Web sites directed toward children. It found that 89 percent of the sites collected personal information from children. However, 46 percent of them did not include any disclosure of their collection and use of such information. As a result, Congress passed the Children's Online Privacy Protection Act, which requires Web site operators targeting children to post privacy policies on their sites. They must also notify parents about the information they're gathering and obtain parental consent before collecting personal information from children under age 13.[82]

Many companies have responded to consumer privacy and security concerns with actions of their own. Companies such as Expedia have conducted voluntary audits of their privacy and security policies. It is important to protect the privacy and rights of consumers. Trust is one of the most important assets of a manager and a company.

■■■ CHAPTER REVIEW

I. Direct and Digital Marketing involves engaging directly with carefully targeted individual consumers and customer communities to both obtain an immediate response and build lasting customer relationships. Companies use direct marketing to tailor their offers and content to the needs and interests of narrowly defined segments or individual buyers. In this way, they build customer engagement, brand community, and sales.

A. The New Direct-Marketing Model. In the spate of online social and mobile media, direct marketing has undergone a dramatic transformation. Direct and digital marketing are more than just supplementary channels or advertising media; they constitute a complete model for doing business.

B. Rapid Growth of Direct and Digital Marketing. Direct and digital marketing have become the fastest-growing form of marketing. Direct marketing continues to become more Internet-based, and digital direct marketing is claiming a surging share of marketing spending and sales.

C. Benefits of Direct and Digital Marketing to Buyers and Sellers. For buyers, direct and digital marketing are convenient, easy, and private. They give buyers anywhere, anytime access to an almost unlimited assortment of goods and a wealth of product and buying information. For sellers, direct marketing often provides low-cost, efficient, speedy alternatives for reaching their markets as well as greater flexibility. Especially in today's digital environment, direct marketing provides opportunities for real-time marketing that links brands to important moments and trending events in customers' lives.

II. Forms of Direct and Digital Marketing. Traditional direct-marketing tools include face-to-face selling, direct-mail marketing, catalog marketing, telemarketing, direct-response TV marketing, and kiosk marketing. In recent years, however, a new set of digital and direct-marketing tools have emerged. These include Web sites, online ads, promotional e-mail, online videos, blogs, social media marketing, and mobile marketing.

III. Digital and Social Media Marketing. Digital marketing tools and platforms directly engage consumers anywhere at any time via their computers, smartphones, tablets, Internet-ready TVs, and other digital devices. The use of the Internet and digital technology impacts both buyers and the marketers who serve them.

   A. Marketing, the Internet, and the Digital Age. The digital age has fundamentally changed customers' notions of convenience, speed, price, product information, service, and brand interactions. As a result, it has given marketers a whole new way to create customer value, engage customers, and build customer relationships. Also, companies that have traditionally operated off-line have now created their own online sales, marketing, and brand community channels.

   B. Online Marketing. Online marketing refers to marketing via the Internet using company Web sites, online advertising and promotions, e-mail marketing, online video, and blogs.

      1. Web Sites and Branded Web Communities. For most companies, the first step in conducting online marketing is to create a Web site. Some Web sites are designed to engage customers and move them closer to a direct purchase or other marketing outcome, while others' primary purpose is to present brand content that engages consumers and creates customer-brand community.

      2. Online Advertising. Online advertising has become a major promotional medium. The main forms of online advertising are display ads and search-related ads. Together, they account for the largest portion of firms' digital marketing budgets.

      3. E-Mail Marketing. E-mail can be the ultimate direct-marketing medium. Marketers can send highly targeted, tightly personalized, relationship-building messages. Many companies also use configurable e-mail systems that let customers choose what they want to get to steer clear of frustration from spam e-mails.

      4. Online Videos. Online videos engage consumers and are a form of inexpensive marketing. Videos can go viral and harbor a vast amount of attention.

      5. Blogs and Other Online Forums. Blogs (or Web logs) are online journals where people and companies post their thoughts and other content, usually related to narrowly defined topics. They usually appeal to specific special-interest groups.

   C. Social Media Marketing. For travel products, it can be argued that social media entails a change from one-to-one recommendations from individuals to many-to-many conversations. In the past, these personal sources often came from talking with a friend, relative, or local resident. Social media has now expanded the conversation, in terms of both breadth and depth.

      1. Using Social Media. Marketers can engage in social media in two ways: They can use existing social media or they can set up their own. Using existing social media seems the easiest. Thus, most brands, large and small, have set up shop on a host of social media sites.

      2. Social Media Marketing Advantages and Challenges. Social media are targeted and personal—they allow marketers to create and share tailored brand content with individual consumers and customer communities. Social media are interactive, making them ideal for starting and participating in customer conversations and listening to customer feedback. Social media are also immediate and timely. Social media can be very cost effective. Social media marketing also presents challenges. First, many companies are still experimenting with how to use them effectively, and results are hard to measure. Second, such social networks are largely user controlled.

      3. Managing User-Generated Social Media Content. UGC is valuable, whether it is positive or negative. The positive comments create community and encourage others to use the product. The negative comments provide feedback on what customers do not like and how we did not meet their expectations. These comments help us improve the service delivery system.

      4. Listening to Customers on Social Media. One of the goals of a company's social media plan should be to engage its customers and create a conversation.

      5. International Social Media. Social media managers working internationally will need to find out which sites are most effective as they move around the world.

      6. Integrated Social Media Marketing. Companies that use social media successfully are integrating a broad range of diverse media to create brand-related social sharing, engagement, and customer community.

   D. Mobile Marketing. Mobile marketing features marketing messages, promotions, and other marketing content delivered to on-the-go consumers through their mobile devices. Marketers use mobile marketing to engage customers anywhere, anytime during the buying and relationship-building processes.

IV. Customer Databases and Traditional Direct Marketing. Effective direct marketing begins with a good customer database. A customer database is an organized collection of comprehensive data about individual customers or prospects, including geographic, demographic, psychographic, and behavioral data. A good customer database can be a potent relationship-building tool.

A. **Database Uses.** Companies use databases to locate good potential customers and to generate sales leads. They can mine their databases to learn about customers in detail and then fine-tune their market offerings and communications to the special preferences and behaviors of target segments or individuals. In all, a company's database can be an important tool for building stronger long-term customer relationships.

V. **Relationship Marketing and Loyalty Programs.** Direct marketing allows companies to develop a strong relationship with their customers, which helps prevent them from switching to competitors. Relationship marketing has a long-term orientation. The goal is to deliver long-term value to customers, and the measure of success is long-term customer satisfaction. Relationship marketing requires that all the company's departments work together with marketing as a team to serve the customer. It involves building relationships at many levels: economic, social, technical, and legal, resulting in high customer loyalty.

A. **Benefits of Customer Relationship Management.** The benefits of CRM comes from building continued patronage of loyal customers, reduced marketing costs, decreased price sensitivity of loyal customers, and partnership activities of loyal customers.

B. **Loyalty Programs.** Loyalty programs were developed as a way to attract and maintain a company's best customers. The biggest change for North American hotel loyalty programs is the shift in the importance of generational trends, with millennials trending and baby boomers fading.

VI. **Traditional Forms of Direct Marketing.** The traditional forms of direct marketing used in the hospitality industry are direct-mail marketing, telephone marketing, kiosk marketing, and iTV.

A. **Direct-Mail Marketing.** Involves sending an offer, announcement, reminder, or other item to a person at a particular address. Using highly selective mailing lists, direct marketers send out millions of mail pieces each year: letters, catalogs, ads, brochures, samples, DVDs, and other "salespeople with wings." Direct mail is by far the largest direct-marketing medium.

B. **Telephone Marketing.** Involves using the telephone to sell directly to consumers and business customers. Telephone marketing now accounts for 22 percent of all direct-marketing–driven sales.

C. **Kiosk Marketing.** As consumers become more and more comfortable with computer and digital technologies, many companies are placing information and ordering machines called kiosks (in contrast to vending machines, which dispense actual products) in stores, airports, and other locations.

D. **Interactive TV.** iTV lets viewers interact with TV programming and advertising using their remote controls.

VII. **Online Privacy and Security.** Marketers have a responsibility to protect the privacy of customer information and make sure personal information such as credit card numbers is secure.

■■■ DISCUSSION QUESTIONS

1. Discuss the benefits of direct marketing to both buyers and sellers.

2. Find an example of a good video for a hospitality or travel company on YouTube. Why do you feel it was effective?

3. Define data warehouse and explain why it is a popular data management tool.

4. Discuss ways an Internet site can collect and use information from its visitors. You may refer to the site of a hotel, restaurant, club, or a destination marketing organization when answering your question.

5. Find an example of a hospitality or travel company effectively using social media.

■■■ EXPERIENTIAL EXERCISE

Do the following:

Sign up for a loyalty program for hospitality or travel organization. What information did it request from you? Did the information seem useful? Is there information it should have asked for but did not? Did it ask you if it was all right if it sent you information? See if you receive any response from the company after signing up.

■■■ INTERNET EXERCISE

Go to two Web sites for the same type of hospitality or tourism organization. For example, go to two restaurants, two destination marketing organizations, and so forth. How is the Web site linked to social media? Visit one of the social media sites linked to the Web site. Do you feel they made good use of the social media site, why or why not?

■■■ REFERENCES

1 Sources: Lauren Johnson, "Southwest Airlines Builds Email Database via Mobile Initiative," *Mobile Marketer*, June 26, 2012, www.mobilemarketer.com/cms/news/email/13177.html; "Southwest Airlines Taps SMS to Streamline Customer Service," *Mobile Marketer*, May 6, 2010, www.mobilemarketer.corn!cms/news/database-crm/6174.html; Samantha Hosenkamp, "How Southwest Manages Its Popular Social Media Sites, "*Ragan's PR Daily*, February 10, 2012, www.prdaily.com/Main/Articles/How_Southwest_manges_its_popular_social_media_sit_l0788.aspx; "Southwest Airlines Rule the Social Atmosphere, Dominating Facebook and Twitter," *PRWeb*, May 23, 2012, www.prweb.com/releases/2012/5/prweb9536405.htm; and information from "Nuts About Southwest," www.blogsouthwest.com; "What Is DING!?," www.southwest.com/ding; and www.southwest.com/iphone (accessed November 2013).

2 See http://mobileapp.marriott.com

3 See http://anyware.dominos.com

4 For these and other direct marketing statistics in this section, see Direct Marketing Association, *The DMA Statistical Fact Book 2014*, 36th ed., April 2014; and a wealth of other information at www.thedma.org, accessed September 2014.

5 Ginger Gonion, "Outlook 2014: Marketing Spending to Rise," *Direct Marketing News*, January 10, 2014, www.dmnews.com/outlook-2014-marketing-spending-to-rise/article/328925/; Thad Reuter, "U.S. e-Commerce to Grow to 13% in 2013," *Internet Retailer*, March 13, 2013, https://www.internetretailer.com/2013/03/13/us-e-commerce-grow-13-2013; Sucharita Mulpuru, "US Online Retail Forecast, 2012 to 2017," March 13, 2013, www.forrester.com/US+Online+Retaii+Forecast+2012+To+2017/fulltext/-/E-RES93281?objectid=RES93281; "Marketing Fact Pack 2014," *Advertising Age* (December 30, 2013): 14; and "Monthly and Annual Retail Trade," U.S. Census Bureau, www.census.gov/retail (accessed September 2014).

6 See Pew Research Center's Internet & American Life Project, "Internet User Demographics," www.pewinternet.org/data-trend/internet-use/latest-stats/ (accessed June 2014); "Digital Set to Surpass IV in Time Spent with US Media," *eMarketer*, August 1, 2013, www.emarketer.com/Article/Digital-Set-Surpass-IV-TimeSpent-with-US-Media/1010096; "ITU Release Latest Tech Figures & Global Rankings," October 7, 2013, www.itu.int/net/pressoffice/pressreleases/2013/41.aspx#.Uumujvad6cC; John Heggestuen, "One in Every 5 People in the World Own a Smartphone, One in Every 17 Own a Tablet," *Business Insider*, December 15, 2013, www.businessinsider.corn/smartphone-and-tablet-penetration-2013-10; and James O'Tolle, "Mobile Apps Overtake PC Internet Usage in U.S.," *CNN Money*, February 28, 2014, http://money.cnn.com/2014/02/28/technology/mobile/mobile-apps-internet//.

7 Ginger Conlon, "Outlook 2014: Marketing Spending to Rise," *Direct Marketing News*, January 10, 2014, www.dmnews.com/outlook-2014-marketing-spending-to-rise/article/328925.

8 Ginger Conlon, "Outlook 2014: Marketing Spending to Rise"; and Google annual reports, http://investor.google.com/proxy.html (accessed September 2014).

9 "Social Media Is the Hot New Thing, but Email Is Still the King," *Advertising Age* (September 30, 2013): 18.

10 See Nora Aufreiter et al., "Why Marketers Keep Sending You Emails," January 2014, www.mckinsey.com/Insights/Marketing_Sales/Why_marketers_should_keep_sending_you_emails; Niti Shah, "18 Email Marketing Stats That'll Make You Better at Your Job," *HubSpot*, December 5, 2013, http://blog.hubspot.com/marketing/email-marketing-stats-list; and Amy Gesenhues, "Report: Marketing Emails Opened on Mobile Devices Jumped 61% to 65% in 04 2013," January 23, 2014, http://marketingland.com/report-65-of-marketing-emails-were-opened-on-mobile-devicesin-q4-2013-71387

11 Larry Bennett, "Worldwide Spam Rate Falls 2.5 Percent but New Tactics Emerge," *ZDNet*, January 23, 2014, www.zdnet.com/worldwide-spam-rate-falls-2-5-percent-but-new-tacticsemerge-7000025517/.

12 Janet Logan, "Dialog Marketing Elevates E-Mail Effectiveness," *Customer Interaction Solutions*, http://prquest.umi.com/pdqweb?Did=000000091700542 (accessed December 30, 2001).

13 Beth Negus Viveiros, "Red Lobster to Upgrade Loyalty Program," *Direct* (July 2004): 10.

14 Carlo Wolff, "Cutting Through the Clutter," Lodging Hospitality (September 1, 2008): 46–48.

15 Linda Moses, "Online Video Ads Have Higher Impact than TV Ads," *Adweek*, May 1, 2013, www.adweek.com/print/148982; and ·comScore Releases December 2013 U.S. Online Video Rankings," January 10, 2014, www.comscore.com/Insights/Press_Releases/2014/1/comScore_Releases_December_2013_US_Online_Video_Rankings.

16 For these and other examples, see "Samsung, Wieden & Kennedy Rule Ad Age's 2013 Viral Video Awards," *Advertising Age*, April 16, 2013, http://adage.com/article/240900/; and Alexander Coolidge, "P&G Aims for Moms' Heart with Latest 'Thank You' Ad," *USA Today*, January 8, 2014, www.usatoday.com/story/money/business/2014/01/08/pg-olympics-thank-youad/4380229/.

17 "Evian: Masters of Online Video," *The Guardian*, www.theguardian.com/media-networklebuzzing-partner-zone/evian-online-videoadvertising-baby-me (accessed June 2014); and Emma Bazilian, "Ad of

the Day: Evian Spins a Familiar Web with a Dancing Baby Spider-Man," *Adweek*, April 3, 2014, www .adweek.com/news/advertising-branding/ad-day-evian-spins-familiar-web-dancingbaby-spider-man-156755.

18 Troy Dreier, "The Force Was Strong with This One," *Streaming Media Magazine* (April/May 2011): 66–68; also see Thales Teixeira, "The New Science of Viral Ads," *Harvard Business Review* (March 2012): 25–28; and Hilary Masell Oswald, "The Biology of a Marketplace Sensation," *Marketing News* (September 2013): 31–35.

19 "State of the Blogging World in 2012," *New Media Expo blog*, July 25, 2012, www.blog-world.com/2012/07/25/state-of-the-blogging-world-in-2012; and "The Blogconomy: Blogging Statistics," *Social Media Today*, August 28, 2013, http://socialmediatoday.com/mikevelocity/1698201/blogging-stats-2013-infographic.

20 Based on information found in Keith O'Brien, "How McDonald's Came Back Bigger Than Ever," *New York Times* (May 6, 2012): MM44.

21 Patrick Landman, "If You Do Not Have a Blog, Your Hotel Website Is Dead," tnooz.com, November 19, 2012, http://www.tnooz.com/article/if-you-do-not-have-a-blog-your-hotel-website-is-dead/ (accessed November 19, 2012).

22 Stuart Feil, "How to Win Friends and Influence People," *Adweek* (September 10, 2013): S1–S2.

23 Trip Advisor, "Fact Sheet," 2015, http://www .tripadvisor.com/PressCenter-c4-Fact_Sheet.html/ (accessed March 17, 2015).

24 Khaldoon "Khal" Nusair, A. Bilgihan, F. Okumus, and C. Cobanoglu, "Generation Y Travelers' Commitment to Online Social Network Websites," *Tourism Management*, 35 (2013): 13–22; E. Walsh, "Looking Ahead: Millennial Travel Trends-Part1," 2014, https://www.turnerpr.com/blog/millennial-travel-trends-part-1/ (accesses July 23, 2014).

25 J. Bowen and S. C. McCain, "Transitioning Loyalty Programs: A Commentary on "The Relationship Between Customer Loyalty and Customer Satisfaction," *International Journal of Contemporary Hospitality Management*, 27, no. 3 (2015): 415–430.

26 Khaldoon "Khal" Nusair, A. Bilgihan, F. Okumus, and C. Cobanoglu, "Generation Y Travelers' Commitment to Online Social Network Websites," *Tourism Management*, 35 (2013): 13–22.

27 G. Bleedorn, "Say Hello to the Millennial Generation," *ABA Bank Marketing* (January–February 2013): 24–28.

28 "How Millennials Use and Control Social Media," American Press Institute, March 16, 2015, http:// www.americanpressinstitute.org/publications/reports/survey-research/millennials-social-media/ (accessed August 27, 2015).

29 For more information see John Bowen, "Trends Affecting Social Media: Implications for Practitioners and Researchers," *Worldwide Hospitality and Tourism Themes*, 7, no. 3 (2015): 221–228.

30 http://newsroom.fb.com/company-info; www.youtube .com/yt/press/statistics.html; and www.statisticbrain .com/twitter-statistics/ (accessed September 2014).

31 Karl Greenberg, "Volvo Uses Twitter Chat for Digital Focus Groups," *Marketing Daily*, May 29, 2013, www.mediapost.com/publications/article/201309/#axzz2UsMXTPXB.

32 Lodging Interactive, "Lodging Interactive Expands Reputation Management and Social Media Marketing to Restaurants," 2015, http://www.hospitalitynet.org/news/4069404.html/ (accessed March 16, 2015).

33 B. Zeng and R. Gerritsen, "What Do We Know About Social Media in Tourism? A Review," *Tourism Management Perspectives*, 10 (2014): 27–36.

34 Jennifer Beese, "Social Hospitality: How 8 Hotels Engage Guests On & Offline," August 27, 2015, http://sproutsocial.com/insights/social-media-and-hospitality/ (accessed August 25, 2105).

35 HyeRyeon Lee and Shane C. Blum, "How Hotel Responses to Online Reviews Differ by Hotel Rating: An Exploratory Study," *Worldwide Hospitality and Tourism Themes*, 7, no. 3 (2015): 242–250.

36 S. Shankman, "What It's Really Like to Be a Hotel Social Media Manager," 2014, http://skift .com/2014/07/29/what-its-really-like-to-be-a-hotel-social-media-manager/ (accessed March 30, 2015).

37 Todd Wasser, "How Hotels and Travel Companies Are Nailing Social Media," October 28, 2011, http://mashable.com/2011/10/28/hotels-travel-social-media/ (accessed June 10, 2012).

38 Jennifer Beese, "Social Hospitality: How 8 Hotels Engage Guests On & Offline," August 27, 2015, http://sproutsocial.com/insights/social-media-and-hospitality/ (accessed August 25, 2015).

39 Mike D'Antonio, "Affinia Hotels Brings Feedback Home," *1 to 1 Magazine* (July/August 2008): 13.

40 Melissa Allison, "Re-Creating the Coffee Klatch Online," *Raleigh News & Observer* (May 6, 2013): 1D; Todd Wassermann, *MAshable*, December 13, 2013, http://lmashable.com/2013/12/05/starbucks-tweet-a-coffee-180000/; and www.facebook.com/Starbucks and https://twitter.com/Starbucks (accessed September 2014).

41 Jargon Julie, Emily Steel, and Joann Lublin, "Taco Bell Makes Spicy Retort to Suit," *Wall Street Journal*, Media Business (Monday, January 31, 2011): B5. Mobile Marketing: The New Frontier, HSMAI Foundation, September 9, 2009. "Social Media for Management Companies and Brands," HSMAI Foundation, June 15, 2010, https://www.facebook.com/sundachicago (accessed August 28, 2015); Anna Washenko, "4 Restaurants Doing Social Media Right," October 19,

2012, http://sproutsocial.com/insights/restaurants-using-social-media/ (accessed August 29, 2015).

42 L. Hejl, "Planning Your 2015 Marketing Budget," 2014, http://socialfactor.com/planning-2015-marketing-budget/ (accessed March 30, 2015); Anna Washenko, 4 Restaurants Doing Social Media Right, October 19, 2012, http://sproutsocial.com/insights/restaurants-using-social-media/ (accessed August 29, 2015).

43 Hotel News Now, "Infographic: Consumer Mobile Booking Habits," 2015, http://www.hotelnewsnow.com/article/15431/Infographic-Consumer-mobile-booking-habits/ (accessed March 16, 2015).

44 R. B. Reilly, "The Travel Industry Is Booming on Smartphones as Mobile Bookings Hit 40 Percent," 2014, http://venturebeat.com/2014/09/19/travel-bookings-by-mobile-devices-in-u-s-now-at-40-percent-and-growing-report/ (accessed March 22, 2015).

45 B. Workman, "The Travel Industry Is Racing to Catch Up with Tourists' and Business Travelers' Mobile Habits," 2014, http://www.businessinsider.com/the-mobile-travel-industry-is-growing-2-2014-2 (accessed March 22, 2015).

46 S. Bennett, "The Impact of Social Media on Travel and Tourism [Infographic]," 2012, http://www.adweek.com/socialtimes/social-media-travel-hospitality/466163 (accessed March 30, 2015).

47 R. Katz, "Top 5 Social Marketing Trends for Brands to Watch in 2015," 2014, http://www.clickz.com/clickz/column/2378721/top-5-social-marketing-trends-for-brands-to-watch-in-2015 (accessed March 15, 2015).

48 R. B. Reilly, "The Travel Industry Is Booming on Smartphones as Mobile Bookings Hit 40 Percent," 2014, http://venturebeat.com/2014/09/19/travel-bookings-by-mobile-devices-in-u-s-now-at-40-percent-and-growing-report/ (accessed March 22, 2015).

49 John Bowen, "Trends Affecting Social Media: Implications for Practitioners and Researchers," *Worldwide Hospitality and Tourism Themes*, 7, no. 3 (2015): 221–228.

50 See Lauren Johnson, "McDonald's Beefs Up Advertising Strategy with Mobile Game," *Mobile Marketer*, March 28, 2013, www.mobilemarketer.com/cms/news/advertising/12447.html; and Rimma Kats, "McDonald's Beefs Up Mobile Efforts via Targeted Campaign," *Mobile Marketing*, August 16, 2013, www.mobilemarketer.com/cms/news/advertising/13553.html.

51 See Judith Acquino, "JetBlue Voice-Activated Ad Teaches People to Speak 'Pigeon,' " *Ad Exchanger*," September 26, 2013, www.adexchanger.com/online-advertising/jetblue-voice-activated-adsteach-people-to-speak-pigeon/; and Lauren Johnson, "Top 10 Mobile Advertising Campaigns of 2013," December 24, 2013, www.mobilemarketer.com/cms/news/advertising/16847.html.

52 Alicia Orr Suman, "Ideas You Can Take to the Bank! 10 Big Things All Direct Marketers Should Be Doing Now," *Target Marketing* (February 2003): 31–33; Mary Ann Kleirzfelter, "Know Your Customer," *Target Marketing* (January 2005): 28–31; and Michele Fitzpatrick, "Socialize the Database Beyond Marketing," www.dmnews.com (accessed January 29, 2007).

53 Daniel Lyons, "Too Much Information," *Forbes* (December 13, 2004): 210; Mike Freeman, "Data Company Helps Wal-Mart, Casinos, Airlines Analyze Data," *Knight Ridder Business Tribune News* (February 24, 2006): 1; and John Foley, "Exclusive: Inside HP's Data Warehouse Gamble," *Information Week* (January 1–8, 2007): 30–35.

54 Martin Baier, Kurtis M. Ruf, and Goutam Chakraborty, *Contemporary Database Management* (Evanston, IL: Racom, 2002).

55 "Hilton Hotels Corp. Takes Lead with OnQ," *Hotels* (August 2003): 14.

56 Ibid.

57 Michael J. A. Berry and Gordon Linoff, *Data Mining Techniques* (New York: Wiley, 1997).

58 Robert Groth, *Data Mining* (Upper Saddle River, NJ: Prentice Hall, 1999).

59 See Rob Jackson and Paul Wang, *Strategic Database Marketing* (Chicago, IL: NTC Publishing Group. 1994).

60 *Making Loyalty the Mission* (Harvard Business School Video, 1995).

61 Edward L. Nash, *Direct Marketing* (New York: McGraw-Hill, 1986).

62 Leonard L. Berry and A. Parasuraman, *Marketing Services: Competing Through Quality* (New York: Free Press, 1991), pp. 136–142.

63 Colleen Dejong, "Loyalty Marketing at a Glance; Hotel Programs," *Colloquy*, http://www.colloquy.com/cont_matrix.asp?industry=Hotel (accessed October 24, 2001), www.marriott.com and www.hilton.com (accessed August 30, 2015).

64 James H. Donnelly, Jr., Leonard L. Berry, and Thomas W. Thompson, *Marketing Financial Services: A Strategic Vision* (Homewood, IL: Dow Jones–Irwin, 1985), p. 113.

65 Thomas E. Caruso, "Kotler: Future Marketers Will Focus on Customer Data Base to Compete Globally," *Marketing News* (June 8, 1992): 21.

66 Allison Perlik, "High Fidelity: Exclusive R&I Research Reveals What Draws Loyal Customers and What Drives Them Away," *Restaurants & Institutions* (February 15, 2003): 44+.

67 Frederick F. Reichheld and W. Earl Sasser, Jr., "Zero Defections: Quality Comes to Services," *Harvard Business Review*, 68 (1990): 105–111.

68 Ibid.

69 Jack Nicas, "Inside United's Secret Club for Top Fliers," August 22, 2013, wsj.com, http://www.wsj.com/articles/SB10001424127887323423804579025120455867410 (accessed August 30, 2015).

70 John Bowen and Stowe Shoemaker, "Relationship in the Luxury Hotel Segment: A Strategic Perspective" (Ithaca, NY: Cornell University, 1997). An overview of this research paper can be found in the February 1998 issue of the *Cornell Hotel and Restaurant Administration Quarterly*.

71 Phil Bligh and Doug Kurk, "Cashing In on Customer Loyalty," *CRM Magazine* (June 2004): 48+; and Matthew Haeberle, "Betting on Customer Loyalty: Harrah's Loyalty Program Is No Gamble—It's a Sure Thing, *"Chain Store Age* (January 2004): 12A+.

72 A. Weissenberg, A. Katz, and A. Narula, "A Restoration in Hotel Loyalty- Developing a Blueprint for Reinventing Loyalty Programs," 2013, http://www.deloitte.com/view/en_US/us/Industries/travel-hospitalityleisure/72ce4f52478ab310VgnVCM1000003256f70aRCRD.htm (accessed July 23, 2014).

73 P. Maycock, "Personalization Equals Loyalty for Millennials," 2014, http://www.hotelnewsnow.com/Article/13067/Personalization-equals-loyalty-for-millennials (accessed July 7, 2014).

74 See DMA, *The Power of Direct Marketing, 2009–2010 Edition*; and "Mail Spend to Rise," *Deliver Magazine*, January 7, 2010, https://www.deUvermagazine.com/the-magazine/2010/01/07/mail-spend-to-rise; Direct Marketing Association, "The DMA 2007 Statistical Fact Book," (June 2007): 224.

75 Julie Liesse, "When Times Are Hard, Mail Works," *Advertising Age* (March 30, 2009): 14; Sarah O'Leary, "Thanks to Spam, It's Not Junk Mail Anymore," *Huffington Post* (April 19, 2010), http://www.huffingtonpost.com/sarah-oleary/thanks-to-spam-its-not-ju_b_542024.html; and for counterpoints, see Gavin O'Malley, "Direct-Mail Doomed, Long Live E-Mail," MediaPost News, May 20, 2009, accessed at www.mediapost.com/publications.

76 DMA, *The Power of Direct Marketing, 2009–2010 Edition*. Direct Marketing Association, "The DMA 2006 Statistical Fact Book," (June 2006): 250.

77 "Off the Hook," *Marketing Management* (January–February 2008): 5; Jeff Gelles, "Consumer 10.0: Calls Persist Despite List," *Philadelphia Inquirer* (January 24, 2010): D2; and www.donotcall.gov (accessed October 2010); Christopher S. Rugaber, "Do Not Call List Expanded 23% to 132M U.S. Phone Numbers in 2006, Federal Agency Says," Associated Press, April 5, 2007.

78 Teinowitz, "Do Not Call Does Not Hurt Direct Marketing," p. 3.

79 Stephanie Rosenbloom, "The New Touch-Face of Vending Machines," *New York Times* (May 25, 2010), accessed at www.nytimes.com/2010/05/26/business/26vending.html; "Interactive: Ad Age Names Finalists," *Advertising Age* (February 27, 1995): 12–14.

80 Shahnaz Mahmud, "Survey: Viewers Crave TV Ad Fusion," *Adweek.com* (January 25, 2008), www.adweek.com; Andrew Hampp, "Addressable Ads Are Here; Who's Ready?" *Advertising Age* (April 13, 2009): 9; and Hampp, "Scorecard: Were We Wrong or Almost Right on LTV?" *Advertising Age*, April 12, 2010, http://adage.com/cabletvlO/article?article_id=143163.

81 See Peter Han and Angus Maclaurin, "Do Consumers Really Care About Online Privacy?" *Marketing Management* (January–February 2002): 35–38.

82 See Jennifer DiSabatino, "FTC OKs Self-Regulation to Protect Children's Privacy," *Computerworld* (February 12, 2001): 32.

Managing Hospitality and Tourism Marketing

IV

Hobbit Hole, New Zealand. Courtesy of Uxozavr/Fotolia.

Objectives

After reading this chapter, you should be able to:

1. Discuss destination marketing system.

2. Identify the components of tourism destination competitiveness.

3. Explain tourism development strategies and different options for creating and investing in tourism attractions.

4. Understand how to segment and identify visitor segments.

5. Discuss the importance of destination image and branding and creating visitor experiences.

6. Explain how central tourist agencies are organized.

Destination Marketing

Why would anyone go to New Zealand for vacation? This was a question begging for an answer before the tourism board launched a new global campaign in international markets in 1999. The bold, simple, and concise statement of the brand campaign headline—"100% Pure New Zealand"—was aligned with images of nature, people, wilderness, activities, and sweeping landscapes in their purity. The key feeding markets were the United States, Australia, England, and Japan. The slogan was simple and straightforward in any language, not needing any translation on a global scale.

This was the first global marketing campaign for New Zealand that had a single message across all of its tourism markets. Interestingly, it resulted largely from a tight budget the tourism bureau, Tourism New Zealand (TNZ), has faced and the decision makers realized that running a separate campaign in each country would be expensive. The umbrella campaign turned out to be an opportunity to communicate a distinctive voice and visitor experience combining landscapes, people, and activities. As part of the campaign, New Zealand also launched a comprehensive, vivid, and interactive Web site as part of its integrated marketing communication to engage potential visitors pre-trip and to sustain relationship and promote storytelling post-trip.

The Lord of the Rings movie trilogy, filmed in New Zealand and released over 2001 to 2003, made a significant contribution to raising New Zealand's profile as an adventure and breathtaking tourist destination in key markets. The campaign has undoubtedly become very successful and helped New Zealand to generate a positive image and brand recognition as a travel destination. Becoming a focal point in many advertising, public relations (PR), online marketing, and special events sponsorships, the international campaign demonstrated the economic and marketing impact of a movie-induced destination branding campaign and helped TNZ take advantage of wide coverage and publicity in local and international media. TNZ also actively worked to leverage the brand by building PR activities around the events such as America's Cup and Rally of New Zealand. Currently, TNZ's international media program hosts around 150 international journalists in New Zealand each year from print, online, and broadcast organizations.

Specific marketing campaigns have been linked to the release of each film and to significant film events such as the Oscars and other award ceremonies. For example, following Oscar nominations and successes, newspaper advertisements, and a poster campaign promoted New Zealand as "Best Supporting Country in a Motion Picture."

Over the years the tagline has been used as "100% pure relaxation," "100% pure welcome," "100% pure adrenalin," and "100% pure you"—all connected back to the core premise of "100% Pure New Zealand." Feeder market-specific campaigns have also taken place under the "100% Pure New Zealand" umbrella brand campaign such as "What's On" in Australia, "What Do You Say UK?" in the United Kingdom, and "The New Zealand Life Back Promise" in the United States. The campaign has recently been extended beyond tourism to doing business, making investments, having education, and working and living in New Zealand (visit http://www.newzealand.com/).

From 1999 to 2004, the number of visitors grew at an average of 7 percent a year. Between 1999 and 2008, visitor arrivals grew 50 percent, from 1.6 million to 2.4 million and foreign exchange earnings from $3.5 billion to almost $6 billion. The International Visitor Survey from 2004 found that 6 percent of visitors to New Zealand cite *The Lord of the Rings* as being one of the main reasons for visiting New Zealand. In 2004, 63,200 visitors participated in a *Lord of the Rings* activity while here, and since then, an average 47,000 visitors each year have visited a film location.

The latest adaption, "100% Middle-earth, 100% Pure New Zealand" campaign, promotes New Zealand as a visitor destination through its association with the upcoming film releases of *The Hobbit* Trilogy. Association with films such as *The Hobbit* movies offers New Zealand a wider opportunity to enhance its international profile. The goal is to show potential travelers that the fantasy of Middle-earth is in fact the reality of New Zealand. Again, TNZ's marketing strategy focuses on stunning landscapes and converting the international attention drawn from starring in *The Hobbit* trilogy into travel demand. The new campaign was named the best destination marketing campaign at the 2012 World Travel Awards.

Research by the New Zealand Institute of Economic Research has found that the marketing of New Zealand as Middle-earth has had a significant and quantifiable impact on growth in visitor arrivals from Western markets. International Visitor Arrivals data for year ending August 2014 show holiday arrivals into New Zealand are up 7.2 percent on last year. Holiday arrivals from the United States, a key target market for the Middle-earth campaign, are up 14.2 percent on the same period last year. The International Visitor Survey shows that 13 percent of all international visitors surveyed in July 2013 to June 2014 say *The Hobbit* was a factor in stimulating their interest in New Zealand as a destination.

The image building "100% Pure New Zealand" campaign has now been broadened, beyond tourism, to attract businesses, trade, talents, employees, and students to further diversify the island country economy. The brand is extended to combine all things associated with the place economy (tourism, business, trade, arts, and education) under one brand.

Film tourism, also called movie-induced or film-induced tourism, consists of visits to a destination or attraction because of the destination's feature on television (TV) or cinema screen. The New Zealand case clearly demonstrates the critical role of movies in developing and communicating a destination image and the power of public and media relations for Destination Marketing Organizations' (DMOs) efforts of marketing and branding tourist destinations.

If you sell the sizzle, you need to deliver the sausage, as well. Once New Zealand set the expectations with the campaign, they also needed to deliver the experience. Therefore, TNZ made sure that the campaign would match the promise and initiated new quality guidelines and high standards for accommodations, tour companies, and visitor information centers. The DMO also partnered with Air New Zealand (ANZ) to develop special "Middle-Earth" fares and travel packages.

DMOs can exploit movie-induced tourism opportunities and engage in four types of marketing activities to promote film tourism: (1) proactive efforts to encourage producers to film at the destination, (2) generation of ongoing publicity around the film and destination, (3) marketing activities promoting the film location after production, and (4) leveraging the film tourism by developing activities.[1]

■■■ The Globalization of the Tourist Industry

Tourism. A stay of one or more nights away from home for leisure or business, except such things as boarding, education, or semipermanent employment.

The word **tourism** has many definitions. We use the World Tourism Organization's (UNWTO) and United Nations Statistics Division's (UNSTAT) definition of tourism: "a trip to a main destination outside usual environment, for less than a year, for any main purpose (business, leisure, or other personal purpose) other than to be employed by a resident entity in the country or place visited."[2] This book uses the words *tourism* and *travel* interchangeably.

The world has become a global community, opening places unimaginable decades earlier: the wonders of Antarctica, the secrets of the Himalayas, the rain forests of the Amazon, the beauty of Tahiti, the Great Wall of China, the dramatic Victoria Falls, the origin of the Nile, and the wilds of the Scottish islands. Travel is a global business with an expanding market. Table 17–1 lists the international tourist arrivals and receipts at the top tourist destinations.

Tourism industry has shown uninterrupted growth in terms of international arrivals over the past six decades, from 250 million in 1950 to almost 1.1 billion in 2014. International tourism receipts reached U.S. $1,245 billion worldwide in 2014, up from U.S. $1,197 billion in 2013.[3] Many new destinations have

Paris, "the City of Lights," attracts more than 15 million international visitors. The largest number comes from Britain, followed by the United States, Germany, Italy, and China. Courtesy of Orpheus26/Fotolia.

TABLE 17–1
The World's Top Tourism Destinations (International Tourist Arrivals and Receipts)

Rank	Country	Arrivals in Millions	Rank	Receipts in U.S. $ Billions
1	France	83.0	3	53.6
2	United States	66.7	1	126.2
3	Spain	57.5	2	56.3
4	China*	57.7	4	50.0
5	Italy	46.4	6	41.2
6	Turkey	35.7	12	25.3
7	Germany	30.4	8	38.1
8	United Kingdom	29.3	7	36.2
9	Russian Federation	25.7	27	11.2
10	Thailand	22.4	9	33.8

Source: From Tourism Highlights 2014. Copyright © 2014 The World Tourism Organization. Reprinted by permission.
*Excludes Hong Kong (23.8 million arrivals, U.S. $33.0 billion receipts) and Macao (13.6 million arrivals, U.S. $43.7 billion receipts).

Tourism accounts for more than 50 percent of Bermuda's foreign exchange. Courtesy of Peter Rooney/Fotolia.

emerged to benefit from tourism development. International arrivals are expected to reach nearly 1.6 billion by the year 2020.

France continued to top the ranking of international tourist arrivals with 83 million tourists, and came fourth in terms of international tourism receipts with U.S. $54 billion. Compared to 2011 arrivals, Thailand has entered the top 10 destinations. Mexico (was tenth in 2011 with 23.3 million arrivals) and Malaysia (ninth in 2011 with 24.7 million arrivals) were replaced by Russian Federation and Thailand. Turkey remained sixth in arrivals.

When ranking top international tourist destinations, one should consider two key tourism indicators—international tourist arrivals and international tourism receipts. Although eight of the top destinations appear in both lists, their rankings show marked differences. These destinations attract different types of tourists with varying average length of stay and spending per trip. Today many industries of the world are dominated by relatively few competitors (oligopolies), who hold major market shares. It is often difficult or impossible for potential new competitors to enter those markets. Market entry in tourism is open, and new destinations can acquire the economic and social benefits of tourism.

Students reading this book today can enter the world tourism industry and plan strategies to help drive tourism growth for their nations, states, and cities. Successful destination planning and marketing can bring hundreds of millions and even billions of dollars in revenue to destinations. New supportive industries and jobs can be created and standards of living can be increased. At the same time, the interchange of cultures assists the quest for world peace. Destination marketing is a career worthy of college and university graduates.

Tourist destinations do not need spectacular attractions such as an Eiffel Tower, Grand Canyon, or Leaning Tower to participate in today's tourism. Regions such as Eastern Europe and countries such as China and India are rapidly developing. They are now generators of tourists, as well as destinations for tourists. Asia and the Pacific recorded the strongest growth with a 6 percent increase in arrivals, followed by Europe and Africa, both 5 percent increase. China has become the number one tourism source market in the world, spending U.S. $129 billion on international tourism. By 2020, China is expected to be the largest inbound and outbound market in the world. China has 2.5 million hotel rooms and in 15 to 20 years is expected to have 5 to 7 million more.

■■■ Marketing Tourism Destinations

The Tourism Destination

Destinations. Places with some form of actual or perceived boundary, such as the physical boundary of an island, political boundaries, or even market-created boundaries.

Infrastructure. The system according to which a company, organization, or other body is organized at the most basic level.

Tourists travel to **destinations**, places with some form of actual or perceived boundary, such as the physical boundary of an island, political boundaries, or even market-created boundaries such as those of a travel wholesaler who defines a South Pacific tour solely as Australia and New Zealand. Central America consists of seven nations, but few, if any, national tourist offices or tour planners view it that way. A commonly packaged tour of Central America includes only two or three nations, such as Costa Rica, Guatemala, and Panama. Others are excluded for reasons of political instability or deficient **infrastructure**.

Although Australia and New Zealand are often packaged together for the North American visitor, Australia has worked hard for many years to make it a single destination rather than share the limited vacation time of visitors. In turn, destinations within Australia, such as the state of Western Australia, or cities such as Perth or Adelaide, believe they must develop a distinct destinations reputation to avoid being left out or used only as overnight stopovers.

The desire to become a recognized destination presents a difficult marketing challenge. Within eastern North Carolina, the town of New Bern has several interesting visitor attractions and events. The remainder of the county offers considerably less, yet visitor promotion funds are collected from a countywide hotel bed tax. Political pressure forced tourism officials to promote Craven County as a destination rather than just the town of New Bern. The promotion of a relatively unfamiliar town poses sufficient problems, but the promotion of a county greatly intensifies the challenge.

Macrodestinations such as the United States contain thousands of microdestinations, including regions, states, cities, towns, and even visitor destinations within a town. It is not unusual to find tourists who view their Hawaiian destination as the Hilton Hawaiian Village in Honolulu and may rarely, if ever, venture outside the perimeter. Thousands of visitors fly to Orlando and proceed directly to Disney World, where most or all of their vacation is spent. These tourists do not view Florida or Orlando as their destinations, but rather Disney World.

For some pleasure travelers, the real destination is the vehicle of travel, such as a cruise ship, river paddle ship, or a special railroad such as the Orient Express. These "moving destinations" offer a variety of events for passengers, and dining is particularly important. Games, gambling, theater, musicals, participatory murder mysteries, seminars, dances, and a host of other onboard events enhance the pleasure of moving destinations. As industrialized societies experience enlarged numbers of senior citizens, these relatively passive moving destinations are likely to receive increased demand.

Macrodestinations.

Destinations such as the United States that contain thousands of microdestinations, including regions, states, cities, towns, and visitor destinations within a town.

Destination Marketing System

Destination marketing is more challenging than marketing other products because a destination is a bundle of highly diverse products, including geographic size, attractions, accommodation, food and beverage, and entertainment. The complexity is augmented by limited control by DMOs and the number of public and private stakeholders involved in delivering a unified brand and destination experience.

Unlike business marketing in which target markets determine product strategy, initial destination marketing efforts usually start with the attractions and resources at hand that determine potential segments to target (except for man-made destinations). Figure 17–1 shows vital linkages between supply and demand in tourism to understand the role of marketing. Destination marketing is systematically linking supply (destination features and benefits) with demand (needs and wants of travelers) and enhancing competitiveness of a destination in a sustainable manner.

Destinations have varying natural, historical, and cultural attractions. To enhance competitiveness, destinations develop and offer facilitating, supporting, and augmented products such as infrastructure, lodging, food and beverage, transportation, tours, entertainment, visitor services, and hospitality of local people to appeal to existing markets or new markets. Therefore, a good knowledge of the demand side—current and potential visitor characteristics and destination selection behavior—is also necessary for successful destination marketing. Destinations need to understand what type of travelers they seek to attract and what they desire from their travel. They can improve their overall marketing effort by developing specific product offerings for specific segments. For example, millennials want customized experience and cocreate their destination experience. They are more interested than older generations in traveling abroad. The United Nations estimates that 20 percent of all international tourists, or nearly 200 million travelers, are young people, and that this demographic generates more than $180 billion in annual tourism revenue.[4]

Typically, DMOs, such as ministries of tourism, national tourism organizations (NTOs), and convention and visitors bureaus (CVBs), are the formal marketing organizations dealing with long-term strategy development. Funding is often provided by sales tax or special room tax receipts. The Las Vegas Convention and Visitors Authority (LVCVA) is the official DMO of Las Vegas funded by county hotel room tax. The LVCVA's responsibilities involve marketing activities, branding, market research, strategic planning, and operating convention and event centers.

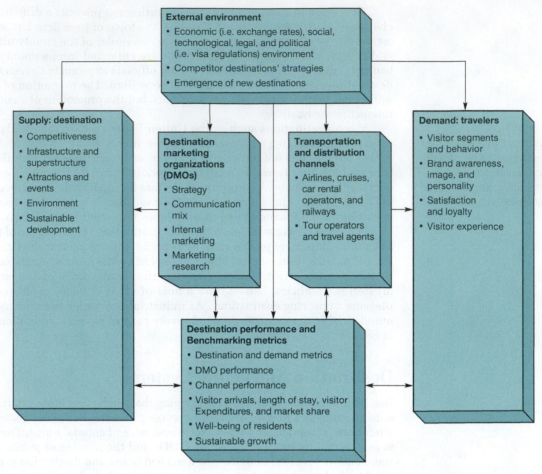

Figure 17–1
Destination marketing system

The responsibility for marketing destinations and delivering a memorable experience on location are generally shared by many diverse public and private organizations including chamber of commerce, hotel/motel associations, environmental organizations, and many more.[5] LVCVA Board of Directors involves both public and private industry members.

The selling function, to a great extent, is carried out by distribution channel and transportation companies such as airlines, tour operators, and travel agents. Distribution channel members and transportation companies play unique roles because they also have bargaining powers and strong influence on destination marketing and competitiveness. Tour operators and travel agents are significant information sources influencing the images and decisions of travelers.[6] Working closely with DMOs or independently, they develop and distribute travel packages and promote a destination. For most European and Mediterranean destinations targeting sun and sea markets, most vacation packages are sold via tour operators that determine "price" for destinations. They decide on destinations to be included in their sales portfolio, determine price quotes for hotels in host destinations as well as prices visitors pay for all-inclusive packages (Kozak and Baloglu, 2011). Transportation companies get involved in developing and selling vacation packages through their own travel companies or strategic alliances. For example, United Vacations owned by United Airlines has its own list of destinations and offers leisure vacation packages that combine airfare with negotiated hotel rates in domestic and international destinations, car rentals, and entertainment.[7]

The trends in external environment will influence all elements of marketing system and destination competitiveness. Dramatic fluctuations in exchange rates (e.g., recent decline in Russian ruble), visa regulations, terrorism attacks (e.g., India, Egypt, Bali, and Middle Eastern countries), disease outbreaks and epidemics (e.g., Ebola in Africa, SARS [severe acute respiratory syndrome] in Hong Kong, bird flu in Asia), and some natural disasters (e.g., tsunami in Thailand) significantly affect destination marketing and competitiveness. An increase in fuel costs makes distant (closer) destinations less (more) price competitive. The practices by destination's competitive set such as new tourism development and brand positioning will also impact the destination's marketing strategy.

Destination benchmarking should include not only outcomes and performance metrics in terms of number of visitors, market share, and revenue generated, but also other elements such as visitor satisfaction and loyalty, brand recognition and image, performances of DMOs, and sustainable growth metrics. There are three main types of benchmarking: internal, external, and generic. Internal benchmarking is to keep track of changes over time (quarterly or annually) and compare current performance of a destination with its previous performances (e.g., changes in visitor satisfaction, brand image, number of arrivals, and tourism receipts). External benchmarking consists of selecting a major competitor and comparing performances in a given period (e.g., comparison of Jamaica and Dominican Republic). Generic benchmarking uses international standards and best practices (e.g., carbon footprints, European "Blue Flag" ecolabeling for beaches and marinas) for comparison. This type of benchmarking would particularly be appropriate for destination DMO performance to learn from best practices in terms of public and media relations, creating events, building partnerships, branding, and organizational effectiveness.[8]

Destination Competitiveness

Destinations have varying but similar resources and attractions. New Zealand has beautiful scenery and nature. Singapore offers multicultural urban attractions. Jamaica has beautiful beaches. So does Thailand. Turkey and Greece are rich in history, culture, nature, and beaches. Bali offers cultural traditions, while Italy has culture, cuisine, art, and fashion. Some destinations are rich in natural resources but seriously disadvantaged in other areas. Some have numerous resources and attractions and the luxury of targeting a wider selection market segments.[9]

Destination competitiveness requires an understanding of two important concepts: comparative and competitive advantages. *Comparative advantage* is possession of resources, natural and/or man-made, critical to tourism development. It may include natural resources (climate, location, natural beauties), historical and cultural resources, factors such as human resources, capital resources, infrastructure (roads, water supply, public services), and tourism superstructure (hotels and restaurants, theme parks, golf courses). But having attractions and resources is not enough. The success in competitive arena lies in turning comparative advantages into strengths relative to competition. *Competitive advantage* is to make use of these resources efficiently and effectively to enhance competitiveness of destination.[10]

Travel and Tourism Competitiveness Index

Numerous, but interrelated, factors determine a place competitiveness in the regional and global marketplace. One comprehensive framework and measure of travel and tourism (T&T) competitiveness on a global scale is the Travel and Tourism Competitiveness Index (TTCI) developed and published each year by World Economic Forum (WEF).

The TTCI "aims to measure the factors and policies that make it attractive to develop the T&T sector in different countries." It is derived from the Executive Opinion Survey, "hard" data from external sources for each country, and input from global agencies such as World Tourism Organization (UNWTO), the Organization for Economic Cooperation and Development (OECD), the World Travel and Tourism Council (WTTC), and Deloitte.

Each country or destination (a total of 140 countries and economies) score is composed of 14 pillars (Figure 17–2). The pillars were grouped under three broad categories or subindex: (1) the T&T regulatory framework subindex (Pillars 1 to 5); (2) the T&T business environment and infrastructure subindex (Pillars 6 to 10); and (3) the T&T human, cultural, and natural resources subindex (Pillars 11 to 14) (see Appendix A for pillar descriptions).

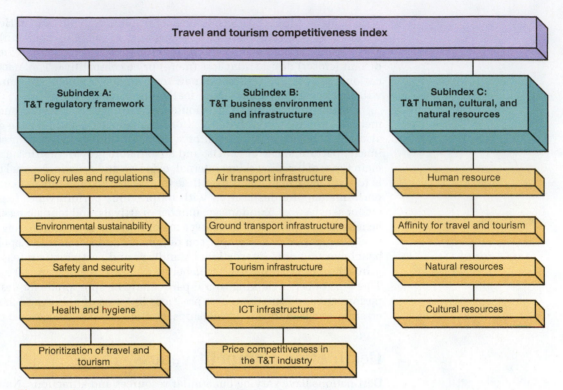

Figure 17–2
Travel and Tourism Competitiveness Index
Source: From Travel and Tourism Competitiveness Report 2014. Copyright © 2014 by World
Economic Forum. Reprinted by permission.

Table 17–2 shows the overall ranking of the 10 countries—regional and world rankings-based three main subindexes: (1) regulatory framework; (2) business environment and infrastructure; and (3) human, cultural, and natural resources. The scores range from 1 (lowest) to 6 (highest). Switzerland maintains its top ranking position in the past five years, along with Germany and Austria. It is a strong leisure tourism destination and an important business travel hub attracting international conventions, fairs, and exhibitions. However, it has relatively low score in Subindex B because its price competitiveness (Pillar 10) is significantly low, the 139th in World rankings. Regional ranking (America, Europe, North Africa, sub-Saharan Africa, Middle-East, and Asia Pacific) is also important because investors and travelers are interested in particular regions. Even though Singapore ranks tenth in world rankings, it has the top ranking position in terms of regional rankings among Asia Pacific countries. The report published by WEF also ranks countries for each of the 14 individual pillar scores. In Europe, Spain leads in cultural resources because of its numerous World Heritage sites, large number of international fairs and exhibitions, significant sports stadium capacity, many hotel rooms, and car rental facilities. Furthermore, its air transport infrastructure is highly developed and ranks among the top 10 worldwide.

The index is a measurement of the factors that make it attractive to develop business in the T&T industry of individual countries, rather than a measure of country attractiveness as a tourist destination. The TTCI serves two purposes. First, it provides a benchmarking tool for 140 countries and economies to understand their strengths and weaknesses for attracting businesses and tourism investment. Second, it provides information for national policymakers and tourism industry to formulate strategic policy and tourism development to enhance T&T competitiveness.

PRICE COMPETITIVENESS Price competitiveness has a particular importance for tourist destinations because lower costs increase the attractiveness of some countries for many travelers. For most European destinations targeting sun and sea markets, tour operators determine prices tourists pay. TUI (Touristik Union International),

TABLE 17–2

Top 10 Countries Based on 2014 Travel and Tourism Competitiveness Index

Country	Regional Rank	World Rank	Subindex A: T&T Regulatory Framework	Subindex B: Business Environment and Infrastructure	Subindex C: T&T Human, Cultural, and Natural Resources
Switzerland	1	1	5.94	5.42	5.63
Germany	2	2	5.57	5.29	5.31
Austria	3	3	5.80	5.11	5.24
Spain	4	4	5.48	5.30	5.36
United Kingdom	5	5	5.44	5.13	5.57
United States	1	6	4.95	5.36	5.65
France	6	7	5.56	5.18	5.20
Canada	2	8	5.27	5.17	5.39
Sweden	7	9	5.54	4.89	5.30
Singapore	1	10	5.74	5.31	4.64

Source: From Travel and Tourism Competitiveness Report 2014. Copyright © 2014 by World Economic Forum. Reprinted by permission.

Thomas Cook, DER Touristik, and Neckermann are major European tour operators. They have bargaining and coercive power because of the oversupply of facilities in Mediterranean region and resorts. In Chapter 11, we covered a variety of pricing strategies. Product bundle pricing is important for tourist destinations because vacation packages are frequently developed and sold through travel agents and online. The Web site sales of traditional vacation packages in the United States hit $5.4 billion in 2012.[11]

The price factors include the cost of transport services such as air travel to the visitor and the cost of ground content such as accommodation, tour services, food and beverage, and entertainment. For international travel, exchange rates and cost of living in origin and destination are major determinants of travel demand and destination competitiveness. "Two types of prices have to be considered in estimating the price competitiveness of a destination. The first one is relative price between the receiving and origin country, the second is relative price between competing destinations, which generates the substitution price effect."[12] For a traveler in the United States, if a similar trip to France and Thailand costs less for Thailand, Thailand is more price competitive (more value for money) and more likely to be selected.

One of the indicators for international comparison of prices is the "Big Mac" index that is invented by *The Economist* in 1986 to guide whether currencies are at their correct levels. For example, the average price of a Big Mac in the United States in July 2014 was $4.80; in China it was only $2.73 at market exchange rates.[13] But, at the end of the day, it only tells us about the price of a burger, not that of a complex tourism product. In today's world, tourists are well informed about and more sensitive to exchange rates rather than price levels and inflation rates.

Sustainable Tourism

Tourism has economic, social/cultural, and environmental impacts on a destination. Therefore, destinations should consider triple bottom line—economic, social/cultural, and environmental (profit, people, and planet)—when it comes to product development, competitiveness, and marketing. **Sustainable tourism** refers to tourism that minimizes the environmental impacts and sociocultural changes, and sustains the longevity of a destination, and creates economic opportunity for local communities.[14] The triple bottom line suggests that a destination is operating in a way so that its economic, society, and environment interests intersect.[15] A sustainable destination will act for the interest of travelers and residents as well as for the protection

Sustainable tourism. Tourism that minimizes the environmental impacts and sociocultural changes, sustains the longevity of a destination, and creates economic opportunity for local communities.

Tanzania is one of the most popular tourist destinations in Africa. In an effort to create sustainable tourism, tourists on safaris now carry cameras instead of guns. Courtesy of Aleksandar Todorovic/Fotolia.

Multiplier effect. Tourist expenditures that are recycled through the local economy, being spent and spent again.

of the resources. From a marketing standpoint, sustainable tourism can mean giving up current revenues from tourism by limiting capacity to ensure there will be demand for tourism in the future.

Economic Effects of Tourism

Tourism's most visible benefit is direct employment in hotels, restaurants, retail establishments, and transportation. A second but less visible benefit consists of support industries. The third benefit of tourism is the **multiplier effect**, as tourist expenditures are recycled through the local economy. Tourism's fourth benefit is state and local revenues derived from taxes on tourism, shifting the tax burden to nonresidents as in Texas, Nevada, and Florida. Tourism accounts for more than half of Bermuda's foreign exchange and tax revenues. It is one of the few developed countries without an income tax. New York's cumulative bed tax on hotel rooms raises hundreds of millions of dollars in annual revenues. Dallas, Los Angeles, and Houston all have bed taxes in excess of 12 percent. Hawaii derives a heavy percent of its total state and county taxes from tourism.

Critics of such taxation contend that these schemes are taxation without representation and eventually lead to careless government spending or spending that has little relevance to promoting tourism and enhancing the travel experience. Hospitality and travel managers must make sure that bed taxes and other tourist-related taxes go back into promoting tourism and developing the infrastructure to support tourism. Approximately 53 percent of all room tax paid by visitors in Las Vegas goes back into the community, translating into hundreds of millions of dollars distributed among community agencies to build roads, parks, schools, and other government programs that benefit the residents.[16]

Tourism also yields a fifth benefit: It stimulates exports of locally made products. Estimates of visitor spending on gifts, clothing, and souvenirs are in the range of 15 to 20 percent of total expenditures. The degree to which these products are made or assembled in a destination affects the economic impact of the local economy.

Destinations dominated by all-inclusive resorts face challenges for sustainable tourism that benefit locals. Critics of the all-inclusive concept in Jamaica observe that little of the revenue generated by the resorts actually goes to improving Jamaica's standard of living. Even though Sandals and Superclubs are locally owned, the considerable presence of foreign-owned resorts generates leakage of money back to the developed countries.[17] "Tourism, long viewed as vile, repressive, and imperialistic by the Castro government, was out of necessity given center stage as the shining star upon which Cuba's hopes for a productive and economically sound future was pinned."[18] This reversal by the Castro government shows the importance of tourism, especially in island countries.

Social/Cultural Effects of Tourism

Tourism growth affects the social/cultural basis of destinations in both positive and negative ways. Cuba offers an extreme example. After Castro opened Cuba's doors to tourism, an unexpected societal phenomenon occurred. The tourism boom resulted in the departure of highly trained professionals from their careers. Physicians, teachers, engineers, and others abandoned their professions to become waiters, bartenders, and bellhops. A teacher earning 180 pesos per month could easily earn that amount in a day in tourism. In addition, individuals with hard currency acquired from tips could shop in the "dollar store" where only foreign currency was accepted. These stores had no shortage of consumer products.

As regulations were relaxed in Cuba, thousands of Cuban citizens opened and operated a multitude of small ventures such as home restaurants and handcrafts.[19]

Las Vegas is a man-made destination attracting over 40 million visitors a year, generating $45 billion in economic impact. Courtesy of Las Vegas News Bureau.

Destinations may not welcome tourists uniformly. Due to location, climate, limited resources, size, and cultural heritage, some places have few economic choices other than to participate in tourism. Some engage in tourism with mixed emotions and, at times, ambivalence. For instance, Bali is concerned that tourism is destroying its culture, as farmland becomes resorts and new jobs unravel family values. "Bali and tourism is not a marriage of love," observed a Bali tourism official, clearly focusing on the dilemma of cultural breakdown.

This is becoming a serious issue in many parts of the United States, particularly the West. The people of Colorado voted against the use of tax revenues for use in tourism promotion. In many small communities, residents are increasingly opposed to the use of sales tax receipts for tourism promotion. Others have mounted opposition to large groups that bring thousands of visitors to the community, such as baseball tournaments, spring vacation students, or motorcycle events. The mixture of full-time residents versus owners of second homes is changing in many resort communities, with part-time residents becoming a greater percentage of the population. These people do not depend on the local economy for employment and often view masses of tourists as a negative factor in their enjoyment of the community.

In Ocho Rios, Jamaica, all-inclusive resorts are owned mostly by foreign investors that target short-stay and big spenders who might never leave the resort itself, which does not help local businesses or cultural understanding.

Environmental Effects of Tourism

Too often, tourism planners focus mostly on destination developments without paying attention to retaining and preserving the attributes that attracted travelers to the destination in the first place. Italy's Adriatic Sea coast has been devastated by the adverse publicity associated with the growth of brown algae that makes swimming nearly impossible. Growing pollution levels at the Grand Canyon and overcrowding in Yosemite Valley may significantly diminish the attractiveness of these great national parks. Some of East Africa's renowned game parks are being turned into dust bowls by tourists ferried around in four-wheel-drive vehicles.

Greece's national treasure, the formerly white marble Parthenon in Athens, stands as a pollution-stained symbol of environmental neglect. Thailand's beautiful beach resorts and temples have been severely damaged by pollution and poor sanitation.

The Wave, a spectacular Jurassic-era Navajo sandstone formation near Big Water, Utah, is one of the most photographed rock formations in North America. It is also popular as a hiking destination that the Bureau of Land Management (BLM) limits daily visits to 20 people, who are selected by a random drawing of numbers.[20]

This may well be a view of things to come, as those responsible for natural and historical attractions throughout the world struggle to protect their properties yet serve increasing numbers of visitors. Sustainable tourism is a concept of tourism management that anticipates and prevents problems that occur when carrying capacity is exceeded.

Ecotourism is one of the fastest-growing niche markets in the travel industry and generally viewed as representing sustainable tourism. In fact, this occurs only when the government and the private industry cooperate in planning and strict enforcement of regulations and laws. Costa Rica is commonly cited as a good example of ecotourism. By contrast, ecotourism in Nepal now resembles mass tourism. Two hundred mountain lodges have been built, with large areas cleared for timber, resulting in erosion. Excessive hiking has also resulted in erosion as well as trash and sewage problems, even on Mount Everest.[21]

Costa Rica attracts ecotourists from around the world. Courtesy of Davey_Rocket/ Fotolia.

MODIFIED ENVIRONMENTS: ECOTOURISM SUBSETS Today, members of the tourism industry such as resorts, ski lodges, golf courses, and city centers have developed habitats on their grounds that encourage wildlife. Peregrine falcons have learned to thrive in U.S. cities.[22]

Rather than provide neatly mani-cured lawns and plants that provide no food value to animals, some resorts are encouraging natural areas, nesting sites, and artificial reefs. Guests are usually thrilled to see wildlife on the grounds. Admittedly, problems can occur as deer populations explode or dangerous pred-ators ranging from poisonous snakes to crocodiles and cougars find the grounds to their liking.

INDUSTRY (PUBLIC AND PRIVATE) AND COMMUNITY COOPERATION Destination tourism depends on public/private partnerships or joint developing in planning, financing, and implementation. Successful long-run tourism destinations require coopera-tion in planning among constituencies. Many communities that directly depend on tourism fail to coordinate important sectors of the economy. Public authority is required to clear, develop, and write down land costs and to make infrastructure investments. The destination must often subsidize or provide tax incentives for private investment in hotels, convention centers, transit, and parking. Restoration is often carried out by nonprofit development corporations from the National Historic Trust to the U.S. Park Service, with private investment promoted through various tax incentives. From airlines to hotels, the tourist industry provides dedicated tax revenues from fuel, leases, bed taxes, and sales taxes to support a long-term bonus for capital construction of tourist-related infrastructure and other public improve-ments. Such steps made it possible for New York City to add the South Street Seaport Museum, Javits Convention Center, and Ellis Island Immigration Museum to its tourist attraction portfolio.

Mega events provide interesting cases to examine for public–private partner-ship models. Cities and regions turn to such partnerships for hosting mega events such as Olympics and World Cups. The 2014 Winter Olympics in Sochi, Russia, and the 2010 World Cup in South Africa are some good examples.[23]

Destination marketing can only be successful if all stakeholders are involved in strategic planning. Therefore, internal marketing principles should be applied to marketing destinations, as well. This includes educating and rewarding stake-holders, sharing critical information with them, coordinating the efforts of all stakeholders and residents, and engaging them in the strategic marketing planning.

In 2014, Ministry of Jamaica partnered with the Jamaica Environment Trust (JET) through a $34 million environmental awareness initiative called the "Clean Coasts Project." The one-year project is intended to educate and encourage Jamaicans and visitors to engage in sustained clean-up activities throughout the year.[24]

CARBON-NEUTRAL VACATIONS As the number of concerns about global warm-ing increases, the demand for carbon-neutral vacations will also increase. Many adjustments lie ahead for hospitality providers and their guests. The challenge is already difficult at some luxurious resorts where energy-intensive amenities are plentiful. Prices at the King Pacific Lodge, a deluxe floating lodge on the remote British Columbia coast, start about $5,000 per head for three nights, including the float plane, spa treatment, and Cuban cigars. Even so, the lodge has said no to guests for requests determined to be environmentally unfriendly, such as one to hire three twin-engine boats to take a party of seven salmon fishing. The guest offered to pay extra for the fuel but was still denied because of concerns about the environment.[25]

Because leisure travel is emotional and discretionary, guests have come to expect amenities and services without questioning the environment. The following are guest privileges formerly taken for granted and now being questioned:

	Results (lbs of CO_2)
Using fresh towels each day	0.5
Jet ski (3 hours)	730
Keeping hotel room cool (24 hours)	105
Eighteen holes of golf in a cart	3
Taking a Coke from minibar	2
45 minutes on treadmill	2
Two hours fishing trip in a boat	420 per passenger
45-minute helicopter ride	350 per passenger

The emphasis on CO_2 emissions will not be popular or acceptable to all guests. A Beverly Hills divorce lawyer who was a guest at King Pacific Lodge said this of such efforts, "It's putting a Band-Aid on a worldwide sore. It's great for liberal people—those who are antagonistic to the wealthy, who are able to afford to ride in a helicopter."

Tourism Development and Investments

Tourist competition is fierce amid a growing and constantly changing tourist market. In addition to strong tourist destinations, declining places upgrade and make new investments, and new places appear. Leavenworth, Washington, an old logging and mining town, experienced revival when it transformed itself into a Bavarian village. Winterset, Iowa, John Wayne's birthplace, is now visited by tourists. Seymour, Wisconsin, lays claim to being home of the first hamburger, hosting August Hamburger Days. Seymour organizers once cooked the world's largest hamburger, weighing 5,520 pounds.

In Shandong province of China, the city of Qufu was the hometown of Confucius, the ancient philosopher and educator. Qufu tourism resources are mainly historical and cultural. Today much of the tourism business is led by the government. Qufu needs to diversify tourism products and develop more accommodation facilities by seeking further cooperation between private and public sector.[26]

With the current U.S. trend toward shorter but more frequent vacations, many places within 200 miles or so of major metropolitan areas have found new opportunities to access the tourist market. Local tourism and convention bureaus tout the theme, "Stay Close to Home." The Louisiana Office of Tourism spent $6 million to market a summer travel bargain program to a 500-mile market.

Cities create many tourist attractions. Darling Harbour in Sydney has developed as a major tourist attraction. It is the location of the Sydney Convention and Exhibition Centre and home to numerous restaurants, retail stores, and attractions, including the Sydney Aquarium, Australian National Maritime Museum, and an Imax theater. The district is also within walking distance of the Star Casino and Sydney's Chinatown. It is easily accessible by monorail, water taxi, or train. By clustering a number of activities into one district, Darling Harbour gives tourists another reason to visit Sydney or stay an extra day to take in the attractions. In addition to attracting tourists, developments like Darling Harbour also provide benefits for local residents.

Marketing HIGHLIGHT 17–1   Cuba Tourism Development: A Time Travel

Shifting political and economic structures have put Cuban tourism on a fluctuating course of development. The most significant setback to Cuba's tourism industry resulted from the 1962 U.S.-declared trade embargo that restricted travel to Cuba by Americans. The Cuban government also resisted developing international tourism in the 1960s and the 1970s because of the corrosive effects it had in the prerevolutionary period. With the fall of the Soviet Union, Cuba shifted its economic and social policy again to rejuvenate tourism and initiated an aggressive tourism campaign to generate foreign exchange and stimulate investment. Since then, international tourism made huge inroads in Cuba's economic landscape, surpassing sugar and nickel exports in 1997 as the single largest earner of hard currency.

Cuba made health care a priority after its 1959 revolution. The fall of the Soviet Union and an expanding trade deficit urged Cuba to give priority to its health industry to boost tourism. The country invested significantly in its health infrastructure and biotechnology and implemented an aggressive public health strategy. This resulted in competitive advantage comparable to or better than even industrialized countries. Indeed, Cuba has a long history in health or medical tourism. Pre-Castro Cuba attracted American women wanting an abortion. The "Havana weekend" was a travel package including airfare, medical care, and hotel accommodation.

Medical or health tourism has now become a worldwide phenomenon and is a growing international trend. The market is segmented by purpose, complexity and type of care, and cost. Medical tourists are motivated by several elements, including a desire for privacy, a desire to avoid long waiting lists in travelers' home countries, and quality of facilities and services. Cuba's success in medical tourism prompted several Asian countries such as Thailand and India, and Caribbean islands such as Jamaica, Barbados, and Puerto Rico to jump on the medical tourism bandwagon. These destinations have differentiated and positioned themselves to develop their own brands of medical tourism and to appeal to various health tourist segments. Cuba portrays itself offering extensive health services, high-quality doctors, quality facilities, and services at a low cost and specializes in rehabilitation, cancer care, dentistry, eye care, and cosmetic surgery. Jamaica is positioning itself in the wellness market, whereas Barbados is positioning itself as a destination for infertility treatments. Puerto Rico is branding itself as a medical destination for U.S. patients seeking lower-priced care particularly for cardiovascular and orthopedic surgeries.

Cuba also showcased its health services by sending its health resources abroad to help the victims of natural disasters. For example, when Kashmir faced a catastrophic earthquake in 2005, Cuba sent 3,000 medical staff and enough equipment to erect 30 field hospitals. Four-hundred Cuban doctors were among the first to place a hospital and provide care to the victims of Haiti's 2010 earthquake.

Another tourism development triggered by the fall of Soviet Union was sports tourism. Marabana is the International Marathon in Havana, with participants from all over the world. Around 3,000 people from over 70 countries feel motivated enough every year to get to the starting line. The development of sports tourism on the island was logical because the majority of visitors to Cuba do not come solely for the sport but also for destination's traditional tourism offerings such as sun, sea, sand, and hedonistic pleasure seeking. U.S. citizens now will be able to travel legally to Cuba to participate in the Marabana Havana Marathon or Half Marathon.

Tourism development in Cuba has primarily focused on mass tourism, with an emphasis on all-inclusive packages. Varadero is a classic destination of mass tourism development and has followed an intensive development strategy. Cuba has vast resources for developing tourism and comparative advantages, which includes its unique history and culture. For example, Havana offers distinctive architecture, heritage, and cultural tourism. The rest of the country has the potential to be marketed for ecotourism, adventure tourism, and nature tourism. A more diversified tourism strategy and development is needed to make Cuba's tourism feasible for the long term.

Investing in the health industry is one way for Cuba to increase gross domestic product, upgrade services, create jobs, generate foreign exchange, and boost tourism. Americans may see appeal of medical tourism in Cuba if the restrictions are further relaxed.

The Hotel Nacional de Cuba is considered a symbol of history, culture, and Cuban identity. Courtesy of Philip Kotler.

A destination audit study revealed that Cuba's strengths were the potential for developing a diverse tourism product, beautiful beaches, many colonial sites, music, culture, good security, friendliness of the host society, and the growth of joint venture hotels that have better service and quality standards. However, the audit also uncovered some weaknesses such as poor transportation system and travel services and the lack of telecommunication and internet access.

In 2015, the popular online home-rental service Airbnb announced that it now lists more than 1,000 accommodation options on the island, which is half of the island's inventory. One of the most developed elements of Cuba's entrepreneurial sector is a network of thousands of privately owned rooms and houses for tourists. The properties range from small apartments in central Havana to multiroom beach houses with top-notch food and maid service.

In 2014, Cuba tourist arrivals hit record 3 million foreign visitors, bringing in over $2.5 billion hard currency. Still, Cuba needs to further diversify and upgrade its tourism products and services and in addition to packaged tourism. Future tourism development strategy for Cuba depends on sustainable tourism, considering long-term tourism impacts (economic, social, and environmental) and the facilitation of cooperation and collaboration between different stakeholders—government, businesses, tourists, and the local residents. For the moment, however, it is the government who continues to lead.

Sources: http://news.yahoo.com/cuba-tourist-arrivals-hit-record-2014-105618176.html (retrieved on December 31, 2014); Annette B. Ramírez de Arellano, "Medical Tourism in the Caribbean" *Signs* (Winter 2011): 289–297; "CUBA: Revival of Interest in Cuban Medical Tourism," *International Medical Travel Journal,* http://www.imtj.com/news/?entryid82=425382 (retrieved on August 1, 2015); Sheryl Marie Elliott and Lisa Delpy Neirotti, "Challenges of Tourism in a Dynamic Island Destination: The Case of Cuba," *Tourism Geographies* (August 2008): 375–402; William Neuman, "Americans May See Appeal of Medical Tourism in Cuba If the Restrictions Are Further Relaxed," *The New York Times,* February 15, 2015, http://www.nytimes.com/2015/02/18/world/americas/americans-may-see-appeal-of-medical-tourism-in-cuba.html?_r=0; John Sugden, "Running Havana: Observations on the Political Economy of Sport Tourism in Cuba," *Leisure Studies,* (2007), 26 No 2: 235–251; http://www.havanamarathon.net/havana-marathon-2014/ (retrieved on August 1, 2015); Michael Weissenstein, "Airbnb in Cuba Is a Reality: Start Your Bookings Now" *Skift Report* (April 02, 2015), http://skift.com/2015/04/02/airbnb-in-cuba-is-a-reality-starting-today.

Destinations must make more than financial or hospitality investments to attract tourists. Places find that they must expand public services, specifically public safety, traffic and crowd control, emergency health, sanitation, and street cleaning. They must also promote tourism internally to their own citizens and business retailers, restaurants, financial institutions, public and private transit, lodging, police, and public servants. They must invest in recruiting, training, licensing, and monitoring tourist-related businesses and employees.

Tourism Events and Attractions

Events and attractions are the two primary strategies used by tourist destinations to attract visitors. To attract tourists, destinations must still respond to the travel basics of cost and convenience. Like other consumers, tourists weigh costs against the benefits of specific destinations and investment of time, effort, and resources against a reasonable return in education, experience, fun, relaxation, and memories. Convenience takes on various meanings in travel decisions: time involved in travel from airport to lodging, language barriers, cleanliness and sanitary concerns, access to interests (beaches, attractions, amenities), and special needs (elderly, disabled, children, dietary, medical care, fax and communication, auto rental).

Events

Events generate economic impact resulting from hotel accommodations, food and beverage expenditures, tourist attractions, entertainment, gasoline, and various shopping purchases. Events vary considerably in their complexity and contribution to a community's tourism base. Potential event segments for a tourist destination are (1) cultural celebrations (e.g., festivals and religious events), (2) political events, (3) arts and entertainment events (e.g., concerts), (4) business and trade (e.g., conventions, meetings, and trade shows), (5) educational and scientific events (e.g., conferences and seminars), (6) sports events (mega events and professional competition), (7) recreational events (sports and games for fun), and (8) private events (e.g., weddings, parties, and social events).[27]

Events may be offered by nearly every community regardless of size. Pukwana, South Dakota, a town of only 287 people, features a Turkey Trot and a lawn mower race, and both have received national publicity. Another South Dakota town hosts the annual Motorcycle Rally, which attracts hundreds of thousands of visitors to Sturgis, a town with a population of 6,442 people.

Organizations commonly responsible for tourism development and promotion are tourism authorities, tourism/visitor bureaus, Chambers of Commerce, convention and visitor bureaus, tourism ministries, and others. These organizations usually have responsibility for planning and organizing events designed to bring visitors to the community. Both business and leisure events should be considered in strategic planning. Las Vegas relies heavily on business and leisure events and offers highly diversified large and small events, including conventions meetings, exhibitions, sport and arts events, concerts, shows, festivals, celebrity visits, and private parties. Las Vegas has more than 10 million square feet of exhibit and meeting space. The International Consumer Electronics Show (International CES), the annual trade show, books 2 million square feet of exhibit space. It brings together over 150,000 retail buyers, distributors, manufacturers, analysts, and media to Las Vegas to preview the newest products and technologies in the $208 billion consumer electronics industry.[28]

Local organizations may have worthy ideas for events to attract visitors and should be supported. In many cases, local organizations plan events designed for the enjoyment of community members. Oftentimes the events occur annually and take the form of a festival, such as a jazz festival or cherry blossom festival. Tourism planners should conduct a careful audit of the existing resources of their communities to determine opportunities for events. Rivers and ski slopes are obvious, but resources like a large vacant piece of land may be overlooked, yet this might lend itself to an event such as a balloon rodeo.

One of the biggest tourism draws in western Pennsylvania is Pymatuning Reservoir, where 400,000 visitors arrive each year to throw stale bread at carp. This has occurred by word of mouth. Thousands of carp swim in such tightly packed groups that ducks walk on top of them. The mayor of nearby Linesville said, "Carp-tourism keeps this town afloat. It supports several restaurants, a high-end gift shop, and vendors of stale bread."[29]

Utah Shakespeare Festival began as a small event and became a multimillion-dollar event creating jobs, generating tax revenue, and enhancing tourism. The initial two-week season attracted an excited 3,276 spectators, yielded a much needed $2,000 on which to build a second season, and demonstrated the cooperative relationship between college and community. The festival is now a year-round operation with a full-time staff of 26 and a budget of over $5 million. The total economic impact of the festival is estimated to be more than $35 million annually in direct and indirect economic impact.[30] Average annual attendance is 120,000 and nonresident visitors spending on lodging, transportation, restaurants, and souvenirs is over $10 million.

Beyond their economic value, events help create an identity for a community. Urban newspapers and suburban weeklies often publish a list of events, festivals, and celebrations occurring within a day's driving distance. State and local tourism offices do the same, making sure that travel agents, restaurants, hotels, airports, and train and bus stations have event-based calendars for posting.

Events can help destinations reduce seasonality problem. The Shakespeare Festival in Stratford, Canada, began as a small regional event and became a North American event for the United States and Canada. Most musical and cultural festivals in Europe followed the same pattern, such as Salzburg, Edinburgh, and Spoleto. Europe's Festival of Arts provides a selection among 50 musical festivals from Norway to Spain, with several dozen dance competitions, major summer art exhibits, and theater from London's West End to Berlin's Festival Weeks. The entire European continent, including Eastern Europe, has exploded in summer-place competition for tourists. Major U.S. cities have summer programs of scheduled events, and some, such as Milwaukee, have well-established year-round events. Milwaukee's June–September lakefront festivals (Festa Italiana, German Fest, Afro Fest, Polish Fest, and others) attract tourists regionally and nationally.

Wine festivals and wine trails and tours have been popular in Europe for generations. These are now occurring in the wine areas of Australia, New Zealand, and the United States. The Napa Valley of California has over 270 vineyards, each offering a unique visitor experience for the 5 million wine tourists annually.[31] Areas not previously known for wine production such as Texas, Missouri, Virginia, and North Carolina have established festivals and wine trails.

A study by the Washington State Wine Commission showed that 2 million visitors a year visit the 135 wineries in that state, generating $19 million in visitor income. The Australian Winemakers Association estimated that by 2025, wine tourism revenue would reach $1.1 billion.[32]

SUSTAINABLE EVENT MARKETING Events that attract a desired market and harmoniously fit with a community's culture can provide beneficial results, particularly if the event regularly reoccurs over a period of years. Events that occur only once or that require substantial capital investment for a community may not offer sufficient economic returns. A common reply by event promoters is that the PR value of the event outweighs cost considerations. This claim must be carefully and objectively analyzed before acceptance. Events must also be examined for the possible effect and cultural/societal impact they may have on the host community. "Destinations must choose their events to fit the needs of the locality, since each event draws on its own type of crowd."[33]

Some events are now marketed as being "green" or "sustainable." Green events can not only save money but also help the event stand out from the crowd. For example, events use downloadable content to decrease the carbon footprint and attract more crowd using online resources in an increasingly digital age.

Professional event planners within tourism agencies commonly establish requirements concerning desirable events. Here are some examples:

- Event must attract a minimum number of visitors.

- Event must complement and enhance the cultural nature of the community.

- Event should be replicable in future years, ideally on an annual basis.

- Workers from the community should be employed if part-time paid employees are needed.

- Events must not create destruction of private or public properties.

- As much as possible, events should use the services of local companies, such as food caterers.

- Events should provide guests for local hotels if hotel bed tax monies are used in their promotions.

- Events should allow/encourage participation by local residents.

SPORTS EVENTS Many communities view sports events as attractive ways to bring visitors to their destinations. These events are often enjoyed by both visitors and residents.

Sports travel in the United States is estimated at $27 billion each year, with 75 million American adults traveling to attend a sports event as spectator or participant.[34] Las Vegas hosts major sports events such as NASCAR (National Association

Sydney, Australia's Darling Harbour is an example of a well-planned tourist center. Courtesy of Roxor/Fotolia.

for Stock Car Auto Racing), the Las Vegas Bowl, and the National Finals Rodeo. The attendees spend more on lodging and non-gaming activities than on gambling. Golf has become a viable new market segment for Las Vegas.

Two very popular sports events are biking and marathons. An example is Ride The Rockies in which 4,000 people apply to ride 409 miles across Colorado. Riders come from all 50 states and many foreign nations. Host cities along the route benefit through travel expenditures from the riders as well as contributions from the sponsors to nonprofit charities in the host cities.[35]

The Walt Disney World Marathon covers a 26.2-mile course and attracts over 17,000 runners. This single event fills Disney World with 110,000 visitors during a normally slow part of the year. The success of this marathon prompted Disney to add a Princess Half Marathon for women. All Disney marathons sell out far in advance, despite comparatively high entry fees. "We literally take over Walt Disney World," said a spokesperson for Disney. "We overwhelm the property with runners."[36]

Attractions

Attractions may be natural, such as Niagara Falls or the Scottish Highlands, or manufactured, such as the shopping areas of Buckingham Palace, Hong Kong, or the Vatican.

Many nations have recognized the value of these natural attractions and have created national or state parks to protect them. However, the sheer numbers of visitors wishing to experience attractions threaten the ability of those in charge to protect them.

The long-run success of tourism will depend on manufactured attractions to satisfy the desire for travel. Historic attractions such as the pyramids of Egypt and Mexico are also at risk with increased visitor numbers. New attractions are continuously needed. This requires tourism investment.

Tourism investment ranges from relatively low-cost market entry for festivals or events to multimillion-dollar infrastructure costs of stadiums, transit systems, airports, and convention centers. Regardless of the cost, urban renewal planners seek to build tourism into the heart of their city's revitalization. Boston's Quincy Market, New York's Lincoln Center, and San Francisco's Fisherman's Wharf are examples. The ability to concentrate attractions, facilities, and services in a convenient, accessible location is essential to create a strong destination pull.

In centrally planned economies, governments control, plan, and direct tourist development. Tourism is necessary to earn hard currencies for trade and development and serves national purposes. Tourist expansion is highly dependent on public investments, which have proved to be woefully inadequate without private investment and market mechanisms to respond to changing consumer needs and wants. Many nations promote private investment through joint ventures, foreign ownership, and time sharing for individual investors. The Mexican Riviera (e.g., Puerto Vallarta, Cancun, and Istapa) is an example of public/private combinations of successful tourism investments, where state investment in infrastructure works with private investment in tourist amenities, from hotels, restaurants, and golf courses to shopping areas.

UNESCO WORLD HERITAGE SITES

Regardless of one's opinion about the United Nations, the designation of World Heritage Sites by the United Nations Educational, Scientific, and Cultural Organization (UNESCO) is important to world tourism and very important to selected sites. This program designates and thereby hopes to help conserve sites of outstanding cultural or natural importance to the common heritage of

Mayan ruin in Chichen Itza is one of the most visited attraction in Mexico and one of the New Seven Wonders of the World. Courtesy of Nikla/Fotolia.

The Diyarbakir Fortress, Turkey was inscribed on UNESCO's World Heritage List in 2015. After the Great Wall of China, the Walls of Diyarbakir are the world's longest and best-preserved medieval walls, which form a shape like turbot and measure 5.5 kilometers in length. Courtesy of Merthan Anik, and Culture and Tourism Department of Diyarbakir Municipality.

humanity. In 2015, a total of 1,031 such sites were listed: 802 cultural, 197 natural, and 32 mixed. Each site belongs to the country in which it is located, but it is considered to be of international interest to preserve and protect these sites.[37]

Tourism authorities view inclusion on this list as very important. In 2008, Dresden, Germany, wanted to build a 2,100-foot-long bridge called Waldschlosschen Bridge over a picturesque river. UNESCO threatened to take Dresden off the list if it built the bridge.

WATERFRONT ATTRACTIONS   Throughout much of the world, cities and towns have finally realized the tremendous value of their river, lake, and ocean waterfronts.[38] Many of these were used for warehouses, docks, power generation facilities, and heavy industry. These were ugly, dangerous, and often polluted areas. Now cities such as Los Angeles and Baltimore, United States; Buenos Aires, Argentina; and Hamburg, Germany, have discovered there is gold in redeveloping these areas for upscale housing, restaurants, hotels, shops, and even maritime commerce all within a relatively small area. HafenCity (Harbor City) of Hamburg is the largest urban development project in Europe. This area is not strictly a tourist attraction. "We want to join economic, social, cultural, and architectural forces in a way that translates into lasting urbanity," said Mr. Bruns-Berentelg, chief planner.

It should not be a surprise that people attract people. The concept of distinct tourist attractions is only a part of tourism planning. New York, London, Paris, and other cities are tourist attractions. The development of areas of cities such as waterfronts for multipurpose living is an extension of the natural attraction that cities have always held for travelers.

Dubai is a good example of a city that has developed a good infrastructure along with tourist attractions. The airport at Dubai is world class and offers excellent duty-free shopping. The highway system is well designed and maintained, making it easy to get from the airport to the resorts. The hotels realize the importance of service and customer satisfaction. Once at the hotel, the guest can select from a variety of activities, including water sports, tennis, golf, or sightseeing tours. Resorts spend a great deal of effort training their employees, who come from all over the world. The employee base also means that guests from almost any country will be able to find an employee speaking their language. Dubai set out on a strategy of using tourism to broaden its economic base and developed a plan to implement that strategy.

Two of the resorts in Dubai are the Burj Al Arab and the Jumeirah Beach Hotel. The Burj Al Arab is not only the world's tallest all-suites hotel but also one of the most luxurious. All of its 202 units are two-story suites. Guests staying at the Burj Al Arab have a choice of airport transportation: a Rolls-Royce limousine or a helicopter. Each floor features a private reception, and there is a personal butler for each suite. The Jumeirah Beach Hotel has 600 rooms and 18 restaurants and features a

The Burj Al Arab in Dubai is one of the world's most luxurious hotels. Courtesy of marrfa/Fotolia.

reef a mile offshore for scuba divers. The hotel also features extensive meeting and conference facilities to attract international meetings.

CASINOS AS ATTRACTIONS   States and municipalities typically look at jobs and tax revenues. Prior to the U.S. recession, commercial casinos employed 366,000 people and paid over $5 billion in direct gaming taxes. Many observers say this is not all good news. They say (1) casinos often take business from other entertainment such as theaters and sports bars, (2) new casinos need fewer employees due to video poker machines, (3) revenues taken from local residents often leave the area as profits for out-of-state corporations, (4) casinos may actually destroy some jobs, (5) casinos don't provide the kind of societal benefits as a biotech firm, a hospital, a university, or other enterprises, and (6) casinos foster societal problems such as pathological gambling.

Research has shown that casinos do not take business away from local restaurants and they do create jobs. However, just as many other businesses, a poorly planned casino can be a determent to the area, whereas a properly planned one can be beneficial to the region. To maximize its benefits, gaming should be incorporated into a strategic plan for the area. From a tourism perspective, gaming works best when it is part of several tourism attractions for the area, not the only tourism attraction for the area. Gaming destinations that include entertainment facilities featuring nationally known performers, golf courses, fine restaurants, hotel rooms, and meeting facilities can attract leisure tourists as well as meetings and conventions. In fact, gaming can be the source of funds to create tourist destinations.

The Greektown Casino project in Detroit shows how a casino can work with the community to create tourism. As part of the casino's effort to create a symbiotic relationship with area business, the casino owners put $200 million into refurbishing Trappers Alley, a historical area around the casino featuring restaurants and clubs, which encouraged businesses to invest their own funds to give their operations a facelift. Greektown also created an innovative loyalty program (players club) that allowed players to redeem their points in over 20 restaurants in the Trappers Alley area, generating revenue for local business owners. In this case, the casino served as the catalyst to revitalize a tourist area that had fallen on hard times.[39]

INDIAN GAMING   Gambling (legalized gambling, mostly casinos) on 227 American Indian reservations has been described as "The Native American Success Story." The gambling operations and the businesses that support them are said to support 600,000 jobs. According to Ernest Stevens, chairman of the National Indian Gaming Association (NIGA), this has had a tremendous impact on reservation economies. Indian casino revenues have been estimated at $22.6 billion.[40]

Not all observers of Indian casinos believe they are healthy for the broader community. Critics say they exist despite the fact that state and neighboring communities do not recognize legalized casinos. Because these locations are often remote rural communities, they attract neighbors who are often bored, lonely, and not wealthy, who become addicted to gambling, thus creating financial hardships for their families.[41]

STOPOVER TOURISM   Many visitor destinations are in fact only stopover destinations for travelers on their way elsewhere. Singapore has more than twice the number of annual visitors than its resident population, but visitors stay less than three days. Twenty-one percent are in transit or stopover guests.

Singapore's visitors shop, dine, and stay in world-class hotels. Sightseeing and entertainment represent only 3 percent of their expenditures. Despite short stays, Singapore ranks second in Asia and eleventh in the world in terms of tourism receipts.[42]

Kansas, Nebraska, Arkansas, Missouri, and many other states recognize the value of stopover visitors to their economies. Cities at the edge of large metroplex

Singapore has been a model of urban tourism in Southeast Asia. Courtesy of MasterLu/Fotolia.

areas such as Lewisville, Texas, north of Dallas, also serve as stopover destinations. Many visitors prefer to stop outside a metroplex at a convenient roadside motel rather than attempt to find lodging in the city center.

Destination Life Cycle: Rejuvenating a Destination

Like a hotel or a restaurant, tourist destinations become dated, tacky, and undesirable for contemporary travelers. A resort destination will experience a life cycle similar to the product life cycle and eventually go into decline, or the destruction stage. Tourism managers must manage their products and make sure that during the growth stage the foundation is built for an infrastructure that will support future tourism demands. In some cases, sustaining tourism in the mature stage may mean limiting the amount of tourists to a number that the infrastructure can handle. Tourist development must balance the temptation to maximize tourist dollars with preservation of the natural tourist attractions and the quality of life for local residents. This is often a difficult task. Those tourist destinations that do not manage their product may have a short life.

Tourist destinations that build solid infrastructures can look for increased business by expanding from a seasonal product to a multiseasonal product or by expanding the geographic base of their product. For example, Aspen, Colorado, expanded from winter skiing to summer recreation, education, and culture. Quebec promotes summer and fall tourism and its winter carnival and skiing. West Virginia is popular in the summer and fall seasons, but it also aggressively promotes the spring and winter seasons.

The Waikiki area on the island of Oahu fell victim to its life cycle. As of mid-2007, $2 billion had been spent to renovate Waikiki, with another $1 billion committed.[43] A 93,000-square-foot retail and restaurant center was built in the heart of Waikiki Beach Walk. Zoning restrictions were removed and Outrigger Enterprises Group tore down five of its older hotels. Many other improvements were made, including the removal of T-shirt and souvenir shops on one street making it the upscale Rodeo Drive of Hawaii.

Even the beach was expanded by back-pumping 10,000 cubic yards of sand from offshore. To prevent Waikiki from becoming another noisy waterfront, banana boats, parasailing, speedboats, and jet skis were prohibited. Ed Fuller, president of Marriott International, said, "The city made a major commitment to bring Waikiki back as a great destination."

Rejuvenating a destination requires the cooperation of various government entities and several sectors of private enterprise including heavy involvement by the hospitality industry.

◼◼◼ Segmenting and Monitoring the Tourist Market

The decision to spend one's disposable income on travel versus furniture, a boat, or other purchase alternatives involves important psychological determinants. Table 17–3 lists some of the major psychological determinants of demand for tourism. These determinants can be used as segmentation variables. Demographics and lifestyles are also important segmentation variables.

Segmenting visitors based on push and pull motivations has been a common practice for benefit segmentation. The push factors are considered to be sociopsychological motivations that predispose the individual to travel, while the pull factors are destination attributes that attract the individual to a specific destination.

TABLE 17–3
Psychological Travel Motivations

Prestige. A level of prestige has always been attached to travelers, particularly long-distance travelers. Marco Polo gained historical fame through travel, as did the heroes of Greek and Roman mythology, such as Ulysses. Travel to Aspen, the Riviera, Switzerland, and many other destinations provides the traveler with a level of prestige, if only in the mind of the traveler.

Escape. The desire to escape momentarily from the day-to-day rhythm of one's life is a basic human need. Travel marketers have long recognized this need, as reflected by glamorous advertisements in which the word *escape* is often mentioned.

Sexual opportunity. This has both a positive and an ugly side. Travel has long been viewed as a means to meet attractive people. This has been part of the heritage of transatlantic ocean travel, the Orient Express, and riverboat travel. Unfortunately, the existence of sex tours to certain Asian nations and the preponderance of houses of prostitution in some destination areas provide examples of a darker side.

Education. Travel in and of itself has historically been viewed as broadening. Many deeper psychological reasons for travel are masked by the rationale that educational benefits outweigh the cost, risks, and stress.

Social interaction. The opportunity to meet and interact with people previously unknown is a powerful motivator. Destination resorts and cruise lines commonly appeal to this need.

Family bonding. Family reunions have become an important market segment for many in the travel industry. In an era of intense pressure on the family, such as two careers, there is a strong need to refocus priorities and bond as a family. Unfortunately, the types of vacations selected by families do not always lead to bonding. If adults participate all day in activities such as diving, skiing, or golf, young children may be relegated to organized kids' programs and experience little bonding with parents.

Relaxation. Observers of human and animal conduct sometimes state that the human being is either alone or among a limited number of species that continue to play into adulthood. Destination resorts and cruise ships best exemplify need fulfillment for play. It is small wonder that cruise line travel has become a "destination" in direct competition with land-bound places.

Self-discovery. For many, travel offers the opportunity to "find oneself." Witness the action of many people following a dramatic event in their lives, such as a divorce or the death of a family member. Throughout recorded history, people have sought self-discovery by "visiting the mountain," "finding solace in the desert," and "losing oneself." Many cultures, including so-called primitive ones, have encouraged or even forced their youth to travel alone to find self-discovery. Youth hotels throughout the world serve a group of travelers, many of whom are seeking self-discovery. Temporary employment opportunities at resorts are often filled by those taking time off to learn more about who they are and wish to be. The concept of "holistic vacations" has been developed for people seeking self-discovery.

Sources: Peter Hawes, "Holistic Vacations," *Hemisphere* (March 1995): 85–87; A. J. Crompton, "Motivations for Pleasure Vacations," *Annals of Tourism Research*, 6 (1974): 408–424; A. Mathieson and G. Wall, *Tourism: Economics, Physical and Social Impacts* (Harlow, Essex, UK: Longman, 1982).

The push–pull model considers both destination-specific characteristics and tourists' individualistic characteristics. A recent study segmented China's long-haul outbound travel market based on their push and pull motivations into three groups: entertainment/adventure seekers, life-seeing experience/culture explorers, and relaxation/knowledge seekers.[44]

The growing percentage of retirees in many nations has vastly expanded the tourism business. An increasing percentage of two-career couples has resulted in a trend toward shorter, more frequent vacations. Longer vacations (10 or more nights) have been declining for years in the United States; shorter vacations (three nights, including weekends) have become increasingly popular. Hotels and airlines have accommodated these trends with low-cost weekend excursion packages. Business travel now includes mixed business and leisure. To capture the trend toward shorter vacations within driving distance of home, new local and regional tourist attractions have been growing, as have family-oriented resorts.

Foreign visitor travel has become an increasingly important segment of the North American travel industry. Since the decline of the U.S. and Canadian dollars, foreign tourism has grown. British Isles visitors seek out New York, Florida, and

Playa del Carmen, while continental visitors have a strong fascination for the U.S. West, particularly California. Hawaii targets Japan because of its high gross national product and spending and because 50 percent of all Japanese visitors to the U.S. mainland spend part of their trip in Hawaii. The Japanese repeat market outspends visitors from the U.S. mainland by a 4:1 margin.

In 2014, 19 percent of the 41 million tourists of Las Vegas were international visitors, or about 8 million.[45] The LVCVA aims to benefit from surge in foreign tourism and has set a goal of making international travelers 30 percent of the Las Vegas total visitors. The average international traveler spends about $1,011 per stay and remains in the Las Vegas longer than four days each trip. Compare that with domestic tourists who spend $645 per visit on average and stay about three days.

About 70 percent of the city's international visitors now come from just three countries: the United Kingdom, Mexico, and Canada. LVCA through its international offices use different market strategies. In the United Kingdom, the office focuses on lifestyle elements of Las Vegas, including shows, nightlife, and dining. Key sporting events such as boxing are also popular in the UK market. Canadians are more interested in food and wine culture, celebrity chefs, and culinary events. The LVCVA sees the emerging markets of Brazil, Russia, India, and China as the regions with the most untapped potential.[46]

Accommodating changing lifestyles and needs is a dynamic challenge for the tourism industry in light of demographic trends and income shifts. Where baby boomers once opted for status destinations and elaborate accommodations, many now opt for all-inclusive resorts and package tours that promise comfort, consistency, and cost effectiveness. Tourism planners must consider how many tourists are desired, which segments to attract, and how to balance tourism with other industries. Choices will be constrained by the destinations' climate, natural topography, resources, history, culture, and facilities. Like other enterprises, tourist marketers must know the actual and potential customers and their needs and wants, determine which target markets to serve, and decide on appropriate products, services, and programs.

The millennial generation is more interested than older generations in traveling abroad. The United Nations estimates that 20 percent of all international tourists, or nearly 200 million travelers, are young people, and that this demographic generates more than $180 billion in annual tourism revenue.[47]

A nationwide survey of millennials provided some insights for tourist destinations. It revealed that millennials are highly influenced by friends and family in selecting places to visit, and they are also more likely to travel with friends or to places friends have visited. Millennials visit online travel agencies as well as visit Web sites of destinations. They have strong preference to learn new things and fun and entertaining experience. Millennials are attracted to authentic destinations. This trend has sprouted into new accommodation concepts including hostels, Airbnb, couch surfing, and home exchanges. Millennials also care about environmental issues and engage in sustainable practices. They will prefer destinations that engage in sustainable practices.[48]

To appeal to millennials, destinations can involve locals in marketing efforts because millennial travelers rely on social media and word-of-mouth recommendations, and trust travel reviews from peers as well as strangers. Destinations can facilitate relationship building. "Visit a Swede" is a good example of this relational marketing. The Web site is designed to connect tourists to Sweden with residents. The result is local residents become

Cave hotels in Cappadocia, Turkey. Cave hotels offer an authentic local experience and would be a more popular destination for millennials.
Courtesy of psvrusso/Fotolia.

involved in the co-creation of the tourist's experience. The resident also become tourism ambassadors for their country and city. BeWelcome has also opened up channels of communication between visitors and locals.[49]

Charleston, South Carolina, has several times won the South Carolina Governor's Cup for Travel and Tourism, been named the "most mannerly" city in the United States 10 times, and has been named a top-10 travel destination by *Conde Nast* magazine readers 11 times. It has also won awards from *National Geographic, Brides*, and *Travel & Leisure* magazines.

Another South Carolina travel destination, Myrtle Beach, attracts many more tourists, but Charleston remains "the Award Winner Jewel in South Carolina's Destination Crown."[50]

How does Charleston prevail as a top destination? The answer is that it does its best to preserve and retain what has historically attracted people to Charleston: history, charming architecture, pleasant and mannerly people, helpfulness, gardens, quaintness, and excellent cuisine.

These winning attributes could quickly disappear if discount shopping areas replaced old homes or if a multimillion-dollar theme park was built in the heart of the city. Vigilance is essential to preserve and further the genuine differentiating factors of a destination. These can disappear in a short period of time to the detriment of residents and visitors.

Not every tourist is interested in a particular destination. A destination would waste its money trying to attract everyone who travels. Instead of a shotgun approach, destinations must take a rifle approach and sharply define target markets. Many visitors to Myrtle Beach would find Charleston stuffy and boring. Attempts to attract those individuals would result in mutual dissatisfaction.

Agritourism

Agritourism. Agriculture-based tourism that includes farms, ranches, and wineries. It provides rural areas with a means to attract tourists.

In an era in which most people in industrialized nations are urban or suburban dwellers, **agritourism** (farm or ranch tourism)—a niche ecotourism—has become one of the fastest-growing segments of the travel industry. This is particularly true in many European nations, North America, and Australia/New Zealand. Agri-destinations offer edutainment, relaxation, outdoor adventures, and dining experiences. It takes many forms, from just visiting a farm to staying and even working at a farm for education and hands-on experience. One can stay in an accommodation on farm premises and enjoy meals of farm produce.[51] Top agritourism destinations include Taiwan "leisure farms," Tuscany (Italy), Mallorca (Spain), Brazil, Hawaii, California for organic farming, and Philippines.[52] In Hawaii, agritourism options range from visiting coffee plantations in the Big Island's Kona region to exploring the plantations on Maui to staying on organic farms on the island of Oahu.

A study by Colorado State University provides evidence of the importance of agritourism. "Summer and fall had the highest agritourism visitation rates," said Dawn Thilmany, professor in Colorado State's Department of Agriculture and Resource Economics, who led the study.

In a state known for its skiing, agricultural activities have shown the potential to provide a real boost to Colorado's tourism efforts outside of winter months. Thilmany said, "Increased visitations during these times help fill the underutilized capacity of lodging and service industries." More than 20 percent of those surveyed took more than three agritourism trips each year, offering great potential for farm and ranch enterprises considering agritourism activities, according to the report.

Tourists from outside Colorado reported spending an average of $860 per trip; in-state tourists reported spending an average of $368, according to the report. Both in-state and out-of-state tourists said they would spend more during their next trip to Colorado ($450 for state residents; $1,023 for out-of-state tourists). Among the more frequent agritourism travelers, about 56 percent were Colorado residents.[53]

"We found there is sufficient interest in agritourism in Colorado to warrant active joint planning by communities and the agritourism enterprises they support," Thilmany said, offering as an example the joint marketing plan of Grand Junction's wine country. "Many regions of Colorado already see significant amounts of visitors to farm- and ranch-based diversions. Through coordinated marketing efforts, these regions can continue to capitalize on agritourism activities."

Space Tourism

In April 2001, Dennis Tito became the first space tourist when he paid $20 million to fly on the *Soyuz* taxi mission to the International Space Station. In October 2008, Richard Garrett paid $30 million to fly on a *Soyuz* mission and become the sixth space tourist. As a result of the Russians willingness to allow space tourists on their missions, there is now a travel agency, Space Adventures, specializing in space tourism.[54]

A number of private companies have been formed to provide trips into space for tourists. The founder of Virgin Atlantic Airline, Sir Richard Branson, has formed Virgin Galactic, with test flights scheduled soon. Commercial space travel for upscale tourists is planned from Las Cruces Spaceport America in New Mexico. Additional sites will be in the United Kingdom, Australia, and Sweden.

Space travelers will have to undergo elite cosmonaut training. They will be in a vehicle named SS2, which will climb to 50,000 feet altitude under a mother ship Space Ship Two. After release, the SS2 will free fall for a few seconds, fire its rockets, and accelerate into a vertical trajectory climbing to an altitude of 360,800 feet. Those aboard the SS2 will enjoy a 1,000-mile horizon of the earth in zero gravity. The entire flight will last about two and a half hours.[55]

NASA (National Aeronautics and Space Administration) is preparing for moon tourism, including developing plans to prevent looting of the six areas where manned space missions landed on the moon between 1969 and 1972. Under its guidelines, people can walk only within 246 feet of the first site where Neil Armstrong first walked on the moon. NASA's concern over protecting the sites was prompted by Google's $30 million prize for the first privately funded team to land a robot on the moon. It appears that NASA feels that people will soon follow robots on the moon. It wants to make sure that tourists don't trample on the footprint of Armstrong's "one small step for man."[56]

Multiday Hiking and Religious Pilgrimages

Many potential tourists are tired of traditional tourism opportunities, such as a beach resort. A huge and growing market exists for multiday trekking (hiking). In some cases, hiking has a religious basis, such as in pilgrimages to significant religious sites such as the Camino de Santiago de Compostela in northern Spain. This trip may be accomplished by foot, horseback, or bicycle and may be as long as a month or just a few days. In 1990, the Cathedral in Santiago registered 4,918 hikers (pilgrims), but today over 100,000 people are recorded each year and that is probably an underestimate.

Christian sites are by no means the only ones that are visited. Millions of pilgrims visit Hindu, Buddhist, Islamic, and other religious sites. Although most visitors arrive by some form of modern transport, many prefer to walk.

In western Japan, a walking pilgrimage to 33 sacred sites and the 1,300-km pilgrimage to the 88 holy sites of Shikoku Island are experienced by hundreds of thousands of hiking pilgrims. Most devotees on these pilgrimages carry a staff bearing the words, "We too walk together." Many of those on the Camino de Santiago carry a staff bearing a seashell.

Perhaps the most publicized pilgrimages are those of the Islamic faith such as that of Hajj, a pilgrimage to Mecca in which millions of Muslims participate, including 12,000 Americans in 2010. The Shrine of Iman Reza in Iran attracts over 12 million visitors each year. Visitors to these shrines arrive via many forms of travel.

Trails are available for special-interest hikers with cultural, scientific, religious, or gastronomical interests such as wine tours. Some trails such as the Milford in New Zealand are so popular that visitor numbers are restricted.

A North Sea Trail is being developed in Europe, which crosses six countries and extends for 3,000 miles and was funded by the European Union with nearly $15 million. The European Union already had 11 long-distance paths from Lapland to Gibraltar and Cyprus.

The 2,175-mile-long Appalachian Trail on the East Coast of the United States from Maine to Georgia has long been popular. Extended hikes such as this are supported by tourism organizations throughout the world as they disperse visitors, lessen the negative aspects of tourism, and provide economic support to rural communities.

Hundreds of cultural routes with tourism potential exist throughout the world, such as The Silk Road that started at the Chinese imperial city of Xian and extended across the Taklimakan desert to the Mediterranean. Long and arduous treks such as this will be completed in entirety by very few tourists, but many are likely to hike portions of the trail.[57]

Medical Tourism

Medical tourism. One of the fastest-growing and most lucrative tourism markets. Tourists spend a large amount on medical treatment, stay in top hotels, and often travel around the country after their surgery.

Medical tourism is one of the fastest-growing and most lucrative segments of tourism, as people travel internationally to gain access to less expensive medical care. In 2003 there were 350,000 medical tourists, by 2010 that number grew to 6 million, and by 2017 the number is expected to grow to 16 million.

The growth in medical tourism is driven by four main factors: low cost, long waiting lines in national health-care services, accessibility to procedures and treatments, and opportunity for a vacation and privacy. Cost is the main driver. For people with no or inadequate insurance, low-cost health care at an international destination may be the only viable solution for health care. In an effort to stay young, baby boomers are seeking cosmetic surgery and dental work. These elective procedures are often not covered by insurance, creating a booming business for these procedures in Mexico, Central America, Asia, and Eastern Europe. In countries with national health care, such as Australia, Canada, and England, people needing elective surgery are often put on a waiting list. To some of those on the waiting list, a low-cost procedure overseas is often preferred to putting up with the malady for months. International health care also provides access to experimental procedures or treatments that are prohibited by law in one's home country. This includes experimental cancer treatments and treatments using stem cells. The privacy of having cosmetic surgery done overseas, recovering on the beach, and coming home healed and looking 10 years younger is a great alternative to hiding out at home while the scars are healing.

In Asia, Thailand is the most popular destination for Western European health-care tourists for cosmetic surgeries. About 2.5 million foreign patients visited Thailand in 2012, representing approximately half of the market share of total foreign tourist arrival in the Asian region. India attracts large number of patients for cardiac surgeries. Brazil (cosmetic surgery) and Mexico (weight loss surgery) receive patients from the United States because of geographic proximity. Turkey witnesses a growth in orthopedic, laser eye, and cosmetic surgeries.[58]

Medical tourism is being blended with the opportunity for a vacation. Some insurance companies in North America are offering their customers, who qualify for health care, the option to have it done at an international location. As an incentive, they will waive the deductible and co-pay, as well as provide airfare and lodging during and after treatment. They sell both the cost savings and the opportunity for a free vacation to their client. The insurance company still comes out over the cost of having the surgery done in the United States. The biggest concern for the patient is the quality of the health care. Countries that want to capture the medical tourism market need to develop standards and accrediting procedures to create a perception of quality and build trust among medical tourists.[59]

Genealogical Tourism

The interest in knowing more about one's ancestors has grown substantially in recent years.[60] Many people plan vacations to visit genealogical research sites.

The Allen County Public Library in Fort Wayne, Indiana, hosts 400,000 visitors annually. The Church of Jesus Christ of Latter-day Saints in Utah has become a "must visit" site for 700,000 annual visitors. This is the world's largest depository of family records.

Other nations that received large numbers of immigrants from Europe such as Australia, New Zealand, Argentina, and Canada have growing numbers of genealogical tourists. Scotland refocused on genealogy tourism after VisitScotland, Scotland's national tourism organization, estimated that ancestral tourism in Scotland is worth more than $600 million a year. The destination initiated a promotion campaign and developed budget "genealogy packages." Malcolm Roughead, VisitScotland's chief executive, said, "We need to do all we can to make sure every visitor will have the experience of a lifetime. In our advertising campaigns we will be inviting people from all over the globe to come home and walk in the footsteps of their ancestors."[61]

Travel to Gallipoli battlefield of the First World War has become a 'rite of passage' for younger Australian generations. The tourist trade is booming on Turkey's Gallipoli peninsula as thousands of Australians make their way to the WWI battlefields for the Anzac Centenary. Many Australians have paid between $7,000 and $10,000 to make the pilgrimage.[62]

Identifying Target Markets

A destination can identify its natural target markets in two ways. One is to collect information about its current visitors. Where do they come from? Why do they come? What are their demographic characteristics? How satisfied are they? How many are repeat visitors? How much do they spend? By examining these and other questions, planners can determine which visitors should be targeted.

The second approach is to audit the destination's events and attractions and select segments that might logically have an interest in them. We cannot assume that current visitors reflect all the potentially interested groups. For example, if Kenya promoted only safaris, it would miss groups interested in native culture, flora, or bird species.

Tourist segments are attracted by different features. The local tourist board or council could benefit by asking questions keyed to segmentation variables. These variables, including attractions sought, market areas or locations, customer characteristics, and/or benefits sought, can help define the best target markets.

After a destination identifies its natural target markets, tourism planners should conduct research to determine where these tourists are found. Which countries contain a large number of citizens who have the means and motivation to enjoy the particular place? For example, Aruba attracts mainly sun-and-fun tourists. The United States, Canada, and certain European countries are good sources. Eastern Europeans have been ruled out because they lack the purchasing power, but this is changing. Australians are ruled out because they have their own nearby sun-and-fun destinations, even though they are frequent travelers. This analysis can uncover many or few natural target markets. If many are identified, the relative potential profit from each should be evaluated. The potential profit of a target tourist segment is the difference between the amount that the tourist segment is likely to spend and the cost of attracting and serving this segment. The promotional cost depends on the budget. The serving cost depends on the infrastructure requirements. Ultimately, potential tourist segments should be ranked and selected in order of their profitability.

If the analysis identifies too few natural tourist segments, investments may be needed in infrastructure and visitor events and attractions. The payoff from these investments may come years later, but this lag is often necessary if the destination is to become an active participant in an increasingly competitive marketplace.

The Irish Tourist Board observed that many young European tourists visited the Emerald Isle to enjoy its natural, unspoiled beauty as backpackers and campers, but they spent little money. A serious question for Ireland was whether its tourism scorecard should be based on the number of tourists attracted (the prevailing standard) or their spending level. A consensus emerged that Ireland should try to attract a relatively small market of high-income tourists who stay longer, spend more, and are culturally and environmentally compatible.

Toward this end, the Irish Tourist Board now touts not only Ireland's mountains, water, and ancient buildings, but also its literary giants, such as Oscar Wilde, George Bernard Shaw, and James Joyce. The board wants to attract high-income, culture-seeking tourists to Dublin, where the sparkling Irish speech and wit can be experienced.

Whatever tourist segment a destination seeks, it needs to be very specific. A ski area attracts skiers. Natural reefs attract snorkelers and divers. Arts and crafts attract the art crowd, and gambling attracts gaming tourists. Yet even with such givens, potential visitors must be segmented by additional characteristics. Sun Valley, Aspen, Vail, and Alta appeal to upper-income and professional skiers, and Keystone, Winter Park, Copper Mountain, and Telluride attract the family market. Tahoe and Squaw Valley draw the skiing and gaming markets. Monte Carlo appeals to an international gaming segment, whereas Deauville, France, promotes a more regional gaming market near Paris.

Tourism marketers know that even though an area may attract an activity-specific segment, there is great potential in providing reasons for others to come. For instance, a ski family or group often contains individuals who do not wish to ski. Why then should they come? If the answer is "we offer only a single activity," the group may decide to go somewhere else that offers broader vacation opportunities.

Las Vegas discovered that shopping, dining, and entertainment could attract nongamblers and also serve as secondary activities for all but the most dedicated gamblers. The Forum shopping mall at Caesars in Las Vegas provides continuous entertainment and a great variety of restaurants, making the retail sales areas some of the most costly and desirable to rent in North America. Today, the top attraction in Las Vegas is shopping and entertainment, not gambling.

Classification of Visitor Segments

Several classifications have been used to describe different visitor destination segments. The most commonly used classifications are based on whether the tourist travels with a group or independently. The common terms are group-inclusive tour (GIT) and independent traveler (IT). National tourism offices, international airlines, and others involved in international travel frequently use these designations.

Here are some classifications describing tourists by their degree of institutionalization and their impact on the destinations:

- *Organized mass tourists.* This corresponds to the GIT. These people have little or no influence over their travel experience other than to purchase one package or another. They commonly travel in a group, view the destination through the windows of a tour bus, and remain in preselected hotels. Shopping in the local market often provides their only contact with the native population.

- *Individual mass tourists.* These people are similar to the previous category but have somewhat more control over their itinerary. For instance, they may rent a car to visit attractions.

- *Explorers.* These people fall in the IT classification. They plan their own itineraries and make their own reservations. They tend to be very sociable people who enjoy interacting with people at the destination.

- *Drifters.* These people, the backpacker group, seldom, if ever, are found in a traditional hotel. They may stay at youth hostels with friends or camp out. They tend to mix with lower socioeconomic native groups and are commonly found riding third-class rail or bus. Most tend to be young.

- *Visiting friends and relatives (VFR).* VFR, as the name suggests, are people who stay in the homes of friends or relatives. For this reason, they are often discounted as important tourists. This is incorrect. They may not spend money on lodging, but they do spend on dining, attending attractions/events, and shopping.

- *Business travelers.* This often encompasses any form of business, including conventions, trade shows, and job seeking.

- *Pleasure travel.* This too is a very wide and all-encompassing classification. It may be of limited use without further segmentation.

- *Bleisure (Business and pleasure travelers).* Many convention and business travelers plan to incorporate a period of relaxation prior to or after their business.

- *Education and religious travel.* This broad category includes students, those on a pilgrimage, missionaries, and a host of others. It may be of limited use in tourism planning unless further segmented.

- *Pass-through tourists.* These are extremely important visitors to states such as Kansas and Nebraska and to cities in Texas that serve as convenient rest or overnight stopping areas.

Another well-known tourist classification system is *Plog's categorization.*[63] Destinations can be placed on the psychographic curve based on the types of people who visit there most. Tourists' personality characteristics determine their travel patterns and preferences. These designations are similar to the groups mentioned previously but range from psychocentric to allocentric. Plog observed that destinations are first discovered by **allocentrics** (backpackers or explorers). As the natives discover the economic benefits of tourism, services and infrastructure are developed. When this occurs, allocentrics are turned off and find another unspoiled destination. The nature of visitors now changes, with each new group somewhat less adventurous than the preceding group, perhaps older, and certainly more demanding of creative comforts and service. Finally, a destination becomes so familiar that the least adventurous group of **psychocentrics** finds it acceptable.

A study of travelers' behaviors and preferences demonstrated that Costa Rica's position is evolving from being a destination for near allocentric to one that attracts mid-centrics. The researchers concluded that Costa Rica had indeed built its infrastructure to the point that adventurers are put off and mid-centrics are attracted, just as Plog's model predicted.

Knowing this, other nations in Central America, Honduras, Belize, and Nicaragua, are pursuing the adventures market. Therefore, preservation of the natural environment in those nations is essential, including the need to set aside particular areas for special protection.

The researchers also noted that parts of Asia, China, Cambodia, Thailand, and Vietnam are rushing into a phase of development that is poorly planned based on the Plog analysis.[64]

Allocentrics. Persons with a need for new experiences, such as backpackers and explorers.

Psychocentrics. Persons who do not desire change when they travel. They like to visit nonthreatening places and stay in familiar surroundings.

Monitoring the Tourist Markets

Tourist markets are dynamic, and a marketing information system is part of any well-run tourist organization. Destinations need to closely monitor the relative popularity of their various attractions by determining the number and type of tourists attracted to each. The popularity of the Metropolitan Museum of Art, Big Ben, or the Coliseum can suddenly or gradually change. Marketing information systems help identify and predict environmental trends that are responsible for these changes. Information should be collected on changes, emerging markets, and potential target markets.

The LVCVA conducts an annual tourist profile. Information for this profile is collected through ongoing customer surveys. Survey results indicate that the majority of visitors spend less than four hours a day gambling. The visitors are coming for entertainment and the non-gaming amenities of the mega-resorts. This information helped to attract a number of new restaurants, such as Spago, Wolfgang Puck's, Cafe Coyote, and Planet Hollywood. Las Vegas has developed a reputation as a restaurant town. This further enhances its image as a diverse destination rather than just a gaming venue.

One job of a tourist organization is to increase the accessibility of a destination. The LVCVA uses information from its survey to identify emerging markets that can support direct airline flights. Armed with current travel patterns and projected travel patterns based on its surveys, the LVCVA makes presentations to airlines, trying to convince them to start new routes, which will be profitable for the airlines and provide another region of the country with direct air service to Las Vegas. The accessibility of Las Vegas by frequently scheduled and relatively inexpensive airfare is in part responsible for it being one of the top convention centers in the United States. This did not happen by accident; it happened as a result of efforts by the LVCVA.

The Steamboat Springs, Colorado, Chamber Resort Association, and other resorts' visitor bureaus also work with airlines to ensure air accessibility to their cities. However, because these areas have a small population base and experience varying snowfall levels, airlines are reluctant to include them in their schedule without a financial guarantee. This means the visitor bureau must assume an active role to ensure that funding is available for the airline guarantees should this be necessary.

Tourist organizations need information to stay competitive. Tourist products must change to meet the needs of the changing market. Emerging markets must be identified and served. New markets that can be served by the existing tourist product must be identified. Tourist organizations trying to accomplish these tasks without good information are at a disadvantage.

First-Time Versus Repeat Visitors

First-time and repeat visitors are important segments for a tourist destination and they should be monitored. Destination wants to have a healthy balance of first-time and repeat visitors. Eighty percent of Las Vegas visitors are repeat visitors, which could create problems in the long-run.

For some destinations, visitor satisfaction would be more important than repeat visitation loyalty because their target markets would seek more variety and are less likely to visit the same destination repeatedly. A study found that less loyal tourists to international destinations are either "Natural Switchers" or "Experiential Switchers." Natural switchers are variety seekers or price-sensitive travelers, whereas experiential switchers are those who are dissatisfied with their visit. These groups should be targeted differently.[65]

Short-Haul Versus Long-Haul Tourists

Tourists who travel short distances tend to stay for short durations. They also show preferences for package tours. Long-haul tourists tend to engage in longer duration, multi-destination trips and seek to fulfill multipurposes, such as city sightseeing, country hikes, attending several cultural events, and participating in events.

■■■ Communicating with the Tourist Market

Competition for Visitors Involves Image Making

Destination images are heavily influenced by pictorial creations used in movies or TV, by music, and, in some cases, by popular entertainers and celebrities.

State media investment to attract tourists has grown rapidly. States such as Texas and Alaska have more than quadrupled their tourism media budgets. Nations and states invade and advertise in each other's markets. For instance, Illinois targets New York, California, Texas, and Japan. It produces multilingual travel guides, DVDs, and radio segments.

Destinations have formed partnerships with travel, recreational, and communication businesses on joint marketing efforts. They advertise in national magazines and travel publications and work with business-travel promotions to link the growing business-leisure segment of the traveling public, and they target travel agencies. Many states have located welcome centers along major interstate highways that include unstaffed two-way video systems to answer questions from a central location or otherwise assist travelers. States also target their own residents with brochures, maps, and a calendar of events.

Finally, effective destination imaging requires congruence between advertising and the destination. Glossy photographs of sunsets, beaches, buildings, and events need to have some relationship to what tourists actually experience; otherwise, destinations run the risk of losing tourist goodwill and generating bad word of mouth.

Many tourist destinations have discovered that it is important to show residents interacting with tourists in their advertisements. Thousands of mountain slopes and beaches exist in the world and most look alike in photos. Very few tourists seek a completely secluded vacation site. People are social creatures by nature and consciously or unconsciously seek the company of fellow humans.

Branding Destinations

Tourist destinations increasingly embrace branding techniques to develop unique positions, images, and personalities in a highly competitive environment. **Destination branding** is creating a differentiated destination image that influences travelers' decision to visit a destination and conveys the promise of a memorable experience that is uniquely associated with the destination.[66] Branding opportunities for destinations exist at geographical levels such as country, city, and town (umbrella and sub-brands), specific attractions such as museums and theme parks, events such as mega-events and festivals, and lifestyle travel packages.

Destination visits or vacations express lifestyle, personality, and status. A study found that visitors who see a closer fit between their personality and Las Vegas's brand personality as a tourist destination are more likely to come back and to engage in positive word-of-mouth communication for the destination.[67]

PR and publicity (movies, news stories, events, and celebrities) are vital to develop brand awareness and image. The branding strategy of Las Vegas historically focuses on special events and appearance in movies.

Visitor-based brand equity measures such as brand recognition, image, loyalty, and brand advocacy are critical benchmarking performance measures for destinations. The Tourism Commission on Nevada launched a rebranded Nevada marketing campaign for other forms of tourism in neighboring states (California, Arizona, and Utah) and international markets. The goal is to promote rural areas and lesser-known sights, including "Wild West" experiences.[68]

Destination branding.
Creating a differentiated destination image that influences travelers' decision to visit a destination and conveys the promise of a memorable experience that is uniquely associated with the destination.

Destination Tourism Slogans

A destination slogan is part of brand identity articulated to position a product. It is a short phrase that communicates descriptive or persuasive information about a brand. Slogans are considered an essential element to build brand awareness and image at country, state, and city levels.[69] Some popular slogans are "What Happens in Vegas Stays in Vegas," "I Love NY," and "Virginia is for Lovers" and "100% Pure New Zealand." Las Vegas actually has several lesser slogans aimed at narrow audiences, including "Not business as usual," aimed at meeting planners; "Overtime guaranteed," to promote special events; and "A world of entertainment," for international audiences.

Destinations can change their slogans as part of their rebranding strategy. Recently, the Greek National Tourism Organization (GNTO) launched a new global tourism campaign under a new slogan "Greece, All Time Classic." Jamaica ditched its longtime slogan "Jamaica—Once you go you know" after 10 years. It has been replaced by "Jamaica—Get All Right" to elicit a message that Jamaica is a place that makes visitors "feel alright." Singapore Tourism Board rebranded tagline "Uniquely Singapore" to "YourSingapore."

Effectiveness of Advertising/Promotion

The success of yesterday's advertising/promotion as a model for today is increasingly being questioned. The results of research on the subject of effectiveness of state expenditures to promote tourism are certain to be controversial.

One study concluded that "states with lower levels of tourism activity can enjoy small benefits from increased spending while states with higher levels of tourism would benefit from decreased spending."[70] Another study concerning the effectiveness of advertising suggested that "there was no significant difference between the control group that was not exposed to anything and the group that saw the advertisement as far as attitude formation and interest in visiting a destination were concerned."[71]

The two studies referred to may be in the vanguard of demonstrating the need for new marketing strategies to effectively market visitor destinations. Society has changed. Traditional media such as TV, newspaper and magazine ads, and AM/FM radio may not be utilized by target markets, particularly younger ones. In today's digital age, savvy DMOs are tapping social and mobile networks, smartphones and tablets, GPS (global positioning system) apps, e-commerce, and booking engines to economically reach consumers 24/7, and globally. Their Web sites can now interactively deploy video, text, audio, booking systems, photos and real-time comments from customers.[72]

New Zealand formed a global partnership with Facebook to build story-driven content together and to market the destination across their platforms of Instagram and Facebook. TNZ's Director of Marketing, Andrew Fraser, said, "It was increasingly important to be able to work effectively across all digital platforms and working directly with Facebook was a great opportunity to ensure the campaign used the most effective best practice techniques. Essentially what we did was go to Facebook and ask them to create a content idea that addressed some of the barriers faced by people who are actively considering coming to New Zealand. Our research showed that while this audience understands the epic landscapes, there are gaps in their knowledge regarding their perceptions of our infrastructure, ease of travelling around New Zealand and the variety of things to do and see." This collaboration resulted in an engaging and natural story of two American tourists missing the train to Wellington from Britomart and embarking on a Kombi road trip where they meet the locals and see the country.[73]

DMOs are usually in charge of developing and measuring the effectiveness of promotion campaigns. One significant outlet is major T&T fairs in Berlin, Las Vegas, and Madrid, which bring destinations, intermediaries, and travel trade together.

Developing Packages of Attractions and Amenities

An effective way of communicating with potential travelers is by offering packages. Tourist organizations must develop a package of attractions and amenities. Travelers make comparisons about the relative advantages and disadvantages of competing destinations. Destinations must provide easy access to attractions by bus, boats, carriages, and planes. They need to distribute brochures, audiotapes, and videotapes to travel agents and individual prospects. City bus companies might prepare half-day, full-day, and evening tours to highlight the destination's major attractions. Concentrating attractions, services, and facilities in a small area creates excitement, adventure, and crowds.

Destinations constantly discover hidden assets that have vast tourist potential. Illinois, for example, has more public and semipublic golf courses per population than any other state except Florida. It now promotes golf tours. Japanese tours responded to a package of golf and Chicago shopping. Pennsylvania has reclaimed old coal mining areas with championship golf courses, expanding its recreational facilities to promote tourism.

Victoria, Canada, "The City of Gardens," is home to The Butchart Gardens, a 55-acre abandoned quarry that was transformed into a beautiful living garden of flowers. The Butchart Garden has become synonymous with Victoria's tourist industry, featuring special events, dining, and gift shopping. When combined with other activities such as golf, shopping, dining, and museums, many packages can be developed for different visitor segments.

The Koshare Indian Museum at La Junta, Colorado, is an example of a cultural tourist attraction. The museum houses one of the largest collections of North American art and artifacts in the world and a library on Native American history. Native American dances are preserved by teaching them to the young men of the community, who perform throughout the nation as the Koshare Indian Dancers.

A destination may promote one, a few, or many of its attractions. Chicago's marketing theme "Chicago's Got It" featured pictures of its famous architecture, lakefront, symphony, world's tallest building, financial exchanges, and Wrigley Field (home of the Chicago Cubs) to suggest that the city had everything: business, culture, entertainment, recreation, and sports. In contrast, San Francisco played off its well-developed image as seductive and mysterious: a photo of a foggy, softly lit Golden Gate Bridge with the copy, "In the Beginning, God Created Heaven and Earth. San Francisco Took a Little Longer."

Competition among destinations extends to restaurants, facilities, sports, cultural amenities, and entertainment. Which place has the most four-star hotels, best culinary fare, most museums and theaters, best wine and drink, best chefs, or best native, cultural, or ethnic flair? Campaigns are carried out in specialty publications. Testimonials and rankings are found in travel brochures, advertising, and travel guides.

Despite the best offers of a destination to portray a positive image through PR and advertising, image building is affected by reports of disturbing societal problems, including human rights abuse.

Charges of human rights abuse from Western governments directly affect tourism development and growth. The government of Myanmar viewed its people as "contributing labor" to the development of the tourism-related infrastructure. International human rights observers viewed this development as forced labor. The U.K.-based Tourism Concern reported that the Myanmar State Law Order Restoration Council (SLORC) is "implementing projects earmarked for tourism through the use of forced labor and the displacement of people."[74] Tourism Concern reported that chained prison gangs and conscripted families had been used to build roads and prepare tourism sites. According to the reports, army members went from house to house taking people for forced labor.

The SLORC denied these reports and stated that people were contributing their voluntary labor happily. Whatever the truth, reports of human rights abuse, crime, disease, and other societal problems have a negative effect on tourism and may persist long after the problem is corrected.

National tourist organizations (NTOs). A national government or quasi-government agency that markets destination tourism.

Making a destination tourist friendly is the task of a central tourist agency, which may be public, quasi-public, nonprofit, or private. These agencies are referred to as **national tourist organizations (NTOs)**. Outside the United States, this agency is often run by the central government, state, or province, together with local government officials. The European Travel Commission, a 24-nation group bent on luring U.S. visitors to Europe, coordinates promotional activity in the United States.

Creating and Managing Visitor Experiences

Attractions alone do not attract visitors. Most places seek to deepen the travel experience by providing greater value and making the experience more significant and rewarding. A destination is an amalgam of diverse products and environments generating a total destination experience.

The experience "clues" are building blocks of a product experience based on sensory information that collectively shape the consumer experience. Anything perceived and sensed (sight, sound, touch, taste, and smell) in the environment is an experience "clue" and must be managed. Unmanaged or random, negative clues can ruin the whole experience by canceling out the positive ones.[75] Applying it to tourism context, a typical international destination experience starts at the airport (or even before if a visitor begins to "experience" the destination by surfing its Web site), continues with taxicab or shuttle service, hotel check-in, dining, sightseeing tours, and shopping and entertainment experiences.

Tourist destinations can create a net positive total experience by arranging the hundreds of clues. For example, negative clues such as smell and pollution that diminish the experience should be eliminated. In some cities, the roads between airport and the city were rerouted because old one included slums and shanty neighborhoods along for many miles. In Singapore, the airport road is always adorned with seasonal flowers and offers a scenic ride for very long miles. Singapore's cab drivers are known for their professional training and service, which include English-language exams, safety programs, and location skills. Some places invest little in that area, even though airport cabs and public transit may be the first encounter points that visitors have with a destination and can be critical to tourist satisfaction.

Specific attractions can also create and manage visitor experiences. Havana Club Museum of Rum, a renovated eighteenth-century colonial house, in the historic district of Old Habana implements some of the experiential marketing principles including a mule-driven cane mill show and tasting in the courtyard, history and real-time experience of rum-making process appealing to senses. A bar

Boulder City, Nevada, offers zip line tours that cover just over a mile and a half of the canyon. Courtesy of Las Vegas News Bureau.

for rum tasting, local food, local live music, and a memorabilia store for rum and cigar is offered to enhance the experience. Destinations should find a delicate balance between designing or managing experiences and keeping the authenticity of the experience.

Cocreation of Destination Experience and Social Media

Developments in new media have transformed the relationship that individuals have with their social network and tourist destinations. Visitors now interact with different elements of destinations and tourism suppliers and cocreate their own experiences. Designing experiences in tourism should pay attention to interactivity, interactions between tourists and physical elements of destination, interactions with social elements of destination (other tourists, locals, employees, and social networks), and interactions with social media. The social platforms have become an integral part before the trip (cocreating), during the trip (sharing experiences real-time), and after the trip in the form of storytelling and helping others cocreate their own experience.[76] A 2014 Chase Marriott Rewards survey reveals that nearly all millennial travelers post on social networks and share experiences with friends while traveling.

DMOs and tourism providers can create interactive platforms for travelers to facilitate the process. Thailand (DMO Web site) focuses on traveler-generated stories and offers a platform, "Real Experiences" for cocreation, which includes exciting travel stories, insider travel tips, and travel videos and photos that showcase the many exciting activities, festivals, and destinations in Thailand.[77]

Live-Like-a-Local Experience

Younger generations want an authentic and "live-like-a-local" destination experience. "Like-a-local" site is an organization that enables visitors to taste and experience the local culture and destination like a local. All kinds of interactive workshops such as gastronomy, art, painting, and dancing are offered by local experts. For example, visitors to Istanbul can arrange a five-hour gastronomic walking tour by a local guide beginning on the European side of Istanbul and ending on the Asian side. One can also arrange bicycle or walking tours in Barcelona, gastronomic tours in Paris, or historical city tours in Prague.[78]

The Withlocals connects visitors with locals through food and experiences in Asian countries. Visitors can contact local guides for customized tours, taste the local culture by dining with a family in their home, and participate in activities and workshops led by locals. For example, they can try Mui Thai boxing, drive a Tuk Tuk, or have a typical Thai dinner in a local's home.[79]

The Canadian Tourism Commission (CTC) recently launched the Explore Canada Like a Local (ECLAL) Web site and mobile device app to facilitate travel research for people traveling in or planning a trip to Canada and to connect locals and travelers.[80]

Couchsurfing is not just about furniture. It is an online cultural exchange community and alternative travel platform for travelers to stay with locals instead of at hotels. Today, Couchsurfing has over 3 million members in more than 200 countries and facilitates tens of thousands of face-to-face encounters across the world each week. Members around the globe locate travel accommodation while traveling by staying in the homes of other members and organizing gatherings with fellow members. Members also use the community to exchange information, advice, stories, and culture. Couchsurfing offers "live-like-local" experience because members can also join local groups that plan social activities like happy hours, camping trips, and other gatherings.[81]

■■■ Organizing and Managing Tourism Marketing

National Tourism Organizations

Countries and states usually have government or quasi-government agencies that market destination tourism. On the national level, these are referred to as NTOs. An NTO has two marketing tasks: (1) The NTO can formulate and develop the tourist product or products of the destination and (2) it can promote them in appropriate markets. It can base its approach to development and promotion on market research and thus achieve a close match between the products and the markets. In doing this, the tourist organization is acting on behalf of the whole destination and is complementary to the development and promotion activities of individual tourist providers. The U.S. Travel Association is the national, nonprofit organization whose mission is to increase travel to and within the United States. It has more than 1,300 member organizations representing all components of the travel industry such as destinations, travel service providers, and travel associations. The association engages in lobbying efforts to further promote T&T and leads national promotion aimed at international travelers such as Brand USA.[82] Brand USA produces the official U.S. T&T Web site, www.DiscoverAmerica.com.

The NTO is responsible for the following functions:

- *Flow of research data.* The NTO coordinates tourism research for the area. Information on origin of visitors, length of stay, type of accommodation used, and expenditures on different tourism products are collected and disseminated to members of the organization. This information helps the NTO evaluate trends and develop marketing strategies. It also provides valuable information to hospitality and travel businesses.

- *Representation in markets.* The NTO often has offices in major markets. These promote the country within the market. The promotion comes in the form of advertising with response mechanisms, such as advertisements in travel magazines featuring a toll-free number to call for additional information. Respondents receive a tour manual. The offices answer questions from prospective visitors and facilitate the development of distribution linkages. They also serve as important sources of information about trends in the market.

- *Organization of workshops and trade shows.* The NTO facilitates the interaction of tourism with members of the distribution channels, such as travel agents and wholesalers. In addition to developing workshops, the NTO purchases space at major travel shows and invites travel industry members to participate in the booth, by either displaying material or having a physical presence. This saves the member the cost of purchasing an individual booth.

Familiarization trip (Fam trip). A trip where travel agents or others who can send business to a tourist destination attraction, cruise, or hotel are invited to visit at a low cost or no cost.

- *Familiarization trips (Fam trips).* The NTO develops **familiarization trips** for key members of the distribution channel and travel writers. A fam trip is a low-cost or no-cost trip sponsored by a travel destination including hotels, cruise lines, and resorts for travel agents or others who can send business to the travel destination.

- *Participation in joint marketing schemes.* Some NTOs provide cooperative advertising support to help members promote to selected markets. The British Tourist Authority, for example, helps support British Airways advertising in the United States. It is hoped these advertisements will develop additional tourists for Britain, thus helping the British hospitality and travel industry.

- *Support for new or small businesses.* NTOs may provide support for new products and small businesses that are important to the overall tourism of the area. For example, rural tourism, regional festivals, and bed and breakfast (B&B) accommodations are often promoted by NTOs.

- *Consumer assistance and protection.* NTOs assist the consumer by providing product information. For example, in some countries there are classification schemes for lodging accommodations. These are designed to educate travelers concerning types of available lodging. Sometimes NTOs influence the design of lodging brochures and menus appropriate for a particular market segment.

- *General education.* NTOs conduct conferences and courses to educate travel industry providers from their nation to understand the needs of foreign markets.

Like other organizations, NTOs must develop a mission statement, goals, and a strategy. The underlying objective of national strategy formulation is to translate current conditions in the region into desired situations. For example, a federal government with the goal of increasing the economic benefits of tourism to a specific subregion may select a strategy to increase visitation to that area. A country that is highly dependent on one specific geographic market for its demand may adopt a strategy of diversification. For example, Mexico, known for its sun and sea destinations, has developed historical sites to attract a different segment of tourists.

Destinations marketers who are able to influence site selection of groups such as associations can expect invaluable visitors' income for the community. To have a chance of being selected as a meeting site, a destination must be included in the initial decision process. Careful study and research is needed of those responsible for site selection. Research of targeted associations and understanding who the real decision makers are within the providence of the site selection committee is needed.[83]

Regional Tourist Organizations: State Associations and Convention and Tourist Bureaus

Many state or provinces have their own tourist organizations. Queensland in Australia has created Tourism Queensland, statutory authority of the Queensland government. State tourist organizations (STOs) perform many of the same functions of an NTO, only on a regional level. They also work with the NTOs, to obtain funds and effectively employ resources in their area. Tourism Queensland, working with other tourism organizations, has developed a 10-year strategic plan for the state.[84] New York State's STO developed the *I Love New York* campaign. Like many STOs, New York divided the state into regions that have a common theme for tourists. For example, some of the names of the regions are New York City, The Catskills, Greater Niagara, and the Thousand-Islands-Seaway Region.[85] The owners and managers of hospitality organizations such as a hotels, restaurants, or attractions that entice tourists should work with STOs to see how they can promote their businesses.

City, county, or area convention and visitors' bureaus (CVB) promote tourism on the local level. Because they promote a specific destination, they are often referred as a **destination marketing organization (DMO)**. A major focus of DMOs is to bring meetings and conventions to the local convention facilities and hotels with meeting space. The convention facilities are often owned by the local government and sometimes built knowing they would not make money off the rental of the facility. The dollars the tourists bring to the city and the sales taxes and hotel occupancy taxes would cover the loss on the convention center. Sometimes the DMO and the convention center management are two separate organizations, which calls for close communication between the two organizations.

Hotels, restaurants with banquet space, and restaurants near convention hotels should work closely with their CVB to make sure they get their fair share of the convention business. The local hotel association and restaurant association usually have board positions on the CVB's board to make sure their interests are represented.[86]

CVBs often work with airlines serving their area and create travel missions to visit markets, domestic and international, that represent opportunities for all tourist industry members within a destination to work together. Large enterprises such as a ski resort or a large attraction such as the Biltmore house in Asheville, North Carolina, may provide a booth with representatives, whereas small members such as a B&B may be able to only provide brochures and support the sponsoring tourist promotion organizations.

Destination marketing organization (DMO). A group that promotes a specific destination. Often a local CVB serves as the DMO.

▰▰▰ CHAPTER REVIEW

I. Globalization of the Tourist Industry. The world has become a global community. Regions such as Eastern Europe and countries such as China and India are rapidly developing. They are now generators of tourists as well as destinations for tourists.

II. Marketing Tourism Destinations
  A. Tourism destination
   1. **Destinations** are places with some form of actual or perceived boundary.
   2. **Macrodestinations** such as the United States contain thousands of microdestinations, including regions, states, cities, towns, and visitor destinations within a town.
  B. Destination marketing system Destination marketing is systematically linking supply (destination features and benefits) with demand (needs and wants of travelers) and enhancing competitiveness of a destination in a sustainable manner.
  C. Destination competitiveness
   1. **Travel and Tourism Competitiveness Index (TTCI)** It aims to measure the factors and policies that make it attractive to develop the T&T sector in different countries. Each country or economy is ranked on a set of indexes.
   2. **Price competitiveness** Price competitiveness has a particular importance for tourist destinations because lower costs increase the attractiveness of some countries for many travelers.
  D. Sustainable tourism It refers to tourism that minimizes the environmental impacts and socio-cultural changes, sustains the longevity of a destination, and creates economic opportunity for local communities.
   1. **Economic effects of tourism** They are direct employment in hospitality and tourism industries, support for other industries, multiplier effect, tax revenue, and exports of locally made products.
   2. **Social/cultural effects of tourism** Tourism growth affects the social/cultural basis of destinations in both positive and negative ways.
   3. **Environmental effects of tourism** Too often, tourism planners focus mostly on tourism development without paying attention to retaining and preserving the destination attributes.

III. Tourism Development and Investments
  A. Tourism events and attractions
   1. **Events** that attract a desired market and harmoniously fit with a community's culture can provide beneficial results, particularly if the event regularly reoccurs over a period of years.
   2. **Attractions** may be natural, such as Niagara Falls or the Scottish Highlands or a beach. They can also be manufactured, such as the shopping areas of Buckingham Palace, Hong Kong, the Vatican, or a casino resort.
  B. Attractions
   1. **UNESCO World Heritage Sites**
   2. **Waterfront attractions**
   3. **Casinos as attractions**
   4. **Indian gaming**
   5. **Stopover tourism.** Many visitor destinations are in fact only stopover destinations for travelers on their way elsewhere.
  C. Destination life cycle: Rejuvenating a destination Destinations will experience a life cycle similar to the product life cycle and eventually go into decline or the destruction stage.

IV. Segmenting and Monitoring the Tourist Market. Tourism planners must consider how many tourists are desired and which segments to attract. Travel motivations, nationality, generational markets such as millennials, and lifestyles are effective segmentation base used by destinations.
  A. Agritourism. Agriculture-based tourism that includes farms, ranches, and wineries. It provides rural areas with a means to attract tourists.
  B. Space tourism. As private companies provide vehicles to send tourists into space, this form of tourism will develop. In the near term, it will just be for the very rich.
  C. Multiday hiking and religious pilgrimages.
  D. Medical tourism. It is one of the fastest-growing and most lucrative tourism markets. Tourists spend a large amount on medical treatment, stay in top hotels, and often travel around the country after their surgery. The aging baby boomers and the growing cost of health care will ensure the growth of medical tourism in the future.
  E. Genealogical tourism.
  F. Identifying target markets.
   1. Collect information about its current visitors
   2. Audit the destination's attractions and select segments that might logically have an interest in them
  G. Classification of visitor segments
   1. Group-inclusive tour (GIT)
   2. Independent traveler (IT; formerly FIT)
  H. Monitoring the tourist markets. Tourist markets are dynamic and a marketing information system is part of any well-run tourist organization.

V. Communicating with the Tourist Market
  A. Competition for visitors requires image making. Tourist destinations largely compete on images held by current and potential travelers.
  B. Branding destinations. Branding opportunities for destinations exist at geographical levels such as country, city, and town (umbrella and sub-brands); specific attractions such as museums and theme parks; events such as mega-events and festivals; and lifestyle travel packages.
  C. Destination tourism slogans. Slogans are considered an essential element to build brand awareness and image at country, state, and city levels.

D. Effectiveness of advertising/promotion. In today's digital age, savvy DMOs are tapping social and mobile networks, smartphones and tablets, GPS apps, e-commerce, and booking engines to economically reach consumers 24/7, and globally. Their Web sites can now interactively deploy video, text, audio, booking systems, photos, and real-time comments from customers.

E. Developing packages of attractions and amenities. An effective way of communicating with potential travelers is by offering packages. Tourist organizations must develop a package of attractions and amenities.

F. Creating and managing visitor experiences. Attractions alone do not attract visitors. Most places seek to deepen the travel experience by providing greater value and making the experience more significant and rewarding.
1. **Cocreation of destination experience and social media**
2. **Live-Like-a-Local experience**

VI. Organizing and Managing Tourism Marketing. Making a destination tourist friendly is the task of a central tourist agency, which may be public, quasi-public, nonprofit, or private. These agencies are referred to as national tourist organizations (NTOs), STOs, CVBs, or destination management organizations.

■■■ DISCUSSION QUESTIONS

1. How does a tourism destination determine what to promote and to whom it should be promoted?

2. What benefits and costs does tourism bring to your area?

3. Choose one of the psychological determinants of demand listed in Table 17–3 and describe a tourism product that is based on the determinant you have chosen.

4. Choose what you believe to be a good tourism promotion for a city, region, state, or country and explain why you think it is a good promotion. In your critique, discuss the media used, target audience, and benefits the destination offers.

5. Choose a visitor experience in a destination. Discuss how you can make it a memorable experience for visitors.

■■■ EXPERIENTIAL EXERCISE

Do the following:

1. Choose an event (festival, concert, play, etc.) in your area that draws tourists. Look into how the event is promoted and the benefits it brings to the community. Is this event effectively promoted? If yes, why? If no, how could it be improved?

■■■ INTERNET EXERCISE

1. Find two different sites of tourism marketing organizations, national, state, or CVB. Evaluate how effective you feel these Web sites are in promoting the destination. Explain your answer.

2. Visit Destination Marketing Association International (DMAI) homepage, http://www.destinationmarketing .org. What are the benefits for a DMO for becoming a member of the association?

■■■ REFERENCES

1 Graham Busby and Callu Haines, "Doc Martin and Film Tourism: Creation of Destination Image," *Tourism*, 61, no. 2 (2013): 105–120; Simon Hudson and J. R. Brent Ritchie, "Promoting Destinations via Film Tourism: An Empirical Identification of Supporting Marketing Initiatives," *Journal of Travel Research*, 44 (2006): 387–396; accessed June 16, 2015, from http://www.tourismnewzealand.com/about-us/what-we-do/campaign-and-activity/; accessed September 28, 2014, from http://www.tourismnewzealand.com/sector-marketing/film-tourism/; Daniela Carl, Sara Kindon, and Karen Smith, "Tourists' Experiences of Film Locations: New Zealand as 'Middle-Earth'," *Tourism Geographies*, 9, no. 1 (2007): 49–63; "Celebrating 10 Years of 100% Pure New Zealand," http://www.tourismnewzealand.com/media/1544/pure-as-celebrating-10-years-of-100-pure-new-zealand.pdf (accessed July 31, 2015).

2 "Understanding Tourism: Basic Glossary," http://media.unwto.org/en/content/understanding-tourism-basic-glossary 2015 (accessed August 5); "International Recommendations for Tourism Statistics 2008: 10," from http://unstats.un.org/unsd/publication/SeriesM/seriesm_83rev1e.pdf.

3 Tourism Highlights 2015, UNWTO (August 2015): 2.

4 Amanda Machado, "How Millennials Are Changing Travel," *The Atlantic*, June 18, 2014, http://www.theatlantic.com/international/print/2014/06/how-millennials-are-changing-international-travel/373007/.

5 Robert Govers and Frank Go, *Place Branding: Gocal, Virtual and Physical Identities, Constructed, Imagined and Experienced* (New York: Palgrave Macmillan, 2009).

6 Seyhmus Baloglu and Mehmet Mangaloglu, "Tourism Destinations Images of Turkey, Egypt, Greece, and Italy as Perceived by US-Based Tour Operators and Travel Agents," *Tourism Management*, 22, no. 1, 1–9.

7 See vacations.united.com.

8 Kozak and Seyhmus Baloglu, *Managing and Marketing Tourist Destinations: Strategies to Gain a Competitive Advantage* (New York, NY: Routledge, 2011), 111–129.

9 Geoffrey. I Crouch and J. R. Brent Ritchie, "Conceptual and theoretical perspectives," in *Competitiveness and Tourism*, Vol. 1. Geoffrey. I Crouch and J. R. Brent Ritchie (Eds.) (Northampton, MA: An Elgar Research Collection, 2012), 75.

10 Geoffrey. I Crouch and J. R. Brent Ritchie, "Introduction," in *Competitiveness and Tourism*, Vol. 1. eds. Geoffrey. I Crouch and J. R. Brent Ritchie (Northampton, MA: An Elgar Research Collection, 2012), pp. xii–xx.

11 "U.S. Consumer Online Travel Spending Surpasses $100 Billion for First Time in 2012," February 20, 2013, http://www.comscore.com/Insights/Press-Releases/2013/2/U.S.-Consumer-Online-Travel-Spending-Surpasses-100-Billion-for-First-Time-in-2012.

12 Peter Forsyth and Larry Dwyer, "Tourism Price Competitiveness," in *Competitiveness and Tourism*, Vol. 2. eds. Geoffrey. I Crouch and J. R. Brent Ritchie (Northampton, MA: An Elgar Research Collection, 2012), p. 78.

13 See www.economist.com/content/big-mac-index.

14 Salah S. Hassan, "Determinants of Market Competitiveness in an Environmentally Sustainable Tourism Industry," *Journal of Travel Research*, 38, no. 3 (2000): 244.

15 Andrew W. Savitz, *Triple Bottom Line* (San Francisco, CA: Jossey-Bass, 2006).

16 Terry Jicinsky and Seyhmus Baloglu, "Las Vegas—A Diversified Destination," in Metin Kozak and Seyhmus Baloglu, *Managing and Marketing Tourist Destinations: Strategies to Gain a Competitive Advantage* (New York, NY: Routledge, 2011), 155.

17 Hawkes, Ethan and Kwortnik, Robert J. Jr, "Connecting with the Culture: A Case Study in Sustainable Tourism," *Cornell Hotel and Restaurant Administration Quarterly*, 47, no. 4 (2006): 369–381.

18 Sergei Khrushckev, Tony L. Henthorne, and Michael S. Latour, "Cuba at the Crossroads," *Cornell Hospitality Quarterly* (November 2007): 402–414.

19 Ibid.

20 Hugo Martin, "Utah's Wave Is a Rock Star Without a Crowd," *The Denver Post* (January 6, 2008): 1T, 6T.

21 Rex S. Toh, Habibullah Kahn, and Karen Kim, "Singapore Tourist Industry: How Its Strengths Offset Economic, Social and Environmental Challenges," *Cornell Hotel and Restaurant Administration Quarterly*, 42, no. 1 (2001): 46.

22 David Bruce Weaver, "Eco-Tourism as Mass Tourism: Contradiction or Reality?" *Cornell Hotel and Restaurant Administration Quarterly*, 42, no. 2 (2001): 112.

23 "Game on - Mega-event infrastructure opportunities," April 2011, from https://www.pwc.com/en_GX/gx/capital-projects-infrastructure/pdf/Mega-Events_with_Abadie_Change.pdf.

24 "Tourism Ministry to Undertake $34 Million 'Clean Coasts Project,'" *Jamaica Observer*, June 27, 2014, http://www.jamaicaobserver.com/news/Tourism-ministry-to-undertake—34-million—Clean-Coasts-Project-_17024117.

25 Jeffrey Ball, "The Carbon Neutral Vacation," *Wall Street Journal* (July 28–29, 2007): P1, P4, P5.

26 Ma Aiping, Si Lina, and Zhang Hongfei, "The Evolution of Cultural Tourism: The Example of Qufu, the Birthplace of Confucius," in *Tourism in China: Destination, Cultures and Communities*, eds. Chris Ryan and Gu Huimin (New York: Routledge, 2009), pp. 187–196.

27 Donald Getz, "Event Tourism: Definition, Evolution, and Research," *Progress in Tourism Management*, 29 (2008): 403–428.

28 Lisa Wirthman, "What to Expect at the 2015 Consumer Electronics Show," November 19, 2014, http://www.forbes.com/sites/lasvegas/2014/11/19/what-to-expect-at-the-2015-consumer-electronics-show/.

29 James R. Hagerty, "Loaves and Fish: Piscine Gluttony in Pennsylvania," *Wall Street Journal* (June 16–17, 2007): A1, A2.

30 http://www.bard.org/about/history.html#.VE1BBvl4pKU (accessed August 9, 2015); "Economic Impact of The Utah Shakespeare Festival," January 4, 2012, from http://www.le.utah.gov/interim/2012/pdf/00003264.pdf.

31 Martin A. O'Neill and Adrian Palmer, "Wine Production and Tourism: Adding Service to a Perfect Partnership," *Cornell Hotel and Restaurant Administration Quarterly*, 45, no. 3 (2004): 271.

32 Ibid.

33 Juergen Gnoth and Syed Aziz Anwar, "New Zealand Bets on Event Tourism," *Cornell Hotel and Restaurant Administration Quarterly*, 41, no. 4 (2000): 80.

34 Eliza Ching-Yick Tse and Suk-Ching Ho, "Targeting Sports Teams," *Cornell Hotel & Restaurant Administrative Quarterly* (February 2006): 49–59.

35 Susan Wargin, "Update," www.9news.com (accessed July 10, 2011).

36 "An Earful of Cheer, Disney Does Marathons the Only Way It Knows How," *Hemispheres Magazine.com* (May 2011).

37 World Heritage Centre, World Heritage List, http://whc .unesco.org/en/list/ (accessed August 11, 2015).

38 Deborah Steinborn, "On the Waterfront," *Wall Street Journal* (June 11, 2007): R11.

39 http://www.greektowncasino.com/Gaming/ ClubGreektown/ (accessed October 11, 2008); R. Ankeny, "Greektown Casino: We'll Bring Neighborhood Firms to Table," *Crain's Detroit Business*, 15, no. 33 (1999): 3–4 (retrieved June 13, 2004, from EBSCOhost online article search engine); T. Lam, "Home Court Advantage: Greektown Casino Owners Are Betting on Metro Detroiters' Affection for the Neighborhood," *Detroit/Windsor Casino Guide* (November 10, 2000), as originally printed in the Detroit Free Press, http:// www.freep.com/casinoguide/greektown/greek.htm (accessed June 14, 2004).

40 www.fortune.com/sections, Special Advertising Feature, "Indian Gaming, The Native American Success Story," 2007.

41 Mark Whitehouse, "Bad Odds," *Wall Street Journal* (June 11, 2007): R5.

42 Rex S. Toh, Habibullah Kahn, and Karen Lim, "Singapore's Tourism Industry: How Its Strength Offsets Economic, Social and Environmental Challenges," *Cornell Hotel and Restaurant Administrative Quarterly*, 42, no. 1 (2001): 42, 48.

43 Norman Skiareivitz, Copley News Service, "Going Places: Waikiki $2 Billion Makeover," *Steamboat Pilot & Today* (November 4, 2007): 1D, 2D.

44 Xiang (Robert) Li, Fang Meng, Muzaffer Uysal, and Brian Mihalik, "Understanding China's Long-Haul Outbound Travel Market: An Overlapped Segmentation Approach," *Journal of Business Research*, 66, no. 6 (2013): 786–793.

45 "Vegas FAQs," from http://www.lvcva.com/includes/ content/images/media/docs/2014-Vegas-FAQs.pdf.

46 Laura Carroll, "Las Vegas Aims to Benefit from Surge in Foreign Tourism," *Las Vegas Review Journal*, January 8, 2012, http://www.reviewjournal.com/business/ tourism/las-vegas-aims-benefit-surge-foreign-tourism; Laura Carroll, "Seeking International Visitors: Tourism Agency Widens Reach," *Las Vegas Review Journal* (February 29, 2012): 1d, 4d.

47 Amanda Machado, "How Millennials Are Changing Travel," *The Atlantic*, June 18, 2014, http://www .theatlantic.com/international/print/2014/06/how- millennials-are-changing-international-travel/373007/.

48 Teresa Lee, "Top Millennial Traveler Trends," *Hotels Interactive*, April 16, 2013, from http://www.hotelin- teractive.com/article.aspx?articleID=28911; "Meet the Millennials: Insights for Destinations," 2011, from www.pgavdestinations.com/images/insights/ Meet_the_Millennials.pdf; "Destination Marketing for Millennials," http://www.adventuretravelnews .com/destination-marketing-for-millennials (accessed November 13, 2014).

49 "Destination Marketing for Millennials," http://www .adventuretravelnews.com/destination-marketing -for-millennials (accessed November 13, 2014).

50 Tom Crosby, "Kiawah Island Joins Charleston as Major South Carolina Destination," *Go Magazine* (March/ April 2004): 29.

51 Sharon Flanigan, Kirsty Blackstock, and Colin Hunter, "Agritourism from the Perspective of Providers and Visitors," *Tourism Management*, 40 (2014): 395.

52 "Top 8 Agritourism Destinations in the World," http:// www.mnn.com/lifestyle/eco-tourism/photos/top-8- agritourism-destinations-in-the-world/cultivate-your- knowledge (accessed August 5, 2015).

53 "Colorado's Agritourism Market Climbing Says New CSU Report," College of Agricultural Sciences, *AG Family* (Fall 2007), Colorado State University, p. 4.

54 *Houston Chronicle*, http://www.chron.com/disp/story .mpl/front/6052360.html (accessed October 11, 2008).

55 See www.virgingalactic.com.

56 Dan Vergano, "NASA Prepares for Moon Tourism," *USA Today* (November 10, 2011): 1.

57 *Centennial Journal* (May 2007): 11C, 12C.

58 "Medical Tourism Market (India, Thailand, Singapore, Malaysia, Mexico, Brazil, Taiwan, Turkey, South Korea, Costa Rica, Poland, Dubai, and Philippines)— Global Industry Analysis, Size, Share, Growth, Trends, and Forecast, 2013–2019," http://www.transparency- marketresearch.com/medical-tourism.html (accessed August 10, 2015); "Medical Tourism in 2013, Facts and Statistics," *Medical Tourism Resource Guide*, http://www.medicaltourismresourceguide.com/ medical-tourism-in-2013 (accessed May 9, 2015).

59 Michael D. Horowitz and Jeffrey A. Rosenweig, "Medical Tourism—Health Care in the Global Economy," *Physician Executive*, 33, no. 6 (2007), 24–30; "Healthcare Cost," *Healthcare Financial Management*, 62, no. 9 (2008): 12.

60 Carla Almeida Santos and Grace Yan, "Genealogical Tourism: A Phenomenological Examination," *Journal of Travel Research*, 49, no. 1 (February 2011).

61 "Scotland Urged to Refocus on Genealogy Tourism," *The Scotsman*, November 25, 2012, from http://www .scotsman.com/lifestyle/arts/news/scotland-urged-to- refocus-on-genealogy-tourism-1-2658576.

62 James Glenday, "Gallipoli 2015: Tourist Trade Booms Ahead of Anzac Centenary," April 20, 2015, from http://www.abc.net.au/news/2015-04- 20/gallipoli-tourist-trade-booms-ahead-of-anzac- centenary/6404628.

63 Stanley C. Plog, "Why Destinations Rise and Fall in Popularity," *Cornell Hotel and Restaurant Quarterly*, 14, no. 4 (1974): 55–59.

64 Zhaoping Liu, Judy A. Siguaw, and Cathy A. Enz, "Using Tourist Travel Habits and Preferences to Assess

Strategic Destination Positioning," *Cornell Hospitality Quarterly*, 49, no. 3 (August 2008): 258–280.

65 Seyhmus Baloglu, "An Investigation of a Loyalty Typology and the Multidestination Loyalty of International Travelers," *Tourism Analysis*, 6, no. 1 (2001): 41–52.

66 Robert Govers and Frank Go, *Place Branding: Glocal, Virtual and Physical Identities, Constructed, Imagined and Experienced* (New York: Palgrave Macmillan, 2009).

67 Ahmet Usakli and Seyhmus Baloglu, "Brand Personality of Tourist Destinations: An Application of Self-Congruity Theory," *Tourism Management* 32 (2011): 114–127.

68 Laura Caroll, "Polishing a Silver Lining," *Las Vegas Business Press* (July 1–14, 2013): 6–9; Laura Carroll, "Seeking International Visitors: Tourism Agency Widens Reach," *Las Vegas Review Journal* (February 29, 2012): 4d.

69 Xinran Y. Lehto, Gwangjin Lee, and Joseph Ismail, "Measuring Congruence of Affective Images of Destinations and Their Slogans," *International Journal of Tourism Research*, 16 (2014): 250.

70 John Deskins and Matthew Seevers, "Are State Expenditures to Promote Tourism Effective?" *Journal of Travel Research*, 50, no. 2 (March 2011): 167.

71 Marsha Coleman and Kenneth F. Backman, "Walking in Memphis: Testing One DMO's Marketing Strategy to Millennials," *Journal of Travel Research*, 49, no. 1 (February 2010).

72 Bill Baker, "The Changing Role of DMOs in the Digital Age," http://destinationbranding.com/dmofuture (accessed December 24, 2014).

73 http://www.tourismnewzealand.com/news/tourisms-global-facebook-campaign-world-class/ Retrieved on July 28, 2015; see www.facebook.com/purenewzealand.

74 J. S. Perry Hobson and Roberta Leung, "Hotel Development in Myanmar," *Cornell Hotel and Restaurant Administration Quarterly*, 38, no. 1 (1997): 60–71. See also F. Doherty, "Come Ye Back to Mandalay," *Tourism in Focus*, 15 (Spring 1995): 8.

75 Lewis P. Carbone, *Clued In: How to Keep Customers Coming Back Again and Again* (Upper Saddle River, NJ: Pearson Education, Inc., 2004).

76 Noel Scott, Eric Laws, and Phillip Boksberger, "The Marketing of Hospitality and Leisure Experiences," *Journal of Hospitality Marketing & Management*, 18, no. 2–3 (2014): 99–110; Iis P. Tussyadiah, "Toward a Theoretical Foundation for Experience Design in Tourism," *Journal of Travel Research*, 53, no. 5 (2014): 543–564; Barbara Neuhofer, Dimitrios Buhalis, and Adele Ladkin, "Conceptualizing Technology Enhanced Destination Experiences," *Journal of Destination Marketing & Management*, 1 (2012): 36–46.

77 See http://www.tourismthailand.org/Real-Experiences.

78 See http://www.likealocalguide.com.

79 See https://www.withlocals.com.

80 See http://matadornetwork.com/goods/how-to-explore-canada-like-a-local.

81 Jennie Germann Molz, "CouchSurfing and Network Hospitality: 'It's Not Just About the Furniture.," *Hospitality & Society*, 1 no. 3 (2011): 215–224; Devan Rosen, Pascale Roy Lafontaine, and Blake Hendrickson, "CouchSurfing: Belonging and Trust in a Globally Cooperative Online Social Network," *New Media & Society*, 13, no. 6 (2011): 981–998.

82 See https://www.ustravel.org.

83 Chris Ryan, *Recreational Tourism: A Social Science Perspective* (New York: Routledge, 1991), pp. 5–34; A. J. Burkhart and S. Medlik, *Tourism: Past, Present, and Future* (London: Heinemann, 1981), p. 256; T. C. Victor Middleton, *Marketing in Travel and Tourism* (Oxford, UK: Butterworth-Heinemann, 1994); Ernie Heath and Geoffrey Wall, *Marketing Tourism Destination* (New York: Wiley, 1992), p. 65; R. C. Mills and A. M. Morrison, *The Tourism System: An Introductory Text* (Upper Saddle River, NJ: Prentice Hall, 1985), p. 248; S. Crystal, "What Is the Meeting Industry Worth?" *Meeting News*, 17, no. 7 (1993): 1, 11.

84 http://www.tq.com.au/ (accessed October 11, 2008).

85 http://www.iloveny.com/home.aspx (accessed October 11, 2008).

86 "Best Practices Convention Center Sales and Convention Center Operations," A report from the Joint Study Committee, Destination Marketing Association International, and International Association of Assembly Managers, August 25, 2007.

■■■ APPENDIX A: 2014 TRAVEL AND TOURISM COMPETITIVENESS INDEX

Subindex A: T&T regulatory framework

1. Policy rules and regulations pillar captures the extent to which the policy environment is conducive to developing the T&T sector in each country.

2. Environmental sustainability pillar measures the stringency and enforcement of the government's environmental regulations in each country, carbon dioxide emissions and the percentage of endangered species in the country, and the extent to which governments prioritize the sustainable development of the T&T industry in their respective economies.

3. Safety and security pillar takes into account the costliness of common crime and violence as well as terrorism, and the extent to which police services can be

relied upon to provide protection from crime as well as the incidence of road traffic accidents in the country.

4. Health and hygiene pillar measures drinking water and sanitation quality as well as the availability of physicians and hospital beds.

5. Prioritization of the T&T sector pillar measures the extent to which the government prioritizes the T&T sector, such as ensuring the country's attendance at international T&T fairs and commissioning high-quality "destination-marketing" campaigns.

Subindex B: T&T business environment and infrastructure

6. Air transport infrastructure pillar measures ease of access to and from countries, as well as movement to destinations within countries based on the quantity of air transport, the number of departures, airport density, the number of operating airlines, and the quality of the air transport infrastructure both for domestic and international flights.

7. Ground transport infrastructure pillar takes into account the quality of roads, railroads, and ports, as well as the extent to which the national transport network as a whole offers efficient, accessible transportation to key business centers and tourist attractions.

8. Tourism infrastructure pillar takes into account the accommodation infrastructure (the number of hotel rooms) and the presence of major car rental companies in the country, as well as a measure of its financial infrastructure for tourists (the availability of automatic teller machines, or ATMs).

9. Information and Communication Technology (ICT) infrastructure pillar measures ICT penetration rates (Internet, telephone lines, and broadband), which provide a sense of the society's online activity as well the Internet use by businesses in carrying out transactions in the economy.

10. Price competitiveness in the T&T industry pillar measures the extent to which goods and services in the country are more or less expensive than elsewhere (purchasing power parity) as well as airfare ticket taxes and airport charges (which can make flight tickets much more expensive), fuel price levels compared with those of other countries, taxation in the country (which can be passed through to travelers), and the relative cost of hotel accommodations.

Subindex C: T&T human, cultural, and natural resources

11. Human resources pillar takes into account the education and training levels in each economy as well as the availability of qualified labor.

12. Affinity for T&T pillar measures the extent to which a country and society are open to tourism and foreign visitors, including the extent to which businesses are focused on customer orientation or satisfaction, the national population's attitude toward foreign travelers, and tourism openness (tourism expenditures and receipts as a percentage of gross domestic product [GDP]).

13. Natural resources pillar consists of a number of environmental attractiveness measures such as the number of UNESCO natural World Heritage sites, the quality of the natural environment, the richness of the fauna in the country as measured by the total known species of animals, and the percentage of nationally protected areas.

14. Cultural resources pillar include the number of UNESCO cultural World Heritage sites, sports stadium seat capacity, the number of international fairs and exhibitions in the country, and its creative industries exports.

Objectives

After reading this chapter, you should be able to:

1. Understand why it is important to have a marketing plan and be able to explain the purpose of a marketing plan.

2. Prepare a marketing plan following the process described in this chapter.

Next Year's Marketing Plan

Hospitality companies know that planning and research go hand in glove. This is particularly true of companies such as Preferred Hotels & Resorts Worldwide that serve the affluent guest, as described by Peter Cass, president and chief executive officer (CEO). Pictured earlier is the Post Ranch Inn in California, which is built on a cliff 1,200 feet above the Pacific Ocean—a member of Preferred's Boutique collection.

The rationale is that the experience of the truly discerning traveler is shaped by the "little things," beyond guaranteeing merely a clean, comfortable room and a desirable package of amenities. In-depth guest input will also be used to shape the criteria that go into defining the on-property guest experience. Through a proprietary customer satisfaction program currently under development, Preferred Hotels & Resorts will refine still further fine points of detail that create a truly memorable and complete "luxury experience."

For example, at the Rittenhouse Hotel in Philadelphia, frequent guests are greeted nightly with an expensive pearl on their pillow instead of the usual chocolate. At Halekulani in Honolulu, named the number-one hotel in the world by *Gourmet* magazine, guests are escorted to their rooms for swift, private check-in and receive a welcoming box of chocolates made by their in-house chocolatier soon afterward.

Although "comment cards" and guest preference sheets remain commonplace at many luxury hotels, no other worldwide lodging brand has built into its core mission the complete and total fulfillment of the guests' individual tastes, requirements, and predilections.

We have found that complete attention to detail—a total commitment to guest satisfaction that saves guest time, energy, and efforts; provides completely personalized and individual service; and creates the experience of "intellectual surprise" for its consumers—is what drives repeat business among the affluent.

To better understand its affluent consumer, Preferred Hotels & Resorts launched a market research effort that "drills down" to the deepest level of guest preference and expectation. Using a prospect identification and lifestyle data collection system, detailed and segmented data are gathered not only about the preferences of luxury travelers but also about unperceived "micromarkets" that make up the luxury travel segment.

At the individual property level, the expectation is that property managers will soon be able to learn not only what kind of room guests prefer when they travel on business, but also what their favorite leisure activities are, what kind of wine they like to drink—even their favorite reading material. At the macrolevel, Preferred targets programs, promotions, and partnerships tailored to the micromarket segments that make up its customer base. Examples are West Coast lawyers who golf or company CEOs who travel with children. Data collected from drilling down into the guest experience enable Preferred to provide the ultimate in guest service. Unique data can assist to discover distribution channels to market to the affluent.

Initial Applications of the Research: "Experiential" Associations and New Marketing Programs

Although affluent guests value individuality and attention to detail, Preferred has begun to identify certain distinct attributes or expectations that define the affluent as a group. More than anything else, affluents tend to flock together around common symbols, expectations, and experiences. In a word, they associate themselves into groups. Membership in the group, in turn, comes to define participation in the affluent experience.

Association is built into the concept of the affluent experience so that Preferred's creation of programs that target the affluent can be understood as a universal affinity program for the discerning consumer. It is the ultimate "affinity program for the affluent."

Preferred has taken the affinity concept a step further by identifying an interlinked series of value and quality associations that respond to the affluent client's desire for unique, memorable experiences and superior service, and by using that information to provide experiences that cater directly and uniquely to that desire.

Seabourn/Windstar

An example of the research in action is a partnership between Preferred and Seabourn/Windstar Cruises. The linkage is the desire of guests who stay at exclusive Preferred hotel properties to take expensive cruises on these two cruise lines, among the world's finest. The customer reward is the ability to translate stays at Preferred hotels into free nights on these cruises. This allows Preferred and Seabourn/Windstar to share guest histories and databases that reveal a guest's preferences and thus guarantees the ability to best service the guest with the expectation of creating return business.

Golf the Preferred Way

Another example of the application of the lifestyle marketing approach is "Preferred Golf," a partnership with Wide World of Golf, a worldwide marketer of upscale golf services. Preferred Golf provides Preferred guests with access to the world's finest golf courses by means of staying at a Preferred hotel or resort.

Engaging New Partners: Travel Agents and the Lifestyle Client Building Program

Lifestyle marketing programs that target the affluent have applications that extend far beyond merely "selling room nights."

For example, through programs such as Wide World of Golf and the cruise redemption program, Preferred properties and travel agents can work together to sell complete "experiential packages" for the affluent traveler. Travel agents enter Preferred's luxury marketing "loop" as partners and build relationships with discerning travelers. This goes well beyond the usual booking of air travel and hotels on the basis of price and availability. Client building is achieved through educational seminars, training programs, and special package promotions. Agents are encouraged to position themselves as key components of Preferred's affluent marketing channel.[1]

Success in the marketplace is not guaranteed by understanding marketing concepts and strategies. Successful marketing requires planning and careful execution. It is easy to become so involved in the day-to-day problems of running a marketing department that little or no time is devoted to planning. When this occurs, the marketing department is probably operating without purpose and is being reactive rather than proactive. Even experienced managers sometimes fail to see that this is occurring until it is too late. This may be one of the root causes for high turnover within hospitality, marketing, and sales departments.

■■■ Purpose of a Marketing Plan

A marketing plan serves several of the following purposes within any hospitality company:

- Provides a road map for all marketing activities of the firm for the next year.

- Ensures that marketing activities are in agreement with the corporate strategic plan.

- Forces marketing managers to review and think through objectively all steps in the marketing process.

- Assists in the budgeting process to match resources with marketing objectives.

- Creates a process to monitor actual against expected results.

The development of a marketing plan is a rigorous process and cannot be accomplished in a few hours. Instead, it is best to set aside one or more days to develop next year's plan. Many marketing managers find it best to leave the office along with their staff and all necessary data while writing the plan. Constant interruptions that occur in the office are detrimental to the planning process.

To be effective, a new marketing plan must be written each year. Marketing plans written for periods longer than a year are generally not effective. At the same time, the annual marketing plan must be written against a longer-term strategic plan that states what the company hopes to achieve, say, three to five years down the road.

Many managers believe that the process of writing a plan is invaluable because it forces those writing it to question, think, and strategize. A plan should be developed with the input and assistance of key members of the marketing department. The discussion and thought process required to produce a plan is stimulating and very helpful in team building. It is also an excellent training device for younger staff members who wish to be managers.

Marketing plans are not created in a vacuum. To develop successful strategies and action programs, marketers need up-to-date information about the environment, the competition, and the market segments to be served. Often, analysis of internal data is the starting point for assessing the current marketing situation, supplemented by marketing intelligence and research investigating the overall market, the competition, key issues, and threats and opportunities. As the plan is put into effect, marketers use a variety of research techniques to measure progress toward objectives and identify areas for improvement if results fall short of projections.

Finally, marketing research helps marketers learn more about their customers' requirements, expectations, perceptions, and satisfaction levels. This deeper understanding provides a foundation for building competitive advantage through well-informed segmenting, targeting, differentiating, and positioning decisions. Thus, the marketing plan should outline what marketing research will be conducted and how the findings will be applied.

The marketing plan shows how the company will establish and maintain profitable customer relationships. In the process, however, it also shapes a number of internal and external relationships. First, it affects how marketing personnel work with each other and with other departments to deliver value and satisfy customers. Second, it affects how the company works with suppliers, distributors, and strategic alliance partners to achieve the objectives listed in the plan. Third, it influences the company's dealings with other stakeholders, including government regulators, the media, and the community at large. All of these relationships are important to the organization's success, so they should be considered when a marketing plan is being developed.

Unlike a business plan, which offers a broad overview of the entire organization's mission, objectives, strategy, and resource allocation, a marketing plan has a more limited scope. It serves to describe how the organization's strategic objectives will be achieved through specific marketing strategies and tactics, with the customer as the starting point. It is also linked to the plans of other departments within the organization. Suppose a marketing plan calls for selling 200,000 units annually. The production department must gear up to make that many units, the finance department must arrange funding to cover the expenses, the human resources department must be ready to hire and train staff, and so on. Without the appropriate level of organizational support and resources, no marketing plan can succeed.

Although the exact length and layout varies from company to company, a marketing plan usually contains the sections described in this chapter. To guide implementation effectively, every part of the plan must be described in considerable detail. Sometimes a company posts its marketing plan on an internal Web site, which allows managers and employees in different locations to consult specific sections and collaborate on additions or changes. We now discuss the following sections of a marketing plan in detail.

   I. Executive Summary

  II. Corporate Connection

 III. Environmental Analysis and Forecasting

 IV. Segmentation and Targeting

  V. Next Year's Objectives and Quotas

 VI. Action Plans: Strategies and Tactics

 VII. Resources Needed to Support Strategies and Meet Objectives

VIII. Marketing Control

 IX. Presenting and Selling the Plan

  X. Preparing for the Future

We examine the role played by each section of the marketing plan.

■■■ Section I: Executive Summary

Executive summary. A short summary of the marketing plan to quickly inform top executives.

The **executive summary** and a few charts or graphs from the body of the plan may be the only parts ever read by top management. Consequently, it is of great importance to write this section carefully, with top management in mind.

The following few tips may assist in writing the executive summary:

- Write it for top executives.

- Limit the number of pages to between two and four.

- Use short sentences and short paragraphs. Avoid using words that are unlikely to be understood.

- Organize the summary as follows: Describe next year's objectives in quantitative terms; briefly describe marketing strategies to meet goals and objectives, including a description of target markets; describe expected results by quarter; and identify the dollar costs necessary, as well as key resources needed.

- Read and reread the executive summary several times. Never write it once and then place it in the plan. Modify and change the summary until it flows well, is easily read, and conveys the central message of the marketing plan.

■■■ Section II: Corporate Connection

Relationship to Other Plans

A marketing plan is not a stand-alone tool. Instead, it must support other plans, such as the firm's strategic plan. Whenever possible, the marketing manager should participate in or provide input to the development of a strategic plan. If this is not practical, it remains imperative to understand the contents of the strategic plan prior to development of next year's marketing plan.

A marketing plan supports the company's strategic plan in several ways. Next year's marketing strategies and tactics must support strategic decisions such as the following:

- Corporate goals with respect to profit, growth, and so on
- Desired market share
- Positioning of the company or of its product lines
- Vertical or horizontal integration
- Strategic alliances
- Product-line breadth and depth
- Customer-relationship management (CRM)

Marketing-Related Plans

In large corporations, marketing-related plans are sometimes developed by people who do not report to marketing. This is usually the result of (1) originally establishing these departments independent of marketing, (2) political maneuvering in which a nonmarketing executive desired control of these areas, and (3) the failure of top management to understand the need to unify marketing-related activities.

Marketing-related areas in which plans are sometimes written independently of marketing include the following:

- Sales
- Advertising and promotion
- Public relations and publicity
- Marketing research
- Pricing
- Customer service

The director of sales works with his/her sales managers on the marketing plan. Courtesy of Antonio Diaz/Fotolia.

If these plans are developed independently of a marketing plan with no consideration as to how they tie together, the result is often chaotic, counterproductive, and a source for continuous infighting among marketing-related areas.

When the organizational design of a company fails to place major marketing activities under the marketing umbrella, the task of writing and implementing a marketing plan is made more complex. Under these conditions, it behooves the marketing manager to invite the managers of other marketing-related areas to participate in the marketing plan development process. This action should then be reciprocated.

The activities of marketing and many other departments within a company are closely intertwined. Operations and finance are two areas that affect and in turn are affected by marketing. If guest experiences are diminished because of problem areas in operations, marketing will be adversely affected. Similarly, if financial projections are unrealistic for certain months or for various product lines, marketing will be called to task.

It is unrealistic to expect perfect harmony between marketing and other departments. It is by no means unrealistic to suggest that relations can usually be greatly improved and that a critical place to begin is by interchanging data, suggestions, and other assistance when department plans are being developed.

Corporate Direction

A good marketing plan begins with the fact that the only purpose of marketing is to support the enterprise. It is good politics and good sense to begin next year's plan by recognizing and restating these corporate elements. Let top management know that the following helped guide the development of next year's plan:

- Mission statement
- Corporate philosophy
- Corporate goals

Hospitality companies are highly sensitive to changes in their social, political, and economic environments. A manufacturer of food or toiletries may not immediately feel the impact of these changes, but airlines, hotels, auto rental firms, and cruise lines witness an instant reaction.

■■■ Section III: Environmental Analysis and Forecasting

After the terrorist attacks of September 11, 2001, U.S. hospitality firms felt the impact. Pleasure travel instantly evaporated as fear of terrorism gripped Americans. Unfortunately, some companies responded without clearly thinking. Several hotel chains quickly offered substantial discounts to guests. This did nothing to increase demand but instead simply gave discounts to people who had to travel for business and would have paid a higher rate. A marketing plan is not a political or economic treatise, and hospitality marketers are not expected to be experts in these fields. They are expected to be aware of major **environmental factors** likely to affect the industry and the company, to consider their possible impact on marketing, and to respond quickly and intelligently to new events and trends.

Environmental factors. Social, political, and economic factors that affect a firm and its marketing program.

Positioning Statement

A marketing plan should provide a positioning statement of how the enterprise intends to differentiate—position itself—in the marketplace. This provides essential guidance to the rest of the plan.

Major airlines such as American Airlines have traditionally positioned themselves as hub-and-spoke carriers serving multimarket segments and as market share companies. Other airlines have positioned themselves as low-price niche carriers, serving point-to-point markets.

Small resort hotels usually position themselves as providers of vacation/holiday service for individuals, couples, and small groups. Larger resort hotels position themselves as serving this market but also serving the corporate seminar, meeting, and conference market.

A limousine service positions itself differently from a taxi cab business. A tour bus business positions itself differently from a sightseeing bus business.

All members of the marketing and sales departments and their service suppliers such as ad agencies, public relations firms, marketing research firms, and others must know the desired positioning of the enterprise. Otherwise, their efforts may result in a confused array of strategies, tactics, and results that may not serve the company well.

Tourist/visitor destinations usually have a more difficult task selecting a single unifying positioning statement usually due to political pressures and end up trying to be all things to all people. It is little wonder that their advertising and sales tactics mimic others.

Major Environmental Factors

Hospitality organizations need to anticipate the influence of these broad environmental factors on their business.

Social

Consider the possible impact of major social factors, such as crime and changing demographics. These factors vary in their intensity and their geographic incidence. Social factors relevant to Los Angeles, California, or Sydney, Australia, may have little relevance to Rapid City, South Dakota.

Social conditions sometimes change rapidly to the benefit of alert marketers. The hotel market within India had long been considered as uninteresting by many hotel chains. Today, India's social and economic structures have become conducive to mid-priced hotel development. The emergence of a potentially gigantic market has attracted many chains, including Holiday Inn Worldwide, Choice Hotels, Carlson Hotels Worldwide, Southern Pacific Hotels (Australia), and Oberoi Hotels and Resorts (India).

Political

Legislation affecting taxation, pension benefits, and casino gambling are only a few examples of political decisions likely to affect marketing directly. International politics is increasingly important to corporate hospitality marketing plans. The opening of Vietnam to investors and tourists after years of being off limits provides risk as well as rewards for the hospitality industry.[2] The same will undoubtedly be true with Cuba.

Economic

Changes in economic variables such as employment and interest rates should be recognized. The hospitality industry, especially the lodging and cruising sectors, is highly sensitive to business-cycle movements.

Terrorism

The horrific terrorist attacks on the Taj Mahal Palace Hotel and the Hotel Oberoi Trident in November 2008 killed 164 people and wounded at least 308.[3] These attacks suddenly brought terrorism to the worldwide hospitality industry. In December 2014, the Lindt Café in Sydney, Australia, was the target of terrorism. In January 2015, the headquarters of Charlie Hebdo and a Jewish Kosher supermarket/deli in Paris also suffered terrorism attacks.

Clearly, all segments of the hospitality industry are at risk as targets of terrorism. A security plan concerning terrorism should be an integral part of the planning process for any company/organization within the hospitality industry. Your employees and guests are at risk in the absence of such a plan. It is not the function of a marketing plan but marketing/sales executives have a responsibility to urge upper management to take this subject seriously if they have not already done so.

Economic Drivers of Growth

Economic drivers of growth have the ability to rapidly affect change. Marketers must be aware of these drivers before, during, and after entry into a market. An example is the Aerotropolis, which has been seriously considered for some communities.

The Aerotropolis

The term *aerotropolis* was developed by Professor John D. Kasarda of the University of North Carolina. An aerotropolis is a transportation and urban development concept built around an airport. An aerotropolis is designed to serve as a powerful economic development force. These centers are built to facilitate the rapid movement of freight and passengers, such as Schiphol Airport in the Netherlands. A huge market for flowers and plants, Bloemenveiling Aalsmeer of Amsterdam, exists in tiny Netherlands as the largest and most important market in Europe. This is due in heavy part to the existence of Schiphol Airport.

Many aerotropolis centers are being built in China, Korea, and other nations where they serve as centers for tourism, transportation, and international business. Hotels, restaurants, and entertainment centers are critical participants in a successful aerotropolis.[4]

Competitive Analysis

Competitive analysis. An analysis of the primary strengths and weaknesses, objectives, strategies, and other information relative to competitors.

It is common practice for hospitality companies to conduct a **competitive analysis**. In some cases, this analysis deals primarily with the observable physical properties of a competitor. For example,

Our Hotel	Their Hotel
500 rooms	600 rooms
One ballroom	Two ballrooms
Executive center	No executive center

An analysis solely of physical differences usually misses major competitive advantages or disadvantages. It is doubtful that most guests know or care about the room count of competitive hotels. They do recognize differences in service level, cleanliness, staff knowledge, and the responsiveness of the sales department. A competitive analysis must extend beyond inventory comparisons. True competitive advantages are factors that are recognized by guests and influence their purchase decisions. A creative and alert marketing manager recognizes competitive variables that are truly of importance to the customers and are controllable. Such a manager develops strategies and tactics to improve areas of weakness and enhance already strong points.

Based strictly on a comparison of physical attributes, many hospitality firms should not exist. Bed and breakfast (B&B) establishments are usually old homes without a swimming pool and may have shared bathrooms, yet they fill a competitive niche. Hertz and Avis may compete head-to-head, offering clean, late-model cars, but Rent-a-Wreck auto rental company successfully offers automobiles that many people would be ashamed to be seen driving.

The single best way to conduct a competitive analysis is to involve members of the marketing sales department, such as the sales force. These people often have difficulty discussing environmental variables such as interest rates, but they can talk knowledgeably for hours about the competition and guest preferences.

Market Trends

Market trends. External trends of many types that are likely to affect the marketing in which a corporation operates.

Market trends are a reflection of environmental competitive variables. Market trend information for the hospitality industry is often available from outside organizations free of charge. Common sources include chambers of commerce, visitors' bureaus, universities, government agencies, banks, trade associations, and commercial organizations such as firms of certified public accountants or consultants who carry public information for publicity purposes.

Useful market trend information for writing a hospitality marketing plan includes the following:

- *Visitor trends:* Origination areas, stopover sites, visitor demographics, spending habits, length of stay, and so on.

- *Competitive trends:* Numbers, location, type of products offered (e.g., all-suite hotels), occupancy levels, average rates, and so on.

- *Related industry trends:* Interdependence of the members of the hospitality industry with airline flights, convention center bookings, new airport construction, and new highways. It is important to study trends for supporting or related industries.

Caterers of in-flight meals were dramatically affected by the trend among U.S. airlines to eliminate or reduce onboard meal service. Companies such as Dobbs International Services, which provided full-course meals, had to find new markets and new products. Caterair International Corporation diversified into the repair of airplane audio headsets, and Sky Chefs explored the private-label business and food preparation for prisons, schools, and hospitals. Randall C. Boyd, senior vice president of marketing and customer service for Sky Chefs, said, "We are good sandwich makers, salad makers, and pasta makers. Whether a prisoner or a college student is eating our sandwich, we don't care."[5]

Select only those trends that are useful in developing the plan. It is of no value to fill a plan with pages of information that have little or no direct relevancy. Unfortunately, it is common to read marketing plans prepared by professionals that are filled with "boilerplate" (statistics, tables, and graphs that are interesting and colorful but have little relevance to the marketing needs of a particular company or organization). Thousands of dollars are spent on so-called marketing plans filled with boilerplate.

Market Potential

Market potential. The total estimated dollars or unit value of a defined market for a defined product, including competitive products.

Estimates of **market potential** often seem to be ignored by those who write hospitality marketing plans. Marketing managers in hotels sometimes feel that the concept has no application to them. "We view all travelers as potential guests" is a frequently heard comment. Others reply that the concept is theoretical for the hospitality industry and applies primarily to consumer-packaged goods.

These opinions are incorrect! Although it is true that measurement of true market potential is impossible, estimates can and should be made. The hospitality industry is notorious for ignoring or misinterpreting market potential estimates, thus leading to overbuilding, overcapacity, price cutting, and frantic advertising and promotion in an attempt to fill rooms or fill seats.

Market potential should be viewed as the total available demand for a hospitality product within a particular geographic market at a given price. It is important not to mix different hospitality products into an estimate of market potential.

It is common to hear individuals speak of the market for hotel rooms in a region as a number of room nights or gross number of travelers. For purposes of writing a marketing plan, such figures are interesting but do not indicate market potential for your products. Most markets consist of a mix of hotel properties, ranging from luxury to budget, with specialty lodging such as all-suites, condominium hotels, and B&Bs.

There has been an explosion of branded hotels in Shanghai and throughout China. Courtesy of Robepco/Fotolia.

Each type of property faces its own peculiar market potential, except for times when a special event fills every bed in town. Estimates of market potential normally begin by examining the market for all hotels but should then shift to specific markets for your hotel and directly competitive properties, often referred to as a competitive set. To be precise, market potential estimates should be shown as demand estimates at various price points; however, this is generally unnecessary for most marketing plans. The average marketing manager for a property such as a hotel finds it impossible to make good quantitative estimates of market potential in room nights or dollars. These people lack marketing research support, and most were not trained in quantitative analysis. Therefore, market potential estimates are often expressed in "guesstimates," such as "The market seems to be growing or declining by about 5 percent a year."

Warning! Even though precise estimates may be beyond the abilities of many hospitality marketing managers, it is essential to go through the thought process of examining market potential. Never assume that market potential is static or unimportant to marketing success. The use of revenue management has created greatly improved estimates of market potential.

By engaging in the process of estimating market potential, those who develop marketing plans become aware of potentially important market conditions and can then adjust marketing strategies appropriately. Remember, the process of developing a marketing plan is not a precise discipline such as engineering or chemistry. The exercise of writing a plan is usually as important to marketing success as the plan itself.

Estimated marketing potential led U.S. ski resort developers to Asia. The world's highest and snowiest mountains remained virtually untapped for snow resorts. Developers estimated that 3 percent of the Chinese population might be potential skiers. This meant 43.3 million people.

The managing director of the project estimated a market potential of 100 million people with sufficient disposable income. Professor Simon Hudson of the University of Calgary said there are 70 million skiers and snowboarders worldwide and that if 3 percent of India's population took up skiing that would be a 36.6 million person market.[6]

Although these estimates of market potential are not very sophisticated, they represent the kind of potential that excite entrepreneurs and investors.

Lodging Market Potential Index (L-MPI©)

A joint research project between the School of Hospitality Business, Michigan State University's Center for International Business Education and Research (MSU-CIBER), and Global Edge developed the Lodging Market Potential Index.

According to the developers of this index, it is useful as a first step in hotel development, investment, and acquisition decisions. They state that this market index identifies market areas that show long-term potential for hotel development and will enable hotel developers and investors to conduct a relative comparison of the 25 largest lodging markets.[7]

Marketing Research

The need for marketing intelligence is ongoing. Much of the information acquired by marketing research in a current calendar or fiscal year serves as the basis for developing next year's marketing plan. Marketing research needs vary considerably by type and size of the hospitality company. Companies such as Hertz or Hilton Hotels have corporate marketing research departments. An individual hotel property or car rental location may have a need for additional marketing information. In these cases, the individual property or location is generally responsible for acquiring these data.

Marketing research needs can usually be divided into macromarket and micromarket information. Macromarket information includes, but is not restricted to, the following:

- Industry trends
- Socioeconomic and political trends
- Competitive information
- Industry-wide customer data

Micromarket information includes, but is not restricted to, the following:

- Guest information
- Product/service information
- New-product analysis and testing

Marketing HIGHLIGHT 18–1   The Indigo Pearl Resort: Facebook Strategy and Planning the Indigo Pearl

The Indigo Pearl Resort is an independent, luxury design property located in Phuket, Thailand. Michael Nurbatlain joined the resort as a sales manager, but this role quickly expanded to include managing digital marketing, e-commerce, and social media.[8]

Indigo Pearl Resort had witnessed a clear shift in its market mix: growing from a heavy reliance on tour operators to direct bookings and online channels. Michael Nurbatlain and the team at Indigo Pearl led this growth by developing a presence in a variety of channels, with Facebook emerging as one of the biggest successes. In just one year, Michael grew the resort's Facebook fan page to more than 8,000 followers. "While Twitter is beginning to gain popularity here in Asia, Facebook has nearly complete market adoption with our customers," said Michael.

It's all about planning. "Have a solid plan when it comes to Facebook, and create an editorial calendar. Be very strict about creating and following deadlines." Too many people just wake up in the morning and try to create content on the fly. "If there is no solid plan for 3–12 months, it's difficult to consistently deliver good quality results."

Facebook Contents: The Key to Growth

"Last year we wanted to give something to our Facebook fans," said Michael. "At the time, we had about 3,000 fans, and decided to create a photo contest around what symbolizes Indigo Pearl."

Fans were asked to post pictures, and then vote on their favorites. But Facebook contacted them, saying the contest setup violated terms and conditions. This forced them to set up an independent voting scheme allowing their fans to vote, which worked even better in the end. The contest generated great interaction among existing fans, strengthening their online community. Additionally, the contest generated a couple of hundred new fans—which was considered a great success at that time.

Latest Facebook Contest: Ultimate Holiday Package

This year's idea was to set up a new system. Rather than just asking fans to submit pictures, Indigo Pearl Resort wanted to add another layer of involvement. Michael and Indigo Pearl Resort asked fans to design their dream three-day holiday package. What would they like to do in Phuket? The resort was not very strict with the guidelines, so that if someone wrote some poetry about the perfect holiday, for example, it was still accepted as an entry.

"I imagined Mercedes running a promotion around designing your dream car," said Michael. "Although I'm a big fan of cars, I wouldn't know what horsepower to put in or the details of the engine. While our guests travel a lot, they are not hoteliers, so it would be somewhat difficult for them to come up with a breakdown package of all the amenities, so we left it very open."

"We didn't buy any Facebook ads or spend much time promoting the content." Michael worked a bit with the local media to get mentioned on their Web sites and sent out some tweets to promote it. But no other public relations or press releases were used. Everything was done through Facebook.

"Within days we had 10–15 entries and then we started to get a snowball effect. We asked fans to send in their pictures, screened them and placed the photos in the album called Ultimate Family Package. Once the photo was approved, the contest participants could ask their friends and family to vote on the entry."

"This is what created a VIRAL MARKETING effect for the resort. One photo had over 1,000 likes. It surpassed our expectations and we could hardly believe it."

Lessons Learned

- You work hard to generate friends and followers. Remember they are important assets of your online community. Treat them with respect and courtesy. Respond to comments whether they are positive or negative. Thank those who post positive comments and thank those that post negative comments for bringing the issue to your attention. Remember that other members of the community will observe how you handle negative comments.

- For online contests have multiple prizes. People realize that winning a contest online is a low probably. Having multiple prizes increases the perception that winning is a possibility and will result in more participation.

- Photos are an essential component of Facebook. Pictures of your guests enjoying your property, tourists enjoying a destination or guests enjoying a trip you planned will receive more likes than a long post. Pictures attract attention and it is often easier to post a picture with a short note than a written post.

- Avoid using Facebook as an advertising medium. Post items that will be of interest to your community. A special promotion may be of interest, but promotions should be infrequent. They should account for less than 10% of your posts.

- There should be consistency between the brand values and brand personality communicated to online communities and the brand values and personality guests observe when the visit your property and/or interact with your employees.

- Intermediary buyer data
- Pricing studies
- Key account information
- Advertising/promotion effectiveness

Print Publications

An enjoyable and worthwhile method of keeping up with trends is to continuously read publications in your field such as hotel, restaurant, cruise line, golfing, all-inclusive resorts, and others. Also worthwhile are general business publications such as *The Wall Street Journal*.

The August 27, 2014, edition of this publication carried news about a new hotel chain (Graduate Hotels) that targeted college towns. College towns were selected since many are located in sometimes overlooked and small towns.

"While the big brands have been obsessive about chasing after the millennial generation, Graduate Hotels aim for an older guest of 35 years of age." This market and even older segments visit college towns with their high-school-age children or grandchildren to attend sporting events or to introduce their alma mater to the next generation. Graduate Hotels each have a bar and restaurant, locally inspired art collections, and 100 to 150 rooms priced slightly above limited-service hotels in the area.[9] Remember that reporters from printed publications do much of the initial market research for you.

Another proven method of collecting marketing information is to personally visit the company's properties, distributors who serve the company, employees, customers, franchisees, and others knowledgeable about the company.

After assuming the position of CEO of CiCi Pizza in 2009, Mr. Mike Shumsky visited many of the company's 650 restaurants, of which only 16 were company owned. Following this trip told CiCi Pizza managers, I have visited your operations and listened to your comments. I have told you how I will react to what I have learned from you. For your part we have to become one brand.[10]

Harrah's Entertainment, Inc. (Harrah's), has proven to the worldwide hospitality industry that CRM combined with technology and management support can provide impressive financial results while extending a close relationship with one's customers (see Chapter 5). Under the leadership of Gary Loveman, a former Harvard professor, this casino company developed Harrah's Winner Information Network. The system required a substantial investment to capture data from the different customer touch points as the customers moved through and between Harrah's casinos and resorts. Harrah's used data mining and experiments using different offers to see what created the most value for their customers.[11]

Harrah's left little to chance. It invested more than $100 million in computers and software to develop what is widely regarded as the industry's most sophisticated "frequent bettor" program. With the Total Rewards program, which contains the world's largest database of casino customers, it has been able to create sustainable loyalty, a dominant competitive advantage.

Harrah's innovative idea was to grow by getting more business from its existing customer base. This approach was in contrast to the strategy of building ever more elaborate and splashy new casinos. Gary W. Loveman refers to its success as "the triumph of software over hardware in gaming."

The Total Rewards program increased traffic in Harrah's casinos. Marketing programs driven by data increased retention. Keeping customers goes right to the bottom line. An increase in retention of just 1 percent is worth $2 million in net profit annually.[12]

The success of Harrah's clearly demonstrated that new strategies and tactics are essential for all members of the hospitality industry. Technology, CRM, and social marketing pose dramatic opportunities to marketers. Traditional support areas such as marketing research and advertising must support management with new concepts and quantitative answers or perish. It is no longer sufficient to be content with customer surveys, in-room questionnaires, and advertising research measuring such nebulous intangibles as "share of mind."

■■■ Section IV: Segmentation and Targeting

Segmentation Analysis

The heart of any marketing plan is careful analysis of available market segments and the selection of appropriate target markets. Not all market segments are appropriate for a hospitality company. The selection of segments is the result of (1) understanding what the company is and what it wishes to be and (2) studying available segments and determining if they fit the capabilities and desires of the company to obtain and secure them.

A common mistake within the hospitality industry is the selection of inappropriate segments. Marketing managers commonly err by allowing or encouraging the acquisition of low-yield segments in an effort to maintain occupancy. At the opposite extreme, companies sometimes feel they are serving "low-class" customers and attempt to attract quite different segments. If this is done in the absence of genuine product/service changes, the chances for success are slim to nonexistent.

In the case of a hotel, "A marketing plan tells you who is using your hotel and where you can look to expand your business."[13] The Los Angeles Biltmore Hotel had been the center of Los Angeles society for many years, but the property began to deteriorate and was sold. The new owners faced the task of restoring life to the hotel. One of the first discoveries by the new owners was that the Biltmore's marketing plan was confused. Some people believed that the hotel catered only to groups and tours, whereas others felt the hotel did not want their business and marketed only to commercial and transient guests. The guest mix was found to be 28 percent commercial, 40 percent groups, and 32 percent leisure. The new management decided that a more appropriate mix was 40 percent commercial, 50 percent groups, and 10 percent leisure. With this directive in mind, the hotel was able to establish a new marketing plan that included repositioning the hotel, changing food and beverage operations, and changing prices.[14]

Analysis of Internal Data	Analysis of External Data
Guest registrations	Published industry information
Credit card receipts	Marketing research
Customer surveys	Guesstimates after talking with competitors, vendors, and others in the industry
Customer database	

When developing a marketing plan, marketers must look to both internal and external data sources for information concerning market segments.

Market-Segment-Profitability Analysis (MSPA)

Information that identifies each of a company's existing customer segments by revenue, cost, and profitability is extremely valuable but information about guests by segment is often not gathered or not analyzed. "Hotel marketers usually focus on customer segments. On the other hand, accountants record and report the operational results by department, not market segments."[15]

Market segment profitability data are even less likely to be available for most restaurants and are virtually nonexistent for tourism marketers such as those with most convention and visitor bureaus.

Targeting

No area of the marketing plan surpasses the selection of target markets in importance. If inappropriate markets are selected, marketing resources will be wasted. A high level of expenditures for advertising or sales promotion cannot compensate for misdirected marketing efforts.

Like the previous example of the Los Angeles Biltmore Hotel, targeting begins by defining the mix of desired guests. Commonly used broad groupings for guests are listed in the following table:

Business	Versus	Pleasure
Individual guests		IT (individuals who make their own reservations)
Conventions		
Seminars/conferences		GIT (group-inclusive tours)

The selection of a customer/guest mix must support the positioning strategy of the company. The mix should also support revenue management. This is not always the case. It is altogether too common for marketing/sales to plan and operate without consulting or working with the revenue management department.

Target markets are selected from the list of available segments. These include segments currently served by the company and newly recognized markets. The selection of target markets is a primary responsibility of marketing management. This requires careful consideration of the variables already discussed in the development of the marketing plan. Far too many marketing managers in the hospitality industry simply select last year's target markets. Although it is normally true that the majority of target markets remain the same, new ones appear and the order of importance can change between years.

Many Asian and Australian hotel managers discovered that their key segments in terms of spending and room nights were no longer American or European guests. Guests from Asian nations surpassed in importance than those from Western nations.

Women travelers represent a solid and growing percentage of travelers. Observation of hotel advertisements shows that hotel marketers realize the importance of this segment.

A study of gender-based lodging preferences showed that "there were several significant differences between male and female business travelers in their hotel selection and use criteria."[16] For instance, women considered security, room service, and low price to be more important, whereas men were more concerned about the availability of suite rooms with separate bed and office spaces.

Marketing planners need to stay abreast of such preferences, relay them to other departments within the hotel, and use this information in the selection of market segments.

An interesting market is couples expecting their first baby. These are people who delayed having children until their mid-thirties and want a "last hurrah" together before the infant arrives. The Bodega Bay Lodge and Spa in California offers a one-night babymoon package. Guest preferences change from champagne and a heated spa to bottled water and a gentle massage.[17]

Tourism Targets

Marketing plans for tourism marketers use a similar format to the hospitality industry for writing a marketing plan but the initial definition of targets may be quite broad. The following example for the Tourism 2020 Strategy, Tourism Australia, provides an example of initially broad targets.

Global Market Strategy—Australia[18]

"To achieve the Tourism 2020 Strategy, Tourism Australia will focus the majority of its global marketing resources on markets which represent the greatest potential for tourism growth to the year 2020. Tourism Australia will also target those emerging markets that have the strongest growth potential, and will continue to support rest-of-world markets.

Key markets have been categorized by the potential of growth in visitor spend by 2020. Visitor spend, tracked by the International Visitor Survey, refers to the amount of Australian dollar (AUD) spent by travelers in Australia."

The following were taken from the Global Market Strategy—Australia.

Visitor spend by the following markets has the potential to be worth over $5 billion by 2020:

- Greater China (China and Hong Kong)
- North America (United States and Canada)
- United Kingdom
- Australia

Visitor spend by the following markets has the potential to be worth over $2.5 billion by 2020:

- New Zealand
- South Korea
- Singapore
- Malaysia

Visitor spend by the following markets has the potential to be worth over $1 billion by 2020:

- Japan
- Indonesia
- India
- Germany

After identifying major macromarkets, tourism planners/marketers tend to look for broad sub-segments such as leisure versus business and then sub-segments within these such as active-passive leisure travelers with more sub-segments such as saltwater sports, mountain bike enthusiasts, or snow skiing under active leisure travelers.

Further sub-segmentation may use postal codes such as those for Los Angeles and San Francisco in the United States. Business travelers may be identified as professional professors, medical doctors, engineers, or managers of corporations.

What are the sources of information for such segmentation? National (federal) tourism planners review travel information cards required by most nations for individuals entering their nations. Beyond that, tourism planners may build a database of studies compiled by universities, private consulting/research firms, airlines, cruise ships, and others. These organizations may also commission researchers to find out more about specific markets/market segments.

Tourism ministries, bureaus, visitor centers, and others responsible for tourism/marketing planning and implementation provide employment for many university/college graduates in business, economics, hospitality, tourism, and other related fields.

■■■ Section V: Next Year's Objectives and Quotas

Objectives

Timetable. Specific dates to accomplish strategies and tactics.

The establishment of objectives provides direction for the rest of the marketing plan. The purpose of marketing strategies and tactics is to support objectives. The marketing budget must be sufficient to ensure adequate resources to achieve objectives and to meet **timetables** that describe the time period in which expected sales results will occur.

Occasionally, there is confusion as to what constitutes an objective. Statements such as "To be the best in our industry" or "To provide excellent guest service" are accepted as objectives. That is always an error because these types of statements are slogans or mottos. They are not objectives. The following are examples of objectives:

- Quantitative (expressed in monetary terms [dollars, pesos] or unit measurements such as room nights, passenger miles, number of cars to rent, or occupancy)

- Time specific (one year, six months)

- Profit/margin specific (e.g., an average margin of 22 percent)

The process of establishing objectives is not an easy task and should not be accomplished by simply adding a random percentage to last year's objectives.

Objectives should be established after carefully considering the areas already discussed.

- Corporate goals
- Corporate resources
- Environmental factors
- Competition
- Market trends
- Market potential
- Available market segments and possible target markets

To ensure profitability and remain competitive in today's marketplace, it has become necessary to establish several sub-objectives. For instance, a hotel with 1,000 rooms undoubtedly will have two broad objectives: average occupancy and average room rate. By themselves, these objectives do not serve as sufficient guides for developing marketing strategies. A set of sub-objectives is needed, as shown in Table 18–1.

Other sub-objectives may also be established by the marketing department. Again, these should support corporate goals and next year's primary objectives. They should never stand alone as objectives, unrelated to the primary function of the marketing department.

Each marketing support area needs to be guided by a set of sub-objectives. This includes areas such as advertising, promotion, public relations, marketing research, and, of course, sales.

Establishing measurable quantitative objectives for these areas is not an easy task, but increasingly, top management is requiring that such be done. Advertising and promotion are areas in which measurement of results is particularly difficult. Management would like to know what the dollar return was for advertising or how much market share or occupancy increased as a result of advertising/promotion. With few exceptions, such as direct advertising, current measurement techniques do not permit accurate measurements of this type. Consequently, objectives for advertising, such as share of mind and awareness level, are commonly used. These are not suitable substitutes.

Rating System Objectives

Some hotels are obsessed with ratings. The management of these hotels may drive corporate behavior, including marketing/sales, to help the hotel achieve another star or diamond or other symbol rating.

Because Internet distribution, companies, and user customers rely on ratings, it is quite possible that many additional hotels will set objectives to attain higher ratings.

TABLE 18–1

Examples of Objectives Common to the Hotel Industry

Objectives	Average Occupancy	Average Room Rate
Sub-objectives	Occupancy per period of time Seasonal: prime, shoulder, trough	Average rate per period of time and by type of room
	Monthly	
	Weekly	
	Daily	
	Weekend	
	Midweek	

	Types of Sleeping Rooms	By Time
	Suites	Seasonal
	Poolside	Monthly
	Regular room	Weekly
		Daily
		Weekend
	Occupancy by type of sleeping room	*Note:* Yield objectives are used by many members of the hospitality industry, such as hotels, rental cars, cruise lines, airlines, and passenger rail.
	Suites	
	Pool side	
	Cabaña	
	Cottage	
	Regular sleeping rooms	
	Occupancy per type of function room	
	Ballroom	
	Seminar room	
	Executive conference room	

Objectives	Annual Sales by	Annual Sales by: Units Dollars
	Time period	
	Seasonal	
	Monthly	
	Weekly	
	Daily	
	Weekend	
	Department	
	Group sales	
	Incentive sales	
	Sales territory	
	Eastern United States	
	Western United States	
	Salesperson	
	Joe	
	Sally	
	June	
	Fred	

Quotas

Quotas. Quantitative and time-specific accomplishment measurements established for members of a sales force.

No word creates more fear within the sales/marketing department than **quotas**. Yet, without quotas, the probability of accomplishing objectives is slim at best. To be effective, quotas must be:

- based on next year's objectives;
- individualized;
- realistic and obtainable;
- broken down to small units, such as each salesperson's quota per week; and
- understandable and measurable (e.g., quota = $10,000 sales for product line x in week 5). An example of a quota that is not understandable or measurable is "to obtain 10 percent increase of market share early in the year."

Communicating the Plan

A sophisticated and brilliantly developed plan is of no use if it is not understood, believed, or used. "A marketing plan should not be just a call to action or a benchmark by which to judge the efficiency and effectiveness of decisions. The plan should also serve as a method for communicating marketing strategy to people whose duty it is to implement or authorize the company's marketing strategies."[19] Several groups may serve as an audience for a marketing plan.

Top Management

This group must be convinced that the plan will accomplish the stated goals and objectives. Top management demonstrates acceptance or denial by its level of monetary support.

Marketing managers should strive for more than budgeting support. If top management buys in and demonstrates visible support, morale within the marketing department will increase, and other departments will be willing to lend support. To the contrary, the company grapevine quickly knows if marketing is only weakly supported by top management. Support from others will be weak at best if there is a perception that management is not solidly behind marketing.

Board of Directors or Group of Investors

Occasionally, a board of directors or an investor's group may ask to be apprised of next year's marketing plan. This group generally does not seek details but instead wants to know the answers to the following questions:

- Does the plan support corporate goals?
- What are the dollars and unit objectives?
- What are the major strategies to achieve these objectives?
- What is the cost?
- When can we expect to see results?
- Does the plan support revenue management objectives?

Subordinates

Members of the marketing and sales departments must understand and support the marketing plan. It is important to develop a group mentality that the marketing plan for next year is a realistic and important road map. Unfortunately, far too many people in hospitality companies believe that the development of a marketing plan is a waste of time because no one will ever pay it any heed.

The InterContinental Playa Bonita Resort and Spa is part of Bern Hotels and Resorts. Bern operates hotels throughout Panama. It is important that each hotel has a marketing plan that fits with the corporate plan. Courtesy by Bern Hotels and Resorts.

Vendors

It is important to transmit some aspects of the marketing plan to selected vendors. This is particularly true as strategic alliances develop. Vendors such as advertising agencies, marketing research firms, computer software providers, public relations firms, and consultants need to know and understand the marketing plan. It may be advisable to include these people in the plan's development. Supply chain management is not generally a responsibility assigned to marketing, but there are strategic alliances between hospitality companies and suppliers that affect the pricing, customer service, and other marketing functions. It is in the best interests of marketing to cooperate closely with those responsible for supply chain management. Advances in this management tool could and probably will affect what marketing will do. Such changes may need to be recognized in the marketing plan.

Supply chain management has been successfully used by manufacturers and by large retail chains for many years. The result has been cost savings and increased efficiencies of operators. Now, the restaurant industry is employing supply chain management.

Joseph O'Reilly provided information in restaurant logistics concerning restaurant supply management. O'Reilly reported that "Darden Restaurants (Olive Garden, Capital Grille, Longhorn Steakhouse) has more than 2,000 restaurants. Darden's supply chain manages more than $3 billion in capital and food product expenditures annually." "Because of its sheer size, Darden initiated a major supply chain overhaul that it expects will save $45 million annually through lower prices and less wasted food."[20] Starbucks decided to use this tool to team with other hospitality companies and purchase basic items such as sugar and milk.

The need for this management tool is the result of worldwide price increases in agricultural commodities. Commodity price increases are the result of increased worldwide demand for food. Unless worldwide production increases sufficiently to meet this demand, restaurants will need to continuously seek new approaches to acquiring foodstuffs in a cost-effective and efficient manner.

Some restaurants (individual and chain) have decided to buy directly from producers. However, farmers are often not prepared to harvest, package, and prepare their crops for direct use by restaurants. The future marketplace for agricultural products could look quite different from the existing market in which producers view their crops as commodities, not table-ready products.[21]

Other Departments

Other departments, such as revenue management, housekeeping, front desk, customer service, and maintenance, will be affected by next year's plan. They have a right to know key elements of the plan.

It is common for marketing managers to be asked to outline the marketing plan briefly and answer questions in a monthly manager's meeting. If a forum such as this does not exist, marketing managers should initiate a review of next year's marketing plan with other department heads after obtaining clearance from the general manager or president.

▪▪▪ Section VI: Action Plans: Strategies and Tactics

Marketing strategies are designed as the vehicle to achieve marketing objectives. In turn, marketing tactics are tools that support strategies. Far too often, strategies

It is important for cooperation between businesses that serve tourists. Shown in the picture is Mykonos, a popular tourist destination in Europe. Courtesy of Panos/Fotolia.

and tactics have little relationship to objectives. This is always an error and is commonly the result of the following:

- Desire to maintain status quo.

- Lazy, incompetent, or unsure management. These people do not wish to risk their positions through new strategies and tactics.

- Failure to engage in marketing planning or to view the processes as serious and meaningful to decision making.

- Undue heavy influence of outside vendors, such as advertising agencies, which do not wish to change direction or try new media such as digital marketing.

- Failure to understand the relationship between objectives, strategies, and tactics.

- Myopic thinking that things are going well and one does not fix something that is not broken. Unfortunately, in the fast-paced, competitive hospitality industry, by the time the product is demonstrably broken, it is beyond repair.

Marketing strategies and tactics use advertising and promotion, sales and distribution, pricing and product. Each must be custom designed to meet the specific needs of a company. It is unwise to follow ratios or industry averages concerning expenditures for advertising, new-product development, or other strategy areas.

Strategies and tactics must always be custom made to fit the needs and culture of a company and to allow it to meet or exceed objectives. A study of marketing strategies and tactics used by restaurants was conducted. It was found that many restaurants use weak strategies, including following the leader, rather than developing individualized, unique strategies and tactics. The authors concluded that restaurants may be able to do well for a number of years, but over time their lack of strategy lead to lower profits and even failure.[22]

Nonqualified Audience: Cluster Marketing

In recent years, some hotel companies have formed cluster marketing groups. These consist of different properties managed by the same management company within a common market area; however, each may represent a separate flag and have different ownership.

In extreme cases, a cluster marketing manager is appointed and each of the different properties is expected to submit otherwise confidential data such as leads and pending contracts to a common pool. This is highly questionable marketing behavior and may place the hotels' marketing/sales departments in a position of violating fiduciary and professional responsibilities to their hotels.

Marketing and sales plans are not to be shared with competitors. Before honoring a request by a cluster marketing group to share any confidential data, the management company must receive a written, dated, and signed statement from the general manager granting permission to do so.

Sales Strategies

The sales force must develop and use sales strategies to support objectives. Examples of sales strategies are as follows:

- Prevent erosion of key accounts.
- Grow key accounts.

- Grow selected marginal accounts.

- Eliminate selected marginal accounts.

- Retain selected marginal accounts but provide lower-cost sales support.

- Obtain new business from selected prospects.

A description of sales strategies should start with these six general strategies and indicate how the sales department is going to implement each one. The general strategy is supported by specific sales tactics, such as the following:

Outside the Company (Examples)

- Sales blitz of all or targeted accounts and projects

- Telephone, direct mail, and personal sales calls to selected decision makers and decision influencers

- Trade booths at selected travel shows

- Sales calls and working with travel intermediaries: tour wholesalers, travel agencies, incentive bonuses, and international sales reps

- Luncheon for key customers, prospects, or decision influencers

- Travel missions and other tactics

Inside the Company (Examples)

- Training of sales staff

- Involvement and support of nonsales personnel

- Motivational and control programs

- Involvement and support of management

Distribution Strategies

The selection of appropriate channels of distribution is basic to the development of successful sales strategies. Hospitality companies must be ever alert to changing distribution channels and the need for change.

Internet reservation systems, online travel agencies (OTAs), and the reduced number of traditional travel agents are important changes in the distribution system. It is critical for a marketing plan to identify each of the major distribution channels that is expected to produce sales and to forecast by week, month, and quarter the expected volume of sales each will provide.

Distribution systems do not provide equal sales volumes and, just as important, they do not provide equal profit margins. Hospitality managers will increasingly be tempted to accept ever greater sales volumes from independent companies such as Expedia, Travelocity, Priceline.com, and Hotels.com. This will almost assuredly erode profit margins.

In the absence of establishing sales and profit goals and sales limits for some distribution channels, hospitality managers may one day awaken to see a particular channel or company dominating their sales volume. Undoubtedly, other channels exist and should be added to a marketing plan if they are important to a company. (See Chapter 12 for a discussion on distribution channels.) Marketing and sales managers should be willing to sample and use new channels.

Advertising and Promotion Strategies

Advertising and promotion strategies should be established by people within the company responsible for these strategies, such as the director of advertising, the sales manager, or the marketing manager. It is critical for this person to work with supporting groups, such as an advertising agency, sales promotion firm, specialty advertising agencies, and consultants directly involved in the establishment and performance of advertising and promotion strategies.

It is inadvisable to give outside firms the sole authority for deriving and implementing these strategies. History has shown that when this occurs, the supporting group, such as an advertising agency, may produce brilliant copy and illustrations placed in well-respected media, only to find that these fail to meet objectives. The reason is that outside groups may not view objectives the same way as the client. Many advertising agencies have won distinguished honors for ads that did little or nothing to increase sales or market share for the client. Outside professionals correctly view their client as the company or the company's management, not the end consumer. Unfortunately, this view leads to pleasing the managers who hired them rather than achieving corporate or marketing objectives. Theoretically, corporate and marketing objectives and those of the manager should be synchronized. In fact, often a wide gap exists between the two. In some cases, outside professionals disdain client corporate or marketing objectives and view these as a detriment or obstacle to the creative process. The ideal is for corporate managers responsible for advertising/promotion to work as a team with selected outside professionals to derive strategies and tactics that satisfy objectives in a timely and cost-effective manner.

When this is accomplished, the team will develop an advertising/promotion mix of vehicles that includes tactics selected to achieve objectives, not simply to provide commissions, make life easy for the professionals, or produce a bland program that probably won't be criticized by management but may accomplish little.

Those who create advertising/promotion strategies have the following responsibilities:

- Select a blend or mix of media that may include commissionable mass media, direct mail, trade shows, billboards, specialty advertising, and social media (Facebook and others).

- Digital and social marketing must be considered as alternative media.

- Select or approve the message. This includes graphics, color, size, copy, and other format decisions.

- Design a media schedule showing when each medium, including noncommissionable media, will be used.

- Design a schedule of events, such as public relations events and familiarization (FAM) trips for travel writers.

- Carefully transmit this information to management.

- Supervise the development and implementation of advertising/promotion programs, with particular care given to timetables and budget constraints.

- Assume responsibility for the outcome. Increasingly, top management is requiring those in charge of advertising/promotion to prove effectiveness and to stand behind results.

Unfortunately, despite decades of marketing teaching and thousands of articles on the subject, many managers in the hospitality industry continue to equate marketing with advertising. They fail to realize that advertising is simply one part of marketing. The authors of the restaurant strategy referred to earlier concluded, "Many firms [restaurants] have attempted to hold market share by increasing advertising expenditures. Advertising alone will not ensure success."[23]

Another area of the advertising/promotion mix that needs consideration in a marketing plan is cooperative advertising/promotion. This requires teamwork and a place in the budget. For example, in the case of a resort, cooperative opportunities exist between the following entities:

- Resort and resort community (e.g., all resorts, restaurants, and attractions in Provincetown, Cape Cod, Massachusetts)

- Resort and tourism promotion groups (e.g., state tourism department or local Chamber of Commerce)

- Resort and suppliers (e.g., Citrus Board or Columbia Coffee)

- Resort and transportation companies (e.g., airlines, motor coach, cruise lines)
- Resort and sister hotels or resorts

An example of cooperative advertising/promotion opportunities is offered by hotels in Mexico. After an examination of the brochures of 10 hotel chains in Mexico, it was found that most made minimal or no reference to other Mexican hotels operated by the chain. Club Med made good use of this marketing tool. Club Med had not only a Mexican brochure for all its properties but also a special supplemental brochure for its properties near prestigious archaeological sites.[24]

Pricing Strategies

Pricing remains a function of marketing. Marketing managers must maintain control of this area; they must interface with revenue management. Marketing and sales departments will continuously be in conflict with pricing if pricing strategies are not understood and considered in marketing and sales plans. Today pricing is more critical than ever before due largely to the role of OTAs.

For instance, sales has responsibility for working with intermediaries such as tour wholesalers and with key customers. Both these customers will ask for price discounts. Commitments for large blocks of rooms, airline seats, autos, or ship berths will inevitably create problems with revenue or yield-management departments. Marketing and sales plans cannot be effective if they are developed without sales forecasts and revenue projections by major market segments. If forecasts and revenue projections are made without the input of the revenue management department, conflict will occur.

Review again the objectives and sub-objectives presented in Table 18–1. These call for average room rate objectives for each product class by season of the year. Using the concepts and practices of revenue management, pricing objectives may be considerably enhanced to include weekly objectives and objectives by sub-segments. Marriott Hotels uses a strategy known as rational pricing. This calls for *fencing*, placing restrictions on customer segments selected due to their perceived level of price elasticity. Fencing restrictions will immediately affect marketing and sales plans. Marketing managers are also advised to work with the reservations department during the planning process. Reservations often have considerable latitude to adjust prices and may account for a significant percentage of sales.

Pricing objectives and strategies affect every facet of marketing and sales. The selection of appropriate target markets and the emphasis to be given to each again depend on pricing.

Marketing and sales managers who view themselves at war with pricing managers are probably doomed to eventual failure. The top managers in most hospitality companies realize that a 10 percent upward adjustment in rates can produce favorable profit results in excess of cost cutting or traditional marketing and sales strategies to increase the number of guests.

Pricing strategies are of great importance to chain restaurants and need to be reviewed constantly. As an example, food-service quality is the predominant influence on guest ratings for family, steakhouse, and casual dining restaurants. Family price appeal enhances a guest's rating for a family restaurant chain but not necessarily for a steakhouse or casual dining.[25]

A marketer who has gained experience in a family restaurant chain might make erroneous pricing decisions when hired by a steakhouse or casual dining chain. Despite the fact that restaurant chains may seem alike, different pricing strategies may need to be developed for each.

Product Strategies

Marketing has an important role to play in the improvement of existing products and the development of new ones. In some hospitality firms, marketing is expected to be heavily involved in the process; in others, marketing assumes only an advisory role; and sadly, in others, marketing is excluded from the process.

Marketing professionals can exert considerable input and strategic direction when planning basic product changes as dramatic as those occurring within the resort industry. Marketing can also help greatly to enhance revenue from product changes as additions to the current product line. Hundreds or thousands of new product opportunities exist in most hospitality companies. The Alexis Park Resort in Las Vegas invented "Cocktail Cruises," which is essentially a motorized cart driven by an employee who offers poolside guests drinks so they can stay by the pool.[26] The Opryland Hotel in Nashville uses a similar concept to sell hotel logo souvenir merchandise. "Whenever there is more to be sold than your customers are buying, profit potential is not being realized. Revenue boosting opportunities abound for the creative operator who is willing to offer facilities, services, and events that will attract customers and to train customer-contact employees to stimulate add-on sales and sales upgrades."[27]

The process of making product line changes requires the input and advice of many individuals and departments. Marketing may identify a need, such as the "neighborhood bakery" concept, for use in fast-food chains, but this product concept directly affects production, finance, and human resources. When McDonald's, Burger King, and Wendy's experimented with fresh biscuits or croissants, they discovered that these products prepared from scratch or frozen dough required additional working space, equipment, and employee training.[28]

Lost or Decline of Iconic Restaurant Brands

"Some of America's once iconic brands are now shells of their former selves." In 10 years, several of the nation's biggest restaurant chains lost more than 50 percent of their sales and have closed hundreds of locations. "As an example, Bennigans sales plunged by more than 90 percent between 2002 and 2012. Nearly all of the declining brands face an aging image and business model," says Darren Tristano, Vice President of TECHNOMIC, a consulting and research firm. Today, if you are not updating your restaurant within five to eight years of the previous update, you are falling out of favor."[29]

Unfortunately, most hotel marketing plans do not list or break down product categories in a marketing plan other than by type of room, catering/banquets, food and beverage, and perhaps a catch-all "other" products category. One reason for this is that many management contracts between owners and management companies place little, if any, emphasis on products other than rooms and food and beverage. Therefore, management pays little attention to lesser product categories. The result is that many marketing plans do not consider cross-selling and upselling opportunities using existing products, to say nothing of new product opportunities.

■■■ Section VII: Resources Needed to Support Strategies and Meet Objectives

Marketing plans must be written with available resources, or those likely to become available, in mind. A common error in writing a marketing plan is to develop strategies that are probably highly workable but for which there is insufficient support. Another error is to assume that top management will not provide additional support regardless of the brilliance of the plan. Marketing plans can and must be sold to top management. A balance between mythical over-the-top plans and total acquiescence to perceived inflexibility of management is needed in any solid marketing plan.

Personnel

Generally, the most costly and difficult resource needed to ensure success with marketing/sales strategies is personnel. The addition of personnel is sometimes viewed as unnecessary, impractical, or unwise, given current budgetary restrictions.

Obviously, sometimes the addition of salespeople, secretaries, analysts, and others is absolutely essential. Be prepared to justify this request, and remember that many people, particularly salespeople, are not instantly productive. Training and recruiting costs must be considered with this resource request, as well as the time required by members of management to interview and work with these people.

The influence of the corporate culture cannot be overlooked in this process. Imagine a company such as the Ritz-Carlton with the philosophy that it not only treats its customers as ladies and gentlemen but also treats its employees as ladies and gentlemen. Fulfillment of this pledge with appropriate new personnel is demanding and may be time consuming.[30]

A marketing plan may need to specify the type of person required for a position if it is not described elsewhere, such as in company policies and procedures. Some hospitality companies operate under the philosophy that "we are always hiring excellent people." Marketing managers must plan personnel needs ahead for seasonal cost differences, such as a month with heavy trade show expenses or several weeks when brochures will be mailed to key customers and prospects. Budgets should reflect careful planning of resource use, such as temporary help on a week-by-week basis. A carefully constructed budget is simply a reflection of a well-thought-out marketing plan.

Other Monetary Support

Monetary support not accounted for by salary, wages, and benefits must be considered carefully and included. This includes travel expenses; motivational costs, such as a trip to Las Vegas; and other monetary needs.

Research, Consulting, and Training

Hospitality companies often have need for outside professionals to assist with marketing research, such as focus groups; training, such as sales training; or consulting to provide objective outside appraisals, advice, and revenue management.

Miscellaneous Costs

This area should not be a source of slush funds. Many expenses, such as subscriptions to professional books and journals, may be included here.

Budgets

In larger organizations, corporate policies and procedures may direct marketing managers as to categories of expenses and items that may be included. Marketing managers of smaller companies may need to develop their own list and to use it each year as a guide to ensure that all essential resources are included.

Budgets should be established to reflect projected costs weekly, monthly, quarterly, and annually. This is not simply to make life easier for the finance/account area personnel next year.

■■■ Section VIII: Marketing Control

This discussion of marketing control presupposes that the sales plan is part of the marketing plan. This is not always the case; some hospitality organizations separate the two functions.

The essentials for writing a sales plan follow the same general procedure as those described for a marketing plan. A sales plan does not need all the aspects of a marketing plan, such as advertising or marketing research, because these may be furnished by support departments. A sales plan should pay particular attention to the sales force and its objectives and to strategies to ensure that sales quotas are met and possibly exceeded.

Sales Objectives

Sales objectives must be established for each sales area, division, region, salesperson, and time period. The broad sales objectives discussed previously serve as the basis for establishing individual objectives. The sum of all sales objectives or quotas for members of the sales force must equal or exceed annual objectives.

One method of establishing annual sales objectives for the company is to begin with sales planning among members of the sales force. Each member should be expected to develop a list of all sales accounts currently served by that person, plus prospects for the coming year. From this, an estimate of potential sales by account and prospect will provide a means of forecasting next year's sales.

Management, beginning with the sales manager and ending with the general manager or other member of top management, then has the responsibility for critically examining these forecasts. Management seldom accepts the forecasts of the sales force without amending them, usually upward. This is known as bottom-up, top-down planning.

Management amends sales force forecasts for the following reasons:

- Sales force members often wish to protect themselves and give lower sales estimates than are actually possible.

- The company has certain sales objectives that it expects based on the needs of the company.

- Management may have access to marketing research information not available to the sales force.

- Management may have a history of dealing with the sales force and realize that forecasts are generally too high or too low by x percent.

- Management may be willing to provide the marketing/sales department with additional resources that are unknown to members of the sales force.

Table 18–2 shows a typical hotel sales forecast for a salesperson. Sales managers have the responsibility to work closely with their salespeople to ensure that sales forecasts are accurate. They must then provide a composite sales forecast for their department and present it to management.

Sales Forecast and Quotas

Eventually, all members of the sales force must be presented with sales quotas. Annual sales quotas should then be broken down into monthly and quarterly sales. Many sales managers and experienced salespeople break monthly quotas into weekly figures.

Sales managers have the responsibility for working with their salespeople to ensure that quotas are met or surpassed. It is important to evaluate sales results continually and develop corrective tactics if it appears that actual sales will not meet forecasts or quotas. Sales managers and salespeople who wait several months before evaluating actual sales against forecasts usually find it is too late to take corrective action.

Expenditures Against Budget

It is also important for marketing/sales managers to monitor actual expenditures continually against budgeted figures. This, too, must be done on a regular basis. As described in the Red Robin case (see Chapter 3), this chain now establishes budgets each quarter.

Periodic Evaluation of All Marketing Objectives

The role of marketing and sales managers is sometimes compared to that of an adult babysitter. A frequent comment made by people in these positions is that they spend a great deal of time simply making sure that people under their direction

TABLE 18–2

Example of a Sales Forecast for a Hotel Salesperson

Salesperson: Janet Chin	SALES CURRENT YEAR			SALES PROJECTED NEXT YEAR		
	Room Nights	Revenue	Avg. Rate	Room Nights	Revenue	Avg. Rate
Major commercial accounts (key accounts)						
1.						
2.						
3.						
4.						
Other commercial accounts						
1.						
2.						
3.						
4.						
Major intermediary accounts						
1.						
2.						
3.						
4.						
Other intermediary accounts						
1.						
2.						
3.						
4.						
Airline accounts						
1.						
2.						
3.						
4.						
Other accounts						
1.						
2.						
3.						
4.						
Prospects for next year						
1.						
2.						
3.						
4.						
Total accounts/prospects	Total current year			Totals projected next year		

perform tasks in a timely fashion. There is much truth in this comment because a critical role of marketing/sales managers is to ensure that all objectives are met or exceeded on time.

Managers responsible for functions such as advertising, promotions, and marketing research also have a responsibility to ensure that all tasks are performed on time. If a summer brochure is printed three weeks after the due date, chances are very good that the sales force may miss the opportunity to send or deliver this advertising medium to prospects and key accounts during the time that they make travel decisions. In turn, the sales force may fail to make summer sales quotas. All marketing/sales tasks are important. If this is not true, the task and the position should be eliminated.

Marketing Activity Timetable

One method commonly used by marketing/sales managers to ensure that tasks are completed on time is the use of a marketing activity timetable. This simple device lists major activities, the dates they must be completed, the person responsible, and a space for checking whether the task has been accomplished.

Readjustments to Marketing Plan

Human beings are incapable of devising a perfect marketing plan. Market conditions change, disasters occur, and many other reasons create a need to refine marketing plans. Generally, refinements should be made in the area of tactics, budgets, and timing of events rather than in major objectives or strategies. Changes in tactics normally do not require top management approval and are viewed as the normal responsibility of marketing/sales managers.

■■■ Section IX: Presenting and Selling the Plan

Changes in major objectives such as annual sales volume and in major strategies always require approval by top management. Marketing/sales managers are advised to refrain from considering changes in major objectives and strategies unless absolutely necessary. Top management will almost certainly view the necessity for change as a reflection of poor management by marketing/sales managers unless the cause was a disaster, such as a major fire in a hotel.

Never assume that a marketing plan is so logical that it will sell itself. A marketing plan must be sold to many people, including the following:

- *Members of marketing/sales department.* Many people within the marketing/sales areas do not believe in planning. They view the process of developing, writing, defending, and using a written plan to be a waste of time. Comments are frequently heard such as, "If management would just let us do our job and quit all this planning, the company would do better." This common sentiment may exist due to poor experience with prior planning, fear of the process, or genuine ignorance about the benefits. Marketing/sales managers need the support of subordinates in the planning process. It is best to sell the benefits of the process rather than to force acquiescence.

- *Vendors/ad agencies and others.* Outside organizations, such as advertising and marketing research agencies, need to be involved in the planning process. They must be made aware that their participation in the marketing planning process is an expected part of their responsibilities as team members.

- *Top management.* Top management must approve the annual marketing plan. It is seldom sufficient to write a lengthy plan, send it through company mail or e-mail to top management, and expect an enthusiastic endorsement. Marketing/sales managers must sell the plan to members of management through meetings, such as friendly luncheons and formalized presentations. Key members of the staff may be expected to participate in formal presentations. These appearances should always be treated with the same careful planning and professionalism that would be expected if a sales presentation were made to a key prospect for $2 million worth of business. Use professional presentation materials when appropriate, such as PowerPoint presentations, overheads, and bound copies of the annual plan. Prepare selected charts, graphs, and tables that are easy to understand and quickly reinforce key points.

▪■▪ Section X: Preparing for the Future

The process of marketing planning is a continuum. The task is never ending. Marketing/sales managers must always be planning. In reality, the development of next year's marketing plan begins the day this year's plan is approved.

Data Collection and Analysis

Marketing plan development depends on the availability of reliable information. This task can always be improved. The process of data collection and analysis from internal and external sources continues each day. Marketing/sales managers must always be alert for methods to improve the process.

Marketing Planning as a Tool for Growth

A good marketing plan will assist your company and department to prosper and grow. What is not so obvious to many is that a good plan will also enable people to prosper and grow. This occurs in the following several ways:

- The participatory planning process allows people to understand the management process.

- People learn to become team players during the process.

- People learn to establish objectives and set timetables to ensure they are met.

- The process of establishing realistic strategies and tactics to meet objectives is learned.

- People who approach the planning process with a receptive mind and use the marketing plan usually find it enhances their professional career.

Many hospitality companies have developed a planning culture in which there is a respect for planning as a positive process. This is a reflection of a corporate culture and top management support. Changes in top management sometimes mean that support for marketing planning will decrease or in some instances planning will be discouraged. A strong corporate culture that emphasizes and encourages planning within all levels of the company will be rewarded. Sometimes management becomes discouraged by the process, particularly when market conditions worsen as a new competitor threatens market share. It is at times like this that a corporate culture of planning provides stability and assurance of purpose and direction.

An example of the need for planning in poor economic times, rather than resorting to reactive "just-do-something" tactics, is offered by the California Country Club (CCC) of Los Angeles. This club, like many others in southern California, had a waiting list of potential members, but suddenly the waiting list changed to members wanting to leave the club.

Instead of panicking and grasping for an immediate marketing cure-all, the management of CCC pursued a process of market planning, starting with an analysis of the market and competitors. The planning process allowed CCC to recognize marketing opportunities, such as pricing strategies, including the elimination of golf-only fees. The need for a customer-directed policy of "just say yes" was also discovered and implemented. These and other changes represented a complete turnover from previous policies and procedures, thus allowing the club to increase market share and revenue.[31]

A study of the process used by hotels to develop marketing plans has shown that "the most important features in the development of a marketing plan appear to be management participation and commitment at all levels, sufficient time for development, specific training in developing a marketing plan, and tying incentives to the achievements of goals and objectives."[32]

In good times or bad, consistency in marketing planning pays good dividends for any hospitality company and its employees.[33]

▪▪▪ CHAPTER REVIEW

I. Purpose of a Marketing Plan
- **A.** Serves as a road map for all marketing activities of the firm for the next year.
- **B.** Ensures that marketing activities are in agreement with the corporate strategic plan.
- **C.** Forces marketing managers to review and think objectively through all steps in the marketing process.
- **D.** Assists in the budgeting process to match resources with marketing objectives.

II. Tips for Writing the Executive Summary
- **A.** Write it for top executives.
- **B.** Limit the number of pages to between two and four.
- **C.** Use short sentences and short paragraphs.
- **D.** Organize the summary as follows: Describe next year's objectives in quantitative terms; briefly describe marketing strategies to meet goals and objectives; identify the dollar costs necessary as well as key resources needed.
- **E.** Read and reread before final submit.

III. Corporate Connection
- **A.** Relationships to other plans
  1. Corporate goals: profit, growth, and others
  2. Desired market share
  3. Positioning of the enterprise or of product lines
  4. Vertical or horizontal integration
  5. Strategic alliances
  6. Product-line breadth and depth
- **B.** Marketing-related plans also include the following:
  1. Sales
  2. Advertising and promotion
  3. Marketing research
  4. Pricing
  5. Customer services
- **C.** Corporate direction
  1. Mission statement
  2. Corporate philosophy
  3. Corporate goals

IV. Environmental Analysis and Forecasting
- **A. Positioning statement (although it should be its own Roman numeral)**
- **B. Analysis of major environmental factors**
  1. Social
  2. Political
  3. Economic
- **C. Economic drivers of growth**
  1. The aerotropolis
- **D. Competitive analysis**
  1. List the major existing competitors confronting your firm next year.
  2. List new competitors.
  3. Describe the major competitive strengths and weaknesses of each competitor.
- **E. Marketing trends:** Monitor visitor trends, competitive trends, related industry trends.
- **F. Market potential**

1. Market potential should be viewed as the total available demand for a firm's product within a particular geographic market at a given price. It is important not to mix different products into an estimate of market potential.
2. Provide an estimate or guesstimate of market potential for each major product line in monetary terms such as dollars and in units such as room nights or passengers.

- **G. Marketing research**
  1. **Macromarket information:** Industry trends, socioeconomic and political trends, competitive information, and industry-wide customer data.
  2. **Micromarket information:** Guest information, product/service information, new-product analysis and testing, intermediary buyer data, pricing studies, key account information, and advertising/promotion effectiveness.

V. Segmentation and Targeting. The selection of segments is the result of the following:
- **A.** Understanding who the company is and what it wishes to be.
- **B.** Studying available segments and determining if they fit the capabilities and desires of the company to obtain and secure them.

VI. Next Year's Objectives and Quotas
- **A. Objectives**
  1. **Quantitative objectives:** Expressed in monetary terms, expressed in unit measurements, time specific and profit/margin specific.
  2. **Other objectives:** Corporate goals, corporate resources, environmental factors, competitions, market trends, market potential, available market segments, and possible target markets.
  3. **Actions**
     - **a.** List primary marketing/sales objectives for next year.
     - **b.** List sub-objectives for next year.
     - **c.** Break down objective by quarter, month, and week.
     - **d.** List other specific sub-objectives by marketing support area, such as advertising/promotion objectives.
- **B. Rating system objectives**
- **C. Quotas**
  1. Based on next year's objectives
  2. Individualized
  3. Realistic and obtainable
  4. Broken down to small units, such as each salesperson's quota per week
  5. Understandable/measurable
- **D. Communicating the plan**
- **E. Top management**
- **F. Board of directors or group of investors**
- **G. Subordinates**
- **H. Vendors**

I. **Other**

J. **Action quotas.** Break down and list quotas for sales departments, sales territories, all sales intermediaries, each sales intermediary, and each salesperson.

VII. **Action Plans: Strategies and Tactics**

A. **Cluster marketing**

B. **Sales strategies**
1. Prevent erosion of key accounts
2. Grow key accounts
3. Grow selected marginal accounts
4. Eliminate selected marginal accounts
5. Retain selected marginal accounts but provide lower-cost sales support
6. Obtain new business from selected prospects
7. Distribution strategies

C. **Advertising/promotion strategies**
1. Select a blend or mix or media.
2. Select or approve the message.
3. Design a media schedule showing when each medium, including noncommissionable media, will be used.
4. Design a schedule of events.
5. Carefully transmit this information to management.
6. Supervise the development and implementation of advertising/promotion programs, with particular care given to timetables and budget constraints.
7. Ensure responsibility for the outcome.

D. **Pricing strategy**
1. Carefully review pricing objective with departments responsible for pricing, planning, and implementation.
2. Refine pricing objectives to reflect sales and revenue forecasts.
3. Describe pricing strategies to be used throughout the year.
4. Make certain that price, sales, and promotion/advertising objectives are synchronized and working in support of corporate objectives.

E. **Product strategies**
1. Describe the involvement of the marketing department in major strategic product development.
2. Describe the role of marketing in new-product acquisition or product development.
3. Describe ongoing or planned product development programs for which marketing has responsibility.

VIII. **Resources Needed to Support Strategies and Meet Objectives**

A. Study and then list the need for new marketing/sales personnel, including temporary help during the next year.

B. Study and list the type and amount of equipment and space that will be needed to support marketing/sales.

C. Study and list the amount of monetary support needed next year.

D. Study and list the amount and type of other costs necessary next year.

E. Study and list the amount of outside research, consulting, and training assistance needed.

F. Prepare a marketing budget for approval by top management.

IX. **Marketing Control**

A. Sales force members often wish to protect themselves and give lower sales estimates than are actually possible.

B. The company has certain sales objectives it expects based on the needs of the company.

C. Management may have access to marketing research information not viewed by the sales force.

D. Management may have a history of dealing with the sales force and realizes that forecasts are generally too high or too low by x percent.

E. Management may be willing to provide the marketing/sales department with additional resources.

X. **Presenting and Selling the Plan**

A. Members of marketing/sales departments

B. Vendor/ad agencies and others

C. Top management

XI. **Preparing for the Future**

A. The participatory planning process allows people to understand the management process.

B. People learn to become team players during the process.

C. People learn to establish objectives and set timetables to ensure they are met.

D. People learn the process of establishing realistic strategies and tactics to meet objectives.

E. People who approach the planning process with a receptive mind and use the marketing plan will usually find it enhances their professional career.

■■■ DISCUSSION QUESTIONS

1. What is the purpose of a marketing plan?
2. What is the relevancy of environmental factors to an annual marketing plan?
3. Why is the determination of market potential so important?
4. How should market segments and targets be described in a marketing plan?
5. Should marketing objectives be described in quantitative terms? Why or why not?
6. What is the relationship, if any, between marketing strategies and marketing objectives?
7. Is marketing control really necessary in a marketing plan, or is it an optional managerial exercise?

■■■ EXPERIENTIAL EXERCISE

Do the following:

Meet with a director of sales of a hotel, a general manager of a hotel, or the director of a tourism marketing organization and ask him or her to go over the organization's marketing plan with you. Have him or her explain the process he or she uses to develop a marketing plan.

■■■ INTERNET EXERCISES

Choose a hospitality or tourism organization in your area. On the Internet find information that would be useful to you if you were developing a marketing plan for the organization. Explain how you would use this information.

■■■ REFERENCES

1 Condensed with permission from Peter Cass, "Luxury Lifestyle Marketing: New Frontier," *Hospitality Business Review*, 2, no. 3 (Fall 1999): 27–30.

2 Perry J. S. Hobson, Henry C. S. Vincent, and Kye-Sung Chon, "Vietnam's Tourism Industry: Can It Be Kept Afloat?" *Cornell Hotel and Restaurant Administration Quarterly*, 35, no. 5 (1994): 42–49.

3 2008 Mumbai Attacks, Wikipedia, http://en.wikipedia.org/wicki/2008_Mumbai_attacks

4 John D. Kasarda and Greg Lindsay, *Aerotropolis: The Way We'll Live Next*, 2011, ISBN 978-03741001193.

5 Richard Gibson, "Flight Caterers Widen Horizons Beyond Airlines," *Wall Street Journal* (January 16, 1995): B1, B8.

6 David O. Williams, "Ski Execs Target Asian Markets," *Rocky Mountain News* (January 4, 2008): 5.

7 Lodging Market Potential Index, August 13, 2012, Global Edge.msu.edu and A.J. Singh, Raymond S. Schmidgall, and Tunga Kiyak, The Lodging Market Potential Index (L-MPI©) Ranking of Major Lodging Markets in the United States, Vol 7, No. 1, 2013.

8 Josiah Mackenzie, Michael Nurbatlian's Photo Contest Gained 2000+ New Faces in Two Weeks for Indigo Pearl Resort, Hotel Marketing Strategies-Technology for Better Guest Experiences, July 17, 2011, www.hotelmarketingstrategies.com

9 Karmin Craig, "New Hotel Chain to Give Its Guests the Old College Try," *The Wall Street Journal*, August 27, 2014, pg. C6.

10 Chad Eric Watt, CiCi's Higher Returns from Revamped Stores, *Dallas Business Journal*, 33, no. 46 (July 2–8, 2010).

11 Hugh J. Watson and Linda Volonino, Case Study: Harrah's High Payoff from Customer Information, www.terry.uga

12 Ibid.

13 Carl K. Link, "Developing a Marketing Plan: Lessons from the Inn at Plum Creek," *Cornell Hotel and Restaurant Administration Quarterly*, 34, no. 5 (1993): 35.

14 L. K. Prevette and Joseph Giudice, "Anatomy of a Turnaround: The Los Angeles Biltmore," *Cornell Hotel and Restaurant Administration Quarterly*, 30, no. 3 (1989): 32.

15 Karady Islam and Woo Gon Kim, "Comparing Market Segment Profitability Analysis with Department Profitability Analysis and Hotel Marketing-Decision Tools," *Cornell Hotel & Restaurant Administration Quarterly*, 47, no. 2 (2006): 155–173.

16 Ron Leiber, "A New Parenting Ritual: The Last Hurrah," *Wall Street Journal* (July 7, 2004): D1.

17 Ibid.

18 From Global Market Strategy Tourism Australia, 2013–2015, Retrieved from www.tourism.australia.com/markets/market-strategy.aspx. Copyright © 2013 by Tourism Australia. Reprinted by permission.

19 Francis Buttle, "The Marketing Strategy Worksheet: A Practical Tool," *Cornell Hotel and Restaurant Administration Quarterly*, 33, no. 3 (1992): 57.

20 Joseph O'Reilly, Restaurant Logistics: Serving Up the Perfect Meal, www.inboundlogistics.com, August 2012.

21 Julie Jargon, "Eateries' New Way to Shop," *Wall Street Journal*, Corporate News (April 1, 2011): B5.

22 Joseph J. West and Michael D. Olsen, "Grand Strategy: Making Your Restaurant a Winner," *Cornell Hotel and Restaurant Administration Quarterly*, 31, no. 2 (1990): 77.

23 Ibid.

24 Hanam Ayala, "Mexican Resorts: A Blueprint with an Expiration Date," *Cornell Hotel and Restaurant Administration Quarterly*, 34, no. 3 (1993): 40.

25 Michael S. Morgan, "Benefit Dimensions of a Midscale Restaurant Chain," *Cornell Hotel and Restaurant Administration Quarterly*, 34, no. 2 (1993): 44–45.

26 Carl K. Link, "Internal Merchandising: Creating Revenue Opportunities," *Cornell Hotel and Restaurant Administration Quarterly*, 30, no. 3 (1989): 56.

27 Ibid., p. 57.

28 Regina Robichald and Mahmood A. Khan, "Responding to Market Changes: The Fast

Food Experience," *Cornell Hotel and Restaurant Administration Quarterly*, 29, no. 3 (1988): 47.

29 Michael B. Sauter and Thomas C. Frohlich, America's Disappearing Restaurant Chains, December 12, 2013, http://247wallst.com/specialreport/2013.

30 William E. Kent, "Putting Up the Ritz: Using Culture to Open a Hotel," *Cornell Hotel and Restaurant Administration Quarterly*, 31, no. 3 (1990): 16–24.

31 Jeffrey L. Pellissier, "Remarketing: One Club's Response to a Changing Market," *Cornell Hotel and Restaurant Administration Quarterly*, 34, no. 4 (1993): 53–58.

32 S. Dev Chekitan, "Marketing Practices at Hotel Chains," *Cornell Hotel and Restaurant Administration Quarterly*, 31, no. 3 (1990): 54–63.

33 For more on developing a marketing plan, see James C. Makens, *The Marketing Plan Workbook* (Upper Saddle River, NJ: Prentice-Hall, 1985); *Hotel Sales and Marketing Plan Workbook* (Winston-Salem, NC: Marion-Clarence, 1990).

The Five-Gap Model of Service Quality

A widely used model of service quality is known as the five-gap model (Figure A–1). This model defines service quality as meeting customer expectations. In the words of those who developed the model, "Knowing what customers expect is the first and possibly the most critical step in delivering service quality. Stated simply, providing service that customers perceive as excellent requires that a firm know what customers expect." This model is closely linked to marketing because it is customer based. The model has five gaps.

■■■ Gap 1: Consumer Expectations Versus Management Perception

Hospitality executives may fail to understand what consumers expect in a service and which features are needed to deliver high-quality service. When management does not understand what its customers want, a gap 1 exists. For example, a manager may develop a system to ensure that all guests wait no longer than 15 minutes to check in. However, if guests start getting upset after 10 minutes, this system will cause dissatisfaction. Talking to guests before developing the check-in system would enable the manager to learn that the critical time is 10 minutes, not 15 minutes. Marriott Hotels observed that guests were not using the complimentary bath crystals provided as a bathroom amenity. They discontinued the bath crystals in favor of cable television, a more important benefit to most guests than bath crystals. Originally, management believed bath crystals would be considered a benefit. However, after observing its guests, management found that guest satisfaction could be increased by offering a different service.

Many firms conduct initial studies to find out what their market wants, but later they become internally focused and oblivious to the fact that customers' needs have changed. If customer needs change but the product does not, the marketing mix becomes less attractive to the target market, and gap 1 has increased. Managers should walk around their operations, talk with customers, and encourage feedback. Management can also gain information on customers from marketing information systems.

■■■ Gap 2: Management Perception Versus Service Quality Specifications

Gap 2 occurs when managers know what their customers want but are unable or unwilling to develop systems that will deliver it. Several reasons have been given for gap 2: (1) inadequate commitment to service quality, (2) lack of perception of feasibility, (3) inadequate task standardization, and (4) absence of goal setting.

Some companies look for short-term profits and are unwilling to invest in people or equipment. This almost inevitably causes service quality problems. Hotel owners who are reluctant to provide enough operating capital can be a cause of gap 2 errors. For example, the hotel owner who budgets for just enough linen to get by may discover that the linen inventory quickly drops below critical levels as

Figure A–1
Conceptual model of service quality: the gap analysis model.
Source: A. Parasuraman, Valarie Zeithaml, and Leonard L. Berry, "A Conceptual Model of Service Quality and Its Implication for Future Research," *Journal of Marketing* (Fall 1985): 44. Reprinted with permission of the American Marketing Association.

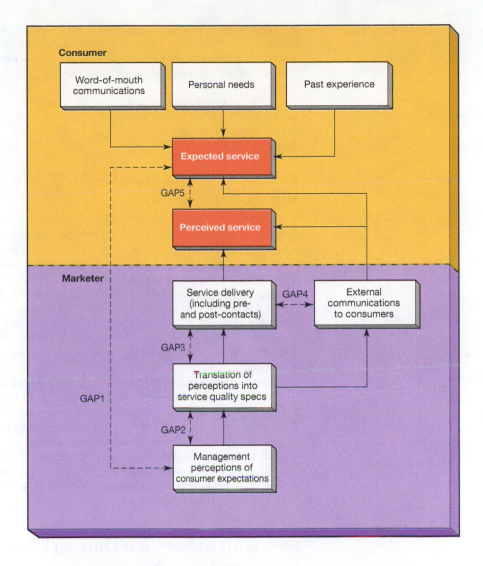

linen is stolen and destroyed. A visitor experienced this in Ft. Lauderdale, Florida. The guest returned from a walk on the beach to a freshly cleaned room, started to get ready to take a shower, and noticed there were no towels in the room. The guest called housekeeping and explained that he had to take a shower to get ready for a business appointment and there were no towels in the room. Housekeeping apologized, saying they were short on towels. In about 15 minutes, a housekeeper arrived with towels, causing the guest to arrive late for the appointment. Incidents such as this detract from a positive guest experience, create unnecessary tasks, and decrease employee morale. In this case, hotel management knew that the linen inventory was low, but the owner either did not want to invest in linen or did not have the money to supply the hotel properly.

Sometimes managers feel that improving an existing problem is not feasible. For example, most business guests want to check out after breakfast. They are usually in a hurry to get started with the day's business. Many hotel managers understand this but accept a 10- to 20-minute wait as the best they can do because they are unwilling to hire extra employees to help during the rush period. Bill Marriott Jr. felt that the problem was important enough to develop a system to solve it and invented express checkouts. Guests receive their bills the evening before. If the bills are accurate, the guests simply drop them off with their keys at the front desk. Today, most hotel chains use some type of express checkout system. Some hotels make use of technology and allow the guest to check the accuracy of bills on their television screens and check out using in-room television equipment. The express checkout system was developed by a person who viewed reducing checkout queues as a challenge rather than a problem that was an inherent part of the system. Bill Marriott eliminated this gap 2 error. He demonstrated that capital is not the only cure for a gap 2 problem. Innovative thinking can also eliminate gap 2 problems. Sometimes we need to look for unconventional solutions to the problem. Translating customer needs into service specifications is critical to service quality.

Finally, goals must be accepted by employees. Management must show its support through measurement of results, communication, and rewarding employees for superior service.

■■■ Gap 3: Service Quality Specifications Versus Service Delivery

Gap 3 is referred to as the service-performance gap. Gap 3 occurs when management understands what needs to be delivered and appropriate specifications have been developed but employees are unable or unwilling to deliver the service. Gap 3 errors occur during moments of truth, when the employee and the customer interact. Employees are expected to act cheerfully and solve the guests' problems. When they do not, guests may perceive a problem with functional quality. Often gap 3 errors occur when management assumes that the employees are delivering excellent service and do not pay attention to detail. It is important for management to inspect service delivery to let employees know it appreciates the job they are doing.

Gap 3 errors can be minimized through internal marketing programs. Management of the human resources functions (hiring, training, monitoring working conditions, and developing reward systems) is important in reducing gap 3 errors. Gap 3 errors are also the result of customer-contact employees being overworked. This can occur when a business is understaffed or an employee is required to work a second shift for an employee who called in sick. Under these conditions employees become tired and stressed. They lose their enthusiasm for the job and become less willing to solve customer problems. This lack of customer orientation leads to gap 3 errors.

■■■ Gap 4: Service Delivery Versus External Communications

Gap 4 is created when the firm promises more in its external communications than it can deliver. Earlier in this book we mentioned the advertising campaign put on by the government of Bermuda, inviting travelers to enjoy the attractions of the island during its uncrowded low season. Visitors were disappointed when they discovered that many attractions were closed during the off season. Marketers must make sure that operations can deliver what they promise.

During the last week of ski season, skiers were surprised to find that only half the runs on one side of the mountain had been groomed. This was particularly annoying and even dangerous because the half grooming occurred on intermediate runs where less-than-expert skiers might suddenly encounter bad conditions. The runs had been perfectly groomed all season until that final week. Late-season arrivals undoubtedly felt they had been slighted.

The Regent of Fiji encountered a severe problem when a military takeover occurred and discouraged tourism. A consultant, Chuck Gee, dean of the School of Travel Industry Management at the University of Hawaii, was hired to advise the hotel during this crisis. Chuck's advice was "Do nothing different. Do not reduce your staff, your lighting, your food quality, or your service." When asked why, Chuck's answer was that the Regent had positioned itself as a luxury resort and must continue to offer that level of service even if only one guest appeared. He further explained that the Regent knew there were risks when it entered this market and must now be prepared to accept them and pay the price to continue as an upscale resort.

Lack of consistency can also cause gap 4 problems. Hotel policies were discussed during a marketing seminar. After the seminar a manager from La Quinta told of a problem with a guest when the cashier refused to cash a personal check. The check was over the limit that La Quinta had set for personal checks. However, the guest had cashed a check for the same amount during a previous stay at a La Quinta Inn. The first desk clerk had given the implicit message that it was all right to cash personal checks for that amount. The clerk may have known the guest, had enough cash, and felt the guest should receive a favor. This clerk did not realize that problems were being developed for the next La Quinta. Customers expect chains to have similar products and policies. Inconsistency results in gap 4 errors.

■■■ Gap 5: Expected Service Versus Perceived Service

Gap 5 is a function of the others. As any of the other gaps increase in size, gap 5 also increases. It represents the difference between expected quality and perceived quality. The expected quality is what the guest expects to receive from the company. The perceived service is what the guest perceives he or she received from the company. If the guest receives less than he or she expected, the guest is dissatisfied.

The five-gap service model provides insights into the delivery of quality service. By studying this model, we can develop an understanding of the potential problem areas related to service quality. This insight will help to close any gaps that may exist in our operations.

Forecasting Market Demand

■■■ Defining the Market

Market demand measurement calls for a clear understanding of the market involved. The term *market* has acquired many meanings over the years. In its original meaning, a market was a physical place where buyers and sellers gathered to exchange goods and services. Medieval towns had market squares where sellers brought their goods and buyers shopped for them. In today's cities, buying and selling occurs in what are called shopping areas rather than markets.

To an economist, the term *market* describes all the buyers and sellers who transact over some good or service. Thus, the limited-service hotel market consists of all the consumers who use limited-service hotels and the companies who supply limited-service hotel rooms. The economist is interested in the structure, conduct, and performance of each market.

To a marketer, a market is the set of all actual and potential buyers of a product or service. A market is the set of buyers, and the industry is the set of sellers. The size of the market hinges on the number of buyers who might exist for a particular market offer. Potential buyers for something have three characteristics: interest, income, and access.

Consider the market for Carnival Cruises. To assess its market, Carnival must first estimate the number of customers who have a potential interest in going on a cruise. To do this, the company could conduct a random sampling of consumers and ask the following question: "Do you have an interest in taking a cruise?" If one person out of ten says *yes*, Carnival can assume that 10 percent of the total number of consumers is the potential market for cruises. The potential market is the set of consumers that professes some level of interest in a particular product or service.

Consumer interest alone is not enough to define the cruise market. Potential consumers must have enough income to afford the product. They must be able to answer *yes* to the following question: "Can you afford to purchase a cruise?" The higher the price, the fewer the number of people who can answer yes to this question. Thus, market size depends on both interest and income.

For some market offers, Carnival might have to restrict sales to certain groups. Carnival requires passengers to be 21 years old, unless they are married; then they can be 18 years old. A particular state might not allow the signing of a contractual agreement by anyone under the age of 21. This eliminates the ability to sell to married couples between 18 and 21. The remaining adults make up the qualified available market: the set of consumers that has interest, income, access, and qualifications for the product.

Carnival now has the choice of going after the whole qualified available market or concentrating on select segments. Carnival's served market is the part of the qualified available market that it decides to pursue. For example, Carnival may decide to concentrate its marketing efforts on the East Coast, the Chicago area, and the Southwest. These areas become its served market. Carnival and its competitors will end up selling a certain number of cruises in their served market. The penetrated market is the set of consumers that has bought cruises.

Figure B–1 brings these market concepts together with some hypothetical numbers. The bar on the left of the figure shows the ratio of the potential market— all those who are interested—to the total market. Here the potential market

Figure B–1
Levels of market definition.

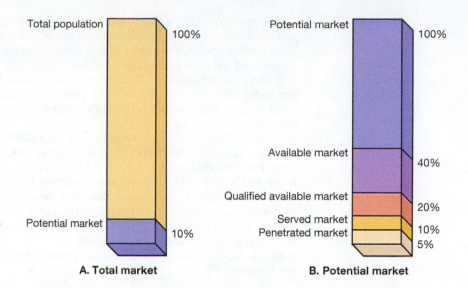

A. Total market

B. Potential market

is 10 percent. The bar on the right shows several possible breakdowns of the potential market. The available market—those who have interest, income, and access—is 40 percent of the potential market. The qualified available market—those who can meet the legal requirements—is 50 percent of the total available market (or 20 percent of the potential market). Carnival concentrates its efforts on 50 percent of the qualified available market—the served market, which is 10 percent of the potential market. Finally, Carnival and its competitors already have penetrated 50 percent of the served market (or 5 percent of the potential market).

These market definitions are a useful tool for marketing planning. Carnival's management can take a number of actions if it is not satisfied with current sales. It can lobby to get the age for signing a legal contract lowered. It can expand its markets in North America or in other areas of the world. Carnival can lower its prices to expand the size of the potential market. It can try to attract more buyers from its served market through stronger promotion or distribution efforts to target current customers. Or it can try to expand the potential market by increasing advertising to convert uninterested consumers into interested consumers. This is what Carnival did when it created the "Fun Ships."

Market Areas for Restaurants

In the restaurant industry, it is common to describe market areas geographically and call them *trade areas*, which vary by type of restaurant and area description. For example, in rural areas it is common for people to make a 100-mile round trip to dine at a favorite restaurant. In contrast, 90 percent of the customers of a fast-food restaurant in a residential area of a major city live within 3 miles of the restaurant. People are not willing to spend a great deal of time getting a fast-food meal. But if they eat at a specialty restaurant such as a Hard Rock Café, they are willing to drive across town. Thus, Hard Rock Café's trade area may encompass a 15-mile radius. A McDonald's in the same town may define its trade area as a 3-mile radius.

John Melaniphy, a restaurant site location expert, describes the trade area of a restaurant as an area that provides 85 percent of the restaurant's business. Restaurants that serve out-of-town guests can examine customers' zip codes and find out where their guests are staying while they are visiting the city. He gives other factors that influence the trade area of a restaurant. Topography defines trade areas. Rivers, lakes, or mountains may set boundaries. Psychological barriers can also exist. For example, expressways, airports, and industrial parks may create barriers. Demographic differences in neighborhoods can also create psychological barriers.

For example, residents of a lower-class neighborhood may feel more comfortable eating in their own neighborhood than eating in a restaurant in an upper-middle-class neighborhood, even though both restaurants are the same distance from their houses and have the same average check.

Competition has a big impact on the trade area. Sometimes competition from the same chain may define a trade area. For example, in a city that has eight McDonald's, an adjacent McDonald's may set the boundaries of the trade area for another.

Traffic flows and road patterns also help define trade areas. Accessibility is an important consideration: The better the access, the more extensive the trade area. People also become accustomed to traveling in certain directions and are more likely to travel 4 miles to a restaurant that they pass every day going to work than 4 miles in a direction that they travel infrequently. Thus, a knowledge of normal traveling routes to major employment and shopping areas is useful in determining a trade area. Freeways can also present a perceived barrier. Even though the freeway may provide turn-around loops without stoplights, the multi-lane roadway will result in some consumers choosing restaurants on their side of the freeway.

■■■ Measuring Current Market Demand

We now turn to some practical methods for estimating current market demand. Marketers want to estimate three different aspects of current market demand: total market demand, area market demand, and actual sales and market shares.

Estimating Total Market Demand

The total market demand for a product or service is the total volume that would be bought by a defined consumer group in a defined geographic area in a defined time period in a defined marketing environment under a defined level and mix of industry marketing effort.

Total market demand is not a fixed number but a function of the stated conditions. One of these conditions, for example, is the level and mix of industry marketing effort. Another is the state of the environment. Part A of Figure B–2 shows the relationship between total market demand and these conditions. The horizontal axis shows different possible levels of industry marketing expenditure in a given period. The vertical axis shows the resulting demand level. The curve represents the estimated level of market demand for varying levels of industry marketing expenditure. Some base sales (called the market minimum) would take place without any marketing expenditures. Greater marketing expenditures would yield higher levels of demand, first at an increasing rate and then at a decreasing rate. Marketing expenditures above a certain level would not cause much more demand, suggesting an upper limit to market demand called the *market potential*. The industry market forecast shows the level of market demand corresponding to the planned level of industry marketing expenditure in the given environment.

The distance between the market minimum and the market potential shows the overall sensitivity of demand to marketing efforts. We can think of two extreme types of markets, the expandable and the nonexpandable. An expandable market, such as the market for air travel, is one whose size is affected by the level of industry marketing expenditures. In terms of Figure B–2, in an expandable market, the distance between Q_1 and Q_2 would be fairly large. A nonexpandable market, such as the market for opera, is one whose size is not much affected by the level of marketing expenditures; the distance between Q_1 and Q_2 would be fairly small. Organizations selling in a nonexpandable market can take primary demand—total demand for all brands of a given product or service—as a given. They concentrate their marketing resources on building selective demand—demand for their brand of the product or service.

Figure B–2
Market demand.

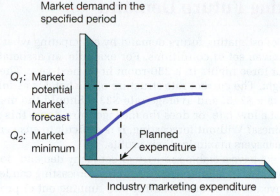

A. Market demand as a function of industry marketing expenditure (assumes a marketing environment of prosperity)

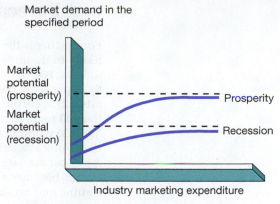

B. Market demand as a function of industry marketing expenditures (under prosperity vs. recession)

Given a different marketing environment, we must estimate a new demand curve. Figure B–2 shows the relationship of market demand to the environment. A given level of marketing expenditure will always result in more demand during prosperity than it would during a recession. Marketers should carefully define the situation for which they are estimating market demand.

Estimating Area Market Demand

Companies face the problem of selecting the best sales territories and allocating their marketing budget optimally among these territories. Therefore, they need to estimate the market potential of different cities, states, and even national markets. Two major methods are available: the market-buildup method and the market-factor index method. The market-buildup method calls for identifying all the potential buyers in each market and estimating their potential purchases. The market-factor index method is used in the fast-food industry. A common method for calculating area market potential is to identify market factors that correlate with market potential and combine them into a weighted index.

Many companies compute additional area demand measures. Marketers now can refine state-by-state and city-by-city measures down to census tracts or zip code centers. Census tracts are small areas about the size of a neighborhood, and zip code centers (designed by the U.S. Postal Service) are larger areas, often the size of small towns. Information on population size, family income, and other characteristics is available for each type of unit. The area demographic information is appended with lifestyle information, such as Experian's Mosaic USA (mentioned in Chapter 8) and PRIZM by Claritas. Marketers can use these data for estimating demand in neighborhoods or other smaller geographic units within large cities.

Estimating Actual Sales and Market Shares

In addition to estimating total and area demand, a company will want to know the actual industry sales in its market. Thus, it must identify its competitors and estimate their sales. The industry's trade association often collects and publishes total industry sales, although it does not list individual company sales separately. In this way, each company can evaluate its performance against the industry as a whole. Suppose that the company's sales are increasing at a rate of 5 percent a year and industry sales are increasing at 10 percent. This company is actually losing its relative standing in the industry.

Forecasting Future Demand

Forecasting is the art of estimating future demand by anticipating what buyers are likely to do under a given set of conditions. For example, an association wants to book 100 rooms for three nights in a 250-room hotel next year. They will pay $225 per room per night. The current rate structure of the hotel is as follows: rack rate $275, corporate rate $245, and average rate $235. Should the manager take the 300 room-nights at a low rate, or does the manager turn down this request for $67,500 worth of business? Without forecasting, it is difficult to answer this question. Forecasts help managers maximize their profits.

Most markets do not have a stable industry or company demand, so good forecasting becomes a key factor in company success. Poor forecasting can lead to overstaffing and excess inventories or understaffing and running out of products. The more unstable the demand, the more the company needs accurate forecasts and elaborate forecasting procedures.

Forecasting Methods

Many firms base their forecasts on past sales. They assume that the causes of past sales can be uncovered through statistical analysis and that analysts can use the causal relations to predict future sales. One popular method, time-series analysis, consists of breaking down the original sales into four components—trend, cycle, season, and erratic components—and then recombining these components to produce the sales forecast. *Trend* is the long-term underlying pattern of growth or decline in sales resulting from basic changes in population, capital formation, and technology. It is found by fitting a straight line through past sales.

Cycle captures the medium-term wave movement of sales resulting from changes in general, economic, and competitive activity. The cyclical component can be useful for medium-range forecasting. Cyclical swings, however, are difficult to predict because they do not occur at regular intervals.

Season refers to a consistent pattern of weekly, monthly, or quarterly sales movements within the year. In the hospitality industry, we usually think of seasonal changes on a yearly basis, but weekly and hourly sales changes are important. The seasonal component can be related to weather factors, holidays, and trade customs. The seasonal pattern provides a norm for forecasting short-range sales. Yield management depends on forecasting demand by day, by flight or cruise, and by hour of the day. Historical sales patterns are carefully analyzed, such as examining sales for Tuesdays of the second week of September or total passengers and the mix of passengers on flight 482 each Wednesday at 3:30 P.M. Forecasting in the airline industry is further complicated by the presence of interconnecting stops. Large hospitality companies, such as hotel chains, and car rental firms, such as Hertz, depend on sophisticated software to analyze huge volumes of data.

Finally, *erratic events* include strikes, snowstorms, earthquakes, riots, fires, and other disturbances. These components, by definition, are unpredictable and should be removed from past data to reveal the more normal behavior of sales. Most of these events cannot be accurately forecasted, but a few, such as snowstorms and strikes, lend themselves to short-run forecasting. Hotel managers in Washington, D.C., know that if a major snowstorm is predicted for the city, room demand will increase. Visitors will be unable to leave the city and will want to retain their rooms. Office workers may be unable to return home and will also want a room. Managers who have a knowledge of the past behavior of demand when erratic events occurred can factor this into their thinking in times of crisis management.

The first step in managing demand is understanding the factors that affect the demand of the firm's market segments. The payday of a major employer may drive area customer demand. For example, in north Dallas the Friday and Saturday nights after a payday at Texas Instruments are much busier than non-payday weekends. There also may be seasonal variations. The Boulders, a resort in Arizona, charges more than $500 a room in season, yet it closes in July and August because of a lack of demand for rooms at less than half this price. Holiday periods have a positive influence on demand at most resorts. Business travel drops off between mid-December and mid-January, during the summer period, and over weekends. Although there is fluctuation in demand, much of the fluctuation can be explained. Managers must understand the factors that drive demand and build it into their forecasts.

Suppose that a 250-room hotel had an occupancy of 76 percent, selling 69,350 room-nights during the year at an average rate of $80. During the last seven years, the number of room-nights sold and average rate have both increased by 5 percent. The hotel has undergone two expansions to keep up with the growth. This information suggests that next year the hotel will sell 72,818 room-nights (69,350 × 1.05) at an average rate of $84 (1.05 × $80). The manager first has to determine whether the hotel has the capacity to handle the increase. If the hotel sold out to business travelers from Tuesday to Thursday during February through May and September through October, it is unrealistic to expect that the growth will continue at a 5-percent rate because it will be constrained by capacity. The only opportunity to increase occupancy is during the low-demand periods.

Let us assume that a recession is expected next year. As a result, the number of room-nights is expected to drop by 10 percent, and the average rate is expected to decrease by 15 percent as competitors cut their rates to attract customers. If the manager did not factor in the recession and projected based solely on past information, the occupancy and average room rate would be greatly overstated. Taking the recession into consideration, the forecast will call for a lower occupancy at a greatly reduced room rate,

When a forecast calls for a decrease in sales, it is important to document the reasons for the decrease. This is especially true of regional recessions. A regional economy with a heavy dependence on one industry can suffer a regional recession when that industry declines while the rest of the country enjoys prosperity. When the hotel management sends its forecast showing a decline in sales to the home office, it will be rejected unless it is well supported. In many cases when a director of sales has presented a marketing plan calling for a decrease in sales without supporting documents to defend the projected decrease, corporate management required the director of sales to increase the forecast. In this scenario, the hotel fails to meet the revised forecast, and the director of sales is fired for not meeting the sales goal. Managers must forecast accurately and provide information to support their forecasts.

Statistical Demand Analysis

Time-series analysis views past and future sales as a function of time rather than as a function of any real demand factors. But many factors affect the sales of any product. Statistical demand analysis is a set of statistical procedures used to discover the most important real factors affecting sales and their relative influence. The factors most commonly analyzed are prices, income, population, and promotion.

Statistical demand analysis consists of expressing sales (Q) as a dependent variable and trying to explain sales as a function of several independent demand variables $X_1, X_2, \ldots, X_n$. That is,

$$Q = f(X_1, X_2 \ldots, X_n)$$

Using a technique called multiple-regression analysis, various equation forms can be statistically fitted to the data in the search for the best predicting factors and equation. For example, a restaurant near Marquette University in Milwaukee, Wisconsin, found that its sales were explained by whether Marquette University was in session and the preceding week's sales:

$$Q = 12750 + 6250X_1 + 0.21X_2$$

where X_1 is a dummy variable indicating whether Marquette was in session, with 1 given when it was in session and 0 used when it was not in session, and X_2 is last week's sales. For example, if Marquette had just finished a term and management wanted to predict sales for next week when last week's sales were $24,000, forecast sales for next week would be as follows:

$$Q = 12750 + 6250X_1 + 0.21X_2$$
$$= 12750 + 6250(0) + 0.21(24000)$$
$$= 12750 + 0 + 5040$$
$$= \$17.790$$

The manager could also expect a decline in sales (because the preceding week's sales will be falling) as activity around the campus slows down. For example, if the restaurant achieved the forecasted sales of $17,790, the next week's projected sales would be $16,486. The decline is due to the drop in the previous week's sales from $24,000 to $17,790 and caused by less people on campus.

Two precautions apply to the use of regression in forecasting. First, the equation just stated will not be sensitive to extraordinary events. For example, on parents' weekend the restaurant may generate very high sales. The equation does not include parents' weekend as a variable; therefore, it is unable to project sales accurately for this event. The sales for the week after parents' weekend will be overstated because the figure for the previous week will be extraordinarily high. Second, it is dangerous to forecast outside the range of the different variables used to build the forecast. For example, if a hotel manager examines the relationship between advertising and room sales, the manager may find that room sales increase $5 for every dollar spent on advertising. If the hotel advertising expenditures had ranged from $75,000 to $150,000, we could not necessarily expect this relationship to hold up for advertising expenditures of $250,000 because this level of advertising has not been tested.

The precautions cited earlier illustrate two types of errors caused by the misuse of regression analysis. Statistical demand analysis can be very complex, and the marketer must take care in designing, conducting, and interrupting such analysis. Yet constantly improving computer technology has made statistical demand analysis an increasingly popular approach to forecasting.

Two other forecasting techniques used in the hospitality industry are moving average and exponential smoothing. A moving average is the average of a set number of previous periods (n); this average is used to predict sales for the next period. For example, if a restaurant had sales of $12,000, $12,500, $13,000, and $12,500 over the last four weeks, using a four-week moving average, the sales forecast for the next week would be $12,500.

$$\frac{\$12,000 + \$12,500 + \$13,000 + \$12,500}{4} = \$12,500$$

A limitation of moving averages is that the latest period used in the average has the same weight as the current period. Exponential smoothing is a simple but useful mathematical technique, which allows recent periods to be weighted.

The forecasting techniques presented in this appendix represent a few of the techniques that managers use. It is not within the scope of this book to provide a detailed explanation of all forecasting techniques. We simply want to illustrate that tools are available to assist managers with their forecasts.

Case Studies

■■■ Case 1 Zipcar: It's Not about Cars—It's About Urban Life

Imagine a world in which no one owns a car. Cars would still exist, but rather than owning cars, people would just share them. Sounds crazy, right? But Scott Griffith,

CEO of Zipcar, the world's largest car-share company, paints a picture of just such an imaginary world. And he has nearly 800,000 passionate customers—or Zipsters, as they are called—who will back him up.

Zipcar specializes in renting out cars by the hour or day. Although this may sound like a minor variation on the established rental car agency business, car sharing—a concept pioneered by Zipcar—is an entirely different concept. As Griffith took the driver's seat of the young start-up company, he knew that if the company was going to achieve cruising speed, it needed to be far more than just another car service. Zipcar needed to be a well-positioned brand that appealed to a customer base with unfulfilled needs.

A Car Rental Company That Isn't About Cars

As Griffith considered what Zipcar had to offer, it was apparent that it couldn't be all things to all people. But the concept seemed particularly well suited to people who live or work in densely populated neighborhoods in cities such as New York, Boston, Atlanta, San Francisco, and London. For these customers, owning a car (or a second or third car) is difficult, costly, and environmentally irresponsible. Interestingly, Zipcar doesn't see itself as a car-rental company. Instead, it's selling a lifestyle, the urban life.

Initially, the Zipcar brand was positioned exclusively round a value system. As an urban lifestyle brand, Zipcar focused on traits that city dwellers have in common. For starters, the lifestyle is rooted in environmental consciousness. At first, Zipcar focused on green-minded customers with promotional pitches such as "We • Earth" and "Imagine a world with a million fewer cars on the road." Zipcar's vibrant green logo reflects this save-the-Earth philosophy. And Zipcar really does deliver on its environmental promises. Studies show that every shared Zipcar takes up to 20 cars off the road and cuts carbon emissions by up to 50 percent per user. On average, Zipsters travel 44 percent fewer miles than when they owned a car, leaving an average of 219 gallons of crude oil in the ground. Multiply all this out by 11,000 cars in Zipcar's fleet, and that's a pretty substantial impact on the environment.

But it wasn't long Zipcar realized that if it was going to grow, it needed to move beyond just being green. So the brand has broadened its positioning to include other urban lifestyle benefits—benefits that Zipcar appeals to on its site in response to the question, "Who exactly is the car-sharing type?" Zipcar provides these most common reasons for car sharing:

- I don't want the hassle of owning a car.

- I want to save money.

- I take public transit, but need a car sometimes.

- Once in a while I need a second car.

- I need a big car for a big job.

- I want to impress my boss.

One of most important benefits Zipcar provides is convenience. Owning a car in a densely populated urban area can be a real hassle. Zipcar lets customers focus on driving, not on the complexities of car ownership. It gives them "Wheels when you want them," in four easy steps: "Join. Reserve. Unlock. Drive."

Fulfilling Consumer Needs

To join, you pay around $60 for an annual membership and receive your personal Zipcard, which unlocks any Zipcar vehicle located in urban areas around the world. Then, when you need a car, reserve one—minutes or months in advance—online, by phone, or using a smartphone app. You can choose the car you want, when and where you want it, and drive it for as little as $7.50 an hour, including gas, insurance, and free miles. When you're ready, walk to the car, hold your Zipcard to the windshield to unlock the doors, and you're good to go. When you're done, you drop the car off at the same parking spot—Zipcar worries about the maintenance and cleaning.

Zipcar not only eliminates the hassle of urban car ownership, it also saves money. By living with less, the average Zipster saves $600 a month on car payments, insurance, gas, maintenance, and other car ownership expenses. That's like getting a $10,000 a year raise after taxes. In an era when consumers have become more frugal, this is a big plus, especially for those looking to live more minimally.

Zipcar isn't for everyone—it doesn't try to be. Instead, it zeros in on a narrowly defined urban lifestyle positioning. For starters, Zipcar "pods" (a dozen or so vehicles located in a given neighborhood) are stocked from a portfolio of over 50 different models that trendy urbanites love. The vehicles are both hip and fuel efficient: Toyota Priuses, Honda CRVs, MINIs, Volvo S60s, BMW 328s, Toyota Tacomas, Toyota Siennas, Subaru Outbacks, and others. And Zipcar now has plug-in hybrids, fully electric vehicles, and full-size vans for big jobs. Each car has its own personality—a name and profile created by a Zipster. For example, Prius Ping "jogs in the morning; doesn't say much," whereas Civic Carlos "teaches yoga; loves to kayak." Such personal touches make it feel like you're borrowing the car from a friend, rather than being assigned whatever piece of metal happens to be available.

To further eliminate hassles and make Zipcar as convenient as possible, company promotional tactics are designed to appeal to city dwellers. The company's goal is for Zipsters to not have to walk more than seven minutes to get to one of its car pods, no easy task. Zipcar's management realizes that even with targeted Web and mobile promotions it is hard to target at a block level. Zipcar sends street teams to understand the urban blocks. They use local ads and transit advertising. They use an on-the-ground guerilla-type marketing approach.

With its eye sharply focused on maintaining the Zipcar image, the company is consistently developing new features that appeal to the tech-savvy urbanites. Recently, the company has shifted its focus a bit from being a Web-based business to being an overwhelmingly mobile concern. Soon, Zipcars will have in-car device holders for smartphones that will allow for easy plug-in and hands-free navigation. The interface between the cars and the users will allow playlists stored on the phone to be played through the car's audio system. Users will be provided with information specific to the vehicle they are in, a personalized deal recommendation service, and a real-time feedback loop where users can report on vehicle cleanliness, damage, and fuel levels.

Fostering Brand Community

Zipcar's orientation around the urban, environmentally conscious lifestyle fosters a tight-knit sense of customer community. Zipsters are as fanatically loyal as the hardcore fans of Harley-Davidson or Apple, brands that have been nurturing customer relationships for decades. Loyal Zipsters serve as neighborhood brand ambassadors; 30 percent of new members join up at the recommendation of existing customers. "When I meet another Zipcar member at a party or something, I feel like we have something in common," says one Brooklyn Zipster. "It's like we're both making intelligent choices about our lives." And just like Harley owners get together on weekends to ride, the Internet is littered with announcements for Zipster parties at bars, restaurants, and comedy clubs, among other places.

As Zipcar has taken off, it has broadened the appeal of its brand to include a different type of urban dweller—businesses and other organizations. Companies such as Google now encourage employees to be environmentally conscious by commuting via a company shuttle and then using Zipcars for both business and personal use during the day. Other companies are using Zipcar as an alternative to black sedans, long taxi rides, and congested parking lots. Government agencies are getting into the game as well. The city of Chicago recently partnered with Zipcar to provide a more efficient and sustainable transportation alternative for city agencies. And Washington, DC, now saves more than $1 million a year using Zipcar. Fleet management has proven to be a good market for Zipcar. As word of mouth spreads on savings that Zipcar can bring, organizations wanting to get rid of their fleet of cars are signing up with Zipcar. How is Zipcar's strategy of positioning itself as an urban lifestyle brand working? By all accounts, the young car-sharing nicher has the pedal to the metal and its tires are smoking. In just the past five years, Zipcar's annual revenues have rocketed nearly fivefold, to more than $270 million.

Zipcar has also reached the milestone of being profitable. And with 10 million people now within walking distance of a Zipcar, there's plenty of room to grow. As more cars are added, Zipcar's reach will only increase.

Zipcar's rapid growth has sounded alarms at the traditional car-rental giants. Enterprise, Hertz, Thrifty, and even U-Haul now have their own car-sharing operations. Avis also had one. But recently, Avis decided to shut down its own service and buy Zipcar for nearly $500 million. The Zipcar brand will now benefit from cost savings that the large-scale rental service enjoys. As for the others, Zipcar has a big head start in terms of size and experience, cozy relationships in targeted neighborhoods, and an urban hipster cred that corporate giants like Hertz will have trouble matching. To Zipsters, Hertz rents cars, but Zipcar is a part of their hectic urban lives.

Sources: Based on information from Mark Clothier, "Zipcar Soars After Profit Topped Analysts' Estimates," Bloomberg.com, November 9, 2012, www.bloomberg,com/ news/20I2-l1-09/zipcar-soars-after-profittopped-analysts-estimates.html; Darrell Etherington, "Zipcar CEO Details In-Car Assistant, Personalized Deals and Member Onboarding for Mobile App," *Techcrunch*, October 9, 2012, www.techcrunch.com/2012/10/09/zipcar-ceo-details-in-car-assistant-personalizeddeals-and-member-onboarding-for-mobile-app/; Jerry Hirsch, "Zipcar CEO Talks About Car Sharing as Lifestyle Choice," *Seattle Times*, May 13, 2012, www .seattletimes.nwsource.com/html/businesstechnoIogy/2018197748_inpersonzipcarl4.html; Paul Keegan, "Zipcar; The Best New Idea in Business," *Fortune*, August 27, 2009, www.moneycnn .com/2009/08/26/news/companies/zipcar_car_rentals.fortune/; Stephanie Clifford, "How Fast Can This Thing Go, Anyway?" *Inc.*, March 1, 2008, www.inc.com/magazine/20080301/ how-fast-can-this-thing-go-anyway.html; www.zipcar.com (accessed May 2013).

◼◼◼ QUESTIONS FOR DISCUSSION

Chapter 4

1. What environmental factors would make Zipcar an attractive acquisition for Avis?

Chapter 6

1. Describe the beliefs and values associated with Zipcar's brand image.

2. How did Zipcar match the values and beliefs, with lifestyle?

Chapter 7

Zipcar was developed for a consumer segment, but found an application for organizational markets. Use the organizational buying decisions presented in Chapter 7 in the text as a reference for your answers to the next two questions.

1. What problem does Zipcar solve for an organization?

2. What need does it fulfill?

3. What type of organization could Zipcar best serve?

Chapter 8

1. Evaluate Zipcar based on benefit-based positioning.

2. Compare Zipcar's positioning based on benefits to Zipcar's positioning based on beliefs and values. Which is stronger?

◼◼◼ Case 2 Cafeteria I.C.E.

The cafeteria for employees of I.C.E. (the national electric company of Costa Rica: Instituto Costarricense de Electricidad) was experiencing difficulties, and top management felt compelled to see what corrective actions could be taken. Responsibility for correcting the problems had been assigned to Antonio F. Caas Mora, assistant manager for telecommunications.

The problems were of two types. First, no one was satisfied with the time required for lunch. The time often extended beyond the allocated half hour, resulting in loss of productivity. The second, related problem was how to change the lunchtime eating habits of the employees. The majority of employees used the main serving line, where they purchased a heavy traditional Latin meal. This required a considerable amount of time and also made the employees sleepy after eating. As a result, afternoon productivity among office personnel declined.

Background on I.C.E. and the Cafeteria

I.C.E. was the largest electric utility and the only telephone company in the nation of Costa Rica. It was owned and operated by the government of Costa Rica.

Although I.C.E. had field office locations throughout Costa Rica, the central administrative offices were located in the city of San José in a modern 15-story building. A total of 4,486 persons were employed by I.C.E. and 1,453 of these worked in the central office building. This group used the cafeteria facilities.

The cafeteria had been in operation for five years. It was under the management of an employee cooperative. This cooperative was managed by an elected board of directors consisting of employees of I.C.E. The board of directors of the cooperative hired a full-time manager who had direct responsibility for the cafeteria operation.

Description of Employees

Employees who worked in the I.C.E. building and used the cafeteria were primarily white-collar personnel. A minority of blue-collar employees such as maintenance personnel used the cafeteria. Employees who worked in the I.C.E. building consisted primarily of administrators, staff specialists, engineers, clerical personnel, secretaries, and receptionists.

The Menu and Eating Habits

The cafeteria consisted of two serving lines; the main serving line was the most popular with the employees and was the one with the long waiting lines. This line served what was known as the *casado*, a typical Latin meal. The menu changed each day. A typical meal consisted of a meat dish such as a small steak, sausage, or liver. This was accompanied with rice, beans, and a vegetable such as corn or, more commonly, potatoes.

The meals served in the main serving line reflected the cultural habits of Costa Ricans with traditional food. The noontime meal historically had been eaten with the family and required two or three hours, including family conversation and sometimes a short nap. This custom was the basis for closing stores during midday. It was still the custom in many parts of Latin America for all types of businesses to close until 2 or 3 P.M. The traditional long lunch hour meant that employees would arrive for work early in the morning, take a long lunch break, return for work, and stay late in the evening until 6 or 6:30 P.M. The management of I.C.E. had decided to break with this tradition to allow as smooth a workday as possible without the interruption of a long lunch break. The I.C.E. system closely paralleled that found in the United States.

There was evidence of change in eating habits in San José. Several U.S.-style restaurants had entered the market and did a brisk business at lunch with hamburgers, pizza, and other quick foods. McDonald's, Hardee's, and Pizza Hut were popular noontime restaurants, especially with younger people. After witnessing the success of restaurants such as McDonald's, the board of directors of the cooperative decided to open a sandwich line in the cafeteria. This was separate from the main serving line. It consisted of a long counter. Plastic food trays were placed on the counter and filled with stacks of unwrapped cold sandwiches such as cheese or ham and cheese. Other trays contained slices of fruits such as papaya or watermelon and cake. Coffee, milk, and carbonated beverages were available from dispensers located on the counter.

Two cash registers were located at the end of the main serving line, and one at the end of the sandwich line. Information was not recorded concerning the number of employees who used each line or the average expenditure per person in the sandwich line. However, it was felt that the average lunch expenditure per employee would probably be about two-thirds of the per-person expenditure in the main serving line.

Working Hours and Office Rules

The office hours at I.C.E. extended from 7:30 A.M. to 3:30 P.M., with half an hour for lunch. Employees were expected to arrive on time. This meant that some employees had to rise as early as 5:30 A.M., and few could rise later than 6:30 A.M.

Coffee breaks were not officially permitted, and there were no vending machines in the building. The policy of no coffee breaks had been instituted because many employees spilled coffee or other liquids on reports. It was also felt that a coffee break was unnecessary because half an hour was given for lunch. Workers would occasionally bring a cake or cookies from home and share them with employees in their work area, even though this was officially frowned upon.

A system had been devised to prevent all employees from crowding into the cafeteria at one time. The doors of the cafeteria were locked until 11 A.M., at which time employees began to arrive on a set schedule by floors. The line closed promptly at 1:30 P.M.

Survey Results

Before attempting to make changes to correct the situation in the cafeteria, management felt it would be wise to conduct a survey among the employees. This was done through the use of a written questionnaire, which was given to all persons using the cafeteria on a selected day. The results of this questionnaire follow.

Opinions Concerning Selected Factors (%)

	OPINION				
FACTOR	VERY GOOD	GOOD	AVERAGE	BAD	NO OPINION
Quality	0.63	16.46	44.78	23.42	14.71
Variety	4.59	35.28	28.96	18.67	12.50
Cleanliness	1.74	18.67	36.55	29.75	13.24
Courtesy	5.38	27.37	39.24	25.16	2.85
Convenience	8.07	30.70	34.65	23.26	3.32
Quality of cooking	8.39	35.28	33.70	18.83	3.80
Quantity	3.16	28.48	39.72	20.41	8.23

Opinions Concerning Type of Food Served (%)

	OPINION				
FOOD	VERY GOOD	GOOD	AVERAGE	BAD	NO OPINION
Chicken w/rice	8.86	43.04	29.59	7.59	10.92
Shrimp w/rice	1.11	12.34	33.23	31.64	21.68
Meatballs	2.37	12.97	31.33	31.65	21.68
Sea bass	10.28	37.18	25.63	8.86	18.04
Breaded steak	4.11	22.47	34.02	18.04	21.36
Flank steak in sauce	3.64	24.68	30.85	15.82	25.06
Tongue in sauce	5.54	26.58	26.42	17.41	24.05
Chicken in sauce	3.32	23.10	29.43	16.30	27.85
Fried chicken	2.37	23.89	30.70	12.97	30.06
Pork chop	3.32	19.15	29.43	21.99	26.11
Spaghetti w/meat	1.90	13.77	29.11	33.07	22.15
Spaghetti w/tuna	2.37	10.92	26.42	34.18	26.11
Chickpeas w/tripe	3.64	17.56	28.80	28.01	21.99
Chop suey	1.90	14.40	24.05	38.76	20.89

Opinions Concerning Diet and Type of Meal (%)

	YES	NO	NO OPINION
Do you believe the diet is well balanced?	17.88	75.63	6.49
Do you feel that the special plate of the day should be eliminated?	27.69	66.61	5.70
Do you believe the *casado* should be eliminated?	26.42	68.04	5.54
Do you believe a lighter meal should be served?	36.23	14.40	49.37

Light Meal Preferences[a] (%)

	YES	NO
Hot dogs	44.46	55.54
Hamburgers	30.85	69.15
Chicken	42.41	57.54
Pastry	36.55	63.45
Fruit	18.99	81.01
Sandwiches	49.53	50.47
Desserts	31.80	68.20
Soup	18.35	81.65
Salads	23.10	76.90
Fruit salads	33.86	66.14
Other	10.28	89.72

[a]If a light meal was served. All respondents answered this.

Answers Concerning Eating Habits (%)

	YES	NO	NO ANSWER
Do you follow a special diet?	14.72	76.58	8.70
Do you usually bring your lunch?	10.76	81.33	7.91

Average Time Taken to Eat Lunch (%)

20–30 minutes	18.83
30–45 minutes	61.87
45–60 minutes	12.50
Over 60 minutes	0.79
No answer	6.01

Observations Concerning Seating in Cafeteria

A series of observations were made in the cafeteria on typical days. The cafeteria held 58 tables with four chairs each, for a total of 232 places. The utilization of this space on the days observed is shown in the tables that follow.

Use of Available Seating Capacity

TIME	AVAILABLE SEATS	PERSONS IN WAITING LINE	THEORETICAL SURPLUS OR SHORTAGE OF SEATS
Wednesday, August 16			
11:45	45	80	235
12:25	16	90	274
12:30	48	90	274
1:05	68	40	128
1:20	88	27	161
Thursday, August 17			
11:15	44	16	128
11:42	68	38	130
11:56	39	43	24
12:00	44	55	211
12:10	80	53	127
12:15	56	37	119
12:30	56	52	24
12:40	56	47	19
12:55	26	46	220
1:15	56	3	153

Tables Occupied by One or Two People

	TABLES OCCUPIED BY ONE	TABLES OCCUPIED BY TWO	TOTAL
Wednesday, August 16			
11:42	12	22	34
11:56	6	26	32
12:00	6	38	44
12:10	3	30	33
12:15	15	18	33
12:30	6	26	32
12:55	15	20	35
1:15	6	14	20

Rate of Flow Through Serving Line

Main line. After two days of observation, it was found that the average time required for a person to pass through the main serving line from the moment a person picked up a tray until leaving the cash register was slightly in excess of 3 minutes, with a range of 2 to 4 minutes. There was never a break in this line from the moment the cafeteria opened at 11 A.M. until it closed at 1:30 P.M. The line moved steadily, yet a waiting line would form between 12:00 P.M. and 12:45 P.M., which at times extended well into the hallway in front of the elevator and caused waiting times of 20 minutes before reaching the actual food line.

Sandwich line. The amount of time required per person to pass through the sandwich line ranged from 0.5 to 4 minutes. The average time for persons who used the sandwich line but did not use a sandwich grill to cook cold sandwiches was 2.10 minutes. The amount of time required in this line when someone used the sandwich grill located beyond the cash register ranged between 3 and 8 minutes, with an average time of 4.5 minutes. At times as many as 8 or 10 persons would be waiting to use the sandwich grill.

■■■ QUESTIONS FOR DISCUSSION

Chapter 3

1. Can the use of marketing concepts/strategies be of use in solving the problem with Cafeteria I.C.E.?

2. What effect can an individual organization such as I.C.E. have on changing ingrained cultural habits such as those of noontime dining?

3. What would you suggest be done to increase patronage of the sandwich and fruit line?

■■■ Case 3 Disney

Few companies have been able to connect with their audience as well as Disney has. From its founding by brothers Walt and Roy Disney in 1923, the Disney brand has always been synonymous with trust, fun, and quality entertainment for the entire family. Walt Disney was interested in bringing laughter to people.

The Walt Disney Company has grown into the worldwide phenomenon that today includes theme parks, feature films, television networks, theatre productions, consumer products, and a growing online presence. In its first two decades, however, it was a struggling cartoon studio that introduced the world to Mickey Mouse, who went on to become its most famous character. Few believed in Disney's vision at the time, but the smashing success of cartoons with sound and of the first full-length animated film, *Snow White and the Seven Dwarfs*, in 1937 led to other animated classics throughout the 1940s, 1950s, and 1960s, including *Pinocchio*, *Bambi*, *Cinderella*, and *Peter Pan*, live-action films such as *Mary Poppins* and the *Love Bug*, and television series like *Davy Crockett*.

When Walt Disney died in 1966, he was considered the best-known person in the world. He had expanded the Disney brand into film, television, consumer products, and Disneyland in southern California, the company's first theme park. After Walt's death, Roy Disney took over as CEO and realized his brother's dream of opening the 24,000-acre Walt Disney World theme park in Florida. Roy died in 1971, and the company stumbled for several years without the leadership of its two founding brothers. It wasn't until the late 1980s that the company reconnected with its audience and restored trust and interest in the Disney brand.

It all started with the release of the *Little Mermaid*, which turned an old fairy tale into a magical animated Broadway-style movie that won two Oscars. Between the late 1980s and 2000, Disney entered an era known as the Disney Renaissance as it released groundbreaking animated films such as *Beauty and the Beast* (1991), *Aladdin* (1992), the *Lion King* (1994), *Toy Story* (with Pixar, 1995), and *Mulan* (1998). In addition, the company thought of creative new ways to target its core family-oriented consumers as well as expand into new areas to reach an older audience. It launched the Disney Channel, Touchstone Pictures, and Touchstone Television. Disney featured classic films during the Disney Sunday Night Movie and sold its classic films on video at extremely low prices, reaching a whole new generation of children. It tapped into publishing, international theme parks, and theatrical productions that helped reach a variety of audiences around the world.

Today, Disney consists of five business segments: Studio Entertainment, which creates films, recording labels, and theatrical performances; Parks and Resorts, which focuses on Disney's 11 theme parks, cruise lines, and other travel-related assets; Consumer Products, which sells all Disney-branded products; Media Networks, which includes Disney's television networks such as ESPN, ABC, and the Disney Channel; and Interactive.

Disney's greatest challenge today is keeping a 90-year-old brand relevant and current with its core audience while staying true to its heritage and core brand values. Disney was faced with showing respect to its heritage, while at the same time maintaining it relevancy through innovation.

Internally, to achieve quality and recognition, Disney has focused on the Disney Difference, which stems from one of Walt Disney's most recognizable quotes: "Whatever you do, do it well." He said if you do people will come back and bring others to show them how well you do it.

Disney works hard to connect with its customers on many levels and through every single detail. For example, at Disney World, "cast members" or employees are trained to be "assertively friendly" and greet visitors by waving big Mickey Mouse hands, hand out maps to adults and stickers to kids, and clean up the park so diligently that it's difficult to find a piece of garbage anywhere.

Every detail matters, right down to the behavior of custodial workers who are trained by Disney's animators to take their simple broom and bucket of water and quietly "paint" a Goofy or Mickey Mouse in water on the pavement. It's a moment of magic for guests that lasts just a minute before it evaporates in the hot sun.

Disney's broad range of businesses allows the company to connect with its audience in multiple ways, efficiently and economically. Hannah Montana provides an excellent example. The company took a tween-targeted television show and moved it across several divisions to become a significant franchise for the company, including millions of CD sales, video games, popular consumer products, box office movies, concerts around the world, and ongoing live performances at international Disneyland resorts in Hong Kong, India, and Russia.

Recently, Disney acquired three huge brands: Pixar, Marvel, and Lucas Films. The company has started to leverage these properties, which include the Star Wars brand and superheroes such as Spiderman, Iron Man, and the Hulk, across many of its businesses in order to create sustainable character brands and new growth opportunities for the company.

Perhaps the most anticipated new product of 2013 was the Disney Infinity gaming platform, which crossed all Disney boundaries. Disney Infinity allowed consumers to play with many of the Disney characters at the same time, interacting and working together on different adventures. For example, Andy from *Toy Story* might join forces with Captain Jack Sparrow from *Pirates of the Caribbean* and several monsters from Monsters, Inc. to fight villains from outer space.

With so many brands, characters, and businesses, Disney uses technology to ensure that a customer's experience is consistent across every platform. The company connects with its consumers in innovative ways through e-mail, blogs, and its Web site. It was one of the first companies to begin regular podcasts of its television shows as well as to post news about its products and interviews with Disney's employees, staff, and park officials. Disney's Web site provides insight into its movie trailers, television clips, Broadway shows, and virtual theme park experiences.

Disney's marketing campaign in recent years has focused on how it helps make unforgettable family memories. The campaign, "Let the Memories Begin," features real guests throughout Disney enjoying different rides and magical experiences. Disney realized that each and every day it is making memories for its guests.

According to internal studies, Disney estimates that consumers spend 13 billion hours "immersed" with the Disney brand each year. Consumers around the world spend 10 billion hours watching programs on the Disney Channel, 800 million hours at Disney's resorts and theme parks, and 1.2 billion hours watching a Disney movie—at home, in the theater, or on their computer. Today, Disney is the 13th most powerful brand in the world, and its revenues topped $45 billion in 2013.

Sources: "Company History," Disney.com; Annual Reports, Disney.com; Richard Siklosc, "The Iger Difference" *Fortune*, April 11, 2008; Brooks Barnes, "After Mickey's Makeover; Less Mr. Nice Guy," *New York Times*, November 4, 2009; "World's Most Powerful Brands," *Forbes*, April 2012; Dorothy Pomerantz, "Five Lessons in Success from Disney's $40 Million CEO," *Forbes*, January 23, 2013; "Disney Launches Infinity Video Game That Costs More Than an iPad Mini," *Daily Mail*, January 6, 2013; Carmine Gallo, "Customer Service the Disney Way," *Forbes*, April 14, 2011; Hugo Martin, "Disney's 2011 Marketing Campaign Centers on Family Memories," *Times*, P. 1A, September 23, 2010; Elena Malydhina, "Disney Parks Campaign Borrows Family Memories," *Adweek*, September 23, 2010.

◼◼◼ QUESTIONS FOR DISCUSSION

Chapter 6

1. What does Disney do best to connect with its core consumers?

2. What are the risks and benefits of expanding the Disney brand in new ways, such as video games or superheroes?

■■ Case 4 JetBlue: Delighting Customers Through Happy Jetting

In the early years, JetBlue was a thriving young airline with a strong reputation for outstanding service. In fact, the low-fare airline referred to itself as a customer service company that just happened to fly planes. But on a Valentine's Day, JetBlue was hit by the perfect storm, literally, of events that led to an operational meltdown. One of the most severe storms of the decade covered JetBlue's main hub at New York's John F. Kennedy International Airport with a thick layer of snow and ice. JetBlue did not have the infrastructure to deal with such a crisis. The severity of the storm, coupled with a series of poor management decisions, left JetBlue passengers stranded in planes on the runway for up to 11 hours. Worse still, the ripple effect of the storm created major JetBlue flight disruptions for six more days.

Understandably, customers were livid. JetBlue's efforts to clean up the mess following the six-day Valentine's Day nightmare cost over $30 million in overtime, flight refunds, vouchers for future travel, and other expenses. But the blow to the company's previously stellar customer-service reputation stung far more than the financial fallout. JetBlue became the butt of jokes by late night talk show hosts. Some industry observers even predicted that this would be the end of JetBlue.

But just three years later, the company is not only still flying, it is growing, profitable, and hotter than ever. During a serious economic downturn competing airlines were cut routes, retiring aircraft, laying off employees, and lost money. JetBlue added planes, expanded into new cities, hired thousands of new employees, and turning profits.

Truly Customer Focused

What's the secret to JetBlue's success? Quite simply, it's an obsession with making sure that every customer experience lives up to the company slogan, "Happy Jetting." Lots of companies say they focus on customers. But at JetBlue, customer well-being is ingrained in the culture.

From the beginning, JetBlue set out to provide features that would delight customers. For example, most air travelers expect to be squashed when flying coach. But JetBlue has configured its seats with three more inches of legroom than the average airline seat. That may not sound like much. But those three inches allow six-foot three-inch Arianne Cohen, author of *The Tall Book: A Celebration of Life from on High*, to stretch out and even cross her legs. If that's not enough, for as little as $10 per flight, travelers can reserve one of JetBlue's "Even More Legroom" seats, which offer even more space and a flatter recline position. Add the fact that every JetBlue seat is well padded and covered in leather, and you already have an air travel experience that rivals first-class accommodations (something JetBlue doesn't offer).

Food and beverage is another perk that JetBlue customers enjoy. The airline doesn't serve meals, but it offers the best selection of free beverages and snacks to be found at 30,000 feet. In addition to the standard soft drinks, juices, and salty snacks, JetBlue flyers enjoy Terra Blues chips, Immaculate Baking's Chocobillys cookies, and Dunkin' Donuts coffee. But it isn't just the selection; it's the fact that customers don't feel like they have to beg for a nibble. One customer describes snacking on JetBlue as an "open bar for snacks. They are constantly walking around offering it. I never feel thirsty. I never feel hungry. It's not 'Here, have a little sip,' and 'Good-bye, that's all you get.'"

Airlines often can't control flight delays, especially at busy airports like JFK. So JetBlue wants to be sure that customers will be entertained even in the event of a delay. That's why every seat has its own LCD entertainment system. Customers can watch any of 36 channels on DirectTV or listen to 100+ channels on Sirius XM Radio, free of charge. If that isn't enough, six bucks will buy a movie or your favorite television show. JetBlue rounds out the amenities with free Wi-Fi in terminals and free sending and receiving of e-mails and instant messages in the air.

Even JetBlue's main terminal, the new state-of-the-art T-5 terminal at JFK, is not the usual airline experience. With more security lanes than any terminal in the United States, travelers scurry right through. High-end dining (tapas, lobster tempura, and Kobe sliders, just to name a few options) can be found among the terminal's 22 restaurants. And its 25 retail stores are characteristic of the latest mall offerings. A children's play zone, comfortable lounge areas, workspaces, and piped in music from Sirius XM Radio make travelers hesitant to leave.

More Than Amenities

Although the tangible amenities that JetBlue offers are likely to delight most travelers, CEO David Barger recognizes that these things are not nearly enough to provide a sustainable competitive advantage. "The hard product—airplanes, leather seats, satellite TVs, bricks and mortar—as long as you have a check book, they can be replicated," Barger tells a group of new hires in training. "It's the culture that can't be replicated. It's how we treat each other. Do we trust each other? Can we push back on each other? The human side of the equation is the most important part of what we're doing."

It's that culture that gives JetBlue customer service unlike that of any other airline. Taking care of customers starts as early as a customer's first encounter with a JetBlue call center. Many callers feel like they are talking to the lady next door. That's because, in all likelihood, they are. JetBlue's founder pioneered a reservation system that employs part-time reps working from home. Mary Driffill is one of 700 at-home reservations agents in Salt Lake City alone. She logs on to her computer and receives calls in her four-year-old daughter's bedroom, under the watchful eye of Raggedy Ann, Potbelly Bear, and Chewy, the family Pomeranian-Chihuahua mix. "It's the best job I've ever had," says Driffill. "Every day I talk to people who love the company as much as I do. That reminds me I'm part of this."

JetBlue employees are well acquainted with the company's core values: safety, integrity, caring, passion, and fun. If that sounds like an awful lot of warm fuzzies, it's intentional. But JetBlue hires the types of employees that fit these values. The values then provide the basis for what Robin Hayes, JetBlue's chief commercial officer, calls the company's S.O.C.I.A.L. currency program. In JetBlue's words:

Standing for something. JetBlue was formed with the idea of bringing humanity back to travel, and our engagement with our customers is central to that mission.

Operationalizing the brand. Whether it is in the airport, on the planes, on the phones, or online, the connection with our customers is a key factor in how we do business.

Conversing with customers, broadly. To be properly in touch with the community, it requires the ability to understand and react to the collective conversation that occurs.

Involving, immersing employees. Social media involvement requires understanding and involvement from all aspects and departments of the company.

Advocating the brand. For JetBlue, we understand the ability to market to a social community is dependent on our customers' willingness to hear and spread those marketing messages.

Listening. Waiving the carry-on bike fee . . . shows we quickly identify and adapt new policies based on feedback we receive through social media channels. It demonstrates our ability to listen and react holistically.

When You Love Your Customers, They Love You Back

Customers who spread positive word of mouth are called many names—true friends, angels, apostles, and evangelists. The religious overtones of such labels come from the idea that loyal customers are like true believers who share the good word like a missionary would. JetBlue has an unusually high ratio of such customers. Most airline customers are loyal because they have frequent flyer points. If not for those points, most couldn't care less with whom they fly. For most, flying is a generally unpleasant experience regardless of who operates the plane.

However, JetBlue customers are so enthralled with what the airline has to offer that they look forward to flying. And they want to keep in touch with the brand even when they aren't flying. JetBlue has 1.1 million followers on Twitter, more than any other company except Whole Foods Market and Zappos.com, two other customer service legends. Twitter even features JetBlue as a case study on smart corporate twittering. More broadly, by the metric of social currency (a fancy term for networks of customers spreading by word of mouth), JetBlue is the strongest U.S. brand, outperforming even Apple.

JetBlue's strong word of mouth has been fueled by the company's ability to delight customers. People love to talk about JetBlue because the experience is so unexpected. Most airline travel has a particular pattern: small seats, bad entertainment, and little (if any) food. JetBlue breaks this pattern: leather seats, your own entertainment system with dozens of channels, and at least some choice of food. People can't stop talking about the experience because they have to express their surprise, especially given the "value" price. They are so used to airline travel being poor, late, or uncomfortable these days that cases where a company seems to care and provide good service seems noteworthy. Satisfaction itself is unexpected.

In 10 short years, JetBlue has proven that an airline can deliver low fares, excellent service, and steady profits. It has shown that even in the airline business, a powerful brand can be built. Few other airlines have been able to write this story. If you're thinking Southwest Airlines, you'd be on target. In fact, JetBlue's founders modeled the airline after Southwest. JetBlue has often been called "the Southwest of the Northeast." JetBlue's on-board crews even greet customers on-board with jokes, songs, and humorous versions of the safety routine, something Southwest has been known for since the 1970s. But where Southwest has made customers happy with no frills, JetBlue is arguably doing it all, including the frills.

Until last year, Southwest and JetBlue steered clear of each other. But then both airlines added a Boston–Baltimore route. Boston is a JetBlue stronghold; Baltimore is Southwest's biggest market. But with JetBlue's younger workforce and newer, more fuel-efficient planes, its cost per available seat mile is 8.88 cents, whereas it's 9.76 cents for Southwest. That has allowed JetBlue to do something that no other airline has done to Southwest; undercut it on price with $39 tickets that are $20 cheaper than Southwest's lowest fare. It's not clear yet how the battle of the low-fare, high-service airlines will play out. But it may well turn out that as JetBlue and Southwest cross paths on more routes, the losers will be the other airlines.

◼◼◼ QUESTIONS FOR DISCUSSION

Chapter 1

1. Give examples of needs, wants, and demands that JetBlue customers demonstrate, differentiating these three concepts. What are the implications of each for JetBlue's practices?

2. Describe in detail all the facets of JetBlue's product. What is being exchanged in a JetBlue transaction?

3. What value does JetBlue create for its customers?

Chapter 2

1. Explain how JetBlue has created a service culture.

2. Do you think JetBlue would be a good company to work for? Explain your answer.

Sources: Stuart Elliott, "JetBlue Asks Its Fliers to Keep Spreading the Word," *New York Times* (May 10, 2010): p. B7; Marc Gunther, "Nothing Blue About JetBlue," *Fortune* (September 14, 2009): p. 114; Chuck Salter, "Calling JetBlue," *Fast Company* (May 1, 2004), www .fastcompany.com/magazine/82/jetblue_agents.html; Kevin Randall, "Red, Hot, and Blue: The Hottest American Brand Is Not Apple," *Fast Company* (June 3, 2010), www.fastcompany .com/1656066/apple-jetblue-social-currency-twitter.

■■■ Case 5 The Hunt Room: Change the Concept or Just the Decor?

The Rolling Hills Country Club is an established club in a major eastern city. Jimmy Johnson, the general manager of the club, had just convened the regular weekly meeting of the executive committee. The first item on the agenda was the Hunt Room.

Hans Krueger, the food and beverage manager, claims that sales have been declining for the last five years. He states the overall concept of the room is excellent. There have been some minor upgrades (replacing the chairs and the carpet), but no major renovation has taken place since 1990. He feels it is time for a major renovation. He claims that the food, service, and pricing are fine, but the atmosphere has grown tired. He claims that the comment cards returned by the guests have been highly favorable. Mr. Krueger has submitted plans for a $500,000 renovation package. His package calls for an updating of the same concept.

Alice Whitaker, the catering manager, claims the concept is no longer viable. She states that patronage of the restaurant has dropped. She says the people who use the Hunt Room may still enjoy it, but a very small percentage of the members use the room. Jimmy Johnson is concerned that if the changes to the room are major he may lose the room's current customers and not be able to replace them with members drawn to the new concept. He is tending to side with Hans, viewing minor changes to the concept as a safe alternative.

The club has three restaurants: the Venetian Room, the Hunt Room, and the Terrace Room. The Venetian Room is the main dining room. It is a light, open room that overlooks the golf course. Its menu is eclectic and includes a selection of European, American, and Asian cuisine. The average check in the Venetian room is $22 for lunch and $45 for dinner. The Hunt Room is the casual dining room. It has rich wood paneling, red leather chairs, and features paintings of hunting scenes on the walls. The Hunt Room's menu features beef, quail, and several seafood items. The average check is $40 for dinner. The Hunt Room closed for lunch in 2007, due to declining lunch sales. The Terrace Room is an informal room with the same menu for lunch and dinner. The menu is similar to one that might be found in a family-oriented restaurant. It is on the ground floor and features a patio that is popular with members using the swimming pool, who want more than the snack bar offers. The average check is $10 for breakfast, $14 for lunch, and $20 for dinner. Dinner business is very slow, except for the summer. In fact, Johnson is thinking of closing this room for dinner.

Referring to the Hunt Room, Alice Whitaker claims the club's members no longer want a heavy beef menu. She has also observed what she feels is a trend: Members are seeking new dining experiences. They want excitement in the menus and would enjoy a room with a casual atmosphere. Additionally, she claims that the restaurant prices have gradually crept up, and the restaurant is no longer considered casual dining. Those guests who want a casual meal usually end up in the Terrace Room or in a local restaurant. Ms. Whitaker feels the local restaurants offer better value for the money.

Mr. Krueger responded by stating that the restaurant offers a much better value than it did when it opened. He claims that beef prices have risen by 140 percent since 2000, but he has absorbed some of these increases and menu prices have only increased by 100 percent. He further stated that he was not in competition with every restaurant in town—the club has prestige and members come here because it is their club. Krueger claims the club gives good value compared with the fine dining restaurants in town.

Jimmy Johnson did not want the discussion to escalate into an argument. He, therefore, tabled the discussion on the Hunt Room until more information could be obtained. He was also proceeding very carefully. He has only been at the club for two years. He has been able to maintain the status quo of the club but has not made any significant changes. The club's membership wait list has continued its downward trend. The club had an average wait of four years in 2005; today the wait is 18 months. Food and beverage sales have remained flat over the last three years, despite an average menu increase of 4 percent per annum. Jimmy feels he has "stabilized the club," but he has not been able to show increases in sales. He feels the turnaround has come, but he also knows some board members are growing impatient. Thus, he feels a mistake with the new concept for the Hunt Room could cost him his job. He also knows many of the older board members enjoy the Hunt Room.

Another problem with the club is that the membership is aging. Most of the young members are sons or daughters of members. The club does not seem to attract members under 40. This makes it hard for Johnson to make changes because many of the older members do not want change, and the younger members who came to the club with their parents have grown used to it. They seem to like the club the way it is, yet they do not use the food and beverage facilities. Most of the younger members use the golf course and drop their children off at the pool. For the most part, their food and beverage sales are limited to the snack bars at the golf course and swimming pool.

Johnson ponders his options: Do nothing, or try to keep things from declining. He knows preventing further declines is a significant accomplishment. However, he feels the board is looking for increases. If he makes a mistake with the Hunt Room, he will quickly lose his job. If he does nothing, he may be able to hang on for several more years but if he does not turn sales around, eventually he will lose his job.

■■■ QUESTIONS FOR DISCUSSION

Chapter 9

1. If you were the general manager, what process would you go through to determine a new concept for the Hunt Room?

2. What information would you seek? Where would you find this information?

3. What makes restaurant concepts grow out of favor? How often should a room be reconcepted?

4. Should club restaurants compete with local restaurants?

5. Brainstorm to come up with possible concepts for the Hunt Room. You should include decor and menu ideas.

■■■ Case 6 In-N-Out Burger: Customer Value the Old-Fashioned Way

In 1948, Harry and Esther Snyder opened the first In-N-Out Burger in Baldwin Park, California. It was a simple double drive-thru setup with the kitchen between two service lanes, a walk-up window, and outdoor seating. The menu consisted of burgers, shakes, soft drinks, and fries. This format was common for the time period. In fact, another burger joint that fit this same description opened up the very same year just 45 minutes away from the first In-N-Out Burger. It was called McDonald's. Today, McDonald's boasts over 34,000 stores worldwide that bring in more than $88 billion every year. In-N-Out has only 281 stores in five states, good for an estimated $625 million a year. Based on the outcomes, it would seem that McDonald's has emerged the clear victor.

But In-N-Out never wanted to be another McDonald's. And despite its smaller size—or perhaps because of it—In-N-Out's customers like the regional chain just the way it is. When it comes to customer satisfaction, In-N-Out beats McDonald's hands down. It regularly posts the highest customer satisfaction scores of any fast-food restaurant in its market areas. Compared to McDonald's customers, patrons of In-N-Out are really "Lovin' it." Just about anyone who has been to an In-N-Out believes it's the best burger they've ever had. It comes as no surprise, then, that the average per-store sales for In-N-Out eclipse those of McDonald's and are double the industry average.

Breaking All the Rules

According to Stacy Perman, author of a definitive book on In-N-Out, the company has achieved unequivocal success by "breaking all the rules." By rules, Ms. Perman refers to the standard business practices for the fast-food industry and even retail in general. In-N-Out has maintained a tenacious focus on customer well-being, but it has done so by doing the unthinkable: not changing. The company's original philosophy is still in place today and best illustrates the basis for the company's rule breaking: "Give customers the freshest, highest quality foods you can buy and provide them with friendly service in a sparkling clean environment." The big burger giants might take exception to the idea that they aren't providing the same customer focus. But let's take a closer look at what these things mean to In-N-Out.

For starters, at In-N-Out, quality food means fresh food. Burgers are made from 100 percent pure beef—no additives, fillers, or preservative s. In-N-Out owns and operates its own patty-making commissaries, ensuring that every burger is fresh and never frozen. Vegetables are sliced and diced by hand in every restaurant. Fries are even made from whole potatoes. And, yes, milkshakes are made from real ice cream. In an industry that has progressively become more and more enamored with processing technologies such as cryogenically freezing foods and preparing all ingredients in off-site warehouses, In-N-Out is indeed an anomaly. In fact, you won't even find a freezer, heating lamp, or microwave oven in an In-N-Out restaurant. From the beginning, the company slogan has been "Quality you can taste." And customers are convinced that they can do just that.

In-N-Out hasn't changed its formula for freshness. But in another deviation from the norm, it also hasn't changed its menu. Unlike McDonald's or Wendy's, which introduce seemingly unending streams of new menu items, In-N-Out stays true to Harry Snyder's original mantra: "Keep it real simple. Do one thing and do it the best you can." This charge from the founder focuses on what the chain has always done well: making really good hamburgers, really good fries, and really good shakes, that's it. While others have focused on menu expansion in constant search of the next hit item to drive traffic, In-N-Out has tenaciously stuck to the basics. In fact, it took 60 years for the company to add 7up and Dr Pepper to its menu.

Although the limited menu might seem restrictive, customers don't feel that way. In another demonstration of commitment to customers, In-N-Out employees will gladly make any of the menu items in a truly customized fashion. From the chain's earliest years, menu modifications became such a norm at In-N-Out that a "secret" menu emerged consisting of code words that aren't posted on regular menu boards. So customers in the know can order their burgers "animal style" (pick les, extra spread, grilled onions, and a mustard-fried patty). Although the "Double-Double" (double meat, double cheese) is on the menu, burgers can also be ordered in 3 × 3 or 4 × 4 configurations. Fries can also be ordered animal style (two slices of cheese, grilled onions, and spread), well done, or light. A Neapolitan shake is a mixture of chocolate, vanilla, and strawberry shakes. The list goes on and on. Knowledge of this secret menu is yet another thing that makes customers feel special.

It's not just In-N-Out's food that pleases customers. The chain also features well-trained employees who deliver unexpectedly friendly service. In-N-Out hires and retains outgoing, enthusiastic, and capable employees and treats them very well. It pays new part-time staff $10.50 an hour and gives them regular raises. Part-timers also receive paid vacations. General managers make over $100,000 a year plus bonuses and receive a full-benefit package that rivals anything in the corporate world. Managers who meet goals are sent on lavish trips with their spouses, often to Europe in first-class seats. For gala events, managers wear tuxedos. Executives believe that the men and women who run In-N-Out stores stand shoulder-to-shoulder with any blue-chip manager, and want them to feel that way. Managers are promoted from within. In fact, 80 percent of In-N-Out managers started at the very bottom. As a result, In-N-Out has one of the lowest turnover rates in an industry infamous for high turnover.

Happy, motivated employees help create loyal, satisfied customers. In fact, words like *loyal* and *satisfied* don't do justice to how customers feel about In-N-Out Burger. The restaurant chain has developed an unparalleled cult following. When a new In-N-Out first opens, the line of cars often stretches out a mile or more, and people stand in line for hours to get a burger, fries, and a shake. Fans have been known to camp overnight to be the first in line. When In-N-Out made its debut in Texas, one woman cried. "Pinch me, it just doesn't feel real," whimpered customer Danielle Deinnocentes, overcome with emotion as the reality of her new-found proximity to the burger chain set in.

Slow Growth Nurtures Fans

Some observers point out that it's probably more than just the food and the service that created In-N-Out's diehard customer base. Because of In-N-Out's slow-growth expansion strategy, you won't find one of the famous red-and-white stores with crisscrossed palm trees on every corner. By 1976, In-N-Out had grown to only 18 southern California stores, whereas McDonald's and Burger King had opened thousands of stores worldwide. It took In-N-Out 40 years to open its first non-California store in Las Vegas. And even as the company expands into Arizona, Utah, and Texas, it sticks tenaciously to its policy of not opening more than about 10 stores per year.

The lack of access to an In-N-Out in most states has created legions of cravers coast to coast. Fans have created countless Facebook pages, filled with posts by consumers begging the family-owned corporation to bring In-N-Out to their states. But In-N-Out's policy is driven by its commitment to quality. It will open a new store only when it has trained management and company-owned distribution centers in place.

The scarcity of In-N-Out stores only adds to its allure. Customers regularly go out of their way and drive long distances to get their fix. Having to drive a little further contributes to the feeling that going to In-N-Out is an event. Out-of-state visitors in the know often put an In-N-Out stop high on their list of things to do. Jeff Rose, a financial planner from Carbondale, Illinois, always stops at In-N-Out first when he visits Las Vegas to see his mother. "You have to pass it when you drive to her house," he says in his defense. "It's not like the time I paid an extra $40 in cab fare to visit an In-N-Out on the way to the San Diego airport."

Consistent with the other elements of its simple-yet-focused strategy, In-N-Out doesn't spend much on advertising—it doesn't have to. In fact, although the company doesn't release financial figures, some estimates place total promotional spending at less than 1 percent of revenues. In-N-Out's small promotional budget is for local billboards and radio ads. But when it comes to really spreading the word, In-N-Out lets its customers do the heavy lifting. Customers truly are apostles for the brand. They proudly wear In-N-Out T-shirts and slap In-N-Out bumper stickers on their cars. Rabid regulars drag a constant stream of new devotees into restaurants, an act often referred to as "the conversion." They can't wait to pass along the secret menu codes and share the sublime pleasures of diving into a 4 × 4 animal style. "When you tell someone else what 'animal style' means," says an analyst, "you feel like you're passing on a secret handshake. People really get into the whole thing."

In-N-Out doesn't use paid endorsers, but word-of-mouth praise regularly flows from the mouths of A-list celebrities. When former *Tonight Show* host Conan O'Brien asked Tom Hanks what he recommended doing in Los Angeles, Hanks replied, "One of the true great things about Los Angeles is In-N-Out Burger." Paris Hilton famously claimed she was on her way to In-N-Out when she was pulled over for a DUI. And paparazzi have snapped shots of scores of celebrities getting an In-N-Out fix, including Miley Cyrus, Selena Gomez, Christian Slater, and Nick Jonas. The fact that such celebrities aren't paid to pay homage to the brand under-scores that In-N-Out is truly a hip place.

A Questionable Future?

Many analysts have questioned whether or not In-N-Out can sustain its unwavering 65-year run. For example, the company that had been run only by Harry, Esther, or one of their two sons for its first 58 years hit a barrier in 2006 when Esther Snyder passed away. The only direct descendant of the Snyder family at that time was 23-year-old Lynsi Martinez, who was not yet in a position to take over the company. That left In-N-Out in the hands of Mark Taylor, the former vice president of operations. But as directed by Esther Snyder's will, granddaughter Lynsi took over as In-N-Out's sixth president in 2010 before her 28th birthday. Often described as shy, Martinez has progressively gained ownership of the company and will have full control in 2017.

The changing of the executive guard has gone largely unnoticed by customers and fans, an indication that the In-N-Out legacy carries on. With long lines still snaking out the door of any location at lunchtime, demand seems as high as ever. "The more chains like McDonald's and Burger King change and expand, the more In-N -Out sticks to its guns," says the analyst. "In a way, it symbolizes the ideal American way of doing business: Treating people well, focusing on product quality, and being very successful." In-N-Out's customers couldn't agree more. When it comes to fast-food chains, delighted customers will tell you, "There's In-N-Out, and then there's everyone else."

Sources: Seth Lubove, "Youngest American Woman Billionaire Found with In-N-Out," *Bloomberg*, February 4, 2013, www.bloomberg.com/news/2013-02-04/youngest-american-woman-billionaire-found-within-n-out.html; Jay Weston, "In-N-Out Burger's 'Secret Menu' Revealed," *Huffington Post*, April 6, 2012, www.huffingtonpost.com/ jay-weston/in-n-out-burgers-secret-menu_b_1407388.html; Meredith Land, "Inside the In-N-Out Burger Empire," NBCDFW, November 17, 2011, www.nbcdfw.com/the-scene/food-drink/Inside-the-In -N-Out Burger-Empire-134008293.html; www.in-n-out.com (accessed May 2013).

■■■ QUESTIONS FOR DISCUSSION

Chapter 3

1. Describe In-N-Out's strengths and weaknesses.

2. Should In-N-Out adopt a high-growth strategy? Why or why not?

■■■ Case 7 The Australian Tourist Commission

The Australian Tourist Commission (ATC) was planning a marketing research study within the United States. The plan had originated in the home office in Melbourne and was sent to regional offices for comment before soliciting bids. These regional offices were located in London, Frankfurt, New York, Los Angeles, Tokyo, and Auckland. Visitor traffic to Australia from the United States had grown at a slower rate than other major market areas. It was apparent that marketing strategies were needed to increase the number of American visitors to Australia. Before developing a new marketing plan, it was felt that a study should be conducted within the United States to identify target markets.

Research Objectives

Objectives had been identified for the study:

1. To identify and quantify groups in the U.S. population with the highest potential for holidaying in Australia.

2. To investigate in detail the factors that determine holiday destination choice among the high-potential groups.

3. To provide information indicating the types of holiday products, taking into account time and cost factors, which would satisfy the holiday needs of the high-potential groups.

4. To investigate the awareness of and preferences for alternative destinations.

5. To provide information to guide publicity agencies as to the type of creative approaches that will appeal to and motivate the high-potential groups.

6. To provide a guide to media patterns that will enable efficient communication to the high-potential groups.

7. To identify the best distribution modes for holiday products aimed at the high-potential groups (e.g., airlines, travel agents, bank travel departments).

8. To investigate the role of the travel trade and its importance in determining holiday destination choice.

9. To determine past and intended future holiday behavior among the high-potential groups and to describe them in socioeconomic terms. Detailed information must be collected on the destinations visited on past trips and the sequence of these visits.

In addition to the objectives, the ATC felt that the study should be designed with the following purposes in mind:

• To enable the development of a comprehensive understanding of the destination selection process—essential if Australia is to be marketed more successfully in the United States.

• To enable the design of products of greatest appeal to the high-potential groups, in terms of cost, length of holiday, preferred standard of accommodation, and domestic transportation.

• To enable Australia to be promoted in a way that will capitalize on its perceived strengths, overcome its perceived weaknesses, and compete more effectively with the strengths and weaknesses of competing long-haul destinations.

• To provide an adequate measurement of the extent of awareness of and interest in various Australian features (e.g., the Barrier Reef, the outback, Sydney Harbour).

• To provide detailed knowledge of the holiday planning process, including the time involved and the sources of information used.

• To enable more efficient communication and distribution of available products to the high-potential groups.

Proposed Methodology

It was the opinion of the ATC that the study should be divided into two stages. The first would be of a "qualitative" nature for the purpose of developing personality and attitudinal questions that would then be used in the second quantitative phase. The general opinion was that face-to-face interviews of 30 to 35 minutes each would be needed for both parts of the study. The use of telephone interviews was considered but rejected because it was feared that they could not provide the depth of answers needed, particularly as "tradeoff" questions were being asked.

Due to the high cost of field research in the United States, it seemed imperative to minimize the sample size. Consequently, a total of a thousand face-to-face interviews during the primary research were considered to be sufficient to provide good precision for estimates from the total sample and from the various subgroups.

The ATC felt that respondents should be selected on the basis of four criteria: (1) past travel experience, (2) future travel intentions, (3) travel desire, and (4) interest in Australia. Those who should be interviewed would include people who had never traveled and had no intention or desire to travel. The term *travel* was defined as long-haul international travel for pleasure purposes, excluding Mexico, Canada, and the Caribbean. In addition, people with immediate family living in Australia were to be excluded.

In the interests of efficiency, it was felt that the sample should overrepresent key markets; hence, a screening process was to be used in the interviews. The screening questions were to be administered in sequential fashion, with the first criterion being "past travel experience." The sample structure emphasized those with extensive travel experience, as research indicated that this was a prime market for Australia. The recommended structure was as follows:

• Past travelers: Traveled in the last five years to a long-haul destination for pleasure, with or without a stated intention to travel.
  $N = 600$ broken down as:
  a. At least 200 "experienced travelers"
  b. At least 200 with "stated travel intention"
  c. At least 200 with "interest in Australia"

- Potential travelers: Stated intention to travel in the next three years to a long-haul destination for pleasure, without past travel experience.
  $N = 300$ broken down as:
  a. At least 100 whose primary intended destination is not UK/Europe
  b. At least 200 with "interest in Australia"

- Non/latent travelers:
  a. $N = 100$ comprising persons with no past travel experience and no stated intention to travel, but who:
  b. Have an expressed desire to travel (to a long-haul destination for pleasure purposes)
  c. Express an interest in visiting Australia

Although a random sampling technique was desired, the sample was to be heavily biased toward upper-income groups and not representative of the general mix of the U.S. population. Further sampling restrictions that were felt to be necessary included the following:

1. No interviews from persons who lived in rural areas or small urban centers.

2. Undersampling from the East Coast, with the exception of New York.

3. Undersampling from the southern states, with the exception of Florida.

4. Oversampling from California, Hawaii, New York, Texas, and Florida. The reason for this was an observation of incidence patterns based on data generated from past international visitor surveys by the ATC.

5. Use of a form of multistage sampling in which cities would be the primary unit. For reasons of cost, no more than 20 cities should be selected. This selection of cities should not be "purposive"; however, it should be a random selection of cities within the constraints specified next.

Responses

100	New York
50	Florida
50	Texas
150	California
100	Hawaii
50	New England
150	Eastern North Central
50	Western North Central
100	Other South Atlantic
50	Other Western South Central and Eastern South Central
100	Mountain
50	Pacific
1,000	

One of the reasons for the suggested sampling procedure was that the ATC had data on a large sample from the United States known as Travel Pulse, plus data from an earlier ATC study known as the International Visitors Survey. It was felt that the new study should provide data that would be cross-comparable with the results from the previous studies.

U.S. Arrivals in Australia by Purpose of Visit (%)	
Holiday	43
Visiting relatives	15
Business	23
Other	19
Total	100

Age of International Visitors to Australia (%)	
0–4	8.3
15–24	14.5
25–34	20.4
35–49	23.5
50–64	22.3
65+	11.0

Occupations of International Visitors to Australia (%)

Professional (excluding teachers)	13.1
Teachers	3.5
Administrative workers	15.9
Clerical and sales workers	9.8
Service workers (including armed services)	3.9
Other	11.1
Inadequately described	5.8
Total (working persons)	63.1
Children (0–14 years)	8.3
Students (15 years and over)	4.8
Home duties	14.8
Independent means, pensioners, etc.	9.0
Total (nonworking persons)	36.9
Total	100.0

Seasonality of Foreign Arrivals to Australia Ranked by Number of Monthly Arrivals

	OCEANIA	AFRICA	AMERICAS	ASIA	EUROPE
January	7	6	5	5	3
February	6	4	3	4	12
March	4	2	4	3	10
April	3	8	7	8	4
May	9	9	11	11	5
June	11	12	12	12	9
July	2	7	10	7	6
August	12	11	8	10	2
September	5	10	9	9	8
October	10	5	6	6	7
November	8	1	1	1	11
December	1	3	2	2	1

Top-Ten Origin Countries of Visitors to Australia (%)

New Zealand	28.9
United Kingdom and Ireland	14.6
United States	13.5
Japan	5.5
Papua New Guinea	4.4
Canada	3.2
Germany	2.7
Netherlands	1.9
Malaysia	1.8
Hong Kong	1.8

Regional Travel Patterns Within the United States (Holiday Visitors per 100,000 Population)

East South Central	3.77	Rhode Island	5.7
Kentucky	3.9	Connecticut	11.8
Tennessee	4.6	Mid Atlantic	10.56
Alabama	3.6	New York	13.3
Mississippi	2.4	New Jersey	10.5
West South Central	9.06	Pennsylvania	6.4
Arkansas	7.4	East North Central	10.57
Louisiana	3.4	Ohio	10.7
Oklahoma	12.6	Indiana	8.6
Texas	10.4	Illinois	13.3
Mountain	29.13	Michigan	9.7
Montana	28.4	Wisconsin	7.3
Idaho	25.1	West North Central	14.67
Wyoming	10.8	Minnesota	18.3
Colorado	28.1	Iowa	14.6
New Mexico	22.8	Missouri	14.5
Arizona	26.2	North Dakota	8.7
Utah	18.6	South Dakota	13.4
Nevada	54.8	Nebraska	10.9
Pacific	43.91	Kansas	13.5
Washington	33.0	South Atlantic	11.12
Oregon	29.9	Delaware	6.6
California	42.5	Maryland	10.0
Alaska	88.7	District of Columbia	52.0
Hawaii	148.5	Virginia	7.3
New England	9.06	West Virginia	3.1
Maine	5.4	North Carolina	4.2
New Hampshire	2.4	South Carolina	4.8
Vermont	8.1	Georgia	5.5
Massachusetts	9.7	Florida	23.7

■■■ QUESTIONS FOR DISCUSSION

Chapter 5

1. What is your opinion of the research objectives and purposes for the study?

2. What is your opinion of the proposed methodology?

3. Why do you suppose that travel to Australia from the United States was lower than desired? In answering this question, consider the cost of travel, time required, and other factors.

4. In your opinion, will information from the survey permit the ATC to address the issues raised in Question 3?

■■■ Case 8 The Witchery by the Castle

Andrew Lloyd Webber commented, "It's the prettiest restaurant ever." "Number Four in the 50 Best Places in the World for Honeymooners" is the Witchery by the Castle in Edinburgh, Scotland, which is consistently recognized as one of the world's great places to dine and stay. It has won numerous awards, such as the prestigious AA Wine Award for Scotland and the Scottish Tourist Board's Thistle Award. The *Sunday Times* rated the luxurious suites at the Witchery as "among the most sought-after romantic hideaways in Scotland," and the *Sunday Herald* described them as a "Jewel Box Setting."

Located at the top of the Royal Mile, close to the gates of Edinburgh Castle, the Witchery sits in the heart of Edinburgh's historic old town. A gilded heraldic metal sign marks the entrance. A short walk away are the Scottish Parliament, the Museum of Scotland, St. Giles, and the National Galleries. The Edinburgh Airport is only eight miles away, and Waverly Rail Station is just a few hundred yards away.

The Witchery was originally built for an Edinburgh merchant in 1595. Edinburgh, like Salem, Massachusetts, went through a period of "witch accusations" and persecutions, which occurred at the site of the current witchery.

By 1979, the building that now houses the Witchery was in total disrepair. James Thomson, an Edinburgh native, saw opportunity beyond the decay in a neglected part of Edinburgh. James began his career as a young man with a Saturday job in Crawford's tearooms and gained an appreciation for history at George Heriot's School. Years later, James became Scotland's youngest hospitality licensee as creator and owner of the Witchery.

Today, witches are a historic oddity, replaced by suites and a restaurant serving some of the finest cuisine in the United Kingdom in a candle-lit ambience in which the only electric light identifies the fire exit.

In 1979, the success of the Witchery led James to open a second restaurant, Secret Garden, in a derelict schoolyard adjacent to the Witchery. James could see opportunity in what others regarded as trash and incorporated a wealth of salvaged building materials into the Secret Garden, including a sixteenth-century doorway from the Duke of Gordon's ceiling, to build the Secret Garden restaurant, named by one reviewer as the "most civilized dining room in Scotland."

Now bookings at the Witchery and the Secret Garden are made weeks in advance because both have become the most popular destination restaurants in Edinburgh and remain fully booked. Annually they serve over 200,000 guests.

Above the Witchery restaurant, atop a winding staircase, are two magical and opulent suites, the Old Rectory and the Inner Sanctum, packed with antiques and enough atmosphere to have pleased Cleopatra and Antony, royalty, or movie stars. Named as one of the United Kingdom's top-10 romantic destinations, these suites stay booked throughout the year at a room rate of £250 per night, including a bottle of champagne, chocolates, a continental breakfast, and a newspaper (who wants to read?).

The success of the original suites led James to develop five more as the "world's greatest places to stay." The Library, Vestry, Guardsroom, and Armory all boast their own individuality. All were designed as perfect romantic hideaways with masses of antiques, opulently draped beds, rich textiles, and huge roll-top baths built for two. These are located in a lavishly restored seventeenth-century building just a few steps from the Witchery in Edinburgh's historic Castlehill. If possible, these suites are even more theatrical and opulent than the original two.

The gothic library suite overlooks the historic Royal Mile and includes masses of antique books, paisley-covered walls, and a book-lined bathroom with an open fire.

The Armory is discreetly located, overlooking a small private courtyard. This huge and glamorous suite is hung with dramatic tapestries and features an oak-paneled bathroom. The Guardroom is exceptionally spacious overlooking the historic old-town rooftops and a romantic bedroom paneled with antique leather.

Fully booked restaurants and suites did not occur without reason. The Witchery developed a worldwide reputation for sensational food in the most indulgent setting. The very best of Scotland's produce, such as Angus beef, lamb, game, and seafood, are served. Scottish lobster and Loch Fyne oysters are regularly featured alongside Witchery classic dishes such as hot smoked salmon with leeks and hollandaise or Angus beef fillet with smoked garlic broth.

The Witchery also developed a reputation for its wines, gaining a prestigious *Wine Spectator* Award for Excellence and many other awards for its cellar.

Its comprehensive list of almost a thousand wines covers all of the great wine-producing areas, varieties, prices, and styles with a special selection of 17 available by the glass. A skilled and enthusiastic wine team, supported by a respected sommelier, constantly taste, source, and buy wines to add to the already extensive cellar. Their extensive knowledge is available to guests in the restaurant.

Along with a large selection of old-world classics from Burgundy and Bordeaux, there are extensive selections from New World producers such as Australia,

Chile, and New Zealand and a comprehensive Spanish and Italian list. Champagne is a Witchery specialty with selections from Pommery to the deluxe cuvées of Krug, Roederer Christa, and Dom Perignon.

An extensive range of malt whiskey, armagnacs, and liqueurs are also available. Mineral water is locally produced by Findlay's in East Lothian, Scotland.

Obviously, much of the success of the Witchery, Secret Garden, and the suites may be attributed to their historic location, the ambience, the quality of the products, and the excitement and theater built into each.

James knows that these factors need to be continuously supported to ensure success. He is well aware of the tendency of hospitality guests to seek new dining and lodging experiences. He also recognizes the importance of word of mouth to deliver new guests. He believes that the product must be supported by staff loyalty and excellence, community involvement, personal leadership, and an appropriate use of technology.

Staff Development

Following attendance at the Disney Institute in Florida, James instituted a new mind-set in the company, encouraging staff to constantly seek to exceed guests' already high expectations. Staff members are empowered to deal with any guest request and are personally responsible for delivering each guest's total satisfaction. James encourages his team to develop rewarding long-term careers within his company, so staff turnover is significantly below the industry norm, and many of his staff have been with him long term. A large proportion have returned to work with him again after gaining experience with other organizations at home and abroad.

Community and Industry Involvement

James believes the hospitality industry offers exciting careers, and he encourages young people to enter. James supports and funds a number of educational initiatives at primary, secondary, and higher education levels, including supporting students in local high schools with cooking competitions, training with restaurant chefs, and work experience within his restaurants. Recently, he was delighted to see a student reach the Scottish final of the *Future Chef of the Year*.

In 1999, he endowed the *James Thomson Award for Outstanding Customer Service*, which annually recognizes and financially assists a student who has shown outstanding commitment to excellence in customer service during his or her studies at Edinburgh's Telford College. He continues to be a significant sponsor of an annual exchange trip between Edinburgh students and the François Rabelais College in Lyon, France, giving up to 20 students and lecturers hands-on experience in Michelin-starred restaurants in France's culinary capital.

A strong believer in rewarding and recognizing the very best led James to sponsor the Scottish tourism "Oscars," the Visit Scotland Thistle Awards, the Caterer .com Best Tourism Website Award, and the recent Caterer.com Web Awards. Frequently asked to lend his expertise to others in the industry, he has judged the Caterer Hospitality Week Innovations Awards over recent years as well as being a regular judge for the Thistle Awards.

As an industry leader, James frequently speaks publicly to promote tourism and hospitality issues, and his restaurants maintain a high media profile in Scotland worldwide. He has written a food column in *The Herald* newspaper and speaks at industry events. Making his restaurants and suites available to the media has promoted a positive quality image of Scottish hospitality in dozens of publications, including *Vogue*, *Hello*, *Elle*, *Cosmopolitan*, and the *New York Times*, as well as on television around the world.

James believes that he has an obligation to assist in the growth of tourism to Scotland and especially to Edinburgh. Aware that visitors to Edinburgh were looking for more information about the historic but neglected Old Town, James supported the creation of the Caddies and Witchery Tours, the city's first customer walking tours. Tours leave from outside the Witchery every evening and have become a memorable part of the visitor experience for thousands of visitors to Edinburgh.

James works closely with several public and private-sector organizations, including the Scottish Enterprise Innovation Group, the Scottish Borders Tourist Board, and the National Museums of Scotland to improve the standards of Scotland's hospitality products. An enthusiast for Disney's approach to customer care, James has encouraged a range of tourism businesses to learn from the best, including leading study tours to the Disney Institute in Florida. He often speaks on the lessons that can be learned from Disney. In 2002, in conjunction with other partners, he launched Castlehill Christmas, a joint initiative to bring business to local tourism enterprises at what was a traditionally quiet time of the year with a dramatic architectural lighting display and a program of events focused on Castlehill. James is a key member of the finance committee, raising over £300,000 in sponsorship to bring the prestigious Meeting Planners International Conference to Edinburgh in 2004, an international event with huge benefits for the city and Scotland.

Supporting the wider community, especially in Edinburgh's historic Old Town, has a place too. James acts as a trustee of the Old Town Charitable Trust, a member of the Board of the Queen's Hall, and support of the advisory group of the local homelessness initiative, the Edinburgh Streetwork Project. He also supports an under-10 football team. The Witchery supports a local community football team and the National Judo Academy. The innovative Just for Starters program that James pioneered as a collaborative venture brought a number of people with difficult backgrounds into the industry by harnessing the resources of a number of public- and private-sector organizations, including the police and army, to support, educate, and mentor them in the transition from homelessness to employment.

As sole shareholder, James is able to commit a significant proportion of the company's profits back to the community through ongoing support of charities, including the Hospitality Industry Trust, Crusaid Shelter, the Army Benevolent Fund, St. Columbia's Hospice, Save the Children, and the Royal Lyceum Theatre. Regular donations of dining or accommodation vouchers from the restaurants are also given to organizations to use for their own fundraising purposes.

Technology

James's basic concept of giving the diner a magical dining experience where each of the elements of food, wine, service, location, and decor all combine to create a magical dining experience was innovative when he established the Witchery, and constant innovation has been a hallmark ever since. He was ahead of other restaurants, installing specialist EPOS systems to process diners' orders and bills discreetly. James established a state-of-the-art mini call center to allow all guest enquiries for his restaurants to be dealt with centrally by a highly skilled team using specially developed reservation software. For guests looking to book online, he was an early investor in Web sites that have given the restaurants and suites a 24-hour worldwide presence with an average of a thousand hits each day. His restaurants were among the first in the United Kingdom to offer real-time table reservations online using his reservations database. James believes that hospitality firms can use the latest technology to provide a truly old-fashioned level of service. He credits much of his success to community and employee support. For James, marketing is far more than advertising or brochure development. He has demonstrated the importance of personal involvement by owners/managers in the community and the industry and strong product differentiation.

■■■ QUESTIONS FOR DISCUSSION

Chapter 4

1. From the preceding discussion, analyze the strengths and weaknesses of the Witchery.

Chapter 14

1. Discuss the Witchery's public relations efforts. Offer any suggestions you have for how the Witchery could gain publicity outside of Scotland.

■■■ Case 9 Mayo Clinic

Mayo Clinic is the first and largest integrated not-for-profit medical group practice in the world. William and Charles Mayo founded the clinic over 100 years ago as a small outpatient facility and pioneered the concept of a medical group practice—a model that is widely used today.

Mayo Clinic provides exceptional medical care and leads the United States in many specialties such as cancer, heart disease, respiratory disorders, and urology. It consistently ranks at the top of *U.S. News & World Report*'s Best Hospitals list and enjoys 85 percent brand recognition among U.S. adults. It has reached this level of success by taking a different approach from most clinics and hospitals and putting a relentless focus on the patient's experience. The clinic's two interrelated core values trace back to its founders and are at the heart of all the organization does: placing the patient's interests above all others and practicing teamwork.

Every aspect of the patient's experience is considered at Mayo Clinic's three campuses in Rochester (MN), Scottsdale (AZ), and Jacksonville (FL). The moment a patient walks into one of Mayo Clinic's facilities, he or she feels the difference. New patients are welcomed by professional greeters who walk them through the administrative processes. Returning patients are greeted by name and with a warm smile. The buildings have been designed so that, in the words of the architect of one, "patients feel a little better before they see their doctors." The 21-story Gonda Building in Rochester has spectacular wide-open spaces with the capability of adding 10 more floors. Fine art hangs on the walls, and doctors' offices are designed to feel cozy and comforting rather than sterile and impersonal.

The lobby of the Mayo Clinic hospital in Scottsdale has an indoor waterfall and a wall of windows overlooking mountains. In pediatric exam rooms, resuscitation equipment is hidden behind a large cheery picture. Hospital rooms feature microwave ovens and chairs that really do convert to beds because, as one staff member explained, "People don't come to the hospital alone." The newest emergency medical helicopter was customized to incorporate high-tech medical equipment and is one of the most advanced aircraft in the world.

The other significant difference in serving patients is Mayo Clinic's concept of teamwork. A patient can come to Mayo Clinic with or without a physician's referral. At that time, the patient's team is assembled, which can include the primary physician, surgeons, radiation oncologists, radiologists, nurses, residents, or other specialists with the appropriate skill, experience, and knowledge.

Teams of medical professionals work together to diagnose patients' medical problems, including debating test results for hours to determine the most accurate diagnosis and best treatments. Once a team consensus has been reached, the leader meets with the patient and discusses his or her options. Throughout the process, patients are encouraged to take part in the discussion. If surgery is necessary, the procedure is often scheduled to take place within 24 hours, a dramatic difference from the long wait patients experience at many hospitals. Mayo Clinic's doctors understand that those who seek their care want action as soon as possible.

Mayo's doctors are put on salary instead of being paid by the number of patients seen or tests ordered. As a result, patients receive more individualized attention and care, and physicians work together instead of against each other. As one pediatrician at Mayo explained, "We're very comfortable with calling colleagues for what I call 'curbside consulting.' I don't have to make a decision about splitting a fee or owing someone something. It's never a case of quid pro quo."

Mayo Clinic is a not-for-profit, so all its operating income is invested back into the clinic's research and education programs. Breakthrough research is quickly implemented into the quality care of the patients. Mayo Clinic offers educational programs through its five schools, and many of its physicians come up through these programs with Mayo's philosophies engrained in their heads, including Mayo's motto: "The best interest of the patient is the only interest to be considered."

Third parties have recognized Mayo Clinic for decades for its independent thinking, outstanding service and performance, and core focus on patient care and satisfaction.

■■■ QUESTIONS FOR DISCUSSION

Chapter 9

1. Explain why Mayo Clinic is so good at customer service. Why has it been so successful practicing medicine differently from other hospitals?

2. How has the Mayo Clinic used tangible elements of the service product to enhance its service delivery?

Sources: Avery Comarow, "Americas Best Hospitals," *U.S. News & World Report* (July 15, 2009); Chen May Yee, "Mayo Clinic Reports 2007 Revenue Grew 10%," *Star Tribune* (March 17, 2008); Leonard L. Berry and Kent D. Seltman, *Management Lessons from Mayo Clinic* (New York; McGraw-Hill, 2008); Leonard L. Berry, "Leadership Lessons from Mayo Clinic," *Organizational Dynamics* 33 (August 2004): 228–242; Leonard L. Berry and Neeli Bendapudi, "Clueing in Customers," *Harvard Business Review* (February 2003): 100–106; John La Forgia, Kent Seltman, and Scott Swanson, "Mayo Clinic: Sustaining a Legacy Brand and Leveraging Its Equity in the 21st-century Market," Presentation at the Marketing Science Institute's Conference on Brand Orchestration, Orlando, FL, December 4–5, 2003; Paul Roberts, "The Agenda—Total Teamwork," *Fast Company* (March 31, 1999).

■■■ Case 10 Hawaiian Sights

After nine months in operation, Hawaiian Sights was struggling to solicit support from tour operators. Despite earlier comments from many that this type of tour was needed and should sell without any problems, sales success had been elusive.

As a walking tour, Hawaiian Sights covered the least explored areas of "Olde Honolulu" ordinarily bypassed by tour buses: (1) the Civic and Historical Center, (2) downtown Honolulu, and (3) Chinatown. The tour allowed tourists to mingle and make friends with Hawaii's "real" people—away from Waikiki—and was viewed as an oral historical excursion.

Tours began with an escort/guide meeting clients at a predetermined location in Waikiki. The group would board the city bus and disembark (20 minutes later) in front of the state capital building. The narration continued for the next four hours. The group spent one hour for lunch and shopping on Fort Street Mall and returned to Waikiki on the city bus. The idea for Hawaiian Sights occurred to Evelyn Wako when she noticed that conventional city tours ignored the most important part of Hawaii: its people. The majority of tourists rode through Honolulu, viewing the city through bus windows. Evelyn felt that if tourists really wanted to learn about Hawaii, they had to get off those buses. Evelyn knew that walking tours were successful in Europe, so why not Hawaii?

The concept of a tour that forced customers to take the city bus and to walk was so different that operators of travel desks and travel agencies gave Hawaiian Sights little encouragement or cooperation. They also said that the original commission structure of 20 percent on a $35 (retail price) item did not produce enough revenue to interest them. Lunch was not included, but clients could eat at any of the restaurants or food concessions around the Fort Street Mall area. Tourists were encouraged to eat with the "natives" on benches in the tree-shaded mall. They could get to meet Hawaiians, observe life in Hawaii, feed the birds, or just be alone to shop in stores that were less expensive than those in Waikiki.

During each tour the escorts would board city buses with their groups at the Historical Center. Prior to boarding, the group was given a short briefing as to what would transpire. They were informed that more than 70 percent of Hawaii's population was "non-Caucasian." The tourists observed how the bus would change from a touristy one into a local bus the farther it moved away from Waikiki.

The unusual nature of Hawaiian Sights enabled it to be included in the tour brochures of several tour operators and two airlines. With sales lower than expected, Evelyn was searching for ways to advertise her tours. She felt that one way might be to distribute brochures to tourists on the street. She was thinking of hiring girls dressed in grass skirts to act as salesgirls. This was sure to bring some negative reaction from certain segments of the Hawaiian population. Evelyn knew that the hotel travel desks remained a key sales tool. Operators of one desk were negative from the beginning. They felt that their clientele were too upscale to ride the city bus.

Tourists who had taken the Hawaiian Sights walking tour rated it far superior to conventional bus tours. Hawaiian Sights offered a "satisfaction guaranteed or money back" guarantee, and so far no customer had expressed dissatisfaction. Despite this, Evelyn had not yet found a way to attract sufficient numbers of tourists to make the new business profitable.

■■■ QUESTIONS FOR DISCUSSION

Chapter 16

1. How could Hawaiian Sights use social media to promote its business?

2. Can Hawaiian Sights use digital marketing to distribute their product? Explain your answer.

■■■ Case 11 The Ritz-Carlton

Few brands attain such a high standard of customer service as the Ritz-Carlton. This luxury hotel chain began with the original Ritz-Carlton Boston, which revolutionized the way U.S. travelers experienced customer service in a hotel. It was the first of its kind to provide a private bath in each guest room, fresh flowers throughout the hotel, and an entire staff dressed in formal white tie, black tie, or morning-coat attire.

In 1983, hotelier Horst Schulze and a four-person development team acquired the rights to the Ritz-Carlton name and created the concept by which it is known today, with its company-wide concentration on both the personal and the functional side of service. The five-star hotel not only provides impeccable facilities but also takes customer service extremely seriously.

The Ritz-Carlton fulfills this promise by providing impeccable training for its employees and executing its Three Steps of Service and 12 Service Values. The Three Steps of Service state that employees must use a warm and sincere greeting always using the guest's name, anticipate and fulfill each guest's needs, and give a warm good-bye, again using the guest's name. Every manager carries a laminated card with the 12 Service Values. A Ritz-Carlton executive explained, "It's all about people. Nobody has an emotional experience with a thing. We're appealing to emotions." The Ritz-Carlton's 35,000 employees in 29 countries go out of their way to create unique and memorable experiences for their guests.

Not only is the company known for training its employees to provide impeccable customer service, but it also reinforces its mission and values with them on a daily basis. Each day, managers gather their employees for a 15-minute "line up" to check in, resolve any impending problems, and read and discuss what the Ritz-Carlton calls "wow stories." These true stories, read to every employee around the world, recognize an individual employee for his or her outstanding customer service and also highlight 1 of the 12 Service Values.

One family staying at the Ritz-Carlton, Bali, needed a particular type of egg and milk for their son who suffered from food allergies. Employees could not find the appropriate items in town, but the executive chef at the hotel remembered a store in Singapore that sold them. He contacted his mother-in-law, who purchased the items and personally flew them more than 1,000 miles to Bali for the family. This example showcased Service Value 6.

In another instance, a waiter overheard a man telling his wheelchair-bound wife that it was too bad he couldn't get her down to the beach. The waiter told the maintenance crew, and by the next day they had constructed a wooden walkway to the beach and pitched a tent at the far end where the couple had dinner.

Wow stories can also be as simple as an employee's remembering how a guest prefers coffee and then preparing it that way without asking for the rest of his or her stay. According to Cooper, the daily wow story is "the best way to communicate what we expect from our ladies and gentlemen around the world. Every story reinforces the actions we are looking for and demonstrates how each and every person in our organization contributes to our service values." Each employee is empowered to spend as much as $2,000 without management approval to help deliver a guest's anticipated need or desire, supporting the company's intention to build lifelong positive relationships with each customer.

Ritz-Carlton measures the success of its customer service efforts through Gallup phone interviews, which ask both functional and emotional questions. Functional questions include: "How was the meal?" or "Was your bedroom clean?" while emotional questions reveal the customer's sense of well-being. The hotel uses these findings as well as day-to-day experiences to continually enhance and improve the experience for its guests.

In less than three decades, Ritz-Carlton has grown from 1 U.S. location to 87 in 29 countries; the company plans to expand further throughout Europe, Africa, Asia, the Middle East, and the Americas. It has also earned two Malcolm Baldrige Quality Awards—the only company ever to win the prestigious award twice.

Sources: Robert Reiss, "How Ritz Carlton Stays at Top," *Forbes*, October 30, 2009; Carmine Gallo, "Employee Motivation the Ritz-Carlton Way," *BusinessWeek*, February 29, 2008; Carmine Gallo, "How Ritz-Carlton Maintains Its Mystique," *BusinessWeek*, February 13, 2007; Jennifer Robison, "How the Ritz-Carlton Manages the Mystique." *Gallup Management Journal*, December 11, 2008; Kelly Kearsley, "Taking a Cue from Ritz-Carlton's Customer Service," *Wall Street Journal*, March 1, 2013; Micah Solomon, "How Four Seasons and Ritz-Carlton Empower Employees and Uphold Customer Service Standards," *Forbes*, October 28, 2013; Micah Solomon, "A Great Customer Experience (Ritz-Carlton Caliber) Requires More than Just Empowered Employees," *Forbes*, September 18, 2013; The Ritz-Carlton, www .RitzCarlton.com.

■■■ QUESTIONS FOR DISCUSSION

Chapter 7

1. What market segments in Chapter 7 do you feel would be the best match for a Ritz Carlton hotel?

Chapter 10

1. Explain how Ritz Carlton applies the internal marketing concepts mentioned in Chapter 10.

Chapter 15

1. You are a sales person for the Ritz-Carlton in Cleveland, Ohio. A pharmaceutical company has contacted you about having a product introduction and information session for a new drug. It expects 100 medical doctors to come to the event. They are considering your hotel and another hotel. The other hotel is an independent brand equivalent to a business hotel such as a Marriott, Hyatt, or Hilton. The bid at the other hotel is 10 percent less. Your manager has told you not to lower your price. How would you overcome the price objection and close the deal?

2. How does the Ritz-Carlton match up to competing hotels? What are the key differences?

3. Discuss the importance of the "wow stories" in maintaining top-quality customer service for a luxury hotel like the Ritz-Carlton.

■■■ Case 12 Grand Targhee*

In the competitive world of ski resorts, the race for profitability is always an uphill battle. But Grand Targhee Resort is carving out an innovative path to success that counters conventional wisdom and rethinks strategies popular with larger resorts. Personalized service gave Targhee the lift it needed.

*Courtesy of Catherine Fredman.

At first glance, Wyoming's Grand Targhee Ski & Summer Resort would seem to have less chance of survival than a ball of its signature talcum-powder snow on a hot summer's day. The crucial element for a successful destination ski resort, according to conventional wisdom, is land. The skiers and snowboarders demand a return on their hefty investment in a roundtrip airline ticket, accommodations, and skyrocketing lift fees in the form of an enormous and varied terrain crisscrossed by numerous high-speed lifts. Off the mountain, it's no longer enough to throw up a couple of pseudo-chalets housing a lodge, a rental shop, and a cafeteria. Today, visitors expect a base village crammed with spiffy shops, luxury hotels, and high-octane restaurants—a destination in itself.

Based on those parameters, Targhee wouldn't appear to have what it takes. Located on the western side of the Grand Tetons about 30 miles from Jackson Hole, Targhee grabs the edge on size—3,000 acres compared to Jackson Hole's 2,500—but accesses it with just four fill-size lifts and a snow card, compared to Jackson Hole's eight lifts, a gondola, and a tram. Similarly, visitors who white-knuckle their way up the long and hairpin approach road to Targhee find a handful of low-slung lodges, shops, and restaurants grouped around a plaza that can be explored thoroughly in 15 minutes, whereas Jackson Hole's crowded base village recently slotted in a Four Seasons hotel, and the town of Jackson is an easy 12 miles away.

Land usage in the base area is traditionally the key to a destination ski area's bottom line. "Real estate has become a huge part of the business plans for all the major ski operations," says Mary McKhann, editor of *The Snow Industry Letter*, a trade publication covering the ski and snowboard industry. That real estate generates hefty rents from shops and restaurants and sizable amounts of income from sales of high-priced single-family homes, townhouse condominiums, and interval ownership (the latest euphemism for time-shares). The sale residential real estate and the sale and/or lease commercial real estate is often is needed to justify the development of the resort. Many times the sales of lift tickets along is not enough to sustain a ski resort.

Targhee's pristine terrain is located in the Targhee National Forest and is subject to strict regulations regarding the usage of public land. It took six years to get permission to build a new lift on Peaked Mountain; further expansion of either the slope system or the base area is unlikely in the near future.

Yet 80 percent of the skiers who have tasted Targhee's powder come back for seconds. Although that figure might not seem notable compared to an average return rate of 77 percent for destination skiers at 79 major areas nationwide, many of those areas are within just an hour or two of a significant urban center. Targhee's nearest city is Idaho Falls, Idaho, 80 miles away.

What Is Targhee's Secret?

Because Targhee literally could not expand into new territory, it was forced to take another look at what it already had. In doing so, it found that it was sitting on a mother lode of resources just waiting to be discovered. The light went on for Larry Williamson seven summers ago. At the time, Targhee's horseback riding concession was run by an outside outfitter that strictly scheduled everything: One-hour rides left at 9:00 A.M., 10:30 A.M., and 1:00 P.M., and two-hour rides went out at 10:00 A.M. and 1:30 P.M. "We couldn't get them to accept the idea that if its 9:30 and you've got guests waiting and two wranglers and fifteen horses sitting down there, why wait half an hour to go on a ride?" Williamson recalls.

Targhee took over the riding program, and Williamson quickly realized that guests didn't want riding lessons per se; they wanted to enjoy being on a horse. The program was changed to accommodate their wishes. The result: "We went from $24,000 to more than $45,000 in one three-month season with no change in marketing, except that when you come in, we'll put you on a horse as soon as possible." Today, the horse concession is pushing $84,000 in revenues.

The next task is to figure out how to satisfy the customer when the snow fell. As a former ski instructor, Williamson knew that the ski school experience could make or break a guest's visit. A University of Idaho survey found that virtually 100 percent of the people who had taken lessons at Targhee's ski school planned on returning, whereas less than half who had not taken lessons were willing to come back. "The obvious answer was that if you're in ski school, you develop a friendship and become part of Targhee," says Williamson.

But there was a less obvious and even more compelling aspect to the lessons. Many ski schools judge their success on how much the student improves. One problem with that method is that success is defined by the instructor's parameters, rather than the guests' preferences.

Williamson came up with a different winning formula. "It really wasn't about how much the guest improved," he concluded. "It was more about how much fun the guest had. People don't like to pay for classes on vacation unless it's something fun. Fun became my focus for the industry."

A key element in Williamson's idea about fun is Mark Hanson, the snow sports school director. Hanson had run the children's program at Targhee for five years before becoming overall director. He knew the secret of a superb program: "If little kids don't have fun, mom's not going to bring them back again. And if they do have fun, mom isn't going to be able to keep them from coming back."

In transferring the successful elements of the kids' program to the adult lessons, Hanson had to take into account the fact that about 80 percent of Targhee's adult clientele is either level II or III skiers, compared to 60 percent at most other resorts. Such advanced skiers are not nearly as inclined to take a lesson as beginners. "We teach, on a percentage basis, far fewer lessons than Vail, so it became a particular challenge to get those advanced skiers into lessons," Williamson says. "Their attraction to powder is part of the answer. Customized options are another. Finding out what people want to accomplish became a priority. Rather than worrying about what they do with their bodies, get them doing things that help develop confidence."

Hanson examined Targhee's liabilities and realized that they could help the company differentiate itself and even provide opportunities. Targhee welcomes about a tenth of those who throng the slopes at Steamboat Springs, a Colorado resort with comparable acreage. But rather than sulk about empty slopes, Hanson says, "The lack of exorbitant volume becomes an advantage. We can be more personal with folks. We can say, 'It's just you and me now, so let's go play and do what you want.'"

Thanks to the small volume, Targhee's snow sports school can afford to be more flexible. At Big Sky, Montana, four hours to the north, semiprivate intermediate lessons go out in the afternoon only; if the snow has turned to slush by 2 P.M., that's tough luck. With so few crowds at Targhee, lessons billed as "group" frequently have attendance that would be more accurately labeled "semiprivate."

But it's the private lessons that best demonstrate Hanson's determination to bend over backward to achieve customer satisfaction. "You can go on a private lesson any time or any day," says public relations director Susie Barnett Bushong. "If you decide you don't want to learn a technical skill, that you just want the instructor to show you secret powder stashes, that's fine. And if you aren't happy with your lessons, you can come back the next day and get a free one."

As the program changed from the standpoint of value and product, the pay strategy changed too. Instead of being paid merely for the cost of their labor, Targhee instructors have a hefty incentive to ensure customer satisfaction through repeat business. "Instructors make much more money from returning mountain tours or returning private lessons than from lessons just assigned to them," Williamson says.

Although an expected amenity, a ski school is often something of a loss leader. Although larger areas amortize the various expenses involved in building up and staffing a school through other revenues, Targhee is too small to afford that kind of luxury. Hence the push to sell private and semiprivate lessons. "Financially, they're a win for us because they generate more revenue, they're a win for the instructors because they can make more money, and they're a win for the guests because they're getting what they want," says Hanson.

Hanson spends a lot of time ensuring he's got the right staff. "They have to be pros at working with people," he says. Again, Targhee's size is an advantage. "We might hire 10 or 12 people every year, whereas some resorts hire 200 each season," he says. "That smaller need allows me to be choosy."

It also enables him to keep a close eye on his staff; no supervisor is in charge of more than 15 instructors. Hanson monitors requests for private and semiprivate lessons and checks responses to guest surveys. "I don't do any formal spying, but I spend a lot of time on the hill myself," he allows. "I can say, 'Hey, I noticed you were doing this. Why?'"

Hanson's attentions have paid off. Grand Targhee's ski school brings in only 4.5 percent of revenue, compared to a national average of 7.5 percent. But in terms of EBITDA (earnings before interest, taxes, depreciation, and amortization), the school contributes a whopping 30.1 percent, whereas the national average is a little more than half that amount.

Targhee also bucks the industry trend by fervently pursuing the local market. "All the research will tell you that the destination guest spends more money, but to be successful, we can't afford to concentrate on that one aspect of our market," says Hanson. To broaden its share of the regional market, Targhee has adopted an all-encompassing approach, sponsoring ski programs in elementary, middle, and high schools, partnering with ski clubs in nearby Idaho Falls and at the University of Idaho at the other end of the state, and organizing programs aimed at niche audiences as narrow as, say, women from southeastern Idaho. Not surprisingly, discounted lessons and instructional weekends are a big part of the perks of membership in those ski clubs. "We get a lot of the same people who come to every instructional they can, and they generate more business for us by telling their friends," says Hanson.*

Targhee's drive for customer satisfaction and repeat business pervades every aspect of its efforts, from the parking lot attendants to the ski patrol. Each department is graded on its performance, with guest satisfaction accounting for a large portion of the rating. Five years ago, the ski patrol had a 44 percent performance rating. Then patrol staff members started to have lunch with guests, give demonstrations with their avalanche dog, and make themselves more visible. Last year, their score hit 88 percent.

Similarly, the parking lot attendants had barely eked out a 40 percent rating. They decided that guests wanted to see them working efficiently, so they donned bright orange vests, worked out a series of hand signals, were friendlier, and boosted their rating up to the 90s. Says Williamson, "The whites of the teeth are the number-one factor."

Williamson knows that Targhee will never be able to compete directly with places like Vail or Jackson Hole. It will never have the same number of chair lifts or the swanky base village that can be subsidized by real estate sales and rentals. "We try to focus not on competing with other resorts but on those features that make Targhee unique," he says. By mining those already existing assets, Williamson's team has figured out a way to turn Targhee's famous effervescent powder into cold, hard cash.

■■■ QUESTIONS FOR DISCUSSION

Chapter 2

1. How did the management of Grand Targhee create a service culture?

2. How does fun relate to establishing a service culture?

3. What product did Grand Targhee focus on to create interaction between the guests and employees? Why was this product successful?

Chapter 10

1. Find evidence from the case to show that Grand Targhee practiced good internal marketing concepts.

■■■ Case 13 The Bleeding Heart Restaurant: Unique Positioning of a Restaurant

The Bleeding Heart Restaurant and Bistro has been a favorite with Londoners (UK) for 30 years. The perennially popular restaurant and Bistro was started in 1983 by Robert and Robyn Wilson, two former journalists, as a tiny basement wine bar in a deserted and derelict cellar that had once been the warehouse of a Victorian clock manufacturer. Despite warnings from fellow members of London's wine trade that

*Reprinted by permission from Catherine Fredman.

a bar so hidden could never succeed, the Bleeding Heart prospered from the start. Today, it serves over a thousand guests per day.

History

Bleeding Heart Yard

The long-established and extremely popular Bleeding Heart restaurant offers superb French food in historical surroundings. The restaurant takes its name from the yard where it is located, which, according to the history books, was named after an eleventh-century beauty, Lady Elizabeth Hatton, who was found murdered there.

The Legend

Lady Elizabeth Hatton was the toast of eleventh-century London society. The widowed daughter-in-law of the famous merchant Sir Christopher Hatton (one-time consort of Queen Elizabeth I), Lady Elizabeth was young, beautiful, and very wealthy. Her suitors were many and varied, and they included a leading London bishop and a prominent European ambassador. Invitations to her soirees in Hatton Garden were much sought after.

Her annual Winter Ball, on January 26, 1626, was one of the highlights of the London social season. Halfway through the evening's festivities, the doors to Lady Hatton's grand ballroom were flung open. In strode a swarthy gentleman, slightly hunched of shoulder, with a clawed right hand. He took her by the hand, danced her once around the room and out through the double doors into the garden. A buzz of gossip arose. Would Lady Elizabeth and the European ambassador (for it was he) kiss and make up, or would she return alone? Neither was to be. The next morning her body was found in the cobblestone courtyard—torn limb from limb, with her heart still pumping blood onto the cobblestones. And from henceforth, the yard was to be known as the Bleeding Heart Yard.

Charles Dickens and the Bleeding Heart

Charles Dickens knew Bleeding Heart well. In *Little Dorrit* he wrote of folks in the yard, saying, "The more practical of the Yard's inmates abided by the tradition of the murder." But he went on to document another Bleeding Heart story: "The gentler and more imaginative inhabitants, including the whole of the tender sex, were loyal to the legend of a young lady imprisoned in her own chamber by a cruel father for remaining true to her own true lover—but it was objected to by the murderous party that this was the invention of a spinster and romantic, still lodging in the Yard."

Today, the Bleeding Heart has grown well beyond that tiny basement wine bar but has preserved and enhanced the architectural, cultural, and historic value of its unique location while serving a multisegment market.

The Tavern has guarded the entrance to the Bleeding Heart Yard since 1746 with a history of conviviality encapsulated in its then boast of "drunk for a penny and dead drunk for two pence." Today, the Tavern offers a traditional neighborhood bar with real ale and a light lunchtime menu for those pressed for time.

Downstairs the Tavern Dining Room with its jolly farmyard illustrations features an open rotisserie and grill and provides a warm and comforting setting in which to enjoy free-range organic British meat, game, and poultry along with an excellent-value wine list.

The Tavern is also open for breakfast, with freshly squeezed orange juice, home-baked croissants, and "The Full English" with tasty Suffolk Bacon.

Early Days

In the early days, the Bleeding Heart's proximity to the headquarters of many of the national dailies—*The Times, The Mirror*, and *The Guardian*—coupled with the media connections (and the media's partiality to a decent bottle of wine) meant that from its inception the wine bar attracted a number of leading journalists and, in their wake, the public relations industry.

The Barristers Chambers of Gray's Inn were also but a corkscrew's throw away, and the Bleeding Heart became a popular lunch spot for this learned group to discuss their briefs over a decent bottle of claret and a platter of charcuterie or cheese.

The increasingly upscale clientele began to demand a more sophisticated menu than the simple wine bar fare originally offered. In response, the bar expanded its horizons into an adjoining basement and its kitchens to include a white tablecloth restaurant with more sophisticated, although still classically French, cuisine.

From that 40-seat bar, the Bleeding Heart expanded, above and around the ancient cobblestoned courtyard to encompass a formal fine-dining restaurant seating 160 with a 30-seat terrace, a 60-seat bistro with its own 40-seat terrace, a 70-seat tavern and bar, and two private dining rooms: the Parlor and the Wine Cellar. Adjoining Bleeding Heart Yard in Ely Place is the stunning medieval function room, the Crypt, and its intimate Crypt Café. The twelfth-century crypt, which seats 120, was the venue for the celebration following the wedding of Henry VIII and Catherine of Aragon.

Marketing

Opening day was December 1, 1983. The Wilsons deployed two French waitresses to hand out "How to Find Us" maps at the local underground station (subway). There was no advertising because there was no budget. As a launch tool, the leaflets were not an instant success; on that first day the restaurant earned only £39.37. However, within a week, word started to spread and turnover tripled. The week-long distribution of those leaflets was Bleeding Heart's only external promotion ever did.

Word of mouth was relied on to reach the right sort of customer. It worked, building a loyal and homogeneous clientele who believe that they have, by finding the tucked-away little Yard and the bustling bistro beneath it, made a personal discovery. The restaurant was a "best kept secret," a secret that, fortunately, lots of people were in on. The Unique Selling Proposition (USP) was their unique location.

Shortly after opening, Bleeding Heart was described by a New York reviewer as "bleeding hard to find but worth it." A London cab driver commented to a lost diner that the reason it was called Bleeding Heart was that it was Bleeding Hard to find. Robert and Robyn used the mantra that you had to discover Bleeding Heart rather than read an advertisement about it. They also worked hard building a database of regular customers, mainly by running monthly prize drawings to garner business cards, which, in those pre-e-mail days, had postal addresses and telephone numbers. It was a labor-intensive task, but they built a customer base of some 5,000 with a shorter list of 500 of those with a special interest in wine.

To the short list they promoted their regular wine and food evenings and any wine-related events such as the New Beaujolais Breakfast. Magnum Night was launched offering a special half-price deal on Friday evenings (the quietest night) for magnums of champagne. The Seagram Company had discovered a large stock of magnums of Heidsieck champagne in Ireland, which they were keen to offload at a very attractive price.

Despite the fact there was no promotion, Magnum Night became a rapid and astonishingly successful draw card. The hours it was available were cut from 5:30 until 7:00 P.M. only to discover that queues were forming in the yard. On one occasion, a journalist from the BBC phoned offering to pay in advance by credit card lest he should miss the 7:00 P.M. cutoff.

However, there was a downside to this promotion. Regular evening diners (long-term bread-and-butter customers) couldn't get in the door past the queues of Johnny-come-lately champagne quaffers, and with much regret, especially from the champagne drinkers; the promotion was stopped after a year. In its place the Magnum Club was created based on the premise that wine tastes better in bigger bottles. Regular customers were invited to join. Initially members were offered a discount on champagne. Then the offer expanded to include invitations to wine tastings and wine making dinners. The Club is still going strong and membership is free but by invitation only, and it is much sought after.

Today, the Wilsons still do no advertising for Bleeding Heart Restaurant, Bistro, or Tavern, but they have begun carefully targeted promotions for special functions in special publications aimed at the corporate event market and the wedding sector. These are always tied to associated editorial features.

Talking to regular customers has become much easier with e-mail, but the Wilsons are hypercautious about invading their e-space. Mailings are used only for major events such as the summer opening of the outdoor terrace when regular customers are given a complimentary glass of rosé wine to celebrate the sunshine.

The Wilsons believe that keeping a low profile has worked in an increasingly crowded marketplace. In 2008, despite the economic slowdown in the financial sector, turnover was still increasing. During this difficult economic period, the *London Evening Standard* newspaper wrote a feature about restaurants feeling the pinch of the recession. Bleeding Heart was one of the few restaurants to be lauded as "fully booked."

The restaurant received a number of favorable comments from both local and international media. The media praised the food, service, and ambiance of the restaurant. This media was more effective than any advertising the restaurant could place, as potential guests viewed it as a credible source of information. Thus, the press coverage proved to be a major factor in driving business to the restaurant.

Awards

During its first six months, the tiny wine bar/bistro was voted one of London's Top Ten Wine Bars by *Time Out* magazine and has continued to win plaudits from national and international press ever since, including "London's most romantic restaurant" from *The Times*, "Best Venue in Europe" from the *Guardian*, and "Best Private Dining."

The *Zagat Guide* put it in the top three restaurants in London for a business lunch. *Hardens*, the most authoritative London restaurant guide, and *Square Meal*, the city of London's eating-out bible, both rate it number one for business. Since its inception, Bleeding Heart has always been known for its extensive and well-priced wine list. The Wilsons have been frequent winners of an annual Award of Excellence for "One of the Best Wine Lists in the World" from *Wine Spectator* magazine.

■■■ QUESTIONS FOR DISCUSSION

Chapter 13

1. Explain the elements of the promotional mix that the Bleeding Heart Restaurant used.

2. Why do you think the Bleeding Heart was so successful with such a small budget for promotion?

Chapter 14

1. If you were hired as a public relations firm for the Bleeding Heart, how would you plan its public relations campaign?

2. There are a number of favorable mentions in popular media about the restaurant. How do you think it was able to get these mentions in the media?

Chapter 16

1. The Bleeding Heart has not changed its promotional strategy since it opened. If you purchased the Bleeding Heart, would you use social media? If you would, explain how you will use it. If not, explain why not.

■■■ Case 14 Pricing Almost Destroys and Then Saves a Local Restaurant

"As I pulled into the gravel parking lot I knew immediately that the Mexicatessan was a warm, friendly Mexican restaurant. There was nothing new here, and I don't mean that in a negative way. Nothing looked new but it all looked comfortable, well worn with the passage of time. Mexican motifs line the walls and ceiling right next to the window air conditioners."

The restaurant, located in a lower-middle-class neighborhood, attracts both locals and Houston's rich and famous. The restaurant's profitability started to drop. The owner, Mr. Herrera, worked long, hard hours producing a high-quality product that his customers enjoyed, but he received very little reward for his time and investment. He had a good product, a good location, and a strong following. The problem was pricing. The prices at the Mexicatessan were far below those of the competition. Herrera wanted to offer good value, and he felt that he had to keep his prices below the chains. He used price to gain a competitive advantage against the chain's expensive buildings and their large regional advertising budgets.

Instead of attracting and maintaining loyal customers, the Mexicatessan's low prices almost destroyed the business. The prices were not high enough to produce sufficient cash flow to keep the restaurant in good repair. Herrera was unable to receive financial reward for his efforts. After several years of struggling, the owner commissioned a research project to see how he could increase his cash flow. The research suggested that his prices were 50 percent less than those of the competition, even though his customers thought the food quality was better. Herrera decided to increase his prices so they were only 10 percent less than the competition. He felt this price difference and his food quality would offset the competitive advantages of the chains. He set out to achieve his strategy through a series of planned price increases. Because achieving his target would mean price increases of 70 percent or more on some items, the first price increase was about 25 percent, with subsequent price increases gradually moving him to his desired pricing levels. Over a three-year period, the menu prices increased by 40 to 70 percent. This was a bold move.

After the price increases, the Mexicatessan's revenues increased at a higher percentage than the price increases, indicating there was little resistance to the price increases. Herrera's customers still thought they were getting good value. The price increases allowed him to put a new roof on the building, hire additional staff, decorate the restaurant's interior, and receive a good return on his investment. This case study demonstrates the importance of price. Operations that charge too little often do not have money to maintain the business, although they have many customers and appear prosperous.

Herrera was lucky. It is easier to move up the price of a product that is underpriced than it is to lower the price of an overpriced product. Companies that overcharge create a negative attitude among those who have tried their products. Even when prices are lowered, customer attitudes may remain unchanged. Pricing must be a carefully planned management process.

■■■ QUESTIONS FOR DISCUSSION

Chapter 11

1. Why was Mr. Herrera reluctant to raise his prices? How did these low prices almost destroy the business?

2. Using this case as an example, explain how the concepts of demand, price, and profits are interrelated.

■■■ Case 15 Company Case Spirit Airlines: The Lowest Possible Price—At All Costs

Customers were tweeting terrible comments about Spirit Airlines. They were complaining about the lack of empathy they received from airline agents when their flight was cancelled. They are complaining about having to pay for extra charges after they had purchased their ticket. One customer tweeted out that one warning others not to fly Spirit Airlines. These comments, tweeted by real Spirit Airlines customers, are not the types of feedback a company generally wants to hear from customers. And at the same time that the airline's operating philosophy has generated lots of negative testimonials in social media, it has also earned Spirit Airlines the dubious distinction as Consumer Reports' lowest-rated airline for the customer experience. In fact, Spirit Airlines received one of the lowest-ever overall scores given by the esteemed consumer watchdog.

With that kind of reputation, you would think that Spirit Airlines is headed down a path to bankruptcy. To the contrary, however, Spirit is one of the fastest-growing U.S. carriers. It fills almost every available seat on every flight. And it turns profits each and every quarter—a difficult feat in the airline industry. In a world filled with companies doing back flips to fill each customer's every desire that kind of financial success seems like an unlikely outcome given such a high level of customer dissatisfaction. How does Spirit do it? And what are customers complaining about? As it turns out, although Spirit Airlines doesn't want its customers to leave its planes unhappy, its philosophy is described perfectly by an old adage—when you make an omelet, you have to break some eggs.

Value Equals Low Price

Spirit Airlines first began scheduled flights in 1990 out of Atlantic City. Over the next 17 years, the airline expanded along the East Coast with limited service to Caribbean and South American destinations. But in 2007, it unveiled an entirely new business model as part of a nationwide expansion plan. Billing itself as an "ultra low-cost carrier," Spirit set its prices lower than any other airline on the routes it flew. In the years since, Spirit has consistently maintained lower prices—in some case up to 90 percent lower than competing airlines.

But to fly so cheap, customers must not only pay the fare, they have to pay the price. When customers buy a ticket on a Spirit flight, they are paying for one thing and one thing only, occupying a seat on a plane from one destination to another. That's because Spirit Airlines has deconstructed airline flight service, charging a fee for each and every service component. Charging fees for various components of flight service is common airline practice these days, but Spirit charges extra for everything. On Spirit Airlines, you really do get what you pay for—and not one peanut more.

For example, although other airlines charge for food, they typically provide free beverages and a basic snack. On Spirit Airlines, a bottle of water or can of soda costs you $3.00. Want a pillow or a blanket? No problem. You can have both for the duration of the flight—for $7.00. Spirit offers no onboard entertainment or Wi-Fi. And seats on a Spirit flight are not only closer together than on other carriers, they don't recline. Spirit packs about 30 more seats in the same space as standard airlines. If customers don't want to be so close to neighbors in front of them—you guessed it—for a fee, they can get a seat in the exit row or the front row, providing some 10 extra inches of legroom.

Spirit refers to its pricing practices as "frill control," and it maintains that such pricing gives customers more control than they get with competing airlines. "We think of it as options that customers choose," says Spirit CEO Ben Baldanza, who cringes at the word *fee*. In support of his "options" theory, he points out that the "free" soda on other airlines isn't really free. Customers pay for it in the price of the ticket, whether they want the beverage or not. Although this approach sounds refreshing, many customers hold a different view, as suggested by the following customer experience:

> Jack had never heard of Spirit Airlines. But as he shopped for a flight from New York City to Chicago to attend a college reunion, he booked a roundtrip flight with Spirit, whose price was $60 cheaper than any other option. Upon checking in at New York's LaGuardia Airport and requesting a seat assignment, the desk agent told him that would cost $15, unless he wanted to pay $25 to $50 for a seat with extra legroom. Jack opted for the $25 option, and was then charged $10 to print his boarding pass. At the gate, the agent told him there would be a fee for his standard carry-on bag—a whopping $100. The soda and snack Jack requested onboard cost him $8.

On the return trip, Jack thought he had the system figured out. By checking in online, the fee for his carry-on bag was only $45 and the boarding pass was free. After checking in at a self-serve kiosk and making his way through security, he approached his gate with 15 minutes to spare. Thinking he had plenty of time, he ducked into a gift shop to pick up a snack and a magazine for the flight. As he handed his boarding pass to the agent at the gate, Jack was told that, because he hadn't arrived at the gate 15 minutes before scheduled departure, his seat on the sold-out flight had been given to a standby passenger. So he paid $150 to stay in an airport hotel, only to wake up at 3:30 A.M. to catch the only morning flight back to LaGuardia. So although he may have saved $60 on his ticket price, in the end his Spirit flight had cost him an additional $328—by itself almost as much as the round-trip fare.

Jack's example may represent a worst-case scenario. But the social media are filled with similar stories by unwary travelers. And because Spirit flies with a small fleet, it has less backup to deal with aircraft problems, causing above-average flight delays and cancellations. As a result of that and its pricing policies, Spirit draws roughly three times more complaints to the U.S. Department of Transportation than any other airline.

The Customer Is Always Wrong

When it comes to responding to customer complaints and requests, Spirit Airlines takes a hardline approach. It seems that no matter how much customers plead for exceptions to its fees, company representatives are trained to stand their ground. Baldanza justifies this by explaining that the extra charges are not mandatory. In other words, passengers can get to and from their destinations without paying for anything more than the price of the ticket. The company further defends its pricing by pointing out that it hides no information from customers—those who take the time to look know what the price of the ticket covers and what it does not.

Spirit doesn't hide from its poor customer service record. In some respects, it wears that record as a badge of honor. When a study was released ranking Spirit Airlines dead last with the most complaints made to the Department of Transportation, Spirit turned it into bragging rights. Although it had the worst record, the airline averaged only eight complaints per 100,000 customers over a five-year period—a number that declined to five by the time the report was released. So Spirit celebrated by offering $24 discounts to customers. They were celebrating that only 1 out of every 20,000 passengers filed a complaint. They said that was OK because they were not the airline for everyone.

The Counterpoint

The subtext of most Spirit hate speech is that its fees are unfair and that customers are being fleeced. However, most customers know exactly what they are getting and seem happy with that. When asked if she resented having to pay $3 for water on a Spirit flight, one passenger replied, "Not at all. They're trying to cover their costs." That seems to be the sentiment of many understanding Spirit customers who are more than happy to sacrifice a few extras in order to get truly cheap airfare.

To see what all the fuss was about, one airline analyst put Spirit to the test, eyes wide open. After paying only $63 for a one-way flight from Detroit to LaGuardia— roughly $300 less than the same fare offered by Delta, American, or United—he reported on his experience. "After we landed I turned to my friend and said, 'I don't get it—what the hell are people complaining about?'" His overall assessment was that customer dissatisfaction stems from misconceptions—that if people are aware of Spirit policies ahead of time, they can avoid unpleasant surprises and not be charged for add-ons unless they want them. His suggestions? If you want entertainment, make sure you have your own movies or music on a mobile device. Plan ahead for snacks or beverages by bringing your own, or budget in buying Spirit's. Add the carry-on or checked bag fees to the price of the ticket to get a true price or, pack very light and jam everything into one small carry-on bag or backpack that all passengers can take on for free. And be mentally prepared to "be able to determine the shampoo used by the person in the row ahead of you." For flights no longer than three hours, being a little squished isn't that bad.

For all those customers who complain that fees add up to more than the savings on the ticket price, official numbers suggest otherwise. Spirit's total flight price (all fees included) is still the lowest in the industry at an average of $102.02, compared to $125.65 for Southwest and $152.97 for Delta. And even with that price difference, Spirit still makes money, thanks to the industry's lowest cost per seat-mile. In the past four years, annual revenue at Spirit Airlines increased from $781 million to $1.7 billion. Net income rose likewise from $72 million to $177 million.

Spirit Airlines is on a tear, and it doesn't plan to slow things down. It currently accounts for only 1.4 percent of the weekly U.S. seat inventory. But if things go as planned, that figure will rise to 5 percent by 2022. And as Baldanza sees it, that growth is good for the industry. He sees Spirit as expanding the demand for air transportation by providing flight at prices that enable people to fly on Spirit that could not afford to fly on the other airlines.

What about all those complaints? Although Spirit isn't saying that it will never improve with respect to the customer experience, it is making one thing very clear: "[We won't] add costs for things that most customers don't value as much as our low fares just to reduce the complaints of a few customers. Doing that would raise prices for everyone, compromising our commitment to what our customers have continuously told us they truly value-the lowest possible price."

Sources: "If Spirit Airlines Is So Unpopular, Why Are Its Flights So Full?" CBS News, March 23, 2014, www.cbsnews.com/news/if-spirit-airlinesis-so-unpopular-why-are-its-flights-so-fuil/; Justin Bachman, "How Spirit Airlines Turned Cheap Seats and Sore Knees into Steady Profits," *Bloomberg Businessweek*, April 29, 2014, www.businessweek.com/articles/2014-04-29/love-or-hate-it-spirit-airlines-has-found-a-solidbusiness-in-cheap-fares; Justin Bachman, "Spirit Airlines Sees All Those Passenger Complaints as Mere Misunderstandings," *Bloomberg Businessweek*, April 18, 2014, www.businessweek.com/articles/2014-04-18/spiritairlines-passenger-complaints-part-of-its-business-model; Jared Blank, "3 Myths about Spirit Airlines," *Online Travel Review*, September 10, 2012, www.onlinetravelreview.com/2012/09/10/3-myths-about-spirit-airlinesor-my-flight-on-spirit-was-perfectly-fine-really/; quotes and other information accessed at www.spirit.com/content/documents/en-us/Contract_of_Carriage.pdf and www.fspiritair.com/spiritairlines_toptweets2.html (accessed July 2014).

■■■ QUESTIONS FOR DISCUSSION

Chapter 1

1. Do you feel Spirit Airlines has a customer orientation? Explain your answer.

2. What is Spirit Airlines' value proposition?

Chapter 11

1. Based on the concept of customer value-based pricing, explain Spirit Airlines' success.

2. Does Spirit Airlines employ good-value pricing or value-added pricing? Explain.

3. Does Spirit's pricing strategy truly differentiate it from the competition?

4. Is Spirit's pricing strategy sustainable? Explain.

5. What changes, if any, would you recommend that Spirit make?

■■■ Case 16 Apollo Hotel

After just 10 months of operation, Ryan Sawyer was proud of what he had accomplished managing the Apollo Hotel, but he knew that much work remained.

The Apollo was owned by the Williams Cosmetic Company and was located in Kentucky. The hotel had originally been built to serve as housing for students who attended the Williams Cosmetology School and was converted to an 82-room hotel in September 2002 to serve the general public.

In addition to the hotel, the complex contained a manufacturing plant for personal care products and the corporate headquarters of the Williams Cosmetic Company.

The Williams Cosmetic Company discontinued the operation of a cosmetology school and decided to concentrate on the manufacture and sale of cosmetics. The hotel was opened to use the existing building.

When the hotel opened, there were very few guests, almost no staff, and a limited budget. The hotel had no brochure, Web site, or even a listing in the yellow pages. Although Ryan had no previous hospitality industry experience, he was told to build the business and turn it into a profitable operation.

Ryan held a bachelor's degree in economics/business management from Colorado State University. He had worked with a large regional bank and with JCPenney Company.

Marketing Strategy

Ryan decided that the hotel should be marketed to a wide spectrum of guests. Over the years Mr. and Mrs. Williams had met many people through their church and community work. These contacts proved useful in promoting the hotel.

The Convention and Visitors Bureau also proved to be helpful and referred many guests. Ryan contacted the Little League and secured contracts for teams to stay in the hotel by offering free lodging to referees on a double occupancy per room basis.

To entice guests during the season, Ryan decided to offer three nights for the price of two if guests would make reservations two months prior to arrival and pay in advance. This proved to be moderately effective.

A large electric utility company was offered very good rates to encourage their crews to stay at the hotel. This resulted in many nights of occupancy.

U.S. military personnel were also encouraged to stay at the hotel through very good rates. Ryan believed that with only 82 rooms, the best opportunity to fill beds was to contact organizations rather than attempt to market to individual travelers.

The hotel seemed to be gaining a reputation as "value lodging" and had experienced 58 percent occupancy on average for the last four months.

Ryan observed that the company's cosmetic items were not used or sold in the hotel even though they were manufactured on the grounds. This was corrected by placing Williams' amenity products in the rooms and opening a gift shop in the hotel, which sold the company's personal care products as well as other traditional gift shop items.

Personnel

As a small, privately owned hotel not operating as a flag property, the management of Apollo could explore different operational strategies. As an example, front-desk employees were paid a commission on business that they brought to the hotel. This encouraged front-desk people to continuously be aware of sales opportunities when someone called or dropped in. It also encouraged them to "sell" the hotel to their friends and to organizations they knew such as churches, schools, and clubs. Ryan said that with commissions, front-desk employees averaged more income than their counterparts in other area hotels.

Ryan believed that his primary responsibility was to "keep the lights on" by marketing the hotel and that operational decisions should be left to those responsible for the operational areas. He held the belief that most people who desired personal growth and responsibility could learn the operational tasks and would find ways to do the job better without top-down micromanagement. He also believed that all employees should be cross-trained and willing temporarily to accept responsibilities outside the primary department. The maintenance man had once been asked to wear a suit and serve as bellboy during a heavy occupancy period. This seemed to work well.

All new employees were expected to learn how to clean rooms and make beds so they could help with that important area in crunch times. The number-one criterion for employment with Apollo was, "Are you willing to learn and willing to work?"

Employees were also expected to constantly improve their professionalism. When decisions were needed by management, department heads were expected to type up their proposal and present it in a professional manner. This forced the department heads to think through the proposal, take it seriously, and be prepared to defend it.

Openness to New Ideas

Ryan said he was open to new ideas from employees and others concerning ways to improve occupancy and operations at the hotel.

■■■ QUESTIONS FOR DISCUSSION

Chapter 9

1. What recommendations would you offer to Ryan to:
   a. Increase occupancy
   b. Improve REVPAR
   c. Improve operations

Chapter 10

1. What would you do to further increase the level of personal responsibility that Ryan developed among employees?

2. Do you believe that employees should be cross-trained to do many tasks in a hotel? Does this alienate applicants who might otherwise be good employees?

Chapter 13

1. Should Ryan hire an ad agency to help position and market the hotel? Explain your answer.

■■■ Case 17 Chuck E. Cheese CEC Entertainment: "Where a Kid Can Be a Kid"

Chuck E. Cheese is going to Latin America. Binvenidos! Mike Magusiak, president and CEO, announced that the company's management and board of directors strongly supported a strategy of developing new entertainment centers in Latin America. Several factors were considered in this decision.

- The demographics of Latin America demonstrate a heavy percentage of kids. CEC understands this market segment and has a proven track record in its 540 entertainment units, which annually entertain 40 million kids.

- According to information provided by CEC Entertainment, Chuck E. Cheese is more popular with kids than Mickey Mouse and Ronald McDonald.

- The mission of Chuck E. Cheese is to bring families together in a wholesome environment for fun, games, and food. This mission fits well with the culture and demographics of Latin America.

- In a magazine article, the author commented parents are always looking for ways to entertain their children. He commented that children are often not patient enough to enjoy the service one receives in a full-service restaurant. Trying to keep the children from bothering other guests becomes an unpleasant experience for the parents and when they are unsuccessful it creates an unpleasant experience for other diners. He states that Chuck E. Cheese provides a product that children enjoy and when children are happy with a dining experience, the parents are happy.[1]

- Despite language differences, Latin America is culturally similar to the United States. Millions of Latin Americans visit the United States each year and many of them head for Disney World, Disneyland, and other entertainment providers.

- Latin Americans are family focused. Parents and grandparents can be expected to visit a Chuck E. Cheese restaurant with children. Repeat visitations are almost guaranteed to occur.

- Many sophisticated investors live in Latin America. In most cases, these people speak English and many studied or worked in the United States.

---

[1]Jackson, Eric, "Forget Kids, Investors Can Go for Chuck E. Cheese," *Breakout Performance*, Thursday, March 4, 2010, http://breakoutperformance.-blogspot.com/2010/03/forget-kids-investors-can-go-for-chuck.html (accessed November 22, 2011).

Chuck E. Cheese has over 30 years of operating success and offers attractive unit profitability. According to Mike Magusiak, the operating margins of 13 percent at Chuck E. Cheese surpass most other chain restaurants.

- Mexico and Central America are only a few hours from major U.S. cities such as Houston, Miami, Los Angeles, and others. This facilitates management support for new restaurants. Although countries such as Chile, Argentina, and Brazil are further away, they are well served by U.S. and international air carriers.

- Latin Americans are a friendly and hospitable people who enjoy working with customers, particularly children.

- Unlike some food dishes that suffer from recipe changes, the menu items of Chuck E. Cheese such as pizza, salads, oven-roasted sandwiches, Buffalo wings, and desserts can easily be modified to meet local food tastes and preferences.

- Little or no direct competition against the Chuck E. Cheese concept exists in most Latin American cities.

- All the food ingredients needed for a Chuck E. Cheese operation are readily available throughout Latin America.

- CEC Entertainment has experience with entertainment centers in Canada, Puerto Rico, Saudi Arabia, Dubai, Guam, and three units in Chile and Guatemala. It was felt that this experience would prove invaluable to the success of multiunit operations in Latin America.

- *Merchandise Sales Opportunities.* Observations of Latin American markets demonstrated that young people are highly attracted to merchandise with logos of consumer products and services. This should provide CEC units within Latin America with excellent opportunities for increased revenue per customer.

- *Fiestas, Birthdays, and Other Celebrations.* Latin Americans have to celebrate birthdays and other special times with the family. Chuck E. Cheese provides over 2 million birthday parties each year.

- Latin American customers, like those in the United States and Canada, are increasingly active in the use of computers. Chuck E. Cheese has experience with online management/marketing and has a database of over 3 million members who receive e-mail updates and specials.

Mike expressed strong optimism that the decision to concentrate international growth in Latin America would eventually provide increased employment opportunities for employees, particularly those fluent in Spanish and Portuguese.

New ideas and concepts might be learned from successful Latin American operations. These might be incorporated into Chuck E. Cheese units elsewhere to the increased entertainment pleasure of kids and thus to profit potential for CEC Entertainment.

■■■ QUESTIONS FOR DISCUSSION

Chapter 6

1. Explain from a consumer behavior standpoint why Chuck E. Cheese appears to be a good fit for Latin America.

2. How do you think consumer behavior in Latin America may differ from consumer behavior in the United States?

Chapter 8

1. Many of the preceding facts suggest that family segment in Latin American will be attracted to Chuck E. Cheese, just as families in the United States are attracted to the entertainment complex. What are the arguments used in the case to defend this argument?

2. What questions do you have that you would want answered before you expanded into Latin America?

◼◼◼ Case 18 Tropicana Fishing Lodge

How does a fishing lodge fit into our operations as a major producer of bananas? This was the question that faced the Costa Rican division of an international banana company.

Location and Description of Tropicana

Tropicana was a fishing lodge located on the Caribbean coast of Costa Rica. It was situated on the banks of the River Pastura. It could be reached by light plane because there was a paved landing strip on the nearby properties of Del Monte. It could also be reached by means of a mountain highway from San José. This road was 98 percent paved and required approximately three to three-and-a-half hours of travel. Fog could be a problem on this road and could impede travel. A small dock had been built to accommodate loading and unloading the boats. A series of steps, including rather steep steel ones with a rope handhold, led to the grassy bank above.

Immediately behind the lodge was a banana plantation. A cement sidewalk separated the plantation from the lodge and homes. The grounds surrounding the lodge were well kept and quite attractive. The beauty was not dramatic or awe inspiring but was instead peaceful and relaxing. Jungle growth could be seen on the opposite bank of the river, and monkeys could be heard howling in the forest.

The lodge was built in the fashion of a jungle building—it was not constructed on the ground but on wooden stilts. This allowed ventilation and helped prevent rotting. It also helped discourage insects and small animals from entering. The lodge was small but would accommodate 22 guests. Guest rooms were contained in a separate cabin that formed an "L" to the main lodge. The rooms were clean and well maintained. Each room had a bathroom with a shower and other bathroom fixtures. Beds were of the single-bed or bunk-bed style. There was no air conditioning in the rooms, but the evening breeze was pleasant. A light blanket was sometimes necessary.

Recreational Facilities

Fishing for tarpon and snook was the primary entertainment offered by Tropicana. This occurred in the intercoastal canal, which runs from Limón to the Nicaraguan border. It was also done in lagoons and the mouths of rivers. The river in front of Tropicana offered little opportunity for fishing; it was necessary to go downstream 30 to 40 minutes by boat to reach fishing sites.

Three principal areas were noted for tarpon and snook. One was in a lagoon 40 minutes downstream and to the south of Tropicana. Another was downstream and north of Tropicana near the village of Parismina. This was 45 minutes to an hour away and near a competitor's lodge. The third was much farther north, in the area of Tortuguero. This was roughly one-and-a-half hours away.

The scenery in the intercoastal canal and along the jungle rivers was beautiful. One could see a variety of bird life, including many rare species. Monkeys could be heard and sometimes seen in the trees. Both Walt Disney and Jacques Cousteau had made movies featuring the region. Crocodiles were difficult to see. Deer, marguary, jaguar, and many small animals also lived there but were rarely seen. Botanists and other nature lovers could find hours of enjoyment in the variety of trees, flowers, orchids, and other plant life, including a perfume tree that filled the air with a beautiful aroma in the evening.

There was little or no opportunity to exploit commercial hunting in the area. The area was not known for ducks or geese, and the deer were quite small. In addition, much of the area was gradually being turned into national parks, and wildlife would be protected. Swimming or water skiing in the lagoons and intercoastal waterway would be dangerous due to submerged logs. There was also the possibility of sharks. The Caribbean coast represented miles of uninhabited dark sandy beach. It had palm trees and was attractive but was not developed. Moreover, it was very difficult to reach the beach from Tropicana. The surf at the mouth of the river was too strong to permit entry into the sea with the flat-bottom boats and motors. Thus, the boats could not be used for ocean fishing.

Any large-scale building projects such as a lodge, modern tennis courts, or a golf course would require land. This would almost certainly have to come from land that was profitably planted in bananas.

Fishing Season

Although Tropicana remained open all year, guests were advised that fishing was impossible from November 1 to January 15. This was the time of year when the heaviest rains occurred. The longest periods of dry weather were from the latter part of January through most of May and then again from August through October. The best time for snook fishing occurred in late August until November 1. A schedule of the best fishing months versus the traditional months of high occupancy at Tropicana follows. This schedule presented certain difficulties in promoting Tropicana as a year-round lodge. During the months of May through August, Tropicana had to compete with vacation areas in the United States. September and October represented excellent months for fishing but relatively weak ones for occupancy due to the fact that school was open in the United States. In addition, these were fall months in the United States, with nice weather conditions there. November and December were winter months in the United States and could be promoted as vacation months, but fishing was impossible during that time. Increased promotion would be necessary to reduce the dependency on three to five months of natural draw. November, December, and half of January would remain poor months due to weather and fishing conditions. Thus, Tropicana would face, at a maximum, nine favorable months.

MONTH	FISHING CONDITIONS	FIVE HIGHEST MONTHS OF OCCUPANCY AT TROPICANA (APPROXIMATELY 80% OF TOTAL OCCUPANCY)
January	Good	
February	Excellent	1
March	Fair	2
April	Fair	3
May	Excellent	
June	Excellent	
July	Good	
August	Good	
September	Excellent	4
October	Excellent	5
November	Poor	
December	Poor	

Value of Lodge

It was difficult to estimate the market value of the lodge, but Eric estimated that it would probably be valued somewhere between $250,000 and $500,000 (United States). A difficulty in appraising the lodge was that its success was tied directly to the banana company, which owned and operated the source of electrical power for the lodge. A buyer might find this factor of concern. However, a generator and an independent well would not be difficult to acquire.

Competitors

- *Azul Grande.* The fishing lodge of Azul Grande was the primary competitor and could accommodate 24 guests. This lodge was located in the fishing village of Parismina and could be reached only by private airplane or boat. It was not as attractive as Tropicana. It was surrounded by poor fishing shacks and older in appearance than Tropicana. However, it was clean and well maintained. A monkey in the front yard greeted all visitors. Clients for this lodge were almost exclusively from the United States. The owners advertised in select outdoor magazines. The owner also appeared on TV talk shows when he was in the United States. Bookings in the United States were handled through an exclusive agent in Chicago who worked on a commission basis.

- *Isla Del Sol.* This fishing lodge was located at the mouth of the San Juan River, which forms a border for Nicaragua and Costa Rica. The manager/owner was a Mr. Laurie from Detroit. This lodge was experiencing difficulty in breaking even and was open six months or less each year.

- *Casa Fantastica.* This fishing lodge was also located at the mouth of the San Juan River and open six months or less each year. There was no information concerning the success of this lodge, but it was apparent that the management was fairly aggressive, as witnessed by advertisements from the outdoor magazine *The Salt Water Sportsman.*

Rates

Rates for competitive fishing lodges on the Caribbean coast ranged from $2,000 to $3,500 per person per week. Tropicana and other lodges did not encourage guests to come for periods of less than five days. This was due to the cost of transportation. It also provided a guest with more opportunities to catch fish. Guests who stayed for shorter periods of time sometimes arrived when fishing was poor and returned to spread stories of poor fishing. All lodges provided competitive services, although Tropicana provided even more individualized attention to guests and was willing to spend more time and money to transport guests to good fishing sites.

Promotion and Client Profile: Las Perla

Promotion for Tropicana was handled primarily through ads in the English-print newspapers in San José. Word-of-mouth advertising seemed to be the primary means by which people heard of the lodge. A review of the guest book indicated that the majority of guests had been from the United States; the second largest group were Costa Ricans.

■■■ QUESTIONS FOR DISCUSSION

Chapter 12

1. What distribution channels would you use for the Tropicana Fishing Lodge?

2. How are distribution and segmentation related?

Chapter 13

1. What promotional strategies/tactics would you suggest for Tropicana?

2. Discuss the differences in management and marketing between a commercial fishing or hunting lodge and a commercial hotel.

3. Could the marketing of diverse hunting/fishing lodges be conducted effectively by an independent group responsible for multiple properties?

■■■ Case 19 Boulder Creek

One of the most difficult marketing tasks in any industry is to reposition a declining product, attract new market segments, and achieve market success. Yet that is exactly what Andrea Lewis did with a former Econo Lodge in a nonhighway location in Boulder, Colorado.

"This was the hardest thing I had ever done," said Andrea. "My husband, Burt and I, purchased the property in 1999 but Burt was busy with real estate in Chicago and left most of the responsibility to me."

Andrea knew nothing about hotels but found that her training and experience supervising 26 salespeople in 19 states as manager of corporate sales for Tiffany & Company was invaluable. Andrea had just been offered a promotion with Tiffany's when Burt called to say they were purchasing an ignored Econo Lodge in Boulder that had great potential. "I need you to quit your job, move to Boulder, and remake this hotel," said Burt. Andrea had recently experienced the death of two young friends and said to herself, "I love Boulder, and I love Colorado. This will be a challenge, but life is short, so let's do it."

Life at Tiffany's was a dream compared to the task that confronted Andrea. The property contained a 100-year-old home suffering from lack of maintenance, a motel complex that had been built in stages with little or no curbside appeal, a lack of landscaping, a rutted parking lot, and a lack of physical amenities such as a swimming pool and exercise room. Located in a student residential area, the property did not easily lend itself to drive-by stopovers.

Employee quality and attitudes matched the property. Several employees were drug dealers or addicts, and an attitude of ignoring the guest prevailed. The management and staff seemed more interested in naked pool parties than guest interaction. One unusual guest service offered at the front desk was a tattoo on the ankle with real tattoo machines. Maintenance and housekeeping were not prepared to provide anything more than a barely acceptable level of guest satisfaction.

"The staff we inherited could not embrace customer service and consistently attracted low-life guests," said Andrea. It was not surprising that the front office was protected by bulletproof glass.

Management practices had discouraged customers from their nearest neighbors, the University of Colorado and Naropa University, a Buddhist institution. The hotel's policy had been, "No we won't direct bill even the most upstanding and desirable commercial clients, including Colorado University."

Turnaround

Within three years, this property changed from despair to being the winner of the gold award and a nomination for Platinum as the only Quality Inn in the United States. Repeat business at Boulder Creek was high and in a period of low hotel occupancy for the industry, Boulder Creek achieved a 78 percent average occupancy compared to 50 percent for Boulder hotels. Simultaneously, the Boulder Creek enjoyed an average daily rate (ADR) of $70, high for its category in 2002.

How did this remarkable turnaround occur?

Flag Change

Burt and Andrea believed that dramatic change was not possible under the Econo Lodge name but felt there was an advantage in remaining within the family of Choice Hotels International. They realized that the brand Quality Inn and Suites had not been used in the Boulder market. Andrea developed a presentation for the management of Choice Hotels that demonstrated the dramatic changes she planned and was granted the right as the first and only Econo Lodge to change to a Quality Inn.

Physical Property

The city of Boulder has very strict building codes and building permits are difficult to acquire. Knowing this, Andrea hired a respected architect with knowledge of the city and the elected officials. Andrea and the architect decided that the century-old home should be preserved and enhanced as a historic building and given multiple uses as front desk, business center, management offices, breakfast room, and two guest rooms upstairs.

A fireplace of colored river rock serves as a focal point near the front desk. The work of Colorado western artists was selected to furnish the historic home and the guest rooms. Curbside appeal was greatly enhanced by improving visibility, particularly of the historic home as a focal point. Landscaping with native wild-flowers and rocks serves as the area of support for an attractive sign announcing the brands Quality Inn and Suites and Boulder Creek.

The 40 guest rooms and 6 suites were remodeled with "casually upscale lodge furnishings." Each room has many of the features expected in an upscale hotel such as Hyatt or Westin.

- Private voice mail with off-site access
- Two-line data port speakerphones
- Internet access
- Twenty-five-inch color TV, microwave, refrigerator
- Coffee maker, coffee, iron, full-size ironing board, hair dryer
- Massage showerhead

Andrea sought local artisans to make Western-style lamps, furniture, and bedspreads.

A fitness center was built and furnished with new state-of-the-art equipment. An inside sauna and a hot tub were built near a refurbished indoor swimming pool and a coin-operated laundry for guest use only.

The breakfast bar offers an assortment far beyond the typical cold cereal and doughnuts of many hotels. Free daily breakfast at Boulder Creek is a deluxe hot breakfast buffet of eggs, sausage, waffles, cereal, bakery goods, fruit, yogurt, and three types of juice, tea, or coffee.

Samantha

Samantha, a soft-coated Wheaton Terrier, is Andrea's personal pet and friend of the staff and guests. When Boulder Creek opened, pets were not accepted. This proved to be a bit awkward as Samantha found the space immediately beneath the No Pets Allowed sign perfect for naps. Several guest rooms are now reserved for guests with pets. Other rooms remain pet free because some guests have allergies to pets.

New Staff

Because retraining staff and changing old attitudes proved much more difficult than changing the physical structure, the entire original staff was fired.

Andrea originally went to an organization called the Boulder Workplace, which placed her in touch with individuals 50 years and older seeking employment. A manager lacked hotel experience but held a degree in operations management and exhibited the correct people skills and positive attitude.

Andrea personally took charge of employee training using a philosophy that if you treat your employees as gold, they will in turn treat you as gold. Although Andrea held an MBA from Vassar, she credited her training at Tiffany's and earlier at Estee Lauder with instilling the concept of "Excellence."

A constant theme of Andrea's that is taught to all employees is "Customer Service Doesn't Get a Day Off." Many of the first hires had to be taught computer skills, but recent hires generally bring these skills to the job.

Marketing/Sales

Unlike some hotels where the guest is expected to step around ladders and paint cans, Andrea refused to open until the hotel was ready. "Sure we needed the cash flow, but it was critical that the guests enjoy a finished product." Many people wanted to come even during remodeling, but were told, "You can't come here now, wait until we are ready; we do not want to disappoint you." Guests waited and were pleased that they did. Andrea said there is something in all of us that says, "If I can't have something, that is exactly what I want."

An initial budget of $60,000 was established for marketing/public relations expenses. Andrea personally visited target organizations in Boulder prior to the grand opening on May 9, 2000. She felt that selected organizations could provide guests who would recognize and appreciate quality lodging. Those seeking only a "cheap sleep" were not viewed as target guests.

The University of Colorado and Naropa University had visiting professors, parents, and many others who visit during the year. Successful corporations, particularly those in technology, could provide many business travelers.

Direct billing was welcomed and individuals from these target organizations who might influence visitor hotel selection were personally given tours of the property. A list of potential guests and gatekeepers was developed and used for extending invitations to launch parties, swim parties, cocktail parties, and other planned events.

Travel writers were invited and given red carpet treatment as well as an honest and interesting story about the development of Boulder Creek. This resulted in many articles written in newspapers and magazines. Many free nights were given to individuals who could influence future business.

Andrea also targeted supportive hospitality businesses in which there might be a possibility of quid pro quo ("You scratch my back; I'll scratch yours"). Packages that supported local businesses such as restaurants were developed. Andrea felt that these built support among "local partners" and also provided the hotel guests with something above and beyond what they expect.

Now after building the business and understanding what is required to market the property successfully, Andrea said she was ready to hire a salesperson to ensure the continuation and growth of business.

Going Green

A majority of Boulder Creek's guests have some affiliation with one of the local universities. These guests ask for services that are regarded as healthy and environmentally friendly. A policy of no smoking was expected, but a recent request had caused Andrea to think creatively. The hotel offered quality amenities in each room such as shampoo, soap, and lotion. Lately many guests had stated these were not environmentally friendly and that amenities should be offered in a liquid dispenser.

Andrea was considering how to comply with this request without resorting to the common institutional look of dispensers and without offending guests who preferred the traditional mini-bottle amenities.

Keeping It Fresh and Different

Andrea knew that her key to future success would depend on keeping the property fresh, upscale, and different. This meant examining details.

Each room featured Boulder Creek's own custom coffee blend created by Wolfgang Puck. Cordless phones in each room permitted guests to walk and talk rather than being tied to a phone by the bed. An outside dog run had been discussed but was not currently possible due to lack of space. Backup bedspreads were also used when a dog had been in the room.

Andrea felt that new windows were needed and would result in considerable energy savings. However, the swimming pool needed freshening. Should she spend the money on windows that would probably not be recognized by the guest or in the pool? This was typical of the type of decision Andrea faced.

Expansion

Andrea and Burt felt comfortable that they understood the Boulder market and had recently purchased another older property in Boulder. This would again require the hands-on skills of Andrea.

Beyond that was Fort Collins with Colorado State University, Greeley with Northern Colorado University, and other Colorado cities. The question of flag affiliation also affected the future. Should Boulder Creek remain a Quality Inn? Only about 10 percent of actual guest reservations came from the parent company, but there was value in the flag. Andrea and Burt felt they could do well as an independent, but then someone else would acquire the Quality Inn brand in the area and benefit from their hard work.

Boulder had been good to Andrea, and many townspeople regularly commented about how much they appreciated what Boulder Creek had done for the neighborhood and the town. The planning and work of Andrea and Burt had paid off, but both realized that they could not relax and would need to remain constantly alert and open to new ideas and concepts.

■■■ QUESTIONS FOR DISCUSSION

Chapter 8

1. Andrea and Burt repositioned Boulder Creek. Explain who the market was before repositioning and who their target market is now.

2. How did they change the marketing mix to fit their new target market?

3. Would you retain the Quality Inn flag? Explain your decision.

■■■ Case 20 International Travel Agency

The owner of International Travel Agency located in Mexico City was concerned about the performance of the sales force. The travel agencies focused on tours to the United States. The tours included airfare, hotel room, and transportation to and from the airport. The most popular tours were sold to families going to Orlando, Houston, or New York.

It was felt that members of the sales force did not really use their sales opportunities but instead thought only about the basic package tour without added benefits. The sales force did not seem to have an interest in maximizing sales and profits by aggressively selling the entire product mix. In the case of tours to Orlando, this would include tickets to Disney World, Epcot Center, and Universal Studios. Rental cars were often used by many of the travelers, because of the distance between the theme parks. Booking reservations for rental cars created another opportunity for the sales force.

In total, the agency had a sales force of seven. Two people called on commercial accounts and were expected to spend more of their time outside the office. The remaining five persons were referred to as travel counselors and worked entirely within the agency selling the tour packages.

None of the travel counselors who worked within the agency was assigned a quota. The executive sales consultants, who worked outside the office, were assigned a sales quota. Failure to meet a quota would be discussed with the salesperson, but no other action was usually taken unless this failure continued for several months. If serious and persistent deficiencies existed, the salesperson could be subject to discharge.

The agency provided five to seven familiarization (fam) trips for members of the sales force each year. This meant that each salesperson could experience at least one trip per year, and they were assigned on a rotating basis. These trips did not reduce time from the salesperson's guaranteed number of days of annual vacation. The purpose of a fam trip was to acquaint travel agents with destination areas and the services of airlines, hotels, restaurants, and so on. It was hoped that when the agents gained experience with the destination, the president felt that the agency could maximize profits by selling more travel services to customers. An analysis of the sales of the three travel counselors revealed that approximately 95 percent of their sales came from the package. The remaining 5 percent consisted items such as theme park tickets, rental cars, room upgrades, tours at the destination, travel insurance, and entertainment tickets.

The agents could answer questions in their customer's native language and make suggestions based on their knowledge of the destination and feedback they received from other guests. Using their knowledge of the destination and the customer they could offer room upgrades such as two-bedroom suites for larger families, or breakfast in the hotel, which if purchased through the agency offered a substantial discount. Guests going to Orlando are going to purchase theme park tickets; those going to New York are likely going to want to go to a Broadway show. If the right products were sold to the right customers, the satisfaction of international customers should increase.

The owner of International Travel had tried to encourage the travel counselors to sell other services but felt that they seemed uninterested in taking the time and effort required. The owner believed that maximizing sales of the complete product mix would lead to increased customer satisfaction and profits. He needs to develop a plan to encourage cross-selling.

■■■ QUESTIONS FOR DISCUSSION

Chapter 15

1. What can be done to encourage the sales force to engage in more cross-selling?

2. Does the current fam trip program serve as a motivational tool for the sales force?

3. Discuss what is needed in terms of sales incentives and sales controls to achieve the objectives of the International Travel Agency.

■■■ Case 21 Superior Hotels

Jan Trible, president of Superior Hotels, was concerned with the future expansion of the company. Superior Hotels had built a strong reputation in the management of time-share resorts in Florida. The company had recently acquired a consulting contract for a ski resort in the Rocky Mountains, which would mark its entrance into a new area of resort management. Now there was serious discussion concerning the advisability of entering the commercial hotel segment of the hotel industry within cities of 100,000 to 200,000 in population.

Management of Time-Share Resorts

The management style of Superior Hotels was exemplified in the management of the company's time-share resorts. Superior managed five time-share resorts, with a total of 240 units. The company maintained a policy of not accepting management contracts for time-share projects that were in trouble. The company philosophy maintained that most of these had been ill planned and probably had little likelihood of long-range success. Jan personally believed that a major shakeup in the time-share industry was coming and that many existing projects would fail.

The Superior Hotel policy was to begin working with the developers of a time-share resort at the beginning of the project. It was felt that developers have a short-run viewpoint, but a management company must think of the long run. The policy was to become involved in the entire planning process of the project, including blueprints and interior decorations. If a developer refused to cooperate, Superior would remove itself from future management. Management believed that a time-share project differed considerably from a conventional hotel or resort development.

1. A time-share project has hundreds or thousands of owners. A conventional hotel or resort has one or a few.

2. Time-share projects receive high-intensity use, with 95 percent occupancy being normal. Furniture, carpeting, and other furnishings can wear out in a third of the time. Therefore, rules of thumb developed for hotels would often not apply in time-share.

3. The guest assumes a proprietary interest in a time-share. Guests are extremely critical because they view the units as theirs and complain about things that a hotel guest would accept.

4. A great deal of hype goes into the sales of a time-share unit, and guests arrive with extreme expectations. Superior has to bring reality into the dreams that the sales department creates.

5. The long-run success of a time-share unit depends on attracting the same guests each year for as long as 20 years or more. If guests became dissatisfied and enough guests decided to drop their ownership, resales can be very difficult and the entire project can be in jeopardy.

Several management practices had been developed by Superior to deal with these complexities.

Owner Feedback

Owner comment sheets were distributed to each owner/guest during each visit. Jan took pride in the fact that she read each one personally. These sheets covered a variety of areas, from general appearance of the unit to any evidence of insects and rodents. If the comments were particularly bad, a member of management, including Jan, would personally contact the owner and report on the steps that had been taken to correct the problem.

Feedback was also received in "owner coffees." These weekly meetings with owners included attendance by one or more members of management. These could include the resort owner, the head of housekeeping, the director of internal management, and others. A quarterly newsletter was published by Superior and sent to all owners. In addition to information of a general nature such as changes in airfares to the resort, the newsletter was personalized to the extent that it reminded all owners of their vacation week.

Recreation Management

Superior Hotels believed that even the most beautiful and best-maintained resort could eventually become boring. To ensure that guests would find something new each year, a recreation program was established with a full-time professional in charge. Programs were designed for all ages. These employed some of the successful concepts of Club Med.

Supervised programs for children allowed parents a freedom they could not enjoy at most resorts. Hot dog parties, beach parties, tennis competitions, seashell classes, and many other programs offered a variety of recreational and educational pursuits. Each recreational program was monitored as to attendance and guest satisfaction, and weak ones were eliminated. A dominant feature of all the programs was the opportunity for interaction among guests. Jan believed that a guest at the average resort could spend a week and never develop new friendships. Ideally, the recreation programs encouraged friendships to develop.

Housekeeping and Maintenance

The turnover of a majority of the guests one day and the mass arrival of an equal number the next provides special housekeeping and maintenance problems for time-share projects. A full-time maintenance crew was employed, and a large inventory of replacement furnishings was carried. If a TV set or electric range had a problem, it was replaced immediately rather than sending a repair technician. With only one vacation week, Jan felt that a guest did not want to share it with a repair person. Housekeeping was performed for the time-share resorts under contract with an independent housekeeping company. Housekeeping managers were responsible for examining each room personally and ensuring that corrections immediately followed discovery of a problem.

The Superior Hotel Image and Philosophy

"All Superior properties must be first class; there is no room in this corporation for mundane or second-class properties." This statement by Jan summed up the company's philosophy. The philosophy concerning quality had led management to change its policy concerning the new properties it would manage. The company recently initiated a policy of holding an equity position in all future properties. This decision was made for two reasons. First, an ownership position would allow Superior to have a stronger voice in the development and management of properties and would help ensure quality. Second, Superior Hotels had no interest in "bringing up" properties to a desired quality and performance level only to find that the managers had decided not to renew the management contract.

Corporate Objectives

The management and ownership of Superior Hotels desired for the company to be recognized as a strong national resort and commercial hotel management company within 10 years. It was felt that resort properties offered limited growth opportunities because others had developed the most desirable locations.

The best strategy for the next five years seemed to lie in the development of first-class commercial properties within Sunbelt cities of 100,000 to 200,000 people. It was felt that the development of three new properties per year in this market was realistic. Sunbelt cities were believed to offer the best potential for growth because of the scarcity of 150- to 200-room high-quality hotels. These second-tier cities remained important industrial and agricultural centers and did not usually offer truly first-class hotel accommodations. In many cases a respected medical complex had been developed in these cities, and it was felt that this factor alone would serve as a magnet for visitors.

■■■ QUESTIONS FOR DISCUSSION

Chapter 18

1. What are the core competencies of Superior Hotels? Management of resorts? Management of time-share resorts? Management of ski resorts? Management of commercial hotels? Other?

2. Do you believe that Superior Hotels should be entering diverse markets such as ski resorts and commercial hotels?

3. Do you believe that Superior Hotels can effectively market and manage a wide diversity of properties?

4. What would you advise Jan Trible to do?

■■■ Case 22 The Cameron Trading Post and Lodge

Travelers who venture 52 miles north of Flagstaff, Arizona, on Highway 89 are surprised and delighted when they stop at the Cameron Trading Post along the Little Colorado River Canyon. In reality, Cameron Trading Post represents most of the commercial activity in the town of Cameron. A decommissioned swayback suspension bridge built in 1911 sits next to the property.

Cameron began as a trading post where Hopi and Navajo residents bartered wool, blankets, and livestock for flour, sugar, canned goods, and household products. A trip to the post would take days of travel by horse-drawn wagon. Customers were always treated as family and fed and housed at the trading post. The local people trusted traders at Cameron because they understood local dialects and customers and explained the confusing American legal and social system.

Today the trading post is owned by the employees and Joe Atkinson, a direct descendent of the original owners. It serves as a stopping point for travelers headed to the Grand Canyon, Lake Powell, the Painted Desert, and Utah.

The Cameron Trading Post and Lodge represent an example of:

Quality

Customer service

Respect for Native American culture

Excellent merchandising

Fair treatment and training of employees

Employee empowerment

Continuous product innovation

Cameron Trading Post may also represent a warning for the entire hospitality industry concerning the delicate balance between natural resource use, particularly water, and commercial growth.

The strength behind Cameron Trading Post is Joe Atkinson, a product and heir of Western pioneers and their attitudes—not the Hollywood version.

Joe's family came to Arizona and New Mexico as Indian traders. One was killed by Paiutes, Navajos, or outlaws in the 1840s as he carried trading goods by horse and mule to his customers.

Joe was born to the business at the Three Hogans Trading Post in Arizona. His uncles, CD and Hubert Richardson, moved to Arizona from Cleburne, Texas, and established a trading post at Cameron in 1916. In 1964, it was leased to Chevron Oil Company and later to the Harvey Corporation, a hospitality company pioneer who had built a successful western hotel, restaurant, and gift shop chain in cooperation with the Santa Fe Railroad.

In 1977, Joe gained control of the Cameron Trading Post as well as Indian jewelry stores in Gallup, Santa Fe, Albuquerque, and Phoenix.

Joe didn't have the advantage of a college education but became an acknowledged expert in Indian jewelry and art and also learned to fly his own twin-engine Cessna. Joe discovered cigars at age four and until recently he and a good cigar were inseparable. That was the second time he had to give up cigars. The first was when he started grade school and the principal would not permit a cigar-smoking first grader.

The Cameron Trading Post serves as a source of southwestern art, souvenirs, and curios. The store features quality handcrafted traditional patterns on weaving, baskets, pottery, jewelry, and carvings. A free gallery of American Southwest Indian art is situated in a historic building of sandstone and log on the property.

Visitors dine in an atmosphere of antique luxury. A huge stone fireplace and beautiful local art provide a southwestern setting for breakfast, lunch, and dinner. The menu features American and Mexican foods as well as a signature "Navajo taco."

The 66-room lodge follows the upscale Southwest theme with exquisite furnishings and impeccable maintenance. Prices are moderate, yet 100 percent occupancy occurs only 25 to 30 nights a year.

ROOM RATES

January–February	$69–$139 + tax
March–April	$89–$169 + tax
May–October	$109–$189 + tax
November–December	$79–$169 + tax

Additionally, the property contains RV sites with full hookup, electricity, sewage, and water.

RV RATES

Nightly	$25 + tax
Monthly	$350 + tax

Joe said that marketing by Cameron Trading Post is almost nonexistent other than information in the AAA guidebook and a few signs. The Southwest has experienced a prolonged drought and the property has been strictly limited to 24 million gallons per year, which it pulls from the Little Colorado River. With current use at 22.5 million gallons, Joe said the management was forced to consider customer tradeoffs. Lodge customers use more water than restaurant guests or stop-by shoppers, yet hotel guests provide cross-sales in the restaurant and in the gift shop.

Prior to 9/11, the property hosted 45 tour buses per day. Forty percent of these were European tourists; the remainder were U.S. and Canadian retirees. The management originally felt that these guests would appreciate a cafeteria line because the stop time was only 30 to 40 minutes. Instead, the guests, particularly the Europeans, wanted sit-down service.

Once this was known, the management and staff found a system to serve all guests hot meals of their choice in 25 minutes. Joe expressed pride in the willingness of his employees to provide such service.

In 2004, bus tours had reached 18 per day, and further gains were expected unless another terrorist attack or unforeseen problem occurred in the United States. The European travelers from Germany, Italy, and France were particularly excited by the Indian products and gallery and the fact that 90 percent or more of the employees are Native American, largely of the Hopi and Navajo cultures.

The Alumni Club of Stanford University also discovered Cameron. Members of this group annually stayed in the RV camp or the lodge and brought their own chef who prepared open-air meals in the garden.

Collector's Auction

Although Joe downplayed his company's marketing activity, he said that tremendous success had been achieved with a collector's auction of Southwest Indian Art, first held in 1985 with only 15 to 18 people in attendance. By 1999, over 300 people attended filling rooms, RV sites, and the restaurant and gift shop. Eventually this was discontinued as the availability of antique Indian art diminished. The front cover of the final auction catalog featured four-year-old Joe sitting in a wooden rocking chair with cigar in hand.

Joe admitted that other promotional events could be organized to help increase occupancy in off-seasons. Typical occupancy percentages follow:

Summer	85%
Winter	30%
Fall/Spring	60–70%

U.S. vacation patterns account for the summer peak, but the best months for cool weather in northern Arizona occur in the trough seasons.

Management Style

Joe personally takes charge of selecting room furnishings, gallery displays, and overseeing future expansion ideas such as the possible construction of Navajo-style Hogans along the rim of the canyon to serve as unique guest rooms.

Mike Davis, general manager, is charged with daily operations, including the critical task of merchandise buying. Mike came from a strong retail background and Joe said he largely takes a hands-off approach yet consults with Mike.

Very little turnover exists among employees, and many retire with a retirement package that is quite good for the area. Joe said the following of his employees:

- They are dedicated to Cameron.

- They offer great input for improving operations.

- They want to learn and improve.

- They are customer friendly and provide good service.

- They are not afraid to say "that's a dumb idea."
- They are cross-trained to work in different areas and willingly do so.
- They look on themselves and management as an extended family.

Joe and his management group realize the many advantages of the Native American workforce, the history of Cameron, and emphasis on quality that has been established. However, they know that the task of balancing customers and product offerings with the natural resource base will grow even more pressing in the future.

At present, merchandise sales represent the largest source of income with food and beverage second, followed by lodging. Joe believes it is important to have a mix of the three product areas and to resist any temptation to overemphasize merchandise. His goal is to maintain the cultural and historical foundation of the Cameron Trading Post and Lodge and provide a secure employment base for the 110 full-time employees who would otherwise be forced to drive or move to Flagstaff or Phoenix to support their families, thus disrupting their centuries-old cultural and societal heritage.

Updated September 2, 2015; http://www.camerontradingpost.com/.

▪▪▪ QUESTIONS FOR DISCUSSION

Chapter 18

1. Discuss the tradeoff issues that Joe and his management team face concerning marketing, growth, natural resources, and the posts' traditional employment base.

2. What would you recommend to the management of Cameron Trading Post and Lodge?

3. What other sensitive resource issues are hospitality companies likely to face in the next 5 to 10 years? In the United States? In other countries?

4. What is the proper role for marketing in resource management?

5. What should Cameron Trading Post and Lodge do about the relatively low occupancy during the nonpeak seasons?

▪▪▪ Case 23 Elk Mountain Hotel

History of Elk Mountain Hotel

When Peter Thieriot first saw Elk Mountain Hotel, it looked like the proverbial money pit, an endless hole into which renovation funds could be thrown. Peter's lawyers strongly advised him to walk away and forget any thought of buying and remodeling this 1905 hotel in Elk Mountain, Wyoming.

Yet its history, its tranquil location in a beautiful grove of cottonwoods, the Old West appearance of the town of Elk Mountain, and the natural charm of the hotel and its proximity to Peter's buffalo ranch served as a magnet, and in 2000 Peter became owner and renovator of Elk Mountain Hotel.

The Garden Spot Pavilion had sat on the grounds of the hotel for decades and attracted big names such as Louis Armstrong, Tex Beneke, Tommy Dorsey, and Les Brown, all popular with crowds in the 1940s and 1950s. Old-timers said, "You didn't have to know how to dance at the Pavilion, the floor would do it for you." Sure enough, the floor moved to the rhythm of the band and the crowd.

Peter Thieriot Renovates Elk Mountain Hotel

Wyoming winters and time took the Pavilion, but Peter believes he can bring it back with modern construction and a special spring floor so once again "you won't need to know dancing to dance real good."

"We stripped the hotel and then built it back again room by room," said Trey Webb, the front-desk clerk and head waiter. Nine layers of wallpaper were removed from the dining room, but a large enough chunk of each remained to frame them and place them in the dining room.

Trey exemplifies the spirit and drive of Wyoming people that helped draw Peter to Elk Mountain from San Francisco. Trey, a high school senior, is headed to the University of Wyoming on a rodeo scholarship to study biology and eventually become a doctor. An expert in "bull dogging and calf roping," Trey knows horses and he knows people. He and other high school kids from the area find part-time employment at the hotel. Their native "Western personalities" and desire to help others makes them popular with guests. They also display a genuine affection for the hotel and pride in its renaissance.

It's easy for employees and guests to love the place because the restoration built warmth and coziness into the 12 guest rooms, the parlor, and the dining room. Peter developed an attic on the third floor into a conference room to host meetings of 16 people around a table with ample wall space for flip-chart pages temporarily held with masking tape, so common to meetings of this size.

Prior to renovations, the hotel served as a watering hole for a sometimes rough bunch of characters from the Medicine Bow area. Ten years before Peter bought the hotel, two of the rowdies took their argument to the hotel's parking lot where they settled it the old-fashioned way with six-shooters. Fortunately, neither of those would-be Wyatt Earps could aim straight, and the sheriff arrived before lead could accidentally find its mark.

Rowdies have been replaced by less colorful, middle-aged professional couples. "A few of the old customers returned looking for a beer and some action after renovations but when they spotted the wine and cheese, the Lexus and Lincoln cars in the parking lot, and heard English spoken without cussin' every other word, they promptly left and never returned," said Peter.

"Half this country loves what we did to this hotel and the other half has a different opinion." That was confirmed by a ranch family in McFadden 30 miles east who placed themselves squarely in the "love" section. Their opinion was that the renovated hotel added much to the community.

There is no fear that guests accustomed to fine dining when traveling and dining out at home will have to settle for less at Elk Mountain Hotel. The menu was designed to "combine a touch of flair, a hint of the Old West, and a big pinch of professionalism." With buffalo and caribou on the menu, there is more than a hint of the Old West. With a good selection of California and imported wines, seafood-based appetizers, and desserts such as crème brulée, compliments, not complaints, are most often heard.

The unanimous opinion of guests is that the hotel was renovated with style. The area on which the hotel sits had once been a stagecoach station for the Overland Trail. Although that building is gone, the Victorian style of the original 1905 building has been enhanced. The original embossed tin ceilings were cleaned and repainted, and the exterior asbestos shingles that used to hide the natural beauty were removed to expose the original cedar lap siding. Peter knew the hotel could be restored to this level of quality.

Susan and Arthur Havers Purchase the Hotel

Arthur and Susan Prescott Havers purchased the hotel 10 years ago. Susan was a marketing consultant in San Francisco, but had a culinary background. She had owned and managed a restaurant and catering company in Belgium and earned a Grand Diplome from Le Cordon Bleu in Paris. Arthur was vice president of international development for E-Trade. It was their dream to open a business together, and although they had this dream for many years they were not able to find the right project. While searching the Internet, Arthur came across the Elk Mountain Hotel. The historic hotel aroused their curiosity. Although the hotel was not for sale they contacted Peter, who also had a residence in San Francisco, to see if he would be interested in selling it. They visited Elk Mountain to see the hotel and the region. They found the people to be friendly, with a sense of humor. In addition to the people they enjoyed the wide-open spaces. A year later the Havers were owners of Elk Mountain Hotel.

Susan's culinary background enabled the restaurant to be turned into a "hidden gem" and customers who discovered it encouraged people driving across I-80 to take the four-mile drive off the Interstate highway to Elk Mountain Hotel. The Havers used their marketing and culinary skills to create special dinners that pair food with wine, beer, or whiskey. They also have created unique events such as a women's handgun training weekend, for $1,100 per person. The fee covers handgun training, meals and three nights lodging, and dinner and breakfast during the stay.

They will be the only guests in the hotel and should be prepared to stay up till 1 A.M. helping track down shadows and bumps in the night. Package price is $250 per couple inclusive of room and dinner but excludes taxes and gratuities. Employees of the hotel swear it has a friendly ghost, and perhaps the guests at the dinner will find it.

Friendly or not, ghosts don't pay bills. That requires live paying guests, and getting more of those, particularly in the low season, requires marketing. Positive word of mouth can't be beaten, but it takes marketing to get enough of those mouths talking.

Peter Thieriot had the vision to renovate the Elk Mountain Resort; the Havers used marketing skills and Susan's culinary skills to turn the hotel into a destination. However, a town of 200 people cannot create the demand necessary to support. Elk Mountain needs to be a destination for people in nearby towns and a place for organizations to hold events and retreats.

Updated September, 2015; Sources accessed 11/20/21011; "Elk Mountain, Wyoming," *MuniNetGuide*, http://www.muninetguide.com/states/wyoming/elk-mountain/; Jackie Borchardt, "Elk Mountain Hotel Offers Serenity, Escape," trib.com (March 27, 2011), http://trib .com/business/article_46602367-c87f-5f72-857b-3867c8734ae2.html; "Historic Elk Mountain Hotel Finding an International Flavor," *Rawlins Daily Times*, undated http://www .elkmountainhotel.com/-attachments/RawlinsDaily.pdf; Elk Mountain Hotel Web site; www .elkmountainhotel.com (accessed September 3, 2015).

■■■ QUESTIONS FOR DISCUSSION

Chapter 8 or Chapter 18

Examine a map of the state of Wyoming and its neighboring states.

1. What percentage of lodging business would you expect from Wyoming residents in the three seasonal periods: peak, summer; shoulder, late fall and early spring; trough, winter? Which Wyoming towns are target markets?

2. From what markets would the remaining occupancy come?

3. What market targets would you select in terms of demographics and lifestyle?

Chapter 14

1. Develop a publicity/public relations campaign appropriate for Elk Mountain Hotel. Include cost estimates.

Remember that free publicity costs something, such as room and board for travel writers.

2. Develop a series of creative packages that might be used to increase occupancy in shoulder and trough periods.

Chapter 16

1. The Havers have linked their site to Tripadvisor, and have posted photos on Flickr. Arthur stated if it was not for the Internet, they would have not survived. How does the Internet help a small hotel like Elk Mountain Hotel?

2. After visiting the hotel's Web site what suggestions would you have for additional uses of the Internet to market the hotel?

■■■ Case 24 IRTRA—Recreational Park XETULUL

Amazing, unbelievable, fantastic! These are words commonly used to describe XETULUL, a Guatemalan recreational park developed and operated for private-sector workers by their employers. It has a rating of five stars on TripAdvisor. This park is located in the province of Quezaltenango (pronounced "kay-sot-in-al-go") near the town of San Martin on the Pacific Coast Highway about 50 miles south of the Mexican border and 100 miles from the capital city of Guatemala City. The park is owned and operated by IRTRA, the Institute of Recreation for Workers of Private Companies in Guatemala, and opened in June 2002.

The XETULUL park instantly reminds one of Disney World with hotels, restaurants, individual cabanas, and three theme parks: an aquatic park with wave pool, superslides, and swimming pools; a sports park under construction; and a theme park. The theme park combines beautiful buildings that replicate historic sites of Europe and the Americas. Gift shops feature quality Guatemalan and imported products, including clothing, cosmetics, footwear, and gifts. Restaurants are sparkling clean and feature Guatemalan, U.S., and European menus. Cafeterias, sit-down restaurants, and snack areas are open to serve 12,000 visitors per day.

A variety of rides include roller coasters, bumper cars, a train, and water rides, including replicas of Venetian gondolas and a waterfall drop.

The park was developed in a former coffee plantation and tropical forest. Huge trees, grass, and shrubs provide shade for tropical birds and animals that share the park with human visitors.

Most Guatemalan workers might never be able to visit the recreational/theme parks of the United States or Europe, but they can enjoy an affordable and unique Guatemalan version.

None of this would be unusual if one of the traditional theme park operators such as Six Flags or Disney owned the park, but instead a unique organization known as IRTRA is the owner/operator. IRTRA was established by the private industry of Guatemala to provide affordable recreation for employees and their families as well as owners and managers of the companies.

The Chamber of Commerce, the Association of Agriculturalists, and the Association of Industry in Guatemala petitioned the Guatemalan Congress to pass a law permitting the establishment of IRTRA and the right to fund it with tax-exempt monies. Thus, the theme park was built and continues to be supported totally by monies from Guatemalan private industry. A small fee is charged for entrance to the park but is purposely kept low. Other costs such as meals and beverages are reasonably priced.

The vision and mission statements of IRTRA include the following:

- To develop a recreation opportunity for Guatemalan workers and employees at international standards.

- To create parks and gardens using the latest technology for the benefit of Guatemalan workers and employees.

- To provide employees opportunities with educational/training to improve their professional and personal lives.

- To assist in the development of Guatemala.

- To create recreational parks that are designed according to the latest technology and operated by the most competent individuals.

- To preserve the ecology of our places of recreation.

Although IRTRA is a secular organization, it has a creed that expresses a faith in God, a belief in serving one's fellows, a belief in work based on courtesy and cleanliness, a belief in working with nature rather than against it, and a belief in the need to inspire and motivate others to achieve happiness.

Personnel

The executive staff of XETULUL includes full-time salaried managers and a staff of medical doctors and nurses. The general manager of lodging, Randolph Brenner, earned an MBA from INCAE, the prestigious Central American affiliate of the Harvard Business School.

The entire staff, including groundskeepers, waiters, front-desk personnel, cashiers, ride operators, gift shop salespeople, and many more, are Guatemalans. Because many lack extensive formal education and cultural experience outside small villages or farms, extensive training programs exist on the grounds of XETULUL. Personnel are instructed in basic skills such as hygiene, guest interaction, handling complaints, and proper dress. Several are given instruction in the use of computers, cash registers, and the operation and maintenance of rides and other machinery.

These skills have allowed many employees to find employment in other sectors of Guatemalan society. The prevailing attitudes among the 1,500 employees of XETULUL are friendliness, helpfulness, and a willingness to listen to guests.

Results

The development of XETULUL created a tourist industry outside the park consisting of hotels, restaurants, retail stores, and auto service.

Since opening, the park has received more than 3.7 million visitors. Although most of these were from Guatemala, a growing percentage comes from other Central American countries and Mexico, with a small percentage from Europe and the United States/Canada. Annually, 1.2 million visitors enjoy the park.

Perhaps the most impressive results are in the mix of guests. The great majority are skilled and unskilled Guatemalan workers, but a large number of mid- and upper-management, including owners of Guatemalan enterprises, mix freely with their employees.

Pricing and Attractions

The price of entrance to the amusement park is $6.50 for children and $13.00 for adults. A water park is adjacent to the park and the admission price is the same. A ticket to both parks costs U.S.$9.00 for children and $18.00 for adults. Both parks are free for an employee of one of the sponsoring organizations and four of their family members. There are three lodging choices at the park ranging from U.S.$12.00 to $212 for employees of an affiliated organization, depending on type of accommodation, day of the week, and season. Lodging for the public a little more than double these rates. These prices seem low; however, the average wage is $1,000 per month and lodging within the park is reasonable and of four-star caliber. Restaurants are open from 7 A.M. until 10 P.M., and the swimming pool is available from 9 A.M. to 9 P.M. Special honeymoon packages are available such as the three-night junior suite package for Q1,685 (approximately U.S.$210), which includes lodging, meals, a bottle of champagne, and a basket of fruit in the room.

Many special attractions are offered to guests such as weekend dancing and fireworks displays on holidays.

Sources: Authors' visit to the Park, Salary Survey in Guatemala, *Salary Explorer*, http://www.salaryexplorer.com/salarysurvey.php?loc=89&loctype=1 (accessed September 3, 2015); IRTA Web site, http://irtra.org.gt/ (accessed September 3, 2015).

■■■ QUESTIONS FOR DISCUSSION

Chapter 17

1. The park was started and continues to be maintained through a contribution from private industries, whose workers and managers can use the park. What benefit does this create for the company?

2. XETULUL not only attracted workers from the companies associated with it, it also created a tourism attraction. What benefits of the park enabled it to become a regional attraction?

■■■ Case 25 Bern Hotels and Resorts Panama

Strategic planning for the leading hotel and resort group in Panama had always been important but 12 new hotels were scheduled to enter their market adding 4,304 additional rooms by 2017. The two new upcoming Westin projects belonged to Bern Hotels and Resorts but the remainder were direct competitors (see Table 1).

Many first-time visitors to Panama are surprised and impressed to witness skyscrapers, multi-lane highways, a modern airport, and condos, apartments, and homes equal to those in the United States and Europe. Economic growth of the country during the late 1990s had been upward to 10 percent and this had fueled the boom in hotel development. The short- to medium-term concern was that hotel supply was quickly going to outpace demand unless the country was able to promote and attract more visitors; a job for both the public and private sectors.

Mr. Glen Champion, vice president of Bern Hotels and Resorts (BHR), had responsibility for strategic planning and direction to ensure that their current operating group of hotels would continue to be strong in an increasingly competitive environment. This group included two Intercontinental Hotels, one Holiday Inn and one Crowne Plaza, owned and operated under franchise agreements with IHG hotels as well as the Le Meridian Panama hotel under a franchise with Starwood hotels. The group also had the Gamboa Rainforest Resort in the jungle alongside the Panama Canal as well as a number of other tourism-related service businesses that were directly or indirectly affected by the hotel business. Further, franchise agreements had been signed with Starwood to open two Westin hotels, the Westin Playa Bonita resort in 2011 and the Westin Panama City, Panama in 2012.

Glen said that enhanced marketing/sales strategies and tactics might be needed but that they would need to support rather than replace the company's basic goals, which had proven to be the mission for the company's success. These were:

- To provide excellent service to guests.

- To provide continuous training and motivation to all employees, including empowerment whenever possible.

- To control expenses and permit continuous improvement through solid financial returns.

Key to supporting as well as building upon the mission that these three goals represented for the company were strategic marketing actions and efforts. A long-term strategy began with the conceptualization of products and services offered. The sales and marketing efforts that followed up with proper systems and analysis since ongoing adjustments were crucial to the success of a multiunit growth company such as BHR. An overview of this follows:

Strategic Plan—Reinforcing the Marketing Efforts

1. **Protect the Product and Service** by offering and delivering consistently high-quality operations in all the businesses, performing renovations on some of the older properties, and refreshing spaces in others. Renew service training in all properties with stronger BHR backbone, ongoing training, and staff certification using the Panama International Hotel School as a driving platform.

2. **Marketing the Brands** and capitalizing on brand distinct initiatives to differentiate properties. Maximize the resources of the brand affiliations with the international chains as much as possible and promote our own internal initiatives consistently, that is, Corporate Marketing Plan, loyalty programs, online Web-based marketing, industry alliances, social media, public relations initiatives, print, television, and other media.

3. **Revenue Management Effectively Performed** working in tune with reservations call centers, sales teams, and hotel front office teams to maximize the yield on the ever-changing demand in the market. Continuously analyze channels regarding sources of business per region. Ensure that our products and services are found on the different reservation systems with accurate information

TABLE 1
Hotel Additions Proposed for Panama

NAME OF HOTEL PROJECT	LOCATION	ROOMS	2011	2012	2013	2014	2015	2016	2017
Under Construction									
Hilton Panama	Balboa		353	351	351	351	351	351	351
DoubleTree by Hilton	Via Espana	156	78	156	156	156	156	156	156
Panamera, a Waldorf Astoria Hotel	Calle 47	130	130	130	130	130	130	130	130
Trump Ocean Club	Punta Pacifica	369	185	369	369	369	369	369	369
Westin Plaza Bonita	Playa Bonita	611	102	611	611	611	611	611	611
Westin	Costa del Este	198		34	198	198	198	198	198
Hyatt Place	Fin. District	167			84	167	167	167	167
Bristol addition	Fin. District	62		62	62	62	62	62	62
Aloft by Starwood	Convention Ctr	312			150	234	312	312	312
Renaissance	Fin. District	300				300	300	300	300
Megapolis—Decameron Ritz Carlton	Balboa	300	300	150	300	300	300	300	300
Subtotal		3,176	364	1863	2,411	2,878	3,176	3,176	3,176
	Annual Additions		364	1,498	548	467	298	0	0
Medium—High Probability (>50%)									
Hilton Garden Inn	Behind the El Panama	176			176	176	176	176	176
Planet Hollywood	Fin. District	309				155	309	309	309
Crowne Plaza—CBT Tocumen Airport	Tocumen	176			176	176	176	176	176
Hyatt Place	Costa del Este	167				84	167	167	167
Embassy Suites by Hilton	Calle 50	300			300	300	300	300	300
Subtotal		1,128	0	0	352	891	1,128	1,128	1,128
	Annual Additions			0	352	539	238	0	0
Total Additional Rooms—UC			364	1,863	2,411	2,878	3,176	3,176	3,176
Total Additional Rooms w/50% Probability			0	0	352	891	1,128	1,128	1,128
Grand Total Additional Rooms UC and Probable			364	1,863	2,763	3,769	4,304	4,304	4,304
	Annual Additions		364	1,498	900	1,006	536	–	–

and are easy to purchase. Ensure that market analysis information is provided to the sales force to make its efforts more effective and focused.

4. **Sales and Prospecting Through Coordinated National and International Sales Teams.** Ensure proper market segmentation follow-up using all internal and external teams and resources to cover all potential areas such as regular trade fair ad exhibition participation to drive sales and improve exposure. Individual properties site inspection and in-house prospecting. Emphasize individual brand and BHR loyalty programs for demand generation. Ensure proper systems control and prospecting for repeat or similar demand generation. Utilize third-party database communication of promotions and targeted mailings.

5. **Vertical Integration.** A unique business model had been adopted by the Bern Group based on vertical integration and the development of corporate-owned and operated supporting companies such as "Sensory Spas by Clarins," a deluxe spa service, retail stores within the hotels, the Panama International Hotel School, GT incentives aimed at corporate incentive group travel, Ocean Business Center, a turnkey short-term office solution and Gamboa Tours, originally designed to offer jungle tours but now offering many tour packages. The company had grown and developed many synergies for handling back of the house operational tasks that were supported by a lean corporate structure of human development, financial control, systems, and sales and marketing.

    The Panama International Hotel School, a division of Bern Hotels and Resorts, was open to multinational qualified students who were free to seek employment wherever they wished following graduation. However, Glen said he hoped to hire as many as possible for employment in the Bern group. This organizational structure of Bern was not present in other hotels within Bern's competitive set. This competitive set agreed to share some data on a daily basis, including:

    • Occupancy—previous night

    • Average daily rate—ADR

6. **Medical Tourism Market Segment.** The Bern management feared that the first response by the Panama hotel community to added competition would be to cut rates. To reduce this risk to Bern properties, Glen and the marketing staff had been working on new strategies such as the development of different segments such as the Caribbean medical market. The Caribbean represented a market of 5 million people with few local secondary care opportunities. This market was accustomed to travel elsewhere for medical treatment such as hip replacement, serious cardiovascular problems, dermatology, and other needs. Glen had been working with a team of Panama medical doctors to evaluate this as a new or expanded market.

    It was well known that the Venezuelan market liked to visit Panama and many had purchased property there. However, under the existing administration, it was difficult to transmit funds from Venezuela.

7. **Sales Force Structure.** The structure of the sales force had been changed to make it more efficient and to better combat the new competition. Previously, the sales force had been divided into national and international. Each salesperson had been expected to call on accounts and then perform all the paperwork and follow-up associated with each account.

    The new organization was divided into Outside-Pro Active salespeople and Inside-Reactive sales support staff. The latter were expected to relieve the Pro Active sales force of most or all of the required paperwork, thus leaving them with more time to make additional sales calls and to perform essential public relations activities associated with their positions.

8. **Sales Force Career Portfolios.** All Bern employees and especially those in the sales force were required to develop and maintain an actual career portfolio. Members of the sales force were encouraged to keep learning new sales skills and to apply them in the field. Evidence of attendance at sales training

sessions and other self-help programs were placed in their BHR career portfolios and were examined during performance review.

9. **Cross-Selling.** Glen felt that improved cross-selling opportunities surely existed between the hotels and the various enterprises owned and operated by Bern such as Royal Card, Panama Rental Solutions, and Gamboa Tours.

As Glen reviewed the company's policies and strategies, he believed that Bern Hotels and Resorts was well positioned in the Panama market to meet the threat of increased competition, yet he was well aware of the importance to remain open to new ideas. For this reason Glen made it a point to attend several seminars and conferences in the United States and Europe that were sponsored by major universities and professional associations. These were not restricted to the hospitality and tourism industries as Glen felt that many ideas and concepts developed for other industries had relevance for the many properties under his direct leadership.

Note: Mr. Glen Champion has indicated that he would welcome suggestions and new ideas from readers of this book. He may be reached at gchampion@-bernhotel spanama.com.

■■■ QUESTIONS FOR DISCUSSION

Chapter 3

1. From information you receive on the Internet (http://www.empresasbern.com/; http://www.bernhotel spanama.com/) do a SWOT analysis of Bern Hotels. There is a language button (idioma) on the top left banner. If the screen is in Spanish, you can choose this button and change to English.

2. From your SWOT analysis how would you prioritize the nine items of the strategic plan?

Chapter 12

1. Bern Hotels and Resorts Panama is a collection of branded and nonbranded properties. How would you develop a distribution system that would promote this group of hotels? Look at using multiple channels; some might be hotel specific, while others could be used for all their brands.

GLOSSARY

Administered VMS. A vertical marketing system coordinates successive stages of production and distribution, not through common ownership or contractual ties, but through the size and power of one of the parties.

Advertising. Any paid form of nonpersonal presentation and promotion of ideas, goods, or services by an identified sponsor.

Agent. A wholesaler who represents buyers or sellers on a more permanent basis, performs only a few functions, and does not take title to goods.

Agritourism. Agriculture-based tourism that includes farms, ranches, and wineries. It provides rural areas with a means to attract tourists.

Alliances. Alliances are developed to allow two organizations to benefit from each other's strengths.

Allocating. Sales representatives decide on which customers to allocate scarce products.

Allocentrics. Persons with a need for new experiences, such as backpackers and explorers.

Ansoff product–market expansion grid. A matrix developed by cell, plotting new products and existing products with new products and existing products. The grid provides strategic insights into growth opportunities.

Approach. The step in which the salesperson meets the customer for the first time.

Aspirational group. A group to which a person wishes to belong.

Atmosphere. Designed environments that create or reinforce a buyer's leanings toward consumption of a product.

Attitude. A person's enduring favorable or unfavorable cognitive evaluations, emotional feelings, and action tendencies toward some object or idea.

Augmented products. Additional consumer services and benefits built around the core and actual products.

Aural. The dimension of atmosphere relating to volume and pitch.

Baby boomers. The 78 million people born between 1946 and 1964.

Backward integration. A growth strategy by which companies acquire businesses supplying them with products or services (e.g., a restaurant chain purchasing a bakery).

Behavioral segmentation. Dividing a market into groups based on consumers' knowledge, attitude, use, or response to a product.

Belief. A descriptive thought that a person holds about something.

Big Data. The huge and complex data sets generated by today's sophisticated information generation, collection, storage, and analysis technologies.

Brand equity. The added value endowed on products and services. It may be reflected in the way consumers think, feel, and act with respect to the brand, as well as in the prices, market share, and profitability the brand commands for the firm.

Brand image. The set of beliefs consumers hold about a particular brand.

Brand promise. The marketer's vision of what the brand must be and do for consumers.

Brand. A name, term, sign, symbol, design, or a combination of these elements that is intended to identify the goods or services of a seller and differentiate them from competitors.

Branding. The process of endowing products and services with the power of a brand. It's all about creating differences between products.

Broker. A wholesaler who does not take title to goods and whose function is to bring buyers and sellers together and assist in negotiations.

Buying center. All those individuals and groups who participate in the purchasing and decision-making process and who share common goals and the risks arising from the decisions.

Buzz marketing. Cultivating opinion leaders and getting them to spread information about a product to others in their community.

Cast members. A term used for employees. It implies that employees are part of a team that is performing for their guests.

Causal research. Marketing research to test hypotheses about cause-and-effect relationships.

Channel conflict. Disagreement among marketing channel members on goals and roles—who should do what and for what rewards.

Channel level. A level of middleman that performs some work in bringing the product and its ownership closer to the final buyer.

Closing. The sales step in which a salesperson asks the customer for an order.

Cognitive dissonance. Buyer discomfort caused by postpurchase conflict.

Communicating. Sales representatives communicate information about the company's products and services.

Competitive advantage. An advantage over competitors gained by offering consumers greater value either through lower prices or by providing more benefits that justify higher prices.

Competitive analysis. An analysis of the primary strengths and weaknesses, objectives, strategies, and other information relative to competitors.

Competitors' strategies. When competitors use segmentation, undifferentiated marketing can be suicidal. Conversely, when competitors use undifferentiated marketing, a firm can gain an advantage by using differentiated or concentrated marketing.

Concentric diversification strategy. A growth strategy whereby a company seeks new products that have technological or marketing synergies with existing product lines.

Confused positioning. Leaving buyers with a confused image of a company.

Conglomerate diversification strategy. A product growth strategy in which a company seeks new businesses that have no relationship to the company's current product line or markets.

Consumption phase. Takes place when the customer consumes the service.

Contests, sweepstakes, and games. Give consumers a chance to win something, such as cash or a trip.

Continuity. Scheduling ads evenly within a given period.

Contractual VMS. A vertical marketing system in which independent firms at different levels of production and distribution join together through contracts to obtain more economies or sales impact than they could achieve alone.

Convention. A specialty market requiring extensive meeting facilities. It is usually the annual meeting of an association and includes general sessions, committee meetings, and special-interest sessions.

Copy testing. A process performed before or after an ad is printed or broadcast.

Core product. Answers the question of what the buyer is really buying. Every product is a package of problem-solving services.

Corporate communications. This activity covers internal and external communications and promotes understanding of an organization.

Corporate meeting. A meeting held by a corporation for its employees.

Corporate mission statement. A guide to provide all the publics of a company with a shared sense of purpose, direction, and opportunity, allowing all to work independently, yet collectively, toward the organization's goals.

Corporate values. A set of corporate priorities and institutional standards of behavior.

Corporate VMS. A vertical marketing system that combines successive stages of production and distribution under single ownership. Channel leadership is established through common ownership.

Cost-plus pricing. Adding a standard markup to the cost of the product.

Counseling. Involves advising management about public issues and company positions and image.

Coupons. Certificates that offer buyers savings when they purchase specified products.

Cross-cultural marketing. This is the practice of including ethnic themes and cross-cultural perspectives within the mainstream marketing of the organization.

Cross-selling. The company's other products that are sold to the guest.

Cross-training. Training employees to do two or more jobs within the organization.

Crowdsourcing. Is an open-innovation new-product idea program.

Culture. The set of basic values, perceptions, wants, and behaviors learned by a member of society from family and other important institutions.

Customer database. An organized collection of comprehensive data about individual customers or prospects, including geographic, demographic, psychographic, and behavioral data.

Customer equity. The discounted lifetime values of all the company's current and potential customers.

Customer expectations. Expectations based on past buying experiences, the opinions of friends, and market information.

Customer relationship management (CRM). It involves managing detailed information about individual customers and carefully managing customer "touch points" in order to maximize customer loyalty.

Customer satisfaction. The extent to which a product's perceived performance matches a buyer's expectations.

Customer touch point. Any occasion on which a customer encounters the brand and product—from actual experience to personal or mass communications to casual observation.

Customer value. The difference between the benefits that the customer gains from owning and/or using a product and the costs of obtaining the product.

Customer-engagement marketing. Fosters direct and continuous customer involvement in shaping brand conversations, experiences, and community.

Customer-perceived value. The customer's evaluation of the difference between all the benefits and all the costs of a market offering relative to those of competing offers.

Data warehouse. A central repository of an organization's customer information.

Decline. The period when sales fall off quickly and profits drop.

Degree of product homogeneity. Undifferentiated marketing is more suited for homogeneous products. Products that can vary in design, such as restaurants and hotels, are more suited to differentiation or concentration.

Demands. Human wants that are backed by buying power.

Demographic segmentation. Dividing the market into groups based on demographic variables such as age, gender, family size, family life cycle, income, occupation, education, religion, race, and nationality.

Demography. The study of human populations in terms of size, density, location, age, sex, race, occupation, and other statistics.

Derived demand. Organizational demand that ultimately comes from (derives from) the demand for consumer goods.

Descriptive research. Marketing research to better describe marketing problems, situations, or markets, such as the market potential for a product or the demographics and attitudes of consumers.

Destination branding. Creating a differentiated destination image that influences traveler's decision to visit a destination and conveys the promise of a memorable experience that is uniquely associated with the destination.

Destination marketing organization (DMO). A group that promotes a specific destination. Often a local CVB serves as the DMO.

Destinations. Places with some form of actual or perceived boundary, such as the physical boundary of an island, political boundaries, or even market-created boundaries.

Detachment phase. When the customer is through using the product and departs.

Digital and social media marketing. Using digital marketing tools such as Web sites, social media, mobile apps and ads, online video, e-mail, and blogs that engage consumers anywhere, at any time, via their digital devices.

Direct marketing channel. A marketing channel that has no intermediary levels.

Direct marketing. Direct communications with carefully targeted individual consumers to obtain an immediate response and cultivate lasting customer relationships.

Direct rating. The advertiser exposes a consumer panel to alternative ads and asks them to rate the ads.

Direct-mail marketing. Direct marketing through single mailings that include letters, ads, samples, foldouts, and other "salespeople with wings" sent to prospects on mailing lists.

Direct-marketing. Connections carefully targeted individual consumers to both obtain an immediate response and cultivate lasting customer relationships: the use of direct mail, the telephone, direct-response television, e-mail, the Internet, and other tools to communicate directly with specific consumers.

Discriminatory pricing. Refers to segmentation of the market and pricing differences based on price elasticity characteristics of the segments.

Disintermediation. The elimination of intermediaries.

Drop. The action taken toward a product that may cause harm or customer dissatisfaction.

Dynamic packaging. A package vacation on a single Web site in which buyers can put together airline flights, lodging, car rental, entertainment, and tours in their own customer-designed packages.

Dynamic pricing. Continually adjusting prices to meet the characteristics and needs of the marketplace.

Echo boomers. See millennials. Born between 1977 and 1994, these children of the baby boomers now number 72 million, dwarfing the Gen Xers and almost equal in size to the baby-boomer segment. Also known as Generation Y.

E-commerce. The general term for a buying and selling process that is supported by electronic means, primarily the Internet.

Economic environment. The economic environment consists of factors that affect consumer purchasing power and spending patterns. Markets require both power and people. Purchasing power depends on current income, price, saving, and credit; marketers must be aware of major economic trends in income and changing consumer spending patterns.

Emotional labor. The necessary involvement of the service provider's emotions in the delivery of the service.

Empowerment. When a firm empowers employees, it moves the authority and responsibility to make decisions to the line employees from the supervisor.

Environmental factors. Social, political, and economic factors that affect a firm and its marketing program.

Environmental management perspective. A management perspective in which a firm takes aggressive actions to affect the publics and forces in its marketing environment rather than simply watching and reacting to it.

Ethnographic research. Trained observers interact with and/or observe consumers in their natural habitat.

Events. Occurrences staged to communicate messages to target audiences, such as news conferences or grand openings.

Exchange. The act of obtaining a desired object from someone by offering something in return.

Executive summary. A short summary of the marketing plan to quickly inform top executives.

Experimental research. The gathering of primary data by selecting matched groups of subjects, giving them different treatments, controlling related factors, and checking for differences in group responses.

Exploratory research. Marketing research to gather preliminary information that will help to better define problems and suggest hypotheses.

Facilitating products. Those services or goods that must be present for the guest to use the core product.

Familiarization trip (Fam trip). A trip where travel agents or others who can send business to a tourist destination attraction, cruise, or hotel are invited to visit at a low cost or no cost.

Family life cycle. The stages through which families might pass as they mature.

Financial intermediaries. Banks, credit companies, insurance companies, and other businesses that help finance transactions or insure against the risks associated with the buying and selling of goods.

Fixed costs. Costs that do not vary with production or sales level.

Follow-up. The sales step in which the salesperson follows up after the sale to ensure customer satisfaction and repeat business.

Forward integration. A growth strategy by which companies acquire businesses that are closer to the ultimate consumer, such as a hotel acquiring a chain of travel agents.

Franchise. A contractual vertical marketing system in which a channel member called a franchiser links several stages in the production distribution process.

Generation X. A generation of 45 million people born between 1965 and 1979; named Generation X because they lie in the shadow of the boomers and lack obvious distinguishing characteristics; other names include "baby busters," "shadow generation," or "yiffies"—young, individualistic, freedom-minded few.

Generation Y. See millennials.

Geographic segmentation. Dividing a market into different geographic units such as nations, states, regions, counties, cities, or neighborhoods.

Going-rate pricing. Setting price based largely on following competitors' prices rather than on company costs or demand.

Group. Two or more people who interact to accomplish individual or mutual goals.

Growth. The product life-cycle stage when a new product's sales start climbing quickly.

Handling objections. The sales step in which the salesperson seeks out, clarifies and overcomes any customer objections to buying.

Horizontal conflict. Conflict between firms at the same level.

Horizontal diversification strategy. A product growth strategy whereby a company looks for new products that could appeal to current customers, which are technologically unrelated to its current line.

Horizontal integration. A growth strategy by which companies acquire competitors.

Horizontal marketing system (HMS). Two or more companies at one level join to follow new marketing opportunities. Companies can combine their capital, production capabilities, or marketing resources to accomplish more than one company working alone.

Hospitality industry. Made up of those businesses that offer one or more of the following: accommodation, prepared food and beverage service, and/or entertainment.

Human need. A state of felt deprivation in a person.

Human want. The form that a human need takes when shaped by culture and individual personality.

Incentive travel. A reward that participants receive for achieving or exceeding a goal.

Income segmentation. Dividing a market into different income groups.

Information gathering. Sales representatives conduct market research and intelligence work and fill in a call report.

Informative advertising. Advertising used to inform consumers about a new product or feature to build primary demand.

Infrastructure. The system according to which a company, organization, or other body is organized at the most basic level.

Inseparability. A major characteristic of services; they are produced and consumed at the same time and cannot be separated from their providers.

Intangibility. A major characteristic of services; they cannot be seen, tasted, felt, heard, or smelled before they are bought.

Integrated marketing communications. Under this concept, the company carefully integrates its many communications channels to deliver a clear, consistent, and compelling message about the organization and its brands.

Interactive marketing. Marketing by a service firm that recognizes perceived service quality depends heavily on the quality of the buyer–seller interaction.

Internal data. Internal data consist of electronic databases and nonelectronic information and records of consumer and market information obtained from within the company.

Internal marketing. Marketing by a service firm to train effectively and motivate its customer-contact employees and all the supporting service people to work as a team to provide customer satisfaction.

Internal marketing. Involves marketing to the firm's internal customers, its employees.

Introduction. The product life-cycle stage when a new product is first distributed and made available for purchase.

Joining stage. The product life-cycle stage when the customer makes the initial inquiry contact.

Junket reps. Serve the casino industry as intermediaries for premium players.

Laboratory test. This test uses equipment to measure consumers' physiological reactions to an ad: heartbeat, blood pressure, pupil dilation, and perspiration.

Learning. Changes in a person's behavior arising from experience.

Lifestyle. A person's pattern of living as expressed in his or her activities, interests, and opinions.

Lifetime value (LTV). The LTV of a customer is the stream of profits a customer will create over the life of his or her relationship to a business.

Lobbying. Dealing with legislators and government officials to promote or defeat legislation and regulation.

Local marketing. Tailoring brands and promotions to the needs and wants of local customer groups—cities, neighborhoods, and specific restaurant/hotel/store locations.

Macrodestinations. Destinations such as the United States that contain thousands of microdestinations, including regions, states, cities, towns, and visitor destinations within a town.

Macroenvironment. The larger societal forces that affect the whole microenvironment: competitive, demographic, economic, natural, technological, political, and cultural forces.

Macroenvironmental forces. Demographic, economic, technological, political, legal, social, and cultural factors.

Market development strategy. Finding and developing new markets for your current products.

Market homogeneity. If buyers have the same tastes, buy a product in the same amounts, and react the same way to marketing efforts, undifferentiated marketing is appropriate.

Market positioning. Formulating competitive positioning for a product and a detailed marketing mix.

Market potential. The total estimated dollars or unit value of a defined market for a defined product, including competitive products.

Market segmentation. Dividing a market into direct groups of buyers who might require separate products or marketing mixes.

Market targeting. Evaluating each market segment's attractiveness and selecting one or more segments to enter.

Market trends. External trends of many types that are likely to affect the marketing in which a corporation operates.

Market. A set of actual and potential buyers of a product.

Marketing concept. The marketing management philosophy that holds that achieving organizational goals depends on determining the needs and wants of target markets and delivering desired satisfactions more effectively and efficiently than competitors.

Marketing environment. The actors and forces outside marketing that affect marketing management's ability to develop and maintain successful transactions with its target customers.

Marketing information system (MIS). A structure of people, equipment, and procedures to gather, sort, analyze, evaluate, and distribute needed, timely, and accurate information to marketing decision makers. The MIS begins and ends with marketing managers, but managers throughout the organization should be involved in the MIS. First, the MIS interacts with managers to assess their information needs. Next, it develops needed information from internal company records, marketing intelligence activities, and the marketing research process. Information analysts process information to make it more useful. Finally, the MIS distributes information to managers in the right form and at the right time to help in marketing planning, implementation, and control.

Marketing intelligence. Everyday information about developments in the marketing environment that helps managers prepare and adjust marketing plans.

Marketing intermediaries. Firms that help the company to promote, sell, and distribute its goods to final buyers; they include middlemen, physical distribution firms, marketing service agencies, and financial intermediaries.

Marketing management. The art and science of choosing target markets and building profitable relationships with them.

Marketing manager. A person who is involved in marketing analysis, planning, implementation, and control activities.

Marketing mix. Elements include product, price, promotion, and distribution. Sometimes distribution is called place and the marketing situation facing a company.

Marketing opportunity. An area of need in which a company can perform profitably.

Marketing research. The systematic design, collection, analysis, and reporting of data and findings relevant to a specific marketing situation facing a company.

Marketing services agencies. Marketing research firms, advertising agencies, media firms, marketing consulting firms, and other service providers that help a company to target and promote its products to the right markets.

Marketing strategy. The marketing logic by which the company hopes to create this customer value and achieve these profitable relationships.

Marketing Web site. Web sites designed to engage consumers in an interaction that will move them closer to a purchase or other marketing outcome.

Marketing. The art and science of finding, retaining, and growing profitable customers.

Maturity. The stage in a product life cycle when sales growth slows or levels off.

Media. Nonpersonal communications channels, including print media (newspapers, magazines, direct mail), broadcast media (radio, television), and display media (billboards, signs, posters).

Medical tourism. One of the fastest-growing and most lucrative tourism markets. Tourists spend a large amount on medical treatment, stay in top hotels, and often travel around the country after their surgery.

Membership groups. Groups that have a direct influence on a person's behavior and to which a person belongs.

Microenvironment. The forces close to a company that affect its ability to serve its customers: the company, market channel firms, customer markets, competitors, and the public.

Microenvironmental forces. Customers, competitors, distribution channels, and suppliers.

Micromarketing. The practice of tailoring products and marketing programs to suit the tastes of specific individuals and locations.

Millennials (also called Generation Y or the echo boomers). Born between 1980 and 2000, these children of the baby boomers number 83 million, dwarfing the Gen Xers and larger even than the baby-boomer segment. This group includes several age cohorts: tweens (ages 8 to 12), teens (13 to 18), and young adults (the 20 somethings).

Mobile marketing. Marketing promotions, messages, and other content delivered to on-the-go consumers through mobile phones, smartphones, tablets, and other mobile devises.

Moment of truth. Occurs when an employee and a customer have contact.

Motivational houses. Provide incentive travel offered to employees or distributors as a reward for their efforts.

Motive. A need that is sufficiently pressing to direct a person to seek satisfaction of that need.

Multichannel marketing distribution. Multichannel distribution, as when a single firm sets up two or more marketing channels to reach one or more customer segments.

Multiplier effect. Tourist expenditures that are recycled through the local economy, being spent and spent again.

Mystery shoppers. Hospitality companies often hire disguised or mystery shoppers to pose as customers and report back on their experience.

National tourist organizations (NTOs). A national government or quasi-government agency that markets destination tourism.

Observational research. The gathering of primary data by observing relevant people, actions, and situations.

Olfactory. The dimension of atmosphere relating to scent and freshness.

Online advertising. Advertising that appears while consumers are surfing the Web, including display ads, search-related ads, and online classifieds.

Online focus groups. Gathering a small group of people online with a trained moderator to chat about a product, service, or organization and gain qualitative insights about consumer attitude and behavior.

Online marketing research. Collecting primary data online through Internet surveys, online focus groups, Web-based experiments, or tracking of consumers' online behavior.

Online marketing. Company efforts to market products and services and build customer relationships over the Internet.

Online social networks. Online social communities—blogs, social networking, Web sites, or even virtual worlds—where people socialize or exchange information and opinions.

Online travel agency (OTA). A travel agency that conducts business through the Internet with no physical locations or stores.

Opinion leaders. People within a reference group who, because of special skills, knowledge, personality, or other characteristics, exert influence on others.

Order-routine specification. The stage of the industry buying process in which a buyer writes the final order with the chosen supplier(s), listing the technical specifications, quantity needed, expected time of delivery, return policies, warranties, and so on.

Organization image. The way a person or group views an organization.

Organizational buying process. The decision-making process by which formal organizations establish the need for purchased products and services and identify, evaluate, and choose among alternative brands and suppliers.

Organizational culture. The pattern of shared values and beliefs that gives members of an organization meaning and provides them with the rules for behavior in that organization.

Overpositioning. Giving buyers a too-narrow picture of the company.

Patronage rewards. Cash or other awards for regular use of a company's products or services.

Performance review. The stage of an industrial buying process in which a buyer rates its satisfaction with

suppliers, deciding whether to continue, modify, or drop the relationship.

Perishability. A major characteristic of services; they cannot be stored for later use.

Personal selling. Personal presentation by the firm's sales force to make sales and build customer relationships.

Personality. A person's distinguishing psychological characteristics that lead to relatively consistent and lasting responses to his or her environment.

Phase-out. The ideal method of removing an unpopular or unprofitable product; it enables a product to be removed in an orderly fashion.

Physical evidence. Tangible clues such as promotional material, employees of the firm, and the physical environment of the firm. Physical evidence is used by a service firm to make its product more tangible to customers.

Point-of-purchase (POP) promotions. Includes displays and demonstrations that take place at the time of sale.

Political environment. Laws, government agencies, and pressure groups that influence and limit the activities of various organizations and individuals in society,

Portfolio tests. Consumers view or listen to a portfolio of advertisements, taking as much time as they need.

Preapproach. The step in which the salesperson or company identifies qualified potential applicants.

Premiums. Goods offered either free or at low cost as an incentive buy a product.

Presentation. The sales step in which the sales persons tells the "value story" to the buyer showing how the company's offer solves the customer's problems.

Press relations. Placing newsworthy information into the news media to attract attention.

Press release. Information released to the media about certain new products or services.

Price. The amount of money charged for a product or service, or the sum of the values that consumers exchange for the benefits of having or using the product or service.

Primary data. Information collected for the specific purpose at hand.

Problem recognition. The stage of the industrial buying process in which someone in a company recognizes a problem or need that can be met by acquiring a good or a service.

Product concept. The idea that consumers will favor products that offer the most quality, performance, and features, and therefore the organization should devote its energy to making continuous product improvements.

Product concept. A detailed version of a product idea stated in meaningful consumer terms.

Product development. Developing the product concept into a physical product to ensure that the product idea can be turned into a workable product.

Product idea. Envisioning a possible product that company managers might offer to the market.

Product image. The way that consumers picture an actual or potential product.

Product publicity. Various efforts to publicize specific products.

Product specification. The stage of an industrial buying process in which the buying organization decides on and specifies the best technical product characteristics for a needed item.

Production concept. Holds that customers will favor products that are available and highly affordable, and therefore management should focus on production and distribution efficiency.

Promotion mix. The specific mix of advertising, personal selling, sales promotion, and public relations a company uses to pursue its advertising and marketing objectives.

Prospecting. The process of searching for new accounts

Psychocentrics. Persons who do not desire change when they travel. They like to visit nonthreatening places and stay in familiar surroundings.

Psychographic segmentation. Dividing a market into different groups based on social class, lifestyle, or personality characteristics.

Public relations. The process by which a positive image and customer preference are created through third-party endorsement.

Public. Any group that has an actual or potential interest in or impact on an organization's ability to achieve its objectives.

Pulsing. Scheduling ads unevenly over a given period.

Purpose of a business. To create and maintain satisfied, profitable customers.

Quotas. Quantitative and time-specific accomplishment measurements established for members of a sales force.

Recall tests. The advertiser asks people who have been exposed to magazines or television programs to recall everything they can about the advertisers and products that they saw.

Recognition tests. The researcher asks readers of, for instance, a given issue of a magazine to point out what they have seen.

Reference groups. Groups that have a direct (face-to-face) or indirect influence on a person's attitude or behavior.

Relationship marketing. Involves creating, maintaining, and enhancing strong relationships with customers and other stakeholders.

Reminder advertising. Advertising used to keep consumers thinking about a product.

Retailer. Business whose sales come primarily from retailing.

Return on marketing investment (or marketing ROI). The net return from a marketing investment divided by the costs of the marketing investment. It measures the profits generated by investments in marketing activities.

Revenue management. A pricing method using price as a means of matching demand with capacity.

Revenue management. Forecasting demand to optimize profit. Demand is managed by adjusting price. Fences are often built to keep all customers from taking advantage of

lower prices. For example, typical fences include making a reservation at least two weeks in advance or staying over a Saturday night.

Role. The activities that a person is expected to perform according to the persons around him or her.

Run-out. Removing a product after existing stock has been depleted; used when sales for an item are low and costs exceed revenues, such as the case of a restaurant serving a crabmeat cocktail with sales of only one or two items per week.

Sales promotion. Consists of short-term incentives to encourage the purchase of sale of a product or service.

Sample. Offers of a trial amount of a product.

Sample. (1) A segment of a population selected for marketing research to represent the population as a whole; (2) offer of a trial amount of a product to consumers.

Search-related advertising (or contextual advertising). Text-based ads and links that appear alongside search engine results on sites such as Google and Yahoo!

Secondary data. Information that already exists somewhere, having been collected for another purpose.

Self-concept. Self-image, the complex mental pictures people have of themselves.

Selling concept. The idea that consumers will not buy enough of an organization's products unless the organization undertakes a large selling and promotion effort.

Selling. Sales representatives know the art of salesmanship: approaching, presenting, answering objections, and closing sales.

Service culture. A system of values and beliefs in an organization that reinforces the idea that providing the customer with quality service is the principal concern of the business.

Service profit chain. A model that shows the relationships between employee satisfaction, customer satisfaction, customer retention, value creation, and profitability.

Servicing. Sales representatives provide various services to the customers: consulting on their problems, rendering technical assistance, arranging financing, and expediting delivery.

Share of customer. The portion of the customer's purchasing that a company gets in its product categories.

SMERF. SMERF states for social, military, educational, religious, and fraternal organizations. This group of specialty market has a common price-sensitive thread.

Social classes. Relatively permanent and order divisions in a society whose members share similar values, interests, and behaviors.

Social media. Independent and commercial online communities where the people congregate, socialize, and exchange views and information.

Social selling. The use of online, mobile, and social media to engage customers, build stronger customer relationships and augment sales performance.

Societal marketing concept. The idea that an organization should determine the needs, wants, and interests of target markets and deliver the desired satisfactions more effectively and efficiently than competitors in a way that maintains or improves the consumer's and society's well-being.

SoLoMo (social+local+mobile). Marketing that targets on-the-go consumers as they come and go in key local market areas.

Spam. Unsolicited, unwanted, commercial e-mail messages.

Specific product attributes. Price and product features can be used to position a product.

Stakeholder. Stakeholders include customers, employees, suppliers, and the communities where their business is located and other people or organizations that have an interest in the success of the business.

Strategic business units (SBUs). A single business or collection of related businesses that can be planned separately from the rest of the company.

Strategic planning. The process of developing and maintaining a strategic fit between the organization's goals and capabilities and its changing marketing opportunities.

Subculture. A group of people with shared value systems based on common life experiences and situations.

Supplier search. The stage of the industrial buying process in which a buyer tries to find the best vendor.

Supplier selection. The stage of the industrial buying process in which a buyer receives proposals and selects a supplier or suppliers.

Suppliers. Firms and individuals that provide the resources needed by a company and its competitors to produce goods and services.

Supply Chain. Upstream and downstream partners. Upstream from the company is a set of firms that supply raw materials, components, parts, information, finances, and expertise needed to create a product. Downstream marketing channel partners, such as wholesalers and retailers, form a vital connection between the firm and its customers.

Supporting products. Extra products offered to add value to the core product and to help differentiate it from the competition.

Survey research. The gathering of primary data by asking people questions about their knowledge, attitudes, preferences, and buying behavior.

Survival. A technique used when a company's or business unit's sales slump, creating a loss that threatens its existence. Because the capacity of a hotel or restaurant is fixed, survival often involves cutting prices to increase demand and cash flow. This can disrupt the market until the firm goes out of business or the economy improves.

Sustainable tourism. Tourism that minimizes the environmental impacts and sociocultural changes, sustains the longevity of a destination, and creates economic opportunity for local communities.

SWOT analysis. Evaluates the company's overall strengths (S), weaknesses (W), opportunities (O), and threats (T).

Tactile. The dimension of atmosphere relating to softness, smoothness, and temperature.

Targeting. Sales representatives decide how to allocate their scarce time among prospects and customers.

Telephone marketing. Using the telephone to sell directly to customers.

Timetable. Specific dates to accomplish strategies and tactics.

Total costs. Costs that are the sum of the fixed and variable costs for any given level of production.

Tourism. A stay of one or more nights away from home for leisure or business, except such things as boarding, education, or semipermanent employment.

Transaction. Consists of a trade of values between two parties; marketing's unit of measurement.

Underpositioning. Failing ever to position the company at all.

Upselling. Training sales and reservation employees to offer continuously a higher-priced product that will better meet the customers' needs, rather than settling for the lowest price.

Value chain. The series of internal departments that carry out value-creating activities to design, produce, market, deliver, and support a firm's products.

Value proposition. The full mix of benefits on which a brand is differentiated and positioned.

Value proposition. The full positioning of a brand—the full mix of benefits upon which it is positioned.

Value-based pricing. Uses the buyer's perceptions of value, not the seller's cost, as the key to pricing.

Variability. A major characteristic of services; their quality may vary greatly, depending on who provides them and when, where, and how they are provided.

Variable costs. Costs that vary directly with the level of production.

Vertical conflict. Conflict between different levels of the same channel.

Vertical marketing systems (VMSs). Distribution channel structures in which producers, wholesalers, and retailers act as a unified system: Either one channel member owns the others, or has contracts with them, or has so much power that they all cooperate.

Viral marketing. The Internet version of word-of-mouth marketing—Web sites, videos, e-mail messages, or other marketing events that are so infectious that customers will want to pass them along to friends.

Visual. The dimension of atmosphere relating to color, brightness, size, and shape.

Wholesaler. Firms engaged primarily in wholesaling activity.

Zaltman Metaphor Elicitation Technique (ZMET). A qualitative technique to uncover both conscious and unconscious motives, thoughts and feelings of consumers.

INDEX